Data Abstraction & Problem Solving with C++

Walls And Mirrors

Seventh Edition

Frank M. Carrano
University of Rhode Island

Timothy M. Henry
New England Institute of Technology

PEARSON

Boston Columbus Indianapolis Hoboken New York San Francisco
Amsterdam Cape Town Dubai London Madrid Milan Munich Paris Montreal Toronto
Delhi Mexico City Sao Paulo Sydney Hong Kong Seoul Singapore Taipei Tokyo

Vice President and Editorial Director, ECS: Marcia J. Horton

Executive Editor: Tracy Johnson (Dunkelberger)

Editorial Assistant: Kristy Alaura

Program Manager: Carole Snyder

Project Manager: Robert Engelhardt

Media Team Lead: Steve Wright

R&P Manager: Rachel Youdelman

R&P Senior Project Manager: William Opaluch

Senior Operations Specialist: Maura Zaldivar-Garcia

Inventory Manager: Meredith Maresca

Marketing Manager: Demetrius Hall

Product Marketing Manager: Bram Van Kempen

Marketing Assistant: Jon Bryant

Cover Designer: Marta Samsel

Cover Art: © Jeremy Woodhouse/Ocean/Corbis

Full-Service Project Management: John Orr, Cenveo Publisher Services / Nesbitt Graphics, Inc.

Pearson Education Ltd., London
Pearson Education Australia Ply. Ltd., Sydney
Pearson Education Singapore, Pte. Ltd.
Pearson Education North Asia Ltd., Hong Kong
Pearson Education Canada, Inc., Toronto
Pearson Education de Mexico, S.A. de C.V.
Pearson Education–Japan, Tokyo
Pearson Education Malaysia, Pte. Ltd.
Pearson Education, Inc., Hoboken, New Jersey

Library of Congress Cataloging-in-Publication Data on file

www.pearsonhighered.com

ISBN-10: 0-13-446397-8
ISBN 13: 978-0-13-446397-1

42 2022

Welcome to the seventh edition of *Data Abstraction & Problem Solving with C++: Walls and Mirrors*. Since the publication of the first edition, we all have gained experience with teaching data abstraction in an object-oriented way using C++. This edition reflects that experience and the many comments and suggestions received from faculty and students alike.

I am pleased to continue working with my co-author, Dr. Timothy Henry, who adds his professional experience with C++ and attention to pedagogy to our presentation. Our goal remains to give students a superior foundation in data abstraction, object-oriented programming, and other modern problem-solving techniques. All C++ code has been updated to use exceptions, follow safe and secure coding techniques such as those described in the SEI CERT Coding Standards, and use C++11 and C++14 features.

We hope that you enjoy reading this book. Like many others before you, you can learn—or teach—data structures in an effective and sustainable way.

Talk to Us

Walls and Mirrors continues to evolve. Your comments, suggestions, and corrections will be greatly appreciated. Here are a few ways to reach us:

- E-mail: carrano@acm.org or thenry@neit.edu

- Facebook: www.facebook.com/makingitreal
- Twitter: twitter.com/Frank_M_Carrano
- Blog: frank-m-carrano.com/makingitreal

The topics that we cover in this book deal with the various ways of organizing data so that a given application can access and manipulate data in an efficient way. These topics are fundamental to your future study of computer science, as they provide you with the foundation of knowledge required to create complex and reliable software. Whether you are interested in designing video games or software for robotic-controlled surgery, the study of data structures is vital to your success. Even if you do not study all of the topics in this book now, you are likely to encounter them later. We hope that you will enjoy reading the book, and that it will serve as a useful reference tool for your future courses.

The walls and mirrors in the title represent two fundamental problem-solving techniques that appear throughout the presentation. Data abstraction isolates and hides the implementation details of a module from the rest of the program, much as a wall can isolate and hide you from your neighbor. Recursion is a repetitive technique that solves a problem by solving exactly the same but smaller problems, much as images in facing mirrors grow smaller with each reflection.

Please be sure to browse the rest of this preface to see the features that will help you in your studies. To help you learn and to review for exams, we have included such learning aids as video tutorials (VideoNotes), checkpoint questions with answers, margin notes, programming tips, chapter summaries, and a glossary. As a help during programming, you will find C++ reference material in the appendixes and inside the covers. You should review the list of this book's features given later in this preface in the section "Features to Enhance Learning."

The presentation makes some basic assumptions about your knowledge of C++. Some of you may need to review this language or learn it for the first time by consulting the appendixes of this book. This book covers C++ classes and other relevant aspects of the language in C++ Interludes that occur throughout the book between certain chapters. These interludes do not assume that you already know their topics. We assume no experience with recursive functions, which are included in Chapters 2 and 5.

All of the C++ source code that appears in this book is available for your use. Later in this preface, the description of supplementary materials tells you how to obtain these files, as well as the VideoNotes and other online documents.

Organization

This book's organization, sequencing, and pace of topic coverage make learning and teaching easier by focusing your attention on one concept at a time, by providing flexibility in the order in which you can cover topics, and by clearly distinguishing between the specification and implementation of abstract data types, or ADTs. To accomplish these goals, we have organized the material into 21 chapters and 8 interludes. Most chapters focus on either the specification and use of an ADT or its various implementations. You can choose to cover the specification of an ADT followed by its implementations, or you can treat the specification and use of several ADTs before you consider any implementation issues. The book's organization makes it easy for you to choose the topic order that you prefer.

Contents at a Glance

The following list shows the overall composition of the book. A further chapter-by-chapter description appears later. Note that gray highlighted sections are available online.

What's New?

This edition of *Walls and Mirrors* is an important enhancement of the previous edition, yet retains a pedagogical approach that makes the material accessible to students at the introductory level. The coverage that you enjoyed in previous editions is still here. As is usual for us, we have read every word of the previous edition and made changes to improve clarity and correctness. No chapter or interlude appears exactly as it did before. In this new edition, we

- Updated the C++ code to follow professional conventions by using
  - □ Exceptions rather than return values to signal unusual situations.
  - □ Safe and secure coding techniques, such as those found in SEI CERT Coding Standards.
  - □ C++11 and C++14 features where applicable.

  Note that we tested the C++ code using the following compilers: GNU g++, clang/LLVM, Xcode 6.x, and Visual Studio 2013 and 2015RC.

- Refined our terminology and presentation to ease understanding.
- Revised figures to improve clarity.
- Replaced technologically dated examples.
- Added Notes and Programming Tips.
- Added programming problems in the areas of gaming, finance, and e-commerce.
- Added Security Notes as a new element.
- Added a new C++ Interlude 4, "Safe Memory Management Using Smart Pointers," midway in the book to introduce smart pointers, a C++11 feature. Chapters subsequent to this interlude use smart pointers.

Chapter-by-Chapter Overview

Readers of this book should have completed a programming course, preferably in C++. Appendix A covers the essentials of C++ that we assume readers will know. You can use this Appendix as a review or as the basis for making the transition to C++ from another programming language. Note that Appendixes K and L offer some help for those who are transitioning from Java or Python, respectively.

- **Chapters 1 through 5:** Chapter 1 introduces object-oriented concepts and discusses problem solving, good programming practices, and ADTs. It then specifies a simple ADT—the bag—and declares the bag's operations within a C++ template interface in a nonthreatening way. Such interfaces enable the client to choose the type of data that the ADT stores.

  Next is C++ Interlude 1, which presents C++ classes. It gives more details about template interfaces—like the one presented in Chapter 1—and shows how to use inheritance to define a class derived from an interface.

  As it did in earlier editions, Chapter 2 introduces recursion, and Chapter 5 develops it as a problem-solving tool. Recursion is revisited often throughout the book.

  We clearly separate the specification, use, and implementation of the bag by dividing the material across several chapters. For example, Chapter 1 specifies the bag and provides several examples of its use. Chapter 3 covers implementations that use arrays. Just before Chapter 4 introduces chains of linked nodes and uses one in the definition of a class of bags, C++ Interlude 2 covers pointers, polymorphism, and dynamic memory allocation. Both Chapters 3 and 4 include recursion in their presentation.

  By introducing the bag as the first ADT we consider, we make the difficult topic of linked data more accessible to students. Adding or removing the first node in a chain of linked nodes is the easiest task, and these simple manipulations are the ones we need to use for a linked implementation of the bag. Subsequent chapters will add to this discussion of linked nodes.

  Chapter 3 does more than simply implement the ADT bag. It shows how to approach the implementation of a class by initially focusing on core methods. When defining a class, it is often useful to implement and test these core methods first and to leave definitions of the other methods for later. Chapter 4 follows this approach in its development of a link-based implementation of the ADT bag.

  We continue to separate specification from implementation throughout most of the book when we discuss various other ADTs. You can choose to cover the chapters that specify and use the ADTs and then later cover the chapters that implement them. Or you can cover the chapters as they appear, implementing each ADT right after studying its specification and use. A list of chapter prerequisites appears later in this preface to help you plan your path through the book.

- **Chapters 6 and 7:** Chapter 6 discusses stacks, giving examples of their use, and Chapter 7 implements the stack using an array and then again using a chain. We manipulate this chain in same way that we do for the ADT bag. Between these chapters is C++ Interlude 3, which discusses C++ exceptions. Chapter 7 then shows how to use an exception in the implementation of the ADT stack, when a client violates a method's precondition.

- **Chapters 8 and 9:** The next two chapters introduce the ADT list. We discuss this container abstractly and then implement it by using an array and then a chain of linked nodes. Adding and removing a node that lies between existing nodes of a chain is easier for students to grasp, now that they have experience with the implementations of the bag and stack. Once again, we use exceptions to enforce method preconditions.

- **C++ Interlude 4:** This new interlude introduces smart pointers, a recent addition to C++. We use smart pointers in linked implementations in subsequent chapters.

- **Chapters 10 and 11:** Chapter 10 introduces the complexity of algorithms, a topic that we integrate into future chapters. Chapter 11 discusses various sorting techniques and their relative complexities. We consider both iterative and recursive versions of these algorithms.

- **Chapter 12:** Chapter 12 introduces the sorted list, and looks at a linked implementation and its efficiency. We then talk about the relationship between a list and a sorted list and show how to use the list as a base class for the sorted list. Note that Chapter 12 is preceded by C++ Interlude 5 that discusses class relationships and the various ways a class can be reused. Chapter 12 puts that discussion into immediate use.
- **Chapters 13 and 14:** Chapter 13 presents the ADTs queue and priority queue, along with some uses of these containers. In doing so, we give an example of simulation that uses both ADTs, and finally summarize the difference between position-oriented and value-oriented ADTs. Chapter 14 implements the queue, and introduces tail pointers, circularly linked chains, and circular arrays. We offer an implementation of a priority queue by using a sorted list, but note that a better approach will come later when we introduce the ADT heap.
- **Chapters 15 through 17:** Before we begin the next chapter, C++ Interlude 6 introduces overloaded operators and friend access. We overload operators when we define classes of trees in this group of chapters. Chapter 15 discusses trees—binary, binary search, and general—and their possible uses. Chapter 16 considers implementations of these trees, and briefly introduces the tree sort. C++ Interlude 7 presents iterators in the context of a list. Chapter 17 introduces the ADT heap and shows how to implement it by using an array. We then use a heap to implement the priority queue and to sort an array.
- **Chapter 18:** This chapter covers the specification and use of the ADT dictionary. We look at implementations of the dictionary that use an array or a binary search tree. We then introduce hashing and use it as a dictionary implementation.
- **Chapter 19:** Chapter 19 introduces balanced search trees. Included in this chapter are the AVL, 2-3, 2-4, and red-black trees. These trees are considered as implementations of the ADT dictionary.
- **Chapter 20:** Next, we discuss graphs, suggest two ways to implement them, and look at several applications.
- **Chapter 21:** This last chapter considers data storage in external direct access files. Merge sort is modified to sort such data, and external hashing and B-tree indexes are used to search it. These searching algorithms are generalizations of the internal hashing schemes and 2-3 trees already developed. Finally, C++ Interlude 8 ends the main presentation by discussing the containers and algorithms available in the C++ Standard Template Library (STL).
- **Appendixes A through L:** The appendixes provide supplemental information. As we mentioned earlier, Appendix A reviews C++ up to but not including classes. Appendixes B, C, D, and F present important aspects of programming, the Unified Modeling Language (UML), the software life cycle, and algorithm verification. Appendix E covers mathematical induction, and Appendix G covers input and output with external files. Appendix H provides a list of C++ header files and standard functions, and Appendix I considers the javadoc commenting style and defines the tags that we use in this book. Appendix J is simply a chart of the ASCII character codes. Finally, Appendixes K and L are brief transition guides to C++ for those who know Java or Python, respectively.

Features to Enhance Learning

The pedagogical features and organization of this book were carefully designed to facilitate learning and to allow instructors to tailor the material easily to a particular course. These features help students not only during their first reading of the material, but also during subsequent review.

 Notes: Important ideas are presented or summarized in highlighted paragraphs and are meant to be read in line with the surrounding text.

 Security Notes: Aspects of safe and secure programming are introduced and highlighted in this new feature.

 Programming Tips: Suggestions to improve or facilitate programming are featured as soon as they become relevant.

 Examples: Numerous examples illuminate new concepts.

 Checkpoint Questions: Questions are posed throughout each chapter and integrated within the text to reinforce the concept just presented. These "checkpoint" questions help readers to understand the material, since answering them requires pause and reflection. Solutions to these questions are provided online.

 VideoNotes: Online tutorials are a Pearson feature that provides visual and audio support to the presentation given throughout the book. They offer students another way to recap and reinforce key concepts by providing additional instruction in a more dynamic form than a static textbook. VideoNotes allow for self-paced instruction with easy navigation, including the ability to select, play, rewind, fastforward, and stop within each video. Unique VideoNote icons appear throughout this book whenever a video is available for a particular concept or problem. A detailed list of the 50 VideoNotes for this text and their associated locations in the book can be found on page xxiii. VideoNotes are free with the purchase of a new textbook. To purchase access to VideoNotes separately, please go to

www.pearsonhighered.com/carrano

Margin Notes: Brief phrases in the margins help you review material or locate particular content.

Chapter Summaries: Each chapter ends with a list of key ideas that summarize what was presented.

Exercises and Programming Problems: Further practice is available by solving the exercises and programming problems at the end of each chapter. Unfortunately, we cannot give readers the answers to these exercises and problems, even if they are not enrolled in a class. Only instructors who adopt the book can receive selected answers from the publisher. For help with these exercises and programming problems, you will have to contact your instructor.

Glossary of Terms: A glossary of all terms introduced in this book is available online.

Accessing Instructor and Student Resource Materials

The following items are available on the publisher's website at

www.pearsonhighered.com/carrano

- C++ source code as it appears in the book
- A link to any misprints that have been discovered since the book was published
- Links to additional online content, which is described next

Instructor Resources

The following protected material is available to instructors who adopt this book by logging onto Pearson's Instructor Resource Center, accessible from

www.pearsonhighered.com/carrano

- PowerPoint lecture slides
- Test bank
- Instructor solutions manual
- Complete C++ source code
- Figures from the book

Additionally, instructors can access the book's Premium Website for the following online premium content, also accessible from

www.pearsonhighered.com/carrano

- Instructional VideoNotes
- Answers to the Checkpoint Questions
- A glossary of terms

Please contact your Pearson sales representative for an instructor access code. Contact information is available at www.pearsonhighered.com/replocator.

Student Resources

The following material is available to students by logging onto the book's Premium Website accessible from www.pearsonhighered.com/carrano:

- Instructional VideoNotes
- Answers to the Checkpoint Questions
- A glossary of terms

Students must use the access card located in the front of the book to register for and then enter the Premium Website. Students without an access code can purchase access to the Premium Website by following the instructions listed there.

Acknowledgments

This book evolved from the original *Intermediate Problem Solving and Data Structures: Walls and Mirrors* by Paul Helman and Robert Veroff (©†1986 by The Benjamin/Cummings Publishing Company, Inc.). Professors Helman and Veroff introduced two powerful analogies, walls and mirrors, that have made it easier for us to teach—and to learn—computer science. This work builds on their organizational framework and overall perspective and includes some technical and textual content, examples, figures, and exercises derived from the original work.

Our sincere appreciation and thanks go to the following reviewers for carefully reading the previous edition and making candid comments and suggestions that greatly improved this edition:

Said Bettayeb	*University of Houston, Clear Lake*
Prabir Bhattacharya	*University of Cincinnati*
Moe Bidgoli Saginaw	*Valley State University*
Andrew Cencini	*Bennington College*
Chia-Chu Chiang	*University of Arkansas, Little Rock*
John Gauch	*University of Arkansas, Fayetteville*
Rania Hodhod	*Columbus State University*
Larry Latour	*University of Maine, Orono*
Logan Mayfield	*Monmouth College*
Dana Vrajitoru	*Indiana University, South Bend*

Special thanks go to our support team at Pearson Education during the lengthy process of revising this book: Tracy Johnson, Scott Disanno, Bob Engelhardt, Carole Snyder, Kelsey Loanes, and Kristy Alaura. Our copy editor, Rebecca Pepper, ensured that our presentation is not only grammatical, but also is clear, correct, and understandable. Our project manager, John Orr, led us from manuscript to finished book calmly and precisely, while adhering to an exceptionally tight schedule.

Previous editions were greatly improved by the special care taken by Steven J. Holtz, who teaches at the University of Minnesota Duluth, and Paul Nagin and Janet Prichard, who also provided valuable material. Their contributions endure in this edition.

Numerous other people provided input for the previous editions of *Walls and Mirrors* at various stages of its development. All of their comments were useful and greatly appreciated. In alphabetical order, they are Karl Abrahamson, Stephen Alberg, Ronald Alferez, Vicki Allan, Jihad Almahayni, James Ames, Andrew Allen Anda, Claude W. Anderson, Andrew Azzinaro, Tony Baiching, Don Bailey, N. Dwight Barnette, Jack Beidler, Wolfgang W. Bein, Sto Bell, David Berard, Brian Bershad, John Black, Richard Botting, Wolfin Brumley, Daryl Carr, Philip Carrigan, Stephen Clamage, Michael Clancy, David Clayton, Michael Cleron, Chris Constantino, Shaun Cooper, Sarp Arda Coskun, Andrew Danner, Charles Denault, Vincent J. DiPippo, Suzanne Dorney, Colleen Dunn, Carl Eckberg, Sebastian Elbaum, Matthew Evett, Karla Steinbrugge Fant, Caroline Fell, Jean Foltz, Max Fomitchev, Mike Fulford, Susan Gauch, Mark Van Gorp, Sarah Gothard, Martin Granier, Sr., Marguerite Hafen, Randy Hale, Ranette H. Halverson, George Hamer, Judy Hankins, Jean Harnett, Andrew Hayden, Michael Hayden, Sarah Hayden, Lisa Hellerstein, Lasse Hellvig, Karsten Henckell, Lesly Hershman, Mary Lou Hines, Michael Hirsch, Jack Hodges, Larry M. Holt, Stephanie Horoschak, Lily Hou, John Hubbard, Tom Irdy, Kris Jensen, Thomas Judson, Edwin J. Kay, Laura Kenney, Roger King, Ladislav Kohout, Jim LaBonte, Jean Lake, Janusz Laski, Elaine Lavallee, Sally Lawrence, Cathie LeBlanc, Greg Lee, Urban LeJeune, Matt Licklider, Adam Lindstrom, John M. Linebarger, Shih Hsi Liu, Marilyn Lloyd, Ken Lord, Paul Luker, Ethan Mallove, Manisha Mande, Pierre-Arnoul de Marneffe, John Marsaglia, Tim Martin, Jane Wallace Mayo, Mark McCormick, Dan McCracken, Vivian McDougal, Shirley McGuire, Sue Medeiros, Jie Hu Meichsner, Waleed Meleis, Carol Melville, Edalin Michael, James R. Miller, Jim Miller, Guy Mills, Rameen Mohammadi, Cleve Moler, Narayan Murthy, David Naff, Paul Nagin, Abhaya Nayak, Douglas

Acknowledgments

Niehaus, Rayno Niemi, Daniel Nohl, Debbie Noonan, John O'Donnell, Andrew Oldroyd, Larry Olsen, Raymond L. Paden, Roy Pargas, Brenda C. Parker, Thaddeus F. Pawlicki, Keith Pierce, Gary Pollock, Albert Prichard, Lucasz Pruski, George B. Purdy, David Radford, Bina Ramamanthy, Steve Ratering, Hal Records, Stuart Regis, Nouhad J. Rizk, Mateen Rizki, J. D. Robertson, Daniel Rosenkrantz, Robert A. Rossi, Jerry Roth, John Rowe, Michael E. Rupp, Sharon Salveter, Charles Saxon, Chandra Sekharan, Linda Shapiro, Yujian Sheng, Mary Shields, Ren-Ben Shiu, Dmitri Slobodin, Ronnie Smith, Carl Spicola, Richard Snodgrass, Neil Snyder, Garth O. Sorenson, Ken Sousa, Chris Spannabel, Paul Spirakis, Clinton Staley, Matt Stallman, Mark Stehlick, Benjamin Schomp, Harriet Taylor, David Teague, Virginia Teller, David Tetreault, Hans-Joerg Tiede, Lindsey Triebel, Dwight Tuinista, John Turner, Karen Van Houten, Robert Vincent, Susan Wallace, James E. Warren, Xiaoqiao Wei, Joyce Wells, Jerry Weltman, Art Werschultz, Nancy Wiegand, Alicia Williams, Howard Williams, Brad Wilson, James Wirth, Wally Wood, Kathie Yerion, Xiaohui Yuan, Salih Yurttas, Wu Yusong, Rick Zaccone, Alan Zaring, and Chao Zhao.

Finally, we thank our families and friends—Doug, Ted, Tom, Nancy, Sue, Joanne, Tita, Bobby, Lorraine, and Marge—for giving us lives away from computers.

Thank you all.
F. M. C.
T. M. H.

Contents

Contents

Contents

Contents

Contents

Contents

Chapter Prerequisites

Each chapter, interlude, and Appendix assumes that the reader has studied certain previous material. This list indicates those prerequisites. Numbers represent chapter numbers, and letters reference appendices. The notation I*x* represents C++ Interlude *x*. Underlined prerequisites indicate an incidental or a partial dependence. You can use this information to plan a path through the book.

		Prequisites
Chapter 1	Data Abstraction: The Walls	A, B, C
C++ Interlude 1	C++ Classes	A, 1
Chapter 2	Recursion: The Mirrors	A, B, C
Chapter 3	Array-Based Implementations	A, 1, I1, 2
C++ Interlude 2	Pointers, Polymorphism, and Memory Allocation	3
Chapter 4	Link-Based Implementations	1, I1, 2, 3, I2
Chapter 5	Recursion as a Problem-Solving Technique	2
Chapter 6	Stacks	1, I1
C++ Interlude 3	Exceptions	I1
Chapter 7	Stack Implementations	3, I2, 4, 6, I3
Chapter 8	Lists	1, I1
Chapter 9	List Implementations	3, I2, 4, I3, 8
C++ Interlude 4	Safe Memory Management Using Smart Pointers	I2, 9
Chapter 10	Algorithm Efficiency	1, 2, 4, 9
Chapter 11	Sorting Algorithms and Their Efficiency	2, 5, 10
C++ Interlude 5	Class Relationships and Reuse	1, I1, I2, 6, 8
Chapter 12	Sorted Lists and Their Implementations	8, 10, I4, 15
Chapter 13	Queues and Priority Queues	6, 8, 12
Chapter 14	Queue Implementations	I4, 13
C++ Interlude 6	Overloaded Operators and Friend Access	4, 8, 9
Chapter 15	Trees	2, 4, 5, 6, 8, I4, 10, 13
Chapter 16	Tree Implementations	4, 5, 6, 9, I4, 10, 12, I6, 15
C++ Interlude 7	Iterators	9, I4, I6
Chapter 17	Heaps	13, 15, 16
Chapter 18	Dictionaries and Their Implementations	4, I4, 10, 11, 12, 16, 17
Chapter 19	Balanced Search Trees	15, 16, 18
Chapter 20	Graphs	5, 6, 16
Chapter 21	Processing Data in External Storage	G, 11, 18, 19
C++ Interlude 8	The Standard Template Library	N/A
Appendix A	Review of C++ Fundamentals	Knowledge of a programming language

Appendix B	Important Themes in Programming	A, 1
Appendix C	The Unified Modeling Language	I4
Appendix D	The Software Life Cycle	A, a general knowledge of software
Appendix E	Mathematical Induction	Ability to prove theorems
Appendix F	Algorithm Verification	E
Appendix G	Files	A
Appendix H	C++ Header Files and Standard Functions	N/A
Appendix I	C++ Documentation Systems	N/A
Appendix J	ASCII Character Codes	N/A
Appendix K	C++ for Java Programmers	Java programming
Appendix L	C++ for Python Programmers	Python programming

VideoNotes Directory

VideoNote

Data Abstraction: The Walls

Chapter

1

Contents

Prerequisites

This chapter summarizes several fundamental principles that serve as the basis for dealing with the complexities of large programs. The discussion both reinforces the basic principles of programming and demonstrates that writing well-designed and well-documented programs is essential. The chapter also introduces algorithms and data abstraction and indicates how these topics relate to the book's main theme of problem solving. Data abstraction is a technique for increasing the modularity of a program—for building "walls" between a program and its data structures. During the design of a solution, you will discover that you need to support several operations on the data and therefore need to define abstract data types (ADTs). Only after you have clearly specified the operations of an ADT should you consider data structures for implementing it. This chapter will introduce a simple ADT and use it to demonstrate the advantages of ADTs in general.

In subsequent chapters, we examine ways of organizing and using data. As we focus on these new ideas, pay attention to how all of the solutions we look at adhere to the basic principles discussed in this chapter.

1.1   Object-Oriented Concepts

Coding without a solution design increases debugging time

Where did you begin when you wrote your last program? After reading the problem specifications and going through the requisite amount of procrastination, most novice programmers simply begin to write code. Obviously, their goal is to get their programs to execute, preferably with correct results. Therefore, they run their programs, examine error messages, insert semicolons, change the logic, remove semicolons, pray, and otherwise torture their programs until they work. Most of their time is probably spent checking both syntax and program logic. Certainly, your programming skills are better now than when you wrote your first program, but are you able to write a really large program by using the approach just described? Maybe, but there are better ways.

VideoNote
Object-oriented concepts

Whereas a first course in computer science typically emphasizes programming issues, the focus of this book is on the broader issues of problem solving. Here the term **problem solving** refers to the entire process of taking the statement of a problem and developing a computer program that solves that problem. This process requires you to pass through many phases, from gaining an understanding of the problem to be solved, through designing a conceptual solution, to implementing the solution as a computer program. In a large software project, problem solving requires not only the development of a computer program, but also the examination of user workflows and possible changes to how a user performs daily tasks.

A solution specifies a system of interacting objects

Object-oriented analysis and design (OOAD) is a process for solving problems. From an object-oriented perspective, a **solution** is a computer program consisting of a system of interacting classes of objects. An **object** has a set of characteristics and behaviors related to the solution. Each object is responsible for some aspect of the solution. A set of objects having the same type is called a **class**. An object of a class is also known as an **instance** of the class. When you create an object of a class, you **instantiate** the object.

An object is an instance of a class

OOAD helps us to discover and describe these objects and classes. These techniques give us a starting place for moving from a problem statement to a solution.

1.1.1   Object-Oriented Analysis and Design

OOA explores a problem, not a solution

Object-oriented analysis (OOA) is the process of understanding what the problem is and what the requirements of a solution are. It is the initial stage in problem solving. During analysis you get an accurate perception of what **end users** expect the solution to be and do. The **requirements**

of a solution give you a description of *what* a solution must be and *what* a solution must do—without imposing *how* to design or implement that solution.

During OOA, you express the problem and the requirements of a solution in terms of relevant objects. These objects may represent real-world objects, software systems, or ideas. Using OOA, you describe these objects and their interactions among one another. Analysis work involves the discovery associated with understanding the problem. It does not involve thinking about a solution to the problem, and instead focuses on thinking about the problem itself.

The results of analysis act as input to the process of design. During **object-oriented design (OOD)**, you describe a solution to the problem, fulfilling the requirements you discovered during analysis. You express the solution in terms of software objects, and you note how those objects will **collaborate**. Objects collaborate when they send each other **messages**; that is, objects call on one another to perform operations. The interactions among objects are as important as the objects themselves and require careful planning. To solve the problem efficiently, the collaborations among objects should be meaningful and minimal.

During OOD, you typically create one or more **models** of a solution for the problem. Some of the models emphasize the interactions among objects; others show the relationships among the objects. Taken together, the models create a design that can be implemented in C++ or any other object-oriented language.

Specify what to do, not how to do it

OOA explores a problem in terms of its objects

OOD explores a solution to a problem

OOD explores a solution's objects and their collaborations

1.1.2   Aspects of an Object-Oriented Solution

Unless otherwise stated, a solution to a problem in this book is a computer program. A program comprises **modules** working together. A module is a self-contained unit of code and could be a single, stand-alone **function**, a class **method**, a class itself, a group of several functions or classes that work closely together, or other blocks of code. Exactly how a module is defined depends on the type and size of the application. Functions and methods implement **algorithms**, which are step-by-step recipes for performing a task within a finite period of time. One action that an algorithm often performs is operating on a collection of data.

When designing a solution, your challenge is to create a good set of modules. These modules must store, move, and alter data. They also use methods to communicate with one another. When constructing a solution, you must organize your data collection so that you can operate on the data easily in the manner that an algorithm requires. In fact, most of this book describes ways of organizing data.

Modules implement algorithms, which often manipulate data

Object-oriented programming languages allow us to build classes of objects. A class combines the **attributes**—or characteristics—of objects of a single type together with the objects' operations—or **behaviors**—into a single unit. The individual data items specified in a class are called **data members**. The operations specified in the class are referred to as methods or **member functions**. Attributes are typically data, and the behaviors, or methods, often operate on that data. In programming languages such as C++, Python, and Java, classes specify the attributes and operations for the objects.

Objects encapsulate attributes (data) and behaviors (operations)

Encapsulation is a technique that hides inner details. Whereas functions encapsulate behavior, objects encapsulate data as well as behavior. For example, a clock encapsulates the time—an attribute—along with certain operations, such as setting or displaying the time. You can request that a clock perform those operations but you cannot see how they are done (unless you have a mechanical clock with see-through sides!).

Encapsulation hides inner details

Classes can inherit properties and operations from other classes. For example, once you have defined a base class of clocks, you can design a subclass of alarm clocks that inherits the properties of a clock but adds operations that provide the functionality of an alarm. You can produce an alarm clock quickly, because the clock portion is done. Thus, **inheritance**—another

Inheritance supports reusing software

object-oriented concept—allows you to reuse classes you defined earlier for a related purpose by extending that implementation or making slight modifications.

Inheritance may make it impossible for the compiler to determine which operation you require in a particular situation. However, **polymorphism**—which literally means *many forms*—enables this determination to be made at execution time. That is, the outcome of a particular operation depends upon the object that performs the operation. For example, you can create a pointer to a clock object, `myClock`, in your program in such a way that it could reference either a clock object or an alarm clock. When `myClock` is asked to display the time, the compiler cannot determine whether it should use the clock implementation to display the time or the alarm clock implementation, since it does not know to which class of clocks the object referenced by `myClock` belongs. Polymorphism allows the compiler to simply note that the meaning of an operation is unknown until execution time.

Note: **Three principles of object-oriented programming**
1. Encapsulation: Objects combine data and operations.
2. Inheritance: Classes can inherit properties from other classes.
3. Polymorphism: Objects can determine appropriate operations at execution time.

1.2   Achieving a Better Solution

The last program you wrote most likely solved the given problem correctly. However, was it the best possible solution? If you spent little—if any—time doing analysis and design, the solution probably left something to be desired. If you were to code the same program again, you would doubtless produce a better solution than your first attempt. However, if you spent some extra time analyzing the problem and designing a solution, you would probably get your best solution.

Time devoted to analysis and design is time well spent

Suppose that you generated three correct but different solutions. Can you identify aspects of each solution that makes it better than the other solutions? What are these aspects? What should you focus on to create better solutions?

Creating a good set of modules for a moderate-sized problem is more art than science. It requires experience on the part of the programmer. A given problem likely has no "best" set of modules. Some sets of modules—and their interactions—might be better than others in light of certain measures. Moreover, for a sufficiently large problem, several different sets of modules could be considered "best," depending upon the measure used. The "better" designs, however, do adhere to certain principles, which we examine next.

1.2.1   Cohesion

A highly cohesive module performs one well-defined task

Each module should perform one well-defined task; that is, it should be highly **cohesive**. A highly cohesive module brings several immediate benefits to a design or solution.

First, the module, if well named, promotes self-documenting, easy-to-understand code. For example, a highly cohesive function called `sort` should do nothing but sort. What this function does is clear from its name: If this function also prints the sorted values, it is not cohesive.

Second, a highly cohesive module is easy to reuse in other software projects. If a solution for another problem is being developed, the highly cohesive `sort` function can be used without change. If this function also prints the sorted values, it is much less likely to be the right sorting routine for the job.

Third, a highly cohesive module is much easier to maintain. Because the highly cohesive sort function does nothing but sort, fixing a logical error is simpler. If this function prints the sorted values, too, the printing code will complicate the function's maintenance. A highly cohesive module has but one task that might need revision.

Fourth, a highly cohesive module is more **robust**; that is, it is less likely to be affected by change. The highly cohesive sort function will require change only if the system requires a different kind of sort. For example, you might need to sort data into descending, rather than ascending, order, or you might need a faster sort.

A robust module performs well under unusual conditions

Like many object-oriented principles, cohesion can be described in human terms. A person with low cohesion has "too many irons in the fire." Such people tend to get bogged down in everything that they need to get done, and nothing they do gets done well. They could become more cohesive by delegating some of their responsibilities to others.

 Note: A guiding principle of OOD is that each class should have a single, well-defined responsibility. The methods of a class should be highly cohesive and related directly to supporting the responsibility of the class. The responsibilities of a class are functionally equivalent to the tasks that the class needs to perform. If a class has too many responsibilities, it should be split into multiple classes, each with a single responsibility taken from the original class.

1.2.2   Coupling

Coupling is a measure of the dependence among modules. This dependence, for example, could involve sharing data structures or calling each other's methods. Ideally, the modules in a design should be independent of one another. However, some degree of coupling is necessary to get work done. That is, modules should be **loosely coupled**, and **highly coupled** modules should be avoided.

A loosely coupled module is independent

Loose coupling benefits a system in several ways. First, a module with loose coupling tends to create a system that is more adaptable to change. If class *A* depends on—that is, is highly coupled to—a class *B* and class *B* is changed, it is very likely that these changes will affect class *A* and break it.

Second, a module with loose coupling creates a system that is easier to understand. If class *A* depends on a class *B*, understanding how class *A* works requires an understanding of class *B*. Thus, class *A* is difficult to understand in isolation. A solution with a high degree of coupling can become nearly impossible to understand.

Third, a module with loose coupling increases the reusability of that module. If class *A* depends on a class *B*, reusing class *A* in another program is complicated by the need to include class *B* in that program as well. Reusing coupled modules requires reusing all of the modules together as a unit. Often this is not desirable, or possible.

Fourth, a module with loose coupling has increased cohesion. Moreover, highly cohesive modules tend to be loosely coupled. As the level of cohesion associated with a module goes down, that module does more unrelated work, as we saw in the previous section. This has the side effect of causing the module to be coupled with many other modules from other areas in the program.

Again, realize that some coupling is required; coupling cannot and should not be eliminated from designs and solutions. To get work done, objects must collaborate. But collaboration requires objects to depend on one another. Tasks that an object has delegated to other objects create coupling between these objects. This coupling is necessary, but it should be kept to a minimum. However, other factors may influence a design. Thus, some designs with more coupling are better than other designs with less coupling because of these other factors.

> **Note:** If, in the past, you have spent little or no time on analysis and design for your programs, you must change this habit! The end result of OOD should be a modular solution that is easy to translate into the constructs of a particular programming language. By spending adequate time with analysis and design, you will spend less time writing and debugging your program.

1.3   Specifications

When you design a modular solution to a problem, each module simply states what it does but not how it does it. No one module may "know" how any other module performs its task—it may know only what that task is. For example, if one part of a solution is to sort some data, one of the modules may be a sorting algorithm, as Figure 1-1 illustrates. The other modules know that the sorting module sorts, but they do not know how it sorts. In this way, the various components of a solution are kept isolated from one another.

Specify each module before implementing it

Using this idea, you can write the modules in relative isolation from one another, knowing what each one will do but not necessarily *how* each will eventually do it. It is essential that a module's specifications be written and understood.

FIGURE 1-1   The task sort is a module separate from the MyProgram module

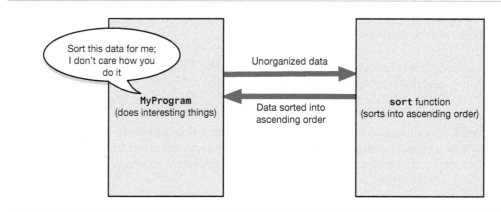

1.3.1   Operation Contracts

A module's contract specifies the module's purpose, assumptions, input, and output

An **operation contract** documents how a method can be used and what limitations it has. You should begin specifying this contract during analysis, finish the specification during design, and then document the contract in your code, particularly within the header files. In this way, programmers who use your code can understand what contract they need to honor for the method to generate correct results.

There is certain information you need to provide for each method. A method's **interface** will specify how to call the method and the number, order, and types of arguments it expects—as already discussed. You also need to specify what should be true before the method is called and what will be true after the method finishes execution.

During design, it is also important that you clearly specify not only the purpose of each module, but also the **data flow** among modules. For example, you should provide answers to these questions for each module:

Specify the data flow among modules

- What data is available to the module before its execution?
- What does the module assume?
- What actions have taken place after the module executes?
- What does the data look like after the module executes?

Thus, you should specify in detail the assumptions, input, and output for each module.

For example, if you as program designer needed to sort an array of integers, you might write the following specifications for a sort function:

The function will receive an array of *num* integers, where *num* > 0.
The function will return the array with the integers sorted.

You can view these specifications as the terms of a contract between your function and the module that calls it.

Specifications are the terms of a contract

This contract helps programmers understand what responsibilities the module will have to the other modules in the solution. Whoever writes the sort function must live up to this contract. After the sort function has been written and tested, the contract tells the rest of the program how to call the sort function properly, as well as the result of doing so.

Notice, however, that a module's contract does not commit the module to a particular way of performing its task. If another part of the program assumes anything about the algorithm, it does so at its own risk. Thus, for example, if at some later date you rewrite your function to use a different sorting algorithm, you should not need to change the rest of the program at all. As long as the new function honors the terms of the original contract, the rest of the program should be oblivious to the change.

An operation contract should not describe how a module will perform its task

This should not be news to you. Although you might not have explicitly used the term *contract* before, the concept should be familiar. You write a contract when you write a function's **precondition**, which is a statement of the conditions that must exist at the beginning of a function, as well as when you write its **postcondition**, which is a statement of the conditions at the end of a function. For example, the sort function that adheres to the previous contract could appear in pseudocode[1] as

Operation contracts should include precise preconditions and postconditions

```
// Sorts an array.
// Precondition: anArray is an array of num integers; num > 0.
// Postcondition: The integers in anArray are sorted.
sort(anArray, num)
```

First-draft specifications

These particular pre- and postconditions actually are deficient, as can be the case in a first-draft contract. For example, does *sorted* mean ascending order or descending order? How large can num be? While implementing this function, you might assume that *sorted* means ascending order and that num will not exceed 100. Imagine the difficulties that can arise when another person tries to use sort to sort an array of 500 integers into descending order. This user will not know your assumptions unless you documented them by revising the contract as follows:

Revised specifications

```
// Sorts an array into ascending order.
// Precondition: anArray is an array of num integers and 1 <= num <= MAX_ARRAY,
```

---

[1] Pseudocode in this book appears in blue.

```
// where MAX_ARRAY is a global constant that specifies the maximum size of anArray.
// Postcondition: anArray[0] <= anArray[1] <= ... <= anArray[num - 1];
// num is unchanged.
sort(anArray, num)
```

When you write a precondition, begin by describing the method or function's input arguments, mention any global named constants that it uses, and finally list any assumptions that it makes. When you write a postcondition, describe what changes the module has made. Note that in the case of a method or function that returns a value—which is technically a part of the postcondition—the value should be described.

Precise documentation is essential

Novice programmers tend to dismiss the importance of precise documentation, particularly when they are simultaneously designer, programmer, and user of a small program. If you design sort but do not write down the terms of the contract, will you remember them when you later implement the function? Will you remember how to use sort weeks after you have written it? To refresh your memory, would you rather examine your program code or read a simple set of pre- and postconditions? As the size of a program increases, good documentation becomes even more important, regardless of whether you are sole author or part of a team.

Note: An operation contract completely specifies a module's purpose, assumptions, input, and output.

Note: The program component that uses a module is the module's **client**. The **user** is a person who uses a program.

1.3.2   Unusual Conditions

You as a class designer need to make decisions about how to treat unusual conditions and include these decisions in your specifications. The documentation for methods and functions should reflect these decisions.

In general, you can address unusual situations in several ways. You can

- **Assume that the invalid situations will not occur.** A method could state as an assumption—that is, a precondition—restrictions to which a client must adhere. It is then up to the client to check that the precondition is satisfied before invoking the method. As long as the client obeys the restriction, the invalid situation will not occur. However, taking this approach is risky: Since the client can ignore the precondition, your method can fail, leaving the program in an unsafe condition. Recall that Section B.5.2 of Appendix B suggests that a function should check its precondition. The same is true for methods.
- **Ignore the invalid situations.** A method could simply do nothing when given invalid data. Doing absolutely nothing, however, leaves the client without knowledge of what happened.
- **Guess at the client's intention.** Like the previous option, this choice can cause problems for the client.
- **Return a value that signals a problem.** For example, a method can return a boolean value that indicates its success or failure.
- **Throw an exception.** Throwing an exception is often the preferred way for a C++ method to react to unusual events that occur during its execution. The method can simply report

a problem without deciding what to do about it. The exception enables each client to act as needed in its own particular situation. For simplicity right now, we will adopt the philosophy that methods should throw exceptions only in truly unusual circumstances, when no other reasonable solution exists. You can learn about exceptions in C++ Interlude 3.

 Security Note: All methods should enforce their preconditions.

 Note: A first draft of a module's specifications often overlooks or ignores situations that you really need to consider. You might intentionally make these omissions to simplify this first draft. Once you have written the major portions of the specifications, you can concentrate on the details that make the specifications complete.

1.3.3   Abstraction

Abstraction separates the purpose of a module from its implementation. Modularity breaks a solution into parts, or modules; abstraction specifies each module clearly *before* you implement it in a programming language. For example, what does the module assume, and what action does it take? What task is this module responsible for when called on? Such specifications clarify the design of your solution, because you can focus on its high-level functionality without the distraction of implementation details. In addition, they help you modify one part of a solution without significantly affecting the other parts. For example, you should be able to change the sorting algorithm in the previous example without affecting the rest of the solution.

Specifications do not indicate how to implement a module

As the problem-solving process proceeds, you gradually refine the modules until eventually you implement their actions by writing code—typically, classes and their methods. Separating the purpose of a module from its implementation is known as **functional** (or **procedural**) **abstraction**. Once a module is written, you can use it without knowing the particulars of its algorithm as long as you have a statement of its purpose and a description of its arguments. Assuming that the module is documented properly, you can use it knowing only its specifications. You do not need to look at its implementation.

Complete specifications enable you to use a module without knowing its implementation

Functional abstraction is essential to team projects. After all, in a team situation, you have to use modules written by others, frequently without knowledge of their algorithms. Can you actually use such a module without studying its code? In fact, you do this each time you use a C++ Standard Library function, such as sqrt in the C++ math library cmath. Because sqrt is precompiled, you do not have access to its source statements. Furthermore, it may be that sqrt was written in a language other than C++! There is so much about sqrt that you do not know; yet you can use it in your program without concern, as long as you know its specifications. If you pass sqrt a floating-point expression, it will return the floating-point square root of the value of that expression. You can use sqrt even though you do not know its implementation.

Consider now a collection of data and a set of operations on the data. The operations might include ones that add new data to the collection, remove data from the collection, or search for some data. **Data abstraction** focuses on what the operations do with the collection of data, instead of on how you implement them. The other modules of the solution "know" *what* operations they can perform, but they do not know *how* the data is stored or *how* the operations are performed.

Specify what a module does, not how to do it

For example, you have used an array, but have you ever stopped to think about what an array actually is? There are many pictures of arrays throughout this book. They might resemble the way a C++ array is implemented on a computer, and then again they might not. In either case, you can use an array without knowing what it "looks like"—that is, how it is implemented. Although different systems may implement arrays in different ways, the differences are transparent to the programmer.

For instance, regardless of how the array `years` is implemented, you can always store the value 1492 in location `index` of the array by using the statement

```
years[index] = 1492;
```

and later display the value by using the statement

```
cout << years[index] << endl;
```

Both functional and data abstraction ask you to think "what," not "how"

Thus, you can use an array without knowing the details of its implementation, just as you can use the function `sqrt` without knowing the details of its implementation. Let's explore this idea in more detail.

1.3.4   Information Hiding

As you have seen, abstraction tells you to write functional specifications for each module that describe its outside, or public, view. However, abstraction also helps you identify details that you should hide from public view—details that should not be in the specifications but rather should be private. The principle of **information hiding** tells you not only to hide such details within a module, but also to ensure that no other module can tamper with these hidden details.

All modules and ADTs should hide something

While writing a module's specifications, you must identify details that you can hide within the module. The principle of information hiding involves not only hiding these details, but also making them *inaccessible* from outside a module. One way to understand information hiding is to imagine walls around the various tasks a program performs. These walls prevent the tasks from becoming entangled. The wall around each task prevents the other tasks from "seeing" how that task is performed.

The isolation of the modules cannot be total, however. Although `MyProgram` does not know *how* the task `sort` is performed, it must know *what* the task `sort` is and how to initiate it. For example, suppose your program needs to operate on a sorted array of names. The program may, for instance, need to search the array for a given name or display the names in alphabetical order. The program thus needs a function `sort` that sorts an array of names. Although the rest of the program knows that `sort` can sort an array, it should not care how `sort` accomplishes its task.

Thus, imagine a tiny slit in the wall, as Figure 1-2 illustrates. The slit is not large enough to allow the outside world to see the function's inner workings, but items can pass through the slit into and out of the function. This slit is the **prototype**, **declaration**, or **header** of the function. The slit comprises the function or method's name, parameter list, and return type. For example, you can pass the array into the function `sort`, and the function can pass the sorted array out to you. What goes in and comes out is governed by the terms of the function's specifications, or contract: *If you use the function in this way, this is exactly what it will do for you.*

Suppose that a faster sort algorithm is developed. Since the function `sort` is isolated from the other modules in the program, the new algorithm can be implemented in the `sort` function without affecting those other modules. Thus, if `MyProgram` uses the task `sort`, and if the algorithm and implementation for performing the sort changes, `MyProgram` will not be affected. As Figure 1-3 illustrates, the wall prevents `MyProgram`'s algorithm from depending on `sort`'s algorithm.

FIGURE 1-2   Tasks communicate through a slit in the wall

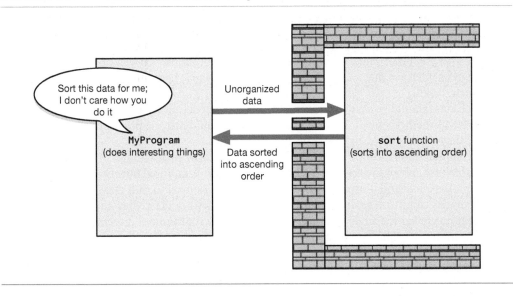

 Note: Information hiding limits the ways in which you need to deal with modules and data. As a user of a module, you do not worry about the details of its implementation. As an implementer of a module, you do not worry about its uses.

FIGURE 1-3   A revised implementation communicates through the same slit in the wall

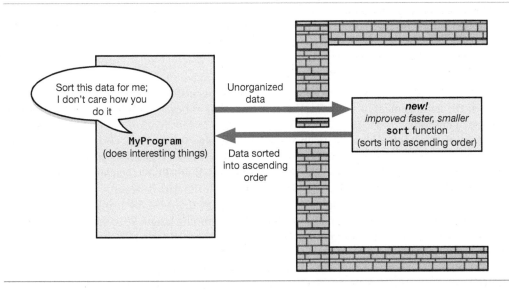

1.3.5   Minimal and Complete Interfaces

A module's interface is the only way to interact with that module

The interface for a class is made up of the publicly accessible methods and data. Typically, a class interface contains only methods, as you will see, because publicly accessible data fields generally cause problems. The interface for a class describes the only way for programmers to interact with that class. Thus, interfaces are where collaboration between objects takes place. It is through its interface that a class is coupled to other classes. Designing good class interfaces is an important skill.

Each class should be easy to understand. Thus, when designing a class, you should keep the number of its methods small. However, your classes should provide programmers the power to do what they need to do easily. These desires are at odds.

A **complete interface** for a class is one that will allow programmers to accomplish any reasonable task, given the responsibilities of that class. A **minimal interface** for a class is one that contains a method if and only if that method is essential to that class's responsibilities. Programmers can more easily learn how to interact with a class that has a minimal interface, as it has fewer methods to understand. Classes with minimal interfaces are also much easier to maintain. Changes to a class with an extensive interface could affect many of its methods.

You should evaluate classes in terms of how complete and minimal their interfaces are. It is important that interfaces be complete. Of somewhat less importance is having a minimal interface; sometimes a nonessential method is just too useful to omit.

The interface to a function or method is more accurately called its **signature**. The signature consists of the module's name; the number, order, and types of its arguments; and any qualifiers such as const that might apply. A signature looks very much like a function's or method's prototype, but does not include a return type. You use the signature to a function or method when you call it, sending it the correct number, order, and type of arguments.

1.4   Abstract Data Types

Often the solution to a problem requires operations on data. Such operations are broadly described in one of three ways:

Typical operations on data

- **Add** data to a data collection.
- **Remove** data from a data collection.
- **Ask questions** about the data in a data collection.

The details of the operations, of course, vary from application to application, but the overall theme is the management of data. Realize, however, that not every problem uses or requires all of these operations.

Most of this book is about data abstraction. To enable you to think abstractly about data, you should define an **abstract data type**, or **ADT**. An ADT is a collection of data *and* a set of operations on the data. You can use an ADT's operations, if you know their specifications, without knowing how the operations are implemented or how the data is stored.

An ADT is not a fancy name for a data structure

Ultimately, someone—perhaps you—will implement the ADT by using a **data structure**, which is a construct that you can define within a programming language to store a collection of data. For example, you might store the data in a C++ array of strings or in an array of other objects or in an array of arrays.

For example, suppose that you need to store a collection of names in a manner that allows you to search rapidly for a given name. *A collection of names providing for rapid searches* is the description of a simple ADT. The description of an ADT's operations must be rigorous enough to specify completely their effect on the data, yet must specify neither how to store the data nor how to carry out the operations. For example, the ADT operations should not specify whether to store the data in consecutive memory locations or in disjoint memory locations. You choose a particular data structure when you **implement** an ADT.

When a program must perform data operations that are not directly supported by the language, you should first design an ADT and carefully specify what the ADT operations are to do (the contract). Then—*and only then*—should you implement the operations with a data structure. If you implement the operations properly, the rest of the program will be able to assume that the operations perform as specified—that is, that the terms of the contract are honored. However, the program must not depend on a particular technique for supporting the operations.

Note: ADTs versus data structures
- An abstract data type is a specification for a group of values and the operations on those values.
- A data structure is an implementation of an ADT within a programming language.

To give you a better idea of the conceptual difference between an ADT and a data structure, consider a refrigerator's ice dispenser, as Figure 1-4 illustrates. It has water as input and produces as output either chilled water, crushed ice, or ice cubes, according to which one of three buttons you push. It also has an indicator that lights when no ice is available. The water is analogous to data; the operations are *chill*, *crush*, *cube*, and *isEmpty* (or *noIce*). At this level of design, the dispenser is analogous to an ADT; you are not concerned with how the dispenser will perform its operations, only that it performs them. If you want crushed ice, do you really care how the dispenser accomplishes its task, as long as it does so correctly? Thus, after you have specified the dispenser's operations, you can design many uses for crushed ice without knowing how the dispenser accomplishes its tasks and without the distraction of engineering details.

FIGURE 1-4   A dispenser of chilled water, crushed ice, and ice cubes

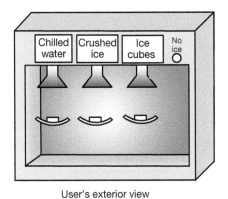

User's exterior view

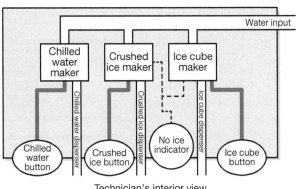

Technician's interior view

Specifications indicate what ADT operations do, but not how to implement them

Carefully specify an ADT's operations before you implement them

ADTs and data structures are not the same

Eventually, however, someone must build the dispenser. Exactly how will this machine produce crushed ice, for example? It could first make ice cubes and then either crush them between two steel rollers or smash them into small pieces by using hammers. Many other techniques are possible. The internal structure of the dispenser corresponds to the implementation of the ADT in a programming language, that is, to a data structure.

Although the owner of the dispenser does not care about its inner workings, he or she does want a design that is as efficient in its operation as possible. Similarly, the dispenser's manufacturer wants a design that is as easy and inexpensive to build as possible. You should have these same concerns when you choose a data structure to implement an ADT. Even if you do not implement the ADT yourself, but instead use an already implemented ADT, you—like the person who buys a refrigerator—should care about at least the ADT's efficiency.

Notice that steel walls surround the dispenser. The only breaks in the walls accommodate the input (water) to the machine and its output (chilled water, crushed ice, or ice cubes). Thus, the machine's interior mechanisms are not only hidden from the user, but also inaccessible. In addition, the mechanism of one operation is hidden from and inaccessible to another operation.

This modular design has benefits. For example, you can improve the operation *crush* by modifying its implementation without affecting the other modules. You could also add an operation to the machine without affecting the original three operations. Thus, both abstraction and information hiding are at work here.

A program should not depend on the details of an ADT's implementation

To summarize, data abstraction results in a wall of ADT operations between data structures and the program that accesses the data within these data structures, as Figure 1-5 illustrates. If you are on the program's side of the wall, you will see an interface that enables you to communicate with the data structure. That is, you ask the ADT operations to manipulate the data in the data structure, and they pass the results of these manipulations back to you.

This process is analogous to using a vending machine. You press buttons to communicate with the machine and obtain something in return. The machine's external design dictates how

FIGURE 1-5   A wall of ADT operations isolates a data structure from the program that uses it

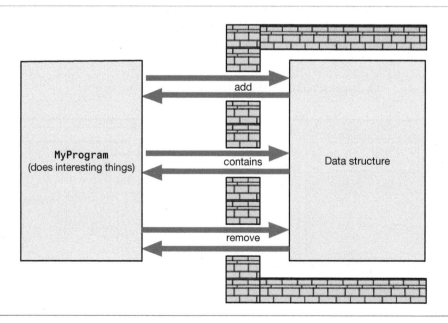

you use it, much as an ADT's specifications govern what its operations are and what they do. As long as you use a vending machine according to its design, you can ignore its inner technology. As long as you agree to access data only by using ADT operations, your program can be oblivious to any change in the data structures that implement the ADT.

Using an ADT is like using a vending machine

The following pages describe several abstract data types, focusing on the specifications of their operations, but not their implementations.

1.4.1 Designing an ADT

VideoNote
Designing an ADT

The design of an abstract data type should evolve naturally during the problem-solving process. As an example of how this process might occur, suppose that you want to display the dates of all the holidays in a given year. One way to do this is to examine a calendar. That is, you could consider each day in the year and ascertain whether that day is a holiday. The following pseudocode is a possible solution to this problem:

```
// Displays the dates of all holidays in a given year.
listHolidays(year)
{
    aDate = date of first day of year
    while (aDate is before the first day of year + 1)
    {
        if (aDate is a holiday)
            write(aDate, " is a holiday")
        aDate = date of next day
    }
}
```

What data is involved here? Clearly, this problem operates on dates, where a date consists of a month, day, and year. What operations will you need to solve the holiday problem? Your ADT must specify and restrict the legal operations on the dates, just as the fundamental data type int restricts you to operations such as addition and comparison. You can see from the previous pseudocode that you must

What data does a problem require?

- Find the date of the first day of a given year.
- Decide whether a date is before another date.
- Decide whether a date is a holiday.
- Get the date of the day that follows a given date.

What operations does a problem require?

Thus, you could specify the following operations for an ADT date in pseudocode that uses the notation of the **Unified Modeling Language (UML)**, as described in Appendix C:

```
// Returns the date of the first day of a given year.
+getFirstDay(year: integer): Date

// Returns true if this date is before the given date; otherwise returns false.
+isBefore(otherDate: Date): boolean

// Returns true if this date is a holiday; otherwise returns false.
+isHoliday(): boolean

// Returns the date of the day after this date.
+getNextDay(): Date
```

The listHolidays pseudocode now appears as follows:

```
// Displays the dates of all holidays in a given year.
listHolidays(year: integer): void
{
```

```
         aDate = getFirstDay(year)
         while (aDate.isBefore(getFirstDay(year + 1)))
         {
            if (aDate.isHoliday())
               write (aDate, " is a holiday ")
            aDate = aDate.getNextDay()
         }
      }
```

Thus, you can design an ADT by identifying data and choosing operations that are suitable to your problem. After specifying the operations, you use them to solve your problem independently of the implementation details of the ADT.

An appointment book. As another example of an ADT design, imagine that you want to create a computerized appointment book that spans a one-year period. Suppose that you make appointments only on the hour and half hour between 8 a.m. and 5 p.m. You want your system to store a brief notation about the nature of each appointment along with the date and time.

To solve this problem, you can define an ADT appointment book. The data items in this ADT are the appointments, where an appointment consists of a date, time, and purpose. What are the operations? Two obvious operations are

* Make an appointment for a certain date, time, and purpose. (You will want to be careful that you do not make an appointment at an already occupied time.)
* Cancel the appointment for a certain date and time.

In addition to these operations, it is likely that you will want to

* Ask whether you have an appointment at a given time.
* Get the purpose of your appointment at a given time.

Finally, ADTs typically have initialization and destruction operations that we assume but do not specify at this stage.

Thus, the ADT appointment book can have the following operations:

```
// Returns true if an appointment exists at the date and time specified,
// false otherwise.
+isAppointment(apptDate: Date, apptTime: Time): boolean

// Adds an appointment for the date, time, and purpose specified as long as
// it does not conflict with an existing appointment.
// Returns true if successful, false otherwise.
+makeAppointment(apptDate: Date, apptTime: Time, apptPurpose: string): boolean

// Removes the appointment at the date and time specified.
// Returns true if successful, false otherwise.
+cancelAppointment(apptDate: Date, apptTime: Time): boolean

// Gets the purpose of the appointment at the given date and time, if one exists.
// Otherwise returns an empty string.
+getAppointmentPurpose(apptDate: Date, apptTime: Time): string
```

You can use these ADT operations to design other operations on the appointments. For example, suppose that you want to change the date or time of a particular appointment within the existing appointment book apptBook. The following pseudocode indicates how to accomplish this task by using the previous ADT operations:

```
// Change the date or time of an appointment.
Get the following data from the user: oldDate, oldTime, newDate, newTime
```

```
// Get purpose of appointment.
oldPurpose = apptBook.getAppointmentPurpose(oldDate, oldTime)
if (oldPurpose is not the empty string)
{
    // See whether the new date/time is available.
    if (apptBook.isAppointment(newDate, newTime))
        // New date/time is booked
        write("You already have an appointment at ", newTime, " on ", newDate)
    else
    {
        // New date/time is available; cancel old appointment; make new one.
        apptBook.cancelAppointment(oldDate, oldTime)
        if (apptBook.makeAppointment(newDate, newTime, oldPurpose))
            write("Your appointment has been rescheduled to ",
                newTime, " on ", newDate)
    }
}
else // No previous appointment existed at the old date and time
    write("You do not have an appointment at ", oldTime, " on ", oldDate)
```

Again notice that you can design applications that use ADT operations without knowing how the ADT is implemented. The exercises at the end of this chapter provide examples of other tasks that you can perform with this ADT.

You can use an ADT without knowledge of its implementation

1.4.2   ADTs That Suggest Other ADTs

Both of the previous examples require you to represent a date; the appointment book example also requires you to represent the time. C++ has date-time objects specified in `ctime` that you can use to represent the date and the time. You can also design ADTs to represent these items in a more object-oriented way. It is not unusual for the design of one ADT to suggest other ADTs. In fact, you can use one ADT to implement another ADT.

This final example also describes an ADT that suggests other ADTs for its implementation. Suppose that you want to design a database of recipes. You could think of this database as an ADT. The recipes are the data items, and some typical operations on the recipes could include the following:

You can use an ADT to implement another ADT

```
// Adds a recipe to the database.
+addRecipe(aRecipe: Recipe): boolean

// Removes a recipe from the database.
+removeRecipe(aRecipe: Recipe): boolean

// Gets the named recipe from the database.
+getRecipe(name: string): Recipe
```

This level of the design does not indicate such details as where `addRecipe` will place a recipe into the database.

Now imagine that you want to design an operation that scales a recipe retrieved from the database: If the recipe is for *n* people, you want to revise it so that it will serve *m* people. Suppose that the recipe contains measurements such as 2½ cups, 1 tablespoon, and ¼ teaspoon. That is, the quantities are given as mixed numbers—integers and fractions—in units of cups, tablespoons, and teaspoons.

This problem suggests another ADT—measurement—with the following operations:

```
// Returns this measure.
+getMeasure(): Measurement
```

```
// Sets this measure to another one.
+setMeasure(m: Measurement)

// Returns this measure multiplied by a fractional scale factor, which has no units.
+scaleMeasure(scaleFactor: double): Measurement

// Returns this measure converted from its old units to new units.
+convertMeasure(oldUnits: MeasureUnit, newUnits: MeasureUnit): Measurement
```

Suppose that you want the ADT measurement to perform exact fractional arithmetic. Because our planned implementation language C++ does not have a data type for fractions, and floating-point arithmetic is not exact, another ADT called fraction is in order. Its operations could include addition, subtraction, multiplication, and division of fractions. For example, you could specify addition as

```
// Returns the sum, reduced to lowest terms, of this fraction and the given fraction.
+add(other: Fraction): Fraction
```

Moreover, you could include operations to convert a mixed number to a fraction and vice versa when feasible. When you finally implement the ADT measurement, you can use the ADT fraction. That is, you can use one ADT to implement another ADT.

1.5   The ADT Bag

Imagine a paper bag, a reusable cloth bag, or even a plastic bag. People use bags when they shop, pack a lunch, or eat potato chips. A bag contains things. We could consider the bag to be an abstract data type.

Let's specify and use the ADT **bag**. Knowing just its interface, you can use a bag in a program. You do not need to know how the entries in the bag are represented or how the bag operations are implemented. These specifics are hidden behind the bag's wall of abstraction, and your program will not depend on these specifics. As you will see, this important program characteristic is what data abstraction is all about.

What distinguishes a bag from other ADTs? A bag doesn't do much more than contain its items. It doesn't order them in a particular way, nor does it prevent duplicate items. While describing the behaviors for the ADT bag that we'll design in this chapter, let's keep in mind that we are specifying an abstraction inspired by an actual physical bag. For example, a paper bag holds things of various dimensions and shapes in no particular order and without regard for duplicates. Our abstract bag will hold unordered and possibly duplicate objects, but let's insist that these objects have the same or related data types.

Note: A bag is an object that contains a finite number of objects having the same data type and in no particular order. A bag can contain duplicate items.

A bag is a container

Note: A **container** is an object that holds a collection of other objects. A bag is an example of a container.

1.5.1   Identifying Behaviors

Since a bag contains a finite number of objects, reporting how many objects it contains could be one of a bag's behaviors:

- Get the number of items currently in the bag.

A related behavior detects if a bag is empty:

- See whether the bag is empty.

We should be able to add and remove objects:

- Add a given object to the bag.
- Remove an occurrence of a specific object from the bag, if possible.
- Remove all objects from the bag.

Note that the add operation does not indicate where in the bag an object should go. Remember that a bag does not order its contents. The remove operation looks for a particular item in the bag. If it finds it, it takes it out. If the bag contains several objects equal to the removed one, they remain in the bag. If the operation can't find the specific object in the bag, it can't remove it, and just says so. Finally, the second remove operation simply empties the bag of all objects.

What is in a particular bag? The answer to this question can be answered by the following operations:

- Count the number of times a certain object occurs in the bag.
- Test whether the bag contains a particular object.
- Look at all objects that are in the bag.

We have enough behaviors for now. At this point, we would have written all the behaviors on a piece of paper or, as Appendix C suggests, on the **class-responsibility-collaboration (CRC) card** pictured in Figure 1-6.

Since a bag is an abstract data type, we only describe its data and specify its operations. We do not indicate how to store the data or how to implement its operations. Don't think about arrays, for example. You first need to clearly know what the bag operations do: Focus on what the operations do, not on how they do them. That is, you need a detailed set of specifications before you can use a bag in a program. In fact, you should specify the bag operations before you even decide on a programming language.

FIGURE 1-6   A CRC card for a class Bag

Bag
Responsibilities
Get the number of items currently in the bag
See whether the bag is empty
Add a given object to the bag
Remove an occurrence of a specific object from the bag, if possible
Remove all objects from the bag
Count the number of times a certain object occurs in the bag
Test whether the bag contains a particular object
Look at all objects that are in the bag
Collaborations
The class of objects that the bag can contain

1.5.2   Specifying Data and Operations

Before we can implement a bag in C++, we need to describe its data and specify in detail the methods that correspond to the bag's behaviors. We'll name the methods, choose their parameters, decide their return types, and write comments to fully describe their effect on the bag's data. Our eventual goal, of course, is to write a C++ header file and comments for each method. However, we first will express the methods in pseudocode and then in UML notation.

The first behavior on our CRC card gives rise to a method that returns a count of the current number of entries in the bag. The corresponding method has no parameters and returns an integer. In pseudocode, we have the following specification, again using UML notation:

Use the UML to describe classes at various stages of their development

```
// Returns the current number of entries in this bag.
+getCurrentSize(): integer
```

We can test whether the bag is empty by using a boolean-valued method, again without parameters. Its specification in pseudocode is

```
// Returns true if this bag is empty.
+isEmpty(): boolean
```

We now want to add a given object to the bag. We can name the method add and give it a parameter to represent the new entry. We could write the following pseudocode:

```
// Adds a new entry to this bag.
add(newEntry)
```

We might be tempted to make add a void method, assuming that the method will always be successful. But if something unexpected happens, such as the bag is full, we cannot add a new entry to it. What should we do in this case?

Here are two options that we can take when add cannot complete its task:

- Do nothing. We cannot add another item, so we ignore it and leave the bag unchanged.
- Leave the bag unchanged, but signal the client that the addition is impossible.

The first option is easy, but it leaves the client wondering what happened. Of course, we could state as a precondition of add that the bag must not already be full. Then the client has the responsibility to avoid adding a new entry to a full bag. However, as Section 1.3.2 stated, trusting the client is not a safe programming practice.

The second option is the better one, and it is not too hard to specify or implement. How can we indicate to the client whether the addition was successful? We could throw an exception if the addition is impossible or otherwise unsuccessful, but we will leave this approach for later. Displaying an error message is not a good choice, as you should let the client dictate all written output. Since the addition is either successful or not, we can simply have the method add return a boolean value.

Thus, we can specify the method add more completely as

```
+add(newEntry: ItemType): boolean
```

where newEntry's data type is ItemType. In C++ Interlude 1, we will discuss the implementation details of using templates and typedef statements to give us flexibility in the type of data our ADT can hold.

Two behaviors involve removing entries from a bag: remove a particular entry and remove all entries. Suppose we name the methods and any parameters and begin to specify them in pseudocode as follows:

// Removes one occurrence of a particular entry from this bag, if possible.
`remove(anEntry)`

// Removes all entries from this bag.
`clear()`

What return types are these methods?

The `remove` method won't be able to remove a given entry if it isn't in the bag. We will have the method return a boolean value, much as `add` does, so it can indicate success or not. Thus, the UML specification for the method is

`+remove(anEntry: ItemType): boolean`

The method `clear` can be a void method: We just want to empty the bag, not get any of its contents. Thus, we refine its specification as follows:

`+clear(): void`

The remaining behaviors do not change the contents of the bag. One of these behaviors counts the number of times a given object occurs within the bag. Its specification in pseudocode is

// Counts the number of times a given entry appears in this bag.
`+getFrequencyOf(anEntry: ItemType): integer`

Another method tests whether the bag contains a given object. We specify it in pseudocode as follows:

// Tests whether this bag contains a given entry.
`+contains(anEntry: ItemType): boolean`

Finally, we want to look at the contents of the bag. Rather than providing a method that displays the entries in the bag, we will define one that places copies of these entries into a vector. The client is then free to display any or all of them in any way desired. Here is the specification for our last method:

// Gets all entries in this bag.
`+toVector( ): vector`

As we developed the previous specifications for the bag's methods, we represented them using UML notation. Figure 1-7 shows the result of doing so.

FIGURE 1-7   UML notation for the class Bag

```
┌─────────────────────────────────────────────────┐
│                      Bag                         │
├─────────────────────────────────────────────────┤
│                                                  │
├─────────────────────────────────────────────────┤
│ +getCurrentSize(): integer                       │
│ +isEmpty(): boolean                              │
│ +add(newEntry: ItemType): boolean                │
│ +remove(anEntry: ItemType): boolean              │
│ +clear(): void                                   │
│ +getFrequencyOf(anEntry: ItemType): integer      │
│ +contains(anEntry: ItemType): boolean            │
│ +toVector(): vector                              │
└─────────────────────────────────────────────────┘
```

Notice that the CRC card and UML diagram do not reflect all of the details, such as assumptions and unusual circumstances. However, after you have identified such conditions, you should specify how your methods will behave under each one. You should write down your decisions about how you want your methods to behave, as we have done in the following table. Later, you can incorporate these informal descriptions into the C++ comments that document your methods.

ABSTRACT DATA TYPE: BAG	
DATA	
• A finite number of objects, not necessarily distinct, in no particular order, and having the same data type. • The number of objects in this collection.	
OPERATIONS	
PSEUDOCODE	DESCRIPTION
`getCurrentSize()`	Task: Reports the current number of objects in this bag. Input: None. Output: The number of objects currently in the bag.
`isEmpty()`	Task: Sees whether this bag is empty. Input: None. Output: True or false according to whether the bag is empty.
`add(newEntry)`	Task: Adds a given object to this bag. Input: `newEntry` is an object. Output: True or false according to whether the addition succeeds.
`remove(anEntry)`	Task: Removes an occurrence of a particular object from this bag, if possible. Input: `anEntry` is an object. Output: True or false according to whether the removal succeeds.
`clear()`	Task: Removes all objects from this bag. Input: None. Output: None.
`getFrequencyOf(anEntry)`	Task: Counts the number of times an object occurs in this bag. Input: `anEntry` is an object. Output: The integer number of times `anEntry` occurs in the bag.
`contains(anEntry)`	Task: Tests whether this bag contains a particular object. Input: `anEntry` is an object. Output: True or false according to whether `anEntry` occurs in the bag.
`toVector()`	Task: Gets all objects in this bag. Input: None. Output: A vector containing copies of all entries currently in the bag.

Security Note: **Dealing with unusual conditions**

As mentioned earlier, you must make decisions about how to treat unusual conditions. The documentation for the ADT bag should reflect both these decisions and the details in the previous discussion. For example, our specification of the method `remove` implies that it will return false if a client tries to remove an entry from an empty bag. Although, we could have given the method the precondition that the bag not be empty, we should not assume that a client will satisfy the precondition before calling the method. When designing an ADT, do not assume that a client will use your methods correctly.

Note: A first draft of an ADT's specifications often overlooks or ignores situations that you really need to consider. You might intentionally make these omissions to simplify this first draft. Once you have written the major portions of the specifications, you can concentrate on the details that make the specifications complete.

Question 1 Write specifications using UML notation for a function that computes the sum of the first five positive integers in an array of n arbitrary integers.

1.5.3 An Interface Template for the ADT

As your specifications become more detailed, they increasingly should reflect your choice of programming language. Ultimately, you can write C++ headers for the bag's methods and organize them into a header file for the class that will implement the ADT.

The C++ header file in Listing 1-1 contains the methods for an ADT bag and detailed comments that describe their behaviors. If you are unfamiliar with C++ classes, templates, and virtual methods, C++ Interlude 1 provides a refresher on C++ classes and discusses C++ templates, virtual methods, and abstract base classes. By using templates and abstract base classes, we can take advantage of the object-oriented design concepts of encapsulation, polymorphism, and inheritance beginning with our first ADT.

Note: To emphasize the distinction between the design of an ADT and its implementation with a data structure, this textbook uses templates and abstract base classes in the description of our ADTs. We will call the header file containing the abstract base class a **client interface**.[2] A programmer should not need anything more than the client interface to use a class in your program, as it completely specifies the methods of the ADT.

---

[2] If you are familiar with Java, the interfaces for our ADTs correspond to Java interfaces. Both provide a public interface consisting of methods that the programmer of our ADT must implement.

As you examine the interface in Listing 1-1, notice the decisions that were made to address the unusual situations mentioned in the previous section. In particular, each of the methods add, remove, and contains returns a value. Note the commenting tags, which begin with @ and are described in Appendix I, that we use to specify the methods.

For now, the items in the bag will be objects of the same class. To accommodate entries of any single class type, the bag methods use a **generic type** ItemType for each entry. To give meaning to the identifier ItemType, we must write template<class ItemType> on the line before the class header. Once the actual data type is chosen by a client, the compiler will use that data type wherever ItemType appears.

The class BagInterface is a C++ abstract base class. An **abstract base class**, or simply an **abstract class**, in C++ contains at least one method that is declared as virtual and has no implementation. An abstract class cannot be instantiated; it can only be used as a base class. The subclass must then implement the methods specified but not defined in the abstract class.

LISTING 1-1 A file containing a C++ interface for bags

```cpp
1   /** @file BagInterface.h */
2   #ifndef BAG_INTERFACE_
3   #define BAG_INTERFACE_
4
5   #include <vector>
6
7   template<class ItemType>
8   class BagInterface
9   {
10  public:
11     /** Gets the current number of entries in this bag.
12      @return  The integer number of entries currently in the bag. */
13     virtual int getCurrentSize() const = 0;
14
15     /** Sees whether this bag is empty.
16      @return  True if the bag is empty, or false if not. */
17     virtual bool isEmpty() const = 0;
18
19     /** Adds a new entry to this bag.
20      @post  If successful, newEntry is stored in the bag and
21         the count of items in the bag has increased by 1.
22      @param newEntry  The object to be added as a new entry.
23      @return  True if addition was successful, or false if not. */
24     virtual bool add(const ItemType& newEntry) = 0;
25
26     /** Removes one occurrence of a given entry from this bag,
27         if possible.
28      @post  If successful, anEntry has been removed from the bag
29         and the count of items in the bag has decreased by 1.
30      @param anEntry  The entry to be removed.
31      @return  True if removal was successful, or false if not. */
32     virtual bool remove(const ItemType& anEntry) = 0;
33
34     /** Removes all entries from this bag.
35      @post  Bag contains no items, and the count of items is 0. */
36     virtual void clear() = 0;
```

```
37
38     /** Counts the number of times a given entry appears in this bag.
39      @param anEntry  The entry to be counted.
40      @return  The number of times anEntry appears in the bag. */
41     virtual int getFrequencyOf(const ItemType& anEntry) const = 0;
42
43     /** Tests whether this bag contains a given entry.
44      @param anEntry  The entry to locate.
45      @return  True if bag contains anEntry, or false otherwise. */
46     virtual bool contains(const ItemType& anEntry) const = 0;
47
48     /** Empties and then fills a given vector with all entries that
49         are in this bag.
50      @return  A vector containing copies of all the entries in the bag. */
51     virtual std::vector<ItemType> toVector() const = 0;
52
53     /** Destroys this bag and frees its assigned memory. (See C++ Interlude 2.) */
54     virtual ~BagInterface() { }
55  }; // end BagInterface
56  #endif
```

The specifications of these operations are the sole terms of the contract for the ADT bag: *If you request that these operations be performed, this is what will happen.* The specifications contain no mention of how to store the bag or how to perform the operations; they tell you only what you can do to the bag. It is of fundamental importance that the specification of an ADT *not* include implementation issues. This restriction on the specification of an ADT is what allows you to build a wall between an implementation of an ADT and the program that uses it—that is, the client. The behavior of the operations is the only thing on which a program should depend.

 Note: Although writing an interface before implementing a class is certainly not required, doing so enables you to document your specifications in a concise way. You then can use the code in the interface as an outline for the actual class. Having an interface also provides a data type for an ADT that is independent of a particular class definition. Chapters 3 and 4 will develop different implementations of a class of bags. Code written with respect to an interface allows you to more easily replace one implementation of a bag with another.

1.5.4   Using the ADT Bag

Imagine that we hire a programmer to implement the ADT bag in C++, given the interface and specifications that we have developed so far. If we assume that these specifications are clear enough for the programmer to complete the implementation, we can use the bag's operations in a program without knowing the details of the implementation. That is, we do not need to know how the programmer implemented the bag to be able to use it. We need to know only what the ADT bag does.

The following example demonstrates how we can use a bag and assumes that we have a C++ class, Bag, that implements the C++ abstract class BagInterface given in Listing 1-1.

Example. Suppose you invited three friends to your home to watch your favorite soccer team on television. To make the commercial breaks more interesting, you make up the following game. From a deck of cards, you remove the entire suit of clubs: the cards Ace, Two, Three, ..., Jack, Queen, and King of clubs. You randomly select six of these cards and place them into a bag. Your friends then guess which cards are in the bag. Each time they correctly guess a card, it is removed from the bag. When the bag is empty, the friend with the most cards wins. Listing 1-2 shows a simple program that plays this game.

LISTING 1-2 A program for a card guessing game

```cpp
1   #include <iostream> // For cout and cin
2   #include <string>   // For string objects
3   #include "Bag.h"     // For ADT bag
4
5   int main()
6   {
7      std::string clubs[] = { "Joker", "Ace", "Two", "Three", "Four",
8                              "Five", "Six", "Seven", "Eight", "Nine",
9                              "Ten", "Jack", "Queen", "King" };
10     // Create our bag to hold cards.
11     Bag<std::string> grabBag;
12
13     // Place six cards in the bag.
14     grabBag.add(clubs[1]);
15     grabBag.add(clubs[2]);
16     grabBag.add(clubs[4]);
17     grabBag.add(clubs[8]);
18     grabBag.add(clubs[10]);
19     grabBag.add(clubs[12]);
20
21     // Get friend's guess and check it.
22     int guess = 0;
23     while (!grabBag.isEmpty())
24     {
25        std::cout << "What is your guess? (1 for Ace to 13 for King):";
26        std::cin >> guess;
27
28        // Is card in the bag?
29        if (grabBag.contains(clubs[guess]))
30        {
31           // Good guess - remove card from the bag.
32           std::cout << "You get the card!\n";
33           grabBag.remove(clubs[guess]);
34        }
35        else
36        {
37           std::cout << "Sorry, card was not in the bag.\n";
38        } // end if
39     } // end while
40     std::cout << "No more cards in the bag. Game over!\n";
41     return 0;
42  }; // end main
```

Programming Tip: After you design a class, try writing some code that uses your class before you implement the class. You will not only see whether your design works for the problem at hand, but also test your understanding of your own design and check the comments that document your specifications. You might discover problems with either your class design or your specifications. If so change your design and specifications, and try using the class again.

Question 2   What is an abstract data type?

Question 3   What steps should you take when designing an ADT?

SUMMARY

1.   Object-oriented analysis (OOA) is used during the initial stage in problem solving to understand what the problem is and what the requirements of a solution are.

2.   During object-oriented design (OOD), you describe a solution to a problem whose requirements are discovered during OOA. You express the solution in terms of software objects.

3.   Encapsulation is a principle of object-oriented programming whereby you hide the inner details of functions, methods, and objects. Functions and methods encapsulate behavior, and objects—that is, instances of a class—encapsulate data as well as behavior.

4.   Inheritance is another concept related to object-oriented programming, allowing you to reuse already defined classes by extending their definitions or making slight modifications.

5.   Polymorphism is the third principle of object-oriented programming, whereby objects determine appropriate operations at execution time.

6.   Each module should be highly cohesive; that is, it should perform one well-defined task.

7.   Coupling is a measure of the dependence among modules. Modules should be loosely coupled. A function or method should be as independent as possible.

8.   UML is a modeling language used to express object-oriented designs. It provides a notation to specify the data and operations and uses diagrams to show relationships among classes.

9.   An operation contract documents how a module can be used and what limitations it has.

10.   A function or method should always include an initial comment that states its purpose, its precondition—that is, the conditions that must exist at the beginning of a module—and its postcondition—the conditions at the end of a module's execution.

11.   For problems that primarily involve data management, encapsulate data with operations on that data by designing classes. Practice abstraction—that is, focus on what a module does instead of how it does it.

12.   Data abstraction is a technique for controlling the interaction between a program and its data structures. It builds walls around a program's data structures, just as other aspects of modularity build walls around a program's algorithms. Such walls make programs easier to design, implement, read, and modify.

13. The specification of a set of data-management operations, together with the data values on which they operate, defines an abstract data type (ADT).

14. Only after you have fully defined an ADT should you think about how to implement it. The proper choice of a data structure to implement an ADT depends both on the details of the ADT operations and on the context in which you will use the operations.

EXERCISES

1. The price of an item you want to buy is given in dollars and cents. You pay for it in cash by giving the clerk *d* dollars and *c* cents. Write specifications for a function that computes the change, if any, that you should receive. Include a statement of purpose, the preconditions and postconditions, and a description of the arguments.

2. A date consists of a month, day, and year. Consider the class Date of such dates. Suppose that Date represents the month, day, and year as integers. For example, July 4, 1776, is month 7, day 4, and year 1776.
   a. Write specifications for a method within Date that advances any given date by one day. Include a statement of purpose, the preconditions and postconditions, a description of the arguments, and a description of any return value.
   b. Write a C++ implementation of this method. Design and specify any other method that you need. Include comments that will be helpful to someone who will maintain your implementation in the future.

3. Write a pseudocode function in terms of the ADT appointment book, described in Section 1.4.1, for each of the following tasks. Do you need to add operations to the ADT to perform these tasks?
   a. Change the purpose of the appointment at a given date and time.
   b. Display all the appointments for a given date.

4. Imagine that you have just left a store with a bag of groceries. You are concerned that the fragile items will not survive the trip home, so when you reach your car, you place those items into their own bag. If Bag is a class of bags, write C++ statements that remove all the items from storeBag and place them into one of two new bags, as follows: Place all occurrences of bread and eggs into fragileBag, and all other items into groceryBag. When you are done, storeBag should be empty. Assume that grocery items are represented by strings.

5. Suppose that a bag contains strings that represent various grocery items. Write a C++ function that removes and counts all occurrences of a given string from such a bag. Your function should return this number. Use comments in javadoc style to fully specify your function. Accommodate the possibility that the given bag is either empty or does not contain any occurrences of the given string.

6. The *union* of two bags is a new bag containing the combined contents of the original two bags. Design and specify a method union for the ADT bag that returns as a new bag the union of the bag receiving the call to the method and the bag that is the method's one argument. Include sufficient comments to fully specify the method.

   Note that the union of two bags might contain duplicate items. For example, if object x occurs five times in one bag and twice in another, the union of these bags contains x seven times. Specifically, suppose that bag1 and bag2 are bags; bag1 contains the strings a, b, and c; and bag2 contains the strings b, b, d, and e. The expression bag1.union(bag2) returns a bag containing the strings a, b, b, b, c, d, and e. Note that union does not affect the contents of bag1 and bag2.

7. The *intersection* of two bags is a new bag containing the entries that occur in both of the original two bags. Design and specify a method intersection for the ADT bag that returns as a new bag the intersection of the bag receiving the call to the method and the bag that is the method's one argument. Include sufficient comments to fully specify the method.

Note that the intersection of two bags might contain duplicate items. For example, if object x occurs five times in one bag and twice in another, the intersection of these bags contains x two times. Specifically, suppose that bag1 and bag2 are bags; bag1 contains the strings a, b, and c; and bag2 contains the strings b, b, d, and e. The expression bag1.intersection(bag2) returns a bag containing only the string b. Note that intersection does not affect the contents of bag1 and bag2.

8. The *difference* of two bags is a new bag containing the entries that would be left in one bag after removing those that also occur in the second. Design and specify a method difference for the ADT bag that returns as a new bag the difference of the bag receiving the call to the method and the bag that is the method's one argument. Include sufficient comments to fully specify the method.

Note that the difference of two bags might contain duplicate items. For example, if object x occurs five times in one bag and twice in another, the difference of these bags contains x three times. Specifically, suppose that bag1 and bag2 are bags; bag1 contains the strings a, b, and c; and bag2 contains the strings b, b, d, and e. The expression bag1.difference(bag2) returns a bag containing only the strings a and c. Note that difference does not affect the contents of bag1 and bag2.

9. Consider the ADT polynomial—in a single variable x—whose operations include the following:

```
degree() // Returns the degree of a polynomial.
coefficient(power) // Returns the coefficient of the x^power term.
changeCoefficient(newCoefficient, power) // Replaces the coefficient of
                                         // the x^power term with newCoefficient.
```

For this problem, consider only polynomials whose exponents are nonnegative integers. For example,

$$p = 4x^5 + 7x^3 - x^2 + 9$$

The following examples demonstrate the ADT operations on this polynomial.

p.degree() is 5 (the highest power of a term with a nonzero coefficient)
p.coefficient(3) is 7 (the coefficient of the x^3 term)
p.coefficient(4) is 0 (the coefficient of a missing term is implicitly 0)
p.changeCoefficient(-3, 7) changes the polynomial p to $-3x^7 + 4x^5 + 7x^3 - x^2 + 9$

Using these ADT operations, write statements to perform the following tasks:

a. Display the coefficient of the term that has the highest power.
b. Increase the coefficient of the x^3 term by 8.
c. Compute the sum of two polynomials.

PROGRAMMING PROBLEMS

1. Consider a program that will read employee data, sort the data by employee identification number, write out the sorted data, and compute various statistics about the data, such as the average age of an employee. Design a modular solution to this problem using UML notation. What classes and methods did you identify during the design of your solution? Write complete specifications, including preconditions and postconditions, for each module.

2. A *matrix* is a rectangular array of numerical values. You can add or multiply two matrices to form a third matrix. You can multiply a matrix by a scalar, and you can transpose a matrix. Design an ADT that represents a matrix that has these operations.

Specify each ADT operation by stating its purpose, by describing its parameters, and by writing a pseudocode version of its header. Then write a C++ interface for the methods of a matrix. Include javadoc-style comments in your code.

3. A *ring* is a collection of items that has a reference to a current item. An operation—let's call it advance—moves the reference to the next item in the collection. When the reference reaches the last item, the next advance operation moves the reference back to the first item. A ring also has operations to get the current item, add an item, and remove an item. The details of where an item is added and which item is removed are up to you.

   Design an ADT to represent a ring of objects. Specify each operation by stating its purpose, by describing its parameters, and by writing a pseudocode version of its header. Then write a C++ interface for a ring's methods. Include javadoc-style comments in your code.

4. A **set** is a special bag that does not allow duplicates. Specify each operation for a set of objects by stating its purpose, by describing its parameters, and by writing preconditions, postconditions, and a pseudocode version of its header. Then write a C++ interface for the set. Include javadoc-style comments in your code.

5. Imagine a pile of books on your desk. Each book is so large and heavy that you can remove only the top one from the pile. You cannot remove a book from under another one. Likewise, you can add another book to the pile only by placing it on the top of the pile. You cannot add a book beneath another one.

   If you represent books by their titles alone, design a class that you can use to track the books in the pile on your desk. Specify each operation by stating its purpose, by describing its parameters, and by writing a pseudocode version of its header. Then write a C++ interface for the pile's methods. Include javadoc-style comments in your code.

6. Exercises 6, 7, and 8 ask you to specify methods for the ADT bag that return the union, intersection, and difference of two bags. Define each of these methods independently of the bag's implementation by using only ADT bag operations.

7. (Gaming) Design an ADT for a one-person guessing game that chooses n random integers in the range from 1 to m and asks the user to guess them. The same integer might be chosen more than once. For example, the game might choose the following four integers that range from 1 to 10: 4, 6, 1, 6.

   The following interaction could occur between the user and the game, after the user has specified the integers m and n:
   Enter your guesses for the 4 integers in the range from 1 to 10 that have been selected:
   1 2 3 4
   2 of your guesses are correct. Guess again.
   Enter your guesses for the 4 integers in the range from 1 to 10 that have been selected:
   2 4 6 8
   2 of your guesses are correct. Guess again.
   1 4 6 6
   You are correct! Play again? **No**
   Good-bye!

8. (Gaming) A system of caves is a group of interconnected underground tunnels. Two, and only two, tunnels can intersect to form a cave. Design an ADT cave and an ADT cave system. An archeologist should be able to add a newly discovered cave to a cave system and to connect two caves together by a tunnel. Duplicate caves—based on GPS coordinates—are not permitted. Archeologists should also be able to list the caves in a given cave system.

9. (Finance) Financial accounts like checking accounts, credit card accounts, and loan accounts have some aspects in common. New transactions—credits and debits—can be posted to the account, and they can be canceled if they have not yet been reconciled. The account can be reconciled, provide its current balance, and display all transactions.
   a. Design the ADT transaction and the ADT financial account.
   b. Draw a UML class diagram that includes the classes Transaction, FinancialAccount, CreditCardAccount, and CheckingAccount.

10. (E-commerce) When shopping online, you select items and add them to a shopping cart. Duplicate items are permitted in a shopping cart, as you can purchase multiples of the same item. You also can remove an item from a shopping cart, if you change your mind about buying it. The shopping cart can show its current contents with their prices and the total cost of these items. Design the ADTs item and shopping cart.

C++ Classes

Contents

Prerequisites

Throughout this book we design abstract data types and implement them as data structures using C++. This C++ Interlude provides a refresher on C++ classes and then introduces additional C++ tools we can use to define our abstract data types in a flexible manner that maintains the wall between our design and the implementation.

    After reviewing classes, we will look at **class templates**. This C++ construct gives us the power to specify the data type of the items contained in a data structure in a very generic way. For example, if you had spent two weeks developing a great class to represent a bag of integers, wouldn't it be great if you could easily use the same code for a bag that holds strings? Class templates allow you to define classes that are independent of the type of data stored in the data structure. When a client is ready to instantiate an object of the class, the client can specify the type of data the object holds.

Header (.h), or **specification, files** in C++ provide a mechanism to partially separate the design of a class from the implementation in the **source**, or **implementation** (.cpp), **file**. The header file must also contain a description of both the data fields for the class and any private methods used by the class. A client does not need to know about the private methods or data fields to use the class in a program. To provide a public interface for an ADT, you can write an abstract base class, thereby separating design from implementation. An abstract base class allows the client to take full advantage of polymorphism when using our class.

To introduce these concepts, let's look at a simple problem that illustrates all three of the fundamental concepts of object-oriented programming: encapsulation, inheritance, and polymorphism.

C1.1 A Problem to Solve

VideoNote
C++ classes

Suppose that a friend who is creating a video game asked you to design and develop a group of classes to represent three types of boxes carried by the characters in the game. Each type of box can only hold one item. A character can put an item in the box or look at the item in the box. The three types of boxes are:

- **Plain box**—a plain old box that holds only one item.
- **Toy box**—a box that has color and holds only one item.
- **Magic box**—a box that holds only one item, but magically changes it to the first item that was ever stored in the box.

Let's begin by designing an ADT plain box. It is the simplest of the three boxes, and we may be able to use aspects of its implementation for the other two boxes. Since game characters can only place items in the box or look at them, the box needs only two public methods, setItem to place an item in the box and getItem to get the stored item. Here is the UML notation for those methods:

```
+setItem(theItem: ItemType)
+getItem(): ItemType
```

We can define ItemType as the type of item stored in the box by using a typedef statement. For example, to have the box hold a double, we can write

```
typedef double ItemType;
```

To have the box hold another type of data, we need only to replace the word double with the new data type. Listing C1-1 shows the declaration of our class PlainBox that would appear in a header file. To save space here, we show only basic comments that describe the class and omit the specifications, preconditions, and postconditions. We have used the object-oriented concept of encapsulation to group together data—the item stored in the box—with the methods that operate on that data: the two constructors, a method setItem to change the item's value, and a method getItem to return the item's value.

LISTING C1-1 The header file for the class PlainBox

```
1   /** @file PlainBox.h */
2
3   #ifndef PLAIN_BOX_
4   #define PLAIN_BOX_
```

```
5
6    // Set the type of data stored in the box
7    typedef double ItemType;
8    // Declaration for the class PlainBox
9    class PlainBox
10   {
11   private:
12      // Data field
13      ItemType item;
14
15   public:
16      // Default constructor
17      PlainBox();
18
19      // Parameterized constructor
20      PlainBox(const ItemType& theItem);
21
22      // Method to change the value of the data field
23      void setItem(const ItemType& theItem);
24
25      // Method to get the value of the data field
26      ItemType getItem() const;
27   }; // end PlainBox
28   #endif
```

Let's look in detail at this C++ class declaration.

C1.1.1 Private Data Fields

The data field item is declared in a private section of the class declaration. Every data field in every class presented in this textbook is in a private section. This restricts access to the data field to only the class in which it is defined. Typically, we provide methods—such as setItem and getItem—to access the data fields. In this way, the class controls how and whether other classes can access the data fields. Additionally, methods such as setItem can ensure that a client does not set a data field to an illegal value. This design principle should lead to programs that not only are easier to debug, but also have fewer logical errors from the beginning.

Clients and derived classes should not have direct access to the data fields of a class. If you, as class designer, believe that a derived class might need to access or modify the data fields of the base class, you should still make the data fields private but provide protected methods so that any derived classes can access or modify the data. More information on access modifiers, such as private and protected, is presented later in C++ Interlude 5.

As we build more complex data structures, we need to guarantee their integrity. This is simpler to do if we restrict access to the data fields to only our class. For example, suppose we have a class that stores items in an array and maintains a count of the number of items used in the array. Each time our class adds or removes an item from the array, the item count needs to be modified to reflect the change. If a client of our class had direct access to the array, the client could add and remove entries in the array and neglect to update the item counter. This counter would not accurately reflect the number of entries in the array, resulting in, for example, the loss of data or an abnormal termination of the program.

C1.1.2 Constructors and Destructors

Classes have two types of special methods, called constructors and destructors. A **constructor** allocates memory for new instances of a class and can initialize the object's data to specified values. A **destructor** destroys an instance of a class when the object's lifetime ends. A typical class has several constructors but only one destructor. For many classes, you can omit the destructor. In such cases, the compiler generates a destructor for you. For the classes in this C++ Interlude, the compiler-generated destructor is sufficient. C++ Interlude 2 discusses how and why you would write your own destructor.

In C++, a constructor has the same name as the class. Constructors have no return type—not even `void`—and cannot use `return` to return a value. A class can have more than one constructor, as is the case for the class `PlainBox`. One of the constructors, the **default constructor**, has no parameters. Typically, a default constructor initializes data fields to values that the class implementor chooses. Other constructors have parameters. These **parameterized constructors** initialize data fields to values chosen by the client but approved by the constructor. The compiler decides which constructor to call by matching the argument list supplied by the client with the parameters of the available constructors. A match occurs when the arguments and parameters correspond in number, data type, and order.

Note: If you do not define any constructors for a class, the compiler creates a default constructor—one without parameters. Once you define a constructor, the compiler does not create any of its own. Therefore, if you define a parameterized constructor but not a default constructor, your class will not have a default constructor.

When you declare an instance of the class, a constructor is invoked implicitly. For example, the statement

```
PlainBox myBox;
```

invokes the default constructor, which creates the object `myBox` and initializes the data field `item` to a value given in the constructor's definition. Notice that you do not include parentheses after `myBox` when invoking the default constructor. The statement

```
PlainBox myBox(specialValue);
```

invokes the parameterized constructor, which, as you will see, initializes the data field `item` to `specialValue`. Thus, `specialValue` is stored in the box.

C1.1.3 Methods

As discussed in Chapter 1, methods implement the algorithms that solve a problem. A method prototype conveys three important pieces of information to a client wishing to use our class: the method name, the number and types of its parameters, and the method's return type. The prototype describes the slit in the wall of abstraction. Prototypes for methods a client can use are in the public section of the class declaration.

An **accessor method** in a class accesses, or gets, the value of a data field. Its name often begins with the word *get*. Accessor methods do not change the data fields of an object. An important part of the `PlainBox` class declaration is the accessor method `getItem`, which is labeled with the keyword `const`:

```
ItemType getItem() const;
```

This keyword is a signal to both the compiler and other programmers that the method does not change the data fields of the object. Such a method is known as a **constant**, or `const`, **method**.

Another way to think of a const method is that the object is the same before and after calling it. Using const in a method declaration enables the compiler to flag any code within the method's definition that modifies the data fields, thereby protecting the programmer from an inadvertent mistake.

Programming Tip: Constant methods can access and use data fields, but cannot modify them. Thus, labeling all accessor methods with the const declaration is a good technique to protect the integrity of your data fields.

A **mutator method** in a class changes the value of a data field. Often, the name of a mutator method begins with the word *set*. The method setItem is an example of a mutator method. Mutator methods cannot be const methods. The same is true for constructors, because they must initialize the data fields of an object.

Passing parameters by constant reference. Passing an argument by reference to a method, especially when the argument is a complex object, saves time and memory, since the method can access or modify the object without copying it. The risk with this technique is that the method has access to data declared outside of its class; the method has "broken through the wall" and can modify an item owned by the client that invoked the method. To keep the efficiency of passing by reference and still protect the data of our client, we use the keyword const before the declaration of that parameter. We say that such a parameter is **passed by constant reference**. The method treats the parameter as a constant that cannot be modified. Using const with parameters passed by reference protects client objects and reduces the chance of side effects. Our method can still access and use an object passed by constant reference, but the compiler flags any modifications to the object as errors. Note that the method setItem and the parameterized constructor both have a parameter theItem that is passed by constant reference, as you can see from their declarations:

```
void setItem(const ItemType& theItem);

PlainBox(const ItemType& theItem);
```

Security Note: **Guidelines to protect the integrity of a class**
* Declare all data fields in the private section of the class declaration.
* Declare as a const method any method that does not change the object's data fields (accessor methods).
* Precede the declaration of any parameter passed by reference with const, unless you are certain it must be modified by the method, in which case the method should be either protected or private.

C1.1.4 Preventing Compiler Errors

You can declare C++ variables only once within each program block. A second declaration, or redefinition, of a variable in the same block results in a compiler error. For example, suppose you have the following loop:

```
for (int index = 0; index < count; index++)
{
   int index = count / 6; // index is redefined in loop - compiler error!
   total += index;
}  // end for
```

Redefining `index` inside the loop results in a compile-time error, since `index` was already defined in the `for` statement. The same restriction on redefinition applies to entire classes. Let's see how we could accidentally redefine our `PlainBox` class.

If we want to use a `PlainBox` object in our program, for instance in our `main` function, we must include `PlainBox.h` in the file containing the `main` function, `main.cpp`, so the compiler knows about the public interface for our class. We also need to include the header file for our `PlainBox` class in `PlainBox.cpp` so the compiler knows about the data fields and methods of the class when it compiles the class's implementation.

These requirements create a problem, since the compiler reads our `PlainBox` definition twice, even though the class needs to be defined only once. We don't know which file the compiler will try to compile first, so both files must include `PlainBox.h`. This duplication results in the class being redefined when the header file is read again. We need a way to prevent the compiler from reading the class definition a second time. The `#ifndef`, `#define`, and `#endif` **preprocessor directives** provide a solution.

You are already familiar with the `#include` directive, which includes the contents of another file in the current file. You use `#ifndef` to conditionally include a class definition. For example, the header file for `PlainBox` in Listing C1-1 contains

```
#ifndef PLAIN_BOX_
#define PLAIN_BOX_
```

as its first two lines. The directive `#ifndef` means "If `PLAIN_BOX_` is not defined, then ..." If the compiler had not defined the name `PLAIN_BOX_`, it would process the code that follows until it reached the `#endif` directive at the end of the file.

The `#define` directive defines the name `PLAIN_BOX_`. If another file includes the class definition of `PlainBox`, the name `PLAIN_BOX_` will already have been defined. That file's `#ifndef` directive will cause the preprocessor to skip any of the code that follows; that is, the code will be hidden from the compiler, and so the compiler will not see our class definition more than once.

In this textbook, all header files use these preprocessor directives to protect against including class definitions multiple times. Though you can use any names in the directives, the name to test in `#ifndef` and the name defined by `#define` must be the same. We write such names in uppercase and end them with an underscore character.

C1.2 Implementing a Solution

After we have designed our solution, the next step is to implement each of the methods we declared in the header file. Listing C1-2 shows the implementation, or source code, file for the class `PlainBox`. The method implementations are simple, but there are a few syntax items we should discuss.

LISTING C1-2 Implementation file for the `PlainBox` class

```
1   /** @file PlainBox.cpp */
2   #include "PlainBox.h"
3
4   PlainBox::PlainBox()
5   {
6   }  // end default constructor
7
8   PlainBox::PlainBox(const ItemType& theItem)
9   {
10      item = theItem;
11  }  // end constructor
```

```
12
13    void PlainBox::setItem(const ItemType& theItem)
14    {
15       item = theItem;
16    }  // end setItem
17
18    ItemType PlainBox::getItem() const
19    {
20       return item;
21    }  // end getItem
```

The header file `PlainBox.h` contains our class declaration. We must use the preprocessor directive `#include` to include the `PlainBox` class declaration so the compiler can validate our method headers and provide access to class data fields. The method headers must match those provided in the class declaration. Including the header file does not tell the compiler that the methods defined here are part of the `PlainBox` class. To do so, you must precede the constructor and method names with the class name followed by two colons—that is,

```
PlainBox::
```

The reason for this requirement is that C++ allows a source file to contain the implementations of methods for several classes and stand-alone functions. The **namespace indicator** `PlainBox::` is a prefix that indicates to the compiler that the method is a part of the `PlainBox` namespace. A C++ **namespace** is a syntax structure, such as a class, that allows you to group together declarations of data and methods under a common name, such as `PlainBox`. Once a method has been defined as part of a namespace, it has access to all the data and methods in that namespace. Thus, the constructor and methods in Listing C1-2 have access to `PlainBox`'s data fields and methods.

 Note: To better modularize our code, the implementation files in this book will contain only methods from a single class.

C1.2.1 Initializers

Although you can simply use an assignment statement to assign a value to a data member, as we have done here, it is preferable to use an **initializer**. Each initializer uses a functional notation that consists of a data member name followed by its initial value enclosed in parentheses—for example, `item(theItem)`. If you write more than one initializer, you separate them with commas. A colon precedes the first (or only) initializer. Thus, a better definition of `PlainBox`'s default constructor is

```
template <class ItemType>
PlainBox::PlainBox(const ItemType& theItem) : item(theItem)
{
}  // end default constructor
```

Often the implementation of a constructor consists only of initializers, so its body is empty, as is the case here. Note that you can use these initializers with constructors but not with other methods.

Programming Tip: When a class has several data members, the constructor initializes them in the order in which they appear in the class definition instead of the order in which the initializers appear in the constructor definition. You should use the same order in both cases to avoid confusion, even if the initialization order does not make a difference.

C1.3 Templates

At this point, our PlainBox class looks similar to many of the classes you probably have implemented in a previous C++ course. The class works well, as long as the characters in the game want to store a double value in a box. But what do we do if one character wants to store a double and a second has a string or MagicWand object to store? Since our current PlainBox class can store only a double, we would need to create new classes—PlainBoxForStrings and PlainBoxForWands, for example—to hold different object types. These classes would function in exactly the same way as the PlainBox class, so we could copy the code with only a few changes. For example, we have to change the typedef in each header file. For the PlainBoxForStrings class, the typedef would be

```
typedef string ItemType;
```

and for the PlainBoxForWands class, the typedef would be

```
typedef MagicWand ItemType;
```

We also would need to change the names of the constructors and the namespace indicators to reflect the new class names. If we had a more complex class, these changes would require a substantial amount of effort and would be an error-prone process. Later, if our friend changed the requirements for PlainBox, we would need to go through each of the PlainBox class variations and make the required changes.

The root of the problem in this scenario is that the programmer must know what types of objects will be stored in the box before the program is built. The programmer must then write a different class for each type of object that is to be stored. The *functionality* of each box is the same, but the *type of data* differs. **Templates** enable the programmer to separate the functionality of an implementation from the type of data used in the class. Listing C1-3 contains the header file for a template version of the class PlainBox.

LISTING C1-3 Template header file for the PlainBox class

```
 1   /** @file PlainBox.h */
 2
 3   #ifndef PLAIN_BOX_
 4   #define PLAIN_BOX_
 5
 6   template<class ItemType> // Indicates this is a template definition
 7
 8   // Declaration for the class PlainBox
 9   class   PlainBox
10   {
11   private:
12      // Data field
13      ItemType item;
```

```
14   public:
15      // Default constructor
16      PlainBox();
17
18      // Parameterized constructor
19      PlainBox(const ItemType& theItem);
20
21      // Mutator method that can change the value of the data field
22      void setItem(const ItemType& theItem);
23
24      // Accessor method to get the value of the data field
25      ItemType getItem() const;
26   }; // end PlainBox
27
28   #include "PlainBox.cpp" // Include the implementation file
29   #endif
```

As you can see from Listing C1-3, changing our earlier definition of the class PlainBox in Listing C1-1 to be a template requires only two changes to our header file. We replace the typedef statement with a statement to indicate that this class is a template:

```
template<class ItemType>
```

We also must include the implementation file just prior to the #endif directive by writing

```
#include "PlainBox.cpp"
```

This addition is necessary because the compiler does not compile a template class until it sees the client's instantiation of the template and knows the actual data type corresponding to the **generic type** ItemType.

 Programming Tip: In your development environment, do not add the implementation file—PlainBox.cpp, for example—to the project. It will automatically be included by the compiler when it is needed.

The implementation file PlainBox.cpp requires a few changes, but these changes all follow a pattern. Prior to *each* method's definition, you write the same template statement

```
template<class ItemType>
```

to indicate that the method is a template. The namespace indicator, PlainBox<ItemType>::, must also precede each method name to reflect that the method's definition is based on the generic type ItemType. These changes are shown in Listing C1-4.

LISTING C1-4 Implementation file for the PlainBox template class

```
1    /** @file PlainBox.cpp */
2    #include "PlainBox.h"
3
4    template<class ItemType>
5    PlainBox<ItemType>::PlainBox()
6    {
7    } // end default constructor
```

```
8
9    template<class ItemType>
10   PlainBox<ItemType>::PlainBox(const ItemType& theItem) : item(theItem)
11   {
12   }  // end constructor
13
14   template<class ItemType>
15   void PlainBox<ItemType>::setItem(const ItemType& theItem)
16   {
17      item = theItem;
18   }  // end setItem
19
20   template<class ItemType>
21   ItemType PlainBox<ItemType>::getItem() const
22   {
23      return item;
24   }  // end getItem
```

To instantiate an instance of PlainBox, you write the data type of the item to be placed in a box between angle brackets, as the following examples show:

```
PlainBox<double> numberBox;      // A box to hold a double
PlainBox<std::string> nameBox;   // A box to hold a string object
PlainBox<MagicWand> wandBox;     // A box to hold a MagicWand object
```

Methods of these box instances are invoked as before:

```
double health = 6.5;
numberBox.setItem(health);
std::string secretName = "Rumpelstiltskin";
nameBox.setItem(secretName);
MagicWand elfWand;
wandBox.setItem(elfWand);
```

 Note: By using templates, you can define a class that involves data of any type, even data types that are created after you designed and implemented your class.

C1.4 Inheritance

Now that the class PlainBox has been written, we will look at the other two boxes. The toy box is very similar to our plain box, but it has an additional characteristic, color, which we can represent with an enumerated type Color. We set the color of our toy box when it is created. The characters in the game can ask about the box's color but cannot change it. Here is the UML notation for those methods:

```
+getColor(): string
+setItem(ItemType theItem)
+getItem(): ItemType
```

The methods setItem and getItem behave exactly the same as the similarly named methods implemented for the PlainBox class. We can reuse the code in PlainBox by using inheritance. Inheritance allows us to reuse and extend work we have already completed and tested.

C1.4.1 Base Classes and Derived Classes

We can use PlainBox as a **base class**, or **superclass**, for our ToyBox class. You can think of a base class as a parent class. The ToyBox class is the **derived class**, or **subclass**, of the PlainBox class. To indicate that ToyBox is derived from PlainBox, we use the following syntax in the class header of ToyBox:

```
class ToyBox : public PlainBox<ItemType>
```

Any instance of the derived class is also considered to be an instance of the base class and can be used in a program anywhere that an instance of the base class can be used. Also, when the keyword public is used with the base class, any of the publicly defined methods or data fields in the base class can be used by clients of the derived class. In C++, a derived class inherits all the members of its base class, except the constructors and destructor. That is, a derived class has the data fields and methods of the base class in addition to the members it defines, though it can access only publicly defined members. A derived class can also revise any inherited public method.

As you can see in Listing C1-5, ToyBox defines only the constructors and new methods specific to it, if it has not needed to revise any methods of the base class. The methods setItem and getItem are inherited from the PlainBox class and can be used in our ToyBox class.

LISTING C1-5 Template header file for the class ToyBox

```
1    /** @file ToyBox.h */
2
3    #ifndef TOY_BOX_
4    #define TOY_BOX_
5    #include "PlainBox.h"
6
7    enum Color {BLACK, RED, BLUE, GREEN, YELLOW, WHITE};
8
9    template<class ItemType>
10   class ToyBox : public PlainBox<ItemType>
11   {
12   private:
13      Color boxColor;
14
15   public:
16      ToyBox();
17      ToyBox(const Color& theColor);
18      ToyBox(const ItemType& theItem, const Color& theColor);
19      Color getColor() const;
20   }; // end ToyBox
21   #include "ToyBox.cpp"
22   #endif
```

An instance of the class ToyBox has two data fields—item, which is inherited, and boxColor, which is new. Because an instance of a derived class can invoke any public method in the base class, an instance of ToyBox has all the methods that PlainBox defines, as well as new constructors; a new, compiler-generated destructor; and a new method getColor. Although an instance of a derived class contains copies of inherited data fields, the code for inherited methods is not copied.

A derived class cannot access the private members of the base class directly, even though they are inherited. *Inheritance does not imply access.* After all, you can inherit a locked vault but be unable to open it. In the current example, the data field item of PlainBox is private, so you can reference it only within the definition of the class PlainBox and not within the definition of ToyBox. However, the class ToyBox can use PlainBox's public methods setItem and getItem to set or obtain the value of item indirectly. ToyBox can also use an initializer to invoke PlainBox's constructor, as its third constructor in Listing C1-6 does.

LISTING C1-6 Implementation file for the class ToyBox

```cpp
1   /** @file ToyBox.cpp */
2
3   #include "ToyBox.h"
4
5   template<class ItemType>
6   ToyBox<ItemType>::ToyBox() : boxColor(BLACK)
7   {
8   }  // end default constructor
9
10  template<class ItemType>
11  ToyBox<ItemType>::ToyBox(const Color& theColor) : boxColor(theColor)
12  {
13  }  // end constructor
14
15  template<class ItemType>
16  ToyBox<ItemType>::ToyBox(const ItemType& theItem, const Color& theColor)
17                          : PlainBox<ItemType>(theItem), boxColor(theColor)
18  {
19  }  // end constructor
20
21  template<class ItemType>
22  Color ToyBox<ItemType>::getColor() const
23  {
24      return boxColor;
25  }  // end getColor
```

Although inheritance enables you to reuse software components when you define a new class, constructors are not inherited from the base class. Instead, the compiler places code to implicitly call the base-class default constructor as the first action of every constructor in the derived class. This ensures that all base-class data fields are properly initialized before any of the code in the derived class executes. Therefore, our ToyBox class does not inherit the constructors from PlainBox, but its constructors call the PlainBox default constructor as their first action. If we need more control over setting base-class data fields, the derived-class constructor can call the appropriate base-class constructor by placing it first in the initializer list, as shown in the third ToyBox constructor. The compiler then inserts code to call the base-class parameterized constructor instead of the base-class default constructor as the first action of the derived class's constructor.

A client of our ToyBox class can create and use a ToyBox object in much the same way that we did for PlainBox:

```cpp
std::string favoriteToy = "Jack-in-the-Box";
ToyBox<string> myToyCase(favoriteToy, RED); // A red toy box
std::string oldToy = myToyCase.getItem();   // oldToy is a Jack-in-the-Box
favoriteToy = "Spinning Top";
myToyCase.setItem(favoriteToy);                   // myToyCase now holds a Spinning Top
```

C1.4.2 Overriding Base-Class Methods

You can add as many new data fields and methods to a derived class as you like. Although you cannot revise a base class's private data fields and should not reuse their names, you can redefine inherited methods; this is called overriding a base-class method. A method in a derived class **overrides**, or redefines, a method in the base class if the two methods have the same name and parameter declarations—that is, if they have the same signatures.

To see an example of when we may need to redefine a base-class method, let's consider the implementation of the class MagicBox. This box magically changes any item placed inside to a copy of the first item it ever held. A simple way to do this is to store only the first item. Future calls to setItem will do nothing. Therefore, every call to getItem returns the first item stored in the box.

As with the toy box, we can derive our class from the PlainBox class, but we also need to define a data field to indicate if an initial item has been stored in our box. We can use a boolean field, firstItemStored, which is set to true once the first item has been stored in the box. We can then check this flag to see what setItem should do. If firstItemStored is false, we know that the argument passed to setItem is the first item we are asked to store. If firstItemStored is true, we know this is not the first item, and we simply do nothing.

Here is the UML notation for our MagicBox methods:

```
+setItem(ItemType theItem)
+getItem(): ItemType
```

These methods are like those in the class PlainBox, but we need a different implementation of setItem to meet the special requirements of this box. Therefore, we need to override the Plain-Box implementation of setItem. Listing C1-7 gives the header file for our class MagicBox. It has the private data field firstItemStored, a default constructor, a parameterized constructor, and the special version of setItem that we need.

LISTING C1-7 Header file for the class MagicBox

```cpp
1   /** @file MagicBox.h */
2
3   #ifndef MAGIC_BOX_
4   #define MAGIC_BOX_
5   #include "PlainBox.h"
6
7   template<class ItemType>
8   class MagicBox: public PlainBox<ItemType>
9   {
10  private:
11     bool firstItemStored;
12
13  public:
14     MagicBox();
15     MagicBox(const ItemType& theItem);
16     void setItem(const ItemType& theItem);
17  }; // end MagicBox
18  #include "MagicBox.cpp"
19  #endif
```

The implementation of the default constructor must call the base-class constructor and then initialize the data field firstItemStored to false to indicate that the first item has not been stored yet. The method setItem must check this data field and, if no item has been stored, call the base-class method setItem to store the parameter in the data field item. You can see these implementations in Listing C1-8.

LISTING C1-8 Implementation file for the class MagicBox

```
1   /** @file MagicBox.cpp */
2
3   #include "MagicBox.h"
4   template<class ItemType>
5   MagicBox<ItemType>::MagicBox() : firstItemStored(false)
6   {
7      // PlainBox constructor is called implicitly.
8      // Box has no magic initially
9   } // end default constructor
10
11  template<class ItemType>
12  MagicBox<ItemType>::MagicBox(const ItemType& theItem) : firstItemStored(false)
13  {
14     // Box has no magic initially
15     setItem(theItem); // Calls MagicBox version of setItem
16     // Box has magic now
17  } // end constructor
18
19  template<class ItemType>
20  void MagicBox<ItemType>::setItem(const ItemType& theItem)
21  {
22     if (!firstItemStored)
23     {
24        PlainBox<ItemType>::setItem(theItem);
25        firstItemStored = true; // Box has magic now
26     } // end if
27  } // end setItem
```

To simplify the parameterized constructor, we can call the setItem method to set the first item stored in the box. However, the MagicBox class has two setItem methods available, its own and the base-class version. As discussed earlier, to use the base-class version of the method, we would precede the method name with the base-class namespace indicator. To use this class's setItem method, we can simply invoke the method as shown in the parameterized constructor. Without a namespace indicator in front of the method name, the compiler assumes that the programmer is referring to the current class and inserts code to call that version of the method.

Question 1 Revise the parameterized constructor to call the base-class's constructor instead of MagicBox's constructor.

C1.5 Virtual Methods and Abstract Classes

When we designed the interface for our ADT bag in Chapter 1, we created an abstract class that describes each of the public methods. Recall that an abstract class in C++ contains at least one method declared as virtual that has no implementation. An abstract class can only serve as a base class; it cannot be instantiated. The derived class must define the methods specified but not already implemented by the abstract class.

C1.5.1 Virtual Methods

Using the keyword `virtual` in front of the prototype, or header, of the method tells the C++ compiler that the code this method executes is determined at runtime, not when the program is compiled. A method declared this way is referred to as a **virtual method**. Why should we declare a method as virtual?

The rules of inheritance allow us to use a derived class anywhere that its base class is used. For example, we could declare a variable that is a plain box:

```
PlainBox<std::string> cardBox;
```

Then we could create a `MagicBox` object and assign it to the variable `cardBox`:

```
cardBox = MagicBox<std::string>("Queen of Hearts");
```

Later, the player might store a different string in the box, and so we execute

```
cardBox.setItem("Jack of Spades");
```

Because the compiler considers the object `cardBox` to be of type `PlainBox<string>`, the `PlainBox` version of the method `setItem` is used in the previous statement. The `PlainBox` implementation of `setItem` stores the value of its parameter in `item`. Thus, a problem arises when our client calls the method `getItem`:

```
std::string myFirstCard = cardBox.getItem();
```

The method `getItem` returns the string `"Jack of Spades"` instead of `"Queen of Hearts"`. This is not the behavior the client desires, because `cardBox` was assigned an instance of `MagicBox`.

If we declare `PlainBox`'s method `setItem` to be virtual in the `PlainBox` header file by writing

```
virtual void setItem(const ItemType& theItem);
```

the version of `setItem` invoked during execution is determined by the specific type of object stored in `cardBox`. In our example, the `MagicBox` version of `setItem` would be called, since that is the type of object most recently stored in `cardBox`. Having this decision delayed until the program executes is an example of polymorphism and is a key benefit of object-oriented programming.

To fully implement our box example as a demonstration of polymorphic code, and to thoroughly discuss virtual methods and abstract classes, we need to use pointers. Pointers are introduced in C++ Interlude 2, and so we will delay further discussion and the completion of this example until then.

C1.5.2 Abstract Classes

The previous example used a virtual method so that a choice could be made during program execution between two implementations of the `setItem` method. We can use this same idea to assist with our goal of designing each ADT as a public interface that describes its functionality and is implementation independent. Declaring our ADT methods as virtual allows an application using our class to take advantage of polymorphism when the ADT's methods are invoked.

One significant difference between such an ADT and the previous example that uses the `PlainBox` class is that we do not want to provide an implementation of the ADT methods. Instead, we want to force the classes derived from the ADT to provide the implementations. Yet if we do not provide an implementation of the ADT, the compiler or linker will issue an error message when we try to build a program using our class.

We can avoid this error by writing our methods as **pure virtual methods**. A pure virtual method is a virtual method that has no implementation. We can now say that an abstract class is one that has at least one pure virtual method. To tell the compiler that a virtual method is a pure virtual method, you write = 0 before the semicolon at the end of the method prototype, as in the following example:

```
virtual void setItem(const ItemType& theItem) = 0;
```

Listing C1-9 defines the template class BoxInterface that provides a public interface for the box classes described earlier in this interlude. BoxInterface is an abstract class, because it contains at least one pure virtual method. Remember that abstract classes cannot be directly instantiated.

LISTING C1-9 An abstract class that is an interface for the ADT box

```
1   /** @file BoxInterface.h */
2
3   #ifndef BOX_INTERFACE_
4   #define BOX_INTERFACE_
5
6   template <class ItemType>
7   class BoxInterface
8   {
9   public:
10     virtual void setItem(const ItemType& theItem) = 0;
11     virtual ItemType getItem() const = 0;
12     virtual ~BoxInterface() {} // C++ Interlude 2 explains virtual destructors
13   }; // end BoxInterface
14   #endif
```

We can indicate that our class PlainBox is derived from BoxInterface by changing its class header to

```
class PlainBox : public BoxInterface<ItemType>
```

In the future when we design the public interface for an ADT, we will express that interface as an abstract class. When we introduce pointers in C++ Interlude 2, we will explore the importance and use of abstract classes in depth. Until then, we will use only abstract classes as a design tool for our ADTs.

PROGRAMMING PROBLEMS

1. Define the classes Cave and CaveSystem that Programming Problem 8 in Chapter 1 asks you to design.
2. Define the classes Transaction and FinancialAccount that Programming Problem 9a in Chapter 1 asks you to design.
3. Define the classes CheckingAccount and SavingsAccount as subclasses of the class FinancialAccount, as defined in the previous programming problem.
4. Define the class Item that Programming Problem 10 in Chapter 1 asks you to design. Then define the classes Clothing and CellPhone as subclasses of Item.

Chapter

2

Recursion: The Mirrors

Contents

Prerequisites

The goal of this chapter is to ensure that you have a basic understanding of recursion, which is one of the most powerful techniques available to the computer scientist. This chapter assumes that you have had little or no previous introduction to recursion. If, however, you have already studied recursion, you can review this chapter as necessary.

By presenting several relatively simple problems, the chapter demonstrates the thought processes that lead to recursive solutions. These problems are diverse and include examples of counting, searching, and organizing data. In addition to presenting recursion from a conceptual viewpoint, this chapter discusses techniques that will help you understand the mechanics of recursion. These techniques are particularly useful for tracing and debugging recursive functions.

Some recursive solutions are far more elegant and concise than the best of their nonrecursive counterparts. For example, the classic Towers of Hanoi problem appears to be quite difficult, yet it has an extremely simple recursive solution. On the other hand, some recursive solutions are terribly inefficient, as you will see, and should not be used.

Chapter 5 continues the formal discussion of recursion by examining more difficult problems. Recursion will play a major role in many of the solutions that appear throughout the remainder of this book.

2.1   Recursive Solutions

Recursion breaks a problem into smaller identical problems

Recursion is an extremely powerful problem-solving technique. Problems that at first appear to be quite difficult often have simple recursive solutions. Like other problem-solving techniques, recursion breaks a problem into several smaller problems. What is striking about recursion is that these smaller problems are of *exactly the same type* as the original problem—mirror images, so to speak.

Did you ever hold a mirror in front of another mirror so that the two mirrors face each other? You will see many images of yourself, each behind and slightly smaller than the other. Recursion is like these mirror images. That is, a recursive solution solves a problem by solving a smaller instance of the same problem! It then solves this new problem by solving an even smaller instance of the same problem. Eventually, the new problem will be so small that its solution will be either obvious or known. This solution will lead to the solution of the original problem.

For example, suppose that you could solve problem P_1 if you had the solution to problem P_2, which is a smaller instance of P_1. Suppose further that you could solve problem P_2 if you had the solution to problem P_3, which is a smaller instance of P_2. If you knew the solution to P_3 because it was small enough to be trivial, you would be able to solve P_2. You could then use the solution to P_2 to solve the original problem P_1.

Some recursive solutions are inefficient and impractical

Recursion can seem like magic, especially at first, but as you will see, it is a very real and important problem-solving approach that is an alternative to **iteration**. An iterative solution involves loops. You should know at the outset that not all recursive solutions are better than iterative solutions. In fact, some recursive solutions are impractical because they are so inefficient. Recursion, however, can provide elegantly simple solutions to problems of great complexity.

Complex problems can have simple recursive solutions

As an illustration of the elements in a recursive solution, consider the problem of looking up a word in a dictionary. Suppose you wanted to look up the word "vademecum." Imagine starting at the beginning of the dictionary and looking at every word in order until you found "vademecum." That is precisely what a **sequential search** does, and for obvious reasons, you want a faster way to perform the search.

One such approach is the **binary search**, which in spirit is similar to the way in which you actually use a printed dictionary. You open the dictionary—maybe to a point near its middle—and by glancing at the page, determine which "half" of the dictionary contains the desired word. The following pseudocode is a first attempt to formalize this process:

```
// Search a dictionary for a word by using a recursive binary search
if (the dictionary contains only one page)
    Scan the page for the word
else
{
    Open the dictionary to a point near the middle
    Determine which half of the dictionary contains the word
    if (the word is in the first half of the dictionary)
        Search the first half of the dictionary for the word
    else
        Search the second half of the dictionary for the word
}
```

A binary search of a dictionary

Parts of this solution are intentionally vague: How do you scan a single page? How do you find the middle of the dictionary? Once the middle is found, how do you determine which half contains the word? The answers to these questions are not difficult, but they would only obscure the solution strategy right now.

The previous search strategy reduces the problem of searching the dictionary for a word to a problem of searching half of the dictionary for the word, as Figure 2-1 illustrates. Notice two important points. First, once you have divided the dictionary in half, you already know how to search the appropriate half: You can use exactly the same strategy that you employed to search the original dictionary. Second, note that there is a special case that is different from all the other cases: After you have divided the dictionary so many times that you are left with only a single page, the halving ceases. At this point, the problem is sufficiently small that you can solve it directly by scanning the single page that remains for the word. This special case is called the **base case** (or **basis** or **degenerate case**).

A base case is a special case whose solution you know

FIGURE 2-1   A recursive solution

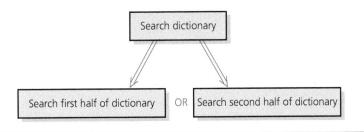

This strategy is called **divide and conquer**. You solve the dictionary search problem by first *dividing* the dictionary into two halves and then *conquering* the appropriate half. You solve the smaller problem by using the same divide-and-conquer strategy. The dividing continues until you reach the base case. As you will see, this strategy is inherent in many recursive solutions.

A binary search uses a divide-and-conquer strategy

To further explore the nature of the solution to the dictionary problem, consider a slightly more rigorous formulation.

```
search(aDictionary: Dictionary, word: string)
{
    if (aDictionary is one page in size)
        Scan the page for word
    else
    {
```

> *Open* aDictionary *to a point near the middle*
> *Determine which half of* aDictionary *contains* word
> if (word *is in the first half of* aDictionary)
>   search(*first half of* aDictionary, word)
> else
>   search(*second half of* aDictionary, word)
> }
> }

Writing the solution as a function allows several important observations:

A recursive function calls itself

1. One of the actions of the function is to call itself; that is, the function search calls the function search. This action is what makes the solution recursive. The solution strategy is to split aDictionary in half, determine which half contains word, and apply the same strategy to the appropriate half.

Each recursive call solves an identical, but smaller, problem

2. Each call to the function search made from within the function search passes a dictionary that is one-half the size of the previous dictionary. That is, at each successive call to search(aDictionary, word), the size of aDictionary is cut in half. The function solves the search problem by solving another search problem that is identical in nature but smaller in size.

A test for the base case enables the recursive calls to stop

3. There is one search problem that you handle differently from all of the others. When aDictionary contains only a single page, you use another approach: You scan the page directly. Searching a one-page dictionary is the base case of the search problem. When you reach the base case, the recursive calls stop and you solve the problem directly.

Eventually, one of the smaller problems must be the base case

4. The manner in which the size of the problem diminishes ensures that you will eventually reach the base case.

These facts describe the general form of a recursive solution. Though not all recursive solutions fit these criteria as nicely as this solution does, the similarities are far greater than the differences. As you attempt to construct a new recursive solution, you should keep in mind the following four questions.

>
> **Note:** **Four questions for constructing recursive solutions**
> 1. How can you define the problem in terms of a smaller problem of the same type?
> 2. How does each recursive call diminish the size of the problem?
> 3. What instance of the problem can serve as the base case?
> 4. As the problem size diminishes, will you reach this base case?

Now consider two relatively simple problems: computing the factorial of a number and writing a string backward. Their recursive solutions further illustrate the points raised by the solution to the dictionary search problem. These examples also illustrate the difference between a recursive **valued function**—which returns a value—and a recursive **void function**.

2.2   Recursion That Returns a Value

VideoNote

Recursion: The mirrors

The mechanics of recursion are clearer when the recursive function returns a value instead of just performing an action, and so we examine one in detail.

2.2.1   A Recursive Valued Function: The Factorial of *n*

Do not use recursion if a problem has a simple, efficient iterative solution

Computing the factorial of an integer *n* is a good first example because its recursive solution is easy to understand and neatly fits the mold described earlier. However, because the problem has a simple and efficient iterative solution, you should not use the recursive solution in practice.

To begin, consider the familiar iterative definition of *factorial*(*n*) (more commonly written as *n*!):

$factorial(n) = n \times (n - 1) \times (n - 2) \times \cdots \times 1$ for an integer $n > 0$
$factorial(0) = 1$

An iterative
definition of factorial

The factorial of a negative integer is undefined. You should have no trouble writing an iterative factorial function based on this definition.

To define *factorial*(*n*) recursively, you first need to define *factorial*(*n*) in terms of the factorial of a smaller number. To do so, simply observe that the factorial of *n* is equal to the factorial of (*n* − 1) multiplied by *n;* that is,

$$factorial(n) = n \times [(n - 1) \times (n - 2) \times \cdots \times 1]$$
$$= n \times factorial(n - 1)$$

A recurrence
relation

The definition of *factorial*(*n*) in terms of *factorial*(*n* − 1), which is an example of a **recurrence relation**, implies that you can also define *factorial*(*n* − 1) in terms of *factorial*(*n* − 2), and so on. This process is analogous to the dictionary search solution, in which you search a dictionary by searching a smaller dictionary in exactly the same way.

The definition of *factorial*(*n*) lacks one key element: the base case. As was done in the dictionary search solution, here you must define one case differently from all the others, or else the recursion will never stop. The base case for the factorial function is *factorial*(0), which you know is 1. Because *n* originally is greater than or equal to zero and each call to *factorial* decrements *n* by 1, you will always reach the base case. With the addition of the base case, the complete recursive definition of the factorial function is

$$factorial(n) = \begin{cases} 1 & \text{if } n = 0 \\ n \times factorial(n - 1) & \text{if } n > 0 \end{cases}$$

A recursive
definition of factorial

To be sure that you understand this recursive definition, apply it to the computation of *factorial*(4). Because 4 > 0, the recursive definition states that

$factorial(4) = 4 \times factorial(3)$

Similarly,

$factorial(3) = 3 \times factorial(2)$
$factorial(2) = 2 \times factorial(1)$
$factorial(1) = 1 \times factorial(0)$

You have reached the base case, and the definition directly states that

$factorial(0) = 1$

At this point, the application of the recursive definition stops and you still do not know the answer to the original question: What is *factorial*(4)? However, the information to answer this question is now available:

Because *factorial*(0) = 1, *factorial*(1) = 1 × 1 = 1
Because *factorial*(1) = 1, *factorial*(2) = 2 × 1 = 2
Because *factorial*(2) = 2, *factorial*(3) = 3 × 2 = 6
Because *factorial*(3) = 6, *factorial*(4) = 4 × 6 = 24

You can think of recursion as a process that divides a problem into a task that you can do and a task that a friend can do for you. For example, if I ask you to compute *factorial*(4), you could first determine whether you know the answer immediately. You know immediately that *factorial*(0) is 1—that is, you know the base case—but you do not know the value of *factorial*(4) immediately. However, if your friend computes *factorial*(3) for you, you could compute *factorial*(4) by multiplying *factorial*(3) and 4. Thus, your task will be to do this multiplication, and your friend's task will be to compute *factorial*(3).

Your friend now uses the same process to compute *factorial*(3) as you are using to compute *factorial*(4). Thus, your friend determines that *factorial*(3) is not the base case, and so asks another friend to compute *factorial*(2). Knowing *factorial*(2) enables your friend to compute *factorial*(3), and when you learn the value of *factorial*(3) from your friend, you can compute *factorial*(4).

Notice that the recursive definition of *factorial*(4) yields the same result as the iterative definition, which gives $4 \times 3 \times 2 \times 1 = 24$. To prove that the two definitions of *factorial* are equivalent for all nonnegative integers, you would use mathematical induction. (See Appendix E.) Chapter 5 discusses the close tie between recursion and mathematical induction.

The recursive definition of the factorial function has illustrated two points. (1) *Intuitively*, you can define *factorial*(n) in terms of *factorial*(n − 1). (2) *Mechanically*, you can apply the definition to determine the value of a given factorial. Even in this simple example, applying the recursive definition required quite a bit of work. That, of course, is where the computer comes in.

Once you have a recursive definition of *factorial*(n), it is easy to construct a C++ function that implements the definition. For simplicity, our function does not verify its precondition:

```
/** Computes the factorial of the nonnegative integer n.
 @pre  n must be greater than or equal to 0.
 @post  None.
 @return  The factorial of n; n is unchanged. */
int fact(int n)
{
   if (n == 0)
      return 1;
   else // n > 0, so n-1 >= 0. Thus, fact(n-1) returns (n-1)!
      return n * fact(n - 1); // n * (n-1)! is n!
} // end fact
```

Suppose that you use the statement

```
std::cout << fact(3);
```

to call the function. Figure 2-2 depicts the sequence of computations that this call would require.

FIGURE 2-2   fact(3)

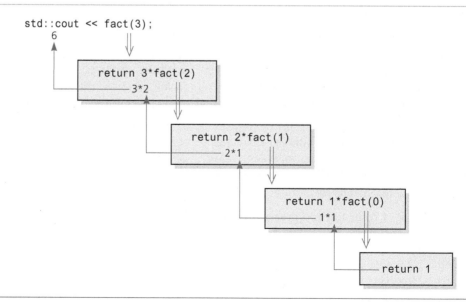

This function fits the model of a recursive solution given earlier in this chapter as follows:

1. One action of `fact` is to *call itself*.
2. At each recursive call to `fact`, the integer whose factorial you need to compute is *diminished by* 1.
3. The function handles the factorial of 0 differently from all the other factorials: It does not generate a recursive call. Rather, you know that `fact(0)` is 1. Thus, the *base case* occurs when *n* is 0.
4. Given that *n* is nonnegative, item 2 of this list assures you that you will always *reach the base case*.

`fact` satisfies the four criteria of a recursive solution

Note: A recursive algorithm must have a base case, whose solution you know directly without making any recursive calls. Without a base case, a recursive function will generate an infinite sequence of calls.

The function `fact` requires as its precondition a nonnegative value of *n*. At the time of the recursive call `fact(n-1)`, *n* is positive, so *n* − 1 is nonnegative. Because the recursive call satisfies `fact`'s precondition, you can expect that `fact(n-1)` will return the factorial of *n* − 1. Therefore, the computation n * `fact(n-1)` is the factorial of *n*. Chapter 5 uses mathematical induction to prove formally that `fact(n)` returns the factorial of *n*.

If you ever violated `fact`'s precondition, the function would not behave correctly. That is, if the calling program ever passed a negative value to `fact`, an infinite sequence of recursive calls—terminated only by a system-defined limit—would occur, because the function would never reach the base case. For example, `fact(-4)` would call `fact(-5)`, which would call `fact(-6)`, and so on.

Violating `fact`'s precondition causes "infinite" recursion

The function ideally should protect itself by testing for a negative *n*. If *n* < 0, the function could, for example, either return 0 or throw an exception. Chapter 1 and Appendix B discuss how to react to errors and unusual conditions; see Sections 1.3.2, B.2.5, and B.5. You might want to review that discussion at this time.

At an intuitive level, it should be clear that the function `fact` implements the recursive definition of *factorial*. Now consider the mechanics of executing this recursive function. The logic is straightforward, except perhaps for the expression in the `else` clause. This expression can be explained as follows:

1. Each operand of the product n * `fact(n-1)` is evaluated.
2. The second operand—`fact(n-1)`—is a call to the function `fact`. Although this is a recursive call (the function `fact` calls the function `fact`), there really is nothing special about it. Imagine substituting a call to another function—the standard function `abs`, for example—for the recursive call to `fact`. The principle is the same: Simply evaluate the function.

In theory, evaluating a recursive function is no more difficult than evaluating a nonrecursive function. In practice, however, manual bookkeeping can quickly get out of hand. The next section introduces a systematic way to trace the actions of a recursive function. For a computer, the bookkeeping is simple but can use more memory than is allocated for such a task.

Question 1 The following function computes the sum of the first *n* ≥ 1 integers. Show how this function satisfies the properties of a recursive function.

```
/** Computes the sum of the integers from 1 through n.
 @pre   n > 0.
 @post  None.
 @param n  A positive integer.
 @return  The sum 1 + 2 + . . . + n. */
```

```
int sumUpTo(int n)
{
   int sum = 0;
   if (n == 1)
      sum = 1;
   else // n > 1
      sum = n + sumUpTo(n - 1);

   return sum;
}  // end sumUpTo
```

2.2.2   The Box Trace

An activation record is created for each function call

You can use a **box trace** both to help you understand recursion and to debug recursive functions. However, such a mechanical device is no substitute for an intuitive understanding of recursion. The box trace illustrates how compilers frequently implement recursion. As you read the following description of the technique, realize that each box roughly corresponds to an **activation record**, which a compiler typically uses in its implementation of a function call. C++ Interlude 2 will discuss activation records further.

The box trace is illustrated here for the recursive function fact, which returns a value.

1. Label each recursive call in the body of the recursive function. Several recursive calls might occur within a function, and it will be important to distinguish among them. These labels help you keep track of the correct place to which you must return after a function call completes. For example, mark the expression fact(n - 1) within the body of the function with the letter A:

Label each recursive call in the function

```
if (n == 0)
   return 1;
else
   return n * fact(n - 1);
                      Ⓐ
```

You return to point A after each recursive call, substitute the computed value for the term fact(n - 1), and continue execution by evaluating the expression n * fact(n - 1).

2. Represent each call to the function during the course of execution by a new box in which you note the **local environment** of the function. More specifically, each box will contain

Each time a function is called, a new box represents its local environment

- The values of the arguments of the argument list.
- The function's local variables.
- A placeholder for the value returned by each recursive call from the current box. Label this placeholder to correspond to the labeling in step 1.
- The value of the function itself.

When you first create a box, you will know only the values of the input arguments. You fill in the other values as you determine them from the function's execution. For example, you would create the box in Figure 2-3 for the call fact(3). (You will see in later examples that you must handle reference arguments somewhat differently than value arguments and local variables.)

FIGURE 2-3 A box

```
n = 3
A: fact(n-1) = ?
return ?
```

3. Draw an arrow from the statement that initiates the recursive process to the first box. Then, when you create a new box after a recursive call, as described in step 2, you draw an arrow from the box that makes the call to the newly created box. Label each arrow

FIGURE 2-4   The beginning of the box trace

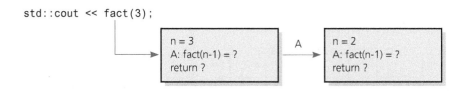

to correspond to the label (from step 1) of the recursive call; this label indicates exactly where to return after the call completes. For example, Figure 2-4 shows the first two boxes generated by the call to fact in the statement std::cout << fact(3).

4. After you create the new box and arrow as described in steps 2 and 3, start executing the body of the function. Each reference to a value in the function's local environment references the corresponding value in the current box, regardless of how you generated the current box.

5. On exiting the function, cross off the current box and follow its arrow back to the box that called the function. This box now becomes the current box, and the label on the arrow specifies the exact location at which execution of the function should continue. Substitute the value returned by the just-terminated function call for the appropriate placeholder in the current box.

Figure 2-5 is a complete box trace for the call fact(3). In the sequence of diagrams in this figure, the current box is the deepest along the path of arrows and is highlighted in blue, whereas crossed-off boxes are dashed and shaded gray.

FIGURE 2-5   Box trace of fact(3)

The initial call is made, and method **fact** begins execution:

n = 3
A: fact(n-1)=?
return ?

At point A a recursive call is made, and the new invocation of the method **fact** begins execution:

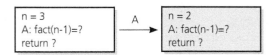

At point A a recursive call is made, and the new invocation of the method **fact** begins execution:

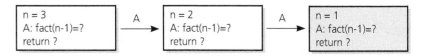

At point A a recursive call is made, and the new invocation of the method **fact** begins execution:

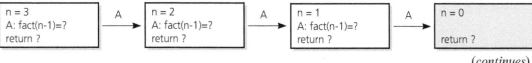

(*continues*)

FIGURE 2-5 Box trace of `fact(3)` (*continued*)

This is the base case, so this invocation of **fact** completes and returns a value to the caller:

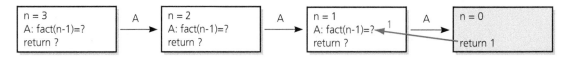

The method value is returned to the calling box, which continues execution:

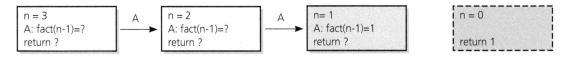

The current invocation of **fact** completes and returns a value to the caller:

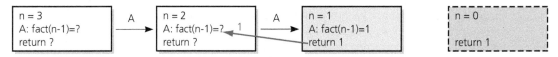

The method value is returned to the calling box, which continues execution:

The current invocation of **fact** completes and returns a value to the caller:

The method value is returned to the calling box, which continues execution:

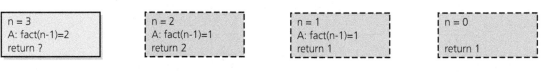

The current invocation of **fact** completes and returns a value to the caller:

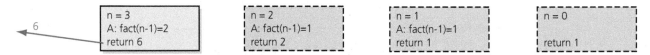

The value 6 is returned to the initial call.

Note: The box trace, in conjunction with well-placed cout statements, can be a good aid in debugging recursive functions. Such statements should report the point in the program from which each recursive call occurs, as well as the values of input arguments and local variables at both entry to and exit from the function. Be sure to remove these cout statements from the final version of the function.

 Question 2 Write a box trace of the function given in Checkpoint Question 1.

2.3   Recursion That Performs an Action

Recursive functions need not return a value; they can be void functions.

2.3.1   A Recursive Void Function: Writing a String Backward

Now consider a problem that is slightly more difficult: Given a string of characters, write it in reverse order. For example, write the string "cat" as "tac". To construct a recursive solution, you should ask the four questions in the Note at the end of Section 2.1.

You can construct a solution to the problem of writing a string of length n backward in terms of the problem of writing a string of length $n - 1$ backward. That is, each recursive step of the solution diminishes by 1 the length of the string to be written backward. The fact that the strings get shorter and shorter suggests that the problem of writing some very short strings backward can serve as the base case. One very short string is the empty string, the string of length zero. Thus, you can choose for the base case the problem

> *Write the empty string backward*

The base case

The solution to this problem is to do nothing at all—a very straightforward solution indeed! (Alternatively, you could use the string of length 1 as the base case.)

Exactly how can you use the solution to the problem of writing a string of length $n - 1$ backward to solve the problem of writing a string of length n backward? This approach is analogous to the one used to construct the solution to the factorial problem, where you specified how to use *factorial*$(n - 1)$ in the computation of *factorial*(n). Unlike the factorial problem, however, the string problem does not suggest an immediately clear way to proceed. Obviously, not any string of length $n - 1$ will do. For example, there is no relation between writing the string "apple" (of length 5) backward and writing "pear" (a string of length 4) backward. You must choose the smaller problem carefully so that you can use its solution in the solution to the original problem.

How can you write an n-character string backward, if you can write an $(n - 1)$-character string backward?

The string of length $n - 1$ that you choose must be a substring (part) of the original string. Suppose that you strip away one character from the original string, leaving a substring of length $n - 1$. For the recursive solution to be valid, the ability to write the substring backward, combined with the ability to perform some minor task, must result in the ability to write the original string backward. Compare this approach with the way you computed *factorial* recursively: The ability to compute *factorial*$(n - 1)$, combined with the ability to multiply this value by n, resulted in the ability to compute *factorial*(n).

You need to decide which character to strip away and which minor task to perform. Consider the minor task first. Because you are writing characters, a likely candidate for the minor task is writing a single character. As for the character that you should strip away from the string, there are several possible alternatives. Two of the more intuitive alternatives are

Strip away the last character

or

Strip away the first character

Consider the first of these alternatives, stripping away the last character, as Figure 2-6 illustrates.

FIGURE 2-6   A recursive solution

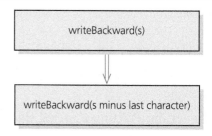

For the solution to be valid, you must write the last character in the string first. Therefore, you must write the last character before you write the remainder of the string backward. A high-level recursive solution, given the string s, is

writeBackward
writes a string
backward

```
writeBackward(s: string)
{
    if (the string is empty)
        Do nothing—this is the base case
    else
    {
        Write the last character of s
        writeBackward(s minus its last character)
    }
}
```

 Note: A recursive solution must involve one or more smaller problems that are each closer to a base case than is the original problem. You must be sure that these smaller problems eventually reach the base case. Failure to do so could result in an algorithm that does not terminate.

This solution to the problem is conceptual. To obtain a C++ function, you must resolve a few implementation issues. Suppose that the function will receive one argument: a string s to be written backward. All characters, including blanks, are part of the string. The C++ function writeBackward appears as follows:

```
/** Writes a character string backward.
 @pre  The string s to write backward.
 @post  None.
 @param s  The string to write backward. */
void writeBackward(std::string s)
{
```

```
    int length = s.size(); // Length of string
    if (length > 0)
    {
        // Write the last character
        std::cout << s.substr(length - 1, 1);

        // Write the rest of the string backward
        writeBackward(s.substr(0, length - 1)); // Point A
    } // end if
    // length == 0 is the base case - do nothing
} // end writeBackward
```

Notice that the recursive calls to writeBackward use successively shorter versions of the string s, ensuring that the base case will be reached. Because the function does nothing when it reaches the base case, it does not deal with the base case explicitly. The base case is implicit.

You can trace the execution of writeBackward by using the box trace. As was true for the function fact, each box contains the local environment of the recursive call—in this case, the input argument s and the local variable length. The trace will differ somewhat from the trace of fact shown in Figure 2-5 because, as a void function, writeBackward does not use a return statement to return a computed value. Figure 2-7 traces the call to the function writeBackward with the string "cat".

writeBackward does not return a computed value

FIGURE 2-7   Box trace of writeBackward("cat")

The initial call is made, and the function begins execution:

```
s = "cat"
length = 3
```

Output line: **t**

Point A (writeBackward(s)) is reached, and the recursive call is made.

The new invocation begins execution:

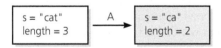

Output line: **ta**

Point A is reached, and the recursive call is made.

The new invocation begins execution:

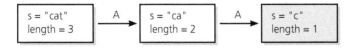

Output line: **tac**

Point A is reached, and the recursive call is made.

The new invocation begins execution:

(continues)

FIGURE 2-7   Box trace of `writeBackward("cat")` (*continued*)

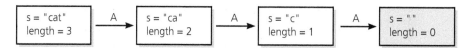

This is the base case, so this invocation completes.

Control returns to the calling box, which continues execution:

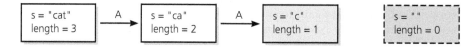

This invocation completes. Control returns to the calling box, which continues execution:

This invocation completes. Control returns to the calling box, which continues execution:

This invocation completes. Control returns to the statement following the initial call.

Another solution. Now consider a slightly different approach to the problem. Recall the two alternatives for the character that you could strip away from the string: the last character or the first character. The solution just given strips away the last character of the string. It will now be interesting to construct a solution based on the second alternative:

Strip away the first character

To begin, consider a simple modification of the previous pseudocode solution that replaces each occurrence of *last* with *first*. Thus, the function writes the first character rather than the last and then recursively writes the remainder of the string backward.

```
writeBackward1(s: string)
{
    if (the string s is empty)
        Do nothing— this is the base case
    else
    {
        Write the first character of s
        writeBackward1(s minus its first character)
    }
}
```

Does this solution do what you want it to? If you think about this function, you will realize that it writes the string in its normal left-to-right direction instead of backward. After all, the steps in the pseudocode are

Write the first character of s
Write the rest of s

These steps simply write the string s. Naming the function writeBackward does not guarantee that it will actually write the string backward—recursion really is not magic!

You can write s backward correctly by using the following recursive formulation:

Write s *minus its first character backward*
Write the first character of s

In other words, you write the first character of s only *after* you have written the rest of s backward. This approach leads to the following pseudocode solution:

```
writeBackward2(s: string)
{
    if (the string s is empty)
        Do nothing—this is the base case
    else
    {
        writeBackward2(s minus its first character)
        Write the first character of s
    }
}
```

The translation of writeBackward2 into C++ is similar to that of the original writeBackward function and is left as an exercise.

It is instructive to carefully trace the actions of the two pseudocode functions writeBackward and writeBackward2. First, add statements to each function to provide output that is useful to the trace, as follows:

```
writeBackward(s: string)
{
    cout << "Enter writeBackward with string: " << s << endl;
    if (the string is empty)
        Do nothing—this is the base case
    else
    {
        cout << "About to write last character of string: " << s << endl;
        Write the last character of s
        writeBackward(s minus its last character)  // Point A
    }
    cout << "Leave writeBackward with string: " << s << endl;
}

writeBackward2(s: string)
{
    cout << "Enter writeBackward2 with string: " << s << endl;
    if (the string is empty)
        Do nothing—this is the base case
    else
    {
        writeBackward2(s minus its first character)  // Point A
        cout << "About to write first character of string: " << s << endl;
        Write the first character of s
    }
    cout << "Leave writeBackward2 with string: " << s << endl;
}
```

*cout statements
can help you trace
the logic of a
recursive function*

Figures 2-8 and 2-9 show the output of the revised pseudocode functions writeBackward and writeBackward2, when initially given the string "cat".

FIGURE 2-8 Box trace of `writeBackward("cat")` in pseudocode

The initial call is made, and the function begins execution:

Output stream:

Enter writeBackward with string: cat
About to write last character of string: cat
t

Point A is reached, and the recursive call is made. The new invocation begins execution:

s = "cat" ─A→ s = "ca"

Output stream:

Enter writeBackward with string: cat
About to write last character of string: cat
t
Enter writeBackward with string: ca
About to write last character of string: ca
a

Point A is reached, and the recursive call is made. The new invocation begins execution:

s = "cat" ─A→ s = "ca" ─A→ s = "c"

Output stream:

Enter writeBackward with string: cat
About to write last character of string: cat
t
Enter writeBackward with string: ca
About to write last character of string: ca
a
Enter writeBackward with string: c
About to write last character of string: c
c

Point A is reached, and the recursive call is made. The new invocation begins execution:

This invocation completes execution, and a return is made.

Output stream:

Enter writeBackward with string: cat
About to write last character of string: cat
t
Enter writeBackward with string: ca
About to write last character of string: ca
a
Enter writeBackward with string: c
About to write last character of string: c
c
Enter writeBackward with string:
Leave writeBackward with string:

This invocation completes execution, and a return is made.

Output stream:

Enter writeBackward with string: cat
About to write last character of string: cat
t
Enter writeBackward with string: ca
About to write last character of string: ca
a
Enter writeBackward with string: c
About to write last character of string: c
c
Enter writeBackward with string:
Leave writeBackward with string:
Leave writeBackward with string: c

This invocation completes execution, and a return is made.

Output stream:

Enter writeBackward with string: cat
About to write last character of string: cat
t
Enter writeBackward with string: ca
About to write last character of string: ca
a
Enter writeBackward with string: c
About to write last character of string: c
c
Enter writeBackward with string:
Leave writeBackward with string:
Leave writeBackward with string: c
Leave writeBackward with string: ca

(continues)

FIGURE 2-8   Box trace of `writeBackward("cat")` in pseudocode (*continued*)

| s = "cat" | s = "ca" | s = "c" | s = "" |

This invocation completes execution, and a return is made.

Output stream:

Enter writeBackward with string: cat
About to write last character of string: cat
t
Enter writeBackward with string: ca
About to write last character of string: ca
a
Enter writeBackward with string: c
About to write last character of string: c
c
Enter writeBackward with string:
Leave writeBackward with string:
Leave writeBackward with string: c
Leave writeBackward with string: ca
Leave writeBackward with string: cat

FIGURE 2-9   Box trace of `writeBackward2("cat")` in pseudocode

The initial call is made, and the function begins execution:

| s = "cat" |

Output stream:

Enter writeBackward2 with string: cat

Point A is reached, and the recursive call is made. The new invocation begins execution:

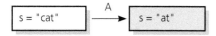

Output stream:

Enter writeBackward2 with string: cat
Enter writeBackward2 with string: at

Point A is reached, and the recursive call is made. The new invocation begins execution:

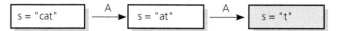

FIGURE 2-9   Box trace of `writeBackward2("cat")` in pseudocode (*continued*)

Output stream:

> Enter writeBackward2 with string: cat
> Enter writeBackward2 with string: at
> Enter writeBackward2 with string: t

Point A is reached, and the recursive call is made. The new invocation begins execution:

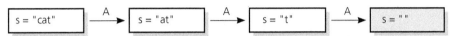

This invocation completes execution, and a return is made.

Output stream:

> Enter writeBackward2 with string: cat
> Enter writeBackward2 with string: at
> Enter writeBackward2 with string: t
> Enter writeBackward2 with string:
> Leave writeBackward2 with string:

This invocation completes execution, and a return is made.

Output stream:

> Enter writeBackward2 with string: cat
> Enter writeBackward2 with string: at
> Enter writeBackward2 with string: t
> Enter writeBackward2 with string:
> Leave writeBackward2 with string:
> About to write first character of string: t
> t
> Leave writeBackward2 with string: t

This invocation completes execution, and a return is made.

Output stream:

> Enter writeBackward2 with string: cat
> Enter writeBackward2 with string: at
> Enter writeBackward2 with string: t
> Enter writeBackward2 with string:
> Leave writeBackward2 with string:
> About to write first character of string: t
> t
>
> Leave writeBackward2 with string: t
> About to write first character of string: at
> a
>
> Leave writeBackward2, string: at

(*continues*)

FIGURE 2-9   Box trace of `writeBackward2("cat")` in pseudocode (*continued*)

| s = "cat" | | s = "at" | | s = "t" | | s = "" |

This invocation completes execution, and a return is made.

Output stream:

> Enter writeBackward2 with string: cat
> Enter writeBackward2 with string: at
> Enter writeBackward2 with string: t
> Enter writeBackward2 with string:
> Leave writeBackward2 with string:
> About to write first character of string: t
> t
> Leave writeBackward2 with string: t
> About to write first character of string: at
> a
> Leave writeBackward2 with string: at
> About to write first character of string: cat
> c
> Leave writeBackward2 with string: cat

You need to be comfortable with the differences between these two functions. The recursive calls that the two functions make generate a different sequence of values for the argument s. Despite this fact, both functions correctly write the string argument backward. They compensate for the difference in the sequence of values for s by writing different characters in the string at different times relative to the recursive calls. In terms of the box traces in Figures 2-8 and 2-9, `writeBackward` writes a character just before generating a new box (just before a new recursive call), whereas `writeBackward2` writes a character just after crossing off a box (just after returning from a recursive call). When these differences are put together, the result is two functions that employ different strategies to accomplish the same task.

This example also illustrates the value of the box trace, combined with well-placed `cout` statements, in debugging recursive functions. The `cout` statements at the beginning, interior, and end of the recursive functions report the value of the argument s. In general, when debugging a recursive function, you should also report both the values of local variables and the point in the function where each recursive call occurred, as in this example:

Well-placed but temporary `cout` statements can help you debug a recursive function

```
abc(. . .)
{
    std::cout << "Calling function abc from point A.\n";
    abc(...) // This is point A
    std::cout << "Calling function abc from point B.\n";
    abc(...); // This is point B
}
```

Remove `cout` statements after you have debugged the function

Realize that the `cout` statements do not belong in the final version of the function.

 Question 3 Given an integer $n > 0$, write a recursive function `countDown` that writes the integers $n, n - 1, \ldots, 1$. *Hint:* What task can you do and what task can you ask a friend to do for you?

2.4   Recursion with Arrays

When you are working with an array, recursion can be a practical and powerful tool. For our first example, we write the contents of an array backward. We then look at several problems that involve searching an array.

VideoNote
Recursion with arrays

2.4.1   Writing an Array's Entries in Backward Order

The solution to this problem is much like our first solution in Section 2.3.1 when we wrote a string backward. We can write the following pseudocode:

```
writeArrayBackward(anArray: char[])
{
    if (the array is empty)
        Do nothing—this is the base case
    else
    {
        Write the last character in anArray
        writeArrayBackward(anArray minus its last character)
    }
}
```

How will we pass anArray minus its last character to writeArrayBackward? We could pass the number of characters left in the array. At each recursive call, we would decrease this number by 1. Alternatively, we could pass the index of the last character. That is, if last is this index, writeArrayBackward would act on the array portion anArray[0] through anArray[last], which we will designate as anArray[0..last].[1] The recursive call would then act on the subarray anArray[0..last – 1]. A more general variation of this idea also passes the index of the first array character. So instead of assuming that this index is 0, we would pass anArray[first.. last] to writeArray-Backward.

We can write the function writeArrayBackward as follows:

```
/** Writes the characters in an array backward.
 @pre  The array anArray contains size characters, where size >= 0.
 @post  None.
 @param anArray  The array to write backward.
 @param first  The index of the first character in the array.
 @param last  The index of the last character in the array. */
void writeArrayBackward(const char anArray[], int first, int last)
{
    if (first <= last)
    {
        // Write the last character
        std::cout << anArray[last];

        // Write the rest of the array backward
        writeArrayBackward(anArray, first, last - 1);
    } // end if

    // first > last is the base case - do nothing

}  // end writeArrayBackward
```

---

[1] You will see this notation in the rest of the book to represent a portion of an array.

Question 4 In the previous definition of `writeArrayBackward`, why does the base case occur when the value of `first` exceeds the value of `last`?

Question 5 Write a recursive function that computes and returns the product of the first $n \geq 1$ real numbers in an array.

Question 6 Show how the function that you wrote for the previous question satisfies the properties of a recursive function.

Question 7 Write a recursive function that computes and returns the product of the integers in the array `anArray[first..last]`.

2.4.2   Searching a Sorted Array: The Binary Search

Searching is an important task that occurs frequently. Often, searches are for a particular entry in an array. We now will examine a few searching problems that have recursive solutions. Our goal is to develop further your understanding of recursion.

This chapter began with an intuitive approach to a binary search algorithm by presenting—at a high level—a way to find a word in a dictionary. We now develop this algorithm fully and illustrate some important programming issues.

A binary search conquers one of its subproblems at each step

Recall the earlier solution to the dictionary problem:

```
search(aDictionary: Dictionary, word: string)
{
    if (aDictionary is one page in size)
        Scan the page for word
    else
    {
        Open aDictionary to a point near the middle
        Determine which half of aDictionary contains word

        if (word is in the first half of aDictionary)
            search(first half of aDictionary, word)
        else
            search(second half of aDictionary, word)
    }
}
```

Now alter the problem slightly by searching an array `anArray` of integers for a given value, the **target**. The array, like the dictionary, must be sorted, or else a binary search is not applicable. Hence, assume that

$$anArray[0] \leq anArray[1] \leq anArray[2] \leq . . . \leq anArray[size - 1]$$

where `size` is the size of the array. A high-level binary search for the array problem is

```
binarySearch(anArray: ArrayType, target: ValueType)
{
    if (anArray is of size 1)
        Determine if anArray's value is equal to target
    else
    {
        Find the midpoint of anArray
        Determine which half of anArray contains target
        if (target is in the first half of anArray)
            binarySearch(first half of anArray, target)
        else
            binarySearch(second half of anArray, target)
    }
}
```

Although the solution is conceptually sound, you must consider several details before you can implement the algorithm:

1. **How will you pass half of `anArray` to the recursive calls to `binarySearch`?** You can pass the entire array at each call but have `binarySearch` search only `anArray[first..last]`, that is, the portion `anArray[first]` through `anArray[last]`. Thus, you would also pass the integers `first` and `last` to `binarySearch`:

   ```
   binarySearch(anArray, first, last, target)
   ```

   With this convention, the new midpoint is given by

   ```
   mid = (first + last) / 2
   ```

   Then `binarySearch(`*first half of* `anArray, target)` becomes

   ```
   binarySearch(anArray, first, mid − 1, target)
   ```

   and `binarySearch(`*second half of* `anArray, target)` becomes

   ```
   binarySearch(anArray, mid + 1, last, target)
   ```

   > The array halves are `anArray[first..mid-1]` and `anArray[mid+1..last]`; neither half contains `anArray[mid]`

2. **How do you determine which half of the array contains `target`?** One possible implementation of

   ```
   if (target is in the first half of anArray)
   ```
   is

   ```
   if (target < anArray[mid])
   ```

   However, there is no test for equality between `target` and `anArray[mid]`. This omission can cause the algorithm to miss `target`. After the previous halving algorithm splits `anArray` into halves, `anArray[mid]` is not in either half of the array. (In this case, two halves do not make a whole!) Therefore, you must determine whether `anArray[mid]` is the value you seek *now,* because later it will not be in the remaining half of the array. The interaction between the halving criterion and the termination condition (the base case) is subtle and is often a source of error. We need to rethink the base case.

   > Determine whether `anArray[mid]` is the target you seek

3. **What should the base case(s) be?** As it is written, `binarySearch` terminates only when an array of size 1 occurs; this is the only base case. By changing the halving process so that `anArray[mid]` *remains in one of the halves*, it is possible to implement the binary search correctly so that it has only this single base case. However, it can be clearer to have two distinct base cases as follows:

   * `first > last`. You will reach this base case when `target` is not in the original array.
   * `target == anArray[mid]`. You will reach this base case when `target` is in the original array.

   These base cases are a bit different from any you have encountered previously. In a sense, the algorithm determines the answer to the problem from the base case it reaches. Many search problems have this flavor.

4. **How will `binarySearch` indicate the result of the search?** If `binarySearch` successfully locates `target` in the array, it could return the index of the array value that is equal to `target`. Because this index would never be negative, `binarySearch` could return a negative value if it does not find `target` in the array.

The C++ function `binarySearch` that follows implements these ideas. The two recursive calls to `binarySearch` are labeled as `X` and `Y` for use in a later box trace of this function.

```
/** Searches the array anArray[first] through anArray[last]
    for a given value by using a binary search.
 @pre  0 <= first, last <= SIZE - 1, where SIZE is the
    maximum size of the array, and anArray[first] <=
    anArray[first + 1] <= ... <= anArray[last].
 @post  anArray is unchanged and either anArray[index] contains
    the given value or index == -1.
 @param anArray  The array to search.
 @param first  The low index to start searching from.
 @param last  The high index to stop searching at.
 @param target  The value to find.
 @return  Either index, such that anArray[index] == target, or -1.*/
int binarySearch(const int anArray[], int first, int last, int target)
{
    int index = 0;
    if (first > last)
        index = -1; // target not in original array
    else
    {
        // If target is in anArray, anArray[first] <= target <= anArray[last]
        int mid = first + (last - first) / 2;
        if (target == anArray[mid])
            index = mid; // target found at anArray[mid]
        else if (target < anArray[mid])
            // Point X
            index = binarySearch(anArray, first, mid - 1, target);
        else
            // Point Y
            index = binarySearch(anArray, mid + 1, last, target);
    }  // end if
    return index;
}  // end binarySearch
```

Notice that if target occurs in the array, it must be in the segment of the array delineated by first and last. That is, the following is true:

anArray[first] ≤ target ≤ anArray[last]

Figure 2-10 shows box traces of binarySearch when it searches the array containing 1, 5, 9, 12, 15, 21, 29, and 31. Notice how the labels X and Y of the two recursive calls to binarySearch appear in the diagram. Exercise 16 at the end of this chapter asks you to perform other box traces with this function.

 Note: When developing a recursive solution, you must be sure that the solutions to the smaller problems really do give you a solution to the original problem. For example, binarySearch works because each smaller array is sorted and the value sought is between its first and last values.

There is another implementation issue—one that deals specifically with C++—to consider. Recall that an array is never passed to a function by value and is therefore not copied. This aspect of C++ is particularly useful in a recursive function such as binarySearch. If the array anArray is large, many recursive calls to binarySearch might be necessary. If each call copied anArray, much memory and time would be wasted. On the other hand, because anArray is not copied, the function can alter the array's values unless you specify anArray as const, as was done for binarySearch.

Because an array argument is always passed by reference, a function can alter it unless you specify the array as const

FIGURE 2-10   Box traces of binarySearch with anArray = <1, 5, 9, 12, 15, 21, 29, 31>

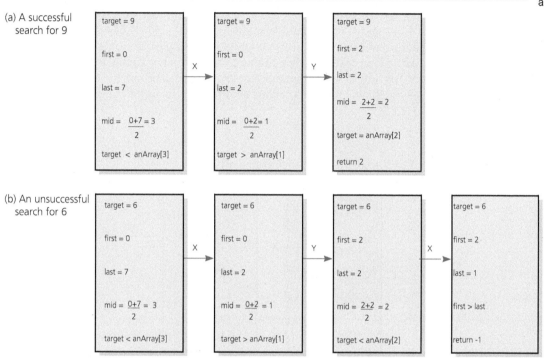

(a) A successful search for 9

(b) An unsuccessful search for 6

A box trace of a recursive function that has an array argument requires a new consideration. Because the array anArray is neither a value argument nor a local variable, it is not a part of the function's local environment, and so the entire array anArray should not appear within each box. Therefore, as Figure 2-11 shows, you represent anArray outside the boxes, and all references to anArray affect this single representation.

Represent reference arguments outside of the boxes in a box trace

Note: Notice that the C++ computation of the midpoint mid is
```
int  mid = first + (last - first) / 2;
```
instead of
```
int  mid = (first + last) / 2;
```
as the pseudocode would suggest. If you were to search an array of at least 2^{30}, or about 1 billion, values, the sum of first and last could exceed the largest possible int value of $2^{30} - 1$. Thus, the computation first + last would overflow to a negative integer and result in a negative value for mid. If this negative value of mid was used as an array index, it would be out of bounds and cause incorrect results. The computation first + (last - first) / 2 is algebraically equivalent to (first + last) / 2 and avoids this error.

Security Note: Overflow and wrapping

In the previous Note, you learned that if a signed integer computation overflows, your program most likely will behave in unexpected ways. A similar situation can occur with unsigned integers. As soon as an unsigned-integer computation exceeds the largest value for its type, it **wraps around** to the type's smallest value. For example, a variable whose data type is unsigned short can have values that range from 0 to 65,535. If the variable has a value of 65,535, and we add 1 to it, we should get 65,536. However, the actual result would be 0, because the computation would wrap around to 0. If we had added 5 to 65,535 instead of 1, the computation would wrap around to 4.

Either overflow or wrapping could cause our code to behave in unexpected ways, thereby giving a malicious attacker control of the system on which our code executes.

FIGURE 2-11   Box trace with a reference argument

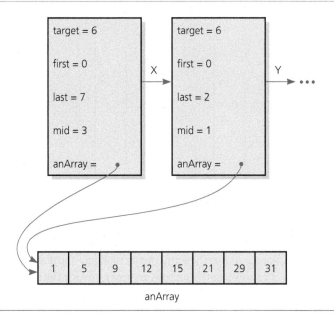

anArray

2.4.3   Finding the Largest Value in a Sorted or Unsorted Array

Suppose that you have an array anArray of integers in any order, and you want to find the largest value. You could construct an iterative solution without too much difficulty, but instead let's consider a recursive formulation:

```
if (anArray has only one entry)
    maxArray(anArray) is the entry in anArray
else if (anArray has more than one entry)
    maxArray(anArray) is the maximum of
        maxArray(left half of anArray) and maxArray(right half of anArray)
```

Notice that this strategy fits the divide-and-conquer model that the previous binary search algorithm used. That is, we proceed by dividing the problem and conquering the subproblems, as Figure 2-12 illustrates. However, there is a difference between this algorithm and the binary search algorithm. Although the binary search algorithm conquers only one of its subproblems at each step, maxArray conquers both. Because both subproblems are solved recursively, this approach is called **multipath recursion**. After maxArray conquers the subproblems, it must reconcile the two solutions—that is, it must find the maximum of the two maximums. Figure 2-13 illustrates the computations that are necessary to find the largest integer in the array that contains 1, 6, 8, and 3 (denoted here by <1, 6, 8, 3>).

maxArray conquers both of its subproblems at each step

Question 8 Define the recursive C++ function maxArray that returns the largest value in an array and adheres to the pseudocode just given.

FIGURE 2-12   Recursive solution to the largest-value problem

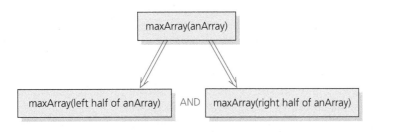

FIGURE 2-13   The recursive calls that maxArray(<1,6,8,3>) generates

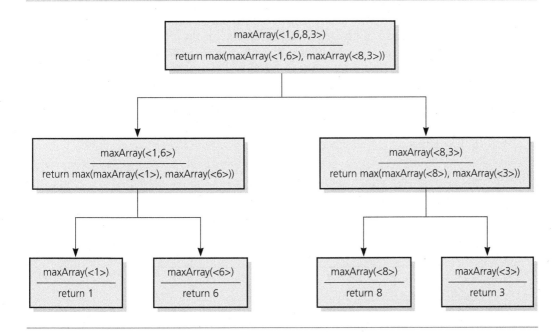

2.4.4   Finding the kth Smallest Value of an Unsorted Array

Our discussion of searching concludes with a more difficult problem. Although you could skip this example now, Chapter 11 uses aspects of it in a sorting algorithm.

The previous two examples presented recursive techniques for finding an arbitrary value in a sorted array and for finding the largest value in an arbitrary array. This example describes a recursive solution for finding the kth smallest value in an arbitrary unsorted array anArray of distinct values. Would you ever be interested in such a value? Statisticians often want the median value in a collection of data. The median value in an ordered collection of data occurs in the middle of the collection. In an unordered collection of data, the number of values that are smaller than the median value is about the same as the number of values that are larger. Thus, if you have 49 values, the 25th smallest value is the median value.

Obviously, you could solve this problem by sorting the array. Then the kth smallest value would be anArray[k-1]. Although this approach is a legitimate solution, it does more than the problem requires; a more efficient solution is possible. The solution outlined here finds the kth smallest value without completely sorting the array.

By now, you know that you solve a problem recursively by writing its solution in terms of one or more smaller problems of the same type in such a way that this notion of *smaller* ensures that you will always reach a base case. For all of the earlier recursive solutions, the reduction in problem size between recursive calls is *predictable*. For example, the factorial function always decreases the problem size by 1; the binary search always halves the problem size. In addition, the base cases for all the previous problems except the binary search have a static, predefined size. Thus, by knowing only the size of the original problem, you can determine the number of recursive calls that are necessary before you reach the base case.

For all previous examples, you know the amount of reduction made in the problem size by each recursive call

The solution that you are about to see for finding the kth smallest value departs from these techniques. Although you solve the problem in terms of a smaller problem, just how much smaller this problem is depends on the values in the array and cannot be predicted in advance. Also, the size of the base case depends on the values in the array, as it did for the binary search. (Recall that you reach one of the base cases for a binary search when the middle value is the one sought.)

You cannot predict in advance the size of either the smaller problems or the base case in the recursive solution to the kth-smallest-value problem

The unpredictable nature of this solution is caused by the problem itself: The relationship between the rankings of the values in any predetermined parts of the array and the ranking of the values in the entire array is not strong enough to determine the kth smallest value. For example, suppose that anArray contains the values shown in Figure 2-14. Notice that 6, which is in anArray[3], is the third-smallest value in the first half of anArray and that 8, which is in anArray[4], is the third-smallest value in the second half of anArray. Can you conclude from these observations anything about the location of the third-smallest value in all of anArray? The answer is no; these facts about parts of the array do not allow you to draw any useful conclusions about the entire array. You should experiment with other fixed splitting schemes as well.

FIGURE 2-14   A sample array

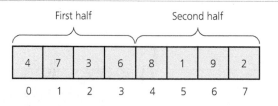

FIGURE 2-15   A partition about a pivot

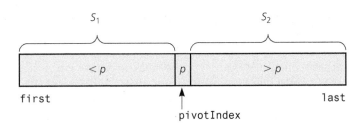

The recursive solution proceeds by

1. Selecting a **pivot** value in the array
2. Cleverly arranging, or **partitioning**, the values in the array about this pivot value
3. Recursively applying the strategy to *one* of the partitions

Suppose that you want to find the kth smallest value in the array segment anArray[first..last]. Let the pivot p be any value of the array segment. (For now, ignore how to choose p.) You can partition the values of anArray[first..last] into three regions: S_1, which contains the values less than p; the pivot p itself; and S_2, which contains the values greater than p. This partition implies that all of the values in S_1 are smaller than all of the values in S_2. Figure 2-15 illustrates this partition.

Partition anArray into three parts: values < p, p, and values > p

All values in the segment anArray[first..pivotIndex-1] are less than p, and all values in the segment anArray[pivotIndex+1..last] are greater than p. Notice that the sizes of the regions S_1 and S_2 depend on both p and the other values of anArray[first..last].

This partition induces three smaller problems, such that the solution to one of the problems will solve the original problem:

1. If S_1 contains k or more values, S_1 contains the k smallest values of the array segment anArray[first..last]. In this case, the kth smallest value must be in S_1. Since S_1 is the array segment anArray[first..pivotIndex-1], this case occurs if $k < $ pivotIndex – first + 1.
2. If S_1 contains $k - 1$ values, the kth smallest value must be the pivot p. This is the base case; it occurs if $k = $ pivotIndex – first + 1.
3. If S_1 contains fewer than $k - 1$ values, the kth smallest value in anArray[first..last] must be in S_2. Because S_1 contains pivotIndex – first values, the kth smallest value in anArray[first..last] is the $(k - ($pivotIndex $ - $ first $ + 1))^{st}$ smallest value in S_2. This case occurs if $k > $ pivotIndex – first + 1.

A recursive definition can summarize this discussion. Let

        kSmall(k, anArray, first, last) = k^{th} smallest value in anArray[first..last]

After you select the pivot value p and partition anArray[first..last] into S_1 and S_2, you have that kSmall(k, anArray, first, last) equals

- kSmall(k, anArray, first, pivotIndex – 1) if k < pivotIndex – first + 1
- p   if k = pivotIndex – first + 1
- kSmall(k – (pivotIndex – first + 1), anArray, pivotIndex + 1, last)
                                             if k > pivotIndex – first + 1

There is always a pivot, and because it is not part of either S_1 or S_2, the size of the array segment to be searched decreases by at least 1 at each step. Thus, you will eventually reach the base case: The desired value is a pivot. A high-level pseudocode solution is as follows.

The kth smallest
value in anArray
[first..last]

```
// Returns the kth smallest value in anArray[first..last].
kSmall(k: integer, anArray: ArrayType, first: integer, last: integer): ValueType
{
    Choose a pivot value p from anArray[first..last]
    Partition the values of anArray[first..last] about p

    if (k < pivotIndex - first + 1)
        return kSmall(k, anArray, first, pivotIndex - 1)
    else if (k == pivotIndex - first + 1)
        return p
    else
        return kSmall(k - (pivotIndex - first + 1), anArray, pivotIndex + 1, last)
}
```

This pseudocode is not far from a C++ function. The only questions that remain are how to choose the pivot value p and how to partition the array about the chosen p. The choice of p is arbitrary. Any p in the array will work, although the sequence of choices will affect how soon you reach the base case. Chapter 11 gives an algorithm for partitioning the values about p. There you will see how to turn the function kSmall into a sorting algorithm.

2.5   Organizing Data

Given some data organized in one way, you might need to organize it in another way. Thus, you will actually change some aspect of the data and not, for example, simply search it. The problem in this section is called the Towers of Hanoi. Although this classic problem probably has no direct real-world application, we consider it because its solution so well illustrates the use of recursion.

2.5.1   The Towers of Hanoi

Many, many years ago, in a distant part of the Orient—in the Vietnamese city of Hanoi—the emperor's wiseperson passed on to join his ancestors. The emperor needed a replacement wiseperson. Being a rather wise person himself, the emperor devised a puzzle, declaring that its solver could have the job of wiseperson.

The emperor's puzzle consisted of n disks (he didn't say exactly how many) and three poles: A (the source), B (the destination), and C (the spare). The disks were of different sizes and had holes in the middle so that they could fit on the poles. Because of their great weight, the disks could be placed only on top of disks larger than themselves. Initially, all the disks were on pole A, as shown in Figure 2-16a. The puzzle was to move the disks, one by one, from pole A to pole B. A person could also use pole C in the course of the transfer, but again a disk could be placed only on top of a disk larger than itself.

As the position of wiseperson was generally known to be a soft job, there were many applicants. Scholars and peasants alike brought the emperor their solutions. Many solutions were thousands of steps long, and many contained deeply nested loops and control structures. "I can't understand these solutions," bellowed the emperor. "There must be an easy way to solve this puzzle."

And indeed there was. A great Buddhist monk came out of the mountains to see the emperor. "My son," he said, "the puzzle is so easy, it almost solves itself." The emperor's security chief wanted to throw this strange person out, but the emperor let him continue.

"If you have only one disk (that is, $n = 1$), move it from pole A to pole B." So far, so good, but even the village idiot could get that part right. "If you have more than one disk (that is, $n > 1$), simply

FIGURE 2-16   Solving the Towers of Hanoi puzzle

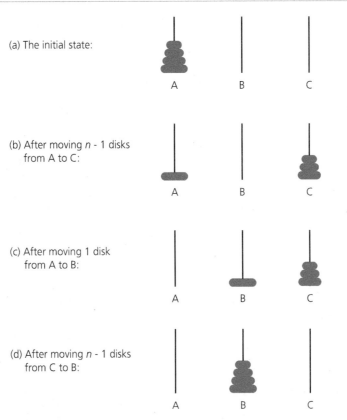

(a) The initial state:

(b) After moving *n* - 1 disks
     from A to C:

(c) After moving 1 disk
     from A to B:

(d) After moving *n* - 1 disks
     from C to B:

1. Ignore the bottom disk and solve the problem for $n - 1$ disks, with the small modification that pole C is the destination and pole B is the spare. (See Figure 2-16b.)
2. After you have done this, $n - 1$ disks will be on pole C, and the largest disk will remain on pole A. So solve the problem for $n = 1$ (recall that even the village idiot could do this) by moving the large disk from A to B. (See Figure 2-16c.)
3. Now all you have to do is move the $n - 1$ disks from pole C to pole B; that is, solve the problem with pole C as the source, pole B as the destination, and pole A as the spare." (See Figure 2-16d.)

There was silence for a few moments, and finally the emperor said impatiently, "Well, are you going to tell us your solution or not?" The monk simply gave an all-knowing smile and vanished.

The emperor obviously was not a recursive thinker, but you should realize that the monk's solution is perfectly correct. The key to the solution is the observation that you can solve the Towers problem of n disks by solving three smaller—in the sense of number of disks —Towers problems. Let towers(count, source, destination, spare) denote the problem of moving count disks from pole source to pole destination, using pole spare as a spare. Notice that this definition makes sense even if there are more than count disks on pole source; in this case, you concern yourself with only the top count disks and ignore the others. Similarly, the poles destination and spare might have disks on them before you begin; you ignore these, too, except that you may place only smaller disks on top of them.

You can restate the emperor's problem as follows: Beginning with *n* disks on pole A and zero disks on poles B and C, solve `towers(n, A, B, C)`. You can state the monk's solution as follows:

Step 1. Starting in the initial state—with all the disks on pole A—solve the problem

`towers(n - 1, A, C, B)`

That is, ignore the bottom (largest) disk and move the top *n* − 1 disks from pole A to pole C, using pole B as a spare. When you are finished, the largest disk will remain on pole A, and all the other disks will be on pole C.

Step 2. Now, with the largest disk on pole A and all others on pole C, solve the problem

`towers(1, A, B, C)`

That is, move the largest disk from pole A to pole B. Because this disk is larger than the disks already on the spare pole C, you really could not use the spare. However, fortunately—and obviously—you do not need to use the spare in this base case. When you are done, the largest disk will be on pole B, and all other disks will remain on pole C.

Step 3. Finally, with the largest disk on pole B and all the other disks on pole C, solve the problem

`towers(n - 1, C, B, A)`

That is, move the *n* − 1 disks from pole C to pole B, using A as a spare. Notice that the destination pole B already has the largest disk, which you ignore. When you are done, you will have solved the original problem: All the disks will be on pole B.

The problem `towers(count, source, destination, spare)` has the following pseudocode solution:

```
solveTowers(count, source, destination, spare)
{
    if (count is 1)
        Move a disk directly from source to destination
    else
    {
        solveTowers(count - 1, source, spare, destination)
        solveTowers(1, source, destination, spare)
        solveTowers(count - 1, spare, destination, source)
    }
}
```

This recursive solution follows the same basic pattern as the recursive solutions you saw earlier in this chapter:

1. You solve a Towers problem by solving other Towers problems.
2. These other Towers problems are smaller than the original problem; they have fewer disks to move. In particular, the number of disks decreases by 1 at each recursive call.
3. When a problem has only one disk—the base case—the solution is easy to solve directly.
4. The way that the problems become smaller ensures that you will reach a base case.

Solving the Towers problem requires you to solve many smaller Towers problems recursively. Figure 2-17 illustrates the resulting recursive calls and their order when you solve the problem for three disks.

Now consider a C++ implementation of this algorithm. Notice that since most computers do not have arms (at the time of this writing), the function moves a disk by giving directions to a human. Thus, the parameters that represent the poles are of type `char`, and the corresponding arguments could be `'A'`, `'B'`, and `'C'`. The call `solveTowers(3, 'A', 'B', 'C')` produces this output:

FIGURE 2-17   The order of recursive calls that results from solveTowers(3, A, B, C)

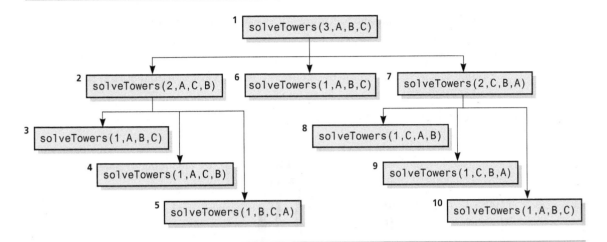

```
Move top disk from pole A to pole B
Move top disk from pole A to pole C
Move top disk from pole B to pole C
Move top disk from pole A to pole B
Move top disk from pole C to pole A
Move top disk from pole C to pole B
Move top disk from pole A to pole B
```

The C++ function follows:

```cpp
void solveTowers(int count, char source, char destination, char spare)
{
   if (count == 1)
   {
      std::cout << "Move top disk from pole " << source
                << " to pole " << destination << std::endl;
   }
   else
   {
      solveTowers(count - 1, source, spare, destination); // X
      solveTowers(1, source, destination, spare);         // Y
      solveTowers(count - 1, spare, destination, source); // Z
   } // end if
} // end solveTowers
```

Question 9 Trace the execution of the function solveTowers to solve the Towers of Hanoi problem for two disks.

2.6   More Examples

The next three problems require you to count certain events or combinations of events or things. They are good examples of recursive solutions with more than one base case. However, these solutions are tremendously inefficient, and so are not practical. Do not let this inefficiency discourage you. Recursion can be useful and efficient, even though it is not always so. Your goal right now is to understand recursion by examining simple problems.

2.6.1   The Fibonacci Sequence (Multiplying Rabbits)

Rabbits are very prolific breeders. If rabbits did not die, their population would quickly get out of hand. Suppose we assume the following "facts," which were obtained in a recent survey of randomly selected rabbits:

* Rabbits never die.
* A rabbit reaches sexual maturity exactly two months after birth; that is, at the beginning of its third month of life.
* Rabbits are always born in male-female pairs. At the beginning of every month, each sexually mature male-female pair gives birth to exactly one male-female pair.

Suppose that you started with a single newborn male-female pair. How many pairs would there be in month 6, counting the births that took place at the beginning of month 6? As 6 is a relatively small number, you can figure out the solution easily:

Month 1: 1 pair, the original rabbits.

Month 2: 1 pair still, because the rabbits are not yet sexually mature.

Month 3: 2 pairs; the original pair has reached sexual maturity and has given birth to a second pair.

Month 4: 3 pairs; the original pair has given birth again, but the pair born at the beginning of month 3 are not yet sexually mature.

Month 5: 5 pairs; all rabbits alive in month 3 (2 pairs) are now sexually mature. Add their offspring to those pairs alive in month 4 (3 pairs) to yield 5 pairs.

Month 6: 8 pairs; 3 newborn pairs from the pairs alive in month 4 plus 5 pairs alive in month 5.

You can now construct a recursive solution for computing *rabbit*(*n*), the number of pairs alive in month *n*. You must determine how you can use *rabbit*(*n* − 1) to compute *rabbit*(*n*). Observe that *rabbit*(*n*) is the sum of the number of pairs alive just prior to the start of month *n* and the number of pairs born at the start of month *n*. Just prior to the start of month *n*, there are *rabbit*(*n* − 1) pairs of rabbits. Not all of these rabbits are sexually mature at the start of month *n*. Only those that were alive in month *n* − 2 are ready to reproduce at the start of month *n*. That is, the number of pairs born at the start of month *n* is *rabbit*(*n* − 2). Therefore, you have the recurrence relation

The number of pairs in month *n*

$$rabbit(n) = rabbit(n - 1) + rabbit(n - 2)$$

Figure 2-18 illustrates this relationship.

FIGURE 2-18   Recursive solution to the rabbit problem

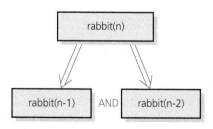

This recurrence relation—like some previous examples—solves a problem by solving more than one smaller problem of the same type. This does not add much conceptual difficulty, but you must be very careful when selecting the base case. The temptation is simply to say that *rabbit*(1) should be the base case because its value is 1 according to the problem's statement. But what about *rabbit*(2)? Applying the recursive definition to *rabbit*(2) would yield

$$rabbit(2) = rabbit(1) + rabbit(0)$$

Thus, the recursive definition would need to specify the number of pairs alive in month 0—an undefined quantity.

One possible solution is to define *rabbit*(0) to be 0, but this approach seems artificial. A slightly more attractive alternative is to treat *rabbit*(2) itself as a special case with the value of 1. Thus, the recursive definition has two base cases, *rabbit*(2) and *rabbit*(1). The recursive definition becomes

Two base cases are necessary because there are two smaller problems

$$rabbit(n) = \begin{cases} 1 & \text{if } n \text{ is 1 or 2} \\ rabbit(n-1) + rabbit(n-2) & \text{if } n > 2 \end{cases}$$

Incidentally, the series of numbers *rabbit*(1), *rabbit*(2), *rabbit*(3), and so on is known as the **Fibonacci sequence**, which models many naturally occurring phenomena.

A C++ function to compute *rabbit*(n) is easy to write from the previous definition:

```
/** Computes a term in the Fibonacci sequence.
 @pre  n is a positive integer.
 @post  None.
 @param n  The given integer.
 @return  The nth Fibonacci number. */
int rabbit(int n)
{
   if (n <= 2)
      return 1;
   else // n > 2, so n - 1 > 0 and n - 2 > 0
      return rabbit(n - 1) + rabbit(n - 2);
}  // end rabbit
```

rabbit computes the Fibonacci sequence but does so inefficiently

Should you actually use this function? Figure 2-19 illustrates the recursive calls that rabbit(7) generates. Think about the number of recursive calls that rabbit(10) generates. At best, the function rabbit is inefficient. Thus, its use is not feasible for large values of n. This problem is discussed in more detail at the end of this chapter, at which time you will see some techniques for generating a more efficient solution from this same recursive relationship.

 Note: A recursive solution that recomputes certain values frequently can be quite inefficient. In such cases, iteration may be preferable to recursion.

2.6.2 Organizing a Parade

You have been asked to organize the Fourth of July parade, which will consist of bands and floats in a single line. Last year, adjacent bands tried to outplay each other. To avoid this problem, the sponsors have asked you never to place one band immediately after another. In how many ways can you organize a parade of length *n*?

FIGURE 2-19   The recursive calls that rabbit(7) generates

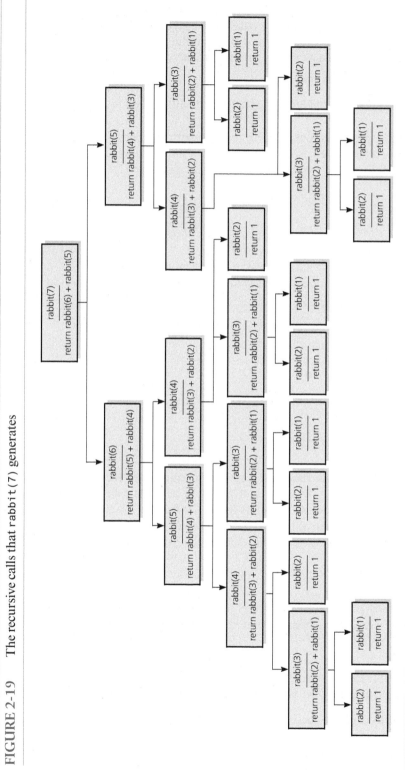

Assume that you have at least n marching bands and n floats from which to choose. Since the parade is of length n, it will not include all of the available bands and floats. When counting the number of ways to organize the parade, assume that the parades *band-float* and *float-band*, for example, are different parades and count as two ways.

The parade can end with either a float or a band. The number of ways to organize the parade is simply the sum of the number of parades of each type. That is, let

$P(n)$ be the number of ways to organize a parade of length n
$F(n)$ be the number of parades of length n that end with a float
$B(n)$ be the number of parades of length n that end with a band

Then

$P(n) = F(n) + B(n)$

First, consider $F(n)$. You will have a parade of length n that ends with a float simply by placing a float at the end of *any* acceptable parade of length $n - 1$. Hence, the number of acceptable parades of length n that end with a float is precisely equal to the total number of acceptable parades of length $n - 1$; that is

$F(n) = P(n - 1)$

The number of acceptable parades of length n that end with a float

Next, consider $B(n)$. The only way a parade can end with a band is if the unit just before the end is a float. (If it is a band, you will have two adjacent bands.) Thus, the only way to organize an acceptable parade of length n that ends with a band is first to organize a parade of length $n - 1$ that ends with a float and then add a band to the end. Therefore, the number of acceptable parades of length n that end with a band is precisely equal to the number of acceptable parades of length $n - 1$ that end with a float:

$B(n) = F(n - 1)$

The number of acceptable parades of length n that end with a band

You use the earlier fact that $F(n) = P(n - 1)$ to obtain

$B(n) = P(n - 2)$

Thus, you have solved $F(n)$ and $B(n)$ in terms of the smaller problems $P(n - 1)$ and $P(n - 2)$, respectively. You then use

$P(n) = F(n) + B(n)$

to obtain

$P(n) = P(n - 1) + P(n - 2)$

The number of acceptable parades of length n

The form of this recurrence relation is identical to the solution for the multiplying rabbits problem.

As you saw in the rabbit problem, two base cases are necessary, because the recurrence relation defines a problem in terms of two smaller problems. As you did for the rabbit problem, you can choose $n = 1$ and $n = 2$ for the base cases. Although both problems use the same values of n for their base cases, there is no reason to expect that they use the same values for these base cases. That is, there is no reason to expect that $rabbit(1)$ is equal to $P(1)$ and that $rabbit(2)$ is equal to $P(2)$.

Two base cases are necessary because there are two smaller problems

A little thought reveals that for the parade problem,

$P(1) = 2$ (The parades of length 1 are *float* and *band*.)
$P(2) = 3$ (The parades of length 2 are *float-float*, *band-float*, and *float-band*.)

In summary, the solution to this problem is

$P(1) = 2$
$P(2) = 3$
$P(n) = P(n - 1) + P(n - 2)$ for $n > 2$

A recursive solution

This example demonstrates the following points about recursion:

- Sometimes you can solve a problem by breaking it up into cases—for example, parades that end with a float and parades that end with a band.
- The values that you use for the base cases are extremely important. Although the recurrence relations for P and *rabbit* are the same, their base cases (when $n = 1$ or 2) are different. This difference causes *rabbit*(n) and $P(n)$ to differ when n is greater than 2. For example, *rabbit*(20) = 6,765, while $P(20)$ = 17,711. The larger the value of n, the larger the discrepancy. You should think about why this is so.

2.6.3   Choosing k Out of n Things

A rock band would like to tour n cities. Unfortunately, time will allow for visits to only k cities. The band's agent considers the different choices for visiting k cities out of the n possibilities. Because time is short, the band members are not concerned about the order in which they visit the same k cities.

Let $g(n, k)$ be the number of groups of k cities chosen from n. If we consider city C, either we visit C or we do not. If we do visit city C, we will have to choose $k - 1$ other cities to visit from the $n - 1$ remaining cities. Thus, the number of groups of cities that include C is $g(n - 1, k - 1)$. On the other hand, if we do not visit city C, we will have to choose k cities to visit from the remaining $n - 1$ cities. The number of groups of cities that do not include C is $g(n - 1, k)$. Thus, we can compute $g(n, k)$ by solving two smaller counting problems of the same type; that is,

The number of ways to choose k out of n things is the sum of the number of ways to choose $k - 1$ out of $n - 1$ things and the number of ways to choose k out of $n - 1$ things

$$g(n, k) = g(n - 1, k - 1) + g(n - 1, k)$$

We still need to find the base case(s) and demonstrate that each of the two smaller problems eventually reaches a base case. First, if the band had time to visit all n cities—that is, if k equals n—there is only one group of all the cities. Thus, the first base case is

$$g(k, k) = 1$$

Just as there is only one group of all the cities ($k = n$), there is also only one group of zero cities ($k = 0$). Thus, the second base case is

$$g(n, 0) = 1$$

(Alternatively, you could define the second base case to be $g(n, 1) = n$.)

Now if $k < n$, the second term $g(n - 1, k)$ in the recursive definition will reach the first base case, because at each successive stage of the recursion, $n - 1$ decreases until it reaches k. However, the first term, $g(n - 1, k - 1)$, does not reach this base case. Since $n - 1$ and $k - 1$ both decrease at the same rate, they will never become equal. The first term, $g(n - 1, k - 1)$, does, in fact, approach the second base case.

 Note: When you solve a problem by solving two (or more) smaller problems, each of the smaller problems must be closer to a base case than the original problem.

For completeness, we add one final part to this recursive solution:

$$g(n, k) = 0 \quad \text{if } k > n$$

Although k could not be greater than n in the context of this problem, the addition of this case makes the recursive solution more generally applicable.

To summarize, the following recursive solution solves the problem of choosing k out of n things:

$$g(n, k) = \begin{cases} 1 & \text{if } k = 0 \\ 1 & \text{if } k = n \\ 0 & \text{if } k > n \\ g(n - 1, k - 1) + g(n - 1, k) & \text{if } 0 < k < n \end{cases}$$

The number of groups of k things recursively chosen out of n things

You can easily derive the following function from this recursive definition:

```
/** Computes the number of groups of k out of n things.
 @pre   n and k are nonnegative integers.
 @post  None.
 @param n  The given number of things.
 @param k  The given number to choose.
 @return  g(n, k). */
int getNumberOfGroups(int n, int k)
{
   if ( (k == 0) || (k == n) )
      return 1;
   else if (k > n)
      return 0;
   else
      return getNumberOfGroups(n - 1, k - 1) + getNumberOfGroups(n - 1, k);
}  // end getNumberOfGroups
```

Like the rabbit function, this function is inefficient and not practical to use. Figure 2-20 shows the number of recursive calls that the computation of g(4, 2) requires.

FIGURE 2-20   The recursive calls that g (4, 2) generates

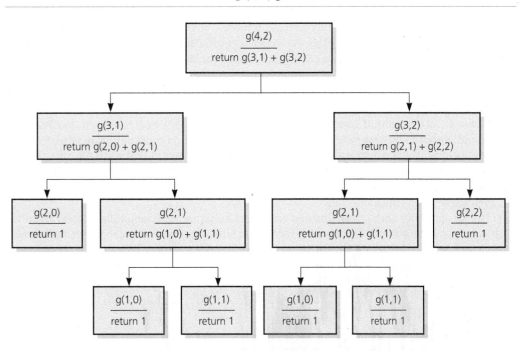

Note: When a recursive function contains more than one recursive call, you often will need more than one base case.

Question 10 Compute $g(4, 2)$.

2.7   Recursion and Efficiency

Recursion is a powerful problem-solving technique that often produces very clean solutions to even the most complex problems. Recursive solutions can be easier to understand and to describe than iterative solutions. By using recursion, you can often write simple, short implementations of your solution.

The overriding concern of this chapter has been to give you a solid understanding of recursion so that you will be able to construct recursive solutions on your own. Most of our examples, therefore, have been simple. Unfortunately, some of the recursive solutions in this chapter are so inefficient that you should not use them. The recursive functions `binarySearch` and `solveTowers` are the notable exceptions, as they are quite efficient.[2]

Two factors contribute to the inefficiency of some recursive solutions:

- The overhead associated with function calls
- The inherent inefficiency of making recursive calls whose arguments are the same as those in earlier recursive calls

The first of these factors does not pertain specifically to recursive functions but is true of functions in general. In most implementations of C++ and other high-level programming languages, a function call incurs a certain amount of bookkeeping overhead. As was mentioned earlier, each function call produces an activation record, which is analogous to a box in the box trace. Recursive functions magnify this overhead because a single initial call to the function can generate a large number of recursive calls. For example, the call *factorial*(*n*) generates *n* recursive calls. On the other hand, the use of recursion, as is true of modularity in general, can greatly clarify complex programs. This clarification frequently more than compensates for the additional overhead.

However, you should not use recursion just for the sake of using recursion. For example, you probably should not use the recursive *factorial* function in practice. You can easily write an iterative *factorial* function, given the iterative definition that was stated earlier in this chapter. The iterative function is almost as clear as the recursive one and is more efficient. There is no reason to incur the overhead of recursion when its use does not gain anything. *Recursion is truly valuable when a problem has no simple iterative solutions.*

The second point about recursion and efficiency is that some recursive algorithms are inherently inefficient. This inefficiency is a very different issue than that of overhead. It has nothing to do with how a compiler happens to implement a recursive function, but rather is related to the technique that the algorithm employs.

Factors that contribute to the inefficiency of some recursive solutions

Recursion can clarify complex solutions

Do not use a recursive solution if it is inefficient and you have a clear, efficient iterative solution

---

[2]Chapters 5 and 11 present other practical, efficient applications of recursion.

As an example, recall the recursive solution for the multiplying rabbits problem that you saw earlier in this chapter:

$$rabbit(n) = \begin{cases} 1 & \text{if } n \text{ is 1 or 2} \\ rabbit(n-1) + rabbit(n-2) & \text{if } n > 2 \end{cases}$$

The recursive version of `rabbit` is inherently inefficient

The diagram in Figure 2-19 illustrated the computation of *rabbit*(7). Earlier, you were asked to think about what the diagram would look like for *rabbit*(10). If you thought about this question, you may have come to the conclusion that such a diagram would fill up most of this chapter. The diagram for *rabbit*(100) would fill up most of this universe!

The fundamental problem with *rabbit* is that it computes the same values over and over again. For example, in the diagram for *rabbit*(7), you can see that *rabbit*(3) is computed five times. When *n* is moderately large, many of the values are recomputed literally trillions of times. This enormous number of computations makes the solution infeasible, even if each computation requires only a trivial amount of work.

However, do not conclude that the recurrence relation is of no use. One way to solve the rabbit problem is to construct an iterative solution based on this same recurrence relation. The iterative solution goes forward instead of backward and computes each value only once. You can use the following iterative function to compute *rabbit*(n) even for very large values of *n*.

You can use `rabbit`'s recurrence relation to construct an efficient iterative solution

```
/** Iterative solution to the rabbit problem. */
int iterativeRabbit(int n)
{
   // Initialize base cases:
   int previous = 1;   // Initially rabbit(1)
   int current = 1;    // Initially rabbit(2)
   int next = 1;       // rabbit(n); initial value when n is 1 or 2

   // Compute next rabbit values when n >= 3
   for (int i = 3; i <= n; i++)
   {
      // current is rabbit(i - 1), previous is rabbit(i - 2)
      next = current + previous;   // rabbit(i)
      previous = current;          // Get ready for next iteration
      current = next;
   }  // end for

   return next;
}  // end iterativeRabbit
```

Thus, an iterative solution can be more efficient than a recursive solution. In certain cases, however, it may be easier to discover a recursive solution than an iterative solution. Therefore, you may need to convert a recursive solution to an iterative solution. This conversion process is easier if your recursive function calls itself once, instead of several times. Be careful when deciding whether your function calls itself more than once. Although the recursive function `rabbit` calls itself twice, the function `binarySearch` calls itself once, even though you see two calls in the C++ code. Those two calls appear within an `if` statement; only one of them will be executed.

Convert from recursion to iteration if it is easier to discover a recursive solution but more efficient to use an iterative solution

Converting a recursive solution to an iterative solution is even easier when the solitary recursive call is the last *action* that the function takes. This situation is called **tail recursion**. For example, the function `writeBackward` exhibits tail recursion because its recursive call is the last action that the function takes. Before you conclude that this is obvious, consider the function `fact`. Although its recursive call appears last in the function definition, `fact`'s last action is the multiplication. Thus, `fact` is not tail-recursive.

A tail-recursive function

Recall the definition of `writeBackward`:

```cpp
void writeBackward(std::string s)
{
   int length = s.size();
   if (length > 0)
   {
      // Write last character
      std::cout << s.substr(length - 1, 1);
      writeBackward(s.substr(0, length - 1)); // Write rest
   } // end if
} // end writeBackward
```

Removing tail
recursion is often
straightforward

Because this function is tail-recursive, its last recursive call simply repeats the function's action with altered arguments. You can perform this repetitive action by using an iteration that will be straightforward and often more efficient. For example, the following definition of `writeBackward` is iterative:

```cpp
/** Iterative version. */
void writeBackward(std::string s)
{
   int length = s.size();
   while (length > 0)
   {
      std::cout << s.substr(length - 1, 1);
      length--;
   } // end while
} // end writeBackward
```

Because tail-recursive functions are often less efficient than their iterative counterparts, and because the conversion of a tail-recursive function to an equivalent iterative function is rather mechanical, some compilers automatically replace tail recursion with iteration. Eliminating other forms of recursion is usually more complex and is a task that *you* would need to undertake, if necessary.

Some recursive algorithms, such as *rabbit*, are inherently inefficient, while other recursive algorithms, such as the binary search,[3] are extremely efficient. You will learn how to determine the relative efficiency of a recursive algorithm in more advanced courses concerned with the analysis of algorithms. Chapter 10 introduces some of these techniques briefly.

Chapter 5 continues the discussion of recursion by examining several difficult problems that have straightforward recursive solutions. Other chapters in this book use recursion as a matter of course.

Question 11 Of the following recursive functions that you saw in this chapter, identify those that exhibit tail recursion: `fact`, `writeBackward`, `writeBackward2`, `rabbit`, *P* in the parade problem, `getNumberOfGroups`, `maxArray`, `binarySearch`, and `kSmall`.

---

[3] The binary search algorithm also has an iterative formulation.

SUMMARY

1. Recursion is a technique that solves a problem by solving a smaller problem of the same type.

2. When constructing a recursive solution, keep the following four questions in mind:

   a. How can you define the problem in terms of a smaller problem of the same type?
   b. How does each recursive call diminish the size of the problem?
   c. What instance of the problem can serve as the base case?
   d. As the problem size diminishes, will you reach this base case?

3. When constructing a recursive solution, you should assume that a recursive call's result is correct if its precondition has been met.

4. You can use the box trace to trace the actions of a recursive function. These boxes resemble activation records, which many compilers use to implement recursion. Although the box trace is useful, it cannot replace an intuitive understanding of recursion.

5. Recursion allows you to solve problems—such as the Towers of Hanoi—whose iterative solutions are difficult to conceptualize. Even the most complex problems often have straightforward recursive solutions. Such solutions can be easier to understand, describe, and implement than iterative solutions.

6. Some recursive solutions are much less efficient than a corresponding iterative solution due to their inherently inefficient algorithms and the overhead of function calls. In such cases, the iterative solution can be preferable. You can use the recursive solution, however, to derive the iterative solution.

7. If you can easily, clearly, and efficiently solve a problem by using iteration, you should do so.

EXERCISES

1. The following recursive function getNumberEqual searches the array x of n integers for occurrences of the integer desiredValue. It returns the number of integers in x that are equal to desiredValue. For example, if x contains the ten integers 1, 2, 4, 4, 5, 6, 7, 8, 9, and 12, then getNumberEqual(x, 10, 4) returns the value 2, because 4 occurs twice in x.

```
int getNumberEqual(const int x[], int n, int desiredValue)
{
   int count = 0;

   if (n <= 0)
      return 0;
   else
   {
      if (x[n - 1] == desiredValue)
         count = 1;

      return getNumberEqual(x, n - 1, desiredValue) + count;
   } // end else
} // end getNumberEqual
```

Demonstrate that this function is recursive by listing the criteria of a recursive solution and stating how the function meets each criterion.

2. Perform a box trace of the following calls to recursive functions that appear in this chapter. Clearly indicate each subsequent recursive call.
   a. rabbit(5)
   b. countDown(5) (You wrote countDown in Checkpoint Question 3.)

3. Write a recursive function that will compute the sum of the first *n* integers in an array of at least *n* integers. *Hint:* Begin with the *n*th integer.

4. Given two integers, *start* and *end*, where *end* is greater than *start*, write a recursive C++ function that returns the sum of the integers from *start* through *end*, inclusive.

5. **a.** Revise the function writeBackward, discussed in Section 2.3.1, so that its base case is a string of length 1.
    b. Write a C++ function that implements the pseudocode function writeBackward2, as given in Section 2.3.1.

6. Describe the problem with the following recursive function:

    ```cpp
    void printNum(int n)
    {
        std::cout << n << std::endl;
        printNum(n - 1);
    }  // end printNum
    ```

7. Given an integer *n* > 0, write a recursive C++ function that writes the integers 1, 2, ..., *n*.

8. Given an integer *n* > 0, write a recursive C++ function that returns the sum of the squares of 1 through *n*.

9. Write a recursive C++ function that writes the digits of a positive decimal integer in reverse order.

10. **a.** Write a recursive C++ function writeLine that writes a character repeatedly to form a line of *n* characters. For example, writeLine('*', 5) produces the line *****.
    b. Now write a recursive function writeBlock that uses writeLine to write *m* lines of *n* characters each. For example, writeBlock('*', 5, 3) produces the output

    ```
    *****
    *****
    *****
    ```

11. What output does the following program produce?

    ```cpp
    int getValue(int a, int b, int n);
    int main()
    {
        std::cout << getValue(1, 7, 7) << std::endl;
        return 0;
    }  // end main

    int getValue(int a, int b, int n)
    {
        int returnValue = 0;
        std::cout << "Enter: a = " << a << " b = " << b << std::endl;
        int c = (a + b)/2;
        if (c * c <= n)
            returnValue = c;
        else
            returnValue = getValue(a, c-1, n);

        std::cout << "Leave: a = " << a << " b = " << b << std::endl;
        return returnValue;
    }  // end getValue
    ```

12. What output does the following program produce?

    ```cpp
    int search(int first, int last, int n);
    int mystery(int n);
    int main()
    {
    ```

```
std::cout << "mystery(30) produces the following output: \n";
int result = mystery(30);
std::cout << "mystery(30) = " << result << "; should be 5\n";
return 0;
} // end main

int search(int first, int last, int n)
{
   int returnValue = 0;
   std::cout << "Enter: first = " << first << " last = "
             << last << std::endl;

   int mid = (first + last)/2;
   if ( (mid * mid <= n) && (n < (mid+1) * (mid+1)) )
      returnValue = mid;
   else if (mid * mid > n)
      returnValue = search(first, mid-1, n);
   else
      returnValue = search(mid+1, last, n);
   std::cout << "Leave: first = "
             << first << " last = " << last << std::endl;
   return returnValue;
} // end search

int mystery(int n)
{
   return search(1, n, n);
} // end mystery
```

13. Consider the following function that converts a positive decimal number to base 8 and displays the result.

```
void displayOctal(int n)
{
   if (n > 0)
   {
      if (n / 8 > 0)
         displayOctal(n / 8);
      std::cout << n % 8;
   } // end if
} // end displayOctal
```

Describe how the algorithm works. Trace the function with $n = 100$.

14. Consider the following program:

```
int f(int n);

int main()
{
   std::cout << "The value of f(8) is " << f(8) << std::endl;
   return  0;
} // end main

/** @pre   n >= 0. */
int f(int n)
{
   std::cout << "Function entered with n = " << n << std::endl;
   switch (n)
   {
      case 0: case 1: case 2:
         return n + 1;
      default:
```

```
                    return f(n-2) * f(n-4);
        }  // end switch
}  // end f
```

Show the exact output of the program. What argument values, if any, could you pass to the function f to cause the program to run forever?

15. Consider the following function:

```
void recurse(int x, int y)
{
    if (y > 0)
    {
        x++;
        y--;
        std::cout << x  << " " << y << std::endl;
        recurse(x, y);
        std::cout << x << " " << y << std::endl;
    }  // end if
}  // end recurse
```

Execute the function with $x = 5$ and $y = 3$. How is the output affected if x is a reference argument instead of a value argument?

16. Perform a box trace of the recursive function binarySearch, which appears in Section 2.4.2, with the array 1, 5, 9, 12, 15, 21, 29, 31 for each of the following search values:

    a. 5
    b. 13
    c. 16

17. The algorithm kSmall, as discussed in Section 2.4.4, assumes that the array contains distinct values. Modify the algorithm so that the array can contain duplicate values. You will need to decide whether the second smallest value in the array 7 7 8 9, for example, is 7 or 8. Although, your choice is arbitrary, it will affect your algorithm.

18. Imagine that you have 101 Dalmatians; no two Dalmatians have the same number of spots. Suppose that you create an array of 101 integers: The first integer is the number of spots on the first Dalmatian, the second integer is the number of spots on the second Dalmatian, and so on. Your friend wants to know whether you have a Dalmatian with 99 spots. Thus, you need to determine whether the array contains the integer 99.

    a. If you plan to use a binary search to look for the 99, what, if anything, would you do to the array before searching it?
    b. What is the index of the integer in the array that a binary search would examine first?
    c. If none of your Dalmatians have 99 spots, exactly how many comparisons will a binary search require to determine that 99 is not in the array?

19. This problem considers several ways to compute x^n for some $n \geq 0$.

    a. Write an iterative function power1 to compute x^n for $n \geq 0$.
    b. Write a recursive function power2 to compute x^n by using the following recursive formulation:

$$x^0 = 1$$
$$x^n = x \times x^{n-1} \text{ if } n > 0$$

c. Write a recursive function `power3` to compute x^n by using the following recursive formulation:

$x^0 = 1$

$x^n = (x^{n/2})^2$ if $n > 0$ and n is even

$x^n = x \times (x^{n/2})^2$ if $n > 0$ and n is odd

d. How many multiplications will each of the functions `power1`, `power2`, and `power3` perform when computing 3^{32}? 3^{19}?

e. How many recursive calls will `power2` and `power3` make when computing 3^{32}? 3^{19}?

20. Modify the recursive `rabbit` function so that it is visually easy to follow the flow of execution. Instead of just adding "Enter" and "Leave" messages, indent the trace messages according to how "deep" the current recursive call is. For example, the call `rabbit(4)` should produce the output

```
Enter rabbit: n = 4
   Enter rabbit: n = 3
      Enter rabbit: n = 2
      Leave rabbit: n = 2 value = 1
      Enter rabbit: n = 1
      Leave rabbit: n = 1 value = 1
   Leave rabbit: n = 3 value = 2
   Enter rabbit: n = 2
   Leave rabbit: n = 2 value = 1
Leave rabbit: n = 4 value = 3
```

Note how this output corresponds to Figure 2-19.

21. Consider the following recurrence relation:

$f(1) = 1; f(2) = 1; f(3) = 1; f(4) = 3; f(5) = 5;$
$f(n) = f(n - 1) + 3 \times f(n - 5)$ for all $n > 5$.

a. Compute $f(n)$ for the following values of n: 6, 7, 12, 15.

b. If you were careful, rather than computing $f(15)$ from scratch (the way a recursive C++ function would compute it), you would have computed $f(6)$, then $f(7)$, then $f(8)$, and so on up to $f(15)$, recording the values as you computed them. This ordering would have saved you the effort of ever computing the same value more than once. (Recall the iterative version of the rabbit function discussed at the end of this chapter.)

Note that during the computation, you never need to remember all of the previously computed values—only the last five. Taking advantage of these observations, write a C++ function that computes $f(n)$ for arbitrary values of n.

22. Write iterative versions of the following recursive functions: `fact`, `writeBackward`, `binarySearch`, and `kSmall`.

23. Prove that the function `iterativeRabbit`, which appears in Section 2.7, is correct by using invariants. (See Appendix F for a discussion of invariants.)

24. Consider the problem of finding the greatest common divisor (gcd) of two positive integers a and b. The algorithm presented here is a variation of Euclid's algorithm, which is based on the following theorem:[4]

Theorem. If a and b are positive integers with $a > b$ such that b is not a divisor of a, then

$gcd(a, b) = gcd(b, a \bmod b)$.

---

[4] This book uses mod as an abbreviation for the mathematical operation modulo. In C++, the modulo operator is %.

This relationship between $gcd(a, b)$ and $gcd(b, a \bmod b)$ is the heart of the recursive solution. It specifies how you can solve the problem of computing $gcd(a, b)$ in terms of another problem of the same type. Also, if b does divide a, then $b = gcd(a, b)$, so an appropriate choice for the base case is $(a \bmod b) = 0$.

This theorem leads to the following recursive definition:

$$gcd(a, b) = \begin{cases} b & \text{if } (a \bmod b) = 0 \\ gcd(b, a \bmod b) & \text{otherwise} \end{cases}$$

The following function implements this recursive algorithm:

```
int gcd(int a, int b)
{
    if (a % b == 0) // Base case
        return b;
    else
        return gcd(b, a % b);
}  // end gcd
```

   a. Prove the theorem.
   b. What happens if $b > a$?
   c. How is the problem getting smaller? (That is, do you always approach a base case?) Why is the base case appropriate?

25. Let $c(n)$ be the number of different groups of integers that can be chosen from the integers 1 through $n - 1$ so that the integers in each group add up to n (for example, $n = 4 = [1 + 1 + 1 + 1] = [1 + 1 + 2] = [2 + 2]$). Write recursive definitions for $c(n)$ under the following variations:

   a. You count permutations. For example, 1, 2, 1 and 1, 1, 2 are two groups that each add up to 4.
   b. You ignore permutations.

26. Consider the following recursive definition:

$$Acker(m, n) = \begin{cases} n + 1 & \text{if } m = 0 \\ Acker(m - 1, 1) & \text{if } n = 0 \\ Acker(m - 1, Acker(m, n - 1)) & \text{otherwise} \end{cases}$$

This function, called *Ackermann's function*, is of interest because it grows rapidly with respect to the sizes of m and n. What is $Acker(1, 2)$? Implement the function in C++ and do a box trace of $Acker(1, 2)$. (*Caution:* Even for modest values of m and n, Ackermann's function requires *many* recursive calls.)

PROGRAMMING PROBLEMS

1. Implement a recursive function that computes a^n, where a is a real number and n is a nonnegative integer.

2. Implement the algorithm maxArray, discussed in Section 2.4.3, as a C++ function. What other recursive definitions of maxArray can you describe?

3. Implement the binarySearch algorithm presented in this chapter for an array of strings.

4. Implement the algorithm kSmall, discussed in Section 2.4.4, as a C++ function. Use the first value of the array as the pivot.

Array-Based Implementations

Contents

Prerequisites

Appendix A	Review of C++ Fundamentals
Chapter 1	Data Abstraction: The Walls
C++ Interlude 1	C++ Classes
Chapter 2	Recursion: The Mirrors (for Section 3.3)

You have seen that during the design of a solution, you must support several operations on data and therefore need to define abstract data types (ADTs). Only after you have clearly specified the operations of an ADT should you consider data structures for implementing it. This chapter explores implementation issues that involve arrays as the underlying data structures.

3.1   The Approach

An ADT is a collection of data and a set of operations on that data

We have said that a collection of data, together with a set of operations on that data, are called an abstract data type, or ADT. For example, suppose that you want to store a collection of names that you can search rapidly. The collection of names, together with operations that add a name, remove a name, and search for a name, can form an ADT that solves this problem.

Specifications indicate what ADT operations do, but not how to implement them

Previously, we emphasized the specification of an abstract data type. When you design an ADT, you concentrate on what its operations do, but you ignore how you will implement them. That is, the description of an ADT's operations must be rigorous enough to specify completely their effect on the data, yet it must not specify how to store the data nor how to carry out the operations. For example, the operations of an ADT should not specify whether to store the data in consecutive memory locations or in disjoint memory locations. The result should be a set of clearly specified ADT operations.

How do you implement an ADT once its operations are clearly specified? That is, how do you store the ADT's data and carry out its operations? You begin by choosing particular data structures to store the data. Recall that a data structure is a construct that you can define within a programming language to store a collection of data. For example, C++ arrays are data structures.

Your first reaction to the implementation question might be to choose a data structure and then to write methods that access it in accordance with the ADT's operations. Although this point of view is not incorrect, hopefully you have learned not to jump right into code. In general, you should refine an ADT through successive levels of abstraction yielding successively more concrete descriptions of the ADT.

The choices that you make during the implementation process can affect the execution time of your code. For now, our analyses will be intuitive, but Chapter 10 will introduce you to quantitative techniques that you can use to weigh the trade-offs involved.

Recall that the client—that is, the program that uses the ADT—should see only a wall of available operations that act on data, as Figure 1-5 in Chapter 1 illustrates. Both the data structure that you choose to contain the data and the implementations of the ADT's operations are hidden behind the wall. By now, you should realize the advantage of this wall and take steps to prevent a client's direct access—either intentional or accidental—to the data structure, as shown in Figure 3-1. Why is such access undesirable? Public data fields allow the client to *go around* the wall of abstraction and access the ADT's data directly. For example, suppose that you use an array items to store an ADT's data. In a program that uses the ADT, you might, for example, accidentally access the first element in the array by writing

```
firstItem = items[0];
```

instead of by invoking an ADT operation. If you changed to another implementation of the ADT, your program would be incorrect. To correct your program, you would need to locate and change all occurrences of items[0]—but first you would have to realize that items[0] is in error! Moreover, by violating the wall, a client could damage the ADT's data. If the data were ordered in a certain way, for example, the ADT's operations would ensure that the order was maintained. But if a client could alter the data directly, that order could be destroyed.

 Note: Implementing an ADT as a C++ class provides a way for you to enforce the wall of an ADT, thereby preventing access of the data structure in any way other than by using the ADT's operations. A client then cannot damage the ADT's data. Moreover, the client is independent of the details of the ADT's implementation, because it adheres only to the ADT's specifications.

FIGURE 3-1   Violating the wall of ADT operations

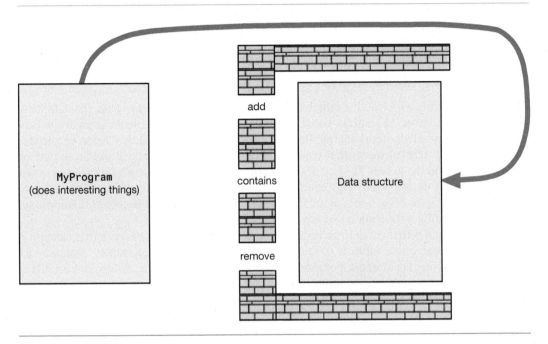

3.1.1 Core Methods

The definition of a class that implements an ADT could be fairly involved. In general, you should not define the entire class and then attempt to test it. Instead, you should identify a group of **core methods** to both implement and test before continuing with the rest of the class definition. By leaving the definitions of the other methods for later, you can focus your attention and simplify your task. But what methods should be part of this group? In general, such methods should be central to the purpose of the class and allow reasonable testing. We sometimes will call a group of core methods a **core group**.

When dealing with a container such as a bag, for example, you cannot test most methods until you have created the container and placed items into it. Thus, adding objects to the container is a fundamental operation. If the method add does not work correctly, testing other methods such as remove would be pointless. Thus, the add method would be part of the group of core methods that we implement first.

To test whether add works correctly, we need a method that allows us to see the container's data. For the ADT bag, the method toVector serves this purpose, and so it is a core method. Any constructors are also fundamental and are in the core group. Similarly, other methods that a core method might call are part of the core group as well. Such methods might be public methods within the ADT or private "helper" methods.

 Programming Tip: Methods such as add and remove that can alter the underlying data structure of a container are likely to have the most involved implementations. In general, you should define such methods before the others in the class. But since you can't test remove before add is correct, you should delay implementing it until after add is completed and thoroughly tested.

> **Programming Tip:** When defining a class, implement and test a group of core methods. Begin with methods that add to a container of objects and/or have involved implementations.

3.1.2   Using Fixed-Size Arrays

When implementing an ADT that represents a data collection, you need to store the data items and track their number. In an **array-based implementation**, you store the items in an array. How much of the array will the items occupy? Possibly all of it, but this is not likely. That is, you need to keep track of the array elements that you have assigned to contain the data and those that are available for use in the future. The maximum length of the array—its physical size—is a known, fixed value such as MAX_SIZE. You can keep track of the current number of items in the collection—that is, the collection's logical size—in a variable. An obvious benefit of this approach is that implementing an operation that reports this value will be easy.

When you add a first entry to an array, you typically place it in the array's first element—that is, the element whose index is 0. Doing so, however, is not a requirement, especially for arrays that implement containers. For example, some container implementations can benefit by ignoring the array element whose index is 0 and using index 1 as the first element in the array. Sometimes you might want to use the elements at the end of the array before the ones at its beginning. For the ADT bag, we have no reason to be atypical, and so the objects in a bag can begin at index 0 of the array.

Another consideration is whether the container's entries should occupy consecutive elements of the array. Requiring the add method to place objects into an array consecutively is certainly reasonable, but why should we care, and is this really a concern? It is a concern, because we need to establish certain truths, or **assertions**, about our planned implementation so that the action of each method is not detrimental to other methods. For example, the method toVector must "know" where add has placed the entries. Our decision now also will affect what must happen later when we remove an entry from the container. If we insist that the bag's entries occupy consecutive array elements, will the method remove ensure that they remain so?

What happens after add places a new entry into the last available array element? A subsequent addition will be impossible unless an entry is first removed from the array. An add method that encounters a full array should either signal its client or allocate a larger array. In this chapter, add will return a boolean value to indicate whether it was successful. In C++ Interlude 2, which follows this chapter, you will learn how to resize the array. Rather than returning a value, a method can signal its client by throwing an exception. C++ Interlude 3 will discuss this approach.

3.2   An Array-Based Implementation of the ADT Bag

VideoNote

Core ArrayBag
methods

We will now make the previous discussion concrete by implementing the ADT bag as a class using an array to store its entries. Recall from Chapter 1 that the ADT bag's operations are

```
+getCurrentSize(): integer
+isEmpty(): boolean
+add(newEntry: ItemType): boolean
+remove(anEntry: ItemType): boolean
+clear(): void
+getFrequencyOf(anEntry: ItemType): integer
+contains(anEntry: ItemType): boolean
+toVector(): vector
```

These operations will become public methods in our class.

Each method will require access to both the array of bag entries and the current number of entries in the bag. Thus, we make the array and a counter data members of the class. Since the length of the array defines the bag's capacity—that is, its maximum size—we will define a constant whose value is this size. To hide these data members from the clients of the class, we make them private. Thus, we define the following private data members within the header file for our class:

A client of the class cannot access the class's private members directly

```
static const int DEFAULT_CAPACITY = 50;
ItemType items[DEFAULT_CAPACITY]; // Array of bag items
int itemCount;                     // Current count of bag items
int maxItems;                      // Max capacity of the bag
```

Figure 3-2 illustrates these data members, assuming a bag of integers.

FIGURE 3-2   An array-based implementation of the ADT bag

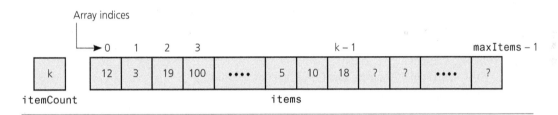

Security Note: Data members should be private

By making a class's data members private, you control how a client can access or change their values. Doing so protects the integrity of the data structure. If the client could manipulate this data directly because the data was public, it could alter the behavior of the ADT operations. Public data members also make debugging a program's logic harder, because you would need to look for errors outside of your class, greatly increasing the number of lines of code you must review.

3.2.1   The Header File

Having chosen the data members, and knowing the details of `BagInterface`, which we developed in Chapter 1, we can write the header file shown in Listing 3-1 for our class of bags. We name the class `ArrayBag` and give it a default constructor, which is sufficient for this example. Notice the small value given to the constant `DEFAULT_CAPACITY`. It enables us to fill a bag completely and easily to verify that our class behaves gracefully in this situation. After you study C++ Interlude 2, you will be able to add another constructor that enables the client to set the capacity of the bag during program execution. We included the data field `maxItems` in anticipation of this enhancement.

Also notice that we declare a private method `getIndexOf`. This method returns the index of the element within the array `items` that contains a given entry. As you will see later, we can use `getIndexOf` to make the methods `contains` and `remove` more time efficient. You most likely would not decide to add `getIndexOf` to the header file until after you began work on the implementation of the public methods.

LISTING 3-1 The header file for the class `ArrayBag`

```
1   /** Header file for an array-based implementation of the ADT bag.
2    @file ArrayBag.h */
3
4   #ifndef ARRAY_BAG_
5   #define ARRAY_BAG_
6
7   #include "BagInterface.h"
8
9   template<class ItemType>
10  class ArrayBag : public BagInterface<ItemType>
11  {
12  private:
13     static const int DEFAULT_CAPACITY = 6;  // Small size to test for a full bag
14     ItemType items[DEFAULT_CAPACITY];        // Array of bag items
15     int itemCount;                           // Current count of bag items
16     int maxItems;                            // Max capacity of the bag
17
18     // Returns either the index of the element in the array items that
19     // contains the given target or -1, if the array does not contain
20     // the target.
21     int getIndexOf(const ItemType& target) const;
22
23  public:
24     ArrayBag();
25     int getCurrentSize() const;
26     bool isEmpty() const;
27     bool add(const ItemType& newEntry);
28     bool remove(const ItemType& anEntry);
29     void clear();
30     bool contains(const ItemType& anEntry) const;
31     int getFrequencyOf(const ItemType& anEntry) const;
32     vector<ItemType> toVector() const;
33  }; // end ArrayBag
34
35  #include "ArrayBag.cpp"
36  #endif
```

[!] Programming Tip: When a method does not alter the class's data members, make it a const method as a safeguard against an implementation error.

[!] Programming Tip: Should the method `getIndexOf` be public or private?

You might think that the method `getIndexOf` would be useful to a client, since it returns the index of an entry in the array `items`. While that might be true, there are important reasons why the method should be private. We declared the array `items` as private because it is a detail of our array-based implementation. The client cannot access the entries in this array without invoking a public method of our class. The indices of these entries are also implementation details that are of no use to the client because it cannot access the array `items` by name. Any method that returns an index to a private array should be declared as private.

3.2.2   Defining the Core Methods

Section 3.1.1 suggests that we consider the methods add and toVector as core methods and define them first. Since we will want to check that add correctly increments the count of the bag's entries, we should also implement getCurrentSize and isEmpty. Thus, we add these two methods to our core group, along with appropriate constructors.

As we define the methods for the class ArrayBag, we place them into the file ArrayBag.cpp, which begins as follows:

```cpp
/** Implementation file for the class ArrayBag.
 @file ArrayBag.cpp */
#include "ArrayBag.h"
```

The constructor. The following default constructor initializes both the current number of items in the bag and the bag's capacity by using initializers, as described in C++ Interlude 1:

```cpp
template<class ItemType>
ArrayBag<ItemType>::ArrayBag(): itemCount(0), maxItems(DEFAULT_CAPACITY)
{
}  // end default constructor
```

The method add. To add a new item to a bag that is not full, we can place it right after the last item in the array by writing the following statement:

```cpp
items[itemCount] = newEntry;
```

If we are adding to an empty bag, itemCount will be zero, and the assignment will be to items[0]. If the bag contains one entry, an additional entry will be assigned to items[1], and so on. In this way, no other items in the array need to move. After each addition to the bag, we increase the counter itemCount. Figure 3-3 depicts this insertion. If add is successful, it returns true. Otherwise—if the bag is full, for example—add returns false, as you can see from its definition:

```cpp
template<class ItemType>
bool ArrayBag<ItemType>::add(const ItemType& newEntry)
{
   bool hasRoomToAdd = (itemCount < maxItems);
   if (hasRoomToAdd)
   {
      items[itemCount] = newEntry;
      itemCount++;
   }  // end if

   return hasRoomToAdd;
}  // end add
```

FIGURE 3-3   Inserting a new entry into an array-based bag

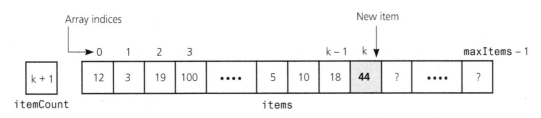

Note: The entries in a bag have no particular order. Thus, the method add can place a new entry into any convenient element of the array items. In the previous definition of add, that element is the one immediately after the last element used.

Note: This array-based implementation of the ADT bag restricts the number of items that a bag can contain. Thus, the implementation should check whether the array has space available before inserting a new item, and the client should take appropriate action if the insertion is impossible.

Programming Tip: Variables that are local to a method's implementation should not have the same name as data members of the class.

The method toVector. The method toVector in our initial core group gets the entries that are in a bag and returns them to the client within a vector. A simple loop within toVector adds the bag's entries to this vector.

```cpp
template<class ItemType>
vector<ItemType> ArrayBag<ItemType>::toVector() const
{
    vector<ItemType> bagContents;
    for (int i = 0; i < itemCount; i++)
        bagContents.push_back(items[i]);
    return bagContents;
}  // end toVector
```

Note: The class vector is in the Standard Template Library (STL) and is described in Appendix A and C++ Interlude 8.

The methods getCurrentSize and isEmpty. The last two methods in our core group have the following straightforward definitions:

```cpp
template<class ItemType>
int ArrayBag<ItemType>::getCurrentSize() const
{
    return itemCount;
}  // end getCurrentSize

template<class ItemType>
bool ArrayBag<ItemType>::isEmpty() const
{
    return itemCount == 0;
}  // end isEmpty
```

Question 1 What happens to the array items when the method add cannot add another entry to it, because it is already full?

Question 2 If a client of ArrayBag creates a bag aBag and a vector v containing five items, what happens to those items after the statement v = aBag.toVector() executes?

3.2.3   Testing the Core Methods

Getting ready. After defining the core methods, you should test them. But what about the other methods in `BagInterface`? Since `ArrayBag`—as given in Listing 3-1—adheres to the specifications in `BagInterface`, the C++ compiler will look for a definition of each method declared in this interface. Should we wait until we complete their definitions to begin testing? Absolutely not! Testing methods as you write them makes finding logical errors easier. However, instead of writing a complete implementation of each method in `BagInterface`, we can provide incomplete definitions of the methods we choose to temporarily ignore.

An incomplete definition of a method is called a **stub**. The stub needs only to keep the syntax checker happy. For example, for each method that returns a value, you can avoid syntax errors by adding a `return` statement that returns a dummy value. Methods that return a boolean value should return false, for example. This result is reasonable, since the method does not perform its specified behavior. On the other hand, void methods can simply have an empty body.

For instance, the method `remove` ultimately will return true or false, so its stub must contain a `return` statement and could appear as follows:

```cpp
template<class ItemType>
bool ArrayBag<ItemType>::remove(const ItemType& anEntry)
{
   return false; // STUB
} // end remove
```

A stub for the void method `clear` could be

```cpp
template<class ItemType>
void ArrayBag<ItemType>::clear()
{
   // STUB
} // end clear
```

Note that if you plan to call a stub within your test program, the stub should report that it was invoked by displaying a message.

 Programming Tip: Do not wait until you complete the implementation of an ADT before testing it. By writing stubs, which are incomplete definitions of required methods, you can begin testing early in the process.

A test program. Listing 3-2 contains a program that tests the core methods `add`, `toVector`, `getCurrentSize`, and `isEmpty` of the class `ArrayBag` at this stage of its development. The `main` function creates an empty bag by using the default constructor and passes it to the function `bagTester`. This function calls another function, `displayBag`, that tests the methods `toVector` and `getCurrentSize`.

LISTING 3-2 A program that tests the core methods of the class `ArrayBag`

```cpp
1   #include <iostream>
2   #include <string>
3   #include "ArrayBag.h"
4
5   using std::cout;
6   using std::endl;
7
```

(continues)

```
8   void displayBag(ArrayBag<std::string>& bag)
9   {
10     cout << "The bag contains " << bag.getCurrentSize()
11          << " items:" << endl;
12     std::vector<std::string> bagItems = bag.toVector();
13
14     int numberOfEntries = bagItems.size();
15     for (int i = 0; i < numberOfEntries; i++)
16     {
17        cout << bagItems[i] << " ";
18     }  // end for
19     cout << endl << endl;
20  }  // end displayBag
21
22  void bagTester(ArrayBag<std::string>& bag)
23  {
24     cout << "isEmpty: returns " << bag.isEmpty()
25          << "; should be 1 (true)" << endl;
26     displayBag(bag);
27
28     std::string items[] = {"one", "two", "three", "four", "five", "one"};
29     cout << "Add 6 items to the bag: " << endl;
30     for (int i = 0; i < 6; i++)
31     {
32        bag.add(items[i]);
33     }  // end for
34
35     displayBag(bag);
36     cout << "isEmpty: returns " << bag.isEmpty()
37          << "; should be 0 (false)" << endl;
38     cout << "getCurrentSize: returns " << bag.getCurrentSize()
39          << "; should be 6" << endl;
40     cout << "Try to add another entry: add(\"extra\") returns "
41          << bag.add("extra") << endl;
42  }  // end bagTester
43
44  int main()
45  {
46     ArrayBag<std::string> bag;
47     cout << "Testing the Array-Based Bag:" << endl;
48     cout << "The initial bag is empty." << endl;
49     bagTester(bag);
50     cout << "All done!" << endl;
51
52     return 0;
53  }  // end main
```

Output

```
Testing the Array-Based Bag:
The initial bag is empty.
isEmpty: returns 1; should be 1 (true)
The bag contains 0 items:

Add 6 items to the bag:
The bag contains 6 items:
one two three four five one
```

```
isEmpty: returns 0; should be 0 (false)
getCurrentSize: returns 6; should be 6
Try to add another entry: add("extra") returns 0
All done!
```

Note: If you define a constructor for a class but do not also define a default constructor, the compiler will not generate one for you. In this case, a statement such as

```
ArrayBag<std::string> aBag;
```

is illegal.

3.2.4 Implementing More Methods

Now that we can add items to a bag successfully, we can define the other methods. Although we will not do so here, you should test each new definition as you complete it.

Programming Tip: Testing each method as you define it is especially important when its logic is not obvious. However, even the simplest method is susceptible to a careless mistake, which can lead to hours of frustrating debugging of other methods that depend on the supposedly correct method.

The method getFrequencyOf. To count the number of times a given object occurs in a bag, we count the number of times the object occurs in the array items. Using a while loop to cycle through the array's indices from 0 to itemCount − 1, we compare the given object to every object in the array. Each time we find a match, we increment a counter. When the loop ends, we simply return the value of the counter.

The method definition follows:

```
template<class ItemType>
int ArrayBag<ItemType>::getFrequencyOf(const ItemType& anEntry) const
{
   int frequency = 0;
   int curIndex = 0; // Current array index
   while (curIndex < itemCount)
   {
      if (items[curIndex] == anEntry)
      {
         frequency++;
      } // end if

      curIndex++; // Increment to next entry
   } // end while

   return frequency;
} // end getFrequencyOf
```

The method contains. One easy way to define the method contains is to have it call the method getFrequencyOf, which we just defined. If the frequency of occurrence of a given entry is greater than zero, the bag must contain that entry. If the frequency is zero, the bag does not contain the entry. Thus, you could define contains as follows:

```cpp
template<class ItemType>
bool ArrayBag<ItemType>::contains(const ItemType& target) const
{
   return getFrequencyOf(target) > 0;
} // end contains
```

Although this method will work, it usually will do more work than necessary. After all, get-FrequencyOf must check every entry in the bag, whereas contains could quit looking at entries as soon as it finds one that is the same as the given entry. That is, its logic can be described by the following pseudocode:

```
contains(anEntry)
{
   while (anEntry is not found and we have more array elements to check)
   {
      if (anEntry equals the next array entry)
         anEntry is found in the array
   }
}
```

This loop terminates under one of two conditions: Either anEntry has been found in the array or the entire array has been searched without success.

Based on this pseudocode, a definition of the method contains follows:

```cpp
template<class ItemType>
bool ArrayBag<ItemType>::contains(const ItemType& anEntry) const
{
   bool found = false;
   int curIndex = 0; // Current array index
   while (!found && (curIndex < itemCount))
   {
      if (anEntry == items[curIndex])

         found = true;
      else
         curIndex++; // Increment to next entry
   } // end while

   return found;
} // end contains
```

Here is another way of defining the method contains:

```cpp
template <class ItemType>
bool ArrayBag<ItemType>::contains(const ItemType& anEntry) const
{
   bool isFound = false;
   int curIndex = 0; // Current array index
   while (!isFound && (curIndex < itemCount))
   {
      isFound = (anEntry == items[curIndex]);
      if (!isFound)
         curIndex++; // Increment to next entry
   } // end while

   return isFound;
} // end contains
```

Question 3 What is an advantage and a disadvantage of calling the method getFrequencyOf from contains?

Programming Tip: **Loop variables**
Many programmers use single-letter names for the variables that control loops. Sometimes we use them also, especially with simple loops that count. For example, the for loops in Listing 3-2 use the variable i as a loop counter. However, we tend to use longer mnemonic names for loop variables to make their intent clearer to you.

Note: **Testing the additional methods**
As you define additional methods for the class ArrayBag, you should test them. While you could focus only on these additional methods, you really should form a test program incrementally. In this way, you test all of the methods you have defined so far. By using a small value for the constant DEFAULT_CAPACITY, you easily can test what happens when a bag becomes full.

Note: **Two kinds of loops**
To count how many times an entry occurs in an array, the method getFrequencyOf uses a loop that cycles through all of the array's entries. In fact, the body of the loop executes itemCount times. In contrast, to indicate whether a given entry occurs in an array, the loop in the method contains ends as soon as the desired entry is discovered. The body of this loop executes between one and itemCount times. You should be comfortable writing loops that execute either a definitive or a variable number of times.

3.2.5   Methods That Remove Entries

VideoNote

Other ArrayBag methods

We have postponed the definition of the method remove until now because it involves more thought than the other methods. The method clear, however, is relatively simple, even though we are leaving it until last.

The method remove. We now want to remove a given entry—call it anEntry—from a bag. If the entry occurs more than once in the bag, we will remove only one occurrence. Exactly which occurrence is removed is unspecified. We will simply remove the first occurrence of anEntry that we encounter while searching for it. Adhering to our specifications in BagInterface, we will return either true or false to indicate whether the removal was successful.

Assuming that the bag is not empty, we search the array items until either we find anEntry in the array or we note where it occurs within the array. Figure 3-4 illustrates the array after a successful search.

FIGURE 3-4   The array items after a successful search for the string "Alice"

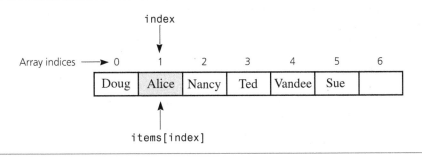

Now consider how to remove the located item from the array. You could blank it out—the entry is removed but the array element remains— but this strategy can lead to gaps in the array, as Figure 3-5a illustrates. An array that is full of gaps has three significant problems:

- itemCount − 1 is no longer the index of the last item in the array. You would need another variable, lastPosition, to contain this index.
- Because the items are spread out, the method contains might have to look at every element of the array, even when only a few items are present.
- When items[maxItems − 1] is occupied, the bag could appear full, even when fewer than maxItems items are present.

FIGURE 3-5   Removing an entry from an array-based bag

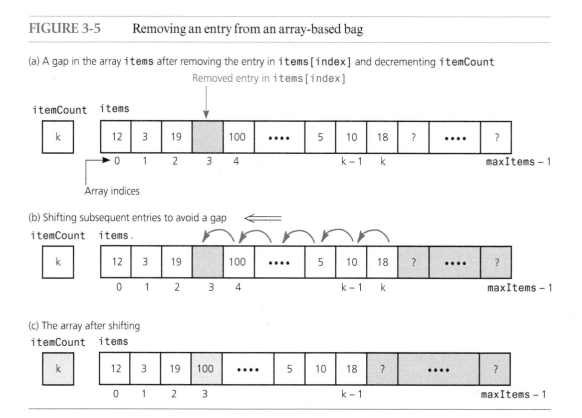

(a) A gap in the array items after removing the entry in items[index] and decrementing itemCount

(b) Shifting subsequent entries to avoid a gap

(c) The array after shifting

We could get rid of that gap by copying each successive entry to the previous element in the array, beginning with the entry after the removed item and ending with the last entry, as shown in Figure 3-5b. The result of shifting these entries is shown in Figure 3-5c. This time-consuming approach is not necessary, however.

Remember that we are not required to maintain any particular order for a bag's entries. So instead of shifting array entries after removing an entry, we can replace the entry being removed with the last entry in the array, as follows. After locating anEntry in items[index], as Figure 3-6a indicates, we copy the entry in items[itemCount − 1] to items[index] (Figure 3-6b). We then ignore the entry in items[itemCount − 1] by decrementing itemCount.

FIGURE 3-6 Avoiding a gap in the array while removing an entry

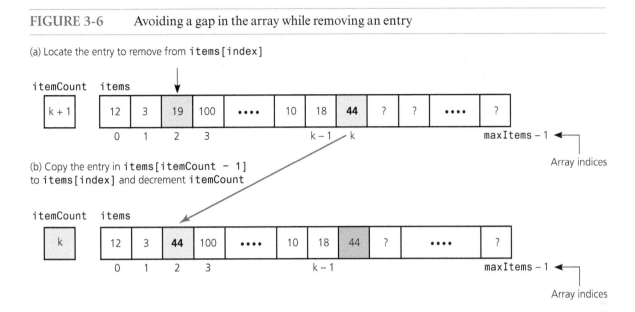

(a) Locate the entry to remove from items[index]

(b) Copy the entry in items[itemCount - 1]
to items[index] and decrement itemCount

The following pseudocode details the steps needed to remove a given entry from a bag. Note that by decrementing itemCount before using it in an index, we compute itemCount – 1 once instead of twice.

```
Search the array items for anEntry
if (anEntry is in the bag at items[index])
{
    Decrement the counter itemCount
    items[index] = items[itemCount]
    return true
}
else
    return false
```

The initial search for anEntry is the same search as done in the method contains. Calling contains here is not much help, as we want to know not only whether the bag contains anEntry but also, if it does, where it occurs in the array. Clearly, we could modify the loop in contains slightly, but a better way places the loop in a private method that both contains and remove can call. This method is getIndexOf, which we declared earlier in the header file and whose definition follows:

```
template<class ItemType>
int ArrayBag<ItemType>::getIndexOf(const ItemType& target) const
{
    bool isFound = false;
    int result = -1;
    int searchIndex = 0;

    // If the bag is empty, itemCount is zero, so loop is skipped
    while (!isFound && (searchIndex < itemCount))
    {
```

```
      isFound = (items[searchIndex] == target);
      if (isFound)
      {
         result = searchIndex;
      }
      else
      {
         searchIndex++;
      }  // end if
   }  // end while

   return result;
}  // end getIndexOf
```

The method remove now has the following definition:

```
template<class ItemType>
bool ArrayBag<ItemType>::remove(const ItemType& anEntry)
{
   int locatedIndex = getIndexOf(anEntry);
   bool canRemoveItem = !isEmpty() && (locatedIndex > -1);
   if (canRemoveItem)
   {
      itemCount--;
      items[locatedIndex] = items[itemCount];
   }  // end if

   return canRemoveItem;
}  // end remove
```

Question 4 Revise the definition of the method contains so that it calls the method getIndexOf.

Question 5 Should we revise the specification of the method contains so that if it locates a given entry within the bag, it returns the index of that entry? Why or Why not?

Question 6 Revise the definition of the method getIndexOf so that it does not use a boolean variable.

The method clear. The method clear can make a bag appear empty simply by setting itemCount to zero. Thus, we have the following definition for this method:

```
template<class ItemType>
void ArrayBag<ItemType>::clear()
{
   itemCount = 0;
}  // end clear
```

3.2.6 Testing

To test our completed class, we can add the following statements to the method bagTester that appears in Listing 3-2:

```
std::cout << "contains(\"three\"): returns " << bag.contains("three")
          << "; should be 1 (true)" << std::endl;
std::cout << "contains(\"ten\"): returns " << bag.contains("ten")
          << "; should be 0 (false)" << std::endl;
```

```
std::cout << "getFrequencyOf(\"one\"): returns "
          << bag.getFrequencyOf("one") << " should be 2" << std::endl;
std::cout << "remove(\"one\"): returns " << bag.remove("one")
          << "; should be 1 (true)" << std::endl;
std::cout << "getFrequencyOf(\"one\"): returns "
          << bag.getFrequencyOf("one") << " should be 1" << std::endl;
std::cout << "remove(\"one\"): returns " << bag.remove("one")
          << "; should be 1 (true)" << std::endl;
std::cout << "remove(\"one\"): returns " << bag.remove("one")
          << "; should be 0 (false)" << std::endl;
std::cout << std::endl;

displayBag(bag);

std::cout << "After clearing the bag, ";
bag.clear();

std::cout << "isEmpty: returns " << bag.isEmpty()
          << "; should be 1 (true)" << std::endl;
```

Note: References such as bag.itemCount and bag.items[4] would be illegal within the client, because itemCount and items are within the private portion of the class.

Note: To implement an ADT, given implementation-independent specifications of the ADT's operations, you first must choose a data structure to contain the data. Next, you declare a class within a header file. The ADT's operations are public methods within the class, and the ADT's data consists of class members that are typically private. You then implement the class's methods within an implementation file. The program that uses the class will be able to access the data only by using the ADT's operations.

Note: In practice, when choosing among implementations of an ADT, you must ask whether the fixed-size restriction of an array-based implementation presents a problem in the context of a particular application. The answer to this question depends on two factors. The obvious factor is whether, for a given application, you can predict in advance the maximum number of items in the ADT at any one time. If you cannot, it is quite possible that an operation—and hence the entire program—will fail because the ADT in the context of a particular application requires more storage than the array can provide.

On the other hand, if for a given application you can predict in advance the maximum number of items in an ADT at any one time, you must explore a more subtle factor: Would you waste storage by declaring an array to be large enough to accommodate this maximum number of items? Consider a case in which the maximum number of items is large, but you suspect that this number rarely will be reached. For example, suppose that a bag could contain as many as 10,000 items, but the actual number of items in the bag rarely exceeds 50. If you declare 10,000 array locations at compilation time, at least 9,950 array locations will be wasted most of the time.

We can avoid both of the previous cases by allocating a larger—or smaller—array during execution. The next C++ Interlude will show you how.

3.3   Using Recursion in the Implementation

The previous chapter gave several examples of how to use recursion to process an array. If you examine the definition of ArrayBag that we have just developed, you will see two loops that can be replaced by recursion: One is in the public method getFrequencyOf, and the other is in the private method getIndexOf. Let's look at the details.

3.3.1   The Method getIndexOf

We begin with the private method that searches the array for a given entry. The iterative definition examines each entry in the array one at a time in sequential order until it either finds the desired one or reaches the end of the array without success. Suppose that searchIndex is the index of the next array element to examine. We have two base cases:

- If items[searchIndex] is the entry we seek, we are done.
- If searchIndex equals itemCount, we are done, because the entry is not in the array.

The recursive step is to search the rest of the array beginning with items[searchIndex + 1].

To accomplish this recursion, we need a way to decrease the size of the problem at each recursive call. The recursive getIndexOf can search fewer and fewer entries at each recursive call by changing the value of searchIndex. Since the method is private, we can simply give it searchIndex as a parameter. To do so, we must revise its declaration in the header file as follows:

```
int getIndexOf(const ItemType& target, int searchIndex) const;
```

We then can write the following recursive definition for this method:

```
template<class ItemType>
int ArrayBag<ItemType>::getIndexOf(const ItemType& target, int searchIndex) const
{
   int result = -1;
   if (searchIndex < itemCount)
   {
      if (items[searchIndex] == target)
      {
         result = searchIndex;
      }
      else
      {
         result = getIndexOf(target, searchIndex + 1);
      }  // end if
   }  // end if

   return result;
}  // end getIndexOf
```

Because we have changed the header of the method, we need to locate and change the calls to getIndexOf within the other methods of ArrayBag. Thus, we will change the calls within the methods remove and contains from

```
getIndexOf(anEntry);
```

to

```
getIndexOf(anEntry, 0);
```

Note that getIndexof begins its recursive search with the entire array.

3.3.2   The Method `getFrequencyOf`

The method `getFrequencyOf` also searches an array, much as `getIndexOf` does, but unlike that method, `getFrequencyOf` must examine every entry in the array. That is, the search does not end if an array entry matches the entry we seek.

Suppose that `searchIndex` is the index of the next array element to examine. A recursive definition for this search has only one base case: If `searchIndex` equals `itemCount`, we are done. However, we have two recursive steps:

- If `items[searchIndex]` is the entry we seek, the frequency of occurrence of this entry is one more than its frequency of occurrence in the rest of the array.
- If `items[searchIndex]` is not the entry we seek, the frequency of occurrence of the entry is the same as its frequency of occurrence in the rest of the array.

Just as we had to add another parameter to `getIndexOf`, the recursive method here needs `searchIndex` as a parameter. However, `getFrequencyOf` is a public method, so we cannot change its signature. Instead, `getFrequencyOf` must call a private method that accomplishes the recursive search. Thus, let's add

```
int countFrequency(const ItemType& target, int searchIndex) const;
```

to the private portion of `ArrayBag`'s declaration in the header file.

The method `getFrequencyOf` simply calls this private method, so its definition is as follows:

```
template<class ItemType>
int ArrayBag<ItemType>::getFrequencyOf(const ItemType& anEntry) const
{
   return countFrequency(anEntry, 0);
}  // end getFrequencyOf
```

The recursive definition of the private method `countFrequency` is

```
template<class ItemType>
int ArrayBag<ItemType>::countFrequency(const ItemType& target,
                                       int searchIndex) const
{
   if (searchIndex < itemCount)
   {
      if (items[searchIndex] == target)
      {
         return 1 + countFrequency(target, searchIndex + 1);
      }
      else
      {
         return countFrequency(target, searchIndex + 1);
      }  // end if
   }
   else
      return 0;  // Base case
}  // end countFrequency
```

Stylistically, we prefer to have only one exit from a method. To revise `countFrequency` so that it has one `return` statement instead of three, we define a local variable, `frequency`, to contain the return value. The method then has the following definition. Note that the base case is implicit.

```
template<class ItemType>
int ArrayBag<ItemType>::countFrequency(const ItemType& target,
                                       int searchIndex) const
{
   int frequency = 0;
   if (searchIndex < itemCount)
   {
      if (items[searchIndex] == target)
      {
         frequency = 1 + countFrequency(target, searchIndex + 1);
      }
      else
      {
         frequency = countFrequency(target, searchIndex + 1);
      }  // end if
   }  // end if

   return frequency;
}  // end countFrequency
```

SUMMARY

1. By using a class to implement an ADT, you encapsulate the ADT's data and operations. In this way, you can hide implementation details from the program that uses the ADT. In particular, by making the class's data members private, you can change the class's implementation without affecting the client.

2. Given an interface that specifies an ADT in an implementation-independent way, derive a class from the interface and declare the class within a header file. Choose a data structure to contain the ADT's data. Then implement the class's methods within an implementation file.

3. You should make a class's data members private so that you can control how a client can access or change the data.

4. An array-based implementation of an ADT stores the ADT's data in an array.

5. Generally, you should not define an entire class and then attempt to test it. Instead, you should identify a group of core methods to both implement and test before continuing with the rest of the class definition.

6. Stubs are incomplete definitions of a class's methods. By using stubs for some methods, you can begin testing before the class is completely defined.

7. A client must use the operations of an ADT to manipulate the ADT's data.

EXERCISES

1. Consider a bag of integers. Write a client function that computes the sum of the integers in the bag aBag.

2. Write a client function replace that replaces a given item in a given bag with another given item. The function should return a boolean value to indicate whether the replacement was successful.

3. The previous exercise describes the function replace. This operation exists outside of the ADT bag; that is, it is not an ADT bag operation. Instead, its implementation is written in terms of the ADT bag's operations.

a. What is an advantage and a disadvantage of the way that `replace` is implemented?

b. What is an advantage and a disadvantage of adding the operation `replace` to the ADT bag?

4. Design and implement an ADT that represents a rectangle. Include typical operations, such as setting and retrieving the dimensions of the rectangle, and finding the area and the perimeter of the rectangle.

5. Design and implement an ADT that represents a triangle. The data for the ADT should include the three sides of the triangle but could also include the triangle's three angles. This data should be in the private section of the class that implements the ADT.

   Include at least two initialization operations: one that provides default values for the ADT's data, and another that sets this data to client-supplied values. These operations are the class's constructors. The ADT also should include operations that look at the values of the ADT's data; change the values of the ADT's data; compute the triangle's area; and determine whether the triangle is a right triangle, an equilateral triangle, or an isosceles triangle.

6. Write a recursive array-based implementation of the method `toVector` for the class `ArrayBag`.

7. Write a client function that merges two bags into a new third bag. Do not destroy the original two bags.

8. Specify and define a method for `ArrayBag` that removes a random entry from the bag.

9. Add a constructor to the class `ArrayBag` that creates a bag from a given array of entries.

PROGRAMMING PROBLEMS

1. Design and implement an ADT that represents the time of day. Represent the time as hours and minutes on a 24-hour clock. The hours and minutes are the private data members of the class that implements the ADT. Include at least two initialization operations: one that provides a default value for the time, and another that sets the time to a client-supplied value. These operations are the class's constructors. Also include operations that set the time, increase the present time by a number of minutes, and display the time in 12-hour and 24-hour notations.

2. Design and implement an ADT that represents a calendar date. You can represent a date's month, day, and year as integers (for example, 4/1/2017). Include operations that advance the date by one day and display the date by using either numbers or words for the months. As an enhancement, include the name of the day.

3. Design and implement an ADT that represents a price in U.S. currency as dollars and cents. After you complete the implementation, write a client function that computes the change due a customer who pays *x* for an item whose price is *y*.

4. Add the methods `union`, `intersection`, and `difference` to the class `ArrayBag`. Exercises 6, 7, and 8 of Chapter 1 describe these operations.

5. Implement the ADT set that you specified in Programming Problem 4 of Chapter 1 by using an array.

6. Implement the ADT pile that you specified in Programming Problem 5 of Chapter 1 by using an array.

7. Implement the ADT polynomial that Exercise 9 in Chapter 1 describes by using an array.

8. Implement the ADT appointment book, described in Section 1.4.1 of Chapter 1. Write a program that demonstrates your new class.

9. Specify and implement an ADT for fractions. Provide operations that add, subtract, multiply, and divide these numbers. The results of all arithmetic operations should be in lowest terms, so include a private method `reduceToLowestTerms`. Exercise 23 in Chapter 2 will help you with the details of this method. To simplify the determination of a fraction's sign, you can assume that the denominator of the fraction is positive.

10. Specify and implement an ADT for mixed numbers, each of which contains an integer portion and a fractional portion in lowest terms. Assume the existence of the ADT fraction, as described in the previous problem. Provide operations that add, subtract, multiply, and divide mixed numbers. The results of all arithmetic operations should have fractional portions that are in lowest terms. Also include an operation that converts a fraction to a mixed number.

11. Implement the ADT recipe book based on the recipe database described in Section 1.4.2 of Chapter 1. In doing so, implement the ADT measurement. Define additional operations as necessary. For example, you should add an operation to the recipe book to scale a recipe.

12. You can use either a set or a bag to create a spell checker. The set or bag serves as a dictionary and contains a collection of correctly spelled words. To see whether a word is spelled correctly, you see whether it is contained in the dictionary. Use this scheme to create a spell checker for the words in an external file. To simplify your task, restrict your dictionary to a manageable size.

13. Repeat the previous project to create a spell checker, but instead place the words whose spelling you want to check into a bag. The difference between the dictionary (the set or bag containing the correctly spelled words) and the bag of words to be checked is a bag of incorrectly spelled words.

14. (Finance) Design and implement an ADT that represents a credit card account. The data of the ADT should include the customer name, the account number, and the account balance. The initialization operation should set the data to client-supplied values. Include operations for a purchase and a payment, the addition of an interest charge to the balance, and the display of the statistics of the account.

15. (Gaming) Implement the guessing game that Programming Problem 7 in Chapter 1 asked you to design. Use a bag to contain the integers chosen by the game.

16. (Gaming) Design and implement an ADT that represents a character in a video game. The data of the ADT should include the character's name, height, weight, tendency, and health. The tendency of a character is the "goodness" of the character and ranges from −1.0 (very bad) to 1.0 (very good) with 0.0 being neutral. The health of the character is represented as a percentage between 0.0 and 1.0 with 1.0 being 100% healthy. Characters begin with a neutral tendency and 100% health. The name, height, and weight should be initialized by the client. Include the following operations:

   - `heal`—Increases a character's health by a client-supplied percentage.
   - `injure`—Decreases a character's health by a client-supplied percentage.
   - `takeAction`—Changes a character's tendency by a random percentage based on a user-supplied parameter. A positive parameter increases the tendency; a negative parameter decreases the tendency.
   - `displayAttributes`—Displays information about a character's data fields.

17. (E-commerce) Design and implement an ADT that represents a product that may be purchased in an online store. The data of the ADT should include a product's name, category, description, local ID, manufacturer ID, price, and quantity on hand. When a product is created, it must have at least a user-supplied name, local ID, and price. Other characteristics can be given later. Define additional operations to display product information and to adjust the quantity on hand based on a user-supplied value.

Pointers, Polymorphism, and Memory Allocation

Contents

Prerequisites

Chapter 3 Array-Based Implementations

This C++ Interlude discusses memory allocation for variables and arrays and introduces you to pointers to complete the discussion on polymorphism begun in the first C++ Interlude. Pointers are a powerful tool for the programmer, but you must be careful to use them correctly. This interlude explains the need for pointers and shows when and how to safely use them. Certain aspects of pointers are not covered in this interlude, but those features either are unnecessary in this textbook or introduce unsafe practices.

We will introduce memory allocation during execution instead of compilation and show how pointers are involved with this process. We will also discuss how to create a new and larger array during execution, if an array becomes full. Our use of pointers and memory management tools, such as the operators new and delete, are traditional. C++ Interlude 4 introduces smart pointers and other tools available in the C11 revision to C++. Although we are moving to a new standard, you should understand the older techniques used in the millions of legacy programs and code libraries that must be maintained.

Throughout our discussion here, and throughout the book, we will stress safe and secure programming practices. To begin our discussion, let's consider how memory is allocated for local variables and parameters.

C2.1　Memory Allocation for Variables and Early Binding of Methods

When you declare an ordinary variable x to have the data type int, the C++ compiler allocates a memory cell that can hold an integer. You use the identifier x to refer to this cell. To put the value 5 in the cell, you could write

```
int x = 5;
```

To display the value that is in the cell, you could write

```
std::cout << "The value of x is " << x << std::endl;
```

As discussed in Chapter 2, a function's locally declared variables such as x are placed into an activation record with its parameters and some bookkeeping data. These activation records are stored in an area of your application's memory called the **run-time stack**. Each time a function is called, an activation record is automatically created on the run-time stack. When the function ends, the activation record is destroyed, freeing the memory used for the local variables and parameters. At that point, the function's local variables and their values are no longer accessible to your program. Your program then returns to where the function was invoked and executes the statement following the function call. This behavior is the same for methods.

When you create an object, the storage for the data members of that object are also placed into an activation record for the currently executing function or method. The statements

```
PlainBox<std::string> myPlainBox;
MagicBox<std::string> myMagicBox = MagicBox<std::string>();
```

show two different ways of invoking default constructors to create instances of PlainBox and MagicBox, respectively. When these objects are instantiated, their data fields are placed on the run-time stack just as primitive data types are. Recall from Listings C1-3 and C1-7 in C++ Interlude 1 that the names of those data fields are item and firstItemStored.

The compiler also knows that if you invoke the setItem method on these objects by writing

```
myPlainBox.setItem("Fun Item");
myMagicBox.setItem("Secret Item");
```

the PlainBox version of the setItem method should be called for myPlainBox, and the MagicBox version of the setItem method should be called for myMagicBox. This choice, which is an example of **early binding**, is made during compilation and cannot be altered during execution.

Most of the time, this automatic memory management and early binding are all you need in your program. However, two situations can arise in which you need to do more:

Two situations when automatic memory management and early binding are insufficient

- You want to take advantage of polymorphism.
- You must access an object outside of the function or method that creates it.

C2.2　A Problem to Solve

Suppose your friend was so impressed with your work on the three boxes discussed in C++ Interlude 1 that she asked you to continue helping with the video game. She would like you to write a function that takes two arguments: an object of any of the three types of boxes and an item of type string. The function should place the item in the box by invoking the box's setItem method.

FIGURE C2-1   UML class diagram for a family of classes

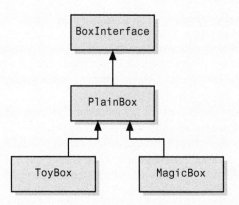

Since ToyBox and MagicBox are derived from PlainBox, as Figure C2-1 illustrates, you may think that the following function definition would suffice:

```
void placeInBox(PlainBox<std::string>& theBox, std::string theItem)
{
    theBox.setItem(theItem);
} // end placeInBox
```

The parameter theBox can accept as an argument any PlainBox object or an object of a class derived from PlainBox. This function could then be used in the following sequence of statements:

```
std::string specialItem = "Riches beyond compare";
std::string hammerItem = "Hammer";

PlainBox<std::string> myPlainBox;
placeInBox(myPlainBox, hammerItem);            // Stores hammerItem
placeInBox(myPlainBox, specialItem);           // Stores specialItem
std::cout << myPlainBox.getItem() << std::endl; // Displays specialItem

MagicBox<std::string> myMagicBox;
placeInBox(myMagicBox, hammerItem);            // Stores hammerItem
placeInBox(myMagicBox, specialItem);           // Stores specialItem
std::cout << myMagicBox.getItem() << std::endl; // Displays specialItem
```

An example of early binding

Although this code compiles, it does not perform as you would expect. Since otherItem has already been stored in the magic box, specialItem should not replace that item. Unfortunately, when the item stored in the magic box is displayed, the output is Riches beyond compare. The reason is that, in our function, the statement

```
theBox.setItem(theItem);
```

invokes the PlainBox version of the setItem method instead of the MagicBox version. In this case, the compiler determined the version of the method to invoke from the type of the parameter theBox instead of from the type of its corresponding argument. The following set of statements has a similar result:

Another example of
early binding

```
PlainBox<std::string> mySpecialBox = MagicBox<std::string>();
mySpecialBox.setItem(hammerItem);              // Stores hammerItem
mySpecialBox.setItem(specialItem);             // Stores specialItem

std::cout << mySpecialBox.getItem() << std::endl; // Displays specialItem
```

In both situations, the version of `setItem` that will be called is determined when the program is compiled. In this second case, even though we instantiated a `MagicBox` object for `mySpecialBox`, the variable `mySpecialBox` is of type `PlainBox`, so the `PlainBox` version of `setItem` is called. The same decision logic applies to our function `placeInBox`.

This code is correct from the compiler's perspective. The compiler assumes it is our intent to have the parameter `theBox` and the variable `mySpecialBox` behave as `PlainBox` objects. We need a way to communicate to the compiler that the code to execute should not be determined until the program is running. This is called **late binding**, which is an aspect of polymorphism. To solve this problem and have both our function and simple-code examples execute as we intend, we need two tools: pointer variables and virtual methods.

VideoNote

C++ memory allocation

The new operator
allocates memory in
the free store

C2.3 Pointers and the Program's Free Store

To take advantage of late binding, we do not want our objects to be in an activation record on the run-time stack. We need another location. When a C++ program begins execution, in addition to the run-time stack, the operating system sets aside memory for the code—called **code storage** or **text storage**—and for any global variables and static variables—called **static storage**. Your program is also given extra memory, called the **free store**, or **application heap**,[1] which a programmer can use to store data. Figure C2-2 illustrates these portions of memory.

We allocate memory for a variable in the free store by using the operator `new`. After allocating memory for the variable, the `new` operator returns the memory address of the variable in the free store so the program can use it. This memory address must be placed in a special type of variable called a **pointer variable**, or simply a **pointer**. A pointer variable contains the location, or

---

FIGURE C2-2   Sample program memory layout

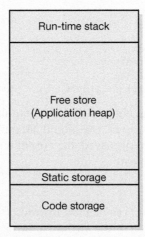

---

[1] Many people call the free store a "heap." Because Chapter 17 introduces the ADT heap—and the free store is not an ADT heap—we offer the term "application heap" instead of "heap" as an alternate way of referring to the free store. This book typically uses "free store" to avoid confusion with the ADT heap.

address in memory, of a memory cell or object. This address is used to reference the memory cell or object, and so is known as a **reference**.

Unlike variables on the run-time stack, which have their memory allocated and deallocated automatically, variables placed in the free store persist in memory even when the function or method that created them ends. This means that when a programmer allocates memory from the free store for a variable, the programmer has the responsibility to deallocate that memory when the variable is no longer needed. Failure to do so often results in a **memory leak**. A memory leak is memory that has been allocated for use but is no longer needed and cannot be accessed or deallocated.

To indicate that a variable is a pointer, we place the character * after the data type that the pointer references.[2] For example, the statement

```
MagicBox<std::string>* myBoxPtr = new MagicBox<std::string>();
```

creates a `MagicBox` object in the free store and places the address of the object in the local variable `myBoxPtr`. We say that `myBoxPtr` points to a `MagicBox` object. We use the notation `->` to call a method of an object that is in the free store:

```
std::string someItem = "Something Free";
myBoxPtr->setItem(someItem);
```

Figure C2-3 shows the state of memory and the local variables after the previous statements execute. Since the variables `myBoxPtr` and `someItem` are local to their function or method, they are on the run-time stack.

Observe that this newly created object has no programmer-defined name. The only way to access its methods is indirectly via the pointer that `new` creates, that is, by using `myBoxPtr->` as in the previous example. Usually we will simplify the diagrams so that only the object in the free store and its pointer are drawn, as in Figure C2-4.

Margin notes:

If you allocate memory in the free store, you eventually must deallocate it

Indicate a pointer type by writing an asterisk after the data type

---

FIGURE C2-3 Run-time stack and free store after `myboxPtr` points to a `MagicBox` object and its data member `item` is set

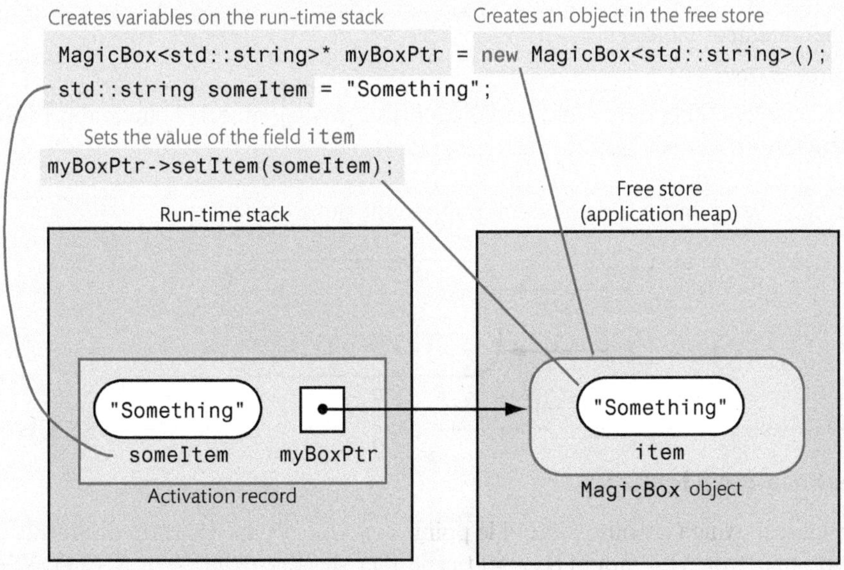

Creates variables on the run-time stack   Creates an object in the free store

```
MagicBox<std::string>* myBoxPtr = new MagicBox<std::string>();
std::string someItem = "Something";
```

Sets the value of the field `item`
```
myBoxPtr->setItem(someItem);
```

Free store (application heap)

Run-time stack

"Something"

someItem   myBoxPtr

Activation record

"Something"

item

MagicBox object

---

[2] Some programmers place the * next to the name of the variable. The authors of this textbook believe placing the * next to the data type more clearly shows that the variable is of a pointer type.

FIGURE C2-4   `myBoxPtr` and the object to which it points

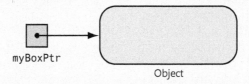

Pointer variables are simply another type of variable and follow the same rules as other variable types. For example, if you declare a pointer variable that points to a `ToyBox<std::string>` object, you can have it point only to `ToyBox<std::string>` objects, not `ToyBox<double>` objects or `MagicBox<std::string>` objects, as the following statements illustrate:

```
ToyBox<std::string>* toyPtr = new ToyBox<std::string>();   // OK
ToyBox<std::string>* gamePtr = new ToyBox<double>();       // Error!
ToyBox<std::string>* boxPtr = new MagicBox<std::string>(); // Error!
```

If you have two pointer variables that can point to the same type of object, you can make them point to the same object by using the assignment operator =. For example, the statement

```
ToyBox<std::string>* somePtr = toyPtr;
```

makes the variable `somePtr` point to the same `ToyBox` object to which `toyPtr` points. In such cases, it is helpful to think of the assignment operator as copying the *value* stored within the pointer variable on its right into the pointer variable on its left. Since pointers store addresses of objects, the value copied is the *location* of an object in the free store. The object itself is not copied. The result is that both pointer variables point to the same object, as shown in Figure C2-5.

If you declare a pointer variable but do not immediately create an object for it to reference, you should set the pointer to `nullptr`. An assignment like the following one is necessary because C++ does not initialize the pointer for you:

```
ToyBox<int>* myToyPtr = nullptr;
```

In contrast, the statement

```
ToyBox<int> myToy;
```

declares an ordinary variable `myToy` and initializes it to a `ToyBox` object by invoking `ToyBox`'s default constructor.

FIGURE C2-5   Two pointer variables that point to the same object

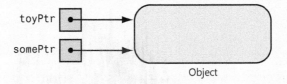

C2.3.1 Deallocating Memory

When the memory to which a pointer variable points is no longer needed, you deallocate it by using the **delete** operator. You should then set the pointer variable to `nullptr` as a signal that it no longer references or points to an object:

```
delete somePtr;
somePtr = nullptr;
```

Security Note If we did not set `somePtr` to `nullptr` in this example, `somePtr` would be an example of a **dangling pointer**, because it would still contain the address of an object that was deallocated. Dangling pointers can be the source of serious errors.

Always remember that if a method of a class uses `new` to create an object, some method of the class must use `delete` eventually to free the object's memory. It is a characteristic of safe and secure programming that any object allocating memory from the free store also assumes responsibility to deallocate that memory when it is no longer needed.

If you use the new operator to allocate memory, you must use the `delete` operator to deallocate it

Pointers give the programmer a great amount of control over how memory is used and when binding occurs, as we will discuss shortly. They also can create severe problems and hard-to-find bugs if not properly used. The two most common errors involving pointers are the memory leak and the dangling pointer. Let's look at how these problems can occur in a program so that you can prevent them in your code. C++ Interlude 4 covers additional techniques that use smart pointers to avoid these issues.

C2.3.2 Avoiding Memory Leaks

Memory leaks occur when an object has been created in the free store, but the program no longer has a way to access it. Because the object cannot be accessed, it cannot be deleted and so takes up memory, even though it cannot be used. A program can quickly run out of memory and crash if it has several memory leaks. Even a single statement that is called multiple times can cause a memory leak.

Consider the following statements:

```
MagicBox<std::string>* myBoxPtr = new MagicBox<std::string>();
MagicBox<std::string>* yourBoxPtr = new MagicBox<std::string>();
yourBoxPtr = myBoxPtr; // Results in an inaccessible object
```

Figure C2-6 traces the execution of these statements. Eventually, `yourBoxPtr` points to the same object as `myBoxPtr`, and so the object to which `yourBoxPtr` originally pointed is no longer accessible, resulting in the memory leak shown in part *c* of the figure.

FIGURE C2-6   An assignment that causes an inaccessible object.

```
// Creating first object
MagicBox<std::string>* myBoxPtr = new MagicBox<std::string>();
```
myBoxPtr → Object

```
// Creating second object
MagicBox<std::string>* yourBoxPtr = new MagicBox<std::string>();
```
yourBoxPtr → Object

myBoxPtr → Object

```
// Assignment causes an inaccessible object
yourBoxPtr = myBoxPtr;
```
yourBoxPtr → Object

Inaccessible object in free store (memory leak)

To prevent this leak, we should not create the second object. Instead, either initialize yourBoxPtr to nullptr or simply set it to myBoxPtr:

```
MagicBox<std::string>* myBoxPtr = new MagicBox<std::string>();
MagicBox<std::string>* yourBoxPtr = myBoxPtr;
```

A more subtle memory leak occurs when a function or method creates an object in the free store and loses the pointer to it by either not returning that pointer to the caller or not storing it in a class data member. That is what happens in the function given in Listing C2-1.

LISTING C2-1 **Poorly written function that allocates memory in the free store**

```
1   void myLeakyFunction(const double& someItem)
2   {
3      ToyBox<double>* someBoxPtr = new ToyBox<double>();
4      someBoxPtr->setItem(someItem);
5   }   // end myLeakyFunction
```

The parameter someItem and the pointer someBoxPtr are both stored in an activation record on the run-time stack and so are automatically destroyed after the function ends. The object created in the free store by new ToyBox<double>() is still in the free store. Since the only reference we had to it was someBoxPtr and that has been destroyed, we no longer have a way to get to that object, and so we have a memory leak.

We have several options to fix this function. The first is to delete the object before the function terminates. We can do this by adding the lines

```
delete someBoxPtr;
someBoxPtr = nullptr;
```

at the end of the function. If the ToyBox object pointed to by someBoxPtr is needed only by this function, a better implementation choice would have been to not allocate memory from the free store, but to use a local variable such as is done in the following statements:

```
ToyBox<double> someBox;   // someBox is not a pointer variable
someBox.setItem(someItem);
```

If the object created in this function is required outside the function, the function can return a pointer to it so that the caller can access the object. To implement this option, we would change the function's return type from void to ToyBox<double>* and return someBoxPtr, which is a pointer to a ToyBox<double> object. The resulting function definition is

```
ToyBox<double>* pluggedLeakyFunction(const double& someItem)
{
   ToyBox<double>* someBoxPtr = new ToyBox<double>();
   someBoxPtr->setItem(someItem);
   return someBoxPtr;
} // end pluggedLeakyFunction
```

You could call this function by writing statements such as

```
double boxValue = 4.321;
ToyBox<double>* toyPtr = pluggedLeakyFunction(boxValue);
```

Now toyPtr points to the object created by the ToyBox constructor in pluggedLeakyFunction. When a function returns a pointer to an object that it created in the free store, the segment of the program using that pointer must take responsibility for deleting the object. Otherwise, a memory leak could still occur. When documenting such a function, you should add comments to indicate this responsibility. For example, you could precede the definition of pluggedLeakyFunction with these comments:

```
/** Creates an object in the free store and returns a pointer to it.
  Caller must delete the object when it is no longer needed. */
```

Of course, this comment does not prevent a memory leak, but it alerts users of your function about the potential for a leak. The function could still be misused and called with a statement such as

```
pluggedLeakyFunction(boxValue); // Misused; returned pointer is lost
```

in which case the returned pointer to the object in the free store is lost and a memory leak occurs.

The best option for preventing a memory leak is to not use a function to return a pointer to a newly created object. Instead, you should define a class that has a method for this task. The class takes responsibility for deleting the object in the free store and ensures that there is no memory leak. At a minimum, such a class will have three parts: a method that creates the object in the free store, a data field that points to the object, and a method—the destructor—that deletes the object when the class instance is no longer needed. C++ Interlude 1 introduced class destructors; we discuss them further now.

Every C++ class has a destructor that has the same name as the class, but is preceded by the tilde (~) character. For objects that are local variables, the destructor is called when the activation record containing the object is removed from the run-time stack. If the object was created using new and is stored in the free store, the destructor is called when the client uses the operator delete to free the memory allocated to the object.

Often, the compiler-generated destructor is sufficient for a class, but if the class itself creates an object in the free store by using the new operator, it is a safe and secure programming practice to implement a destructor to ensure that the memory for that object is freed.

Listing C2-2 gives the header file for a GoodMemory class that demonstrates how to avoid a memory leak. The pointer variable in our previous function pluggedLeakyFunction is now a data field in GoodMemory. As long as this field points to an existing object in the free store, we will have access to the object.

To prevent a memory leak, do not use a function to return a pointer to a newly created object

LISTING C2-2 Header file for the class GoodMemory

```
/** @file GoodMemory.h */
#ifndef GOOD_MEMORY_
#define GOOD_MEMORY_
#include "ToyBox.h"

class GoodMemory
{
private:
   ToyBox<double>* someBoxPtr;
public:
   GoodMemory();            // Default constructor
   virtual ~GoodMemory(); // Destructor
   void unleakyMethod(const double& someItem);
}; // end GoodMemory
#endif
```

Because the class `GoodMemory` has a pointer variable for a data field, we should define a default constructor to initialize the pointer to `nullptr`. The destructor for this class simply needs to delete the object to which the pointer points. Listing C2-3 shows the implementation file for this class.

LISTING C2-3   Implementation file for the class `GoodMemory`

```
1   /** @file GoodMemory.cpp */
2   #include "GoodMemory.h"
3
4   GoodMemory::GoodMemory() : someBoxPtr(nullptr)
5   {
6   }  // end default constructor
7
8   GoodMemory::~GoodMemory()
9   {
10      delete someBoxPtr;
11  }  // end destructor
12
13  void GoodMemory::unleakyMethod(const double& someItem)
14  {
15      someBoxPtr = new ToyBox<double>();
16      someBoxPtr->setItem(someItem);
17  }  // end unleakyMethod
```

Unlike the original function `myLeakyFunction`, as presented in Listing C2-1, the following client function uses the class `GoodMemory` to guarantee that no memory leak occurs:

```
void goodFunction()
{
    double boxValue = 4.321;              // Original statement
    GoodMemory gmObject;                   // Create a safe memory object
    gmObject.unleakyMethod(boxValue);     // Perform the task
}  // end goodFunction
```

The compiler greatly helps us here. First, the compiler can check to ensure that a `GoodMemory` object has been created before calling the method `unleakyMethod`. This guarantees a safe memory allocation and deallocation. Then, since the variable `gmObject` is a local variable, the compiler automatically calls the `GoodMemory` destructor when execution of the function `goodFunction` ends. Thus, the memory allocated in the free store is freed.

C2.3.3   Avoiding Dangling Pointers

As mentioned earlier, a dangling pointer is a pointer variable that no longer references a valid object. Four situations can cause dangling pointers, but we will cover only three of them because we consider the fourth one to be an unsafe practice.[3]

Situations that can cause a dangling pointer

- Situation 1: As Section C2.3.1 discusses, if you do not set a pointer variable to `nullptr` after using `delete`, you leave the pointer dangling since it contains the address of a previously used object that was deallocated.

---

[3] We do not use & as the "address of" operator in this textbook. As a result, pointer variables can be assigned only to variables in the free store, so a function cannot return a pointer to a local variable that no longer exists.

- Situation 2: Similarly, if you declare a pointer variable but do not assign it a value, the result is a dangling pointer. As with any C++ variable, when C++ creates a pointer variable, its value is undefined. That is, C++ does not automatically initialize or clear the memory that a variable represents. The compiler and the programmer have no way to check that the value in the pointer variable actually points to an object in the free store. That value might simply be whatever was in the memory when the pointer was created. For example, suppose that you write statements such as

```
MagicBox<int>* myMagicBoxPtr;
myMagicBoxPtr->getItem();
```

Here, the pointer variable myMagicBoxPtr is not assigned an object to point to. When the method getItem is called, the program will abort—usually with a segment fault error—because the program treats the value in myMagicBoxPtr as the address of a MagicBox<int> object and tries to find the getItem method at that address. Since it is very unlikely that a MagicBox<int> object happens to be there, the program ends abnormally.

If you need to create a pointer variable but do not have an object for it to point to, you should always set it to nullptr:

```
MagicBox<int>* myMagicBoxPtr = nullptr;
```

Then your code can compare the pointer variable to nullptr to see whether it points to a valid object in the free store, as in the following example:

```
if (myMagicBoxPtr != nullptr)
    myMagicBoxPtr->getItem();
```

If the pointer is not nullptr, you can use the pointer to call a method.

- Situation 3: The third situation that can cause a dangling pointer is subtle, and the best way to guard against it is careful programming. Consider the following statements that we saw earlier when discussing memory leaks:

```
MagicBox<std::string>* myBoxPtr = new MagicBox<std::string>();
MagicBox<std::string>* yourBoxPtr = myBoxPtr;
```

Executing this code results in the memory configuration shown in Figure C2-7, where both yourBoxPtr and myBoxPtr point to the same object. We say that yourBoxPtr is an **alias** of myBoxPtr since they both refer to the same object. There is nothing wrong with this code so far, and it does not have any memory leaks.

Suppose we then execute the following statements:

```
delete myBoxPtr;
myBoxPtr = nullptr;
yourBoxPtr->getItem();
```

FIGURE C2-7   Aliases: Two pointers referencing (pointing to) the same object

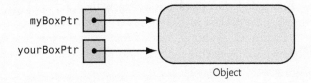

Object

Here we try to practice safe and secure programming by setting `myBoxPtr` to `nullptr` after deleting the object that it points to. But the call `yourBoxPtr->getItem()` results in the program aborting. What happened? Figure C2-8 shows the state of memory just prior to this call. As you can see, the object pointed to by `myBoxPtr` was deleted, as it should have been. The problem arises because `yourBoxPtr` still references the object's location in the free store, even though the object no longer exists. Since the object no longer exists, `yourBoxPtr` is a dangling pointer and the program aborts when we try to call a method on that object.

FIGURE C2-8   Example of a dangling pointer

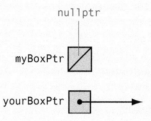

 Programming Tip: How to avoid dangling pointers

- Set pointer variables to `nullptr` either initially or when you no longer need them. If a class has a pointer variable as a data field, the constructor should always initialize that data field, to point either to an object or to `nullptr`. For example, the class `GoodMemory` in Listing C2-3 demonstrates this safeguard.
- Test whether a pointer variable contains `nullptr` before using it to call a method.
- Try to reduce the use of aliases in your program. As you will see, that is not always possible or desirable in certain situations.
- Do not delete an object in the free store until you are certain that no other alias needs to use it.
- Set all aliases that reference a deleted object to `nullptr` when the object is deleted.

C2.4 Virtual Methods and Polymorphism

Now that we have some of the basics of pointers behind us, we can dive into the implementation of polymorphism. To allow the compiler to perform the late binding necessary for polymorphism, you must declare the methods in the base class as virtual. In C++ Interlude 1, we began a discussion of virtual methods—methods that use the keyword `virtual` to indicate that they can be overridden. In the example in Section C2.2, `PlainBox` is the base class, which we defined in Listing C1-3 of C++ Interlude 1. The code that we wrote then did not behave as we desired. To correct that problem, we must declare as virtual the methods of `PlainBox` that we want other classes to override, as Listing C2-4 shows. Notice that only the header file of the base class (`PlainBox`) needs to be revised. Declaring the methods `setItem` and `getItem` as virtual makes it possible for the method code to be bound late.

LISTING C2-4   Revised header file for the class `PlainBox`

```
1    /** @file PlainBox.h */
2    #ifndef PLAIN_BOX_
3    #define PLAIN_BOX_
4
5    template<class ItemType> // Indicates this is a template
6
7    // Declaration for the class PlainBox
8    class PlainBox
9    {
10   private:
11      // Data field
12      ItemType item;
13
14   public:
15      // Default constructor
16      PlainBox();
17
18      // Parameterized constructor
19      PlainBox(const ItemType& theItem);
20
21      // Mutator method that can change the value of the data field
22      virtual void setItem(const ItemType& theItem);
23
24      // Accessor method to get the value of the data field
25      virtual ItemType getItem() const;
26   }; // end PlainBox
27
28   #include "PlainBox.cpp" // Include the implementation file
29   #endif
```

To fully implement late binding, we must create the variables in the free store and use pointers to reference them. Thus, we must also change the code from our first example of early binding in Section C2.2 to

```
std::string specialItem = "Riches beyond compare!";
std::string hammerItem = "Hammer";

PlainBox<std::string>* myPlainBoxPtr = new PlainBox<std::string>();
placeInBox(myPlainBoxPtr, hammerItem);           // Stores hammerItem
placeInBox(myPlainBoxPtr, specialItem);          // Stores specialItem
std::cout << myPlainBoxPtr->getItem() << std::endl; // Displays specialItem

MagicBox<std::string>* myMagicBoxPtr = new MagicBox<std::string>();
placeInBox(myMagicBoxPtr, hammerItem);           // Stores hammerItem
placeInBox(myMagicBoxPtr, specialItem);          // Ignores specialItem
std::cout << myMagicBoxPtr->getItem() << std::endl; // Displays hammerItem
```

An example of late binding

Next, we must change the function `placeInBox` to accept a pointer to a `PlainBox<string>` object:

```
void placeInBox(PlainBox<std::string>* theBox, std::string theItem)
{
    theBox->setItem(theItem);
} // end placeInBox
```

Our function `placeInBox` now will call the correct version of `setItem` according to the type of box pointed to by its first argument.

The last change is to free the memory used by the variables in the free store by adding the following statements to the program:

```cpp
delete myPlainBoxPtr;
myPlainBoxPtr = nullptr;
delete myMagicBoxPtr;
myMagicBoxPtr = nullptr;
```

The use of virtual methods has a significant impact on the future use of a class. Imagine that you had compiled the class `PlainBox` and its implementation before you wrote the derived class `MagicBox`. If you then wrote `MagicBox`, assuming access to the compiled class `PlainBox`, you could override `getItem` because it is virtual in `PlainBox`. As a result, you would change the behavior of `getItem` for instances of `MagicBox`, even though `PlainBox` was already compiled. That is, classes that define virtual methods are **extensible**: You can add capabilities to a derived class without having access to the ancestor's source statements.

Note: **Key points about virtual methods**

- A virtual method is one that a derived class can override.
- You must implement a class's virtual methods. (Pure virtual methods are not included in this requirement.)
- A derived class does not need to override an existing implementation of an inherited virtual method.
- Any of a class's methods may be virtual. However, if you do not want a derived class to override a particular method, the method should not be virtual.
- Constructors cannot be virtual.
- Destructors can and should be virtual. Virtual destructors ensure that future descendants of the object can deallocate themselves correctly.
- A virtual method's return type cannot be overridden.

Programming Tip The class `GoodMemory` in Listing C2-2 has a virtual destructor. Anytime you explicitly declare a class's destructor, you should include the keyword `virtual`. In this way, the correct destructor will be called, and all objects in the free store will be deleted. For example, if the class `FunMemory` is derived from `GoodMemory`, and `FunMemory`'s constructor allocates an object in the free store, `FunMemory`'s destructor has the responsibility to delete this object. If `GoodMemory`'s destructor is not virtual, `FunMemory`'s destructor might not be called, as would be the case in the following example:

```cpp
GoodMemory* recentMemory = new FunMemory();
. . .
delete recentMemory;
```

C2.5 Dynamic Allocation of Arrays

When you declare an array in C++ by using statements such as

An ordinary C++
array is statically
allocated

```cpp
const int MAX_SIZE = 50;
double myArray[MAX_SIZE];
```

the compiler reserves a specific number—MAX_SIZE, in this case—of memory cells for the array. This memory allocation occurs before your program executes, so it is not possible to wait until execution to give MAX_SIZE a value. We have already discussed the problem this fixed-size data structure causes when your program has more than MAX_SIZE items to place into the array.

You just learned how to use the new operator to allocate memory dynamically—that is, during program execution. Although Section C2.3 showed you how to allocate memory for a single variable or object, you actually can allocate memory for many at one time. If you write

```
int arraySize = 50;
double* anArray = new double[arraySize];
```

Use the new operator to allocate an array dynamically

the pointer variable anArray will point to the first item in an array of 50 items. Unlike MAX_SIZE, arraySize can change during program execution. You can assign a value to arraySize at execution time and thus determine how large your array is. That is good, but how do you use this array?

Regardless of how you allocate an array—statically, as in the first example, or dynamically, as in the second—you can use an index and the familiar array notation to access its elements. For example, anArray[0] and anArray[1] are the first two items in the array anArray.

When you allocate an array dynamically, you need to return its memory cells to the system when you no longer need them. As described earlier, you use the delete operator to perform this task. To deallocate the array anArray, you write

```
delete [ ] anArray;
```

delete returns a dynamically allocated array to the system for reuse

Note that you include brackets when you apply delete to an array.

Now suppose that your program uses all of the array anArray, despite having chosen its size during execution. You can allocate a new and larger array, copy the old array into the new array, and finally deallocate the old array. Doubling the size of the array each time it becomes full is a reasonable approach. The following statements double the size of anArray:

```
double* oldArray = anArray;                     // Copy pointer to array

anArray = new double[2 * arraySize];            // Double array size

for (int index = 0; index < arraySize; index++) // Copy old array
    anArray[index] = oldArray[index];

delete [ ] oldArray;                            // Deallocate old array
```

You can increase the size of a dynamically allocated array

Subsequent discussions in this book will refer to both statically allocated and dynamically allocated arrays. We will refer to dynamically allocated arrays as **resizable**.

C2.5.1 A Resizable Array-Based Bag

We can use a resizable array to implement the ADT bag so that the bag never becomes full—within the bounds of the particular computer, of course. If we look at the header file for the class ArrayBag, as given in Listing 3-1 of Chapter 3, and the implementation of the various methods, we see that the declaration of the array items in the header file, as well as the definitions of the constructor and the add method within the implementation file, need to be changed. We also must add a destructor to both files.

The declaration of the fixed-size array items of bag entries, as given in listing 3-1 of Chapter 3 is

```
ItemType items[DEFAULT_CAPACITY];
```

Recall that this array will be allocated during compilation. Now that we want to be able to resize the array during execution, we will declare items in the header file as follows:

```
ItemType* items;
```

We then allocate the array initially by writing the following statement within the body of the constructor:

```
items = new ItemType[DEFAULT_CAPACITY];
```

We declare the destructor in the header file as

```
virtual ~ArrayBag();
```

and then define it in the implementation file as follows:

```
template<class ItemType>
ArrayBag<ItemType>::~ArrayBag()
{
   delete [] items;
} // end destructor
```

The method add increases the capacity of the array items as necessary. When the array becomes full, add can double its capacity instead of failing to add the item and returning false. The revised method follows. Since the bag is never full, this version of the add method can always return true.

```
template<class ItemType>
bool ArrayBag<ItemType>::add(const ItemType& newEntry)
{
   bool hasRoomToAdd = (itemCount < maxItems);
   if (!hasRoomToAdd)
   {
      ItemType* oldArray = items;
      items = new ItemType[2 * maxItems];
      for (int index = 0; index < maxItems; index++)
         items[index] = oldArray[index];
      delete [ ] oldArray;
      maxItems = 2 * maxItems;
   } // end if

   // We can always add the item
   items[itemCount] = newEntry;
   itemCount++;
   return true;
} // end ResizableArrayBag add
```

Doubling the array items each time the bag is full is not as attractive as it might first seem. Each time you expand the size of an array, you must copy its contents. When the array is a small 50-element array, you copy the 50-element array to a 100-element array before completing the addition. The next 49 additions then can be made quickly without copying the array.

If you have a 50,000-element array that is full, you must allocate memory for 100,000 entries before copying the 50,000 entries in the current array. This takes considerably longer to do and a significantly greater amount of memory. It is possible that you needed storage for only 50,001 entries and will have 49,999 unused array elements wasting memory. Once you realize that your array is too large, you could reduce its size by allocating a smaller array and copying the entries to this new array. However, there is no way to predict whether or not you should do so. The application might need the extra array elements in the future.

In Chapter 4, we consider another implementation of the ADT bag that does not have this memory-allocation problem and that never becomes full.

Chapter 4

Link-Based Implementations

Contents

Prerequisites

Chapter 1	Data Abstraction: The Walls
C++ Interlude 1	C++ Classes
Chapter 2	Recursion: The Mirrors (for Section 4.3)
Chapter 3	Array-Based Implementations (incidental dependence)
C++ Interlude 2	C++ Pointers, Polymorphism, and Memory Allocation

This chapter introduces you to a link-based data structure using C++ pointers, which were described in C++ Interlude 2. You will learn how to work with such structures and how to use one to implement a class of bags. The material in this chapter is essential to much of the presentation in the chapters that follow.

VideoNote

Linked chain
concepts

4.1 Preliminaries

As the previous chapter shows, you can organize data items by placing them into the elements of an array. These items occur one after the other, but are accessible in any order. Another way to organize the data items is to place them within objects—usually called **nodes**—that are linked together into a "chain," one after the other.

To understand how this chain can hold our data items, imagine a freight train like the one in Figure 4-1. Each box car in the train can contain cargo and is linked to another car. The engine is special, since it does not contain any cargo, but it is linked to the train's first car. The first car is linked to the second car, which is linked to the third car, and so on.

FIGURE 4-1   A freight train

The door at the back end of the locomotive and each car opens in one direction only, toward the back of the train. The door at the back of the last car is locked. If you begin at the engine, you can travel to the first car, and then to the second car, and so on until you reach the last car. Since the doors in each car open in only one direction, you can move from one car to the next one, but you cannot go back from where you came.

Like our train cars, a node contains both data (cargo) and a link, or reference, to another node. Figure 4-2 illustrates a single node. It has two data fields: item, which in this example contains a string, and next, which is a pointer variable.

FIGURE 4-2   A node

Figure 4-3 shows several nodes linked together. We use arrows to represent the pointers, but what type of pointer should you use within a node, and to what will it point? You might guess that the pointer should point to a string, but actually it must point to a node that contains the string. Because pointers can point to data of any type—and since nodes are objects—pointers can, in fact, point to nodes. Thus, a node of type Node, for example, will have as one of its members a pointer to another node of type Node. For example, the statement

Defining a pointer to
a node

```
Node<std::string>* nodePtr;
```

defines a pointer variable nodePtr that can point to a node of type Node that contains a string as its data item. Nodes should be dynamically allocated. For example,

Dynamically
allocating a node

```
nodePtr = new Node<std::string>();
```

allocates a node to which nodePtr points.

FIGURE 4-3   Several nodes linked together

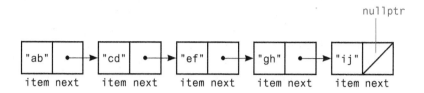

To access the members of a node, you use the pointer nodePtr and the –> notation introduced in C++ Interlude 2, because the node does not have a user-defined name. Suppose our class of nodes has an accessor method, getItem, that returns the value of the data member item. To get a copy of the data in the node to which nodePtr points, you write nodePtr->getItem().[1] Likewise, if our class of nodes has the method getNext to access the data member next, the expression nodePtr->getNext() represents the pointer next. For example, if nodePtr points to the second node in Figure 4-3, nodePtr->getItem() returns the string "cd" and nodePtr->getNext() returns a pointer to the third node. We can save this new pointer in nodePtr itself by writing

```
nodePtr = nodePtr->getNext();
```

If we execute the previous statement again, nodePtr will point to the fourth node in Figure 4-3. Executing the statement one more time makes nodePtr point to the last node shown in Figure 4-3. What is the value of the member next in this last node? That is, what value does nodePtr->getNext() return? We want this value to be a signal that we have reached the last of the linked nodes. If this value is nullptr, we easily can detect when we have reached the end of the linked nodes.

We have one more detail to consider: Nothing so far points to the first node. If you cannot get to the first node, you cannot get to the second node; and if you cannot get to the second node, you cannot get to the third node; and so on. The solution is to have an additional pointer whose sole purpose is to point to the first of several linked nodes. Such a pointer is called the **head pointer** or simply the head of the data structure.

The head pointer points to the first node

Figure 4-4 illustrates a **linked chain** of nodes with a head pointer. Observe that the head pointer headPtr is different from the other pointers in the diagram in that it is not within one of the nodes and does not contain any data. It contains only a link, or reference, to the first node in the chain. That is, the variable headPtr simply enables you to access the chain's beginning. The head pointer is like the locomotive in Figure 4-1. The locomotive has no cargo, but is linked to the first car in the train. What value should headPtr contain if there are no nodes for it to point to? Assigning headPtr the value nullptr is a logical choice in this case.

If headPtr is nullptr, it points to nothing

FIGURE 4-4   A head pointer to the first of several linked nodes

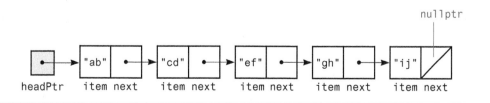

---

[1] An alternative notation, (*nodePtr).getItem(), is possible, but this book will not use it. Although this notation is analogous to the use of the dot operator to reference the members of a named structure, the –> operator is more suggestive of pointers.

Note: Although all of the pointers shown in Figure 4-4 point to nodes, the head pointer is a simple pointer variable, whereas the `next` fields are within nodes.

 Programming Tip: It is a common mistake to think that before you can assign `headPtr` a value, you first must create a new `Node` object. This misconception is rooted in the belief that the variable `headPtr` does not exist if it does not point to a node. This is not at all true; `headPtr` is a pointer variable waiting to be assigned a value. Thus, for example, you can assign `nullptr` to `headPtr` without first using `new`. In fact, the sequence

```
headPtr = new Node<std::string>(); // An incorrect use of new
headPtr = nullptr;
```

destroys the content of the only pointer—`headPtr`—to the newly created node, as Figure 4-5 illustrates. Thus, you have needlessly created a new node and then made it inaccessible. This action creates a memory leak in your program and should be avoided!

FIGURE 4-5   A lost node

```
headPtr = new Node<std::string>();
```
headPtr


```
headPtr = nullptr;
```
headPtr

4.1.1   The Class Node

Before we continue, let's examine the C++ code for the class `Node`. Listing 4-1 gives the header file for the class. In addition to the data members `item` and `next` that we introduced earlier, the class declares three constructors, two accessor methods—one each for `item` and `next`—and two mutator methods—again one each for `item` and `next`. Notice that within this class, a pointer to a node has the data type `Node<ItemType>*`.

LISTING 4-1 The header file for the template class Node

```
1   /** @file Node.h */
2
3   #ifndef NODE_
4   #define NODE_
5
6   template<class ItemType>
7   class Node    .
8   {
9   private:
10     ItemType        item; // A data item
11     Node<ItemType>* next; // Pointer to next node
12   public:
13     Node();
```

```
14      Node(const ItemType& anItem);
15      Node(const ItemType& anItem, Node<ItemType>* nextNodePtr);
16      void setItem(const ItemType& anItem);
17      void setNext(Node<ItemType>* nextNodePtr);
18      ItemType getItem() const;
19      Node<ItemType>* getNext() const;
20   }; // end Node
21   #include "Node.cpp"
22   #endif
```

Listing 4-2 shows the implementation file for Node.

LISTING 4-2 The implementation file for the class Node

```
1    /** @file Node.cpp */
2    #include "Node.h"
3    template<class ItemType>
4    Node<ItemType>::Node() : next(nullptr)
5    {
6    }  // end default constructor
7
8    template<class ItemType>
9    Node<ItemType>::Node(const ItemType& anItem) : item(anItem), next(nullptr)
10   {
11   }  // end constructor
12
13   template<class ItemType>
14   Node<ItemType>::Node(const ItemType& anItem, Node<ItemType>* nextNodePtr)
15                       : item(anItem), next(nextNodePtr)
16   {
17   }  // end constructor
18
19   template<class ItemType>
20   void Node<ItemType>::setItem(const ItemType& anItem)
21   {
22      item = anItem;
23   }  // end setItem
24
25   template<class ItemType>
26   void Node<ItemType>::setNext(Node<ItemType>* nextNodePtr)
27   {
28      next = nextNodePtr;
29   }  // end setNext
30
31   template<class ItemType>
32   ItemType Node<ItemType>::getItem() const
33   {
34      return item;
35   }  // end getItem
36
37   template<class ItemType>
38   Node<ItemType>* Node<ItemType>::getNext() const
39   {
40      return next;
41   }  // end getNext
```

4.2   A Link-Based Implementation of the ADT Bag

Now that we have a class of nodes to use when defining link-based data structures, we will use it to define a link-based implementation of the ADT bag. Doing so will allow us to examine some of the basic practices for creating such implementations. Subsequent chapters will expand on these ideas.

Unlike array-based implementations, a link-based implementation does not impose a fixed maximum size on the data structure—except, of course, as imposed by the storage limits of the system. Additionally, an ADT's insertion and removal operations do not need to move any data items.

As was true for ArrayBag, we need to represent the items in the bag and its size. Figure 4-6 indicates one possible way to represent this data by using nodes. Here headPtr points to a linked chain of nodes containing the items in the bag. The integer itemCount is the current number of items in the bag. Both headPtr and itemCount will be private data members of our class.

FIGURE 4-6   A link-based implementation of the ADT bag

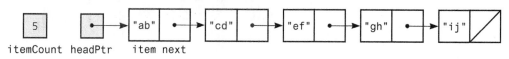

From Chapter 1, recall the interface BagInterface that describes the operations of the ADT bag. Also remember that we should use this interface when developing any implementation of this ADT. The bag operations in this interface, given in UML notation, are as follows:

```
+getCurrentSize(): integer
+isEmpty(): boolean
+add(newEntry: ItemType): boolean
+remove(anEntry: ItemType): boolean
+clear(): void
+getFrequencyOf(anEntry: ItemType): integer
+contains(anEntry: ItemType): boolean
+toVector(): vector
```

These operations correspond to the public methods in our class.

4.2.1   The Header File

The header file given in Listing 4-3 declares the class LinkedBag. The private data members are headPtr, which points to the first node in the linked chain that contains the items in the bag, and itemCount, which counts these items. The private section of the class also declares a private method, whose purpose will become clear shortly. The public section declares a default constructor, a copy constructor—whose purpose is discussed near the end of Section 4.2.3—a destructor, and the public methods of the class. The public method declarations are identical to those in the class ArrayBag as given in Chapter 3. As you will see, the compiler-generated copy constructor and destructor are not sufficient for link-based implementations.

Recall from C++ Interlude 2 that destructors should be virtual. We have tagged LinkedBag's destructor with the keyword virtual in the header file. Failure to do so will result in a warning from the compiler and, if your class is used as a base class, a possible memory leak.

LISTING 4-3 The header file for the class LinkedBag

```cpp
/** ADT bag: Link-based implementation.
 @file LinkedBag.h */

#ifndef LINKED_BAG_
#define LINKED_BAG_

#include "BagInterface.h"
#include "Node.h"

template<class ItemType>
class LinkedBag : public BagInterface<ItemType>
{
private:
   Node<ItemType>* headPtr; // Pointer to first node
   int itemCount;           // Current count of bag items
   // Returns either a pointer to the node containing a given entry
   // or the null pointer if the entry is not in the bag.
   Node<ItemType>* getPointerTo(const ItemType& target) const;

public:
   LinkedBag();                                   // Default constructor
   LinkedBag(const LinkedBag<ItemType>& aBag);    // Copy constructor
   virtual ~LinkedBag();                          // Destructor is virtual
   int getCurrentSize() const;
   bool isEmpty() const;
   bool add(const ItemType& newEntry);
   bool remove(const ItemType& anEntry);
   void clear();
   bool contains(const ItemType& anEntry) const;
   int getFrequencyOf(const ItemType& anEntry) const;
   vector<ItemType> toVector() const;
}; // end LinkedBag

#include "LinkedBag.cpp"
#endif
```

4.2.2 Defining the Core Methods

Just as we did when we defined an array-based implementation of the ADT bag in Chapter 3, we begin our new implementation by defining the same core methods: the default constructor, add, toVector, getCurrentSize, and isEmpty. We will write stubs for the remaining methods, including the copy constructor and destructor.

The default constructor. The following default constructor initializes the head pointer and the current number of items in the bag:

```cpp
template<class ItemType>
LinkedBag<ItemType>::LinkedBag() : headPtr(nullptr), itemCount(0)
{
} // end default constructor
```

The method add. A bag does not order its entries, so the method `add` can insert a new item at any convenient location within the linked chain of nodes that contains the bag's entries. The most convenient place for us to make this insertion is at the beginning of the chain, because the first node is the only one that we can access directly. Figure 4-7 illustrates how we add a new node to the beginning of an existing chain of nodes.

You must make `headPtr` point to the new node, and the new node must point to the node that had been at the beginning of the chain. Note how the following definition of the method `add` accomplishes this:

Inserting a node at the beginning of a linked chain

```
template<class ItemType>
bool LinkedBag<ItemType>::add(const ItemType& newEntry)
{
    // Add to beginning of chain: new node references rest of chain;
    // (headPtr is nullptr if chain is empty)
    Node<ItemType>* newNodePtr = new Node<ItemType>();
    newNodePtr->setItem(newEntry);
    newNodePtr->setNext(headPtr);   // New node points to chain
    headPtr = newNodePtr;           // New node is now first node
    itemCount++;

    return true;                    // The method is always successful
}  // end add
```

FIGURE 4-7　Inserting at the beginning of a linked chain

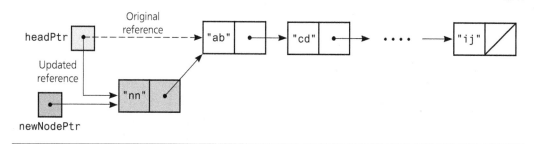

Insertion into an empty chain is really an insertion at the beginning of the chain

Observe that if the bag is empty before the insertion `headPtr` is `nullptr`, so the `next` pointer of the new node is set to `nullptr`. This step is correct because the new item is the last item—as well as the first item—in the chain. Also note that the `add` method always returns true, since an addition to a bag is always possible. That is, the bag never gets full.

 Programming Tip: Our method `add` uses the operator `new` to create a new node object and place it on the application heap. Because C++ does not automatically deallocate unreferenced objects as Java and Python do, it is our class's responsibility to ensure that the object is removed from the application heap using the operator `delete`. As discussed in C++ Interlude 2, the class destructor is one method where we do this. Since we created this node to contain the entry that we are adding to the bag, it follows that another opportunity to delete the node is when we remove the item from the bag.

Question 1 Consider a linked chain of three nodes, such that each node contains a string. The first node contains "A", the second node contains "B", and the third node contains "C".

    a. Write C++ statements that create the described linked chain. Beginning with a head pointer `headPtr` that contains `nullptr`, create and attach a node for "C", then create and attach a node for "B", and finally create and attach a node for "A".

    a. Repeat part *a*, but instead create and attach nodes in the order "A", "B", "C".

The method `toVector`. Recall that the method `toVector` retrieves the entries that are in a bag and returns them to the client within a vector. A loop within `toVector` adds the bag's entries to this vector. In the array-based implementation, this loop simply accesses an array of these entries. Here we must retrieve the entries from the nodes in a chain. To do that, we must move from node to node; that is, we must **traverse** the chain. As we **visit** each node, we copy its data item into the vector.

> *A traverse operation visits each node in the linked chain*

Let's write some high-level pseudocode for this loop, given the linked chain pictured in Figure 4-6.

> *Let a current pointer reference the first node in the chain*
> `while` (*the current pointer is not the null pointer*)
> *{*
>   *Assign the data portion of the current node to the next element in a vector*
>   *Set the current pointer to the next pointer of the current node*
> *}*

This solution requires that you keep track of the current position within the chain. Thus, you need a pointer variable—let's call it `curPtr`—that references the current node.

Note: The pointer variable `curPtr` is analogous to the integer variable `curIndex` that we used in Section 3.2.4 of Chapter 3 to keep track of the current entry in an array.

Initially, `curPtr` must reference the first node. Because `headPtr` references the first node, simply copy `headPtr` into `curPtr` by writing

```
Node<ItemType>* curPtr = headPtr;
```

Then you can use the expression `curPtr->getItem()` to access the data portion of the current node. After copying the data into the vector, you advance the current pointer to the next node by writing

```
curPtr = curPtr->getNext();
```

Figure 4-8 illustrates this action. If the previous assignment statement is not clear, consider

```
Node<ItemType>* temp = curPtr->getNext();
curPtr = temp;
```

and then show that the intermediate variable `temp` is not necessary.

FIGURE 4-8   The effect of the assignment `curPtr = curPtr->getNext()`

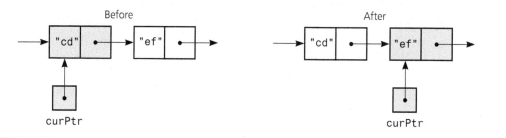

These ideas lead to the following definition of `toVector`:

```
template<class ItemType>
std::vector<ItemType> LinkedBag<ItemType>::toVector() const
{
    std::vector<ItemType> bagContents;
    Node<ItemType>* curPtr = headPtr;
    int counter = 0;
    while ((curPtr != nullptr) && (counter < itemCount))
    {
        bagContents.push_back(curPtr->getItem());
        curPtr = curPtr->getNext();
        counter++;
    } // end while
    return bagContents;
} // end toVector
```

Here `curPtr` points to each node in a nonempty chain during the course of the loop's execution, and so the data portion of each node is accessed and added to the end of the vector. After the last node is accessed, `curPtr` becomes `nullptr`, and the loop terminates. For an empty bag, `headPtr` is `nullptr`, so the loop is correctly skipped. Note that the variable `counter`, while not necessary, provides a defense against going beyond the end of the chain.

 Programming Tip: A common error in writing a loop used to traverse a linked chain is to compare `curPtr->getNext()` instead of `curPtr` with `nullptr`. When `curPtr` points to the last node of a nonempty chain, `curPtr->getNext()` is `nullptr`, and so the loop would terminate before accessing the data in the last node. In addition, when the chain is empty, `headPtr`—and therefore `curPtr`—are `nullptr`, making the value of `curPtr->getNext()` undefined. Such references are incorrect and should be avoided.

The methods `isEmpty` and `getCurrentSize`. The last two methods in our core group have the following definitions, which are like the ones in the array-based implementation given in Chapter 3.

```
template<class ItemType>
bool LinkedBag<ItemType>::isEmpty() const
{
    return itemCount== 0;
} // end isEmpty

template<class ItemType>
int LinkedBag<ItemType>::getCurrentSize() const
{
    return itemCount;
} // end getCurrentSize
```

Note: Testing the core methods

Just as we did in the previous chapter, you should test each method as you define it. In fact, with little change, you can revise the program given in Listing 3-2 and use it to test the core methods that we have just defined. The bag in that program became full, but it will not here. In Section 4.4, we will examine how to change that program so that it can test multiple bag implementations.

Question 2 Why are only a few changes necessary to reuse the code in Listing 3-2? How would you implement the changes using the "find and replace" functionality of a text editor or IDE?

Question 3 Why is a LinkedBag object not concerned about becoming full?

4.2.3   Implementing More Methods

Having successfully defined the core methods, we will continue to define the remaining ones in our class.

The method getFrequencyOf. To count the number of times a given object occurs in a bag, we count the number of times the object occurs in the linked chain. To do so, we need to traverse the chain and compare each of its data items with the given object. Each time we find a match, we increment a counter. When the traversal ends, we return the value of the counter.

The loop we will use is like the one we wrote in the method toVector. Here is the definition of getFrequencyOf:

```cpp
template<class ItemType>
int LinkedBag<ItemType>::getFrequencyOf(const ItemType& anEntry) const
{
   int frequency = 0;
   int counter = 0;
   Node<ItemType>* curPtr = headPtr;
   while ((curPtr != nullptr) && (counter < itemCount))
   {
      if (anEntry == curPtr->getItem())
      {
         frequency++;
      }  // end if

      counter++;
      curPtr = curPtr->getNext();
   }  // end while

   return frequency;
}  // end getFrequencyOf
```

Question 4 Suppose that the ADT bag had an operation that displayed its contents. Write a C++ definition for such a method for the class LinkedBag.

Question 5 How many assignment operations does the method that you wrote for the previous question require?

The method `contains`. The discussion in Chapter 3 about the method `contains` applies here as well. Although the method could call the method `getFrequencyOf`, which we just defined, doing so usually will involve more work than is necessary. Whereas `getFrequencyOf` must check every entry in the bag, `contains` exits as soon as it finds an entry in the bag that is the same as the given one.

We observed in the previous chapter that the methods `contains` and `remove` perform the same search for a specific entry. Thus, to avoid duplicate code, we perform this search in a private method that both `contains` and `remove` can call. We declared this private method in the header file, and its definition follows.

```cpp
// Returns either a pointer to the node containing a given entry
// or the null pointer if the entry is not in the bag.
template<class ItemType>
Node<ItemType>* LinkedBag<ItemType>::
                getPointerTo(const ItemType& target) const
{
   bool found = false;
   Node<ItemType>* curPtr = headPtr;
   while (!found && (curPtr != nullptr))
   {
      if (target == curPtr->getItem())
         found = true;
      else
         curPtr = curPtr->getNext();
   }  // end while

   return curPtr;
}  // end getPointerTo
```

The definition of the method `contains` is straightforward:

```cpp
template<class ItemType>
bool LinkedBag<ItemType>::contains(const ItemType& anEntry) const
{
   return (getPointerTo(anEntry) != nullptr);
}  // end contains
```

Question 6 If the pointer variable `curPtr` becomes `nullptr` in the method `getPointerTo`, what value does the method `contains` return when the bag is not empty?

Question 7 Trace the execution of the method `contains` when the bag is empty.

Question 8 Revise the definition of the method `getPointerTo` so that the loop is controlled by a counter and the value of `itemCount`.

Question 9 What is a disadvantage of the definition of the method `getPointerTo`, as described in the previous question, when compared to its original definition?

Question 10 Why should the method `getPointerTo` not be made public?

The method `remove`. Recall that the method `remove` deletes one occurrence of a given entry and returns either true or false to indicate whether the removal was successful. Just as adding a new node to a linked chain is easiest at its beginning, so is removing the first node. But the entry that we need to remove is not always in the chain's first node.

Suppose that we locate the entry to remove in node *n*. We can replace that entry with the entry in the first node, and then delete the first node. Thus, we can describe the logic for remove with the following pseudocode:

```
remove(anEntry)
{
    Find the node that contains anEntry
    Replace anEntry with the entry that is in the first node
    Delete the first node
}
```

By using the private method getPointerTo to locate the entry that we want to remove, we can define the method remove as follows:

```
template<class ItemType>
bool LinkedBag<ItemType>::remove(const ItemType& anEntry)
{
    Node<ItemType>* entryNodePtr = getPointerTo(anEntry);
    bool canRemoveItem = !isEmpty() && (entryNodePtr != nullptr);
    if (canRemoveItem)
    {
        // Copy data from first node to located node
        entryNodePtr->setItem(headPtr->getItem());

        // Disconnect first node
        Node<ItemType>* nodeToDeletePtr = headPtr;
        headPtr = headPtr->getNext();

        // Return node to the system
        nodeToDeletePtr->setNext(nullptr);
        delete nodeToDeletePtr;
        nodeToDeletePtr = nullptr;

        itemCount--;
    }  // end if

    return canRemoveItem;
}  // end remove
```

After the method remove deletes a node, the system can use this returned memory and possibly even reallocate it to your program as a result of the new operator. Suppose that this reallocation actually occurs when you ask for a new node for your linked chain. You can be sure that your new node does not still point to your linked chain, because you executed the statement nodeToDeletePtr->setNext(nullptr) before you deallocated the node. Doing this and setting the variable nodeToDeletePtr to nullptr are examples of defensive programming that can avoid devastating, subtle errors later in the program. We take these steps, even though nodeToDeletePtr is a local variable that we do not use again, to secure our code from a malicious hacker.

 Programming Tip: Remember that any time you allocate memory by using new, you must eventually deallocate it by using delete.

 Note: For a pointer p, delete p deallocates the node to which p points; it does not deallocate p. The pointer p still exists, but it contains an undefined value. You should not reference p or any other pointer variable that still points to the deallocated node. To help you avoid this kind of error, and to protect your code from malicious use, you can assign nullptr to p after executing delete p. However, if variables other than p point to the deallocated node, the possibility of error still exists.

Question 11 Given the previous definition of the method `remove`, which entry in a bag can be removed in the least time? Why?

Question 12 Given the previous definition of the method `remove`, which entry in a bag takes the most time to remove? Why?

The method `clear`. The method `clear` cannot simply set `ItemCount` to zero, thereby ignoring all of the entries in the linked chain. Because the nodes in the chain were allocated dynamically, `clear` must deallocate them. Thus, we have the following definition for this method:

```
template<class ItemType>
void LinkedBag<ItemType>::clear()
{
   Node<ItemType>* nodeToDeletePtr = headPtr;
   while (headPtr != nullptr)
   {
      headPtr = headPtr->getNext();

      // Return node to the system
      nodeToDeletePtr->setNext(nullptr);
      delete nodeToDeletePtr;
      nodeToDeletePtr = headPtr;
   } // end while
   // headPtr is nullptr; nodeToDeletePtr is nullptr

   itemCount = 0;
} // end clear
```

The destructor. Each class has only one destructor. The destructor destroys an instance of the class, that is, an object, when the object's lifetime ends. Typically, the destructor is invoked implicitly at the end of the block in which the object was created.

You must write a destructor if your class allocates memory dynamically

Classes that use only statically allocated memory can depend on the compiler-generated destructor, as was the case for the class `ArrayBag` in Chapter 3. However, when a class uses dynamically allocated memory, as in the present link-based implementation, you need to write a destructor that deallocates this memory by using `delete`. The destructor for `LinkedBag` can simply call the method `clear`, as it uses `delete` to deallocate each node in the linked chain containing the bag's entries. The destructor's definition follows:

```
template<class ItemType>
LinkedBag<ItemType>::~LinkedBag()
{
   clear();
} // end destructor
```

A destructor's name is a tilde (~) followed by the class name. A destructor cannot have arguments, has no return type—not even `void`—and cannot use `return` to return a value.

Question 13 Revise the destructor in the class `LinkedBag` so that it does not call `clear`, but it instead directly deletes each node of the underlying linked chain.

The copy constructor. The second constructor in `LinkedBag` is the copy constructor:

```
LinkedBag(const LinkedBag<ItemType>& aBag);
```

The **copy constructor** makes a copy of an object. It is invoked implicitly when you either

- Use the assignment operator to assign an object to a variable,
- Pass an object to a function by value,
- Return an object from a valued function, or
- Define and initialize an object, as in

```
LinkedBag bag2(bag1);
```

where bag1 exists already.

Situations that invoke the copy constructor

When copying an object involves only copying the values of its data members, the copy is called a **shallow copy**. If a shallow copy is sufficient, you can omit the copy constructor, in which case the compiler generates a copy constructor that performs a shallow copy. Such was the case in Chapter 3 for the class ArrayBag, although we did not mention it. That array-based implementation of the ADT bag used a compiler-generated copy constructor to copy both the array of bag items and the number of items.

A compiler-generated copy constructor performs a shallow copy

For our new link-based implementation, a compiler-generated copy constructor would copy only the data members itemCount and headPtr. For example, Figure 4-9a pictures a linked chain and the result of this shallow copy. Both the original pointer headPtr and its copy point to the same linked chain. In other words, the chain's nodes are not copied. If you need to create a copy of the linked chain, you must write your own copy constructor. That is, a **deep copy** is needed, as Figure 4-9b illustrates.

FIGURE 4-9   (a) A linked chain and its (b) shallow copy; (c) deep copy

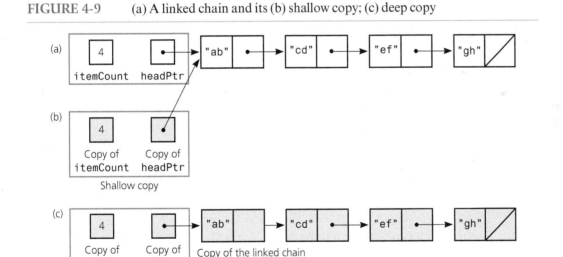

Thus, the copy constructor appears as follows.

```
template<class ItemType>
LinkedBag<ItemType>::LinkedBag(const LinkedBag<ItemType>& aBag)
{
    itemCount = aBag.itemCount;
    Node<ItemType>* origChainPtr = aBag.headPtr;
```

```
      if (origChainPtr == nullptr)
        headPtr = nullptr; // Original bag is empty; so is copy
      else
      {
        // Copy first node
        headPtr = new Node<ItemType>();
        headPtr->setItem(origChainPtr->getItem());

        // Copy remaining nodes
        Node<ItemType>* newChainPtr = headPtr;    // Last-node pointer
        origChainPtr = origChainPtr->getNext();   // Advance pointer
        while (origChainPtr != nullptr)
        {
           // Get next item from original chain
           ItemType nextItem = origChainPtr->getItem();

           // Create a new node containing the next item
           Node<ItemType>* newNodePtr = new Node<ItemType>(nextItem);

           // Link new node to end of new chain
           newChainPtr->setNext(newNodePtr);

           // Advance pointers
           newChainPtr = newChainPtr->getNext();
           origChainPtr = origChainPtr->getNext();
        }  // end while

        newChainPtr->setNext(nullptr); // Flag end of new chain
      }  // end if
   }  // end copy constructor
```

As you can see, the copy constructor is an expensive operation. It requires traversing the original linked chain and duplicating each node visited.

4.3   Using Recursion in Link-Based Implementations

It is possible, and sometimes desirable, to process linked chains recursively. This section examines how to write the iterative methods given previously as recursive ones. Such recursive methods will require the chain's head pointer as an argument. Therefore, they should not be public, because the head pointer is a private data member of the class and the client does not—and should not—have access to it. Otherwise, clients could access the linked nodes directly, thereby violating the ADT's wall.

4.3.1   Recursive Definitions of Methods in LinkedBag

As an introduction to this topic, we will revise two methods in the class LinkedBag to use recursion. These methods simply traverse a chain of linked nodes without making any changes to it.

The method toVector. We begin with the method toVector because it has a straightforward recursive implementation. This operation requires us to traverse the linked chain of nodes as we copy data from the nodes into a vector. Traversal of a linked chain is an operation that occurs in many situations.

We have established that the method performing the recursion must be private and must have the head pointer as a parameter. Since the method will copy data into a vector as it traverses the linked chain, the vector must also be a parameter. We can declare this method in the private section of the class LinkedBag, as follows:

```
// Fills the vector bagContents with the data in the nodes of
// the linked chain to which curPtr points.
void fillVector(std::vector<ItemType>& bagContents,
                Node<ItemType>* curPtr) const;
```

Given a definition of this method, we could implement toVector as follows:

```
template<class ItemType>
std::vector<ItemType> LinkedBag<ItemType>::toVector() const
{
   std::vector<ItemType> bagContents;
   fillVector(bagContents, headPtr);
   return bagContents;
} // end toVector
```

Thus, after creating a vector, toVector fills it—by calling fillVector—with the data in the chain of linked nodes whose head pointer is headPtr. Finally, toVector returns the vector to the client.

To define fillVector, we need to think recursively. If the chain is empty—that is, if curPtr is nullptr—we have nothing to do. This is the base case. In the recursive step, we first add the data curPtr->getItem() to the vector and then recursively fill the vector with the chain that begins at curPtr->getNext(). The method then has the following definition:

```
template<class ItemType>
void LinkedBag<ItemType>::fillVector(std::vector<ItemType>& bagContents,
                                     Node<ItemType>* curPtr) const
{
   if (curPtr != nullptr)
   {
      bagContents.push_back(curPtr->getItem());
      fillVector(bagContents, curPtr->getNext());
   } // end if
} // end fillVector
```

Even though fillVector has a reference parameter, the method is safe because it is private. A similar situation occurs in Chapter 16 and is discussed further in a Note in Section 16.3.1.

The private method getPointerTo. The method getPointerTo locates a given entry within the linked chain. To do so, it traverses the linked chain, but unlike fillVector's traversal, this traversal stops if it locates the node that contains the given entry, that is, the target. The iterative version of getPointerTo has one parameter, which is the target. We could define a private method to perform the recursion—as we did for toVector—that has two parameters: the target entry and a head pointer. Then getPointerTo could call this new private method. However, since getPointerTo is itself a private method, we can revise it to have the necessary two parameters. That is the approach we will take here. Of course, we also will have to revise the calls to the method that appear in the rest of the class.

We begin by replacing the declaration of getPointerTo in the header file for the class LinkedBag with the following statements:

```
// Locates a given entry within this bag.
// Returns either a pointer to the node containing a given entry or
// the null pointer if the entry is not in the bag.
Node<ItemType>* getPointerTo(const ItemType& target,
                             Node<ItemType>* curPtr) const;
```

Before we forget to do so, let's revise the calls to this method that occur in the methods remove and contains. The original calls are getPointerTo(anEntry), but each one now needs a second argument as follows: getPointerTo(anEntry, headPtr).

The recursive definition of this method has two base cases. One case occurs when the chain is empty, causing the method to return `nullptr`. The other base case occurs when we locate the desired entry at `curPtr->getItem()`. In this case, the method returns `curPtr`. The recursive step searches the chain beginning at `curPtr->getNext()`. Thus, the method has the following definition:

```cpp
template<class ItemType>
Node<ItemType>* LinkedBag<ItemType>::getPointerTo(const ItemType& target,
                                                  Node<ItemType>* curPtr) const
{
   Node<ItemType>* result = nullptr;
   if (curPtr != nullptr)
   {
      if (target == curPtr->getItem())
         result = curPtr;
      else
         result = getPointerTo(target, curPtr->getNext());
   } // end if

   return result;
} // end getPointerTo
```

Other methods that can have a recursive definition are left for you as exercises.

Question 14 Revise the method `getPointerTo` so that it does not use the local variable `result`, but instead executes a `return` statement after each test is completed.

Question 15 Revise the method `clear` so that it calls a recursive method to deallocate the nodes in the chain.

4.4   Testing Multiple ADT Implementations

In Chapter 3, we developed a short program, shown in Listing 3-2, that tested the core methods of our array-based bag implementation. Because we used ADT bag methods when we tested our implementation, we can use the same code—with a few changes—to test our linked implementation. You need only to change each occurrence of `ArrayBag` to `LinkedBag` and recompile the program.

But what if later you change the array-based implementation and want to retest it? You would need to change each occurrence of `LinkedBag` back to `ArrayBag`. Let's examine a way we can revise the test program to let the user decide which bag implementation needs testing. By taking advantage of polymorphism, we can do this without needing to duplicate the test code.

In Chapter 1, we described our ADT bag in the abstract class `BagInterface`. Since both `ArrayBag` and `LinkedBag` share public methods defined in that class, we made each a subclass of `BagInterface`. In our test program, if we declare the variable `bagPtr` as a pointer to an object that implements the methods in `BagInterface`, we can use an instance of either `ArrayBag` or `LinkedBag` as the object `bagPtr` references. We define `bagPtr` as

```cpp
BagInterface<std::string>* bagPtr = nullptr;
```

We then ask the user which implementation to test, and if we assign either 'A' or 'L' to the `char` variable `userChoice`, we can instantiate an instance of the requested bag type and run the test by writing the following code:

```
   if (userChoice == 'A')
   {
      bagPtr = new ArrayBag<std::string>();
      std::cout << "Testing the Array-Based Bag:" << std::endl;
   }
   else
   {
      bagPtr = new LinkedBag<std::string>();
      std::cout << "Testing the Link-Based Bag:" << std::endl;
   } // end if

   std::cout << "The initial bag is empty." << std::endl;
   bagTester(bagPtr);
   delete bagPtr;
   bagPtr = nullptr;
```

To accommodate the data type of bagPtr, we need to change the parameter lists of the functions in our test program as follows:

```
void displayBag(BagInterface<std::string>* bagPtr)
```

and

```
void bagTester(BagInterface<std::string>* bagPtr)
```

Finally, we must change the notation used to call the ADT bag methods, since bagPtr is a pointer. For example, we change the expression

```
bag.isEmpty()
```

to

```
bagPtr->isEmpty()
```

Listing 4-4 is a complete listing of the modified test program for core methods of classes that are implementations of the ADT bag.

LISTING 4-4 **A program that tests the core methods of classes that are derived from the abstract class BagInterface**

```
1  #include "BagInterface.h"
2  #include "ArrayBag.h"
3  #include "LinkedBag.h"
4  #include <iostream>
5  #include <string>
6
7  void displayBag(BagInterface<std::string>* bagPtr)
8  {
9     std::cout << "The bag contains " << bagPtr->getCurrentSize()
10              << " items:" << std::endl;
11    std::vector<std::string> bagItems = bagPtr->toVector();
12    int numberOfEntries = bagItems.size();
13    for (int i = 0; i < numberOfEntries; i++)
14    {
15       std::cout << bagItems[i] << " ";
16    } // end for
17    std::cout << std::endl << std::endl;
18  } // end displayBag
```

(*continues*)

```
19
20   void bagTester(BagInterface<std::string>* bagPtr)
21   {
22      std::cout << "isEmpty: returns " << bagPtr->isEmpty()
23               << "; should be 1 (true)" << std::endl;
24      std::string items[] = {"one", "two", "three", "four", "five", "one"};
25      std::cout << "Add 6 items to the bag: " << std::endl;
26      for (int i = 0; i < 6; i++)
27      {
28         bagPtr->add(items[i]);
29      }  // end for
30
31      displayBag(bagPtr);
32      std::cout << "isEmpty: returns " << bagPtr->isEmpty()
33               << "; should be 0 (false)" << std::endl;
34      std::cout << "getCurrentSize returns : " << bagPtr->getCurrentSize()
35               << "; should be 6" << std::endl;
36      std::cout << "Try to add another entry: add(\"extra\") returns "
37               << bagPtr->add("extra") << std::endl;
38   }  // end bagTester
39
40   int main()
41   {
42      BagInterface<std::string>* bagPtr = nullptr;
43      char userChoice;
44      std::cout << "Enter 'A' to test the array-based implementation\n"
45               << " or 'L' to test the link-based implementation: ";
46      std::cin >> userChoice;
47      if (toupper(userChoice) == 'A')
48      {
49         bagPtr = new ArrayBag<std::string>();
50         std::cout << "Testing the Array-Based Bag:" << std::endl;
51      }
52      else
53      {
54         bagPtr = new LinkedBag<std::string>();
55         std::cout << "Testing the Link-Based Bag:" << std::endl;
56      }  // end if
57
58      std::cout << "The initial bag is empty." << std::endl;
59      bagTester(bagPtr);
60      delete bagPtr;
61      bagPtr = nullptr;
62      std::cout << "All done!" << std::endl;
63
64      return 0;
65   }  // end main
```

Sample Output 1

```
Enter 'A' to test the array-based implementation
or 'L' to test the link-based implementation: A
Testing the Array-Based Bag:
```

```
The initial bag is empty.
isEmpty: returns 1; should be 1 (true)
Add 6 items to the bag:
The bag contains 6 items:
one two three four five one

isEmpty: returns 0; should be 0 (false)
getCurrentSize returns : 6; should be 6
Try to add another entry: add("extra") returns 0
All done!
```

Sample Output 2

```
Enter 'A' to test the array-based implementation
or 'L' to test the link-based implementation: L
Testing the Link-Based Bag:
The initial bag is empty.
isEmpty: returns 1; should be 1 (true)
Add 6 items to the bag:
The bag contains 6 items:
one five four three two one

isEmpty: returns 0; should be 0 (false)
getCurrentSize returns : 6; should be 6
Try to add another entry: add("extra") returns 1
All done!
```

Question 16 Revise the program in Listing 4-4 so that it tests first the link-based implementation and then the array-based implementation. Ensure that the program does not have a memory leak.

4.5 Comparing Array-Based and Link-Based Implementations

Typically, the various implementations that a programmer contemplates for a particular ADT have advantages and disadvantages. When you must select an implementation, you should weigh these advantages and disadvantages before you make your choice. As you will see, the decision among possible implementations of a container is one that you must make often. As an example of how you should proceed in general, we compare the two implementations of the ADT bag that you have seen.

The array-based implementation that you saw in Chapter 3 appears to be a reasonable approach. Arrays are easy to use, but as was already mentioned, an array has a fixed size, and it is possible for the number of items in the bag to exceed this fixed size. In practice, when choosing among implementations of a container, you must ask the question of whether the fixed-size restriction of an array-based implementation presents a problem in the context of a particular application. The answer to this question depends on two factors. One obvious factor is whether, for a given application, you can predict in advance the maximum number of items in your data collection at any one time. If you cannot, it is quite possible that an operation—and hence the entire program—will fail because the container requires more storage than the array can provide.

On the other hand, if for a given application you can predict in advance the maximum number of items in your data collection at any one time, you must explore a more subtle factor: Would you waste storage by declaring an array to be large enough to accommodate this

Arrays are easy to use, but they have a fixed size

Can you predict the maximum number of items in the ADT?

Will an array waste storage?

maximum number of items? Consider a case in which the maximum number of items is large, but you suspect that this number rarely will be reached. For example, suppose that your bag could contain as many as 10,000 items, but the actual number of items in the bag rarely exceeds 50. If you declare 10,000 array locations at compilation time, at least 9,950 of them will be wasted most of the time. In both of the previous cases, the array-based implementation given in Chapter 3 is not desirable.

Increasing the size of a dynamically allocated array can waste storage and time

What if you use a dynamically allocated array? Because you would use the new operator to allocate storage dynamically, you will be able to provide as much storage as the bag needs (within the bounds of the particular computer, of course). Thus, you do not have to predict the maximum size of the bag. However, if you double the size of the array each time you reach the end of the array—which is a reasonable approach to enlarging the array—you still might have many unused array locations. In the example just given, you could allocate an array of 50 locations initially. If you actually have 10,000 items in your bag, doubling the array as necessary will eventually give you an array of 12,800 locations, which is 2,800 more than you need. Remember also that you waste time by copying the array and then deallocating it each time you need more space.

An array-based implementation is a good choice for a small bag

Now suppose that your application uses a bag to hold the names of at most 200 countries. You could allocate enough storage in the array for the bag and know that you would waste little storage when the bag contains only a few names. With respect to its size, an array-based implementation is perfectly acceptable in this case.

Linked chains do not have a fixed size

A link-based implementation can solve any difficulties related to the fixed size of an array-based implementation. You use the new operator to allocate storage dynamically, so you do not need to predict the maximum size of the bag. Because you allocate memory one item at a time, the bag will be allocated only as much storage as it needs. Thus, you will not waste storage.

The item after an array item is implied; in a chain of linked nodes, an item points explicitly to the next item

Array-based and link-based implementations have other differences, and these differences affect both the time and memory requirements of the implementations. Any time you store a collection of data in an array or a linked chain, the data items become ordered; that is, there is a first item, a second item, and so on. This order implies that a typical item has a predecessor and a successor. In an array anArray, the location of the next item after the item in anArray[i] is *implicit*—it is in anArray[i+1]. In a linked chain, however, you *explicitly* determine the location of the next item by using the reference in the current node. This notion of an implicit versus explicit next item is one of the primary differences between an array and a linked chain. Therefore, an advantage of an array-based implementation is that it does not have to store explicit information about where to find the next data item, thus requiring less memory than a link-based implementation.

An array-based implementation requires less memory than a link-based implementation

Another, more important advantage of an array-based implementation is that it can provide **direct access** to a specified item. For example, if you use the array items to implement the ADT bag, you know that accessing either items[0] or items[49] takes the same amount of time. That is, the **access time** is constant for an array.

You can access array items directly with equal access time

On the other hand, if you use a link-based implementation, you have no way of immediately accessing the node that contains the ith item. To get to the appropriate node, you use the next pointers to traverse the linked chain from its beginning until you reach the ith node. That is, you access the first node and get the pointer to the second node, access the second node and get the pointer to the third node, and so on until you finally access the ith node. Clearly, the time it takes you to access the first node is less than the time it takes to access the 50th node. The access time for the ith node depends on i. The type of implementation chosen will affect the efficiency of the ADT's operations.

You must traverse a linked chain to access its ith node

The time to access the ith node in a linked chain depends on i

We will continue to compare various solutions to a problem throughout this book. Chapter 10 introduces a more formal way to discuss the efficiency of algorithms. Until then, our discussions will be informal.

SUMMARY

1. You can link objects—called nodes—to one another to form a chain of linked data. Each node contains a data item and a pointer to the next node in the chain. A pointer variable external to the chain—called the head pointer—references the first node. The last node in the chain has nullptr in its pointer portion, so it references no other node.

2. You use the new operator to dynamically allocate a new node, whereas you use the delete operator to deallocate a node.

3. Inserting a new node at the beginning of a linked chain or deleting the first node of a linked chain are easier to perform than insertions and deletions anywhere else in the chain. The insertion requires a change to two pointers: the pointer within the new node and the head pointer. The deletion requires a change to the head pointer and an application of the delete operator to the removed node.

4. Unlike an array, which enables you direct access to any of its elements, a linked chain requires a traversal to access a particular node. Therefore, the access time for an array is constant, whereas the access time for a linked chain depends on the location of the node within the chain.

5. When traversing a linked chain using the pointer variable curPtr, you must be careful not to reference curPtr after it has "passed" the last node in the chain, because curPtr will have been set to the value nullptr. For example, the loop

   ```
   while (value > curPtr->getItem())
      curPtr = curPtr->getNext();
   ```

   is incorrect if value is greater than all the data values in the linked chain, because curPtr becomes nullptr. Instead you should write

   ```
   while ((curPtr != nullptr) && (value > curPtr->getItem()))
      curPtr = curPtr->getNext();
   ```

   Because C++ uses short-circuit evaluation (see Appendix A) of logical expressions, if curPtr becomes nullptr, the expression curPtr->getItem() will not be evaluated.

6. A class that allocates memory dynamically needs an explicit copy constructor that copies an instance of the class. The copy constructor is invoked implicitly when you either use the assignment operator to assign an object to a variable, pass an object to a function by value, return an object from a valued function, or define and initialize an object. If you do not define a copy constructor, the compiler will generate one for you. A compiler-generated copy constructor is sufficient only for classes that use statically allocated memory.

7. A class that allocates memory dynamically needs an explicit destructor. The destructor should use delete to deallocate the memory associated with the object. If you do not define a destructor, the compiler will generate one for you. A compiler-generated destructor is sufficient only for classes that use statically allocated memory.

8. Although you can use the new operator to allocate memory dynamically for either an array or a linked chain, you can increase the size of a linked chain one node at a time more efficiently than you can increase the size of an array. When you increase the size of a dynamically allocated array, you must copy the original array entries into the new array and then deallocate the original array.

EXERCISES

1. If `headPtr` is a pointer variable that points to the first node of a linked chain of at least two nodes, write C++ statements that delete the second node and return it to the system.

2. Revise the public method `add` in the class `LinkedBag` so that the new node is inserted at the end of the linked chain.

3. Suppose that the class `LinkedBag` did not have the data member `itemCount`. Revise the public method `getCurrentSize` so that it counts the number of nodes in the linked chain
    a. Iteratively
    b. Recursively

4. Revise the public method `getFrequencyOf` in the class `LinkedBag` so that it is recursive.

5. Add a constructor to the class `LinkedBag` that creates a bag from a given array of entries.

6. Specify and define a method for `LinkedBag` that removes a random entry from the bag.

7. Compare the number of operations required to display the data in each of the *n* nodes in a linked chain with the number of operations required to display each of the *n* items in an array.

8. Compare the number of operations required to display the data in the *n*th node in a linked chain with the number of operations required to display the *n*th item in an array.

9. Compare the work required by the array-based and link-based implementations of the ADT bag operation `remove(anEntry)`. Consider the various locations of `anEntry` within the array or chain.

10. In a **doubly linked chain**, each node can point to the previous node as well as to the next node. Figure 4-10 shows a doubly linked chain and its head pointer. Define a class to represent a node in a doubly linked chain.

11. List the steps necessary to add a node to the beginning of the doubly linked chain shown in Figure 4-10.

12. List the steps necessary to remove the first node from the doubly linked chain shown in Figure 4-10.

FIGURE 4-10   A doubly linked chain

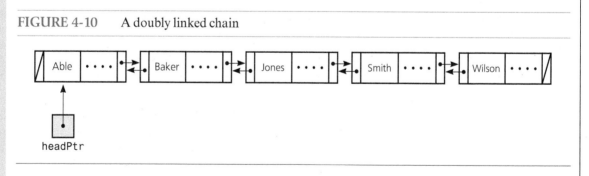

PROGRAMMING PROBLEMS

1. Add the methods `union`, `intersection`, and `difference` to the class `LinkedBag`. Exercises 6, 7, and 8 of Chapter 1 describe these operations.

2. Implement the ADT set that you specified in Programming Problem 4 of Chapter 1 by using a linked chain.

3. Implement the ADT pile that you specified in Programming Problem 5 of Chapter 1 by using a linked chain.

4. Implement the ADT polynomial that Exercise 9 in Chapter 1 describes by using a linked chain.

5. Consider a sparse implementation of the ADT polynomial that stores only the terms with nonzero coefficients. For example, you can represent the revised polynomial p in Exercise 9 of Chapter 1 with the linked chain shown in Figure 4-11.
    a. Complete the sparse implementation.
    b. Define a traverse operation for the ADT polynomial that will allow you to add two sparse polynomials without having to consider terms with zero coefficients explicitly.

FIGURE 4-11   A sparse polynomial

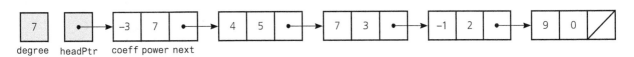

6. Define a class DoublyLinkedBag that implements the ADT bag by using a doubly linked chain, as shown in Figure 4-10. Use the class of nodes that Exercise 10 defines.

7. Use the classes for a set or a bag, as defined in this chapter or described in the previous projects, to create a spell checker. Consult the details given in Programming Problems 12 and 13 of Chapter 3.

8. Specify and implement an ADT character string by using a linked chain of characters. Include typical operations such as finding its length, appending one string to another, finding the index of the leftmost occurrence of a character in a string, and testing whether one string is a substring of another.

9. (Finance) Repeat Programming Problem 14 in Chapter 3, but use link-based implementations instead of array-based ones.

10. (Gaming) Repeat Programming Problem 15 in Chapter 3, but use a link-based implementation instead of an array-based one.

11. (Gaming) When you play a board or card game or when you use a shared computing resource, you get a turn and then wait until everyone else has had a turn. Although the number of players in a game remains relatively static, the number of users of a shared computing service fluctuates. Let's assume that this fluctuation will occur.

    Design an ADT that keeps track of turns within a group of people. You should be able to add or remove people and determine whose turn occurs now.

    Begin with a given group of people; assign these people an initial order. (This order can be random or specified by the user.) The first new person joining the group should get a turn after all others have had an equal number of turns. Each subsequent new person should get a turn after the person who joined the group most recently has had a turn.

    Also design an ADT to represent a person. (You can be conservative with the amount of data that this ADT contains.) The data that your first ADT stores is made up of instances of the ADT person.

    Implement your ADTs as C++ classes. Write a program that uses—and therefore tests—your ADTs completely. Your program should process several additions and removals, and demonstrate that people are given turns correctly.

12. (E-commerce) Repeat Programming Problem 16 in Chapter 3, but use a link-based implementation instead of an array-based one.

13. Occasionally, a link-based structure that does not use pointers is useful. One such structure uses an array whose items are "linked" by array indexes. Figure 4-12a illustrates an array of nodes that represents the linked chain whose first node contains the string "B", second node contains "E", and third node contains "J". Each node has two members, item and next. The next member is an integer index to the array element that contains the next node in the linked chain. Note that the next member of the last node contains −1. The integer variable head contains the index of the first node in the chain.

The array elements that currently are not a part of the linked chain make up a *free list* of available nodes. These nodes form another linked chain, with the integer variable free containing the index of the first free node. To insert an item into the beginning of the original linked chain, you take a free node from the beginning of the free list and insert it into the linked chain (Figure 4-12b). When you remove an item from the linked chain, you add the node to the beginning of the free list (Figure 4-12c). In this way, you can avoid shifting data items.

Implement the ADT bag by using this array-based linked chain.

FIGURE 4-12   An array-based implementation of a linked chain

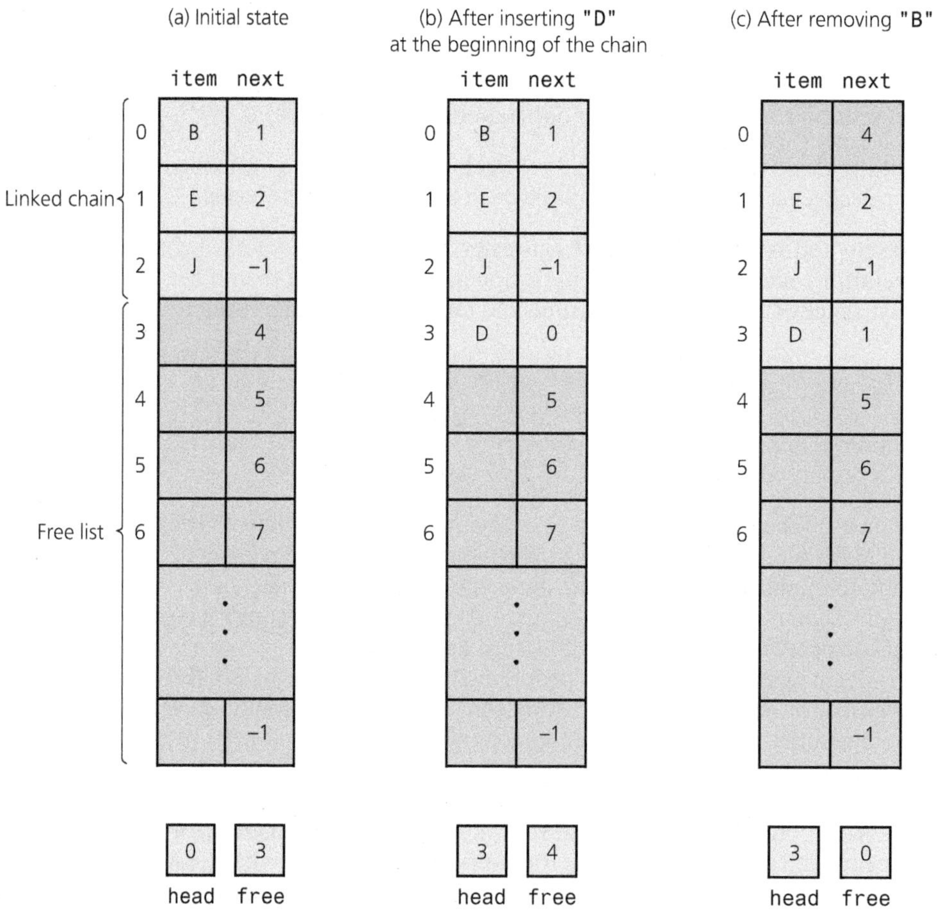

Recursion as a Problem-Solving Technique

Contents

Prerequisites

    Chapter 2   Recursion: The Mirrors

Chapter 2 presented the basic concepts of recursion, and now this chapter moves on to some extremely useful and somewhat complex applications in computer science. The recursive solutions to the problems you will see are far more elegant and concise than the best of their nonrecursive counterparts.

This chapter introduces two new concepts: formal grammars and backtracking. Formal grammars enable you to define, for example, syntactically correct algebraic expressions, which we explore in some detail. Backtracking is a problem-solving technique that involves guesses at a solution. The chapter concludes with a discussion of the close relationship between recursion and mathematical induction; you will learn how to use mathematical induction to study properties of algorithms.

More applications of recursion appear in subsequent chapters.

5.1   Defining Languages

English and C++ are two languages with which you are familiar. A **language** is nothing more than a set of strings of symbols from a finite alphabet. For example, if you view a C++ program as one long string of characters, you can define the set of all syntactically correct C++ programs. This set is the language

$$C++Programs = \{\text{string } s : s \text{ is a syntactically correct C++ program}\}$$

Notice that whereas all programs are strings, not all strings are programs. A C++ compiler is a program that, among other things, sees whether a given string is a member of the language *C++Programs*; that is, the compiler determines whether the string is a syntactically correct C++ program. Of course, this definition of *C++Programs* is not descriptive enough to allow the construction of a compiler. The definition specifies a characteristic of the strings in the set *C++Programs*: The strings are syntactically correct C++ programs. However, this definition does not give the rules for determining whether a string is in the set; that is, the definition does not specify what is meant by a syntactically correct C++ program.

The word "language" does not necessarily mean a programming language or a communication language. For example, the set of algebraic expressions forms a language

$$AlgebraicExpressions = \{\text{string } s : s \text{ is an algebraic expression}\}$$

The language *AlgebraicExpressions* is the set of strings that meets certain rules of syntax; however, the set's definition does not give these rules.

In both examples, the rules for forming a string within the language are missing. A **grammar** states the rules of a language. The grammars that you will see in this chapter are recursive in nature. One of the great benefits of using such a grammar to define a language is that you can often write a straightforward recursive algorithm, based on the grammar, that determines whether a given string is in the language. Such an algorithm is called a **recognition algorithm** for the language.

A grammar states the rules for forming the strings in a language

As it is a complex task to present a grammar for the set *C++Programs*, we will look instead at grammars for some simpler languages, including several common languages of algebraic expressions.

5.1.1   The Basics of Grammars

A grammar uses several special symbols:

Symbols that grammars use

- $x \mid y$ means x or y.
- $x \cdot y$ or $x\,y$ means x followed by y.
- $<\,word\,>$ means any instance of *word*, where *word* is a symbol that must be defined elsewhere in the grammar.

We'll use these symbols to write a simple grammar, one for the following language:

$$C++Identifiers = \{\text{string } s : s \text{ is a legal C++ identifier}\}$$

As you know, a legal C++ identifier begins with a letter and is followed by zero or more letters and digits. In this context, the underscore (_) is a letter. One way to represent this definition of an identifier is with a syntax diagram, as shown in Figure 5-1.

FIGURE 5-1   A syntax diagram for C++ identifiers

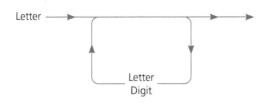

A syntax diagram is convenient for people to use, but a grammar is a better starting point if you want to write a function that will recognize an identifier. A grammar for the language *C++Identifiers* is

$$<identifier> = <letter> | <identifier><letter> | <identifier><digit>$$

$$<letter> = a | b | \ldots | z | A | B | \ldots | Z | \_$$

$$<digit> = 0 | 1 | \ldots | 9$$

A grammar for the language of C++ identifiers

The definition reads as follows:

> *An identifier is a letter, or an identifier followed by a letter, or an identifier followed by a digit.*

The most striking aspect of this definition is that *identifier* appears in its own definition: This grammar is recursive, as are many grammars.

Many grammars are recursive

Given a string *s*, you can determine whether it is in the language *C++Identifiers* by using the grammar to construct the following recognition algorithm:

- If *s* is of length 1, it is in the language if the character is a letter. (This statement is the base case, so to speak.)
- If *s* is of length greater than 1, it is in the language if the last character of *s* is either a letter or a digit, and *s* minus its last character is an identifier.

The pseudocode for a recursive valued function that determines whether a string is in the language *C++Identifiers* follows:

```
// Returns true if s is a legal C++ identifier, otherwise returns false.
isId(s: string): boolean
{
   if (s is of length 1)                    // Base case
      if (s is a letter)
         return true
      else
         return false
   else if (the last character of s is a letter or a digit)
      return isId(s minus its last character)  // Point X
   else
      return false
}
```

A recognition algorithm for C++ identifiers

Figure 5-2 contains a trace of this function for the string "A2B".

FIGURE 5-2   Trace of isId("A2B")

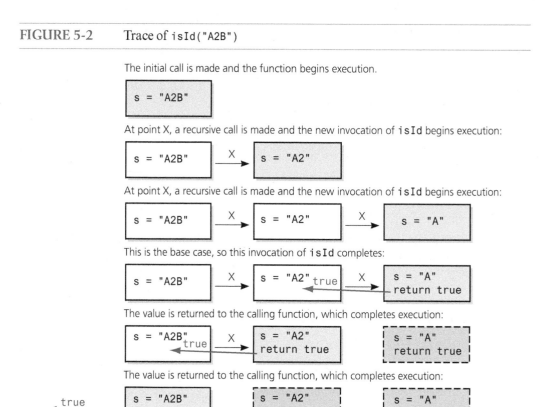

5.1.2   Two Simple Languages

Now consider two more examples of simple languages, their grammars, and resulting recognition algorithms.

Palindromes.   A *palindrome* is a string that reads the same from left to right as it does from right to left. For example, "radar" and "deed" are both palindromes. You can define the language of palindromes as follows:

Palindromes = {string *s* : *s* reads the same left to right as right to left}

How can you use a grammar to define the language *Palindromes*? You need to devise a rule that allows you to determine whether a given string *s* is a palindrome. In the spirit of recursive definitions, you should state this rule in terms of determining whether a smaller string is a palindrome. Your first instinct might be to choose *s* minus its last (or first) character for the smaller string. However, this approach does not work, because there is no relationship between the statements

   s is a palindrome

and

   s minus its last character is a palindrome

That is, *s* might be a palindrome, although *s* minus its last character is not, as is the case for "deed." Similarly, *s* minus its last character might be a palindrome, although *s* is not, as is the case for "deeds."

A little thought reveals that you must consider characters in pairs: There *is* a relationship between the statements

s is a palindrome

and

s minus its first and last characters is a palindrome

Specifically, *s* is a palindrome if and only if

A recursive
description of a
palindrome

* The first and last characters of *s* are the same

and

* s minus its first and last characters is a palindrome

You need a base case that you will reach after stripping away enough pairs of characters. If *s* has an even number of characters, you will eventually be left with two characters, and then, after you strip away another pair, you will be left with zero characters. A string of length 0 is called the **empty string** and is a palindrome. If *s* has an odd number of characters, you will eventually be left with one character, after which you cannot strip away another pair. Hence, you must have a second base case: A string of length 1 is a palindrome.

Strings of length 0
or 1 are the base
cases

This discussion leads to the following grammar for the language of palindromes:

A grammar for the
language of
palindromes

$$<pal> = \text{empty string} \mid <ch> \mid a <pal> a \mid b <pal> b \mid \ldots \mid Z <pal> Z$$

$$<ch> = a \mid b \mid \ldots \mid z \mid A \mid B \mid \ldots \mid Z$$

Based on this grammar, you can construct a recursive valued function for recognizing palindromes. The pseudocode for such a function follows:

A recognition
algorithm for
palindromes

```
// Returns true if the string s of letters is a palindrome; otherwise returns false.
isPalindrome(s: string): boolean
{
    if (s is the empty string or s is of length 1)
        return true
    else if (the first and last characters of s are the same letter)
        return isPalindrome(s minus its first and last characters)
    else
        return false
}
```

Strings of the form A^nB^n. The notation A^nB^n represents the string that consists of *n* consecutive *A*'s followed by *n* consecutive *B*'s. Another simple language consists of such strings:

$$AnBn = \{\text{string } s : s \text{ is of the form } A^nB^n \text{ for some } n \geq 0\}$$

The grammar for this language is actually very similar to the grammar for palindromes. You must strip away both the first and last characters and check to confirm that the first character is an *A* and the last character is a *B*. Thus, the grammar for the language *AnBn* is

A grammar for the
language of strings
A^nB^n

$$<legal\_word> = \text{empty string} \mid A <legal\_word> B$$

The pseudocode for a recognition function for this language follows:

A recognition
algorithm for strings
A^nB^n

```
// Returns true if the string s is of the form A^nB^n; otherwise returns false.
isAnBn(s: string): boolean
{
    if (the length of s is zero)
        return true
```

```
        else if (s begins with the character A and ends with the character B)
            return isAnBn(s minus its first and last characters)
        else
            return false
}
```

Note: Grammars, like recursive algorithms, must have carefully chosen base cases. You must ensure that, when a string is decomposed far enough, it will always reach the form of one of the grammar's base cases.

Question 1 Consider the language of the following character strings: $, cc$d, cccc$dd, cccccc$ddd, and so on. Write a recursive grammar for this language.

5.2 Algebraic Expressions

VideoNote

Processing
expressions

One of the tasks a compiler must perform is to recognize and evaluate algebraic expressions. For example, consider the C++ assignment statement

```
y = x + z * (w / k + z * (7 * 6));
```

A C++ compiler must determine whether the right side is a syntactically legal algebraic expression; if so, the compiler must then indicate how to compute the expression's value.

There are several common definitions for a "syntactically legal" algebraic expression. Some definitions force an expression to be fully parenthesized—that is, to have parentheses around each pair of operands together with their operator. Thus, you would have to write ((a * b) * c) rather than a * b * c. In general, the stricter a definition, the easier it is to recognize a syntactically legal expression. On the other hand, conforming to overly strict rules of syntax is an inconvenience for programmers.

This section presents three different languages for algebraic expressions. The expressions in these languages are easy to recognize and evaluate but are generally inconvenient to use. However, these languages provide us with good, nontrivial applications of grammars. We will see other languages of algebraic expressions whose members are difficult to recognize and evaluate but are convenient to use. To avoid unnecessary complications, assume that you have only the binary operators +, −, *, and / (no unary operators or exponentiation). Also, assume that all operands in the expression are single-letter identifiers.

5.2.1 Kinds of Algebraic Expressions

The algebraic expressions you learned about in school are called **infix expressions**. The term "infix" indicates that every binary operator appears *between* its operands. For example, in the expression

$a + b$

the operator + is between its operands a and b. This convention necessitates associativity rules, precedence rules, and the use of parentheses to avoid ambiguity. For example, the expression

$a + b * c$

is ambiguous. What is the second operand of the +? Is it b or is it $(b * c)$? Similarly, the first operand of the * could be either b or $(a + b)$. The rule that * has higher precedence than + removes the ambiguity by specifying that b is the first operand of the * and that $(b * c)$ is the second operand of the +. If you want another interpretation, you must use parentheses:

$(a + b) * c$

Even with precedence rules, an expression like

$a / b * c$

is ambiguous. Typically, / and * have equal precedence, so you could interpret the expression either as $(a / b) * c$ or as $a / (b * c)$. The common practice is to *associate from left to right*, thus yielding the first interpretation.

Two alternatives to the traditional infix convention are **prefix expressions** and **postfix expressions**. Under these conventions, an operator appears either before its operands (prefix) or after its operands (postfix). Thus, the infix expression

$a + b$

is written in prefix form as

$+ a b$

and in postfix form as

$a b +$

To further illustrate the conventions, consider the two interpretations of the infix expression $a + b * c$ just considered. You write the expression

$a + (b * c)$

in prefix form as

$+ a * b c$

The + appears before its operands a and $(* b c)$, and the * appears before its operands b and c. The same expression is written in postfix form as

$a b c * +$

The * appears after its operands b and c, and the + appears after its operands a and $(b c *)$.
Similarly, you write the expression

$(a + b) * c$

in prefix form as

$* + a b c$

The * appears before its operands $(+ a b)$ and c, and the + appears before its operands a and b. The same expression is written in postfix form as

$a b + c *$

The + appears after its operands a and b, and the * appears after its operands $(a b +)$ and c.
If the infix expression is fully parenthesized, converting it to either prefix or postfix form is straightforward. Because each operator then corresponds to a pair of parentheses, you simply move the operator to the position marked by either the open parenthesis "("—if you want to

---

In a prefix expression, an operator precedes its operands

In a postfix expression, an operator follows its operands

convert to prefix form—or the close parenthesis ")"—if you want to convert to postfix form. This position either precedes or follows the operands of the operator. All parentheses would then be removed.

For example, consider the fully parenthesized infix expression

$$((a + b) * c)$$

To convert this expression to prefix form, you first move each operator to the position marked by its corresponding open parenthesis:

Converting to prefix form

$$((a\ b)\ c)$$
$$\downarrow\downarrow$$
$$*+$$

Next, you remove the parentheses to get the desired prefix expression:

$$*+a\ b\ c$$

Similarly, to convert the infix expression to postfix form, you move each operator to the position marked by its corresponding close parenthesis:

Converting to postfix form

$$((ab)\ c)$$
$$\downarrow\ \downarrow$$
$$+\ *$$

Then you remove the parentheses:

$$a\ b + c*$$

When an infix expression is not fully parenthesized, these conversions are more complex. Chapter 6 discusses the general case of converting an infix expression to postfix form.

Prefix and postfix expressions never need precedence rules, association rules, or parentheses

The advantage of prefix and postfix expressions is that they never need precedence rules, association rules, or parentheses. Therefore, the grammars for prefix and postfix expressions are quite simple. In addition, the algorithms that recognize and evaluate these expressions are relatively straightforward.

5.2.2   Prefix Expressions

A grammar that defines the language of all prefix expressions is

$$<prefix> = <identifier>\ |\ <operator><prefix><prefix>$$
$$<operator> = +\ |\ -\ |\ *\ |\ /$$
$$<identifier> = a\ |\ b\ |\ \ldots\ |\ z$$

From this grammar, you can construct a recursive algorithm that recognizes whether a string is a prefix expression. If the string is of length 1, it is a prefix expression if and only if the string is a single lowercase letter. Strings of length 1 can be the base case. If the length of the string is greater than 1, then for it to be a legal prefix expression, it must be of the form

$$<operator>\ <prefix>\ <prefix>$$

Thus, the algorithm must check to see whether

- The first character of the string is an operator

and

- The remainder of the string consists of two consecutive prefix expressions

The first task is trivial, but the second is a bit tricky. How can you tell whether you are looking at two consecutive prefix expressions? A key observation is that if you add *any* string of nonblank characters to the end of a prefix expression, you will no longer have a prefix expression. That is, if E is a prefix expression and Y is any nonempty string of nonblank characters, then $E\,Y$ cannot be a prefix expression. This is a subtle point; Exercise 17 at the end of this chapter asks you to prove it.

If E is a prefix expression, $E\,Y$ cannot be

Given this observation, you can begin to determine whether you have two consecutive prefix expressions by identifying a first prefix expression. If you find one, the previous observation implies that only one endpoint is possible for this first expression.

If you find that the first prefix expression ends at position endPos, you then attempt to find a second prefix expression beginning at position endPos + 1. If you find the second expression, you must check whether you are at the end of the string in question.

By using these ideas, you can show, for example, that +*ab–cd is a prefix expression. For +*ab–cd to be a prefix expression, it must be of the form $+E_1E_2$, where E_1 and E_2 are prefix expressions. Now you can write

$E_1 = *E_3E_4$, where
$E_3 = a$
$E_4 = b$

Because E_3 and E_4 are prefix expressions, E_1 is a prefix expression. Similarly, you can write

$E_2 = -E_5E_6$, where
$E_5 = c$
$E_6 = d$

and see that E_2 is a prefix expression.

You can write a function to test whether an expression is a prefix expression by first constructing a recursive valued function endPre(strExp, first) to examine the expression that begins at position first of the string strExp and to locate the end of the first prefix expression it finds. If successful, the function returns the index of the end of the prefix expression. If no such prefix expression exists, endPre returns −1. The function appears in pseudocode as follows.

endPre determines the end of a prefix expression

```
// Finds the end of a prefix expression, if one exists.
// Precondition: The substring of strExp from the index first through the end of
// the string contains no blank characters.
// Postcondition: Returns the index of the last character in the prefix expression that
// begins at index first of strExp, or −1 if no such prefix expression exists.
endPre(strExp: string, first: integer): integer
{
    last = strExp.length() − 1
    if (first < 0 or first > last)
        return −1

    ch = character at position first of strExp
    if (ch is an identifier)
        return first            // Index of last character in simple prefix expression
    else if (ch is an operator)
    {
        // Find the end of the first prefix expression
        endPos = endPre(strExp, first + 1)    // Point X
```

```
            // If the end of the first prefix expression was found, find the end of the second
            // prefix expression
            if (endPos > -1)
                return endPre(strExp, endPos + 1) // Point Y
            else
                return -1
      }
      else
          return -1
}
```

Figure 5-3 contains a trace of endPre when the initial expression is + * a b – c d.

FIGURE 5-3   Trace of endPre("+*ab-cd", 0)

The initial call endPre("+*ab-cd", 0) is made, and endPre begins execution:

```
first              = 0
last               = 6
```

First character of strExp is +, so at point X, a recursive call is made and the new invocation of endPre begins execution:

```
first              = 0       X    first              = 1
last               = 6   ───►     last               = 6
X: endPre("+*ab-cd", 1)
```

Next character of strExp is *, so at point X, a recursive call is made and the new invocation of endPre begins execution:

```
first              = 0       X    first              = 1       X    first              = 2
last               = 6   ───►     last               = 6   ───►     last               = 6
endPos             = ?            endPos             = ?
X: endPre("+*ab-cd", 1)          X: endPre("+*ab-cd", 2)
```

Next character of strExp is a, which is a base case. The current invocation of endPre completes execution and returns its value:

```
first              = 0       X    first              = 1            ┌ first              = 2 ┐
last               = 6   ───►     last               = 6       2    │ last               = 6 │
endPos             = ?            endPos             = 2   ◄────────┤ return 2               │
X: endPre("+*ab-cd", 1)                                            └────────────────────────┘
```

Because endPos > –1, a recursive call is made from point Y and the new invocation of endPre begins execution:

Next character of strExp is b, which is a base case. The current invocation of endPre completes execution and returns its value:

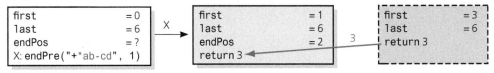

The current invocation of `endPre` completes execution and returns its value:

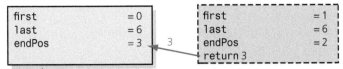

Because `endPos > -1`, a recursive call is made from point Y and the new invocation of `endPre` begins execution:

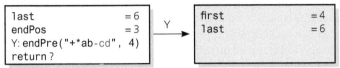

Next character of `strExp` is -, so at point X, a recursive call is made and the new invocation of `endPre` begins execution:

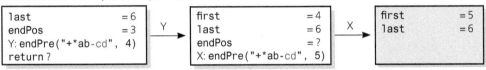

Next character of `strExp` is c, which is a base case. The current invocation of `endPre` completes execution and returns its value:

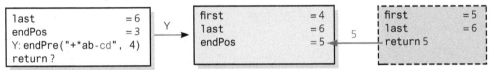

Because `endPos > -1`, a recursive call is made from point Y and the new invocation of `endPre` begins execution:

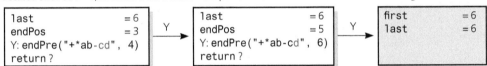

Next character of `strExp` is d, which is a base case. The current invocation of `endPre` completes execution and returns its value:

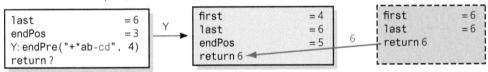

The current invocation of `endPre` completes execution and returns its value:

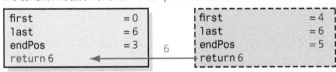

The current invocation of `endPre` completes execution and returns its value to the original call to `endPre`:

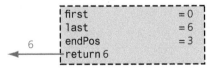

Now you can use the function `endPre` to determine whether a string contains a prefix expression as follows:

```
// Sees whether an expression is a prefix expression.
// Precondition: strExp contains a string with no blank characters.
// Postcondition: Returns true if the expression is in prefix form; otherwise returns false.
```

A recognition algorithm for prefix expressions

```
isPrefix(strExp: string): boolean
{
   lastChar = endPre(strExp, 0)
   return (lastChar >= 0) and (lastChar == strExp.length() - 1)
}
```

Having determined that a string is a prefix expression, how can you evaluate it? Because each operator is followed by its two operands, you can look ahead in the expression for them. However, such operands can themselves be prefix expressions, which you must evaluate first. These prefix expressions are subexpressions of the original expression and must therefore be "smaller." A recursive solution to this problem seems natural.

The following function, which appears in pseudocode, evaluates a prefix expression. This algorithm is simpler than one that evaluates infix expressions.

An algorithm to evaluate a prefix expression

```
// Returns the value of a given prefix expression.
// Precondition: strExp is a string containing a valid prefix expression with no blanks.
evaluatePrefix(strExp: string): float
{
   strLength = the length of strExp
   if (strLength == 1)
      return value of the identifier   // Base case—single identifier
   else
   {
      op = strExp[0]                // strExp begins with an operator

      // Find the end of the first prefix expression—will be the first operand
      endFirst = endPre(strExp, 1)

      // Recursively evaluate this first prefix expression
      operand1 = evaluatePrefix(strExp[1..endFirst]);

      // Recursively evaluate the second prefix expression—will be the second operand
      endSecond = strLength - endFirst + 1
      operand2 = evaluatePrefix(strExp[endFirst + 1..endSecond])

      // Evaluate the prefix expression
      return operand1 op operand2
   }
}
```

Question 2 Write the prefix expression that represents the following infix expression: $(a/b) * c - (d + e) * f$

Question 3 Write the infix expression that represents the following prefix expression: $--a/b + c * d e f$

Question 4 Is the following string a prefix expression? $+-/a\ b\ c * + d\ e\ f * g\ h$

5.2.3   Postfix Expressions

A grammar that defines the language of all postfix expressions is

$$<postfix> = <identifier>\,|\,<postfix><postfix><operator>$$
$$<operator> = +\,|-\,|*\,|\,/$$
$$<identifier> = a\,|\,b\,|\,\ldots\,|\,z$$

Some calculators require that you enter two numbers before you enter the operation that you want to perform. Such calculators, in fact, require you to enter postfix expressions.

Here we shall develop an algorithm for converting a prefix expression to a postfix expression. Chapter 6 presents a nonrecursive algorithm for evaluating postfix expressions. Together, these two algorithms give you another technique for evaluating a prefix expression. To simplify the conversion algorithm, assume that, by using the prefix recognition algorithm, you have a syntactically correct prefix expression.

If you think recursively, the conversion from prefix form to postfix form is straightforward. If the prefix expression *exp* is a single letter, then

$$postfix(exp) = exp$$

Otherwise *exp* must be of the form

$$<operator><prefix1><prefix2>$$

The corresponding postfix expression is then

$$<postfix1><prefix2><operator>$$

where $<prefix1>$ converts to $<postfix1>$ and $<prefix2>$ converts to $<postfix2>$ Therefore,

$$postfix(exp) = postfix(prefix1) \bullet postfix(prefix2) \bullet <operator >^1$$

Thus, at a high level, the conversion algorithm is

```
if (exp is a single letter)
    return exp
else
    return postfix(prefix1) • postfix(prefix2) • <operator>
```

An algorithm that converts a prefix expression to postfix form

The following pseudocode function convert refines this algorithm. The string preExp contains the prefix expression.

```
// Converts a prefix expression to postfix form.
// Precondition: The string preExp is a valid prefix expression with no blanks.
// Postcondition: Returns the equivalent postfix expression.
convertPreToPost(preExp: string): string
{
    preLength = the length of preExp
    ch = first character in preExp
    postExp = an empty string

    if (ch is a lowercase letter)
        // Base case—single identifier
        postExp = postExp • ch           // Append to end of postExp
    else // ch is an operator
    {
        // pre has the form <operator> <prefix1> <prefix2>
        endFirst = endPre(preExp, 1)     // Find the end of prefix1

        // Recursively convert prefix1 into postfix form
        postExp = postExp • convert(preExp[1..endFirst])

        // Recursively convert prefix2 into postfix form
        postExp = postExp • convert(preExp[endFirst + 1..preLength - 1))

        postExp = postExp • ch           // Append the operator to the end of postExp
    }
    return postExp
}
```

A recursive algorithm that converts a prefix expression to postfix form

---
[1] Recall that the symbol • means to join the expressions.

Question 5 Write the postfix expression that represents the following infix expression:
$(a*b - c)/d+(e - f)$

5.2.4   Fully Parenthesized Expressions

Most programmers would object to using prefix or postfix notation for their algebraic expressions, so most programming languages use infix notation. However, infix notation requires precedence rules, rules for association, and parentheses to avoid ambiguity within the expressions.

You can make precedence and association rules unnecessary by placing parentheses around each pair of operands together with their operator, thereby avoiding any ambiguity. A grammar for the language of all fully parenthesized infix expressions is

A grammar for the language of fully parenthesized algebraic expressions

$$<infix> = <identifier> \,|\, (<infix><operator><infix>)$$
$$<operator> = \, + \,|-|*|\,/$$
$$<identifier> = a\,|\,b\,|\ldots|\,z$$

Although the grammar is simple, the language is rather inconvenient for programmers.

Therefore, most programming languages support a definition of algebraic expressions that includes both precedence rules for the operators and rules of association so that fully parenthesized expressions are not required. However, the grammars for defining such languages are more involved and the algorithms for recognizing and evaluating their expressions are more difficult than those you have seen in this section. Programming Problem 9 at the end of this chapter describes such a grammar without left-to-right association rules and asks you to write a recognition algorithm. Programming Problem 8 at the end of Chapter 6 presents a nonrecursive evaluation algorithm for algebraic expressions that use both precedence and left-to-right association rules.

5.3   Backtracking

VideoNote

Backtracking

This section considers an organized way to solve a problem by making successive guesses at its solution. If a particular guess leads to a dead end, you back up to that guess and replace it with a different guess. This strategy of retracing steps in reverse order and then trying a new sequence of steps is called **backtracking**. You can combine recursion and backtracking to solve the following problem.

Backtracking is a strategy for guessing at a solution and backing up when an impasse is reached

5.3.1   Searching for an Airline Route

This example will introduce you to a general type of search problem. In this particular problem, you must find a path from some point of origin to some destination point. We shall solve this problem by using recursion. In the next chapter, we will solve it again without recursion.

Determine whether HPAir flies from one city to another

The High Planes Airline Company (HPAir) wants a program to process customer requests to fly from some origin city to some destination city. So that we can focus on recursion, we will simplify the problem by just indicating whether a sequence of HPAir flights from the origin city to the destination city exists.

Imagine three input text files that specify all of the flight information for the airline as follows:

- The names of cities that HPAir serves
- Pairs of city names, each pair representing the origin and destination of one of HPAir's flights
- Pairs of city names, each pair representing a request to fly from some origin to some destination

The program should then produce output such as

```
Request is to fly from Providence to San Francisco.
HPAir flies from Providence to San Francisco.

Request is to fly from Philadelphia to Albuquerque.
Sorry. HPAir does not fly from Philadelphia to Albuquerque.

Request is to fly from Salt Lake City to Paris.
Sorry. HPAir does not serve Paris.
```

Representing the flight data. The flight map in Figure 5-4 represents the routes that HPAir flies. An arrow from city C_1 to city C_2 indicates a flight from C_1 to C_2. In this case, C_2 is adjacent to C_1 and the path from C_1 to C_2 is called a **directed path**. Notice that if C_2 is adjacent to C_1, it does not follow that C_1 is adjacent to C_2. For example, in Figure 5-4, the airline has a flight from city R to city X, but not from city X to city R. As you will see in Chapter 20, the map in Figure 5-4 is called a **directed graph**.

C_2 is adjacent to C_1 if there is a directed path from C_1 to C_2

FIGURE 5-4   Flight map for HPAir

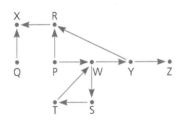

The nature of the search. When processing a customer's request to fly from some origin city to some destination city, you must determine from the flight map whether there is a route from the origin to the destination. For example, by examining the flight map in Figure 5-4, you can see that a customer could fly from city P to city Z by flying first to city W, then to city Y, and finally to city Z; that is, there is a directed path from P to Z: $P \rightarrow W$, $W \rightarrow Y$, $Y \rightarrow Z$. Thus, you must develop an algorithm that searches the flight map for a directed path from the origin city to the destination city. Such a path might involve either a single flight or a sequence of flights. The solution developed here performs an **exhaustive search**. That is, beginning at the origin city, the solution will try every possible sequence of flights until either it finds a sequence that gets to the destination city or it discovers that no such sequence exists.

First consider how you might perform the search by hand. One approach is to start at the origin city C_0 and select an arbitrary flight that departs from the origin city. This flight will lead you to a new city, C_1. If city C_1 happens to be the destination city, you are done; otherwise, you must attempt to get from C_1 to the destination city. To do this, you select a path to travel out of C_1. This flight will lead you to city C_2. If C_2 is the destination, you are done; otherwise, you must attempt to get from C_2 to the destination city, and so on.

A recursive strategy. To fly from the origin city to the destination city by first flying from the origin city to a city C and then by flying from C to the destination has a distinct recursive flavor. We can restate this strategy as follows:

A recursive search strategy

To fly from the origin to the destination
{
    Select a city `C` *adjacent to the origin*
    Fly from the origin to city `C`
    `if` (`C` *is the destination city*)
        Terminate— the destination is reached
    `else`
        Fly from city `C` *to the destination*
}

Possible outcomes of the exhaustive search strategy

Consider the possible outcomes of applying the previous strategy:

1. You eventually reach the destination city and can conclude that it is possible to fly from the origin to the destination.
2. You reach a city C from which there are no departing flights.
3. You go around in circles. For example, from C_1 you go to C_2, from C_2 you go to C_3, and from C_3 you go back to C_1. You might continue this tour of the three cities forever; that is, the algorithm might not terminate.

If you always obtained the first outcome, everyone would be happy. This outcome corresponds to a base case of the recursive algorithm. If you ever reach the destination city, no additional problems of the form "fly from city C to the destination" are generated, and the algorithm terminates. However, because HPAir does not fly between all pairs of cities, you certainly cannot expect that the algorithm will always find a path from the origin city to the destination. For example, if city P in Figure 5-4 is the origin city and city Q is the destination city, the algorithm could not possibly find a path from city P to city Q.

Even if there were a sequence of flights from the origin city to the destination, it would take a bit of luck for the previous strategy to discover it—the algorithm would have to select a "correct" flight at each step. For example, even though there is a way to get from city P to city Z in Figure 5-4, the algorithm might not find it and instead might reach outcome 2 or 3. That is, suppose that from city P the algorithm chose to go to city R. From city R the algorithm would have to go to city X, from which there are no flights out (outcome 2). On the other hand, suppose that the algorithm chose to go to city W from city P. From city W, the algorithm might choose to go to city S. It would then have to go to city T and then back to W. From W, it might once again choose to go to city S and continue to go around in circles (outcome 3).

Use backtracking to recover from a wrong choice

You thus need to make the algorithm more sophisticated, so that it always finds a path from the origin to the destination, if such a path exists, and otherwise terminates with the conclusion that there is no such path. Suppose that the earlier strategy results in outcome 2: You reach a city C from which there are no departing flights. This certainly does not imply that there is no way to get from the origin to the destination; it implies only that there is no way to get from city C to the destination. In other words, it was a mistake to go to city C. After discovering such a mistake, the algorithm can retrace its steps, or *backtrack*, to the city C' that was visited just before city C was visited. Once back at city C', the algorithm can select a flight to some city other than C. Notice that it is possible that there are no other flights out of city C'. If this were the case, it would mean that it was a mistake to visit city C', and thus, you would want to backtrack again—this time to the city that was visited just before city C'.

For example, you saw that, in trying to get from city P to city Z in Figure 5-4, the algorithm might first choose to go from city P to city R and then on to city X. As there are no departing flights from city X, the algorithm must backtrack to city R, the city visited before city X. Once back at city R, the algorithm would attempt to go to some city other than city X but would discover that this is not possible. The algorithm would thus backtrack once more, this time to city P, which was visited just before city R. From city P, the algorithm would choose to go to city W, which is a step in the right direction!

We can resolve these problems by refining our strategy: We mark visited cities and never fly to a city that has been visited already.

```
// Discovers whether a sequence of flights from originCity to destinationCity exists.
searchR(originCity: City, destinationCity: City): boolean
{
    Mark originCity as visited
    if (originCity is destinationCity)
        Terminate—the destination is reached
    else
        for (each unvisited city C adjacent to originCity)
            searchR(C, destinationCity)
}
```

A refinement of the recursive search algorithm

Now consider what happens when the algorithm reaches a city that has no unvisited city adjacent to it. For example, consider the piece of a flight map in Figure 5-5. When searchR reaches city M—that is, when the argument originCity has the value M—the for loop will not be entered, because no unvisited cities are adjacent to M. Hence, the searchR algorithm returns. This return has the effect of backtracking to city L, from which the flight to M originated. In terms of the previous pseudocode, the return is made to the point from which the call searchR(M, destinationCity) occurred. This point is within the for loop, which iterates through the unvisited cities adjacent to L; that is, the argument originCity has the value L.

FIGURE 5-5   A piece of a flight map

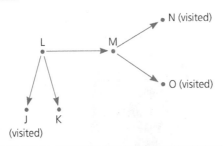

After backtracking from M to L, the for loop will again execute. This time the loop chooses city K, resulting in the recursive call searchR(K, destinationCity). From this point, the algorithm will either eventually reach the destination city—and terminate—or backtrack once again to city L. If it backtracks to L, the for loop will terminate, because there are no more unvisited cities adjacent to L, and a return from searchR will occur. The effect is to backtrack to the city where the flight to L originated. If the algorithm ever backtracks to the origin city and no remaining unvisited cities are adjacent to it, the algorithm will terminate, and you can conclude that no sequence of flights from the origin to the destination exists. Notice that the algorithm will always terminate in one way or another, because it will either reach the destination city or run out of unvisited cities to try.

> **Note: Searching a map**
>
> When searching for a sequence of flights between cities, you must take into account the possibility that the algorithm will make wrong choices. For example, the algorithm must be able to backtrack when it hits a dead end, and you must eliminate the possibility that the algorithm will cycle.

Operations on the flight map.   Now consider the operations that the search algorithm must perform on the flight map. The algorithm marks cities as it visits them, sees whether a city has been visited, and finds an unvisited city that is adjacent to a given city. You can treat the flight map as an ADT that has *at least* these operations in addition to the search operation itself. Other desirable operations include placing data into the flight map, inserting a city adjacent to another city, displaying the flight map, displaying the names of all cities, and displaying the cities that are adjacent to a given city. Thus, the ADT flight map could include the following operations, given here in UML notation.

ADT flight map
operations

```
//  Reads flight information into the flight map.
+readFlightMap(cityFileName: string, flightFileName: string): void

//  Displays flight information.
+displayFlightMap(): void

//  Displays the names of all cities that HPAir serves.
+displayAllCities(): void

//  Displays all cities that are adjacent to a given city.
+displayAdjacentCities(aCity: City): void

//  Marks a city as visited.
+markVisited(aCity: City): void

//  Clears marks on all cities.
+unvisitAll(): void

//  Sees whether a city was visited.
+isVisited(aCity: City): boolean

//  Inserts a city adjacent to another city in a flight map.
+insertAdjacent(aCity: City, adjCity: City): void

//  Returns the next unvisited city, if any, that is adjacent to a given city.
//  Returns a sentinel value if no unvisited adjacent city was found.
+getNextCity(fromCity: City): City

//  Tests whether a sequence of flights exists between two cities.
+isPath(originCity: City, destinationCity: City): boolean
```

The latter operation isPath uses the searchR algorithm to make its determination. If the class Map is the implementation of the ADT flight map, its method isPath has the following C++ definition. Note that NO_CITY is a City object that Map defines as a constant for getNextCity to return in case it cannot find an unvisited adjacent city.

```
/** Tests whether a sequence of flights exists between two cities.
 @pre  originCity and destinationCity both exist in the flight map.
 @post  Cities visited during the search are marked as visited
    in the flight map.
 @param originCity  The origin city.
 @param destinationCity  The destination city.
 @return  True if a sequence of flights exists from originCity
    to destinationCity; otherwise returns false. */
bool Map::isPath(City originCity, City destinationCity)
{
   // Mark the current city as visited
   markVisited(originCity);

   bool foundDestination = (originCity == destinationCity);
   if (!foundDestination)
   {
      // Try a flight to each unvisited city
      City nextCity = getNextCity(originCity);
      while (!foundDestination && (nextCity != NO_CITY))
      {
         foundDestination = isPath(nextCity, destinationCity);
         if (!foundDestination)
            nextCity = getNextCity(originCity);
      }  // end while
   }  // end if

   return foundDestination;
}  // end isPath
```

 Note: The subproblems that a recursive solution generates eventually must reach a base case. Failure to do so could result in an algorithm that does not terminate. Solutions that involve backtracking are particularly subject to this kind of error.

 Question 6 Trace the method `isPath` with the map in Figure 5-6 for the following requests. Show the recursive calls and the returns from each.
- Fly from *A* to *B*.
- Fly from *A* to *D*.
- Fly from *C* to *G*.

FIGURE 5-6   Flight map for Checkpoint Question 6

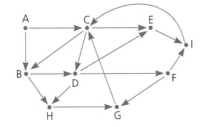

5.3.2 The Eight Queens Problem

Place eight queens on the chessboard so that no queen can attack any other queen

A chessboard contains 64 squares that form eight rows and eight columns. The most powerful piece in the game of chess is the queen, because it can attack any other piece within its row, within its column, or along its diagonal. The Eight Queens problem asks you to place eight queens on the chessboard so that no queen can attack any other queen.

One strategy is to guess at a solution. However, according to Section 2.6.3 of Chapter 2, there are $g(64, 8) = 4,426,165,368$ ways to arrange eight queens on a chessboard of 64 squares—so many that it would be exhausting to check all of them for a solution to this problem. Nevertheless, a simple observation eliminates many arrangements from consideration: Each row and column can contain exactly one queen. Thus, attacks along rows or columns are eliminated, leaving only $8! = 40,320$ arrangements of queens to be checked for attacks along diagonals. A solution now appears more feasible.

Place queens one column at a time

Suppose that you provide some organization for the guessing strategy by placing one queen per column, beginning with the first square of column 1. Figure 5-7a shows this queen and its range of attack, as indicated by the blue dots. When you consider column 2, you eliminate its first square because row 1 contains a queen, you eliminate its second square because of a

FIGURE 5-7   Placing one queen at a time in each column, showing the placed queens' range of attack (newly placed queens can attack squares marked in blue)

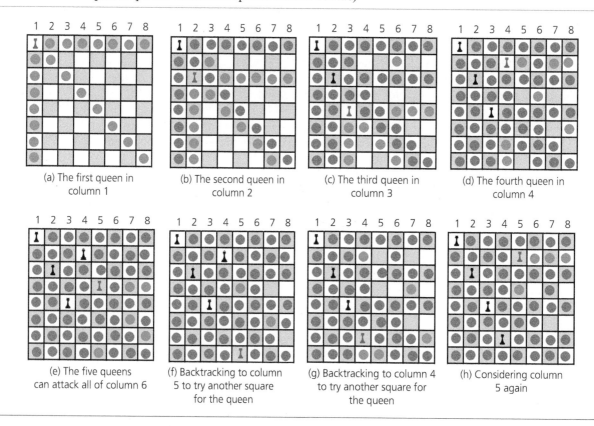

(a) The first queen in column 1

(b) The second queen in column 2

(c) The third queen in column 3

(d) The fourth queen in column 4

(e) The five queens can attack all of column 6

(f) Backtracking to column 5 to try another square for the queen

(g) Backtracking to column 4 to try another square for the queen

(h) Considering column 5 again

diagonal attack, and you finally place a queen in the third square of column 2, as Figure 5-7b illustrates. The black dots in the figure indicate squares that are rejected because a queen in that square is subject to attack by another queen in an earlier column. The blue dots indicate the additional squares that the new queen can attack.

We continue to place queens in this manner until we get to column 6, as Figure 5-7e shows. Although the five placed queens cannot attack each other, they can attack any square in column 6, and therefore, you cannot place a queen in column 6. You must back up to column 5 and move its queen to the next possible square in column 5, which is in the last row, as Figure 5-7f indicates. When you consider column 6 once again, there are still no choices for a queen in that column. Because you have exhausted the possibilities in column 5, you must back up to column 4. As Figure 5-7g shows, the next possible square in column 4 is in row 7. You then consider column 5 again and place a queen in row 2 (Figure 5-7h).

How can you use recursion in the process that was just described? Consider an algorithm that places a queen in a column, given that you have placed queens correctly in the preceding columns. First, if there are no more columns to consider, you are finished; this is the base case. Otherwise, after you successfully place a queen in the current column, you need to consider the next column. That is, you need to solve the same problem with one fewer column; this is the recursive step. Thus, you begin with eight columns, consider smaller problems that decrease in size by one column at each recursive step, and reach the base case when you have a problem with no columns.

This solution appears to satisfy the criteria for a recursive solution. However, you do not know whether you can successfully place a queen in the current column. If you can, you recursively consider the next column. If you cannot place a queen in the current column, you need to backtrack, as has already been described.

The following pseudocode describes the algorithm for placing queens in columns, given that the previous columns contain queens that cannot attack one another:

> *If you reach an impasse, backtrack to the previous column*

```
// Places queens in eight columns.
placeQueens(queen: Queen, row: integer, column: integer): boolean
{
    if (column > BOARD_SIZE)
        The problem is solved
    else
    {
        while (unconsidered squares exist in the given column and
               the problem is unsolved)
        {
            Find the next square in the given column that is
             not under attack by a queen in an earlier column
            if (such a square exists)
            {
                Place a queen in the square

                // Try next column
                if (!placeQueens(a new queen, firstRow, column + 1))
                {
                    // No queen is possible in the next column
                    Remove the new queen
                    Move the last queen that was placed on the board
                     to the next row in that column
                }
```

> *The solution combines recursion with backtracking*

```
            else
            {
                Remove the new queen
                return true
            }
        }
    }
}
}
```

The Eight Queens problem is initiated by the method doEightQueens, which calls placeQueens with a new queen in the upper-left corner of the board:

```
doEightQueens()
{
    placeQueens(a new queen, firstRow, firstColumn)
}
```

After doEightQueens has completed, we can display the board, if a solution was found.

FIGURE 5-8   A solution to the Eight Queens problem

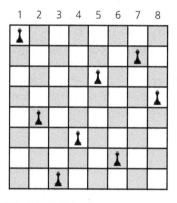

Figure 5-8 indicates the solution that the previous algorithm finds. By modifying the arguments to placeQueens, you can discover other solutions to the Eight Queens problem. The Programming Problems at the end of this chapter ask you to consider other solutions to this algorithm, as well as additional modifications.

Question 7 Consider a Four Queens problem, which has the same rules as the Eight Queens problem but uses a 4 × 4 board. Find all solutions to this new problem by applying backtracking by hand.

Implementing a solution to the Eight Queens problem. You can write a solution to the Eight Queens problem in a variety of ways. For example, you can define two classes: a Board class to represent the chessboard and a Queen class to represent a queen on the board. A Queen object could keep track of its row and column placement and be able to move to the next row. A Board object keeps track of the Queen objects currently on the board and contains operations—such as placeQueens—to solve the Eight Queens problem and display the solution.

The Board class in the solution described thus far may be represented in a number of ways. The simplest representation would be a two-dimensional array; however, such an array wastes space because only eight squares out of 64 are used. Another approach would be to use a vector or a one-dimensional array of only the squares that contain a queen. Because the algorithm uses backtracking, a dynamic array is the optimal choice. The `vector` container in the STL is often used in place of an array type, because it allows the number of elements to vary dynamically and provides several built-in methods. Indexing is provided with array-type subscripting or with the `at` method, which provides range checking as well. Programming Problem 1 at the end of this chapter asks to complete an implementation of the solution to this problem.

5.4   The Relationship Between Recursion and Mathematical Induction

A very strong relationship exists between recursion and mathematical induction. Recursion solves a problem by specifying a solution to one or more base cases and then demonstrating how to derive the solution to a problem of an arbitrary size from the solutions to smaller problems of the same type. Similarly, mathematical induction proves a property about the natural numbers by proving the property about a base case—usually 0 or 1—and then proving that the property must be true for an arbitrary natural number n if it is true for the natural numbers smaller than n.

Given the similarities between recursion and mathematical induction, it should not be surprising that induction is often employed to prove properties about recursive algorithms. What types of properties? You can, for example, prove that an algorithm actually performs the task that you intended. As an illustration, we will prove that the recursive factorial algorithm of Chapter 2 does indeed compute the factorial of its argument. Another use of mathematical induction is to prove that a recursive algorithm performs a certain amount of work. For example, we will prove that the solution to the Towers of Hanoi problem—also from Chapter 2— makes exactly $2^N - 1$ moves when it starts with N disks.

You can use induction to prove that a recursive algorithm either is correct or performs a certain amount of work

5.4.1   The Correctness of the Recursive Factorial Function

The following pseudocode describes a recursive function that computes the factorial of a non-negative integer n:

```
fact(n: integer): integer
{
    if (n is 0)
        return 1
    else
        return n * fact(n - 1)
}
```

You can prove that the function `fact` returns the values

$factorial(0) = 0! = 1$

$factorial(n) = n! = n \times (n - 1) \times (n - 2) \times \ldots \times 1$ if $n > 0$

The proof is by induction on n.

Basis. *Show that the property is true for $n = 0$.* That is, you must show that `fact(0)` returns 1. But this result is simply the base case of the function: `fact(0)` returns 1 by its definition.

You now must establish that

property is true for an arbitrary $k \Rightarrow$ property is true for $k + 1$

Inductive hypothesis. *Assume that the property is true for n = k.* That is, assume that

$$factorial(k) = k! = k \times (k-1) \times (k-2) \times \ldots \times 1$$

Inductive conclusion. *Show that the property is true for n = k + 1.* That is, you must show that `fact(k + 1)` returns the value

$$(k+1) \times k \times (k-1) \times (k-2) \times \ldots \times 2 \times 1$$

By definition of the function `fact`, `fact(k + 1)` returns the value

$$(k+1) \times factorial(k)$$

But by the inductive hypothesis, `fact(k)` returns the value

$$k \times (k-1) \times (k-2) \times \ldots \times 2 \times 1$$

Thus, `fact(k + 1)` returns the value

$$(k+1) \times k \times (k-1) \times (k-2) \times \ldots \times 2 \times 1$$

which is what you needed to show.

The inductive proof is thus complete.

5.4.2   The Cost of Towers of Hanoi

In Chapter 2, you saw the following pseudocode solution to the Towers of Hanoi problem:

```
solveTowers(count, source, destination, spare)
{
    if (count is 1)
        Move a disk directly from source to destination
    else
    {
        solveTowers(count - 1, source, spare, destination)
        solveTowers(1, source, destination, spare)
        solveTowers(count - 1, spare, destination, source)
    }
}
```

We now pose the following question: If you begin with *N* disks, how many moves does `solveTowers` make to solve the problem?

Let *moves*(*N*) be the number of moves made starting with *N* disks. When *N* = 1, the answer is easy:

$$moves(1) = 1$$

When *N* > 1, the value of *moves*(*N*) is not so apparent. An inspection of the `solveTowers` algorithm, however, reveals three recursive calls. Therefore, if you knew how many moves `solveTowers` made starting with *N* − 1 disks, you could figure out how many moves it made starting with *N* disks; that is,

$$moves(N) = moves(N-1) + moves(1) + moves(N-1)$$

Thus, you have a recurrence relation for the number of moves required for *N* disks:

A recurrence relation for the number of moves that `solveTowers` requires for N disks

$$moves(1) = 1$$
$$moves(N) = 2 \times moves(N-1) + 1 \qquad \text{if } N > 1$$

For example, you can determine *moves*(3) as follows:

$$moves(3) = 2 \times moves(2) + 1$$
$$= 2 \times (2 \times moves(1) + 1) + 1$$
$$= 2 \times (2 \times 1 + 1) + 1$$
$$= 7$$

Although the recurrence relation gives you a way to compute *moves*(N), a **closed-form formula**—such as an algebraic expression—would be more satisfactory, because you could substitute any given value for N and obtain the number of moves made. However, the recurrence relation is useful because there are techniques for obtaining a closed-form formula from it. Because these techniques are not relevant to us right now, we simply pull the formula out of the blue and use mathematical induction to prove that it is correct.

The solution to the previous recurrence relation is

$$moves(N) = 2^N - 1 \quad \text{for all } N \geq 1$$

> A closed-form formula for the number of moves that solveTowers requires for N disks

Notice that $2^3 - 1$ agrees with the value 7 that was just computed for *moves* (3).

The proof that *moves*(N) = $2^N - 1$ is by induction on N.

Basis. *Show that the property is true for $N = 1$.* Here $2^1 - 1 = 1$, which is consistent with the recurrence relation's specification that *moves* (1) = 1.

You now must establish that

property is true for an arbitrary k $\Rightarrow$ *property is true for $k + 1$*

Inductive hypothesis. *Assume that the property is true for $N = k$.* That is, assume

$$moves(k) = 2^k - 1$$

Inductive conclusion. *Show that the property is true for $N = k + 1$.* That is, you must show that *moves* ($k + 1$) = $2^{k+1} - 1$. Now

$$moves(k + 1) = 2 \times moves(k) + 1 \qquad \text{from the recurrence relation}$$
$$= 2 \times (2^k - 1) + 1 \qquad \text{by the inductive hypothesis}$$
$$= 2^{k+1} - 1$$

which is what you needed to show. The inductive proof is thus complete.

Do not get the false impression that proving properties of programs is an easy matter. These two proofs are about as easy as any will be. However, well-structured programs are far more amenable to these techniques than are poorly structured programs.

Appendix E provides more information about mathematical induction.

 Note: The subtleties of some of the algorithms you encountered in this chapter indicate the need for mathematical techniques to prove their correctness. The application of these techniques during the design of the various components of a solution can help to eliminate errors in logic before they appear in the program. One such technique is mathematical induction; another is the use of loop invariants, which Appendix F discusses.

SUMMARY

1. A grammar is a device for defining a language, which is a set of strings of symbols. By using a grammar to define a language, you often can construct a recognition algorithm that is directly based on the grammar. Grammars are frequently recursive, thus allowing you to describe vast languages concisely.

2. To illustrate the use of grammars, we defined several different languages of algebraic expressions. These languages have their relative advantages and disadvantages. Prefix and postfix expressions, though difficult for people to use, have simple grammars and eliminate ambiguity. On the other hand, infix expressions are easier for people to use but require parentheses, precedence rules, and rules of association to eliminate ambiguity. Therefore, the grammar for infix expressions is more involved.

3. Backtracking is a solution strategy that involves both recursion and a sequence of guesses that ultimately lead to a solution. If a particular guess leads to an impasse, you retrace your steps in reverse order, replace that guess, and try to complete the solution again.

4. A close relationship between mathematical induction and recursion exists. You can use induction to prove properties about a recursive algorithm. For example, you can prove that a recursive algorithm is correct, and you can derive the amount of work it requires.

EXERCISES

1. Trace the following recursive functions:
   a. isPalindrome with the string abcdeba
   b. isAnBn with the string AABB
   c. endPre with the expression $-*/abcd$

2. Consider the language that the following grammar defines:
   $$<S> = \$ \,|\, <W>\,|\, \$<S>$$
   $$<W> = \text{abb} \,|\, \text{a}<W>\text{bb}$$
   Write all strings that are in this language and that contain seven or fewer characters.

3. Write a recursive grammar for the language of strings of one or more letters. The first letter of each string must be uppercase, and all other letters in the string must be lowercase.

4. Consider a language of character strings that contain only dots and dashes. All strings in this language contain at least four characters and begin with either two dots or two dashes. If the first two characters are dots, the last one must be a dash; if the first two characters are dashes, the last one must be a dot. Write a recursive grammar for this language.

5. Consider a language of strings that contains only X's, Y's, and Z's. A string in this language must begin with an X. If a Y is present in a string, it must be the final character of the string.
   a. Write a recursive grammar for this language.
   b. Write all the possible two-character strings of this language.

6. Consider a language of words, where each word is a string of dots and dashes. The following grammar describes this language:
   $$<word> = <dot> \,|\, <dash><word> \,|\, <word><dot>$$
   $$<dot> \;\; = \bullet$$
   $$<dash> = -$$

    a. Write all three-character strings that are in this language.

    b. Is the string • • • – – in this language? Explain.

    c. Write a seven-character string that contains more dashes than dots and is in the language. Show how you know that your answer is correct.

    d. Write pseudocode for a recursive recognition function `isIn(str)` that returns true if the string `str` is in this language and returns false otherwise.

7. Consider the following grammar:

$$<word> = R\,|\,<D>\,|\,<D><word><S>$$
$$<D> \quad = Q\,|\,P$$
$$<S> \quad = 1$$

Write pseudocode for a recursive function that returns true if a string is in this language and returns false otherwise.

8. Consider the following grammar:

$$<G> = \text{empty string}\,|\,<E>\,|\,<V><E>\,|\,<E><G><V>$$
$$<E> = \&\,|\,\#$$
$$<V> = W\,|\,A$$

    a. Write pseudocode for a recursive function that returns true if a string is in this language and returns false otherwise.

    b. Is the string &W#W in this language?

9. Let L be the language

$$L = \{S : S \text{ is the form } A^n B^{2n}, \text{ for some } n > 0\}$$

Thus, a string is in L if and only if it starts with a sequence of A's and is followed by a sequence of twice as many B's. For example, AABBBB is in L, but ABBB, ABBABB, and the empty string are not.

    a. Give a grammar for the language L.

    b. Write a recursive function that decides whether the string `strExp` is in L.

10. Is $+*a-b/c++de-fg$ a prefix expression? Explain in terms of the grammar for prefix expressions.

11. Is $ab/c*efg*h/+d-+$ a postfix expression? Explain in terms of the grammar for postfix expressions.

12. Consider the language that the following grammar defines:

$$<S> = <L>\,|\,<D><S><S>$$
$$<L> = A\,|\,B$$
$$<D> = 1\,|\,2$$

    a. Write all three-character strings that are in this language.

    b. Write one string in this language that contains more than three characters.

13. Consider a language of the following character strings: The letter A, the letter B, the letter C followed by a string that is in the language, and the letter D followed by a string in the language. For example, these strings are in this language: A, CA, CCA, DCA, B, CB, CCB, DB, and DCCB.

    a. Write a grammar for this language.

    b. Is CAB in this language? Explain.

    c. Write a recursive recognition algorithm for this language.

14. Consider the language that the following grammar defines:

$$<word> = \$\,|\,a<word>a\,|\,b<word>b\,|\cdots|\,y<word>y\,|\,z<word>z$$

Equivalently,

$$L = \{s\$ \text{ reverse}(s) : s \text{ is a string of letters of length} \geq 0\}$$

Note that this language is very similar to the language of palindromes, but there is a special middle character here. This language has the following characteristics:
- A string with no characters is not in the language.
- A string with exactly one character is in the language if the character is a $.
- A longer string is in the language if the ends are identical letters and the inner substring (from the second character to the next-to-last character of str) is in the language.

Describe a recursive recognition algorithm that processes the string from left to right, reading one character at a time without saving the string for future reference. Write a C++ function that implements your algorithm.

15. Consider the following recursive function:

```cpp
int p(int x)
{
    if (x <= 3)
        return x;
    else
        return p(x-1) * p(x-3);
}  // end p
```

Let $m(x)$ be the number of multiplication operations that the execution of p(x) performs.
a. Write a recursive definition of $m(x)$.
b. Prove that your answer to part *a* is correct by using mathematical induction.

16. Consider palindromes that consist only of lowercase letters, such as "level" and "deed," but not "RadaR," "ADA," or "101." Let $c(n)$ be the number of palindromes of length n.
a. Write a recursive definition of $c(n)$.
b. Prove that your answer to part *a* is correct by using mathematical induction.

17. Prove the following for single-letter operands: If E is a prefix expression and Y is a nonempty string of nonblank characters, then $E\ Y$ cannot be a legal prefix expression. (*Hint*: Use a proof by induction on the length of E.)

18. Chapter 2 gave the following definition for $g(n, k)$, where n and k are assumed to be nonnegative integers:

$$g(n, k) = \begin{cases} 1 & \text{if } k = 0 \\ 1 & \text{if } k = n \\ 0 & \text{if } k > n \\ g(n-1, k-1) + g(n-1, k) & \text{if } 0 < k < n \end{cases}$$

Prove by induction on n that the following is a closed form for $g(n, k)$:

$$g(n, k) = \frac{n!}{(n-k)!k!}$$

PROGRAMMING PROBLEMS

1. Complete the classes Queen and Board for the Eight Queens problem.

2. Revise the program that you just wrote for the Eight Queens problem so that it answers the following questions:

    a. How many backtracks occur? That is, how many times does the program remove a queen from the board?

    b. How many calls to isUnderAttack are there?

    c. How many recursive calls to placeQueens are there?

*3. You can begin the Eight Queens problem by placing a queen in the second square of the first column instead of in the first square. You can then call placeQueens to begin with the second column. This revision should lead you to a new solution. Write a program that finds all solutions to the Eight Queens problem.[2]

4. Write a program that will recognize and evaluate prefix expressions. First design and implement a class of prefix expressions. This class should contain methods to recognize and evaluate prefix expressions. This chapter discusses the algorithms you will need to implement these methods.

5. Write a program that will recognize and evaluate postfix expressions. First design and implement a class of postfix expressions. This class should contain methods to recognize and evaluate postfix expressions.

6. Implement the algorithm described in this chapter to convert a prefix expression to postfix form. Involve the classes that Programming Problems 4 and 5 describe.

7. Implement a recognition algorithm for the language in Exercise 5.

8. The following is a grammar that allows you to omit parentheses in infix algebraic expressions when the precedence rules remove ambiguity. For example, $a + b * c$ means $a + (b * c)$. However, the grammar requires parentheses when ambiguity would otherwise result. That is, the grammar does not permit left-to-right association when several operators have the same precedence. For example, $a / b * c$ is illegal. Notice that the definitions introduce factors and terms.

$$<expression> = <term > | <term> + <term > | <term> - <term>$$
$$<term> = <factor> | <factor >*<factor> | <factor>/<factor>$$
$$<factor> = < letter> | (<expression>)$$
$$<letter> = a | b | \ldots | z$$

The recognition algorithm is based on a recursive chain of subtasks: *find an expression → find a term → find a factor*. What makes this a recursive chain is that *find an expression* uses *find a term*, which in turn uses *find a factor*. *Find a factor* either detects a base case or uses *find an expression*, thus forming the recursive chain. The pseudocode for the recognition algorithm follows:

```
FIND AN EXPRESSION
// The grammar specifies that an expression is either a single term or
// a term followed by a + or a -, which then must be followed by a second term.
{
    Find a term
    if (the next symbol is + or -)
        Find a term
}
```

---

[2] Especially challenging projects in this book are indicated with an asterisk.

FIND A TERM
// The grammar specifies that a term is either a single factor or
// a factor followed by a * or a /, which must then be followed by a second factor.
{
    Find a factor
    `if` (*the next symbol is * or /*)
        Find a factor
}

FIND A FACTOR
// The grammar specifies that a factor is either a single letter (the base case) or
// an expression enclosed in parentheses.
{
    `if` (*the first symbol is a letter*)
        Done
    `else if` (*the first symbol is a* '(')
    {
        Find an expression starting at the character after '('
        Check for ')'
    }
    `else`
        No factor exists
}

Design and implement a class of infix expressions, as described by the given grammar. Include a method to recognize a legal infix expression.

9. Do you know how to find your way through a maze? After you write this program, you will never be lost again!

Assume that a maze is a rectangular array of squares, some of which are blocked to represent walls. The maze has one entrance and one exit. For example, if *x*'s represent the walls, a maze could appear as follows:

```
xxxxxxxxxxxxxxxxx x
x       x        xxxx x
x xxxxx   xxxxx   xx x
x xxxxx xxxxxxx  xx x
x x             xx xx x
x xxxxxxxxx xx      x
xxxxxxxxxxxxxoxxxxxxx
```

A creature, indicated in the previous diagram by *o*, sits just inside the maze at the entrance (bottom row). Assume that the creature can move in only four directions: north, south, east, and west. In the diagram, north is up, south is down, east is to the right, and west is to the left. The problem is to move the creature through the maze from the entrance to the exit (top row), if possible. As the creature moves, it should mark its path. At the conclusion of the trip through the maze, you should see both the correct path and incorrect attempts. Write a program to solve this problem.

Squares in the maze have one of several states: CLEAR (the square is clear), WALL (the square is blocked and represents part of the wall), PATH (the square lies on the path to the exit), and VISITED (the square was visited, but going that way led to an impasse).

This problem uses two ADTs that must interact. The ADT creature represents the creature's current position and contains operations that move the creature. The creature should be able to move north, south, east, and west one square at a time. It should also be able to report its position and mark its trail.

The ADT maze represents the maze itself, which is a two-dimensional rectangular arrangement of squares. You could number the rows of squares from the top beginning with zero, and number the columns of squares from the left beginning with zero. You could then use a row number and a column number to uniquely identify any square within the maze. The ADT clearly needs a data structure to represent the maze. It also needs such data as the height and width of the maze given in numbers of squares and the row and column coordinates of both the entrance to and the exit from the maze.

The ADT maze should also contain, for example, operations that create a specific maze given descriptive data that we will detail to display a maze, determine whether a particular square is part of the wall, determine whether a particular square is part of the path, and so on.

The search algorithm and its supporting functions are outside both of the ADTs creature and maze. Thus, the maze and the creature will be arguments that you must pass to these functions. If you are at the maze's entrance, you can systematically find your way out of the maze by using the following search algorithm. This involves backtracking—that is, retracing your steps when you reach an impasse.

Step 1. First check whether you are at the exit. If you are, you're done (a very simple maze); if you are not, go to step 2.

Step 2. Try to move to the square directly to the north by calling the function goNorth (step 3).

Step 3. If goNorth was successful, you are done. If it was unsuccessful, try to move to the square directly to the west by calling the function goWest (step 4).

Step 4. If goWest was successful, you are done. If it was unsuccessful, try to move to the square directly to the south by calling the function goSouth (step 5).

Step 5. If goSouth was successful, you are done. If it was unsuccessful, try to move to the square directly to the east by calling the function goEast (step 6).

Step 6. If goEast was successful, you are done. If it was unsuccessful, you are still done, because no path exists from the entrance to the exit.

The function goNorth will examine all the paths that start at the square to the north of the present square as follows. If the square directly to the north is clear, is inside the maze, and has not been visited before, move into this square and mark it as part of the path. (Note that you are moving from the south.) Check whether you are at the exit. If you are, you're done. Otherwise, try to find a path to the exit from here by trying all paths leaving this square except the one going south (going south would put you back in the square from which you just came) as follows. Call goNorth; if it is not successful, call goWest and, if it is not successful, call goEast. If goEast is not successful, mark this square as visited, move back into the square to the south, and return.

The following pseudocode describes the goNorth algorithm:

```
goNorth(maze, creature)
{
    if (the square to the north is clear, inside the maze, and unvisited)
    {
        Move to the north
        Mark the square as part of the path
        if (at exit)
            success = true
    else
    {
        success = goNorth(maze, creature)
        if (!success)
        {
            success = goWest(maze, creature)
            if (!success)
            {
                success = goEast(maze, creature)
                if (!success)
                {
```

```
                          Mark square visited
                          Backtrack south
                     }
                   }
                 }
               }
             }
           else
               success = false

           return success
       }
```

The goWest function will examine all the paths that start at the square to the west of the present square as follows. If the square directly to the west is clear, is inside the maze, and has not been visited before, move into this square and mark it as part of the path. (Note that you are moving from the east.) Check whether you are at the exit. If you are, you're done. Otherwise, try to find a path to the exit from here by trying all paths leaving this square except the one going east (this would put you back in the square from which you just came) as follows. Call goNorth; if it is not successful, call goWest; and if it is not successful, call goSouth. If goSouth is not successful, mark this square as visited, move back into the square to the east, and return. The functions goEast and goSouth are analogous to goWest and goNorth.

The input data to represent a maze is simple. For example, the previously given maze is represented by the following lines of input, which can be in a text file:

```
20   7              ← width and height of the maze in squares
   0  18            ← row and column coordinate of maze exit
   6  12            ← row and column coordinate of maze entrance

xxxxxxxxxxxxxxxxxx x
x       x      xxxx x
x xxxxx  xxxxx  xx x
x xxxxx xxxxxxx xx x
x x           xx xx x
x xxxxxxxxxx xx     x
xxxxxxxxxxxx xxxxxxx
```

After the first three lines of numeric data in the file, each of the next lines corresponds to a row in the maze, and each character in a line corresponds to a column in the maze. An *x* indicates a blocked square (part of the wall), and a blank indicates a clear square. This notation is convenient, because you can see what the maze looks like as you design it.

Stacks

Contents

Prerequisites

Chapter 1   Data Abstraction: The Walls
C++ Interlude 1   C++ Classes

So far in this book, we have discussed data abstraction as it relates to the design of a solution, introduced C++ classes as a way to hide a solution's implementation, introduced resizable arrays and linked nodes as data structures used in many ADT implementations, and developed recursion as a problem-solving technique that is useful in the construction of algorithms. The primary concerns of the remainder of this book are the aspects of problem solving that involve the management of data—that is, the identification and implementation of some of the more common data-management operations. Our earlier discussions will prove useful in simplifying and solving these data management problems.

Our study of data management has three goals. The first is to identify useful sets of operations—that is, to identify abstract data types. The second goal is to examine applications that use these abstract data types. The third goal is to construct implementations for the abstract data types—that is, to develop data structures and classes. As you will discover, the nature of the operations of an abstract data type, along with the application in which you will use it, greatly influences the choice of its implementation.

The ADT bag discussed in Chapter 1 does not organize its data. However, you can organize data either by position or by value. In general, these organizations are appropriate for applications of rather different natures. For example, if an application needs to ask a question about the first person in a line, you should organize the data by position. On the other hand, if an application needs to ask a question about the employee named Smith, you should organize the data by value. Throughout the rest of this book, you will see several ADTs that use these two data organizations.

This chapter introduces a well-known ADT called a stack. You will see how the operations on a stack give it a last-in, first-out behavior. Two of the several applications of a stack that the chapter considers are evaluating algebraic expressions and searching for a path between two points. Finally, the chapter discusses the important relationship between stacks and recursion. We leave the implementations of the stack to the next chapter.

6.1   The Abstract Data Type Stack

VideoNote
The ADT stack

The specification of an abstract data type that you can use to solve a particular problem can emerge during the design of the problem's solution. The ADT developed in the following example happens to be an important one: the ADT stack.

6.1.1   Developing an ADT During the Design of a Solution

When you type a line of text on a keyboard, you are likely to make mistakes. If you use the Backspace key to correct these mistakes, each backspace erases the previous character entered. Consecutive backspaces are applied in sequence and so erase several characters. For instance, if you type the line

    abcc←ddde←←←eg←fg

where ← represents the backspace character, the corrected input would be

    abcdefg

How can a program read the original line and get the correct input? In designing a solution to this problem, you eventually must decide how to store the input line. In accordance with the ADT approach, you should postpone this decision until you have a better idea of what operations you will need to perform on the data.

A first attempt at a solution leads to the following pseudocode:

Initial draft of a solution

```
// Read the line, correcting mistakes along the way
while (not end of line)
{
    Read a new character ch
    if (ch is not a '←')
        Add ch to the ADT
    else
        Remove from the ADT (and discard) the item that was added most recently
}
```

This solution calls to attention two of the operations that the ADT will have to include:

- Add a new item to the ADT.
- Remove from the ADT and discard the item that was added most recently.

Two ADT operations
that are required

Notice that potential trouble lurks if you type a ← when the ADT is empty—that is, when the ADT contains no characters. If this situation should occur, you have three options: (1) have the program terminate and write an error message, (2) throw an exception, or (3) have the program ignore the ← and continue. Any of these options is reasonable, so let's suppose that you decide to ignore the ← and continue. Therefore, the algorithm becomes

```
// Read the line, correcting mistakes along the way
while (not end of line)
{
    Read a new character ch
    if (ch is not a '←')
        Add ch to the ADT
    else if (the ADT is not empty)
        Remove from the ADT and discard the item that was added most recently
    else
        Ignore the '←'
}
```

The "read and
correct" algorithm

From this pseudocode, you can identify a third operation required by the ADT:

- See whether the ADT is empty.

Another required
ADT operation

This solution places the corrected input line in the ADT. Now suppose that you want to display the line. At first, it appears that you can accomplish this task by using the ADT operations already identified, as follows:

```
// Display the line
while (the ADT is not empty)
{
    Remove from the ADT and discard the item that was added most recently
    Display . . . . Uh-oh!
}
```

A false start at
writing the line

This pseudocode is incorrect for two reasons:

- When you remove and discard an item from the ADT, the item is gone, so you cannot display it. What you should have done was to *look at* the item that was added to the ADT most recently. Since we cannot see inside an ADT, we use an accessor operation to return a copy of the item added most recently, enabling us to look at it. Note that an accessor operation does not change the ADT's data, so after getting and displaying the item, you remove it from the ADT.
- The last character of the input line is the item most recently added to the ADT. You certainly do not want to write it first. The resolution of this particular difficulty is left to you as an exercise.

Reasons why the
attempted solution
is incorrect

If we address only the first difficulty, the following pseudocode displays the input line in reverse order:

The write-backward
algorithm

```
// Display the line in reverse order
while (the ADT is not empty)
{
    Get a copy of the item that was added to the ADT most recently and assign it to ch
    Display ch
    Remove from the ADT and discard the item that was added most recently
}
```

Another required
ADT operation

Thus, a fourth operation is required by the ADT:

- Get a copy of the item that was added to the ADT most recently.

Although you have yet to think about an implementation of the ADT, you know that you must be able to perform four specific operations.[1] These operations define the required ADT, which happens to be well known: It is usually called a **stack**.

6.1.2 Specifications for the ADT Stack

We have identified the following operations for the ADT stack:

- See whether a stack is empty.
- Add a new item to the stack.
- Remove from the stack and discard the item that was added most recently.
- Get a copy of the item that was added to the stack most recently.

The term "stack" is intended to conjure up visions of things encountered in daily life, such as a stack of plates in the school cafeteria, a stack of books on your desk, or a stack of assignments that you need to work on. In common English usage, "stack of" and "pile of" are synonymous. To computer scientists, however, a stack is not just any old pile. A stack has the property that the last item placed on the stack will be the first item removed. This property is commonly referred to as **last in, first out** or simply **LIFO**.

LIFO: The last item
inserted onto a
stack is the first item
out

A stack of plates in a cafeteria makes a very good analogy of the abstract data type stack, as Figure 6-1 illustrates. As new plates are added, the old ones drop farther into the well beneath the surface. At any particular time, only the plate last placed on the stack is above the surface and visible. This plate is at the **top of the stack** and is the one that must be removed next. In general, the plates are removed in exactly the opposite order from that in which they were added.

The LIFO property of stacks seems inherently unfair. Think of the poor person who finally gets the last plate on the cafeteria's stack, one that may have been placed there six years ago. Or how would you like to be the first person to arrive on the stack for a movie—as opposed to the line for a movie. You would be the last person allowed in! These examples demonstrate the reason that stacks are not especially prevalent in everyday life. The property that we usually desire in our daily lives is *first in, first out*, or *FIFO*. A *queue*, which you will learn about in Chapter 13, is the ADT with the FIFO property. Most people would much prefer to wait in a movie queue— as a line is called in Britain—than in a movie stack. However, while the LIFO property of stacks is not appropriate for very many everyday situations, it is precisely what is needed for a large number of problems that arise in computer science.

FIGURE 6-1   A stack of cafeteria plates

---

[1] The final algorithm to write the line correctly instead of in reverse order does not require additional ADT operations.

Notice how well the analogy holds between the ADT stack and the stack of cafeteria plates. The operations that manipulate data on the ADT stack are the *only* such operations, and they correspond to the only things that you can do to a stack of plates. You can determine whether the stack of plates is empty but not how many plates are on the stack; you can inspect the top plate but no other plate; you can place a plate on top of the stack but at no other position; and you can remove a plate from the top of the stack but from no other position. If you were not permitted to perform any of these operations, or if you were permitted to perform any other operations, the ADT would not be a stack.

Although the stack of cafeteria plates suggests that, as you add or remove plates, the other plates move, do not have this expectation of the ADT stack. The stack operations involve only the top item and imply only that the other items in the stack remain in sequence. Implementations of the ADT stack operations might or might not move the stack's items. The implementations given in the next chapter do not move data items.

Refining the specification of the ADT stack. The following summary of the ADT stack provides some detail about how we wish to specify its operations. The names given here for stack operations are conventional.

ABSTRACT DATA TYPE: STACK

DATA

* A finite number of objects, not necessarily distinct, having the same data type and ordered by when they were added.

OPERATIONS

PSEUDOCODE	DESCRIPTION
isEmpty()	Task: Sees whether this stack is empty. Input: None. Output: True if the stack is empty; otherwise false.
push(newEntry)	Task: Adds newEntry to the top of this stack. Input: newEntry. Output: True if the operation is successful; otherwise false.
pop()	Task: Removes the top of this stack. That is, it removes the item that was added most recently. Input: None. Output: True if the operation is successful; otherwise false.
peek()	Task: Returns a copy of the top of this stack. That is, it gets the item that was added most recently. The operation does not change the stack. Input: None. Output: A copy of the top of the stack.

Figure 6-2 shows a UML diagram for a class of stacks.

Using the ADT stack in a solution. Recall that Chapter 1 urged you to focus on the specification of a module before you considered its implementation. After writing an ADT's operations in

FIGURE 6-2　　UML diagram for the class Stack

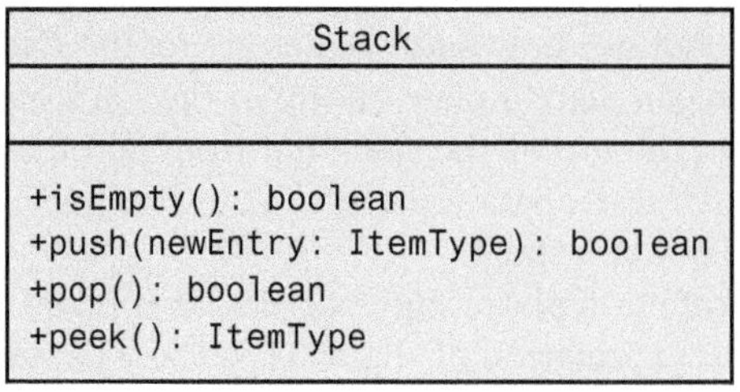

```
                    Stack


+isEmpty(): boolean
+push(newEntry: ItemType): boolean
+pop(): boolean
+peek(): ItemType
```

pseudocode, you should try to use them as a check of your design. Such a test can highlight any deficiencies in your specifications or design. For example, you can use the previous stack operations to refine the algorithms developed earlier in this chapter.

The refined algorithms

```
// Reads an input line, recognizing the character '←' as a backspace that erases the
// previously typed character.
// Returns a stack of the corrected characters read.
readAndCorrect(): Stack
{
    aStack = a new empty stack
    Read newChar
    while (newChar is not the end-of-line symbol)
    {
        if (newChar is not a '←')
            aStack.push(newChar)
        else if (!aStack.isEmpty())
            aStack.pop()
        Read newChar
    }
    return aStack
}

// Displays the input line in reverse order by writing the contents of the stack aStack.
displayBackward(aStack: Stack)
{
    while (!aStack.isEmpty())
    {
        newChar = aStack.peek()
        aStack.pop()
        Write newChar
    }
    Advance to new line
}
```

You should be able to use the stack operations without knowing their implementations or even what a stack looks like. Because working with an ADT involves building a wall around the implementation, your program can use a stack independently of the stack's implementation. As long as the program correctly uses the ADT's operations—that is, as long as it honors the operation contract—it will work regardless of how you implement the ADT.

For the program to do this, however, the operation contract must be written precisely. That is, before you implement any operations of the ADT, you should specify in detail both their requirements before use and their ultimate effect. Realize, however, that during program design, the first attempt at specification is often informal and is only later made precise by the writing of preconditions and postconditions. For example, the previous specifications of the ADT stack leave the following questions unanswered:

* How will pop affect an empty stack?
* What will peek do when the stack is empty?

Questions that the informal specifications of the stack leave unanswered

 Note: Specifications for pop and peek should accommodate an empty stack.

An interface. The interface given in Listing 6-1 formalizes our specification of the ADT stack.

LISTING 6-1   A C++ interface for stacks

```cpp
1   /** @file StackInterface.h */
2   #ifndef STACK_INTERFACE_
3   #define STACK_INTERFACE_
4
5   template<class ItemType>
6   class StackInterface
7   {
8   public:
9      /** Sees whether this stack is empty.
10      @return  True if the stack is empty, or false if not. */
11     virtual bool isEmpty() const = 0;
12
13     /** Adds a new entry to the top of this stack.
14      @post  If the operation was successful, newEntry is at the top of the stack.
15      @param newEntry  The object to be added as a new entry.
16      @return  True if the addition is successful or false if not. */
17     virtual bool push(const ItemType& newEntry) = 0;
18
19     /** Removes the top of this stack.
20      @post  If the operation was successful, the top of the stack
21         has been removed.
22      @return  True if the removal is successful or false if not. */
23     virtual bool pop() = 0;
24
25     /** Returns a copy of the top of this stack.
26      @pre  The stack is not empty.
27      @post  A copy of the top of the stack has been returned, and
28         the stack is unchanged.
29      @return  A copy of the top of the stack. */
30     virtual ItemType peek() const = 0;
31
32     /** Destroys this stack and frees its assigned memory. */
33     virtual ~StackInterface() { }
34   }; // end StackInterface
35   #endif
```

Question 1 If you push the letters *A*, *B*, *C*, and *D* in order onto a stack of characters and then pop them, in what order will they be removed from the stack?

Question 2 What do the initially empty stacks `stack1` and `stack2` "look like" after the following sequence of operations?

```
stack1.push(1)
stack1.push(2)
stack2.push(3)
stack2.push(4)
stack1.pop()
stackTop = stack2.peek()
stack1.push(stackTop)
stack1.push(5)
stack2.pop()
stack2.push(6)
```

Axioms (optional). Most people will understand intuitive specifications, such as those given previously for the stack operations. However, some ADTs are much more complex and less intuitive than a stack. For such ADTs, you should use a more rigorous approach to defining the behavior of their operations: You must supply a set of mathematical rules—called **axioms**—that precisely specify the behavior of each operation of an ADT.

An axiom is a mathematical rule

An axiom is a true statement for an ADT's operation. For example, you are familiar with axioms for algebraic operations; in particular, you know the following rules for multiplication:

Axioms for multiplication

$$(a \times b) \times c = a \times (b \times c)$$
$$a \times b = b \times a$$
$$a \times 1 = a$$
$$a \times 0 = 0$$

These rules, or axioms, are true for any numeric values of *a*, *b*, and *c*, and describe the behavior of the multiplication operator $\times$.

Axioms specify the behavior of an ADT

In a similar fashion, you can write a set of axioms that completely describes the behavior of the operations for the ADT stack. For example,

A newly created stack is empty

is an axiom because it is true for all newly created stacks. We can state this axiom succinctly in terms of the ADT stack operations as follows, if we represent a newly created stack by the pseudocode expression `Stack()`:

An example of an axiom

```
(Stack()).isEmpty() = true
```

Note that our notation for an axiom represents a sequence of actions, and the equal sign denotes algebraic equality.

To formally capture the intuitive notion that the last item inserted into the stack `aStack` is the first item to be removed, you could write an axiom such as

```
(aStack.push(newItem)).pop() ⇒ aStack
```

That is, if you push `newItem` onto `aStack` and then pop it, you are left with the original stack `aStack`.

The following axioms formally define the ADT stack.

> **Note:** **Axioms for the ADT stack**
>
> ```
> (Stack()).isEmpty() = true
> (Stack()).pop() = false
> (Stack()).peek() = error
> (aStack.push(item)).isEmpty() = false
> (aStack.push(item)).peek() = item
> (aStack.push(item)).pop() = true
> (aStack.push(item)).pop() ⇒ aStack
> ```

6.2   Simple Uses of a Stack

VideoNote
Using the ADT stack

Once you have satisfactorily specified the behavior of an ADT, you can design applications that access and manipulate the ADT's data solely in terms of its operations and without regard for its implementation. Thus, we can use the operations of the ADT stack even though we have not discussed their implementations yet. This section presents two rather simple examples for which the LIFO property of stacks is appropriate.

6.2.1   Checking for Balanced Braces

C++ uses curly braces, "{" and "}", to delimit groups of statements. For example, braces begin and end a method's body. If you treat a C++ program as a string of characters, you can use a stack to verify that a program contains balanced braces. For example, the braces in the string

```
abc{defg{ijk}{l{mn}}op}qr
```

are balanced, while the braces in the string

```
abc{def}}{ghij{kl}m
```

are not balanced. You can see whether a string contains balanced braces by traversing it from left to right and checking that each successive close brace "}" matches with the most recently encountered unmatched open brace "{"; that is, the "{" must be to the left of the current "}". The braces are balanced if

1. Each time you encounter a "}", it matches an already encountered "{".
2. When you reach the end of the string, you have matched each "{".

Requirements for
balanced braces

The solution requires that you keep track of each unmatched "{" and discard one each time you encounter a "}". One way to perform this task is to push each "{" encountered onto a stack and pop one off each time you encounter a "}". Thus, a first-draft pseudocode solution is

```
for  (each character in the string)
{
   if (the character is a '{')
      aStack.push('{')
   else if (the character is a '}')
      aStack.pop()
}
```

Initial draft of a
solution

Although this solution correctly keeps track of braces, missing from it are the checks that conditions 1 and 2 are met—that is, that the braces are indeed balanced. To verify condition 1 when a "}" is encountered, you can check to see whether the stack is empty before popping from it.

If it is empty, you terminate the loop and report that the string is not balanced. To verify condition 2, you check that the stack is empty when the end of the string is reached.

Thus, the pseudocode solution to check for balanced braces in aString becomes

A detailed pseudocode solution to check a string for balanced braces

```
// Checks the string aString to verify that braces match.
// Returns true if aString contains matching braces, false otherwise.
checkBraces(aString: string): boolean
{
    aStack = a new empty stack
    balancedSoFar = true
    i = 0                          // Tracks character position in string

    while (balancedSoFar and i < length of aString)
    {
        ch = character at position i in aString
        i++

        // Push an open brace
        if (ch is a '{')
            aStack.push('{')

        // Close brace
        else if (ch is a '}')
        {
            if (!aStack.isEmpty())
                aStack.pop()       // Pop a matching open brace
            else                   // No matching open brace
                balancedSoFar = false
        }
        // Ignore all characters other than braces
    }

    if (balancedSoFar and aStack.isEmpty())
        aString has balanced braces
    else
        aString does not have balanced braces
}
```

Figure 6-3 shows the stacks that result when this algorithm is applied to several simple examples.

FIGURE 6-3   Three traces of the algorithm that checks for balanced braces

---

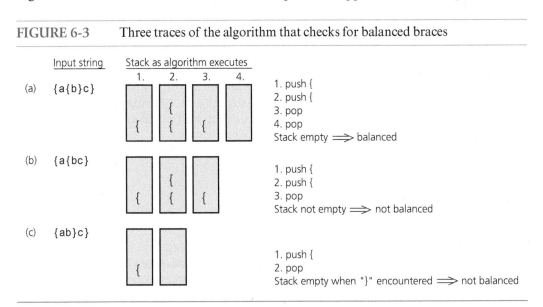

Question 3 For each of the following strings, trace the execution of the balanced-braces algorithm and show the contents of the stack at each step.

    a. x{{yz}}}

    b. {x{y{{z}}}

    c. {{{x}}}

Note: The push operation can fail for implementation-dependent reasons. For example, push fails if the array in an array-based implementation is full. In the spirit of fail-safe programming, a function that implements this balanced-braces algorithm should check push's return value.

Aside: A solution without stacks

It may have occurred to you that a simpler solution to this problem is possible. You need only keep a count of the current number of unmatched open braces.[2] You need not actually store the open braces in a stack. However, the stack-based solution is conceptually useful as it previews more legitimate uses of stacks. For example, Exercise 7 at the end of this chapter asks you to extend the algorithm given here to check for balanced parentheses and square brackets in addition to braces.

6.2.2   Recognizing Strings in a Language

Consider the problem of recognizing whether a particular string is in the language

$$L = \{s\$s' : s \text{ is a possibly empty string of characters other than } \$, s' = \text{reverse}(s)\}$$

For example, the strings A\$A, ABC\$CBA, and \$ are in L, but AB\$AB and ABC\$CB are not. (Exercise 14 in Chapter 5 introduced a similar language.) This language is like the language of palindromes that you saw in Chapter 5, but strings in this language have a special middle character.

    A stack is useful in determining whether a given string is in L. Suppose you traverse the first half of the string and push each character onto a stack. When you reach the \$ you can undo the process: For each character in the second half of the string, you pop a character off the stack. However, you must match the popped character with the current character in the string to ensure that the second half of the string is the reverse of the first half. The stack must be empty when—and only when—you reach the end of the string; otherwise, one "half" of the string is longer than the other, and so the string is not in L.

    The following algorithm uses this strategy. To avoid unnecessary complications, assume that aString contains exactly one \$.

---

[2] Each time you encounter an open brace, you increment the count; each time you encounter a close brace, you decrement the count. If this count ever falls below zero, or if it is greater than zero when the end of the string is reached, the string is unbalanced.

```
// Checks the string aString to verify that it is in language L.
// Returns true if aString is in L, false otherwise.
recognizeString(aString: string): boolean
{
    aStack = a new empty stack

    // Push the characters that are before the $ (that is, the characters in s) onto the stack
    i = 0                              // Tracks character position in string
    ch = character at position i in aString
    while (ch is not a '$')
    {
        aStack.push(ch)
        i++
        ch = character at position i in aString
    }

    // Skip the $
    i++

    // Match the reverse of s
    inLanguage = true                  // Assume string is in language
    while (inLanguage and i < length of aString)
    {
        if (!aStack.isEmpty())
        {
            stackTop = aStack.peek()
            aStack.pop()
            ch = character at position i in aString
            if (stackTop equals ch)
                i++                    // Characters match
            else
                inLanguage = false  // Characters do not match (top of stack is not ch)
        }
        else
            inLanguage = false        // Stack is empty (first half of string is shorter
                                      // than second half)
    }
    if (inLanguage and aStack.isEmpty())
        aString is in language
    else
        aString is not in language
}
```

You can use an ADT's operations in an application without the distraction of implementation details

Note: In both of the preceding examples, notice how you can focus on the task at hand without the distraction of implementation details such as arrays. With less to worry about, you are less likely to make an error in your logic when you use the ADT's operations in applications such as checkBraces and recognizeString. Likewise, when you finally implement the ADT's operations in C++, you will not be distracted by these applications. In addition, because checkBraces and recognizeString do not depend on any implementation decisions that you make, they are not altered by your decisions. These remarks assume that you do not change the specifications of the ADT's operations when you implement them. However, developing software is not a linear process. You may realize during implementation that you need to refine your specifications. Clearly, changes to the specification of any module affect any already-designed uses of that module.

To summarize, you can specify the behavior of an ADT independently of its implementation. Given such a specification, and without any knowledge of how the ADT will be implemented, you can design applications that use the ADT's operations to access its data.

Question 4 Trace the execution of the language-recognition algorithm described in the previous section for each of the following strings, and show the contents of the stack at each step.

    a. a$a
    b. ab$ab
    c. ab$a
    d. ab$ba

6.3 Using Stacks with Algebraic Expressions

This section contains two more problems that you can solve neatly by using the ADT stack. Keep in mind throughout that you are using the ADT stack to solve the problems. You can use the stack operations, but you may not assume any particular implementation. You choose a specific implementation only as a last step.

Your use of an ADT's operations should not depend on its implementation

    Chapter 5 presented recursive grammars that specified the syntax of algebraic expressions. Recall that prefix and postfix expressions avoid the ambiguity inherent in the evaluation of infix expressions. We will now consider stack-based solutions to the problems of evaluating infix and postfix expressions. To avoid distracting programming issues, we will allow only the binary operators *, /, +, and −, and we will disallow exponentiation and unary operators.

    The strategy we shall adopt here is first to develop an algorithm for evaluating postfix expressions and then to develop an algorithm for transforming an infix expression into an equivalent postfix expression. Taken together, these two algorithms provide a way to evaluate infix expressions. This strategy eliminates the need for an algorithm that directly evaluates infix expressions, which is a somewhat more difficult problem that Programming Problem 8 considers.

To evaluate an infix expression, first convert it to postfix form and then evaluate the postfix expression

6.3.1 Evaluating Postfix Expressions

As we mentioned in Chapter 5, some calculators require you to enter postfix expressions. For example, to compute the value of

    2 * (3 + 4)

by using a postfix calculator, you would enter the sequence 2, 3, 4, +, and *, which corresponds to the postfix expression

    2 3 4 + *

Recall that an operator in a postfix expression applies to the two operands that immediately precede it. Thus, the calculator must be able to retrieve the operands entered most recently. The ADT stack provides this capability. In fact, each time you enter an operand, the calculator pushes it onto a stack. When you enter an operator, the calculator applies it to the top two operands on the stack, pops the operands from the stack, and pushes the result of the operation onto the stack. Figure 6-4 shows the action of the calculator for the previous sequence of operands and operators. The final result, 14, is on the top of the stack.

    You can formalize the action of the calculator to obtain an algorithm that evaluates a postfix expression, which is entered as a string of characters. To avoid issues that cloud the algorithm with programming details, assume that

- The string is a syntactically correct postfix expression
- No unary operators are present
- No exponentiation operators are present
- Operands are single lowercase letters that represent integer values

Simplifying assumptions

FIGURE 6-4   The effect of a postfix calculator on a stack when evaluating the postfix expression 2 3 4 + *

Key entered	Calculator action		Stack (top to bottom)
2	push 2		2
3	push 3		3 2
4	push 4		4 3 2
+	operand2 = peek	(4)	4 3 2
	pop		3 2
	operand1 = peek	(3)	3 2
	pop		2
	result = operand1 + operand2	(7)	
	push result		7 2
*	operand2 = peek	(7)	7 2
	pop		2
	operand1 = peek	(2)	2
	pop		
	result = operand1 * operand2	(14)	
	push result		14

A pseudocode algorithm that evaluates postfix expressions

The pseudocode algorithm is then

```
for (each character ch in the string)
{
    if (ch is an operand)
        Push the value of the operand ch onto the stack
    else // ch is an operator named op
    {
        // Evaluate and push the result
        operand2 = top of stack
        Pop the stack

        operand1 = top of stack
        Pop the stack

        result = operand1 op operand2
        Push result onto the stack
    }
}
```

Upon termination of the algorithm, the value of the expression will be on the top of the stack. Programming Problem 5 at the end of this chapter asks you to implement this algorithm.

Question 5 By using a stack, evaluate the postfix expression *a b − c +*. Assume the following values for the identifiers: *a* = 7, *b* = 3, and *c* = −2. Show the status of the stack after each step.

6.3.2   Converting Infix Expressions to Equivalent Postfix Expressions

Now that you know how to evaluate a postfix expression, you will be able to evaluate an infix expression if you first can convert it into an equivalent postfix expression. The infix expressions here are the familiar ones, such as $(a+b) * c / d - e$. They allow parentheses, operator precedence, and left-to-right association.

Will you ever want to evaluate an infix expression? Certainly—you have written such expressions in programs. The compiler that translated your programs had to generate machine instructions to evaluate the expressions. To do so, the compiler first transformed each infix expression into postfix form. Knowing how to convert an expression from infix to postfix notation not only will lead to an algorithm to evaluate infix expressions, but also will give you some insight into the compilation process.

If you manually convert a few infix expressions to postfix form, you will discover three important facts:

- The operands always stay in the same order with respect to one another.
- An operator will move only "to the right" with respect to the operands; that is, if in the infix expression the operand x precedes the operator op, it is also true that in the postfix expression the operand x precedes the operator op.
- All parentheses are removed.

Facts about converting from infix to postfix

As a consequence of these three facts, the primary task of the conversion algorithm is determining where to place each operator.

The following pseudocode describes a first attempt at converting an infix expression to an equivalent postfix expression postfixExp:

First draft of an algorithm to convert an infix expression to postfix form

Initialize postfixExp *to the empty string*
for (*each character* ch *in the infix expression*)
{
    switch (ch)
    {
        case ch *is an operand*:
            Append ch *to the end of* postfixExp
            break
        case ch *is an operator*:
            Save ch *until you know where to place it*
            break
        case ch *is a* '(' *or a* ')':
            Discard ch
            break
    }
}

You may have guessed that you really do not want simply to discard the parentheses, as they play an important role in determining the placement of the operators. In any infix expression, a set of matching parentheses defines an isolated subexpression that consists of an operator and its two operands. Therefore, the algorithm must evaluate the subexpression independently of the rest of the expression. Regardless of what the rest of the expression looks like, the operator within the subexpression belongs with the operands in that subexpression. The parentheses tell the rest of the expression that

> *You can have the value of this subexpression after it is evaluated; simply ignore everything inside.*

Parentheses, operator precedence, and left-to-right association determine where to place operators in the postfix expression

Parentheses are thus one of the factors that determine the placement of the operators in the postfix expression. The other factors are precedence and left-to-right association.

In Chapter 5, you saw a simple way to convert a fully parenthesized infix expression to postfix form. Because each operator corresponded to a pair of parentheses, you simply moved each operator to the position marked by its close parenthesis and finally removed the parentheses.

The actual problem is more difficult, however, because the infix expression is not always fully parenthesized. Instead, the problem allows precedence and left-to-right association, and therefore requires a more complex algorithm. The following is a high-level description of what you must do when you encounter each character as you read the infix string from left to right. To hold the operators, we use a stack named `operatorStack`.

Five steps in the process to convert from infix to postfix form

1. When you encounter an operand, append it to the output string `postfixExp`.
   Justification: The order of the operands in the postfix expression is the same as the order in the infix expression, and the operands that appear to the left of an operator in the infix expression also appear to its left in the postfix expression.
2. Push each "(" onto the stack.
3. When you encounter an operator, if the stack is empty, push the operator onto the stack. However, if the stack is not empty, pop operators of greater or equal precedence from the stack and append them to `postfixExp`. You stop when you encounter either a "(" or an operator of lower precedence or when the stack becomes empty. You then push the current operator in the expression onto the stack. Thus, this step orders the operators by precedence and in accordance with left-to-right association. Notice that you continue popping from the stack until you encounter an operator of strictly lower precedence than the current operator in the infix expression. You do not stop on equality, because the left-to-right association rule says that in case of a tie in precedence, the leftmost operator is applied first—and this operator is the one that is already on the stack.
4. When you encounter a ")", pop operators off the stack and append them to the end of `postfixExp` until you encounter the matching "(".
   Justification: Within a pair of parentheses, precedence and left-to-right association determine the order of the operators, and step 3 has already ordered the operators in accordance with these rules.
5. When you reach the end of the string, you pop the remaining contents off the stack and append them to the end of `postfixExp`.

For example, Figure 6-5 traces the action of the algorithm on the infix expression $a - (b + c * d)/e$, assuming that the stack `operatorStack` and the string `postfixExp` are initially empty. At the end of the algorithm, `postfixExp` contains the resulting postfix expression $a\,b\,c\,d * + e/-$.

FIGURE 6-5   A trace of the algorithm that converts the infix expression $a - (b + c * d)/e$ to postfix form

ch	operatorStack (top to bottom)	postfixExp	
a		a	
–	–	a	
(	(–	a	
b	(–	a b	
+	+ (–	a b	
c	+ (–	a b c	
*	* + (–	a b c	
d	* + (–	a b c d	
)	+ (–	a b c d *	Move operators from stack to
	(–	a b c d * +	`postfixExp` until "("
	–	a b c d * +	
/	/ –	a b c d * +	
e	/ –	a b c d * + e	
	–	a b c d * + e /	Copy operators from
		a b c d * + e / –	stack to `postfixExp`

You can use the previous five-step description of the algorithm to develop a fairly concise pseudocode solution, which follows. The symbol • in this algorithm means concatenate (join), so postfixExp • x means concatenate the string currently in postfixExp and the character x—that is, follow the string in postfixExp with the character x.

```
for (each character ch in the infix expression)
{
    switch (ch)
    {
        case operand:        // Append operand to end of postfix expression—step 1
            postfixExp = postfixExp • ch
            break
        case '(':            // Save '(' on stack—step 2
            operatorStack.push(ch)
            break
        case operator:       // Process stack operators of greater precedence—step 3
            while (!operatorStack.isEmpty() and operatorStack.peek() is not a '(' and
                    precedence(ch) <= precedence(operatorStack.peek()))
            {
                Append operatorStack.peek() to the end of postfixExp
                operatorStack.pop()
            }
            operatorStack.push(ch) // Save the operator
            break
        case ')':                  // Pop stack until matching '('—step 4
            while (operatorStack.peek() is not a '(')
            {
                Append operatorStack.peek() to the end of postfixExp
                operatorStack.pop()
            }
            operatorStack.pop()    // Remove the open parenthesis
            break
    }
}
// Append to postfixExp the operators remaining in the stack—step 5
while (!operatorStack.isEmpty())
{
    Append operatorStack.peek() to the end of postfixExp
    operatorStack.pop()
}
```

A pseudocode algorithm that converts an infix expression to postfix form

Because this algorithm assumes that the given infix expression is syntactically correct, it can ignore the return values of the stack operations. Programming Problem 7 at the end of this chapter asks you to remove this assumption.

Note: Algorithms that evaluate an infix expression or transform one to postfix form must determine which operands apply to a given operator. Doing so allows for precedence and left-to-right association so that you can omit parentheses.

Question 6 Convert the infix expression $a\ /\ b\ *\ c$ to postfix form by using a stack. Be sure to account for left-to-right association. Show the status of the stack after each step.

Question 7 Explain the significance of the precedence tests in the infix-to-postfix conversion algorithm. Why is a $\geq$ test used rather than a $>$ test?

6.4   Using a Stack to Search a Flight Map

The previous chapter described the HPAir problem, whereby we searched an airline's flight map to see whether we could fly from some origin city to some destination city. At that time, we found a recursive solution to the problem. We now will solve the problem again using a stack instead of recursion. Doing so will bring to light the close relationship between stacks and recursion.

Let's recall some of the discussion about this problem from the previous chapter. Given HPAir's flight map shown in Figure 6-6, you can fly from city P to city Z by flying first to city W, then to city Y, and finally to city Z. We need to find this path by trying every possible sequence of flights until we either find a sequence that gets to the destination city or determine that no such sequence exists. You will see that the ADT stack is useful in organizing this search.

If we were to perform the search by hand, we could start at the origin city C_0 and select an arbitrary departing flight to a new city, C_1. If city C_1 happens to be the destination city, we are done; otherwise, we must try to fly from C_1 to the destination city. By repeating this strategy, we will encounter three possible outcomes, just as you saw in the previous chapter.

Possible outcomes of the exhaustive search strategy

1. You eventually reach the destination city.
2. You reach a city C from which there are no departing flights.
3. You go around in circles forever.

Even if a sequence of flights exists from the origin city to the destination city, we might not find it and instead reach outcome 2 or 3. Just as we did in the recursive solution, if we reached a city C from which there are no departing flights—that is outcome 2—we would *backtrack* to the city C' that we visited just before we visited city C. Once back at city C', we would select a flight to some city other than C. If there were no other flights out of city C', we would backtrack again—this time to the city that was visited just before city C'. To avoid outcome 3, we mark the cities as we visit them, just as we did in Chapter 5, and never visit a city more than once.

Use backtracking to recover from a wrong choice

For the algorithm to implement this strategy, it must maintain information about the order in which it visits the cities. First notice that when the algorithm backtracks from a city C, it must retreat to the city that it visited most recently before C. This observation suggests that you maintain the sequence of visited cities in a stack. That is, each time you decide to visit a city, you push its name onto the stack. For example, if you want to fly from city P to city Z in Figure 6-6, the algorithm might first choose to go from city P to city R and then on to city X. Parts a, b, and c of Figure 6-7 illustrate the stack for these flights. You select the next city to visit from those adjacent to the city on the top of the stack. When you need to backtrack from the city at the top of the stack (for example, because there are no flights out of city X), you simply pop a city from the stack, as shown in Figure 6-7d. After the pop, the city on the top of the stack—R—is the

Use a stack to organize an exhaustive search

FIGURE 6-6   A flight map

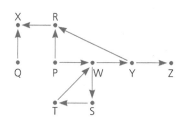

FIGURE 6-7   The stack of cities as you travel from *P* to *W*

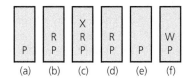

city on the current path that you visited most recently before *X*. It is not possible to fly out of city *R* to some city other than city *X,* so you backtrack once more, this time to city *P*, by popping the stack, as Figure 6-7e illustrates. Figure 6-7f shows the stack after the subsequent flight to city *W*.

The algorithm, as developed so far, is as follows.

```
cityStack = a new empty stack
cityStack.push(originCity)  //  Push origin city onto cityStack

while (a sequence of flights from the origin to the destination has not been found)
{
    if (you need to backtrack from the city on the top of the stack)
        cityStack.pop()
    else
    {
        Select a destination city C for a flight from the city on the top of the stack
        cityStack.push(C)
    }
}
```

Notice that, at any point in the algorithm, the contents of the stack correspond to the sequence of flights currently under consideration. The city on the top of the stack is the city you are visiting currently, directly "below" it is the city visited previously, and so forth down to the bottom city, which is the first city visited in the sequence—that is, the origin city. In other words, within the `while` loop,

> *The stack contains a directed path from the origin city at the bottom of the stack to the city at the top of the stack.*[3]

You can, therefore, always retrace your steps as far back through the sequence as needed.

Now consider the question of when to backtrack from the city on the top of the stack. You have already seen one case when backtracking is necessary. You must backtrack from the city on the top of the stack when there are no flights out of that city. Another time when you need to backtrack is related to the problem of going around in circles, described previously as the third possible outcome of the original strategy. You never want to visit a city that the search has already visited. As a consequence, you must backtrack from a city whenever there are no more unvisited cities to fly to. To see why, consider two cases:

Backtrack when there are no more unvisited cities

- If you have visited city *C* and it is still somewhere in the stack—that is, it is part of the sequence of cities that you are exploring currently—you do not want to visit *C* again.

---

[3] A statement such as this one is called a loop invariant. It is a condition that is true before and after each execution of an algorithm's loop. Invariants are discussed further in Appendix F.

Two reasons for not
visiting a city more
than once

Any sequence that goes from C through $C_1, C_2, \ldots, C_k$, back to C, and then to C' might just as well skip the intermediate cities and go from C directly to C'.

For example, suppose that the algorithm starts at P in Figure 6-6 and, in trying to find a path to Y, visits W, S, and T. There is now no reason for the algorithm to consider the flight from T to W because W is already in the stack. Any city you could fly to by going from W to S, from S to T, and then back to W—such as city Y—you could fly to directly from W without first going through S and T. Because you do not allow the algorithm to visit W a second time, it will backtrack from S and T to W and then go from W directly to Y. Figure 6-8 shows how the stack would appear if revisits were allowed and how it looks after backtracking when revisits are not allowed. Notice that backtracking to W is very different from visiting W for a second time.

- If you have visited city C, but it is no longer in the stack—because you backtracked from it and popped it from the stack—you do not want to visit C again. This situation is subtle; consider two cases that depend on why you backtracked from the city.

  If you backtracked from C because there were no flights out of it, then you certainly do not ever want to try going through C again. For example, if, starting at P in Figure 6-6, the algorithm goes to R and then to X, it will backtrack from X to R. At this point, although X is no longer in the stack, you certainly do not want to visit it again, because you know there are no flights out of X.

  Now suppose that you backtracked from city C because all cities adjacent to it had been visited. This situation implies that you have already tried all possible flights from C and have failed to find a way to get to the destination city. There is thus no reason to go to C again. For example, suppose that starting from P in Figure 6-6, the algorithm executes the following sequence: Visit R, visit X, backtrack to R (because there are no flights out of X), backtrack to P (because there are no more unvisited cities adjacent to R), visit W, visit Y. At this point, the stack contains P-W-Y with Y on top, as Figure 6-8b shows. You need to choose a flight out of Y. You do not want to fly from Y to R, because you have visited R already and tried all possible flights out of R.

  In both cases, visiting a city a second time does not gain you anything, and in fact, it may cause you to go around in circles.

FIGURE 6-8   The effect of revisits on the stack of cities

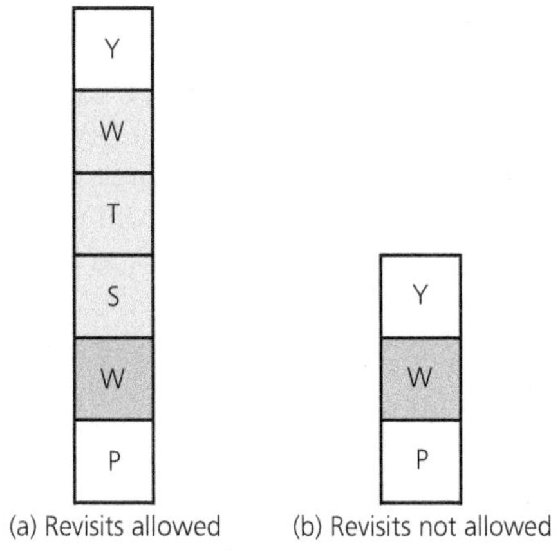

(a) Revisits allowed   (b) Revisits not allowed

To implement the rule of not visiting a city more than once, you simply mark a city when it has been visited. When choosing the next city to visit, you restrict consideration to unmarked cities adjacent to the city on the top of the stack. The algorithm thus becomes

Mark the visited cities

```
cityStack = a new empty stack
Clear marks on all cities

cityStack.push(originCity) // Push origin city onto the stack
Mark the origin as visited

while (a sequence of flights from the origin to the destination has not been found)
{
    // Loop invariant: The stack contains a directed path from the origin city at
    // the bottom of the stack to the city at the top of the stack
    if (no flights exist from the city on the top of the stack to unvisited cities)
        cityStack.pop()         // Backtrack
    else
    {
        Select an unvisited destination city C for a flight from the city on the top of the stack
        cityStack.push(C)
        Mark C as visited
    }
}
```

Next draft of the search algorithm

Finally, you need to refine the condition in the `while` statement. That is, you need to refine the algorithm's final determination of whether a path exists from the origin to the destination. The loop invariant, which states that the stack contains a directed path from the origin city to the city on the top of the stack, implies that the algorithm can reach an affirmative conclusion if the city at the top of the stack is the destination city. On the other hand, the algorithm can reach a negative conclusion only after it has exhausted all possibilities—that is, after the algorithm has backtracked to the origin and has no unvisited cities to fly to from the origin. At that point, the algorithm will pop the origin city from the stack and the stack will become empty.

With this refinement, the algorithm appears as follows:

```
// Searches for a sequence of flights from originCity to destinationCity
searchS(originCity: City, destinationCity: City): boolean
{
    cityStack = a new empty stack
    Clear marks on all cities

    cityStack.push(originCity) // Push origin onto the stack
    Mark the origin as visited

    while (!cityStack.isEmpty() and destinationCity is not at the top of the stack)
    {
        // Loop invariant: The stack contains a directed path from the origin city at
        // the bottom of the stack to the city at the top of the stack
        if (no flights exist from the city on the top of the stack to unvisited cities)
            cityStack.pop()         // Backtrack
        else
        {
            Select an unvisited destination city C for a flight from the city on the top of the stack
            cityStack.push(C)
            Mark C as visited
        }
    }
    if (cityStack.isEmpty())
        return false // No path exists
    else
        return true  // Path exists
}
```

The final version of the search algorithm

FIGURE 6-9   A trace of the search algorithm, given the flight map in Figure 6-6

Action	Reason	Contents of stack (top to bottom)
Push P	Initialize	P
Push R	Next unvisited adjacent city	R P
Push X	Next unvisited adjacent city	X R P
Pop X	No unvisited adjacent city	R P
Pop R	No unvisited adjacent city	P
Push W	Next unvisited adjacent city	W P
Push S	Next unvisited adjacent city	S W P
Push T	Next unvisited adjacent city	T S W P
Pop T	No unvisited adjacent city	S W P
Pop S	No unvisited adjacent city	W P
Push Y	Next unvisited adjacent city	Y W P
Push Z	Next unvisited adjacent city	Z Y W P

Notice that the algorithm does not specify the order of selection for the unvisited cities. It really does not matter what selection criteria the algorithm uses, because the choice will not affect the final outcome: Either a sequence of flights exists or it does not. The choice, however, will affect the specific flights that the algorithm considers. For example, suppose that the algorithm always flies to the alphabetically earliest unvisited city from the city on the top of the stack. Under this assumption, Figure 6-9 contains a trace of the algorithm's action, given the map in Figure 6-6, with *P* as the origin city and *Z* as the destination city. The algorithm terminates with success.

Recall from Chapter 5 the following operations that the search algorithm must perform on the flight map.

ADT flight map operations

```
// Marks a city as visited.
markVisited(aCity: City): void

// Clears marks on all cities.
unvisitAll(): void

// Returns the next unvisited city, if any, that is adjacent to a given city.
// Returns a sentinel value if no unvisited adjacent city was found.
getNextCity(fromCity: City): City

// Tests whether a sequence of flights exists between two cities.
isPath(originCity: City, destinationCity: City): boolean
```

Assuming that the class `Map` implements the ADT flight map and the class `Stack` implements the stack operations, the definition of `Map`'s method `isPath` is as follows and uses the `searchS` algorithm. As we mentioned in Chapter 5, `NO_CITY` is a `City` object that `Map` defines as a constant for `getNextCity` to return in case it cannot find an unvisited adjacent city.

C++ implementation of searchS

```
/** Tests whether a sequence of flights exists between two cities.
    Nonrecursive stack version.
 @pre  originCity and destinationCity both exist in the flight map.
 @post  Cities visited during the search are marked as visited
    in the flight map.
 @param originCity  The origin city.
 @param destinationCity  The destination city.
 @return  True if a sequence of flights exists from originCity
    to destinationCity; otherwise returns false. */
```

```cpp
bool Map::isPath(City originCity, City destinationCity)
{
   Stack cityStack;

   unvisitAll(); // Clear marks on all cities

   // Push origin city onto cityStack and mark it as visited
   cityStack.push(originCity);
   markVisited(originCity);

   City topCity = cityStack.peek();
   while (!cityStack.isEmpty() && (topCity != destinationCity))
   {
      // The stack contains a directed path from the origin city
      // at the bottom of the stack to the city at the top of the stack

      // Find an unvisited city adjacent to the city on the top of the stack
      City nextCity = getNextCity(topCity);

      if (nextCity == NO_CITY)
         cityStack.pop(); // No city found; backtrack
      else                // Visit city
      {
         cityStack.push(nextCity);
         markVisited(nextCity);
      }  // end if

      if (!cityStack.isEmpty())
         topCity = cityStack.peek();
   }  // end while

   return !cityStack.isEmpty();
}  // end isPath
```

Programming Problem 11 at the end of this chapter provides implementation details that will enable you to complete the solution to the HPAir problem.

Question 8 Trace the method isPath with the map in Figure 6-10 for the following requests. Show the state of the stack after each step.

   a. Fly from *A* to *B*.
   b. Fly from *A* to *D*.
   c. Fly from *C* to *G*.

FIGURE 6-10   Flight map for Checkpoint Question 8

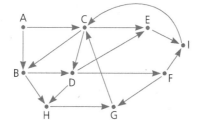

> **Note: The STL class `stack`**
>
> The Standard Template Library (STL) contains the container `stack`, which is a template class. However, some methods of this class have slightly different names than the ones we have used here. You can use the STL `stack` to implement the algorithms given in this chapter until we write our own implementations in the next chapter. Alternatively, you can use the class `OurStack`, as described in Programming Problem 1 at the end of this chapter. You can learn more about the STL in C++ Interlude 8.

6.5   The Relationship Between Stacks and Recursion

We have solved the HPAir problem twice, once in the previous chapter by using recursion and again in the previous section by using the ADT stack. We now want to look at the ways that these two approaches organize the search for a sequence of flights. You will see that the ADT stack has a hidden presence in the concept of recursion and, in fact, that stacks have an active role in most computer implementations of recursion.

Consider how the two search algorithms implement three key aspects of their common strategy.

A comparison of key aspects of two search algorithms

- **Visiting a new city.** The recursive algorithm `searchR` visits a new city *C* by making the call `searchR(C, destinationCity)`. The algorithm `searchS` visits city *C* by pushing *C* onto a stack. Notice that if you were to use the box trace to trace the execution of `searchR`, the call `searchR(C, destinationCity)` would generate a box in which the city *C* is associated with the parameter `originCity` of `searchR`.

  For example, Figure 6-11 shows both the state of the box trace for `searchR` and the stack for `searchS` at corresponding points of the search for a path from city *P* to city *Z* in Figure 6-6.

- **Backtracking.** Both search algorithms attempt to visit an unvisited city that is adjacent to the current city. Notice that this current city is the value associated with the parameter `originCity` in the deepest (rightmost) box of `searchR`'s box trace. Similarly, the current city is on the top of `searchS`'s stack. In Figure 6-11, this current city is *X*. If no unvisited cities are adjacent to the current city, the algorithms must backtrack to the previous city. The algorithm `searchR` backtracks by returning from the current recursive call. You represent this action in the box trace by crossing off the deepest box. The algorithm `searchS` backtracks by explicitly popping from its stack. For example, from the state depicted in Figure 6-11, both algorithms backtrack to city *R* and then to city *P*, as Figure 6-12 illustrates.

FIGURE 6-11   Visiting city *P*, then *R*, then *X*: (a) box trace versus (b) stack

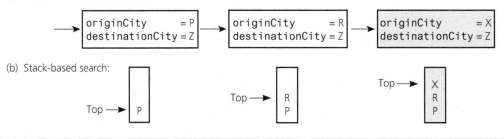

(a) Box trace of recursive search:

(b) Stack-based search:

FIGURE 6-12   Backtracking from city X to R to P: (a) box trace versus (b) stack

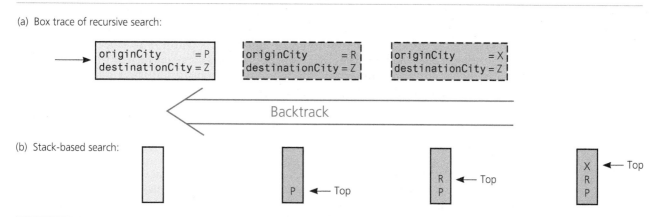

(a) Box trace of recursive search:

(b) Stack-based search:

- **Termination.** The search algorithms terminate either when they reach the destination city or when they exhaust all possibilities. All possibilities are exhausted when, after backtracking to the origin city, no unvisited adjacent cities remain. This situation occurs for searchR when all boxes have been crossed off in the box trace and a return occurs to the point of the original call to the algorithm. For searchS, no unvisited cities are adjacent to the origin when the stack becomes empty.

Thus, the two search algorithms really do perform the identical action. In fact, provided that they use the same rule to select an unvisited city—for example, traverse the current city's list of adjacent cities alphabetically—they will always visit the identical cities in the identical order. The similarities between the algorithms are far more than coincidence. In fact, it is always possible to capture the actions of a recursive function by using a stack.

An important context in which the close tie between stacks and recursion is explicitly utilized is a compiler's implementation of a recursive function. It is common for a compiler to use a stack to implement a recursive function in a manner that greatly resembles the box trace. When a recursive call to a function occurs, the implementation must remember certain information. This information consists essentially of the same local environment that you place in the boxes—values of both arguments and local variables and a reference to the point from which the recursive call was made.

> Typically, stacks are used to implement recursive functions

During execution, the compiled program must manage these boxes of information, or activation records, just as you must manage them on paper. As the HPAir example has indicated, the operations needed to manage the activation records are those that a stack provides. When a recursive call occurs, a new activation record is created and pushed onto a stack. This action corresponds to the creation of a new box at the deepest point in the sequence. When a return is made from a recursive call, the stack is popped, bringing the activation record that contains the appropriate local environment to the top of the stack. This action corresponds to crossing off the deepest box and following the arrow back to the preceding box. Although we have greatly simplified the process, most implementations of recursion are based on stacks of activation records.

> Each recursive call generates an activation record that is pushed onto a stack

You can use a similar strategy to implement a nonrecursive version of a recursive algorithm. You might need to recast a recursive algorithm into a nonrecursive form to make it more efficient, as mentioned in Chapter 2. The previous discussion should give you a taste of the techniques for removing recursion from a program. You will encounter recursion removal as a formal topic in more advanced courses, such as compiler construction.

> You can use stacks when implementing a nonrecursive version of a recursive algorithm

SUMMARY

1. The ADT stack operations have a last-in, first-out (LIFO) behavior.

2. Algorithms that operate on algebraic expressions are an important application of stacks. The LIFO nature of stacks is exactly what the algorithm that evaluates postfix expressions needs to organize the operands. Similarly, the algorithm that transforms infix expressions to postfix form uses a stack to organize the operators in accordance with precedence rules and left-to-right association.

3. You can use a stack to determine whether a sequence of flights exists between two cities. The stack keeps track of the sequence of visited cities and enables the search algorithm to backtrack easily. However, displaying the sequence of cities in their normal order from origin to destination is awkward, because the origin city is at the bottom of the stack and the destination is at the top.

4. A strong relationship between recursion and stacks exists. Most implementations of recursion maintain a stack of activation records in a manner that resembles the box trace.

5. The formal mathematical study of ADTs uses systems of axioms to specify the behavior of ADT operations.

EXERCISES

1. Write pseudocode statements that create a stack of the strings "Jamie", "Jane", and "Jill" in that order with "Jamie" at the top.

2. Given the stack created in Exercise 1, in what order will three pop operations remove the strings from the stack?

3. Suppose that you have a stack aStack and an empty auxiliary stack auxStack. Show how you can do each of the following tasks by using only the ADT stack operations.
   a. Display the contents of aStack in reverse order; that is, display the top last.
   b. Count the number of items in aStack, leaving aStack unchanged.
   c. Remove every occurrence of a specified item from aStack, leaving the order of the remaining items unchanged.

4. The diagram of a railroad switching system in Figure 6-13 is commonly used to illustrate the notion of a stack. Identify three stacks in the figure and show how they relate to one another. How can you use this system to construct any possible permutation of railroad cars?

FIGURE 6-13   Railroad switching system for Exercise 4

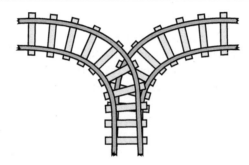

5. Suppose that the ADT stack included a method remove(n) that removes the topmost n entries from a stack. Specify this method by writing comments and a header. Consider the various ways that the method could behave when the stack does not contain at least n entries.

6. Section 6.1.1 described an algorithm that reads a string of characters, correcting mistakes along the way.
   a. For the following input line, trace the execution of the algorithm and show the contents of the stack at each step:

   abc←de←←fg←h

   b. Implement the read-and-correct algorithm as a C++ function, but make the stack local to the function instead of an argument. Let the function construct a string that contains the corrected input characters in forward order, and return it.

7. Revise the solution to the balanced-braces problem so that the expression can contain three types of delimiters: ( ), [ ], and { }. Thus, {ab(c[d])e} is valid, but {ab(c)) is not.

8. For each of the following strings, trace the execution of the language-recognition algorithm described in Section 6.2.2, and show the contents of the stack at each step.
   a. xy$xy   **b.** y$yx   **c.** xy$y
   d. xy$x   **e.** xx$xx

9. Write a pseudocode function that uses a stack to determine whether a string is in the language L, where
   a. $L = \{s : s$ contains equal numbers of A's and B's$\}$
   b. $L = \{s : s$ is of the form $A^n B^n$ for some $n \geq 1\}$
   c. $L = \{s\, s' : s$ is a string of characters, $s' = \text{reverse}\, (s)\, \}$
   Note: The following strings are not in any of the languages: The empty string and a string with an odd number of characters.

10. Implement in C++ the pseudocode functions that your wrote for Exercise 9.

11. Evaluate the following postfix expressions by using the algorithm given in this chapter. Show the status of the stack after each step of the algorithm. Assume the following values for the identifiers: $a = 7, b = 3,$ $c = 12, d = -5, e = 1.$
   a. $a\, b\, c + -$
   b. $a\, b\, c - d * +$
   c. $a\, b + c - d\, e * +$

12. Convert the following infix expressions to postfix form by using the algorithm given in this chapter. Show the status of the stack after each step of the algorithm.
   a. $a - b + c$ **b.** $a - (b / c * d)$
   c. $a / (b * c)$ **d.** $a / b / c - (d + e) * f$
   e. $(a + b) * c$ **f.** $a * (b / c / d) + e$
   g. $a - (b + c)$ **h.** $a - (b + c * d) / e$

13. Execute the HPAir algorithm with the map in Figure 6-10 (see Checkpoint Question 8) for the following requests. Show the state of the stack after each step.
   a. Fly from A to F.   **b.** Fly from A to G.
   c. Fly from F to H.   **d.** Fly from D to A.
   e. Fly from I to G.

14.   Section 5.1.2 of Chapter 5 defines "palindrome." Write a pseudocode algorithm that uses a stack to test whether a given string is a palindrome.

*15.   You can use the axioms for a stack to prove that the stack defined by the sequence of operations

> *Create an empty stack*
> *Push a 5*
> *Push a 7*
> *Push a 3*
> *Pop (the 3)*
> *Push a 9*
> *Push a 4*
> *Pop (the 4)*

which you can write as

```
(((((((Stack()).push(5)).push(7)).push(3)).pop()).push(9)).push(4)).pop()
```

is exactly the same as the stack defined by the sequence

> *Create an empty stack*
> *Push a 5*
> *Push a 7*
> *Push a 9*

which you can write as

```
(((Stack()).push(5)).push(7)).push(9)
```

Similarly, you can use the axioms to show that

```
(((((((Stack()).push(1)).push(2)).pop()).push(3)).pop()).pop()).isEmpty()
```

is true.

a. The following representation of a stack as a sequence of push operations without any pop operations is called a *canonical form*:

```
(...(Stack()).push()).push())...).push()
```

Prove that any stack is equal to a stack that is in canonical form.

b. Prove that the canonical form is unique. That is, a stack is equal to exactly one stack that is in canonical form.

c. Use the axioms to show formally that

```
((((((((((Stack()).push(6)).push(9)).pop()).pop()).push(2)).pop()).push(3)).
 push(1)).pop()).peek()
```

equals 3.

PROGRAMMING PROBLEMS

1. Using the class stack in the Standard Template Library, define and test the class OurStack that is derived from StackInterface, as given in Listing 6-1. The class stack has the following methods that you can use to define the methods for OurStack.

```
stack();                              // Default constructor
bool empty() const;                   // Tests whether the stack is empty
ItemType& top();                      // Returns a reference to the top of the stack
void push(const ItemType& newEntry);  // Adds newEntry to the top of the stack
void pop();                           // Removes the top of the stack
```

To access stack, use the following include statement:

```
#include <stack>
```

Whenever you need a stack for any of the following problems, use the class OurStack *that Programming Problem* 1 *asks you to write.*

2. Implement the solution to the expanded balanced-braces problem in Exercise 7.

3. Write a function that uses a stack to test whether a given string is a palindrome. Exercise 14 asked you to write an algorithm for such a function.

4. Section 6.2.2 describes a recognition algorithm for the language

   $L = \{s\$s' : s$ is a possibly empty string of characters other than $\$, s' = $ reverse$(s)\}$

   Implement this algorithm.

5. Design and implement a class of postfix calculators. Use the algorithm given in this chapter to evaluate postfix expressions as entered into the calculator. Use only the operators +, −, *, and /. Assume that the postfix expressions are syntactically correct.

6. Consider simple infix expressions that consist of single-digit operands; the operators +, −, *, and /; and parentheses. Assume that unary operators are illegal and that the expression contains no embedded spaces. Design and implement a class of infix calculators. Use the algorithms given in this chapter to evaluate infix expressions as entered into the calculator. You must first convert the infix expression to postfix form and then evaluate the resulting postfix expression.

7. The infix-to-postfix conversion algorithm described in this chapter assumes that the given infix expression is syntactically correct. Modify Programming Problem 6 without this assumption.

8. Repeat Programming Problem 6, but use the following algorithm to evaluate an infix expression infixExp. The algorithm uses two stacks: One stack opStack contains operators, and the other stack valStack contains values of operands and intermediate results. Note that the algorithm treats parentheses as operators with the lowest precedence.

```
for (each character ch in infixExp)
{
   switch (ch)
   {
      case ch is an operand, that is, a digit
         valStack.push(ch)
         break
      case ch is a '('
         opStack.push(ch)
         break
```

```
        case ch is an operator
            if (opStack.isEmpty())
                opStack.push(ch)
            else if (precedence(ch) > precedence(opStack.peek()))
                opStack.push(ch)
            else
            {
                while (!opStack.isEmpty() and
                        precedence(ch) <= precedence(opStack.peek())
                    performOperation()
                opStack.push(ch)
            }
            break
        case ch is a ')'
            while (opStack.peek() is not a '(')
                performOperation()
            opStack.pop()
            break
    }
}
while (!opStack.isEmpty())
    Execute
result = valStack.peek()
```

Note that `performOperation()` means:

```
operand2 = valStack.peek()
valStack.pop()
operand1 = valStack.peek()
valStack.pop()
op = opStack.peek()
opStack.pop()
result = operand1 op operand2
valStack.push(result)
```

Choose one of the following two approaches for your implementation:

- The operator stack `opStack` contains characters, but the operand stack `valStack` contains integers.
- The stack `opStack` contains integer codes that represent the operators, so both stacks contain integers.

9. The infix evaluation algorithm given in Programming Problem 8 assumes that the given infix expression is syntactically correct. Repeat Programming Problem 8 without this assumption.

10. Using stacks, write a nonrecursive version of the function `solveTowers`, as defined in Chapter 2.

11. Complete the solution to the HPAir problem. Three text files are input to the program, as follows:

`cityFile`	Each line contains the name of a city that HPAir serves. The names are in alphabetical order.
`flightFile`	Each line contains a pair of city names that represent the origin and destination of one of HPAir's flights.
`requestFile`	Each line contains a pair of city names that represent a request to fly from some origin to some destination.

You can make the following assumptions:

- Each city name contains at most 15 characters. Pairs of city names are separated by a comma.
- HPAir serves at most 20 cities.
- The input data is correct.

For example, the input files could appear as

```
cityFile:              Albuquerque
                       Chicago
                       San Diego

flightFile:            Chicago,        San Diego
                       Chicago,        Albuquerque
                       Albuquerque,    Chicago

requestFile:           Albuquerque,    San Diego
                       Albuquerque,    Paris
                       San Diego,      Chicago
```

For this input, the program should produce the following output:

```
Request is to fly from Albuquerque to San Diego.
HPAir flies from Albuquerque to San Diego.

Request is to fly from Albuquerque to Paris.
Sorry. HPAir does not serve Paris.

Request is to fly from San Diego to Chicago.
Sorry. HPAir does not fly from San Diego to Chicago.
```

Begin by implementing the ADT flight map as the C++ class FlightMap. Use the stack version of isPath. Because getNextCity is the primary operation that the search algorithm performs on the flight map, you should choose an implementation that will efficiently determine which cities are adjacent to a given city. If there are n cities numbered $1, 2, \ldots, n$, you can use n chains of linked nodes to represent the flight map. You place a node in chain i for city j if and only if there is a directed path from city i to city j. Such a data structure is called an adjacency list; Figure 6-14 illustrates an adjacency list for the flight map in Figure 6-6. Chapter 20 discusses adjacency lists further when it presents ways to represent graphs. At that time, you will learn why an adjacency list is a good choice for the present program.

To simplify reading the input text files, define a class that includes the following methods:

// Returns a name from the next line in a text file.
+getName(): string

// Returns a pair of two names from the next line in a text file.
+getNamePair(): Pair

12. In the implementation of the HPAir problem (see the previous programming problem), the search for the next unvisited city adjacent to a city i always starts at the beginning of the ith chain in the adjacency list. This approach is actually a bit inefficient, because once the search visits a city, the city can never become unvisited. Modify the program so that the search for the next city begins where the last search left off. That is, maintain an array of try-next pointers into the adjacency list.

FIGURE 6-14   Adjacency list for the flight map in Figure 6-6 for Programming Problem 11

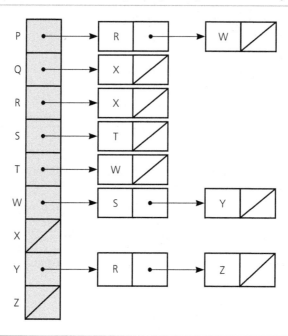

13. Implement an expanded version of the HPAir problem. In addition to the "from" and "to" cities, each line of input contains a flight number (an integer) and the cost of the flight (an integer). Modify the HPAir program so that it will produce a complete itinerary for each request, including the flight number of each flight, the cost of each flight, and the total cost of the trip.

For example, the input files could appear as

```
cityFile:        Albuquerque
                 Chicago
                 San Diego

flightFile:      Chicago,         San Diego    703  325
                 Chicago,         Albuquerque  111  250
                 Albuquerque,     Chicago      178  250

requestFile:     Albuquerque,     San Diego
                 Albuquerque,     Paris
                 San Diego,       Chicago
```

For this input, the program should produce the following output:

```
Request is to fly from Albuquerque to San Diego.
Flight #178 from Albuquerque to Chicago  Cost: $250
Flight #703 from Chicago to San Diego    Cost: $325
Total Cost .............. $575
Request is to fly from Albuquerque to Paris.
Sorry. HPAir does not serve Paris.
Request is to fly from San Diego to Chicago.
Sorry. HPAir does not fly from San Diego to Chicago.
```

When the nonrecursive isPath method finds a sequence of flights from the origin city to the destination city, its stack contains the corresponding path of cities. The stumbling block to reporting this path is that the cities appear in the stack in reverse order; that is, the destination city is at the top of the stack and the origin city is at the bottom. For example, if you use the program to find a path from city P to city Z in Figure 6-6, the final contents of the stack will be P-W-Y-Z with Z on top. You want to display the origin city P first, but it is at the bottom of the stack. If you restrict yourself to the stack operations, the only way that you can write the path in its correct order is first to reverse the stack by popping it onto a temporary stack and then to write the cities as you pop them off the temporary stack. Note that this approach requires that you process each city on the path twice. Programming Problem 11 in Chapter 7 will ask you to write a more efficient way of implementing this task.

14. What modifications to the previous programming problem are required to find a least-cost trip for each request? How can you incorporate time considerations into the problem?

15. (Finance) Imagine that you invest in the stock market. The value of each stock can vary daily, and it might differ from its original purchase cost. The net worth of your stock portfolio is the difference between its original cost and its current value.

   Design and implement a system to track your investments. Include algorithms that purchase stock, sell stock from your portfolio, and calculate the current net worth of the portfolio. When you sell a stock, you sell the most recently purchased one first.

   Hint: Each purchase you make consists of n shares of stock, each at a cost of d dollars. You can place each purchase on a stack. If only a portion of a particular purchase is sold, remove the purchase entry from the stack, modify it to reflect the remaining shares, and place it back onto the stack.

16. (Gaming) Consider the system of caves that Programming Problem 8 in Chapter 1 describes. Suppose that you can enter this system through only one cave and exit the system through only a different cave. Now imagine that you wake up in a cave somewhere within this system of caves. A sign indicates that an exit exists within five caves from your present location. Modify the HPAir search algorithm to find the exit.

17. (E-commerce) Consider a company that maintains an inventory of one kind of fitness tracker, whose costs can vary daily. The value of an item in the inventory is its current cost, which might differ from its original purchase cost. The selling price of a fitness tracker is 120% of its current cost. The company sells the most recently purchased trackers first. The current net worth of the company is the difference between the original cost and the current selling price of its entire inventory.

   Design and implement an inventory system for this company. Include algorithms that purchase items for the inventory, sell items from the inventory, and calculate the current net worth of the company.

   Hint: Each purchase made by the company consists of n fitness trackers, each at a cost of d dollars. You can place each purchase on a stack. If only a portion of a purchase is sold, remove the purchase entry from the stack, modify it to reflect the remaining inventory, and place it back onto the stack.

Exceptions

Contents

Prerequisites

C++ Interlude 1   C++ Classes

Exceptions provide a mechanism in C++ and other programming languages for interrupting program execution when errors, unusual circumstances, or other events occur. An **exception** is an object that signals the rest of the program that something unexpected has happened. Our code can react appropriately to the exception based on its type and what the exception can tell us via its methods. We **handle** the exception when we detect and react to it.

Some exceptions indicate mistakes in your code. By correcting those mistakes, you avoid the exceptions and no longer have to worry about them. Your final code gives no indication that an exception could occur. Furthermore, if your code is entirely correct, an exception will not occur. On the other hand, you can intentionally cause an exception. In fact, the programmers who wrote the code for the C++ Standard Library did so. At the very least, we need to know about exceptions so we can use the methods in the Standard Library.

What should we do when an exception occurs? Should we ever intentionally cause an exception in our own programs, and if so, how would we do so? These are some of the questions that this interlude will answer. This knowledge will be particularly important when we implement the ADT stack in the next chapter.

C3.1 Background

It would be great if every time a method was called, its preconditions were met. As you have seen, that does not always happen. The client could ask a method to remove an item from a container, but the container might be empty. How do we deal with this unusual or exceptional condition? In our implementations so far, a method returns false to indicate that it is unable to perform its task. This value tells the client that some precondition was not met, or that the method has failed for some other reason. It is then the client's responsibility to check the return value to ensure that the method completed its task before continuing.

Sometimes it is not possible for a method to return a boolean value when an unusual situation prevents it from completing its task. For example, the ADT stack's method peek returns a copy of the top item on the stack. Its prototype is

```
virtual ItemType peek() const = 0;
```

What should this method do if the stack is empty? Returning a boolean value would be possible only if the stack contained boolean values, that is, if ItemType was of type bool. Regardless of the type of data in the stack, the return value will indicate a problem only if it is a special value not contained in the stack. We need a consistent mechanism to let the client know that the method could not perform its task—one that does not depend on the type of data stored in the stack. Before we get into the details of such mechanisms, let's look at another example.

C3.1.1 A Problem to Solve

Recall from the previous C++ Interludes the video game that we are creating for our friend. Our next task is to create a function that searches for a given string in a number of boxes. The function has three parameters: an array of PlainBox<std::string> objects, an integer that represents the number of PlainBox objects in the array, and the string to be located in each box. The function will return a copy[1] of the box that contains the string. As a precondition, the function assumes that the given string is in one of the boxes. Listing C3-1 shows our first attempt at this function.

LISTING C3-1 First try at the function findBox

```
1   PlainBox<std::string> findBox(PlainBox<std::string> boxes[], int size,
2                                 std::string target)
3   {
4       int index = 0;
5       bool found = false;
6       while (!found && (index < size))
7       {
8           found = (target == boxes[index].getItem());
9           if (!found)
10              index++; // Look at next entry
11      } // end while
12      return boxes[index];
13  } // end findBox
```

---

[1] Recall that the return statement returns a copy of its argument.

This version of `findBox` meets the basic requirements: It searches the array of boxes and returns the box containing the target string. We encounter a problem if a box containing the target string is not in the array, that is, if the function's precondition is not satisfied. If the target is not found, the function's `while` loop ends when `index` is equal to `size`, which is the number of entries in the array. The function would then return `boxes[size]`, which is undefined. Problems will occur when the client tries to use this "box."

We can repair our code by testing `found` to make sure we found the target before returning a box from the array. Using a simple `if` statement is insufficient, as we still would have the problem of what to return when the target is not found. The next section gives one way to fix our code.

C3.2 Assertions

Chapter 3 and Appendix B define an assertion as a statement of truth about some aspect of a program's logic. You can express an assertion either as a comment or by using the C++ function `assert`. By using `assert`, you can make assertions about variables and objects in a program. Such assertions are in the form of a boolean expression that should be true at a specific point in the program. If the assertion is false, the `assert` function halts execution of the program. Assertions can be used to validate method preconditions before trying to execute the body of a function or method.

To use `assert` in a program, you first must include its header file:

```
#include <cassert>
```

To call the `assert` function, you provide a boolean condition as its argument:

```
assert(someBooleanCondition);
```

When program execution reaches this statement, the boolean condition—that is, the assertion—is tested. If the assertion is true, the program continues to execute normally. If the assertion is false, the program halts and an error message is displayed.

The `assert` statement is an easy way to verify a method's preconditions or postconditions. For example, when implementing the stack method `peek`, we could execute

```
assert(!isEmpty());
```

before trying to return the top of the stack.

Our `findBox` function can test whether the box was found before returning `boxes[index]` by calling `assert`:

```
assert(found);
```

If the target is not found, the assertion is false and the program halts. This prevents the program from trying to use a box that does not exist. Listing C3-2 shows the revised `findBox` function using assertions.

Use an assert statement to test a precondition or postcondition

 Note: The `assert` function is a debugging tool, not a substitute for the `if` statement.

LISTING C3-2 **Revised findBox function with assertions**

```
1   PlainBox<std::string> findBox(PlainBox<std::string> boxes[], int size,
2                                    std::string target)
3   {
4      int index = 0;
5      bool found = false;
6      while (!found && (index < size))
7      {
8         found = (target == boxes[index].getItem());
9         if (!found)
10           index++;    // Look at next entry
11      } // end while
12      assert(found);    // Verify that there is a box to return
13      return boxes[index];
14   } // end findBox
```

Assertions are good to use when you are testing and debugging your program. They can prevent the execution of any function or method if the preconditions have not been met. Halting your program as soon as a problematic condition becomes evident is a good debugging technique that narrows the focus of your search for errors.

As useful as they are, assertions may not be the best solution for a final shipping program. A violation of a function's preconditions may be a simple mistake that the client can fix. Such a situation does not warrant terminating program execution. We need another way to let the client know that an error or unusual condition has occurred and permit it to fix or handle the situation. We should use exceptions here.

 Programming Tip: A statement of truth about some aspect of a program's logic is known as an assertion. You can express an assertion either as a comment or by using the assert function. By including assertions in your program, you facilitate the debugging process.

C3.3 Throwing Exceptions

VideoNote
C++ exceptions

The examples we've looked at in this C++ Interlude have a common problem—how to let the client know that an error, unusual circumstance, or event occurred during execution. The two solutions presented so far—returning a boolean value or using assert to halt the program—are vastly different techniques.

Returning a boolean value requires that the client check the return value of the function to see whether the function was successful. We have no way to force the client to do so. If the client fails to check the return value, execution could continue even though the function did not complete its task. Even if the client checks the return value and finds that the function was unsuccessful, the client has no information about why the function failed. The client knows only that the function failed.

A function that uses assertions can alleviate the need for the client to check whether it completed successfully. With assertions, the program halts when there is an error, and the client cannot perform any further tasks. For an error that either is unimportant to the client's goals or is simple for the client to fix, assertions are an extreme solution.

However, an alternate way of communicating or returning information to a function's client is to **throw an exception**. A thrown exception bypasses normal execution, and control immediately returns to the client. The exception can contain information about the error or unusual condition that helps the client resolve the issue and possibly try the function again.

You can throw an exception by executing a `throw` statement with the following form:

`throw` *ExceptionClass* (*stringArgument*) ;

Here *ExceptionClass* is the type of exception you want to throw, and *stringArgument* is an argument to the constructor of *ExceptionClass* that provides a more detailed description of what may have caused the exception. When a `throw` statement executes, an object of type *ExceptionClass* is created, the exception is thrown and propagated back to the point where the function was called, and the statements in the function that follow the `throw` statement do not execute.

> Use a `throw` statement to throw an exception

C++ has two families of exceptions that a function can throw. You can select one of these or derive a class of your own. Although the exception class in a `throw` statement does not need to be derived from a standard C++ exception class, it is a good programming practice to do so. Figure C3-1 shows the family of exception classes provided by C++.

FIGURE C3-1   Hierarchy of C++ exception classes

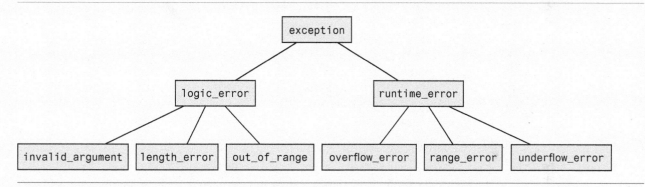

Exceptions derived from `runtime_error` or one of its derived classes are thrown by errors that are detectable only at runtime, such as division by zero or numeric overflow. If such an exception is thrown, the program will halt, just as it will when an assertion fails. Unlike assertions, however, when a `runtime_error` exception is thrown, the exception can contain a message that is displayed to the user giving details about the error and the reason the program halted.

Classes derived from the `logic_error` exception class represent errors in the logic of the program, such as an unmet precondition or the failure to satisfy an invariant or assertion, that you could detect before the program executes. In our `findBox` example, if we wanted to throw an exception to indicate the failure to find the target string, we could write:

```
if (!found)
    throw std::logic_error("Target not found in a box!");
```

When we throw exceptions, we first test for an error or unusual condition using an `if` statement. Then, if one occurred, we use the `throw` statement to throw an exception containing a message to our client.

To restrict the exceptions that a function or method can throw, you include a `throw` clause in its header. This also lets the client know that the function might throw an exception. A `throw` clause consists of the keyword throw followed by a list of exception types separated by commas and enclosed within parentheses. For example, here is the prototype of our findBox function with a throw clause added:

```
PlainBox<std::string> findBox(PlainBox<std::string> boxes[], int size,
                              std::string target) throw(std::logic_error);
```

Listing C3-3 shows the complete findBox function that throws a logic_error exception. Later in this interlude, we will derive an exception class to handle this specific error. First, however, we will look at how a client can deal with a thrown exception.

LISTING C3-3 Revised findBox function that throws an exception

```
1   PlainBox<std::string> findBox(PlainBox<std::string> boxes[], int size,
2                                 std::string target) throw(std::logic_error)
3   {
4      int index = 0;
5      bool found = false;
6      while (!found && (index < size))
7      {
8         found = (target == boxes[index].getItem());
9         if (!found)
10           index++; // Look at next entry
11     } // end while
12
13     if (!found)
14        throw std::logic_error("Target not found in a box!");
15     return boxes[index];
16  } // end findBox
```

Programming Tip: Including a throw clause in a function specification ensures that the function can throw only those exceptions. An attempt by the function to throw any other exception will result in a runtime error. Omitting a throw clause allows a function to throw any exception.

Note: Standard exceptions

The header <stdexcept> defines several standard exceptions that can be thrown by the functions defined in the C++ Standard Library. This header contains two kinds of exceptions—logic exceptions and runtime exceptions:

- Logic exceptions

logic_error	An error occurred in the program's internal logic
invalid_argument	An invalid argument was used in a function call
length_error	An attempt was made to create an object that was too large
out_of_range	An attempt was made to access an element outside the range of a container

- Runtime exceptions

`runtime_error`	An error occurred that is detectable only at runtime
`overflow_error`	An arithmetic overflow has occurred
`range_error`	A computation's result could not be represented by the desired type
`underflow_error`	An arithmetic underflow has occurred

Note: The `javadoc` tag `@throws`

A `javadoc` comment that precedes a method's header should contain a separate line for each exception the method might throw. Each of these lines begins with the tag `@throws`, and they should be ordered alphabetically by the names of the exceptions.

Note: **Whether to throw an exception**

- If several resolutions to an abnormal occurrence are possible, and you want the client to choose one, you should throw an exception.
- If you detect that a programmer has used your method incorrectly, you can throw a runtime exception. Recall that this action will halt program execution.
- If you can resolve the unusual situation in a reasonable manner, your code should do so instead of throwing an exception.

Security Note: A constructor should throw an exception if it cannot complete its execution successfully. In this way, a client will be unable to use a malformed object. Before throwing the exception, however, the constructor must avoid a memory leak by returning any memory it has allocated from the free store.

C3.4 Handling Exceptions

In the previous section, we looked at how you can cause an exception when an error or unusual condition occurs. In this section, we look at exceptions from the point of view of a client and present how to react to or **handle** an exception.

Note: You cannot handle an exception of the standard class `runtime_error` or any of its descendant classes. You can handle only exceptions of the class `logic_error` and its derived classes.

Note: You should not throw a runtime exception simply so that the client does not have to handle it.

To handle an exception, you write code that consists of two pieces. The first piece, the **try block**, contains the statements that might cause or throw an exception. The second piece consists of one or more **catch blocks** that must immediately follow the try block. Each catch block contains code to react to or **catch** a particular type of exception.

Here is the general syntax for a try block followed by one catch block:

```
try
{
    < statement(s) that might throw an exception >
}
catch (ExceptionClass   identifier)
{
    < statement(s) that react to an exception of type ExceptionClass >
}
```

The statements within the try block execute just as they would if the block was not there. If no exception occurs and the try block completes, execution continues with the statement after the last catch block. However, if a statement within a try block causes an exception of the type specified in the catch block, the remainder of the try block is abandoned, and execution immediately transfers to the statements in the catch block. The exception now has been caught. The statements in the catch block execute, and upon their completion, execution continues with the statement immediately after the last catch block.

Note: If an exception has no applicable catch block, the execution of the method or function ends, and the exception propagates to the client of this method or function. If the client does not handle the exception, the exception propagates to the code that invoked the client, and so on. If no method or function handles the exception, the program terminates abnormally.

Note: If an exception occurs in the middle of a try block, the destructors of all objects local to that try block are called. This ensures that all resources allocated in that block are released, even if the block is not completely executed. In general, you should not use the new operator inside of a try block. An exception will complicate knowing whether memory was allocated and, if it was, whether it was deallocated.

Security Note: An important implementation detail of a try block is that it should contain as few statements as possible—ideally, only the statement that could throw an exception. Keeping the try block small reduces the risk of either not executing important code or not deallocating allocated memory if an exception is thrown.

The syntax for a catch block resembles that of a function definition. It specifies both the type of exception the catch block will handle and an identifier. This identifier—called a **catch block parameter**—provides a name for the caught exception that can be used within the catch block. Although a catch block is not a function, throwing an exception is like calling a catch block as if it were a function. The catch block parameter represents the actual exception object provided by the throw statement.

The steps taken in the catch block vary from situation to situation and can be as simple as either doing nothing or displaying an error message, or as elaborate as tasks that update variables and retry the function that threw the exception. Every exception class in the C++ Standard

Library defines the accessor method `what`, which returns a descriptive string created when the exception is thrown. The body of the `catch` block can display this string to provide an indication of the nature of the exception.

Note: A `catch` block whose parameter has the type *ExceptionClass* can catch exceptions of the class *ExceptionClass* and any of *ExceptionClass*'s descendant classes. Specifying a `catch` block with a parameter of type `exception` catches any exception that can be thrown.

Security Note: When a function or method has a `try` block that allocates memory from the free store, the corresponding `catch` block must deallocate that memory. This is especially important if the `try` block calls a constructor. For example, suppose the `try` block contains the statement

```
SomeClass* myPtr = new SomeClass();
```

and `SomeClass`'s default constructor fails. We would have memory allocated for the new object, but it would not be initialized properly. Since constructors should throw an exception if they are unsuccessful, execution would continue with the `try` block's corresponding `catch` block. It is here that the newly allocated memory must be deallocated.

Listing C3-4 shows sample code that calls our `findBox` function and catches any `logic_error` exception thrown. The `catch` block displays a message to the user that something unusual has happened and creates a `PlainBox` object for `foundBox` so that the statement following the `catch` block executes correctly.

LISTING C3-4   Trying the function `findBox`

```
1   // Create and initialize an array of boxes
2   PlainBox<std::string> myBoxes[5];              // Array of PlainBox objects
3   myBoxes[0] = PlainBox<std::string>("ring");
4   myBoxes[1] = PlainBox<std::string>("hat");
5   myBoxes[2] = PlainBox<std::string>("shirt");
6   myBoxes[3] = PlainBox<std::string>("sock");
7   myBoxes[4] = PlainBox<std::string>("shoe");
8   PlainBox<std::string> foundBox;
9
10  // Try to find a box containing glasses
11  try
12  {
13      foundBox = findBox(myBoxes, 5, "glasses");
14  }
15  catch(std::logic_error logErr)
16  {
```

(continues)

```
17      std::cout << logErr.what() << std::endl;  // Display error message
18      foundBox = PlainBox<std::string>("nothing"); // Fix problem
19   }  // end try-catch
20   // Because we catch the exception and fix the problem, the following
21   // statement should work even if the target is not found
22   std::cout << foundBox.getItem() << std::endl;
```

Output

```
Target not found in a box!
nothing
```

C3.4.1 Multiple catch Blocks

A try block might cause more than one type of exception, even if it contains only one statement. Thus, a try block can have many catch blocks associated with it. When more than one catch block follows a try block, the first one—in order of appearance—whose parameter matches the thrown exception in type executes. Thus, the catch blocks must be ordered so that the most specific exception classes are caught before the more general exception classes. For example, the following catch blocks are in the wrong order:

```
std::string str = "Sarah";
try
{
   str.substr(99, 1);
}
catch (std::exception e)                 // WRONG ORDER!!
{
   std::cout << "Something else was caught" << std::endl;
}
catch (std::out_of_range e)
{
   std::cout << "out_of_range exception caught" << std::endl;
}  // end try-catch
```

The compiler may issue a warning message similar to the following one:

```
'class std::out_of_range' : is caught by base class ('class exception') on line n
```

This warning means that any out_of_range exception thrown in the try block will be caught by the first catch block—with the parameter of type exception—so the second catch block will never be reached. To get the code to compile without warnings, you must interchange the two catch blocks.

 Security Note: Arrange catch blocks in order of specificity, catching the most specific one first. Since all exception classes have exception as an ancestor, try to avoid using exception in a catch block. If you must catch exceptions of type exception, do so in the last catch block.

C3.4.2 Uncaught Exceptions

Let's see what happens when an exception is thrown but not caught. The program in Listing C3-5 encodes a string by doing a simple substitution. It replaces each letter in a string with the character that appears three positions later in the alphabet. When it reaches the end of the alphabet, it wraps around to the beginning. For example, *a* is replaced by *d, b* is replaced by *e,* and *w* is replaced by *z*. At this point, it gets replacement letters by wrapping around to the beginning of the alphabet. Thus, *x* is replaced by *a, y* is replaced by *b*, and *z* is replaced by *c*.

LISTING C3-5 A program with an uncaught exception

```cpp
1   #include <iostream>
2   #include <string>
3
4   // Encodes the character at index i of the string str.
5   void encodeChar(int i, std::string& str)
6   {
7      int base = static_cast<int>('a');
8      if (isupper(str[i]))
9         base = int('A');
10
11     char newChar = (static_cast<int>(str[i]) - base + 3) % 26 + base;
12     str.replace(i, 1, 1, newChar); // Method replace can throw exception
13  } // end encodeChar
14
15  // Encodes numChar characters within a string.
16  void encodeString(int numChar, std::string& str)
17  {
18     for (int j = numChar - 1; j >= 0; j--)
19        encodeChar(j, str);
20  } // end encodeString
21
22  int main()
23  {
24     std::string str1 = "Sarah";
25     encodeString(99, str1);
26     return 0;
27  } // end main
```

Figure C3-2 shows the flow of control when an exception occurs in this code. When the function encodeChar makes the call str.replace(99, 1, 1, newChar) in an attempt to access the 99th character in str, an out_of_range exception is thrown. Because encodeChar does not handle the exception, the function terminates, and the exception propagates back to encodeString at the point where encodeChar was called. The function encodeString also does not handle the exception, so it too terminates and the exception propagates back to main. Because main is the main function of the program, it does not handle the exception, and the program execution terminates abnormally with an error message.

FIGURE C3-2 Flow of control for an uncaught exception

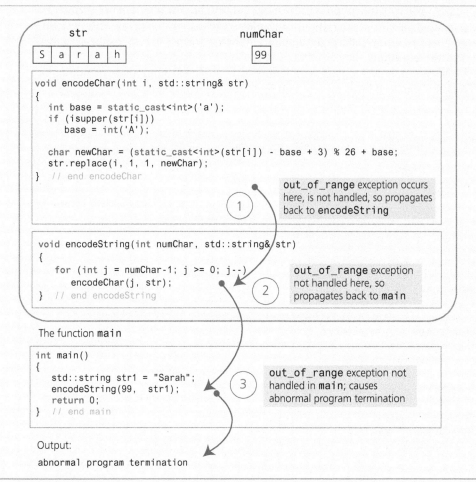

The function **main**

Output:

```
abnormal program termination
```

Security Note: Your code should handle any possible exception

If the function `encodeString` allocated memory on the free store before it called the function `encodeChar`, and if `encodeChar` then threw an exception, a memory leak would occur because `encodeString` does not catch the exception. Thus, it has no opportunity to deallocate that memory. This situation is an example of the importance of handling all known exceptions.

This code contains no indication that the function `encodeChar` could throw the exception `out_of_range`. However, the documentation of `encodeChar` should indicate any exceptions it might throw. Thus, when documenting a function or method, you should also include any possible exceptions that could occur.

C3.4.3 Where to Handle Exceptions

The previous section shows what happens when an `out_of_range` exception occurs, but is not caught, during the execution of the program in Listing C3-5. We can catch this exception at any point in the sequence of function calls. For example, we could rewrite the function `encodeChar` as follows to catch the exception.

```cpp
void encodeChar(int i, std::string& str)
{
    int base = static_cast<int>('a');
    if (isupper(str[i]))
        base = int('A');
    char newChar = (static_cast<int>(str[i]) - base + 3) % 26 + base;
    try
    {
        str.replace(i, 1, 1, newChar);
    }
    catch (std::out_of_range e)
    {
        std::cout << "No character at position " << i << std::endl;
    } // end try-catch
} // end encodeChar
```

The call `encodeString(99, str)` within `main` causes 99 calls to `encodeChar`, and hence the exception is thrown 98 – `str.length()` times. The following output from `encodeChar` is the result.

```
No character at position 99
No character at position 98
No character at position 97
. . .
```

When the exception was not handled, the program terminated the first time the exception occurred. Handling the exception allows the code to continue execution.

Although the `out_of_range` exception is thrown in the function `encodeChar`, that is not necessarily the best place to handle the exception. For example, if the client had made the call `encodeString(10000, str)`, the message printed by `encodeChar` would have appeared 9999 minus `str.length()` times! In this case, it makes more sense for the `try` and `catch` blocks to appear in the function `encodeString` and not in `encodeChar`, as follows:

```cpp
void encodeString(int numChar, std::string& str)
{
    try
    {
        for (int i = numChar - 1; i >= 0; i--)
            encodeChar(i, str);
    }
    catch (std::out_of_range e)
    {
        std::cout << "The string does not contain " << numChar;
        std::cout << " characters." << std::endl;
        std::cout << e.what() << std::endl;
    } // end try-catch
} // end encodeString
```

Now when `encodeChar` throws the exception `out_of_range`, the exception propagates back to the function `encodeString`, which ends execution of the statements in the `try` block and executes the statements in the `catch` block. The expression `e.what()` invokes the method `what` for the exception e, and so it represents a string that describes the exception. For example, the following output would be displayed after the call `encodeString(99, str)`:

```
The string does not contain 99 characters.
invalid string position
```

The message is printed only once, since the `for` loop is inside the `try` block, which is abandoned when the exception occurs. If the `try`/`catch` blocks had been placed inside the `for` loop, `encodeChar` would be called—and therefore the exception would be thrown and handled—at each iteration of the loop. The result would be multiple copies of the message.

 Programming Tip: When an exception can occur within a loop, you must decide whether to place a `try` block within the body of the loop—in which case an exception will be caught each time the loop cycles (as in the first example)—or place the entire loop within a `try` block—in which case the exception would be caught only once (as in the second example). Neither choice is better than the other, but if you make the wrong choice, the client might not get the best information to resolve the exception.

 Note: Sometimes a `catch` block will intentionally terminate program execution. When the block does not do so, but rather completes its execution, any statements that appear after the last `catch` block execute next.

C3.5 Programmer-Defined Exception Classes

You may find that the C++ Standard Library has an exception class already defined that suits the exception needs of your program. You may also want to define your own exception class. Usually, the C++ exception class `exception`, or one of its derived classes, is the base class for programmer-defined exception classes. Adhering to this practice provides a standardized interface for working with exceptions.

An exception class typically consists of a constructor that has a string parameter. For example, you can define the class `TargetNotFoundException` as

```cpp
#include <stdexcept>
#include <string>
class TargetNotFoundException: public std::exception
{
public :
   TargetNotFoundException(const std::string& message = "")
                     : std::exception("Target not found: " + message)
   {
   } // end constructor
}; // end TargetNotFoundException
```

The constructor provides a way for a `throw` statement to identify the condition that caused the exception. For example, the statement

```cpp
throw TargetNotFoundException(target + " not found in a box!");
```

invokes the constructor of `TargetNotFoundException`. The message given to the constructor is returned by the method `what` that is inherited from the class `exception`. Thus, a `catch` block, such as the following one, can access the message:

```
catch(TargetNotFoundException except)
{
    std::cout << except.what() << std::endl;
}
```

If `target` has the value `"glasses"` when this block executes, the output is

```
Target not found: glasses not found in a box!
```

While the string message is helpful, sometimes we want to return additional information to the client to help resolve the problem. We could add a private data field to our exception class to store additional error details. A second parameter in the constructor to receive an initial value for those details, as well as a public accessor method so that the client can retrieve them, are also needed. When a method throws this exception, it would call the constructor and send it the extra data and the message as its two arguments.

Programming Tip: Using exceptions

To throw an exception in a function:

- Determine what errors, preconditions, postconditions, and unusual conditions you must check and where they should be checked, so your function can correctly perform its task. Usually this is done with an `if` statement.
- If an error condition has occurred, throw an exception using the `throw` statement. As an argument to the exception class constructor, pass a string description of the reason for the error.
- Add a `throw` clause to the function header indicating the exceptions thrown by the function.
- Derive a custom exception class to better identify the conditions that caused the error. Although doing so is optional, it is desirable.

To handle an exception or use a method or function that could throw an exception:

- Place the statement that might throw an exception in a `try` block. The fewer statements in the `try` block the better. Do not use `new` to create an object in a `try` block, unless you have a corresponding `delete` in the `catch` block to deallocate the object.
- After the `try` block, place `catch` blocks for each type of exception that can be thrown by the statements in the `try` block. Place the `catch` blocks in order from the most specific exception classes to the more general exception classes.

Implementations of the ADT Stack

Contents

Prerequisites

This chapter implements the ADT stack using the techniques we described in Chapters 3 and 4 for the ADT bag. We first will use an array and then a chain of linked nodes to store the stack's entries. You should be happy to discover the simplicity and efficiency of these implementations. We then will modify these implementations to use exceptions as a way for a method to signal an unusual occurrence, such as an attempt to get an entry from an empty stack.

7.1   An Array-Based Implementation

Figure 7-1a shows a sketch of an array that contains the entries in a stack. Where in the array should the top entry be? Since entries are added or removed at the top of the stack, we can avoid shifting the current entries if we anchor the bottom of the stack at index 0 and track the location of the stack's top using an index top. Then if items is the array and items[top] is the top entry, items and top can be the private data members of our class of stacks. Figure 7-1b illustrates these details. Notice that the top of the stack in this figure is at index 2. We can either add a new entry at index[3] and then increment top or remove the top entry in index[2] by decrementing top to 1.

Our class will have a default constructor to initialize the private data members items and top. Moreover, since we plan to store a stack's entries in statically allocated memory, the compiler-generated destructor and copy constructor will be sufficient. If, on the other hand, we were to use a dynamically allocated array, we would have to define a destructor and a copy constructor.

Listing 7-1 shows the header file for an array-based implementation of the ADT stack. Comments describing the methods are in Listing 6-1 of Chapter 6.

FIGURE 7-1   Using an array to store a stack's entries

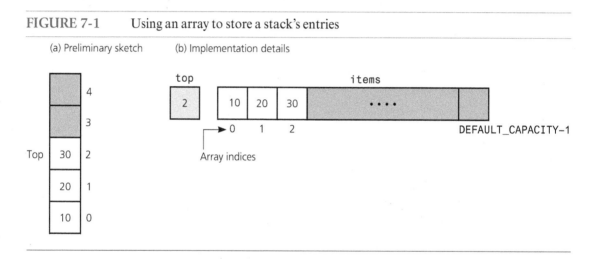

LISTING 7-1   The header file for an array-based stack

```cpp
/** ADT stack: Array-based implementation.
 @file ArrayStack.h */

#ifndef ARRAY_STACK_
#define ARRAY_STACK_

#include "StackInterface.h"

template<class ItemType>
class ArrayStack : public StackInterface<ItemType>
{
private:
   static const int DEFAULT_CAPACITY = maximum-size-of-stack;
   ItemType items[DEFAULT_CAPACITY]; // Array of stack items
   int      top;                     // Index to top of stack
```

```
16   public:
17      ArrayStack();                        // Default constructor
18      bool isEmpty() const;
19      bool push(const ItemType& newEntry);
20      bool pop();
21      ItemType peek() const;
22   }; // end ArrayStack
23
24   #include "ArrayStack.cpp"
25   #endif
```

The implementations of the methods that the previous header file declares are given in Listing 7-2. These definitions are straightforward, but notice that the method peek uses assert to enforce its precondition that the stack contain at least one entry. Later in this chapter, we will improve peek by revising it to throw an exception if the client calls it when the stack is empty.

LISTING 7-2   The implementation file for an array-based stack

```
1    /** @file ArrayStack.cpp */
2
3    #include <cassert>                // For assert
4    #include "ArrayStack.h"           // Header file
5
6    template<class ItemType>
7    ArrayStack<ItemType>::ArrayStack() : top(-1)
8    {
9    }  // end default constructor
10
11   // Copy constructor and destructor are supplied by the compiler
12
13   template<class ItemType>
14   bool ArrayStack<ItemType>::isEmpty() const
15   {
16      return top < 0;
17   }  // end isEmpty
18
19   template<class ItemType>
20   bool ArrayStack<ItemType>::push(const ItemType& newEntry)
21   {
22      bool result = false;
23      if (top < DEFAULT_CAPACITY - 1) // Does stack have room for newEntry?
24      {
25         top++;
26         items[top] = newEntry;
27         result = true;
28      }  // end if
29
30      return result;
31   }  // end push
```

(continues)

```
32    template<class ItemType>
33    bool ArrayStack<ItemType>::pop()
34    {
35       bool result = false;
36       if (!isEmpty())
37       {
38          top--;
39          result = true;
40       } // end if
41
42       return result;
43    } // end pop
44
45    template<class ItemType>
46    ItemType ArrayStack<ItemType>::peek() const
47    {
48       assert (!isEmpty()); // Enforce precondition during debugging
49
50       // Stack is not empty; return top
51       return items[top];
52    } // end peek
53    // end of implementation file
```

A program that uses a stack could begin as follows:

```
#include <iostream>
#include <string>
#include "ArrayStack.h"

int main()
{
   StackInterface<std::string>* stackPtr = new ArrayStack<std::string>();
   std::string anItem;
   std::cout << "Enter a string: ";
   std::cin >> anItem;              // Read an item
   stackPtr->push(anItem);          // Push item onto stack
   . . .
```

Private data members are hidden from the client

By implementing the stack as a class, and by declaring items and top as private, you ensure that the client cannot violate the ADT's walls. If you did not hide your implementation within a class, or if you made the array items public, the client could access the entries in items directly instead of by using the ADT stack operations. Thus, the client could access any entries in the stack, not just its top entry. You might find this capability attractive, but in fact it violates the specifications of the ADT stack. If you truly need to access all the items of your ADT randomly, do not use a stack!

Finally, note that push receives newEntry as a constant reference argument. Therefore, push uses newEntry as an alias to its actual argument, and no copy is made.

Question 1 In Chapter 6, the algorithms that appear in Section 6.2 involve strings. Under what conditions would you choose an array-based implementation for the stack in these algorithms?

Question 2 Describe the changes to the previous stack implementation that are necessary to replace the fixed-size array with a resizable array.

7.2   A Link-Based Implementation

VideoNote
Overview of
LinkedStack

Many applications require a link-based implementation of a stack so that the stack can grow and shrink dynamically. Figure 7-2 illustrates such an implementation, where topPtr is a pointer to the head of the linked nodes.

FIGURE 7-2   A link-based implementation of a stack

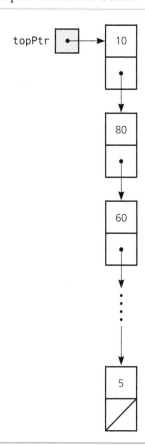

As we did for the array-based implementation, we begin this link-based implementation with a header file based upon StackInterface, as you can see in Listing 7-3. The pointer topPtr points to an instance of the class Node that we used in the implementation of the class LinkedBag in Chapter 4.

Because memory for the nodes is allocated dynamically from the free store, you must write both a copy constructor and a virtual destructor for the link-based stack implementation. As you saw in Chapter 4, if a shallow copy of the stack is sufficient, you can omit the copy constructor, in which case the compiler generates a copy constructor that performs a shallow copy. Such was the case for the array-based implementation.

If we did not write our own copy constructor for the LinkedStack class, the compiler-generated copy constructor would copy only the pointer topPtr. Thus, both topPtr and its copy would point to the same linked nodes; the stack itself would not be copied. You must write a copy constructor that explicitly makes a copy of all the nodes in a linked stack.

LISTING 7-3   The header file for the class `LinkedStack`

```
1    /** ADT stack: Link-based implementation.
2     @file LinkedStack.h */
3
4    #ifndef LINKED_STACK_
5    #define LINKED_STACK_
6
7    #include "StackInterface.h"
8    #include "Node.h"
9
10   template<class ItemType>
11   class LinkedStack : public StackInterface<ItemType>
12   {
13   private:
14      Node<ItemType>* topPtr; // Pointer to first node in the chain;
15                              // this node contains the stack's top
16
17   public:
18   // Constructors and destructor:
19      LinkedStack();                                        // Default constructor
20      LinkedStack(const LinkedStack<ItemType>& aStack); // Copy constructor
21      virtual ~LinkedStack();                               // Destructor
22
23   // Stack operations:
24      bool isEmpty() const;
25      bool push(const ItemType& newItem);
26      bool pop();
27      ItemType peek() const;
28   }; // end LinkedStack
29
30   #include "LinkedStack.cpp"
31   #endif
```

You need an explicit copy constructor and a virtual destructor

Listing 7-4 gives the implementation file for `LinkedStack`. Note the similarity between the copy constructors of `LinkedStack` and `LinkedBag` as given in Chapter 4.

LISTING 7-4   The implementation file for the class `LinkedStack`

```
1    /** @file LinkedStack.cpp */
2    #include <cassert>              // For assert
3    #include "LinkedStack.h"        // Header file
4
5    template<class ItemType>
6    LinkedStack<ItemType>::LinkedStack() : topPtr(nullptr)
7    {
8    }  // end default constructor
9
10   template<class ItemType>
11   LinkedStack<ItemType>::LinkedStack(const LinkedStack<ItemType>& aStack)
12   {
13      // Point to nodes in original chain
14      Node<ItemType>* origChainPtr = aStack.topPtr;
```

```cpp
15      if (origChainPtr == nullptr)
16         topPtr = nullptr;              // Original stack is empty
17      else
18      {
19         // Copy first node
20         topPtr = new Node<ItemType>();
21         topPtr->setItem(origChainPtr->getItem());
22
23         // Point to first node in new chain
24         Node<ItemType>* newChainPtr = topPtr;
25
26         // Advance original-chain pointer
27         origChainPtr = origChainPtr->getNext();
28
29         // Copy remaining nodes
30         while (origChainPtr != nullptr)
31         {
32            // Get next item from original chain
33            ItemType nextItem = origChainPtr->getItem();
34
35            // Create a new node containing the next item
36            Node<ItemType>* newNodePtr = new Node<ItemType>(nextItem);
37
38            // Link new node to end of new chain
39            newChainPtr->setNext(newNodePtr);
40
41            // Advance pointer to new last node
42            newChainPtr = newChainPtr->getNext();
43
44            // Advance original-chain pointer
45            origChainPtr = origChainPtr->getNext();
46         }  // end while
47         newChainPtr->setNext(nullptr); // Flag end of chain
48      }  // end if
49   }  // end copy constructor
50
51   template<class ItemType>
52   LinkedStack<ItemType>::~LinkedStack()
53   {
54      // Pop until stack is empty
55      while (!isEmpty())
56         pop();
57   }  // end destructor
58
59   template<class ItemType>
60   bool LinkedStack<ItemType>::push(const ItemType& newItem)
61   {
62      Node<ItemType>* newNodePtr = new Node<ItemType>(newItem, topPtr);
63      topPtr = newNodePtr;
64      newNodePtr = nullptr;
65      return true;
66   }  // end push
67
```

(continues)

```cpp
68   template<class ItemType>
69   bool LinkedStack<ItemType>::pop()
70   {
71      bool result = false;
72      if (!isEmpty())
73      {
74         // Stack is not empty; delete top
75         Node<ItemType>* nodeToDeletePtr = topPtr;
76         topPtr = topPtr->getNext();
77
78         // Return deleted node to system
79         nodeToDeletePtr->setNext(nullptr);
80         delete nodeToDeletePtr;
81         nodeToDeletePtr = nullptr;
82
83         result = true;
84      }  // end if
85
86      return result;
87   }  // end pop
88
89   template<class ItemType>
90   ItemType LinkedStack<ItemType>::peek() const
91   {
92      assert(!isEmpty());  // Enforce precondition during debugging
93
94      // Stack is not empty; return top
95      return topPtr->getItem();
96   }  // end peek
97
98   template<class ItemType>
99   bool LinkedStack<ItemType>::isEmpty() const
100  {
101     return topPtr == nullptr;
102  }  // end isEmpty
103  // end of implementation file
```

Question 3 In Chapter 6, the algorithms that appear in Section 6.2 involve strings. Under what conditions would you choose a link-based implementation?

Note: Comparing implementations

You have seen two implementations of the ADT stack, one that uses an array and another that uses linked nodes to contain the items in a stack. The discussion in Section 4.5 of Chapter 4 applies here as well. The array-based implementation is a reasonable choice if the number of items in the stack does not exceed the fixed size of the array. For example, when we read and correct an input line, if the system allows a line length of only 80 characters, you reasonably could use a statically allocated array to represent the stack. For stacks that might be large, but often are not, the array-based implementation will waste storage. In that case, the link-based implementation is a better choice.

Security Note: **Initializers versus set methods for constructors**

C++ Interlude 1 suggested that you use initializers instead of assignment statements in constructors to initialize the values of a class's data members. That is still good advice, and initializers clearly show the initialization. However, if you write set methods to alter the values of the data members, you have the opportunity to ensure that the values assigned are valid. Doing so is especially important when those values are supplied by the client. In such cases, constructors can call the set methods to initialize the data members. Thus, we have the following advice when you initialize the values of data members in constructors:

- Use an initializer if the value of the data member has no restrictions.
- Use a set method if the value of the data member needs validation.

Note that even if you do not want a public set method for a particular data member, you can either define a private one for the constructor to call or have the constructor perform its own validation.

Validate any data a client gives you

Security Note: **Constructors and destructors should call only private methods or final public methods**

Constructors and destructors should not call a virtual public method. For example, consider a base class whose constructor calls a virtual public set method and a derived class that overrides this set method. A constructor in the derived class will first call the base-class constructor, which now calls the overridden set method in the derived class. As a result, the base-class constructor may not be able to complete its initialization fully.

To prevent this possibility, you can declare the set method as final. This is a simple solution and the one we recommend. Another solution is to use a class namespace specifier, such as `PlainBox<ItemType>::`, when a constructor calls a method. Doing so will guarantee the consistent behavior of the constructor.

7.3   Implementations That Use Exceptions

Our specifications of the ADT stack appear to handle all eventualities. If you try to add an item to a full stack, the method `push` returns false. If you try to remove an entry from an empty stack, the method `pop` returns false. What happens when you try to look at the top of an empty stack? The method `peek` expects that you will not do this, as stated in its precondition. Our implementations, however, deal with the misuse of this method by beginning its definition with the statement

```
assert(!isEmpty());
```

If the stack is empty, `assert` will issue an error message and halt execution.

Instead of using `assert`, `peek` could throw an exception if its precondition is violated—that is, if it is called when the stack is empty. Let's define the class `PrecondViolatedExcept` that `peek` can use. Listings 7-5 and 7-6 show this class.

LISTING 7-5 The header file for the class `PrecondViolatedExcept`

```
1   /** @file PrecondViolatedExcept.h */
2   #ifndef PRECOND_VIOLATED_EXCEPT_
3   #define PRECOND_VIOLATED_EXCEPT_
4
5   #include <stdexcept>
6   #include <string>
7
8   class PrecondViolatedExcept: public std::logic_error
9   {
10  public:
11     PrecondViolatedExcept(const std::string& message = "");
12  }; // end PrecondViolatedExcept
13
14  #endif
```

LISTING 7-6 The implementation file for the class `PrecondViolatedExcept`

```
1   /** @file PrecondViolatedExcept.cpp */
2   #include "PrecondViolatedExcept.h"
3
4   PrecondViolatedExcept::PrecondViolatedExcept(const std::string& message)
5      : std::logic_error("Precondition Violated Exception: " + message)
6   {
7   }  // end constructor
```

We now add a `throw` clause to both declarations of `peek` in the header files `ArrayStack.h` and `LinkedStack.h` as follows:

```
ItemType peek() const throw(PrecondViolatedExcept);
```

In the implementation files, we add the same `throw` clause to the header of `peek` and then replace the `assert` statement in both definitions of `peek` with the following `if` statement:

```
if (isEmpty())
   throw PrecondViolatedExcept("peek() called with empty stack");
```

Thus, the definition of `peek` in `LinkedStack`, for example, is

```
template<class ItemType>
ItemType LinkedStack<ItemType>::peek() const throw(PrecondViolatedExcept)
{
   // Enforce precondition
   if (isEmpty())
      throw PrecondViolatedExcept("peek() called with empty stack");
   else // Stack is not empty; return top
      return topPtr->getItem();
}  // end peek
```

The previous revisions to `peek` are the same for both the array-based and link-based implementations of the stack.

Note: In the link-based implementation of the stack, both the method push and the copy constructor allocate new nodes. This allocation could fail if the system has no spare memory available. In such a case, the standard exception bad_alloc is thrown. However, in our simple examples, such an occurrence is unlikely to occur unless your computing system has a severely restricted memory size. For simplicity, we will not worry about this situation.

 Question 4 Define the exception class MemoryAllocationExcept and then revise the definition of the method push in the class LinkedStack so that it throws this exception if it cannot allocate a new node.

SUMMARY

1. You can implement a stack by using an array. If the bottom of the stack is in the first element of the array, no stack entries are moved when you add or remove entries.
2. You can implement a stack by using a chain of linked nodes that has a head pointer. The first node of the chain should contain the top of the stack to provide the easiest and fastest addition and removal operations.
3. You should throw an exception to enforce the precondition for the method peek.

EXERCISES

1. Discuss the advantages and disadvantages of an array-based implementation of the ADT stack as compared to a link-based implementation.

2. Consider the ADT bag, as described in Chapters 1, 3, and 4.
    a. Would you be able to implement the ADT stack by using a bag to contain its entries? Why, or why not?
    b. Would you be able to implement the ADT bag by using a stack to contain its entries? Why, or why not?

3. An operation that displays the contents of a stack can be useful during program debugging. Add a display method to the ADT stack such that
    a. The method uses only ADT stack operations; that is, it is independent of the stack's implementation.
    b. The method assumes and uses the link-based implementation of the ADT stack.
    c. The method assumes and uses the array-based implementation of the ADT stack.

4. Repeat the previous exercise, but define the method toVector instead of the method display.

5. To the ADT stack given in this chapter, add a void method remove(n) that removes and discards the topmost n entries from a stack. Write a link-based implementation for this method.

6. Repeat the previous exercise, but write an array-based implementation instead.

7. The destructor given for the link-based implementation of the ADT stack calls pop. Although easy to write, this destructor can be inefficient due to repeated method calls. Write another implementation for the destructor that deallocates the linked nodes directly without calling pop.

8. Imagine an array-based implementation of the ADT stack that stores the stack's entries beginning at the end of an array. Describe how you can define the stack operations so that the push and pop operations do not require you to move existing entries in the array.

9. Imagine a link-based implementation of the ADT stack that stores the stack's top entry at the end of a chain of linked nodes. Describe how you can define the stack operations so that a traversal of the chain is not necessary.

10. Although we do not usually throw our own exception when a method or constructor in LinkedStack fails to allocate a new node, you could do so. Define the exception MemoryAllocationExcept, and revise the copy constructor of LinkedStack so that it throws a MemoryAllocationExcept when the new operator fails to allocate memory. Throwing exceptions from constructors requires great care, since you must be sure to properly deallocate any memory allocated by the constructor before throwing the exception.
    Test your revised version of LinkedStack.

PROGRAMMING PROBLEMS

1. Write an implementation of the ADT stack that uses a resizable array to represent the stack items. Anytime the stack becomes full, double the size of the array. Maintain the stack's bottom entry at the beginning of the array.

2. Repeat Programming Problem 1, but maintain the stack's bottom entry at the end of the array.

3. Repeat Programming Problem 1, but maintain the stack's top entry at the beginning of the array.

4. Repeat Programming Problem 1, but maintain the stack's top entry at the end of the array.

5. Repeat any of the previous four programming problems, but after the first doubling of the array, halve the size of the array anytime fewer than half of the array's locations contain current stack entries.

6. Suppose that instead of doubling the size of an array-based stack when it becomes full, you increase the size of the array by some positive integer k. Implement and demonstrate such a stack that allows the client to specify k when the stack is created.

7. Repeat the previous programming problem, but each time the stack becomes full, increase the size of the array by the next value in this sequence: $3k$, $5k$, $7k$, … for a client-specified positive integer k.

8. Write the implementation of the ADT stack that Exercise 9 describes.

9. The ADT stack lets you peek at its top entry without removing it. For some applications of a stack, you need to also peek at the entry beneath the top entry without removing it. Let's name such an operation peek2. If peek2 fails because the stack contains fewer than two entries, it should throw an exception. Write a link-based implementation of the ADT stack that includes both peek and peek2.

10. Repeat any of the programming problems in Chapter 6, except the first one, using an implementation of the ADT stack that this chapter describes.

11. Repeat Programming Problem 13 in Chapter 6. However, a stack is not the appropriate ADT for the problem of writing the path of cities in the correct order; the appropriate ADT is a *traversable stack*. In addition to the standard stack operations isEmpty, push, pop, and peek, a traversable stack includes the operation traverse. The traverse operation begins at one end of the stack and visits each item in the stack until it reaches the other end of the stack. For this problem, you want traverse to begin at the bottom of the stack and move toward the top.

12. Repeat either Programming Problem 15, 16, or 17 in Chapter 6. The performance of your solution depends in part on whether the stack you use is an instance of the class ArrayStack or an instance of the class LinkedStack. Compare these performances.

Lists

Contents

Prerequisites

An everyday list provides a way for us to organize our thoughts, plans, or tasks. Each list has a first entry, a last entry, and often entries in between. The entries have a position within the list, and therefore they are ordered. In computer science, an ADT list provides another way to organize data. Like an everyday list, the entries in an ADT list have a position and are ordered. This order is not determined by the list itself, but rather by its client.

This chapter specifies the ADT list and gives some examples of how to use it.

VideoNote
The ADT list

8.1   Specifying the ADT List

Consider a list that you might encounter, such as a list of chores, a list of important dates, a list of addresses, or the grocery list pictured in Figure 8-1. As you write a grocery list, where do you put new items? Assuming that you write a neat one-column list, you probably add new items to the end of the list. You could just as well add items to the beginning of the list or add them so that your list is sorted alphabetically. Regardless, the items on a list appear in a sequence. The list has one first item and one last item. Except for the first and last items, each item has a unique **predecessor** and a unique **successor**. The first item—the **head** or **front** of the list—does not have a predecessor, and the last item—the **tail** or **back** of the list—does not have a successor.

Although the six items on the list in Figure 8-1 have a sequential order, they are not necessarily sorted by name. Perhaps the items appear in the order in which they occur on the grocer's shelves, but more likely they appear in the order in which you thought of them as you wrote the list.

Lists contain items of the same type: You can have a list of grocery items or a list of phone numbers. What can you do to the items on a list? You might count the items on the list, add an item to the list, remove an item from the list, or look at (retrieve) an item. The items on a list, together with operations that you can perform on the items, form an ADT: the ADT **list**.

> **Note:** The ADT list is simply a container of items of the same type whose order you indicate and whose position you reference by number. The first entry in a list is at position 1.[1]

You reference list items by their position

You must specify the behavior of the list's operations without thinking about how you could implement them. For example, you need to decide where to add a new item and which item to retrieve or remove. The various possible decisions lead to several kinds of lists. You might decide to add, remove, and retrieve items only at the end of the list, only at the front, or at both the front and the end. The specifications of these lists, which manipulate items at one or both ends, are left as an exercise, as they are not really adequate for an actual grocery list. Instead we will discuss a more general list, one that allows you to access items anywhere on the list. That is, you might look at the item at position *i*, remove the item at position *i,* or insert an item at position *i* on the list. Such operations are part of the ADT list. Other operations that see whether a list is empty or return the length of the list are also useful.

FIGURE 8-1   A grocery list

---

[1] Some designers place a list's first entry at position 0 to match the index numbering of an array. This tradition actually blurs the distinction between abstract specification and actual implementation. Everyday lists have a first entry, so our ADT specification reflects this.

Note: ADT list operations
- Test whether a list is empty.
- Get the number of entries on a list.
- Insert an entry at a given position on the list.
- Remove the entry at a given position from the list.
- Remove all entries from the list.
- Look at (get) the entry at a given position on the list.
- Replace (set) the entry at a given position on the list.

Figure 8-2 shows the UML diagram for this ADT and provides more detail for its operations.

FIGURE 8-2   UML diagram for the ADT list

```
                                    List

 +isEmpty(): boolean
 +getLength(): integer
 +insert(newPosition: integer, newEntry: ItemType): boolean
 +remove(position: integer): boolean
 +clear(): void
 +getEntry(position: integer): ItemType
 +replace(position: integer, newEntry: ItemType): ItemType
```

To get a more precise idea of how the operations work, let's apply them to the following grocery items:

milk, eggs, butter, apples, bread, chicken

Milk will be the first item on the list, and chicken will be the last item. To begin, consider how you can construct this list by using the ADT list operations. One way is first to create an empty list aList and then use a series of insertion operations to append the items to the list one at a time, as follows:

```
aList = a new empty list
aList.insert(1, milk)
aList.insert(2, eggs)
aList.insert(3, butter)
aList.insert(4, apples)
aList.insert(5, bread)
aList.insert(6, chicken)
```

We assume for this simple example that the list can contain all of the items we add to it.

In the previous example, we in effect have inserted each new item at the end of the list. Nevertheless, the list's insertion operation can place new items into any position of the list, not just at its front or end. The effect of an insertion between existing items, however, is not apparent from the previous example. For instance, if you start with the previous grocery list and you perform the operation

```
aList.insert(4, nuts)
```

the list aList should become

milk, eggs, butter, nuts, apples, bread, chicken

All items that had position numbers greater than or equal to 4 before the insertion now have their position numbers increased by 1 after the insertion. In general, if a new item is inserted into position *i*, the position of each item that was at or after position *i* is increased by 1.

Similarly, the removal operation specifies that if an item is removed from position *i*, the position of each item that was at a position greater than *i* is decreased by 1. Thus, for example, if aList is the list

milk, eggs, butter, nuts, apples, bread, chicken

and you perform the operation

aList.remove(5)

the list becomes

milk, eggs, butter, nuts, bread, chicken

All items that had position numbers greater than 5 before the removal now have their position numbers decreased by 1 after the deletion.

These examples illustrate that we can specify the effects of an ADT's operations without having to indicate how to store the data. The following summary of the ADT list provides more details for its operation contract. As usual, the specifications of these operations are the sole terms of the operation contract for the ADT list. The behavior of the operations is the only thing on which a program should depend.

ABSTRACT DATA TYPE: LIST

DATA

- A finite number of objects, not necessarily distinct, having the same data type and ordered by their positions, as determined by the client.

OPERATIONS

PSEUDOCODE	DESCRIPTION
isEmpty()	Task: Sees whether this list is empty. Input: None. Output: True if the list is empty; otherwise false.
getLength()	Task: Gets the current number of entries in this list. Input: None. Output: The integer number of entries currently in the list.
insert(newPosition, newEntry)	Task: Inserts an entry into this list at a given position. An insertion before existing entries causes the renumbering of entries that follow the new one. Input: newPosition is an integer indicating the position of the insertion, and newEntry is the new entry. Output: True if $1 \le$ newPosition $\le$ getLength() $+ 1$ and the insertion is successful; otherwise false.

`remove(position)`	Task: Removes the entry at a given position from this list. A removal before the last entry causes the renumbering of entries that follow the removed one. Input: `position` is the position of the entry to remove. Output: True if $1 \leq$ `newPosition` $\leq$ `getLength()` and the removal is successful; otherwise false.
`clear()`	Task: Removes all entries from this list. Input: None. Output: None. The list is empty.
`getEntry(position)`	Task: Gets the entry at the given position in this list. Input: `position` is the position of the entry to get; $1 \leq$ `position` $\leq$ `getLength()`. Output: The desired entry.
`replace(position, newEntry)`	Task: Replaces the entry at the given position in this list. Input: `position` is the position of the entry to replace; $1 \leq$ `position` $\leq$ `getLength()`. The replacement entry is `newEntry`. Output: The replaced entry.

Note that the return values of the insertion and removal operations provide the ADT with a simple mechanism to communicate operation failure to its client. For example, if you try to remove the tenth item from a five-item list, `remove` will return false. Likewise, `insert` will return false if, for example, the list is full or `position` is out of range. In this way, the client can deal with error situations in an implementation-independent way.

Note: The list operations fall into the three broad categories presented earlier in this book:

- The operation `insert` adds data to a data collection.
- The operation `remove` removes data from a data collection.
- The operations `isEmpty`, `getLength`, and `getEntry` ask questions about the data in a data collection.

The operation `replace` replaces existing data in a data collection, so you can think of it as removing and then adding data.

Question 1 The specifications of the ADT list do not mention the case in which two or more items have the same value. Are these specifications sufficient to cover this case, or must they be revised?

Question 2 Write specifications for a list whose operations `insert`, `remove`, `getEntry`, and `replace` always act at the end of the list.

Axioms (optional). The previous specifications for the operations of the ADT list have been stated rather informally. For example, they rely on your knowing the meaning of "an item is at position *i*" in a list. However, you can write a set of axioms that completely describes the behavior of the list operations. For example,

> *A newly created list is empty*

is an axiom because it is true for all newly created lists. You can state this axiom succinctly in terms of the ADT list operations as follows: [2]

```
(List()).isEmpty() = true
```

The statement

> *If you insert an item into the ith position of a list, you can retrieve it from the ith position of the list*

Use axioms to determine the effect of a sequence of ADT operations

is true for all lists, and so it is an axiom. You can state this axiom in terms of the ADT list operations as follows:

```
(aList.insert(i, item)).getEntry(i) = item
```

That is, getEntry returns the item that insert has put at position i of aList.
The following axioms formally define the ADT list:

> **Note: Axioms for the ADT list**
>
> 1. `(List()).isEmpty() = true`
> 2. `(List()).getLength() = 0`
> 3. `aList.getLength() = (aList.insert(i, item)).getLength() - 1`
> 4. `aList.getLength() = (aList.remove(i)).getLength() + 1`
> 5. `(aList.insert(i, item)).isEmpty() = false`
> 6. `(List()).remove(i) = false`
> 7. `(aList.insert(i, item)).remove(i) = true`
> 8. `(aList.insert(i, item)).remove(i) = aList`
> 9. `(List()).getEntry(i) => error`
> 10. `(aList.insert(i, item)).getEntry(i) = item`
> 11. `aList.getEntry(i) = (aList.insert(i, item)).getEntry(i + 1)`
> 12. `aList.getEntry(i + 1) = (aList.remove(i)).getEntry(i)`
> 13. `(List()).replace(i, item) => error`
> 14. `(aList.replace(i, item)).getEntry(i) = item`

A set of axioms does not make the preconditions and postconditions for an ADT's operations unnecessary. For example, the previous axioms do not describe insert's behavior when you try to insert an item into position 50 of a list of two items. One way to handle this situation is to include the restriction

```
1 <= position <= getLength() + 1
```

in insert's precondition. Another way—which we used in our previous specifications of the ADT list—does not restrict position, but rather has the method return false if position is outside the previous range. Thus, you need both a set of axioms and a set of preconditions and postconditions to define the behavior of an ADT's operations completely.

---

[2] The = notation within these axioms denotes algebraic equality.

You can use axioms to ascertain the outcome of a sequence of ADT operations. For example, if aList is a list of strings and s and t are strings, how does the sequence of operations

```
aList.insert(1, t)
aList.insert(1, s)
```

affect aList? We will show that s is the first item in this list and that t is the second item by using getEntry to look at these items.

You can write the previous sequence of operations in another way as

```
(aList.insert(1, t)).insert(1, s)
```

or

```
tempList = aList.insert(1, t)
tempList.insert(1, s)
```

Now get the first and second items in the list tempList.insert(1, s), as follows:

```
(tempList.insert(1, s)).getEntry(1) = s        by axiom 10
```

and

```
(tempList.insert(1, s)).getEntry(2)
        = tempList.getEntry(1)                by axiom 11
        = (aList.insert(1, t)).getEntry(1)    by definition of tempList
        = t                                   by axiom 10
```

Thus, s is the first item in the list and t is the second item.

8.2   Using the List Operations

VideoNote
Using the ADT list

We now consider some simple examples of how you can use the operations of the ADT list. Recall that exploring such uses is a way to confirm your understanding of an ADT's specifications and gives you an opportunity to change your mind about your design choices prior to implementing the ADT. You can write client functions in terms of the operations that define the ADT list, even though you do not know how the list's data is stored.

An implementation-independent application of the ADT list

Displaying the items on a list. Suppose that you want to display the items on a list. Since this task is not an ADT list operation, we write pseudocode for a client function displayList that uses the ADT operations as follows:

```
// Displays the items on the list aList.
displayList(aList)
{
    for (position = 1 through aList.getLength())
    {
        dataItem = aList.getEntry(position)
        Display dataItem
    }
}
```

Notice that as long as the ADT list is implemented correctly, the displayList function will perform its task. In this case, getEntry successfully retrieves each list item, because position's value is always valid.

Replacing an item. Now suppose that we did not include the operation `replace` in our specification of the ADT list. To replace the entry at a given position in the list with a new one, we would need to write a client function. The following pseudocode defines such a function `replace`:

```
// Replaces the ith entry in the list aList with newEntry.
// Returns true if the replacement was successful; otherwise return false.
replace(aList, i, newEntry)
{
    success = aList.remove(i)
    if (success)
        success = aList.insert(i, newEntry)

    return success
}
```

If `remove` is successful, it sets `success` to true. By testing `success`, `replace` will attempt the insertion only if the removal actually occurred. Then `insert` sets `success`, which `replace` returns to the function that called it. If `remove` is unsuccessful for any reason, including an incorrect value of `i`, it sets `success` to false. The `replace` function then ignores the insertion and returns false.

 Note: Notice that the two previous algorithms depend only on the specifications of the list operations and not on their implementations. The algorithms do not depend on *how* you implement the list. They will work regardless of whether you use an array or some other data structure to store the list's data. This feature is a definite advantage of abstract data types. In addition, by thinking in terms of the available ADT operations, you will not be distracted by implementation details.

 Creating a list of names in alphabetical order. Let's create a list of our friends' names as we think of them. Moreover, let's place the names on the list in alphabetical order. It is up to us to place each name into its correct position in the list. The ADT list does not choose the order of its entries.

The following pseudocode statements place the names Amy, Katsu, Brinda, Drew, Aaron, and Carlos in an alphabetical list. The comment at the end of each statement shows the list after the statement executes.

```
alphaList = a new empty list
alphaList.insert(1, "Amy")      // Amy
alphaList.insert(2, "Katsu")    // Amy Katsu
alphaList.insert(2, "Brinda")   // Amy Brinda Katsu
alphaList.insert(3, "Drew")     // Amy Brinda Drew Katsu
alphaList.insert(1, "Aaron")    // Aaron Amy Brinda Drew Katsu
alphaList.insert(4, "Carlos")   // Aaron Amy Brinda Carlos Drew Katsu
```

After initially placing Amy at the beginning of the list and Katsu at the end of the list (at position 2), we insert

- Brinda between Amy and Katsu at position 2
- Drew between Brinda and Katsu at position 3
- Aaron before Amy at position 1
- Carlos between Brinda and Drew at position 4

Later in Chapter 11, you will learn that this way of inserting each name into a collection of alphabetized names is called an insertion sort.

If we now remove the entry at position 4—Carlos—by writing

```
alphaList.remove(4)
```

Drew and Katsu will be at positions 4 and 5, respectively. Thus, `alphaList.getEntry(4)` would return Drew.

Finally, suppose that we want to replace a name in this list. We cannot replace a name with just any name and expect that the list will remain in alphabetical order. Replacing Brinda with Ben by writing

```
alphaList.replace(3, "Ben");
```

would maintain alphabetical order, but replacing Brinda with Nancy would not. The list's alphabetical order resulted from our original decisions about where to place names on the list. The order did not come about automatically as a result of list operations. That is, the client, not the list, maintains the order. We could, however, design an ADT that maintains its data in alphabetical order. You will see an example of such an ADT in Chapter 12.

Question 3 Write a pseudocode function `swap(aList, i, j)` that interchanges the items currently in positions *i* and *j* of a list. Define the function in terms of the ADT list operations, so that it is independent of any particular implementation of the list. Assume that the list, in fact, has items at positions *i* and *j*. What impact does this assumption have on your solution? (See Exercise 2 at the end of this chapter.)

Question 4 What grocery list results from the following sequence of ADT list operations?

```
aList = a new empty list
aList.insert(1, "butter")
aList.insert(1, "eggs")
aList.insert(1, "milk")
```

Question 5 Suppose that `myList` is a list that contains the five objects a b c d e.

  a. What does `myList` contain after executing `myList.insert(5, w)`?
  b. Starting with the original five entries, what does `myList` contain after executing `myList.insert(6, w)`?
  c. Which, if any, of the operations in parts *a* and *b* of this question require entries in the list to shift positions?

8.3   An Interface Template for the ADT List

We now will formalize our specification of the ADT list by writing a C++ interface, which is given in Listing 8-1.

LISTING 8-1 A C++ interface for lists

```
1   /** Interface for the ADT list
2    @file ListInterface.h */
3
4   #ifndef LIST_INTERFACE_
5   #define LIST_INTERFACE_
6
7   template<class ItemType>
8   class ListInterface
```
(continues)

```
9
10   {
11   public:
12      /** Sees whether this list is empty.
13       @return  True if the list is empty; otherwise returns false. */
14      virtual bool isEmpty() const = 0;
15
16      /** Gets the current number of entries in this list.
17       @return  The integer number of entries currently in the list. */
18      virtual int getLength() const = 0;
19
20      /** Inserts an entry into this list at a given position. .
21       @pre   None.
22       @post  If 1 <= position <= getLength() + 1 and the insertion is
23          successful, newEntry is at the given position in the list,
24          other entries are renumbered accordingly, and the returned
25          value is true.
26       @param newPosition  The list position at which to insert newEntry.
27       @param newEntry  The entry to insert into the list.
28       @return  True if the insertion is successful, or false if not. */
29      virtual bool insert(int newPosition, const ItemType& newEntry) = 0;
30
31      /** Removes the entry at a given position from this list.
32       @pre   None.
33       @post  If 1 <= position <= getLength() and the removal is successful,
34          the entry at the given position in the list is removed, other
35          items are renumbered accordingly, and the returned value is true.
36       @param position  The list position of the entry to remove.
37       @return  True if the removal is successful, or false if not. */
38      virtual bool remove(int position) = 0;
39
40      /** Removes all entries from this list.
41       @post  The list contains no entries and the count of items is 0. */
42      virtual void clear() = 0;
43
44      /** Gets the entry at the given position in this list.
45       @pre   1 <= position <= getLength().
46       @post  The desired entry has been returned.
47       @param position  The list position of the desired entry.
48       @return  The entry at the given position. */
49      virtual ItemType getEntry(int position) const = 0;
50
51      /** Replaces the entry at the given position in this list.
52       @pre   1 <= position <= getLength().
53       @post  The entry at the given position is newEntry.
54       @param position  The list position of the entry to replace.
55       @param newEntry  The replacement entry.
56       @return  The replaced entry. */
57      virtual ItemType replace(int position, const ItemType& newEntry) = 0;
58
59      /** Destroys this list and frees its assigned memory. */
60      virtual ~ListInterface() { }
61   }; // end ListInterface
62   #endif
```

Summary

1. The ADT list maintains its data by position. Each entry in a list is identified by its position, which is given by an integer, beginning with 1. Thus, the data in a list has an order, but that order is determined by the list's client, not the list itself.

2. You can insert a new entry into a list at a position that ranges from 1 to the current length of the list plus 1. Thus, you can insert a new entry before the first entry, after the last entry, or between two current entries.

3. Inserting a new entry into a list renumbers any existing entries that follow the new one in the list.

4. You can remove an entry that is currently at a position that ranges from 1 to the current length of the list. Thus, you can remove the first entry, the last entry, or any interior entry.

5. Removing an entry from a list renumbers any existing entries that follow the one removed from the list.

Exercises

1. Consider an ADT list of integers. Write a pseudocode function that computes the sum of the integers in the list aList. The definition of your function should be independent of the list's implementation.

2. Implement the function swap, as described in Checkpoint Question 3, but remove the assumption that the ith and j^{th} items on the list exist. Return a value that indicates whether the swap was successful.

3. Use the function swap that you wrote in Exercise 2 to write a function that reverses the order of the items in a list aList.

4. Section 8.2 describes the functions displayList and replace. Their definitions are written in terms of the ADT list operations.
   a. What is an advantage and a disadvantage of the way that displayList and replace are implemented?
   b. What is an advantage and a disadvantage of defining displayList and replace as operations of the ADT list?

5. Suppose that the ADT list has a method getPosition that returns the position of a given entry within the list. Write specifications for such a method.

6. Write a pseudocode function getPosition at the client level that returns the position of a given entry within a given list.

7. Suppose that the ADT list has a method contains that tests whether the list contains a given entry. Write specifications for such a method.

8. Write a pseudocode function contains at the client level that tests whether a given list contains a given entry.

9. The ADT list method remove removes from the list the entry at a given position. Suppose that the ADT list has another method remove that removes a given entry from the list. Write specifications for such a method. What does your method do if the list contains duplicate entries?

10. Write a pseudocode function remove at the client level that removes a given entry from a given list.

11. Use the axioms for the ADT list, as given in "Axioms" in Section 8.1 of this chapter, to prove that the sequence of operations

> *Insert A into position 2*
>
> *Insert B into position 2*
>
> *Insert C into position 2*

has the same effect on a nonempty list of characters as the sequence

> *Insert C into position 2*
>
> *Insert B into position 3*
>
> *Insert A into position 4*

12. Repeat Exercise 21 in Chapter 2, using the ADT list to implement the function $f(n)$.

PROGRAMMING PROBLEMS

1. Write pseudocode implementations of the ADT polynomial operations, as defined in Exercise 9 of Chapter 1, in terms of the ADT list operations.

2. Santa Claus allegedly keeps lists of those who are naughty and those who are nice. On the naughty list are the names of those who will get coal in their stockings. On the nice list are those who will receive gifts. Each object in this list contains a name (a string) and a list of that person's gifts (an instance of an ADT list). Design an ADT for the objects in the nice list. Specify each ADT operation by stating its purpose, describing its parameters, and writing preconditions, postconditions, and a pseudocode version of its header. Then write a template interface for the ADT that includes javadoc-style comments.

3. The local runner's club wants an application that provides the order of the runners during its annual marathon. This order is recorded in real time by a system much like that used at highway toll plazas. Each milepost marker transmits a radio-frequency signal as a runner passes by. This signal is received by a small transponder, which each runner wears, and then broadcasts identifying information back to the milepost. Though this gives the position at the current milepost, the club wants live, up-to-the-second updates. To achieve this, they have modified the runners' transponders to signal when a runner passes another runner. This system then sends the current placement of each runner as an integer to your application. Design an application that uses a list to record the current place of each runner. The application should

- Create the initial placement of the runners in the list as they reach mile marker 5. (This delay gives the runners time to spread out.)
- Update the positions of the runners whenever one runner passes another and at each mile marker.
- Fix a runner's position in the list as soon as the runner crosses the finish line.

4. (Gaming) Design an ADT starting gate for a horse race. Suppose that n horses enter the race and are assigned post positions 1 through n. If one horse fails to enter the starting gate and is disqualified, the other horses do not change positions. Implement your design in pseudocode using the operations of the ADT list.

5. (Finance) The checks in a checkbook are numbered sequentially. Design an ADT check and an ADT checkbook. The first check in a particular checkbook can begin at any given positive integer. Implement your design for the checkbook in pseudocode using the operations of the ADT list.

6. (E-commerce) Some online stores offer their customers a gift registry, where they can enter items that they would like to receive as gifts for a special event. Design an ADT for a gift registry that enables the client to rank the gifts in order of preference.

List
Implementations

Contents

Prerequisites

Chapter 3   Array-Based Implementations
C++ Interlude 2   Pointers, Polymorphism, and Memory Allocation
Chapter 4   Link-Based Implementations
C++ Interlude 3   Exceptions
Chapter 8   Lists

Having clearly specified the operations of an ADT list in the previous chapter, we now consider data structures for implementing it. This chapter explores two implementations of the list and compares their advantages and disadvantages.

9.1 An Array-Based Implementation of the ADT List

When you design an abstract data type, you concentrate on what its operations do, but you ignore how you will implement them. Now that we have clearly specified operations for the ADT list, we can implement it as a C++ class. Recall that the list operations in their UML form are

```
+isEmpty(): boolean
+getLength(): integer
+insert(newPosition: integer, newEntry: ItemType): boolean
+remove(position: integer): boolean
+clear(): void
+getEntry(position: integer): ItemType
+replace(position: integer, newEntry: ItemType): ItemType
```

You need to represent the items on a list and its length. Your first thought is probably to store the list's items in an array items. In fact, you might believe that "list" is simply a fancy name for an array. This belief is not quite true, however. An array-based implementation is a natural choice because both an array and a list identify their items by number. However, the ADT list has operations such as getLength that an array does not. Later in this chapter, you will see an implementation of the ADT list that does not use an array.

With an array-based implementation, you can store a list's entries in an array items. How much of the array will the list occupy? Possibly all of it, but probably not. That is, you need to keep track of the array elements that you have assigned to the list and those that are available for use in the future. The maximum length of the array—its physical size—is a known, fixed value. You can keep track of the current number of entries on the list—that is, the list's length or logical size—in a variable itemCount. An obvious benefit of this approach is that implementing the operation getLength will be easy.

In the previous chapter, we decided to number the entries in a list intuitively, that is, the first entry is at position 1. Which array element should contain this first entry? We could place it in items[0], so that the list's kth entry is in items[k - 1]. Doing so, however, requires that we subtract 1 from an entry's position in a list to obtain the index of the array location that contains the entry. To reduce the chance of confusion and error, we will place a list's first entry in items[1] and its kth entry in items[k]. Thus, we will not use—and will ignore—the array element items[0]. Doing so results in a minor waste of space, but leads to a more intuitive implementation.

We will use the following statements to define the data members for an array-based implementation of the ADT list:

The data members

```
static const int DEFAULT_CAPACITY = 100;   // Default capacity of the list
ItemType items[DEFAULT_CAPACITY + 1];      // Array of list items (ignore items[0])
int itemCount;                             // Current count of list items
int maxItems;                              // Maximum capacity of the list
```

Figure 9-1 illustrates these data members. To hide them from the clients of the class, we will make these data members private.

9.1.1 The Header File

Now that we have chosen the data members for our class ArrayList, we can write its header file, as given in Listing 9-1. We derive ArrayList from the template interface ListInterface that we developed in the previous chapter. We provide a default constructor, and since we plan to use a statically allocated array, the compiler-generated destructor and copy constructor will be sufficient. The only other detail that ListInterface does not specify is the behavior of the methods getEntry and

FIGURE 9-1   An array-based implementation of the ADT list

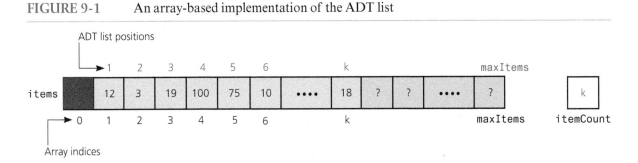

replace should their caller violate their precondition. That is, what should we do if these methods are given an out-of-bounds list position? We can throw an exception in this case, and to this end, we use the class PrecondViolatedExcept as defined in Listings 7-5 and 7-6 of Chapter 7.

 Note: By defining the data member maxItems for ArrayList, we enable the class implementer to allocate the array items dynamically instead of statically as we have done here. Thus, the programmer could easily define a constructor that allows the client to choose the size of the array.

LISTING 9-1 The header file for the class ArrayList

```
1   /** ADT list: Array-based implementation.
2    @file ArrayList.h */
3
4   #ifndef ARRAY_LIST_
5   #define ARRAY_LIST_
6
7   #include "ListInterface.h"
8   #include "PrecondViolatedExcept.h"
9
10  template<class ItemType>
11  class ArrayList : public ListInterface<ItemType>
12  {
13  private:
14     static const int DEFAULT_CAPACITY = 100; // Default capacity of the list
15     ItemType items[DEFAULT_CAPACITY + 1];     // Array of list items (ignore items[0])
16     int itemCount;                            // Current count of list items
17     int maxItems;                             // Maximum capacity of the list
18
19  public:
20     ArrayList();
21     // Copy constructor and destructor are supplied by compiler
22
23     bool isEmpty() const;
24     int getLength() const;
25     bool insert(int newPosition, const ItemType& newEntry);
26     bool remove(int position);
27     void clear();
28
```
(continues)

```
29      /** @throw  PrecondViolatedExcept if position < 1 or position > getLength(). */
30      ItemType getEntry(int position) const throw(PrecondViolatedExcept);
31
32      /** @throw  PrecondViolatedExcept if position < 1 or position > getLength(). */
33      ItemType replace(int position, const ItemType& newEntry)
34                                    throw(PrecondViolatedExcept);
35   }; // end ArrayList
36
37   #include "ArrayList.cpp"
38   #endif
```

VideoNote
Overview of
ArrayList

9.1.2   The Implementation File

As usual, we will begin our implementation with the method or methods that add new entries to our container and any methods that help us to verify the correctness of those additions. For ArrayList, we want to define the method insert. The methods isEmpty and getLength will be easy to define and will be useful while testing insert. We also will want to call the method getEntry to check the contents of the list. And, of course, we need to define the constructor. Let's begin with these methods as our core group.

The constructor and the methods isEmpty and getLength. The default constructor initializes the data members itemCount to zero and maxItems to DEFAULT_CAPACITY:

```
template<class ItemType>
ArrayList<ItemType>::ArrayList() : itemCount(0), maxItems(DEFAULT_CAPACITY)
{
}  // end default constructor
```

The method isEmpty tests whether itemCount is zero, and getLength simply returns the value of itemCount:

```
template<class ItemType>
bool ArrayList<ItemType>::isEmpty() const
{
   return itemCount == 0;
}  // end isEmpty

template<class ItemType>
int ArrayList<ItemType>::getLength() const
{
   return itemCount;
}  // end getLength
```

Shift array entries to insert an item

The method insert. To insert a new entry at a given position in the array items, you must create room for the new entry by shifting the entries at and beyond this position toward the end of array. Figure 9-2 depicts this insertion. Part *a* shows the list prior to adding a new entry at position 3. Starting at the end of the list—*not* the end of the array—we copy the entry in items[i] to items[i + 1] for values of i ranging from itemCount down to 3, as Figure 9-2b illustrates. Finally, we insert the new entry into items[newPosition], or items[3] in this example. Figure 9-2c shows the list after this step.

The definition of the method insert follows:

```
template<class ItemType>
bool ArrayList<ItemType>::insert(int newPosition, const ItemType& newEntry)
{
   bool ableToInsert = (newPosition >= 1) && (newPosition <= itemCount + 1)
                              && (itemCount < maxItems);
   if (ableToInsert)
   {
```

FIGURE 9-2   Shifting items for insertion at list position 3

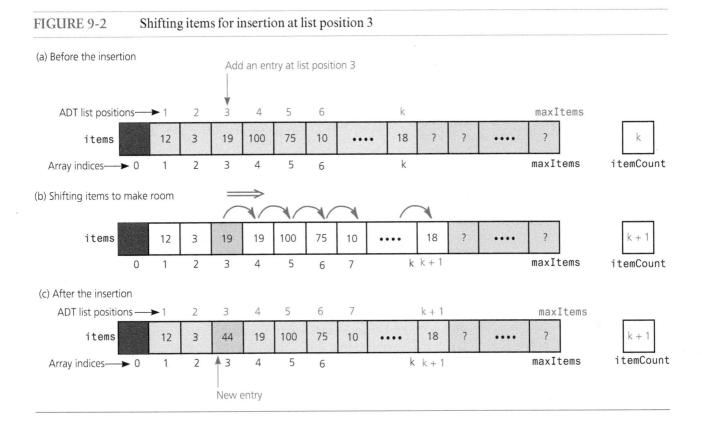

```
            // Make room for new entry by shifting all entries at
            // positions from itemCount down to newPosition
            // (no shift if newPosition == itemCount + 1)
            for (int pos = itemCount; pos >= newPosition; pos--)
                items[pos + 1] = items[pos];

            // Insert new entry
            items[newPosition] = newEntry;
            itemCount++; // Increase count of entries
        } // end if

        return ableToInsert;
    } // end insert
```

We can begin testing these methods once we write stubs for the remaining methods. To thoroughly test insert, however, we need the method getEntry, which we define next.

Question 1 Given a nonempty list that is an instance of ArrayList, at what position does an insertion of a new entry require the fewest operations? Explain.

Question 2 Describe an implementation of the method insert for ArrayList that places the entry in position 1 in the last element of the array, the entry in position 2 in the next-to-last element, and so on.

Question 3 How does the original version of insert given previously compare with the one described in Question 2 with respect to the number of operations required?

The method `getEntry`. This method simply needs to return the value in `items[position]`, but we decided to enforce the method's precondition by throwing an exception if `position` is out of bounds. For the purpose of testing the method `insert`, you could write a temporary version of `getEntry` that does not throw an exception but just returns the desired list entry. After testing `insert`, you would then complete `getEntry`'s definition as follows:

```cpp
template<class ItemType>
ItemType ArrayList<ItemType>::getEntry(int position) const
                              throw(PrecondViolatedExcept)
{
   // Enforce precondition
   bool ableToGet = (position >= 1) && (position <= itemCount);
   if (ableToGet)
      return items[position];
   else
   {
      std::string message = "getEntry() called with an empty list or ";
      message = message + "invalid position.";
      throw(PrecondViolatedExcept(message));
   } // end if
} // end getEntry
```

A client. At this point, and after writing stubs for the remaining methods, you should test the core group of methods. The following `main` function demonstrates how you can test the methods `insert` and `getEntry`, but it assumes that you change the value of `DEFAULT_CAPACITY` to 5 in the class definition given in Listing 9-1:

```cpp
const int ITEM_COUNT = 6;
int main()
{
   ListInterface<std::string>* listPtr = new ArrayList<std::string>();
   std::string data[] = {"one", "two", "three", "four", "five", "six"};
   std::cout << "isEmpty: returns " << listPtr->isEmpty()
             << "; should be 1 (true)" << std::endl;
   for (int i = 0; i < ITEM_COUNT; i++)
   {
      if (listPtr->insert(i + 1, data[i]))
      {
         try
         {
            std::cout << "Inserted " << listPtr->getEntry(i + 1)
                      << " at position " << (i + 1) << std::endl;
         }
         catch (std::logic_error except)
         {
            std::cout << "Failed to get entry at position "
                      << (i + 1) << std::endl;
         }
      }
      else
         std::cout << "Cannot insert " << data[i] << " at position " << (i + 1)
                   << std::endl;
   } // end for

   return 0;
} // end main
```

Note that the client cannot contain references such as `listPtr->itemCount` or `listPtr->items[4]`, because `itemCount` and `items` are within the private portion of `ArrayList`.

The method `replace`. The definition of the method `replace` is similar to the one for `getEntry`, so we implement it next:

A client of the class cannot access the class's private members directly

```
template<class ItemType>
ItemType ArrayList<ItemType>::replace(int position, const ItemType& newEntry)
                        throw(PrecondViolatedExcept)
{
    // Enforce precondition
    bool ableToSet = (position >= 1) && (position <= itemCount);
    if (ableToSet)
    {
        ItemType oldEntry = items[position];
        items[position] = newEntry;
        return oldEntry;
    }
    else
    {
        std::string message = "replace() called with an empty list or ";
        message = message + "invalid position.";
        throw(PrecondViolatedExcept(message));
    } // end if
} // end replace
```

The method `remove`. Now consider how to remove an entry from the list. You could blank it out, but this strategy can lead to gaps in the array, as Figure 9-3a illustrates. An array that is full of gaps has three significant problems:

- `itemCount` is no longer the index of the last entry in the array. You need another variable, `lastPosition`, to contain this index.
- Because the items are spread out, the method `getEntry` might have to look at every cell of the array even when only a few entries are present.
- When `items[maxItems]` is occupied, the list could appear full, even when fewer than `maxItems` entries are present.

Thus, what you really need to do is shift the entries in the array so that a removal does not leave a gap, as shown in parts *b* an *c* of Figure 9-3. This data movement is like the one done by the method `insert`, but it occurs in the opposite direction.

FIGURE 9-3   Shifting items to remove an entry

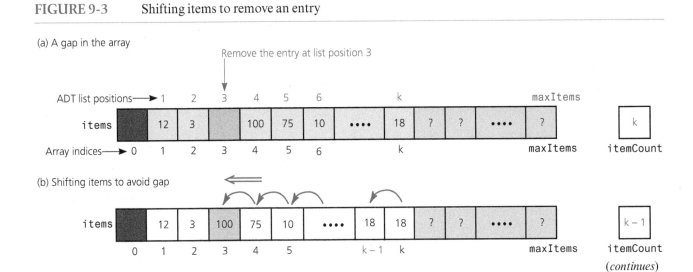

(a) A gap in the array

(b) Shifting items to avoid gap

(continues)

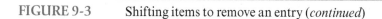

FIGURE 9-3   Shifting items to remove an entry (*continued*)

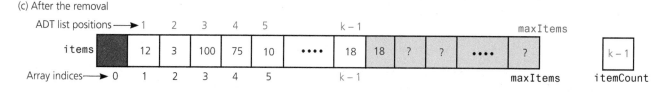

(c) After the removal

The definition of `remove` follows:

```
template<class ItemType>
bool ArrayList<ItemType>::remove(int position)
{
    bool ableToRemove = (position >= 1) && (position <= itemCount);
    if (ableToRemove)
    {
        // Remove entry by shifting all entries after the one at
        // position toward the beginning of the array
        // (no shift if position == itemCount)
        for (int pos = position; pos < itemCount; pos++)
            items[pos] = items[pos + 1];

        itemCount--; // Decrease count of entries
    } // end if

    return ableToRemove;
} // end remove
```

The method `clear`. To clear all of the entries from a list, our last method simply sets `itemCount` to zero:

```
template<class ItemType>
void ArrayList<ItemType>::clear()
{
    itemCount = 0;
} // end clear
```

The entire implementation file for the class `ArrayList` is available online from the book's website.

Question 4 Although the method `remove` cannot remove an entry from an empty list, it does not explicitly check for one. How does this method avoid an attempted removal from an empty list?

9.2   A Link-Based Implementation of the ADT List

We now consider how we can use C++ pointers instead of an array to implement the ADT list. Unlike the array-based implementation, a link-based implementation does not shift items during insertion and removal operations. It also does not impose a fixed maximum length on the list—except, of course, as imposed by the storage limits of the system.

Once again, we need to represent the items in the list and its length. Figure 9-4 indicates one possible way to represent this data by using pointers. Here `headPtr` points to the linked nodes containing the items in the list, where the first node contains the entry at position 1 in the list, and so on. The integer itemCount is the current number of entries in the list. Both headPtr and itemCount will be private data members of our class.

FIGURE 9-4   A link-based implementation of the ADT list

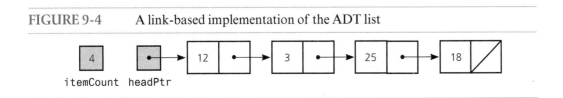

9.2.1   The Header File

Let's name our class of lists LinkedList and write its header file as shown in Listing 9-2. This file has similarities to the header file for ArrayList, as given in Listing 9-1, but let's point out the differences. Here we include the header files for the classes Node and PrecondViolatedExcept, as defined in Listing 4-1 of Chapter 4 and Listing 7-5 of Chapter 7, respectively.

The private section declares the two data members—headPtr and itemCount—as well as a private method getNodeAt that we will use to locate any node within the chain of linked nodes, given its position in the chain. While you could write the necessary loop in the method getEntry, you would soon discover that the methods insert and remove will need the same loop. At that time, you should realize that defining a private method to perform the traversal would be convenient. Although we declare getNodeAt now, adding the declarations of private methods to the header file after you begin the implementation file is not unusual.

 Note: Although you have direct access to any of an array's elements, you must traverse a chain of linked nodes to locate a specified node. A list's retrieval, insertion, and removal operations require such a traversal.

LISTING 9-2 **The header file for the class LinkedList**

```
1   /** ADT list: Link-based implementation.
2    @file LinkedList.h */
3
4   #ifndef LINKED_LIST_
5   #define LINKED_LIST_
6
7   #include "ListInterface.h"
8   #include "Node.h"
9   #include "PrecondViolatedExcept.h"
10
11  template<class ItemType>
12  class LinkedList : public ListInterface<ItemType>
13  {
14  private:
15     Node<ItemType>* headPtr; // Pointer to first node in the chain
16                              // (contains the first entry in the list)
17     int itemCount;          // Current count of list items
```
(continues)

```
18        // Locates a specified node in a linked list.
19        // @pre  position is the number of the desired node;
20        //       position >= 1 and position <= itemCount.
21        // @post  The node is found and a pointer to it is returned.
22        // @param position  The number of the node to locate.
23        // @return  A pointer to the node at the given position.
24        Node<ItemType>* getNodeAt(int position) const;
25
26     public:
27        LinkedList();
28        LinkedList(const LinkedList<ItemType>& aList);
29        virtual ~LinkedList();
30
31        bool isEmpty() const;
32        int getLength() const;
33        bool insert(int newPosition, const ItemType& newEntry);
34        bool remove(int position);
35        void clear();
36
37        /** @throw  PrecondViolatedExcept if position < 1 or
38                                           position > getLength(). */
39        ItemType getEntry(int position) const throw(PrecondViolatedExcept);
40
41        /** @throw  PrecondViolatedExcept if position < 1 or
42                                           position > getLength(). */
43        ItemType replace(int position, const ItemType& newEntry)
44                                           throw(PrecondViolatedExcept);
45     }; // end LinkedList
46
47     #include "LinkedList.cpp"
48     #endif
```

getNodeAt is a private method

The method getNodeAt is not an ADT operation, because it returns a pointer to a node; since nodes are an implementation detail, you would not want any client to call it. Clients should be able to use the ADT without knowledge of the nodes that the implementation uses. It is perfectly reasonable for the implementation of an ADT to define variables and methods that the rest of the program should not access. You could think of the method getNodeAt as marked "for internal use only." Therefore, getNodeAt is a private method that only the implementations of the ADT's operations call.

A copy constructor and a destructor are necessary for a link-based implementation

Because we are declaring a link-based implementation, we must provide a copy constructor and a destructor for our class. The declarations of the other public methods are the same as for the class ArrayList.

9.2.2 The Implementation File

VideoNote
Overview of
LinkedList

Our core methods include the same ones that we defined earlier for ArrayList—namely, the constructor and the methods insert, getEntry, isEmpty, and getLength. The latter two methods have the same bodies as their ArrayList versions, since they involve only the data field itemCount. As we have mentioned, the methods getEntry and insert will call the private method getNodeAt.

The constructor. Because the compiler-generated default constructor would not necessarily initialize headPtr and itemCount to appropriate values, you must provide your own default constructor. Initializers are sufficient to set the values of `headPtr` and `itemCount`, since we, not the client, choose these values. The constructor's definition follows:

```
template<class ItemType>
LinkedList<ItemType>::LinkedList() : headPtr(nullptr), itemCount(0)
{
} // end default constructor
```

The method `getEntry`. Like `getEntry` in `ArrayList`, we will have this method enforce its precondition by throwing an exception if `position` is out of bounds. Note the similarity of its definition to the array-based version given earlier in this chapter:

```
template<class ItemType>
ItemType LinkedList<ItemType>::getEntry(int position) const
                              throw(PrecondViolatedExcept)
{
   // Enforce precondition
   bool ableToGet = (position >= 1) && (position <= itemCount);
   if (ableToGet)
   {
      Node<ItemType>* nodePtr = getNodeAt(position);
      return nodePtr->getItem();
   }
   else
   {
      std::string message = "getEntry() called with an empty list or ";
      message = message + "invalid position.";
      throw(PrecondViolatedExcept(message));
   } // end if
} // end getEntry
```

The method `getNodeAt`. The private method `getNodeAt` locates the node at a given position by traversing the chain. It then returns a pointer to the located node. The traversal begins at the first node of the chain and moves from node to node, counting as it goes, until it reaches the desired one:

```
template<class ItemType>
Node<ItemType>* LinkedList<ItemType>::getNodeAt(int position) const
{
   // Debugging check of precondition
   assert( (position >= 1) && (position <= itemCount) );

   // Count from the beginning of the chain
   Node<ItemType>* curPtr = headPtr;
   for (int skip = 1; skip < position; skip++)
      curPtr = curPtr->getNext();

   return curPtr ;
} // end getNodeAt
```

Security Note: Trusted code

Up to this point, our methods have taken responsibility for enforcing preconditions. If preconditions were not met, the method would fail to complete its action or throw an exception. We did not trust our client to enforce the preconditions of our public methods. As a private method, `getNodeAt` is called only by other methods within the

(continues)

class and not by an unknown client. We consider these calling methods to be **trusted code**, that is, code that presumably functions correctly. Moreover, `getNodeAt` can trust that any calling method will honor its preconditions. This trust is possible since the methods of the class are designed to work together. Still, when we are developing and debugging our code, unexpected problems might arise. Thus, we simply use an assertion during debugging to validate `getNodeAt`'s precondition.

The method `insert`. As you know, you can insert a new entry into a list right before its first entry, right after its last entry, or between two adjacent entries. For the link-based implementations of the ADT bag in Chapter 4 and the ADT stack in Chapter 7, we always inserted a new node into the chain of linked nodes at the chain's beginning. The ADT list requires us to manipulate the chain in additional ways. Let's explore those ways.

Since we know how to insert a new node at the beginning of a chain of nodes, let's consider inserting a node between two existing, adjacent nodes to which the pointer variables `prevPtr` and `curPtr` point, as Figure 9-5a illustrates. If the pointer variable `newNodePtr` points to the new node, you make the new node point to the node that `curPtr` currently points to (Figure 9-5b). You also must alter the value of the pointer in the node that will precede the new node so that it points to the new node, as shown in Figure 9-5c. As the diagram suggests, you can accomplish the insertion by using the pair of statements

Inserting a node between nodes

```
newNodePtr->setNext(curPtr);
prevPtr->setNext(newNodePtr);
```

Now, how did the variables `curPtr` and `prevPtr` get appropriate values? Given `newPosition`, the desired position of the new entry in the list, you traverse the chain until you find the proper position for the new item. The private method `getNodeAt` will perform this traversal for you. Thus,

```
prevPtr = getNodeAt(newPosition - 1);
curPtr = prevPtr->getNext();
```

You then use the `new` operator to create a new node, to which `newNodePtr` points. You initialize its data portion and then insert the node into the chain, as was just described.

Figure 9-6 shows the insertion of a new node at the end of a chain. This insertion is potentially a special case because the intention of the pair of statements

If curPtr is nullptr, inserting at the end of a chain is not a special case

```
newNodePtr->setNext(curPtr);
prevPtr->setNext(newNodePtr);
```

is to insert the new node *between* the nodes to which `curPtr` and `prevPtr` point. If you are to insert the new node at the end of the chain, to what node should `curPtr` point? In this situation, it makes sense to view the value of `curPtr` as `nullptr` because, as you traverse the list, `curPtr` becomes `nullptr` as it moves past the end of the chain. Observe that if `curPtr` has the value `nullptr` and `prevPtr` points to the last node in the chain, the previous pair of assignment statements will indeed insert the new node at the end of the chain. Thus, insertion at the end of a chain is not a special case.

To summarize, the insertion process requires three high-level steps:

Three steps to insert a new node into a chain

1. Create a new node and store the new data in it.
2. Determine the point of insertion.
3. Connect the new node to the linked chain by changing pointers.

FIGURE 9-5   Inserting a new node between existing nodes of a linked chain

(a) Before the insertion of a new node

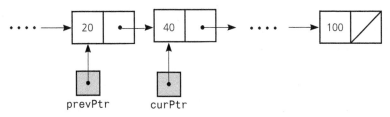

(b) After `newNodePtr->setNext(curPtr)` executes

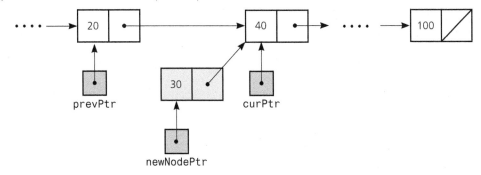

(c) After `prevPtr->setNext(newNodePtr)` executes

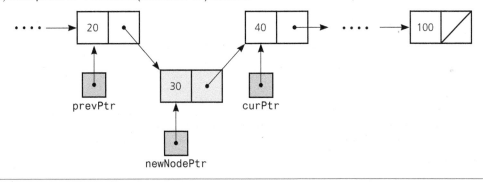

FIGURE 9-6   Inserting a new node at the end of a chain of linked nodes

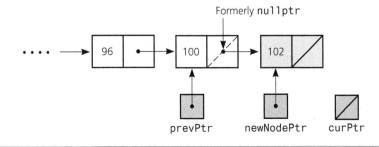

These steps and the previous discussion are implemented in the following definition of insert:

```cpp
template<class ItemType>
bool LinkedList<ItemType>::insert(int newPosition, const ItemType& newEntry)
{
   bool ableToInsert = (newPosition >= 1) && (newPosition <= itemCount + 1);
   if (ableToInsert)
   {
      // Create a new node containing the new entry
      Node<ItemType>* newNodePtr = new Node<ItemType>(newEntry);

      // Attach new node to chain
      if (newPosition == 1)
      {
         // Insert new node at beginning of chain
         newNodePtr->setNext(headPtr);
         headPtr = newNodePtr;
      }
      else
      {
         // Find node that will be before new node
         Node<ItemType>* prevPtr = getNodeAt(newPosition - 1);

         // Insert new node after node to which prevPtr points
         newNodePtr->setNext(prevPtr->getNext());
         prevPtr->setNext(newNodePtr);
      }  // end if

      itemCount++; // Increase count of entries
   }  // end if

   return ableToInsert;
}  // end insert
```

If you have not already begun to test the methods in the core group, you should do so now.

Question 5   Given a nonempty list that is an instance of LinkedList, at what position does an insertion of a new entry require the fewest operations? Explain.

Question 6   In the previous method insert, the second if statement tests the value of newPosition. Should the boolean expression it tests be isEmpty() || (newPosition == 1)? Explain.

Question 7   How does the insert method enforce the precondition of getNodeAt?

The method remove.   To remove any entry from a list, you must be able to remove any node from a chain of linked nodes. Let's consider the removal of an interior node.

As Figure 9-7 indicates, you can remove the node *N* to which curPtr points by altering the value of the pointer in the node that precedes *N*. You need to set this pointer so that it points to the node that follows *N*, thus bypassing *N* on the chain. (The dashed line indicates the old pointer value.) Notice that this pointer change does not directly affect node *N*. Node *N* remains in existence, and it points to the same node that it pointed to before the removal. However, the node has effectively been removed from the chain. For example, a traversal of the chain would never reach node *N*.

FIGURE 9-7 Removing a node from a chain

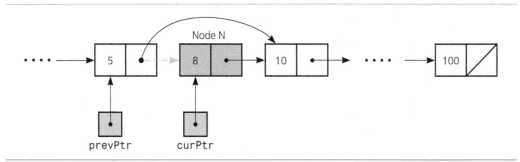

To accomplish this pointer change, notice first that if you had only the pointer `curPtr` pointing to N, you would have no direct way to access the node that precedes N. After all, you cannot follow the links in the chain backward. Thus, you must have the pointer variable `prevPtr` in Figure 9-7. It points to the node that precedes N and makes it possible for you to alter that node's `next` pointer, thereby removing node N from the chain. The following statement is all that you need to remove the node to which `curPtr` points:

```
prevPtr->setNext(curPtr->getNext());
```

Removing an interior node

Does the previous technique work for any node N, regardless of where in the linked chain it appears? No, it does not work if the node to be removed is the *first* node in the chain, but it does work for the last node in the chain. Thus, removing the first node in a chain is a special case, but removing the last node is not, as you will now see.

Figure 9-8 shows the removal of the node to which `curPtr` points, which happens to be the last node. That pointer alone is insufficient, as you must have the variable `prevPtr` point to the next-to-last node. You set the pointer within the next-to-last node to `nullptr`. The same statement that we just used to remove an interior node will make this pointer change, since the value of `curPtr->getNext()` is `nullptr`:

```
prevPtr->setNext(curPtr->getNext());
```

To remove a chain's first node, recall from the link-based implementations of the ADT bag in Chapter 4 and the ADT stack in Chapter 7, that you must change the value of `headPtr` to point to the second node. Thus, the second node becomes the chain's new first node. You make this change to `headPtr` by using the assignment statement

Removing the first node is a special case

```
headPtr = headPtr->getNext();
```

FIGURE 9-8 Removing the last node

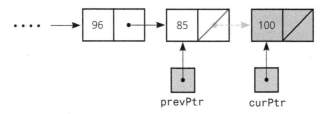

As was the case for the removal of an interior node, the pointers bypass the old first node, although it still exists. Notice also that if the node to be removed is the *only* node in the chain—and thus it is both the first node and the last node—the previous assignment statement assigns the value nullptr to the variable headPtr. Recall that the value nullptr in headPtr indicates an empty chain, and so this assignment statement handles the removal of the only node in a chain correctly.

The removed node still exists, however. Assuming that curPtr points to it, changing the value of curPtr will place the removed node in a state of limbo. It will still require storage space, and the program will no longer be able to access it. You would have a memory leak. Therefore, before you change the value of curPtr, you should use the statements

Return removed nodes to the system by using delete

```
curPtr->setNext(nullptr);
delete curPtr;
curPtr = nullptr;
```

to return the removed node's memory to the system.

To summarize, removing a node from a chain has three high-level steps:

Three steps to remove a node from a chain

1. Locate the node that you want to remove.
2. Disconnect this node from the linked chain by changing pointers.
3. Return the node to the system.

You will see these steps and the previous discussion implemented in the following definition of remove:

```cpp
template<class ItemType>
bool LinkedList<ItemType>::remove(int position)
{
   bool ableToRemove = (position >= 1) && (position <= itemCount);
   if (ableToRemove)
   {
      Node<ItemType>* curPtr = nullptr;
      if (position == 1)
      {
         // Remove the first node in the chain
         curPtr = headPtr; // Save pointer to node
         headPtr = headPtr->getNext();
      }
      else
      {
         // Find node that is before the one to remove
         Node<ItemType>* prevPtr = getNodeAt(position - 1);

         // Point to node to remove
         curPtr = prevPtr->getNext();

         // Disconnect indicated node from chain by connecting the
         // prior node with the one after
         prevPtr->setNext(curPtr->getNext());
      }  // end if

      // Return node to system
      curPtr->setNext(nullptr);
      delete curPtr;
      curPtr = nullptr;

      itemCount--; // Decrease count of entries
   }  // end if

   return ableToRemove;
}  // end remove
```

The method `clear`. To remove all entries from a list, you can use the method `remove`. Because the easiest entry to remove is the first one, the method `clear` can invoke `remove(1)` repeatedly until the list is empty. This action works because, after you remove the first entry in the list, the remaining entries are renumbered. Therefore, to remove all entries, you can repeatedly remove the first entry. Thus, `clear` has the following definition:

```
template<class ItemType>
void LinkedList<ItemType>::clear()
{
   while (!isEmpty())
      remove(1);
}  // end clear
```

Question 8 The link-based implementation of the method `clear` contains the following loop:

```
while (!isEmpty())
   remove(1);
```

a. Can you correctly replace the loop with

```
for (int position = getLength(); position >= 1; position--)
   remove(1);
```

b. Does your answer to part *a* differ if you replace `remove(1)` with `remove(position)`?
c. Do your answers to parts *a* and *b* differ if you replace the `for` statement with

```
for (int position = 1; position <= getLength(); position++)
```

The destructor. Because the method `clear` invokes `remove` repeatedly until the list is empty, and `remove` deallocates the nodes it removes, the destructor can simply call `clear`:

```
template<class ItemType>
LinkedList<ItemType>::~LinkedList()
{
   clear();
}  // end destructor
```

Question 9 Revise the destructor in the class `LinkedList` so that it directly deletes each node of the underlying linked chain without calling either `clear` or `remove`.

The remaining methods. This link-based implementation of the ADT list cannot use a compiler-generated copy constructor, as it would copy only the data members `headPtr` and `itemCount`. Instead, it must also copy the nodes and their contents. The link-based implementations of the ADT bag in Chapter 4 and the ADT stack in Chapter 7 have copy constructors that are quite similar to the one we require for the list. Thus, we leave its definition to you as an exercise, along with the method `replace`.

9.2.3   Using Recursion in LinkedList Methods

Using recursion in the implementation of some of the methods in the class LinkedList can be an attractive alternative to an iterative approach. Section 4.3 of Chapter 4 developed the recursive methods fillVector and getPointerTo for the class LinkedBag. Both methods considered a chain's first node and then recursively considered the rest of the chain. In general, we can state that you can process a linked chain by processing its first node and then the rest of the chain recursively. Thus, to add a new node to a chain of linked nodes at a given position, you use the following logic:

> if (*the insertion position is 1*)
> *Add the new node to the beginning of the chain*
> else
> *Ignore the first node and add the new node to the rest of the chain*

Adding to the beginning of a chain—or subchain—is the base case of this recursion. Happily, the beginning of a chain is the easiest place to make an addition.

If position is the desired position of the new node, newNodePtr points to the new node, and subChainPtr initially points to the chain and later points to the rest of the chain, we can add some detail to the previous logic, as follows:

> if (position == 1)
> {
>   newNodePtr->setNext(subChainPtr)
>   subChainPtr = newNodePtr
>   *Increment* itemCount
> }
> else
>   *Using recursion, add the new node at position* position - 1 *of the subchain pointed to by* subChainPtr->getNext()

The method insert. Let's look at the recursive implementation of the insertion operation before we describe why it works. You learned in Section 4.3 that you write a private method to perform the recursion and you write a public method—typically the one that implements the ADT's operation—to invoke this private method. Thus, the following definition of the public method insert calls the private recursive method insertNode:

```cpp
// The public method insert:
template<class ItemType>
bool LinkedList<ItemType>::insert(int newPosition, const ItemType& newEntry)
{
    bool ableToInsert = (newPosition >= 1) && (newPosition <= itemCount + 1);
    if (ableToInsert)
    {
        // Create a new node containing the new entry
        Node<ItemType>* newNodePtr = new Node<ItemType>(newEntry);
        headPtr = insertNode(newPosition, newNodePtr, headPtr);
    } // end if

    return ableToInsert;
} // end insert
```

The following private recursive method insertNode adds the new node to the subchain to which subChainPtr points at the given position:

```cpp
// The private method insertNode:

// Adds a given node to the subchain pointed to by subChainPtr
// at a given position. Returns a pointer to the augmented subchain.
```

```
template<class ItemType>
Node<ItemType>* LinkedList<ItemType>::insertNode(int position,
                Node<ItemType>* newNodePtr, Node<ItemType>* subChainPtr)
{
   if (position == 1)
   {
      // Insert new node at beginning of subchain
      newNodePtr->setNext(subChainPtr);
      subChainPtr = newNodePtr;
      itemCount++; // Increase count of entries
   }
   else
   {
      Node<ItemType>* afterPtr =
              insertNode(position - 1, newNodePtr, subChainPtr->getNext());
      subChainPtr->setNext(afterPtr);
   } // end if

   return subChainPtr;
} // end insertNode
```

We will trace and explain its logic next.

Tracing an addition to the list's beginning. Consider the list that the chain in Figure 9-9a represents. Let's add a new entry at the beginning of the chain by using an invocation such as

```
myList->insert(1, newEntry);
```

The public method insert will create a new node containing newEntry (Figure 9-9b) and then call the private method insertNode with the invocation

```
insertNode(1, newNodePtr, headPtr);
```

The reference in the argument headPtr is copied to the parameter subChainPtr, and so it also points to the first node in the chain, as Figure 9-9c illustrates.

The new node is linked to the beginning of the original chain, as Figure 9-9d shows. Notice that subChainPtr now points to the new node at the beginning of the chain. However, headPtr is unchanged, even though it is the argument that corresponds to the parameter subChainPtr. The private method now returns the value of subChainPtr, and the public method insert assigns that value to headPtr. The chain with the completed addition appears as in Figure 9-9e.

Tracing an addition to the list's interior. What happens when the addition is not at the beginning of the original chain? Let's trace what happens when we add a new third node to the chain given in Figure 9-9a. The public method insert creates a new node and calls the private method insertNode with the invocation

```
insertNode(3, newNodePtr, headPtr);
```

As in the previous example, the argument headPtr is copied to the parameter subChainPtr, and so it also points to the first node in the chain, as Figure 9-10a illustrates. Since the insertion is not at position 1, another recursive call occurs:

```
insertNode(2, newNodePtr, subChainPtr->getNext());
```

The third argument is a pointer to the chain's second node. This reference is copied to the parameter subChainPtr, as Figure 9-10b depicts. We still have not reached the insertion point, so the recursive process is repeated again:

```
insertNode(1, newNodePtr, subChainPtr->getNext());
```

FIGURE 9-9   Recursively adding a node at the beginning of a chain

(a) The list before any additions

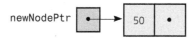

(b) After the public method `insert` creates a new node and before it calls `insertNode`

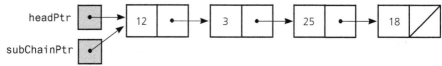

(c) As `insertNode(1, newNodePtr, headPtr)` begins execution

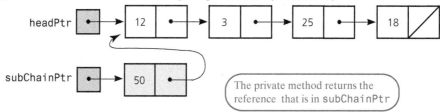

(d) After the new node is linked to the beginning of the chain (the base case)

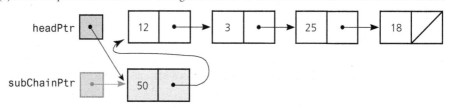

(e) After the public method `insert` assigns to `headPtr` the reference returned from `insertNode`

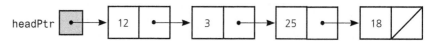

Now `subChainPtr` points to the chain's third node, as shown in Figure 9-10c, and we are at the desired position for the insertion into the chain. No other recursive call occurs, as this is the base case.

The given new node is inserted at the beginning of the subchain to which `subChainPtr` points, as Figure 9-10d illustrates, and then the private method `insertNode` returns a reference to the new node.

The statement

```
Node<ItemType>* afterPtr = insertNode(1, newNodePtr, subChainPtr->getNext());
```

FIGURE 9-10   Recursively adding a node between existing nodes in a chain

(a) As `insertNode(3, newNodePtr, headPtr)` begins execution

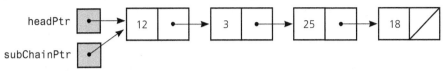

(b) As the recursive call `insertNode(2, newNodePtr, subChainPtr->getNext())` begins execution

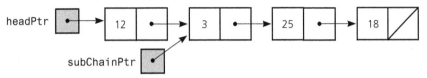

(c) As the recursive call `insertNode(1, newNodePtr, subChainPtr->getNext())` begins execution

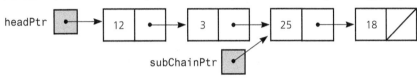

(d) After a new node is linked to the beginning of the subchain (the base case)

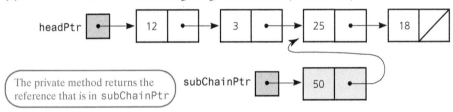

(e) After the returned reference is assigned to `afterPtr`

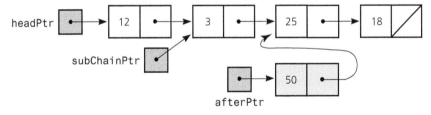

(f) After `subChainPtr->setNext(afterPtr)` executes

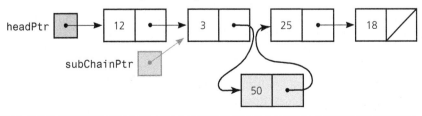

in insertNode now resumes execution. The reference to the new node returned by insertNode is assigned to afterPtr, as Figure 9-10e illustrates. At this time, subChainPtr references the second node, as it did in part *b* of the figure. The next statement to execute in insertNode is

```
subChainPtr->setNext(afterPtr);
```

This statement changes the next pointer in the second node to reference the new node, as shown in Figure 9-10f. The private method insertNode now returns a reference to the second node. If we continue the trace, we will see that the method makes the first node point to the second node and headPtr point to the first node, even though these pointers are already in place.

> **Note:** A recursive addition to a chain of nodes locates and remembers the nodes prior to the insertion point. After the portion of the chain that follows the insertion point is linked to the new node, the recursion links the remembered nodes back into the chain.

Question 10 Using recursion, revise the destructor in the class LinkedList so that it deletes each node of the underlying linked chain.

9.3   Comparing Implementations

The reasons for choosing an array-based implementation or a link-based implementation are the same as discussed in earlier chapters. Although the array-based implementation given in this chapter seems reasonable—after all, an array behaves like a list, and arrays are easy to use—it uses statically allocated memory. As such, it prevents the insert operation from adding an entry to the list if the array is full. If this restriction is not acceptable, you must either resize the array or use a link-based implementation.

The time to access the ith node in a chain of linked nodes depends on i

The array-based and link-based implementations have other differences as well, which affect their time and memory requirements. As we discussed in Section 4.5 of Chapter 4, the time to access an array element is constant, whereas you have no way of immediately accessing the ith node in a linked chain. Thus, the array-based getEntry method, for example, is almost instantaneous regardless of which list item you access. A link-based getEntry, however, requires i steps to access the ith item in the list.

You can access array items directly with equal access time

You already know that the array-based implementation of the ADT list requires you to shift the data when you add entries to or remove entries from the list. For example, if you remove the first entry of a 20-entry list, you must shift 19 entries. In general, removing the ith entry from a list of n entries requires $n - i$ shifts. Thus, remove requires $n - 1$ shifts to remove the first entry, but zero shifts to remove the last one. The method insert has similar requirements.

Insertions and removals with a link-based implementation do not require you to shift data but require a traversal

In contrast, you do not need to shift the data when you add entries to or remove entries from a chain of linked nodes. Thus, if the ADT list has a link-based implementation, the methods insert and remove require essentially the same effort—regardless of the length of the list or the position of the operation within the list—once you know the point of insertion or removal. Finding this point, however, requires a list traversal, the time for which will vary depending on where in the list the operation occurs. Recall that the private method getNodeAt performs this traversal. If you examine the definition of getNodeAt, you will see that getNodeAt(i) requires i assignment operations. Thus, getNodeAt's effort increases with i.

SUMMARY

1. Using an array results in a straightforward implementation of the ADT list, but it is somewhat more involved than the implementations of either the ADT bag or the ADT stack.

2. An array provides direct access to any of its elements, so a method such as getEntry can quickly retrieve any entry in a list.

3. Adding an entry to or removing an entry from an array-based list typically requires that other entries shift by one position within the array. This data movement degrades the time efficiency of these operations, particularly when the list is long and the position of the addition or removal is near the beginning of the list.

4. Adding entries to or removing entries from a chain of linked nodes does not require data to shift. Thus, the methods insert and remove of a link-based implementation of the ADT list require essentially the same effort—regardless of the length of the list or the position of the operation within the list—once the point of insertion or removal is known. Finding this point, however, requires a list traversal, the time for which will vary depending on where in the list the operation occurs.

5. Adding or removing an entry at the beginning of a link-based list is a special case.

6. Adding or removing an entry at the end of a link-based list requires a traversal of the underlying chain.

7. Adding or removing an entry anywhere within a link-based list requires a change of at most two pointers within the underlying chain.

8. The array-based getEntry method is almost instantaneous regardless of which list item you access. A link-based getEntry, however, requires i steps to access the ith item in the list.

EXERCISES

1. Add a constructor to each of the classes ArrayList and LinkedList that creates a list containing the entries in a given array.

2. Define the method replace for the class LinkedList.

3. Define the copy constructor for the class LinkedList.

4. Repeat the previous exercise, but use recursion in your definition.

5. For each of the classes ArrayList and LinkedList, implement the method getPosition, as described in Exercise 5 of Chapter 8.

6. Repeat the previous exercise, but use recursion in your definitions.

7. For each of the classes ArrayList and LinkedList, implement the method contains, as described in Exercise 7 of Chapter 8.

8. Repeat the previous exercise, but use recursion in your definitions.

9. For each of the classes ArrayList and LinkedList, implement the method remove, as described in Exercise 9 of Chapter 8.

10. Repeat the previous exercise, but use recursion in your definition.

11. Write a recursive definition of the private method getNodeAt for the class LinkedList.

12. The method clear for the class LinkedList repeatedly calls remove(1). Although easy to write, this method can be inefficient due to repeated method calls. Write another implementation for this method that deallocates the linked chain directly without calling remove.

13. A *double-ended list* has operations that operate at its beginning and end, in addition to the operations of the list, as given in Section 8.1 of Chapter 8. For example, you can add, remove, and get the first and last entries in a double-ended list. Write a C++ interface for the ADT double-ended list.

PROGRAMMING PROBLEMS

1. Write a program that thoroughly tests the classes ArrayList and LinkedList. During its execution, your program should give the user a choice of which class to test. After the results are displayed, the user should have the opportunity to choose the other class or quit.

2. Write an array-based implementation of the ADT list that expands the size of the array of list entries as needed so that the list can always accommodate a new entry.

3. Repeat the previous programming problem, but also reduce the size of the array as needed to accommodate several removals. When the size of the array is greater than 20 and the number of entries in the list is less than half the size of the array, reduce the size of the array so that it is three quarters of its current size.

4. Revise the array-based implementation of the ADT list to use recursion wherever you can.

5. Revise the link-based implementation of the ADT list to use recursion wherever you can.

6. Adding nodes to or removing nodes from a chain of linked nodes requires a special case when the operation is at the beginning of the chain. To eliminate the special case, you can add a **dummy node** at the beginning of the chain. The dummy node is always present but does not contain a list entry. The chain, then, is never empty, and so the head pointer never contains nullptr, even when the list is empty. Modify the class LinkedList, as presented in this chapter, by adding a dummy node to the chain.

7. Implement the ADT polynomial that Exercise 9 in Chapter 1 describes by using a list. Then write a program that adequately demonstrates your new class.

8. Implement a class of bags, as specified in Chapter 1, by using a list to contain the bag's entries. Then write a program that adequately demonstrates your new class.

9 Implement a class of stacks, as specified in Chapter 6, by using a list to contain the stack's entries. Then write a program that adequately demonstrates your new class.

10. Implement the ADT for the objects on Santa Claus's nice list, as described in Programming Problem 2 of Chapter 8. Then write a program for Santa that maintains his two lists of those who are naughty and those who are nice.

11. The popular social network Facebook was founded by Mark Zuckerberg and his classmates at Harvard University in 2004. At the time, he was a sophomore studying computer science.

    Design and implement an application that maintains the data for a simple social network. Each person in the network should have a profile that contains the person's name, optional image, current status, and a list of friends. Your application should allow a user to join the network, leave the network, create a profile, modify the profile, search for other profiles, and add friends.

12. A **tail pointer** is a pointer variable to the last node in a chain of linked nodes. Write a link-based implementation for a class of double-ended lists, as specified in Exercise 12, that uses both a head pointer and a tail pointer.

13. The solution to the HPAir problem described in Programming Problem 11 of Chapter 6 uses an adjacency list to represent the flight map. Repeat the solution to this problem, but define the adjacency list as a list of lists instead of an array of linked chains. Use lists that have a link-based implementation.

14. Define a class that implements the interface for the ADT double-ended list, as Exercise 13 describes. Use an implementation that is
    a. Array-based
    b. Link-based

15. (Gaming) Repeat Programming Problem 12 in Chapter 4 using a list to implement the ADT that tracks the turns of the players.

16. (Gaming) Use a list to implement the ADT starting gate, as described in Programming Problem 4 in Chapter 8. Write a program that thoroughly tests your class.

17. (Finance) Use a list to implement the ADT checkbook, as described in Programming Problem 5 in Chapter 8. Write a program that thoroughly tests your class.

18. (E-commerce) Use a list to implement the ADT gift registry, as described in Programming Problem 6 in Chapter 8.

Safe Memory Management Using Smart Pointers

Contents

Prerequisites

C++ Interlude 2   Pointers, Polymorphism, and Memory Allocation
Chapter 9   List Implementations

C++ is one of the few high-level programming languages that allow you to reference memory locations. While this ability enables you to finely tune the application's memory management, you need to know when and how to return an object's memory to the operating system. The techniques for these actions are error-prone and, if done improperly, can lead to crashed programs and security vulnerabilities. Smart pointers take care of these memory management details for you.

C4.1 Raw Pointers

Traditional pointers
are raw pointers

C++ Interlude 2 introduced you to traditional memory management techniques using pointers, which we now refer to as **raw pointers**. You allocate memory in the free store by using the new operator, which returns a reference to a newly created object in memory. You store this reference to the object in a pointer variable and use it to access the object. You can copy this reference to another pointer variable, thereby creating an alias to the same object. Later you must use the delete operator to deallocate the object's memory. You also must set to nullptr any pointer variables or aliases that referenced the object and are still in scope. By testing these pointers and aliases, you can avoid using them accidentally to reference the deleted object.

However, you need to keep track of the number of aliases that reference an object. Failure to perform this activity correctly can result in dangling pointers, memory leaks, and other errors, any of which can cause the program to crash, waste memory, or otherwise fail. These are challenging tasks when you are working alone on a program, but they become even more difficult to track when working on a team.

An object's
reference count is
the number of
aliases that
reference it

To avoid these issues, many programming languages, such as Java and Python, do not allow programmers to directly reference objects. These languages use **reference counting** to track the number of aliases that reference an object. This number of aliases is known as the **reference count**. In this way, such languages can detect when an object no longer has references to it and then periodically deallocate such objects using a process known as **garbage collection**. The algorithms that determine which objects to delete are quite complex—and can degrade application performance—since they must not only count references, but also identify situations in which two objects reference each other. If the only reference to each of these objects is the other object, the objects can be deleted even though their reference counts would not be zero.

Note: When a pointer can access a dynamically allocated object, the pointer is said to **own** the object, since it is responsible for deleting the object. For example, the raw pointer headPtr in the class LinkedList, as described in Chapter 9, owns the first node in the chain of linked nodes. That first node contains a pointer that owns the second node in the chain, and so on. LinkedList's destructor uses these pointers to deallocate all of the nodes in the chain.

Since the nodes are a private implementation detail of LinkedList, tracking their ownership might seem like a relatively easy task. However, challenges exist. For example, to remove a value from the middle of a list, you locate the value's node. You will have a pointer, curPtr, to the node and a pointer, prevPtr, to the preceding node. Moreover, each node contains a reference to another node. When you delete the designated node, you must update all necessary references to avoid a dangling pointer.

VideoNote
C++ Smart Pointers

C4.2 Smart Pointers

Many C++ programmers do not want to give up the control over memory allocation that raw pointers provide, nor sacrifice the performance penalties of garbage collection, even though they realize that C++ needs a safer model for managing memory. To this end, C++ now supports smart pointers. A **smart pointer**, or **managed pointer**, is an object that acts like a raw pointer but also provides some automatic memory management features. Memory deallocation with smart pointers occurs as soon as it can be determined that an object is no longer needed. Typically, this action happens when either the last reference to the object goes out of scope—often when a method or function ends—or the smart pointer is set to nullptr. As a result, some of the performance issues of garbage collection are avoided and as much unused memory as possible is made available for the application.

When you declare a smart pointer, it is placed on the application stack. When a smart pointer references an object, we say the object is **managed**. When the smart pointer goes out of scope, its destructor automatically invokes the destructor of the referenced object. Thus, when you use a smart pointer to reference an object, you do not need to use the `delete` operator. By design, the syntax of a smart pointer is almost like that of a raw pointer. In many cases, adapting our code to use smart pointers requires changes only to memory allocation statements.

A managed object is referenced by a smart pointer

You use standard class templates to provide smart pointers. To incorporate them into your program, you need the following directive:

```
#include <memory>
```

We cover three of the types of smart-pointer templates available in C++ here:

`shared_ptr`—Provides shared ownership of an object. Several instances of this class can reference the same object. These instances, which we will call **shared pointers**, use reference counting to detect when an object is no longer reachable by a smart pointer.

`unique_ptr`—Provides unique ownership of an object. During the time that an instance of this class, known as a **unique pointer**, references an object, no other smart pointer can reference the same object. A unique pointer uses a simplified form of reference counting to maintain a reference count of either 0 or 1 for its managed object.

`weak_ptr`—Provides a "weak," or non-owning, reference to an object that is already managed by a shared pointer. Since a **weak pointer** does not have ownership of the object, it cannot affect the object's lifetime. That is, you cannot use this type of pointer to delete the object. As you will see, you can use it when you want two objects to reference each other. Weak pointers do not use reference counting.

Aside

When smart pointers were first added to C++, they were called *smart* pointers. When they were formally added to the C++ Standard, they were named *managed* pointers. The term "smart pointer," however, persists in most documentation, and that is the terminology we will use.

C4.2.1 Using Shared Pointers

Because C++ does not have any restriction on the number of aliases that can reference an object, traditional raw pointers enable shared ownership of objects. Shared pointers also enable multiple references to an object, and they count these references for us. When a managed object is assigned to a shared pointer, the object's reference count is increased by 1.

Each shared pointer owns the object and, if it provides the last reference to the object, has the responsibility to delete the object. However, you do not need to explicitly use the `delete` operator to destroy the managed object. Each time a shared pointer goes out of scope or no longer references its original managed object, it decreases the object's reference count by 1. When the reference count becomes 0, the object's destructor is called for us.

For example, if we wanted to use a raw pointer to create and manipulate a `MagicBox` object—as described in C++ Interlude 1—we could define a function like the following one:

```
void magicFunctionRaw()
{
    MagicBox<std::string>* myMagicPtr = new MagicBox<std::string>();
    std::cout << myMagicPtr->getItem() << std::endl;
    delete myMagicPtr;
    myMagicPtr = nullptr;
} // end magicFunctionRaw
```

In contrast, we could use a shared pointer in a similar function as follows:

```
void magicFunction()
{
    std::shared_ptr<MagicBox<std::string>>
                                  myMagicPtr(new MagicBox<std::string>());
    std::cout << myMagicPtr->getItem() << std::endl;
    // The MagicBox object will be deleted automatically when
    // myMagicPtr goes out of scope.
} // end magicFunction
```

Let's examine the syntax of the statement that creates the shared pointer and allocates memory for our `MagicBox` managed object. We still use the variable `myMagicPtr` to reference a dynamically created `MagicBox` object; however, the type of `myMagicPtr` is now

```
std::shared_ptr<MagicBox<std::string>>
```

As mentioned previously, `shared_ptr` is a class template. In this case, the template type is `MagicBox<std::string>`. The expression

```
myMagicPtr(new MagicBox<std::string>());
```

sends to `shared_ptr`'s constructor the reference returned by the `new` operator and the default `MagicBox` constructor `MagicBox<std::string>()`.

When you dynamically create an object and make the first shared pointer reference—and thereby manage—it, `shared_ptr`'s constructor dynamically allocates a **manager object**. The shared pointer then references the manager object. The manager object has both a reference to the **managed object** and a reference count of the shared pointers that reference the managed object, as Figure C4-1 illustrates. Since three shared pointers reference the manager object in this figure, the reference count is 3.

> A shared pointer references a manager object, which references the managed object

---

FIGURE C4-1   Shared pointers and the manager object referencing a managed object

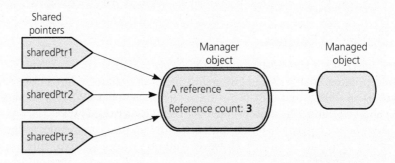

In the previous function `magicFunction`, two memory allocations occur, one when the `MagicBox` object is created explicitly with `new` and a second implicit allocation for the manager object. If you use the standard library function `make_shared` as follows to create both the `MagicBox` object and its manager object, only one memory allocation will occur:

```
std::shared_ptr<MagicBox<std::string>> myMagicPtr =
                        std::make_shared<MagicBox<std::string>>();
```

The code generated by the compiler makes one dynamic memory allocation to create both the managed object and the manager object at the same time. Deletion of both objects will be done for you as well. The result is faster code and better overall memory management.

The C++ Standards Committee realized that the previous syntax is complicated and might hide the true intent of the code, and so it provided a tool to simplify the code. As a result, you can use the keyword `auto` when declaring a variable, function, or method, and let the compiler determine the variable type or return type. For example, you can revise our previous statement as follows:

Use auto when possible to declare a variable, function, or method

```
auto myMagicPtr = std::make_shared<MagicBox<std::string>>();
```

We can now simplify `magicFunction` as follows:

```
void magicFunction()
{
    auto myMagicPtr = std::make_shared<MagicBox<std::string>>();
    std::cout << myMagicPtr->getItem() << std::endl;
} // end magicFunction
```

Note: **The keyword `auto`**

The keyword `auto`
* Tells the compiler to determine the type of a variable from its initializer
* Tells the compiler to determine the return type of a function or method (C++14 and later only)
* Cannot be used as the data type of a parameter of a function or method

Note: To use `auto` successfully, you must write an expression whose data type is clear to the compiler. In our previous statement, the expression

```
std::make_shared<MagicBox<std::string>>()
```

returns a shared pointer to a dynamically allocated `MagicBox<std:string>` object. Thus, the complier can deduce the data type of `myMagicPtr`. We prefer to use `auto` whenever possible.

You can create a shared pointer that does not yet reference an object. For example, the following statement creates a shared pointer that can reference a `PlainBox` object, but it does not create the object:

```
std::shared_ptr<PlainBox<std::string>> myPlainPtr;
```

Because we have used `PlainBox`'s default constructor, the resulting pointer `myPlainPtr` contains `nullptr`, and the associated reference count is 0. When you either use an assignment statement to define an alias for an existing shared pointer or pass a shared pointer by value as an argument to a function or method, the `shared_ptr` copy constructor will make a shallow copy of the shared pointer and increment the managed object's reference count.

Note: Shared pointers

A shared pointer
- Provides a safe mechanism to implement shared object ownership
- Maintains a count of aliases to an object
- Increases the reference count of its managed object by 1 each time the shared pointer's copy constructor is called
- Decreases the reference count of its managed object by 1 when the shared pointer goes out of scope
- Decreases the reference count of its managed object by 1 when the shared pointer is assigned `nullptr`
- Calls the destructor of the managed object when the reference count of this object reaches 0

C4.2.2 Revised `Node` and `LinkedList` Classes

We can use shared pointers in our earlier `Node` and `LinkedList` classes to help ensure that we handle memory correctly. We begin by revising the `Node` class originally found in Listings 4-1 and 4-2 of Chapter 4. We replace the raw pointer type `Node<ItemType>*` of the data field `next` with a shared pointer type `std::shared_ptr<Node<ItemType>>`. Since the default constructor of `shared_ptr` initializes `next` to `nullptr`, we do not need to include `next` in the initializer list of our default constructor. The `getNext` method returns the data field `next`, so the compiler can easily determine the method's return type from `next`'s data type. Listings C4-1 and C4-2 reflect our revised `Node` class.

LISTING C4-1 The revised header file for the class `Node`, originally given in Listing 4-1

A revised class `Node` that uses smart pointers

```
1   #include <memory>
2   template<class ItemType>
3   class Node
4   {
5   private:
6       ItemType item;                          // A data item
7       std::shared_ptr<Node<ItemType>> next; // Pointer to next node
8
9   public:
10      Node();
11      Node(const ItemType& anItem);
12      Node(const ItemType& anItem,
13          std::shared_ptr<Node<ItemType>> nextNodePtr);
14      void setItem(const ItemType& anItem);
15      void setNext(std::shared_ptr<Node<ItemType>> nextNodePtr);
16      ItemType getItem() const;
17      auto getNext() const;
18  }; // end Node
```

LISTING C4-2 The revised implementation file for the class `Node`, originally given in Listing 4-2

```cpp
1    #include "Node.h"
2
3    template<class ItemType>
4    Node<ItemType>::Node()
5    { } // end default constructor
6
7    template<class ItemType>
8    Node<ItemType>::Node(const ItemType& anItem): item(anItem)
9    { } // end constructor
10
11   template<class ItemType>
12   Node<ItemType>::Node(const ItemType& anItem,
13                        std::shared_ptr<Node<ItemType>> nextNodePtr)
14                        : item(anItem), next(nextNodePtr)
15   { } // end constructor
16
17   template<class ItemType>
18   void Node<ItemType>::setItem(const ItemType& anItem)
19   {
20      item = anItem;
21   }  // end setItem
22
23   template<class ItemType>
24   void Node<ItemType>::setNext(std::shared_ptr<Node<ItemType>> nextNodePtr)
25   {
26      next = nextNodePtr;
27   }  // end setNext
28
29   template<class ItemType>
30   ItemType Node<ItemType>::getItem() const
31   {
32      return item;
33   }  // end getItem
34
35   template<class ItemType>
36   auto Node<ItemType>::getNext() const
37   {
38      return next;
39   }  // end getNext
```

Chapter 9 discussed an implementation of the class `LinkedList` using raw pointers. Let's now revise that implementation to use smart pointers and our revised `Node` class. The public interface `ListInterface`, which appears in Listing 8-1 of Chapter 8, does not need to change. After all, pointers are an implementation detail of `LinkedList`. We do need to make some revisions to the header file for `LinkedList` that is given in Listing 9-2 of Chapter 9. We make the head pointer a shared pointer instead of a raw pointer by declaring it as follows:

```cpp
std::shared_ptr<Node<ItemType>> headPtr;
```

In addition, we either can explicitly declare the return type of the private method `getNodeAt` or use the `auto` keyword as we do here:

```
auto getNodeAt(int position) const;
```

Note: **Why are we using shared pointers in `Node` and `LinkedList` instead of a different smart pointer?**

The methods in `LinkedList` require aliases to various nodes in the chain of linked nodes. Since more than one pointer will reference a node, we must use shared pointers.

Listing C4-3 shows a definition for `LinkedList`'s `insert` method using smart pointers. If the position is valid and we are able to insert a new node into the linked chain, we create a managed object of type `Node` with `newEntry` as its data and let the shared pointer `newNodePtr` reference it. The reference count for this new node is 1, since the node's only reference is in `newNodePtr`.

If we are inserting the new entry at the beginning of the list, we make the new node reference the current first node in the chain and let `headPtr` reference this new node. Here, the reference count for our new node is 2, since both `newNodePtr` and `headPtr` reference it, as Figure 4-7 in Chapter 4 shows.

If the insertion position, k, of the new entry is not at the beginning of the list, we let the node at position $k - 1$ reference the new node, and let the new node reference the node originally at position k. Here again, our new node has two references, `newNodePtr` and the `next` field in the preceding node, as Figure 9-5c in Chapter 9 illustrates.

In both of the previous cases, when the `insert` method ends, `newNodePtr` goes out of scope and is destroyed. Therefore, the reference count for our inserted node reduces to 1, because either `headPtr` or the `next` field of its preceding node still references it. When `insert` terminates, all nodes in the linked chain should have a reference count of 1.

Note: When the method `insert` terminates, local pointer variables, such as `newNodePtr`, `prevPtr`, and `curPtr` in Figure 9-5, go out of scope. However, the nodes they referenced are not destroyed, because either other nodes in the list or `headPtr` reference them.

LISTING C4-3 **The `insert` method for `LinkedList`**

```
 1   template<class ItemType>
 2   bool LinkedList<ItemType>::insert(int newPosition,
 3                                     const ItemType& newEntry)
 4   {
 5      bool ableToInsert = (newPosition >= 1) &&
 6                          (newPosition <= itemCount + 1);
 7      if (ableToInsert)
 8      {
 9         // Create a new node containing the new entry
10         auto newNodePtr = std::make_shared<Node<ItemType>>(newEntry);
11
12         // Attach new node to chain
13         if (newPosition == 1)
14         {
```

```
15            // Insert new node at beginning of chain
16            newNodePtr->setNext(headPtr);
17            headPtr = newNodePtr;
18         }
19         else
20         {
21            // Find node that will be before new node
22            auto prevPtr = getNodeAt(newPosition - 1);
23
24            // Insert new node after node to which prevPtr points
25            newNodePtr->setNext(prevPtr->getNext());
26            prevPtr->setNext(newNodePtr);
27         }  // end if
28
29         itemCount++; // Increase count of entries
30      }  // end if
31
32      return ableToInsert;
33   }  // end insert
```

Next, consider LinkedList's remove method using smart pointers, as given in Listing C4-4. Let's look at the automatic reference counting provided by smart pointers. When we enter the remove method, each node in our list has a reference count of 1. The first node is referenced only by headPtr, and each subsequent node is referenced only by its preceding node. To remove a node, we need to sever this reference and then link the part of the chain before the node to the section following the node. When the method terminates, all nodes remaining in the linked chain will still have a reference count of 1.

If we want to remove the node at the beginning of the list, we make headPtr reference the second node in the linked chain. The reference count of the original first node is automatically decremented to 0. The reference count of the new first node in the chain is incremented to 2. When the method terminates, the old first node is deleted since it has a reference count of 0. The destructor also deletes the next field of this node, which reduces the reference count of the new first node to 1.

If we want to remove a node from the interior of the list, we let curPtr reference this node and let prevPtr reference the node before it, as Figure 9-7 in Chapter 9 illustrates. These actions increase the reference count of each of these two nodes to 2. When we make prevPtr's node reference the node after the one to remove, the reference count of the latter node increases to 2 and the reference count of the removed node decreases to 1, as only curPtr references it. When the remove method ends, curPtr goes out of scope, which decreases the reference count of the removed node to 0. Therefore, this node is deleted. As before, the removed node no longer references the node that had followed it, so that node's reference count is again 1. The local pointer prevPtr also goes out of scope, which makes the reference count of the node it referenced decrease to 1. As with insert, when remove terminates, all nodes in the linked chain will have a reference count of 1.

The remove method behaves in a similar way when it removes a node from the end of the linked chain.

LISTING C4-4 The remove method for LinkedList

```cpp
1   template<class ItemType>
2   bool LinkedList<ItemType>::remove(int position)
3   {
4      bool ableToRemove = (position >= 1) && (position <= itemCount);
5      if (ableToRemove)
6      {
7         if (position == 1)
8         {
9            // Remove the first node in the chain
10           headPtr = headPtr->getNext();
11        }
12        else
13        {
14           // Find node that is before the one to delete
15           auto prevPtr = getNodeAt(position - 1);
16
17           // Point to node to delete
18           auto curPtr = prevPtr->getNext();
19
20           // Disconnect indicated node from chain by connecting the
21           // prior node with the one after
22           prevPtr->setNext(curPtr->getNext());
23        } // end if
24
25        itemCount--; // Decrease count of entries
26     } // end if
27
28     return ableToRemove;
29  } // end remove
```

Finally, let's look at the clear method, as given in Chapter 9:

```cpp
template<class ItemType>
void LinkedList<ItemType>::clear()
{
   while (!isEmpty())
      remove(1);
} // end clear
```

Because this implementation uses raw pointers, we must explicitly delete each node in the linked chain. Since the remove method does this, clear calls it instead of repeating the code to perform the deletions. Using smart pointers, we can write the clear method as follows:

The use of smart pointers allows a simple definition of the method clear

```cpp
template<class ItemType>
void LinkedList<ItemType>::clear()
{
   headPtr = nullptr;
   itemCount = 0;
} // end clear
```

By setting headPtr to nullptr, we reduce the reference count of the first node to 0. When the first node is deallocated, the reference count of the second node will be reduced to 0 and thus this node will be deallocated, and so on until the entire chain has been deallocated.

By using smart pointers in our LinkedList class, we no longer have to manually count references and explicitly delete nodes.

C4.2.3 Using Unique Pointers

When several shared pointers reference an object, each of them owns the object. Shared ownership is necessary for many operations on a linked chain, such as traversing its nodes or adding and removing nodes. When implementing each of these operations, we need multiple references—that is, aliases—to the nodes. One reference to a particular node is the next field of the previous node in the chain. Other references are by the aliases that indicate whether the node represents a previous node or a current node.

Sometimes, however, we need to control a managed object's lifetime with extra care, and so we will not want to share the object's ownership. In these cases, we can use a unique pointer. When a unique pointer references a managed object, it can be the only smart pointer that owns the managed object.

Many aspects of a unique pointer are similar to those of a shared pointer, but some differences set unique pointers apart. Unique ownership occurs because unique_ptr does not have a copy constructor. Therefore, two unique pointers can never reference the same managed object in memory. Although a unique pointer does not have a reference count, it behaves as if it has a reference count of 0 or 1. Lastly, if a unique pointer references a managed object, the object is deleted when the pointer goes out of scope.

We can create a unique pointer in several ways, as each of the following statements demonstrates:

```
std::unique_ptr<MagicBox<std::string>> myMagicPtr(new MagicBox<std::string>());
auto myToyPtr = std::make_unique<ToyBox<std::string>>(); // C++14 and later
std::unique_ptr<MagicBox<std::string>> myFancyPtr;        // Empty unique_ptr
```

> Some ways to create a unique pointer

The unique pointer myMagicPtr references and owns a new MagicBox object. Likewise, the unique pointer myToyPtr references and owns a new ToyBox object. Lastly, the unique pointer myFancyPtr contains nullptr.

Since unique_ptr has no copy constructor, you cannot assign one unique pointer to another. For example, the following statement is illegal:

```
myFancyPtr = myMagicPtr; // Error: copy assignment is not permitted
```

Instead, you must transfer ownership of the managed object by using unique_ptr's move function:

```
myFancyPtr = std::move(myMagicPtr); // myMagicPtr now owns nothing
```

The unique pointer myMagicPtr that previously referenced the managed object in this example now references nothing and is set to nullptr. Attempting to invoke a method using myMagicPtr would result in an error.

Note: Although you cannot assign one unique pointer to another unique pointer, you can **transfer its ownership** to another unique pointer by using the standard library function move. Once ownership is transferred, the original unique pointer no longer owns any object and is set to nullptr. Therefore, you should not use that pointer until it manages another object.

Because unique pointers do not have a copy constructor, passing a unique pointer to a function or method must be done either by reference or by using the standard library function move. For example, the following function has a parameter whose type is unique_ptr and that is passed by reference:

> Unique pointers do not have a copy constructor

```
void showBoxItem(std::unique_ptr<PlainBox<std::string>>& theBox)
{
   std::cout << theBox->getItem() << std::endl;
} // end showBoxItem
```

We could call `showBoxItem` by passing it the unique pointer `myFancyPtr` from the previous example, as follows:

```
showBoxItem(myFancyPtr);
```

Since `myFancyPtr` is passed by reference, the caller retains ownership of the managed object that the pointer references.

When returning an object from a function or method, C++ moves the object into the receiving variable. We can use this fact to our advantage and create a function that accepts ownership of an object and then returns it to the caller. The following function does just that:

```
// This method's return type is the type of the object returned.
auto changeBoxItem(std::unique_ptr<PlainBox<std::string>> theBox,
                   std::string theItem)
{
   theBox->setItem(theItem);
   return theBox; // theBox surrenders ownership
} // end changeBoxItem
```

Suppose that we call this function with the unique pointer `myFancyPtr` from our earlier examples:

```
myFancyPtr = changeBoxItem(std::move(myFancyPtr), "Hammer");
```

We use the method `move` to pass the argument to the function and then reassign the returned object to the original unique pointer `myFancyPtr`. If we did not reassign the object to `myFancyPtr`, the pointer would own nothing.

 Note: **Unique pointers**

A unique pointer
- Has solitary ownership of its managed object
- Behaves as if it maintains a reference count of either 0 or 1 for its managed object
- Cannot be assigned to another unique pointer
- Can transfer its unique ownership of its managed object to another unique pointer using the method `move`

C4.2.4 Using Weak Pointers

A weak pointer stores a reference to an object managed only by shared pointers, but does not increment the reference count for the object. We say that a weak pointer only *observes* the managed object but does not have ownership and, therefore, cannot affect its lifetime.

For example, consider the following statements:

```
auto sharedPtr1 = std::make_shared<MagicBox<std::string>>();
auto sharedPtr2 = sharedPtr1;
auto sharedPtr3 = sharedPtr1;
```

```
std::weak_ptr<MagicBox<std::string>> weakPtr1 = sharedPtr1;
auto weakPtr2 = weakPtr1;
```

After these statements execute, the reference count for the object managed by `sharedPtr1` is 3, as Figure C4-2 illustrates, because three shared pointers reference it.

FIGURE C4-2   Weak and shared ownership of a managed object

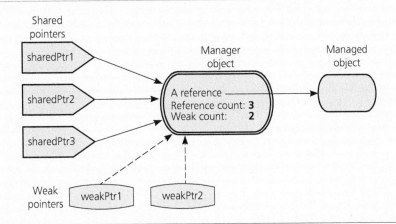

You cannot use a weak pointer such as `weakPtr1` to work with our `MagicBox` object. For example, you cannot use * or -> with a weak pointer, and therefore you cannot write an expression such as `weakPtr1->setItem("Rabbit")`. However, the class `weak_ptr` has the method `lock`; it checks to see whether the managed object still exists and, if it does, returns a shared pointer to the object. This action increments the reference count for the object, "locking" it into existence for as long as the newly created shared pointer is in scope. Thus, we can invoke `setItem` by writing the following statements:

```
// Get a shared pointer
shared_ptr<MagicBox<std::string>> sharedPtr = weakPtr1.lock();
sharedPtr->setItem("Rabbit"); // Correct access
```

Although `weakPtr1`, as a weak pointer, cannot access the object it references, we can use the `lock` method to get a shared pointer to the object and then access it. Note that when `sharedPtr` goes out of scope, the reference count of the managed object returns to its previous value.

Because a weak pointer does not affect the reference count of a managed object, it might still reference the object after the object has been deallocated. In this case, the pointer's `lock` method will return `nullptr`, enabling you to detect this issue. Another way to check whether a managed object has been deleted is to call `weak_ptr`'s `expired` method. This method returns true if the managed object has been deleted.

Exercise 10 of Chapter 4 introduced the doubly linked chain whose nodes can each point to the previous node in the chain as well as the next node. Suppose that `DoubleNode` is a class of such nodes that defines its data fields `next` and `previous` as shared pointers. Figure 4-10 depicts such a chain. Note that the `previous` field of the first node and the `next` field of the last node each contain `nullptr`. Except for the last node, each node in this chain has a reference count of 2.

Suppose that we wanted to write a method to deallocate the entire chain. In the previous section, the method `clear` for the class `LinkedList` sets the chain's head pointer to `nullptr` to deallocate the entire chain. However, doing so here will not work. If we set `headPtr` to `nullptr`, the first node in the doubly linked chain would still have a reference count of 1, because the second node's `previous` field references it. As a result, the first node would not be deleted, nor would the rest of the chain.

To solve this problem, we define the `previous` field as a weak pointer, as shown in Listing C4-5. Now the references to previous nodes are all weak pointers, so they do not affect the reference count of the managed objects. Therefore, each of our doubly linked nodes has a reference count of 1—the reference in either `headPtr` or the node's preceding node. Now, if we set `headPtr` to `nullptr`, the first node will have a reference count of 0 and the sequence of destructors will be called, as occurs in our method `clear` with a singly linked chain.

LISTING C4-5   **Partial header file for the class `DoubleNode`**

```
1    template<class ItemType>
2    class DoubleNode
3    {
4    private:
5       ItemType item;                                  // A data item
6       std::shared_ptr<DoubleNode<ItemType>> next;     // Pointer to next node
7       std::weak_ptr<DoubleNode<ItemType>> previous;   // Pointer to previous node
8    public:
9       // Constructors, destructors, and methods
10   }; // end DoubleNode
```

Note: **Weak pointers**

A weak pointer
- References but does not own an object that is referenced by a shared pointer
- Cannot affect the lifetime of the managed object
- Does not affect the reference count of the managed object
- Has the method `lock` to provide a shared-pointer version of its reference
- Has the method `expired` to detect whether its reference object no longer exists

C4.3   Other Smart Pointer Features

As objects themselves, smart pointers have several member functions. Section C4.2.4 presented the member functions `lock` and `expired` that are specific to weak pointers. Some methods that are common to more than one kind of smart pointer are `reset`, `get`, and `operator bool`.

C4.3.1 A Method Common to All Smart Pointers

The `reset` method gives the smart pointer ownership of the managed object passed as an argument. For example, if `mySmartPtr` and `myOtherPtr` are smart pointers,

```
mySmartPtr.reset(myOtherPtr);
```

is equivalent to the assignment statement

```
mySmartPtr = myOtherPtr;
```

If reset has no argument, the smart pointer is set to nullptr. Thus,

```
mySmartPtr2.reset();
```

has the same effect as

```
mySmartPtr2 = nullptr;
```

When mySmartPtr2 is a unique pointer, its previously managed object is deleted and the unique pointer set to nullptr. When it's a shared pointer, the reference count of the previously managed object is decreased by 1; if this was the last pointer to the object, the object will be destroyed. Lastly, if the pointer was a weak pointer, the lifetime of the previously managed object is not affected.

C4.3.2 A Method Common to All Shared and Unique Pointers

Both unique_ptr and shared_ptr have a member method get that returns the reference to the managed object in a raw pointer. The reference count of the managed object is not changed by this method, so ownership of the object is not released or shared. For example, after the following statements execute, myMagicPtr is a shared smart pointer that manages the MagicBox object, and myRawPtr is a raw pointer that references the same object.

```
auto myMagicPtr = std::make_shared<MagicBox<std::string>>();
MagicBox<std::string>* myRawPtr = myMagicPtr.get();
```

Use of the method get is recommended only for times when a library or legacy code may not work properly with smart pointers. Mixing raw pointers and smart pointers is dangerous, because a dangling pointer could result. Such would be the case if the managed object is deleted while a raw pointer remains in scope and references it. Note that raw pointers are not included in the reference count maintained by the manager object.

Using both raw pointers and smart pointers in the same code is dangerous

You can also use * to dereference a smart pointer, as in the following statement:

```
MagicBox<std::string> myMagicBox = *myMagicPtr;
```

As with other standard library objects in C++, you can test whether a smart pointer references a valid object, as in the following example:

```
if (myMagicPtr)
{
    std::cout << myMagicPtr->getItem() << std::endl;
}
```

C4.3.3 Methods Exclusive to Shared Pointers

Because the object managed by a shared pointer can have multiple owners, two methods can assist in object management:

- unique—Returns true if this shared pointer is the only owner of the managed object
- use_count—Returns the reference count for the managed object

The following statements demonstrate these two methods:

```
auto myMagicPtr = std::make_shared<MagicBox<std::string>>();
std::cout << myMagicPtr.unique() << std::endl;     // Displays true
std::cout << myMagicPtr.use_count() << std::endl;  // Displays 1

auto myOtherPtr = myMagicPtr;
std::cout << myMagicPtr.unique() << std::endl;      // Displays false
std::cout << myMagicPtr.use_count() << std::endl;  // Displays 2
```

C4.3.4 A Method Exclusive to Unique Pointers

If you want a unique pointer to release ownership of a managed object, but you want the object to persist after the unique pointer goes out of scope, you can use the member method `release`. Typically, you would call `release` after getting a raw pointer to the managed object by calling `get`. Remember that after you call `release`, the object is no longer managed and you now have the responsibility of deleting it.

C4.3.5 Unique Pointers with Arrays

You can use a unique pointer to manage a dynamic array. For example, you can rewrite the statement

```
MagicBox<std::string>* magicArray[] = new MagicBox<std::string>[MAX_SIZE];
```

as

```
std::unique_ptr<MagicBox<std::string>[]> magicArray =
                        std::make_unique<MagicBox<std::string>>[MAX_SIZE];
```

Notice the location of the [] in the previous statement. The use of a unique pointer here causes the compiler to insert code that will deallocate the dynamically created array, when `magicArray` goes out of scope.

Algorithm Efficiency

Contents

Prerequisites

This chapter will show you how to analyze the efficiency of algorithms. The basic mathematical techniques for analyzing algorithms are central to more advanced topics in computer science and give you a way to formalize the notion that one algorithm is significantly more efficient than another. As examples, you will see analyses of some algorithms that you have studied before, including those that search data. The next chapter presents sorting algorithms, and they provide additional examples of analyzing efficiency.

10.1 What Is a Good Solution?

In this textbook a computer program is the final form your solutions take, so we should consider what constitutes a good computer program. Presumably, you write a program to perform some task. While performing that task, the program incurs a real and tangible **cost**. This cost includes such factors as the computing time and memory that the program requires, the difficulties encountered by those who use the program, and the consequences of a program that does not behave correctly.

However, the costs just mentioned do not give the whole picture. They pertain only to the life of the solution after it has been developed. In assessing whether a solution is good, you also must consider the effort required to develop the solution as well as any changes—bug fixes or extensions—to the program that are made after the program has been deployed. Each of these incurs costs, too. The total cost of a solution must take into account the value of the time of the people who analyzed, designed, coded, debugged, and tested it. A solution's cost must also include the cost of maintaining, modifying, and expanding it.

Thus, when calculating the overall cost of a solution, you must include a diverse set of factors. If you adopt such a multidimensional view of cost, it is reasonable to evaluate a solution against the following criterion:

A solution is good if the total cost it incurs over all phases of its life is minimal.

Suppose two algorithms perform the same task, such as searching. What does it mean to compare the algorithms and conclude that one is better? The faster one is not necessarily better. Several components contribute to the cost of a computer program, including the cost of human time—the time of the people who develop, maintain, and use the program—and the cost of program execution—that is, its efficiency—measured by the amount of computer time and memory that the program requires to execute.

Today's programs are larger and more complex than ever before. Typically, many people are involved in their development. Good structure and documentation are thus of the utmost importance. In addition, the costs associated with malfunctions are high. People should not have to entrust their livelihoods—or their lives—to a program that only its authors can understand and maintain. Thus, society needs both well-structured programs and techniques for formally verifying their correctness.

At the same time, do not get the impression that a solution's execution time is no longer important. To the contrary, many situations occur for which efficiency is the prime determinant of whether a solution is even usable. However, a solution's efficiency is only one of many aspects that you must consider. If two solutions have approximately the same efficiency, other factors should dominate the comparison. However, when the efficiencies of solutions differ significantly, this difference can be the overriding concern.

Efficiency is only one aspect of a solution's cost

You should be most concerned about efficiency when you develop the underlying algorithm. The choice of a solution's components—the objects and the design of the interactions between those objects—rather than the code you write, has the most significant impact on efficiency. This book advocates a problem-solving philosophy that views the cost of a solution as multidimensional. This philosophy is important to the overall strategy of a successful software project.

 Note: The relative importance of the various components of a solution's cost has changed since the early days of computing. In the beginning, the cost of computer time relative to human time was extremely high. In this type of environment, one cost clearly overshadowed all others: computer resources. If two programs performed the same task, the one that required less time and memory was better.

Computing costs have dropped dramatically since the early days of computers. Thus, the value of the designers' and programmers' time is a much more significant factor than computing time in the cost of a solution. These developments have made obsolete the notion that the fastest-executing solution is always the best. However, some solutions require more computing time than is practical, so knowing how to reduce this time remains important.

10.2 Measuring the Efficiency of Algorithms

VideoNote
Measuring algorithmic efficiency

Well-designed algorithms reduce the human costs of writing a program to implement the algorithm, of maintaining the program, and of modifying the program. Developing good problem-solving skills and programming style has been and continues to be important. However, the efficiency of algorithms is also important. Efficiency is a criterion that you should consider when selecting an algorithm and its implementation.

Consider efficiency when selecting an algorithm

The comparison of algorithms is a topic central to computer science. Measuring an algorithm's efficiency is quite important because your choice of algorithm for a given application often has a great impact. Responsive word processors, grocery checkout systems, automatic teller machines, video games, and life support systems all depend on efficient algorithms.

The **analysis of algorithms** is the area of computer science that provides tools for contrasting the efficiency of different algorithms. Notice the use of the term "algorithms" rather than "programs"; it is important to emphasize that the analysis concerns itself primarily with *significant* differences in efficiency—differences that you can usually obtain only through superior algorithms and rarely through clever tricks in coding. Reductions in computing costs due to clever coding tricks are often more than offset by reduced program readability, which increases human costs. An analysis should focus on gross differences in the efficiency of algorithms that are likely to dominate the overall cost of a solution. To do otherwise could lead you to select an algorithm that runs a small fraction of a second faster than another algorithm yet requires many more hours of your time to implement and maintain.

A comparison of algorithms should focus on significant differences in efficiency

The efficient use of both time and memory is important. The techniques for analyzing time efficiency and space efficiency are similar. However, none of the algorithms covered in this text has significant space requirements, so our focus is primarily on time efficiency.

How do you compare the time efficiency of two algorithms that solve the same problem? One possible approach is to implement the two algorithms and run the programs. This approach has at least three fundamental problems:

Three difficulties with comparing programs instead of algorithms

- **How are the algorithms coded?** If algorithm A runs faster than algorithm B, it could be the result of better programming. Thus, if you compare the running times of the programs, you are really comparing implementations of the algorithms rather than the algorithms themselves. You should not compare implementations, because they are sensitive to factors such as programming style that tend to cloud the issue of which algorithm is inherently more efficient.
- **What computer should you use?** The particular operations that the algorithms require can cause A to run faster than B on one computer, while the opposite is true on another computer. You should compare the efficiency of the algorithms independently of a particular computer.
- **What data should the programs use?** Perhaps the most important difficulty on this list is the selection of the data for the programs to use. There is always the danger that you could select instances of the problem for which one of the algorithms runs uncharacteristically fast. For example, when comparing a sequential search and a binary search of a

sorted array, you might search for an item that happens to be the smallest item in the array. In such a case, the sequential search finds the item more quickly than the binary search because the item is first in the array and is thus the first item that the sequential search examines. Any analysis of efficiency must be independent of specific data.

Algorithm analysis should be independent of specific implementations, computers, and data

To overcome these difficulties, computer scientists employ mathematical techniques that analyze algorithms independently of specific implementations, computers, or data. You begin this analysis by counting the number of significant operations in a particular solution, as the next section describes.

 Note: In general, you should avoid analyzing an algorithm solely by studying the running times of a specific implementation. Running times are influenced by such factors as programming style, the particular computer, and the data on which the program is run.

10.2.1 The Execution Time of Algorithms

Counting an algorithm's operations is a way to assess its efficiency

Previous chapters have informally compared different solutions to a given problem by looking at the number of operations that each solution required. For example, Chapter 9 compared array-based and link-based implementations of the ADT list. An array-based list can access its ith item directly in one step, because the item is stored in `items[i]`. A link-based list, however, must traverse a chain of linked nodes from its beginning until the ith node is reached and would therefore require i steps.

An algorithm's execution time is related to the number of operations it requires. This is usually expressed in terms of the number, n, of items the algorithm must process. Counting an algorithm's operations—if possible—is a way to assess its efficiency. Let's consider a few other examples.

 Traversal of linked nodes. As an example of traversing a chain of linked nodes, consider displaying the data in such a chain. If `headPtr` points to the first node in the chain, the following C++ statements display its data:

```
auto curPtr = headPtr;                          ← 1 assignment
while (curPtr != nullptr)                        ← n + 1 comparisons
{
    std::cout << curPtr->getItem() << std::endl; ← n writes
    curPtr = curPtr->getNext();                  ← n assignments
}  // end while
```

Displaying the data in a linked chain of n nodes requires time proportional to n

If we have n nodes, these statements require $n + 1$ assignments, $n + 1$ comparisons, and n write operations. If each assignment, comparison, and write operation requires, respectively, a, c, and w time units, the statements require $(n + 1) \times (a + c) + n \times w$ time units.[1] Thus, the time required to write n nodes is proportional to n. This conclusion makes sense intuitively: It takes longer to display, or traverse, a linked chain of 100 nodes than it does a linked chain of 10 nodes.

---

[1] Although omitting multiplication operators is common in algebra, we indicate them explicitly here to facilitate counting them.

Note: You must traverse a linked chain to access its ith node. The access time is, therefore, directly proportional to i. On the other hand, you can access array items directly, with equal access time for each item.

 The Towers of Hanoi. Chapter 2 proved recursively that the solution to the Towers of Hanoi problem with n disks requires $2^n - 1$ moves. If each move requires the same time m, the solution requires $(2^n - 1) \times m$ time units. As you will soon see, this time requirement increases rapidly as the number of disks increases.

 Nested loops. Consider an algorithm that contains nested loops of the following form:

```
for (i = 1 through n)
    for (j = 1 through i)
        for (k = 1 through 5)
            Task T
```

If task T requires t time units, the innermost loop on k requires $5 \times t$ time units. The loop on j requires $5 \times t \times i$ time units, and the outermost loop on i requires

$$\sum_{i=1}^{n}(5 \times t \times i) = 5 \times t \times (1 + 2 + \cdots + n) = 5 \times t \times n \times (n + 1)/2$$

time units.[1]

 Question 1 How many comparisons of array items do the following loops contain?

```
for (j = 1; j <= n - 1; j++)
{
    i = j + 1;
    do
    {
        if (theArray[i] < theArray[j])
            swap(theArray[i], theArray[j]);
        i++;
    } while (i <= n);
}  // end for
```

Question 2 Repeat Question 1, replacing the statement i = j + 1 with i = j.

10.2.2 Algorithm Growth Rates

As you can see, the previous examples derive an algorithm's time requirement as a function of the problem size. The way to measure a problem's size depends on the application—typical examples are the number of nodes in a linked chain, the number of disks in the Towers of Hanoi problem, the size of an array, or the number of items in a stack. Thus, we reached conclusions such as

Algorithm A requires $n^2 / 5$ time units to solve a problem of size n
Algorithm B requires $5 \times n$ time units to solve a problem of size n

Measure an algorithm's time requirement as a function of the problem size

---

[1] The formula used here for the sum of the first n integers is given in Example 2 of Appendix E.

The time units in the previous two statements must be the same before you can compare the efficiency of the two algorithms. If we had written

Algorithm A requires $n^2 / 5$ seconds to solve a problem of size n

our earlier discussion indicates the difficulties with such a statement: On what computer does the algorithm require $n^2 / 5$ seconds? What implementation of the algorithm requires $n^2 / 5$ seconds? What data caused the algorithm to require $n^2 / 5$ seconds?

What specifically do you want to know about the time requirement of an algorithm? The most important thing to learn is how quickly the algorithm's time requirement grows as a function of the problem size. Statements such as

Algorithm A requires time proportional to n^2
Algorithm B requires time proportional to n

Compare algorithm efficiencies for large problems

each express an algorithm's proportional time requirement, or **growth rate**, and enable you to compare algorithm *A* with another algorithm *B*. Although you cannot determine the exact time requirement for either algorithm *A* or algorithm *B* from these statements, you can determine that for large problems, *B* requires significantly less time than *A*. That is, *B*'s time requirement—as a function of the problem size *n*—increases at a slower rate than *A*'s time requirement, because *n* increases at a slower rate than n^2. Even if *B* actually requires $5 \times n$ seconds and *A* actually requires $n^2 / 5$ seconds, *B* eventually requires significantly less time than *A*, as *n* increases. Figure 10-1 illustrates this fact. Thus, a conclusion such as "*A* requires time proportional to n^2" is exactly the kind of statement that characterizes the inherent efficiency of an algorithm independently of such factors as particular computers and implementations.

FIGURE 10-1   Time requirements as a function of the problem size *n*

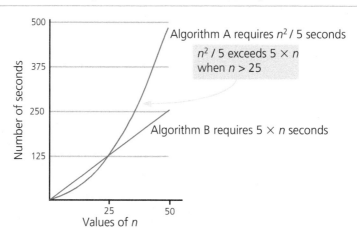

Figure 10-1 also shows that *A*'s time requirement does not exceed *B*'s until *n* exceeds 25. Algorithm efficiency is typically a concern for large problems only. The time requirements for small problems are generally not large enough to matter. Thus, our analyses assume large values of *n*.

 Note: When comparing the efficiency of various solutions, look only at significant differences. This rule is consistent with a multidimensional view of the cost of a computer program.

10.2.3 Analysis and Big O Notation

If

Algorithm A requires time proportional to f(n)

Algorithm A is said to be **order $f(n)$**, which is denoted as **O($f(n)$)**. The function $f(n)$ is called the algorithm's **growth-rate function**. Because the notation uses the capital letter O to denote *order*, it is called the **Big O notation**. If a problem of size n requires time that is directly proportional to n, the problem is O(n)—that is, order n. If the time requirement is directly proportional to n^2, the problem is O(n^2), and so on.

The following definition formalizes these ideas:

> **Note: Definition of the order of an algorithm**
>
> Algorithm A is order $f(n)$—denoted O($f(n)$)—if constants k and n_0 exist such that A requires no more than $k \times f(n)$ time units to solve a problem of size $n \geq n_0$.

The requirement $n \geq n_0$ in the definition of O($f(n)$) formalizes the notion of sufficiently large problems. In general, many values of k and n can satisfy the definition.

The following examples illustrate the definition:

 • Suppose that an algorithm requires $n^2 - 3 \times n + 10$ seconds to solve a problem of size n. If constants k and n_0 exist such that

$$k \times n^2 > n^2 - 3 \times n + 10 \text{ for all } n \geq n_0$$

the algorithm is O(n^2). In fact, if k is 3 and n_0 is 2,

$$3 \times n^2 > n^2 - 3 \times n + 10 \text{ for all } n \geq 2$$

as Figure 10-2 illustrates. Thus, the algorithm requires no more than $k \times n^2$ time units for $n \geq n_0$ and so is O(n^2).

FIGURE 10-2   The graphs of $3 \times n^2$ and $n^2 - 3 \times n + 10$

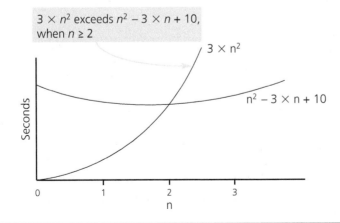

- Previously in Section 10.2.1, we found that displaying a linked chain's first n items requires

$$(n + 1)(a + c) + n \times w$$

time units. Because $2 \times n \geq n + 1$ for $n \geq 1$,

$$(2 \times n) \times (a + c) + n \times w \geq (n + 1) \times (a + c) + n \times w \text{ for } n \geq 1$$

After factoring n on the left side of the inequality, we have

$$(2 \times a + 2 \times c + w) \times n \geq (n + 1) \times (a + c) + n \times w \text{ for } n \geq 1$$

Thus, this task is $O(n)$. Here, k is $2 \times a + 2 \times c + w$ and n_0 is 1.

- Similarly, the solution to the Towers of Hanoi problem requires $(2^n - 1) \times m$ time units. Because

$$m \times 2^n > (2^n - 1) \times m \text{ for } n \geq 1$$

the solution is $O(2^n)$.

The requirement $n \geq n_0$ in the definition of $O(f(n))$ means that the time estimate is correct for sufficiently large problems. In other words, the time estimate is incorrect for at most a finite number of problem sizes. For example, the function $\log n$ takes on the value 0 when n is 1. Thus, the fact that $k \times \log 1$ is 0 for all constants k implies an unrealistic time requirement; presumably, all algorithms require more than 0 time units, even to solve a problem of size 1. Thus, you can discount problems of size $n = 1$ if $f(n)$ is $\log n$.

To dramatize further the significance of an algorithm's proportional growth rate, consider the table in Figure 10-3. The table gives, for various values of n, the approximate values of some common growth-rate functions, which are listed in order of growth:

Order of growth of some common functions

$$O(1) < O(\log_2 n) < O(n) < O(n \times \log_2 n) < O(n^2) < O(n^3) < O(2^n)$$

The table demonstrates the relative speed at which the values of the functions grow. Figure 10-4 represents the growth-rate functions graphically.

FIGURE 10-3   A comparison of growth-rate functions

Function	\multicolumn{6}{c}{n}
	10	100	1,000	10,000	100,000	1,000,000
1	1	1	1	1	1	1
$\log_2 n$	3	6	9	13	16	19
n	10	10^2	10^3	10^4	10^5	10^6
$n \times \log_2 n$	30	664	9,965	10^5	10^6	10^7
n^2	10^2	10^4	10^6	10^8	10^{10}	10^{12}
n^3	10^3	10^6	10^9	10^{12}	10^{15}	10^{18}
2^n	10^3	10^{30}	10^{301}	$10^{3,010}$	$10^{30,103}$	$10^{301,030}$

FIGURE 10-4   A graphical comparison of growth-rate functions[2]

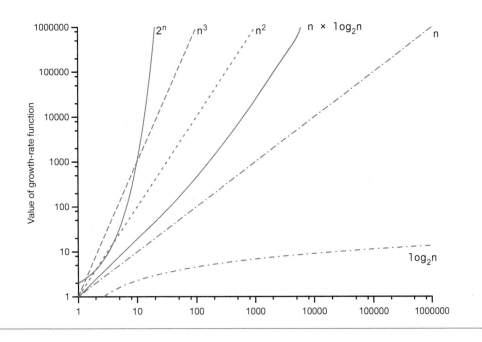

These growth-rate functions have the following intuitive interpretations:

1   A growth-rate function of 1 implies a problem whose time requirement is constant
           and, therefore, independent of the problem's size n.

$\log_2 n$ The time requirement for a logarithmic algorithm increases slowly as the problem size
           increases. If you square the problem size, you only double its time requirement. Later
           you will see that the recursive binary search algorithm that you studied in Chapter 2
           has this behavior. Recall that a binary search halves an array and then searches one of
           the halves. Typical logarithmic algorithms solve a problem by solving a smaller
           constant fraction of the problem.

           The base of the log does not affect a logarithmic growth rate, so you can omit it in
           a growth-rate function. Exercise 8 at the end of this chapter asks you to show why this
           is true.

n The time requirement for an O(n), or **linear**, algorithm increases directly with the size
           of the problem. If you square the problem size, you also square its time requirement.

$n \times \log_2 n$ The time requirement for an O($n \times \log_2 n$) algorithm increases more rapidly than a
           linear algorithm. Such algorithms usually divide a problem into smaller problems that
           are each solved separately. The next chapter examines an example of this algorithm
           type—the merge sort.

---

[2] The graph of $f(n) = 1$ is omitted because the scale of the figure makes it difficult to draw. It would, however, be a
straight line parallel to the x axis through $y = 1$.

n^2 The time requirement for an O(n^2), or **quadratic**, algorithm increases rapidly with the size of the problem. Algorithms that use two nested loops are often quadratic. Such algorithms are practical only for small problems. The next chapter covers several quadratic sorting algorithms.

n^3 The time requirement for an O(n^3), or **cubic**, algorithm increases more rapidly with the size of the problem than the time requirement for a quadratic algorithm. Algorithms that use three nested loops are often cubic, and are practical only for small problems.

2^n The time requirement for an **exponential** algorithm usually increases too rapidly with the size of the problem to be practical.

If algorithm A requires time that is proportional to function f and algorithm B requires time that is proportional to a slower-growing function g, it is apparent that B is always significantly more efficient than A for large enough problems. For large problems, the proportional growth rate dominates all other factors in determining an algorithm's efficiency.

Properties of growth-rate functions.   Several mathematical properties of Big O notation help to simplify the analysis of an algorithm. As we discuss these properties, you should keep in mind that O($f(n)$) means "is of order $f(n)$" or "has order $f(n)$." O is not a function.

Some properties of growth-rate functions

1. **You can ignore low-order terms in an algorithm's growth-rate function.** For example, if an algorithm is O($n^3 + 4 \times n^2 + 3 \times n$), it is also O($n^3$). By examining the table in Figure 10-3, you can see that the n^3 term is significantly larger than either $4 \times n^2$ or $3 \times n$, particularly for large values of n. For large n, the growth rate of $n^3 + 4 \times n^2 + 3 \times n$ is the same as the growth rate of n^3. It is the growth rate of $f(n)$, not the value of $f(n)$, that is important here. Thus, even if an algorithm is O($n^3 + 4 \times n^2 + 3 \times n$), we say that it is simply O(n^3). In general, you can usually conclude that an algorithm is O($f(n)$), where f is a function similar to the ones listed in Figure 10-3.
2. **You can ignore a multiplicative constant in the high-order term of an algorithm's growth-rate function.** For example, if an algorithm is O($5 \times n^3$), it is also O(n^3). This observation follows from the definition of O($f(n)$), if you let $k = 5$.
3. **O($f(n)$) + O($g(n)$) = O($f(n) + g(n)$).** You can combine growth-rate functions. For example, if an algorithm is O(n^2) + O(n), it is also O($n^2 + n$), which you write simply as O(n^2) by applying property 1. Analogous rules hold for multiplication.

These properties imply that you need only an estimate of the time requirement to obtain an algorithm's growth rate; you do not need an exact statement of an algorithm's time requirement, which is fortunate because deriving the exact time requirement is often difficult and sometimes impossible.

An algorithm can require different times to solve different problems of the same size

Worst-case and average-case analyses.   A particular algorithm might require different times to solve different problems of the same size. For example, the time that an algorithm requires to search n items might depend on the nature of the items. Usually you consider the maximum amount of time that an algorithm can require to solve a problem of size n—that is, the worst case. A **worst-case analysis** concludes that algorithm A is O($f(n)$) if, in the worst case, A requires no more than $k \times f(n)$ time units to solve a problem of size n for all but a finite number of values of n. Although a worst-case analysis can produce a pessimistic time estimate, such an estimate does not mean that your algorithm is always slow. Instead, you have shown that the algorithm is never slower than your estimate. Realize, however, that an algorithm's worst case might happen rarely, if at all, in practice.

An **average-case analysis** attempts to determine the average amount of time that an algorithm requires to solve problems of size n. In an average-case analysis, A is $O(f(n))$ if the average amount of time that A requires to solve a problem of size n is no more than $k \times f(n)$ time units for all but a finite number of values of n. Average-case analysis is, in general, far more difficult to perform than worst-case analysis. One difficulty is determining the relative probabilities of encountering various problems of a given size; another is determining the distributions of various data values. Worst-case analysis is easier to calculate and is thus more common.

 Note: While manipulating the Big O notation, remember that $O(f(n))$ represents an inequality. It is not a function but simply a notation that means "is of order $f(n)$" or "has order $f(n)$."

 Question 3 What order is an algorithm that has as a growth-rate function

    a. $8 \times n^3 - 9 \times n$
    b. $7 \times \log_2 n + 20$
    c. $7 \times \log_2 n + n$

10.2.4 Keeping Your Perspective

Before continuing with additional analyses of specific algorithms, a few words about perspective are appropriate. You know that you can access the nth item in an array directly. This access is independent of n: accessing the 100th item takes the same time as it does to access the first item in the array. For an ADT list of n items, the array-based implementation of the retrieval operation `getEntry` is $O(1)$. However, the link-based implementation of `getEntry` requires n steps to traverse a chain until it reaches the nth item, and so is $O(n)$.

> An array-based `getEntry` is $O(1)$
>
> A link-based `getEntry` is $O(n)$

    Throughout the course of an analysis, you should always keep in mind that you are interested only in *significant* differences in efficiency. Is the difference in efficiency for the two implementations of `getEntry` significant? As the size of the list grows, the link-based implementation might require more time to retrieve the desired entry, because its node can be farther away from the beginning of the chain. In contrast, regardless of how large the list is, the array-based implementation always requires the same constant amount of time to retrieve any particular item. Thus, no matter what time difference is significant to you, it is reached if the list is large enough. In this example, observe that the difference in efficiency for the two implementations is worth considering only when the problem is large enough. If the list never has more than 25 items, for example, the difference in the implementations is not significant at all.

    Now consider an application—such as a word processor's spelling checker—that frequently retrieves items from a list but rarely inserts or removes an item. Because `getEntry` for an array-based list is faster than a link-based list's `getEntry`, you should choose an array-based implementation of the list for the application. On the other hand, if an application requires frequent insertions and removals but rarely retrieves an item, you should choose a link-based implementation of the list. The most appropriate implementation of an ADT for a given application strongly depends on how frequently the application performs these operations. More examples of this point are presented in the next chapter.

> When choosing an implementation of an ADT, consider how frequently particular ADT operations occur in a given application

    The response time of some ADT operations, however, can be crucial, even if you seldom use them. For example, an air traffic control system could include an emergency operation to resolve the impending collision of two airplanes. Clearly, this operation must occur

> Some seldom-used but critical operations must be efficient

quickly, even if it is rarely used. Thus, before you choose an implementation for an ADT, you should know what operations a particular application requires, approximately how often the application performs each operation, and the response times that the application requires of each operation.

In the next section we compare a searching algorithm that is $O(n)$ with one that is $O(\log_2 n)$. While it is true that an $O(\log_2 n)$ searching algorithm requires significantly less time on large arrays than an $O(n)$ algorithm requires, on small arrays—say $n < 25$—the time requirements might not be significantly different at all. In fact, it is entirely possible that, because of factors such as the size of the constant k in the definition of Big O, the $O(n)$ algorithm runs faster on small problems. It is only on large problems that the slower growth rate of an algorithm necessarily gives it a significant advantage. Figure 10-1 illustrated this phenomenon.

If the problem size
is always small, you
can probably ignore
an algorithm's
efficiency

Weigh the trade-offs
between an
algorithm's time
requirements and its
memory
requirements

Thus, in general, if the maximum size of a given problem is small, the time requirements of any two solutions for that problem likely will not differ significantly. If you know that your problem size will always be small, do not overanalyze; simply choose the algorithm that is easiest to understand, verify, and code.

Frequently, when evaluating an algorithm's efficiency, you have to weigh carefully the trade-offs between a solution's execution time requirements and its memory requirements. You are rarely able to make a statement as strong as "This approach is the best one for performing the task." A solution that requires a relatively small amount of computer time often also requires a relatively large amount of memory. It may not even be possible to say that one solution requires less time than another. Solution A may perform some components of the task faster than solution B, while solution B performs other components of the task faster than solution A. Often you must analyze the solutions in light of a particular application.

Compare algorithms
for both style and
efficiency

In summary, it is important to examine an algorithm for both style and efficiency. The analysis should focus only on gross differences in efficiency and not reward coding tricks that save milliseconds. Any finer differences in efficiency are likely to interact with coding issues, which you should not allow to interfere with the development of your programming style. If you find an algorithm that is significantly more efficient than others, you should select it, unless you know that the maximum problem size is quite small. If you are solving only small problems, it is possible that a less efficient algorithm would be more appropriate. That is, other factors, such as the simplicity of the algorithm, could become more significant than minor differences in efficiency. In fact, analyzing the time efficiency of an algorithm implicitly assumes that an algorithm is used to solve large problems. This assumption allows you to focus on growth rates, because regardless of other factors, an algorithm with a slow growth rate requires less time than an algorithm with a fast growth rate, provided that the problems to be solved are sufficiently large.

Analysis of an
algorithm's time
efficiency focuses
on large problems

 Note: If a problem is small, do not overanalyze it. In such a situation, the primary concern should be simplicity. For example, if you are searching an array that contains only a small number of items—say, fewer than 25—a simple $O(n)$ algorithm such as a sequential search can be appropriate.

10.2.5 The Efficiency of Searching Algorithms

As another example of analyzing the time efficiency of an algorithm, consider the efficiency of two search algorithms: the sequential search and the binary search of an array.

Sequential search. In a sequential search of an array of *n* items, you look at each item in turn, beginning with the first one, until either you find the desired item or you reach the end of the data collection. In the best case, the desired item is the first one that you examine, so only one comparison is necessary. Thus, in the best case, a sequential search is O(1). In the worst case, the desired item is the last one you examine, so *n* comparisons are necessary. Thus, in the worst case, the algorithm is O(*n*). In the average case, you find the desired item in the middle of the collection, making *n* / 2 comparisons. Thus, the algorithm is O(*n*) in the average case.

Sequential search. Worst case: O(*n*); average case: O(*n*); best case: O(1)

What is the algorithm's order when you do not find the desired item? Does the algorithm's order depend on whether the initial data is sorted? These questions are left for you in Checkpoint Question 4 at the end of this section.

Binary search. Is a binary search of an array more efficient than a sequential search? The binary search algorithm, which Chapter 2 presented, searches a sorted array for a particular item by repeatedly dividing the array in half. The algorithm determines which half the item must be in— if it is indeed present—and discards the other half. Thus, the binary search algorithm searches successively smaller arrays: The size of a given array is approximately one-half the size of the array previously searched.

At each division, the algorithm makes a comparison. How many comparisons does the algorithm make when it searches an array of *n* items? The exact answer depends, of course, on where the sought-for item resides in the array. However, you can compute the maximum number of comparisons that a binary search requires—that is, the worst case. The number of comparisons is equal to the number of times that the algorithm divides the array in half. Suppose that $n = 2^k$ for some *k*. The search requires the following steps:

1. Inspect the middle item of an array of size *n*.
2. Inspect the middle item of an array of size *n* / 2.
3. Inspect the middle item of an array of size $n / 2^2$, and so on.

To inspect the middle item of an array, you must first divide the array in half. If you halve an array of *n* items, then divide one of those halves in half, and continue dividing halves until only one item remains, you have performed *k* divisions. This is true because $n / 2^k$ is 1. (Remember, we assumed that $n = 2^k$.) In the worst case, the algorithm performs *k* divisions and, therefore, *k* comparisons. Because $n = 2^k$, we know that

$$k = \log_2 n$$

Thus, the algorithm is O($\log_2 n$) in the worst case when $n = 2^k$.

What if *n* is not a power of 2? You can easily find the smallest *k* such that

$$2^{k-1} < n < 2^k$$

(For example, if *n* is 30, then $k = 5$, because $2^4 = 16 < 30 < 32 = 2^5$.) The algorithm still requires at most *k* divisions to obtain a subarray with one item. Now it follows that

$$k - 1 < \log_2 n < k$$
$$k < 1 + \log_2 n < k + 1$$
$$k = 1 + \log_2 n \text{ rounded down}$$

Thus, the algorithm is still O($\log_2 n$) in the worst case when $n \neq 2^k$. In general, the algorithm is O($\log_2 n$) in the worst case for any *n*.

Binary search is O($\log_2 n$) in the worst case

Is a binary search faster than a sequential search? Much faster! For example $\log_2 1,000,000 \approx 19$, so a binary search of 1 million sorted items requires at most 20 comparisons, but a sequential search of the same items can require 1 million comparisons! For large arrays, the binary search has an enormous advantage over a sequential search.

Realize, however, that maintaining the array in sorted order requires an overhead cost, which can be substantial. The next chapter examines the cost of sorting an array.

> **Note:** If you are searching a very large array, an O(n) algorithm is probably too inefficient to use.

Question 4 Consider a sequential search of n data items.

    a. If the data items are sorted into ascending order, how can you determine that your desired item is not in the data collection without always making n comparisons?

    b. What is the order of the sequential search algorithm when the desired item is not in the data collection? Do this for both sorted and unsorted data, and consider the best, average, and worst cases.

    c. Show that if the sequential search algorithm finds the desired item in the data collection, the algorithm's order does not depend upon whether or not the data items are sorted.

SUMMARY

1. Using Big O notation, you measure an algorithm's time requirement as a function of the problem size by using a growth-rate function. This approach enables you to analyze the efficiency of an algorithm without regard for such factors as computer speed and programming skill that are beyond your control.

2. When you compare the inherent efficiency of algorithms, you examine their growth-rate functions when the problems are large. Only significant differences in growth-rate functions are meaningful.

3. Worst-case analysis considers the maximum amount of work an algorithm requires on a problem of a given size, while average-case analysis considers the expected amount of work that it requires.

4. Analyzing an algorithm's time requirement will help you to choose an implementation for an abstract data type. If your application frequently uses particular ADT operations, your implementation should be efficient for at least those operations.

EXERCISES

1. Using Big O notation, indicate the time requirement of each of the following tasks in the worst case. Describe any assumptions that you make.

    a. After arriving at a party, you shake hands with each person there.

    b. Each person in a room shakes hands with everyone else in the room.

    c. You climb a flight of stairs.

    d. You slide down the banister.

    e. After entering an elevator, you press a button to choose a floor.

    f. You ride the elevator from the ground floor up to the *n*th floor.

    g. You read a book twice.

2. Describe a way to climb from the bottom of a flight of stairs to the top in time that is at least $O(n^2)$.

3. Using Big O notation, indicate the time requirement of each of the following tasks in the worst case.

    a. Computing the sum of the first *n* even integers by using a for loop

    b. Displaying all *n* integers in an array

    c. Displaying all *n* integers in a sorted linked chain

    d. Displaying all names in an array of *n* linked chains

    e. Displaying one array element

    f. Displaying the last integer in a linked chain

    g. Searching an array of *n* items for a particular value by using a sequential search

    h. Searching an array of *n* items for a particular value by using a binary search

    i. Adding an item to a stack of *n* items

    j. Adding an item to a bag of *n* items

4. Suppose that your implementation of a particular algorithm appears in C++ as

```
for (int pass = 1; pass <= n; pass++)
{
   for (int index = 0; index < n; index++)
   {
      for (int count = 1; count < 10; count++)
      {
         . . .
      }  // end for
   }  // end for
}  // end for
```

The previous code shows only the repetition in the algorithm, not the computations that occur within the loops. These computations, however, are independent of *n*. What is the Big O of the algorithm? Justify your answer.

5. Consider the following C++ function f, which calls the function swap. Assume that swap exists and simply swaps the contents of its two arguments. Do not be concerned with f's purpose. How many comparisons does f perform?

```
void f(int theArray[], int n)
{
   for (int j = 0; j < n; j++)
   {
      int i = 0;
      while (i <= j)
      {
         if (theArray[i] < theArray[j])
            swap(theArray[i], theArray[j]);
         i++;
      }  // end while
   }  // end for
}  // end f
```

6. For large arrays, is a sequential search faster than a binary search in the worst case? Explain.

7. Show that any polynomial $f(x) = c_n x^n + c_{n-1} x^{n-1} + \cdots + c_1 x + c_0$ is $O(x^n)$.

8. Show that for all constants $a, b > 1$, $f(n)$ is $O(\log_a n)$ if and only if $f(n)$ is $O(\log_b n)$. Thus, you can omit the base when you write $O(\log n)$. *Hint:* Use the identity $\log_a n = \log_b n / \log_b a$ for all constants $a, b > 1$.

9. Show that $7n^2 + 5n$ is not $O(n)$.

10. Consider an array of length n containing positive and negative integers in random order. Write C++ code that rearranges the integers so that the negative integers appear before the positive integers. Your solution should use
    a. $O(n^2)$ operations
    b. $O(n)$ operations

PROGRAMMING PROBLEMS

For the following programming problems, you need to time a section of code in C++. For example, the following statements time the execution of the function doSomething:

```
#include <ctime>
clock_t start = clock();
doSomething();
clock_t finish = clock();
double overallTime = static_cast<double>(finish - start) / CLOCKS_PER_SEC;³
```

1. Consider the following two loops:

```
// Loop A
for (i = 1; i <= n; i++)
   for (j = 1; j <= 10000; j++)
      sum = sum + j;

// Loop B
for (i = 1; i <= n; i++)
   for (j = 1; j <= n; j++)
      sum = sum + j;
```

What is the Big O of each loop? Design and implement an experiment to find a value of n for which Loop B is faster than Loop A.

2. Repeat the previous project, but use the following for Loop B:

```
// Loop B
for (i = 1; i <= n; i++)
   for (j = 1; j <= n; j++)
      for (k = 1; k <= j; k++)
         sum = sum + k;
```

---

[3] CLOCKS_PER_SEC is a C++ predefined constant.

3. Write a C++ program that implements the following three algorithms and times them for various values of *n*. The program should display a table of the run times of each algorithm for various values of *n*.

```
// Algorithm A          // Algorithm B          // Algorithm C
sum = 0                 sum = 0                 sum = n * (n + 1) / 2
for i = 1 to n          for i = 1 to n
   sum = sum + i        {
                            for j = 1 to i
                               sum = sum + 1
                        }
```

For each of the following problems, you will need an implementation of the ADT bag whose method remove *removes a random entry instead of a specific one.*

4. Suppose that you have several numbered billiard balls on a pool table. At each step you remove a billiard ball from the table. If the ball removed is numbered *n*, you replace it with *n* balls whose number is *n* / 2, where the division is truncated to an integer. For example, if you remove the 5 ball, you replace it with five 2 balls. Using Big O notation, predict the time requirement for this algorithm when initially the pool table contains only the *n* ball.

   Write a program that simulates this process. Use a bag of positive integers to represent the balls on the pool table. Time the actual execution of the program for various values of *n* and plot its performance as a function of *n*. Compare your results with your predicted time requirements.

5. Repeat the previous project, but instead replace the *n* ball with *n* balls randomly numbered less than *n*.

6. (Gaming) In mythology, the Hydra was a monster with many heads. Every time the hero chopped off a head, two smaller heads would grow in its place. Fortunately for the hero, if the head was small enough, he could chop it off without two more growing in its place. To kill the Hydra, all our hero needed to do was to chop off all the heads.

   Write a program that simulates the Hydra. Instead of heads, we will use strings. A bag of strings, then, represents the Hydra. Every time you remove a string from the bag, erase the first letter of the string and put two copies of the remaining string back into the bag. For example, if you remove HYDRA, you add two copies of YDRA to the bag. If you remove a one-letter word, you add nothing to the bag. To begin, read one word from the keyboard and place it into an empty bag. The Hydra dies when the bag becomes empty.

   Using Big O notation, predict the time requirement for this algorithm in terms of the number *n* of characters in the initial string. Then time the actual execution of the program for various values of *n* and plot its performance as a function of *n*.

7. Programming Problem 6 of Chapter 1 asks you to define the ADT bag methods `union`, `intersection`, and `difference` by using only ADT bag operations. Programming Problem 4 of Chapter 3 asks you to define these methods specifically for the class `ArrayBag`, and Programming Problem 1 of Chapter 4 asks you to define these methods specifically for the class `LinkedBag`. Compare the runtimes of these nine methods for large, randomly generated bags.

Sorting Algorithms and Their Efficiency

Contents

Prerequisites

This chapter examines the important topic of sorting data. You will study some simple algorithms, which you may have seen before, and some more sophisticated recursive algorithms. Sorting algorithms provide varied and relatively easy examples of the analysis of efficiency.

VideoNote

Basic sorting
algorithms

11.1　Basic Sorting Algorithms

Sorting is a process that organizes a collection of data into either ascending[1] or descending order. The need for sorting arises in many situations. You may simply want to sort a collection of data before including it in a report. Often, however, you must perform a sort as an initialization step for other algorithms. For example, searching for data is one of the most common tasks performed by computers. When the collection of data to be searched is large, an efficient technique for searching—such as the binary search algorithm—is desirable. However, the binary search algorithm requires that the data be sorted. Thus, sorting the data is a step that must precede a binary search on a collection of data that is not already sorted. Good sorting algorithms, therefore, are quite valuable.

The sorts in this chapter are internal sorts

You can organize sorting algorithms into two categories. An **internal sort** requires that the collection of data fit entirely in the computer's main memory. The algorithms in this chapter are internal sorting algorithms. You use an **external sort** when the collection of data will not fit in the computer's main memory all at once but must reside in secondary storage, such as on a disk. Chapter 21 examines external sorts.

The data items to be sorted might be integers, character strings, or even objects. It is easy to imagine the results of sorting a collection of integers or character strings, but consider a collection of objects. If each object contains only one data member, sorting the objects is really no different from sorting a collection of integers. However, when each object contains several data members, you must know which data member determines the order of the entire object within the collection of data. This data member is called the **sort key**. For example, if the objects represent people, you might want to sort on their names, their ages, or their zip codes. Regardless of your choice of sort key, the sorting algorithm orders entire objects based on only one data member, the sort key.

For simplicity, the examples in this chapter sort quantities such as numbers or strings. All algorithms in this chapter sort the data into ascending order. Modifying these algorithms to sort data into descending order is simple. Finally, each example assumes that the data resides in an array.

11.1.1　The Selection Sort

Select the largest item

Imagine some data that you can examine all at once. To sort it, you could select the largest item and put it in its place, select the next largest and put it in its place, and so on. For a card player, this process is analogous to looking at an entire hand of cards and ordering it by selecting cards one at a time in their proper order. The **selection sort** formalizes these intuitive notions. To sort an array into ascending order, you first search it for the largest item. Because you want the largest item to be in the last position of the array, you swap the last item with the largest item, even if these items happen to be identical. Now, ignoring the last—and largest—item of the array, you search the rest of the array for its largest item and swap it with its last item, which is the next-to-last item in the original array. You continue until you have selected and swapped $n - 1$ of the n items in the array. The remaining item, which is now in the first position of the array, is in its proper order, so it is not considered further.

Figure 11-1 provides an example of a selection sort. Beginning with five integers, you select the largest—37—and swap it with the last integer—13. (As the items in this figure are ordered, they are shaded in blue. This convention will be used throughout this chapter.) Next you select the largest integer—29—from among the first four integers in the array and swap it with the next-to-last integer in the array—13. Notice that the next selection—14—is already in its proper position, but the algorithm ignores this fact and performs a swap of 14 with itself. It is more efficient in general to occasionally perform an unnecessary swap than it is to continually ask whether the swap is necessary. Finally, you select the 13 and swap it with the item in the second position of the array—10. The array is now sorted into ascending order.

---

[1] To allow for duplicate data items, *ascending* is used here to mean nondecreasing and *descending* to mean nonincreasing.

FIGURE 11-1   A selection sort of an array of five integers

Gray elements are selected;
blue elements comprise the sorted portion of the array.

Initial array:	29	10	14	37	13
After 1st swap:	29	10	14	13	**37**
After 2nd swap:	13	10	14	**29**	**37**
After 3rd swap:	13	10	**14**	**29**	**37**
After 4th swap:	**10**	**13**	**14**	**29**	**37**

Question 1 Trace the selection sort as it sorts the following array into ascending order:
20 80 40 25 60 30

Question 2 Repeat the previous question, but instead sort the array into descending order.

Listing 11-1 gives a C++ function, and the two functions it calls, that performs a selection sort on an array theArray of *n* items, assuming that ItemType is the data type of the array's entries.

LISTING 11-1 **An implementation of the selection sort**

```
1   /** Finds the largest item in an array.
2    @pre   The size of the array is >= 1.
3    @post  The arguments are unchanged.
4    @param theArray  The given array.
5    @param size  The number of elements in theArray.
6    @return  The index of the largest entry in the array. */
7   template <class ItemType>
8   int findIndexOfLargest(const ItemType theArray[], int size);
9
10  /** Sorts  the items in an array into ascending order.
11   @pre   None.
12   @post  The array is sorted into ascending order; the size of the array
13      is unchanged.
14   @param theArray  The array to sort.
15   @param n  The size of theArray. */
16  template <class ItemType>
17  void selectionSort(ItemType theArray[], int n)
18  {
19     // last = index of the last item in the subarray of items yet
20     //        to be sorted;
21     // largest = index of the largest item found
```

(continues)

```
22      for (int last = n - 1; last >= 1; last--)
23      {
24         // At this point, theArray[last+1..n-1] is sorted, and its
25         // entries are greater than those in theArray[0..last].
26         // Select the largest entry in theArray[0..last]
27         int largest = findIndexOfLargest(theArray, last+1);
28
29         // Swap the largest entry, theArray[largest], with
30         // theArray[last]
31         std::swap(theArray[largest], theArray[last]);
32      }  // end for
33   }  // end selectionSort
34
35   template <class ItemType>
36   int findIndexOfLargest(const ItemType theArray[], int size)
37   {
38      int indexSoFar = 0;  // Index of largest entry found so far
39      for (int currentIndex = 1; currentIndex < size; currentIndex++)
40      {
41         // At this point, theArray[indexSoFar] >= all entries in
42         // theArray[0..currentIndex - 1]
43         if (theArray[currentIndex] > theArray[indexSoFar])
44            indexSoFar = currentIndex;
45      }  // end for
46
47      return indexSoFar;  // Index of largest entry
48   }  // end findIndexOfLargest
```

Analysis. As you can see from the previous algorithm, sorting in general compares, exchanges, or moves items. As a first step in analyzing such algorithms, you should count these operations. Generally, such operations are more expensive than ones that control loops or manipulate array indexes, particularly when the data to be sorted is more complex than integers or characters. Thus, our approach ignores these incidental operations. You should convince yourself that by ignoring such operations we do not affect our final result. (See Exercise 1.)

The for loop in the function selectionSort executes $n - 1$ times. Thus, selectionSort calls each of the functions findIndexOfLargest and swap $n - 1$ times. Each call to findIndexOfLargest causes its loop to execute last times (that is, size - 1 times when size is last + 1). Thus, the $n - 1$ calls to findIndexOfLargest, for values of last that range from $n - 1$ down to 1, cause the loop in findIndexOfLargest to execute a total of

$$(n - 1) + (n - 2) + \cdots + 1 = n \times (n - 1)/2$$

times.[1] Because each execution of findIndexOfLargest's loop performs one comparison, the calls to findIndexOfLargest require

$$n \times (n - 1)/2$$

comparisons.

The $n - 1$ calls to swap result in $n - 1$ exchanges. Each exchange requires three assignments, or data moves. Thus, the calls to swap require

$$3 \times (n - 1)$$

moves.

---

[1] See Example 2 in Appendix E for the formula used here.

Together, a selection sort of n items requires

$$n \times (n-1)/2 + 3 \times (n-1) = n^2/2 + 5 \times n/2 - 3$$

major operations. By applying the properties of the growth-rate functions given in Chapter 10, you can ignore low-order terms to get $O(n^2 / 2)$ and then ignore the multiplier $1/2$ to get $O(n^2)$. Thus, the selection sort is $O(n^2)$.

Although a selection sort does not depend on the initial arrangement of the data, which is an advantage of this algorithm, it is appropriate only for small n because $O(n^2)$ grows rapidly. While the algorithm requires $O(n^2)$ comparisons, it requires only $O(n)$ data moves. A selection sort could be a good choice over other approaches when data moves are costly but comparisons are not. Such might be the case if each data item is large but the sort key is short or an integer.

Selection sort is $O(n^2)$

 Note: If you are sorting a very large array, an $O(n^2)$ algorithm is probably too inefficient to use.

11.1.2 The Bubble Sort

The next sorting algorithm is one that you may have seen already. The **bubble sort** compares adjacent items and exchanges them if they are out of order. Like the selection sort, this sort usually requires several passes over the data. During the first pass, you compare the first two items in the array. If they are out of order, you exchange them. You then compare the items in the next pair—that is, in positions 2 and 3 of the array. If they are out of order, you exchange them. You proceed in the same manner, comparing and exchanging items two at a time, until you reach the end of the array.

Figure 11-2a illustrates the first pass of a bubble sort of an array of five integers. You compare the items in the first pair—29 and 10—and exchange them because they are out of order. Next you consider the second pair—29 and 14—and exchange these items because they are out of order. The items in the third pair—29 and 37—are in order, and so you do not exchange them. Finally, you exchange the items in the last pair—37 and 13.

Although the array is not sorted after the first pass, the largest item has "bubbled" to its proper position at the end of the array. During the second pass of the bubble sort, you return to the beginning of the array and consider pairs of items in exactly the same manner as the first

When you order successive pairs of items, the largest item bubbles to the top (end) of the array

FIGURE 11-2   The first two passes of a bubble sort of an array of five integers

(a) Pass 1

(b) Pass 2

Initial array:

| 29 | 10 | 14 | 37 | 13 |

| 10 | 29 | 14 | 37 | 13 |

| 10 | 14 | 29 | 37 | 13 |

| 10 | 14 | 29 | 37 | 13 |

| 10 | 14 | 29 | 13 | **37** |

| 10 | 14 | 29 | 13 | **37** |

| 10 | 14 | 29 | 13 | **37** |

| 10 | 14 | 29 | 13 | **37** |

| 10 | 14 | 13 | **29** | **37** |

The bubble sort
usually requires
several passes
through the array

pass. You do not, however, include the last—and largest—item of the array. That is, the second pass considers the first $n − 1$ items of the array. After the second pass, the second-largest item in the array will be in its proper place in the next-to-last position of the array, as Figure 11-2b illustrates. Now, ignoring the last two items, which are in order, you continue with subsequent passes until the array is sorted.

Although a bubble sort requires at most $n − 1$ passes to sort the array, fewer passes might be possible to sort a particular array. Thus, you could terminate the process if no exchanges occur during any pass. The following C++ function bubbleSort uses a boolean variable to signal when an exchange occurs during a particular pass. The function uses the previous swap function.

LISTING 11-2 An implementation of the bubble sort

```cpp
/** Sorts the items in an array into ascending order.
 @pre  None.
 @post  theArray is sorted into ascending order; n is unchanged.
 @param theArray  The given array.
 @param n  The size of theArray. */
template <class ItemType>
void bubbleSort(ItemType theArray[], int n)
{
   bool sorted = false;       // False when swaps occur
   int pass = 1;
   while (!sorted && (pass < n))
   {
      // At this point, theArray[n+1-pass..n-1] is sorted
      // and all of its entries are > the entries in theArray[0..n-pass]
      sorted = true;          // Assume sorted
      for (int index = 0; index < n - pass; index++)
      {
         // At this point, all entries in theArray[0..index-1]
         // are <= theArray[index]
         int nextIndex = index + 1;
         if (theArray[index] > theArray[nextIndex])
         {
            // Exchange entries
            std::swap(theArray[index], theArray[nextIndex]);
            sorted = false; // Signal exchange
         }  // end if
      }  // end for
      // Assertion: theArray[0..n-pass-1] < theArray[n-pass]

      pass++;
   }  // end while
}  // end bubbleSort
```

Question 3 Trace the bubble sort as it sorts the following array into ascending order: 25 30 20 80 40 60.

Question 4 Repeat the previous question, but instead sort the array into descending order.

Analysis. As was noted earlier, the bubble sort requires at most $n - 1$ passes through the array. Pass 1 requires $n - 1$ comparisons and at most $n - 1$ exchanges; pass 2 requires $n - 2$ comparisons and at most $n - 2$ exchanges. In general, pass i requires $n - i$ comparisons and at most $n - i$ exchanges. Therefore, in the worst case, a bubble sort will require a total of

$$(n - 1) + (n - 2) + \cdots + 1 = n \times (n - 1)/2$$

comparisons and the same number of exchanges. Recall that each exchange requires three data moves. Thus, altogether there are

$$2 \times n \times (n - 1) = 2 \times n^2 - 2 \times n$$

major operations in the worst case. Therefore, the bubble sort algorithm is $O(n^2)$ in the worst case.

> Bubble sort:
> Worst case: $O(n^2)$
> Best case: $O(n)$

The best case occurs when the original data is already sorted: bubbleSort uses one pass, during which $n - 1$ comparisons and no exchanges occur. Thus, the bubble sort is $O(n)$ in the best case.

11.1.3 The Insertion Sort

Imagine once again arranging a hand of cards, but now you pick up one card at a time and insert it into its proper position; in this case, you are performing an **insertion sort**. Chapter 8 introduced the insertion sort algorithm in the context of a list of alphabetical names. In that example, we repeatedly called the method insert to add a string into its proper sorted order in a list.

> Take each item from the unsorted region and insert it into its correct order in the sorted region

You can use the insertion sort strategy to sort items that reside in an array. This version of the insertion sort partitions the array into two regions: sorted and unsorted, as Figure 11-3 depicts. Initially, the entire array is the unsorted region, just as the cards dealt to you sit in an unsorted pile on the table. At each step, the insertion sort takes the first item of the unsorted region and places it into its correct position in the sorted region. This step is analogous to taking a card from the table and inserting it into its proper position in your hand. The first step, however, is trivial: Moving theArray[0] from the unsorted region to the sorted region really does not require moving data. Therefore, you can omit this first step by considering the initial sorted region to be theArray[0] and the initial unsorted region to be theArray[1..n-1]. The fact that the items in the sorted region are sorted among themselves is an assertion[2] of the algorithm. Because at each step the size of the sorted region grows by 1 and the size of the unsorted region shrinks by 1, the entire array will be sorted when the algorithm terminates.

Figure 11-4 illustrates an insertion sort of an array of five integers. Initially, the sorted region is theArray[0], which is 29, and the unsorted region is the rest of the array. You take the first item in the unsorted region—the 10—and insert it into its proper position in the sorted region. This insertion requires you to shift array entries to make room for the inserted item. You

FIGURE 11-3   An insertion sort partitions the array into two regions

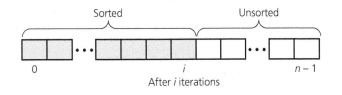

---

[2] As Appendix F discusses, this particular assertion is an invariant.

FIGURE 11-4   An insertion sort of an array of five integers

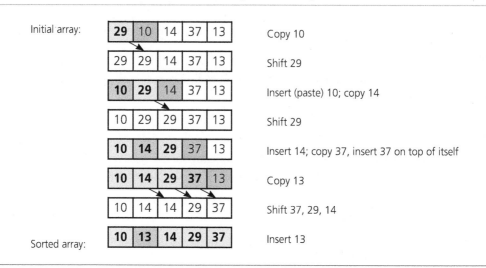

then take the first item in the new unsorted region—the 14—and insert it into its proper position in the sorted region, and so on.

Question 5 Trace the insertion sort as it sorts the array in Checkpoint Question 3 into ascending order.

Question 6 Repeat the previous question, but instead sort the array into descending order.

Listing 11-3 contains a C++ function that performs an insertion sort on an array of *n* items.

LISTING 11-3 An implementation of the insertion sort

```
1    /** Sorts the items in an array into ascending order.
2     @pre  None.
3     @post  theArray is sorted into ascending order; n is unchanged.
4     @param theArray  The given array.
5     @param n  The size of theArray. */
6    template<class ItemType>
7    void insertionSort(ItemType theArray[], int n)
8    {
9       // unsorted = first index of the unsorted region,
10      // loc = index of insertion in the sorted region,
11      // nextItem = next item in the unsorted region.
12      // Initially,  sorted region is theArray[0],
13      //             unsorted region is theArray[1..n-1].
14      // In general, sorted region is theArray[0..unsorted-1],
15      //             unsorted region theArray[unsorted..n-1]
```

```
16     for (int unsorted = 1; unsorted < n; unsorted++)
17     {
18        // At this point, theArray[0..unsorted-1] is sorted.
19        // Find the right position (loc) in theArray[0..unsorted]
20        // for theArray[unsorted], which is the first entry in the
21        // unsorted region; shift, if necessary, to make room
22        ItemType nextItem = theArray[unsorted];
23        int loc = unsorted;
24        while ((loc > 0) && (theArray[loc - 1] > nextItem))
25        {
26           // Shift theArray[loc - 1] to the right
27           theArray[loc] = theArray[loc - 1];
28           loc--;
29        } // end while
30        // At this point, theArray[loc] is where nextItem belongs
31        theArray[loc] = nextItem; // Insert nextItem into sorted region
32     } // end for
33  } // end insertionSort
```

Analysis. The outer `for` loop in the function `insertionSort` executes $n - 1$ times. This loop contains an inner `while` loop that executes at most `unsorted` times for values of `unsorted` that range from 1 to $n - 1$. Thus, in the worst case, the algorithm's comparison occurs

$$1 + 2 + \cdots + (n - 1) = n \times (n - 1)/2$$

times. In addition, the inner loop moves data items at most the same number of times.

The outer loop moves data items twice per iteration, or $2 \times (n - 1)$ times. Together, there are

$$n \times (n - 1) + 2 \times (n - 1) = n^2 + n - 2$$

major operations in the worst case.

Therefore, the insertion sort algorithm is $O(n^2)$ in the worst case. For small arrays—say, fewer than 25 items—the simplicity of the insertion sort makes it an appropriate choice. For large arrays, however, an insertion sort can be prohibitively inefficient—unless the array is already sorted. In that case, the inner `while` loop exits immediately, making the sort $O(n)$ in its best case.

The insertion sort is $O(n^2)$ in the worst case

The insertion sort is $O(n)$ in the best case

11.2 Faster Sorting Algorithms

The previous sorting algorithms are all you really need if you have to sort small arrays or if you need to sort a large array once. For extremely large arrays—particularly ones that must be updated and sorted again—you need faster algorithms. We now examine a few of these more sophisticated techniques.

VideoNote

Faster sorting algorithms

11.2.1 The Merge Sort

Two important divide-and-conquer sorting algorithms, **merge sort** and **quick sort**, have elegant recursive formulations and are highly efficient. The presentations here are in the context of sorting

Divide and conquer

FIGURE 11-5   A merge sort with an auxiliary temporary array

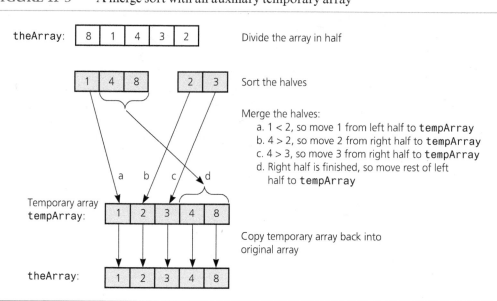

theArray: | 8 | 1 | 4 | 3 | 2 | Divide the array in half

| 1 | 4 | 8 | | 2 | 3 | Sort the halves

Merge the halves:
    a. 1 < 2, so move 1 from left half to `tempArray`
    b. 4 > 2, so move 2 from right half to `tempArray`
    c. 4 > 3, so move 3 from right half to `tempArray`
    d. Right half is finished, so move rest of left
       half to `tempArray`

Temporary array
tempArray: | 1 | 2 | 3 | 4 | 8 |

Copy temporary array back into original array

theArray: | 1 | 2 | 3 | 4 | 8 |

arrays, but—as you will see in Chapter 21—the merge sort easily generalizes to external files. For our discussion, it is convenient to express the algorithms in terms of the array `theArray[first..last]`.

> Halve the array, recursively sort its halves, and then merge the halves

    The merge sort is a recursive sorting algorithm that always gives the same performance, regardless of the initial order of the array items. Suppose that you divide the array into halves, sort each half, and then merge the sorted halves into one sorted array, as Figure 11-5 illustrates. In the figure, the halves <1, 4, 8> and <2, 3> are merged to form the array <1, 2, 3, 4, 8>. This merge step compares an item in one half of the array with an item in the other half and moves the smaller item to a temporary array. This process continues until there are no more items to

> The merge sort requires a second array as large as the original array

consider in one half. At that time, you simply move the remaining items to the temporary array. Finally, you copy the temporary array back into the original array.

    Although the merge step of the merge sort produces a sorted array, how do you sort the array halves prior to the merge step? The merge sort sorts the array halves by using a merge sort—that is, by calling itself recursively. Thus, the pseudocode for the merge sort is

```
// Sorts theArray[first..last] by
//    1. Sorting the first half of the array
//    2. Sorting the second half of the array
//    3. Merging the two sorted halves
mergeSort(theArray: ItemArray, first: integer, last: integer)
{
    if (first < last)
    {
        mid = (first + last) / 2        // Get midpoint

        // Sort theArray[first..mid]
        mergeSort(theArray, first, mid)

        // Sort theArray[mid+1..last]
        mergeSort(theArray, mid + 1, last)
```

```
// Merge sorted halves theArray[first..mid] and theArray[mid+1..last]
        merge(theArray, first, mid, last)
    }
    // If first >= last, there is nothing to do
}
```

Clearly, most of the effort in the merge sort algorithm is in the merge step, but does this algorithm actually sort? The recursive calls continue dividing the array into pieces until each piece contains only one item; obviously an array of one item is sorted. The algorithm then merges these small pieces into larger sorted pieces until one sorted array results. Figure 11-6 illustrates both the recursive calls and the merge steps in a merge sort of an array of six integers.

FIGURE 11-6   A merge sort of an array of six integers

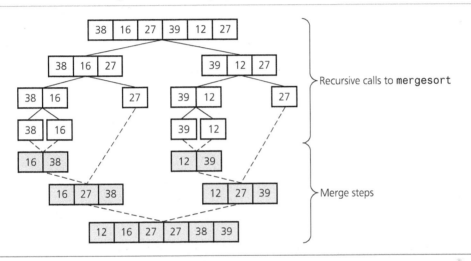

The C++ functions in Listing 11-4 implement the merge sort algorithm. To sort an array theArray of *n* items, you would invoke the function mergeSort by writing

```
mergeSort(theArray, 0, n - 1);
```

LISTING 11-4 **An implementation of merge and mergeSort**

```
1    const int MAX_SIZE = maximum-number-of-items-in-array;
2
3    /** Merges two sorted array segments theArray[first..mid] and
4        theArray[mid+1..last] into one sorted array.
5    @pre  first <= mid <= last. The subarrays theArray[first..mid] and
6        theArray[mid+1..last] are each sorted in increasing order.
7    @post  theArray[first..last] is sorted.
8    @param theArray  The given array.
9    @param first  The index of the beginning of the first segment in
10       theArray.
11   @param mid  The index of the end of the first segment in theArray;
12       mid + 1 marks the beginning of the second segment.
13   @param last  The index of the last element in the second segment in
14       theArray.
```

(continues)

```cpp
15    @note  This function merges the two subarrays into a temporary
16       array and copies the result into the original array theArray. */
17    template <class ItemType>
18    void merge(ItemType theArray[], int first, int mid, int last)
19    {
20       ItemType tempArray[MAX_SIZE]; // Temporary array
21
22       // Initialize the local indices to indicate the subarrays
23       int first1 = first;              // Beginning of first subarray
24       int last1 = mid;                 // End of first subarray
25       int first2 = mid + 1;            // Beginning of second subarray
26       int last2 = last;                // End of second subarray
27
28       // While both subarrays are not empty, copy the
29       // smaller item into the temporary array
30       int index = first1;              // Next available location in tempArray
31       while ((first1 <= last1) && (first2 <= last2))
32       {
33          // At this point, tempArray[first..index-1] is in order
34          if (theArray[first1] <= theArray[first2])
35          {
36             tempArray[index] = theArray[first1];
37             first1++;
38          }
39          else
40          {
41             tempArray[index] = theArray[first2];
42             first2++;
43          }   // end if
44          index++;
45       }  // end while
46       // Finish off the first subarray, if necessary
47       while (first1 <= last1)
48       {
49          // At this point, tempArray[first..index-1] is in order
50          tempArray[index] = theArray[first1];
51          first1++;
52          index++;
53       }  // end while
54       // Finish off the second subarray, if necessary
55       while (first2 <= last2)
56       {
57          // At this point, tempArray[first..index-1] is in order
58          tempArray[index] = theArray[first2];
59          first2++;
60          index++;
61       }  // end for
62
63       // Copy the result back into the original array
64       for (index = first; index <= last; index++)
65          theArray[index] = tempArray[index];
66    }  // end merge
```

```
67   /** Sorts the items in an array into ascending order.
68    @pre  theArray[first..last] is an array.
69    @post  theArray[first..last] is sorted in ascending order.
70    @param theArray  The given array.
71    @param first  The index of the first element to consider in theArray.
72    @param last  The index of the last element to consider in theArray.*/
73   template<class ItemType>
74   void mergeSort(ItemType theArray[], int first, int last)
75   {
76      if (first < last)
77      {
78         // Sort each half
79         int mid = first + (last - first) / 2; // Index of midpoint
80
81         // Sort left half theArray[first..mid]
82         mergeSort(theArray, first, mid);
83
84         // Sort right half theArray[mid+1..last]
85         mergeSort(theArray, mid + 1, last);
86
87         // Merge the two halves
88         merge(theArray, first, mid, last);
89      } // end if
90   } // end mergeSort
```

Question 7 By drawing a diagram like the one shown in Figure 11-6, trace the merge sort as it sorts the following array into ascending order: 25 30 20 80 40 60.

Question 8 Show that the merge sort algorithm satisfies the four criteria of recursion that Chapter 2 describes.

Analysis. Because the merge step of the algorithm requires the most effort, let's begin the analysis there. Each merge step merges theArray[first..mid] and theArray[mid+1..last]. Figure 11-7 provides an example of a merge step that requires the maximum number of comparisons. If the total number of items in the two array segments to be merged is n, then merging the segments requires at most $n - 1$ comparisons. (For example, in Figure 11-7 six items

FIGURE 11-7   A worst-case instance of the merge step in a merge sort

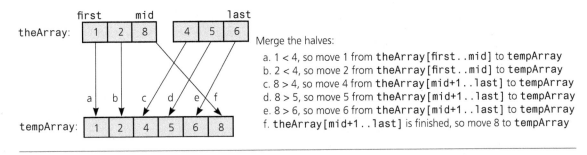

Merge the halves:

a. 1 < 4, so move 1 from theArray[first..mid] to tempArray
b. 2 < 4, so move 2 from theArray[first..mid] to tempArray
c. 8 > 4, so move 4 from theArray[mid+1..last] to tempArray
d. 8 > 5, so move 5 from theArray[mid+1..last] to tempArray
e. 8 > 6, so move 6 from theArray[mid+1..last] to tempArray
f. theArray[mid+1..last] is finished, so move 8 to tempArray

FIGURE 11-8   Levels of recursive calls to mergeSort, given an array of eight items

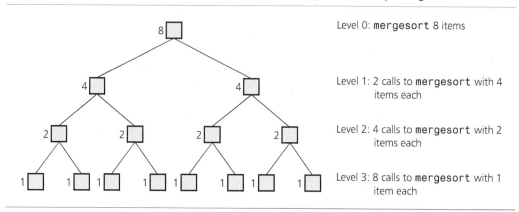

Level 0: **mergesort** 8 items

Level 1: 2 calls to **mergesort** with 4 items each

Level 2: 4 calls to **mergesort** with 2 items each

Level 3: 8 calls to **mergesort** with 1 item each

are in the segments and five comparisons are required.) In addition, there are n moves from the original array to the temporary array, and n moves from the temporary array back to the original array. Thus, each merge step requires $3 \times n - 1$ major operations.

Each call to mergeSort recursively calls itself twice. As Figure 11-8 illustrates, if the original call to mergeSort is at level 0, two calls to mergeSort occur at level 1 of the recursion. Each of these calls then calls mergeSort twice, so four calls to mergeSort occur at level 2 of the recursion, and so on. How many levels of recursion are there? We can count them, as follows.

Each call to mergeSort halves the array. Halving the array the first time produces two pieces. The next recursive calls to mergeSort halve each of these two pieces to produce four pieces of the original array; the next recursive calls halve each of these four pieces to produce eight pieces, and so on. The recursive calls continue until the array pieces each contain one item—that is, until there are n pieces, where n is the number of items in the original array. If n is a power of 2 ($n = 2^k$), the recursion goes $k = \log_2 n$ levels deep. For example, in Figure 11-8, there are three levels of recursive calls to mergeSort because the original array contains eight items and $8 = 2^3$. If n is not a power of 2, there are $1 + \log_2 n$ (rounded down) levels of recursive calls to mergeSort.

The original call to mergeSort (at level 0) calls merge once. Then merge merges all n items and requires $3 \times n - 1$ operations, as was shown earlier. At level 1 of the recursion, two calls to mergeSort, and hence to merge, occur. Each of these two calls to merge merges $n / 2$ items and requires $3 \times (n / 2) - 1$ operations. Together these two calls to merge require $2 \times (3 \times (n / 2) - 1)$ or $3 \times n - 2$ operations. At level m of the recursion, 2^m calls to merge occur; each of these calls merges $n / 2^m$ items and so requires $3 \times (n / 2^m) - 1$ operations. Together the 2^m calls to merge require $3 \times n - 2^m$ operations. Thus, each level of the recursion requires $O(n)$ operations. Because there are either $\log_2 n$ or $1 + \log_2 n$ levels, the merge sort is $O(n \times \log n)$ in both the worst and average cases. You should look at Figure 10-3 in the previous chapter to convince yourself that $O(n \times \log n)$ is significantly faster than $O(n^2)$.

The merge sort is $O(n \times \log n)$

Although the merge sort is an extremely efficient algorithm with respect to time, it does have one drawback: The merge step requires an auxiliary array. This extra storage and the necessary copying of entries are disadvantages.

11.2.2 The Quick Sort

Another divide-and-conquer algorithm

Consider the first two steps of the pseudocode function kSmall that solves the problem of finding the kth smallest item of the array theArray[first..last] and was discussed in Section 2.4.4 of Chapter 2:

FIGURE 11-9   A partition about a pivot

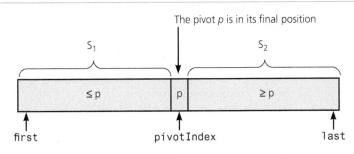

Choose a pivot value p from `anArray[first..last]`
Partition the values of `anArray[first..last]` *about p*

Recall that this partition, which is pictured again in Figure 11-9, has the property that all items in S_1, that is, `theArray[first..pivotIndex - 1]`, are less than or equal to the pivot p, and all items in S_2, that is, `theArray[pivotIndex + 1..last]`, are greater than or equal to p. Though this property does not imply that the array is sorted, it does imply an extremely useful fact: The items within S_1 remain within S_1 when the array is properly sorted, although their positions relative to one another may change. Similarly, the items within S_2 will remain within S_2 when the array is sorted, although their relative positions may change. Finally, the pivot item remains in its position in the final, sorted array.

The partition induces relationships among the array items that are the ingredients of a recursive solution. Arranging the array items around the pivot p generates two smaller sorting problems—sort the left section of the array (S_1), and sort the right section of the array (S_2). The relationships between the pivot and the array items imply that once you solve the left and right sorting problems, you will have solved the original sorting problem. That is, partitioning the array before making the recursive calls places the pivot in its correct position and ensures that when the smaller array segments are sorted their items will be in the proper relation to the rest of the array. Also, the quick sort algorithm will eventually terminate: The left and right sorting problems are indeed smaller problems and are each closer than the original sorting problem to the base case—which is an array containing one item—because the pivot is not part of either S_1 or S_2.

A first draft of pseudocode for the quick sort algorithm follows:

> The quick sort partitions an array into items that are less than or equal to the pivot and those that are greater than or equal to the pivot

> Partitioning places the pivot in its correct position within the array

```
// Sorts theArray[first..last].
quickSort(theArray: ItemArray, first: integer, last: integer): void
{
    if (first < last)
    {
        Choose a pivot item p from theArray[first..last]
        Partition the items of theArray[first..last] about p
        // The partition is theArray[first..pivotIndex..last]

        quickSort(theArray, first, pivotIndex - 1) // Sort S₁

        quickSort(theArray, pivotIndex + 1, last)  // Sort S₂
    }
    // If first >= last, there is nothing to do
}
```

Partitioning the array. Now consider the partition function that both `kSmall` and `quickSort` must call. Partitioning an array section about a pivot item is actually the most difficult part of these two problems.

The partition function will receive an array segment `theArray[first..last]` as an argument. The function must arrange the items of the array segment into two regions: S_1 contains the items less than or equal to the pivot and S_2 contains the items greater than or equal to the pivot. Thus, as you saw in Figure 11-9, S_1 is the segment `theArray[first..pivotIndex - 1]`, and S_2 is the segment `theArray[pivotIndex + 1..last]`.

Place your chosen pivot in theArray[last] before partitioning

What pivot should you use? Various strategies exist for making this choice, as you will see later, so let's assume for now that we have chosen a pivot and go on to develop the partition algorithm. Regardless of which pivot you choose, let's swap it with the last entry `theArray[last]` to get it out of the way while we partition the array. Figure 11-10a shows an array after this step. Starting at the beginning of the array and moving toward the end (left to right in the figure), look for the first entry that is greater than or equal to the pivot. In Figure 11-10b, that entry is 5 and occurs at the index `indexFromLeft`. In a similar fashion, starting at the next-to-last entry

FIGURE 11-10   A partitioning of an array during a quick sort

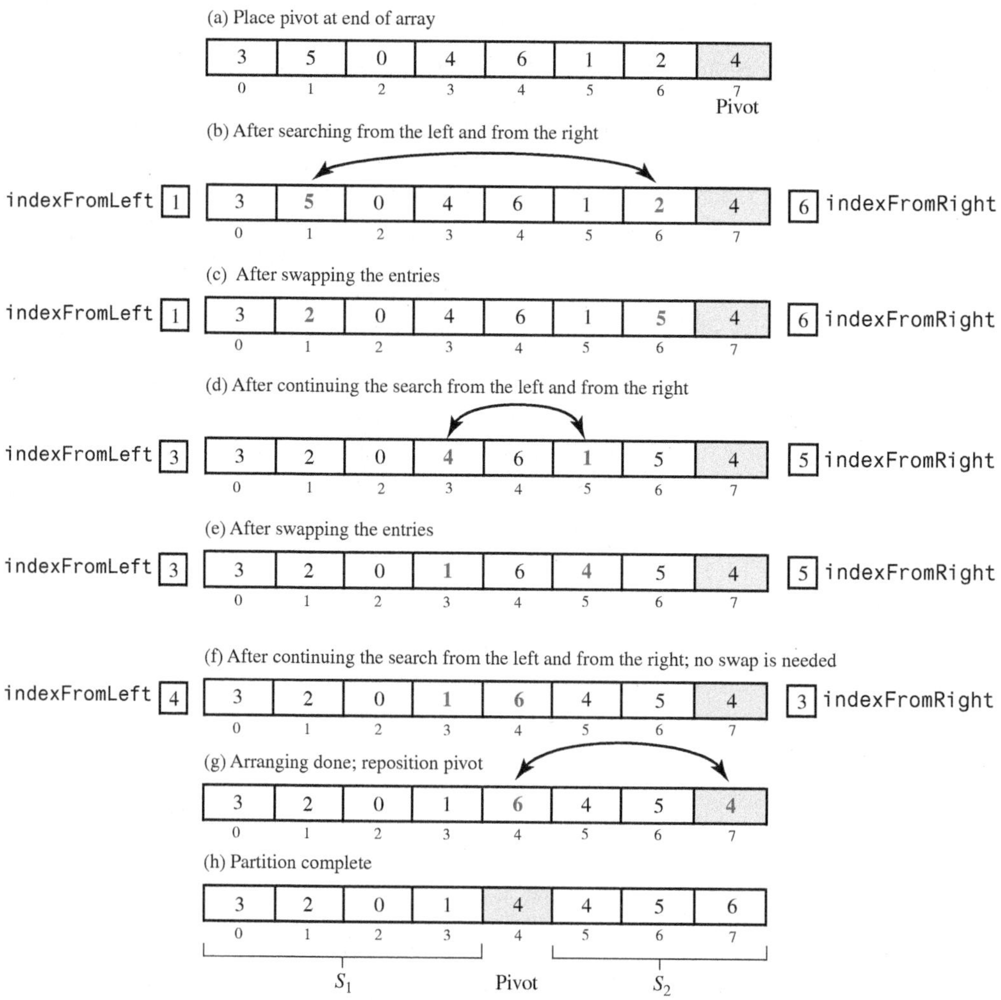

(a) Place pivot at end of array

(b) After searching from the left and from the right

(c) After swapping the entries

(d) After continuing the search from the left and from the right

(e) After swapping the entries

(f) After continuing the search from the left and from the right; no swap is needed

(g) Arranging done; reposition pivot

(h) Partition complete

and moving toward the beginning of the array (right to left in the figure), look for the first entry that is less than or equal to the pivot. In Figure 11-10b, that entry is 2 and occurs at the index `indexFromRight`. Now, if `indexFromLeft` is less than `indexFromRight`, swap the two entries at those indices. Figure 11-10c shows the result of this step. The 2, which is less than the pivot, has moved toward the beginning of the array, while the 5, which is greater than the pivot, has moved in the opposite direction.

Continue the searches from the left and from the right. Figure 11-10d shows that the search from the left stops at 4 and the search from the right stops at 1. Since `indexFromLeft` is less than `indexFromRight`, swap 4 and 1. The array now appears as in Figure 11-10e. Entries equal to the pivot are allowed in either piece of the partition.

Continue the searches again. Figure 11-10f shows that the search from the left stops at 6, while the search from the right goes beyond the 6 to stop at 1. Since `indexFromLeft` is not less than `indexFromRight`, no swap is necessary and the searches end. The only remaining step is to place the pivot between the subarrays S_1 and S_2 by swapping `a[indexFromLeft]` and `a[last]`, as Figure 11-10g shows. The completed partition appears in Figure 11-10h.

Note that the previous searches must not go beyond the ends of the array. Soon you will see a convenient way to implement this requirement.

Entries equal to the pivot.   Notice that both of the subarrays S_1 and S_2 can contain entries equal to the pivot. This might seem a bit strange to you. Why not always place any entries that equal the pivot into the same subarray? Such a strategy would tend to make one subarray larger than the other. However, to enhance the quick sort's performance, we want the subarrays to be as nearly equal in size as possible.

Notice that both the search from the left and the search from the right stop when they encounter an entry that equals the pivot. This means that rather than leaving such entries in place, they are swapped. It also means that such an entry has a chance of landing in each of the subarrays.

Selecting a pivot.   Ideally, the pivot should be the median value in the array, so that the subarrays S_1 and S_2 each have the same—or nearly the same—number of entries. One way to find the median value is to sort the array and then get the value in the middle. But sorting the array is the original problem, so this circular logic is doomed. So instead of getting the best pivot by finding the median of all values in the array, we will at least try to avoid a bad pivot.

We will take as our pivot the median of three entries in the array: the first entry, the middle entry, and the last entry. One way to accomplish this task is to sort only those three entries and use the middle entry of the three as the pivot. Figure 11-11 shows an array both before and after its first, middle, and last entries are sorted. The pivot is the 5. This pivot selection strategy is called **median-of-three pivot selection**, and it assumes that the array has at least three entries. If you have only three entries, the pivot selection sorts them, so there is no need for the partition method or for a quick sort. Thus, we now assume that the array contains at least four entries.

The following pseudocode describes how to sort the first, middle, and last entries in an array of at least four entries. For example, it will transform the array in Figure 11-11a to the one in Figure 11-11b.

```
// Arranges the first, middle, and last entries in an array into ascending order.
sortFirstMiddleLast(theArray: ItemArray, first: integer, mid: integer,
                    last: integer): void
{
    if (theArray[first] > theArray[mid])
        Interchange theArray[first] and theArray[mid]
```

```
    if (theArray[mid] > theArray[last])
        Interchange theArray[mid] and theArray[last]

    if (theArray[first] > theArray[mid])
        Interchange theArray[first] and theArray[mid]

}
```

FIGURE 11-11   Median-of-three pivot selection

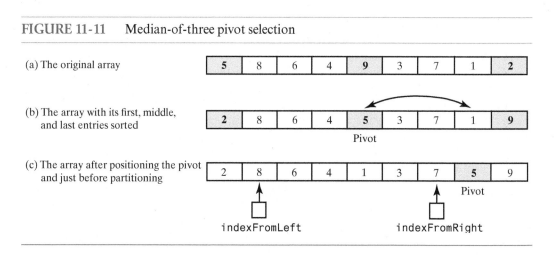

(a) The original array

(b) The array with its first, middle, and last entries sorted

(c) The array after positioning the pivot and just before partitioning

Adjusting the partition algorithm. Median-of-three pivot selection suggests some minor adjustments to our partitioning scheme. Previously, we swapped the pivot with the last entry in the array prior to partitioning. But here the first, middle, and last entries in the array are sorted, so we know that the last entry is at least as large as the pivot. Thus, the last entry belongs in the subarray S_2. We can simply leave the last entry in place. To get the pivot out of the way, we can swap it with the next-to-last entry, a[last - 1], as Figure 11-11b shows. Therefore, the partition algorithm can begin its search from the right at index last - 2.

Also notice that the first entry is at least as small as the pivot, and so it belongs in the subarray S_1. Thus, we can leave the first entry in place and have the partition algorithm begin its search from the left at index first + 1. Figure 11-11c shows the status of the array at this point, just prior to partitioning.

This scheme provides a side benefit that simplifies the loops for the two searches. The search from the left looks for an entry that is greater than or equal to the pivot. That search will terminate because, at worst, it will stop at the pivot. The search from the right looks for an entry that is less than or equal to the pivot. That search will terminate because, at worst, it will stop at the first entry. Thus, the loops need not do anything special to prevent the searches from going beyond the ends of the array.

After the search loops end, we need to position the pivot between the subarrays S_1 and S_2. We do this by swapping the entries a[indexFromLeft] and a[last - 1].

Note: The quick sort rearranges the entries in an array during the partitioning process. Each partition places one entry—the pivot—in its correct sorted position. The entries in each of the two subarrays that are before and after the pivot will remain in their respective subarrays.

The following pseudocode describes the partitioning algorithm for an array of at least four entries:

The partition
algorithm

```
// Partitions theArray[first..last].
partition(theArray: ItemArray, first: integer, last: integer): integer
{
    // Choose pivot and reposition it
    mid = first + (last - first) / 2
    sortFirstMiddleLast(theArray, first, mid, last)
    Interchange theArray[mid] and theArray[last - 1]
    pivotIndex = last - 1
    pivot = theArray[pivotIndex]

    // Determine the regions S₁ and S₂
    indexFromLeft = first + 1
    indexFromRight = last - 2

    done = false
    while (not done)
    {
        // Locate first entry on left that is ≥ pivot
        while (theArray[indexFromLeft] < pivot)
            indexFromLeft = indexFromLeft + 1

        // Locate first entry on right that is ≤ pivot
        while (theArray[indexFromRight] > pivot)
            indexFromRight = indexFromRight - 1

        if (indexFromLeft < indexFromRight)
        {
            Interchange theArray[indexFromLeft] and theArray[indexFromRight]
            indexFromLeft = indexFromLeft + 1
            indexFromRight = indexFromRight - 1
        }
        else
            done = true
    }
    // Place pivot in proper position between S₁ and S₂, and mark its new location
    Interchange theArray[pivotIndex] and theArray[indexFromLeft]
    pivotIndex = indexFromLeft

    return pivotIndex
}
```

Question 9 Trace the quick sort's partitioning algorithm as it partitions the following array: 38 16 40 39 12 27

A function for the quick sort. Before completing the C++ code for the quick sort, we need to think about small arrays. You have seen that the array should contain at least four entries before you call the partition method. But simply agreeing to use the quick sort only on large arrays is not enough. The pseudocode just given for the quick sort shows that partitioning even a large array will eventually lead to a recursive call that involves an array as small as two entries. The code for the quick sort needs to screen out these small arrays and use another way to sort them. An insertion sort is a good choice for small arrays. In fact, using it instead of the quick sort on arrays of as many as ten entries is reasonable. The function in Listing 11-5 implements the quick sort with these observations in mind. It assumes a constant MIN_SIZE that specifies the size of the smallest array on which we will use a quick sort.

LISTING 11-5 **A function that performs a quick sort**

```
1   /** Sorts an array into ascending order. Uses the quick sort with
2       median-of-three pivot selection for arrays of at least MIN_SIZE
3       entries, and uses the insertion sort for other arrays.
4    @pre   theArray[first..last] is an array.
5    @post  theArray[first..last] is sorted.
6    @param theArray  The given array.
7    @param first  The index of the first element to consider in theArray.
8    @param last  The index of the last element to consider in theArray. */
9   template <class ItemType>
10  void quickSort(ItemType theArray[], int first, int last)
11  {
12     if ((last - first + 1) < MIN_SIZE)
13     {
14        insertionSort(theArray, first, last);
15     }
16     else
17     {
18        // Create the partition: S1 | Pivot | S2
19        int pivotIndex = partition(theArray, first, last);
20
21        // Sort subarrays S1 and S2
22        quickSort(theArray, first, pivotIndex - 1);
23        quickSort(theArray, pivotIndex + 1, last);
24     }  // end if
25  }  // end quickSort
```

Analysis. The major effort in the quickSort function occurs during the partitioning step. Partitioning will require no more than n comparisons, and so, like merging, it will be an $O(n)$ task. The ideal situation occurs when the pivot moves to the center of the array, so the two subarrays that the partition forms are the same size. If every recursive call to quickSort forms a partition with equal-sized subarrays, the quick sort will be like a merge sort in that the recursive calls halve the array. As in the previous analysis of the merge sort, you can conclude that there are either $\log_2 n$ or $1 + \log_2 n$ levels of recursive calls to quickSort. Thus, fewer recursive calls to quickSort occur. Each call to quickSort involves m comparisons and at most m exchanges, where m is the number of items in the subarray to be sorted. Clearly $m \le n - 1$. Thus, a quick sort would be $O(n \log n)$, and this would be its best case.

Quick sort: Worst case: $O(n^2)$; average case: $O(n \log n)$

This ideal situation might not always occur, however. It is possible that each partition has one empty subarray. Although one recursive call will have nothing to do, the other call must sort $n - 1$ entries instead of $n / 2$. This occurrence is the worst case because the nonempty subarray decreases in size by only 1 at each recursive call to quickSort, and so the maximum number of recursive calls to quickSort will occur. The result is n levels of recursive calls instead of $\log n$. Thus, in the worst case, quick sort is $O(n^2)$.

A formal analysis of the average-case behavior of a quick sort would show that it is $O(n \log n)$. While the merge sort is always $O(n \log n)$, the quick sort can be faster in practice and does not require the additional memory that merge sort needs for merging. Moreover, on large arrays, you can expect a quick sort to run significantly faster than an insertion sort. However, in its worst case, a quick sort will require roughly the same amount of time as an insertion sort.

The fact that the quick sort's average-case behavior is far better than its worst-case behavior distinguishes it from the other sorting algorithms considered in this chapter. If the original arrangement of data in the array is "random," the quick sort performs at least as well as any known sorting algorithm that involves comparisons.

The efficiency of a merge sort is somewhere between the possibilities for a quick sort: Sometimes the quick sort is faster, and sometimes the merge sort is faster. While the worst-case behavior of a merge sort is of the same order of magnitude as a quick sort's average-case behavior, in most situations a quick sort will run somewhat faster than a merge sort. However, in its worst case, the quick sort will be significantly slower than the merge sort.

Note: The quick sort
- The choice of pivots affects the quick sort's efficiency. Some pivot-selection schemes can lead to worst-case behavior if the array is already sorted or nearly sorted. In practice, nearly sorted arrays can occur more frequently than you might imagine. Fortunately, median-of-three pivot selection avoids worst-case behavior for sorted arrays.
- The quick sort is often used to sort large arrays, as it is usually extremely fast in practice, despite its unimpressive theoretical worst-case behavior. Although a worst-case situation is not typical, even if the worst case occurs, the quick sort's performance is acceptable for moderately large arrays.
- The quick sort is appropriate when you are confident that the data in the array to be sorted is arranged randomly. Although the quick sort's worst-case behavior is $O(n^2)$, the worst case rarely occurs in practice.

ASIDE: Quick sort versus merge sort and kSmall

The quickSort and mergeSort algorithms are similar in spirit, but whereas quickSort does its work before its recursive calls, mergeSort does its work after its recursive calls. That is, while quickSort has the form

```
quickSort(theArray, first, last): void
{
    if (first < last)
    {
        Prepare array for recursive calls
        quickSort(S₁ region of theArray)
        quickSort(S₂ region of theArray)
    }
}
```

mergeSort has the general form

```
mergeSort(theArray, first, last): void
{
    if (first < last)
    {
        mergeSort(Left half of theArray)
        mergeSort(Right half of theArray)
        Tidy up array after the recursive calls
    }
}
```

The preparation in quickSort is to partition the array into regions S_1 and S_2. The algorithm then sorts S_1 and S_2 independently, because every item in S_1 belongs to the left of every item in S_2. In mergeSort, on the other hand, no work is done before the recursive calls: The algorithm sorts each half of the array with respect to itself. However, the algorithm

(continues)

must still deal with the interaction between the items in the two halves. That is, the algorithm must merge the two halves of the array after the recursive calls.

Now recall the pseudocode function kSmall, described in Chapter 2, that returns the kth smallest value in an array:

```
kSmall(k, theArray, first, last): ItemType
{
    Choose a pivot value p from anArray[first..last]
    Partition the values of anArray[first..last] about p

    if (k < pivotIndex - first + 1)
        return kSmall(k, anArray, first, pivotIndex - 1)
    else if (k == pivotIndex - first + 1)
        return p
    else
        return kSmall(k - (pivotIndex - first + 1), anArray,
                      pivotIndex + 1, last)
}
```

The recursive calls to kSmall act only on the section of the array that contains the desired item, and it is not called at all if the desired item is the pivot. On the other hand, quickSort is called recursively on both unsorted sections of the array. Figure 11-12 illustrates this difference.

Question 10 Suppose that you sort a large array of integers by using a merge sort. Next you use a binary search to determine whether a given integer occurs in the array. Finally, you display all of the integers in the sorted array.

    a. Which algorithm is faster, in general: the merge sort or the binary search? Explain in terms of Big O notation.

    b. Which algorithm is faster, in general: the binary search or displaying the integers? Explain in terms of Big O notation.

FIGURE 11-12   kSmall versus quickSort

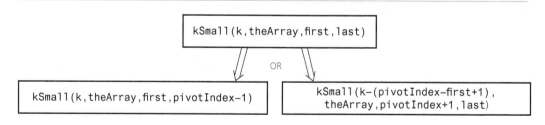

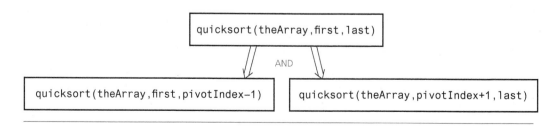

11.2.3 The Radix Sort

The **radix sort** is included here because it is quite different from the other sorts we've described, as it does not compare the array's entries.

Imagine that you are sorting a deck of cards. As you examine the cards one at a time, you place them by rank into 13 possible groups in this order: 2, 3, ..., 10, J, Q, K, A. Combine these groups in order into one pile on the table so that the 2s are on top and the aces are on the bottom. Now take each card from the top of the pile and place it by suit into one of four possible groups in this order: clubs, diamonds, hearts, and spades. When taken together, the groups result in a sorted deck of cards.

A radix sort uses this idea of forming groups and then combining them to sort a collection of data. The sort treats each data item as a character string. As a first simple example of a radix sort, consider this collection of three-letter strings:

ABC, XYZ, BWZ, AAC, RLT, JBX, RDT, KLT, AEO, TLJ

The sort begins by organizing the data according to the rightmost (least significant) letters. Although none of the strings ends in *A* or *B*, two strings end in *C*. Place those two strings into a group. Continuing through the alphabet, you form the following groups:

(ABC, AAC) (TLJ) (AEO) (RLT, RDT, KLT) (JBX) (XYZ, BWZ)   Group strings by their rightmost letter

The strings in each group end with the same letter, and the groups are ordered by that letter. In addition, the strings within each group retain their relative order from the original list of strings.

Now combine the groups into one as follows. Take the items in the first group in their present order, follow them with the items in the second group in their present order, and so on. The following group results:

ABC, AAC, TLJ, AEO, RLT, RDT, KLT, JBX, XYZ, BWZ   Combine the groups

Next, form new groups as you did before, but this time use the middle letter of each string instead of the last letter:

(AAC) (ABC, JBX) (RDT) (AEO) (TLJ, RLT, KLT) (BWZ) (XYZ)   Group the strings by their middle letter

Now the strings in each group have the same middle letter, and the groups are ordered by that letter. As before, the strings within each group retain their relative order from the previous group of all strings.

Combine these groups into one group, again preserving the relative order of the items within each group:

AAC, ABC, JBX, RDT, AEO, TLJ, RLT, KLT, BWZ, XYZ   Combine the groups

Now form new groups according to the first letter of each string:

(AAC, ABC, AEO) (BWZ) (JBX) (KLT) (RDT, RLT) (TLJ) (XYZ)   Group the strings by their first letter

Finally, combine the groups, again maintaining the relative order within each group:

AAC, ABC, AEO, BWZ, JBX, KLT, RDT, RLT, TLJ, XYZ   Sorted strings

The strings are now in sorted order.

In the previous example, all character strings had the same length. If the character strings have varying lengths, you can treat them as if they were the same length by padding them on the right with blanks as necessary.

To sort numeric data, the radix sort treats a number as a character string. You can treat numbers as if they were padded on the left with zeros, making them all appear to be the same length. You then form groups according to the right-most digits, combine the groups, form groups according to the next-to-last digits, combine them, and so on, just as you did in the previous example. Figure 11-13 shows a radix sort of eight integers.

FIGURE 11-13   A radix sort of eight integers

0123, 2154, 0222, 0004, 0283, 1560, 1061, 2150	Original integers
(1560, 2150) (1061) (0222) (0123, 0283) (2154, 0004)	Grouped by fourth digit
1560, 2150, 1061, 0222, 0123, 0283, 2154, 0004	Combined
(0004) (0222, 0123) (2150, 2154) (1560, 1061) (0283)	Grouped by third digit
0004, 0222, 0123, 2150, 2154, 1560, 1061, 0283	Combined
(0004, 1061) (0123, 2150, 2154) (0222, 0283) (1560)	Grouped by second digit
0004, 1061, 0123, 2150, 2154, 0222, 0283, 1560	Combined
(0004, 0123, 0222, 0283) (1061, 1560) (2150, 2154)	Grouped by first digit
0004, 0123, 0222, 0283, 1061, 1560, 2150, 2154	Combined (sorted)

The following pseudocode describes the algorithm for a radix sort of *n* decimal integers of *d* digits each:

```
// Sorts n d-digit integers in the array theArray.
radixSort(theArray: ItemArray, n: integer, d: integer): void
{
   for (j = d down to 1)
   {
      Initialize 10 groups to empty
      Initialize a counter for each group to 0
      for (i = 0 through n - 1)
      {
         k = jth digit of theArray[i]
         Place theArray[i] at the end of group k
         Increase kth counter by 1
      }
      Replace the items in theArray with all the items in group 0,
         followed by all the items in group 1, and so on.
   }
}
```

 Question 11   Trace the radix sort as it sorts the following array into ascending order: 3812 1600 4012 3934 1234 2724 3333 5432

Analysis. From the pseudocode for the radix sort, you can see that this algorithm requires *n* moves each time it forms groups and *n* moves to combine them again into one group. The algorithm performs these $2 \times n$ moves *d* times. Therefore, the radix sort requires $2 \times n \times d$ moves to sort *n* strings of *d* characters each. However, notice that no comparisons are necessary. Thus, radix sort is O(*n*).

Despite its efficiency, the radix sort has some difficulties that make it inappropriate as a general-purpose sorting algorithm. For example, to perform a radix sort of strings of uppercase letters, you need to accommodate 27 groups—one group for blanks and one for each letter. If the original data collection contains n strings, each group must be able to hold n strings. For large n, this requirement demands substantial memory if you use arrays for both the original data and the resulting groups. However, you can save memory by using a chain of linked nodes for each of the 27 groups. Thus, a radix sort is more appropriate for a chain than for an array.

> Even though the radix sort is O(n), it is not appropriate as a general-purpose sorting algorithm

11.3 A Comparison of Sorting Algorithms

Figure 11-14 summarizes the time required in the worst case and average case for the sorting algorithms that appear in this chapter. For reference purposes, two other algorithms—the tree sort and heap sort—are included here, even though you will not study them until Chapters 15 and 17, respectively.

FIGURE 11-14 Approximate growth rates of time required for eight sorting algorithms

	Worst case	Average case
Selection sort	n^2	n^2
Bubble sort	n^2	n^2
Insertion sort	n^2	n^2
Merge sort	$n \times \log n$	$n \times \log n$
Quick sort	n^2	$n \times \log n$
Radix sort	n	n
Tree sort	n^2	$n \times \log n$
Heap sort	$n \times \log n$	$n \times \log n$

Note: The Standard Template Library (STL) provides several sort functions in the library header `<algorithm>`. Consult C++ Interlude 8 for more information about the STL and these functions.

SUMMARY

1. The selection sort, bubble sort, and insertion sort are all O(n^2) algorithms. Although in a particular case one might be faster than another, for large problems they all are slow. For small arrays, however, the insertion sort is a good choice.

2. The quick sort and merge sort are two very efficient recursive sorting algorithms. In the average case, the quick sort is among the fastest known sorting algorithms. However, the quick sort's worst-case behavior is significantly slower than the merge sort's. Fortunately, the quick sort's worst case rarely occurs in practice. The merge sort is not quite as fast as the quick sort in the average case, but its performance is consistently good in all cases. The merge sort has the disadvantage of requiring extra storage equal to the size of the array to be sorted.

3. The radix sort is unusual in that it does not sort the array entries by comparing them. Thus, it is not always applicable, making it inappropriate as a general-purpose sorting algorithm. However, when the radix sort is applicable, it is an O(n) algorithm.

EXERCISES

1. This chapter's analysis of the selection sort ignored operations that control loops or manipulate array indices. Revise this analysis by counting *all* operations, and show that the algorithm is still $O(n^2)$.

2. Trace the insertion sort as it sorts the following array into ascending order:

    20 80 40 25 60 40

3. Trace the selection sort as it sorts the following array into ascending order:

    7 12 24 4 19 32

4. Trace the bubble sort as it sorts the following array into descending order:

    12 23 5 10 34

5. Sort each of the following arrays into ascending order by using the selection sort, bubble sort, and insertion sort:

    a. 8 6 4 2
    b. 2 4 6 8

6. How many comparisons would be needed to sort an array containing 25 entries using the bubble sort in

    a. The worst case?
    b. The best case?

7. Find an array that makes the bubble sort exhibit its worst behavior.

8. Revise the function `selectionSort` so that it sorts an array of instances of a class according to one `int` data member, which is the sort key. Assume that the class contains a member method `getSortKey` that returns the integer sort key.

9. Write recursive versions of `selectionSort`, `bubbleSort`, and `insertionSort`.

10. Trace the merge sort algorithm as it sorts the following array into ascending order. List the calls to `merge-Sort` and to `merge` in the order in which they occur.

    20 80 40 25 60 30

11. When sorting an array by using a merge sort,

    a. Do the recursive calls to `mergeSort` depend on the values in the array, the number of items in the array, or both? Explain.
    b. In what step of `mergeSort` are the items in the array actually swapped (that is, sorted)? Explain.

12. Trace the quick sort algorithm as it sorts the following array into ascending order. List the calls to `quick-sort` and to `partition` in the order in which they occur. Since the given array is small, give `MIN_SIZE` a value of 3 instead of the suggested 10.

    20 80 40 25 60 10 15

13. Suppose that you remove the call to `merge` from the merge sort algorithm to obtain

```
// Mystery algorithm for theArray[0..n-1].
mystery(theArray: ItemArray, n: integer): void
{
   if (n > 1)
   {
      mystery(lefthalf(theArray))
      mystery(righthalf(theArray))
   }
}
```

What does this new algorithm do?

14. How many recursive calls are necessary when `quickSort` sorts an array of size n if you use median-of-three pivot selection?

15. Describe an iterative version of `mergeSort`.

16. One criterion used to evaluate sorting algorithms is stability. A sorting algorithm is **stable** if it does not exchange items that have the same sort key. Thus, items with the same sort key (possibly differing in other ways) will maintain their positions relative to one another. For example, you might want to take an array of students sorted by name and re-sort it by year of graduation. Using a stable sorting algorithm to sort the array by year will ensure that within each year the students will remain sorted by name. Some applications mandate a stable sorting algorithm. Others do not. Which of the sorting algorithms described in this chapter are stable?

17. When we discussed the radix sort, we sorted a deck of cards by first ordering the cards by rank and then by suit. To implement a radix sort for this example, you could use two characters to represent a card, if you used the letter T to represent a 10. For example, S2 is the 2 of spades and HT is the 10 of hearts.

   a. Trace the radix sort for the following cards: S2, HT, D6, S4, C9, CJ, DQ, ST, HQ, DK.
   b. Suppose that you did not use T to represent a 10—that is, suppose that H10 is the 10 of hearts—and that you padded the two-character strings on the right with a blank to form three-character strings. How would a radix sort order the entire deck of cards in this case?

PROGRAMMING PROBLEMS

1. Add a counter to the functions `insertionSort` and `mergeSort` that counts the number of comparisons that are made. Run the two functions with arrays of various sizes. At what size does the difference in the number of comparisons become significant? How does this size compare with the size that the orders of these algorithms predict?

2. Revise the function `quickSort` so that it always chooses the first item in the array as the pivot. Add a counter to the function `partition` that counts the number of comparisons that are made. Compare the behavior of the revised function with the original one, using arrays of various sizes. At what size array does the difference in the number of comparisons become significant? For which pivot selection strategy does the difference in the number of comparisons become significant?

3. Various partitioning strategies are possible for quick sort. What other strategies can you think of ? How do they compare to the two studied in the previous programming problem?

4. Consider the ADT list, as described in Chapters 8 and 9. Add a method `sort` to the list.

5. Repeat Programming Problem 4, but assume a link-based implementation of the ADT list. Use a merge sort in the definition of the method `sort`. Implement any other sorting algorithms that are appropriate for this implementation of a list.

6. Repeat Programming Problem 5, but use a radix sort in the definition of the method `sort` instead of a merge sort.

7. You can sort a large array of integers that are in the range 1 to 100 by using an array count of 100 items to count the number of occurrences of each integer in the array. Fill in the details of this sorting algorithm, which is called a **bucket sort**, and write a C++ function that implements it. What is the order of the bucket sort? Why is the bucket sort not useful as a general sorting algorithm?

8. The **Shell sort** (named for its inventor, Donald Shell) is an improved insertion sort. Rather than always exchanging adjacent items—as in an insertion sort—the Shell sort can exchange items that are far apart in the array. The Shell sort arranges the array so that every h^{th} item forms a sorted subarray in a decreasing sequence of values. For example, if h is 5, every fifth item forms a sorted subarray. Ultimately, if h is 1, the entire array will be sorted.

One possible sequence of h's begins at $n/2$ and halves n until it becomes 1. By using this sequence, and by replacing 1 with h and 0 with $h-1$ in insertionSort, we get the following function for the Shell sort:

```cpp
template <class ItemType>
void shellSort(ItemType theArray[], int n)
{
   for (int h = n / 2; h > 0; h = h / 2)
   {
      for (int unsorted = h; unsorted < n; unsorted++)
      {
         ItemType nextItem = theArray[unsorted];
         int loc = unsorted;
         while ( (loc >= h) && (theArray[loc - h] > nextItem) )
         {
            theArray[loc] = theArray[loc - h];
            loc = loc - h;
         }  // end while
         theArray[loc] = nextItem;
      } // end for
   }  // end for
}  // end shellSort
```

Add a counter to the functions insertionSort and shellSort that counts the number of comparisons that are made. Run the two functions with arrays of various sizes. At what size does the difference in the number of comparisons become significant?

9. Write a program to display the running time of the sorts described in this chapter. Test the sorts on arrays of various sizes. Arrays of the same size should contain identical entries. Use the function clock from <ctime> to time each sort. See the beginning of the programming problems in Chapter 10 for an example of how to time code.

10. Write an in-place merge sort algorithm that does not require a temporary array to merge the two halves. What is the efficiency of your solution?

Class Relationships and Reuse

Contents

Prerequisites

Chapter 1   Data Abstraction: The Walls
C++ Interlude 1   C++ Classes
C++ Interlude 2   Pointers, Polymorphism, and Memory Allocation
Chapter 6   Stacks
Chapter 8   Lists

C++ classes provide a way to enforce the walls of data abstraction by encapsulating an abstract data type's data and operations. An object-oriented approach, however, goes well beyond encapsulation. Inheritance, polymorphism, and containment allow you to define new classes from existing classes. This interlude describes techniques that make collections of reusable software components possible. Realize that much more can and should be said about these techniques. Consider this interlude to be a refinement and expansion of the introduction to this material begun in C++ Interlude 1.

C5.1 Inheritance Revisited

When you think of inheritance, you might imagine a bequest of one million dollars from some long-lost wealthy relative. In the object-oriented world, however, inheritance describes the ability of a class to derive properties from a previously defined class. These properties are like the genetic characteristics you received from your parents: Some traits are the same, some are similar but different, and some are new.

FIGURE C5-1   Inheritance: Relationships among timepieces

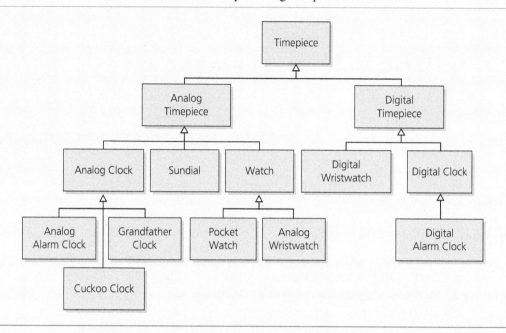

Inheritance, in fact, is a relationship among classes. One class can derive the behavior and structure of another class. For example, Figure C5-1 illustrates some relationships among various timepieces. Digital clocks, for example, include the clock in the dashboard of your car, the clock on the sign of the downtown bank, and the clock on your microwave oven. All digital clocks have the same underlying structure and perform operations such as

> *Set the time*
> *Advance the time*
> *Display the time*

A digital alarm clock is a digital clock that also has alarm methods, such as

> *Set the alarm*
> *Enable the alarm*
> *Sound the alarm*
> *Silence the alarm*

That is, a digital alarm clock has the structure and operations of a digital clock and, in addition, has an alarm and operations to manipulate the alarm.

You can think of the group of digital clocks and the group of digital alarm clocks as classes. The class of digital alarm clocks is a derived class, or subclass, of the class of digital clocks. The class of digital clocks is a base class, or superclass, of the class of digital alarm clocks. Inheritance enables you to reuse software components when you define a new class. For example, you can reuse your design and implementation of an analog clock when you design a cuckoo clock.

In C++, a derived class inherits all of the members of its base class, except the constructors and destructor. That is, a derived class has the data members and methods of the base class in addition to the members it defines. A derived class can also revise any inherited method. For example, according to Figure C5-1, a cuckoo clock is a descendant of an analog clock, like the

A class can derive the behavior and structure of another

A digital alarm clock is a digital clock

Inheritance enables the reuse of existing classes

A derived class inherits the members of its base

FIGURE C5-2   Multiple inheritance

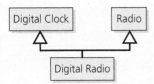

one on a classroom wall. The cuckoo clock inherits the structure and behavior of the analog clock, but revises the way it reports the time each hour by adding a cuckoo.

Sometimes a derived class has more than one base class. For example, as Figure C5-2 illustrates, you can derive a class of clock radios from the class of digital clocks and the class of radios. This type of relationship is known as **multiple inheritance**. Multiple inheritance must be used with care, since it is possible for the base classes to have similarly named methods. For example, suppose that both digital clocks and radios implemented a method turnOn. When the client calls the turnOn method in the digital clock radio, you have no way to know which turnOn method is called. In this textbook, if multiple inheritance is used, the derived class inherits code from only one base class; any other bases classes should be abstract base classes.

In C++ Interlude 1, we used plain boxes, toy boxes, and magic boxes as objects. While designing the class of toy boxes, ToyBox, we decided that a toy box is simply a plain box with a color. This realization is significant in that PlainBox—the class of plain boxes—already existed. Thus, we could let PlainBox be a base class of ToyBox, and we implemented ToyBox without reinventing the basic box. Toward that end, Listing C5-1 recalls the definition of the class PlainBox from Listing C1-3.

> *Inheritance reduces the effort necessary to add features to an existing object*

LISTING C5-1   The class PlainBox, originally given in Listing C1-3

```
1   template<class ItemType>
2   class PlainBox
3   {
4   private:
5       ItemType item;
6
7   public:
8       PlainBox();
9       PlainBox(const ItemType& theItem);
10      void setItem(const ItemType& theItem);
11      ItemType getItem() const;
12  }; // end PlainBox
```

Our derived class ToyBox inherited all the members of the class PlainBox—except the constructors and destructor—and made some changes. We added both a data member that held the box's color and methods to access and set the color.

> *A derived class can add new members to those it inherits*

You can add as many new members to a derived class as you like. Although you cannot revise an ancestor's private data members and should not reuse their names, you can **redefine** inherited methods. A method in a derived class redefines a nonvirtual method in the base class if the two methods have the same name and parameter declarations.

> *A derived class can redefine an inherited method of its base class*

When the derived class MagicBox was implemented in C++ Interlude 1, we redefined the method getItem so that it always returns the first item stored in the box. Figure C5-3 illustrates the relationship between PlainBox and MagicBox.

FIGURE C5-3   The derived class `MagicBox` inherits members of the base class `PlainBox` and redefines and adds members

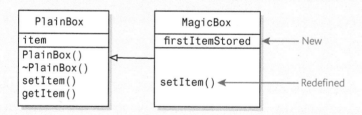

Listing C5-2 shows the declaration of the class `MagicBox`, which was originally given in Listing C1-7 of C++ Interlude 1.

LISTING C5-2 **The class `MagicBox`, originally given in Listing C1-7**

```
1   template<class ItemType>
2   class MagicBox : public PlainBox<ItemType>
3   {
4   private:
5       bool firstItemStored;
6
7   public:
8       MagicBox();
9       MagicBox(const ItemType& theItem);
10      void setItem(const ItemType& theItem);
11  }; // end MagicBox
```

Adding a colon and `public PlainBox<ItemType>` after `class MagicBox` indicates that `PlainBox` is a base class of `MagicBox` or, equivalently, that `MagicBox` is a derived class of `PlainBox`.

An instance of a derived class has all the behaviors of its base class

An instance of the class `MagicBox` has two data members—`item`, which is inherited, and `firstItemStored`, which is new. Because an instance of a derived class can invoke any public method in the base class, an instance of `MagicBox` has all of the methods that `PlainBox` defines; new constructors; a new, compiler-generated destructor; and a redefined method `setItem`. Although an instance of a derived class contains copies of inherited data members, the code for inherited methods is not copied.

A derived class inherits private members from the base class, but cannot access them directly

A derived class cannot access the private members of the base class directly by name, even though they are inherited. Inheritance does not imply access. After all, you can inherit a locked vault but be unable to open it. In the current example, `PlainBox`'s data member `item` is private, so you can reference it only within the definition of the class `PlainBox` and not within the definition of `ToyBox` or `MagicBox`. However, the class `ToyBox` or `MagicBox` can use `PlainBox`'s public methods `setItem` and `getItem` to set or obtain the value of `item` indirectly.

A derived class's methods can call the base class's public methods

Within the implementation of `MagicBox`, you can use the public methods that `MagicBox` inherits from `PlainBox`. For example, the redefined method `setItem` calls the inherited version of the method `setItem`, which you indicate by writing `PlainBox<ItemType>::setItem`. This notation is necessary to differentiate between the two versions of the method. Thus, you can use the scope resolution operator `::` to access a base-class method, even when the method has been redefined in the derived class. The implementation of `MagicBox`'s `setItem` method is then

```
template<class ItemType>
void MagicBox<ItemType>::setItem(const ItemType& theItem)
{
   if (!firstItemStored)
   {
      PlainBox<ItemType>::setItem(theItem);
      firstItemStored = true; // Box now has magic
   } // end if
} // end setItem
```

Clients of a derived class also can invoke the public members of the base class. For example, if you write

```
MagicBox<std::string> myMagicBox("Volleyball");
std::string magicBoxItem = myMagicBox.getItem();
```

myMagicBox's item, "Volleyball", is returned by the method getItem that MagicBox inherits from PlainBox. If a new method has the same name as an ancestor method—setItem, for example—instances of the new class will use the new method, while instances of the ancestor class will use the original method. If myPlainBox is a PlainBox object, the call myPlainBox.setItem(...) will invoke PlainBox's setItem, whereas myMagicBox.setItem(...) will invoke MagicBox's setItem, as Figure C5-4 illustrates. Because the compiler can determine which form of setItem to use at compilation time—as opposed to at execution time—this situation is called early binding, as introduced in C++ Interlude 2. Another term for early binding is **static binding**.

Clients of a derived class can invoke the base class's public methods

Note: Inheritance and the execution order of constructors and destructors

A derived class's constructor executes after the base class's constructor. For example, if you define an instance of MagicBox, its constructor executes after PlainBox's constructor. The destructor of a derived class executes before the destructor of the base class. For example, MagicBox's destructor executes before PlainBox's destructor. This is true for constructors and destructors that you write as well as those generated by the compiler.

FIGURE C5-4   Early, or static, binding: The compiler determines which version of a
               method to invoke

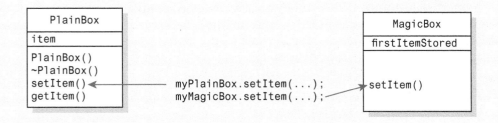

Early binding can lead to problems. For example, the statements

Early binding can cause problems

```
PlainBox<std::string>* cardBoxPtr = new PlainBox<std::string>("Queen of Hearts");
cardBoxPtr->setItem("Jack of Spades");
```

invoke PlainBox's version of setItem. Unfortunately, if cardBoxPtr points to an instance of MagicBox—for example, if you wrote

```
PlainBox<std::string>* cardBoxPtr = new MagicBox<std::string>("Queen of Hearts");
```

the statement

```
cardBoxPtr->setItem("Jack of Spades");
```

still invokes PlainBox's version of setItem, instead of MagicBox's version. In this case, the compiler chose the version of setItem to invoke from the type of the pointer variable cardBoxPtr instead of from the type of object to which cardBoxPtr points.

Simply redefining setItem in MagicBox—as we did earlier—is insufficient. As was briefly discussed in Section C1.5 of C++ Interlude 1 and Section C2.4 of C++ Interlude 2, you also need to tell the compiler that derived classes of PlainBox might revise setItem so that the compiler can make accommodations for such an occurrence. You do this by making setItem a virtual method in PlainBox. Recall that to make a particular method virtual, you simply write the keyword virtual before the method's declaration within the definition of the base class. For example, the class PlainBox appears as

```
class PlainBox
{
public:
   // Everything as before, except setItem
   . . .
   virtual void setItem(const ItemType& theItem);
   . . .
}; // end PlainBox
```

The implementation of setItem is the same as given earlier.

Now, when cardBoxPtr points to an instance of MagicBox, the statement

```
cardBoxPtr->setItem("Jack of Spades");
```

invokes MagicBox's version of setItem. Thus, the appropriate version of a method is decided at execution time, instead of at compilation time, based on the type of object to which cardBoxPtr points. Recall from C++ Interlude 2 that this situation is called late binding. Another term for late binding is **dynamic binding**. A method such as setItem is called **polymorphic**. That is, the outcome of a particular operation depends upon the objects on which the operation acts. We also say that MagicBox's version of setItem **overrides** PlainBox's version.

A virtual method in a derived class can override a virtual method in the base class if they have the same declarations. Overriding a method is similar to redefining a method. However, you can override only virtual methods. Note that you can omit virtual in the derived class. Any method in a derived class that has the same declaration as an ancestor's virtual method—such as setItem—is also virtual without explicit identification, although tagging it with virtual is desirable stylistically. It is also desirable to tag an overriding method with the identifier override, as in the following example:

```
class MagicBox : public PlainBox<ItemType>
{
   // Everything as before, except setItem
   . . .

public:
   . . .
   void setItem(const ItemType& theItem) override;
}; // end MagicBox
```

Late binding means that the appropriate version of a method is decided at execution time

A polymorphic method has multiple meanings

A virtual method is one that you can override

A method that is virtual in a base class is virtual in any derived class

This identifier signals both the reader of your program and the compiler of your intent. The compiler then can ensure that you are correctly overriding a method.

To prevent anyone from overriding a method, you can declare that method as final. For example, if a programmer defines a class using our MagicBox class as a base class, to prevent that derived class from overriding MagicBox's method setItem, you would declare setItem as a final method, as you can see here:

```cpp
class MagicBox : public PlainBox<ItemType>
{
    // Everything as before, except setItem
    . . .

public:
    . . .
    void setItem(const ItemType& theItem) override final;
}; // end MagicBox
```

Now, setItem overrides its base-class version, but cannot itself be overridden. The order of override and final in the declaration of setItem is not important. Also, note that these two identifiers can appear by themselves.

Every class has a compiler-generated **virtual method table (VMT)**, which remains invisible to the programmer. For each method in the class, the VMT contains a pointer to the actual instructions that implement the method. For a method that is not virtual, the compiler can establish this pointer, since it knows the method's definition. For a virtual method, the compiler can not complete the VMT. Instead, a call to a constructor during program execution sets the pointer, as Figure C5-5 illustrates. That is, the constructor establishes pointers—within the VMT—to the versions of the virtual methods that are appropriate for the object. Thus, the VMT is the mechanism that enables late binding.

FIGURE C5-5   Virtual method tables when cardBoxPtr points to an instance of either PlainBox or MagicBox

---

(a) PlainBox<std::string>* cardBoxPtr = new PlainBox<std::string>("Queen of Hearts");

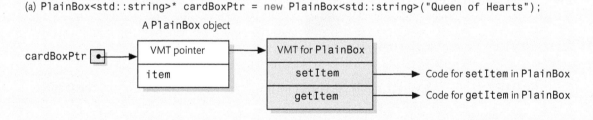

(b) PlainBox<std::string>* cardBoxPtr = new MagicBox<std::string>("Queen of Hearts");

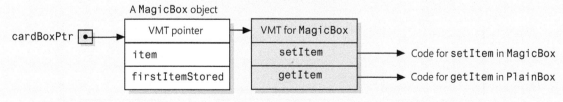

> **Note:** **The identifiers** `override` **and** `final`
>
> The identifier `override` indicates that a virtual method overrides another virtual method in the base class. It appears at the end of the method's prototype. The identifier `final` indicates that a method cannot be overriden by a method in a derived class.

VideoNote

C++ inheritance and
access

C5.1.1 Public, Private, and Protected Sections of a Class

In addition to its public and private sections, a class can have a **protected section**. By creating a protected section, a class designer can hide members from a class's clients but make them available to a derived class. That is, a derived class can reference the protected members of its base class directly, but clients of the base class or derived class cannot.

For example, `PlainBox` has a private member `item`, which the derived class `MagicBox` cannot reference directly. If instead you declared `item` as protected, `MagicBox` would be able to access `item` directly by name. Clients of `MagicBox` or `PlainBox`, however, would not have direct access to `item`. We could then revise our implementation of `MagicBox`'s `setItem` method as follows:

```cpp
template<class ItemType>
void MagicBox<ItemType>::setItem(const ItemType& theItem)
{
   if (!firstItemStored)
   {
      PlainBox<ItemType>::item = theItem; // item has protected access
      firstItemStored = true;             // Box now has magic
   } // end if
} // end setItem
```

The following summary distinguishes among the public, private, and protected sections of a class, and Figure C5-6 illustrates their access.

FIGURE C5-6   Access to public, private, and protected sections of a class by a client and a derived class

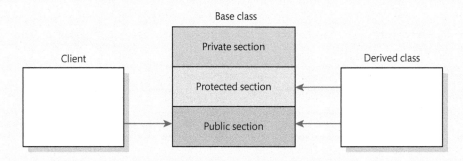

Note: Access categories of a class
- Public members can be used by anyone.
- Private members can be used only by methods of the class.
- Protected members can be used only by methods of the class and its derived classes.

Note: Stylistic guideline

As a general stylistic guideline to maintain information hiding and to keep derived classes from coupling directly to base class data members, you should make all data members of a class private and, if required, provide indirect access to them by defining accessor or mutator methods that are either public or protected. Although a class's public members are available to anyone, its protected members are available exclusively to either its own methods or the methods of a derived class.

In general, a class's data members should be private

C5.1.2 Public, Private, and Protected Inheritance

Several kinds of inheritance are possible. Regardless of the kind of inheritance, a derived class can access all of the base class's public and protected members, but not its private members. You can control how a class's inherited members are passed to subsequent derived classes by specifying one of three kinds of inheritance. You begin the definition of the derived class as

```
class DerivedClass : kindOfInheritance BaseClass
```

where *kindOfInheritance* is one of `public`, `private`, or `protected`. The inheritance that you saw earlier in this interlude is public inheritance. The following summary describes the three kinds of inheritance.

Note: Kinds of inheritance
- **Public inheritance:** Public and protected members of the base class remain, respectively, public and protected members of the derived class.
- **Protected inheritance:** Public and protected members of the base class are protected members of the derived class.
- **Private inheritance:** Public and protected members of the base class are private members of the derived class.

In all cases, private members of a base class remain private to the base class and cannot be accessed directly by a derived class.

Of the three types of inheritance, public inheritance is the most important and the one that we will use most often in subsequent chapters. You use public inheritance to extend the definition of a class. You use private inheritance to implement one class in terms of another class. Protected inheritance is not often used, so we will not cover it.

The following section describes when it is appropriate to use public and private inheritance.

C5.1.3 *Is-a* and *As-a* Relationships

As you just saw, inheritance provides for ancestor/descendant relationships among classes. Other relationships are also possible. When designing new classes from existing ones, it is important to identify their relationship so that you can determine whether to use inheritance and, if so, the kind of inheritance that best reflects the relationship. Three basic kinds of relationships are possible. In this section we discuss *is-a* and *as-a* relationships, which involve inheritance. We discuss an important third relationship, *has-a*, in Section C5.2.

***Is-a* relationships**. Earlier in this interlude, we used public inheritance to derive the class MagicBox from PlainBox. You should use public inheritance only when an ***is-a* relationship** exists between two classes of objects. In this example, a magic box *is a* plain box, as Figure C5-7 illustrates. That is, whatever is true of the base class PlainBox is also true of the derived class MagicBox. Wherever you can use an object of type PlainBox, you can also use an object of type MagicBox. This feature is called **object type compatibility**. In general, a derived class is type-compatible with all of its ancestor classes. Thus, you can use an instance of a derived class instead of an instance of its base class, but not the other way around.

FIGURE C5-7   A magic box *is a* plain box

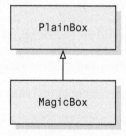

In particular, the object type of an argument in a call to a method can be a descendant of the object type of the corresponding parameter. For example, suppose your program uses the classes PlainBox and MagicBox and contains the following ordinary function, which is not a member of any class:

```cpp
void displayBoxItem(PlainBox<std::string> thing)
{
    std::cout << "The item stored in the box is "
              << thing.getItem() << ".\n";
}  // end displayBoxItem
```

If you define myPlainBox and myMagicBox as

```cpp
PlainBox<std::string> myPlainBox("Basketball");
MagicBox<std::string> myMagicBox("Volleyball");
```

the following calls to displayBoxItem are legal:

```cpp
displayBoxItem(myPlainBox);  // myPlainBox's item is displayed
displayBoxItem(myMagicBox);  // myMagicBox's item is displayed
```

The first call is unremarkable because both the argument myPlainBox and the parameter thing have the same data type. The second call is more interesting: The data type of the argument myMagicBox is a descendant of the data type of the parameter thing. Because a magic box is a plain box, it can behave like a plain box. That is, myMagicBox can perform plain-box behaviors, so you can use myMagicBox anywhere you can use myPlainBox. Note that object type compatibility applies to both value and reference arguments.

***As-a* relationships.** Consider the relationship between the class Stack, which implements the ADT stack, and the class List, which implements the ADT list. Because a Stack object should not be able to have List behaviors, public inheritance is inappropriate in this case. A stack is not a list. When public inheritance is inappropriate, if your class needs access to the protected members of another class or if you need to redefine methods in that class, you can form an ***as-a* relationship** between your classes; that is, you can use private inheritance.

If the relationship between two classes is not *is-a*, you should not use public inheritance

To derive Stack from List using private inheritance, you begin the definition of the class Stack with the header

```
class Stack : private List
```

List's public members—and protected members, if List has any—would be private members of Stack. Thus, within the implementation of Stack, you would be able to use a list to store the stack's entries and manipulate them by using List's methods. We say that Stack implements the ADT stack *as a* list. Both the descendants and clients of Stack are unable to access any members of List. Thus, the underlying list is hidden from the clients of the stack.

If public inheritance is inappropriate and your class does not need access to the protected members of another class, or if you do not need to redefine methods in that class, a *has-a* relationship is preferable and simpler to use than an *as-a* relationship. We consider that next.

C5.2 Containment: *Has-a* Relationships

A ball-point pen *has a* ball as its point, as Figure C5-8 illustrates. Although you would want to use Ball in your definition of a class Pen, you should not use public inheritance, because a pen is not a ball. In fact, you do not use inheritance at all to implement a ***has-a* relationship**. Instead, you can define a data member point—whose type is Ball—within the class Pen as

---

FIGURE C5-8   A pen *has a* or *contains* a ball

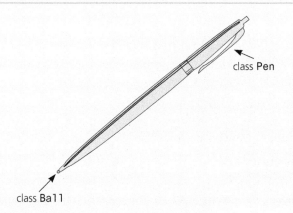

class Pen

class Ball

```
class Pen
{
private:
   Ball point;
   ...
}; // end Pen
```

Has-a, or
containment, means
a class has an
object as a data
member

Recall that a data member can be an instance of any class other than the one currently being defined—Pen, in this example. An instance of Pen has, or *contains*, an instance of Ball. Thus, another name for the *has-a* relationship is **containment**.

As you continue to examine the ball's relationship to the pen, you may realize that if the pen is destroyed, the ball should also be destroyed, since it no longer has a purpose. When an instance of an object cannot exist independently of the containing class, this type of containment is called **composition**. We have seen this in our link-based implementations of an ADT. For example, when an instance of LinkedBag, LinkedStack, or LinkedList is destroyed, the nodes used to store the container's objects are no longer needed and are destroyed also. In the array-based implementations of our ADTs, the array containing the items is destroyed.

Another form of containment is **aggregation**. In an aggregate relationship the contained item can exist independently of the containing class. Our PlainBox class has an instance of ItemType named item. If our plain box is destroyed, the program can continue to use item. Another example of aggregation can be found in the implementations of our ADT bag, ADT stack, and ADT list: The items stored in a bag, stack, or list continue to exist even after we are finished using the container and it has been destroyed.

Programming Tip: Favor containment over inheritance. Use public inheritance when an *is-a* relationship exists, that is, when an instance of a derived class can substitute for an instance of the base class. Use private inheritance when you want to reuse a part of another class's implementation.

Note: Containment and the execution order of constructors and destructors

The constructors for a class's member objects execute in the order listed in the class definition before the class's constructor. For example, Ball's constructor executes before Pen's constructor. The destructors of a class's member objects execute after the class's destructor. For example, Ball's destructor executes after Pen's.

Note: Execution order of constructors and destructors

Considering both inheritance and containment, a class's constructors execute in the following order:

1. Its base class constructor executes.
2. Constructors of its member objects execute in the declaration order.
3. The body of its constructor executes.

A class's destructors execute in the opposite order:

1. The body of its destructor executes.
2. Destructors of its member objects execute in the declaration order.
3. Its base class destructor executes.

C5.3 Abstract Base Classes Revisited

Chapter 1 defined an abstract base class as a class that contains at least one virtual method that has no implementation. C++ Interlude 1 restated that definition as a class that contains at least one pure virtual method. An abstract base class cannot have instances—that is, cannot be instantiated—and is used only as the basis of other classes. Any derived class that fails to implement all of the pure virtual methods is also an abstract base class and cannot have instances.

An abstract base class can provide a constructor, which cannot be pure because constructors cannot be virtual. A destructor in an abstract base class should not be pure, because derived classes will call it, and thus, it should be implemented even if it simply has an empty body. Generally, virtual destructors are recommended.

As you have seen, an abstract base class is a great place to specify an ADT. By defining the methods that make up the ADT's public interface as pure virtual methods, we force any derived class to implement these methods, ensuring a common interface across implementations. For example, Listing C5-3 contains the abstract base class for boxes from C++ Interlude 1.

> A class that contains at least one pure virtual method is an abstract base class

> An abstract base class has descendants but no instances

LISTING C5-3 An abstract class that is an interface for the ADT box

```
1   template <class ItemType>
2   class BoxInterface
3   {
4   public:
5      virtual void setItem(const ItemType& theItem) = 0;
6      virtual ItemType getItem() const = 0;
7      virtual ~BoxInterface() { } // Empty implementation
8   }; // end BoxInterface
```

We can indicate that our class PlainBox is derived from BoxInterface by changing its class header to

```
class PlainBox : public BoxInterface<ItemType>
```

We can also define a new class, JewelryBox, that provides an alternate implementation of the methods in BoxInterface. Its class header would be

```
class JewelryBox : public BoxInterface<ItemType>
```

Figure C5-9 shows the family of box classes.

If we define several pointer variables of type BoxInterface, we can have them point to instances of any of the derived classes:

```
BoxInterface<std::string>* someBoxPtr = new PlainBox<std::string>("Ace");
BoxInterface<std::string>* anotherBoxPtr = new JewelryBox<std::string>("Emerald");
BoxInterface<std::string>* funBoxPtr = new MagicBox<std::string>("Stone");
```

For each of the objects created, we can call the setItem or getItem method, and the implementation specific to the instantiated class will execute, even though the pointers are of type BoxInterface:

```
std::cout << someBoxPtr->getItem() << std::endl;      // Uses PlainBox getItem
std::cout << anotherBoxPtr->getItem() << std::endl;   // Uses JewelryBox getItem
std::cout << funBoxPtr->getItem() << std::endl;       // Uses MagicBox getItem, which
                                                      // is PlainBox getItem
```

FIGURE C5-9   UML class diagram of the family of box classes

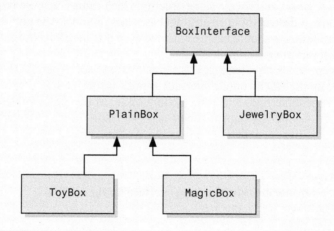

The key points about abstract base classes are summarized next.

 Note: Abstract base classes

An abstract base class:

- By definition is a class that contains at least one pure virtual method.
- Is used only as the basis for derived classes and thus defines a minimum interface for its descendants.
- Cannot have instances, that is, cannot be instantiated.
- Should, in general, omit implementations except for the destructor and methods that provide access to private data members. That is, virtual methods in an abstract base class usually should be pure.
- Must implement any virtual method that is not pure, thereby providing a default implementation if a derived class chooses not to supply its own.

Sorted Lists and Their Implementations

Contents

Prerequisites

One of the most frequently performed computing tasks is the maintenance of a collection of data in some specified order. Many examples immediately come to mind, such as students placed in order by their names, baseball players listed in order by their batting averages, and corporations listed in order by their assets. The items in these examples are in **sorted order**. In contrast, the items on a grocery list might occur in the order in which they appear on the grocer's shelves, but they are probably not sorted by name. These items are ordered simply by their positions within the list.

The ADT sorted list maintains items in sorted order

The ADT **sorted list** maintains its entries in sorted order. The problem of maintaining sorted data involves more than simply sorting the data. Often you need to insert some new data item into its proper, sorted place. Similarly, you often need to remove some data item. For example, suppose your university maintains an alphabetical list of the students who are currently enrolled. The registrar must add names to and remove names from this list because students constantly enroll in and leave school. These operations should preserve the sorted order of the data.

This chapter specifies the ADT sorted list and then implements it in several ways. A major goal of this chapter is to show you how we can develop a class of sorted lists from an existing class of lists.

12.1   Specifying the ADT Sorted List

The ADT list leaves it up to the client to arrange the entries in a given collection. The client can maintain the entries in any order that meets its needs. Recall that to use the insert operation of the ADT list, you must specify both the new entry and its desired position within the list. The ADT sorted list differs from the ADT list in that a sorted list inserts and removes items by their values and not by their positions. For example, the sorted list insertion operation determines the proper position for the new entry according to its value. Since a sorted list takes responsibility for organizing its entries, it does not give the client an operation that inserts a new entry by position. If you were allowed to specify a new entry's position, you might destroy the order of the sorted list's entries.

Note: The ADT sorted list is a container of items that determines and maintains the order of its entries by their values. For simplicity, we will allow the sorted list to contain duplicate items. Insisting that the sorted list contain only unique items is somewhat more complicated, and we will leave this variation as an exercise.

What other operations do we want for this ADT? We've already mentioned that you can add an entry to the sorted list. Since the sorted list determines the position of a new entry, you could ask the ADT for this position. That is, you could ask for the position of an existing entry or for the position in which a proposed entry would occur if you added it to the list. You could also ask the ADT for the entry at a particular position. And clearly you should be able to remove an entry. We could remove a particular entry given its value, but we could also remove an entry given its position in the sorted list. We will include both of these removal operations.

Let's itemize the sorted list's operations—including common ones like getting the current number of entries—and specify them more carefully. Note that none of the operations on a sorted list that involve the position of an entry destroys the list's sorted order.

Note: ADT sorted list operations
- Test whether a sorted list is empty.
- Get the number of entries in a sorted list.
- Insert an entry into a sorted list.
- Remove a given entry from a sorted list.
- Remove the entry at a given position from a sorted list.
- Remove all entries from a sorted list.
- Look at (get) the entry at a given position in a sorted list.
- Get the position of a given entry in a sorted list.

FIGURE 12-1   UML diagram for the ADT sorted list

```
                    SortedList
┌─────────────────────────────────────────────────────┐
│                                                       │
├─────────────────────────────────────────────────────┤
│ +isEmpty(): boolean                                   │
│ +getLength(): integer                                 │
│ +insertSorted(newEntry: ItemType): boolean            │
│ +removeSorted(newEntry: ItemType): boolean            │
│ +remove(position: integer): boolean                   │
│ +clear(): void                                        │
│ +getEntry(position: integer): ItemType                │
│ +getPosition(newEntry: ItemType): integer             │
└─────────────────────────────────────────────────────┘
```

Figure 12-1 shows the UML diagram for this ADT, and the following summary of its operations provides even more details for its operation contract:

ABSTRACT DATA TYPE: SORTED LIST

DATA

- A finite number of objects, not necessarily distinct, having the same data type and ordered by their values.

OPERATIONS

PSEUDOCODE	DESCRIPTION
insertSorted(newEntry)	Task: Inserts an entry into this sorted list in its proper order so that the list remains sorted. Input: newEntry is the new entry. Output: True if insertion is successful, or false if not.
removeSorted(anEntry)	Task: Removes the first or only occurrence of anEntry from this sorted list. Input: anEntry is the entry to remove. Output: Returns true if anEntry was located and removed, or false if not. In the latter case, the list remains unchanged.
getPosition(anEntry)	Task: Gets the position of the first or only occurrence of anEntry in this sorted list. Input: anEntry is the entry to be located. Output: Returns the position of anEntry if it occurs in the sorted list. Otherwise, returns the position where anEntry would occur in the list, but as a negative integer.

The following operations behave as they do for the ADT list and are described in Chapter 8:
```
    isEmpty()
    getLength()
    remove(position)
    clear()
    getEntry(position)
```

Understanding the behavior of the first two methods is straightforward, but let's look more closely at getPosition. Given an entry in the sorted list, the method getPosition returns the entry's position number within the list, as you would expect. We number the entries beginning with 1, just as we do for the ADT list. But what if the given entry is not in the sorted list? In this case, getPosition returns the position number where the entry belongs in the list. The returned number is negative, however, to signal that the entry is not in the list. For example, if missingObject is not in the sorted list but would belong at position 3, getPosition(missingObject) will return –3.

The sorted list also has some, but not all, of the operations of an ADT list. We have already mentioned that adding an entry at a given position is not possible, because otherwise the client could destroy the order of the sorted list. For the same reason, the list's replace method is not available to a sorted list. The other operations of the ADT list, however, are useful for a sorted list as well, including the ones that retrieve or remove the entry at a given position. The methods getEntry and remove each have a position number as a parameter, but they will not alter the relative order of the entries in the sorted list.

Question 1 The specifications of the ADT sorted list do not mention the case in which two or more items have the same value. Are these specifications sufficient to cover this case, or must they be revised?

Question 2 Write specifications for the operation insertSorted when the sorted list must not contain duplicate entries.

12.1.1 An Interface Template for the ADT Sorted List

The C++ interface given in Listing 12-1 formalizes our initial specifications of the ADT sorted list.

LISTING 12-1 A C++ interface for sorted lists

```
1    /** Interface for the ADT sorted list
2     @file SortedListInterface.h */
3
4    #ifndef SORTED_LIST_INTERFACE_
5    #define SORTED_LIST_INTERFACE_
6
7    template<class ItemType>
8    class SortedListInterface
9    {
10   public:
11      /** Inserts an entry into this sorted list in its proper order
12          so that the list remains sorted.
13       @pre  None.
14       @post  newEntry is in the list, and the list is sorted.
15       @param newEntry  The entry to insert into the sorted list.
16       @return  True if insertion is successful, or false if not. */
17      virtual bool insertSorted(const ItemType& newEntry) = 0;
18
19      /** Removes the first or only occurrence of the given entry from this
20          sorted list.
```

```
21        @pre  None.
22        @post  If the removal is successful, the first occurrence of the
23           given entry is no longer in the sorted list, and the returned
24           value is true. Otherwise, the sorted list is unchanged and the
25           returned value is false.
26        @param anEntry  The entry to remove.
27        @return  True if removal is successful, or false if not. */
28     virtual bool removeSorted(const ItemType& anEntry) = 0;
29
30     /** Gets the position of the first or only occurrence of the given
31          entry in this sorted list. In case the entry is not in the list,
32          determines where it should be if it were added to the list.
33        @pre  None.
34        @post  The position where the given entry is or belongs is returned.
35           The sorted list is unchanged.
36        @param anEntry  The entry to locate.
37        @return  Either the position of the given entry, if it occurs in the
38           sorted list, or the position where the entry would occur, but as a
39           negative integer. */
40     virtual int getPosition(const ItemType& anEntry) const = 0;
41
42  // The following methods are the same as those given in ListInterface
43  // in Listing 8-1 of Chapter 8 and are completely specified there.
44
45     /** Sees whether this list is empty. */
46     virtual bool isEmpty() const = 0;
47
48     /** Gets the current number of entries in this list. */
49     virtual int getLength() const = 0;
50
51     /** Removes the entry at a given position from this list. */
52     virtual bool remove(int position) = 0;
53
54     /** Removes all entries from this list. */
55     virtual void clear() = 0;
56
57     /** Gets the entry at the given position in this list. */
58     virtual ItemType getEntry(int position) const = 0;
59
60     /** Destroys this sorted list and frees its assigned memory. */
61     virtual ~SortedListInterface() { }
62  }; // end SortedListInterface
63  #endif
```

12.1.2 Using the Sorted List Operations

 Example. To demonstrate the operations of the ADT sorted list that the previous section specifies, we first create a sorted list of strings. We begin by declaring and allocating a sorted list,
where we assume that SortedList is an implementation of the operations specified by the interface SortedListInterface:

```
std::unique_ptr<SortedListInterface<std::string>> nameListPtr =
                    std::make_unique<SortedList<std::string>>();
```

Next, we add names in an arbitrary order, realizing that the ADT will organize them alphabetically:

```
nameListPtr->insertSorted("Jamie");
nameListPtr->insertSorted("Brenda");
nameListPtr->insertSorted("Sarah");
nameListPtr->insertSorted("Tom");
nameListPtr->insertSorted("Carlos");
```

The sorted list now contains the following entries:

> Brenda
> Carlos
> Jamie
> Sarah
> Tom

Assuming the list just given, here are some examples of the operations on the sorted list:

```
nameListPtr->getPosition("Jamie") returns 3, the position of Jamie in the list
nameListPtr->getPosition("Jill") returns –4, because Jill belongs at position 4 in the list
nameListPtr->getEntry(2) returns Carlos, because he is at position 2 in the list
```

Now remove Tom and the first name in the list by writing

```
nameList.remove("Tom");
nameList.remove(1);
```

The list now contains

> Carlos
> Jamie
> Sarah

Removing the last entry, Tom, did not change the positions of the other entries in the list, but removing the first entry did. Carlos is now at position 1, instead of 2.

Note: The ADT sorted list can add, remove, or locate an entry, given the entry as an argument. The sorted list has several operations that are the same as ADT list operations, namely getEntry (by position), remove (by position), clear, getLength, and isEmpty. However, a sorted list will not let you add or replace an entry by position.

Question 3 Suppose that wordListPtr points to an unsorted list of words. Using the operations of the ADT list and the ADT sorted list, create a sorted list of these words.

Question 4 Assuming that the sorted list you created in the previous question is not empty, write C++ statements that

    a. Display the last entry in the sorted list.
    b. Add the sorted list's first entry to the sorted list again.

12.2 A Link-Based Implementation

As with all ADTs, you have a choice of several ways in which to implement the sorted list. You could store a sorted list's entries in, for example, an array, a chain of linked nodes, an instance of a vector, or an instance of an ADT list. We first will consider a chain of linked nodes and then an instance of an ADT list. Finally, we will use inheritance to develop a completely different implementation.

12.2.1 The Header File

VideoNote

The ADT sorted list

Our implementation that uses a chain of linked nodes to store the entries in a sorted list has several details in common with the link-based implementation of the ADT list that you studied in Chapter 9. In particular, it has the same data fields, similar constructors, several methods that are the same, and the same definition of the class Node, but all revised to use smart pointers, as described in C++ Interlude 4. Let's begin with the header file, which is given in Listing 12-2. The class LinkedSortedList declares three new public methods for the sorted list—insertSorted, removeSorted, and getPosition—each of which takes a list entry as its argument. As you will see, to implement these methods, you will need the private method getNodeBefore. It accepts an entry as its argument and returns a pointer to the node just prior to the one that contains—or should contain—the entry. Since the definitions of the remaining methods are like those in LinkedList, as given in Chapter 9, and two of them involve the position of an entry, you will also need the private method getNodeAt as defined in Chapter 9 but revised to use smart pointers. As you will see, we will use the private method copyChain to provide a recursive implementation for the copy constructor.

LISTING 12-2 The header file for the class LinkedSortedList.

```
1   /** ADT sorted list: Link-based implementation.
2    @file LinkedSortedList.h */
3
4   #ifndef LINKED_SORTED_LIST_
5   #define LINKED_SORTED_LIST_
6   #include <memory>
7   #include "SortedListInterface.h"
8   #include "Node.h"
9   #include "PrecondViolatedExcept.h"
10
11  template<class ItemType>
12  class LinkedSortedList : public SortedListInterface<ItemType>
13  {
14  private:
15     std::shared_ptr<Node<ItemType>> headPtr; // Pointer to first node in chain
16     int itemCount;                            // Current count of list items
17
18     // Locates the node that is before the node that should or does
19     // contain the given entry.
20     // @param anEntry  The entry to find.
21     // @return  Either a pointer to the node before the node that contains
22     //   or should contain the given entry, or nullptr if no prior node exists.
```

(continues)

```
23        auto getNodeBefore(const ItemType& anEntry) const;
24
25        // Locates the node at a given position within the chain.
26        auto getNodeAt(int position) const;
27
28        // Returns a pointer to a copy of the chain to which origChainPtr points.
29        auto copyChain(const std::shared_ptr<Node<ItemType>>& origChainPtr);
30
31    public:
32        LinkedSortedList();
33        LinkedSortedList(const LinkedSortedList<ItemType>& aList);
34        virtual ~LinkedSortedList();
35        bool insertSorted(const ItemType& newEntry);
36        bool removeSorted(const ItemType& anEntry);
37        int getPosition(const ItemType& newEntry) const;
38
39        // The following methods are the same as given in ListInterface:
40        bool isEmpty() const;
41        int getLength() const;
42        bool remove(int position);
43        void clear();
44        ItemType getEntry(int position) const throw(PrecondViolatedExcept);
45    }; // end LinkedSortedList
46    #include "LinkedSortedList.cpp"
47    #endif
```

12.2.2 The Implementation File

The default constructor and destructor for our class LinkedSortedList have practically the same definitions as they do in the class LinkedList. We will, therefore, leave them to you to implement. You could also model the copy constructor after the one in LinkedList, but we will use recursion in our definition here. We begin by having the copy constructor call the private method copyChain, which will have a recursive definition:

```
template<class ItemType>
LinkedSortedList<ItemType>::
                    LinkedSortedList(const LinkedSortedList<ItemType>& aList)
{
    headPtr = copyChain(aList.headPtr);
    itemCount = aList.itemCount;
} // end copy constructor
```

The private method copyChain begins by testing its pointer argument. If it contains nullptr, the orignal sorted list is empty, so the method returns nullptr. Otherwise, the method creates a new node containing the data from the first node of the given chain. The method then recursively inserts the new node into the copy of the chain. After each insertion, the method returns a pointer to the new chain. The definition of copyChain is

```
template<class ItemType>
auto LinkedSortedList<ItemType>::
    copyChain(const std::shared_ptr<Node<ItemType>>& origChainPtr)
{
   std::shared_ptr<Node<ItemType>> copiedChainPtr; // Initial value is nullptr
   if (origChainPtr != nullptr)
   {
      // Build new chain from given one
      // Create new node with the current item
      copiedChainPtr = std::make_shared<Node<ItemType>>(origChainPtr->getItem());
      // Make the node point to the rest of the chain
      copiedChainPtr->setNext(copyChain(origChainPtr->getNext()));
   }  // end if

   return copiedChainPtr;
}  // end copyChain
```

The method `insertSorted`. Adding an entry to a sorted list requires that you find where in the list the new entry belongs. Since the entries are sorted, you compare the new entry with the entries in the sorted list until you reach an entry that is not smaller than the new entry. Figure 12-2 depicts a chain of linked nodes, each containing a string that is sorted alphabetically. The figure shows where the additional strings "Ally", "Cathy", "Luke", "Sue", and "Tom" would be inserted into the chain and the comparisons that would have to occur to arrive at those locations.

You can see from the figure that, in a string comparison, Ally is less than Bob, and so it would be inserted at the beginning of the chain. To see where to insert Luke, you would find that Luke is greater than both Bob and Jill but less than Mike. Thus, Luke belongs before Mike in the chain. Sue, on the other hand, is already in one of the nodes. You would discover that Sue is greater than Bob, Jill, and Mike but not greater than Sue. So you would insert the new entry Sue just before the existing entry Sue. Finally, Tom is greater than all the current names in the list, so you would add it to the end of the chain.

 Note: Given a sorted list with entries in ascending order, you insert a new entry just before the first entry that is not smaller than the new entry.

Recall from earlier chapters that you add a new node to the beginning of a chain differently than at other points in the chain. Adding to the beginning is easy, since `headPtr` references the first node in the chain. To add anywhere else, you need a pointer to the node that will ultimately occur before the new node. Thus, while you traverse the chain of linked nodes to discover where the new entry belongs, you must retain a reference to the node prior to the one under consideration.

FIGURE 12-2 Places to insert strings into a sorted chain of linked nodes

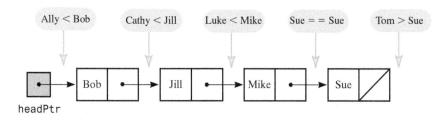

The following high-level algorithm describes our strategy:

```
// Adds a new entry to the sorted list.
insertSorted(newEntry)
{
    Allocate a new node containing newEntry
    Search the chain until either you find a node containing newEntry or you pass
        the point where it should be
    Let prevPtr point to the node before the insertion point
    if (the chain is empty or the new node belongs at the beginning of the chain)
        Add the new node to the beginning of the chain
    else
        Insert the new node after the node referenced by prevPtr

    Increment the length of the sorted list
}
```

Assuming the private method getNodeBefore that we specified in the header file, we can use the previous algorithm to define the insertSorted method, as follows:

```cpp
template<class ItemType>
void LinkedSortedList<ItemType>::insertSorted(const ItemType& newEntry)
{
    auto newNodePtr(std::make_shared<Node<ItemType>>(newEntry));
    auto prevPtr = getNodeBefore(newEntry);

    if (isEmpty() || (prevPtr == nullptr)) // Add at beginning
    {
        newNodePtr->setNext(headPtr);
        headPtr = newNodePtr;
    }
    else                                   // Add after node before
    {
        auto aftPtr = prevPtr->getNext();
        newNodePtr->setNext(aftPtr);
        prevPtr->setNext(newNodePtr);

    }  // end if

    itemCount++;
    return true;
}  // end insertSorted
```

The private method getNodeBefore. We still need to implement the private method getNodeBefore to locate the node that is before the node that should or does contain the given entry. We will need two pointers as we traverse the list. Clearly, we need a pointer to the current node so we can compare its entry to the desired entry. But we also must retain a pointer to the previous node, because it is this pointer that the method returns. In the following implementation, these pointers are curPtr and prevPtr.

```cpp
template<class ItemType>
auto LinkedSortedList<ItemType>::
     getNodeBefore(const ItemType& anEntry) const
{
    auto curPtr = headPtr;
    std::shared_ptr<Node<ItemType>> prevPtr;
```

```
   while ( (curPtr != nullptr) && (anEntry > curPtr->getItem()) )
   {
      prevPtr = curPtr;
      curPtr = curPtr->getNext();
   }  // end while

   return prevPtr;
}  // end getNodeBefore
```

The programming problems at the end of this chapter ask you to complete this implementation of the sorted list.

Note: Since the ADTs sorted list and list share many of the same operations, portions of their implementations are identical.

Question 5 In the `while` statement of the method `getNodeBefore`, how important is the order of the two boolean expressions that the operator `&&` joins? Explain.

Question 6 What does `getNodeBefore` return if the sorted list is empty? How can you use this fact to simplify the implementation of the method `insertSorted` given previously?

Question 7 Suppose that you use the previous method `insertSorted` to add an entry to a sorted list. If the entry is already in the list, where in the list will the method insert it? Before the first occurrence of the entry, after the first occurrence of the entry, after the last occurrence of the entry, or somewhere else?

Question 8 What would be the answer to the previous question if you changed `>` to `>=` in the `while` statement of the method `getNodeBefore`?

12.2.3 The Efficiency of the Link-Based Implementation

The performance of `insertSorted` depends on the efficiency of the method `getNodeBefore`. The latter method locates the insertion point by traversing the chain of nodes. This traversal is O(n), making the addition to a sorted list an O(n) operation. With the exception of `isEmpty` and `getLength`, which are O(1) operations, the sorted-list methods are O(n). We leave these observations for you to show as Exercise 11.

12.3   Implementations That Use the ADT List

As we noted earlier in this chapter, the link-based implementation of the ADT sorted list repeats much of the corresponding implementation of the ADT list. Can we avoid this duplication of effort and reuse portions of the list's implementation?

You can use the ADT list to create and maintain an alphabetical list of strings, but the client must maintain the sorted alphabetical order. It is natural, then, to consider using the ADT list when implementing the ADT sorted list. Basically, you can do this using one of three techniques:

VideoNote

ADT sorted list implementations

- Containment
- Public inheritance
- Private inheritance

FIGURE 12-3   An instance of a sorted list that contains a list of its entries

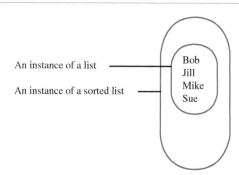

An instance of a list ———

An instance of a sorted list ———

Bob
Jill
Mike
Sue

In most cases, one or more of these three approaches will not be applicable to a particular problem; usually, one of the approaches will be best. However, we will use the sorted list to demonstrate all three techniques.

12.3.1 Containment

A sorted list can maintain its entries within a list, as Figure 12-3 illustrates. You use a list as a data field within the class that implements the sorted list. As noted in C++ Interlude 5, this approach uses a type of containment called composition and illustrates the *has-a* relationship between the class of sorted lists and the class of lists. If we name our new class `SortedListHasA` and use an instance of `LinkedList`, as given in Listing 9-2 of Chapter 9, Figure 12-4 illustrates the relationship between these two classes using UML notation.

FIGURE 12-4   `SortedListHasA` is composed of an instance of the class `LinkedList`

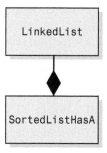

```
LinkedList
```

```
SortedListHasA
```

The header file. Listing 12-3 declares the class `SortedListHasA` so that it *has a* private data member that is an instance of `LinkedList` containing the items in the sorted list. Our class will derive from the interface `SortedListInterface`, as given earlier in Listing 12-1. Note that `listPtr` is a unique pointer, since we will not define aliases to the list. In this way, the sorted list controls ownership of the list. You should use a unique pointer instead of a shared pointer whenever you can.

LISTING 12-3   The header file for the class `SortedListHasA`

```cpp
 1  /** ADT sorted list using the ADT list.
 2   @file SortedListHasA.h */
 3  #ifndef SORTED_LIST_HAS_A_
 4  #define SORTED_LIST_HAS_A_
 5  #include <memory>
 6  #include "SortedListInterface.h"
 7  #include "ListInterface.h"
 8  #include "Node.h"
 9  #include "PrecondViolatedExcept.h"
10
11  template<class ItemType>
12  class SortedListHasA : public SortedListInterface<ItemType>
13  {
14  private:
15     std::unique_ptr<ListInterface<ItemType>> listPtr;
16
17  public:
18     SortedListHasA();
19     SortedListHasA(const SortedListHasA<ItemType>& sList);
20     virtual ~SortedListHasA();
21
22     bool insertSorted(const ItemType& newEntry);
23     bool removeSorted(const ItemType& anEntry);
24     int getPosition(const ItemType& newEntry) const;
25
26     // The following methods have the same specifications
27     // as given in ListInterface in Chapter 8:
28     bool isEmpty() const;
29     int getLength() const;
30     bool remove(int position);
31     void clear();
32     ItemType getEntry(int position) const throw(PrecondViolatedExcept);
33  }; // end SortedListHasA
34  #include "SortedListHasA.cpp"
35  #endif
```

The constructors and destructor.   The constructor creates an instance of `LinkedList` and assigns a reference to it to the pointer variable `listPtr`:

```cpp
template<class ItemType>
SortedListHasA<ItemType>::SortedListHasA()
                       : listPtr(std::make_unique<LinkedList<ItemType>>())
{
} // end default constructor
```

The copy constructor creates a new list and then copies the entries in the given sorted list to the new list:

```cpp
template<class ItemType>
SortedListHasA<ItemType>::
        SortedListHasA(const SortedListHasA<ItemType>& sList)
                       : listPtr(std::make_unique<LinkedList<ItemType>>())
{
```

```
      for (int position = 1; position <= sList.getLength(); position++)
         listPtr->insert(position, sList.getEntry(position));
}   // end copy constructor
```

Note that we call LinkedList's method insert. While this particular definition is not very efficient, a recursive O(*n*) implementation is possible. Exercise 7 at the end of this chapter asks you to investigate this possibility.

The destructor simply calls the method clear, which will deallocate the list:

```
template<class ItemType>
SortedListHasA<ItemType>::~SortedListHasA()
{
   clear();
}   // end destructor
```

The method insertSorted. The implementations of the remaining methods of the ADT sorted list are brief, as the list does most of the work. To add a new entry to the sorted list, we first use the method getPosition, which is an operation of the sorted list. We assume that it is already implemented, even though we have not written it yet. Recall that getPosition finds the position of an existing entry within a sorted list, or the position at which we should insert a new entry that does not occur in the sorted list. The method sets the sign of the integer it returns to indicate whether the entry exists in the list already. Since we allow duplicate entries in our sorted list, we can ignore this sign. Notice that the following implementation uses the standard method abs to discard this sign. It also uses the insert method of the ADT list.

```
template<class ItemType>
bool SortedListHasA<ItemType>::insertSorted(const ItemType& newEntry)
{
   int newPosition = std::abs(getPosition(newEntry));
   return listPtr->insert(newPosition, newEntry);
}   // end insertSorted
```

The method removeSorted. The method removeSorted can call getPosition to determine where in the sorted list the given entry exists or belongs. This time, however, we do need to know whether the entry exists in the list. If it does not exist, we cannot remove it, so removeSorted will return false when this is the case. If the entry is in the sorted list, however, the returned position will be positive, and removeSorted can call the list's method remove to remove the entry. We leave the implementation of removeSorted to you in Checkpoint Question 12.

The method getPosition. Implementing getPosition is somewhat harder than implementing the previous two methods. To decide where in a sorted list an entry is or belongs, we need to compare it to the entries already in the list, beginning with the first one. If the given entry is in the list, we obviously compare entries until we find a match. However, if it is not in the list, we want to stop the search at the point where it belongs in the sorted list. We take advantage of the sorted order of the objects by using logic similar to that described in Section 12.2.2.

Checkpoint Question 9 asks you to define getPosition. You can do so by using the methods getLength and getEntry.

Question 9 Define the method getPosition for the class SortedListHasA.

Question 10 Repeat Checkpoint Question 7 using the method insertSorted of the class SortedListHasA.

Question 11 Can a client of SortedListHasA invoke the method insert of the ADT list? Explain.

Question 12 Define the method removeSorted for the class SortedListHasA.

The remaining methods. Each of the methods isEmpty, getLength, remove, clear, and getEntry of the ADT sorted list has the same specifications as in the ADT list. Each can simply invoke the corresponding list method. For example, the method remove has the following implementation in SortedListHasA:

```
template<class ItemType>
bool SortedListHasA<ItemType>::remove(int position)
{
    return listPtr->remove(position);
} // end remove
```

Efficiency issues. Except perhaps for some subtle logic in getPosition, you can write the previous implementation quickly and with few, if any, errors. Saving human time is an attractive feature of using an existing class to build another. But does the implementation use computer time efficiently? In this particular implementation, several methods invoke getPosition, so their efficiency depends on getPosition's efficiency.

The method getPosition calls the list method getLength, which is an O(1) operation. Therefore, we need not be concerned with it. On the other hand, a loop examines the entries in the list one at a time by invoking getEntry until the desired entry is located. Thus, getPosition's efficiency depends in part on the efficiency of getEntry. However, the efficiency of getEntry depends upon which implementation of the ADT list you use. For the link-based implementation, getEntry is O(n). Since getPosition invokes getEntry within a loop, getPosition is O(n²) in the worst case. Note that each time getEntry retrieves the next entry in the list, it starts its search at the beginning of the chain. This is the cause of getPosition's inefficiency.

Question 13 Suppose that instead of using LinkedList in the implementation of SortedListHasA, you used ArrayList. What Big O would describe the performance of the method getPosition?

Question 14 Give an advantage and a disadvantage of using containment in the implementation of the class SortedListHasA.

Figures 12-5 and 12-6 summarize the efficiencies of the operations for array-based and link-based implementations of the ADTs list and sorted list. Confirmation of these results is left as an exercise. As you can see, the implementation of the sorted list using containment is easy to write but is not very efficient if the underlying list uses a chain of linked nodes.

FIGURE 12-5   The worst-case efficiencies of ADT list operations for array-based and link-based implementations

ADT List Operation	Array-based	Link-based
insert(newPosition, newEntry)	O(n)	O(n)
remove(position)	O(n)	O(n)
getEntry(position)	O(1)	O(n)
replace(position, newEntry)	O(1)	O(n)
clear()	O(1)	O(n)
getLength(), isEmpty()	O(1)	O(1)

FIGURE 12-6   The worst-case efficiencies of the ADT sorted list operations when implemented using an instance of the ADT list

ADT Sorted List Operation	List Implementation	
	Array-based	Link-based
insertSorted(newEntry)	O(n)	O(n^2)
removeSorted(anEntry)	O(n)	O(n^2)
getPosition(anEntry)	O(n)	O(n^2)
getEntry(position)	O(1)	O(n)
remove(givenPosition)	O(n)	O(n)
clear()	O(1)	O(n)
getLength(), isEmpty()	O(1)	O(1)

Note: Using containment to implement the ADT sorted list

When you use an instance of the ADT list to contain the entries in the ADT sorted list, you must use the list's operations to access the sorted list's entries, instead of accessing them directly. Such an implementation of the sorted list is easy to write but is inefficient when the underlying list uses a chain of linked nodes to store its entries.

12.3.2 Public Inheritance

A list is a container of items that you reference by position number. If you maintained those items in sorted order, would you have a sorted list? Ignoring name differences, most operations for the ADT list are *almost* the same as the corresponding operations for the ADT sorted list. The insertion and removal operations differ, however, and the ADT sorted list has an additional operation, getPosition.

You can insert an item into a sorted list by first using getPosition to determine the position in the sorted list where the new item belongs. You then use the list's insert operation to insert the item into that position in the list. You use a similar approach to remove an item from a sorted list.

An is-a relationship implies public inheritance

Thus it appears that a sorted list *is a* list, so let's see whether we can use public inheritance. Figure 12-7 shows the class SortedListIsA as a descendant of the class LinkedList. This diagram represents an implementation in C++ using public inheritance. SortedListIsA inherits LinkedList's members, adds the method getPosition, and revises the insertion and removal operations.

The class SortedListIsA now has useful operations of the ADT list, such as getEntry, remove, clear, isEmpty, and getLength—which it inherits from the class LinkedList—in addition to the methods insertSorted, removeSorted, and getPosition. However, it also inherits insert and replace from LinkedList. By using either of these two position-oriented methods, a client could destroy the order of a sorted list. To prevent this from occurring, SortedListIsA must override them.

FIGURE 12-7   SortedListIsA as a descendant of LinkedList

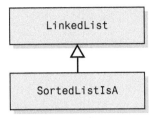

The header file. Listing 12-4 shows a header file for the class SortedListIsA. Note again that we are using public inheritance. You might wonder why we are not using SortedListInterface. Doing so would require us to use multiple inheritance, which, while possible, is beyond our present scope. Since LinkedList is derived from ListInterface, you can think of SortedListIsA as a grandchild of ListInterface.

LISTING 12-4   A header file for the class SortedListIsA

```
1   /** ADT sorted list using ADT list.
2    @file SortedListIsA.h */
3   #ifndef SORTED_LIST_IS_A_
4   #define SORTED_LIST_IS_A_
5   #include <memory>
6   #include "LinkedList.h"
7   #include "Node.h"
8   #include "PrecondViolatedExcept.h"
9
10  template<class ItemType>
11  class SortedListIsA : public LinkedList<ItemType>
12  {
13  public:
14     SortedListIsA();
15     SortedListIsA(const SortedListIsA<ItemType>& sList);
16     virtual ~SortedListIsA();
17
18     bool insertSorted(const ItemType& newEntry);
19     bool removeSorted(const ItemType& anEntry);
20     int getPosition(const ItemType& anEntry) const;
21
22     // The inherited methods remove, clear, getEntry, isEmpty, and
23     // getLength have the same specifications as given in ListInterface.
24
25     // The following methods must be overridden to disable their
26     // effect on a sorted list:
27     bool insert(int newPosition, const ItemType& newEntry) override;
28     void replace(int position, const ItemType& newEntry)
29         throw(PrecondViolatedExcept) override;
30  }; // end SortedListIsA
31  #include "SortedListIsA.cpp"
32  #endif
```

Method definitions. Let's examine the implementations of the sorted list methods. The default constructor and destructor are straightforward; the copy constructor invokes LinkedList's copy constructor by using an initializer:

```
template<class ItemType>
SortedListIsA<ItemType>::SortedListIsA()
{
} // end default constructor

template<class ItemType>
SortedListIsA<ItemType>::SortedListIsA(const SortedListIsA<ItemType>& sList)
                                         : LinkedList<ItemType>(sList)
{
} // end copy constructor

template<class ItemType>
SortedListIsA<ItemType>::~SortedListIsA()
{
} // end destructor
```

The method insertSorted first calls getPosition to get the intended position of the new entry, ignores the sign of this position, and uses the result and LinkedList's insert method to complete its task. Note that since we will override insert in SortedListIsA, we must be careful not to call that implementation, but to call the base class implementation instead.

```
template<class ItemType>
bool SortedListIsA<ItemType>::insertSorted(const ItemType& newEntry)
{
    int newPosition = std::abs(getPosition(newEntry));
    // We need to call the LinkedList version of insert, since the
    // SortedListIsA version does nothing but return false
    return LinkedList<ItemType>::insert(newPosition, newEntry);
} // end insertSorted
```

Call LinkedList's version of insert

The method removeSorted uses an approach similar to that of insertSorted, but it does not ignore the sign of the position returned by getPosition. Insertion happens regardless of whether the new entry is a duplicate of another one already in the sorted list. However, you cannot remove an entry that is not in the list!

```
template<class ItemType>
bool SortedListIsA<ItemType>::removeSorted(const ItemType& anEntry)
{
    int position = getPosition(anEntry);
    bool ableToRemove = position > 0;
    if (ableToRemove)
        ableToRemove = LinkedList<ItemType>::remove(position);

    return ableToRemove;
} // end removeSorted
```

The method getPosition uses the list's method getEntry to access each entry in the list sequentially until it either finds a match or reaches the point where the entry being sought would belong if it were in the list.

```
template<class ItemType>
int SortedListIsA<ItemType>::getPosition(const ItemType& anEntry) const
{
    int position = 1;
    int length = LinkedList<ItemType>::getLength();
```

```
   while ( (position <= length) &&
           (anEntry > LinkedList<ItemType>::getEntry(position)) )
   {
      position++;
   }  // end while

   if ( (position > length) ||
        (anEntry != LinkedList<ItemType>::getEntry(position)) )
   {
      position = -position;
   }  // end if

   return position;
}  // end getPosition
```

Question 15 After determining the position where an entry should occur, the method getPosition calls getEntry to see whether the value at that position matches the target. Revise getPosition to avoid calling getEntry a second time within the if statement.

Programming Tip: Notice that we have preceded the calls to methods inherited from LinkedList with the LinkedList<Item>:: namespace reference. When we called insert from insertSorted, we had to ensure that we called LinkedList's version of insert and not the overriding version in SortedListIsA. After all, the latter method does nothing but return false. Notice, however, that we do not override the methods remove, clear, getEntry, isEmpty, and getLength. Because these methods do not appear explicitly in the header file for SortedListIsA, if you were to call them without the qualifier LinkedList<Item>::, the C++ compiler would assume that they were client functions instead of class methods. You would get a syntax error.

An alternate way of calling these methods is to precede their calls by this-> instead of LinkedList<Item>::. For example, you could write

```
   if (!this->getEntry(somePosition))
```

instead of

```
   if (!LinkedList<ItemType>::getEntry(somePosition))
```

Overridden methods. Recall that we have inherited two methods—insert and replace—from LinkedList that we do not want as public methods of the ADT sorted list. Although we called insert in our definition of insertSorted, we do not want clients to be able to destroy the sorted order of our entries by inserting an item at any specific position within a sorted list. To this end, we override insert so that it always returns false:

```
template<class ItemType>
bool SortedListIsA<ItemType>::insert(int newPosition, const ItemType& newEntry)
{
   return false;
}  // end insert
```

Overriding insert prevents insertions into a sorted list by position

This approach ensures that a client of `SortedListIsA` can never add items by position to an object of `SortedListIsA`. We override `replace` in a similar manner.

A sorted list is *not* a list; do not use public inheritance

Note: Recall that public inheritance enables you to use a derived-class object anywhere that you can use a base-class object. But you cannot use a sorted list in the same way that you can use a list and expect to maintain the values stored in the sorted list in sorted order. Moreover, the value-oriented nature of a sorted list does not support all of a list's operations. Therefore, a sorted list is not really a list, and hence public inheritance is not appropriate.

Programming Tip: You should use public inheritance only when two classes have an *is-a* relationship.

Question 16 What would have happened if you preceded the call to `insert` in the method `insertSorted` by `this->` instead of `LinkedList<ItemType>::`? Explain.

Question 17 What would have happened if you preceded the call to `getEntry` in the method `getPosition` by `this->` instead of `LinkedList<ItemType>::`? Explain.

Efficiency issues. If you compare the implementation of `SortedListIsA` with the one for `SortedListHasA`, you will notice slight differences in the syntax, but the basic logic of the methods is the same. Both classes use methods of the ADT list to define their operations. The performance of corresponding methods is virtually the same.

12.3.3 Private Inheritance

If you do not have an *is-a* relationship between your new class and an existing class, you should not use public inheritance. Instead, if you want to inherit members from the existing class, you can use private inheritance. Private inheritance enables you to use the methods of a base class without giving a client access to them.

The header file in Listing 12-5 declares the class `SortedListAsA`. Note that it is derived from the class `LinkedList` using private inheritance. Except for this addition and the name of the class, this header file is identical to the one in Listing 12-3 for `SortedListHasA`.

LISTING 12-5 The header file for the class `SortedListAsA`

```
1   /** ADT sorted list using ADT list.
2    @file SortedListAsA.h */
3   #ifndef SORTED_LIST_AS_A_
4   #define SORTED_LIST_AS_A_
5   #include <memory>
6   #include "SortedListInterface.h"
7   #include "ListInterface.h"
```

```
8    #include "Node.h"
9    #include "PrecondViolatedExcept.h"
10
11   template<class ItemType>
12   class SortedListAsA : public SortedListInterface<ItemType>,
13                         private LinkedList<ItemType>
14   {
15   public:
16      SortedListAsA();
17      SortedListAsA(const SortedListAsA<ItemType>& sList);
18      virtual ~SortedListAsA();
19      <The rest of the public section is the same as in SortedListHasA in Listing 12-3.>
20      . . .
21
22   }; // end SortedListAsA
23   #include "SortedListAsA.cpp"
24   #endif
```

Because clients of SortedListAsA do not have access to the methods of the base class LinkedList, you need to provide a complete set of sorted list operations. This was not necessary for public inheritance. However, this lack of access also means that we do not have to override inherited methods such as replace that we do not want clients to have.

The implementation of SortedListAsA can use the public[1] members of LinkedList. In fact, the methods insertSorted, removeSorted, and getPosition have the same implementations as they did with public inheritance. The remaining methods simply call the corresponding methods in LinkedList. For example, the method getEntry has the following definition:

```
template<class ItemType>
ItemType SortedListAsA<ItemType>::getEntry(int position) const
                                  throw(PrecondViolatedExcept)
{
   return LinkedList<ItemType>::getEntry(position);
} // end getEntry
```

With both private inheritance (*as-a*) and containment (*has-a*), LinkedList is hidden from the clients of the sorted list. That is, you can use either private inheritance or containment to hide the underlying list in the implementation of the sorted list. Realize, however, that unlike public inheritance, private inheritance does not allow you to use an instance of SortedListAsA wherever you can use an instance of LinkedList; that is, SortedListAsA and LinkedList are not object-type compatible. The UML diagram in Figure 12-8 shows the inheritance relationship between the two classes. The notation <<implementation>> is a **stereotype** and is used to indicate that the SortedListAsA class is implemented in terms of the LinkedList class. You can use a stereotype to identify a unique characteristic of an element in any UML diagram.

---

[1] If LinkedList had protected methods, SortedListAsA could call those, too.

FIGURE 12-8   The SortedListAsA class implemented in terms of the LinkedList class

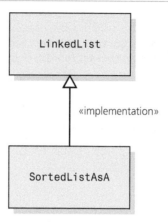

SUMMARY

1. The ADT sorted list maintains its entries in sorted order. It, not the client, determines where to place an entry.

2. The ADT sorted list can add, remove, or locate an entry, given the entry as an argument.

3. The ADT sorted list has several operations that are the same as the corresponding operations of the ADT list. However, a sorted list will not let you add or replace an entry by position.

4. A chain of linked nodes provides a reasonably efficient implementation of the sorted list.

5. A class of sorted lists that has a list as a data field is said to use containment. Although such a class is easy to write, its efficiency can suffer if the implementation of the ADT list is inefficient.

6. Although it seems like a sorted list is a list, deriving a class of sorted lists from a class of lists using public inheritance is not appropriate. Doing so requires you to override some methods of the ADT list that a client of the sorted list class should not be able to use. Additionally, public inheritance would make the two classes object-type compatible, but you cannot use a sorted list anywhere that a list is used.

7. Private inheritance provides a reasonable alternative to containment as an approach to using the ADT list in the implementation of the ADT sorted list. Usually, however, containment is preferable.

EXERCISES

1. Consider the classes Sphere and Ball, as outlined here:

```
class Sphere
{
public:
   . . .
   double getArea() const; // Surface area
   void displayStatistics() const;
   . . .
}; // end Sphere
```

```
class Ball : public Sphere
{
public:
   . . .
   double getArea() const; // Cross-sectional area
   void displayStatistics() const;
   . . .
}; // end Ball
```

Suppose that the implementation of each version of displayStatistics invokes the method getArea.

a. If mySphere is an instance of Sphere and myBall is an instance of Ball, which version of getArea does each of the following calls to displayStatistics invoke? Explain your answer.

```
mySphere.displayStatistics();
myBall.displayStatistics();
```

b. If the statements

```
std::shared_ptr<Sphere> spherePtr;
std::shared_ptr<Ball> ballPtr;
```

declare spherePtr and ballPtr, which version of getArea does each of the following calls to displayStatistics invoke? Explain your answer.

```
spherePtr->displayStatistics();
spherePtr = ballPtr;
spherePtr->displayStatistics();
ballPtr->displayStatistics();
```

2. Define and implement a class Pen that has an instance of Ball as one of its members. Provide several members for the class Pen, such as the data member color and methods isEmpty and write.

3. Consider the following classes:

   * LandVehicle represents a vehicle that travels on land. Its public methods include getWheelCount and getSpeed.
   * MotorizedLandVehicle is a descendant of LandVehicle and represents a land vehicle that has a motor. Its public methods include getEngineCapacity and getFuelType.

   a. Which of the methods mentioned previously can the implementation of getSpeed invoke?
   b. Which of the methods mentioned previously can the implementation of getEngineCapacity invoke?

4. Assume the classes described in Exercise 3 and consider a main method that contains the following statements:

```
LandVehicle landVeh;
MotorizedLandVehicle motorVeh;
```

   a. Which of these objects can invoke the method getWheelCount?
   b. Which of these objects can invoke the method getFuelType?

5. Consider the following classes:

```
class Expr
{
private:
   std::string expression;
public:
   . . .
   int getLength() const;
   virtual void display() const;
   . . .
}; // end Expr

class AlgExpr : public Expr
{
public:
   . . .
   bool isExpression() const;
   bool isBlank(int first, int last) const;
}; // end AlgExpr

class InfixExpr : public AlgExpr
{
public:
   . . .
   bool isExpression() const;
   int valueOf() const;
   void display() const;
   . . .
protected:
   int endFactor(int first, int last) const;
   int endTerm(int first, int last) const;
   int endExpression(int first, int last) const;

private:
   Stack<int> values;
   Stack<char> operators;
}; // end InfixExpr
```

The class AlgExpr represents algebraic expressions, including prefix, postfix, and infix expressions. Its method isExpression simply examines the expression for valid characters but does not consider the order of the characters.

The class InfixExpr represents infix expressions. Its isExpression calls isBlank, and its display calls valueOf.

a. Note that isBlank is public. Should it instead be protected or private? Explain.

b. If inExp is an instance of InfixExpr in the main method, can inExp invoke endExpression? Explain.

c. What small change(s) would you make to the classes to ensure that the correct version of isExpression is called?

6. Assume the classes described in Exercise 5 and consider a main method that contains the statements

```
Expr exp;
AlgExpr aExp;
InfixExpr inExp;
```

    a. Which of these objects can correctly invoke the method `getLength`?
    b. Which of these objects can correctly invoke the method `isExpression`?
    c. Which of these objects can correctly invoke the method `valueOf`?
    d. Give an example of object-type compatibility by writing a method declaration and a call to it that could appear in this main method.

7. Recall from Section 12.3.1 the copy constructor for the class `SortedListHasA`. Its definition uses a loop. Replace that definition with a recursive one, and show that it is O(*n*).

8. Consider an ADT *front list*, which restricts insertions, removals, and retrievals to the first item in the list. Define and implement a class for the ADT stack that is a descendant of `FrontList`.

9. Define an abstract base class `Person` that describes a typical person. Next, define a derived class `Student` that describes a typical student. Finally, derive from `Student` a class `GradStudent` for a typical graduate student.

10. Design and implement the following classes:
    a. An abstract base class `Employee` that represents a generic employee. Include methods to retrieve information about an employee. Derive `Employee` from the class `Person`, as described in Exercise 9.
    b. A subclass of `Employee` called `HourlyEmployee` that describes an employee who gets paid by the hour. Include a public method called `getPay` that returns the pay of the employee for that month and any other relevant methods.
    c. A subclass of `Employee` called `SalariedEmployee` that describes an employee who gets paid a fixed salary every month. Include a public method called `getPay` that returns the pay of the employee for that month. Include any other relevant methods.

11. Confirm the results in Figures 12-5 and 12-6.

12. Imagine an unknown implementation of an ADT sorted list of integers. This ADT organizes its items into ascending order. Suppose that you have just read *n* integers into a one-dimensional array of integers called `data`. Write some C++ statements that use the ADT sorted list operations to sort the array into ascending order.

13. Write pseudocode that merges two sorted lists into a new third sorted list by using only ADT sorted list operations.

14. Define a set of axioms for the ADT sorted list and use them to prove that the sorted list of characters, which is defined by the sequence of operations

```
sList = an empty sorted list
sList.insertSorted('S')
sList.insertSorted('T')
sList.insertSorted('R')
sList.removeSorted('T')
```

is exactly the same as the sorted list defined by the sequence

```
sList = an empty sorted list
sList.insertSorted('T')
sList.insertSorted('R')
sList.removeSorted('T')
sList.insertSorted('S')
```

PROGRAMMING PROBLEMS

1. Complete the implementation of the class `LinkedSortedList`, and write a driver program to fully test it.

2. Define a class for an array-based implementation of the ADT sorted list. Consider a recursive implementation for `getPosition`. Should `insertSorted` and `removeSorted` call `getPosition`?

3. Complete the implementation of the class `SortedListHasA`.

4. Complete the implementation of the class `SortedListAsA`.

5. Consider the class `FrontList` that Exercise 8 describes. Implement `FrontList` in each of the following ways:

    a. Store the list's entries in an instance of `LinkedList`.
    b. Derive `FrontList` from `LinkedList` using public inheritance.
    c. Derive `FrontList` from `LinkedList` using private inheritance.

6. The class `LinkedList`, as described in Sections 9.2.1 and 9.2.2 of Chapter 9, does not contain a method `getPosition` that returns the position number of a given entry. Define a descendant of `LinkedList` that has a method `getPosition` as well as methods that insert and remove items by their values instead of their positions. This new insertion method should always insert the new entry at the beginning of the list. Although the items in this list are not sorted, the new ADT is analogous to the ADT sorted list, which contains the method `getPosition`.

7. Consider an ADT *circular list*, which is like the ADT list but treats its first entry as if it were immediately after its last entry. For example, if a circular list contains six items, retrieval or removal of the eighth item actually involves the list's second item. Let insertion into a circular list, however, behave exactly like insertion into a list. Define and implement the ADT circular list as a derived class of `LinkedList`.

8. Consider an ADT *traversable stack*. In addition to the standard stack operations—`isEmpty`, `push`, `pop`, and `peek`—a traversable stack includes the operation `traverse`. This operation begins at the bottom of the stack and displays each item in the stack until it reaches the top of the stack. Define and implement the ADT traversable stack as a derived class of `ArrayStack`, as given in Section 7.1 of Chapter 7.

9. Define a template interface for the ADT sorted list that is derived from `ListInterface`. Then define the class `SortedListHasA` that is derived from your new interface.

10. Because algebraic expressions are character strings, you can derive a class of algebraic expressions from a class of strings. Define such a class. Include an `isExpression` operation that uses the recognition algorithm given in Programming Problem 9 of Chapter 5 and a `valueOf` operation that uses the evaluation algorithm given in Programming Problem 8 of Chapter 6.

Queues and Priority Queues

Contents

Prerequisites

Chapter 6   Stacks
Chapter 8   Lists (incidental)
Chapter 12   Sorted Lists and Their Implementations (incidental)

Whereas a stack's behavior is characterized as last in, first out, a queue's behavior is characterized as first in, first out. This chapter defines the queue's operations and discusses several uses of them. As you will see, queues are common in everyday life. Their first-in, first-out behavior makes them appropriate ADTs for situations that involve waiting. Queues are also important in simulation, a technique for analyzing the behavior of complex systems. This chapter uses a queue to model the behavior of people in a line.

Sometimes the importance of an object depends on criteria other than when it is placed into a container. In such cases, you can assign each object a priority and organize them according to their priorities instead of chronologically. The priority queue will do this for you.

This chapter explores the two ADTs queue and priority queue. We will consider their implementations in the next chapter.

VideoNote
The ADT queue

13.1   The ADT Queue

FIFO: The first item inserted into a queue is the first item out

A **queue** is like a line of people. The first person to join a line is the first person served, that is, the first to leave the line. New items enter a queue at its **back**, and items leave a queue from its **front**. Operations on a queue occur only at its two ends. This characteristic gives a queue its first-in, first-out (FIFO) behavior. In contrast, you can think of a stack as having only one end, because all operations are performed at the top of the stack. This characteristic gives a stack its last-in, first-out behavior.

As an abstract data type, the queue has the following operations:

> **Note: ADT queue operations**
> - Test whether a queue is empty.
> - Add a new entry to the back of the queue.
> - Remove the entry at the front of the queue (the entry that was added earliest).
> - Get the entry that was added earliest to the queue.

Queues occur in everyday life

Queues are appropriate for many real-world situations. You wait in a queue—that is, a line—to buy a movie ticket, to check out at the bookstore, or to use an automatic teller machine. The person at the front of the queue is served, while new people join the queue at its back. Even when you call an airline to change your flight, your call actually enters a queue while you wait for the next available agent.

Queues many have applications in computing systems

Queues also have applications in computing systems. When you print an essay, the computer sends lines faster than the printer can print them. The lines are held in a queue for the printer, which removes them in FIFO order. If you share the printer with other computers, your request to print enters a queue to wait its turn.

Since all of these applications involve waiting, people study them to see how to reduce the wait. Such studies are called **simulations**, and they typically use queues. Later, this chapter examines a simulation of a line of customers at a bank.

Figure 13-1 shows a UML diagram for the class Queue, and the operation contract that follows specifies the ADT queue in more detail. Note that the conventional names of the operations that add or remove an entry are, respectively, enqueue (pronounced "N-Q") and dequeue (pronounced "D-Q").

FIGURE 13-1   UML diagram for the class Queue

Queue
+isEmpty(): boolean +enqueue(newEntry: ItemType): boolean +dequeue(): boolean +peekFront(): ItemType

ABSTRACT DATA TYPE: QUEUE	

DATA

- A finite number of objects, not necessarily distinct, having the same data type and ordered by when they were added.

OPERATIONS

PSEUDOCODE	DESCRIPTION
isEmpty()	Task: Sees whether this queue is empty. Input: None. Output: True if the queue is empty; otherwise false.
enqueue(newEntry)	Task: Adds newEntry at the back of this queue. Input: newEntry. Output: True if the operation is successful; otherwise false.
dequeue()	Task: Removes the front of this queue. That is, removes the item that was added earliest. Input: None. Output: True if the operation is successful; otherwise false.
peekFront()	Task: Returns the front of this queue. That is, gets the item that was added earliest. The operation does not change the queue. Input: None. Output: The front of the queue.

Figure 13-2 illustrates the effect of these operations on a queue of integers. Notice that enqueue adds an item at the back of the queue and that peekFront looks at the item at the front of the queue, whereas dequeue removes the item at the front of the queue.

FIGURE 13-2   Some queue operations

Operation	Front	Queue after operation
aQueue = *an empty queue*		
aQueue.enqueue(5)		5
aQueue.enqueue(2)		5 2
aQueue.enqueue(7)		5 2 7
aQueue.peekFront()		5 2 7 (Returns 5)
aQueue.dequeue()		2 7
aQueue.dequeue()		7

Question 1 If you add the letters *A*, *B*, *C*, and *D* in sequence to a queue of characters and then remove them, in what order will they leave the queue?

Question 2 What do the initially empty queues queue1 and queue2 "look like" after the following sequence of operations?

```
queue1.enqueue(1)
queue1.enqueue(2)
queue2.enqueue(3)
queue2.enqueue(4)
queue1.dequeue()
queueFront = queue2.peekFront()
queue1.enqueue(queueFront)
queue1.enqueue(5)
queue2.dequeue()
queue2.enqueue(6)
```

Compare these results with Checkpoint Question 2 in Chapter 6.

An interface. Listing 13-1 contains a C++ template that completes our specification of the ADT queue.

LISTING 13-1   A C++ interface for queues

```
1   /** @file QueueInterface.h */
2   #ifndef QUEUE_INTERFACE_
3   #define QUEUE_INTERFACE_
4
5   template<class ItemType>
6   class QueueInterface
7   {
8   public:
9      /** Sees whether this queue is empty.
10       @return  True if the queue is empty, or false if not. */
11      virtual bool isEmpty() const = 0;
12
13      /** Adds a new entry to the back of this queue.
14       @post  If the operation was successful, newEntry is at the
15          back of the queue.
16       @param newEntry  The object to be added as a new entry.
17       @return  True if the addition is successful or false if not. */
18      virtual bool enqueue(const ItemType& newEntry) = 0;
19
20      /** Removes the front of this queue.
21       @post  If the operation was successful, the front of the queue
22          has been removed.
23       @return  True if the removal is successful or false if not. */
24      virtual bool dequeue() = 0;
25
26      /** Returns the front of this queue.
27       @pre  The queue is not empty.
28       @post  The front of the queue has been returned, and the
29          queue is unchanged.
30       @return  The front of the queue. */
31      virtual ItemType peekFront() const = 0;
32
33      /** Destroys this queue and frees its memory. */
34      virtual ~QueueInterface() { }
35   }; // end QueueInterface
36   #endif
```

13.2 Simple Applications of the ADT Queue

This section presents two simple applications of the ADT queue. The applications use the ADT queue operations independently of their implementations.

13.2.1 Reading a String of Characters

VideoNote
Using the ADT queue

When you enter characters at a keyboard, the system must retain them in the order in which you typed them. It could use a queue for this purpose, as the following pseudocode indicates:

A queue can retain characters in the order in which you type them

```
// Read a string of characters from a single line of input into a queue
aQueue = a new empty queue
while (not end of line)
{
    Read a new character into ch
    aQueue.enqueue(ch)
}
```

Once the characters are in a queue, the system can process them as necessary. For example, if you had typed the integer 247—without any mistakes, but possibly preceded or followed by blanks—the queue would contain digits and possibly blanks. The system could convert the digits 2, 4, and 7 into the decimal value 247 by computing $10 \times (10 \times 2 + 4) + 7$.

The following pseudocode function performs this conversion in general:

```
// Converts digits in a queue aQueue into a decimal integer.
getInteger(aQueue: Queue): integer
{
    // Get first digit, ignoring any leading blanks
    do
    {
        ch = aQueue.peekFront()
        aQueue.dequeue()
    } while (ch is blank)
    // Assertion: ch contains first digit

    // Compute the integer n from digits in queue
    n = 0
    done = false
    do
    {
        n = 10 * n + (integer that ch represents)
        done = aQueue.isEmpty()
        if (!done)
        {
            ch = aQueue.peekFront()
            aQueue.dequeue()
        }
    } while (!done and ch is a digit)
    return n
}
```

13.2.2 Recognizing Palindromes

Recall from Section 5.1.2 in Chapter 5 that a palindrome is a string of characters that reads the same from left to right as it does from right to left. In Chapter 6, you learned that you could use a stack to reverse the order of occurrences. You should realize by now that you can use a queue to preserve the order of occurrences. Thus, you can use both a queue and a stack to see whether a string is a palindrome.

You can use a queue in conjunction with a stack to recognize palindromes

FIGURE 13-3   The results of inserting the characters *a, b, c, b, d* into both a queue and a stack

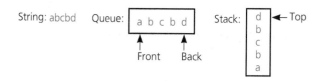

As you traverse a string from left to right, you can add each character to both a queue and a stack. Figure 13-3 illustrates the result of this action for the string "abcbd", which is not a palindrome. You can see that the first character in the string is at the front of the queue and the last character in the string is at the top of the stack. Thus, characters removed from the queue will occur in the order in which they appear in the string, and characters removed from the stack will occur in the opposite order.

Knowing this, you can compare the characters at the front of the queue and the top of the stack. If the two characters are the same, you can remove them. You repeat this process until either the stack and the queue become empty, in which case the original string is a palindrome, or the two characters are not the same, in which case the string is not a palindrome.

The following is a pseudocode version of a nonrecursive recognition algorithm for the language of palindromes:

```
// Tests whether a given string is a palindrome.
isPalindrome(someString: string): boolean
{
    // Create an empty queue and an empty stack
    aQueue = a new empty queue
    aStack = a new empty stack

    // Add each character of the string to both the queue and the stack
    length = length of someString
    for (i = 1 through length)
    {
        nextChar = ith character of someString
        aQueue.enqueue(nextChar)
        aStack.push(nextChar)
    }

    // Compare the queue characters with the stack characters
    charactersAreEqual = true
    while (aQueue is not empty and charactersAreEqual)
    {
        queueFront = aQueue.peekFront()
        stackTop = aStack.peek()
        if (queueFront equals stackTop)
        {
            aQueue.dequeue()
            aStack.pop()
        }
        else
            charactersAreEqual = false
    }
    return charactersAreEqual
}
```

Question 3 Trace the palindrome-recognition algorithm described in this section for each of the following strings of characters:

    a. abcda

    b. radar

Question 4 The palindrome-recognition algorithm checks for an empty queue but not an empty stack. Why is this check sufficient?

Question 5 Improve the palindrome-recognition algorithm described in this section by adding the first `length / 2` characters to the queue and then pushing the remaining characters onto the stack.

13.3 The ADT Priority Queue

Imagine a person who visits a hospital's emergency room (ER). When any patient enters the hospital, the staff creates a record about that person in a database for later retrieval by nurses, doctors, and the billing department. In addition, the staff must keep track of the ER patients and decide when each person will receive care.

What ADT should the ER staff use for their patients? The ADT sorted list would facilitate the treatment of ER patients in alphabetical order by name or in numerical order by ID number. A queue would enable treatment of patients in the order of arrival. In either case, Ms. Zither, who was just rushed to the ER with acute appendicitis, would have to wait for Mr. Able to have a splinter removed. Clearly, the ER staff should assign some measure of urgency, or priority, to the patients waiting for treatment. The next available doctor should treat the patient with the highest priority. The ADT that the ER staff needs should produce this patient on request.

You can organize data by priorities

Another example of the use of priorities is your list of daily or weekly tasks. Suppose that your "to do" list for this week contains the following items:

    Send a birthday card to Aunt Mabel.
    Start the research paper for world history.
    Finish reading Chapter 13 of *Walls and Mirrors.*
    Make plans for Saturday night.

You usually prioritize your list of tasks

When you consult your list, you most likely will attend to the task that, for you, has the highest priority.

A **priority value** indicates, for example, a patient's priority for treatment or a task's priority for completion. What quantity should you use for this priority value? Many reasonable possibilities exist, including a simple ranking from 1 to 10. Let's arbitrarily decide that the largest priority value indicates the highest priority. The priority value becomes a part of the item that you insert into an ADT. You then ask the ADT for the item that has the highest priority.

Such an ADT is known as a **priority queue**. More formally, a priority queue is an ADT that provides the following operations:

Note: ADT priority queue operations

- Test whether a priority queue is empty.
- Add a new entry to the priority queue in its sorted position based on priority value.
- Remove from the priority queue the entry with the highest priority value.
- Get the entry in the priority queue with the highest priority value.

Although priority queues and sorted lists both order their entries by values, these ADTs differ in how their removal operations behave. When you remove an entry from a priority queue, you get the entry with the highest priority value. In contrast, you can remove any entry from a sorted list.

A priority queue orders by priority values

The following operation contract specifies the ADT priority queue in more detail, and Figure 13-4 shows a UML diagram for the class `PriorityQueue`.

ABSTRACT DATA TYPE: PRIORITY QUEUE

DATA

- A finite number of objects, not necessarily distinct, having the same data type and ordered by priority.

OPERATIONS

PSEUDOCODE	DESCRIPTION
`isEmpty()`	Task: Sees whether this priority queue is empty. Input: None. Output: True if the priority queue is empty; otherwise false.
`enqueue(newEntry)`	Task: Adds `newEntry` to this priority queue. Input: `newEntry`. Output: True if the operation is successful; otherwise false.
`dequeue()`	Task: Removes the entry with the highest priority from this priority queue. Input: None. Output: True if the operation is successful; otherwise false.
`peekFront()`	Task: Returns the entry in this priority queue with the highest priority. The operation does not change the priority queue. Input: None. Output: The entry with the highest priority.

FIGURE 13-4   UML diagram for the class `PriorityQueue`

```
            PriorityQueue

+isEmpty(): boolean
+enqueue(newEntry: ItemType): boolean
+dequeue(): boolean
+peekFront(): ItemType
```

13.3.1 Tracking Your Assignments

Professors and bosses like to assign tasks for us to do by certain dates. Using a priority queue, we can organize these assignments in the order in which we should complete them. Suppose that we order the assignments by their due dates. A task with the earliest due date will have the highest priority. We can define a class `Assignment` of tasks that includes a data field `date` representing a task's due date. Figure 13-5 shows a diagram of such a class.

FIGURE 13-5   UML diagram for the class `Assignment`

Assignment
`course`—the course code `task`—a description of the assignment `date`—the due date

`+getCourseCode(): string`
`+getTask(): string`
`+getDueDate(): string`

The following pseudocode shows how you could use a priority queue to organize your assignments and other responsibilities so that you know which one to complete first:

```
assignmentLog = a new priority queue using due date as the priority value
project = a new instance of Assignment
essay = a new instance of Assignment
quiz = a new instance of Assignment
errand = a new instance of Assignment
assignmentLog.enqueue(project)
assignmentLog.enqueue(essay)
assignmentLog.enqueue(quiz)
assignmentLog.enqueue(errand)
cout << "I should do the following first: "
cout << assignmentLog.peekFront()
```

13.4 Application: Simulation

Simulation—a major application area for computers—is a technique for modeling the behavior of both natural and human-made systems. Generally, the goal of a simulation is to generate statistics that summarize the performance of an existing system or to predict the performance of a proposed system. In this section we will consider a simple example that illustrates one important type of simulation.

Simulation models the behavior of systems

A problem to solve. Ms. Simpson, president of the First City Bank of Springfield, has heard her customers complain about how long they have to wait for service at the branch located in a downtown grocery store. Because she fears losing those customers to another bank, she is considering whether to hire a second teller for that branch.

Before Ms. Simpson hires another teller, she would like an approximation of the average time a customer has to wait for service from that branch's only teller. Ms. Simpson heard you were great at solving problems and has come to you for help. How can you obtain this information for her?

Considerations. You could stand with a stopwatch in the bank's lobby all day, but that task is not particularly exciting. Besides, you should use an approach that also allows Ms. Simpson to predict how much improvement she could expect if the bank hired a given number of additional tellers. She certainly does not want to hire the tellers on a trial basis and then monitor the bank's performance before making her final decision.

You conclude that the best way to obtain the information needed is to use a computer model to simulate the behavior of the bank. The first step in simulating a system such as a bank is to construct a mathematical model that captures the relevant information about the system. For example, how many tellers does the bank employ? How often do customers arrive? How long do the customers' transactions take?

If the model accurately describes the real-world system, a simulation can derive accurate predictions about the system's overall performance. For example, a simulation could predict the average time a customer has to wait before receiving service. A simulation can also evaluate proposed changes to the real-world system, such as predicting the effect of hiring more tellers at the bank. A large decrease in the time predicted for the average wait of a customer might justify the cost of hiring additional tellers.

After discussing the problem with Ms. Simpson, you decide that you want the simulation to determine

- The average time a customer waits before receiving service from the current single teller
- The decrease in customer wait time with each new teller added

Simulated time

Simulation time and events.   Central to a simulation is the concept of simulated time. Envision a stopwatch that measures time elapsed during a simulation. For example, suppose that the model of the bank specifies only one teller. At time 0, which is the start of the banking day, the simulated system would be in its initial state with no customers. As the simulation runs, the stopwatch ticks away units of time—perhaps minutes—and certain events occur. At time 20, the bank's first customer arrives. Because there is no line, the customer goes directly to the teller and begins her transaction, which will take about 6 minutes to complete. At time 22, a second customer arrives. Because the first customer has not yet completed her transaction, the second customer must wait in line. At time 26, the first customer completes her transaction and the second customer can begin his. Figure 13-6 illustrates these four times in the simulation.

To gather the information you need, you run this simulation for a specified period of simulated time. During the course of the run, you need to keep track of certain statistics, such as the average time a customer has to wait for service. Notice that in the small example of Figure 13-6, the first customer had to wait 0 minutes to begin a transaction and the second customer had to wait 4 minutes to begin a transaction—an average wait of 2 minutes.

One point not addressed in the previous discussion is how to determine when certain events occur. For example, why did we say that the first customer arrived at time 20 and the second at time 22? After studying real-world systems like our bank, mathematicians learned to model events such as the arrival of people by using techniques from probability theory. This statistical information is incorporated into the mathematical model of the system and is used to generate events in a way that reflects the real world. The simulation uses these events and is thus called an **event-driven simulation**. Note that the goal is to reflect the long-term average behavior of the system rather than to predict occurrences of specific events. This goal is sufficient for the needs of our simulation.

Although the techniques for generating events to reflect the real world are interesting and important, they require a good deal of mathematical sophistication. Therefore, we simply assume that we already have a list of events available for our use. In particular, for the bank problem, we assume that a file contains the time of each customer's arrival—an *arrival event*—and the duration of that customer's transaction once the customer reaches the teller. For example, the data

Sample arrival and transaction times

Arrival time	Transaction length
20	6
22	4
23	2
30	3

FIGURE 13-6   A bank line at time (a) 0; (b) 20; (c) 22; (d) 26

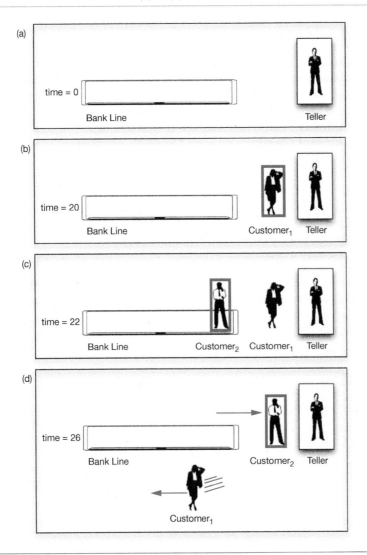

indicates that the first customer arrives 20 minutes into the simulation and her transaction—once begun—requires 6 minutes; the second customer arrives 22 minutes into the simulation, and his transaction requires 4 minutes; and so on. Assume that the input file is ordered by arrival time.

The use of a data file with predetermined event information is common in simulations. It allows us to try many different scenarios or bank teller configurations with the same set of events to ensure a fair comparison.

Notice that the file does not contain *departure events*; the data does not specify when a customer will complete the transaction and leave. In fact, the departure time of a customer cannot be determined until the simulation is run, so the simulation must determine when departures occur. By using the arrival time and the transaction length, the simulation can easily determine the time at which a customer departs. To compute the departure time, we add the length of the transaction to the time when the customer begins the transaction.

For example, if we run the simulation by hand with the previous data, we would compute the departure times as follows:

The results of a simulation

Time	Event
20	Customer 1 enters bank and begins transaction
	Determine customer 1 departure event is at time 26
22	Customer 2 enters bank and stands at end of line
23	Customer 3 enters bank and stands at end of line
26	Customer 1 departs; customer 2 begins transaction
	Determine customer 2 departure event is at time 30
30	Customer 2 departs; customer 3 begins transaction
	Determine customer 3 departure event is at time 32
30	Customer 4 enters bank and stands at end of line
32	Customer 3 departs; customer 4 begins transaction
	Determine customer 4 departure event is at time 35
35	Customer 4 departs

A customer's wait time is the elapsed time between arrival in the bank and the start of the transaction, that is, the amount of time the customer spends in line. The average of this wait time over all the customers is the statistic that you want to obtain.

To summarize, this simulation is concerned with two kinds of events:

Note: Kinds of events in an event-driven simulation

- Arrival events indicate the arrival at the bank of a new customer. The input file specifies the times at which the arrival events occur. As such, they are *externally generated events*. When a customer arrives at the bank, one of two things happens. If the teller is idle when the customer arrives, the customer goes to the teller and begins the transaction immediately. If the teller is busy, the new customer must stand at the end of the line and wait for service.
- Departure events indicate the departure from the bank of a customer who has completed a transaction. The simulation determines the times at which the departure events occur. Thus, they are *internally generated events*. When a customer completes the transaction, he or she departs and the next person in line—if there is one—begins a transaction.

Event loop. The main tasks of an algorithm that performs a simulation are to repeatedly determine the times at which events occur and to process the events when they do occur. In simulation and gaming applications, this process is referred to as the **event loop**. Our algorithm is stated at a high level as follows:

A first attempt at a simulation algorithm

```
// Initialize
currentTime = 0
Initialize the line to "no customers"

while (currentTime <= time of the final event)
{
```

```
if (an arrival event occurs at time currentTime)
    Process the arrival event
if (a departure event occurs at time currentTime)
    Process the departure event

// When an arrival event and departure event occur at the same time,
// arbitrarily process the arrival event first
currentTime++
}
```

But do you really want to increment currentTime by 1? You would for a **time-driven simulation**, where you would determine arrival and departure times at random and compare those times to currentTime. Video games use this approach, since events can occur or need to be processed in almost every unit of time, which is typically a video frame. In such a case, you would increment currentTime by 1 to simulate the ticking of a clock.

A time-driven simulation simulates the ticking of a clock

Recall, however, that this simulation is event driven, so you have a file of predetermined arrival times and transaction times. Because you are interested only in those times at which arrival and departure events occur, and because no action is required between events, you can advance currentTime from the time of one event directly to the time of the next.

An event-driven simulation considers only the times of certain events, in this case, arrivals and departures

Thus, you can revise the pseudocode solution as follows:

Initialize the line to "no customers"
```
while (events remain to be processed)
{
    currentTime = time of next event
    if (event is an arrival event)
        Process the arrival event
    else
        Process the departure event

    // When an arrival event and a departure event occur at the same time,
    // arbitrarily process the arrival event first
}
```

First revision of the simulation algorithm

You must determine the time of the next arrival or departure so that you can implement the statement

currentTime = *time of next event*

To make this determination, you must maintain an **event queue**. An event queue contains all arrival and departure events that will occur but have not occurred yet. The times of the events in the event queue are in ascending order, and thus the next event to be processed is always at the beginning of the queue. The algorithm simply gets the event from the beginning of the queue, advances to the time specified, and processes the event. The difficulty, then, lies in successfully managing the event queue.

An event queue contains all future arrival events and departure events

Managing and processing customers and events. As customers arrive, they go to the back of the line. The current customer, who was at the front of the line, is being served, and it is this customer that you remove from the system next. It is thus natural to use a queue, bankLine, to represent the line of customers in the bank. For this problem, the only information that you must store in the queue about each customer is the time of arrival and the length of the transaction.

Arrival events and departure events are ordered by time, and we always want to remove and process the next event that should occur—the highest-priority event. The ADT priority queue is used in this way. Our events can be stored in the priority queue eventPriorityQueue. We can initialize eventPriorityQueue with the arrival events in the simulation data file and later add the departure events as they are generated.

The event queue is actually a priority queue

But how can you determine the times for the departure events? Observe that the next departure event always corresponds to the customer that the teller is currently serving. As soon as a customer begins service, the time of his or her departure is simply

time of departure = time service begins + length of transaction

Recall that the length of the customer's transaction is in the event queue, along with the arrival time. Thus, as soon as a customer begins service, you place a departure event corresponding to this customer in the event queue. Figure 13-7 illustrates a typical instance of an arrival event and a departure event used in this simulation.

FIGURE 13-7 A typical instance of (a) an arrival event; (b) a departure event

(a) Arrival event

Type	Time	Length
A	20	6

(b) Departure event

Type	Time	Length
D	26	–

Now consider how you can process an event when it is time for the event to occur. You must perform two general types of actions:

Two tasks are required to process each event

- Update the bank line: Add or remove customers.
- Update the event queue: Add or remove events.

To summarize, you process an arrival event as follows:

The algorithm for arrival events

```
// TO PROCESS AN ARRIVAL EVENT

// Update the event queue
Remove the arrival event for customer C from the event queue

// Update the bank line
if (bank line is empty and teller is available)
{
   Departure time of customer C is current time + transaction length
   Add a departure event for customer C to the event queue
   Mark the teller as unavailable
}
else
   Add customer C to the bank line
```

A new customer always enters the bank line and is served while at the front of the line

When customer *C* arrives at the bank, if the line is empty and the teller is not serving another customer, customer *C* can go directly to the teller. The wait time is 0 and you insert a departure event into the event queue. If other customers are in line, or if the teller is assisting another customer, customer *C* must go to the end of the line.

You process a departure event as follows:

The algorithm for departure events

```
// TO PROCESS A DEPARTURE EVENT

// Update the event queue
Remove the departure event from the event queue
```

```
    // Update the bank line
if (bank line is not empty)
{
    Remove customer C from the front of the bank line
    Customer C begins transaction
    Departure time of customer C is current time + transaction length
    Add a departure event for customer C to the event queue
}
else
    Mark the teller as available.
```

When a customer finishes a transaction and leaves the bank, if the bank line is not empty, the next customer C leaves the line and goes to the teller. You insert a departure event for customer C into the event queue.

You can now combine and refine the pieces of the solution into an algorithm that performs the simulation by using the ADTs queue and priority queue:

```
    // Performs the simulation.
simulate(): void
{
    bankLine = a new empty queue  // Bank line
    eventPriorityQueue = a new empty priority queue  // Event queue

    tellerAvailable = true

    // Create and add arrival events to event queue
    while (data file is not empty)
    {
        Get next arrival time a and transaction time t from file
        newArrivalEvent = a new arrival event containing a and t
        eventPriorityQueue.enqueue(newArrivalEvent)
    }

    // Event loop
    while (eventPriorityQueue is not empty)
    {
        newEvent = eventPriorityQueue.peekFront()

        // Get current time
        currentTime = time of newEvent

        if (newEvent is an arrival event)
            processArrival(newEvent, eventPriorityQueue, bankLine)
        else
            processDeparture(newEvent, eventPriorityQueue, bankLine)
    }
}


    // Processes an arrival event.
processArrival(arrivalEvent: Event, eventPriorityQueue: PriorityQueue,
               bankLine: Queue)
{
    // Remove this event from the event queue
    eventPriorityQueue.dequeue()

    customer = customer referenced in arrivalEvent
    if (bankLine.isEmpty() && tellerAvailable)
    {
        departureTime = currentTime + transaction time in arrivalEvent
        newDepartureEvent = a new departure event with departureTime
        eventPriorityQueue.enqueue(newDepartureEvent)
```

The final pseudocode for the event-driven simulation

```
                    tellerAvailable = false
        }
        else
            bankLine.enqueue(customer)
    // Processes a departure event.
    +processDeparture(departureEvent: Event, eventPriorityQueue: PriorityQueue,
                        bankLine: Queue)
    {
        // Remove this event from the event queue
        eventPriorityQueue.dequeue()

        if (!bankLine.isEmpty())
        {
            // Customer at front of line begins transaction
            customer = bankLine.peekFront()
            bankLine.dequeue()
            departureTime = currentTime + transaction time in customer
            newDepartureEvent = a new departure event with departureTime
            eventPriorityQueue.enqueue(newDepartureEvent)
        }
        else
            tellerAvailable = true
    }
```

Figure 13-8 traces this algorithm for the data given earlier and shows the changes to the queue and priority queue. Note that the notation C_i represents a customer who arrived at time i. There are several more implementation details that must be decided, such as how to represent customers and events. Programming Problem 6 at the end of this chapter asks you to complete the implementation of this simulation.

FIGURE 13-8   A trace of the bank simulation algorithm for the data 20 6, 22 4, 23 2, 30 3. (The blue events are events that change or are created at each point in time.)

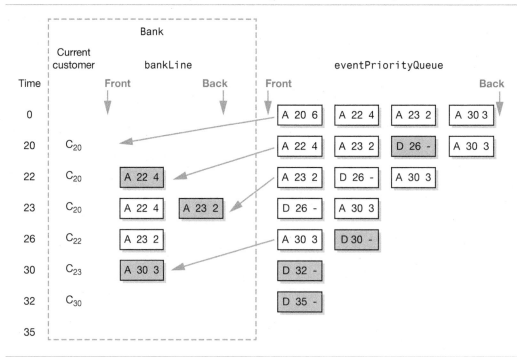

Question 6 In the bank simulation problem, why is it impractical to read the entire input file and create a list of all the arrival and departure events before the simulation begins?

Question 7 Hand-trace the bank-line simulation using the following data:

2	3
4	2
6	3
8	5

Each line of data contains an arrival time and a transaction time. Show the state of the queue and the priority queue at each step.

13.5 Position-Oriented and Value-Oriented ADTs

Of the abstract data types that we have seen so far, the stack, the list, and the queue have operations defined in terms of the positions of their data items. We call them **position-oriented ADTs**. Stacks and queues greatly restrict the positions that their operations can affect; only their end positions can be accessed. The list removes this restriction.

> *Operations for the ADTs list, stack, and queue involve the position of items*

The ADT sorted list is an example of a **value-oriented ADT**. When a new item is added to a sorted list, the sorted list determines the item's placement according to its value. Unlike a list, a sorted list cannot be told where to place its items. The same is true of a priority queue, since it orders its entries according to their priorities, which are values that are a part of each entry.

Although stacks and queues order their entries, and you do not specify where a stack or a queue should place its items, the entries' positions are not determined according to their values. Thus, we do not classify stacks and queues as value oriented.

>
> **Note:** The ADTs stack, queue, list, sorted list, and priority queue all order their entries. The stack, queue, and list are position oriented; the sorted list and priority queue are value oriented. The ADT bag does not order its entries; it is neither position oriented nor value oriented.

Stacks are really quite similar to queues. This similarity becomes apparent if you pair off their operations, as follows:

- Stack `isEmpty` and queue `isEmpty` see whether any items exist in the ADT.
- `push` and `enqueue` insert a new item into one end (the top and back, respectively) of the ADT.
- `pop` and `dequeue`: The `pop` operation removes the most recent item, which is at the top of the stack, and `dequeue` removes the first item, which is at the front of the queue.
- Stack `peek` and queue `peekFront`: The `peek` operation retrieves the most recent item, which is at the top of the stack, and `peekFront` retrieves the first item at the front of the queue.

> *A comparison of stack and queue operations*

The ADT list allows you to insert into, remove from, and inspect an item at any position of the list. Thus, it has the most flexible operations of the three position-oriented ADTs. You can view the list operations as general versions of the stack and queue operations as follows:

ADT list operations generalize stack and queue operations

- `getLength`: If you relax the restriction that the stack and queue versions of `isEmpty` can tell only when an item is present, you obtain an operation that can count the number of items that are present.
- `insert`: If you relax the restriction that `push` and `enqueue` can insert new items into only one position, you obtain an operation that can insert a new item into any position of the list.
- `remove`: If you relax the restriction that `pop` and `dequeue` can remove items from only one position, you obtain an operation that can remove an item from any position of the list.
- `getEntry`: If you relax the restriction that `peek` and `peekFront` can retrieve items from only one position, you obtain an operation that can retrieve the item from any position of the list.

Question 8 For each of the following situations, which of these ADTs (1 through 6) would be most appropriate? (1) a queue; (2) a stack; (3) a list; (4) a sorted list; (5) a priority queue; (6) none of these

    a. The customers at a deli counter who take numbers to mark their turn
    b. An alphabetic list of names
    c. Integers that need to be sorted
    d. The boxes in a box trace of a recursive function
    e. A grocery list ordered by the occurrence of the items in the store
    f. The items on a cash register tape
    g. A word processor that allows you to correct typing errors by using the Backspace key
    h. A program that uses backtracking
    i. A list of ideas in chronological order
    j. Airplanes that stack above a busy airport, waiting to land
    k. People who are put on hold when they call for customer service
    l. An employer who fires the most recently hired person

SUMMARY

1. The definition of the queue operations gives the ADT queue first-in, first-out (FIFO) behavior.

2. Models of real-world systems often use queues. The event-driven simulation in this chapter used a queue to model a line of customers in a bank.

3. Central to a simulation is the notion of simulated time. In a time-driven simulation, simulated time is advanced by a single time unit, whereas in an event-driven simulation, simulated time is advanced to the time of the next event. To implement an event-driven simulation, you maintain a priority queue that contains events that have not yet occurred. The priority queue is ordered by the time of the events, so that the next event to occur is always at the front of the priority queue.

4. A priority queue has operations to retrieve or remove the item with the highest priority.

5. ADTs are classified as either position oriented or value oriented. A position-oriented ADT organizes its items according to their positions, whereas a value-oriented ADT organizes items by their values.

EXERCISES

1. Consider the palindrome-recognition algorithm described in Section 13.2.2. Is it necessary for the algorithm to look at the entire queue and stack? That is, can you reduce the number of times that the loop must execute?

2. Consider the language

$$L = \{s\$s' : s \text{ is a possibly empty string of characters other than } \$, s' = \text{reverse}(s)\}$$

   as defined in Chapter 6. Write a recognition algorithm for this language that uses both a queue and a stack. Thus, as you traverse the input string, you insert each character of s into a queue and each character of s' into a stack. Assume that each input string contains exactly one $\$$.

3. What is the output of the following pseudocode, where num1, num2, and num3 are integer variables?

```
aQueue = a new empty queue
num1 = 5
num2 = 1
num3 = 4
aQueue.enqueue(num2)
aQueue.enqueue(num3)
aQueue.dequeue()
aQueue.enqueue(num1 - num2)
num1 = aQueue.peekFront()
aQueue.dequeue()
num2 = aQueue.peekFront()
aQueue.dequeue()
std::cout << num2 << " " << num1 << " " << num3 << std::endl
```

4. Revise the infix-to-postfix conversion algorithm of Chapter 6 so that it uses a queue to represent the postfix expression.

5. Write a client function that returns the back of a queue while leaving the queue unchanged. This function can call any of the methods of the ADT queue. It can also create new queues. The return type is ItemType, and it accepts a queue as a parameter.

6. An operation that displays the contents of a queue can be useful during program debugging. Add such a display operation to the ADT queue such that display uses only ADT queue operations, so it is independent of the queue's implementation.

7. Write a C++ template interface PriorityQueueInterface for the ADT priority queue.

8. Consider a slight variation of the ADT queue. In this variation, new items can be added to and removed from either end. This ADT is commonly called a **double-ended queue**, or **deque**. Specify each method of the deque by stating the method's purpose; by describing its parameters; and by writing preconditions, postconditions, and a pseudocode version of its header. Then write a C++ template interface for these methods that includes javadoc-style comments.

9. Use a deque, as described in the previous exercise, to solve the read-and-correct problem given in Section 6.1.1 of Chapter 6. In that problem, you enter text at a keyboard and correct typing mistakes by using the Backspace key. Each backspace erases the most recently entered character. Your pseudocode solution should provide a corrected string of characters in the order in which they were entered at the keyboard.

10. With the following data, hand-trace the execution of the bank-line simulation that this chapter describes. Each line of data contains an arrival time and a transaction time. Show the state of the queue and the priority queue at each step.

5	9
7	5
14	5
30	5
32	5
34	5

Note that at time 14, there is a tie between the execution of an arrival event and a departure event.

11. In the solution to the bank simulation problem, can the event queue be a queue instead of a priority queue? Can it be a list or sorted list?

12. Consider the stack-based search of the flight map in the HPAir problem of Chapter 6. You can replace the stack that searchS uses with a queue. That is, you can replace every call to push with a call to enqueue, every call to pop with a call to dequeue, and every call to peek with a call to peekFront. Trace the resulting algorithm when you fly from *P* to *Z* in the flight map in Figure 6-6. Indicate the contents of the queue after every operation on it.

13. As Chapter 6 pointed out, you can define ADT operations in a mathematically formal way by using axioms. Consider the following axioms for the ADT queue, where aQueue is an arbitrary queue and item is an arbitrary queue item:

```
(Queue()).isEmpty() = true
(Queue()).dequeue() = false
(Queue()).peekFront() = error
(Queue().enqueue(item)).dequeue() ⇒ Queue()
(Queue().enqueue(item)).peekFront() = item
(aQueue.enqueue(item)).isEmpty() = false
(aQueue.enqueue(item)).dequeue() = true
```

If aQueue is not empty,

```
(aQueue.enqueue(item)).dequeue() ⇒ (aQueue.dequeue()).enqueue(item)
```

and

```
(aQueue.enqueue(item)).peekFront() = aQueue.peekFront()
```

a. Note the recursive nature of the definition of peekFront. What is the base case? What is the recursive step? What is the significance of the isEmpty test? Why is the queue operation peekFront recursive in nature while the stack operation peek for the ADT stack is not?

b. The representation of a stack as a sequence of push operations without any pop operations is called a canonical form. (See Exercise 15 in Chapter 6.) Is there a canonical form for the ADT queue? That is, can you represent a queue as a sequence of enqueue operations without any dequeue operations? Prove your answer.

PROGRAMMING PROBLEMS

1. Using the class queue in the Standard Template Library, define and test the class OurQueue that is derived from QueueInterface, as given in Listing 13-1. The class queue has the following methods that you can use to define the methods for OurQueue:

```
queue<ItemType>();                        // Default constructor
bool empty() const;                       // Tests whether the queue is empty
void push(const ItemType& newEntry);      // Adds newEntry to the back of the queue
void pop();                               // Removes the front of the queue
ItemType& front();                        // Returns a reference to the front of the queue
```

To access queue, use the following include statement:

```
#include <queue>;
```

2. Using the class priority_queue in the Standard Template Library, define and test the class OurPriorityQueue that is derived from PriorityQueueInterface, as developed in Exercise 7. The class priority_queue has the following methods that you can use to define the methods for OurPriorityQueue:

```
priority_queue<ItemType>();               // Default constructor
bool empty() const;                       // Tests whether the priority queue is empty
void push(const ItemType& newEntry);      // Adds newEntry to the priority queue
void pop();                               // Removes the entry having the highest priority
ItemType& top();                          // Returns a reference to the entry having the
                                          // highest priority
```

To access priority_queue, use the following include statement:

```
#include <priority_queue>;
```

Whenever you need a queue or a priority queue for any of the following problems, use the classes OurQueue and OurPriorityQueue that Programming Problems 1 and 2 ask you to write.

3. Implement the palindrome-recognition algorithm described in Section 13.2.2.

4. Implement the recognition algorithm that you wrote to solve Exercise 2 using the classes OurQueue, as described in Programming Problem 1, and OurStack, as described in Programming Problem 1 of Chapter 6.

5. Implement the radix sort of an array by using a queue for each group. The radix sort is discussed in Section 11.2.3 of Chapter 11.

6. Implement the event-driven simulation of a bank that this chapter described. A queue of arrival events will represent the line of customers in the bank. Maintain the arrival events and departure events in a priority queue, sorted by the time of the event. Use a link-based implementation for the priority queue.

   The input is a text file of arrival and transaction times. Each line of the file contains the arrival time and required transaction time for a customer. The arrival times are ordered by increasing time.

   Your program must count customers and keep track of their cumulative waiting time. These statistics are sufficient to compute the average waiting time after the last event has been processed. Display a trace of the events executed and a summary of the computed statistics (the total number of arrivals and average time spent waiting in line). For example, the input file shown in the left columns of the following table should produce the output shown in the right column.

Input file		Output from processing file on left	
1	5	Simulation Begins	
2	5	Processing an arrival event at time:	1
4	5	Processing an arrival event at time:	2
20	5	Processing an arrival event at time:	4
22	5	Processing a departure event at time:	6
24	5	Processing a departure event at time:	11
26	5	Processing a departure event at time:	16
28	5	Processing an arrival event at time:	20
30	5	Processing an arrival event at time:	22
88	3	Processing an arrival event at time:	24
		Processing a departure event at time:	25
		Processing an arrival event at time:	26
		Processing an arrival event at time:	28
		Processing an arrival event at time:	30
		Processing a departure event at time:	30
		Processing a departure event at time:	35
		Processing a departure event at time:	40
		Processing a departure event at time:	45
		Processing a departure event at time:	50
		Processing an arrival event at time:	88
		Processing a departure event at time:	91
		Simulation Ends	

```
Final Statistics:

    Total number of people processed: 10
    Average amount of time spent waiting: 5.6
```

7. Modify and expand the event-driven simulation program that you wrote in Programming Problem 6.

   a. Add an operation that displays the event queue, and use it to check your hand trace in Exercise 10.

   b. Add some statistics to the simulation. For example, compute the maximum wait in line, the average length of the line, and the maximum length of the line.

   c. Modify the simulation so that it accounts for three tellers, each with a distinct line. You should keep in mind that there should be

      • Three queues, one for each teller
      • A rule that chooses a line when processing an arrival event (for example, enter the shortest line)
      • Three distinct departure events, one for each line
      • Rules for breaking ties in the event queue

      Run both this simulation and the original simulation on several sets of input data. How do the statistics compare?

   d. The bank is considering the following change: Instead of having three distinct lines (one for each teller), there will be a single line for the three tellers. The person at the front of the line will go to the first available teller. Modify the simulation of part *c* to account for this variation. Run both simulations on several sets of input data. How do the various statistics compare (averages and maximums)? What can you conclude about having a single line as opposed to having distinct lines?

8. The people who run the Motor Vehicle Department (MVD) have a problem. They are concerned that people do not spend enough time waiting in lines to appreciate the privilege of owning and driving an automobile. The current arrangement is as follows:

   • When people walk in the door, they must wait in a line to sign in.
   • Once they have signed in, they are told either to stand in line for registration renewal or to wait until they are called for license renewal.

- Once they have completed their desired transaction, they must go and wait in line for the cashier.
- When they finally get to the front of the cashier's line, if they expect to pay by check, they are told that all checks must get approved. To do this, it is necessary to go to the check-approver's table and then reenter the cashier's line at the end.

Write an event-driven simulation to help the MVD gather statistics. Each line of input will contain

- A desired transaction code (*L* for license renewal, *R* for registration renewal)
- A method-of-payment code (*$* for cash, *C* for check)
- An arrival time (integer)
- A name

Write out the specifics of each event (when, who, what, and so on). Then display these final statistics:

- The total number of license renewals and the average time spent in MVD (arrival until completion of payment) to renew a license
- The total number of registration renewals and the average time spent in MVD (arrival until completion of payment) to renew a registration

Incorporate the following details into your program:

- Define the following events: arrive, sign in, renew license, renew registration, and cope with the cashier (make a payment or find out about check approval).
- In the case of a tie, let the order of events be determined by the list of events just given—that is, arrivals have the highest priority.
- Assume that the various transactions take the following amounts of time:

Sign in	10 seconds
Renew license	90 seconds
Register automobile	60 seconds
See cashier (payment)	30 seconds
See cashier (check not approved)	10 seconds

- As ridiculous as it may seem, the people waiting for license renewal are called in alphabetical order. Note, however, that people are not pushed back once their transactions have started.
- For the sake of this simulation, you can assume that checks are approved instantly. Therefore, the rule for arriving at the front of the cashier's line with a check that has not been approved is to go to the back of the cashier's line with a check that has been approved.

9. (Gaming) Repeat Programming Problem 12 in Chapter 4, using a queue to implement the ADT that tracks the turns of the players.

Queue and Priority Queue Implementations

Chapter

14

Contents

Prerequisites

C++ Interlude 4   Safe Memory Management Using Smart Pointers
Chapter 13   Queues and Priority Queues

The previous chapter discussed the ADT queue at length and introduced the ADT priority queue. This chapter will present several implementations of the queue and compare their advantages and disadvantages.

We will consider an implementation of the priority queue, but we can write a much more efficient implementation later, after we explore the ADT heap in Chapter 17.

14.1 Implementations of the ADT Queue

Like stacks, queues can have an array-based or a link-based implementation. However, we also can use an implementation of the ADT list to define a class of queues. Such a class is easy to write, as most of the work is done by the class of lists. If you needed a class of queues right away, you could use this approach. The result would not be as time efficient as possible, however.

We will begin by using an instance of the class LinkedList, as given in Listing 9-2 of Chapter 9, to store the queue's entries. We will then write a link-based implementation, as it is a bit more straightforward than the array-based one, which we will investigate last.

VideoNote
Overview of
LinkedQueue

14.1.1 An Implementation That Uses the ADT List

You can use the ADT list to contain the items in a queue. This approach is especially useful if you need to define a class of queues quickly and already have a class of lists. Figure 14-1 illustrates such a queue. If the item in position 1 of a list represents the front of the queue, you can implement the method dequeue as the list operation remove(1) and the method peekFront as the list operation getEntry(1). Similarly, if you let the item at the end of the list represent the back of the queue, you can implement the operation enqueue(newEntry) as the list operation insert(getLength() + 1, newEntry).

FIGURE 14-1 An implementation of the ADT queue that stores its entries in a list

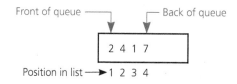

The header file containing such a class definition for the ADT queue appears in Listing 14-1, and the implementation file is in Listing 14-2. Note that we use smart pointers here, and we assume that LinkedList also uses smart pointers as discussed in C++ Interlude 4.

LISTING 14-1 The header file for the class ListQueue

```
1   /** ADT queue: ADT list implementation.
2    @file ListQueue.h */
3
4   #ifndef LIST_QUEUE_
5   #define LIST_QUEUE_
6
7   #include "QueueInterface.h"
8   #include "LinkedList.h"
9   #include "PrecondViolatedExcept.h"
10  #include <memory>
11
12  template<class ItemType>
13  class ListQueue : public QueueInterface<ItemType>
14  {
```

```
15   private:
16      std::unique_ptr<LinkedList<ItemType>> listPtr; // Pointer to list of queue items
17
18   public:
19      ListQueue();
20      ListQueue(const ListQueue& aQueue);
21      ~ListQueue();
22      bool isEmpty() const;
23      bool enqueue(const ItemType& newEntry);
24      bool dequeue();
25
26      /** @throw  PrecondViolatedExcept if this queue is empty. */
27      ItemType peekFront() const throw(PrecondViolatedExcept);
28   }; // end ListQueue
29   #include "ListQueue.cpp"
30   #endif
```

LISTING 14-2 The implementation file for the class ListQueue

```
1    /** ADT queue: ADT list implementation.
2     @file ListQueue.cpp */
3    #include "ListQueue.h" // Header file
4    #include <memory>
5
6    template<class ItemType>
7    ListQueue<ItemType>::ListQueue()
8                        : listPtr(std::make_unique<LinkedList<ItemType>>())
9    {
10   }   // end default constructor
11
12   template<class ItemType>
13   ListQueue<ItemType>::ListQueue(const ListQueue& aQueue)
14                        : listPtr(aQueue.listPtr)
15   {
16   }   // end copy constructor
17
18   template<class ItemType>
19   ListQueue<ItemType>::~ListQueue()
20   {
21   }   // end destructor
22
23   template<class ItemType>
24   bool ListQueue<ItemType>::isEmpty() const
25   {
26      return listPtr->isEmpty();
27   }   // end isEmpty
28
29   template<class ItemType>
30   bool ListQueue<ItemType>::enqueue(const ItemType& newEntry)
31   {
32      return listPtr->insert(listPtr->getLength() + 1, newEntry);
33   }   // end enqueue
34
```

(continues)

```
35   template<class ItemType>
36   bool ListQueue<ItemType>::dequeue()
37   {
38      return listPtr->remove(1);
39   } // end dequeue
40
41   template<class ItemType>
42   ItemType ListQueue<ItemType>::peekFront() const throw(PrecondViolatedExcept)
43   {
44      if (isEmpty())
45         throw PrecondViolatedExcept("peekFront() called with empty queue.");
46
47      // Queue is not empty; return front
48      return listPtr->getEntry(1);
49   } // end peekFront
50   // end of implementation file
```

Of particular note in the implementation file are the definitions of the constructor, copy constructor, and destructor. The constructor creates a new instance of a list. Omitting this step is an easy oversight to make, leading to incorrect execution instead of a syntax error. The copy constructor uses an initializer, listPtr(aQueue.listPtr), to copy the value of aQueue.listPtr to listPtr. Thus, this copy constructor makes a shallow copy of the queue. Exercise 8 at the end of this chapter asks you to revise this copy constructor so that it makes a deep copy. Finally, even though the destructor has an empty body, the list's destructor will be invoked.

Exercise 9 at the end of this chapter asks you to consider the efficiency of this implementation of ListQueue.

14.1.2 A Link-Based Implementation

A link-based implementation of a queue uses a chain of linked nodes, much like the other link-based implementations that you have seen. However, the queue presents a challenge, since we must be able to not only remove entries from its front but also add them to its back. Removing a node from the beginning of a linked chain is easy, but to add a new node to the chain's end, we need a pointer to the chain's last node. One way to accomplish this is to begin at the first node and traverse the chain until we reach the last one. A much more efficient approach uses a **tail pointer** to reference the end of the chain—just as the head pointer references the beginning of the chain. Figure 14-2 illustrates a chain of linked nodes that has both head and tail pointers. Like the head pointer frontPtr, backPtr is external to the chain.

FIGURE 14-2   A chain of linked nodes with head and tail pointers

A linear linked chain can represent a queue

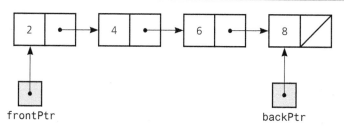

Note: If you use a linear chain with only a head pointer to implement a queue, the enqueue operation will be inefficient. Each addition to the queue requires a traversal to the end of the chain. As the queue increases in length, the traversal time—and hence enqueue's time requirement—will increase.

Listing 14-3 shows the header file for our class definition.

LISTING 14-3   The header file for the class LinkedQueue

```
1   /** ADT queue: Link-based implementation.
2    @file LinkedQueue.h */
3
4   #ifndef LINKED_QUEUE_
5   #define LINKED_QUEUE_
6
7   #include "QueueInterface.h"
8   #include "Node.h"
9   #include "PrecondViolatedExcept.h"
10  #include <memory>
11
12  template<class ItemType>
13  class LinkedQueue : public QueueInterface<ItemType>
14  {
15  private:
16     // The queue is implemented as a chain of linked nodes that has
17     // two external pointers, a head pointer for the front of the queue
18     // and a tail pointer for the back of the queue.
19     std::shared_ptr<Node<ItemType>> frontPtr;
20     std::shared_ptr<Node<ItemType>> backPtr;
21
22  public:
23     LinkedQueue();
24     LinkedQueue(const LinkedQueue& aQueue);
25     ~LinkedQueue();
26
27     bool isEmpty() const;
28     bool enqueue(const ItemType& newEntry);
29     bool dequeue();
30
31     /** @throw  PrecondViolatedExcept if the queue is empty */
32     ItemType peekFront() const throw(PrecondViolatedExcept);
33  }; // end LinkedQueue
34  #include "LinkedQueue.cpp"
35  #endif
```

The method enqueue. Inserting a new node, to which newNodePtr points, at the back of the chain that represents the queue requires two pointer changes: the next pointer in the current back node and the external pointer backPtr. Figure 14-3 illustrates these changes during the addition of an item to a nonempty queue and indicates the order in which they can occur. After creating a new node to which newNodePtr points, the following statements perform this addition:

```
backPtr->setNext(newNodePtr);
backPtr = newNodePtr;
```

FIGURE 14-3   Adding an item to a nonempty queue

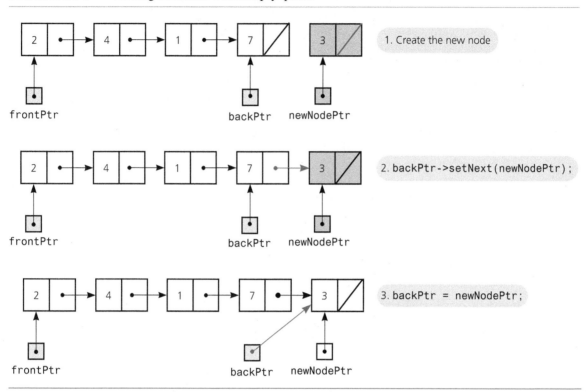

The addition of an item to an empty queue is a special case, as Figure 14-4 illustrates. If newNodePtr points to the new node, the following statements add the node to the empty chain:

```
frontPtr = newNodePtr;
backPtr = newNodePtr;
```

These statements easily follow from the realization that the chain has only one node, which is both the first and last node in the chain.

FIGURE 14-4   Adding an item to an empty queue

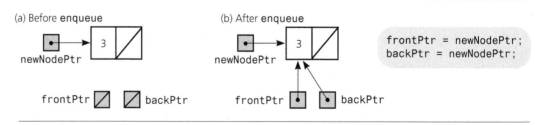

Thus, we have the following definition for the method enqueue:

```
template<class ItemType>
bool LinkedQueue<ItemType>::enqueue(const ItemType& newEntry)
{
```

```
        auto newNodePtr = std::make_shared<Node<ItemType>>(newEntry);

        // Insert the new node
        if (isEmpty())
            frontPtr = newNodePtr;          // The queue was empty
        else
            backPtr->setNext(newNodePtr);   // The queue was not empty

        backPtr = newNodePtr;               // New node is at back
        return true;
    }   // end enqueue
```

The method dequeue. Removing the front of the queue involves deleting the first node of the chain. This is an easier operation than removing the last node, which, fortunately, we do not have to do. Figure 14-5 illustrates the removal of the front item from a queue that contains more than one item. Notice that you need to change only the external pointer frontPtr. Removal from a queue of one item is a special case that sets the external pointers backPtr and frontPtr to nullptr.

FIGURE 14-5   Removing an item from a queue of more than one item

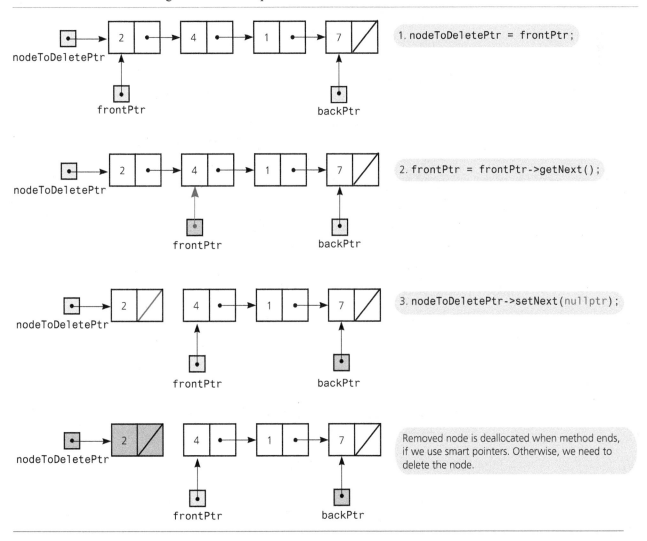

The following definition of the method dequeue shows how to implement these two cases:

```cpp
template<class ItemType>
bool LinkedQueue<ItemType>::dequeue()
{
   bool result = false;
   if (!isEmpty())
   {
      // Queue is not empty; remove front
      auto nodeToDeletePtr = frontPtr;
      if (frontPtr == backPtr)
      {  // Special case: one node in queue
         // Set frontPtr and backPtr to nullptr
         frontPtr.reset();
         backPtr.reset();
      }
      else
         frontPtr = frontPtr->getNext();

      // Maintain an accurate reference count for first node
      nodeToDeletePtr->setNext(nullptr);
      // Removed node will be deallocated when method ends

      result = true;
   }  // end if

   return result;
}  // end dequeue
```

Retrieval. The method peekFront simply returns the value frontPtr->getItem() after checking that the queue is not empty. We leave the rest of this implementation to you as an exercise. (See Exercises 1 through 3 at the end of this chapter.)

A circular linked chain can represent a queue

A circular link-based implementation. We will refer to a chain like the one in Figure 14-2 as a **linear chain**, regardless of how many external pointers it has. The last node in such a chain has a next pointer that is nullptr. Rather than using head and tail pointers, as just described and as shown in Figure 14-2, you can actually get by with one external pointer—to the back—if you make the last node point to the first one. Figure 14-6 illustrates this approach. This data structure is a **circular chain** of linked nodes. Notice that the nodes in a circular chain have next pointers that never contain nullptr. Programming Problem 1 at the end of the chapter asks you to consider the details of the circular chain implementation.

FIGURE 14-6   A circular chain of linked nodes with one external pointer

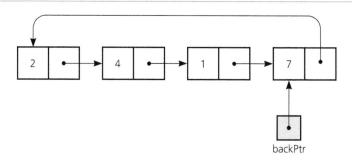

Question 1 Why is a tail pointer desirable when you use a linear chain of linked nodes to implement a queue?

Question 2 If you use a circular chain that has only a tail pointer, as Figure 14-6 illustrates, how do you access the data in the first node?

Question 3 If the ADT queue had a method `clear` that removed all entries from a queue, what would its definition be in the previous link-based implementation?

14.1.3 An Array-Based Implementation

For applications in which a fixed-sized queue does not present a problem, you can use an array to represent a queue. A naive array-based implementation of a queue might include the following definitions, as Figure 14-7a illustrates:

A naive array-based implementation of a queue

VideoNote
Overview of
ArrayQueue

```
static const int DEFAULT_CAPACITY = 50;  // Maximum size of queue;
. . .
ItemType items[DEFAULT_CAPACITY];        // Array of queue items
int       front;                         // Index to front of queue
int       back;                          // Index to back of queue
```

Here `front` and `back` are the indices of the front and back entries, respectively, in the queue. Initially, `front` is 0 and `back` is –1. To add a new item to the queue, you increment `back` and place the item in `items[back]`. To remove an item, you simply increment `front`. The queue is empty whenever `back` is less than `front`. The queue is full when `back` equals `DEFAULT_CAPACITY` – 1.

The problem with this strategy is **rightward drift**—that is, after a sequence of additions and removals, the items in the queue will drift toward the end of the array, making it appear full. In other words, `back` could equal `DEFAULT_CAPACITY` – 1 even when the queue contains only a few items. Figure 14-7b illustrates this situation.

Rightward drift can cause a queue-full condition even though the queue contains few entries

One possible solution to this problem is to shift array entries to the left, either after each removal from the queue or whenever `back` equals `DEFAULT_CAPACITY` – 1. This solution guarantees that the queue can always contain up to `DEFAULT_CAPACITY` items. Shifting is not practical, however, as it would dominate the cost of the implementation.

Shifting entries to compensate for rightward drift is expensive

FIGURE 14-7   A naive array-based implementation of a queue for which rightward drift can cause the queue to appear full

(a) A queue after four **enqueue** operations

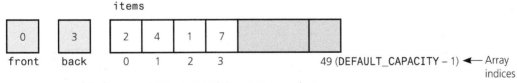

(b) The queue appears full after several **enqueue** and **dequeue** operations

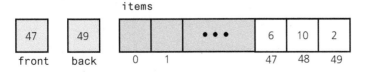

Question 4 Suppose that we change the naive array-based implementation of a queue pictured in Figure 14-7 so that the back of the queue is in items[0]. Although repeated removals from the front would no longer cause rightward drift, what other problem would this implementation cause?

A circular array eliminates rightward drift

A much more elegant solution is possible by viewing the array as circular, as Figure 14-8 illustrates. To remove an item, you increment the queue index front, and to insert an item, you increment back. Figure 14-9 illustrates the effect of a sequence of three queue operations on front, back, and the array. Notice that front and back "advance" clockwise around the array.

FIGURE 14-8   A circular array as an implementation of a queue

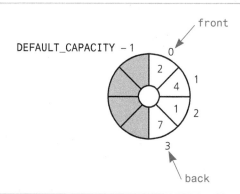

When either front or back advances past DEFAULT_CAPACITY − 1, it should wrap around to 0. This wrap-around eliminates the problem of rightward drift, which occurred in the previous naive implementation, because here the circular array has no end. You obtain the wraparound effect of a circular queue by using modulo arithmetic (that is, the % operator) when incrementing front and back. For example, you can add newEntry to the queue by using the statements

Adding to a queue

```
back = (back + 1) % DEFAULT_CAPACITY;
items[back] = newEntry;
```

FIGURE 14-9   The effect of three consecutive operations on the queue in Figure 14-8

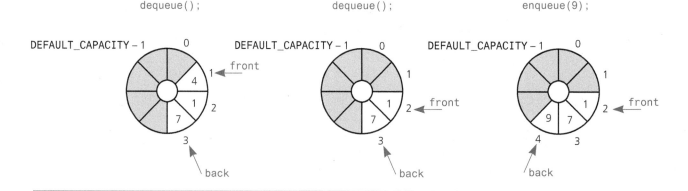

Notice that if `back` equaled `DEFAULT_CAPACITY – 1` before the addition of `newItem`, the first statement, `back = (back + 1) % DEFAULT_CAPACITY`, would have the effect of wrapping `back` around to index 0. Similarly, you can remove the entry at the front of the queue by using the statement

```
front = (front + 1) % DEFAULT_CAPACITY;
```

Removing from a queue

To initialize the queue, you set `front` to 0 and `back` to `DEFAULT_CAPACITY – 1`.

The only difficulty with this scheme is detecting when the queue is empty or full. It seems reasonable to select as the queue-empty condition

`front` is one slot ahead of `back`

as this appears to indicate that `front` "passes" `back` when the queue becomes empty, as Figure 14-10a depicts. However, it is also possible that this condition signals a full queue: Because the queue is circular, `back` might in fact "catch up" with `front` as the queue becomes full. Figure 14-10b illustrates this situation.

Using `front` and `back` will not indicate whether a queue is empty or full

Obviously, you need a way to distinguish between the two situations. One way is to keep a count of the number of items in the queue. Before adding an item to the queue, you check whether the count is equal to `DEFAULT_CAPACITY`; if it is, the queue is full. Before removing an item from the queue, you check whether the count is equal to zero; if it is, the queue is empty.

By counting queue items, you can detect queue-full and queue-empty conditions

FIGURE1 4-10   `front` and `back` as the queue becomes empty and as it becomes full

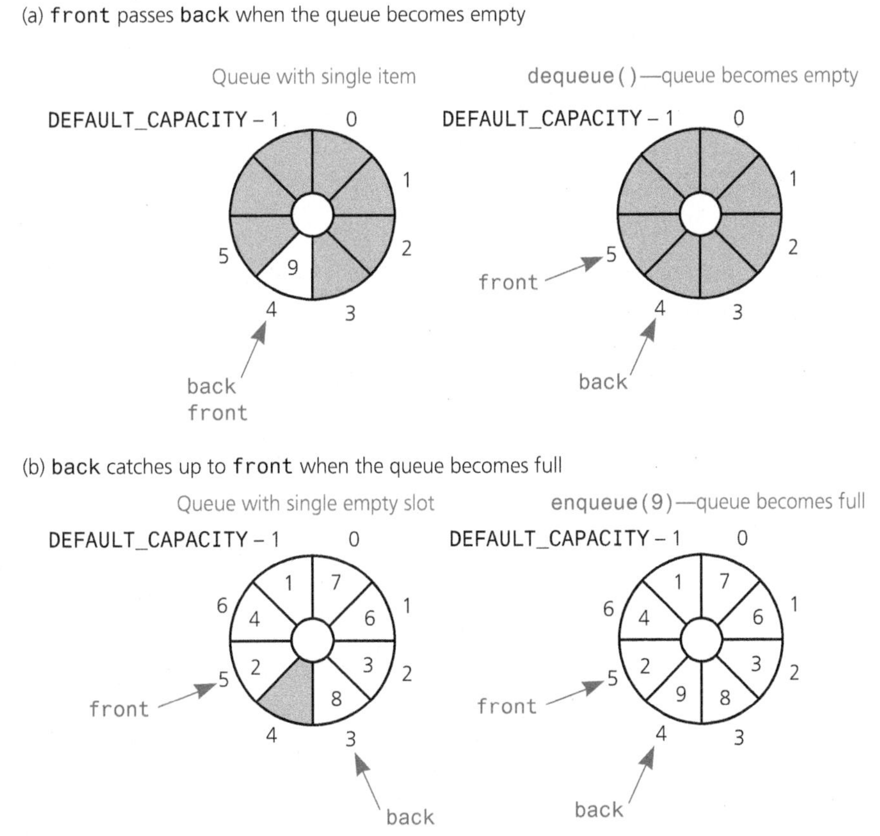

(a) `front` passes `back` when the queue becomes empty

(b) `back` catches up to `front` when the queue becomes full

The header file. Listing 14-4 contains the header file for an array-based implementation of the ADT queue that uses a circular array as just described. Because the data is stored in statically allocated memory, the compiler-generated copy constructor is sufficient.[1] Note that the destructor is inherited from QueueInterface.

LISTING 14-4   The header file for the class ArrayQueue

```cpp
1   /** ADT queue: Circular array-based implementation.
2    @file ArrayQueue.h */
3   #ifndef ARRAY_QUEUE_
4   #define ARRAY_QUEUE_
5   #include "QueueInterface.h"
6   #include "PrecondViolatedExcept.h"
7
8   template<class ItemType>
9   class ArrayQueue : public QueueInterface<ItemType>
10  {
11  private:
12     static const int DEFAULT_CAPACITY = 50;
13     ItemType items[DEFAULT_CAPACITY]; // Array of queue items
14     int      front;                   // Index to front of queue
15     int      back;                    // Index to back of queue
16     int      count;                   // Number of items currently in the queue
17
18  public:
19     ArrayQueue();
20     // Copy constructor supplied by compiler; destructor is inherited
21     bool isEmpty() const;
22     bool enqueue(const ItemType& newEntry);
23     bool dequeue();
24
25     /** @throw  PrecondViolatedExcept if queue is empty. */
26     ItemType peekFront() const throw(PrecondViolatedExcept);
27  }; // end ArrayQueue
28  #include "ArrayQueue.cpp"
29  #endif
```

The implementation file. Listing 14-5 contains the definitions of ArrayQueue's methods as they appear in the implementation file.

LISTING 14-5   The implementation file for the class ArrayQueue

```cpp
1   /** ADT queue: Circular array-based implementation.
2    @file ArrayQueue.cpp */
3   #include "ArrayQueue.h" // Header file
4
```

---

[1] If you use a dynamically allocated array, you must provide a copy constructor.

```
5    template<class ItemType>
6    ArrayQueue<ItemType>::ArrayQueue()
7                         : front(0), back(DEFAULT_CAPACITY - 1), count(0)
8    {
9    }   // end default constructor
10
11   template<class ItemType>
12   bool ArrayQueue<ItemType>::isEmpty() const
13   {
14      return count == 0;
15   }   // end isEmpty
16
17   template<class ItemType>
18   bool ArrayQueue<ItemType>::enqueue(const ItemType& newEntry)
19   {
20      bool result = false;
21      if (count < DEFAULT_CAPACITY)
22      {
23         // Queue has room for another item
24         back = (back + 1) % DEFAULT_CAPACITY;
25         items[back] = newEntry;
26         count++;
27         result = true;
28      }   // end if
29
30      return result;
31   }   // end enqueue
32
33   template<class ItemType>
34   bool ArrayQueue<ItemType>::dequeue()
35   {
36      bool result = false;
37      if (!isEmpty())
38      {
39         front = (front + 1) % DEFAULT_CAPACITY;
40         count--;
41         result = true;
42      }   // end if
43
44      return result;
45   }   // end dequeue
46
47   template<class ItemType>
48   ItemType ArrayQueue<ItemType>::peekFront() const throw(PrecondViolatedExcept)
49   {
50      // Enforce precondition
51      if (isEmpty())
52         throw PrecondViolatedExcept("peekFront() called with empty queue");
53
54      // Queue is not empty; return front
55      return items[front];
56   }   // end peekFront
57   // End of implementation file.
```

> ? **Question 5** If the ADT queue had a method clear that removed all entries from a queue, what would its definition be in the previous array-based implementation?

An isFull flag can replace the counter

Variations. Several commonly used variations of the previous circular-array approach do not require a count of the number of entries in the queue. One approach uses a boolean variable isFull to distinguish between the full and empty conditions. The expense of maintaining this variable is about the same as that of maintaining a counter, however. A faster implementation declares DEFAULT_CAPACITY + 1 locations for the array items, but uses only DEFAULT_CAPACITY of them for queue items. You sacrifice one array location and let front be the index of the location before the front of the queue. As Figure 14-11 illustrates, the queue is full if

    front equals (back + 1) % (DEFAULT_CAPACITY + 1)

but the queue is empty if

    front equals back

Using an extra array location is more time efficient

This approach does not have the overhead of maintaining a counter or boolean variable, and so is more efficient of time. Programming Problems 3 and 4 discuss these two alternate implementations further.

FIGURE 14-11 A circular array having one unused location as an implementation of a queue

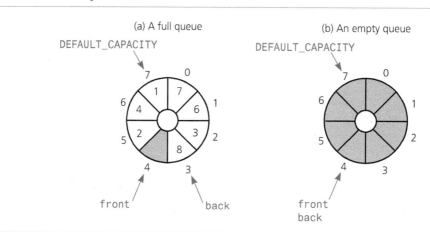

14.1.4 Comparing Implementations

We have suggested implementations of the ADT queue that store the queue's entries in either an instance of the ADT list, a chain of linked nodes that has both a head pointer and a tail pointer, a circular chain that has only one external pointer, an array, or a circular array. You have seen the details of three of these implementations. All of our implementations of the ADT queue are ultimately either array based or link based.

The reasons for making the choice between array-based and link-based implementations are the same as those discussed in earlier chapters. The discussion here is similar to the one in Section 4.5 of Chapter 4. We repeat the highlights here in the context of queues.

Fixed size versus dynamic size

An implementation based on a statically allocated array prevents the enqueue operation from adding an item to the queue if the array is full. Such a queue is appropriate for many data structures, such as buffers, within an operating system. If this restriction is not acceptable, you must use either a dynamically allocated array or a link-based implementation.

Suppose that you decide to use a link-based implementation. Should you choose the implementation that uses a linked chain or the one that uses a link-based implementation of the ADT list? Because a linked chain actually represents the items in the ADT list, using the ADT list to represent a queue is not as efficient as using a linked chain directly. However, the ADT list approach is much simpler to write.

If you decide to use a linked chain instead of the ADT list to represent the queue, should you use a linear chain or a circular chain? We leave this question for you to answer in Programming Problem 1.

Reuse of an already implemented class saves you time

14.2 An Implementation of the ADT Priority Queue

While we could place the entries of a priority queue into either an array or a chain of linked nodes, doing so would be like implementing the ADT sorted list, which we did in Chapter 12. Rather than repeating those implementations, we can use a sorted list to contain the entries of a priority queue. The header file in Listing 14-6 defines a class of priority queues that has as a private data member an instance of the class LinkedSortedList, as given in Listing 12-2 of Chapter 12.

LISTING 14-6 A header file for the class SL_PriorityQueue.

```
1   /** ADT priority queue: ADT sorted list implementation.
2    @file SL_PriorityQueue.h */
3   #ifndef PRIORITY_QUEUE_
4   #define PRIORITY_QUEUE_
5
6   #include "PriorityQueueInterface.h"
7   #include "LinkedSortedList.h"
8   #include "PrecondViolatedExcept.h"
9   #include <memory>
10
11  template<class ItemType>
12  class SL_PriorityQueue : public PriorityQueueInterface<ItemType>
13  {
14  private:
15     std::unique_ptr<LinkedSortedList<ItemType>> slistPtr; // Ptr to sorted list
16                                                           // of items
17
18  public:
19     SL_PriorityQueue();
20     SL_PriorityQueue(const SL_PriorityQueue& pq);
21     ~SL_PriorityQueue();
22
23     bool isEmpty() const;
24     bool enqueue(const ItemType& newEntry);
25     bool dequeue();
26
27     /** @throw  PrecondViolatedExcept if priority queue is empty. */
28     ItemType peekFront() const throw(PrecondViolatedExcept);
29  }; // end SL_PriorityQueue
30  #include "SL_PriorityQueue.cpp"
31  #endif
```

Before we can implement the class SL_PriorityQueue, we need to consider how the sorted list behaves. LinkedSortedList maintains the entries in a sorted list in sorted order. It does so by comparing the entries with each other. For a priority queue, we want these comparisons to be based on the priorities of the entries. Let's assume that each entry is an object that has its priority as a data member. You will learn in C++ Interlude 6 how to make a comparison operator, such as >, base its comparison on specific aspects of its two operands. For now, let's assume that the comparisons are made according to priority. Note that the highest-priority value can be either the largest value or the smallest value, according to the application at hand.

To give you an idea of how to implement this class, let's look at the definitions of the enqueue and dequeue operations:

```cpp
template<class ItemType>
bool SL_PriorityQueue<ItemType>::enqueue(const ItemType& newEntry)
{
   return slistPtr->insertSorted(newEntry);
}  // end enqueue

template<class ItemType>
bool SL_PriorityQueue<ItemType>::dequeue()
{
   // The highest-priority item is at the end of the sorted list
   return slistPtr->remove(slistPtr->getLength());
}  // end dequeue
```

We will leave the remainder of this implementation to you as an exercise. Note, however, that we will discuss a more time-efficient implementation in Chapter 17, when we introduce the ADT heap.

 Question 6 Define the method peekFront for the sorted list implementation of the ADT priority queue.

SUMMARY

1. The enqueue and dequeue operations for a queue require efficient access to both ends of the queue. Therefore, a link-based implementation of a queue uses a linear linked chain that has both a head pointer and a tail pointer. Alternatively, you can use a circular linked chain that has a tail pointer.

2. An array-based implementation of a queue is prone to rightward drift. This phenomenon can make a queue look full when it really is not. Shifting the items in the array is one way to compensate for rightward drift. A more efficient solution uses a circular array.

3. If you use a circular array to implement a queue, you must be able to distinguish between the queue-full and queue-empty conditions. You can make this distinction by counting the number of items in the queue, using a boolean variable isFull, or leaving one array location empty.

4. You can use an array, a chain of linked nodes, or a sorted list to contain the entries in a priority queue. A more time-efficient implementation is possible by using the ADT heap, which we will consider later in this book.

EXERCISES

1. Implement the copy constructor for the class LinkedQueue that is declared in Listing 14-3. *Hint:* Look at the copy constructor for the ADT stack in Listing 7-4 of Chapter 7, but use smart pointers.

2. Repeat the previous exercise, but implement a memory-safe copy constructor instead. If a memory allocation fails, this constructor should release all memory that was allocated prior to the failure and then throw an exception.

3. Imagine an implementation of the class LinkedQueue that uses raw pointers. The destructor for this class could repeatedly call dequeue. Although easy to write, this destructor can be inefficient due to repeated method calls. Write another implementation for the destructor that deallocates the linked chain directly without calling dequeue.

4. An operation that displays the contents of a queue can be useful during program debugging. Add a display operation to the ADT queue such that display assumes and uses the link-based implementation of the ADT queue.

5. Consider a method called getNumberOfEntries that returns the number of entries in a queue without changing the queue. The return type is int, and it does not accept any parameters.
   a. Add getNumberOfEntries to the array-based ADT queue given in this chapter.
   b. Add getNumberOfEntries to the link-based ADT queue given in this chapter.

6. Show that the implementation of a queue that uses an extra array element as described in Section 14.1.3 is more efficient than the counter variation, even though it appears to perform two extra additions in the test:

   ```
   front equals (back + 1) % (DEFAULT_CAPACITY + 1)
   ```

7. Consider the class ListQueue, as given in Listings 14-1 and 14-2. It implements the ADT queue by using the ADT list to represent the items in the queue. Discuss the efficiency of the queue's enqueue and dequeue operations when the ADT list's implementation is
   a. Array based
   b. Link based

8. Revise the definition of ListQueue's copy constructor, as given in Listing 14-2, so that it performs a deep copy instead of a shallow copy.

9. The class ListQueue, as given in Listings 14-1 and 14-2, maintains the queue's back at the end of a list of the queue's entries and has the front of the queue at the beginning of that list. Note that the list is an object of the class LinkedList. What is the impact on the efficiency of the operations enqueue and dequeue if we were to maintain the queue's back at the beginning of the list and the queue's front at the list's end?

10. Complete the implementation of the class SL_PriorityQueue, as described in Section 14.2.

11. Implement the class SL_PriorityQueue, assuming that low values indicate a higher priority. Such a priority queue is useful within operating systems and other similar applications. When the underlying sorted list has a link-based implementation, using the lowest value for the highest priority makes the priority queue operations more efficient. Describe why this benefit is true.

PROGRAMMING PROBLEMS

1. Write a link-based implementation of a queue that uses a circular linked chain to represent the items in the queue. You will need a single tail pointer. When you are done, compare your implementation to the one given in this chapter that uses a linear linked chain with two external pointers. Which implementation is easier to write? Which is easier to understand? Which is more efficient?

2. Write an array-based implementation of a queue that uses a resizable, circular array to represent the items in the queue.

3. Revise the array-based implementation of a queue given in this chapter. Instead of counting the number of items in the queue, use a boolean variable isFull to distinguish between the full and empty conditions.

4. This chapter described another array-based implementation of a queue that uses no special data member—such as count or isFull (see the previous programming problem)—to distinguish between the full and empty conditions. In this implementation, you declare DEFAULT_CAPACITY + 1 locations for the array items, but use only DEFAULT_CAPACITY of them for queue items. You sacrifice one array location by making front the index of the location before the front of the queue. The queue is full if front equals (back + 1) % (DEFAULT_CAPACITY + 1), but the queue is empty if front equals back. Implement this array-based approach.

5. Exercise 8 in the previous chapter defined the double-ended queue, or deque. Implement the ADT deque by using a circular array to contain the items in the deque.

6. Repeat the previous programming problem, but maintain the deque's entries in a linked chain.

7. Implement the ADT deque, as described in Exercise 8 of the previous chapter, as a derived class of ArrayQueue, as given in Listings 14-4 and 14-5.

Overloaded Operators and Friend Access

Contents

Prerequisites

    Chapter 4 Link-Based Implementations
    Chapter 8 Lists
    Chapter 9 List Implementations

C++ provides many operators, such as +, −, =, ==, >, <, and <<, that are defined for primitive data types. For instance, when working with integers, the symbol + represents the addition operation, = is used for the assignment operation, and == is used for equality comparisons. When we define new C++ data types using classes, these symbols do not have a definition that addresses how to add or compare two objects of the class. This C++ Interlude describes the tools that C++ provides you for extending the current operator definitions so that they can be applied to classes you have created.

C6.1 Overloaded Operators

VideoNote
C++ operator
overloading

The standard arithmetic operators in C++ actually have multiple meanings. Although the addition operators in the expressions 2 + 3 and 2.0 + 3.0 appear to be the same, they in fact are not. Because integers such as 2 and 3 have internal representations that differ from floating-point numbers such as 2.0 and 3.0, the algorithm to add two integers must differ from the algorithm to add two floating-point numbers. C++ could use two different symbols to designate integer addition and floating-point addition, but instead it uses only one symbol, +. The actual meaning of the + operator—that is, the type of addition it designates—is implied by the data type of its operands. An operator with more than one meaning is **overloaded** and is an example of a simple form of polymorphism.

An overloaded
operator has more
than one meaning

You saw earlier that you define new data types within C++ by using classes. Clients of such data types should be able to use them as naturally as the standard data types of the language. In particular, a client should be able to combine instances of a class with C++ operators in meaningful ways. To enable a particular operator to operate correctly on instances of a class, you typically must define a new meaning for the operator; that is, you must overload it.

Suppose that myList and yourList are two instances of LinkedList, as given in either Chapter 9 in Listing 9-2 or C++ Interlude 4, and you write

```
if (myList == yourList)
   std::cout << "The lists are equal.\n";
```

You must provide LinkedList with a definition of ==, since the compiler will not provide a default interpretation. Suppose we say that the list myList is equal to the list yourList if

Two lists are
equal if they have
identical lengths
and items

- myList and yourList have the same size, and
- Every item on myList is the same as the corresponding item on yourList

To overload an operator, you define an **operator method** whose name has the form

operator*symbol*

where *symbol* is the operator that you want to overload. For the == operator, you name the method operator== and declare one argument: the object that will appear on the right-hand side of the operator. The current object represents the object on the left-hand side of the operator. For LinkedList, you would add the declaration

```
bool operator==(const LinkedList<ItemType>& rightHandSide) const;
```

to the class definition in the header file.

To understand this notation, realize that we may also have declared a client function isEqualTo that compares a parameter of type LinkedList with the current object to determine equality. The declaration for such a function would look like this:

```
bool isEqualTo(const LinkedList<ItemType>& rightHandSide) const;
```

To use isEqualTo to compare the lists myList and yourList, you would write

```
if (myList.isEqualTo(yourList))
   std::cout << "The lists are equal.\n";
```

You can treat operator== exactly as you do isEqualTo; that is, you can write

```
if (myList.operator==(yourList))
   std::cout << "The lists are equal.\n";
```

because operator== is simply a method name. However, you can also use the more natural shorthand notation myList == yourList, and the compiler will understand that you mean the operator== method.

The LinkedList implementation of this method is

```
template <class ItemType>
bool LinkedList<ItemType>::operator==(const
                            LinkedList<ItemType>& rightHandSide) const
{
   bool isEqual = true; // Assume equal
```

```
      // First check whether the number of items is the same
   if (itemCount != rightHandSide.getLength())
      isEqual = false;
   else
   {  // Then compare items
      auto leftSidePtr = headPtr;
      auto rightSidePtr = rightHandSide.headPtr;

      while ((leftSidePtr != nullptr) && (rightSidePtr != nullptr) && isEqual)
      {
         ItemType leftItem = leftSidePtr->getItem();
         ItemType rightItem = rightSidePtr->getItem();
         isEqual = (leftItem == rightItem);

         leftSidePtr = leftSidePtr->getNext();
         rightSidePtr = rightSidePtr->getNext();
      }  // end while
   }  // end if

   return isEqual;
}  // end operator==
```

The operator == must be defined for ItemType

Note that this method depends on the == operator for items in the list. If these items are themselves instances of a class, that class must overload ==. You can overload the relational operators (<, <=, >, >=) in a similar manner.

Now suppose that you want all implementations of ListInterface, as given in Listing 8-1 of Chapter 8, to provide an implementation of the operator ==. You would need to add the declaration

```
virtual bool operator==(const ListInterface<ItemType>& rightHandSide) const = 0;
```

to the interface ListInterface. Each implementation of ListInterface would then provide a definition of ==, allowing you to compare any two ListInterface objects. The challenge of making the comparison in this case is that only ListInterface methods can be used for the list on the right-hand side, thereby affecting the efficiency of the equality check when comparing lists having two different implementations. For example, if we had an array-based list that we wished to compare to a link-based list, we could not take advantage of the node structure of the underlying linked chain when we accessed the entries. Instead, we would need to use getEntry to access entries, but each call to getEntry would iterate through the list from its beginning until it reaches the desired entry.

The implementation of other relational operators, such as < and >, is completed in a similar way.

C6.1.1 Overloading = for Assignment

Overloading the assignment operator (=) is similar to overloading the equality operator, but it presents additional concerns. Once again, suppose that myList and yourList are two instances of LinkedList. If you place several items in the list yourList and then write

```
myList = yourList;
```

you would expect myList to be an exact copy of yourList. Without an overloaded assignment operator, however, you would get a shallow copy of yourList instead of a deep copy, as Figure 4-9 in Chapter 4 illustrates. Although a shallow copy might be sufficient for a statically allocated data

Without an overloaded assignment operator, you get a shallow copy

structure, a deep copy is necessary for a dynamically allocated one such as the chain of linked nodes in the link-based implementation `LinkedList`. A shallow copy of a `LinkedList` object—`yourList`— would copy only the data members `itemCount` (the length of the list `yourList`) and `headPtr` (the pointer to `yourList`'s first item). The items in the list would not be copied.

To provide an assignment operator for the class `LinkedList`, you would add the declaration

```
LinkedList<ItemType>& operator=(const LinkedList<ItemType>& rightHandSide);
```

to the class definition in `LinkedList`'s header file. The argument `rightHandSide` represents the object to be copied—that is, the object that will appear on the right-hand side of the assignment operator. The method is not void, but instead returns a value to accommodate assignments such as

```
myList = yourList = theirList
```

As you will see, the method returns a reference to the receiving object.

In implementing this method, you must deal with a few subtleties. Suppose that `myList` and `yourList` each contain several items. If you write

```
myList = yourList;
```

The assignment operator must first deallocate `myList`, the object on the left-hand side

what happens to the items that were in `myList`? You might not care, as long as `myList` ultimately contains a copy of the items in `yourList`. You should care, however, if you have a link-based list. Before you can copy the items in `yourList` to `myList`, you need to deallocate the nodes in `myList`. Failure to do so results in a memory leak—that is, memory that was allocated to `myList` is not returned to the system and is inaccessible. Thus, the assignment of `yourList` to `myList` must take these steps:

> *Deallocate memory assigned to* `myList`
> `for` (*each item in* `yourList`)
> {
>   *Allocate a new node for* `myList`
>   *Set the node's data portion to a copy of the item in* `yourList`
> }

The tasks here are like those that you implemented when you wrote the destructor and copy constructor for `LinkedList`. To deallocate memory currently used by `LinkedList` nodes, you can call `clear`. When copying the underlying linked chain of nodes, you can avoid redundancy with the copy constructor by defining a private or protected method, `copyListNodes`, that both the copy constructor and the assignment operator can call.

Make the assignment operator fail-safe by checking for a special case

Now suppose you write

```
myList = myList;
```

Notice what our previous pseudocode tells you to do here: Deallocate `myList` and then make a copy of `myList`. After you have deallocated `myList`, there is nothing left to copy! Your implementation should test for this special case by asking whether the object on the left side of the = operator is the same as the object on the right. If it is, your assignment operator should do nothing—it should be fail-safe.

You can make this test by comparing the addresses of the two list objects rather than by comparing the items on the lists. In C++, `this` is a pointer to the receiving object. Thus, you write

```
if (this != &rightHandSide)
```

to compare the addresses of the objects on the left and right side of the =. Notice the placement of the & symbol; when used in this manner, it means "the address of." We would then read the above statement as "if the address of `this` object is not equal to the address of `rightHandSide`, then . . .". In this textbook, this is the only time when it is necessary to use the & symbol as the "address of" operator.

The link-based implementation of the overloaded assignment operator for `LinkedList` follows:

```cpp
template <class ItemType>
LinkedList<ItemType>& LinkedList<ItemType>::operator=(const
                                    LinkedList<ItemType>& rightHandSide)
{
    // Check for assignment to self
    if (this != &rightHandSide)
    {
        this->clear();                          // Deallocate left-hand side
        copyListNodes(rightHandSide);           // Copy list nodes
        itemCount = rightHandSide.itemCount;    // Copy size of list
    }   // end if

    return *this;
}  // end operator=
```

The assignment operator = requires that we return an object of the same type as `rightHandSide`, so we must return a `LinkedList` object. The returned object is placed into the left-hand side of the assignment statement. Since our implementation of the operator = places a copy of the object referenced by `rightHandSide` into the current, or receiving, object on the left-hand side, we should return the current object, which is represented by `*this`.

Note: In C++, `this` is a pointer to the receiving object. Therefore, `*this` is the receiving object.

If you declare and initialize an object in the same statement, the compiler will invoke the copy constructor and not the = operator. For example, the declaration of `myList` in

```cpp
LinkedList<string> myList = yourList;
```

constructs the object `myList`. This statement is equivalent to:

```cpp
LinkedList<string> myList(yourList);
```

C6.1.2 Overloading + for Concatenation

As we discussed in the previous section, the + operator is used for both integer and floating-point addition. In C++, the + operator is also used as a concatenation operator to append strings. This ability illustrates one of the concerns some programmers have about overloading operators—a symbol can represent several different operations. These operations need not be closely related to each other, so reading code that uses overloaded operators can be difficult.

Suppose you were asked to maintain code someone else wrote and found the following statement in a method:

```
theThing = myThing + yourThing;
```

Can you quickly determine whether the + performs scalar addition—adding two integers or floating-point numbers—or concatenates two strings? Without knowing the data type of the variables myThing and yourThing, you cannot determine what operation + performs. In a well-written program, most variables are declared close to their use, thus helping to clarify the statement, but this is not always the case.

When you choose to overload an operator, you should not change the meaning of the symbol. Your definition should extend the symbol's current operation only for use with a new data type—your class. When working with lists, the concatenation definition of the + symbol applies better than scalar addition, so let's see what is involved in appending one list onto another. Let's assume that theThing, myThing, and yourThing in the previous statement are list objects.

Link-based lists. If we choose to overload the + operator for the link-based implementation of the ADT list, we would add the following declaration to the class definition:

```
LinkedList<ItemType>&
         operator+(const LinkedList<ItemType>& rightHandSide) const;
```

The implementation of this concatenation operator has the following logic:

```
concatList = a new, empty instance of LinkedList
leftChain = a copy of the chain of nodes in this list
rightChain = a copy of the chain of nodes in the list rightHandSide
Set the last node of leftChain to point to the first node of rightChain
concatList.headPtr = leftChain.headPtr
concatList.itemCount = itemCount + rightHandSide.itemCount
return concatList
```

Now, the statement

```
theThing = myThing + yourThing;
```

assigns the returned list concatList to theThing using the assignment operator defined in the previous section.

After implementing the + operator, we should also implement the += operator, since it provides a shorthand for self-assignment using the + operator. This can be a more efficient method, as we do not need to make a copy of our list before appending the copy of right-HandSide.

Array-based lists. An implementation of the + operator for array-based lists has different challenges. For example, we must choose the capacity of the array that will contain the entries of the resulting list. Some possible choices are

- The sum of the capacities of the two lists that are operands
- The capacity of the first (left-hand) list
- The number of actual items stored in the combined lists
- Twice the number of actual items stored in the combined lists to allow for growth

After the new ArrayList object has been created, we can copy the entries from the first list into the first array elements and then place the entries in the second list into the elements that follow.

Note: **Some guidelines for overloading operators**

- Overloading an operator is the same as writing a method whose name is

  `operator`*symbol*

  where *symbol* is the operator that you want to overload.
- Overloaded operators are typically placed in the public section of the class declaration.
- When you decide to overload an operator, be sure that the new operation closely matches how the operator is already used. If that is not possible, consider creating a method whose name is not `operator`*symbol* to perform the operation.
- Commonly overloaded operators are the assignment (=), equality (== and !=), and relational (<, <=, >, >=) operators.
- You can overload any C++ operator except

  `. .* :: ?: sizeof`

- You cannot define new operators by overloading symbols that are not already C++ operators.
- You cannot change the standard precedence of a C++ operator.
- You cannot change the number of arguments for an overloaded operator, since they represent the operator's operands.
- At least one operand of an overloaded operator must be an instance of a class.

C6.2 Friend Access and Overloading <<

In C++, a class can provide additional access to its private and protected parts by declaring other functions and classes as **friends**. Declaring a nonmember function as a friend to a class allows that function to access all of the private and protected members of the class. Let's look at an example in which we need to declare a function as a friend of our class.

Functions and classes can be friends of a class

The output stream operator << is used to output a stream of data to either the display or a file. We commonly stream integers, floating-point numbers, and strings using <<. Occasionally, you may even have streamed a pointer to help with troubleshooting or just to see what happened. C++ has defined the stream operator's action for each of those data types.

Trying to stream a list to the display using statements such as

```
LinkedList<std::string> myList;
std::cout << myList;
```

results in a syntax error because there is no << operation defined for the LinkedList class. Notice that the syntax of the previous cout statement differs from the syntax of previous binary operators we have overloaded. The expression `std::cout << myList` is shorthand for

```
std::cout.operator<<(myList)
```

Thus, when we define << for our LinkedList class, we are actually overloading the method `operator<<` in the ostream class of which cout is an instance. Therefore, we need to define an operation for << in a different manner than the way we overloaded previous operators.

Before discussing how to overload the output stream operator, let's consider what our list should look like if it is displayed or written to a file. If our list contained the four items Ace, Jack, Queen, and King, we could display them on a single line

```
Ace Jack Queen King
```

or on multiple lines with a position label:

```
1 Ace
2 Jack
3 Queen
4 King
```

For our example, let's choose the second form of output. We could use public methods to display the list in this form, but we would need to call getEntry—which iterates through the list from the beginning—to display each item. It is more efficient to access the data directly. Thus, in defining << for our LinkedList class, we should grant the operator<< method in the ostream class access to the private and protected data of LinkedList.

We grant this access by making the operator<< method a friend of LinkedList by placing the following two statements in its declaration in the header file:

```
template<class friendItemType>
friend std::ostream& operator<<(std::ostream& outputStream,
                                const LinkedList<friendItemType>& outputList);
```

The keyword friend indicates that this method has access to private and protected data members and methods of our class as well as to those that are public. Notice that the method returns an ostream object and that the first parameter is also an ostream object. This is because we are overloading an operator method from the ostream class. Also, since the operator is not part of the LinkedList class, we cannot use the same template type ItemType in the declaration; we must declare another template type—friendItemType in our example.

We again must use the different template type when we implement the method:

A friend method

```
template<class friendItemType>
std::ostream& operator<<(std::ostream& outStream,
                         const LinkedList<friendItemType>& outputList)
{
    int position = 1;
    auto curPtr = outputList.headPtr;
    while (curPtr != nullptr)
    {
        outStream << position << "\t" << curPtr->getItem() << std::endl;
        curPtr = curPtr->getNext();
        position++;
    }  // end while

    return outStream;
}  // end operator<<
```

Because the operator<< method is already part of the ostream class, we don't need to include it in our namespace by writing LinkedList<ItemType>:: before the method name.

Note that the method accesses the private data member `headPtr` of the class `LinkedList`. Although this access violates the principle of information hiding, it is done in a controlled fashion: The class `LinkedList` explicitly grants this access by declaring the method as a friend.

We can extend the concept of friend methods to create friend classes. Granting a class access as a friend of another class allows all of the methods contained in the friend class to have access to the private and protected parts of the granting class. This feature is particularly useful when one class is used in the implementation of another class. For example, we have seen link-based implementations of ADTs that have a node declared as a separate class. For example, the `LinkedList` class uses the class `Node`. An alternative is to implement the node as a class whose data members and methods are private and to declare the `LinkedList` class as a friend class. For example, you could define a node for the ADT list as follows:

Friend classes

```
template<class ItemType>
class ListNode                          // A node on the list
{
private:
    ItemType item;                      // A data item on the list
    std::shared_ptr<Node<ItemType>> next; // Pointer to next node

    Node();
    Node(const ItemType& nodeItem, std::shared_ptr<Node<ItemType>> nextNode);

    // Friend class - can access private parts
    template<class friendItemType>
    friend class LinkedList<friendItemType>;
}; // end ListNode
```

The class LinkedList is a friend of ListNode

The class `LinkedList` has the same access privileges to the node's data members `item` and `next` as `ListNode` does. Friends of a base class do not have access to the private and protected parts added by a derived class—only to the private and protected members that appear in the base class.

A friend of a base class is not a friend of a derived class

Note: Some key points about friends

- Friend methods can access the private and protected parts of the class.
- Friend methods are not members of the class.
- When a class is declared as a friend of a class *C*, all of its methods have access to the private and protected parts of the class *C*.
- Friendship is not inherited. The private and protected members declared in a derived class are not accessible by friends of the base class.

Contents

Prerequisites

The previous chapters discussed ADTs whose operations fit into at least one of these general categories:

- Operations that add data to a data collection
- Operations that remove data from a data collection
- Operations that retrieve the data in a data collection

The ADTs list, stack, and queue are all position oriented, and their operations have the form

- Add a data item at the ith position of a data collection.
- Remove a data item from the ith *position* of a data collection.
- Retrieve the data item at the ith *position* of a data collection.

As you have seen, the ADT list allows the value of i to range from 1 to the number of items in the list, while the ADTs stack and queue are more restrictive. For example, the operations of the ADT stack are limited to adding to, removing from, and retrieving one end—the top—of the stack. Thus, although they differ with respect to the flexibility of their operations, lists, stacks, and queues manage an association between data items and positions.

As Section 13.5 of Chapter 13 discussed, the ADT sorted list is value oriented. Its operations are of the form

- Insert a data item containing the value x.
- Remove a data item containing the value x.
- Retrieve a data item containing the value x.

Although these operations, like position-oriented operations, fit into the three general categories of operations listed earlier—they insert data, remove data, and retrieve data—they are based on the values of data items instead of their positions.

Lists, stacks, and queues are linear in their organization of data, in that items are one after another. In this chapter, we organize data in a nonlinear, hierarchical form, whereby an item can have more than one immediate successor. We present two major ADTs: the binary tree and the binary search tree. As you will see, the binary tree is a position-oriented ADT, but it is not linear. Thus, you will not reference items in a binary tree by using a position number. Our discussion of the ADT binary tree provides an important background for the more useful binary search tree, which is a value-oriented ADT. Although a binary search tree is also not linear, it has operations similar to those of a sorted list, which is linear.

VideoNote
Tree concepts

15.1 Terminology

You use **trees** to represent relationships. Previous chapters informally used tree diagrams to represent the relationships between the calls of a recursive algorithm. For example, the diagram of the *rabbit* algorithm's recursive calls in Figure 2-19 of Chapter 2 is actually a tree. Each call to *rabbit* is represented by a box, or node, or **vertex**, in the tree. The lines between the nodes (boxes) are called **edges**. For this tree, the edges indicate recursive calls. For example, the edges from *rabbit*(7) to *rabbit*(6) and *rabbit*(5) indicate that subproblem *rabbit*(7) makes calls to *rabbit*(6) and *rabbit*(5).

Trees are
hierarchical

All trees are **hierarchical** in nature. Intuitively, "hierarchical" means that a "parent-child" relationship exists between the nodes in the tree. If an edge is between node n and node m, and node n is above node m in the tree, then n is the **parent** of m, and m is a **child** of n. In the tree in Figure 15-1a, nodes B and C are children of node A. Children of the same parent—for example, B and C—are called **siblings**. The three children D, E, and F of node B, for example, are siblings. The leftmost child D is called the **oldest child**, or **first child**, of B.

FIGURE 15-1   A tree and one of its subtrees

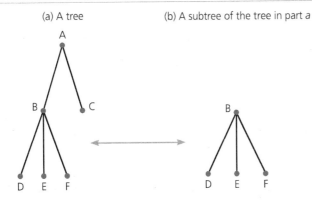

(a) A tree

(b) A subtree of the tree in part *a*

Each node in a tree has at most one parent, and exactly one node—called the **root** of the tree—has no parent. Node *A* is the root of the tree in Figure 15-1a. A node that has no children is called a **leaf** of the tree. The leaves of this tree are *C*, *D*, *E*, and *F*.

The parent-child relationship between the nodes is generalized to the relationships **ancestor** and **descendant**. In Figure 15-1a, *A* is an ancestor of *D*, and thus *D* is a descendant of *A*. Not all nodes are related by the ancestor or descendant relationship: *B* and *C*, for instance, are not so related. However, the root of any tree is an ancestor of every node in that tree. A **subtree** in a tree is any node in the tree together with all of its descendants. A **subtree of a node** *n* is a subtree rooted at a child of *n*. For example, Figure 15-1b shows a subtree of the tree in Figure 15-1a. This subtree has *B* as its root and is a subtree of the node *A*.

> A subtree is any node and its descendants

Because trees are hierarchical in nature, you can use them to represent information that itself is hierarchical in nature—for example, organization charts and family trees, as Figure 15-2 depicts. It may be disconcerting to discover, however, that the nodes in the family tree in Figure 15-2b that represent Bart's parents (Homer and Marge) are the children of the node that represents Bart. That is, the nodes that represent Bart's ancestors in a family tree are the descendants of Bart's node in one of our trees!

FIGURE 15-2   Representations of everyday hierarchical data as trees

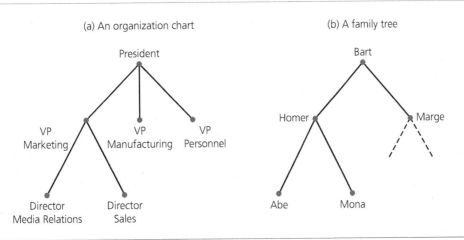

(a) An organization chart

(b) A family tree

15.1.1 Kinds of Trees

Formally, a **general tree** is a set T of one or more nodes such that T is partitioned into disjoint subsets:

- A single node r, the root
- Sets that are general trees, called subtrees of r

Thus, the trees in Figures 15-1 and 15-2a are general trees.

An ***n*-ary tree** is a set T of nodes that is either empty or partitioned into disjoint subsets:

- A single node r, the root
- n possibly empty sets that are n-ary subtrees of r

Each node can have no more than n children. The tree in Figure 15-1 is an n-ary tree with $n = 3$. An n-ary tree is not a special kind of general tree, because an n-ary tree can be empty, whereas a general tree cannot.

If an n-ary tree has the restriction that every node has at most two children, it is a **binary tree**. The primary focus of this chapter will be on binary trees. Formally, a binary tree is a set T of nodes that is either empty or partitioned into disjoint subsets:

Formal definition of a binary tree

- A single node r, the root
- Two possibly empty sets that are binary trees, called **left** and **right subtrees** of r

The trees in Figures 2-19 and 15-2b are binary trees. Notice that each node in a binary tree has no more than two children.

The following intuitive restatement of the definition of a binary tree is useful:

Intuitive definition of a binary tree

T is a binary tree if either

- T has no nodes, or
- T is of the form

where r is a node and T_L and T_R are both binary trees.

Notice that the formal definition agrees with this intuitive one: If r is the root of T, then the binary tree T_L is the left subtree of node r and T_R is the right subtree of node r. If T_L is not empty, its root is the **left child** of r, and if T_R is not empty, its root is the **right child** of r. Notice that if both subtrees of a node are empty, that node is a **leaf**.

Note: Although various kinds of trees are possible, they are either general trees or n-ary trees.

Example: Algebraic expressions. As an example of how you can use a binary tree to represent data in a hierarchical form, consider Figure 15-3. The binary trees in this figure represent algebraic expressions that involve the binary operators $+$, $-$, $\times$, and $/$. To represent an expression such as $a - b$, you place the operator in the root node and the operands a and b into left and right children, respectively, of the root. (See Figure 15-3a.) Figure 15-3b represents the expression $a - b\,/\,c$; a subtree represents the subexpression b/c. A similar situation exists in Figure 15-3c, which represents $(a - b) \times c$. The leaves of these trees contain the expression's operands, while other tree nodes contain the operators. Parentheses do not appear in these trees. The binary tree provides a hierarchy for the operations—that is, the tree specifies an unambiguous order for evaluating an expression. Operators lower in the tree are evaluated first.

FIGURE 15-3   Binary trees that represent algebraic expressions

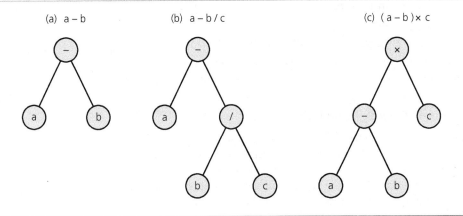

The nodes of a tree typically contain values. **A binary search tree** is a binary tree that is, in a sense, sorted according to the values in its nodes. For each node n, a binary search tree satisfies the following three properties:

- n's value is greater than all values in its left subtree T_L.
- n's value is less than all values in its right subtree T_R.
- Both T_L and T_R are binary search trees.

Properties of a binary search tree

Figure 15-4 is an example of a binary search tree. As its name suggests, a binary search tree organizes data in a way that facilitates searching it for a particular data item. Chapter 16 will discuss binary search trees in detail, and Chapter 19 will present several other trees that improve searching data.

FIGURE 15-4   A binary search tree of names

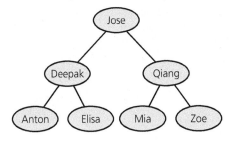

Question 1   What kind of tree is the tree in Figure 15-1a?

Question 2   What kind of tree is the tree in Figure 15-3c?

Question 3   Given the tree in Figure 15-3c, what node or nodes are

    a. Ancestors of *b*?
    b. Descendants of ×?
    c. Leaves?

Question 4 Given the tree in Figure 15-4, what node or nodes are

    a. The tree's root?
    b. Parents?
    c. Children of the parents in part *b* of this question?
    d. Siblings?

15.1.2 The Height of Trees

Trees come in many shapes. For example, although the binary trees in Figure 15-5 all contain the same nodes, their structures are quite different. Although each of these trees has seven nodes, some are "taller" than others. The **height of a tree** is the number of nodes on the longest **path** from the root to a leaf. For example, the trees in Figure 15-5 have respective heights of 3, 5, 7, and 7. Many people's intuitive notion of height would lead them to say that these trees have heights of 2, 4, 6, and 6. Indeed, many authors define height to agree with this intuition. However, the definition of height used in this book leads to a cleaner statement of many algorithms and properties of trees.

There are other equivalent ways to define the height of a tree T. One way uses the following definition of the **level of a node** *n*:

Level of a node

- If n is the root of T, it is at level 1.
- If n is not the root of T, its level is 1 greater than the level of its parent.

For example, in Figure 15-5a, node A is at level 1, node B is at level 2, and node D is at level 3. The height of a tree T in terms of the levels of its nodes is defined as follows:

Height of a tree in terms of levels

- If T is empty, its height is 0.
- If T is not empty, its height is equal to the maximum level of its nodes.

By applying this definition to the trees in Figure 15-5, you will find that their heights are, respectively, 3, 5, and 7, as was stated earlier.

FIGURE15-5   Binary trees with the same nodes but different heights

---

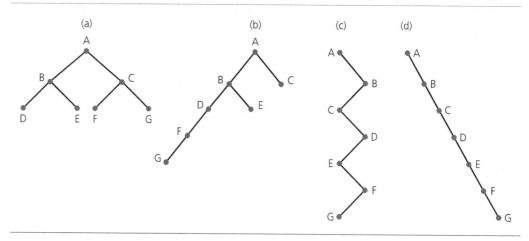

For binary trees, it is often convenient to use an equivalent recursive definition of height:

Recursive definition for height of a binary tree

- If T is empty, its height is 0.
- If T is a nonempty binary tree, then because T is of the form

the height of T is 1 greater than the height of its root's taller subtree; that is, $height(T)$ is equal to $1 + max\{height(T_L), height(T_R)\}$

Question 5 What are the levels of all nodes in the trees in parts b, c, and d of Figure 15-5?

Question 6 What is the height of the tree in Figure 15-4?

15.1.3 Full, Complete, and Balanced Binary Trees

In a **full binary tree** of height h, all nodes that are at a level less than h have two children each. Figure 15-6 depicts a full binary tree of height 3. Each node in a full binary tree has left and right subtrees of the same height. Among binary trees of height h, a full binary tree has as many leaves as possible, and they all are at level h. Intuitively, a full binary tree has no missing nodes.

FIGURE 15-6 A full binary tree of height 3

When proving properties about full binary trees—such as how many nodes they have—the following recursive definition of a full binary tree is convenient:

- If T is empty, T is a full binary tree of height 0.
- If T is not empty and has height $h > 0$, T is a full binary tree if its root's subtrees are both full binary trees of height $h - 1$.

A full binary tree

This definition closely reflects the recursive nature of a binary tree.

A **complete binary tree** of height h is a binary tree that is full down to level $h - 1$, with level h filled in from left to right, as Figure 15-7 illustrates. More formally, a binary tree T of height h is complete if

1. All nodes at level $h - 2$ and above have two children each, and
2. When a node at level $h - 1$ has children, all nodes to its left at the same level have two children each, and
3. When a node at level $h - 1$ has one child, it is a left child

A complete binary tree

Parts 2 and 3 of this definition formalize the requirement that level h be filled in from left to right. Note that a full binary tree is complete.

Full binary trees are complete

FIGURE 15-7   A complete binary tree

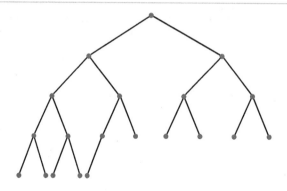

Finally, a binary tree is **height balanced**, or simply **balanced**, if the height of any node's right subtree differs from the height of the node's left subtree by no more than 1. The binary trees in Figures 15-7 and 15-5a are balanced, but the other trees in Figure 15-5 are not balanced. A complete binary tree is balanced.

Note: Summary of tree terminology

General tree	A set of one or more nodes, partitioned into a root node and subsets that are general subtrees of the root.
Parent of node n	The node directly above node n in the tree.
Child of node n	A node directly below node n in the tree.
Root	The only node in the tree with no parent.
Leaf	A node with no children.
Height	The number of nodes on the longest path from the root to a leaf.
Siblings	Nodes with a common parent.
Ancestor of node n	A node on the path from the root to n.
Descendant of node n	A node on a path from n to a leaf.
Subtree of node n	A tree that consists of a child (if any) of n and the child's descendants.
Left (right) child of node n	A node directly below and to the left (right) of node n in a binary tree.
Left (right) subtree of node n	In a binary tree, the left (right) child (if any) of node n plus its descendants.
n-ary tree	A set of nodes that is either empty or partitioned into a root node and at most n subsets that are n-ary subtrees of the root. Each node has at most n children.
Binary tree	A set of nodes that is either empty or partitioned into a root node and one or two subsets that are binary subtrees of the root. Each node has at most two children, the left child and the right child.

Binary search tree	A binary tree in which the value in any node n is greater than the value in every node in n's left subtree but less than the value in every node in n's right subtree.
Full binary tree	A binary tree of height h with no missing nodes. All leaves are at level h, and all other nodes each have two children.
Complete binary tree	A binary tree of height h that is full to level $h - 1$ and has level h filled in from left to right.
Balanced binary tree	A binary tree in which the left and right subtrees of any node have heights that differ by at most 1.

15.1.4 The Maximum and Minimum Heights of a Binary Tree

You can maximize the height of a binary tree with n nodes simply by giving each internal node (nonleaf) exactly one child, as shown earlier in parts c and d of Figure 15-5. This process will result in a tree of height n. The n-node tree with height n in Figure 15-5d strikingly resembles a chain of linked nodes.

n is the maximum height of a binary tree with n nodes

 Note: The maximum height of an n-node binary tree is n.

A minimum-height binary tree with n nodes is a bit more difficult to obtain. As a first step, consider the number of nodes that a binary tree with a given height h can have. For example, if $h = 3$, the possible binary trees include those in Figure 15-8. Thus, binary trees of height 3 can have between three and seven nodes. In addition, Figure 15-8 shows that 3 is the minimum height for a binary tree with four, five, six, or seven nodes. Similarly, binary trees with more than seven nodes require a height greater than 3.

Intuitively, to minimize the height of a binary tree given n nodes, you must fill each level of the tree as completely as possible. A complete tree meets this requirement. In fact, except for the tree in part a, the trees in Figure 15-8 are complete trees and of minimum height. If a complete binary tree of a given height h is to have the maximum possible number of nodes, it should be full, as in part e of the figure. Although complete trees fill their last level from left to right, this order is not necessary for a minimum-height binary tree.

Except for the last level, each level of a minimum-height binary tree must contain as many nodes as possible

FIGURE 15-8   Binary trees of height 3

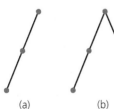   

(a)   (b)   (c)   (d)   (e)

Question 7 What binary trees other than those pictured in Figure 15-8 have a height of 3?

FIGURE 15-9   Counting the nodes in a full binary tree of height h

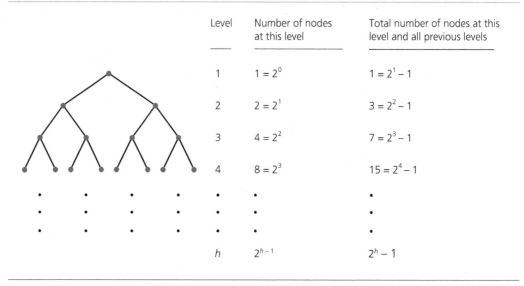

Level	Number of nodes at this level	Total number of nodes at this level and all previous levels
1	$1 = 2^0$	$1 = 2^1 - 1$
2	$2 = 2^1$	$3 = 2^2 - 1$
3	$4 = 2^2$	$7 = 2^3 - 1$
4	$8 = 2^3$	$15 = 2^4 - 1$
⋮	⋮	⋮
h	2^{h-1}	$2^h - 1$

Figure 15-9 counts the nodes of a full tree by level and demonstrates the following facts, whose proof is left as an exercise:

 Note: Facts about full binary trees
- A full binary tree of height $h \geq 0$ has $2^h - 1$ nodes.
- You cannot add nodes to a full binary tree without increasing its height.
- The maximum number of nodes that a binary tree of height h can have is $2^h - 1$.

We now can determine the minimum height of an n-node binary tree.

Note: The minimum height of a binary tree with n nodes is $\lceil \log_2(n + 1) \rceil$.[1]

To prove the previous fact, we let h be the smallest integer such that $n \leq 2^h - 1$ and establish the following assertions:

1. *A binary tree whose height is less than or equal to $h - 1$ has fewer than n nodes.*
   We know that a binary tree of height $h - 1$ has at most $2^{h-1} - 1$ nodes. If it is possible that $n \leq 2^{h-1} - 1$, then h is not the smallest integer such that $n \leq 2^h - 1$. Therefore, n must be

---

[1] The **ceiling of x**, which $\lceil x \rceil$ denotes, is x rounded up. For example, $\lceil 6 \rceil = 6$, $\lceil 6.1 \rceil = 7$, and $\lceil 6.8 \rceil = 7$.

greater than $2^{h-1} - 1$ or, equivalently, $2^{h-1} - 1 < n$. Because a binary tree of height $h - 1$ has at most $2^{h-1} - 1$ nodes, it must have fewer than n nodes.

2. *An n-node complete binary tree whose height is h exists.*

Consider a full binary tree of height $h - 1$. It must have $2^{h-1} - 1$ nodes. As you just saw, $n > 2^{h-1} - 1$ because h was selected so that $n \leq 2^h - 1$. You can thus add nodes to the full tree from left to right until you have n nodes, as Figure 15-10 illustrates. Because a binary tree of height h cannot have more than $2^h - 1$ nodes and $n \leq 2^h - 1$, you will reach n nodes by the time level h is filled up.

3. *The minimum height of a binary tree with n nodes is the smallest integer h such that $n \leq 2^h - 1$.*

If h is the smallest integer such that $n \leq 2^h - 1$, and if a binary tree has height $\leq h - 1$, then by fact 1 it has fewer than n nodes. Because by fact 2 there is a binary tree of height h that has exactly n nodes, h must be as small as possible.

FIGURE 15-10   Filling in the last level of a tree

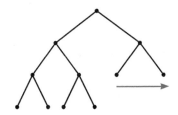

The previous discussion implies that

$$2^{h-1} - 1 < n \leq 2^h - 1$$
$$2^{h-1} < n + 1 \leq 2^h$$
$$h - 1 < \log_2(n + 1) \leq h$$

Now h is either $\log_2(n + 1)$ or satisfies the inequality $h - 1 < \log_2(n + 1) < h$. In the latter case, $\log_2(n + 1)$ cannot be an integer, so we round it up to get h. In either case, we have that h is $\lceil \log_2(n + 1) \rceil$. Thus, we have established that $\lceil \log_2(n + 1) \rceil$ is the minimum height of a binary tree with n nodes.

 Note: Complete trees and full trees with n nodes have heights of $\lceil \log_2(n + 1) \rceil$, which, as you just saw, is the theoretical minimum.

Complete trees and full trees have minimum height

 Question 8 Consider the binary trees in Figure 15-8.

a. Which are complete?
b. Which are full?
c. Which are balanced?
d. Which have minimum height?
e. Which have maximum height?

15.2 The ADT Binary Tree

As an abstract data type, the binary tree has operations that add and remove nodes, set or retrieve the data in the root of the tree, and test whether the tree is empty. By using these basic operations, you can build a binary tree.

Traversal operations that visit every node in a binary tree are important to many algorithms and so are included in this ADT. Visiting a node means "doing something with or to" the node. Chapter 4 introduced the concept of traversal for a linear chain of linked nodes: Beginning with the chain's first node, you visit each node sequentially until you reach the end of the chain. Traversal of a binary tree, however, can visit the tree's nodes in one of several different orders. We examine the details of the traversal operations next.

15.2.1 Traversals of a Binary Tree

A traversal algorithm for a binary tree visits each node in the tree. While visiting a node, you do something with or to either the node's data—such as displaying or modifying it—or the node itself—such as removing it from the tree. For the purpose of this discussion, assume that visiting a node simply means displaying the data portion of the node.

With the recursive definition of a binary tree in mind, you can construct a recursive traversal algorithm as follows. According to the definition, the binary tree T is either empty or is of the form

If T is empty, the traversal algorithm takes no action—an empty tree is the base case. If T is not empty, the traversal algorithm must perform three tasks: It must display the data in the root r, and it must traverse the two subtrees T_L and T_R, each of which is a binary tree smaller than T. We can summarize this logic using the following pseudocode:

The general form of a recursive traversal algorithm

```
if (T is not empty)
{
    Display the data in T's root
    Traverse T's left subtree
    Traverse T's right subtree
}
```

Although we arbitrarily chose to visit the tree's root before traversing its subtrees, the algorithm actually has three choices of when to visit r: It can visit r

Three choices for when to visit the root

- Before it traverses both of r's subtrees—as we just did
- After it has traversed r's left subtree T_L but before it traverses r's right subtree T_R
- After it has traversed both of r's subtrees

These choices result in **preorder**, **inorder**, and **postorder traversals**, respectively. Figure 15-11 shows the results of these traversals for a given binary tree.

Traversal is O(n)

Each of these traversals visits every node in a binary tree exactly once. Thus, n visits occur for a tree of n nodes. Each visit performs the same operations on each node, independently of n, so it must be O(1). Thus, each traversal is O(n).

Preorder traversal. The recursive preorder traversal algorithm is as follows:

```
// Traverses the given binary tree in preorder.
// Assumes that "visit a node" means to process the node's data item.
preorderTraverse(binTree: BinaryTree): void
{
   if (binTree is not empty)
   {
      Visit the root of binTree
      preorderTraverse(Left subtree of binTree's root)
      preorderTraverse(Right subtree of binTree's root)
   }
}
```

FIGURE 15-11   Three traversals of a binary tree

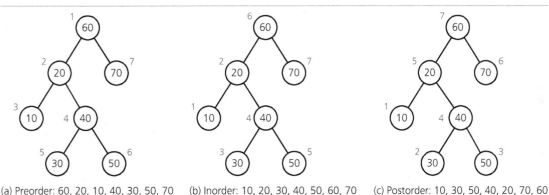

(a) Preorder: 60, 20, 10, 40, 30, 50, 70   (b) Inorder: 10, 20, 30, 40, 50, 60, 70   (c) Postorder: 10, 30, 50, 40, 20, 70, 60

(Numbers beside nodes indicate traversal order.)

The preorder traversal of the tree in Figure 15-11a visits the nodes in this order: 60, 20, 10, 40, 30, 50, 70. If you apply preorder traversal to a binary tree that represents an algebraic expression, such as any tree in Figure 15-3, and display the nodes as you visit them, you will obtain the prefix form of the expression.[2]

Inorder traversal. The recursive inorder traversal algorithm is as follows:

```
// Traverses the given binary tree in inorder.
// Assumes that "visit a node" means to process the node's data item.
inorderTraverse(binTree: BinaryTree): void
{
   if (binTree is not empty)
   {
      inorderTraverse(Left subtree of binTree's root)
      Visit the root of binTree
      inorderTraverse(Right subtree of binTree's root)
   }
}
```

---

[2] The prefix expressions are (a) –*ab*; (b) –*a*/*bc*; (c) ×–*abc*.

The result of the inorder traversal of the tree in Figure 15-11b is 10, 20, 30, 40, 50, 60, 70. If you apply inorder traversal to a binary search tree, you will visit the nodes in order according to their data values. Such is the case for the tree in Figure 15-11b.

Postorder traversal. Finally, the recursive postorder traversal algorithm is as follows:

Postorder traversal

```
// Traverses the given binary tree in postorder.
// Assumes that "visit a node" means to process the node's data item.
postorderTraverse(binTree: BinaryTree): void
{
    if (binTree is not empty)
    {
        postorderTraverse(Left subtree of binTree's root)
        postorderTraverse(Right subtree of binTree's root)
        Visit the root of binTree
    }
}
```

The result of the postorder traversal of the tree in Figure 15-11c is 10, 30, 50, 40, 20, 70, 60. If you apply postorder traversal to a binary tree that represents an algebraic expression, such as any tree in Figure 15-3, and display the nodes as you visit them, you will obtain the postfix form of the expression.[3]

 Note: Although traversal means to visit each item in the ADT, traversal can be more difficult than you might imagine if you do more than simply display each item when you visit it. For example, you might copy the item into another data structure or even alter it. The details of traversal are thus quite application dependent, which makes traversal a difficult operation to define within the framework of an ADT.

Visiting a node. You could have a different traversal operation for each desired task during a visit to a node, such as `preorderTraverseAndDisplay`, `preorderTraverseAndCopy`, and so on. Or the traversal methods for the ADT binary tree could call a function, which the client defines and passes as an argument, when it visits a node. We will take this latter approach, as it is more general.

For example, if the ADT binary tree has the operation `preorderTraverse`, you can invoke it for the binary tree `binTree` as follows:

A client-defined function, which the traversal methods call, defines the meaning of "visit"

```
bintree.preorderTraverse(display);
```

where `display` is a client function that displays the data passed to it as an argument. Suppose the binary tree `binTree` stores `string` objects. You would define the function `display` to display data of type `string`:

```
void display(std::string someItem)
{
    std::cout << someItem << std::endl;
} // end display
```

Now the call `bintree.preorderTraverse(display)` will call `display` each time it visits a node in the tree.

---

[3] The postfix expressions are (a) $a\,b-$; (b) $a\,b\,c/-$; (c) $a\,b-c\times$.

Despite the fact that the ADT operation `preorderTraverse` calls a client-supplied function, the wall between the program and the implementation of the ADT has not been violated. Because `display` is on the client's side of the wall, the function can access the data only by using the ADT operations.

The next chapter will discuss the implementation details of the traversal operations.

Question 9 What are the preorder, inorder, and postorder traversals of the binary trees in parts *a*, *b*, and *c* of Figure 15-5?

15.2.2 Binary Tree Operations

The ADT binary tree has the following operations:

> **Note: ADT binary tree operations**
> - Test whether a binary tree is empty.
> - Get the height of a binary tree.
> - Get the number of nodes in a binary tree.
> - Get the data in a binary tree's root.
> - Set the data in a binary tree's root.
> - Add the given data to a binary tree.
> - Remove the specified data from a binary tree.
> - Remove all data from a binary tree.
> - Retrieve the specified data in a binary tree.
> - Test whether a binary tree contains specific data.
> - Traverse the nodes in a binary tree in preorder, inorder, or postorder.

The following contract specifies these operations in more detail, and a UML diagram for a class of binary trees appears in Figure 15-12.

ABSTRACT DATA TYPE: BINARY TREE	
DATA	
• A finite number of objects in hierarchical order.	
OPERATIONS	
PSEUDOCODE	DESCRIPTION
`isEmpty()`	Task: Tests whether this binary tree is empty. Input: None. Output: True if the binary tree is empty; otherwise false.
`getHeight()`	Task: Gets the height of this binary tree. Input: None. Output: The height of the binary tree.
`getNumberOfNodes()`	Task: Gets the number of nodes in this binary tree. Input: None. Output: The number of nodes in the binary tree.

(continues)

PSEUDOCODE	DESCRIPTION
getRootData()	Task: Gets the data that is in the root of this binary tree. Input: None. Assumes the tree is not empty. Output: The root's data.
setRootData(newData)	Task: Replaces the data item in the root of this binary tree with newData, if the tree is not empty. However, if the tree is empty, inserts a new root node whose data item is newData into the tree. Input: newData is the data item. Output: None.
add(newData)	Task: Adds a given data item to this binary tree. Input: newData is the data item. Output: True if the addition is successful, or false if not.
remove(target)	Task: Removes the specified data item from this binary tree. Input: target is the data item to remove. Output: True if the removal is successful, or false if not.
clear()	Task: Removes all data items from this binary tree. Input: None. Output: None. (The binary tree is empty.)
getEntry(target)	Task: Retrieves a specific data item in this binary tree. Input: target is the desired data item. Output: The entry in the binary tree that matches target.
contains(target)	Task: Tests whether the specified data item occurs in this binary tree. Input: target is the data item to find. Output: True if the binary tree contains a data item that matches target, or false if not.
preorderTraverse(visit)	Task: Traverses this binary tree in preorder and calls the function visit once for each node. Input: visit is a client-defined function that performs an operation on or with the data in each visited node. Output: None.
inorderTraverse(visit)	Task: Traverses this binary tree in inorder and calls the function visit once for each node. Input: visit is a client-defined function that performs an operation on or with the data in each visited node. Output: None.
postorderTraverse(visit)	Task: Traverses this binary tree in postorder and calls the function visit once for each node. Input: visit is a client-defined function that performs an operation on or with the data in each visited node. Output: None.

FIGURE 15-12   UML diagram for the class BinaryTree

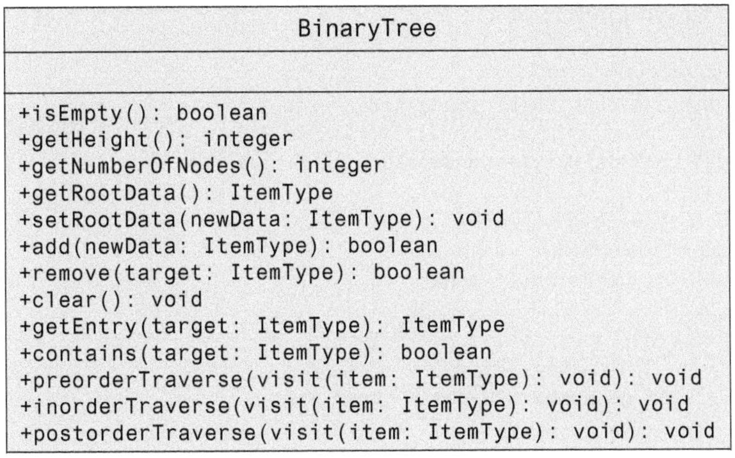

```
+-----------------------------------------------------------+
|                       BinaryTree                          |
+-----------------------------------------------------------+
|                                                           |
+-----------------------------------------------------------+
| +isEmpty(): boolean                                       |
| +getHeight(): integer                                     |
| +getNumberOfNodes(): integer                              |
| +getRootData(): ItemType                                  |
| +setRootData(newData: ItemType): void                     |
| +add(newData: ItemType): boolean                          |
| +remove(target: ItemType): boolean                        |
| +clear(): void                                            |
| +getEntry(target: ItemType): ItemType                     |
| +contains(target: ItemType): boolean                      |
| +preorderTraverse(visit(item: ItemType): void): void      |
| +inorderTraverse(visit(item: ItemType): void): void       |
| +postorderTraverse(visit(item: ItemType): void): void     |
+-----------------------------------------------------------+
```

Example. You can use the add operation to build the binary tree in Figure 15-5a, where the node labels represent character data:

Using ADT binary tree operations to build a binary tree

```
tree = a new empty binary tree
tree.add('A')
tree.add('B')
tree.add('C')
tree.add('D')
tree.add('E')
tree.add('F')
tree.add('G')
```

Given the specification of the add method, you have no reason to expect that the previous statements, in fact, produce the binary tree in the figure. Assuming that the operations are successful, you will know only that the binary tree has seven nodes containing the given data. Our specification of add is intentionally vague and gives the programmer who implements the class BinaryTree flexibility. It also makes BinaryTree more useful as a base class, as you will see in the next chapter.

15.2.3 An Interface Template for the ADT Binary Tree

We formalize our specifications for the ADT binary tree by writing the interface template given in Listing 15-1.

LISTING 15-1 **An interface template for the ADT binary tree**

```
1  /** Interface for the ADT binary tree.
2   @file BinaryTreeInterface.h */
3
4  #ifndef BINARY_TREE_INTERFACE_
5  #define BINARY_TREE_INTERFACE_
6  #include "NotFoundException.h"
```

(continues)

```cpp
template<class ItemType>
class BinaryTreeInterface
{
public:
   /** Tests whether this binary tree is empty.
    @return  True if the binary tree is empty, or false if not. */
   virtual bool isEmpty() const = 0;

   /** Gets the height of this binary tree.
    @return  The height of the binary tree. */
   virtual int getHeight() const = 0;

   /** Gets the number of nodes in this binary tree.
    @return  The number of nodes in the binary tree. */
   virtual int getNumberOfNodes() const = 0;

   /** Gets the data that is in the root of this binary tree.
    @pre  The binary tree is not empty.
    @post  The root's data has been returned, and the binary tree is unchanged.
    @return  The data in the root of the binary tree. */
   virtual ItemType getRootData() const = 0;

   /** Replaces the data in the root of this binary tree with the given data,
       if the tree is not empty. However, if the tree is empty, inserts a new
       root node containing the given data into the tree.
    @pre  None.
    @post  The data in the root of the binary tree is as given.
    @param newData  The data for the root. */
   virtual void setRootData(const ItemType& newData) = 0;

   /** Adds the given data to this binary tree.
    @param newData  The data to add to the binary tree.
    @post  The binary tree contains the new data.
    @return  True if the addition is successful, or false if not. */
   virtual bool add(const ItemType& newData) = 0;

   /** Removes the specified data from this binary tree.
    @param target  The data to remove from the binary tree.
    @return  True if the removal is successful, or false if not. */
   virtual bool remove(const ItemType& target) = 0;

   /** Removes all data from this binary tree. */
   virtual void clear() = 0;

   /** Retrieves the specified data from this binary tree.
    @post  The desired data has been returned, and the binary tree
       is unchanged. If no such data was found, an exception is thrown.
    @param target  The data to locate.
    @return  The data in the binary tree that matches the given data.*/
   virtual ItemType getEntry(const ItemType& target) const = 0;
```

```
57        /** Tests whether the specified data occurs in this binary tree.
58         @post   The binary tree is unchanged.
59         @param target  The data to find.
60         @return  True if data matching the target occurs in the tree, or false if not. */
61        virtual bool contains(const ItemType& target) const = 0;
62
63        /** Traverses this binary tree in preorder (inorder, postorder) and
64            calls the function visit once for each node.
65        @param visit  A client-defined function that performs an operation on
66           either each visited node or its data. */
67        virtual void preorderTraverse(void visit(ItemType&)) const = 0;
68        virtual void inorderTraverse(void visit(ItemType&)) const = 0;
69        virtual void postorderTraverse(void visit(ItemType&)) const = 0;
70
71        /** Destroys this tree and frees its assigned memory. */
72        virtual ~BinaryTreeInterface() {  }
73     }; // end BinaryTreeInterface
74     #endif
```

15.3 The ADT Binary Search Tree

VideoNote

The ADT binary search tree

Searching for a particular item is one operation for which the ADT binary tree is ill suited since we may need to visit every node to discover our target entry. The binary search tree is a binary tree that corrects this deficiency by organizing its data by value. Recall that each node n in a binary search tree satisfies the following three properties:

- n's value is greater than all values in its left subtree T_L.
- n's value is less than all values in its right subtree T_R.
- Both T_L and T_R are binary search trees.

A recursive definition of a binary search tree

This organization of data enables you to search a binary search tree for a particular data item, given its value instead of its position, as we did for the ADT list.

 Example. Let's consider a binary search tree whose nodes contain people's names. Suppose that these names are Anton, Deepak, Elisa, Jose, Mia, Qiang, and Zoe. Figure 15-13 illustrates one binary search tree that we can form with these names.

FIGURE 15-13   A binary search tree of names

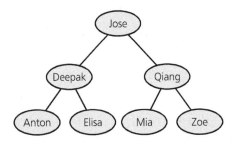

Several different
binary search trees
are possible for the
same data

Many different binary search trees can contain the same data, however. For example, in addition to the tree in Figure 15-13, each tree in Figure 15-14 is a valid binary search tree for the same names. Although these trees have different shapes, each one satisfies the requirements of a binary search tree.

FIGURE 15-14   Binary search trees with the same data as in Figure 15-13

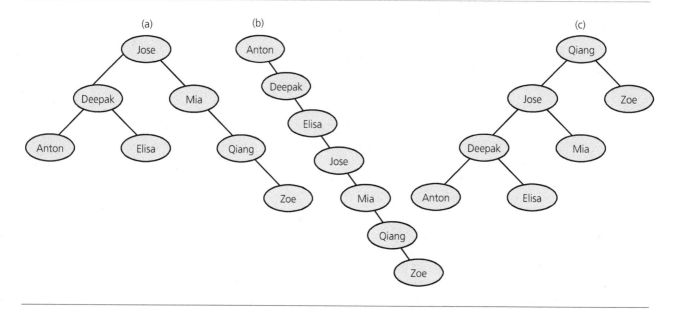

15.3.1 Binary Search Tree Operations

As an ADT, the binary search tree has operations that are like the operations for the ADTs you studied in previous chapters, in that they involve adding, removing, and retrieving data. Unlike the position-oriented ADTs stack, list, and queue, but like the ADT sorted list, the addition, removal, and retrieval operations are by value, not by position. On the other hand, the other operations—including the traversal operations—that you just saw for a binary tree apply to a binary search tree without change, because a binary search tree is a binary tree.

The operations that define the ADT binary search tree are as follows:

Note: ADT binary search tree operations

- Test whether a binary search tree is empty.
- Get the height of a binary search tree.
- Get the number of nodes in a binary search tree.
- Get the data in a binary search tree's root.
- Add the given data item to a binary search tree.
- Remove the specified data item from a binary search tree.
- Remove all data items from a binary search tree.
- Retrieve the specified data item in a binary search tree.
- Test whether a binary search tree contains specific data.
- Traverse the nodes in a binary search tree in preorder, inorder, or postorder.

For simplicity, we will insist that a binary search tree contain unique data. The following contract specifies the addition and removal operations in more detail. The UML diagram for a class of binary search trees will be almost the same as the one for a class of binary trees, so we do not write one here.

ABSTRACT DATA TYPE: BINARY SEARCH TREE

DATA

- A finite number of objects in hierarchical order.

OPERATIONS

PSEUDOCODE	DESCRIPTION
add(newEntry)	Task: Adds a given data item to this binary search tree such that the properties of a binary search tree are maintained. Input: newEntry is the data item to be added. Assumes the entries in the tree are distinct and differ from newEntry. Output: True if the operation is successful, or false if not.
remove(target)	Task: Removes the specified data item from this binary search tree such that the properties of a binary search tree are maintained. Input: target is the data item to remove. Output: True if the operation is successful, or false if not.

The methods isEmpty, getHeight, getNumberOfNodes, getRootData, clear, getEntry, contains, preorderTraverse, inorderTraverse, and postorderTraverse have the same specifications as for a binary tree.

Example. If nameTree is any one of the binary search trees in Figures 15-13 and 15-14, and if their nodes contain strings, the statement

```
std::string name = nameTree.getEntry(mia);
```

where mia is a string variable containing "Mia", locates the node containing "Mia" and assigns its data to name. It doesn't matter which one of the four trees getEntry searches; the result will be the same. The time it takes for getEntry to find "Mia", however, does depend on the shape of the tree, as you will see.

If the string variable hal contains "Hal" and you add it to nameTree by invoking

```
nameTree.add(hal)
```

you will be able to retrieve "Hal" later and still be able to retrieve "Qiang". If you remove "Jose" by using

```
nameTree.remove(jose)
```

you will still be able to retrieve the strings "Qiang" and "Hal". Finally, if displayName is a client function that displays its string argument,

```
nameTree.inorderTraverse(displayName)
```

will display in alphabetical order the names of the people that nameTree represents. Again, it does not matter which one of the four trees you traverse.

?
CHECK POINT

Question 10 Show that each tree in Figures 15-13 and 15-14 is a binary search tree.

Question 11 Show that the inorder traversals of each binary search tree in Figures 15-13 and 15-14 are the same.

Question 12 What are the preorder and postorder traversals of each binary search tree in Figures 15-13 and 15-14? Are the preorder traversals the same? Are the postorder traversals the same?

15.3.2 Searching a Binary Search Tree

Consider again the binary search tree in Figure 15-13. Each node in the tree contains a person's name. Suppose that you want to locate Elisa in the binary search tree. The root node of the tree contains Jose, so if Elisa is present in the tree, it must be in Jose's left subtree, because the string `"Elisa"` is before the string `"Jose"` alphabetically. Because a binary search tree is recursive by nature, it is natural to formulate recursive algorithms for operations on the tree. Thus, you know that Jose's left subtree is also a binary search tree, so you use exactly the same strategy to search this subtree for Elisa. The root of this binary search tree contains Deepak, and, because the string `"Elisa"` is greater than the string `"Deepak"`, Elisa must be in Deepak's right subtree. That right subtree is also a binary search tree, and it happens that Elisa is in the root node of this tree. Thus, the search has located Elisa.

The following pseudocode summarizes this search strategy:

A search algorithm for a binary search tree

```
// Searches the binary search tree for a given target value.
search(bstTree: BinarySearchTree, target: ItemType)
{
    if (bstTree is empty)
        The desired item is not found
    else if (target == data item in the root of bstTree)
        The desired item is found
    else if (target < data item in the root of bstTree)
        search(Left subtree of bstTree, target)
    else
        search(Right subtree of bstTree, target)
}
```

As you will see, this `search` algorithm is the basis of the other operations on a binary search tree.

The shape of the tree in no way affects the validity of the `search` algorithm. The algorithm requires only that a tree be a binary search tree. However, the `search` algorithm works more efficiently on some trees than on others. For example, with the tree in Figure 15-14b, `search` inspects every node before locating Zoe. In fact, this binary search tree really has the same structure as a link-based representation of a sorted list and offers no advantage in efficiency. In contrast, with the full tree in Figure 15-13, the `search` algorithm inspects only the nodes that contain the names Jose, Qiang, and Zoe. These names are exactly the names that a binary search of the sorted array in Figure 15-15 would inspect.

FIGURE 15-15   An array of names in sorted order

Anton	Deepak	Elisa	Jose	Mia	Qiang	Zoe
0	1	2	3	4	5	6

The shape of a binary search tree affects the efficiency of its operations. The more balanced a binary search tree is, the farther it is from a linear structure and the closer the behavior of the search algorithm will be to a binary search of an array (and the farther it will be from the behavior of a linear search). Later in this chapter, you will learn more about how the shape of a binary search tree affects search's efficiency and how adding and removing entries affects this shape.

Question 13 Using the tree in Figure 15-14c, trace the algorithm that searches a binary search tree for

a. Elisa
b. Kyle

In each case, list the nodes in the order in which the search visits them.

15.3.3 Creating a Binary Search Tree

Suppose that you want to add a record for Finn to the binary search tree of Figure 15-13. As a first step, imagine that you instead want to *search* for the string "Finn". The search algorithm first searches the tree rooted at Jose, then the tree rooted at Deepak, and then the tree rooted at Elisa. It then searches the tree rooted at the right child of Elisa. Because this tree is empty, as Figure 15-16 illustrates, the search algorithm has reached a base case and will terminate with the report that Finn is not present. What does it mean that search looked for Finn in the right subtree of Elisa? For one thing, it means that if Finn were the right child of Elisa, search would have found Finn there.

This observation indicates that a good place to put Finn is as the right child of Elisa. Because Elisa has no right child, the placement is simple, requiring only the addition of a new leaf node. More important, Finn belongs in this location—search will look for Finn here. Specifically, adding Finn as the right child of Elisa will preserve the tree's binary search tree property. Because search, when searching for Finn, would follow a path that leads to the right child of Elisa, you are assured that Finn is in the proper relation to the names above it in the tree.

Note: Using search to determine where in the tree to place a new name always leads to an easy addition, because the tree has unique entries. No matter what new item you add to the tree, search will always terminate at an empty subtree. Thus, search always tells you to place the item as a new leaf.

Use search to determine the insertion point

FIGURE 15-16   Empty subtree where the search algorithm terminates when looking for Finn

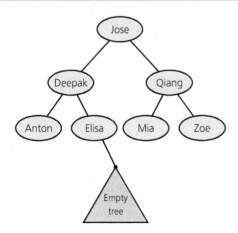

Example. Let's create the binary search tree shown in Figure 15-13. The following pseudocode statements begin with an empty binary search tree and add entries one at time until we get the desired tree:

```
nameTree = a new, empty binary search tree
nameTree.add("Jose")
nameTree.add("Deepak")
nameTree.add("Anton")
nameTree.add("Elisa")
nameTree.add("Qiang")
nameTree.add("Mia")
nameTree.add("Zoe")
```

Once we add Jose to the empty tree, Jose becomes the tree's root. Adding Deepak to the tree leaves the root untouched, and so the only binary search tree that is possible places Deepak as the left child of the root. Why? Because `"Deepak"` is less than `"Jose"`. When we add the next name, Anton, it becomes the left child of Deepak. Note that each addition creates a new leaf of the tree at that point in time. However, it might not remain a leaf in the final tree.

Question 14 Beginning with an empty binary search tree, what binary search tree is formed when you add the following letters in the order given? J, N, B, A, W, E, T

Question 15 Arrange nodes that contain the letters A, C, E, F, L, V, and Z into two binary search trees: one that has maximum height and one that has minimum height. For each tree, indicate the sequence of additions that produce it.

15.3.4 Traversals of a Binary Search Tree

The traversals of a binary search tree are the same as the traversals of a binary tree. The inorder traversal of a binary search tree, however, is of special note. Recall its algorithm from earlier in this chapter:

```
// Traverses the given binary tree in inorder.
// Assumes that "visit a node" means to process the node's data item.
inorder(binTree: BinaryTree): void
{
    if (binTree is not empty)
    {
        inorder(Left subtree of binTree's root)
        Visit the root of binTree
        inorder(Right subtree of binTree's root)
    }
}
```

Note: The inorder traversal of a binary search tree visits the tree's nodes in sorted order.

Use inorder traversal to visit nodes of a binary search tree in sorted order

The proof of the previous fact is by induction on h, the height of the tree. Let T represent the tree. *Basis:* $h = 0$. When T is empty, the algorithm does not visit any nodes. This is the proper sorted order for the zero names that are in the tree!
Inductive hypothesis: Assume that the theorem is true for all k, $0 < k < h$. That is, assume for all k $(0 < k < h)$ that the inorder traversal visits the nodes in sorted order.

Inductive conclusion: You must show that the theorem is true for $k = h > 0$. T has the form

Because T is a binary search tree, all the entries in the left subtree T_L are less than the entry in the root r, and all the entries in the right subtree T_R are greater than the entries in r. The inorder algorithm will visit all the nodes in T_L, then visit r, and then visit all the nodes in T_R. Thus, the only concern is that inorder visit the nodes within each of the subtrees T_L and T_R in the correct sorted order. But because T is a binary search tree of height h, each subtree is a binary search tree of height less than h. Therefore, by the inductive hypothesis, inorder visits the nodes in each subtree T_L and T_R in the correct sorted order. The proof is now complete.

15.3.5 The Efficiency of Binary Search Tree Operations

You have seen binary search trees in many shapes. For example, even though the binary search trees in Figures 15-13 and 15-14 have seven nodes each, they have different shapes and heights. You saw that to locate Zoe in Figure 15-14b, you would have to inspect all seven nodes, but you can locate Zoe in Figure 15-13 by inspecting only three nodes (Jose, Qiang, and Zoe). Consider now the relationship between the height of a binary search tree and the efficiency of the retrieval, addition, and removal operations.

Each of these operations compares a specified value v to the entries in the nodes along a path through the tree. This path always starts at the root of the tree and, at each node n, follows the left or right branch, depending on the comparison of v to the value in n. The path terminates at the node that contains v or, if v is not present, at an empty subtree. Thus, each retrieval, addition, or removal operation requires a number of comparisons equal to the number of nodes along this path. This means that the maximum number of comparisons that each operation can require is the number of nodes on the longest path through the tree. In other words, the maximum number of comparisons that these operations can require is equal to the height of the binary search tree.

The maximum number of comparisons for a retrieval, addition, or removal is the height of the tree

>
> **Note: The height of a binary tree**
> Recall that the height of an n-node binary tree ranges from $\lceil \log_2(n + 1) \rceil$ to n.

If the height of the binary search tree is $\log_2(n + 1)$, the efficiency of its operations is $O(\log n)$. However, what will the height of a binary search tree actually be? The factor that determines the height of a binary search tree is the order in which you add entries to and remove entries from the tree. Recall that, starting with an empty tree, if you add names in the order Anton, Deepak, Elisa, Jose, Mia, Qiang, Zoe, you would obtain a binary search tree of maximum height, as shown in Figure 15-14b. On the other hand, if you add names in the order Jose, Deepak, Qiang, Anton, Elisa, Mia, Zoe, you would obtain a binary search tree of minimum height, as shown in Figure 15-13.

Adding entries in sorted order produces a maximum-height binary search tree

Which of these situations should you expect to encounter in the course of a real application? It can be proven mathematically that if the additions and removals occur in a random order, the height of the binary search tree will be quite close to $\log_2 n$. Thus, in this sense, the previous analysis is not unduly optimistic. However, in a real-world application, is it realistic to expect the additions and removals to occur in random order? In many applications, the answer is yes. There are, however, applications in which this assumption would be dubious.

Adding entries in random order produces a near-minimum-height binary search tree

For example, the person preparing the previous sequence of names to add to the tree might well decide to "help you out" by arranging the names into sorted order. This arrangement, as has been mentioned, would lead to a tree of maximum height. Thus, while in many applications you can expect the behavior of a binary search tree to be excellent, you should be wary of the possibility of poor performance due to some characteristic of a given application.

Is there anything you can do if you suspect that the operations might not occur in a random order? Similarly, is there anything you can do if you have an enormous number of items and need to ensure that the height of the tree is close to $\log_2 n$? Chapter 19 presents variations of the basic binary search tree that are guaranteed always to remain balanced and therefore be of minimum height.

Figure 15-17 summarizes the order of the retrieval, addition, removal, and traversal operations for the ADT binary search tree.

FIGURE 15-17 The Big O for the retrieval, addition, removal, and traversal operations of the ADT binary search tree

Operation	Average case	Worst case
Retrieval	$O(\log n)$	$O(n)$
Addition	$O(\log n)$	$O(n)$
Removal	$O(\log n)$	$O(n)$
Traversal	$O(n)$	$O(n)$

SUMMARY

1. Binary trees provide a hierarchical organization of data, which is important in many applications.

2. Traversing a tree is a useful operation. Intuitively, traversing a tree means to visit every node in the tree. Because the meaning of "visit" is application dependent, you can pass a client-defined visit function to the traversal operation.

3. The binary search tree allows you to use a binary search-like algorithm to search for an item with a specified value.

4. Binary search trees come in many shapes. The height of a binary search tree with n nodes can range from a minimum of $\lceil \log_2(n + 1) \rceil$ to a maximum of n. The shape of a binary search tree determines the efficiency of its operations. The closer a binary search tree is to a balanced tree (and the farther it is from a linear structure), the closer the behavior of the search algorithm will be to a binary search (and the farther it will be from the behavior of a linear search).

5. An inorder traversal of a binary search tree visits the tree's nodes in sorted search-key order.

EXERCISES

1. Consider the tree in Figure 15-18. What node or nodes are
   a. The tree's root?
   b. Parents?
   c. Children of the parents in part *b*?

   d. Siblings?
   e. Ancestors of 50?
   f. Descendants of 20?
   g. Leaves?

2. What is the height of the tree in Figure 15-18?

3. Starting with an empty binary search tree, in what order should you add items to get the binary search tree in Figure 15-18?

4. Using the binary search tree in Figure 15-18, trace the `search` algorithm when it searches for
   a. 30
   b. 15

In each case, list the entries in the order in which the search visits them.

5. Suppose that you traverse the binary search tree in Figure 15-18 and write the data item in each node visited to a file. You plan to read this file later and create a new binary search tree by using the ADT binary search tree operation add. In creating the file, in what order should you traverse the tree so that the new tree will have exactly the same shape and nodes as the original tree?

6. Consider the binary search tree in Figure 15-18. What tree results after you add the entries 80, 65, 75, 45, 35, and 25, in that order?

7. What are the preorder, inorder, and postorder traversals of the binary tree in Figure 15-19?

8. Is the tree in Figure 15-19 a binary search tree? Explain.

9. Write preconditions and postconditions for the ADT binary search tree operations.

10. Beginning with an empty binary search tree, what binary search tree is formed when you add the following values in the order given?
   a. W, T, N, J, E, B, A
   b. W, T, N, A, B, E, J
   c. A, B, W, J, N, T, E
   d. B, T, E, A, N, W, J

FIGURE 15-18   A tree for Exercises 1 through 6

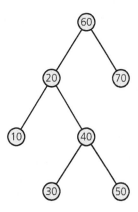

FIGURE 15-19   A tree for Exercises 7 and 8

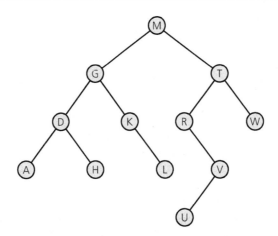

11. Consider the binary search tree in Figure 15-20. The numbers simply label the nodes so that you can reference them; they do not indicate the contents of the nodes.
    a. Without performing an inorder traversal, which node must contain the value that comes immediately after the value in the root? Explain.
    b. In what order will an inorder traversal visit the nodes of this tree? Indicate this order by listing the labels of the nodes in the order that they are visited.

12. Consider a method isLeaf that returns true if a binary tree is a one-node tree—that is, if it consists of only a leaf—and returns false otherwise.
    a. Specify the method isLeaf.
    b. If isLeaf were not a method of a class of binary trees, would a client of the class be able to implement isLeaf? Explain.

13. If duplicates are allowed in a binary search tree, it is important to have a convention that determines the relationship between the duplicates. Items that duplicate the root of a tree should either all be in the left subtree or all be in the right subtree, and, of course, this property must hold for every subtree. Why is this convention critical to the effective use of the binary search tree?

FIGURE 15-20   A binary search tree for Exercise 11

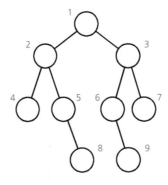

14. Consider a nonempty binary tree with two types of nodes: *min nodes* and *max nodes*. Each node has an integer value initially associated with it. This tree is a *minimax tree* and has a value, which we define as follows:

   - If the root is a min node, the value of the tree is equal to the *minimum* of
     - The integer stored in the root
     - The value of the left subtree, but only if it is nonempty
     - The value of the right subtree, but only if it is nonempty
   - If the root is a max node, the value of the tree is equal to the *maximum* of the above three values.
     a. Compute the value of the minimax tree in Figure 15-21. Each node is labeled with its initial value.
     b. Design a general solution for representing and evaluating these trees.

15. A binary search tree with a given set of data items can have several different structures that conform to the definition of a binary search tree.
    a. If you are given a list of data items, does at least one binary search tree whose preorder traversal matches the order of the items on your list always exist?
    b. Is there ever more than one binary search tree that has the given preorder traversal?

*16. How many differently shaped *n*-node trees are possible when the trees are
    a. Binary trees
    b. Binary search trees

17. Write pseudocode for a binary search tree method that visits all nodes whose data lies within a given range of values (such as all values between 100 and 1,000).

18. By using mathematical induction, prove that a full binary tree of height $h \geq 0$ has $2^h - 1$ nodes.

19. By using mathematical induction, prove that the maximum number of nodes in a binary tree of height h is $2^h - 1$.

20. For a binary tree
    a. What is the maximum number of nodes that a binary tree can have at level *n*?
    b. Prove your answer by using mathematical induction.

FIGURE 15-21 A minimax tree for Exercise 14

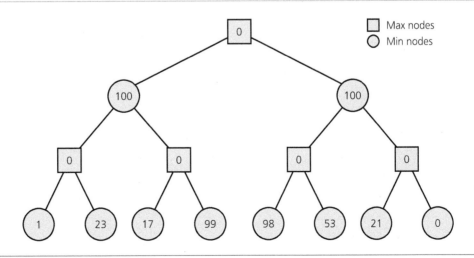

c. Using your answer to part *a*, revise the definition of a complete tree of height *h*.

d. Derive a closed form for the formula

$$\sum_{i=1}^{h} 2^{i-1}$$

What is the significance of this sum?

21. Prove by mathematical induction that a binary tree with *n* nodes has exactly *n* + 1 empty subtrees.

22. A binary tree is *strictly binary* if every nonleaf node has exactly two children. Prove by mathematical induction on the number of leaves that a strictly binary tree with *n* leaves has exactly 2*n* − 1 nodes.

23. Consider two algorithms for traversing a binary tree. Both are nonrecursive algorithms that use an extra container *C* for bookkeeping. Both algorithms have the following basic form:

```
Put the root of the tree in C
while  (C is not empty)
{
    Remove a node from C and name it N
    Visit N
    if  (N has a left child)
        Put the child in C
    if  (N has a right child)
        Put the child in C
}
```

The difference between the two algorithms is the approach for choosing a node *N* to remove from the container *C*:

- Algorithm 1: Remove the newest (most recently added) node from *C*.
- Algorithm 2: Remove the oldest (earliest added) node from *C*.
    a. In what order would each algorithm visit the nodes of the tree in Figure 15-13?
    b. For each algorithm, describe an appropriate ADT for the bookkeeping container *C*. What data should the ADT have? Be conservative with the amount of memory needed for the ADT. Also, note that the traversal of a tree should not alter the tree in any way.

PROGRAMMING PROBLEMS

1. Develop a program that can be used to test an implementation of `BinaryTreeInterface`.

2. Repeat the previous problem, but assume that the implementation represents a binary search tree.

3. Develop an interface template for a general tree. What methods are reasonable for a general tree?

4. Repeat the previous problem, but consider an *n*-ary tree instead.

Contents

Prerequisites

T he previous chapter discussed various kinds of trees, but it focused on the ADTs binary tree and binary search tree. This chapter will show you how to implement these two ADTs by using the constructs of C++. In each case, the data structures will be private data members of a class of trees.

16.1 The Nodes in a Binary Tree

VideoNote
Representing
tree nodes

The first step in implementing a tree is to choose a data structure to represent its nodes. Since each node must contain both data and "pointers" to the node's children—which are other nodes in the tree—it is natural to make each node an object. Thus, we will use a C++ class to define the nodes in the tree. If we place these nodes in an array, the "pointers" in the nodes are array indices. However, if the nodes are a part of a linked chain, we use C++ pointers to link them together.

16.1.1 An Array-Based Representation

Let's name our class of nodes TreeNode. An array-based implementation of a tree uses an array of nodes, so a class of such trees could have the following data members:

```
TreeNode<ItemType>  tree[MAX_NODES];  // Array of tree nodes
int                 root;             // Index of root
int                 free;             // Index of free list
```

The variable root is an index to the tree's root node within the array tree. If the tree is empty, root is −1.

As the tree changes due to additions and removals of its data, its nodes may not be in contiguous elements of the array. Therefore, this implementation requires you to establish a collection of available nodes, which is called a **free list**. To insert a new node into the tree, you first obtain an available node from the free list. If you remove a node from the tree, you place it into the free list so that you can reuse the node at a later time. The data member free is the index to the first node in the free list. We will talk about the free list in a moment.

A free list keeps track of available nodes

Although these data members are appropriate for any tree, we want to restrict our conversation to binary trees and consider a class of its nodes. The class TreeNode, as given in Listing 16-1, is such a class.

LISTING 16-1 The class `TreeNode` for an array-based implementation of the ADT binary tree

```
1   template<class ItemType>
2   class TreeNode
3   {
4   private:
5      ItemType item;         // Data portion
6      int      leftChild;    // Index to left child
7      int      rightChild;   // Index to right child
8
9   public:
10     TreeNode();
11     TreeNode(const ItemType& nodeItem, int left, int right);
12
13  // Declarations of the methods setItem, getItem, setLeft, getLeft,
14  // setRight, and getRight are here.
15
16     . . .
17  }; // end TreeNode
```

Each node in the array-based binary tree has a data item and two array indices, one to each child. Both `leftChild` and `rightChild` within a node are indices to the children of that node. If a node has no left child, `leftChild` is −1; if a node has no right child, `rightChild` is −1. Since `root` is the index of the root r of a binary tree, `tree[root].getLeft()` is `leftChild`, the index of the root of the left subtree of r; `tree[root].getRight()` is `rightChild`, the index of the root of the right subtree of r.

The free list. Even though the data member `free` is the index of the first node in the free list, the next available node is not necessarily at index `free + 1`. When a node is removed from a tree and returned to the free list, it could be anywhere in the array. Thus, we "link" the available nodes together by arbitrarily making the `rightChild` member of each node be the index of the next node in the free list. Thus, both the free list and the tree itself are array-based, but the nodes are linked by array indices instead of C++ pointers. While the free list is a linear data structure, the tree is not.

Figure 16-1 contains a binary tree and its data members for this array-based implementation. Note how the nodes in the tree are linked. For example, Deepak in `tree[1]` has Elisa as its right child. Elisa is in `tree[4]`, and `tree[1].rightChild` is 4. Since Elisa is in a leaf of the tree, its links in `tree[4].leftChild` and `tree[4].rightChild` are each −1. Likewise, Anton and Mia are in leaf nodes. The nodes in the free list are linked, but since this tree has not undergone removals, the free list happens to be in contiguous array elements.

An array-based implementation of a binary tree is much more attractive when the tree is complete. In such cases, indices that link parents and their children are not stored, so the data structure is simpler than if the tree is not complete. In Chapter 17, you will see that an array-based representation of a complete binary tree is useful in the implementation of the ADT priority queue. We will not use any other array-based implementation of a tree.

FIGURE 16-1   (a) A binary tree of names; (b) its implementation using the array `tree`

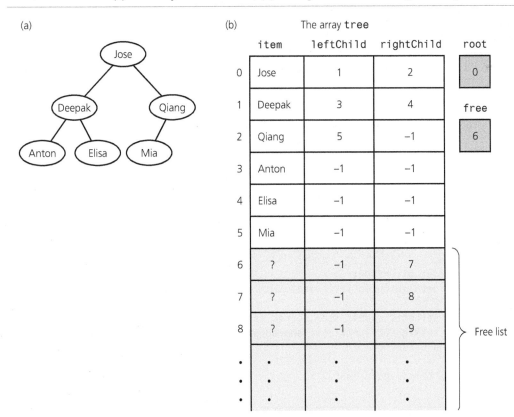

> **Note:** If you use an array-based implementation of a complete binary tree, you must be sure that the tree remains complete as a result of additions or removals.

Question 1 Represent the binary tree in Figure 15-18 of Chapter 15 with an array.

16.1.2 A Link-Based Representation

You can use C++ pointers to link the nodes in the tree. Doing so is the most common way of implementing a tree. Listing 16-2 shows the class `BinaryNode` for a link-based implementation of the ADT binary tree.

LISTING 16-2 The header file containing the class `BinaryNode` for a link-based implementation of the ADT binary tree

```
1   /** A class of nodes for a link-based binary tree.
2    @file BinaryNode.h */
3
4   #ifndef BINARY_NODE_
5   #define BINARY_NODE_
6   #include <memory>
7
8   template<class ItemType>
9   class BinaryNode
10  {
11  private:
12     ItemType                                  item;        // Data portion
13     std::shared_ptr<BinaryNode<ItemType>> leftChildPtr;  // Pointer to left child
14     std::shared_ptr<BinaryNode<ItemType>> rightChildPtr; // Pointer to right child
15
16  public:
17     BinaryNode();
18     BinaryNode(const ItemType& anItem);
19     BinaryNode(const ItemType& anItem,
20                std::shared_ptr<BinaryNode<ItemType>> leftPtr,
21                std::shared_ptr<BinaryNode<ItemType>> rightPtr);
22
23     void setItem(const ItemType& anItem);
24     ItemType getItem() const;
25
26     bool isLeaf() const;
27
28     auto getLeftChildPtr() const;
29     auto getRightChildPtr() const;
30
31     void setLeftChildPtr(std::shared_ptr<BinaryNode<ItemType>> leftPtr);
32     void setRightChildPtr(std::shared_ptr<BinaryNode<ItemType>> rightPtr);
33  }; // end BinaryNode
34
35  #include "BinaryNode.cpp"
36  #endif
```

FIGURE 16-2   A link-based implementation of a binary tree

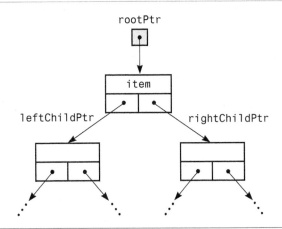

Given the class `BinaryNode` in Listing 16-2, a class of link-based binary trees will declare one data member—a pointer `rootPtr`—to point to the tree's root node. If the tree is empty, `rootPtr` contains `nullptr`. For a binary tree that is not empty, `rootPtr->getLeftChildPtr()` points to the root's left subtree, and `rootPtr->getRightChildPtr()` points to the root's right subtree. If either of these subtrees is empty, the pointer to it would be `nullptr`. Figure 16-2 illustrates the root of a binary tree and its two children.

16.2 A Link-Based Implementation of the ADT Binary Tree

We will derive our class of link-based binary trees from `BinaryTreeInterface`, which specifies the public methods for the ADT binary tree and appears in Listing 15-1 of Chapter 15. The nodes in the tree will be instances of the class `BinaryNode` as given previously in Listing 16-2.

16.2.1 The Header File

The header file in Listing 16-3 declares the class `BinaryNodeTree` in anticipation of its link-based implementation. Note the protected methods that the public methods will call to perform their operations recursively. These methods require pointers as arguments. As such, they should not be public and available to clients of the class. After all, clients should not have access to node pointers. Although these methods could be private, they are protected so that a derived class can use them.

> Some methods should not be public

The public section declares more constructors than we have in the past, allowing a client to define binary trees in a variety of circumstances. For example, you can construct a binary tree

- That is empty
- From data for its root, which is its only node
- From data for its root and from its two subtrees

For example, the following statements invoke these three constructors:

```
BinaryNodeTree<std::string> tree1;
auto tree2Ptr = std::make_shared<BinaryNodeTree<std::string>>("A");
auto tree3Ptr = std::make_shared<BinaryNodeTree<std::string>>("B");
auto tree4Ptr = std::make_unique<BinaryNodeTree<std::string>>("C",
                                                    tree2Ptr, tree3Ptr);
```

> Sample uses of public constructors

In this example, tree1 is an empty binary tree; tree2Ptr and tree3Ptr each point to binary trees that have only a root node. These two roots contain the strings "A" and "B", respectively; and tree4Ptr points to a binary tree whose root contains "C" and has subtrees pointed to by tree2Ptr and tree3Ptr.

Programming Tip: In the previous example, if you were to use BinaryTreeInterface instead of BinaryNodeTree in the data type of either tree2Ptr or tree3Ptr, you would have to cast the variable to BinaryNodeTree before you could call the third constructor. For example, suppose you defined treePtr2 as follows:

```
BinaryTreeInterface<std::string> tree2Ptr = std::make_shared<BinaryNodeTree<std::string>>("A");
```

You would then define treePtr4 as follows:

```
auto arg2 = std::dynamic_pointer_cast<BinaryNodeTree<std::string>>(tree2Ptr);
auto tree4Ptr = std::make_unique<BinaryNodeTree<std::string>>("C", arg2, tree3Ptr);
```

LISTING 16-3   A header file for the link-based implementation of the class BinaryNodeTree

```
1   /** ADT binary tree: Link-based implementation.
2    @file BinaryNodeTree.h */
3
4   #ifndef BINARY_NODE_TREE_
5   #define BINARY_NODE_TREE_
6
7   #include "BinaryTreeInterface.h"
8   #include "BinaryNode.h"
9   #include "PrecondViolatedExcept.h"
10  #include "NotFoundException.h"
11  #include <memory>
12
13  template<class ItemType>
14  class BinaryNodeTree : public BinaryTreeInterface<ItemType>
15  {
16  private:
17     std::shared_ptr<BinaryNode<ItemType>> rootPtr;
18
19  protected:
20  //-------------------------------------------------------------
21  //      Protected Utility Methods Section:
22  //      Recursive helper methods for the public methods.
23  //-------------------------------------------------------------
24     int getHeightHelper(std::shared_ptr<BinaryNode<ItemType>> subTreePtr) const;
25     int getNumberOfNodesHelper(std::shared_ptr<BinaryNode<ItemType>> subTreePtr) const;
26
27     // Recursively adds a new node to the tree in a left/right fashion to keep tree balanced.
28     auto balancedAdd(std::shared_ptr<BinaryNode<ItemType>> subTreePtr,
29                      std::shared_ptr<BinaryNode<ItemType>> newNodePtr);
```

```
30
31       // Removes the target value from the tree.
32       virtual auto removeValue(std::shared_ptr<BinaryNode<ItemType>> subTreePtr,
33                                          const ItemType target, bool& isSuccessful);
34
35       // Copies values up the tree to overwrite value in current node until
36       // a leaf is reached; the leaf is then removed, since its value is stored in the parent.
37       auto moveValuesUpTree(std::shared_ptr<BinaryNode<ItemType>> subTreePtr);
38
39       // Recursively searches for target value.
40       virtual auto findNode(std::shared_ptr<BinaryNode<ItemType>> treePtr,
41                                          const ItemType& target, bool& isSuccessful) const;
42
43       // Copies the tree rooted at treePtr and returns a pointer to the root of the copy.
44       auto copyTree(const std::shared_ptr<BinaryNode<ItemType>> oldTreeRootPtr) const;
45
46       // Recursively deletes all nodes from the tree.
47       void destroyTree(std::shared_ptr<BinaryNode<ItemType>> subTreePtr);
48
49       // Recursive traversal helper methods:
50       void preorder(void visit(ItemType&), std::shared_ptr<BinaryNode<ItemType>> treePtr) const;
51       void inorder(void visit(ItemType&), std::shared_ptr<BinaryNode<ItemType>> treePtr) const;
52       void postorder(void visit(ItemType&), std::shared_ptr<BinaryNode<ItemType>> treePtr) const;
53
54   public:
55       //-------------------------------------------------------------
56       //       Constructor and Destructor Section.
57       //-------------------------------------------------------------
58       BinaryNodeTree();
59       BinaryNodeTree(const ItemType& rootItem);
60       BinaryNodeTree(const ItemType& rootItem,
61                      const std::shared_ptr<BinaryNodeTree<ItemType>> leftTreePtr,
62                      const std::shared_ptr<BinaryNodeTree<ItemType>> rightTreePtr);
63       BinaryNodeTree(const std::shared_ptr<BinaryNodeTree<ItemType>>& tree);
64       virtual ~BinaryNodeTree();
65
66       //-------------------------------------------------------------
67       //       Public BinaryTreeInterface Methods Section.
68       //-------------------------------------------------------------
69       bool isEmpty() const;
70       int getHeight() const;
71       int getNumberOfNodes() const;
72       ItemType getRootData() const throw(PrecondViolatedExcept);
73       void setRootData(const ItemType& newData);
74       bool add(const ItemType& newData); // Adds an item to the tree
75       bool remove(const ItemType& data); // Removes specified item from the tree
76       void clear();
77       ItemType getEntry(const ItemType& anEntry) const throw(NotFoundException);
78       bool contains(const ItemType& anEntry) const;
```

(continues)

```
79
80    //-------------------------------------------------------------
81    //        Public Traversals Section.
82    //-------------------------------------------------------------
83      void preorderTraverse(void visit(ItemType&)) const;
84      void inorderTraverse(void visit(ItemType&)) const;
85      void postorderTraverse(void visit(ItemType&)) const;
86
87    //-------------------------------------------------------------
88    //        Overloaded Operator Section.
89    //-------------------------------------------------------------
90      BinaryNodeTree& operator=(const BinaryNodeTree& rightHandSide);
91    }; // end BinaryNodeTree
92
93    #include "BinaryNodeTree.cpp"
94    #endif
```

An overloaded
assignment
operator

BinaryNodeTree declares an overloaded assignment operator. You could also, of course, overload other operators.

16.2.2 The Implementation

Although we will not provide a complete implementation file here, we will examine its most significant portions.

The constructors. The public constructors have the following definitions in the implementation file:

```
template<class ItemType>
BinaryNodeTree<ItemType>::BinaryNodeTree() : rootPtr(nullptr)
{
} // end default constructor

template<class ItemType>
BinaryNodeTree<ItemType>::
BinaryNodeTree(const ItemType& rootItem)
     :rootPtr(std::make_shared<BinaryNode<ItemType>>(rootItem, nullptr, nullptr))
{
}   // end constructor

template<class ItemType>
BinaryNodeTree<ItemType>::
BinaryNodeTree(const ItemType& rootItem,
               const std::shared_ptr<BinaryNodeTree<ItemType>> leftTreePtr,
               const std::shared_ptr<BinaryNodeTree<ItemType>> rightTreePtr)
  :rootPtr(std::make_shared<BinaryNode<ItemType>>(rootItem,
                                                  copyTree(leftTreePtr->rootPtr),
                                                  copyTree(rightTreePtr->rootPtr))

{
}   // end constructor
```

The default constructor sets the value of rootPtr to nullptr. The second constructor sets root-Ptr to point to a new node containing the given data item. The third constructor also makes rootPtr point to a new node, but the node contains the given data item and pointers to copies of the given subtrees. We talk about the method copyTree next during our discussion of the copy constructor.

The copy constructor and destructor. The copy constructor and the destructor implicitly use traversal. Since traversal is a recursive operation, the copy constructor and destructor each call a recursive method. As we have mentioned before, public ADT methods usually are not themselves recursive, but rather call a recursive method that is either private or protected. We do this to hide the underlying data structure from the client.

The protected method `copyTree`, which the copy constructor calls, uses a recursive preorder traversal to copy each node in the tree. By copying each node as soon as the traversal visits it, `copyTree` can make an exact copy of the original tree. To make the copy distinct from the original tree, the new nodes must be linked together by using new pointers. That is, you cannot simply copy the pointers in the nodes of the original tree. The result is a deep copy of the tree.

Thus, `copyTree` has the following definition:

> To copy a tree, traverse it in preorder and add each data item visited to a new node

```cpp
template<class ItemType>
std::shared_ptr<BinaryNode<ItemType>> BinaryNodeTree<ItemType>::copyTree(
      const std::shared_ptr<BinaryNode<ItemType>> oldTreeRootPtr) const
{
   std::shared_ptr<BinaryNode<ItemType>> newTreePtr;

   // Copy tree nodes during a preorder traversal
   if (oldTreeRootPtr != nullptr)
   {
      // Copy node
      newTreePtr = std::make_shared<BinaryNode<ItemType>>(oldTreeRootPtr->getItem(),
                                             nullptr, nullptr);
      newTreePtr->setLeftChildPtr(copyTree(oldTreeRootPtr->getLeftChildPtr()));
      newTreePtr->setRightChildPtr(copyTree(oldTreeRootPtr->getRightChildPtr()));
   } // end if
   // Else tree is empty (newTreePtr is nullptr)

   return newTreePtr;
} // end copyTree
```

The copy constructor then looks like this:

```cpp
template<class ItemType>
BinaryNodeTree<ItemType>::
                  BinaryNodeTree(const BinaryNodeTree<ItemType>& treePtr)
{
   rootPtr = copyTree(treePtr.rootPtr);
} // end copy constructor
```

Similarly, the protected method `destroyTree`, which the destructor calls, uses a recursive postorder traversal to delete each node in the tree. A postorder traversal is appropriate here because you can delete a node only after you have first traversed and deleted both of its subtrees. Thus, `destroyTree` has the following definition:

```cpp
template<class ItemType>
void BinaryNodeTree<ItemType>::
   destroyTree(std::shared_ptr<BinaryNode<ItemType>> subTreePtr)
{
   if (subTreePtr != nullptr)
   {
      destroyTree(subTreePtr->getLeftChildPtr());
      destroyTree(subTreePtr->getRightChildPtr());
      subTreePtr.reset(); // Decrement reference count to node
   } // end if
} // end destroyTree
```

The destructor then only needs to make the call `destroyTree(rootPtr)`.

The method getHeight. The public method getHeight calls the protected, recursive method getHeightHelper. The height of a subtree rooted at a particular node is 1—for the node itself—plus the height of the node's tallest subtree. Thus, we define the protected method getHeightHelper as follows:

```
template<class ItemType>
int BinaryNodeTree<ItemType>::
    getHeightHelper(std::shared_ptr<BinaryNode<ItemType>> subTreePtr) const
{
    if (subTreePtr == nullptr)
        return 0;
    else
        return 1 + max(getHeightHelper(subTreePtr->getLeftChildPtr()),
                       getHeightHelper(subTreePtr->getRightChildPtr()));
}  // end getHeightHelper
```

The public method getHeight contains just the statement

```
return getHeightHelper(rootPtr);
```

The method getNumberOfNodes has a similar definition.

Question 2 What are the definitions of the public method getNumberOfNodes and the protected helper method getNumberOfNodesHelper?

Question 3 What is the definition of the public method setRootData?

Question 4 What is the definition of the public method getRootData? Recall that this method has a precondition.

The method add. The specification of the public method add says to add a given data item to a binary tree. It does not indicate where that new data should be in the tree. Thus, we have flexibility in how we define the method. Moreover, derived classes of BinaryNodeTree can both override add to change its behavior and adhere to its specification.

Let's place the given data item in a new node and add this node to the tree so that the resulting tree is balanced. Once again, we can use recursion to achieve our goal. The public method add can create a new node containing the data passed to it as an argument. Then the method can pass this node to a protected, recursive method that adds it in an appropriate place in the tree. The protected method must then return a pointer to the tree's root. If we name the protected method balancedAdd, the public add method has the following definition:

```
template<class ItemType>
bool BinaryNodeTree<ItemType>::add(const ItemType& newData)
{
    auto newNodePtr = std::make_shared<BinaryNode<ItemType>>(newData);
    rootPtr = balancedAdd(rootPtr, newNodePtr);

    return true;
}  // end add
```

Now we need to define the protected method balancedAdd. Notice that the add method passes two arguments to balancedAdd: a pointer to the root of the tree—or subtree—to which we will add a node and a pointer to the new node. To add a node to the tree, we add the node to the root's shorter subtree. This is the recursive step, since the subtree is a binary tree. The base case occurs when a subtree is empty.

Here is the definition of balancedAdd:

```cpp
template<class ItemType>
auto BinaryNodeTree<ItemType>::
    balancedAdd(std::shared_ptr<BinaryNode<ItemType>> subTreePtr,
                std::shared_ptr<BinaryNode<ItemType>> newNodePtr)
{
   if (subTreePtr == nullptr)
      return newNodePtr;
   else
   {
      auto leftPtr = subTreePtr->getLeftChildPtr();
      auto rightPtr = subTreePtr->getRightChildPtr();

      if (getHeightHelper(leftPtr) > getHeightHelper(rightPtr))
      {
         rightPtr = balancedAdd(rightPtr, newNodePtr);
         subTreePtr->setRightChildPtr(rightPtr);
      }
      else
      {
         leftPtr = balancedAdd(leftPtr, newNodePtr);
         subTreePtr->setLeftChildPtr(leftPtr);
      } // end if

      return subTreePtr;
   } // end if
} // end balancedAdd
```

For example, the following statements in balancedAdd add a new node to a right subtree:

```cpp
rightPtr = balancedAdd(rightPtr, newNodePtr);
subTreePtr->setRightChildPtr(rightPtr);
```

The recursive call to balancedAdd adds the new node and returns a pointer to the revised subtree. However, we need to link this subtree to the rest of the tree. The call to setRightChildPtr accomplishes this. The addition of a new node to a left subtree is performed in a similar manner. Note that such additions are analogous to the recursive addition of a new node to a linear chain of linked nodes, as discussed in Section 9.2.3 of Chapter 9. Reviewing that section will give you insight into the process here.

Figure 16-3 shows the effect of a sequence of add operations on an initially empty binary tree.

Question 5 Where would a new node be placed next in the binary tree shown in Figure 16-3?

The traversals. Since the traversals are recursive, the public traversal methods each call a protected method that performs the actual recursion. For example, the public method inorder-Traverse calls the protected method inorder. Like inorderTraverse, inorder has the function visit as a parameter. This function specifies the tree item as a reference parameter, which enables the client not only to examine the item but also to modify it. The second parameter of

Implement traversals so that visit remains on the client's side of the wall

FIGURE 16-3   Adding nodes to an initially empty binary tree

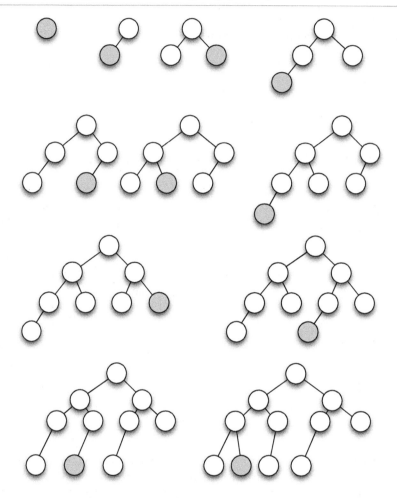

inorder is the pointer `treePtr`, which, due to the recursive calls, eventually points to every node in the tree. The definition of inorder follows:

Protected methods that enable recursive traversals

```
template<class ItemType>
void BinaryNodeTree<ItemType>::
    inorder(void visit(ItemType&),
            std::shared_ptr<BinaryNode<ItemType>> treePtr) const
{
   if (treePtr != nullptr)
   {
      inorder(visit, treePtr->getLeftChildPtr());
      ItemType theItem = treePtr->getItem();
      visit(theItem);
      inorder(visit, treePtr->getRightChildPtr());
   }  // end if
}  // end inorder
```

Now the definition of the public method `inorderTraverse` contains only the call

```
inorder(visit, rootPtr);
```

The other traversals have similar definitions.

Programming Tip: Why did we write

```
ItemType theItem = treePtr->getItem();
visit(theItem);
```

instead of

```
visit(treePtr->getItem());
```

in the definition of `inorder`? Because `visit` has a reference parameter, we need an lvalue to reference. The variable `theItem` serves this purpose.

Note: The client's `visit` method can modify the tree's data but not its structure. The client always owns the data it stores, therefore `visit` does not break the wall between the client and the tree. The integrity of the tree is not damaged.

Question 6 Define the protected method `postorder`.

Nonrecursive traversal (optional). Before leaving the topic of traversals, let's develop a nonrecursive traversal algorithm to illustrate further the relationship between stacks and recursion that was discussed in Chapter 6. In particular, we will develop a nonrecursive inorder traversal for the link-based implementation of a binary tree.

The conceptually difficult part of a nonrecursive traversal is determining where to go next after a particular node has been visited. To gain some insight into this problem, consider how the recursive `inorder` method works:

```
if (treePtr != nullptr)
{
   inorder(visit, treePtr->getLeftChildPtr());   // Point 1
   ItemType theItem = treePtr->getItem();
   visit(theItem);
   inorder(visit, treePtr->getRightChildPtr()); // Point 2
}  // end if
```

Recursive calls from points 1 and 2

The method has its recursive calls marked as points 1 and 2.

During the course of the method's execution, the value of the pointer `treePtr` actually marks the current position in the tree. Each time `inorder` makes a recursive call, the traversal moves to another node. In terms of the stack that is implicit to recursive methods, a call to `inorder` pushes the new value of `treePtr`—that is, a pointer to the new current node—onto the stack. At any given time, the stack contains pointers to the nodes along the path from the tree's root to the current node

Recursive
inorder's implicit
stack gives insight
into a nonrecursive
traversal

n, with the pointer to *n* at the top of the stack and the pointer to the root at the bottom. Note that *n* is possibly "empty"—that is, it may be indicated by a nullptr value for treePtr at the top of the stack. Such an occurrence corresponds to the base case of the recursion.

Figure 16-4 partially traces the execution of inorder and shows the contents of the implicit stack. The first four steps of the trace show the stack as treePtr points first to 60, then to 20, then to 10, and then becomes nullptr. The recursive calls for these four steps are from point 1 in inorder.

FIGURE 16-4 Contents of the implicit stack as treePtr progresses through a given tree during a recursive inorder traversal

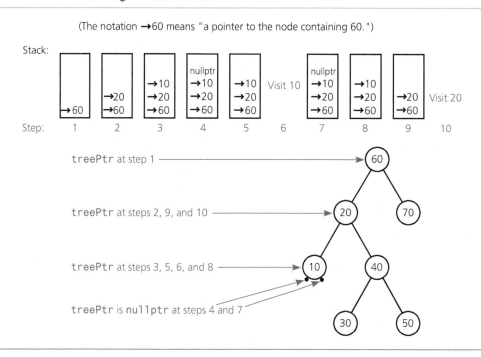

Now consider what happens when inorder returns from a recursive call. The traversal retraces its steps by backing up the tree from a node *n* to its parent *p*, from which the recursive call to *n* was made. Thus, the pointer to *n* is popped from the stack and the pointer to *p* comes to the top of the stack, as occurs in step 5 of the trace in Figure 16-4. In this case, *n* happens to be empty, so nullptr is popped from the stack.

What happens next depends on which subtree of *p* has just been traversed. If you have just finished traversing *p*'s left subtree—that is, if *n* is the left child of *p* and thus the return is made to point 1 in inorder—control is returned to the statement that visits node *p*. Such is the case for steps 6 and 10 of the trace in Figure 16-4. Figure 16-5a illustrates steps 9 and 10 in more detail.

After node *p* has been visited, a recursive call is made from point 2 and the right subtree of *p* is traversed. However, if, as Figure 16-5b illustrates, you have just traversed *p*'s right subtree—that is, if *n* is the right child of *p* and thus the return is made to point 2—control is returned to the end of the method. As a consequence another return is made, the pointer to *p* is popped off the stack, and you go back up the tree to *p*'s parent, from which the recursive call to *p* was made. In this latter case, node *p* is not visited—it was visited before the recursive call to *n* was made from point 2.

FIGURE 16-5   Steps during an inorder traversal of the subtrees of 20

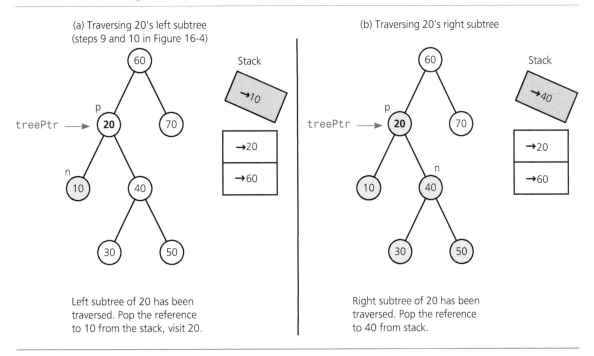

(a) Traversing 20's left subtree
(steps 9 and 10 in Figure 16-4)

Left subtree of 20 has been
traversed. Pop the reference
to 10 from the stack, visit 20.

(b) Traversing 20's right subtree

Right subtree of 20 has been
traversed. Pop the reference
to 40 from stack.

Thus, two facts emerge from the recursive version of inorder when a return is made from a recursive call:

> Actions upon a return from a recursive call to inorder

- The implicit recursive stack of pointers is used to find the node p that the traversal must go back to.
- Once the traversal backs up to node p, it either visits p (for example, displays its data) or backs farther up the tree. It visits p if p's left subtree has just been traversed; it backs up if its right subtree has just been traversed. The appropriate action is taken simply as a consequence of the point—1 or 2—to which control is returned.

You could directly mimic this action by using an iterative method and an explicit stack, as long as some bookkeeping device kept track of which subtree of a node had just been traversed. However, you can use the following observation both to eliminate the need for the bookkeeping device and to speed up the traversal somewhat. Consider the tree in Figure 16-6. After you have finished traversing the subtree rooted at node R, there is no need to return to nodes C and B, because the right subtrees of these nodes have already been traversed. You can instead return directly to node A, which is the nearest ancestor of R whose right subtree has not yet been traversed.

This strategy of not returning to a node after its right subtree has been traversed is simple to implement: You place a pointer to a node in the stack only before the node's left subtree is traversed, but not before its right subtree is traversed. Thus, in Figure 16-6, when you are at node R, the stack contains A and R, with R on top. Nodes B and C are not in the stack, because you have visited them already and are currently traversing their right subtrees. On the other hand, A is in the stack because you are currently traversing its left subtree. When you return from node R, nodes B and C are thus bypassed because you have finished with their right subtrees and do not need to return to these nodes. Thus, you pop R's pointer from the stack and go directly to node A, whose left subtree has just been traversed. You then visit A, pop its pointer from the stack, and traverse A's right subtree.

FIGURE 16-6   Avoiding returns to nodes *B* and *C*

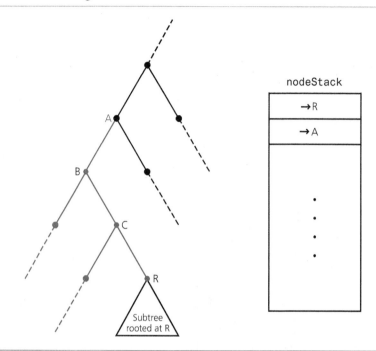

Nonrecursive
inorder traversal

This nonrecursive traversal strategy is captured by the following pseudocode, assuming a link-based implementation. Exercise 9 at the end of this chapter asks you to trace this algorithm for the tree in Figure 16-4.

```
// Nonrecursively traverses a binary tree in inorder.
traverse(visit(item: ItemType): void): void
{
    // Initialize
    nodeStack = A new, empty stack
    curPtr = rootPtr // Start at root
    done = false

    while (!done)
    {
        if (curPtr != nullptr)
        {
            // Place pointer to node on stack before traversing the node's left subtree
            nodeStack.push(curPtr)

            // Traverse the left subtree
            curPtr = curPtr->getLeftChildPtr()
        }
        else  // Backtrack from the empty subtree and visit the node at the top of
              // the stack; however, if the stack is empty, you are done
        {
            done = nodeStack.isEmpty()
```

```
            if (!done)
            {
                curPtr = nodeStack.peek()
                visit(curPtr->getItem())
                nodeStack.pop()

                // Traverse the right subtree of the node just visited
                curPtr = curPtr ->getRightChildPtr()
            }
        }
    }
}
```

Eliminating recursion can be more complicated than the example given here. However, the general case is beyond the scope of this book.

16.3 A Link-Based Implementation of the ADT Binary Search Tree

VideoNote
Overview of
BinarySearchTree

Since a binary search tree is a binary tree, its implementation can use the same node objects as for a binary-tree implementation. As we plan a link-based implementation, we will use the class BinaryNode, as given earlier in Listing 16-2.

The recursive search algorithm that we presented in Section 15.3.2 of Chapter 15 is the basis of the addition, removal, and retrieval operations on a binary search tree. The algorithms that follow for the binary search tree operations assume the link-based implementation of a binary tree that was discussed earlier in this chapter. Also keep in mind the assumption that the data items in the binary search tree are unique.

16.3.1 Algorithms for the ADT Binary Search Tree Operations

Adding a new entry. As Section 15.3.3 of Chapter 15 demonstrated, you add a new entry to a binary search tree in the same place that the search algorithm would look for it. For example, if

Use search to determine where to add data

FIGURE 16-7   Adding Kody to a binary search tree

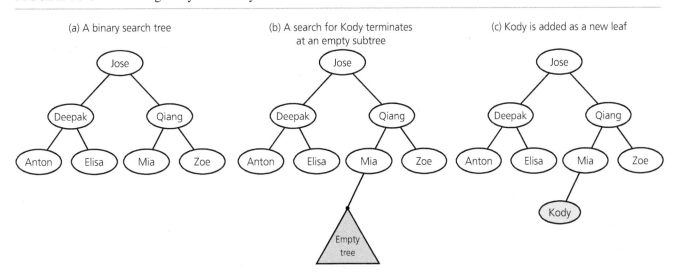

you want to add Kody to the binary search tree shown in Figure 16-7a, you would first search the tree for Kody. The `search` algorithm would terminate at Mia's empty left subtree, as Figure 16-7b illustrates. You would then place Kody as Mia's left child, as Figure 16-7c shows.

Because Mia has no left child, the addition is simple, requiring only that Mia's left-child pointer point to a new node that contains Kody. Because searching for an entry that is not in the binary search tree always ends at an empty subtree, you always add a new data item in a new leaf. Because adding a leaf requires only a change of the appropriate pointer in the parent, the work required for an addition is virtually the same as that for the corresponding search.

We begin by defining the public method `add` as follows:

```
template<class ItemType>
bool BinarySearchTree<ItemType>::add(const ItemType& newData)
{
    auto newNodePtr = std::make_shared<BinaryNode<ItemType>>(newData);
    rootPtr = placeNode(rootPtr, newNodePtr);

    return true;
}  // end add
```

The method creates a new node and passes pointers to the tree and the new node to a recursive method that actually adds the node to the tree. The following high-level pseudocode describes this process:

First draft of the addition algorithm

```
// Places a given new node at its proper position in a binary search tree.
placeNode(subTreePtr: BinaryNodePointer,
          newNodePtr: BinaryNodePointer): BinaryNodePointer
{
    Search the tree to which subTreePtr points for the item in the node pointed
        to by newNodePtr
    if (the search terminates at the left subtree of the node to which parentNode points)
        Set leftChildPtr of parentNode to newNodePtr
    else
        Set rightChildPtr of parentNode to newNodePtr
}
```

The appropriate pointer—`leftChildPtr` or `rightChildPtr`—of node `parentNode` must be set to point to the new node. The recursive nature of the `search` algorithm provides an elegant means of setting the pointer, provided that you return this possibly changed pointer. The situation is quite similar to the recursive `add` method for the ADT list that you saw in Chapter 9. If the tree was empty before the addition, the external pointer to the root of the tree would be `nullptr` and the method would not make a recursive call. Thus, you would return a pointer to the new node. Our pseudocode is refined as follows:

Refinement of the addition algorithm

```
// Recursively places a given new node at its proper position in a binary search tree.
placeNode(subTreePtr: BinaryNodePointer,
          newNodePtr: BinaryNodePointer): BinaryNodePointer
{
    if (subTreePtr is nullptr)
        return newNodePtr
    else if (subTreePtr->getItem() > newNodePtr->getItem())
    {
        tempPtr = placeNode(subTreePtr->getLeftChildPtr(), newNodePtr);
        subTreePtr->setLeftChildPtr(tempPtr);
    }
    else
    {
```

```
        tempPtr = placeNode(subTreePtr->getRightChildPtr(), newNodePtr)
        subTreePtr->setRightChildPtr(tempPtr)
    }
    return subTreePtr
}
```

When `subTreePtr` is `nullptr`, `placeNode` returns a pointer to the new node. For an initially empty tree, `add` assigns the returned pointer to `rootPtr`, as Figure 16-8a illustrates. For a tree that is not empty, `add` assigns the returned pointer to either of the pointers `leftChildPtr` or `rightChildPtr`—whose current value is `nullptr`—in the parent of the empty subtree. Thus, the appropriate pointer within the parent is set to point to the new node. Parts *b* and *c* of Figure 16-8 illustrate the general case of an addition.

You can use the public method `add` to create a binary search tree. For example, beginning with an empty tree, if you add the names Jose, Deepak, Anton, Elisa, Qiang, Mia, and Zoe in order, you will get the binary search tree in Figure 15-13 of Chapter 15. It is interesting to note that the names Jose, Deepak, Anton, Elisa, Qiang, Mia, and Zoe constitute the preorder traversal of the tree in Figure 15-13. Thus, if you take the output of a preorder traversal of a binary search tree and use it with `placeNode` to create a binary search tree, you will obtain a duplicate tree. This result should not surprise you, as the copy constructor for the ADT binary tree used a preorder traversal to copy the tree.

By adding the previous names in a different order, you will get a different binary search tree. For example, by adding the previous names in alphabetical order, you will get the binary search tree in Figure 15-14b of Chapter 15.

 Question 7 Starting with an empty binary search tree, in what order should you add data items to get the binary search tree in Figure 15-18 of Chapter 15?

FIGURE 16-8   Adding new data to a binary search tree

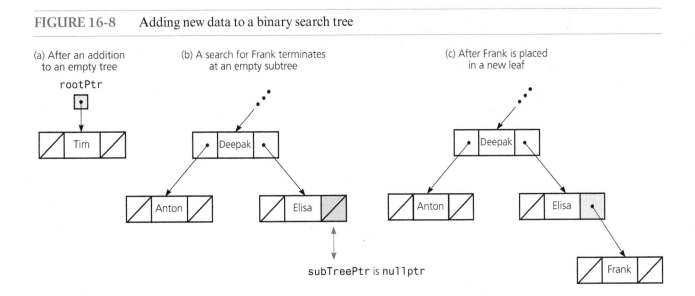

First draft of the
removal algorithm

Removing an entry. Removing an entry from a binary search tree is a bit more involved than adding one. First, you use the search algorithm to locate the specified item and then, if it is found, you must remove it from the tree. A first draft of the algorithm follows:

```
// Removes the given target from a binary search tree.
// Returns true if the removal is successful or false otherwise.
removeValue(target: ItemType): boolean
{
    Locate the target by using the search algorithm
    if (target is found)
    {
        Remove target from the tree
        return true
    }
    else
        return false
}
```

The essential task here is to remove the target from the tree. Assuming that removeValue locates the target in a particular node N, there are three cases to consider:

Three cases for the
node N containing
the item to be
removed

- N is a leaf
- N has only one child
- N has two children

Case 1: Set the
pointer in a leaf's
parent to nullptr

Case 1. The first case is the easiest. To remove the leaf containing the target, you need only set the pointer in its parent to nullptr.

Case 2: Two
possibilities for a
node with one child

Case 2. The second case is a bit more involved. If N has only one child, you have two possibilities:

- N has only a left child
- N has only a right child

Let N's parent adopt
N's child

The two possibilities are symmetrical, so it is sufficient to illustrate the solution for a left child. In Figure 16-9a, L is the left child of N and P is the parent of N. N can be either the left or right child of P. If you removed N from the tree, L would be without a parent and P would be without one of its children. Suppose you let L take the place of N as one of P's children, as in Figure 16-9b. Does this adoption preserve the binary search tree property?

If N is the left child of P, for example, all data items in the subtree rooted at N are less than the item in P. Thus, all data items in the subtree rooted at L are less than the item in P. Therefore, after N is removed and L is adopted by P, all items in P's left subtree are still less than the item in P. This strategy thus preserves the binary search tree property. A parallel argument holds if N is a right child of P, and therefore the binary search tree property is preserved in either case.

Case 3: N has two
children

Case 3. The most difficult of the three cases occurs when the item to be removed is in a node N that has two children, as in Figure 16-10. As you just saw, when N has only one child, the child replaces N. However, when N has two children, these children cannot both replace N: N's parent has room for only one of N's children as a replacement for N. A different strategy is necessary.

In fact, you will not remove N at all. You can find another node that is easier to remove and remove it instead of N. This strategy may sound like cheating, but remember that the client expects only a certain entry to be removed from the ADT. It has no right, because of the wall between the program and the ADT implementation, to expect a particular *node* in the tree to be removed.

Consider, then, an alternate strategy. To remove from a binary search tree a data item that resides in a node N that has two children, take the following steps:

Removing a data
item whose node
has two children

1. Locate another node M that is easier to remove from the tree than the node N.
2. Copy the item that is in M to N, thus effectively removing from the tree the item originally in N.
3. Remove the node M from the tree.

FIGURE 16-9   Case 2 for `removeValue`: The data item to remove is in a node *N* that has only a left child and whose parent is node *P*

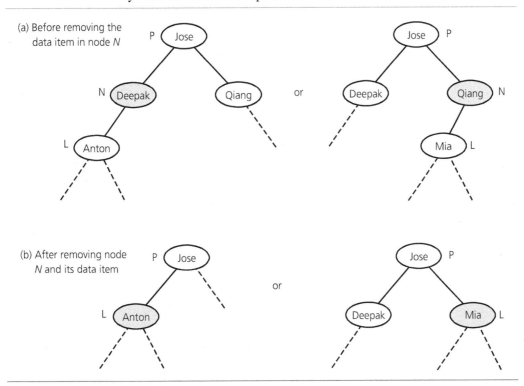

(a) Before removing the data item in node *N*

or

(b) After removing node *N* and its data item

or

What kind of node *M* is easier to remove than the node *N*? Because you know how to remove a node that has either no children or one child, *M* could be such a node. You have to be careful, though. Can you choose any node and copy its data into *N*? No, because you must preserve the tree's status as a binary search tree. For example, if in the tree of Figure 16-11a, you copied the data from *M* to *N*, the result in Figure 16-11b would no longer be a binary search tree.

What data item, when copied into the node *N*, will preserve the tree's status as a binary search tree? All of the entries in the left subtree of *N* are less than the entry in *N*, and all of the entries in the right subtree of *N* are greater than the entry in *N*. You must retain this property when you replace the

FIGURE 16-10   Case 3: The data item to remove is in a node *N* that has two children

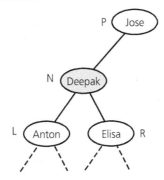

FIGURE16-11   Not any node will do

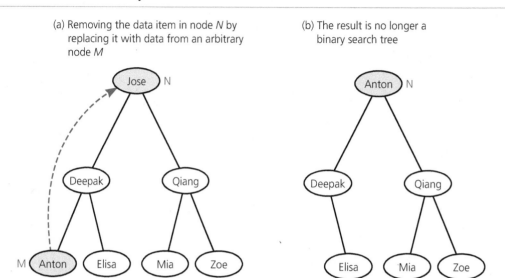

(a) Removing the data item in node *N* by replacing it with data from an arbitrary node *M*

(b) The result is no longer a binary search tree

entry x in node N with the entry y. There are two suitable possibilities for the value y: It can come immediately after or immediately before x in the sorted order of entries. If y comes immediately after x, clearly all entries in the left subtree of N are smaller than y, because they are all smaller than x, as Figure 16-12 illustrates. Further, all entries in the right subtree of N are greater than or equal to y, because they are greater than x and, by assumption, there are no entries in the tree between x and y. A similar argument illustrates that if y comes immediately before x in the sorted order, it is greater than or equal to all entries in the left subtree of N and smaller than all entries in the right subtree of N.

> **The inorder successor of *N*'s entry is in the leftmost node in *N*'s right subtree**

You can thus copy into N either the data item that is immediately after N's entry or the data item that is immediately before it. Suppose that, arbitrarily, you decide to use the node whose entry y comes immediately after N's entry x. This entry is called x's **inorder successor**.[1] How can you locate this node? Because N has two children, the inorder successor of its data item is in the leftmost node of N's right subtree. That is, to find the node that contains y, you follow N's right-child pointer to its right child C, which must be present because N has two children. You then

FIGURE 16-12   Removing the data item x in node N by replacing it with its inorder successor y

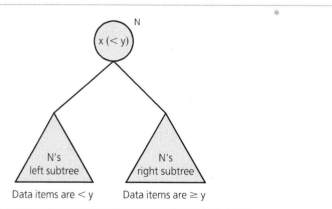

---

[1] We also will use the term *N*'s **inorder successor** to mean the inorder successor of *N*'s entry.

FIGURE 16-13   Replacing the data item in node *N* with its inorder successor

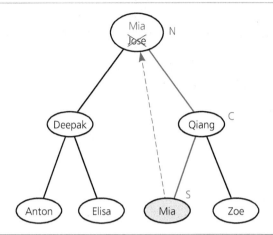

descend the tree rooted at *C* by taking left branches at each node until you encounter a node *S* with no left child. You copy the item in this node *S* into node *N* and then, because *S* has no left child, you can remove *S* from the tree as one of the two easy cases, as Figure 16-13 illustrates.

A more detailed high-level description of the removal algorithm follows:

Second draft of the
removal algorithm

```
// Removes the given target from a binary search tree.
// Returns true if the removal is successful, or false otherwise.
removeValue(subTreePtr: BinaryNodePointer, target: ItemType): boolean
{
    Locate the target by using the search algorithm; it occurs in node N
    if (target is found in node N)
    {
        removeNode(N)  // Defined next
        return true
    }
    else
        return false
}

// Removes the item in a given node of a binary search tree.
removeNode(N: BinaryNode)
{
    if (N is a leaf)
        Remove N from the tree
    else if (N has only one child C)
    {
        if (N was a left child of its parent P)
            Make C the left child of P
        else
            Make C the right child of P
    }
    else  // Node has two children
    {
        Find S, the node that contains N's inorder successor
        Copy the item from node S into node N
        Remove the node S from the tree as you would a leaf or a node with one child
    }
}
```

In the following refinement, search's algorithm is adapted and inserted directly into removeValue. Also, the method removeNode uses the method findSuccesorNode to find the node, *S*, that contains the inorder successor of node *N*. The method findSuccesorNode returns the data item in *S* and then removes node *S* from the tree. The returned item then replaces the data item in node *N*, thus removing it from the binary search tree.

Final draft of the removal algorithm

```
// Removes the given target from the binary search tree to which subTreePtr points.
// Returns a pointer to the node at this tree location after the value is removed.
// Sets isSuccessful to true if the removal is successful, or false otherwise.
removeValue(subTreePtr: BinaryNodePointer, target: ItemType,
            isSuccessful: boolean&): BinaryNodePointer
{
    if (subTreePtr == nullptr)
    {
        isSuccessful = false
    }
    else if (subTreePtr->getItem() == target)
    {
        // Item is in the root of some subtree
        subTreePtr = removeNode(subTreePtr) // Remove the item
        isSuccessful = true
    }
    else if (subTreePtr->getItem() > target)
    {
        // Search the left subtree
        tempPtr = removeValue(subTreePtr->getLeftChildPtr(), target, isSuccessful)
        subTreePtr->setLeftChildPtr(tempPtr)
    }
    else
    {
        // Search the right subtree
        tempPtr = removeValue(subTreePtr->getRightChildPtr(), target, isSuccessful)
        subTreePtr->setRightChildPtr(tempPtr)
    }
    return subTreePtr
}

// Removes the data item in the node, N, to which nodePtr points.
// Returns a pointer to the node at this tree location after the removal.
removeNode(nodePtr: BinaryNodePointer): BinaryNodePointer
{
    if (N is a leaf)
    {
        // Remove leaf from the tree
        Delete the node to which nodePtr points (done for us if nodePtr is a smart pointer)
        return nodePtr
    }
    else if (N has only one child C)
    {
        // C replaces N as the child of N's parent
        if (C is a left child)
            nodeToConnectPtr = nodePtr->getLeftChildPtr()
        else
            nodeToConnectPtr = nodePtr->getRightChildPtr()

        Delete the node to which nodePtr points (done for us if nodePtr is a smart pointer)
        return nodeToConnectPtr
    }
```

```
    else  // N has two children
    {
        // Find the inorder successor of the entry in N: it is in the left subtree rooted
        // at N's right child
        tempPtr = removeLeftmostNode(nodePtr->getRightChildPtr(), newNodeValue)
        nodePtr->setRightChildPtr(tempPtr)
        nodePtr->setItem(newNodeValue)  // Put replacement value in node N
        return nodePtr
    }
}

// Removes the leftmost node in the left subtree of the node pointed to by nodePtr.
// Sets inorderSuccessor to the value in this node.
// Returns a pointer to the revised subtree.
removeLeftmostNode(nodePtr: BinaryNodePointer,
                   inorderSuccessor: ItemType&): BinaryNodePointer
{
    if (nodePtr->getLeftChildPtr() == nullptr)
    {
        // This is the node you want; it has no left child, but it might have a right subtree
        inorderSuccessor = nodePtr->getItem()
        return removeNode(nodePtr)
    }
    else
    {
        tempPtr = removeLeftmostNode(nodePtr->getLeftChildPtr(), inorderSuccessor)
        nodePtr->setLeftChildPtr(tempPtr)
        return nodePtr
    }
}
```

Now the public method `remove` calls `removeValue` and assigns the pointer it receives back from this call to `rootPtr`, as the following pseudocode indicates:

```
// Removes the given data from this binary search tree.
remove(target: ItemType): boolean
{
    isSuccessful = false
    rootPtr = removeValue(rootPtr, target, isSuccessful)
    return isSuccessful
}
```

Let's see how the recursive calls work. Suppose that we have the tree in Figure 16-14a, and we want to remove Dave. We call `remove`, which calls `removeValue`. Assuming that `removeValue` recursively locates Dave in Node *N*, it calls `removeNode` to remove *N*. Any change that `removeNode` makes to its parameter `nodePtr`, is returned by `removeNode` (Figure 16-14b) and then by `removeValue`. Because Dave isn't in the tree's root, the return from `removeValue` is due to a recursive call. The method now assigns the pointer returned by `removeNode`—and the recursive call to `removeValue`—to the left child pointer of node *N*'s parent. The result is shown in Figure 16-14c.

Observe that in the case of the `removeNode` method, the argument that corresponds to its parameter `nodePtr` is either one of the pointers of the parent of *N*, as Figure 16-14 depicts, or the external pointer to the root, in the case where *N* is the root of the original tree. In either case, `nodePtr` points to *N*. Thus, any change you make to `nodePtr` by calling the method `removeNode` with the argument `nodePtr` must be returned so you can change either a pointer in the parent of node *N* or the root pointer.

FIGURE 16-14 Recursive removal of node *N*

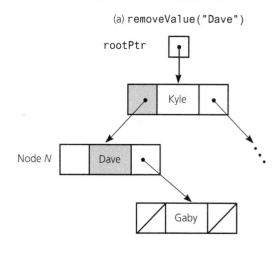

(a) removeValue("Dave")

rootPtr

Kyle

Node *N* Dave

Gaby

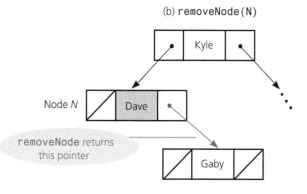

(b) removeNode(N)

Kyle

Node *N* Dave

removeNode returns
this pointer

Gaby

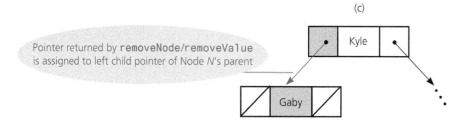

(c)

Pointer returned by removeNode/removeValue
is assigned to left child pointer of Node *N*'s parent

Kyle

Gaby

Security Note: The methods removeValue, removeNode, and removeLeftmostNode
are behind the wall of abstraction, since they are protected. Therefore they can use
pointers as parameters, and if necessary, a reference parameter (isSuccessful or

inorderSuccessor). Each method receives as an argument a pointer to the root of the subtree on which it is to perform its process. When that process is complete, the method returns a pointer to the node that is now the root of that subtree, and the calling method places this pointer in the node's parent.

Note that what we have done is safe programming:

- Only one reference parameter is used in a method, and the argument passed to it is local to the calling method. Thus, any change to the argument's value will be restricted to the method, and will not directly impact the structure of the ADT.
- The calling method has a choice of whether or not to replace the pointer it has passed as an argument with the one returned—which it should do here.
- Each of the three methods performs a single, clearly defined task.

The recursive method removeLeftmostNode, which is called by removeNode if *N* has two children, also uses this strategy to remove the inorder successor of the node containing the item to be removed.

Exercise 12 at the end of this chapter describes an easier removal algorithm. However, that algorithm tends to increase the height of the tree, and, as you will see later, an increase in height can decrease the efficiency of searching the tree.

Question 8 Given the binary search tree in Figure 15-18 of Chapter 15, trace the removal algorithms when removing each of the following values from the tree. Begin with the original tree each time.

    a. 70
    b. 20
    c. 60

Retrieving an entry. By refining the search algorithm, you can implement the operation getEntry. Recall from Section 15.3.2 of Chapter 15 that the search algorithm is

```
// Searches a binary search tree for a given target value.
search(binTree: BinarySearchTree, target: ItemType)
{
   if (binTree is empty)
      The desired item is not found
   else if (target == data item in the root of binTree)
      The desired item is found
   else if (target < data item in the root of binTree)
      search(Left subtree of binTree, target)
   else
      search(Right subtree of binTree, target)
}
```

We can refine this algorithm as follows:

```
// Locates the node in the binary search tree to which subTreePtr points and that contains
// the value target. Returns either a pointer to the located node or nullptr if such a
// node is not found.
findNode(subTreePtr: BinaryNodePointer, target: ItemType): BinaryNodePointer
{
   if (subTreePtr == nullptr)
      return nullptr                        // Not found
```

findNode is a refinement of search

```
        else if (subTreePtr->getItem() == target)
           return subTreePtr;                          // Found
        else if (subTreePtr->getItem() > target)
           // Search left subtree
           return findNode(subTreePtr->getLeftChildPtr(), target)
        else
           // Search right subtree
           return findNode(subTreePtr->getRightChildPtr(), target)
   }
```

The operation getEntry must return the data item with the desired value if it exists; otherwise it must throw an exception NotFoundException. The method, therefore, calls findNode and checks its return value. If the desired target is found, getEntry returns it. If findNode returns nullptr, getEntry throws an exception.

> **Note: Traversals**
>
> The traversals of a binary search tree are the same as the traversals of a binary tree. Recall from Chapter 15 that an inorder traversal of a binary search tree will visit the tree's data items in sorted order.

16.3.2 The Class BinarySearchTree

A C++ link-based definition of the class BinarySearchTree is given in Listing 16-4. Notice the protected methods that implement the recursive algorithms. These methods are not public, because clients do not have access to node pointers. The methods could be private instead, but making them protected enables a derived class to use them directly.

The ADT binary tree and the ADT binary search tree have many methods in common, as Section 15.3.1 of Chapter 15 noted. This observation should not surprise you, as a binary search tree is a binary tree. For this reason, we have derived BinarySearchTree from BinaryNodeTree.

LISTING 16-4   A header file for the link-based implementation of the class BinarySearchTree

```
1   /** Link-based implementation of the ADT binary search tree.
2    @file BinarySearchTree.h */
3
4   #ifndef BINARY_SEARCH_TREE_
5   #define BINARY_SEARCH_TREE_
6
7   #include "BinaryTreeInterface.h"
8   #include "BinaryNode.h"
9   #include "BinaryNodeTree.h"
10  #include "NotFoundException.h"
11  #include "PrecondViolatedExcept.h"
12  #include <memory>
13
14  template<class ItemType>
15  class BinarySearchTree : public BinaryNodeTree<ItemType>
16  {
17  private:
18     std::shared_ptr<BinaryNode<ItemType>> rootPtr;
```

```
19    protected:
20        //----------------------------------------------------------------
21        //      Protected Utility Methods Section:
22        //      Recursive helper methods for the public methods.
23        //----------------------------------------------------------------
24        // Places a given new node at its proper position in this binary
25        // search tree
26        auto placeNode(std::shared_ptr<BinaryNode<ItemType>> subTreePtr,
27                       std::shared_ptr<BinaryNode<ItemType>> newNode);
28
29        // Removes the given target value from the tree while maintaining a
30        // binary search tree.
31        auto removeValue(std::shared_ptr<BinaryNode<ItemType>> subTreePtr,
32                                    const ItemType target,
33                                    bool& isSuccessful) override;
34
35        // Removes a given node from a tree while maintaining a binary search tree.
36        auto removeNode(std::shared_ptr<BinaryNode<ItemType>> nodePtr);
37
38        // Removes the leftmost node in the left subtree of the node
39        // pointed to by nodePtr.
40        // Sets inorderSuccessor to the value in this node.
41        // Returns a pointer to the revised subtree.
42        auto removeLeftmostNode(std::shared_ptr<BinaryNode<ItemType>>subTreePtr,
43                                            ItemType& inorderSuccessor);
44
45        // Returns a pointer to the node containing the given value,
46        // or nullptr if not found.
47        auto findNode(std::shared_ptr<BinaryNode<ItemType>> treePtr,
48                                const ItemType& target) const;
49
50    public:
51        //----------------------------------------------------------------
52        //      Constructor and Destructor Section.
53        //----------------------------------------------------------------
54        BinarySearchTree();
55        BinarySearchTree(const ItemType& rootItem);
56        BinarySearchTree(const BinarySearchTree<ItemType>& tree);
57        virtual ~BinarySearchTree();
58
59        //----------------------------------------------------------------
60        //      Public Methods Section.
61        //----------------------------------------------------------------
62        bool isEmpty() const;
63        int getHeight() const;
64        int getNumberOfNodes() const;
65        ItemType getRootData() const throw(PrecondViolatedExcept);
66        void setRootData(const ItemType& newData);
67        bool add(const ItemType& newEntry);
68        bool remove(const ItemType& target);
69        void clear();
70        ItemType getEntry(const ItemType& anEntry) const throw(NotFoundException);
```

(continues)

```
71      bool contains(const ItemType& anEntry) const;

72

73      //-------------------------------------------------------------
74      //    Public Traversals Section.
75      //-------------------------------------------------------------
76      void preorderTraverse(void visit(ItemType&)) const;
77      void inorderTraverse(void visit(ItemType&)) const;
78      void postorderTraverse(void visit(ItemType&)) const;

79

80      //-------------------------------------------------------------
81      //    Overloaded Operator Section.
82      //-------------------------------------------------------------
83      BinarySearchTree<ItemType>&
84              operator=(const BinarySearchTree<ItemType>& rightHandSide);
85   }; // end BinarySearchTree
86   #include "BinarySearchTree.cpp"
87   #endif
```

16.4 Saving a Binary Search Tree in a File

Imagine a program that maintains the names, addresses, and telephone numbers of your friends and relatives. While the program is running, you can enter a name and get the person's address and phone number. If you terminate program execution, the program must save its database of people in a form that it can recover at a later time.

 If the program uses a binary search tree to represent the database, it must save the tree's data in a file so that it can later restore the tree. Two different algorithms for saving and restoring a binary search tree will be considered here. The first algorithm restores a binary search tree to its original shape. The second restores a binary search tree to a shape that is balanced.

Saving a binary search tree and then restoring it to its original shape. The first algorithm restores a binary search tree to exactly the same shape it had before it was saved. For example, consider the tree in Figure 16-15. If you save the tree in preorder, you get the sequence 60, 20, 10, 40, 30, 50, 70. If you then use the add method to add these values to a binary search tree that is initially empty, you will get the original tree.

> Use a preorder traversal to save a binary search tree in a file; restore it to its original shape by using add

FIGURE 16-15 An initially empty binary search tree after the addition of 60, 20, 10, 40, 30, 50, and 70

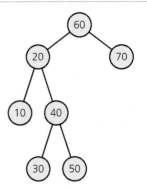

Saving a binary search tree and then restoring it to a balanced shape. After you save a binary search tree in a file, do you necessarily want the restored tree to have its original shape? Recall that you can use a given set of data items to create several binary search trees with different shapes. Although the shape of a binary search tree has no effect whatsoever on the correctness of the ADT operations, it will affect the efficiency of those operations. Efficient operations are ensured if the binary search tree is balanced.

> A balanced binary search tree increases the efficiency of the ADT operations

The algorithm that restores a binary search tree to a balanced shape is surprisingly simple. In fact, you can even guarantee a restored tree of minimum height—a condition stronger than balanced. To gain some insight into the solution, consider a full tree, because it is balanced. If you save a full tree in a file by using an inorder traversal, the file will be in sorted order, as Figure 16-16 illustrates.

A full tree with exactly $n = 2^h - 1$ nodes for some height h has the exact middle of the data items in its root. The left and right subtrees of the root are full trees of $2^{h-1} - 1$ nodes each (that is, half of $n - 1$, as n is odd or, equivalently, $n/2$). Thus, you can use the following recursive algorithm to create a full binary search tree with n nodes, provided you either know or can determine n beforehand.

> Building a full binary search tree

```
// Builds a full binary search tree from n sorted values in a file.
// Returns a pointer to the tree's root.
readFullTree(treePtr: BinaryNodePointer, n: integer): BinaryNodePointer
{
   if (n > 0)
   {
      treePtr = pointer to new node with nullptr as its child pointers

      // Construct the left subtree
      leftPtr = readFullTree(treePtr->getLeftChildPtr(), n / 2)
      treePtr->setLeftChildPtr(leftPtr)

      // Get the data item for this node
      rootItem = next data item from file
      treePtr->setItem(rootItem)

      // Construct the right subtree
      rightPtr = readFullTree(treePtr->getRightChildPtr(), n / 2)
      treePtr->setRightChildPtr(rightPtr)

      return treePtr
   }
   else
      return nullptr
}
```

Surprisingly, you can construct the tree directly by reading the sorted data sequentially from the file.

FIGURE 16-16   A full tree saved in a file by using inorder traversal

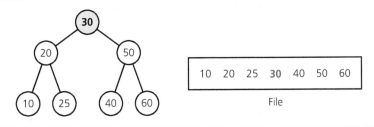

This algorithm for building a full binary search tree is simple, but what can you do if the tree to be restored is not full—that is, if it does not have $n = 2^h - 1$ nodes for some h? The first thing that comes to mind is that the restored tree should be complete—full up to the last level, with the last level filled in from left to right. Actually, because you care only about minimizing the height of the restored tree, it does not matter where the nodes on the last level go, as Figure 16-17 shows.

The method `readFullTree` is essentially correct even if the tree is not full. However, you do have to be a bit careful when computing the sizes of the left and right subtrees of the tree's root. If n is odd, both subtrees are of size $n / 2$, as before, and the root is automatically accounted for. If n is even, however, you have to deal with the root and the fact that one of the root's subtrees will have one more node than the other. In this case, you can arbitrarily choose to put the extra node in the left subtree. The following algorithm makes these compensations:

Building a minimum-height binary search tree

```
// Builds a minimum-height binary search tree from n sorted values in a file.
// Returns a pointer to the tree's root.
readTree(treePtr: BinaryNodePointer, n: integer): BinaryNodePointer
{
    if (n > 0)
    {
        treePtr = pointer to new node with nullptr as its child pointers

        // Construct the left subtree
        leftPtr = readTree(treePtr->getLeftChildPtr(), n / 2)
        treePtr->setLeftChildPtr(leftPtr)

        // Get the data item for this node
        rootItem = next data item from file
        treePtr->setItem(rootItem)

        // Construct the right subtree
        rightPtr = readTree(treePtr->getRightChildPtr(), (n - 1) / 2)
        treePtr->setRightChildPtr(rightPtr)

        return treePtr
    }
    else
        return nullptr
}
```

You should trace this algorithm and convince yourself that it is correct for both even and odd values of n.

To summarize, you can easily restore a tree as a balanced binary search tree if the data is sorted—that is, if it has been produced from the inorder traversal—and you know the number n of nodes in the tree. You need n so that you can determine the middle item and, in turn, the number of nodes in the left and right subtrees of the tree's root. Knowing these numbers is a simple matter of counting nodes as you traverse the tree and then saving the number in a file that the restore operation can read.

Note that `readTree` would be an appropriate protected method of `BinarySearchTree`, if you also had a public method to call it.

 Note: You can use the `readTree` algorithm to restore an out-of-balance binary search tree. Exercise 18 asks you to try it using an array instead of a file.

FIGURE 16-17   A tree of minimum height that is not complete

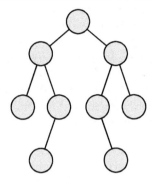

Question 9 Consider the pseudocode operation `readTree`.

   a. What binary search tree results when you execute `readTree` with a file of the six
   integers 2, 4, 6, 8, 10, 12?

   b. Is the resulting tree's height a minimum? Is the tree complete? Is it full?

16.5 Tree Sort

You can use the ADT binary search tree to sort an array efficiently. To simplify the discussion, we will
sort an array of integers into ascending order, as we did with the sorting algorithms in Chapter 11.
   The basic idea of the algorithm is simple:

```
// Sorts the integers in an array into ascending order.
treeSort(anArray: array, n: integer)
{
    Add anArray's entries to a binary search tree bst
    Traverse bst in inorder. As you visit bst's nodes, copy their data items into successive
        locations of anArray
}
```

Tree sort uses a
binary search tree

An inorder traversal of the binary search tree `bst` visits the integers in `bst`'s nodes in ascending
order.
   A tree sort can be quite efficient. As Figure 15-17 in Chapter 15 indicates, each addition to a
binary search tree requires $O(\log n)$ operations in the average case and $O(n)$ operations in the
worst case. Thus, tree sort's n additions require $O(n \times \log n)$ operations in the average case and
$O(n^2)$ operations in the worst case. The traversal of the tree involves one copy operation for each
of the n entries and so is $O(n)$. Because $O(n)$ is less than $O(n \times \log n)$ and $O(n^2)$, tree sort in the
average case is $O(n \times \log n)$ and $O(n^2)$ in the worst case.

Tree sort in the
average case is
$O(n \times \log n)$ and
$O(n^2)$ in the worst
case

Question 10 Trace the tree sort algorithm as it sorts the following array into ascending
order: 20 80 40 25 60 30.

16.6   General Trees

This chapter ends with a brief discussion of general trees and their relationship to binary trees. Consider the general tree in Figure 16-18. The three children *B, C,* and *D* of node *A,* for example, are siblings. The leftmost child *B* is the oldest child, or first child, of *A,* as mentioned in Section 15.1 of Chapter 15. One way to implement this tree uses the `BinaryNode` objects that we used for a link-based binary tree. That is, each node has two pointers: The left pointer points to the node's oldest child and the right pointer points to the node's next sibling. Thus, you can use the data structure in Figure 16-19a to implement the tree in Figure 16-18. Notice that the structure in Figure 16-19a also represents the binary tree pictured in Figure 16-19b.

Recall from Chapter 15 that an *n*-ary tree is a generalization of a binary tree whose nodes each can have no more than *n* children. The tree in Figure 16-18 could be an *n*-ary tree with *n* = 3 instead of a general tree. You can, of course, use the implementation just described for an *n*-ary

FIGURE 16-18   A general tree or an *n*-ary tree when *n* is 3

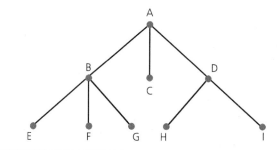

FIGURE 16-19   An implementation of a general tree and its equivalent binary tree

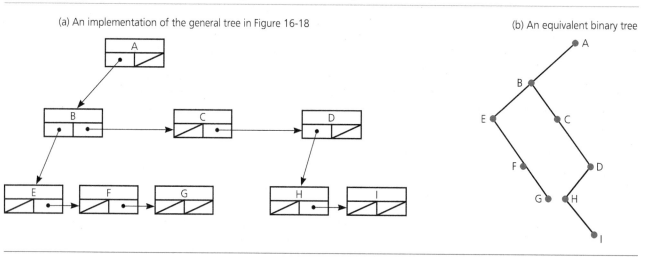

(a) An implementation of the general tree in Figure 16-18

(b) An equivalent binary tree

FIGURE 16-20   An implementation of the *n*-ary tree in Figure 16-18

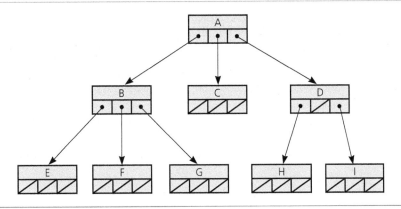

tree. However, because you know the maximum number of children for each node, you can let each node point directly to its children. Figure 16-20 illustrates such a representation for the tree in Figure 16-18. This tree is shorter than the tree in Figure 16-19b.

Exercise 17 discusses general trees further.

SUMMARY

1. The implementation of a binary tree is usually link based. However, if the binary tree is complete, an efficient array-based implementation is possible.

2. A node in a binary tree contains a data item and is connected to at most two descendant nodes. In a linked implementation, a node has two pointers to other nodes in addition to its data item.

3. Because a binary tree has a recursive nature, recursion is useful in the implementation of its operations. As is typical, the recursive methods are not public, since they require parameters that are a part of the underlying data structure. Those methods can be either private or protected, but as protected methods, they are available to classes derived from the class of binary trees.

4. The ADT binary search tree has several methods that are the same as those in the ADT binary tree. However, its addition, removal, and retrieval operations have different definitions than those for the ADT binary tree.

5. Operations on a binary search tree can be quite efficient. In the worst case, however—when the tree approaches a linear shape—the performance of its operations degrades and is comparable to that of a linear linked chain. If you must avoid such a situation for a given application, you should use the balancing methods presented in Chapter 19.

6. The tree sort algorithm efficiently sorts an array by using the binary search tree's addition and traversal operations.

7. If you save a binary search tree's data in a file while performing an inorder traversal of its nodes, you can restore the tree as a binary search tree of minimum height. If you save a binary search tree's data in a file while performing a preorder traversal of its nodes, you can restore the tree to its original form.

8. You can use a binary tree to represent a general tree or an *n*-ary tree. However, since you know the number of nodes in an *n*-ary tree, its nodes can point to all of its children.

EXERCISES

1. Consider the binary search tree in Figure 15-20 of Chapter 15. The numbers simply label the nodes so that you can reference them; they do not indicate the contents of the nodes.

    a. Which node must contain the inorder successor of the value in the root? Explain.

    b. Which node must contain the inorder predecessor of the value in the root? Explain.

2. Arrange nodes that contain the letters *A, C, E, F, L, V,* and *Z* into two binary search trees: one that has maximum height and one that has minimum height.

3. Consider the binary search tree in Figure 15-18a of Chapter 15.

    a. What tree results after you add the entries 80, 65, 75, 45, 35, and 25, in that order?

    b. After you add the nodes mentioned in part *a*, what tree results when you remove the entries 50 and 20?

4. Consider the binary search tree in Figure 16-21. What does the tree look like after you remove *M, D, G,* and *T*, in that order?

FIGURE 16-21   A binary search tree for Exercise 4

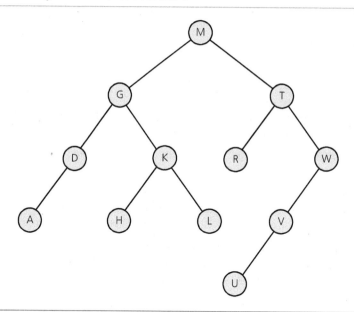

5. If you remove a data item from a binary search tree and then add it back to the tree, will you ever change the shape of the tree?

6. Suppose that the ADT binary tree has the operation

    ```
    replace(item: ItemType, replacementItem: ItemType): boolean
    ```

    It locates, if possible, the node in a binary tree that contains `item` and replaces `item` with `replacementItem`.

    a. Add the operation `replace` to the link-based implementation of the ADT binary tree given in this chapter. The operation should replace an item without altering the tree structure.

    b. Add the operation `replace` to the link-based implementation of the ADT binary search tree. Be sure that the tree remains a binary search tree. Do not use any public methods of the binary search tree.

    c. Implement a method `replace` within a client of `BinarySearchTree`.

7. Consider an array-based implementation of a binary search tree bst. Figure 16-1 presents such a repre-
    sentation for a particular binary search tree.
    a. Depict the array in an array-based implementation for the binary search tree in Figure 15-14a of
    Chapter 15. Assume that tree items are strings.
    b. Show the effect of each of the following sequential operations on the array in part *a* of this
    exercise.

    ```
    bst.add("Doug");
    bst.remove("Mia");
    bst.remove("Deepak");
    bst.add("Samara");
    ```

    c. Repeat parts *a* and *b* of this exercise for the tree in Figure 15-14c.
    d. Write an inorder traversal algorithm for this array-based implementation.

8. Duplicates in an ADT could mean either identical items or, more subtly, objects that match because their
    class overloads the equality operator so that it compares only certain fields, while differences exist in other
    fields. If duplicates are allowed in a binary search tree, it is important to have a convention that determines
    the relationship between the duplicates. Items that duplicate the root of a tree should either all be in the left
    subtree or all be in the right subtree, and, of course, this property must hold for every subtree.
    a. Why is this convention critical to the effective use of the binary search tree?
    b. This chapter stated that you can remove an item from a binary search tree by replacing it with the
    item that either immediately follows or immediately precedes the item to be removed. If dupli-
    cates are allowed, however, the choice between inorder successor and inorder predecessor is no
    longer arbitrary. How does the convention of putting duplicates in either the left or right subtree
    affect this choice?

9. Trace the nonrecursive inorder traversal algorithm for the binary search tree in Figure 16-4. Show the
    contents of the stack as the traversal progresses.

10. Implement in C++ the nonrecursive inorder traversal algorithm for a binary tree that was presented in
    this chapter.

11. Exercise 14 in Chapter 15 introduced the minimax tree. It has min nodes and max nodes. Part *b* of the
    exercise asked you to design a solution for representing and evaluating these trees. Implement your design
    in C++.

12. Design another algorithm to remove items from a binary search tree. This algorithm differs from the
    one described in this chapter when a node *N* has two children. First let *N*'s right child take the place of
    the removed node *N* in the same manner in which you remove a node that has one child. Next recon-
    nect *N*'s left child (along with its subtree, if any) to the left side of the node containing the inorder suc-
    cessor of the value in *N*.

13. Write iterative versions of the methods add and remove for a binary search tree.

14. A **level-order traversal** of a tree processes (visits) nodes one level at a time, from left to right, beginning
    with the root. Design an algorithm that performs a level-order traversal of a binary tree.

15. If you know in advance that you often access a given data item in a binary search tree several times in suc-
    cession before accessing a different item, you will end up searching for the same item repeatedly. One way
    to avoid this problem is to add an extra bookkeeping component to your implementation. That is, you
    can maintain a last-accessed pointer that will always reference the last data item that any binary search
    tree operation accessed. Whenever you perform such an operation, you can check the item most recently
    accessed before performing the operation.

    Revise the implementation of the ADT binary search tree to add this new feature by adding the data
    member lastAccessed to the class.

16. Exercise 10 in Chapter 4 introduced the doubly linked chain. The analogy for a binary search tree is to maintain parent pointers in each binary node in addition to the pointers to the node's children. That is, every node except the root will have a pointer to its parent in the tree. This type of binary tree is called a *doubly linked binary tree*, and such a tree is a part of Figure 16-22. Write addition and removal operations for this tree.

17. A node in a general tree can have an arbitrary number of children.
    a. Describe a C++ implementation of a general tree in which every node contains an array of child pointers. Write a recursive preorder traversal method for this implementation. What are the advantages and disadvantages of this implementation?
    b. Consider the implementation of a general tree that is illustrated in Figure 16-19. Each node has two pointers: The left pointer points to the node's oldest child and the right pointer points to the node's next sibling. Write a recursive preorder traversal method for this implementation.
    c. Every node in a binary tree *T* has at most two children. Compare the oldest-child/next-sibling representation of *T*, as part *b* describes, to the left-child/right-child representation of a binary tree, as this chapter describes. Does one representation simplify the implementation of the ADT operations? Are the two representations ever the same?

18. Given an unbalanced binary search tree, use an inorder traversal to copy its data to an array. Then create a balanced binary search tree using the readTree algorithm given in Section 16.4, but use your array instead of a file.

*19. Add an overloaded == operator to the class BinaryNodeTree.

PROGRAMMING PROBLEMS

1. Complete the implementation of the class BinaryNodeTree that was begun in Section 16.2.2 of this chapter.

2. Implement the class BinarySearchTree, as given in Listing 16-4.

3. Write an array-based implementation of the ADT binary tree that uses dynamic memory allocation. Use a data structure like the one in Figure 16-1.

4. Repeat the previous problem, but define a binary search tree instead.

5. Write a program that maintains a database containing data, such as name and birthday, about your friends and relatives. You should be able to enter, remove, modify, or search this data. Initially, you can assume that the names are unique. The program should be able to save the data in a file for use later.

    Design a class to represent the database and another class to represent the people. Use a binary search tree of people as a data member of the database class.

    You can enhance this problem by adding an operation that lists everyone who satisfies a given criterion. For example, you could list people born in a given month. You should also be able to list everyone in the database.

*6. Many applications require a data organization that simultaneously supports several different data-management tasks. One simple example involves a waiting list of customers, that is, a queue of customer records. In addition to requiring the standard queue operations isEmpty, enqueue, dequeue, and getFront, suppose that the application frequently requires a listing of the customer records in the queue. This listing is more useful if the records appear sorted by customer name. You thus need a traverse operation that visits the customer records in sorted order.

This scenario presents an interesting problem. If you simply store the customer records in a queue, they will not, in general, be sorted by name. If, on the other hand, you just store the records in sorted order, you will be unable to process the customers on a first-come, first-served basis. Apparently, this problem requires you to organize the data in two different ways.

One solution is to maintain two independent data structures, one organized to support the sorted traversal and the other organized to support the queue operations. Figure 16-22 depicts a sorted linked list of customer records and a pointer-based implementation of the queue. The pointer-based data structures are a good choice because they do not require a good estimate of the maximum number of customer records that must be stored.

Implement the ADT queue operations as well as a sorted traversal operation for a queue that points into a doubly linked binary search tree, as shown in Figure 16-22. Doubly linked binary trees are explained in Exercise 16. You will need the addition and removal operations for a binary search tree that contains parent pointers.

FIGURE 16-22   A queue that points into a doubly linked binary search tree

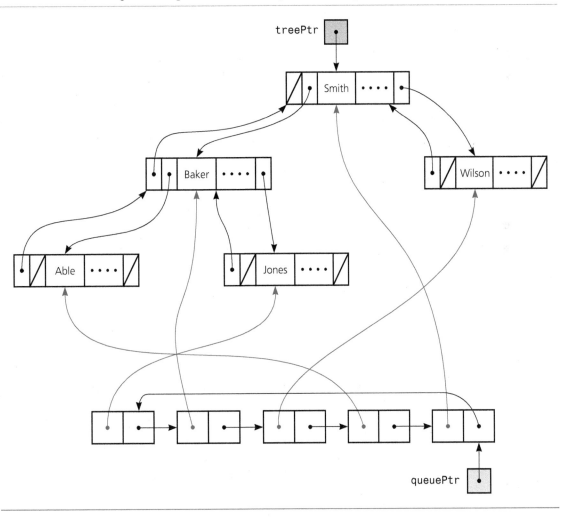

Chapter

17

Heaps

Contents

Prerequisites

Chapter 15 introduced the ADTs binary tree and binary search tree. This chapter will present the ADT heap, which is a special kind of complete binary tree that provides an efficient implementation of the ADT priority queue. You can also use a heap to sort an array as efficiently as you can by using either a quick sort or a merge sort.

17.1   The ADT Heap

A **heap** is a complete binary tree that either is empty or whose root

A heap is a special complete binary tree

VideoNote
The ADT heap

- Contains a value greater than or equal to the value in each of its children, and
- Has heaps as its subtrees

A heap is similar to a binary search tree, although it differs from a binary search tree in two significant ways:

- While you can view a binary search tree as sorted, a heap is ordered in a weaker sense.
- While binary search trees come in many different shapes, heaps are always complete binary trees.

In our definition of a heap, the root contains the item with the largest value. Such a heap is also known as a **maxheap**. **A minheap**, on the other hand, places the item with the smallest value in its root. An example of a maxheap and a minheap are given in Figure 17-1. Exercises 1 and 8 and Programming Problem 3 consider the minheap further.

FIGURE 17-1   (a) A maxheap and (b) a minheap

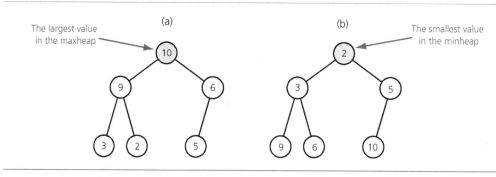

The ADT heap has the following operations:

   Note: ADT heap operations
- Test whether a heap is empty
- Get the number of nodes in a heap
- Get the height of a heap
- Get the data item in the heap's root
- Add a new data item to the heap
- Remove the data item in the heap's root
- Remove all data from the heap

Depending on whether the heap is a maxheap or a minheap, the removal and retrieval operations respectively involve either the largest or the smallest data item in the heap.

The following contract specifies these operations in more detail, and a UML diagram for a class of heaps appears in Figure 17-2.

ABSTRACT DATA TYPE: HEAP	
DATA	
• A finite number of objects in hierarchical order.	
OPERATIONS	
PSEUDOCODE	DESCRIPTION
isEmpty()	Task: Sees whether this heap is empty.
	Input: None.
	Output: True if the heap is empty; otherwise false.
getNumberOfNodes()	Task: Gets the number of nodes in this heap.
	Input: None.
	Output: The number of nodes in the heap.
getHeight()	Task: Gets the height of this heap.
	Input: None.
	Output: The height of the heap.
peekTop()	Task: Gets the data that is in the root (top) of this heap.
	Input: None. Assumes the heap is not empty.
	Output: The data item in the root of the heap. If the heap is a maxheap, this data is the largest value in the heap. For a minheap, the data is the smallest value.
add(newData)	Task: Adds a new data item to this heap.
	Input: newData is the data item to be added.
	Output: True if the addition is successful, or false if not.
remove()	Task: Removes the data item in the root of this heap.
	Input: None.
	Output: True if the removal is successful, or false if not.
clear()	Task: Removes all data from this heap.
	Input: None.
	Output: The heap is empty.

FIGURE 17-2   UML diagram for the class Heap

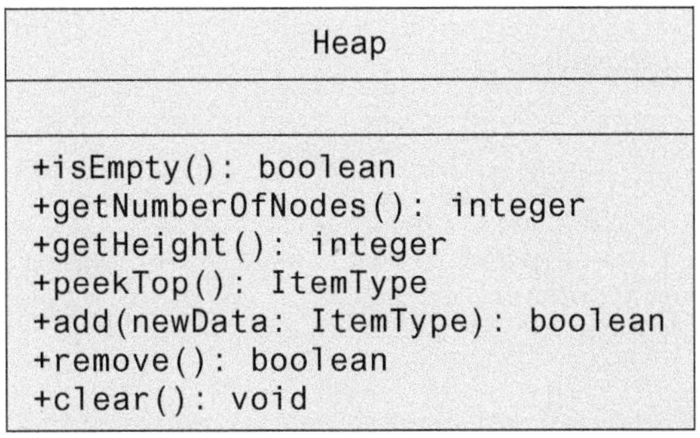

```
                    Heap

    +isEmpty(): boolean
    +getNumberOfNodes(): integer
    +getHeight(): integer
    +peekTop(): ItemType
    +add(newData: ItemType): boolean
    +remove(): boolean
    +clear(): void
```

An interface that finalizes the operation contract for the ADT heap appears in Listing 17-1.

LISTING 17-1 An interface for the ADT heap

```cpp
 1  /** Interface for the ADT heap.
 2   @file HeapInterface.h */
 3
 4  #ifndef HEAP_INTERFACE_
 5  #define HEAP_INTERFACE_
 6
 7  template<class ItemType>
 8  class HeapInterface
 9  {
10  public:
11     /** Sees whether this heap is empty.
12      @return  True if the heap is empty, or false if not. */
13     virtual bool isEmpty() const = 0;
14
15     /** Gets the number of nodes in this heap.
16      @return  The number of nodes in the heap. */
17     virtual int getNumberOfNodes() const = 0;
18
19     /** Gets the height of this heap.
20      @return  The height of the heap. */
21     virtual int getHeight() const = 0;
22
23     /** Gets the data that is in the root (top) of this heap.
24         For a maxheap, the data is the largest value in the heap;
25         for a minheap, the data is the smallest value in the heap.
26      @pre  The heap is not empty.
27      @post  The root's data has been returned, and the heap is unchanged.
28      @return  The data in the root of the heap. */
29     virtual ItemType peekTop() const = 0;
30
31     /** Adds a new data item to this heap.
32      @param newData  The data to be added.
33      @post  The heap has a new node that contains newData.
34      @return  True if the addition is successful, or false if not. */
35     virtual bool add(const ItemType& newData) = 0;
36
37     /** Removes the data that is in the root (top) of this heap.
38      @return  True if the removal is successful, or false if not. */
39     virtual bool remove() = 0;
40
41     /** Removes all data from this heap. */
42     virtual void clear() = 0;
43
44     /** Destroys this heap and frees its assigned memory. */
45     virtual ~HeapInterface() {  }
46  }; // end HeapInterface
47  #endif
```

> **Note:** Do not confuse the ADT heap with the collection of memory cells available for allocation to your program from the free store when you use the `new` operator. This memory is known as a heap, but it is not an instance of the ADT heap.

Question 1 Is the full binary tree in Figure 16-16 of Chapter 16 a heap? Why?

17.2 An Array-Based Implementation of a Heap

VideoNote
Overview of `ArrayHeap`

Because a heap is a binary tree, you can use the array-based implementation of a binary tree discussed in Section 16.1.1 of Chapter 16, if you know the maximum size of the heap. However, because a heap is a complete binary tree, you can use a simpler array-based implementation that saves memory. As you saw in Chapter 15, a complete tree of height h is full to level $h - 1$ and has level h filled from left to right.

Figure 17-3a shows a complete binary tree with its nodes numbered according to a level-by-level scheme. The root is numbered 0, and the children of the root—which are at the next level of the tree—are numbered, left to right, 1 and 2. The nodes at the next level are numbered, left to right, 3, 4, and 5. You place these nodes into the array `items` in numeric order. That is, `items[i]` contains the node numbered i, as Figure 17-3b illustrates. Now, given any node `items[i]`, you can easily locate both of its children and its parent:

If the binary tree is complete and remains complete, you can use a memory-efficient array-based implementation

- Its left child, if it exists, is `items[2 * i + 1]`
- Its right child, if it exists, is `items[2 * i + 2]`
- Its parent, if it exists, is `items[(i - 1) / 2]`

Remember that only the root in `items[0]` does not have a parent.

This array-based representation requires a complete binary tree. If nodes were missing from the middle of the tree, the numbering scheme would be thrown off, and the parent-child relationship among nodes would be ambiguous. This requirement implies that any changes to the heap must maintain its completeness.

As you will see, an array-based representation of a heap is useful in the implementation of the ADT priority queue.

FIGURE 17-3   A complete binary tree and its array-based implementation

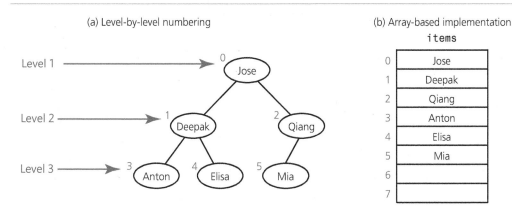

Question 2 What array represents the maxheap shown in Figure 17-1a?

Question 3 What array represents the minheap shown in Figure 17-1b?

Question 4 What criterion can you use to tell whether the node in `items[i]` is a leaf?

Question 5 What complete binary tree does the following array represent?

5	1	2	8	6	10	3	9	4	7
0	1	2	3	4	5	6	7	8	9

Question 6 Does the array in the previous question represent a heap?

17.2.1 Algorithms for the Array-Based Heap Operations

Let's assume that our class of heaps has the following private data members:

> The data members for an array-based implementation of a heap

- `items`: an array of heap items
- `itemCount`: an integer equal to the number of items in the heap
- `maxItems`: an integer equal to the maximum capacity of the heap

The array `items` corresponds to the array-based representation of a complete binary tree, such as the array shown in Figure 17-3b. We will assume that we are working with a maxheap of integers.

Retrieving an item from a heap. First consider the heap's `peekTop` operation. Where is the largest item in the heap? Because the item in every tree node is greater than or equal to the item in either of its children, the largest item must be in the root of the tree—that is, at the top of the heap. Thus, the `peekTop` operation needs to take only the following step:

> peekTop's logic

```
// Return the item in the root
return items[0]
```

Removing an item from a heap. While the `peekTop` operation returns the largest item in the heap—which we know is in its root—the heap operation `remove` must remove it. Removing the root of the heap leaves two disjoint heaps, as Figure 17-4 indicates. Therefore, you do not want to actually remove the root. Instead, you remove the last node of the tree and place its item in the root, as parts *a* and *b* of Figure 17-5 show. The result of this step is *not* necessarily a heap. It is, however, a complete binary tree whose left and right subtrees are both heaps. The only problem is that the item in the root usually is out of place. Such a structure is called a **semiheap**.

> remove's first step produces a semiheap

You thus need a way to transform a semiheap into a heap. One strategy allows the item in the root to *trickle down* the tree until it reaches a node in which it will not be out of place; that is, the item will

FIGURE 17-4   Disjoint heaps after removing the heap's root

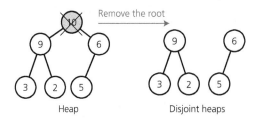

FIGURE 17-5 Removing the data item from a heap's root

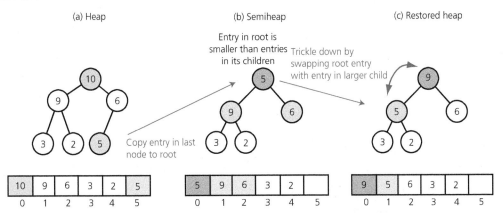

come to rest in the first node where it would be greater than or equal to the item in each of its children. To accomplish this, you first compare the item in the root of the semiheap to the items in its children. If the root's item is smaller than the larger of the items in its children, you swap the item in the root with that larger item. For convenience, we will refer to the child containing the larger item as the *larger child*. The result of this step is shown in Figure 17-5c. Although the value 5 trickles down in this example to its correct position after only one swap, in general more swaps may be necessary.

We need to remember that an array represents the original heap before we remove its root. The remove operation will simply move items within this array, as Figure 17-5 shows. The transformation from the heap in Figure 17-5a to the semiheap in Figure 17-5b is accomplished by the following steps:

```
// Copy the item from the last node and place it into the root
items[0] = items[itemCount - 1]

// Remove the last node
itemCount--
```

The transformation from the semiheap in Figure 17-5b to the heap in Figure 17-5c is accomplished by the following recursive algorithm. Note that the algorithm will not work if it does not begin with a semiheap.

```
// Converts a semiheap rooted at index nodeIndex into a heap.
heapRebuild(nodeIndex: integer, items: ArrayType, itemCount: integer): void
{
    // Recursively trickle the item at index nodeIndex down to its proper position by
    // swapping it with its larger child, if the child is larger than the item.
    // If the item is at a leaf, nothing needs to be done.
    if (the root is not a leaf)
    {
        // The root must have a left child; find larger child
        leftChildIndex = 2 * rootIndex + 1
        rightChildIndex = leftChildIndex + 1
        largerChildIndex = rightChildIndex // Assume right child exists and is the larger

        // Check whether right child exists; if so, is left child larger?
        // If no right child, left one is larger
        if ((largerChildIndex >= itemCount) ||
                            (items[leftChildIndex] > items[rightChildIndex]))
            largerChildIndex = leftChildIndex; // Assumption was wrong
```

remove's final step transforms the semiheap into a heap

Every nonleaf in a complete tree has a left child

```
        if (items[nodeIndex] < items[largerChildIndex])
        {
            Swap items[nodeIndex] and items[largerChildIndex]

            // Transform the semiheap rooted at largerChildIndex into a heap
            heapRebuild(largerChildIndex, items, itemCount)
        }
    }
    // Else root is a leaf, so you are done
}
```

Figure 17-6 illustrates heapRebuild's recursive calls.

FIGURE17-6 Recursive calls to heapRebuild

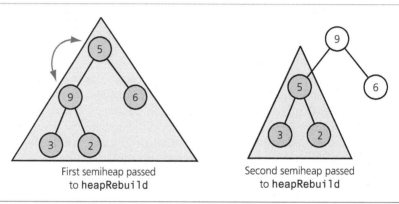

First semiheap passed
to heapRebuild

Second semiheap passed
to heapRebuild

Now the heap's remove operation uses heapRebuild as follows:

```
// Copy the item from the last node into the root
items[0] = items[itemCount - 1]

// Remove the last node
itemCount--

// Transform the semiheap back into a heap
heapRebuild(0, items, itemCount)
```

remove's efficiency

Consider briefly the efficiency of remove. Because the tree is stored in an array, the removal of a node requires you to swap array entries rather than simply to change a few pointers. These swaps may concern you, but they do not necessarily indicate that the algorithm is inefficient. At most, how many array entries will you have to swap? After remove copies the item in the last node of the tree into the root, heapRebuild trickles this item down the tree until its appropriate place is found. This item travels down a single path from the root to, at worst, a leaf. Therefore, the number of array items that heapRebuild must swap is no greater than the height of the tree. The height of a complete binary tree with n nodes is always $\lceil \log_2(n + 1) \rceil$, as you know from Chapter 15. Because each swap requires three data moves, remove requires

remove is O(log n)

$$3 \times \lceil \log_2 (n + 1) \rceil + 1$$

data moves. Thus, remove is O(log n), which is quite efficient.

Adding a data item to a heap. The strategy for the add algorithm is the opposite of that for remove. A new data item is placed at the bottom of the tree, and it *bubbles up* to its proper place,

FIGURE 17-7   Adding 15 to a heap

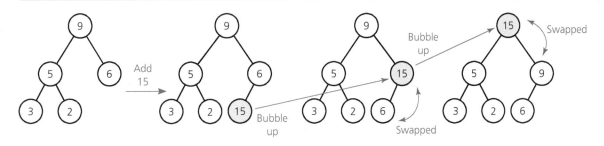

as Figure 17-7 illustrates. Making a node bubble up is easy, because the parent of the node in items[i] is always stored in items[(i - 1) / 2]—unless, of course, the node is the root.

The pseudocode for add follows:

Addition strategy

```
add(newData: itemType): boolean
{
    // Place newData at the bottom of the tree
    items[itemCount] = newData

    // Make new item bubble up to the appropriate spot in the tree
    newDataIndex = itemCount
    inPlace = false
    while ((newDataIndex >= 0) and !inPlace)
    {
        parentIndex = (newDataIndex - 1) / 2
        if (items[newDataIndex] <= items[parentIndex])
            inPlace = true
        else
        {
            Swap items[newDataIndex] and items[parentIndex]
            newDataIndex = parentIndex
        }
    }
    itemCount++
    return inPlace
}
```

add is O(log n)

The efficiency of add is like that of remove. At worst, add has to swap array entries on a path from a leaf to the root. The number of swaps, therefore, cannot exceed the height of the tree. Because the height of the tree, which is complete, is always $\lceil \log_2 (n + 1) \rceil$, add is also O(log n).

Question 7 Is the full binary tree in Figure 16-16 of Chapter 16 a semiheap?

Question 8 Consider the maxheap in Figure 17-1a. Draw the heap after you add 12 and then remove 12.

Question 9 What does the initially empty heap myHeap contain after the following sequence of pseudocode operations?

```
myHeap.add(2)
myHeap.add(3)
myHeap.add(4)
myHeap.add(1)
```

(continues)

```
myHeap.add(9)
myHeap.remove()
myHeap.add(7)
myHeap.add(6)
myHeap.remove()
myHeap.add(5)
```

17.2.2 The Implementation

The header file for the class `ArrayMaxHeap`, which is an array-based implementation of the ADT heap, is in Listing 17-2. This heap is a maxheap.

LISTING 17-2 The header file for the class `ArrayMaxHeap`

```cpp
1   /** Array-based implementation of the ADT heap.
2    @file ArrayMaxHeap.h */
3   #ifndef ARRAY_MAX_HEAP_
4   #define ARRAY_MAX_HEAP_
5   #include  <memory>
6   #include "HeapInterface.h"
7   #include "PrecondViolatedExcept.h"
8
9   template<class ItemType>
10  class ArrayMaxHeap : public HeapInterface<ItemType>
11  {
12  private:
13     static const int ROOT_INDEX = 0;        // Helps with readability
14     static const int DEFAULT_CAPACITY = 21; // Small capacity for testing
15     std::unique_ptr<ItemType[]> items;      // Array of heap items
16     int itemCount;                          // Current count of heap items
17     int maxItems;                           // Maximum capacity of the heap
18
19     // --------------------------------------------------------------------
20     // Most of the private utility methods use an array index as a parameter
21     // and in calculations. This should be safe, even though the array is an
22     // implementation detail, since the methods are private.
23     // --------------------------------------------------------------------
24
25     // Returns the array index of the left child (if it exists).
26     int getLeftChildIndex(const int nodeIndex) const;
27
28     // Returns the array index of the right child (if it exists).
29     int getRightChildIndex(int nodeIndex) const;
30
31     // Returns the array index of the parent node.
32     int getParentIndex(int nodeIndex) const;
33
34     // Tests whether this node is a leaf.
35     bool isLeaf(int nodeIndex) const;
36
```

```
37        // Converts a semiheap to a heap.
38        void heapRebuild(int nodeIndex);
39
40        // Creates a heap from an unordered array.
41        void heapCreate();
42
43   public:
44        ArrayMaxHeap();
45        ArrayMaxHeap(const ItemType someArray[], const int arraySize);
46        virtual ~ArrayMaxHeap();
47
48        // HeapInterface Public Methods:
49        bool isEmpty() const;
50        int getNumberOfNodes() const;
51        int getHeight() const;
52        ItemType peekTop() const throw(PrecondViolatedExcept);
53        bool add(const ItemType& newData);
54        bool remove();
55        void clear();
56   }; // end ArrayMaxHeap
57   #include "ArrayMaxHeap.cpp"
58   #endif
```

Some method definitions. Let's examine the definitions of some of the methods in ArrayMaxHeap, beginning with the private ones. To make our code more readable, we established the private methods getLeftChildIndex, getRightChildIndex, and getParentIndex. The implementations of these methods follow from our observations at the beginning of Section 17.2. For example, the left child of node items[i] is items[2 * i + 1], so the method getLeftChildIndex has the following definition:

```
template<class ItemType>
int ArrayMaxHeap<ItemType>::getLeftChildIndex(const int nodeIndex) const
{
   return (2 * nodeIndex) + 1;
}  // end getLeftChildIndex
```

The recursive private method heapRebuild closely follows the pseudocode given earlier in this chapter, so let's assume that we have coded it and look at a method that uses it. The second constructor creates a heap from an array of entries. To do so, this constructor can call the private method heapCreate, which in turn will need to call heapRebuild. Consider the details.

Notice that heapCreate has no parameters, but it does have access to our class's private data. In particular, heapCreate can use the array items and the counter itemCount. These two data members will serve as both the input to and the output from heapCreate. So if the constructor places values into itemCount and the array items, it can call heapCreate to rearrange the values in the array into a heap.

Thus, we can define the constructor as follows:

```
template<class  ItemType>
ArrayMaxHeap<ItemType>::
ArrayMaxHeap(const ItemType someArray[], const int arraySize):
             itemCount(arraySize), maxItems(2 * arraySize)
{
```

```
    // Allocate the array
    items = std::make_unique<ItemType[]>(maxItems);

    // Copy given values into the array
    for (int i = 0; i < itemCount; i++)
        items[i] = someArray[i];

    // Reorganize the array into a heap
    heapCreate();
}   // end constructor
```

We use initializers to set the initial values of `itemCount` and `maxItems`. After allocating the array `items`, we copy the values from the given array `someArray` into `items`. Finally, we call `heapCreate`.

Now `heapCreate` must form a heap from the values in the array `items`. One way to accomplish this transformation is to use the heap's `add` method to add the data items to the heap one by one. However, a more efficient technique of building a heap out of the items in an array is possible.

For example, assume that the initial contents of an array are as shown in Figure 17-8a. First you imagine the array as a complete binary tree by assigning the array's entries to the tree's nodes, beginning with the root and proceeding left to right down the tree. Figure 17-8b shows the resulting tree. Next, you transform this tree into a heap by calling `heapRebuild` repeatedly. Each call to `heapRebuild` transforms a semiheap—a tree whose subtrees are both heaps but whose root may be out of place—into a heap. But are there any semiheaps in the tree for `heapRebuild` to work on? Although the tree in Figure 17-8b is not a semiheap, each leaf is a semiheap. In fact, each leaf is a heap, but for the sake of simplicity, ignore this fact.

FIGURE 17-8 An array and its corresponding complete binary tree

---

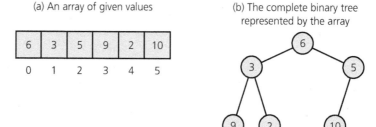

(a) An array of given values

(b) The complete binary tree represented by the array

You first call `heapRebuild` on the leaves from right to left. You then move up the tree, knowing that by the time you reach a node *N*, its subtrees are heaps, and thus `heapRebuild` will transform the semiheap rooted at *N* into a heap. The following pseudocode transforms the array `items` of `itemCount` entries into a heap:

Building a heap from an array of data

```
for (index = itemCount - 1 down to 0)
{
    // Assertion: The tree rooted at index is a semiheap
    heapRebuild(index)
    // Assertion: The tree rooted at index is a heap
}
```

Actually, you can replace `itemCount` with `itemCount / 2` in the previous `for` statement. Thus, our pseudocode becomes

```
for (index = itemCount / 2 - 1 down to 0)
{
    // Assertion: The tree rooted at index is a semiheap
    heapRebuild(index)
    // Assertion: The tree rooted at index is a heap
}
```

Exercise 11 at the end of this chapter asks you to explain why this improvement is possible. Figure 17-9 traces this algorithm for the array in Figure 17-8a. Since the array contains six items, index in the for statement begins at $6 / 2 - 1$, or 2.

FIGURE 17-9   Transforming an array into a heap

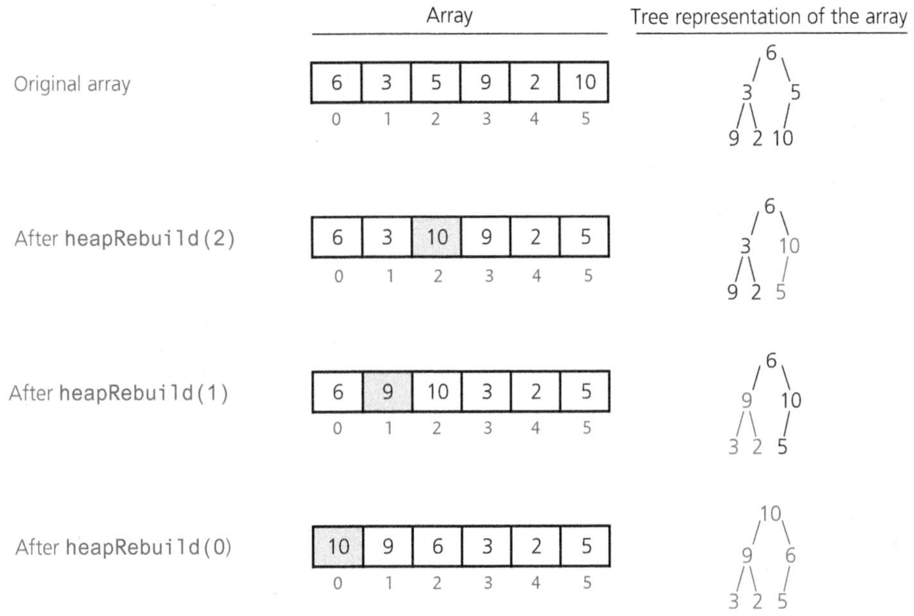

We now translate the previous pseudocode into C++ to get the method heapCreate:

```cpp
template<class ItemType>
void ArrayMaxHeap<ItemType>::heapCreate()
{
    for (int index = itemCount / 2 - 1; index >= 0; index--)
        heapRebuild(index);
}  // end heapCreate
```

Finally, we will define the method peekTop, since it must throw an exception if the heap is empty. Although you might be tempted to simply return items[0], since it always contains the top of the heap, if you do, peekTop will return a value even when the heap might be empty. Thus, you need to have peekTop test for an empty heap, as in the following definition:

```cpp
template<class ItemType>
ItemType ArrayMaxHeap<ItemType>::peekTop() const throw(PrecondViolatedExcept)
{
```

```
        if (isEmpty())
           throw PrecondViolatedExcept("Attempted peek into an empty heap.");
        return items[0];
   }   // end peekTop
```

Programming Problem 1 asks you to complete the implementation file for the class ArrayMaxHeap.

 Question 10 Execute the following pseudocode statements on the array shown in Checkpoint Question 5.

```
     for (index = n – 1 down to 0)
        heapRebuild(index)
```

17.3   A Heap Implementation of the ADT Priority Queue

Priority-queue operations and heap operations are analogous

Section 13.3 of Chapter 13 introduced the ADT priority queue, and Section 14.2 of Chapter 14 offered an implementation based on a sorted list. At that time, we mentioned that using a heap to define a priority queue results in a more time-efficient implementation.

Once you have implemented the ADT heap, the implementation of the ADT priority queue is straightforward, because priority queue operations are exactly analogous to heap operations. The priority value in a priority queue item corresponds to an item in a heap. Thus, the implementation of the priority queue can reuse ArrayMaxHeap. To do so, we could use an instance of ArrayMaxHeap as a data member of the class of priority queues, or we could consider inheritance. Although a heap provides an excellent implementation of a priority queue, a priority queue is not a heap. Since an *is-a* relationship does not exist between ArrayMaxHeap and the class of priority queues, public inheritance is not appropriate. But we can use private inheritance, and that is what we will do. Let's assume that we have an interface for the ADT priority queue, as Exercise 7 in Chapter 13 asked you to write, so that we can derive our new class from it as well.

Listing 17-3 contains a header file for a class of priority queues.

Header file

LISTING 17-3   A header file for the class HeapPriorityQueue

```
1    /** ADT priority queue: Heap-based implementation.
2     @file HeapPriorityQueue.h */
3    #ifndef HEAP_PRIORITY_QUEUE_
4    #define HEAP_PRIORITY_QUEUE_
5    #include "ArrayMaxHeap.h"
6    #include "PriorityQueueInterface.h"
7
8    template<class ItemType>
9    class HeapPriorityQueue : public PriorityQueueInterface<ItemType>,
10                             private ArrayMaxHeap<ItemType>
11   {
12   public:
13      HeapPriorityQueue();
14      bool isEmpty() const;
15      bool enqueue(const ItemType& newEntry);
16      bool dequeue();
17
18      /** @pre  The priority queue is not empty. */
19      ItemType peekFront() const throw(PrecondViolatedExcept);
20   };  // end HeapPriorityQueue
```

```
21
22   #include "HeapPriorityQueue.cpp"
23   #endif
```

Each of the method definitions in Listing 17-4 calls the corresponding method in ArrayMax-Heap. Notice how the method peekFront handles the exception thrown by the heap's peekTop method, so that the message given mentions the priority queue and not the underlying heap.

LISTING 17-4 An implementation of the class HeapPriorityQueue

```
1    /** Heap-based implementation of the ADT priority queue.
2     @file HeapPriorityQueue.cpp */
3
4    #include "HeapPriorityQueue.h"
5
6    template<class ItemType>
7    HeapPriorityQueue<ItemType>::HeapPriorityQueue()
8    {
9       ArrayMaxHeap<ItemType>();
10   } // end constructor
11
12   template<class ItemType>
13   bool HeapPriorityQueue<ItemType>::isEmpty() const
14   {
15      return ArrayMaxHeap<ItemType>::isEmpty();
16   } // end isEmpty
17
18   template<class ItemType>
19   bool HeapPriorityQueue<ItemType>::enqueue(const ItemType& newEntry)
20   {
21      return ArrayMaxHeap<ItemType>::add(newEntry);
22   } // end add
23
24   template<class ItemType>
25   bool HeapPriorityQueue<ItemType>::dequeue()
26   {
27      return ArrayMaxHeap<ItemType>::remove();
28   } // end remove
29
30   template<class ItemType>
31   ItemType HeapPriorityQueue<ItemType>::peekFront() const throw(PrecondViolatedExcept)
32   {
33      try
34      {
35         return ArrayMaxHeap<ItemType>::peekTop();
36      }
37      catch (PrecondViolatedExcept e)
38      {
39         throw PrecondViolatedExcept("Attempted peek into an empty priority queue.");
40      } // end try/catch
41   } // end peekFront
```

The heap implementation requires knowledge of the priority queue's maximum size

A heap versus a binary search tree as a priority queue. How does a heap compare to a binary search tree as an implementation of a priority queue? If you know the maximum number of items in the priority queue, the heap is the better implementation.

Because a heap is complete, it is always balanced, which is its major advantage. If the binary search tree is balanced, both implementations will have the same average performance for n items: They both will be O(log n). A binary search tree, however, can grow taller and become unbalanced during the addition and removal of entries, degrading the implementation's efficiency to O(n) in the worst case. The heap implementation avoids this decrease in performance. In Chapter 19, you will see how to keep a search tree balanced, but the operations that do this are far more complex than the heap operations.

A heap is always balanced

Finite, distinct priority values. If you have a finite number of distinct priority values, such as the integers 1 through 5, many items will likely have the same priority value. You could place items whose priority values are the same in the order in which you encounter them.

A heap of queues

A heap of queues accommodates this situation, one queue for each distinct priority value. To add a data item to the priority queue, you add a queue for the item's priority value to the heap, if it is not already there. Then you add the data item to the corresponding queue. To remove data from a priority queue, you remove the data item at the front of the queue that corresponds to the highest priority value in the heap. If this removal leaves the queue empty, you remove the queue from the heap. Programming Problem 7 at the end of this chapter treats distinct priority values further.

Question 11 Consider a heap-based implementation of the ADT priority queue. What does the underlying heap contain after the following sequence of pseudocode operations, assuming that pQueue is an initially empty priority queue?

```
pQueue.enqueue(5)
pQueue.enqueue(9)
pQueue.enqueue(6)
pQueue.enqueue(7)
pQueue.enqueue(3)
pQueue.enqueue(4)
pQueue.dequeue()
pQueue.enqueue(9)
pQueue.enqueue(2)
pQueue.dequeue()
```

17.4 Heap Sort

As its name implies, the **heap sort** algorithm uses a heap to sort an array of items that are in no particular order. Suppose that we have a heap and an empty array whose size is the number of items in the heap. A call to peekTop gets the largest item in the heap, and we can place that item at the end of the array. A call to remove then removes that item from the heap. By repeatedly calling peekTop and remove, we can move the items from the heap in descending order and place them into sequentially decreasing positions in the array. The result is an array sorted into ascending order.

While this approach would work, it uses more memory and time than is necessary. Let's start over with an array of unsorted values. Our first step would be to transform the array into a heap. Recall the private method heapCreate from our implementation of the ADT heap in

Section 17.2.2. This method transformed the array `items`, which is a data member of the class of heaps, into a heap. The body of `heapCreate` is simply the following loop:

```
for (int index = itemCount / 2 - 1; index >= 0; index--)
    heapRebuild(index);
```

Building a heap from an array of items

As members of the class `ArrayMaxHeap`, both `heapCreate` and `heapRebuild` have access to the class's data members, including the array `items` and its number of entries, `itemCount`. To use `heapRebuild` in a heap sort, we must revise it so that it has the array and its size as parameters. Let's declare `heapRebuild` as a function outside of `ArrayMaxHeap`, as follows:

```
void heapRebuild(int startIndex, ItemType& anArray[], int n)
```

This version of `heapRebuild` is not in `ArrayMaxHeap`

After transforming the array into a heap, heap sort partitions the array into two regions—the Heap region and the Sorted region—as Figure 17-10 illustrates. The Heap region is in `anArray[0..last]`, and the Sorted region is in `anArray[last + 1..n - 1]`. Initially, the Heap region is all of `anArray` and the Sorted region is empty.

FIGURE 17-10 Heap sort partitions an array into two regions

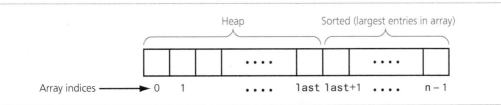

Each step of the algorithm moves an item *I* from the Heap region to the Sorted region. During this process, the following statements are true—they are the algorithm's invariant:

- The Sorted region contains the largest values in `anArray`, and they are in sorted order—that is, `anArray[n - 1]` is the largest item, `anArray[n - 2]` is the second largest, and so on.
- The items in the Heap region form a heap.

Invariant for heap sort

So that the invariant holds, *I* must be the item that has the largest value in the Heap region, and therefore *I* must be in the root of the heap. To accomplish the move, you exchange the item in the root of the heap with the last item in the heap—that is, you exchange `anArray[0]` with `anArray[last]`—and then decrement the value of `last`. As a result, the item just swapped from the root into `anArray[last]` becomes the smallest item in the Sorted region (and is in the first position of the Sorted region). After the move, you must transform the Heap region back into a heap because the new root may be out of place. You can accomplish this transformation by using `heapRebuild` to make the item now in the root trickle down so that the Heap region is once again a heap.

The following algorithm summarizes these steps:

```
// Sorts anArray[0..n-1].
heapSort(anArray: ArrayType, n: integer)
{
    // Build initial heap
    for (index = n / 2 - 1 down to 0)
    {
        // Assertion: The tree rooted at index is a semiheap
        heapRebuild(index, anArray, n)
```

```
    //  Assertion: The tree rooted at index is a heap
}
//  Assertion: anArray[0] is the largest item in heap anArray[0..n–1]

//  Move the largest item in the Heap region—the root anArray[0]—to the beginning
//  of the Sorted region by swapping items and then adjusting the size of the regions
Swap anArray[0] and anArray[n – 1]
heapSize = n – 1 //  Decrease the size of the Heap region, expand the Sorted region

while (heapSize > 1)
{
    //  Make the Heap region a heap again
    heapRebuild(0, anArray, heapSize)

    //  Move the largest item in the Heap region—the root anArray[0]—to the beginning
    //  of the Sorted region by swapping items and then adjusting the size of the regions
    Swap anArray[0] and anArray[heapSize – 1]
    heapSize-- //  Decrease the size of the Heap region, expand the Sorted region
}
}
```

If we begin with the array shown in Figure 17-9, the first steps of heap sort are the same as those shown in the figure, and they transform the array into a heap. Figure 17-11 traces the heap sort from that point on. The C++ implementation of heap sort is left as an exercise.

Heap sort is
O($n \times \log n$)

The analysis of heap sort's efficiency is similar to that of merge sort, as given in Chapter 11. Both algorithms are O($n \times \log n$) in both the worst and average cases. Heap sort has an advantage over merge sort in that it does not require a second array. Quick sort is also O($n \times \log n$) in the average case but is O(n^2) in the worst case. Even though quick sort has poor worst-case efficiency, it is generally the preferred sorting algorithm.

Question 12 Trace the heap sort as it sorts the following array into ascending order: 25 30 20 80 40 60

FIGURE 17-11   A trace of heap sort, beginning with the heap in Figure 17-9

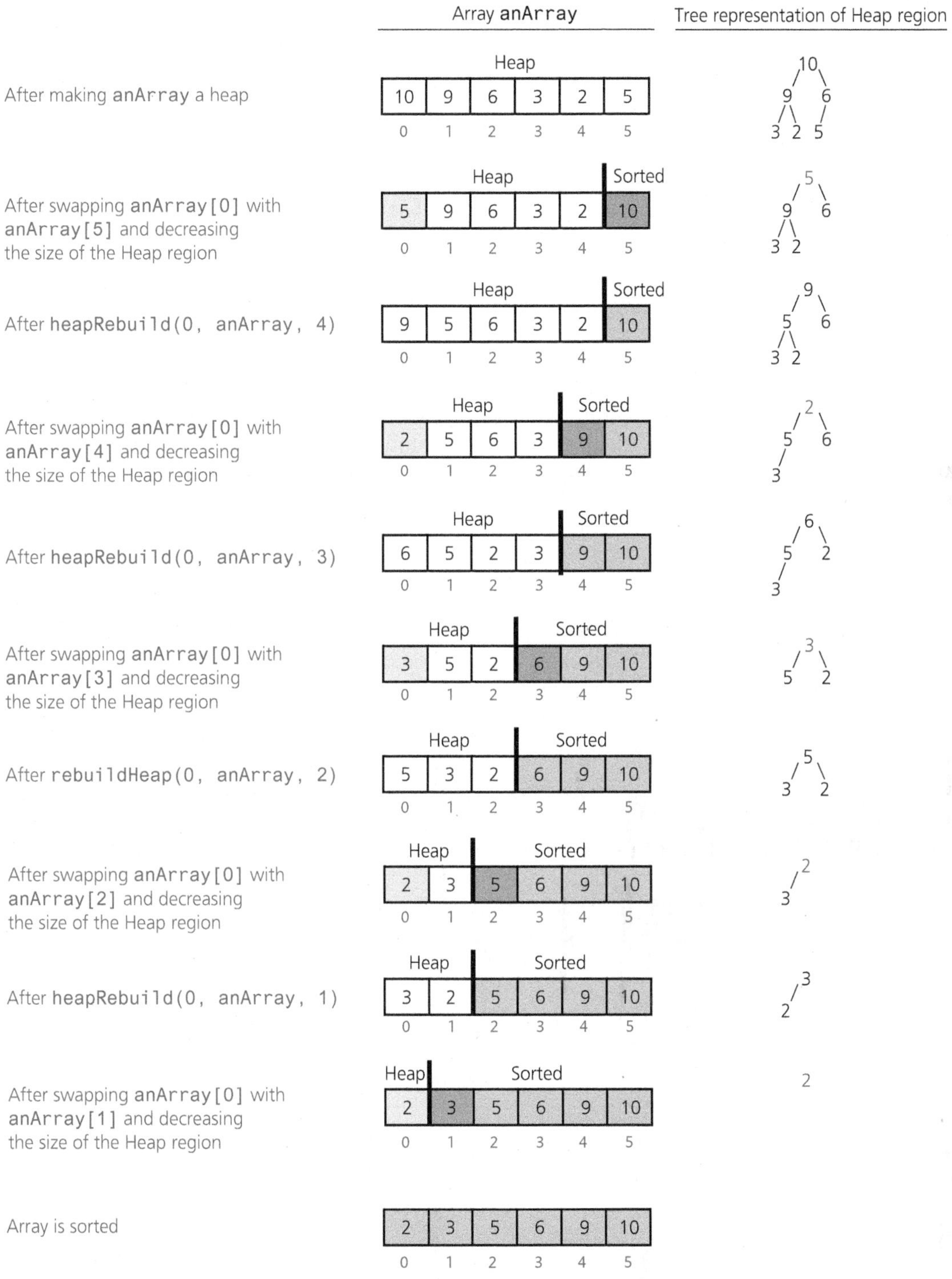

SUMMARY

1. Since a heap is a complete binary tree, it has an efficient array-based implementation.

2. The root of a maxheap contains the heap's largest value. The root of a minheap contains the heap's smallest value.

3. To remove the value in the root of a heap, you first replace the value with the value in the last node of the heap. This step likely results in a semiheap. After removing the last node, you convert the semiheap to a heap by a trickle-down step.

4. To add an item to a heap, you add a new leaf to the heap so that it remains a complete binary tree. You then use a bubble-up step to reposition the new value.

5. A heap that uses an array-based representation of a complete binary tree is a good implementation of a priority queue when you know the maximum number of items that will be stored at any one time.

6. Heap sort converts an array into a heap to locate the array's largest item. This step enables the heap sort to sort an array in an efficient manner.

7. Heap sort, like merge sort, has good worst-case and average-case behaviors, but neither algorithm is as good in the average case as quick sort. Heap sort has an advantage over merge sort in that it does not require a second array.

EXERCISES

1. Given the minheap myHeap in Figure 17-12, show what it would look like after each operation in the following sequence of pseudocode operations:

   ```
   myHeap.add(8)
   myHeap.add(5)
   myHeap.remove()
   ```

   FIGURE 17-12   Minheap for Exercise 1

   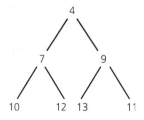

2. Given the maxheap myHeap in Figure 17-13, show what it would look like after each operation in the following sequence of pseudocode operations:

   ```
   myHeap.add(16)
   myHeap.add(14)
   myHeap.remove()
   ```

FIGURE 17-13   Maxheap for Exercise 2

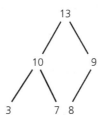

3. Repeat Checkpoint Question 10, but instead use the array 9, 12, 4, 8, 3, 11, 6, 15.

4. Prove that the root of a maxheap contains the largest value in the tree.

5. Does the order in which you add data items to a heap affect the heap that results? Explain.

6. Revise the pseudocode for the ADT heap methods add and heapRebuild so that they do not swap items.

7. Suppose that you have two items with the same priority value. How does the order in which you add these items to a priority queue affect the order in which they will be removed? What can you do if you need entries whose priority values are equal to be served on a first-come, first-served basis?

8. Suppose that you wanted the remove operation of a priority queue to remove the entry whose priority value is smallest instead of largest. You would then use a minheap. Convert the maxheap implementation to a minheap implementation.

9. Suppose that you wanted to maintain the index of the item with the smallest value in an array-based maxheap. That is, in addition to a peekTop operation, you might want to support a getMin operation. How difficult would it be to maintain this index within the add and remove operations?

10. Suppose that after you have placed several items into a priority queue, you need to adjust one of their priority values. For example, a particular task in a priority queue of tasks could become either more or less urgent. How can you adjust a heap if a single value changes?

11. Show that within the pseudocode for the method heapCreate you can replace the statement

```
for (index = itemCount - 1 down to 0)
```

with

```
for (index = itemCount / 2 - 1 down to 0)
```

12. Trace the action of heapSort on the array given in Checkpoint Question 5.

13. Implement heapSort in C++.

14. Revise heapSort so that it sorts an array into descending order.

PROGRAMMING PROBLEMS

1. Complete the implementation file for the class `ArrayMaxHeap` that is described in Section 17.2.2.

2. Use a binary search tree in the implementation of `HeapInterface`. Where in the tree will the largest entry occur? How efficient is this implementation?

3. Implement a class of minheaps using an array. Name your class `ArrayMinHeap`.

4. Consider the problem of combining two heaps together into a single heap.

   a. Write an efficient algorithm for combining two heaps, one with size n and the other with size 1. What is the Big O performance of your algorithm?
   b. Write an efficient algorithm for combining two heaps of equal size n. What is the Big O performance of your algorithm?
   c. Write an efficient algorithm for combining two arbitrary-sized heaps into one heap. What is the Big O performance of your algorithm?
   d. Implement the algorithm that you wrote in part c.

5. Section 2.4.4 of Chapter 2 discussed the problem of finding the kth smallest value in an array of n values. Design an algorithm that uses a minheap to solve this problem. Using the class `ArrayMinHeap` defined in Programming Problem 3, implement your algorithm as a function at the client level.

6. Implement the to-do list that is described at the beginning of Section 13.3 in Chapter 13. Use the class `HeapPriorityQueue` as given in Listings 17-3 and 17-4.

7. Suppose that you wanted to implement a priority queue whose priority values are integers 1 through 5.

   a. Implement the priority queue as a heap of queues, as described in this chapter.
   b. Another solution uses an array of 5 queues, one for each priority value. Use this approach to implement the priority queue.

8. Write an interactive program that will monitor the flow of patients in a large hospital. The program should account for patients who check in and out of the hospital and should allow access to information about a given patient. In addition, the program should manage the scheduling of three operating rooms. Doctors make a request that includes a patient's name and a priority value between 1 and 10 that reflects the urgency of the operation. Patients are chosen for the operating room by priority value, and patients with the same priority are served on a first-come, first-served basis.

   The user should use either one-letter or one-word commands to control the program. As you design your solution, try to identify the essential operations (excuse the pun) that you must perform on the data, and only then choose an appropriate data structure for implementation. This approach will allow you to maintain the wall between the main part of the program and the implementations.

9. Implement a class of priority queues using a binary search tree to contain its items. Discuss the appropriateness and efficiency of this implementation.

Iterators

Contents

Prerequisites

Chapter 9   List Implementations
C++ Interlude 4   Safe Memory Management Using Smart Pointers
C++ Interlude 6   Overloaded Operators and Friend Access

An iterator is an object that traverses a collection of data. During the traversal, you can look at the data entries and process them. You can compare iterators to see if they point to the same entry in a collection, and C++ provides special functions that let you perform other actions with collections, such as searching and counting, when using iterators. Iterators are commonly implemented by overloading operators that correspond to the behaviors an iterator has. A container can instantiate an iterator and give it to a client to use to traverse the contained data collection.

C7.1 Iterators

VideoNote
C++ iterators

How would you count the number of lines on this page? You could use your finger to point to each line as you counted it. Your finger would keep your place on the page. If you paused at a particular line, your finger would be on the current line, and there would be a previous line and a next line. If you think of this page as a list of lines, you would be traversing the list as you counted the lines.

An **iterator** is an object that enables you to traverse a collection of data, such as the data in a list, beginning with the first entry. During one complete traversal, or iteration, each data item is considered once. You control the progress of the iteration by repeatedly asking the iterator to give you a reference to the next entry in the

An iterator is an
object that traverses
a collection of like
objects

collection. You also can modify the collection as you traverse it by adding, removing, or simply changing entries.

You are familiar with iteration because you have written loops. For example, if `nameList` is a list of strings, you can write the following `for` loop to display the entire list:

```
int listSize = nameList.getLength();
for (int position = 1; position <= listSize; position++)
    std::cout << nameList.getEntry(position) << std::endl;
```

Here the loop traverses, or iterates, through the entries in the list. Instead of simply displaying each entry, we could do other things to or with it.

Notice that the previous loop is at the client level, since it uses the ADT operation `getEntry` to access the list. For an array-based implementation of the list, `getEntry` can retrieve the desired array entry directly and quickly. But if a chain of linked nodes represents the list's entries, `getEntry` must move from node to node until it locates the desired one. For example, to retrieve the nth entry in the list, `getEntry` would begin at the first node in the chain and then move to the second node, the third node, and so on until it reached the nth node. At the next repetition of the loop, `getEntry` would retrieve the $n + 1^{st}$ entry in the list by beginning again at the first node in the chain and stepping from node to node until it reached the $n + 1^{st}$ node. This wastes time.

Note: Iterators

An iterator is a program component that steps through, or traverses, a collection of data. The iterator keeps track of its progress during the traversal, or iteration. It can tell you whether a next entry exists and, if so, return a reference to it. During one cycle of the iteration, each data item is considered once.

Iteration is such a common operation that we could include it as part of the ADT list. Doing so would enable a more efficient implementation than you could achieve at the client level. Notice that the operation `toVector` of the ADT bag in Chapters 3 and 4 performs a traversal and is an example of a traversal controlled by the ADT. A client can invoke `toVector` but cannot control its traversal once it begins.

But `toVector` only returns the list's entries. What if we want to do something else with them as we traverse them? We do not want to add another operation to the ADT each time we think of another way to use an iteration. We need a way for a client to step through a collection of data and retrieve or modify the entries. The traversal should keep track of its progress; that is, it should know where it is in the collection and whether it has accessed each entry. An iterator provides such a traversal.

C++ provides a rich library of tools to build iterators, but in this Interlude we focus on the capabilities necessary to implement simple iterators that traverse a collection of items, retrieve an item in a collection, and compare two iterators to see whether they access the same entry in the collection. Such iterators are known as **input iterators**.

C7.1.1 Common Iterator Operations

Though not required, iterators in C++ typically provide basic functionality by using overloaded operators. An iterator operation that accesses the item it currently references is usually implemented by overloading the C++ dereferencing operator `*`. For example, you can define the `*` operator for an iterator `i` so that `*i` is the item that `i` references.

Iterators also have operations that move the iterator forward through the collection. Often, these operations take the form of the overloaded operator `++`. Bidirectional iterators also overload the -- operator to allow you to move backward through the collection. Lastly, the operators == and != are usually overloaded to compare iterators for equality.

Note: **Common iterator operations**

Operation	Description
*	Return the item that the iterator currently references
++	Move the iterator to the next item in the collection
--	Move the iterator to the previous item in the collection (used only for bidirectional or random iterators)
==	Compare two iterators for equality
!=	Compare two iterators for inequality

By enabling you to overload these operators for your iterator class, C++ gives you the advanced iterator operations covered in the next section without further programming. To enable this functionality, however, you must derive your iterator class from the C++ template class `iterator`. This template does not have any methods. Instead, you use it with an **iterator category tag** as the template type to identify the category of your iterator.

For example, the following lines declare an input iterator for the class `LinkedList`:

```
template <class ItemType>
class LinkedIterator : public std::iterator<std::input_iterator_tag, int>
```

where `input_iterator_tag` indicates that this iterator implements input-iterator functionality. The second template type specified, `int`, identifies the type of value used to measure the distance between two iterators. These values are normally integers. The **distance** between two iterators is the number of positions between the current positions of the two iterators. For example, if an iterator points to the first item in a list and another iterator points to the fifth item in the same list, their distance is 4.

Note: **C++ iterator categories**

All of the following iterators support a copy or assign (=) operation and an increment (++) operation in addition to the ones listed next:

Category	Tag	Supported Operations
Input iterator	input_iterator_tag	Equality/inequality (==, !=), access collection entry (*)
Output iterator	output_iterator_tag	Change a collection entry (*)
Forward iterator	forward_iterator_tag	Same as the input and output iterators and has a default constructor
Bidirectional iterator	bidirectional_ iterator_tag	Same as the forward iterator, but also can traverse the collection backward (--)
Random-access iterator	random_iterator_tag	Same as the bidirectional iterator and adds support for arithmetic (+, -, +=, -=) and relational (<, <=, >, >=) operations between iterators. Supports the [ ] operator to directly access collection entries.

C7.1.2 Using Iterator Operations

Before discussing the details of a class of iterators and its implementation, we should examine how clients of `LinkedList` would use these iterators. Standard containers in C++ implement two special methods, `begin` and `end`, that return an iterator to the first entry and last entry respectively. These iterators should have an order of magnitude in performance of O(1) as they move from entry to entry. Let's see how a client could use these methods if we implemented them in our `LinkedList` class.

Up to this point, if we want to display all the entries in a list `myList`, we need to perform this O(n^2) action:

```cpp
int currentPosition = 1;
while (currentPosition <= myList.getLength())
{
    std::cout << myList.getEntry(currentPosition) << " "; // O(n) operation
    currentPosition++;
} // end while
```

Now assume that `LinkedIterator` is a class of iterators for `LinkedList`, and `LinkedList` defines the methods `begin` and `end` and declares them as follows:

```cpp
LinkedIterator<ItemType> begin() const;
LinkedIterator<ItemType> end() const;
```

We can rewrite the previous loop using `LinkedIterator` objects:

```cpp
LinkedIterator<std::string> currentIterator = myList.begin();
while (currentIterator != myList.end())
{
    std::cout << *currentIterator << " "; // O(1) operation
    ++currentIterator;
} // end while
```

The first line creates a `LinkedIterator` object, `currentIterator`, that points to the first entry in the list. The statements in the `while` loop check whether `currentIterator` points to the entry that is at the end of the list. Then, for each entry in the list, we dereference the iterator using the * operator to access and display the entry at the iterator's current position. The iterator is then incremented to reference the next entry in the list for the following iteration.

Notice that the ++ operator precedes the name of the iterator. We use this prefix operator to differentiate it from an arithmetic increment of an integer, which uses the postfix ++ operator. Iterators may implement the postfix ++ operator, but we have chosen not to do this to avoid possible confusion in reading the code.

Note: **Using the ++ and -- operators**

In C++, the operators ++ and -- can be used in either prefix or postfix form to represent incrementing or decrementing the corresponding variable. To differentiate between incrementing or decrementing arithmetic variables from iterator positions, we use ++ and -- as postfix operators for arithmetic operations and as prefix operators for iterator operations.

The implementation of the methods `begin` and `end` in the `LinkedList` class are straightforward:

```cpp
template <class ItemType>
LinkedIterator<ItemType> LinkedList<ItemType>::begin()
{
    return LinkedIterator<ItemType>(this, headPtr);
}  // end begin

template <class ItemType>
LinkedIterator<ItemType> LinkedList<ItemType>::end()
{
    return LinkedIterator<ItemType>(this, nullptr);
}  // end end
```

In the `begin` method, we send the iterator references to the list object and the first node in the chain that contains the list items. Giving the iterator direct access to `LinkedList`'s data members must be done with care. Well-designed iterators only traverse the collection and access the items stored in the collection; they should not change the structure of a collection.

C7.1.3 Implementing an Iterator

Listing C7-1 is the header file for the class, `LinkedIterator`, of input iterators designed to work with our `LinkedList` class. It is a distinct class separate from `LinkedList`. The constructor has two parameters, the list traversed by the iterator and an initial node for the iterator to reference. The second parameter is used by the `LinkedList` class methods `begin` and `end` to initialize the iterator's position.

LISTING C7-1   The header file for the class `LinkedIterator`

```cpp
 1   #ifndef LINKED_ITERATOR_
 2   #define LINKED_ITERATOR_
 3
 4   #include <iterator>
 5   #include "Node.h"
 6
 7   template<class ItemType>
 8   class LinkedList;
 9
10   template <class ItemType>
11   class LinkedIterator : public std::iterator<std::input_iterator_tag, int>
12   {
13   private:
14      // ADT associated with iterator
15      const std::shared_ptr<LinkedList<ItemType>> containerPtr;
16
17      // Current location in collection
18      std::shared_ptr<Node<ItemType>> currentItemPtr;
19
```

(continues)

```
20   public:
21      LinkedIterator(std::shared_ptr<LinkedList<ItemType>> someList,
22                     std::shared_ptr<Node<ItemType>> nodePtr = nullptr);
23
24      /** Overloaded dereferencing operator.
25       @return  The item at the position referenced by iterator. */
26      const ItemType operator*();
27
28      /** Overloaded prefix increment operator.
29       @return  The iterator referencing the next position in the list. */
30      LinkedIterator<ItemType> operator++();
31
32      /** Overloaded equality operator.
33       @param LinkedList  The iterator for comparison.
34       @return  True if this iterator references the same list and
35          the same position as rightHandSide, false otherwise. */
36      bool operator==(const LinkedIterator<ItemType>& rightHandSide) const;
37
38      /** Overloaded inequality operator.
39       @param LinkedList  The iterator for comparison.
40       @return  True if this iterator does not reference the same list and the
41          same position as rightHandSide, false otherwise. */
42      bool operator!=(const LinkedIterator<ItemType>& rightHandSide) const;
43   }; // end LinkedIterator
44
45   #include "LinkedIterator.cpp"
46   #endif
```

In addition to the base class specification and class constructor, there are two other lines in this header file that differ from previous header files. Before we declare the LinkedIterator class, we write a forward declaration of the class LinkedList:

```
template<class ItemType>
class LinkedList;
```

These lines are necessary because the begin and end methods that we added to LinkedList must instantiate an object of the class LinkedIterator<ItemType>, but the LinkedIterator class must have a complete declaration of LinkedList<ItemType> to instantiate itself. To resolve these circular references, we include this forward declaration. When the compiler begins to compile the LinkedIterator class, it will read these statements and know that LinkedList<ItemType> is also a class. The compiler can then use placeholders for the details of LinkedList.

The implementation of LinkedIterator is shown in Listing C7-2.

LISTING C7-2   The implementation file for the class LinkedIterator

```
1   #include "LinkedIterator.h"
2
3   template <class ItemType>
4   LinkedIterator<ItemType>::
```

```
5    LinkedIterator(std::shared_ptr<LinkedList<ItemType>> someList,
6                    std::shared_ptr<Node<ItemType>> nodePtr)
7                       : containerPtr(someList), currentItemPtr(nodePtr)
8    {
9    }   // end constructor
10
11   template <class ItemType>
12   const ItemType LinkedIterator<ItemType>::operator*()
13   {
14      return currentItemPtr->getItem();
15   }   // end operator*
16
17   template <class ItemType>
18   LinkedIterator<ItemType> LinkedIterator<ItemType>::operator++()
19   {
20      currentItemPtr = currentItemPtr->getNext();
21      return *this;
22   }   // end prefix operator++
23
24   template <class ItemType>
25   bool LinkedIterator<ItemType>::operator==(const
26                       LinkedIterator<ItemType>& rightHandSide) const
27   {
28      return ((containerPtr == rightHandSide.containerPtr) &&
29             (currentItemPtr == rightHandSide.currentItemPtr));
30   }   // end operator==
31
32   template <class ItemType>
33   bool LinkedIterator<ItemType>::operator!=(const
34                       LinkedIterator<ItemType>& rightHandSide) const
35   {
36      return ((containerPtr != rightHandSide.containerPtr) ||
37             (currentItemPtr != rightHandSide.currentItemPtr));
38   }   // end operator!=
```

The implementations of the iterator methods use the methods of the Node class. For example, the dereferencing * operator returns the result of calling getItem on the current node, and the ++ operator uses getNext to advance the iterator to the next position. Notice that the ++ operator returns the current object to the caller. This is part of the C++ standard for the ++ operator, but clients seldom use the return value.

Although you could define iterators that have access to public methods of your data structure, you would lose the efficiencies gained by directly accessing the structure. The best approach is to design your ADT and its iterator at the same time, so that you can coordinate their features and ensure that the iterator does not change the class's structure.

C7.2 Advanced Iterator Functionality

Deriving our iterator from the C++ template class iterator enables us to use the iterator with several standard functions provided by C++. These functions simplify many common processes, such as displaying the items in a collection, searching a collection, and counting the number of occurrences of an item in a collection.

The function for_each. Earlier, Section C7.1.2 of this C++ Interlude presented a `while` loop that uses iterators to access and display each item in a list of strings. The C++ standard function `for_each` can accomplish this task in a simpler manner. The syntax of the `for_each` function is:

> for_each(*start_iterator*, *end_iterator*, *function_to_perform*);

where *start_iterator* and *end_iterator* are iterators to the first and last positions in the collection that should be processed, and *function_to_perform* is a function with a single parameter of the same type as the entries stored in the collection. This function is called by `for_each` and is applied to each of the items in the collection from *start_iterator* to *end_iterator*. It is similar to the `visit` function we used in Chapter 15 with binary tree traversals.

To use the `for_each` function, we must create a function to be applied to each of the items in the collection. In this case, the items are strings, and we want to display each one:

```cpp
void displayOneItem(std::string itemToDisplay)
{
    std::cout << itemToDisplay << std::endl;
} // end displayOneItem
```

We can then call the `for_each` function to display all items in the collection as follows:

```cpp
for_each(myList.begin(), myList.end(), displayOneItem);
```

This one statement takes care of all the details involved in displaying the entries in `myList`. Beginning at the first position of `myList`, the statement passes each list item to be displayed to the function `displayOneItem`, until all items have been processed.

Note: The syntax used to call most of the special functions that use iterators to process collections has the form

> *function_name(start_iterator, end_iterator, special_parameters);*

where *special_parameters* represents one or more parameters that the function needs to perform its task.

The function find. To search a collection for a specified target entry, you use the function `find`. This function returns an iterator to the target if it exists in the collection. If the target is not in the collection, `find` returns an iterator to the last position. For example, the following statement searches `myList` for the string `"Ace"`:

```cpp
// Find the entry "Ace" in the collection myList
LinkedIterator<std::string> myCard = find(myList.begin(), myList.end(), "Ace");
```

The function count. Another useful function is `count`. This function returns an integer that represents the number of times a specified value occurs in the collection between the starting iterator and ending iterator:

```cpp
// Count the number of occurrences of "Ace" in collection myList
long aceCount = count(myList.begin(), myList.end(), "Ace");
```

The function advance. To move an iterator forward by a specific number of positions, you can use the `advance` function. It has a slightly different form than most standard functions that use iterators:

> advance(*someIterator*, *distanceToAdvance*);

For example, if we needed to advance an iterator to the fifth entry in myList, we would use the following statements:

```
// Iterator to first position in myList
LinkedIterator<std::string> myIterator = myList.begin();

// Advance from first position to fifth (4 positions ahead)
advance(myIterator, 4);
```

The function distance. To see how many entries remain to be processed in an iteration, we can use the distance function to get the distance from our current position to the end of the collection:

```
long numberRemaining = distance(myIterator, myList.end());
```

The function equal. If you want to test whether the entries in two lists are the same, either for the entire first list or for a subrange within the lists, you can use the equal function. Suppose myList and yourList are two instances of LinkedList<string>. To see whether all entries in myList are equal to the first entries in yourList, you would write:

```
bool same = equal(myList.begin(), myList.end(), yourList.begin());
```

This function is concerned only with a range of positions. The number of entries to compare, *n*, is determined by the distance between the first two iterator parameters. The third iterator parameter specifies a starting location in the second collection for the comparison. If the second collection contains fewer than *n* entries, the function returns false. Otherwise, only *n* entries are compared.

Note: **Some useful C++ functions that use iterators**

- Process entries in a collection from *start_iterator* position to *end_iterator* position by passing each one to the function *function_to_perform*:

  `for_each(start_iterator, end_iterator, function_to_perform);`

- Return an iterator to the position of the first occurrence of *target* between *start_iterator* and *end_iterator*:

  `iteratorType someIterator = find(start_iterator, end_iterator, target);`

- Return the number of occurrences of *target* between *start_iterator* and *end_iterator*:

  `int numberOccur = count(start_iterator, end_iterator, target);`

- Compare entries in collection 1 from *start1_iterator* through *end1_iterator* to those in collection 2 beginning at *start2_iterator*:

  `bool result = equal(start1_iterator, end1_iterator, start2_iterator);`

- Advance *someIterator* from its current position by *distanceToAdvance* positions:

  `advance(someIterator, distanceToAdvance);`

- Find the distance, or number of positions, from *someIterator* to *anotherIterator*:

  `int theDistance = distance(someIterator, anotherIterator);`

Contents

Prerequisites

This chapter considers the ADT dictionary, which is appropriate for problems that must manage data by value. Several dictionary implementations—which use arrays, linked chains, binary search trees, and a new technique known as hashing—will be presented, along with their advantages and disadvantages.

To make an intelligent choice among the various possible dictionary implementations, you must analyze the efficiency with which each of the implementations supports the dictionary operations. For example, we analyze the time-efficiency of array-based and link-based dictionary implementations and conclude that, in many applications, the implementations do not support the dictionary operations as efficiently as possible. This conclusion motivates the use of more sophisticated dictionary implementations.

VideoNote
The ADT dictionary

18.1 The ADT Dictionary

When we began our discussion of sorting a collection of data in Chapter 11, we introduced the notion of a sort key. For example, you might want to sort a collection of data about people based on their names, their ages, or their zip codes. The criterion you choose is known as the sort key. Similarly, you might want to search the same collection of data for a name, an address, or a phone number. The criterion you choose for this search is known as a **search key**.

Applications that require value-oriented operations are extremely prevalent, as you might imagine. For example, the tasks

- Find the phone number of John Smith
- Erase all the information about the employee with ID number 12908

involve values instead of positions. We first encountered a value-oriented ADT, the sorted list, in Chapter 12. Chapter 15 presented the binary search tree, which is also a value-oriented ADT. This section describes yet another value-oriented ADT, the dictionary.

Consider the data given in Figure 18-1 for some major cities in the world. Each city has certain information listed, and the design of the data collection enables you to look up this information. For example, if you wanted to know the population of London, you could scan the

FIGURE 18-1 A collection of data about certain cities

City	Country	Population
Buenos Aires	Argentina	13,639,000
Cairo	Egypt	17,816,000
Johannesburg	South Africa	7,618,000
London	England	8,586,000
Madrid	Spain	5,427,000
Mexico City	Mexico	19,463,000
Mumbai	India	16,910,000
New York City	U.S.A.	20,464,000
Paris	France	10,755,000
Sydney	Australia	3,785,000
Tokyo	Japan	37,126,000
Toronto	Canada	6,139,000

column of city names, starting at the top, until you came to London. Because the cities are listed in alphabetical order, you could also mimic a binary search. You could begin the search near the middle of the column, determine in which half London lies, and recursively apply the binary search to the appropriate half. As you know, a binary search is far more efficient than scanning the entire column of city names from the beginning.

If, however, you wanted to find out which cities in the data collection are in Spain, you would have no choice but to scan the entire data collection. The alphabetical order of the city names does not help you for this problem at all. The data arrangement facilitates the search for a given city, but other types of questions require a complete scan of the data.

The ADT **dictionary**, or **map**, or **table**, also allows you to look up information easily and has a special operation for this purpose. Typically, the entries in the ADT dictionary are objects that contain several pieces of data. You can facilitate the retrieval of this data by basing the search on a specified search key. In the dictionary of cities, for example, you could designate City as the search key if you often needed to retrieve the information about a city.

The ADT dictionary uses a search key to identify its entries

Each entry in a dictionary pairs a search key with a specific piece of data, or **value**. We sometimes will characterize such an entry as a **key-value pair**. For simplicity, we will insist that a dictionary have distinct search keys.

You can devise implementations of a dictionary that allow the rapid retrieval of an entry based on its search key. However, if you need to retrieve an entry based on something other than its search key, you will have to inspect the entire dictionary. Therefore, the choice of a search key sends the ADT implementer the following message:

Arrange the dictionary to facilitate the search for an entry, given its search key.

The basic operations that define the ADT dictionary are as follows:

Note: ADT dictionary operations
- Test whether a dictionary is empty.
- Get the number of entries in a dictionary.
- Add a new entry to a dictionary.
- Remove the entry with a given search key from a dictionary.
- Remove all entries from a dictionary.
- Retrieve the entry in a dictionary that corresponds to a given search key.
- Test whether a dictionary contains an entry with a given search key.
- Traverse the entries in a dictionary in sorted search-key order.

As we refine the specification for the dictionary operation that adds new entries, we should ask this question: What should the operation do if the new entry's search key already exists in the dictionary? We could treat this situation in one of several ways: The operation can

Our dictionary assumes distinct search keys

- Deny the attempt to add the new entry
- Ignore the attempt to add the new entry
- Replace the existing entry with the new entry

The second option is a poor one, as the status of the dictionary would be unknown. Either of the other two options is a reasonable choice; we will choose the first option.

The following operation contract specifies in more detail an ADT dictionary whose entries each have a distinct search key and an associated value. Figure 18-2 shows a UML diagram for a class of dictionaries.

ABSTRACT DATA TYPE: DICTIONARY	
DATA	
• A finite number of objects, each having a unique search key and an associated value.	
OPERATIONS	
PSEUDOCODE	DESCRIPTION
isEmpty()	Task: Sees whether this dictionary is empty. Input: None. Output: True if the dictionary is empty; otherwise false.
getNumberOfEntries()	Task: Gets the number of entries in this dictionary. Input: None. Output: The number of entries in the dictionary.
add(searchKey, newValue)	Task: Adds a search key and its associated value to this dictionary. Input: newValue is the data item to be added; searchKey is the value's associated search key and differs from all search keys presently in the dictionary. Output: True if the addition is successful, or false if not.
remove(searchKey)	Task: Removes the entry with the given search key from this dictionary. Input: searchKey is the search key of the entry to be removed. Output: True if the removal is successful, or false if not.
clear()	Task: Removes all entries from this dictionary. Input: None. Output: None.
getValue(searchKey)	Task: Retrieves the value in this dictionary whose search key is given. Input: searchKey is the search key of the value to be retrieved. Output: The value associated with the given search key.
contains(searchKey)	Task: Sees whether this dictionary contains an entry with a given search key. Input: searchKey is the given search key. Output: True if the dictionary contains the designated entry, or false if not.
traverse(visit)	Task: Traverses this dictionary and calls a given client function once for each entry. Input: The client function visit, which exists outside of the ADT implementation. Output: visit's action occurs once for each entry in the dictionary and possibly alters the entry.

Note: Search keys

The concept of a search key for the ADT dictionary is essential to the implementation of the dictionary. Changing the search key of an existing entry in the dictionary could make that entry or other dictionary entries impossible to find. The client should not be able to modify an entry's search key once that entry is in the dictionary.

FIGURE 18-2   UML diagram for a class of dictionaries

```
Dictionary

+isEmpty(): boolean
+getNumberOfEntries(): integer
+add(searchKey: KeyType, newValue: ValueType): boolean
+remove(targetKey: KeyType): boolean
+clear(): void
+getValue(targetKey: KeyType): ValueType
+contains(targetKey: KeyType): boolean
+traverse(visit(value: ValueType): void): void
```

You should realize that these operations are only one possible set of dictionary operations. The client may require either a subset of these operations or other operations not listed here to fit the application at hand. It may also be convenient to modify the definitions of some of the operations. For example, these operations assume that no two dictionary entries have the same search keys. However, in many applications it is quite reasonable to expect duplicate search keys. If this is the case, you must redefine several of the operations to eliminate the ambiguity that would arise from duplicate search keys. For example, which value should getValue return if several entries have the specified search key? You should tailor your definition of the ADT dictionary to the problem at hand.

> Various sets of dictionary operations are possible

> Other dictionaries could allow duplicate search keys

Although just the operations add, remove, and getValue in the previous set of operations are sufficient for some applications, you cannot do several significant things without additional operations. For instance, you cannot display all of the key-value pairs in the dictionary, because you cannot retrieve a value unless you know its search key. Thus, you cannot display the entire dictionary unless you can traverse the dictionary.

The traverse operation visits each entry in the dictionary once. In defining this operation, you must specify the order in which the traversal should visit the entries. One common specification is to visit them in sorted order by search key, but perhaps you do not care about the order in which the entries are visited. As you will see, the way you define traverse—if you request it at all—can affect the way you implement the dictionary.

> traverse visits all dictionary entries

Like the traversal operations for the ADT binary tree, traverse has a visit function as its argument. Because visit can do any number of things—including access the dictionary via the ADT operations—traverse is a versatile operation. We illustrate this versatility with two brief examples, in which the dictionary contains the data for the cities listed in Figure 18-1.

 Examples: Each of the following tasks will use the city's name as the search key. The class City contains all the information for a city, including its name, country, and population. The class has accessor and mutator methods for each of these pieces of data. An instance of City is the value in the dictionary's key-value pairs.

> Tasks that use the city's name as the search key

- **Display, in alphabetical order, the name of each city and its population.** This task requires you to write the city names in alphabetical order. Since the city names are the search keys, traverse must visit entries alphabetically by search key. You pass the method the name of the function display, which appears in pseudocode as follows:

```
display(aCity: City): void
{
    Display aCity.getName()
    Display aCity.getPopulation()
}
```

Although the visitation order of traverse is significant for this first task, it is immaterial for the next one.

- **Increase the population of each city by 10 percent.** To perform this task, you pass to traverse the name of the function updatePopulation, which we define in pseudocode as follows:

```
updatePopulation(aCity: City): void
{
    aCity.setPopulation(1.1 * aCity.getPopulation())
}
```

18.1.1 An Interface for the ADT Dictionary

To complete our specification of the ADT dictionary, we write the interface shown in Listing 18-1. This interface specifies two data-type parameters—KeyType and ValueType—in the statement

```
template<class KeyType, class ValueType>
```

These parameters make it possible for the data type of the values in a dictionary to differ from the data type of their search keys.

LISTING 18-1 An interface for the ADT dictionary

```
1   /** An interface for the ADT dictionary.
2    @file DictionaryInterface.h */
3
4   #ifndef DICTIONARY_INTERFACE_
5   #define DICTIONARY_INTERFACE_
6
7   #include "NotFoundException.h"
8
9   template<class KeyType, class ValueType>
10  class DictionaryInterface
11  {
12  public:
13     /** Sees whether this dictionary is empty.
14      @return  True if the dictionary is empty;
15         otherwise returns false. */
16     virtual bool isEmpty() const = 0;
17
18     /** Gets the number of entries in this dictionary.
19      @return  The number of entries in the dictionary. */
20     virtual int getNumberOfEntries() const = 0;
```

```
21
22      /** Adds a new search key and associated value to this dictionary.
23       @pre  The new search key differs from all search keys presently
24         in the dictionary.
25       @post  If the addition is successful, the new key-value pair is in its
26         proper position within the dictionary.
27       @param searchKey  The search key associated with the value to be added.
28       @param newValue  The value to be added.
29       @return  True if the entry was successfully added, or false if not. */
30      virtual bool add(const KeyType& searchKey, const ValueType& newValue) = 0;
31
32      /** Removes a key-value pair from this dictionary.
33       @post  If the entry whose search key equals searchKey existed in the
34         dictionary, the entry was removed.
35       @param searchKey  The search key of the entry to be removed.
36       @return  True if the entry was successfully removed, or false if not. */
37      virtual bool remove(const KeyType& searchKey) = 0;
38
39      /** Removes all entries from this dictionary. */
40      virtual void clear() = 0;
41
42      /** Retrieves the value in this dictionary whose search key is given
43       @post  If the retrieval is successful, the value is returned.
44       @param searchKey  The search key of the value to be retrieved.
45       @return  The value associated with the search key.
46       @throw  NotFoundException if the key-value pair does not exist. */
47      virtual ValueType getValue(const KeyType& searchKey) const
48                          throw (NotFoundException) = 0;
49
50      /** Sees whether this dictionary contains an entry with a given search key.
51       @post  The dictionary is unchanged.
52       @param searchKey  The given search key.
53       @return  True if an entry with the given search key exists in the
54         dictionary. */
55      virtual bool contains(const KeyType& searchKey) const = 0;
56
57      /** Traverses this dictionary and calls a given client function once
58         for each entry.
59       @post  The given function's action occurs once for each entry in the
60         dictionary and possibly alters the entry.
61       @param visit  A client function. */
62      virtual void traverse(void visit(ValueType&)) const = 0;
63      /** Destroys this dictionary and frees its assigned memory. */
64
65      virtual ~DictionaryInterface(){ }
66  }; // end DictionaryInterface
67  #endif
```

Question 1 Using the ADT dictionary operations, write pseudocode for a `replace` function at the client level that replaces the dictionary entry whose search key is *x* with another entry whose search key is also *x*.

18.2 Possible Implementations

In previous chapters, ADT implementations often were either array based or link based. That is, you used either an array or a chain of linked nodes to store the ADT's entries. Such implementations are called **linear** because they represent entries one after another in a data structure and thus mirror the flat, list-like appearance of the city data given in Figure 18-1.

Four categories of linear implementations

Linear implementations of a dictionary are certainly possible and fall into four categories:

- Sorted (by search key) array-based
- Sorted (by search key) link-based
- Unsorted array-based
- Unsorted link-based

The unsorted implementations store the key-value pairs in no particular order; they can place a new entry into any convenient location. Notice that the add operation has two parameters: a data value and the value's search key. The sorted implementations must place a new entry into its proper position as determined by its search key. Whether sorted or unsorted, the dictionary must not only store both pieces of data—search key and data value—but also form an association between the two. To do so, we will encapsulate each value with its search key into an object of a new class, Entry, as pictured in Figure 18-3.

FIGURE 18-3   A dictionary entry

Search key	Data value

The array-based and link-based linear implementations have the basic structures shown in Figure 18-4. Both implementations maintain a count of the present number of key-value pairs in the dictionary. The two implementations in this figure happen to be sorted. As you will see, the unsorted and sorted implementations have their relative advantages and disadvantages.

FIGURE 18-4   Data members for two sorted linear implementations of the ADT dictionary for the data in Figure 18-1

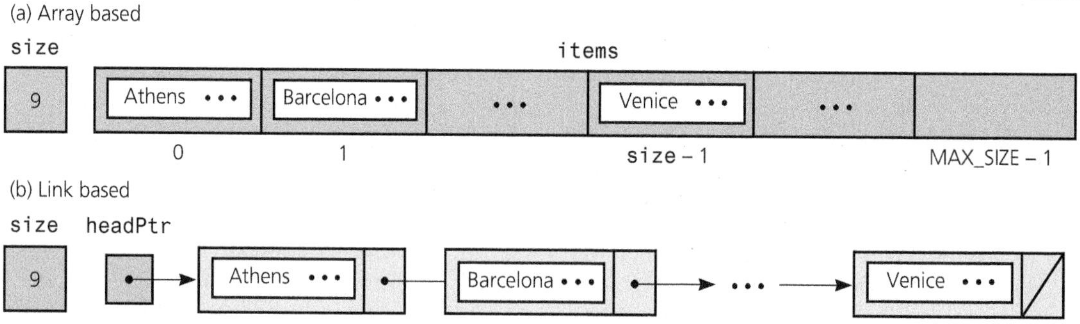

(a) Array based

(b) Link based

Note: A sorted linear array-based implementation of the ADT dictionary must shift data during an addition and when removing an entry. These shifts can be expensive, particularly for large dictionaries.

Although a linear link-based implementation of the ADT dictionary eliminates the need to shift data, it does not support the addition and removal operations any more efficiently than does an array-based implementation, because you cannot perform a binary search in a reasonable fashion.

The header file for the class Entry is in Listing 18-2. Notice that, like DictionaryInterface, the class Entry specifies two data-type parameters. We leave Entry's implementation for you as an exercise.

LISTING 18-2 A header file for a class of dictionary entries

```
1   /** A class of entries to add to an array-based implementation of the
2    ADT dictionary.
3    @file Entry.h */
4
5   #ifndef ENTRY_
6   #define ENTRY_
7
8   template <class KeyType, class ValueType>
9   class Entry
10  {
11  private:
12     KeyType key;
13     ValueType value;
14
15  protected:
16     void setKey(const KeyType& searchKey);
17
18  public:
19     Entry();
20     Entry(const KeyType& searchKey, const ValueType& newValue);
21     ValueType getValue() const;
22     KeyType getKey() const;
23     void setValue(const ValueType& newValue);
24
25     bool operator==(const Entry<KeyType, ValueType>& rightHandValue) const;
26     bool operator>(const Entry<KeyType, ValueType>& rightHandValue) const;
27  }; // end Entry
28  #include "Entry.cpp"
29  #endif
```

Note: Observations about the class Entry

The class Entry has two data members, a dictionary value and an associated search key. It also has a set method and a get method for the value portion, but only a public get method for the search key. This design prevents us from accidentally changing an

(continues)

Entry object's search key, as doing so would destroy the integrity of the dictionary. However, Entry does have a protected method setKey. This method is necessary so that the constructor of any derived class of Entry can initialize the search key.

Notice that the class overloads the operators == and >. While we will not need these overloaded operators for the array-based dictionary, we will use them when we store the dictionary's entries in a binary search tree.

A binary search tree implementation is nonlinear

At this point in your study of ADTs, you have other choices for a dictionary implementation. For instance, you can implement the ADT dictionary by using the ADT list, sorted list, or binary search tree. The binary search tree implementation, as illustrated in Figure 18-5, is an example of a **nonlinear implementation** and offers several advantages over linear implementations. Among these advantages is the opportunity to reuse the implementation of the ADT binary search tree discussed in Chapter 16. Implementations based on the ADTs list and sorted list also share this advantage, and they are left for you to consider as exercises.

FIGURE 18-5 The data members for a binary search tree implementation of the ADT dictionary for the data in Figure 18-1

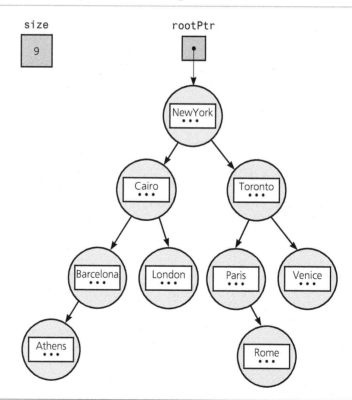

We also will consider an important unsorted implementation that uses a technique known as hashing. Although based on an array, this implementation is unlike any you have seen in this book.

18.2.1 A Sorted Array-Based Implementation of the ADT Dictionary

Whether a dictionary organizes its entries in sorted order by search key or leaves them unsorted, an array-based implementation has data members that are similar to those in array-based implementations of other ADTs that you have seen, namely an array of data items, a count of the items, and a maximum number of items. We have already seen that the data items will be Entry objects that contain both a search key and some other data.

For a sorted dictionary, the operation traverse should visit the dictionary's data values in an order such that their search keys are in sorted order. Note that we have specified this behavior in the header file for the class of dictionaries given in Listing 18-3. Notice also that this dictionary requires that its search keys be unique. This requirement will simplify our implementation, but Exercises 7 and 8 at the end of this chapter ask you to remove this restriction.

The declaration of the class ArrayDictionary contains nothing unusual, but it does declare two private methods—destroyDictionary and findEntryIndex. The former method can be called by both the destructor and the public method clear. The latter method locates the entry in the array entries that has a given search key. This method is useful for the public methods remove, getValue, and contains. Notice that both private methods perform operations needed by more than one public method, enabling us to avoid repetitive code in the definitions of the public methods.

LISTING 18-3 A header file for the class ArrayDictionary

```cpp
1   /** An array-based implementation of the ADT dictionary
2    that organizes its entries in sorted search-key order.
3    Search keys in the dictionary are unique.
4    @file ArrayDictionary.h */
5
6   #ifndef ARRAY_DICTIONARY_
7   #define ARRAY_DICTIONARY_
8
9   #include "DictionaryInterface.h"
10  #include "Entry.h"
11  #include "NotFoundException.h"
12  #include "PrecondViolatedExcept.h"
13
14  template <class KeyType, class ValueType>
15  class ArrayDictionary : public DictionaryInterface<KeyType, ValueType>
16  {
17  private:
18     static const int DEFAULT_CAPACITY = 21; // Small capacity to test for a full dictionary
19     std::unique_ptr<Entry<KeyType, ValueType>[]> entries; // Array of dictionary entries
20     int entryCount;                                    // Current count of dictionary entries
21     int maxEntries;                                    // Maximum capacity of the dictionary
22
23     void destroyDictionary();
24     int findEntryIndex(int firstIndex, int lastIndex, const KeyType& searchKey) const;
25
26  public:
27     ArrayDictionary();
```

(continues)

```
28     ArrayDictionary(int maxNumberOfEntries);
29     ArrayDictionary(const ArrayDictionary<KeyType, ValueType>& dictionary);
30
31     virtual ~ArrayDictionary();
32
33     bool isEmpty() const;
34     int getNumberOfEntries() const;
35     bool add(const KeyType& searchKey, const ValueType& newValue) throw(PrecondViolatedExcept);
36     bool remove(const KeyType& searchKey);
37     void clear();
38     ValueType getValue(const KeyType& searchKey) const throw(NotFoundException);
39     bool contains(const KeyType& searchKey) const;
40
41     /** Traverses the entries in this dictionary in sorted search-key order
42         and calls a given client function once for the value in each entry. */
43     void traverse(void visit(ValueType&)) const;
44   }; // end ArrayDictionary
45   #include "ArrayDictionary.cpp"
46   #endif
```

The requirement that we traverse the dictionary in sorted search-key order provides one reason to sort the array items according to the search key. While we could sort items each time traverse is called, maintaining this array in sorted order has advantages other than avoiding a sorting step. One important advantage of a sorted array is that the private method findEntryIndex can perform a recursive binary search when looking for a particular search key. Notice that the declaration of this method in Listing 18-3 provides two indices as parameters to indicate the portion of the array to search.

The public method add bears the responsibility for keeping the array items sorted. Let's examine its definition:

```
template <class KeyType, class ValueType>
bool ArrayDictionary<KeyType, ValueType>::add(const KeyType& searchKey,
                                              const ValueType& newValue)
                                              throw(PrecondViolatedExcept)
{
    bool ableToInsert = (itemCount < maxItems);
    if (ableToInsert)
    {
        // Make room for new entry by shifting all entries at
        // positions >= newPosition toward the end of the array
        // (no shift if newPosition == itemCount + 1). Performing
        // a binary search doesn't help here, because we need to
        // shift the entries while looking for the location of the addition.
        int index = itemCount;

        // Short-circuit evaluation is important
        while ( (index > 0) && (searchKey < items[index-1].getKey()) )
        {
            items[index] = items[index-1];
            index--;
        } // end while

        // Enforce precondition: Ensure distinct search keys
        if (searchKey != items[index - 1].getKey())
```

```
      {
         // Insert new entry
         items[index] = Entry<KeyType, ValueType>(searchKey, newValue);
         itemCount++; // Increase count of entries
      }
      else
      {
         auto message = "Attempt to add an entry whose search key exists in dictionary.";
         throw(PrecondViolatedExcept(message));
      } // end if
   } // end if

   return ableToInsert;
} // end add
```

Programming Problem 1 at the end of this chapter asks you to complete the implementation of `ArrayDictionary`.

Question 2 Explain how the `while` loop in the previous definition of the method `add` locates the insertion point for the new entry in the array `items`.

Question 3 Why is short-circuit evaluation important in the `while` loop of the previous definition of the method `add`?

Question 4 We mentioned that the `remove` method calls the private method `findEntryIndex` to locate the entry to remove. Assuming that the entry is located, what does `remove` need to do after it gets the index of this entry?

Question 5 What is the definition of the method `traverse` for `ArrayDictionary`?

18.2.2 A Binary Search Tree Implementation of the ADT Dictionary

Although linear implementations of the ADT dictionary are fine for specific applications, they are not suitable as general-purpose classes. The following nonlinear link-based implementation uses a binary search tree to represent the entries in the ADT dictionary. That is, the dictionary class will use composition and thus will have a binary search tree as one of its data members. In this way, our class reuses the class `BinarySearchTree` from Chapter 16.

> This dictionary implementation has a binary search tree as a data member

The header file. The header file in Listing 18-4 declares the class `TreeDictionary`, which like `ArrayDictionary`, stores `Entry` objects that encapsulate data values with their corresponding search keys. Much of this class is the same as or is similar to `ArrayDictionary`, except for the private section. It is there that we declare the binary search tree, `itemTree`, along with a method to help with the traversal operation.

LISTING 18-4 A header file for the class `TreeDictionary`

```
1   /** A binary search tree implementation of the ADT dictionary
2    that organizes its data in sorted search-key order.
3    Search keys in the dictionary are unique.
4    @file TreeDictionary.h */
5
6   #ifndef TREE_DICTIONARY_
7   #define TREE_DICTIONARY_
8                                                              (continues)
```

```
 9   #include "DictionaryInterface.h"
10   #include "BinarySearchTree.h"
11   #include "Entry.h"
12   #include "NotFoundException.h"
13   #include "PrecondViolatedExcept.h"
14
15   template <class KeyType, class ValueType>
16   class TreeDictionary : public DictionaryInterface<KeyType, ValueType>
17   {
18   private:
19      // Binary search tree of dictionary entries
20      BinarySearchTree<Entry<KeyType, ValueType> > entryTree;
21
22   public:
23      TreeDictionary();
24      TreeDictionary(const TreeDictionary<KeyType, ValueType>& dictionary);
25
26      virtual ~TreeDictionary();
27
28      // The declarations of the public methods appear here and are the
29      // same as given in Listing 18-3 for the class ArrayDictionary.
30      ...
31   }; // end TreeDictionary
32   #include "TreeDictionary.cpp"
33   #endif
```

The method implementations. Several of the methods in `TreeDictionary` simply call the analogous method in `BinarySearchTree`. For example, the dictionary method `add` creates an `Entry` object from the value and search key passed to it and then passes that object to the `add` method in `BinarySearchTree`. Recall that we want the dictionary method `add` to throw an exception if it attempts to add an entry whose search key is the same as the search key of an entry already in the dictionary. If the `add` method in `BinarySearchTree` prevented duplicate entries by throwing an exception, we could define the dictionary's `add` method as follows:

```
template <class KeyType, class ValueType>
bool TreeDictionary<KeyType, ValueType>::add(const KeyType& searchKey,
                                             const ValueType& newValue)
                                             throw(PrecondViolatedExcept)
{
   return itemTree.add(Entry<KeyType, ValueType>(searchKey, newValue));
} // end add
```

When we developed the class `BinarySearchTree` in Chapter 16, we considered only trees without duplicate entries. However, the `add` method in this class does not prevent duplicate entries. Although we could revise the class `BinarySearchTree` to behave in the way we need it to now, doing so is not the best course of action. After all, the class might be a part of a library whose source code you do not have. Instead, we will make the dictionary's `add` method prevent duplicate search keys. The following definition of `add` does just that:

```
template <class KeyType, class ValueType>
bool TreeDictionary<KeyType, ValueType>::add(const KeyType& searchKey,
                                             const ValueType& newValue)
                                             throw(PrecondViolatedExcept)
{
```

```
        Entry<KeyType, ValueType> newEntry(searchKey, newValue);
        // Enforce precondition: Ensure distinct search keys
        if (!itemTree.contains(newEntry))
        {
            // Add new entry and return boolean result
            return itemTree.add(Entry<KeyType, ValueType>(searchKey, newValue));
        }
        else
        {
            auto message = "Attempt to add an entry whose search key exists in dictionary.";
            throw(PrecondViolatedExcept(message)); // Exit the method
        } // end if
    } // end add
```

> **Note:** **Using an existing class**
>
> When you have a class that has been carefully designed and thoroughly debugged by either yourself or the developer of a library, you certainly can use it as a part of a new project. However, what if the class does not do exactly what you need? If you wrote the class yourself, you might be tempted to revise it to suit your present situation. But as a finished class, it could be a part of other projects, so you really should not change it. If possible, you should use the class in its present form and make your new class accommodate the aspect that does not suit you. This is what we did when we used the existing class BinarySearchTree in our new class TreeDictionary.

Each of the methods remove, getValue, and contains is passed a search key as its only argument. Each method must search the binary search tree for an Entry object that has a particular search key. How will TreeDictionary's method remove, for example, call BinarySearchTree's method remove? After all, it requires an Entry object as its argument.

The methods of BinarySearchTree compare Entry objects by using either of the operators == or >. These operators are the same ones that Entry overloads. Thus, we can control how BinarySearchTree will make these comparisons. Because we are searching for a specific search key, we overload == and > to examine only the search-key portion of an Entry object. For example, the definition of the overloaded operator == in Entry is

```
template <class KeyType, class ValueType>
bool Entry<KeyType, ValueType>::operator==(
                const Entry<KeyType, ValueType>& rightHandEntry) const
{
    return (searchKey == rightHandEntry.getKey());
} // end operator==
```

Now that BinarySearchTree can compare Entry objects based only on their search keys, how does TreeDictionary's method remove call BinarySearchTree's remove? Because Binary-SearchTree's remove expects an Entry object as an argument, TreeDictionary's remove creates an Entry object that has a specific search key and any value portion, and passes it to the invoked method. To create this Entry object, you can write the following expression:

```
Entry<KeyType, ValueType>(searchKey, ValueType())
```

The outcome is a call to Entry's second constructor with these two arguments: the search key that was passed to TreeDictionary's remove as an argument and the result of a call to ValueType's default constructor. Thus, the remove method in TreeDictionary has the following definition:

```
template <class KeyType, class ValueType>
bool TreeDictionary<KeyType, ValueType>::remove(const KeyType& searchKey)
{
   return itemTree.remove(Entry<KeyType, ValueType>(searchKey, valueType()));
} // end remove
```

We leave the rest of this implementation for you to complete as an exercise.

 Note: Usually a binary search tree can support the ADT dictionary operations quite efficiently. However, in the worst case, when the tree approaches a linear shape, the performance of the dictionary operations is comparable to that of a linear link-based implementation. If a given application cannot tolerate poor performance, you should use the dictionary implementations presented either in Section 18.4 of this chapter or in Chapter 19.

18.3 Selecting an Implementation

Perspective, efficiency, and motivation are reasons for studying the linear implementations

A major goal of this chapter is to indicate how the requirements of a particular application influence the selection of an implementation. The discussion here elaborates on the comments made in Section 10.2.4 of Chapter 10. Some applications require all of the ADT dictionary operations given earlier; others require either a subset of them or additional operations. Before choosing an implementation of the ADT dictionary, you as problem solver should carefully analyze which operations you really need for the application at hand. It is tempting to want all possible operations, but this strategy is a poor one, because often one implementation supports some of the operations more efficiently than another implementation does. Therefore, if you include an operation that you never use, you might end up with an implementation of the ADT that does not best suit your purpose.

What operations are needed?

In addition to knowing what operations are needed for a given application, the ADT implementer should know approximately how often the application will perform each operation. Although some applications may require many occurrences of every operation, other applications may not. For example, if you maintained a dictionary of major cities—such as those in Figure 18-1—you would expect to perform many more retrieval operations than additions or removals. Thus, if you seldom add entries to a dictionary, you can tolerate an implementation that results in an inefficient add operation, as long as frequently used operations are efficient. Of course, as Chapter 10 mentioned, if an ADT operation is to be used in a life-or-death situation, that operation must be efficient even if you rarely need it. The necessary operations, their expected frequency of occurrence, and their required response times are therefore some factors that influence which implementation of an ADT you should select for a particular application. You should, however, remain conscious of factors other than efficiency, as discussed in Chapter 10.

How often is each operation required?

18.3.1 Three Scenarios

Consider now several different application scenarios, each of which requires a particular mix of the dictionary operations. The analysis of various implementations of the ADT dictionary will illustrate some of the basic concerns of the analysis of algorithms. You will see, given an application, how to select an implementation that supports in a reasonably efficient manner the required mix of dictionary operations.

Scenario A: Addition and traversal in no particular order. Mary's sorority plans to raise money for a local charity. Tired of previous fund-raisers, Mary suggests a brainstorming session to discover a new money-making strategy. As each sorority member states her single best idea, Mary adds the member's name and her idea to a dictionary. Later, she will print a report of all the ideas currently in the dictionary. Assume that the organization of the report is irrelevant—the entries can be sorted or unsorted. Also assume that operations such as retrieval, removal, or traversal in sorted order either do not occur or occur so infrequently that they do not influence your choice of an implementation.

For this application, maintaining the search keys in a sorted order has no advantage. In fact, by not maintaining a sorted order, the add operation can be quite efficient. For either unsorted linear implementation, you can add a new key-value pair to any convenient location. For an unsorted array-based implementation, you can easily place a new entry after the last entry in the array—that is, at location entries[itemCount]. Figure 18-6a shows the result of this addition after entryCount has been updated. For a link-based implementation, you can place a new entry in a new node at the beginning of the linked chain. As Figure 18-6b illustrates, the head pointer points to the new node, and the new node points to the node that was previously first in the chain. Thus, you can add a new entry quickly into either unsorted implementation of a dictionary; in fact, the add operation is O(1): It requires a constant time for either implementation regardless of the dictionary size.

Should you choose the array-based or the link-based implementation? As you have seen with other ADTs, an implementation that uses dynamically allocated memory is appropriate if you do not have a good estimate of the maximum possible size of the dictionary. Mary's brainstorming session does not fall into this category, since she knows the dictionary's expected size;[1] her choice is mostly a matter of style. An array-based implementation requires less space than a link-based

An unsorted order is efficient

Array-based versus pointer-based

FIGURE 18-6   Adding an entry for unsorted linear implementations

(a) Array based

entryCount

entries

Place new entry in next available array location

| k + 1 | | Entry | Entry | · · · · | Entry | New entry | ? | · · · · | ? |

0   1   k − 1   k   k + 1   maxEntries − 1

(b) Link based

entryCount headPtr

| k + 1 |

Old reference

New reference

Entry → Entry → · · · → Entry

New entry

Place new node at beginning of chain

---

[1] Section 4.5 of Chapter 4 discussed how the expected and maximum number of items in an ADT affect an array-based implementation.

implementation, because no explicit pointer is stored. The extra cost of this pointer relative to the size of the data items, however, is insignificant in most situations because large data items are typical.

Should you use a binary search tree in the dictionary implementation for this application? Because such an implementation orders the dictionary entries, it does more work than the application requires. In fact, as you saw in Chapter 15, adding data to a binary search tree is $O(\log n)$ in the average case; it is slower than the $O(1)$ linear implementations.

 Scenario B: Retrieval. When you use a word processor's thesaurus to look up synonyms for a word, you use a retrieval operation. If an ADT dictionary represents the thesaurus, each dictionary entry is a record that contains both the word—which is the search key—and the word's synonyms. Frequent retrieval operations require a dictionary implementation that allows you to search efficiently for a word. Typically, you cannot alter the thesaurus, so no addition or removal operations are necessary.

A sorted array-based implementation can use a binary search

For an array-based implementation, you can use a binary search to retrieve a particular word's synonyms, if the array is sorted. On the other hand, for a link-based implementation, you must traverse the linked chain from its beginning until you encounter the word. The binary search performs this retrieval in significantly less time than is required to traverse a linked chain. Two questions come to mind at this point:

Questions

- Is a binary search of a linked chain possible?
- How much more efficient is a binary search of an array than a sequential search of a linked chain?

Can you perform a binary search of a linked chain? Yes, but too inefficiently to be practical. Consider the very first step of the binary search algorithm:

Look at the "middle" entry in the dictionary

A binary search is impractical with a link-based implementation

If n nodes are in a linked chain, how can you possibly get to the middle one? You can traverse the chain from its beginning until you have visited $n / 2$ nodes. But, as you will see in the answer to the second question posed before, just this first step will often take longer than the entire binary search of an array. Further, you would have the same problem of finding the "middle" node at each recursive step. It is thus not practical to perform a binary search for the linear link-based implementation. This observation is extremely significant.

If you know the dictionary's maximum size, a sorted array-based implementation is appropriate for frequent retrievals

On the other hand, if n entries are in an array `entries`, the middle entry is at location $n / 2$ and can be accessed directly. Thus, a binary search of an array requires considerably less time than an algorithm that must inspect every entry in the dictionary. What does "considerably less time" mean? As you know, without the ability to perform a binary search, you may have to inspect every entry in the dictionary, either to locate an entry with a particular search key or to detect that such an entry is not present. In other words, if a dictionary has size n, you will have to inspect as many as n entries; thus, such a search is $O(n)$. How much better can you do with a binary search? Recall from Chapter 10 that a binary search is $O(\log_2 n)$ in its worst case and that an $O(\log_2 n)$ algorithm is substantially more efficient than an $O(n)$ algorithm. For example, $\log_2 1,024 = 10$ and $\log_2 1,048,576 = 20$. For a large dictionary, the binary search has an enormous advantage.

If you do not know the dictionary's maximum size, use a binary search tree in the implementation

Because a thesaurus is probably large, you must choose an implementation for which a binary search is practical. As you have just seen, this observation eliminates the linear link-based implementations. The sorted array-based implementation is fine here, because you know the size of the thesaurus.

An implementation using a binary search tree is also a good choice for retrieval-dominated applications. As you saw in Chapter 15, searching a binary search tree is $O(\log n)$ if the tree is balanced. Because the thesaurus does not change, you can create a balanced tree that remains balanced and be assured of an efficient search. Although the pointers in a binary search tree add a space cost, as scenario A mentioned, this cost is relatively insignificant when the data items are large.

Scenario C: Addition removal, retrieval, and traversal in sorted order. Your local library has a computerized catalog of its books. This catalog is actually a dictionary. To simplify this scenario, let's assume that the search keys are the books' titles and that they are all distinct. You perform a retrieval operation when you access this catalog. The library staff uses addition and removal operations to update the catalog and a traversal to save the entire catalog in a file. Presumably, retrieval is the most frequent operation, but the other operations are not infrequent enough to ignore. If they were, this scenario would be the same as scenario B.

To add to a dictionary an entry whose search key is X, you must first determine where the entry belongs in the dictionary's sorted order. Similarly, to remove from the dictionary an entry that has X as its search key, you must first locate the entry. Thus, both the add and remove operations perform the following steps:

1. Find the appropriate position in the dictionary.
2. Add to (or remove from) this position.

> Both add and remove perform these two steps

Step 1 is far more efficient if the dictionary implementation is array based instead of link based. For an array-based implementation, you can use a binary search to determine—in the case of addition—where the new search key X belongs and—in the case of removal—where the search key is located. On the other hand, for a link-based implementation, you know from the discussion in scenario B that a binary search is impractical, and so you must traverse the chain from its beginning. You also saw in scenario B that it takes significantly less time to perform a binary search of an array than it does to traverse a linked chain.

> Use an array-based implementation for step 1

Thus, because it facilitates a binary search, the array-based implementation is superior with respect to step 1 of add and remove. However, as you may have guessed, the link-based implementation is better for step 2, the actual addition or removal of the entry. Under the array-based implementation, add must shift array entries to make room for the new entry, as Figure 18-7a illustrates. The worst case would require that every array entry be shifted. On the other hand, under the link-based implementation, you can accomplish this second step simply by changing

> Use a link-based implementation for step 2

FIGURE 18-7   Adding an entry for sorted linear implementations

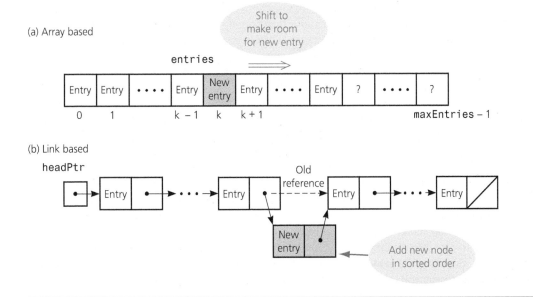

A sorted array-based implementation shifts data during additions and removals

at most two pointers, as Figure 18-7b indicates. Similar comments are true for the `remove` operation. It must shift array entries to fill in the gap created when an entry is removed, but it needs to change only two pointers at most to remove an entry from a linked chain.

When you take steps 1 and 2 together, you will find that the sorted array-based and sorted link-based implementations of `add` or `remove` both require roughly the same amount of time—they are both O(n). Neither implementation supports these two operations particularly well. The binary search tree implementation, however, combines the best features of the two linear implementations. Because it is link based, you avoid shifting data, and the dictionary can grow dynamically as needed. You can also retrieve data from a binary search tree efficiently.

The sorted linear implementations are comparable here, but none is suitable

Note: When designing an ADT to solve a particular problem, do not include unnecessary operations. The proper choice of an implementation depends on the mix of requested operations, and if you request an operation that you do not need, you might get an implementation that does not best support what you are really doing.

Despite certain difficulties, linear implementations of a dictionary can be appropriate

Summary. Although linear implementations of a dictionary are less sophisticated and generally require more time to perform their operations than a binary search tree implementation, they are nevertheless useful for many applications. Because linear implementations are easy to understand conceptually, they are appropriate for dictionaries that will contain only a small number of entries. In such cases efficiency is not as great a concern as are simplicity and clarity. Even when a dictionary is large, a linear implementation may still be appropriate for applications that can use an unsorted dictionary and have few removals.

Note: Comparing linear implementations of the ADT dictionary
- An unsorted array-based implementation of the ADT dictionary can efficiently add an entry at the end of an array. A removal, however, will usually require shifting data so that no gap remains in the array. Because the entries are unsorted, retrieval will require a sequential search.
- A sorted array-based implementation usually requires shifting data during both additions and removals. Retrieval, however, can use an efficient binary search because the entries are sorted.
- An unsorted link-based implementation can efficiently add an entry at the beginning of a linked chain. A removal will require a sequential search but no data shifts. Retrieval will also require a sequential search.
- A sorted link-based implementation requires a sequential search but no data shifts during both additions and removals. Retrieval will also require a sequential search.

A binary search tree implementation is a better choice than a linear implementation, in general

The nonlinear, binary search tree implementation of the ADT dictionary can be a better choice than a linear implementation, in general. If an n-node binary search tree has minimum height—that is, has height $\lceil \log_2 (n + 1) \rceil$—the binary search tree implementation of the ADT dictionary certainly succeeds where the linear implementations failed: You can, with efficiency comparable to that of a binary search, locate an entry in both the retrieval operation and the first steps of the `add` and `remove` operations. In addition, the link-based implementation of the binary search tree permits dynamic allocation of its nodes, so that it can handle a dictionary whose maximum size is unknown.

This implementation also efficiently performs the second step of the addition and removal operations: The actual addition or removal of a node requires only a few pointer changes—plus a short traversal to the inorder successor if the node containing the entry to be removed has two children—rather than the possible shifting of all the dictionary entries, as the array-based implementations require. The binary search tree implementation therefore combines the best aspects of the two linear implementations, yet avoids their disadvantages.

As Chapter 15 showed, however, the height of a binary search tree depends on the order in which you perform the add and remove operations on the tree and can be as large as n. If the addition and removal operations occur in a random order, the height of the binary search tree will be quite close to its minimum value. You do need to watch for a possible increase in the tree's height, however, and the resulting decrease in performance. If instead you use a variation of the binary search tree that remains balanced—as the next chapter will describe—you can keep the height of the tree near $\log_2 n$.

A balanced binary search tree increases the efficiency of the ADT dictionary operations

Figure 18-8 summarizes the order of the addition, removal, retrieval, and traversal operations for the dictionary implementations discussed so far in this chapter.

FIGURE 18-8   The average-case order of the ADT dictionary operations for various implementations

	Addition	Removal	Retrieval	Traversal
Unsorted array-based	O(1)	O(n)	O(n)	O(n)
Unsorted link-based	O(1)	O(n)	O(n)	O(n)
Sorted array-based	O(n)	O(n)	O($\log n$)	O(n)
Sorted link-based	O(n)	O(n)	O(n)	O(n)
Binary search tree	O($\log n$)	O($\log n$)	O($\log n$)	O(n)

Note: Perspective

You might wonder why, if the binary search tree implementation of the ADT dictionary is so good, we studied the linear implementations at all. There are three reasons. The first and foremost reason is perspective. Section 10.2.4 of Chapter 10 spoke of the dangers of overanalyzing a problem. If the size of the problem is small, the difference in efficiency among the possible solutions is likely insignificant. In particular, if the size of the dictionary is small, a linear implementation is adequate and simple to understand.

The second reason is efficiency: A linear implementation can be quite efficient for certain situations. For example, a linear implementation was best for scenario A, where the predominant operations are addition and traversal in no particular order. For scenario B, where the predominant operation is retrieval, the sorted array-based implementation is adequate, if the maximum number of entries is known. For these situations, a concern for simplicity suggests that you use a linear implementation and not a binary search tree, even for large dictionaries.

The third reason is motivation. By seeing scenarios for which the linear implementations are not adequate, you are forced to look beyond arrays and consider other implementations, such as the binary search tree. Actually looking at both a linear implementation and a binary search tree implementation allows you to see these inadequacies more clearly.

18.4 Hashing as a Dictionary Implementation

The binary search tree provides an excellent implementation of the ADT dictionary, as do the balanced search trees that Chapter 19 will discuss. They allow you to perform all of the dictionary operations quite efficiently. If, for example, a dictionary contains 10,000 entries, the operations getValue, add, and remove each require approximately $\log_2 10{,}000 \approx 13$ steps. As impressive as this efficiency may be, situations do occur for which the search-tree implementations are not adequate.

Dictionary operations without searches

As you know, time can be vital. For example, when a person calls the 911 emergency system, the system detects the caller's telephone number and searches a database for the caller's address. Similarly, an air traffic control system searches a database of flight information, given a flight number. Clearly these searches must be rapid.

A radically different strategy is necessary to locate (and add or remove) data virtually instantaneously. Imagine an array `table` of N elements—with each array element capable of holding a single dictionary entry—and a seemingly magical box called an "address calculator." Whenever you have a new entry that you want to add to the dictionary, the address calculator will tell you where you should place it in the array. Figure 18-9 illustrates this scenario.

FIGURE 18-9   Address calculator

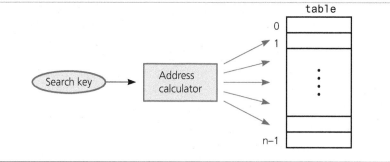

You can thus easily add a new key-value pair to the dictionary as follows:

```
add(searchKey: KeyType, newValue: ValueType): boolean
{
    i = the array index that the address calculator gives you for searchKey
    table[i] = an object that encapsulates searchKey and newValue
}
```

This add operation is O(1); that is, it requires constant time.

You also use the address calculator for the getValue and remove operations. If you want to retrieve an entry that has a particular search key, you simply ask the address calculator to tell you where it would store such an entry, because you would have placed it there earlier by using the add algorithm just given. If the desired entry is present in the dictionary, it will be in the array location that the address calculator specifies.

Thus, the getValue operation appears in pseudocode as follows:

```
getValue(searchKey: KeyType): ValueType throw NotFoundException
{
    i = the array index that the address calculator gives you for searchKey
    if (table[i].getKey() == searchKey)
        return table[i]
    else
        Throw NotFoundException
}
```

Similarly, the pseudocode for the `remove` operation is

```
remove(searchKey: KeyType): boolean
{
    i = the array index that the address calculator gives you for searchKey
    isFound = (table[i].getKey() == searchKey)
    if (isFound)
        Remove the entry from table[i]
    return isFound
}
```

It thus appears that you can perform the operations `getValue`, `add`, and `remove` virtually instantaneously. You never have to search for an entry; instead, you simply let the address calculator tell you where the entry should be. The amount of time required to carry out the operations is O(1) and depends only on how quickly the address calculator can perform this computation.

If you are to implement such a scheme, you must, of course, be able to construct an address calculator that can, with very little work, tell you where a given entry should be. Address calculators are actually not as mysterious as they seem; in fact, many exist that can approximate the idealized behavior just described. Such an address calculator is usually referred to as a **hash function**. The scheme just described is an idealized description of a technique known as **hashing**, and the array `table` is called the **hash table**.

A hash function tells you where to place an entry in an array called a hash table

To understand how a hash function works, consider the 911 emergency system mentioned earlier. If, for each person, the system had a record whose search key was the person's telephone number, it could store these records in an array `table`, as follows. You store the record for a person whose telephone number is t into `table[t]`. Retrieval of the record, then, is almost instantaneous given its search key t. For example, you can store the record for the telephone number 555-1234 in `table[5551234]`. If you can spare 10 million memory locations for `table`, this approach is fine. You need not use memory so extravagantly, however, because 911 systems are regional. If you consider only one telephone exchange, for example, you can store the record for the number 555-1234 in `table[1234]` and get by with an array `table` of 10,000 locations.

The transformation of 5551234 into an array index 1234 is a simple example of a hash function. A hash function h must take an arbitrary integer x and map it into an integer that you can use as an array index. In our example, such indices would be in the range 0 through 9999. That is, h is a function such that for any integer x,

$h(x) = i$, where i is an integer in the range 0 through 9999

Because the database contains entries for every telephone number in a particular exchange, the array `table` is completely full. In this sense, our example is not typical of hashing applications and serves only to illustrate the idea of a hash function. What if many fewer entries were in the array? Consider, for example, an air traffic control system that stores an entry for each current flight according to its four-digit flight number. You could store an entry for Flight 1234 in `table[1234]`, but you still would need an array of 10,000 locations, even if only 50 flights were current.

A hash function maps an integer into an array index

A different hash function would save memory. If you allow space for a maximum of 101 flights, for example, so that the array `table` has indices 0 through 100, the necessary hash function h should map any four-digit flight number into an integer in the range 0 through 100.

If you have such a hash function h—and you will see several suggestions for hash functions later—the dictionary operations are easy to write. For example, in the `getValue` algorithm, the step

i = *the array index that the address calculator gives you for* searchKey

is implemented simply as

```
i = h(searchKey)
```

In the previous example, searchKey would be the flight number.

Although the dictionary operations appear to be virtually instantaneous, is hashing really as good as it sounds? If it really was this good, there would have been little reason for developing all those other dictionary implementations. Hashing would beat them hands down!

Why is hashing not quite as simple as it seems? You might first notice that since the hashing scheme stores data in an array, it would appear to suffer from the familiar problems associated with a fixed-size implementation. Obviously, the hash table must be large enough to contain all of the entries that you want to store. This requirement is not the crux of the implementation's difficulty, however, for—as you will see later—there are ways to allow the hash table to grow dynamically. But the implementation does have a major pitfall, even given the assumption that the number of entries to be stored will never exceed the size of the hash table.

A perfect hash function maps each search key into a unique location of the hash table

Ideally, you want the hash function to map each search key x into a unique integer i. The hash function in the ideal situation is called a **perfect hash function**. In fact, it is possible to construct perfect hash functions if you know all of the possible search keys that *actually* occur in the dictionary. You have this knowledge for the 911 example, since everyone is in the database, but not for the air traffic control example. Usually, you will not know the values of the search keys in advance.

A perfect hash function is possible if you know all the search keys

In practice, a hash function might map two or more search keys x and y into the *same* integer. That is, the hash function tells you to store two or more entries in the same array location table[i]. This occurrence is called a **collision**. Thus, even if fewer than 101 entries were present in the hash table table[0..100], h could very well tell you to place more than one entry into the same array location. For example, if two entries have search keys 1234 and 5678, and if

Collisions occur when the hash function maps more than one entry into the same array location

$$h(1234) = h(5678) = 22$$

h will tell you to place the two entries into the same array location, table[22]. That is, the search keys 1234 and 5678 have collided.

Even if the number of entries that can be in the array at any one time is small, the only way to avoid collisions completely is for the hash table to be large enough that each possible search key can have its own location. If, for example, Social Security numbers were the search keys, you would need an array location for each integer in the range 000000000 through 999999999. This situation would certainly require a good deal of storage! Because reserving vast amounts of storage is usually not practical, collision-resolution schemes are necessary to make hashing feasible. Such schemes usually require that the hash function place entries evenly throughout the hash table.

To summarize, a typical hash function must

Requirements for a hash function

- Be easy and fast to compute
- Place entries evenly throughout the hash table

Note that the size of the hash table affects the ability of the hash function to distribute the entries evenly throughout the table. The requirements of a hash function will be discussed in more detail later in this chapter.

Consider now several hash functions and **collision-resolution schemes**.

18.4.1 Hash Functions

It is sufficient to consider hash functions that have an arbitrary integer as an argument. Why? If a search key is not an integer, you can simply map the search key into an integer, which you then hash. At the end of this section, you will see one way to convert a string into an integer.

It is sufficient for hash functions to operate on integers

There are many ways to convert an arbitrary integer into an integer within a certain range, such as 0 through 100. Thus, there are many ways to construct a hash function. Many of these functions, however, will not be suitable. Here are several simple hash functions that operate on positive integers.

Selecting digits. If your search key is the nine-digit employee ID number 001364825, you could select the fourth digit and the last digit, to obtain 35 as the index to the hash table. That is,

$h(001364825) = 35$ (*select the fourth and last digits*)

Therefore, by using **digit selection** to define your hash function, you would store the entry whose search key is 001364825 in `table[35]`.

You do need to be careful about which digits you choose in a particular situation. For example, the first three digits of a Social Security number are based on the geographic region in which the number was assigned. If you select only these digits, you will map all people from the same region into the same location of the hash table.

Digit-selection hash functions are simple and fast, but generally they do not evenly distribute the entries in the hash table. A hash function really should utilize the entire search key.

Digit selection does not distribute entries evenly in the hash table

Folding. One way to improve on the previous approach of selecting digits is to add the digits. The resulting process is known as **folding**. For example, you can add all of the digits in 001364825 to obtain

$0 + 0 + 1 + 3 + 6 + 4 + 8 + 2 + 5 = 29$ (*add the digits*)

Therefore, you would store the entry whose search key is 001364825 in `table[29]`. Notice that if you add all of the digits from a nine-digit search key,

$0 \leq h(search\ key) \leq 81$

That is, you would use only `table[0]` through `table[81]` of the hash table. To change this situation or to increase the size of the hash table, you can group the digits in the search key and add the groups. For example, you could form three groups of three digits from the search key 001364825 and add them as follows:

$001 + 364 + 825 = 1,190$

For this hash function,

$0 \leq h(search\ key) \leq 3 \times 999 = 2,997$

Clearly, if 2,997 is larger than the size of the hash table that you want, you can alter the groups that you choose. Perhaps not as obvious is that you can apply more than one hash function to a search key. For example, you could select some of the digits from the search key before adding them, or you could either select digits from the previous result 2,997 or apply folding to it once again by adding 29 and 97.

Applying more than one hash function to a single search key

Modulo arithmetic. Modulo arithmetic provides a simple and effective hash function that we will use in the rest of this chapter. For example, consider the function[2]

$h(x) = x \bmod tableSize$

where the hash table has *tableSize* elements. In particular, if *tableSize* is 101, $h(x) = x \bmod 101$ maps any integer x into the range 0 through 100. For example, h maps 001364825 into 12.

For $h(x) = x \bmod tableSize$, many x's map into `table[0]`, many x's map into `table[1]`, and so on. That is, collisions occur. However, you can distribute the dictionary entries evenly over all of `table`—thus reducing collisions—by choosing a prime number as *tableSize*. For instance, 101 in the previous example is prime. The choice of table size will be discussed in more detail

The dictionary size should be prime

---

[2] Remember that this book uses "mod" as an abbreviation for the mathematical operation modulo. In C++, the modulo operator is %.

later in this chapter. For now, realize that 101 is used here as a simple example of a prime table size. For the typical hash table, 101 is much too small.

Converting a character string to an integer. If your search key is a character string—such as a name—you could convert it into an integer before applying the hash function $h(x)$. To do so, you could first assign an integer value to each character in the string. For example, for the word "NOTE" you could assign the ASCII values 78, 79, 84, and 69, to the letters *N*, *O*, *T*, and *E*, respectively. Or, if you assign the values 1 through 26 to the letters *A* through *Z*, you could assign 14 to *N*, 15 to *O*, 20 to *T*, and 5 to *E*.

If you now simply add these numbers, you will get an integer, but it will not be unique to the character string. For example, the word "TONE" will give you the same result. Instead, you can write the numeric value for each character in binary and concatenate the results. If you assign the values 1 through 26 to the letters *A* through *Z*, you obtain the following result for the word "NOTE":

> *N* is 14, or 01110 in binary
> *O* is 15, or 01111 in binary
> *T* is 20, or 10100 in binary
> *E* is 5, or 00101 in binary

Concatenating the binary values gives you the binary integer

> 01110011111010000101

which is 474,757 in decimal. You can apply the hash function x mod *tableSize* for $x = 474,757$.

Now consider a more efficient way to compute 474,757. Rather than converting the previous binary number to decimal, you can evaluate the expression

$$14 \times 32^3 + 15 \times 32^2 + 20 \times 32^1 + 5 \times 32^0$$

This computation is possible because we have represented each character as a 5-bit binary number, and 2^5 is 32.

Horner's rule minimizes the number of computations

By factoring this expression, you can minimize the number of arithmetic operations. This technique is called **Horner's rule** and results in

$$((14 \times 32 + 15) \times 32 + 20) \times 32 + 5$$

Although both of these expressions have the same value, the result in either case could very well be larger than a typical computer can represent; that is, an overflow can occur. If you use the hash function

$$h(x) + x \text{ mod } tableSize$$

you can prevent an overflow by applying the modulo operator after computing each parenthesized expression in Horner's rule. The implementation of this algorithm is left as an exercise.

  Programming Tip: You can use the following method in your dictionary implementations as a hash function. C++ Interlude 8 will discuss the Standard Template Library (STL) and clarify the way that this method uses the STL.

```cpp
template <class KeyType, class ValueType>
int HashedDictionary<KeyType, ValueType>::
                    getHashIndex(const KeyType& searchKey) const
{
```

```
// We are creating a hash function type called hashFunction that hashes
// a search key. First we create an unordered_map object for our KeyType
// and ValueType.
std::unordered_map<KeyType, ValueType> mapper;

// Then we invoke the method hash_function to return the hash function
// for the KeyType and assign it to 'hashFunction'.
typename std::unordered_map<KeyType, ValueType>::
            hasher hashFunction = mapper.hash_function();

// Need static_cast because hashFunction returns an unsigned long.
return static_cast<int>(hashFunction(searchKey) % hashTableSize);
}  // end getHashIndex
```

18.4.2 Resolving Collisions Using Open Addressing

Consider the problems caused by a collision. Suppose that you want to add an entry whose search key is 5678 to the hash table table, as was described previously. The hash function $h(x) = x$ mod 101 tells you to place the new entry in table[22], because 5678 mod 101 is 22. Suppose, however, that table[22] already contains an entry, as Figure 18-10 illustrates.[3] If earlier you had placed an entry whose search key is 1234 into table[22] because 1234 mod 101 equals 22, where do you place the new entry? You certainly do not want to disallow the addition on the grounds that the dictionary is full: You could have a collision even when adding to a dictionary that contains only one entry!

Two general approaches to collision resolution are common. One approach places the new entry into another location within the hash table. A second approach changes the structure of the hash table so that each location table[i] can accommodate more than one entry. We begin with the first approach.

Two approaches to collision resolution

FIGURE 18-10   A collision

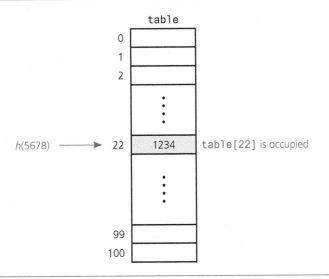

---

[3] Our figures show only the search-key portion of an entry in the hash table.

During an attempt to add a new entry to a dictionary, if the hash function indicates a location in the hash table that is already occupied, you look—or **probe**—for some other empty, or **open**, location in which to place the entry. The sequence of locations that you examine is called the **probe sequence**.

Such schemes are said to use **open addressing**. The concern, of course, is that you must be able to find a dictionary entry efficiently after you have added it. That is, the remove and getValue operations must be able to reproduce the probe sequence that add used, and they must do so efficiently.

The difference among the various open-addressing schemes is the technique used to probe for an empty location. We briefly describe three such techniques.

Linear probing. In this simple scheme to resolve a collision, you search the hash table sequentially, starting from the original hash location. More specifically, if table[h(searchKey)] is occupied, you check the dictionary locations table[h(searchKey)+1], table[h(searchKey)+2], and so on until you find an available location. Figure 18-11 illustrates the placement of four entries that all hash into the same location table[22] of the hash table, assuming a hash function $h(x) = x$ mod 101. Typically, you *wrap around* from the last array location to the first array location if necessary.

> Begin at the hash location and search the dictionary sequentially

In the absence of removals, the implementation of getValue under this scheme is straightforward. You need only follow the same probe sequence that add used until you either find the entry you are searching for; reach an empty location, which indicates that the entry is not present; or visit every table location.

Removals, however, complicate matters slightly. The remove operation itself is no problem. You merely find the desired entry—just as getValue does—and remove it from the hash table, making the location empty. But now what happens when getValue needs to locate another entry? The new empty locations that remove created along a probe sequence could cause getValue to stop prematurely, incorrectly indicating a failure. You can solve this problem by placing a table location into one of three states: occupied (currently in use), empty (has not been used), or removed (was once occupied but is now available). You then modify the getValue operation to continue probing when it encounters a location in the removed state. Similarly, you modify add to place entries into locations that are in either the empty or removed states.

> Three states: occupied, empty, removed

FIGURE 18-11 Linear probing with $h(x) = x$ mod 101

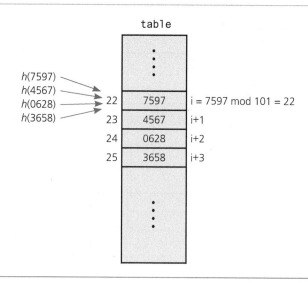

One of the problems with the linear-probing scheme is that entries tend to **cluster** together in the hash table. That is, the table contains groups of consecutively occupied locations. This phenomenon is called **primary clustering**. Clusters can get close to one another and, in fact, merge into a larger cluster. Large clusters tend to get even larger. Thus, one part of the hash table might be densely populated, even though another part has relatively few entries.

Clustering can be a problem

 Note: Primary clustering causes long probe searches and therefore decreases the overall efficiency of hashing.

 Question 6 Write the pseudocode for the `remove` operation when linear probing is used to implement the hash table.

Quadratic probing. You can avoid primary clusters simply by adjusting the linear probing scheme just described. Instead of probing consecutive table locations from the original hash location `table[h(searchKey)]`, you check locations `table[h(searchKey)+1²]`, `table[h(searchKey)+2²]`, `table[h(searchKey)+3²]`, and so on until you find an available location. Figure 18-12 illustrates this open-addressing scheme—which is called **quadratic probing**—for the same hash keys that appear in Figure 18-11.

Unfortunately, when two search keys hash into the same location, quadratic probing uses the same probe sequence for each one. The resulting phenomenon—called **secondary clustering**—delays the resolution of the collision. Although the research of quadratic probing remains incomplete, it appears that secondary clustering is not a problem.

Double hashing. Double hashing, which is yet another open-addressing scheme, drastically reduces clustering. The probe sequences that both linear probing and quadratic probing use are **key independent**. For example, linear probing inspects the locations in the hash table

FIGURE 18-12 Quadratic probing with $h(x) = x \bmod 101$

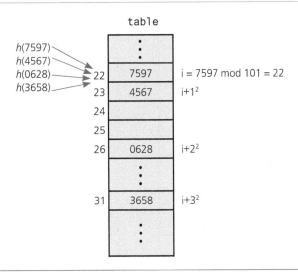

A hash address and a step size determine the probe sequence

sequentially no matter what the search key is. In contrast, double hashing defines probe sequences that are **key-dependent**. In this scheme the probe sequence still searches the hash table in a linear order, starting at the location $h_1(key)$, but a second hash function h_2 determines the size of the steps taken.

Although you choose h_1 as usual, you must follow these guidelines for h_2:

Guidelines for the step-size function h_2

$$h_2(key) \neq 0$$

$$h_2 \neq h_1$$

Clearly, you need a nonzero step size $h_2(key)$ to define the probe sequence. In addition, h_2 must differ from h_1 to avoid clustering.

For example, let h_1 and h_2 be the primary and secondary hash functions defined as

Primary and secondary hash functions

$$h_1(key) = key \bmod 11$$

$$h_2(key) = 7 - (key \bmod 7)$$

where a hash table of only 11 elements is assumed, so that you can readily see the effect of these functions on the hash table. If $key = 58$, h_1 hashes key to dictionary location 3 (58 mod 11), and h_2 indicates that the probe sequence should take steps of size 5 (7 – 58 mod 7). In other words, the probe sequence will be 3, 8, 2 (wraps around), 7, 1 (wraps around), 6, 0, 5, 10, 4, 9. On the other hand, if $key = 14$, h_1 hashes key to table location 3 (14 mod 11), and h_2 indicates that the probe sequence should take steps of size 7 (7 – 14 mod 7), and so the probe sequence would be 3, 10, 6, 2, 9, 5, 1, 8, 4, 0.

Each of these probe sequences visits *all* the table locations. This phenomenon always occurs if the size of the hash table and the size of the probe step are relatively prime, that is, if their greatest common divisor is 1. Because the size of a hash table is commonly a prime number, it will be relatively prime to all step sizes.

Figure 18-13 illustrates the addition of 58, 14, and 91 to an initially empty hash table. Because $h_1(58)$ is 3, you place 58 into table[3]. You then find that $h_1(14)$ is also 3, so to avoid a collision, you step by $h_2(14) = 7$ and place 14 into table[3 + 7], or table[10]. Finally, $h_1(91)$ is 3 and $h_2(91)$

FIGURE 18-13 Double hashing during the addition of 58, 14, and 91

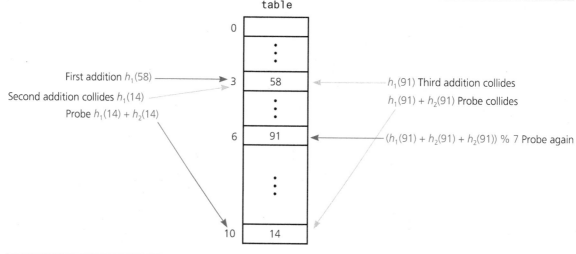

is 7. Because `table[3]` is occupied, you probe `table[10]` and find that it, too, is occupied. You finally store 91 in `table[(10 + 7) % 11]`, or `table[6]`.

While more than two hash functions can be desirable, such schemes are difficult to implement.

Question 7 What is the probe sequence that double hashing uses when $h_1(key) = key$ mod 11, $h_2(key) = 7 - (key$ mod 7), and $key = 19$?

Increasing the size of the hash table. With any of the open-addressing schemes, as the hash table fills, the probability of a collision increases. At some point, a larger hash table becomes desirable. If you use a dynamically allocated array for the hash table, you can increase its size whenever the dictionary becomes too full.

You cannot simply double the size of the array, as we did in earlier chapters, because the size of the hash table must remain prime. In addition, you do not simply move the data from the original hash table to the new hash table. If your hash function is x mod *tableSize*, it changes as *tableSize* changes. Thus, you need to apply your new hash function to every entry in the old hash table before placing it into the new hash table.

Note: Rehashing

After creating a new, larger hash table of an appropriate size, you use the dictionary method add to add each entry in the original hash table to the new table. The method computes the hash index using the size of the new table and handles any collisions. This process of enlarging a hash table and computing new hash indices for its contents is called **rehashing**. You can see that increasing the size of a hash table requires considerably more work than increasing the size of an ordinary array. Rehashing is a task that you should not do often.

18.4.3 Resolving Collisions By Restructuring the Hash Table

Another way to resolve collisions is to change the structure of the array `table`—the hash table—so that it can accommodate more than one entry in the same location. We describe two such ways to alter the hash table.

Each hash-table location can accommodate more than one entry

Buckets. If you define the hash table so that each location `table[i]` is itself an array—called a **bucket**—you can store the entries that hash into `table[i]` in this array. The problem with this approach, of course, is choosing the size b of each bucket. If b is too small, you will only have postponed the problem of collisions until $b + 1$ entries map into some array location. If you attempt to make b large enough so that each array location can accommodate the largest number of entries that might map into it, you are likely to waste a good deal of storage.

A bucket is an element of a hash table that is itself an array

Separate chaining. A better approach than using buckets is to design the hash table as an array of linked chains. In this collision-resolution technique, known as **separate chaining**, each table location `table[i]` points to a chain of linked nodes containing the entries that the hash function has mapped into location i, as Figure 18-14 illustrates. Separate chaining provides a successful approach to resolving collisions. With separate chaining, the size of the dictionary is dynamic and can exceed the size of the hash table, because each linked chain can be as long as necessary. As you will see in the next section, the length of these chains affects the efficiency of retrievals and removals. Even so, separate chaining is the most time-efficient collision-resolution scheme.

Each hash-dictionary location is a linked chain

Separate chaining successfully resolves collisions

FIGURE 18-14   Separate chaining

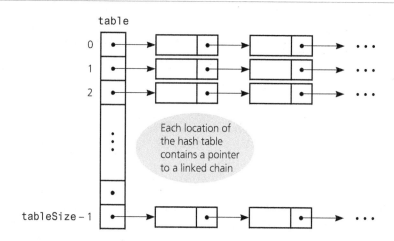

We will discuss an implementation of the ADT dictionary using hashing and separate chaining in Section 18.4.7 of this chapter.

 Question 8 If $h(x) = x$ mod 7 and separate chaining resolves collisions, what does the hash table look like after the following additions occur: 8, 10, 24, 15, 32, 17? Assume that each entry contains only a search key.

18.4.4 The Efficiency of Hashing

An analysis of the average-case efficiency of hashing involves the **load factor** alpha (α), which is the ratio of the current number of entries in the dictionary to the maximum size of the array dictionary. That is,

The load factor measures how full a hash table is

$$\alpha = \frac{Current\ number\ of\ table\ entries}{tableSize}$$

α is a measure of how full the hash table is. As the table fills, α increases and the chance of collision increases, so search times increase. Thus, hashing efficiency decreases as α increases.

Unlike the efficiency of earlier dictionary implementations, the efficiency of hashing does not depend solely on the number n of entries in the dictionary. While it is true that for a fixed *tableSize* efficiency decreases as n increases, for a given n you can choose *tableSize* to increase efficiency. Thus, when choosing the size of the hash table, you should estimate the largest possible n and select *tableSize* so that α is small. As you will see shortly, α should not exceed 2/3.

Unsuccessful searches generally require more time than successful searches

Hashing efficiency for a particular search also depends on whether the search is successful. An unsuccessful search requires more time in general than a successful search. The following analyses[4] enable a comparison of collision-resolution techniques.

---

[4] D. E. Knuth, *Searching and Sorting*, vol. 3 of *The Art of Computer Programming* (Menlo Park, CA: Addison-Wesley, 1973).

Linear probing. For linear probing, the approximate average number of comparisons that a search requires is

$$\frac{1}{2}\left[1 + \frac{1}{1 - \alpha}\right] \quad \text{for a successful search, and}$$

$$\frac{1}{2}\left[1 + \frac{1}{(1 - \alpha)^2}\right] \quad \text{for an unsuccessful search}$$

As collisions increase, the probe sequences increase in length, causing increased search times. For example, for a dictionary that is two-thirds full ($\alpha = 2/3$), an average unsuccessful search might require at most five comparisons, or probes, while an average successful search might require at most two comparisons. To maintain efficiency, it is important to prevent the hash table from filling up.

Do not let the hash table get too full

Quadratic probing and double hashing. The efficiency of both quadratic probing and double hashing is given by

$$\frac{-\log_e(1 - \alpha)}{\alpha} \quad \text{for a successful search, and}$$

$$\frac{1}{1 - \alpha} \quad \text{for an unsuccessful search}$$

On average, both techniques require fewer comparisons than linear probing. For example, for a dictionary that is two-thirds full, an average unsuccessful search might require at most three comparisons, or probes, while an average successful search might require at most two comparisons. As a result, you can use a smaller hash table for both quadratic probing and double hashing than you can for linear probing. However, because they are open-addressing schemes, all three approaches suffer when you are unable to predict the number of additions and removals that will occur. If your hash table is too small, it will fill up, and search efficiency will decrease.

Open-addressing schemes require a good estimate of the number of additions and removals

Separate chaining. Because the dictionary's add operation places the new entry at the beginning of a linked chain within the hash table, it is O(1). The getValue and remove operations, however, are not as fast. They each require a search of the linked chain, so ideally you would like for these chains to be short.

Addition is instantaneous

For separate chaining, *tableSize* is the number of chains, not the maximum number of dictionary entries. Thus, it is entirely possible, and even likely, that the current number of dictionary entries n exceeds *tableSize*. That is, the load factor α, or $n / tableSize$, can exceed 1. Because *tableSize* is the number of linked chains, $n / tableSize$—that is, α—is the average length of each linked chain.

Some searches of the hash table are unsuccessful because the relevant chain is empty. Such searches are virtually instantaneous. For an unsuccessful search of a nonempty chain, however, getValue and remove must examine the entire chain, or α entries in the average case. On the other hand, a successful search must examine a nonempty chain. In the average case, the desired entry will be in the middle of the chain. That is, after finding that the linked chain is not empty, the search will examine $\alpha / 2$ entries.

Thus, the efficiency of the retrieval and removal operations under the separate-chaining approach is

Average-case efficiency of retrievals and removals

$$1 + \frac{\alpha}{2} \quad \text{for a successful search, and}$$

$$\alpha \quad \text{for an unsuccessful search}$$

Even if the linked chains typically are short, you should still estimate the worst case. If you seriously underestimate *tableSize*, or if most of the dictionary entries happen to hash into the same location, the number of entries in a chain could be quite large. In fact, in the worst case, all *n* entries in the dictionary could be in the same linked chain!

As you can see, the time that a retrieval or removal operation requires can range from almost nothing—if the linked chain to be searched either is empty or has only a couple of entries in it—to the time required to search a chain that contains all the entries in the dictionary, if they all hashed into the same location.

Comparing techniques. Figure 18-15 plots the relative efficiency of the collision-resolution schemes just discussed. When the hash table is about half full—that is, when α is 0.5—the techniques are nearly equal in efficiency. As the dictionary fills and α approaches 1, separate chaining is the most efficient technique. Does this mean that we should discard all other search algorithms in favor of hashing with separate chaining?

In the worst case, a hashing implementation of a dictionary can be much slower than other implementationsNo. The analyses here are average-case analyses. Although an implementation of the ADT dictionary that uses hashing might often be faster than one that uses a search tree, in the worst case it can be much slower. If you can afford both an occasional slow search and a large *tableSize*—that is, a small α—then hashing can be an attractive dictionary implementation. However, if you are performing a life-and-death search for your city's poison control center, a search-tree implementation would at least provide you with a guaranteed limit on its worst-case behavior.

Furthermore, while separate chaining is the most time-efficient collision-resolution scheme, you do have the storage overhead of the pointers in the linked chain. If the data entries in the dictionary are small, the pointers add a significant overhead in storage, and

FIGURE 18-15 The relative efficiency of four collision-resolution methods

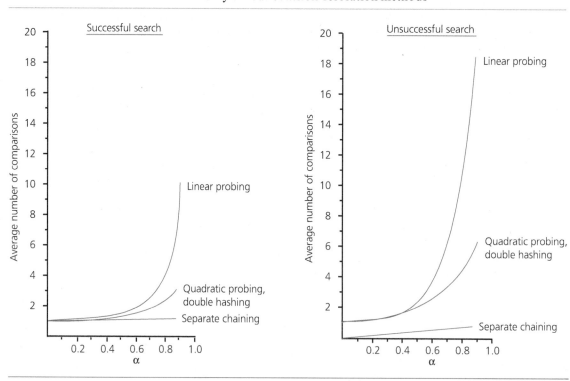

you may want to consider a simpler collision-resolution scheme. On the other hand, if the entries are large, the addition of a pointer is insignificant, so separate chaining is a good choice.

 Note: Maintaining the performance of hashing

Collisions and their resolution typically cause the load factor α to increase and the efficiency of the dictionary operations to decrease. To maintain efficiency, you should restrict the size of α as follows:

- $\alpha < 0.5$ for open addressing
- $\alpha < 1.0$ for separate chaining

If the load factor exceeds these bounds, you must increase the size of the hash table using rehashing.

18.4.5 What Constitutes a Good Hash Function?

Before we conclude this introduction to hashing, consider in more detail the issue of choosing a hash function to perform the address calculations for a given application. A great deal has been written on this subject, most of which is beyond the mathematical level of this book. However, this section will present a brief summary of the major concerns.

- **Is the hash function easy and fast to compute?** If a hashing scheme is to perform dictionary operations almost instantaneously and in constant time, you certainly must be able to calculate the hash function rapidly. Most of the common hash functions require only a single division (like the modulo operation), a single multiplication, or some kind of "bit-level" operation on the internal representation of the search key. In all these cases, the requirement that the hash function be easy and fast to compute is satisfied.

- **Does the hash function scatter the data evenly throughout the hash table?** Unless you use a perfect hash function—which is usually impractical to construct—you typically cannot avoid collisions entirely. For example, to achieve the best performance from a separate-chaining scheme, each `table[i]` should point to a chain containing approximately the same number of entries; that is, each chain should contain approximately $n / tableSize$ entries (and thus no chain should contain significantly more than $n / tableSize$ entries). To accomplish this goal, your hash function should scatter the search keys evenly throughout the hash table.

  > You cannot avoid collisions entirely

- **How well does the hash function scatter random data?** If every search key is equally likely, will the hash function scatter them evenly? For example, consider nine-digit employee ID numbers as the search keys, a hash table `table[0..39]`, and a hash function $h(x) =$ (first two digits of x) mod 40. If all employee ID numbers are equally likely, does a given ID number x have equal probability of hashing into any one of the 40 array locations? For this hash function, the answer is no. Only ID numbers that start with 19, 59, and 99 map into `table[19]`, while only ID numbers that start with 20 and 60 map into `table[20]`. In general, three different ID *prefixes*—that is, the first two digits of an ID number—map into each array location 0 through 19, while only two different prefixes map into each array location 20 through 39. Because all ID numbers are equally likely—and thus all prefixes 00 through 99 are equally likely—a given ID number is 50 percent more likely to hash into one of the locations 0 through 19 than it is to hash into one of the locations 20 through 39. As a result, each array location 0 through 19 would contain, on average, 50 percent more entries than each location 20 through 39.

Thus, the hash function

A function that does not scatter random data evenly

$$h(x) = \text{(first two digits of } x) \bmod 40$$

does not scatter random data evenly throughout the array `table[0..39]`. On the other hand, it can be shown that the hash function

A function that does scatter random data evenly

$$h(x) = x \bmod 101$$

does, in fact, scatter random data evenly throughout the array `table[0..100]`.

- **How well does the hash function scatter nonrandom data?** Even if a hash function scatters random data evenly, it may have trouble with nonrandom data. In general, no matter what hash function you select, it is always possible that the data will have some unlucky pattern that will result in uneven scattering. Although there is no way to guarantee that a hash function will scatter all data evenly, you can greatly increase the likelihood of this behavior.

As an example, consider a hash table `table[0..39]` and a hash function $h(x) = $ first two digits of x. If every ID number is equally likely, h will scatter the search keys evenly throughout the array. But what if every ID number is not equally likely? For instance, a company might assign employee IDs according to department, as follows:

10xxxxx	Sales
20xxxxx	Customer Relations
...	
90xxxxx	Data Processing

Under this assignment, only 9 out of the 100 array locations would contain any entries at all. Further, those locations corresponding to the largest departments (Sales, for example, which corresponds to `table[10]`) would contain more entries than those locations corresponding to the smallest departments. This scheme certainly does not scatter the data evenly.

Much research has been done into the types of hash functions you should use to guard against various types of patterns in the data. The results of this research are really in the province of more advanced courses, but two general principles can be noted here:

General requirements of a hash function

- ☐ The calculation of the hash function should involve the *entire search key*. Thus, for example, computing a modulo of the entire ID number is much safer than using only its first two digits.
- ☐ If a hash function uses modulo arithmetic, the *base should be prime;* that is, if h is of the form

$$h(x) = x \bmod tableSize$$

then *tableSize* should be a prime number. This selection of *tableSize* is a safeguard against many subtle kinds of patterns in the data (for example, search keys whose digits are likely to be multiples of one another). Although each application can have its own particular kind of patterns and thus should be analyzed on an individual basis, choosing a prime number for *tableSize* is an easy way to safeguard against some common types of patterns in the data.

18.4.6 Dictionary Traversal: An Inefficient Operation Under Hashing

For many applications, hashing provides the most efficient implementation of the ADT diction-ary. One important dictionary operation—traversal in sorted order—performs poorly when hashing implements the dictionary. As was mentioned previously, a good hash function scatters entries as randomly as possible throughout the array, so that no ordering relationship exists between a search key that hashes into `table[i]` and one that hashes into `table[i + 1]`. As a consequence, if you must traverse the dictionary in sorted order, you first would have to sort the entries. If sorting were required frequently, hashing would be a far less attractive implementa-tion than a search tree.

Entries hashed into
`table[i]` and
`table[i+1]` have
no ordering
relationship

Traversing a dictionary in sorted order is really just one example of a whole class of operations that hashing does not support well. Many similar operations that you often wish to perform on a dictionary require that the entries be ordered. For example, consider an operation that must find the dictionary entry whose search key is the smallest or largest. If you use a search-tree implementation, these entries are in the leftmost and rightmost nodes of the tree, respectively. If you use a hashing implementation, however, you do not know where these entries are—you would have to search the entire dictionary. A similar type of operation is a **range query**, which requires that you retrieve all entries whose search keys fall into a given range of values. For example, you might want to retrieve all entries whose search keys are in the range 129 to 755. This task is relatively easy to perform by using a search tree (see Exercise 3 in the next chapter), but if you use hashing, there is no efficient way to answer the range query.

In general, if an application requires any of these ordered operations, you should probably use a search tree. Although the `getValue`, `add`, and `remove` operations are somewhat more efficient when you use hashing to implement the dictionary instead of a balanced search tree, the balanced search tree supports these operations so efficiently itself that, in most contexts, the difference in speed for these operations is negligible (whereas the advantage of the search tree over hashing for the ordered operations is significant).

Hashing versus
balanced search
trees

In the context of external storage, however, the story is different. For data that is stored externally, the difference in speed between hashing's implementation of `getValue` and a search tree's implementation may well be significant, as you will see in Chapter 21. In an external set-ting, it is not uncommon to see a hashing implementation of the `getValue` operation and a search-tree implementation of the ordered operations used simultaneously.

18.4.7 Using Hashing and Separate Chaining to Implement the ADT Dictionary

Let's now use hashing to implement the ADT dictionary. We will resolve collisions by using separate chaining.

The hash table. Recall from Figure 18-14 that to use separate chaining, you create a hash table of pointers to chains of linked nodes that represent entries in the dictionary. Although each node in a chain could contain an object of the class `Entry`, as given earlier in Listing 18-2—and as you might do in any of the linked-based implementations mentioned earlier in this chapter—we will derive a new class, `HashedEntry`, from `Entry` and add a pointer field, as Figure 18-16 illustrates. Listing 18-5 shows the declaration of this new class. Notice that `HashedEntry` is like a combination of the classes `Node`—which we have used in previous link-based implementations—and `Entry`. In particular, it inherits the data members and meth-ods of `Entry`, and adds the pointer data field and the methods `getNext` and `setNext` of `Node`.

FIGURE 18-16   A dictionary entry when separate chaining is used

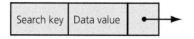

LISTING 18-5 The class HashedEntry

```
1   /** A class of entry objects for a hashing implementation of the
2       ADT dictionary.
3    @file HashedEntry.h */
4
5   #ifndef HASHED_ENTRY_
6   #define HASHED_ENTRY_
7
8   #include "Entry.h"
9
10  template<class KeyType, class ValueType>
11  class HashedEntry : public Entry<KeyType, ValueType>
12  {
13  private:
14     std::shared_ptr<HashedEntry<KeyType, ValueType>> nextPtr;
15  public:
16     HashedEntry();
17     HashedEntry(KeyType searchKey, ValueType newValue);
18     HashedEntry(KeyType searchKey, ValueType newValue,
19               std::shared_ptr<HashedEntry<KeyType, ValueType>> nextEntryPtr);
20
21     void setNext(std::shared_ptr<HashedEntry<KeyType, ValueType>>
22                                                  nextEntryPtr);
23     auto getNext() const;
24  }; // end HashedEntry
25
26  #include "HashedEntry.cpp"
27  #endif
```

Now the data members of our dictionary class, HashedDictionary, are

```
// Creates a unique pointer to an array of shared HashedEntry pointers
std::unique_ptr<std::shared_ptr<HashedEntry<KeyType, ValueType>>[]>
                          hashTable; // Array of pointers to entries
int entryCount;                      // Count of dictionary entries
int hashTableSize;                   // Table size must be prime
static const int DEFAULT_CAPACITY = 101;
```

The array hashTable contains pointers to the itemCount entries in the dictionary. The field
hashTableSize is the size of this array. The constructors will set the value of this field, either to
DEFAULT_CAPACITY or to a value given by the client. We note again that this value must be a prime
number. Any value given to the constructor will need to be checked to determine whether it is
prime and, if not, replaced by a prime number.

Note:

To declare the data member `hashTable` in the class `HashedDictionary`, we wrote

```
std::unique_ptr<std::shared_ptr<HashedEntry<KeyType, ValueType>>[]> hashTable;
```

We can simplify this statement by writing it as

```
std::unique_ptr<hashTableType<KeyType, ValueType>> hashTable;
```

where `hashTableType` is defined just before the class declaration for `HashedDictionary` as follows:

```
template <class KeyType, class ValueType>
using hashTableType = std::shared_ptr<HashedEntry<KeyType, ValueType>>[];
```

Thus, the header file for `HashedDictionary` contains the following statements:

```
template <class KeyType, class ValueType>
using hashTableType = std::shared_ptr<HashedEntry<KeyType, ValueType>>[];

template <class KeyType, class ValueType>
class HashedDictionary : public DictionaryInterface<KeyType, ValueType>
{
private:
   // Creates a unique pointer to an array of shared HashedEntry pointers
   std::unique_ptr<hashTableType<KeyType, ValueType>> hashTable; // Array of entry pointers
   int entryCount;                                                // Count of entries
   int hashTableSize;                                             // Table size must be prime
   static const int DEFAULT_CAPACITY = 101;
   ...
```

The method add. To add a new entry to the dictionary, you place it at the beginning of the chain that the hash function indicates. Assuming that the initial values of the pointers in the hash table are each `nullptr`, the following pseudocode describes the algorithm for the `add` operation:

```
add(searchKey: KeyType, newValue: ValueType): boolean
{
   p = pointer to a new HashedEntry object containing searchKey and newValue
   i = h(searchKey)
   if (hashTable[i] == nullptr)
      hashTable[i] = p
   else
   {
      // Add new entry to beginning of chain
      p->setNext(hashTable[i])
      hashTable[i] = p
   }
   return true
}
```

Recall that we assume that the search key given to `add` is not already in the dictionary.

The definition of `add` in the implementation file for `HashedDictionary` is

```
template <class KeyType, class ValueType>
bool HashedDictionary<KeyType, ValueType>::add(const KeyType& searchKey,
                                               const ValueType& newValue)
{
   // Create entry to add to dictionary
   auto entryToAddPtr =
      std::make_shared<HashedEntry<KeyType, ValueType>>(searchKey, newValue);
```

```
    // Compute the hashed index into the array
    int hashIndex = getHashIndex(searchKey);

    // Add the entry to the chain at hashIndex
    if (hashTable[hashIndex] == nullptr)
    {
        hashTable[hashIndex] = entryToAddPtr;
    }
    else
    {
        entryToAddPtr->setNext(hashTable[hashIndex]);
        hashTable[hashIndex] = entryToAddPtr;
    }  // end if

    return true;
}  // end add
```

The method remove. To remove an entry, given its search key, from the dictionary, you proceed as the following pseudocode indicates:

```
remove(searchKey: KeyType): boolean
{
    i = h(searchKey)
    if (hashTable[i] != nullptr)
    {
        Search the chain pointed to by hashTable[i] for searchKey
        if (searchKey is in the first node)
        {
            hashTable[i] = hashTable[i]->getNext()
            return true
        }
        else
        {
            curPtr = pointer to the entry containing searchKey
            prevPtr = pointer to the previous entry in the chain
            prevPtr->setNext(curPtr->getNext())
            return true
        }
    }
    else
        return false
}
```

HashedDictionary's definition of remove follows:

```
template <class KeyType, class ValueType>
bool HashedDictionary<KeyType, ValueType>::remove(const KeyType& searchKey)
{
    bool isSuccessful = false;

    // Compute the hashed index into the array
    int hashIndex = getHashIndex(searchKey);
    if (hashTable[hashIndex] != nullptr)
    {
        // Special case - first node has target
        if (searchKey == hashTable[hashIndex]->getKey())
        {
            hashTable[hashIndex] = hashTable[hashIndex]->getNext();
            isSuccessful = true;
        }
        else // Search the rest of the chain
```

```
    {
        auto prevPtr = hashTable[hashIndex];
        auto curPtr = prevPtr->getNext();
        while ((curPtr != nullptr) && !isSuccessful )
        {
            if (searchKey == curPtr->getKey())
            {
                // Found item in chain so remove that node
                prevPtr->setNext(curPtr->getNext());
                isSuccessful = true;
            }
            else // Look at next entry in chain
            {
                prevPtr = curPtr;
                curPtr = curPtr->getNext();
            }  // end if
        }  // end while
    }  // end if
}  // end if

    return isSuccessful;
}  // end remove
```

The rest of the implementation of the class `HashedDictionary` is left as an exercise.

SUMMARY

1. The ADT dictionary supports value-oriented operations, such as "Retrieve all the information about John Smith."

2. The linear implementations (array-based and link-based) of a dictionary are adequate only in limited situations, such as when the dictionary is small or for certain operations. In those situations, the simplicity of a linear implementation may be an advantage. A linear implementation of a dictionary, however, is not suitable as a general-purpose, reusable class.

3. A nonlinear link-based (binary search tree) implementation of the ADT dictionary provides the best aspects of the two linear implementations. The link-based implementation allows the dictionary to grow dynamically and allows additions and removals of data to occur through pointer changes instead of data movement. In addition, the binary search tree allows you to use a binary-search-like algorithm when searching for an entry with a specified search key. These characteristics make a nonlinear dictionary implementation far superior to the linear implementations in many applications.

4. Hashing as a dictionary implementation calculates where data should be rather than searching for it. Hashing allows for very efficient retrievals, additions, and removals.

5. The hash function should be extremely easy to compute—it should require only a few operations—and it should scatter the search keys evenly throughout the hash table.

6. A collision occurs when two different search keys hash into the same array location. Two ways to resolve collisions are through probing and chaining.

7. Separate chaining is the most time-efficient collision-resolution scheme.

8. Hashing does not efficiently support operations that require the table entries to be ordered—for example, traversing the table in sorted order.

9. When dictionary operations such as traversal are not important to a particular application, if you know the maximum number of dictionary entries, and if you have ample storage, hashing is an implementation for a dictionary that is simpler and faster than balanced search tree implementations. Tree implementations, however, are dynamic and do not require you to estimate the maximum number of entries.

EXERCISES

1. Implement the class Entry, as given in Listing 18-2.

2. Consider an operation replace(searchKey, replacementValue) that locates, if possible, the entry in a dictionary with the given search key. If the dictionary contains such an entry, the method replaces its value with replacementValue.

   a. Write implementations of replace for the classes ArrayDictionary, TreeDictionary, and Hashed-Dictionary, as described in this chapter.
   b. For TreeDictionary, under what circumstances can replace replace an entry without altering the structure of the binary search tree?

3. Imagine an application program that behaves like an English dictionary. The user types a word and the program provides the word's definition. Thus, the dictionary needs only a retrieval operation. Which implementation of the ADT dictionary would be most efficient as an English dictionary?

4. When you use a word processor's spell checker, it compares the words in your document with words in a dictionary. You can add new words to the dictionary as necessary. Thus, this dictionary needs frequent retrievals and occasional additions. Which implementation of the ADT dictionary would be most efficient as a spell checker's dictionary?

5. A C++ compiler uses a *symbol table* to keep track of the identifiers that a program uses. When the compiler encounters an identifier, it searches the symbol table to see whether that identifier has already been encountered. If the identifier is new, it is added to the table. Thus, the symbol table needs only addition and retrieval operations. Which implementation of the ADT dictionary would be most efficient as a symbol table?

6. Consider adding operations to the ADT dictionary to form the union and intersection of two given dictionaries. Each operation returns a new dictionary. The union should combine all of the entries in both dictionaries into a third dictionary. The intersection should be a dictionary of the entries common to both of the two dictionaries.

   Within each given dictionary, search keys are not duplicated. However, an entry in one dictionary could have the same search key as an entry in the second dictionary. Propose and discuss ways to specify these two operations for this case.

7. The implementations of the ADT dictionary given in this chapter make the following assumption: At any time, a dictionary contains at most one entry with a given search key. Although the definition of the ADT required for a specific application may not allow duplicates, it is wise to test for them rather than simply to assume that they will not occur. Why?

   Modify the dictionary implementations so that they test for—and disallow—any duplicates. What dictionary operations are affected? What are the implications for the unsorted linear implementations?

8. Although disallowing duplicate search keys in the ADT dictionary is reasonable for some applications, it is just as reasonable to have an application that will allow duplicates. What are the implications of adding entries that are not identical but have the same search key? Specifically, what would the implementations of add, remove, and getValue do?

9. Suppose that you want to support two `remove` operations for the ADT dictionary—for example, `removeByName` and `removeByID`. Describe an efficient implementation for these operations.

10. Can you use a heap instead of a binary search tree as an implementation of the ADT dictionary?

11. Write pseudocode for the dictionary operations `add`, `remove`, and `getValue` when the implementation uses hashing and linear probing to resolve collisions.

12. Write the pseudocode for the `remove` operation when the implementation uses hashing and separate chaining to resolve collisions.

13. The success of a hash-table implementation of the ADT dictionary is related to the choice of a good hash function. A good hash function is one that is easy to compute and will evenly distribute the possible data. Comment on the appropriateness of the following hash functions. What patterns would hash to the same location?

    a. The hash table has size 2,048. The search keys are English words. The hash function is

    $h(key)$ = (Sum of positions in alphabet of $key's$ letters) mod 2048

    b. The hash table has size 2,048. The keys are strings that begin with a letter. The hash function is

    $h(key)$ = (position in alphabet of first letter of key) mod 2048

    Thus, "BUT" maps to 2. How appropriate is this hash function if the strings are random? What if the strings are English words?

    c. Repeat parts a and b, but change the size of the hash table to 2039.

    d. The hash table is 10,007 entries long. The search keys are integers in the range 0 through 9999. The hash function is

    $h(key)$ = ($key * random$) truncated to an integer

    where $random$ represents a sophisticated random-number generator that returns a real value between 0 and 1.

    e. The hash table is 10,007 entries long (`HASH_TABLE_SIZE` is 10007). The search keys are integers in the range 0 through 9999. The hash function is given by the following C++ function:

    ```cpp
    int hashIndex(int x)
    {
       for (int i = 1; i <= 1000000; i++)
          x = (x * x) % HASH_TABLE_SIZE;

       return x;
    }  // end hashIndex
    ```

PROGRAMMING PROBLEMS

1. Complete the implementation of the class `ArrayDictionary` as given in Listing 18-3.

2. Develop a program that can be used to test an implementation of the ADT dictionary.

3. Complete the implementation of the class `TreeDictionary` as given in Listing 18-4.

4. Write the sorted link-based, unsorted array-based, and unsorted link-based implementations of the ADT dictionary described in this chapter.

5. Write unsorted and sorted implementations of the ADT dictionary that use, respectively, the ADTs list and sorted list, which Chapters 8 and 12 described.

6. Repeat Programming Problem 5 of Chapter 16, using the ADT dictionary as the database.

7. Consider any collection of data that you can organize in at least two ways. For example, you can order employees by name or by Social Security number and books by title or by author. Note that other information about the employees or books is present in the database but is not used to organize these items. This program assumes that the search keys (for example, book title or book author) are unique and are strings. Thus, in the previous examples, the Social Security number must be a string instead of an integer, and only one book per author is permitted. Choose any set of data that conforms to these requirements, and create a text file.

Program behavior. When your program begins execution, it should read your text file. It then should provide some typical database management operations, all under user control via an interface of your design. For example, you should be able to add an entry, remove an entry, display (that is, retrieve) an entry, and display all of the entries in search-key order. You should be able to use either of two search keys to designate the entry to be removed or displayed.

Implementation notes. The entries in the database should be objects that contain two search keys and additional data, all of which appear in the text file. Thus, you need to design and implement a class of these objects.

Although your program could create two dictionaries from these objects—one organized by one search key (such as the employee name) and the other organized by another search key (such as the Social Security number)—this approach could waste a substantial amount of memory due to the duplication of all of the data in both dictionaries.

A better approach revises the ADT dictionary to provide operations according to two search keys. For example, you want to be able to remove by name and by Social Security number. The underlying data structure for the dictionary's implementation should be a binary search tree. Actually, you will want two binary search trees so that you can organize the data in two ways: by name and by Social Security number, for example.

To avoid duplicated data, store the data in an ADT list and let each node in the binary search trees contain the position of the actual data in the list, instead of the data itself.

Your program can be specific to the type of database (employees, books, and so on), or it can be more general. For example, you could determine the search-key descriptions that the user interface displays by requiring that they be in the text file.

8. Implement the symbol table described in Exercise 5 by reusing the class `TreeDictionary`, as described in Section 18.2.2 of this chapter.

9. Repeat Programming Problem 8, but use the class `HashedDictionary`, as described in Section 18.4.7, which uses separate chaining to resolve collisions. Use the hash function $h(x) = x$ mod *tableSize* and the algorithm that involves Horner's rule, as described in Section 18.4.1 about hash functions, to convert a variable into an integer x.

Because you add an entry to the dictionary only if its search key is not already present, does the time required for an addition increase?

10. Repeat Programming Problem 9, but this time

   a. Use linear probing as the collision-resolution scheme.
   b. Use double hashing as the collision-resolution scheme.
   c. Use quadratic probing as the collision-resolution scheme.

11. Repeat Programming Problem 9, but allocate the hash table dynamically. If the hash table becomes more than half full, increase its size to the first prime number greater than $2 \times$ *tableSize*.

12. Repeat Programming Problem 9, but experiment with variations of chaining. For example, the hash table could point to binary search trees instead of chains of linked entries.

Balanced Search Trees

Contents

Prerequisites

Although Chapter 18 described the advantages of using the binary search tree to implement the ADT dictionary, the efficiency of this implementation suffers when the tree loses its balance. This chapter introduces various other search trees, which remain balanced in all situations and thus enable dictionary operations whose efficiency is comparable to a binary search.

19.1 Balanced Search Trees

As you saw in the previous chapter, the efficiency of the binary search tree implementation of the ADT dictionary is related to the tree's height. The operations add, remove, and getValue follow a path from the root of the tree to the node that contains the desired search key (or, in the case of the add operation, to the node that is to become the parent of the new node). At each node along the path, you compare a given value to the search key in the node and determine which subtree to search next. Because the maximum number of nodes on such a path is equal to the height of the tree, the maximum number of comparisons that the dictionary operations can require is also equal to this height.

As you know, the height of a binary search tree of n nodes ranges from a maximum of n to a minimum of $\lceil \log_2(n + 1) \rceil$. As a consequence, locating a particular data item in a binary search tree requires between n and $\lceil \log_2(n + 1) \rceil$ comparisons. Thus, a search of a binary search tree can be as inefficient as a sequential search of a chain of linked nodes or as efficient as a binary search of a sorted array. Efficiency was the primary reason for developing the binary search tree implementation of the dictionary: We wanted to perform a search of a linked structure as efficiently as we could perform a binary search of an array. Thus, we certainly want the optimum behavior of the binary search tree.

> The height of a binary search tree is sensitive to the order of additions and removals

What affects the height of a binary search tree? As you learned in Chapters 15 and 16, the height of the tree is quite sensitive to the order in which you add or remove data items. For example, consider a binary search tree that contains the data items 10, 20, 30, 40, 50, 60, and 70. If you added the items to the tree in ascending order, you would obtain a binary search tree of maximum height, as shown in Figure 19-1a. If, on the other hand, you added the items in the order 40, 20, 60, 10, 30, 50, 70, you would obtain a balanced binary search tree of minimum height, as shown in Figure 19-1b.

> Various search trees can retain their balance despite additions and removals

As you can see, if you use the algorithms in Chapter 16 to maintain a binary search tree, additions and removals can cause the tree to lose its balance and approach a linear shape. Such a

FIGURE 19-1   The tallest and shortest binary search trees containing the same data

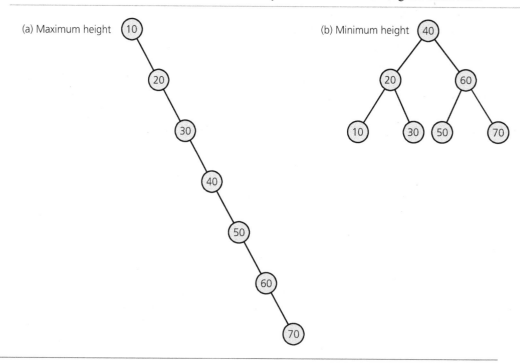

tree is no better than a linear chain of linked nodes. For this reason, it is desirable in many applications to use one of several variations of the basic binary search tree. Such trees can absorb additions and removals without a deterioration of their balance and are easier to maintain than a minimum-height binary search tree. Moreover, you can search these trees almost as efficiently as you can search a minimum-height binary search tree. This chapter discusses the better-known search trees to give you a sense of the possibilities. We continue to assume that the entries in a tree are unique—that is, that there are no duplicates.

19.2 AVL Trees

An **AVL tree**—named for its inventors, Adel'son-Vel'skii and Landis—is a balanced binary search tree. Because the heights of the left and right subtrees of any node in a balanced binary tree differ by no more than 1, you can search an AVL tree almost as efficiently as a minimum-height binary search tree. This section will simply introduce you to the notion of an AVL tree—which is the oldest form of balanced binary tree—and leave the details for another course.

An AVL tree is a balanced binary search tree

It is, in fact, possible to rearrange any binary search tree of n nodes to obtain a binary search tree with the minimum possible height $\lceil \log_2(n+1) \rceil$. Recall, for example, the algorithms developed in Section 16.4 of Chapter 16 that use a file to save and restore a binary search tree. You can start with an arbitrary binary search tree, save its values in a file, and then construct from these same values a new binary search tree of minimum height. Although this approach may be appropriate in the context of a dictionary that occasionally is saved and restored, it requires too much work to be performed every time an addition or removal makes the tree unbalanced. The cost of repeatedly rebuilding the tree could very well outweigh the benefit of searching a tree of minimum height.

The AVL algorithm is a compromise. It maintains a binary search tree whose height is close to the minimum, but it is able to do so with far less work than would be necessary to keep the height of the tree exactly equal to the minimum. The basic strategy of the AVL algorithm is to monitor the shape of the binary search tree. You add or remove nodes just as you would for any binary search tree, but after each addition or removal, you check that the tree is still an AVL tree. That is, you see whether any node in the tree has left and right subtrees whose heights differ by more than 1. For example, suppose that the binary search tree in Figure 19-2a is the result of a sequence of additions and removals. The heights of the left and right subtrees of the root <30> differ by 2. You can restore this tree's AVL property—that is, its balance—by rearranging its nodes. For instance, you can make the node <20> become the root, with left child <10> and right child <30>, as in Figure 19-2b. This action requires changes to the nodes' references and is called a **rotation**. The result is a shorter tree. Notice that you cannot arbitrarily rearrange the tree's nodes, because you must take care not to destroy the search tree's ordering property in the course of the rebalancing.

An AVL tree maintains its height close to the minimum

FIGURE 19-2   An unbalanced binary search tree that becomes balanced by a rotation and remains balanced after an addition

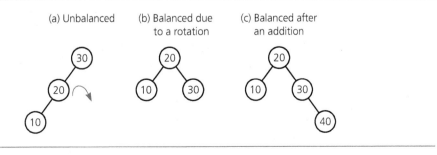

Rotations are not necessary after every addition or removal. For example, you can add 40 to the AVL tree in Figure 19-2b and still have an AVL tree, as Figure 19-2c shows. However, when a rotation is necessary to restore a tree's AVL property, the rotation will be one of two possible types. Let's look at an example of each type.

Suppose that you insert a new node containing 60 into an AVL tree to get the tree in Figure 19-3a. An imbalance occurs at the node <20>; that is, this node's left and right subtrees differ in height by more than 1. A *single rotation* to the left is necessary to obtain the balanced tree in Figure 19-3b: <40> becomes the parent of <20>, which adopts <30> as its right child. Figure 19-3c shows this rotation in a more general form. It shows, for example, that before the rotation the left and right subtrees of the node <40> have heights h and $h + 1$, respectively. After the rotation, the tree is balanced and, in this particular case, has decreased in height from $h + 3$ to $h + 2$.

Figure 19-4 shows examples of a single left rotation that restores a tree's balance but does not affect its height. An analogous single right rotation would produce mirror images of these examples.

FIGURE 19-3   Correcting an imbalance in an AVL tree due to an addition by using a single rotation to the left

---

(a) The addition of 60 to an
    AVL tree destroys its balance

(b) A single left rotation
    restores the tree's balance

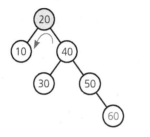

(c) The general case for a single left rotation
    in an AVL tree whose height decreases

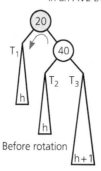

Before rotation

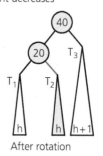

After rotation

FIGURE 19-4   A single rotation to the left that does not affect the height of an AVL tree

---

(a) Unbalanced

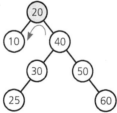

(b) After a single left rotation
    that restores the tree's balance

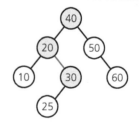

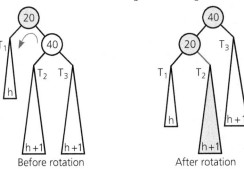

(c) The general case for a single left rotation in an AVL tree whose height is unchanged

Before rotation   After rotation

In some situations, a more complex rotation might be necessary. For example, consider the tree in Figure 19-5a, which is the result of nodes being added to or removed from an AVL tree. The left and right subtrees of the node <40> differ in height by more than 1. A double rotation

FIGURE 19-5   A double rotation that decreases the height of an AVL tree

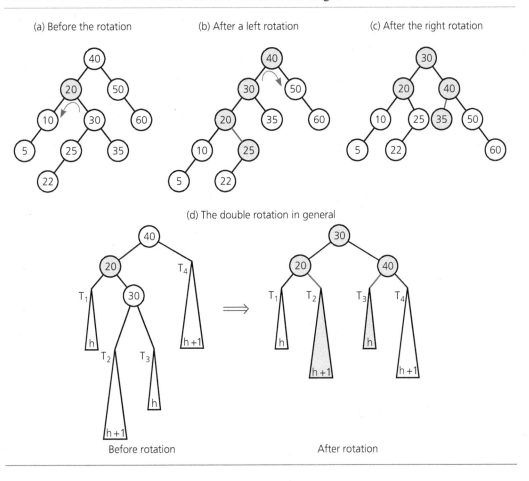

(a) Before the rotation

(b) After a left rotation

(c) After the right rotation

(d) The double rotation in general

Before rotation   After rotation

is necessary to restore this tree's balance. Figure 19-5b shows the result of a left rotation about <20>, and Figure 19-5c shows the result of a right rotation about <40>. Figure 19-5d illustrates this double rotation in a more general form. Mirror images of these figures would provide examples of other possible double rotations.

> **Note: When and where to perform a rotation in an AVL tree**
>
> Operations such as retrieval and traversal do not change the structure of an AVL tree and proceed just as they would for an unbalanced binary search tree. That is, no rotations occur. However, when we add data to an AVL tree, we add a node, and when we remove data from an AVL tree, we delete a node. In either case, the tree might become unbalanced. We need to detect when and where this unbalance occurs, so that we can restore the tree's balance by using rotations.
>
> A binary tree is balanced if the heights of its two subtrees differ by at most 1. We call this difference in heights the **balance factor** of the tree's root. Since any node is the root of a subtree, we define the balance factor as follows:
>
> The balance factor of node N = height(N's left subtree) − height(N's right subtree)
>
> Each node in an AVL tree has a balance factor of either −1, 0, or +1, since the tree is balanced. We record a node's balance factor in the node itself.
>
> The addition and removal operations—like those for any binary search tree—follow a path through the tree that begins at the root and ends at a leaf, which is either the new added node or the node that will be deleted. Let's consider adding data to an AVL tree. The new leaf has a balance factor of 0, because it has no children. That is, we can consider a leaf to have subtrees of height 0. To see whether this new leaf has disturbed the balance of the AVL tree, we look at the balance factor of each of the leaf's ancestors. Since the height of the tree is either unchanged by the addition of a new node or increases by 1, the balance factor of these ancestors is either unchanged or ranges from −2 to +2. As we consider each of the leaf's ancestors, we recompute its balance factor. If this factor is no longer in the range from −1 to +1, we must perform a rotation to correct its balance. The process of moving from the leaf to each of its ancestors and ultimately to the root follows the same path that the insertion took, but in reverse. We refer to this process as **retracing**. The removal operation uses a similar retracing step to correct the tree's balance after a node is deleted.

An AVL tree implementation of a dictionary is more difficult than other implementations

It can be proven that the height of an AVL tree with n nodes will always be very close to the theoretical minimum of $\lceil \log_2(n + 1) \rceil$. The AVL tree implementation of a dictionary is, therefore, one implementation that guarantees a binary search-like efficiency. Usually, however, implementations that use either a 2-3-4 tree or a red-black tree, which we discuss in Sections 19.4 and 19.5, will be simpler.

19.3 2-3 Trees

VideoNote
2-3 trees

A **2-3 tree** is a tree in which each internal node (nonleaf) has either two or three children and all leaves are at the same level. For example, Figure 19-6 shows a 2-3 tree of height 3. A node with two children is called a **2-node**—the nodes in a binary tree are all 2-nodes—and a node with three children is called a **3-node**.

A 2-3 tree is not a binary tree, because a node can have three children; nevertheless, a 2-3 tree does resemble a full binary tree. If a particular 2-3 tree contains only 2-nodes—a possibility,

FIGURE 19-6   A 2-3 tree of height 3

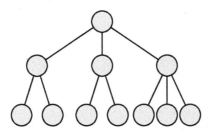

according to the definition—it is like a full binary tree, because all of its internal nodes have two children and all of its leaves are at the same level. If, on the other hand, some of the internal nodes of a 2-3 tree do have three children, the tree will contain more nodes than a full binary tree of the same height. Therefore, a 2-3 tree of height h always has at least as many nodes as a full binary tree of height h; that is, it always has at least $2^h - 1$ nodes. To put this another way, a 2-3 tree with n nodes never has height greater than $\lceil \log_2(n + 1) \rceil$, the minimum height of a binary tree with n nodes.

A 2-3 tree is not a binary tree

A 2-3 tree is never taller than a minimum-height binary tree

Given these observations, a 2-3 tree might be useful as an implementation of the ADT dictionary. Indeed, this is the case if the 2-3 tree orders its nodes to make it useful as a search tree. Just as we distinguish between a binary tree and a binary search tree, we could distinguish between a "2-3 tree" and a "2-3 search tree." The previous description would define a 2-3 tree, and the recursive definition given next would define a 2-3 search tree. Most people, however, do not make such a distinction and use the term "2-3 tree" to mean "2-3 search tree;" we will do so as well. The following recursive definition of a 2-3 tree specifies the order of its nodes, making it a search tree:

 Note: 2-3 trees

T is a 2-3 tree of height h if one of the following is true:

- T is empty, in which case h is 0.
- T is of the form

where r is a node that contains one data item and T_L and T_R are both 2-3 trees, each of height $h - 1$. In this case, the item in r must be greater than each item in the left subtree T_L and smaller than each item in the right subtree T_R.

- T is of the form

where r is a node that contains two data items and T_L, T_M, and T_R are 2-3 trees, each of height $h - 1$. In this case, the smaller item in r must be greater than each item in the left subtree T_L and smaller than each item in the middle subtree T_M. The larger item in r must be greater than each item in the middle subtree T_M and smaller than each item in the right subtree T_R.

> **Note: Rules for placing data items in the nodes of a 2-3 tree**
> The previous definition of a 2-3 tree implies the following rules for how you may place data items in its nodes:
> - A 2-node, which has two children, must contain a single data item that is greater than the left child's item(s) and less than the right child's item(s), as Figure 19-7a illustrates.
> - A 3-node, which has three children, must contain two data items, *S* and *L*, that satisfy the following relationships, as Figure 19-7b illustrates: *S* is greater than the left child's item(s) and less than the middle child's item(s); *L* is greater than the middle child's item(s) and less than the right child's item(s).
> - A leaf may contain either one or two data items.

FIGURE 19-7   Nodes in a 2-3 tree

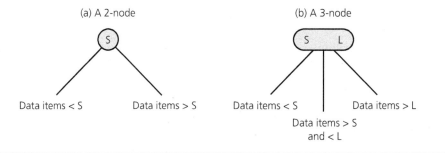

Data items in a 2-3 tree are ordered

Thus, the data items in a 2-3 tree are ordered. For example, the tree in Figure 19-8 is a 2-3 tree.

FIGURE 19-8   A 2-3 tree

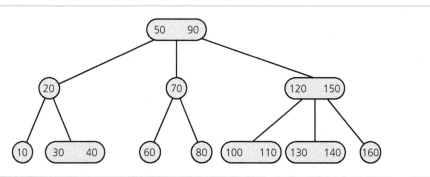

Listing 19-1 declares a class of nodes for a 2-3 tree. When a node contains only one data item, you can place it in `smallItem` and use `leftChildPtr` and `midChildPtr` to point to the node's children. To be safe, you can place `nullptr` in `rightChildPtr`.

LISTING 19-1 A header file for a class of nodes for a 2-3 tree

```cpp
1   /** A class of nodes for a link-based 2-3 tree.
2    @file TriNode.h */
3
4   #ifndef TRI_NODE_
5   #define TRI_NODE_
6
7   template<class ItemType>
8   class TriNode
9   {
10  private:
11     ItemType smallItem;                              // Data portion
12     ItemType largeItem;                              // Data portion
13     std::shared_ptr<TriNode<ItemType>> leftChildPtr;   // Left-child pointer
14     std::shared_ptr<TriNode<ItemType>> midChildPtr;    // Middle-child pointer
15     std::shared_ptr<TriNode<ItemType>> rightChildPtr;  // Right-child pointer
16
17  public:
18     TriNode();
19
20     bool isLeaf() const;
21     bool isTwoNode() const;
22     bool isThreeNode() const;
23
24     ItemType getSmallItem() const;
25     ItemType getLargeItem() const;
26
27     void setSmallItem(const ItemType& anItem);
28     void setLargeItem(const ItemType& anItem);
29     auto getLeftChildPtr() const;
30     auto getMidChildPtr() const;
31     auto getRightChildPtr() const;
32
33     void setLeftChildPtr(std::shared_ptr<TriNode<ItemType>> leftPtr);
34     void setMidChildPtr(std::shared_ptr<TriNode<ItemType>> midPtr);
35     void setRightChildPtr(std::shared_ptr<TriNode<ItemType>> rightPtr);
36  }; // end TriNode
37  #include "TriNode.cpp"
38  #endif
```

19.3.1 Traversing a 2-3 Tree

The algorithms for the traversal, retrieval, addition, and removal operations on a 2-3 tree are recursive. You can avoid distracting implementation details by defining the base case for these recursive algorithms to be a leaf rather than an empty subtree. As a result, the algorithms must assume that they are not passed an empty tree as an argument.

You can traverse a 2-3 tree in sorted order by performing the analogue of an inorder traversal on a binary tree:

Inorder traversal

```
// Traverses a nonempty 2-3 tree in sorted order.
inorder(23Tree: TwoThreeTree): void
{
    if (23Tree's root node r is a leaf)
        Visit the data item(s)
    else if (r has two data items)
    {
        inorder(left subtree of 23Tree's root)
        Visit the first data item
        inorder(middle subtree of 23Tree's root)
        Visit the second data item
        inorder(right subtree of 23Tree's root)
    }
    else // r has one data item
    {
        inorder(left subtree of 23Tree's root)
        Visit the data item
        inorder(right subtree of 23Tree's root)
    }
}
```

19.3.2 Searching a 2-3 Tree

The ordering of data items in a 2-3 tree is analogous to the ordering for a binary search tree and allows you to search a 2-3 tree efficiently for a particular item. In fact, the retrieval operation for a 2-3 tree is quite similar to the retrieval operation for a binary search tree, as you can see from the following pseudocode:

Searching a 2-3 tree is efficient

```
// Locates the value target in a nonempty 2-3 tree. Returns either the located
// entry or throws an exception if such a node is not found.
findItem(23Tree: TwoThreeTree, target: ItemType): ItemType
{
    if (target is in 23Tree's root node r)
    {   // The data item has been found
        treeItem = the data portion of r
        return treeItem // Success
    }
    else if (r is a leaf)
        throw NotFoundException   // Failure

    // Else search the appropriate subtree
    else if (r has two data items)
    {
        if (target < smaller data item in r)
            return findItem(r's left subtree, target)
        else if (target < larger data item in r)
            return findItem(r's middle subtree, target)
        else
            return findItem(r's right subtree, target)
    }
    else // r has one data item
    {
        if (target < r's data item)
            return findItem(r's left subtree, target)
        else
            return findItem(r's right subtree, target)
    }
}
```

You can search the 2-3 tree and the shortest binary search tree with approximately the same efficiency, because

- A binary search tree with n nodes cannot be shorter than $\lceil \log_2(n + 1) \rceil$
- A 2-3 tree with n nodes cannot be taller than $\lceil \log_2(n + 1) \rceil$
- A node in a 2-3 tree has at most two data items

Searching a 2-3 tree is not more efficient than searching a binary search tree, however. This observation may surprise you because, after all, the nodes of a 2-3 tree can have three children, and hence a 2-3 tree might indeed be shorter than the shortest possible binary search tree. Although true, this advantage in height is offset by the extra time required to compare a given value with two values instead of only one. In other words, although you might visit fewer nodes when searching a 2-3 tree, you might have to make more comparisons at each node. As a consequence, the number of comparisons that you need to search a 2-3 tree for a given data item is approximately equal to the number of comparisons required to search a binary search tree that is as balanced as possible. This number is approximately $\log_2 n$.

If you can search a 2-3 tree and a balanced binary search tree with approximately the same efficiency, why then should you use a 2-3 tree? Because although maintaining the balance of a binary search tree is difficult in the face of addition and removal operations, maintaining the shape of a 2-3 tree is relatively simple. For example, consider the two trees in Figure 19-9. The first tree is a binary search tree and the second is a 2-3 tree. Both trees contain the same data items. The binary search tree is as balanced as possible, and thus you can search both it and the 2-3 tree for a data item with approximately the same efficiency. If, however, you add several data items to the binary search tree—by using the addition algorithm of Chapter 16—the tree can quickly lose its balance, as Figure 19-10a indicates. In this example, we have added the values 32 through 39 in reverse numerical order. As you soon will see, you can perform the same additions to the 2-3 tree without a degradation in the tree's shape—it will retain its structure, as Figure 19-10b shows.

Searching a 2-3 tree is O(log n)

Maintaining the shape of a 2-3 tree is relatively easy

FIGURE 19-9   A balanced binary search tree and a 2-3 tree that contain the same entries

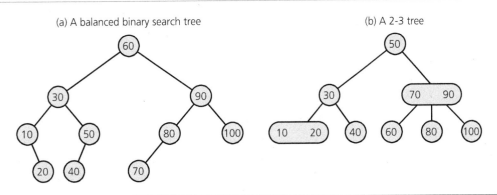

(a) A balanced binary search tree   (b) A 2-3 tree

The new values that we added to the binary search tree of Figure 19-9a appear along a single path in Figure 19-10a. These additions increased the height of the binary search tree from 4 to 12—an increase of 8. On the other hand, the new values in the 2-3 tree in Figure 19-10b are spread throughout the tree. As a consequence, the height of the resulting tree is only 1 greater than the height of the original 2-3 tree in Figure 19-9b. We demonstrate these additions into the original 2-3 tree next.

FIGURE 19-10   The trees of Figure 19-9 after adding the values 39 down to 32

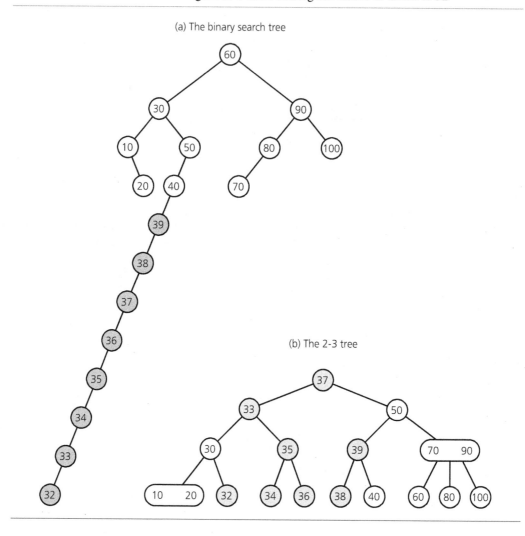

(a) The binary search tree

(b) The 2-3 tree

19.3.3 Adding Data to a 2-3 Tree

Because the nodes of a 2-3 tree can have either two or three children and can contain one or two values, you can add data to the tree while maintaining its shape. The following paragraphs informally describe the sequence of additions that produced the 2-3 tree shown in Figure 19-10b from the original tree in Figure 19-9b.

Ading data to a 2-node leaf is simple

Add 39. As is true with a binary search tree, the first step in inserting a node into a 2-3 tree is to locate the node at which the search for the value to be added would terminate. To do this, you can use the search strategy of the `findItem` algorithm given in the previous section; an unsuccessful search will always terminate at a leaf. With the tree in Figure 19-9b, the search for 39 terminates at the leaf <40>. (We will use this angle-bracket notation to denote a node and its contents.) Because this node contains only one data item, you can simply place the new item into this node. The result is the 2-3 tree in Figure 19-11.

FIGURE 19-11   After adding 39 to the tree in Figure 19-9b

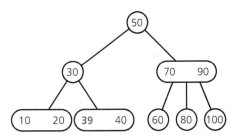

Add 38. In a similar manner, you would search the tree in Figure 19-11 for 38 and find that the search terminates at the node <39 40>. You cannot place 38 in this node, as Figure 19-12a illustrates, because a node cannot contain three values. You can arrange these three values, however, into the smallest (38), middle (39), and largest (40) values. You then move the middle value (39) up to the node's parent *p* and separate the remaining values, 38 and 40, into two nodes that you attach to *p* as children, as Figure 19-12b indicates. You can think of this process as folding the node with three values into an upside-down V that is then attached to the parent node at the V's point. Because the middle value of <38 39 40> moves up, the parent correctly separates the values of its children; that is, 38 is less than 39, which is less than 40. The result of the addition is the 2-3 tree in Figure 19-12c.

Adding data to a 3-node causes it to divide

FIGURE 19-12   The steps for adding 38 to the tree in Figure 19-11

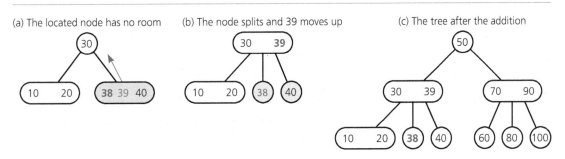

Add 37. The addition of 37 to the tree in Figure 19-12c is easy because 37 belongs in a leaf that currently contains only one value, 38. The result of this addition is the 2-3 tree in Figure 19-13.

FIGURE 19-13   After adding 37 to the tree in Figure 19-12c

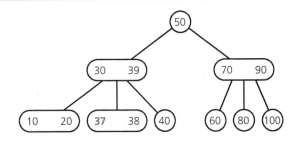

Add 36. The search for 36 terminates at the node <37 38> of the tree in Figure 19-13, but the node has no room for 36, as Figure 19-14a indicates. Thus, you arrange the three values 36, 37, and 38 into the smallest (36), middle (37), and largest (38) values, as you did previously. You then try to move the middle value (37) up to the node's parent <30 39> and give the parent children containing the smallest (36) and largest (38) values, as Figure 19-14b illustrates. However, the node <30 39> cannot contain three values and have four children. This situation is familiar, with the slight difference that the overcrowded node is not a leaf but rather has four children. As you did before, you divide the node into the smallest (30), middle (37), and largest (39) values and then move the middle value up to the node's parent.

Because you are splitting an internal node, you now must account for its four children—that is, what happens to nodes <10 20>, <36>, <38>, and <40>? The solution is to attach the left pair of children—<10 20> and <36>—to the smallest value (30) and attach the right pair of children—<38> and <40>—to the largest value (39), as shown in Figure 19-14c. The final result of this addition is the 2-3 tree in Figure 19-14d.

FIGURE 19-14   The steps for adding 36 to the tree in Figure 19-13

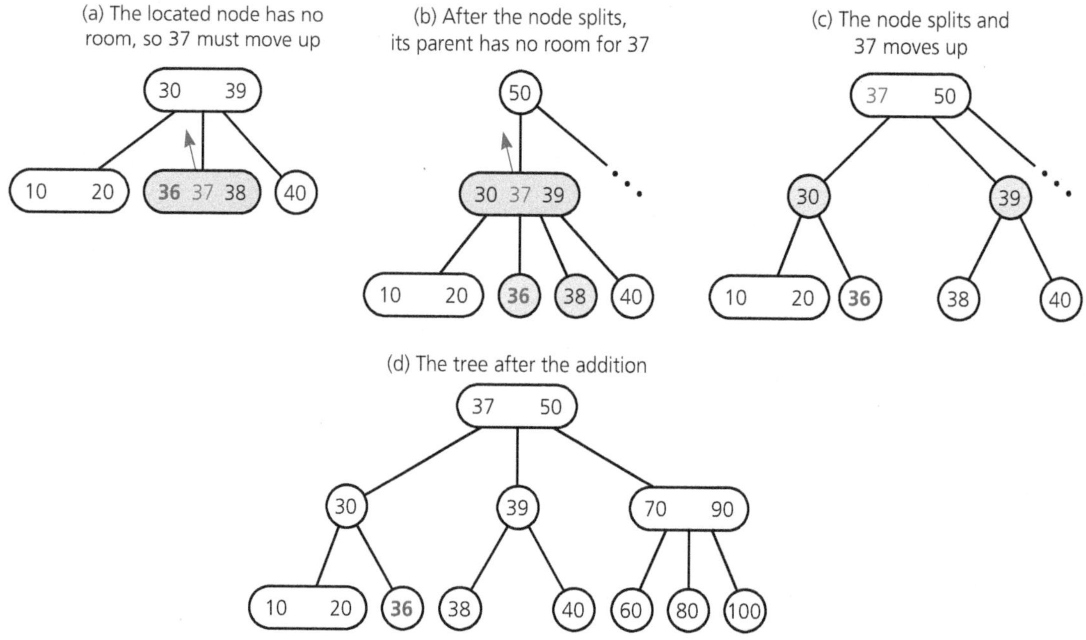

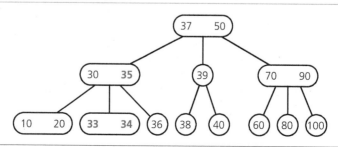

(a) The located node has no room, so 37 must move up

(b) After the node splits, its parent has no room for 37

(c) The node splits and 37 moves up

(d) The tree after the addition

Add 35, 34, and 33. Each of these additions is similar to the previous ones. Figure 19-15 shows the tree after the three additions.

FIGURE 19-15   The tree after the addition of 35, 34, and 33 to the tree in Figure 19-14d

Question 1 To be sure that you fully understand the addition algorithm, add 32 to the 2-3 tree in Figure 19-15. The result should be the tree shown in Figure 19-10b. Once again, compare this tree with the binary search tree in Figure 19-10a and notice the dramatic advantage of the 2-3 tree's addition strategy.

The addition algorithm. Let's consider the general strategy for adding a data item to a 2-3 tree. To begin, you locate the leaf at which the search for the new data item would terminate. If the leaf does not contain two data items, you add the new item to the leaf, and you are done. However, if the leaf already contains two data items, you must split it into two nodes, n_1 and n_2. As Figure 19-16 illustrates, you place the smallest item S into n_1, place the largest item L into n_2, and try to move the middle item M up to the original leaf's parent. If the parent has room for a new item—as is true here—nodes n_1 and n_2 become children of the parent, and you are finished. The parent now has only three children and contains two data items.

When a leaf would contain three data items, split it into two nodes

FIGURE 19-16 Splitting a leaf in a 2-3 tree in general and in a specific example

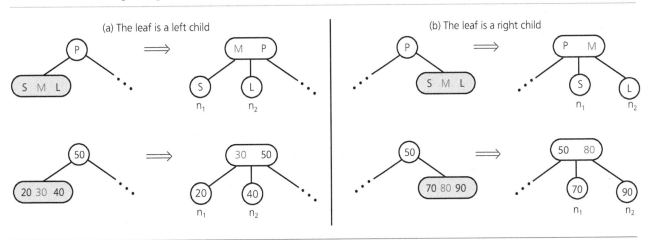

On the other hand, if the parent cannot accommodate the data item moving up, you must split the parent, as follows. You split an internal node n that contains three data items by using the process just described for a leaf, except that you must also take care of n's four children. As Figure 19-17 illustrates, you split n into n_1 and n_2, place n's smallest item S into n_1, attach n's two leftmost children to n_1, place n's largest item L into n_2, attach n's two rightmost children to n_2, and move n's middle item M up to n's parent.

After this, the process of splitting a node and moving a data item up to the parent continues recursively until a node is reached that had only one data item before the addition and thus has only two data items after the addition. Notice in the previous sequence of additions that the tree's height never increased from its original value of 3. In general, an addition will not increase the height of the tree as long as there is at least one node containing only one data item on the path from the root to the leaf that will accommodate the new item. The addition strategy of a 2-3 tree thus postpones the growth of the tree's height much more effectively than does the strategy of a basic binary search tree.

When an internal node would contain three data items, split it into two nodes and accommodate its children

FIGURE 19-17 Splitting an internal node in a 2-3 tree in general and in a specific example

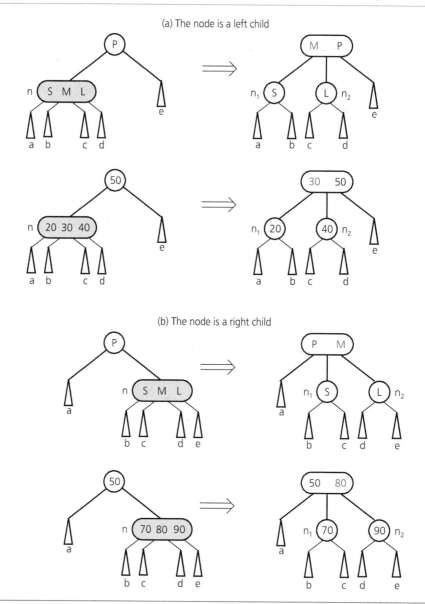

(a) The node is a left child

(b) The node is a right child

When the height of a 2-3 tree does grow, it does so from the top. An increase in the height of a 2-3 tree will occur if every node on the path from the root of the tree to the leaf that will accommodate the new data item contains two items. In this case, the recursive process of splitting a node and moving an item up to the node's parent will eventually reach the root r. When this occurs you must split r into r_1 and r_2 exactly as you would any other internal node. However, you must create a new node that contains the middle item of r and becomes the parent of r_1 and r_2. Thus, the new node is the new root of the tree, as Figure 19-18 illustrates.

FIGURE 19-18   Splitting the root of a 2-3 tree in general and in a specific example

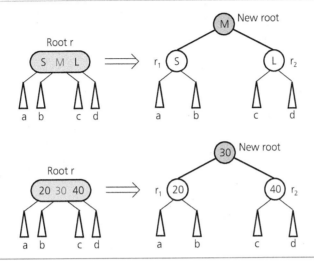

The following high-level algorithm summarizes the entire addition strategy:

2-3 tree addition
algorithm

```
// Adds a new data item to a 2-3 tree whose items are distinct and differ from the
// new item.
add(23Tree: TwoThreeTree, newItem: ItemType): boolean
{
    Locate the leaf, leafNode, in which newItem belongs
    Add newItem to leafNode

    if (leafNode has three data items)
        split(leafNode)
    return true
}

// Splits node n, which contains two data items. Note: If n is
// not a leaf, it has four children.
split(n: TwoThreeNode): void
{
    if (n is the root)
        Create a new node p
    else
        Let p be the parent of n

    Replace node n with two nodes, n1 and n2, so that p is their parent
    Give n1 the smallest data item in n
    Give n2 the largest data item in n

    if (n is not a leaf)
    {
        n1 becomes the parent of n's two leftmost children
        n2 becomes the parent of n's two rightmost children
    }
    Move the middle-valued item in n up to p
    if (p now has three data items)
        split(p)
}
```

Question 2 What is the result of adding 5, 40, 10, 20, 15, and 30—in the order given— to an initially empty 2-3 tree? Note that the addition of one data item to an empty 2-3 tree will result in a one-node tree.

Question 3 What is the result of adding 3 and 4 to the 2-3 tree that you created in the previous question?

19.3.4 Removing Data from a 2-3 Tree

The removal strategy for a 2-3 tree is the inverse of its strategy to add data. Just as a 2-3 tree spreads additions throughout the tree by splitting nodes when they would become too full, it spreads removals throughout the tree by merging nodes when they become empty. As an illustration of the 2-3 tree's removal strategy, consider the removal of 70, 100, and 80 from the tree in Figure 19-19a.

Swap the value to be removed with its inorder successor

Remove 70. By searching the tree in Figure 19-19a, you discover that 70 is in the node <70 90>. Because you always want to begin the removal process at a leaf, the first step is to swap 70 with its inorder successor—the value that follows it in the sorted order. Because 70 is the smaller of

FIGURE 19-19 The steps for removing 70 from the 2-3 tree in Figure 19-9b

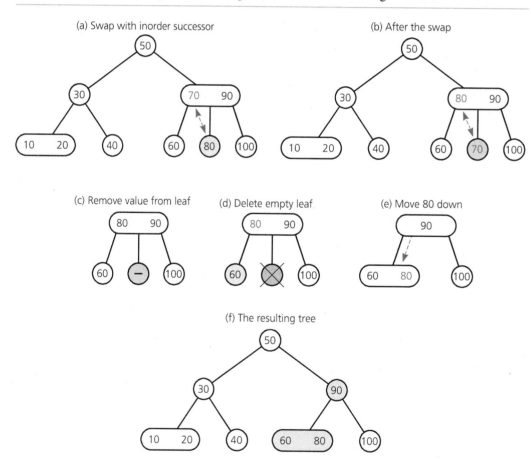

the two values in the node, its inorder successor (80) is the smallest value in the node's middle subtree. Note that the inorder successor of a data item in an internal node will always be in a leaf. After the swap, the tree appears as shown in Figure 19-19b. The value 80 is in a legal position of the search tree because it is larger than all the values in its node's left subtree and smaller than all the values in its node's right subtree. The value 70 is not in a legal position, but this is of no concern, because the next step is to remove this value from the leaf.

In general, after you remove a value from a leaf, another value might remain in the leaf (because the leaf contained two values before the removal). If this is the case, you are done, because a leaf of a 2-3 tree can contain a single value. In this example, however, once you remove 70 from the leaf, the node is left without a value, as Figure 19-19c indicates.

You then delete the node, as Figure 19-19d illustrates. At this point you see that the parent of the deleted node contains two values (80 and 90) but has two children (60 and 100). This situation is not allowed in a 2-3 tree. You can remedy the problem by moving the smaller value (80) down from the parent into the left child, as Figure 19-19e illustrates. Deleting the leaf node and moving a value down to a sibling of the leaf is called *merging* the leaf with its sibling. The 2-3 tree that results from this removal operation is shown in Figure 19-19f.

Merge nodes

Remove 100. The search strategy discovers that 100 is in the leaf <100> of the tree in Figure 19-19f. When you remove the value from this leaf, the node becomes empty, as Figure 19-20a indicates. In this case, however, no merging of nodes is required, because the sibling <60 80> can spare a value. That is, the sibling has two values, whereas a 2-3 tree requires only that it have at least one value. However, if you simply move the value 80 into the empty node—as Figure 19-20b illustrates—you find that the search-tree order is destroyed: The value in 90's right child should be greater than 90, but it is 80. Instead, you move the larger value (80) from <60 80> into the parent and move the value 90 down from the parent into the node that had been empty, as Figure 19-20c shows. This distribution preserves the search-tree order, and you have thus completed the removal. The resulting 2-3 tree is shown in Figure 19-20d.

Redistribute values

FIGURE 19-20   The steps for removing 100 from the tree in Figure 19-19f

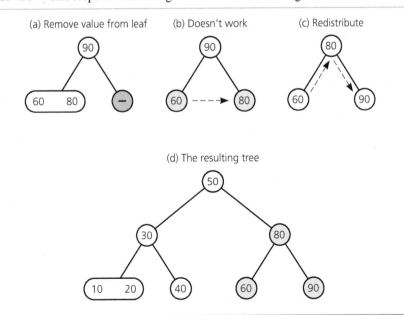

Remove 80.   The search strategy finds that 80 is in an internal node of the tree in Figure 19-20d. You thus must swap 80 with its inorder successor, 90, as Figure 19-21a illustrates. When you remove 80 from the leaf, the node becomes empty, as Figure 19-21b shows. Because the sibling of the empty node has only one value, you cannot redistribute as you did in the previous removal of 100. Instead you must merge the nodes, bringing the value 90 down from the parent and deleting the empty leaf, as Figure 19-21c indicates.

You are not yet finished, however, because the parent contains no data and has only one child. You must recursively apply the removal strategy to this internal node without a value. First, you should check to see whether the node's sibling can spare a value. Because the sibling <30> contains only the single value 30, you cannot redistribute—you must merge the nodes. The merging of two internal nodes is identical to the merging of leaves, except that the child <60 90> of the empty node must be adopted. Because the sibling of the empty node contains

---

FIGURE 19-21   The steps for removing 80 from the 2-3 tree in Figure 19-20d

(a) After swap with inorder successor

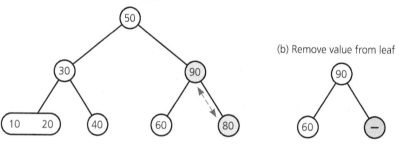

(b) Remove value from leaf

(c) Merge by moving 90 down and removing empty leaf

(d) Merge: move 50 down, adopt empty node's child, delete empty node

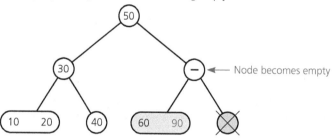

(e) Delete empty root

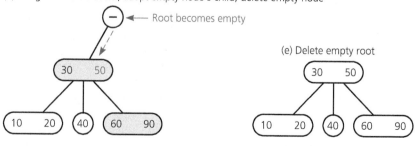

only one value—and hence can have only two children, as stated in the rule for 2-nodes—it can become the parent of <60 90> only if you bring the value 50 down from the sibling's parent. The tree now appears as shown in Figure 19-21d. Note that this operation preserves the search property of the tree.

Now the parent of the merged nodes is left without a data item and only a single child. Usually, you would apply the recursive removal strategy to this node, but this case is special because the node is the root. Because the root is empty and has only one child, you can simply delete it, allowing <30 50> to become the root of the tree, as Figure 19-21e illustrates. This deletion has thus caused the height of the tree to shrink by 1.

To summarize, we have removed 70, 100, and 80 from the 2-3 tree in Figure 19-19a and obtained the 2-3 tree in Figures 19-21e and 19-22a. In contrast, after removing 70, 100, and 80 from the balanced binary search tree in Figure 19-9a, you are left with the tree in Figure 19-22b. Notice that the removals affected only one part of the binary search tree, causing it to lose its balance. The left subtree has not been affected at all, and thus the overall height of the tree has not been diminished.

FIGURE 19-22   Results of removing 70, 100, and 80 from a 2-3 tree and a binary search tree, both which contain the same values

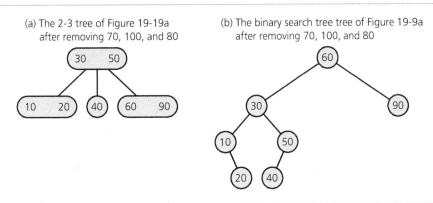

(a) The 2-3 tree of Figure 19-19a after removing 70, 100, and 80

(b) The binary search tree tree of Figure 19-9a after removing 70, 100, and 80

The removal algorithm. In summary, to remove a data item *I* from a 2-3 tree, you first locate the node *n* that contains it. If *n* is not a leaf, you find *I*'s inorder successor and swap it with *I*. As a result of the swap, the removal always begins at a leaf. If the leaf contains an item in addition to *I*, you simply remove *I* and you are done. On the other hand, if the leaf contains only *I*, removing *I* would leave the leaf without a data item. In this case you must perform some additional work to complete the removal.

You first check the siblings of the now-empty leaf. If a sibling has two data items, you redistribute the items among the sibling, the empty leaf, and the leaf's parent, as Figure 19-23a illustrates. If no sibling of the leaf has two items, you merge the leaf with an adjacent sibling by moving an item down from the leaf's parent into the sibling—it had only one item before, so it has room for another—and deleting the empty leaf. This case is shown in Figure 19-23b.

Redistribute values

By moving an item down from a node *n*, as just described, you might cause *n* to be left without a data item and with only one child. If so, you recursively apply the removal algorithm to *n*. Thus, if *n* has a sibling with two items—and three children—you redistribute the items among *n*, the sibling, and *n*'s parent. You also give *n* one of its sibling's children, as Figure 19-23c indicates.

If *n* has no sibling with two data items, you merge *n* with a sibling, as Figure 19-23d illustrates. That is, you move an item down from the parent and let the sibling adopt *n*'s one child.

Merge nodes

FIGURE 19-23   Possible situations during the removal of a data item from a 2-3 tree

(a) Redistributing values to fill an empty leaf

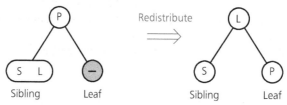

(b) Deleting an empty leaf and merging its sibling with its parent

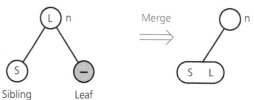

(c) Redistributing values and children to fill an empty node

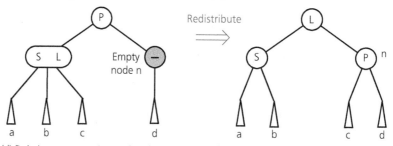

(d) Deleting an empty internal node and merging others

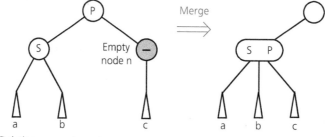

(e) Deleting an empty root

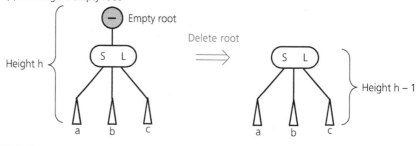

(At this point you know that the sibling previously had only one item and two children.) You then delete the empty leaf. If the merge causes *n*'s parent to be without a data item, you recursively apply the removal process to it.

If the merging continues so that the root of the tree is without a data item—and has only one child—you simply delete the root. When this step occurs, the height of the tree is reduced by 1, as Figure 19-23e illustrates.

A high-level statement of the algorithm for removing data from a 2-3 tree follows:

// Removes the given data item from a 2-3 tree. Returns true if successful
// or false if no such item exists.

2-3 tree removal
algorithm

```
remove(23Tree: TwoThreeTree, dataItem: ItemType): boolean
{
    Attempt to locate dataItem
    if (dataItem is found)
    {
        if (dataItem is not in a leaf)
            Swap dataItem with its inorder successor, which will be in a leaf leafNode

        // The removal always begins at a leaf
        Remove dataItem from leaf leafNode
        if (leafNode now has no data items)
            fixTree(leafNode)
        return true
    }
    else
        return false
}

// Completes the removal when node n is empty by either deleting the root,
// redistributing values, or merging nodes. Note: If n is internal, it has one child.
fixTree(n: TwoThreeNode): void
{
    if (n is the root)
        Delete the root
    else
    {
        Let p be the parent of n
        if (some sibling of n has two data items)
        {
            Distribute items appropriately among n, the sibling, and p
            if (n is internal)
                Move the appropriate child from sibling to n
        }
        else  // Merge the node
        {
            Choose an adjacent sibling s of n
            Bring the appropriate data item down from p into s
            if (n is internal)
                Move n's child to s
            Delete node n
            if (p is now empty)
                fixTree(p)
        }
    }
}
```

The details of the C++ implementation of the preceding addition and removal algorithms for 2-3 trees are rather involved. The implementation is left as a challenging exercise (Programming Problem 2).

You might be concerned about the overhead that the addition and removal algorithms incur in the course of maintaining the 2-3 structure of the tree. That is, after the search strategy locates either the desired data item or the position for a new item, the addition and removal algorithms sometimes have to perform extra work, such as splitting and merging nodes. However, this extra work is not a real concern. A rigorous mathematical analysis would show that the extra work required to maintain the structure of a 2-3 tree after an addition or a removal is not significant. In other words, when analyzing the efficiency of the add and remove algorithms, it is sufficient to consider only the time required to locate the item (or the position for the addition). Given that a 2-3 tree is always balanced, you can search a 2-3 tree in all situations with the logarithmic efficiency of a binary search.

A 2-3 tree is always balanced

Thus, a 2-3 tree implementation of the ADT dictionary is guaranteed to have efficient operations. Although a binary search tree that is as balanced as possible minimizes the amount of work required by the ADT dictionary operations, its balance is difficult to maintain. A 2-3 tree is a compromise: Although searching it may not be quite as efficient as searching a binary search tree of minimum height, it is relatively simple to maintain.

A 2-3 tree implementation of a dictionary is O(log n) for all of its operations

 Question 4 What is the result of removing the 10 from the 2-3 tree that you created in Checkpoint Question 2?

 VideoNote
2-3-4 and red-black trees

19.4   2-3-4 Trees

If a 2-3 tree is so good, are trees whose nodes can have more than three children even better? To some extent, the answer is yes. A **2-3-4 tree** is like a 2-3 tree, but it also allows **4-nodes**, which are nodes that have four children and three data items. For example, Figure 19-24 shows a 2-3-4 tree of height 3 that has the same items as the 2-3 tree in Figure 19-10b. As you will see, you can perform additions and removals on a 2-3-4 tree with fewer steps than a 2-3 tree requires.

FIGURE 19-24   A 2-3-4 tree with the same data items as the 2-3 tree in Figure 19-10b

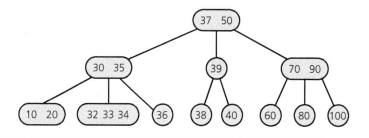

A 2-3-4 tree

 Note: 2-3-4 trees

T is a 2-3-4 tree of height *h* if one of the following is true:

- *T* is empty, in which case *h* is 0.
- *T* is of the form

where r is a node that contains one data item and T_L and T_R are both 2-3-4 trees, each of height $h - 1$. In this case, the item in r must be greater than each item in the left subtree T_L and smaller than each item in the right subtree T_R.

- T is of the form

where r is a node that contains two data items and T_L, T_M, and T_R are 2-3-4 trees, each of height $h - 1$. In this case, the smaller item in r must be greater than each item in the left subtree T_L and smaller than each item in the middle subtree T_M. The larger item in r must be greater than each item in T_M and smaller than each item in the right subtree T_R.

- T is of the form

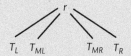

where r is a node that contains three data items and T_L, T_{ML}, T_{MR}, and T_R are 2-3-4 trees, each of height $h - 1$. In this case, the smallest item in r must be greater than each item in the left subtree T_L and smaller than each item in the middle-left subtree T_{ML}. The middle item in r must be greater than each item in T_{ML} and smaller than each item in the middle-right subtree T_{MR}. The largest item in r must be greater than each item in T_{MR} and smaller than each item in the right subtree T_R.

 Note: Rules for placing data items in the nodes of a 2-3-4 tree

The previous definition of a 2-3-4 tree implies the following rules for how you may place data items in its nodes:

- A 2-node, which has two children, must contain a single data item that satisfies the relationships pictured earlier in Figure 19-7a.
- A 3-node, which has three children, must contain two data items that satisfy the relationships pictured earlier in Figure 19-7b.
- A 4-node, which has four children, must contain three data items S, M, and L that satisfy the following relationships, as Figure 19-25 illustrates: S is greater than the left child's item(s) and less than the middle-left child's item(s); M is greater than the middle-left child's item(s) and less than the middle-right child's item(s); L is greater than the middle-right child's item(s) and less than the right child's item(s).
- A leaf may contain either one, two, or three data items.

FIGURE 19-25   A 4-node in a 2-3-4 tree

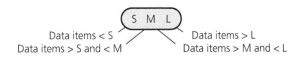

A 2-3-4 tree requires more storage than a 2-3 tree

Although a 2-3-4 tree has more efficient addition and removal operations than a 2-3 tree, a 2-3-4 tree has greater storage requirements due to the additional data members in its 4-nodes, as the beginning of the class QuadNode indicates:

A node in a 2-3-4 tree

```cpp
template<class ItemType>
class QuadNode
{
private:
    ItemType smallItem;                                    // Data portion
    ItemType middleItem;
    ItemType largeItem;
    std::shared_ptr<QuadNode<ItemType>> leftChildPtr;      // Left-child pointer
    std::shared_ptr<QuadNode<ItemType>> leftMidChildPtr;   // Middle-left-child pointer
    std::shared_ptr<QuadNode<ItemType>> rightMidChildPtr;  // Middle-right-child pointer
    std::shared_ptr<QuadNode<ItemType>> rightChildPtr;     // Right-child pointer

    // Constructors, accessor methods, and mutator methods are here.


    . . .

}; // end QuadNode
```

As you will see later, however, you can transform a 2-3-4 tree into a special binary tree that reduces the storage requirements.

19.4.1 Searching and Traversing a 2-3-4 Tree

The search algorithm and the traversal algorithm for a 2-3-4 tree are simple extensions of the corresponding algorithms for a 2-3 tree. For example, to search the tree in Figure 19-24 for 31, you would search the left subtree of the root, because 31 is less than 37; search the middle subtree of the node <30 35>, because 31 is between 30 and 35; and terminate the search at the left child pointer of <32 33 34>, because 31 is less than 32—deducing that 31 is not in the tree. Exercise 8 asks you to complete the details of searching and traversing a 2-3-4 tree.

19.4.2 Adding Data to a 2-3-4 Tree

The addition algorithm for a 2-3-4 tree, like the addition algorithm for a 2-3 tree, splits a node by moving one of its data items up to its parent node. For a 2-3 tree, the search algorithm traces a path from the root to a leaf and then backs up from the leaf as it splits nodes. To avoid this return path after reaching a leaf, the addition algorithm for a 2-3-4 tree splits 4-nodes as soon as it encounters them on the way down the tree from the root to a leaf. As a result, when a 4-node is split and a data item moves up to the node's parent, the parent cannot possibly be a 4-node, and so it can accommodate another item.

Split 4-nodes as they are encountered

As an example of the algorithm, consider the tree in Figure 19-26a. This one-node tree is the result of adding 60, 30, and 10 to an initially empty 2-3-4 tree. We will now add more data to this tree.

Add 20. To find where 20 belongs in the tree, you begin at the root and encounter the 4-node <10 30 60>, which you split by moving the middle value 30 up. Because the node is the root, you create a new root, move 30 into it, and attach two children, as Figure 19-26b illustrates. You continue the search for 20 by examining the left subtree of the root, because 20 is less than 30. The addition results in the tree in Figure 19-26c.

FIGURE 19-26   Adding 20 to a one-node 2-3-4 tree

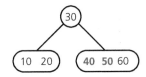

(a) The original tree   (b) After splitting the node   (c) After adding 20

Add 50 and 40. The additions of 50 and 40 do not require split nodes and result in the tree in Figure 19-27.

FIGURE 19-27   After adding 50 and 40 to the tree in Figure 19-26c

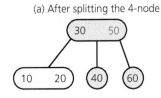

Add 70. While searching the tree in Figure 19-27 to see where 70 belongs in the tree, you encounter the 4-node <40 50 60>, because 70 is greater than 30. You split this 4-node by moving 50 up to the node's parent, <30>, to get the tree in Figure 19-28a. You then add 70 to the leaf <60>, as Figure 19-28b illustrates.

FIGURE 19-28   The steps for adding 70 to the tree in Figure 19-27

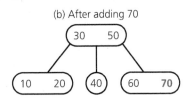

(a) After splitting the 4-node   (b) After adding 70

Add 80 and 15. These additions do not require split nodes and result in the tree in Figure 19-29.

FIGURE 19-29   After adding 80 and 15 to the tree in Figure 19-28b

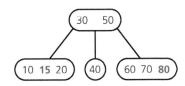

Add 90. As you search the tree in Figure 19-29 for 90's place in the tree, you traverse the root's right subtree, because 90 is greater than 50, and encounter the 4-node <60 70 80>. You split this

4-node into two nodes and move 70 up to the root, as Figure 19-30a indicates. Finally, because 90 is greater than 70, you add 90 to the leaf <80> to get the tree in Figure 19-30b.

FIGURE 19-30 The steps for adding 90 to the tree in Figure 19-29

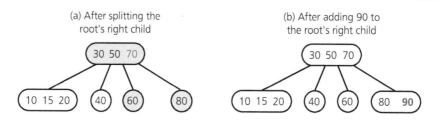

Add 100. As you begin to search the tree in Figure 19-30b for 100, you immediately encounter a 4-node at the tree's root. You split this node into two nodes and move 50 up to a new root, as Figure 19-31a indicates. After continuing the search, you add 100 to <80 90> to get the tree in Figure 19-31b.

FIGURE 19-31 The steps for adding 100 to the tree in Figure 19-30b

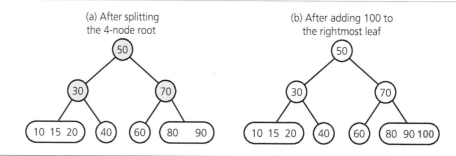

Splitting 4-nodes during additions. As you have just seen, you split each 4-node as soon as you encounter it during your search from the root to the leaf that will accommodate the additonal data item. As a result, each 4-node either will

* Be the root,
* Have a 2-node parent, or
* Have a 3-node parent

Figure 19-32 illustrates how to split a 4-node that is the tree's root. You have seen two previous examples of this: We split <10 30 60> in Figure 19-26a, resulting in the tree in Figure 19-26b.

FIGURE 19-32 Splitting a 4-node root when adding data to a 2-3-4 tree

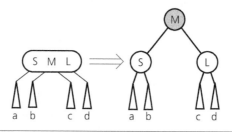

We also split <30 50 70> when adding 100 to the tree in Figure 19-30b, giving us the tree in Figure 19-31a.

Figure 19-33 illustrates the two possible situations that can occur when you split a 4-node whose parent is a 2-node. For example, when you split <40 50 60> during the addition of 70 into the tree in Figure 19-27, you get the tree in Figure 19-28a.

FIGURE 19-33   Splitting a 4-node whose parent is a 2-node when adding data to a 2-3-4 tree

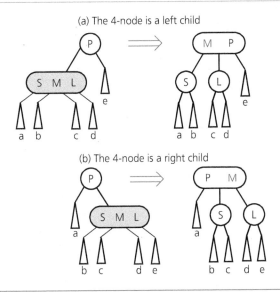

Figure 19-34 illustrates the three possible situations that can occur when you split a 4-node whose parent is a 3-node. For example, when you split <60 70 80> during the addition of 90 to the tree in Figure 19-29, you get the tree in Figure 19-30a.

Question 5 Add 25 to the 2-3-4 tree in Figure 19-31b.

Question 6 Add 3 and 4 to the 2-3-4 tree that you created in the previous question.

19.4.3 Removing Data from a 2-3-4 Tree

The removal algorithm for a 2-3-4 tree has the same beginning as the removal algorithm for a 2-3 tree. You first locate the node n that contains the data item I that you want to remove. You then find I's inorder successor and swap it with I so that the removal will always be at a leaf. If that leaf is either a 3-node or a 4-node, you simply remove I. If you can ensure that I does not occur in a 2-node, you can perform the removal in one pass through the tree from root to leaf, unlike removal from a 2-3 tree. That is, you will not have to back away from the leaf and restructure the tree.

In fact, you can guarantee that I does not occur in a 2-node by transforming each 2-node that you encounter during the search for I into either a 3-node or a 4-node. Several cases are possible, depending on the configuration of the 2-node's parent and its nearest sibling. (Arbitrarily, a node's nearest sibling is its left sibling, unless the node is a left child, in which case its nearest sibling is to its right.) That is, either the parent or the sibling could be a 2-node, a 3-node, or a

Transform each 2-node into a 3-node or a 4-node

FIGURE 19-34 Splitting a 4-node whose parent is a 3-node when adding data to a 2-3-4 tree

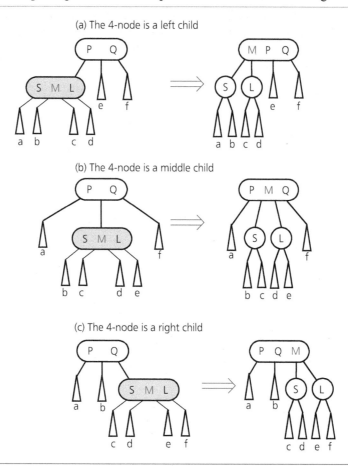

4-node. For example, if the next node that you encounter is a 2-node and both its parent and nearest sibling are 2-nodes, apply the transformation that Figure 19-32 illustrates, but in reverse; however, if the parent is a 3-node, apply the transformation that Figure 19-33 illustrates, but in reverse; and if the parent is a 4-node, apply the transformation that Figure 19-34 illustrates, but in reverse.

The details of removal from a 2-3-4 tree are left to you as a challenging exercise (Exercise 9).

2-3 and 2-3-4 trees are attractive because their balance is easy to maintain

The algorithms for adding data to and removing data from a 2-3-4 tree require fewer steps than those for a 2-3 tree

Note: **2-3 trees versus 2-3-4 trees**

The advantage of both 2-3 and 2-3-4 trees is their easy-to-maintain balance, not their shorter height. Even if a 2-3 tree is shorter than a balanced binary search tree, the reduction in height is offset by the increased number of comparisons that the search algorithm might require at each node. The situation is similar for a 2-3-4 tree, but its addition and removal algorithms require only one pass through the tree and so are more efficient than those for a 2-3 tree. This decrease in effort makes the 2-3-4 tree more attractive than the 2-3 tree.

Note: Nodes with more than four children?

Should we consider trees whose nodes have even more than four children? Although a tree whose nodes can each have 100 children would be shorter than a 2-3-4 tree, its search algorithm would require more comparisons at each node to determine which subtree to search. Thus, allowing the nodes of a tree to have many children is counterproductive. Such a search tree is appropriate, however, when it is implemented in external storage, because moving from node to node is far more expensive than comparing the data values in a node. In such cases, a search tree with the minimum possible height is desirable, even at the expense of additional comparisons at each node. Chapter 21 will discuss external search trees further.

Allowing nodes with more than four children is counterproductive

19.5 Red-Black Trees

A 2-3-4 tree is appealing because it is balanced and because its addition and removal operations use only one pass from root to leaf. On the other hand, a 2-3-4 tree requires more storage than a binary search tree that contains the same data because a 2-3-4 tree has nodes that must accommodate up to three data items. A typical binary search tree, however, might not be balanced.

A 2-3-4 tree requires more storage than a binary search tree

You can use a special binary search tree—a **red-black tree**—to represent a 2-3-4 tree that retains the advantages of a 2-3-4 tree without the storage overhead. The idea is to represent each 3-node and 4-node in a 2-3-4 tree as an equivalent binary search tree. To distinguish between 2-nodes that appeared in the original 2-3-4 tree and 2-nodes that were generated from 3-nodes and 4-nodes, you use red and black child pointers. Let all the child pointers in the original 2-3-4 tree be black, and use red child pointers to link the 2-nodes that result when you split 3-nodes and 4-nodes.

A red-black tree has the advantages of a 2-3-4 tree but requires less storage

Note: In a red-black tree, **red pointers** link the 2-nodes that now contain the values that were in a 3-node or a 4-node. A red pointer references a **red node**, and a **black pointer** references a **black node**.

Figure 19-35 indicates how to represent a 4-node and a 3-node as binary trees. Because there are two possible ways to represent a 3-node as a binary tree, a red-black representation of a 2-3-4 tree is not unique. Figure 19-36 gives a red-black representation for the 2-3-4 tree in Figure 19-24. In all of these figures, a dashed blue line represents a red pointer and a solid black line represents a black pointer.

FIGURE 19-35   Red-black representations of a 4-node and a 3-node

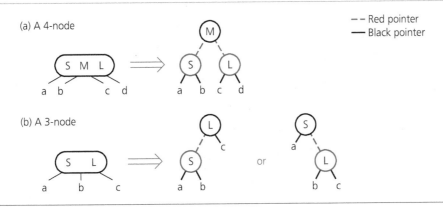

FIGURE 19-36   A red-black tree that represents the 2-3-4 tree in Figure 19-24

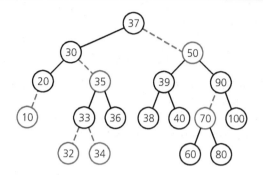

Note: **Properties of a red-black tree**

1. The root is black.
2. Every red node has a black parent.
3. Any children of a red node are black; that is, a red node cannot have red children.
4. Every path from the root to a leaf contains the same number of black nodes.

A node in a red-black tree is similar to a node in a binary search tree, but it must also store the pointer colors. Thus, we derive the class of red-black nodes from the class `BinaryNode` of 2-nodes, as the following C++ statements indicate:

```
enum Color {RED, BLACK};

template<class ItemType>
class RedBlackNode : public BinaryNode<ItemType>
{
private:
   Color leftColor;
   Color rightColor;
public:
   // Get and set methods for leftColor and rightColor
   // . . .

}; // end RedBlackNode
```

A node in a red-black tree

Note: Even with the pointer colors, a node in a red-black tree requires less storage than a node in a 2-3-4 tree. Keep in mind that the transformations in Figure 19-35 imply a change in the structure of the nodes.

Question 7 Why does a node in a red-black tree require less memory than a node in a 2-3-4 tree?

19.5.1 Searching and Traversing a Red-Black Tree

Because a red-black tree is a binary search tree, you can search and traverse it by using the algorithms for a binary search tree. You simply ignore the color of the pointers.

19.5.2 Adding to and Removing from a Red-Black Tree

Because a red-black tree actually represents a 2-3-4 tree, you simply need to adjust the 2-3-4 addition algorithms to accommodate the red-black representation. Recall that while searching a 2-3-4 tree, you split each 4-node that you encounter, so it is sufficient to reformulate that process in terms of the red-black representation. For example, Figure 19-35a shows the red-black representation of a 4-node. Thus, to identify a 4-node in its red-black form, you look for a node that has two red pointers.

Suppose that the 4-node is the root of the 2-3-4 tree. Figure 19-32 shows how to split the 4-node root into 2-nodes. By comparing this figure with Figure 19-35a, you see that to perform an equivalent operation on a red-black tree, you simply change the color of its root's pointers to black, as Figure 19-37 illustrates.

FIGURE 19-37   Splitting a red-black representation of a 4-node root

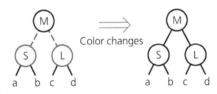

Previously, Figure 19-33 showed how to split a 4-node whose parent is a 2-node. If you reformulate this figure by using the red-black notation given in Figure 19-35, you get Figure 19-38. Notice that this case also requires only color changes within the red-black tree.

Finally, Figure 19-34 showed how to split a 4-node whose parent is a 3-node. Figure 19-39 shows this process for a red-black tree, using the transformations that Figure 19-35 describes. Note that each of the configurations before the split in Figure 19-34 has two red-black representations, using the transformation shown in Figure 19-39b. As you can see, each pair of representations transforms into the same red-black configuration. Of the six possibilities given in Figure 19-39, only two require simple color changes. The others also require **rotations**, that is, changes to the pointers themselves.

The removal algorithm is derived in an analogous fashion from the 2-3-4 tree removal algorithm. Because addition and removal operations on a red-black tree frequently require only color changes, they are more efficient than the corresponding operations on a 2-3-4 tree.

Exercise 11 asks you to complete the details of the addition and removal algorithms.

Splitting the equivalent of a 4-node requires only simple color changes

Pointer changes called rotations result in a shorter tree

Question 8 What red-black tree represents the 2-3-4 tree in Figure 19-31a?

FIGURE 19-38   Splitting a red-black representation of a 4-node whose parent is a 2-node

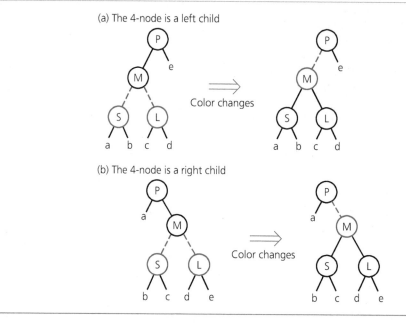

FIGURE 19-39   Splitting a red-black representation of a 4-node whose parent is a 3-node

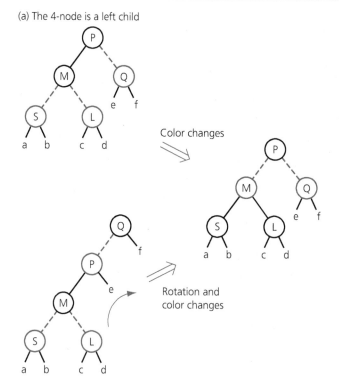

(b) The 4-node is a middle child

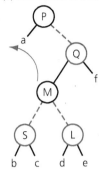

Rotation and
color changes

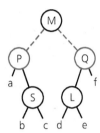

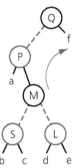

Rotation and
color changes

(c) The 4-node is a right child

Rotation and
color changes

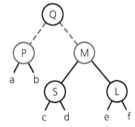

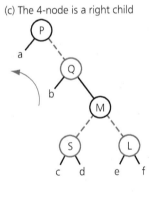

Color changes

SUMMARY

1. An AVL tree is a binary search tree that is guaranteed to remain balanced. The addition and removal algorithms perform rotations in the event that the tree starts to stray from a balanced shape.

2. A 2-3 tree and a 2-3-4 tree are variants of a binary search tree. The internal nodes of a 2-3 tree can have either two or three children. The internal nodes of a 2-3-4 tree can have either two, three, or four children. Allowing the number of children to vary permits the addition and removal algorithms to maintain the balance of the tree easily.

3. The addition and removal algorithms for a 2-3-4 tree require only a single pass from root to leaf and, thus, are more efficient than the corresponding algorithms for a 2-3 tree.

4. A red-black tree is a binary tree representation of a 2-3-4 tree that requires less storage than a 2-3-4 tree. Additions and removals for a red-black tree are more efficient than the corresponding operations on a 2-3-4 tree.

EXERCISES

1. Consider the following sequence of operations on an initially empty search tree:

    Add 10
    Add 100
    Add 30
    Add 80
    Add 50
    Remove 10
    Add 60
    Add 70
    Add 40
    Remove 80
    Add 90
    Add 20
    Remove 30
    Remove 70

    What does the tree look like after these operations execute if the tree is
    a. A binary search tree?   **d.** A red-black tree?
    b. A 2-3 tree?   **e.** An AVL tree?
    c. A 2-3-4 tree?

2. What are the advantages of implementing the ADT dictionary with a 2-3 tree instead of a binary search tree? Why do you not, in general, maintain a completely balanced binary search tree?

3. If your application of the ADT dictionary involves only retrieval—such as searching a thesaurus—what tree would provide for the most efficient table implementation: a minimum-height binary search tree, a 2-3 tree, a 2-3-4 tree, a red-black tree, or an AVL tree? Why?

4. Write a pseudocode function that performs a range query for a 2-3 tree. That is, the function should visit all data items that are within a given range of values. For example, your function should visit all values between 100 and 1,000.

5.   Given the 2-3 tree in Figure 19-40, draw the tree that results after adding *k, b, c, y,* and *w* to the tree.

FIGURE 19-40   A 2-3 tree for Exercise 5

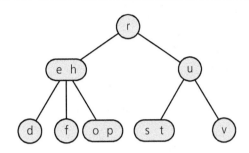

6.   Given the 2-3 tree in Figure 19-41, draw the tree that results after removing *t, e, k,* and *d* from the tree.

FIGURE 19-41   A 2-3 tree for Exercise 6

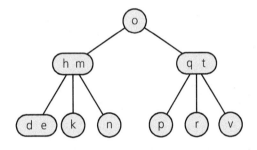

7.   Draw the 2-3-4 tree that results from adding *o, d, j, h, s, g,* and *a,* in the order given, to a 2-3-4 tree that contains a single node whose value is *n.*

8.   Assume that the tree in Figure 19-9b is a 2-3-4 tree, and add 39, 38, 37, 36, 35, 34, 33, and 32 to it. What 2-3-4 tree results?

*9.   Write pseudocode for the addition, removal, retrieval, and traversal operations for a 2-3-4 tree.

10.   Figure 19-36 is a red-black tree that represents the 2-3-4 tree in Figure 19-24. Draw another red-black tree that also represents the same 2-3-4 tree.

11.   What 2-3-4 tree does the red-black tree in Figure 19-42 represent?

12.   Write pseudocode for the addition, removal, retrieval, and traversal operations for a red-black tree.

13.   Write a C++ function that converts a 2-3-4 tree to a red-black tree.

FIGURE 19-42   A red-black tree for Exercise 11

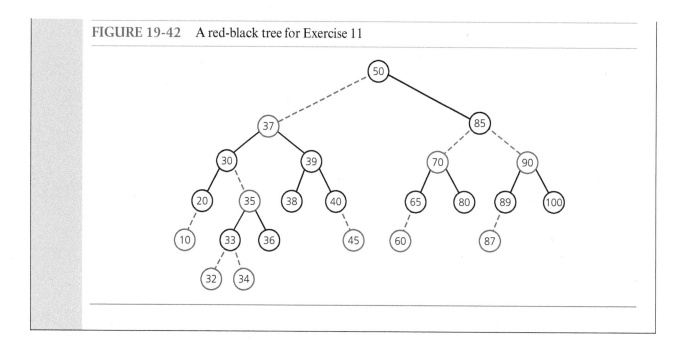

Programming Problems

1. Implement the ADT dictionary by using a 2-3-4 tree.

*2. Implement the ADT dictionary by using a 2-3 tree. (This implementation is more difficult than the 2-3-4 implementation.)

3. Implement the ADT dictionary by using a red-black tree.

4. Repeat Programming Problem 5 of Chapter 16 using a dictionary implemented with a balanced search tree.

Contents

Prerequisites

G raphs are an important mathematical concept with significant applications not only in computer science, but also in many other fields. You can view a graph as a mathematical construct, a data structure, or an abstract data type. This chapter provides an introduction to graphs that allows you to view a graph in any of these three ways. It also presents the major operations and applications of graphs that are relevant to the computer scientist.

20.1 Terminology

You are undoubtedly familiar with graphs: Line graphs, bar graphs, and pie charts are in common use. The simple line graph in Figure 20-1 is an example of the type of graph that this chapter considers: a set of points that are joined by lines. Clearly, graphs provide a way to illustrate data. However, graphs also represent the relationships among data items, and it is this feature of graphs that is important here.

A **graph** G consists of two sets: a set V of vertices, or nodes, and a set E of edges that connect the vertices. For example, the campus map in Figure 20-2a is a graph whose vertices represent buildings and whose edges represent the sidewalks between the buildings. This definition of a graph is more general than the definition of a line graph. In fact, a line graph, with its points and lines, is a special case of the general definition of a graph.

$G = \{V, E\}$; that is, a graph is a set of vertices and a set of edges

FIGURE 20-1 An ordinary line graph

FIGURE 20-2 A graph and one of its subgraphs

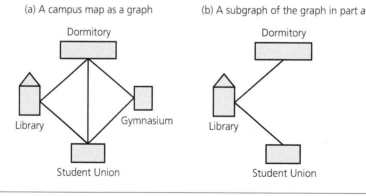

(a) A campus map as a graph

(b) A subgraph of the graph in part a

Adjacent vertices are joined by an edge

A path between two vertices is a sequence of edges

A **subgraph** consists of a subset of a graph's vertices and a subset of its edges. Figure 20-2b shows a subgraph of the graph in Figure 20-2a. Two vertices of a graph are **adjacent** if they are joined by an edge. In Figure 20-2b, the Library and the Student Union are adjacent. A **path** between two vertices is a sequence of edges that begins at one vertex and ends at another vertex. For example, there is a path in Figure 20-2a that begins at the Dormitory, leads first to the Library, then to the Student Union, and finally back to the Library. Although a path may pass

FIGURE 20-3   Examples of graphs that are either connected, disconnected, or complete

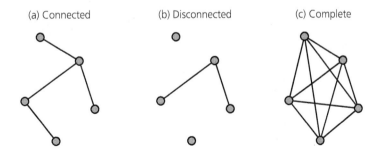

(a) Connected   (b) Disconnected   (c) Complete

through the same vertex more than once, as the path just described does, a **simple path** may not. The path Dormitory–Library–Student Union is a simple path. A **cycle** is a path that begins and ends at the same vertex; a **simple cycle** is a cycle that does not pass through other vertices more than once. The path Library–Student Union–Gymnasium–Dormitory–Library is a simple cycle in the graph in Figure 20-2a. A graph is **connected** if each pair of distinct vertices has a path between them. That is, in a connected graph you can get from any vertex to any other vertex by following a path. Figure 20-3a shows a connected graph. Notice that a connected graph does not necessarily have an edge between every pair of vertices. Figure 20-3b shows a **disconnected** graph.

In a **complete graph**, each pair of distinct vertices has an edge between them. That is, a complete graph has as many edges as possible. The graph in Figure 20-3c is complete. Clearly, a complete graph is also connected, but the converse is not true; notice that the graph in Figure 20-3a is connected but is not complete.

A graph with n vertices can have at most $n \times (n - 1) / 2$ edges; a complete graph has this maximal number of edges. For example, n is 5 for the complete graph in Figure 20-3c, and the graph has $5 \times 4 / 2$, or 10 edges. A graph that has almost the maximum number of edges is said to be **dense**. Conversely, a **sparse** graph has relatively few, or $O(n)$, edges.

Because a graph has a *set* of edges, a graph cannot have duplicate edges between vertices. However, a **multigraph**, as illustrated in Figure 20-4a, does allow multiple edges. Thus, a multigraph is not a graph. A graph's edges cannot begin and end at the same vertex. Figure 20-4b shows such an edge, which is called a **self edge** or **loop**.

You can label the edges of a graph. When these labels represent numeric values, the graph is called a **weighted graph**. The graph in Figure 20-5a is a weighted graph whose edges are labeled with the distances between cities.

A simple path passes through a vertex only once

A cycle is a path that begins and ends at the same vertex

A connected graph has a path between each pair of distinct vertices

A complete graph has an edge between each pair of distinct vertices

A complete graph is connected

A multigraph has multiple edges and so is not a graph

The edges of a weighted graph have numeric labels

FIGURE 20-4   Graph-like structures that are not graphs

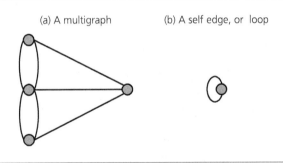

(a) A multigraph   (b) A self edge, or loop

FIGURE 20-5   Examples of two kinds of graphs

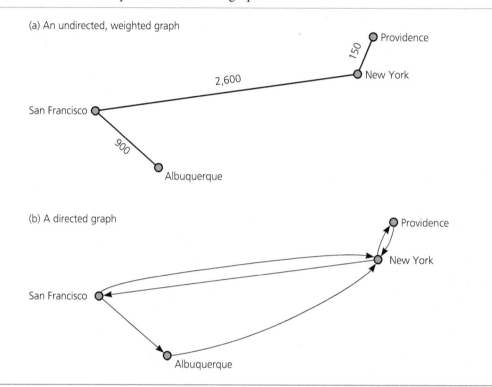

All of the previous graphs are examples of **undirected graphs**, because the edges do not indicate a direction. That is, you can travel in either direction along the edges between the vertices of an undirected graph. In contrast, each edge in a **directed graph**, or **digraph**, has a direction and is called a **directed edge**. Although each distinct pair of vertices in an undirected graph has only one edge between them, a directed graph can have two edges between a pair of vertices, one in each direction. For example, the airline flight map in Figure 20-5b is a directed graph. There are flights in both directions between Providence and New York, but, although there is a flight from San Francisco to Albuquerque, there is no flight from Albuquerque to San Francisco. You can convert an undirected graph to a directed graph by replacing each edge with two directed edges that point in opposite directions.

The definitions just given for undirected graphs apply also to directed graphs, with changes that account for direction. For example, a **directed path** is a sequence of directed edges between two vertices, such as the directed path in Figure 20-5b that begins in Providence, goes to New York, and ends in San Francisco. However, the definition of adjacent vertices is not quite as obvious for a digraph. If there is a directed edge from vertex *x* to vertex *y*, then *y* is adjacent to *x*. (Alternatively, *y* is a **successor** of *x*, and *x* is a **predecessor** of *y*.) It does not necessarily follow, however, that *x* is adjacent to *y*. Thus, in Figure 20-5b, Albuquerque is adjacent to San Francisco, but San Francisco is not adjacent to Albuquerque.

Each edge in a directed graph has a direction

In a directed graph, vertex *y* is adjacent to vertex *x* if there is a directed edge from *x* to *y*

Question 1 Describe the graphs in Figure 20-6. For example, are they directed? Connected? Complete? Weighted?

Question 2 Is it possible for a connected undirected graph with five vertices and four edges to contain a simple cycle? Explain.

FIGURE 20-6   Graphs for Checkpoint Questions 1, 3, 4, and 5

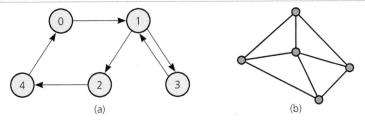

20.2 Graphs as ADTs

You can treat graphs as abstract data types. Addition and removal operations are somewhat different for graphs than for other ADTs that you have studied, in that they apply to either vertices or edges. You can define the ADT graph so that its vertices either do or do not contain values. A graph whose vertices do not contain values represents only the relationships among vertices. Such graphs are not unusual, because many problems have no need for vertex values. However, the following ADT graph operations do assume that the graph's vertices contain values.

Vertices can have values

Note: ADT graph operations
- Test whether a graph is empty.
- Get the number of vertices in a graph.
- Get the number of edges in a graph.
- See whether an edge exists between two given vertices.
- Add a new vertex to a graph whose vertices have distinct values that differ from the new vertex's value.
- Add an edge between two given vertices in a graph.
- Remove a particular vertex from a graph and any edges between the vertex and other vertices.
- Remove the edge between two given vertices in a graph.
- Retrieve from a graph the vertex that contains a given value.

Several variations of this ADT are possible. For example, if the graph is directed, you can replace occurrences of "edges" in the previous operations with "directed edges." You can also add traversal operations to the ADT. Graph-traversal algorithms are discussed in Section 20.3.

Listing 20-1 contains an interface that specifies in more detail the ADT operations for an undirected graph.

LISTING 20-1 A C++ interface for undirected, connected graphs

```cpp
 1  /** An interface for the ADT undirected, connected graph.
 2   @file GraphInterface.h */
 3  #ifndef GRAPH_INTERFACE_
 4  #define GRAPH_INTERFACE_
 5
 6  template<class LabelType>
 7  class GraphInterface
 8  {
 9  public:
10     /** Gets the number of vertices in this graph.
11      @return  The number of vertices in the graph. */
12     virtual int getNumVertices() const = 0;
13
14     /** Gets the number of edges in this graph.
15      @return  The number of edges in the graph. */
16     virtual int getNumEdges() const = 0;
17
18     /** Creates an undirected edge in this graph between two vertices
19         that have the given labels. If such vertices do not exist, creates
20         them and adds them to the graph before creating the edge.
21      @param start  A label for the first vertex.
22      @param end  A label for the second vertex.
23      @param edgeWeight  The integer weight of the edge.
24      @return  True if the edge is created, or false otherwise. */
25     virtual bool add(LabelType start, LabelType end, int edgeWeight) = 0;
26
27     /** Removes an edge from this graph. If a vertex is left with no other edges,
28         it is removed from the graph since this is a connected graph.
29      @param start  A label for the vertex at the beginning of the edge.
30      @param end  A label for the vertex at the end of the edge.
31      @return  True if the edge is removed, or false otherwise. */
32     virtual bool remove(LabelType start, LabelType end) = 0;
33
34     /** Gets the weight of an edge in this graph.
35      @return  The weight of the specified edge.
36         If no such edge exists, returns a negative integer. */
37     virtual int getEdgeWeight(LabelType start, LabelType end) const = 0;
38
39     /** Performs a depth-first search of this graph beginning at the given
40         vertex and calls a given function once for each vertex visited.
41      @param start  A label for the beginning vertex.
42      @param visit  A client-defined function that performs an operation on
43         or with each visited vertex. */
44     virtual void depthFirstTraversal(LabelType start, void visit(LabelType&)) = 0;
45
46     /** Performs a breadth-first search of this graph beginning at the given
47         vertex and calls a given function once for each vertex visited.
48      @param start  A label for the beginning vertex.
49      @param visit  A client-defined function that performs an operation on
50         or with each visited vertex. */
```

```
51      virtual void breadthFirstTraversal(LabelType start, void visit(LabelType&)) = 0;
52
53      /** Destroys this graph and frees its assigned memory. */
54      virtual ~GraphInterface() {   }
55   }; // end GraphInterface
56   #endif
```

20.2.1 Implementing Graphs

The two most common implementations of a graph are the adjacency matrix and the adjacency list. An **adjacency matrix** for a graph with n vertices numbered 0, 1, ..., $n-1$ is an n by n array matrix such that matrix[i][j] is 1 (true) if there is an edge from vertex i to vertex j, and 0 (false) otherwise. Figure 20-7 shows a directed graph and its adjacency matrix. Notice that the diagonal entries matrix[i][i] are 0, although sometimes it can be useful to set these entries to 1. You should choose the value that is most convenient for your application.

An adjacency matrix can represent a graph

FIGURE 20-7   (a) A directed graph and (b) its adjacency matrix

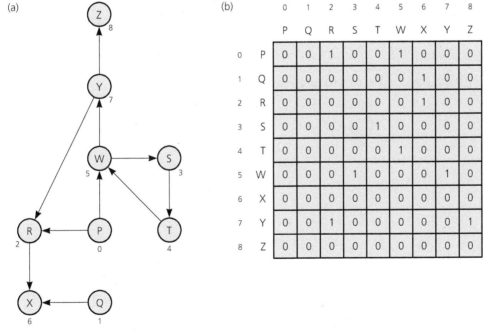

When the graph is weighted, you can let matrix[i][j] be the weight that labels the edge from vertex i to vertex j, instead of simply 1, and let matrix[i][j] equal ∞ instead of 0 when there is no edge from vertex i to vertex j. For example, Figure 20-8 shows a weighted undirected graph and its adjacency matrix. Notice that the adjacency matrix for an undirected graph is symmetrical; that is, matrix[i][j] equals matrix[j][i].

FIGURE 20-8   (a) A weighted undirected graph and (b) its adjacency matrix

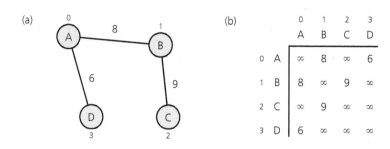

Our definition of an adjacency matrix does not mention the value, if any, in a vertex. If you need to associate values with vertices, you can use a second array, `values`, to represent the n vertex values. The array `values` is one-dimensional, and `values[i]` is the value in vertex i.

An adjacency list
can represent a
graph

An **adjacency list** for a graph with n vertices numbered 0, 1, ..., $n - 1$ consists of n linked chains. The ith linked chain has a node for vertex j if and only if the graph contains an edge from vertex i to vertex j. This node can contain the vertex j's value, if any. If the vertex has no value, the node needs to contain some indication of the vertex's identity. Figure 20-9 shows a directed graph and its adjacency list. You can see, for example, that vertex 0 (P) has edges to

FIGURE 20-9   (a) A directed graph and (b) its adjacency list

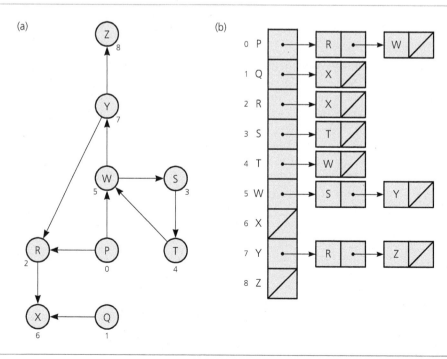

vertex 2 (*R*) and vertex 5 (*W*). Thus, the first linked chain in the adjacency chain contains nodes for *R* and *W*.

Figure 20-10 shows an undirected graph and its adjacency list. The adjacency list for an undirected graph treats each edge as if it were two directed edges in opposite directions. Thus, the edge between *A* and *B* in Figure 20-10a appears as edges from *A* to *B* and from *B* to *A* in Figure 20-10b. The graph in 20-10a happens to be weighted; you can include the edge weights in the nodes of the adjacency list, as shown in Figure 20-10b.

FIGURE 20-10   (a) A weighted undirected graph and (b) its adjacency list

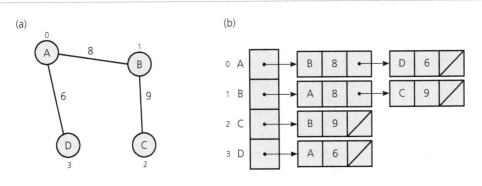

Which of these two implementations of a graph—the adjacency matrix or the adjacency list—is better? The answer depends on how your particular application uses the graph. For example, the two most commonly performed graph operations are

1. See whether there is an edge from vertex *i* to vertex *j*
2. Find all vertices adjacent to a given vertex *i*

Two common operations on graphs

The adjacency matrix supports the first operation somewhat more efficiently than does the adjacency list. To see whether there is an edge from *i* to *j* by using an adjacency matrix, you need only examine the value of `matrix[i][j]`. If you use an adjacency list, however, you must traverse the *i*th linked chain to discover whether a vertex corresponding to vertex *j* is present.

An adjacency list often requires less space than an adjacency matrix

The second operation, on the other hand, is supported more efficiently by the adjacency list. To find all vertices adjacent to a given vertex *i*, given the adjacency matrix, you must traverse the *i*th row of the array; however, given the adjacency list, you need only traverse the *i*th linked chain. For a graph with *n* vertices, the *i*th row of the adjacency matrix always has *n* entries, whereas the *i*th linked chain has only as many nodes as there are vertices adjacent to vertex *i*, a number typically far less than *n*.

An adjacency matrix supports operation 1 more efficiently

Consider now the space requirements of the two implementations. On the surface it might appear that the adjacency matrix requires less memory than the adjacency list, because each entry in the matrix is simply an integer, whereas each list node contains both a value to identify the vertex and a pointer. The adjacency matrix, however, always has n^2 entries, whereas the number of nodes in an adjacency list equals the number of edges in a directed graph or twice that number for an undirected graph. Even though the adjacency list also has *n* head pointers, it often requires less storage than an adjacency matrix, especiallly when the graph is sparse.

An adjacency list supports operation 2 more efficiently

Thus, when choosing a graph implementation for a particular application, you must consider such factors as what operations you will perform most frequently on the graph and the number of edges that the graph is likely to contain. For example, Chapters 5 and 6 presented the HPAir problem, which was to see whether an airline provided a sequence of flights from an origin city to a destination city. The flight map for that problem is in fact a directed graph and appeared earlier in this chapter in Figure 20-9a. Figures 20-7b and 20-9b show, respectively, the adjacency matrix and adjacency list for this graph. Because the most frequent operation was to find all cities (vertices) adjacent to a given city (vertex), the adjacency list would be the more efficient implementation of the flight map. The adjacency list also requires less storage than the adjacency matrix, which you can demonstrate as an exercise.

Question 3 Write the adjacency matrix and the adjacency list for the graph in Figure 20-6a.

VideoNote
Graph operations

20.3 Graph Traversals

The solution to the HPAir problem in Chapter 6 involved an exhaustive search of the graph in Figure 20-9a to find a directed path from the origin vertex (city) to the destination vertex (city). The algorithm searchS started at a given vertex and traversed edges to other vertices until it either found the desired vertex or discovered that no (directed) path existed between the two vertices.

What distinguishes searchS from a standard graph traversal is that searchS stops when it first encounters the designated destination vertex. A **graph-traversal** algorithm, on the other hand, will not stop until it has visited all of the vertices *that it can reach*. That is, a graph traversal that starts at vertex *v* will visit all vertices *w* for which there is a path between *v* and *w*. Unlike a tree traversal, which always visits *all of the nodes* in a tree, a graph traversal does not necessarily visit all of the vertices in the graph unless the graph is connected. In fact, a graph traversal visits every vertex in the graph if and only if the graph is connected, regardless of where the traversal starts. (See Exercise 18.) Thus, you can use a graph traversal to test whether a graph is connected.

> A graph traversal visits all of the vertices that it can reach

> A graph traversal visits all vertices if and only if the graph is connected

If a graph is not connected, a graph traversal that begins at vertex *v* will visit only a subset of the graph's vertices. This subset is called the **connected component** containing *v*. You can find all of the connected components of a graph by repeatedly starting a traversal at an unvisited vertex.

> A connected component is the subset of vertices visited during a traversal that begins at a given vertex

If a graph contains a cycle, a graph-traversal algorithm can loop indefinitely. To prevent such a misfortune, the algorithm must mark each vertex during a visit and must never visit a vertex more than once.

Two basic graph-traversal algorithms, which apply to either directed or undirected graphs, are presented next. These algorithms visit the vertices in different orders, but if they both start at the same vertex, they will visit the same set of vertices. Figure 20-11 shows the traversal order for the two algorithms when they begin at vertex *v*.

20.3.1 Depth-First Search

> DFS traversal goes as far as possible from a vertex before backing up

From a given vertex *v*, the **depth-first search (DFS)** strategy of graph traversal proceeds along a path from *v* as deeply into the graph as possible before backing up. That is, after visiting a vertex, a DFS visits, if possible, an unvisited adjacent vertex.

FIGURE 20-11   Visitation order for two graph-traversal strategies

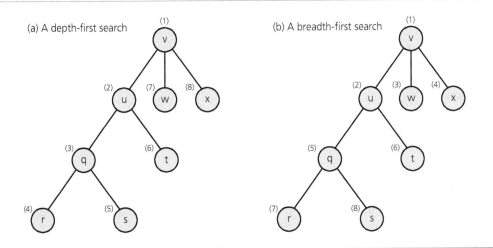

(a) A depth-first search

(b) A breadth-first search

Recursive DFS
traversal algorithm

The DFS strategy has a simple recursive form:

```
// Traverses a graph beginning at vertex v by using a
// depth-first search: Recursive version.
dfs(v: Vertex)
{
    Mark v as visited
    for (each unvisited vertex u adjacent to v)
        dfs(u)
}
```

Choose an order in
which to visit
adjacent vertices

The depth-first search algorithm does not completely specify the order in which it should visit the vertices adjacent to v. One possibility is to visit the vertices adjacent to v in sorted (that is, alphabetic or numerically increasing) order. This possibility is natural either when an adjacency matrix represents the graph or when the nodes in each linked chain of an adjacency list are linked in sorted order.

As Figure 20-11a illustrates, the DFS traversal algorithm marks and then visits each of the vertices v, u, q, and r. When the traversal reaches a vertex—such as r—that has no unvisited adjacent vertices, it backs up and visits, if possible, an unvisited adjacent vertex. Thus, the traversal backs up to q and then visits s. Continuing in this manner, the traversal visits vertices in the order given in the figure.

An iterative version of the DFS algorithm is also possible by using a stack:

An iterative DFS
traversal algorithm
uses a stack

```
// Traverses a graph beginning at vertex v by using a
// depth-first search: Iterative version.
dfs(v: Vertex)
{
    s = a new empty stack

    // Push v onto the stack and mark it
    s.push(v)
    Mark v as visited
```

```
// Loop invariant: there is a path from vertex v at the
// bottom of the stack s to the vertex at the top of s
while (!s.isEmpty())
{
    if (no unvisited vertices are adjacent to the vertex on the top of the stack)
        s.pop() // Backtrack
    else
    {
        Select an unvisited vertex u adjacent to the vertex on the top of the stack
        s.push(u)
        Mark u as visited
    }
}
}
```

The `dfs` algorithm is similar to `searchS` of Chapter 6, but the `while` statement in `searchS` terminates when the top of the stack is `destinationCity`.

For another example of a DFS traversal, consider the graph in Figure 20-12. Figure 20-13 shows the contents of the stack as the previous function `dfs` visits vertices in this graph, beginning at vertex *a*. Because the graph is connected, a DFS traversal will visit every vertex. In fact, the traversal visits the vertices in this order: *a, b, c, d, g, e, f, h, i*.

FIGURE 20-12   A connected graph with cycles

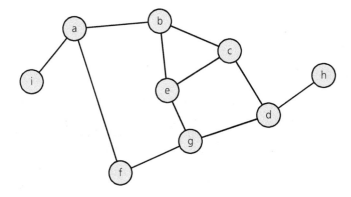

The vertex from which a depth-first traversal embarks is the vertex that it visited most recently. This *last visited, first explored* strategy is reflected both in the explicit stack of vertices that the iterative `dfs` uses and in the implicit stack of vertices that the recursive `dfs` generates with its recursive calls.

Question 4 Use the depth-first strategy to traverse the graph in Figure 20-6a, beginning with vertex 0. List the vertices in the order in which the traversal visits them.

FIGURE 20-13   The results of a depth-first traversal, beginning at vertex *a*, of the graph in Figure 20-12

Node visited	Stack (top to bottom)
a	a
b	a b
c	a b c
d	a b c d
g	a b c d g
e	a b c d g e
(backtrack)	a b c d g
f	a b c d g f
(backtrack)	a b c d g
(backtrack)	a b c d
h	a b c d h
(backtrack)	a b c d
(backtrack)	a b c
(backtrack)	a b
(backtrack)	a
i	a i
(backtrack)	a
(backtrack)	*(empty)*

20.3.2 Breadth-First Search

After visiting a given vertex *v*, the **breadth-first search (BFS)** strategy of graph traversal visits every vertex adjacent to *v* that it can before visiting any other vertex. As Figure 20-11b illustrates, after marking and visiting *v*, the BFS traversal algorithm marks and then visits each of the vertices *u*, *w*, and *x*. Since no other vertices are adjacent to *v*, the BFS algorithm visits, if possible, all unvisited vertices adjacent to *u*. Thus, the traversal visits *q* and *t*. Continuing in this manner, the traversal visits vertices in the order given in the figure.

> BFS traversal visits all vertices adjacent to a vertex before going forward

A BFS traversal will not embark from any of the vertices adjacent to *v* until it has visited all possible vertices adjacent to *v*. Whereas a DFS is a *last visited, first explored* strategy, a BFS is a *first visited, first explored* strategy. It is not surprising, then, that a breadth-first search uses a queue. An iterative version of this algorithm follows.

> An iterative BFS traversal algorithm uses a queue

```
// Traverses a graph beginning at vertex v by using a
// breadth-first search: Iterative version.
bfs(v: Vertex)
{
   q = a new empty queue

   // Add v to queue and mark it
   q.enqueue(v)
   Mark v as visited

   while (!q.isEmpty())
   {
      q.dequeue(w)
```

```
    //  Loop invariant: there is a path from vertex w to every vertex in the queue q
    for (each unvisited vertex u adjacent to w)
    {
        Mark u as visited
        q.enqueue(u)
    }
  }
}
```

Figure 20-14 shows the contents of the queue as bfs visits vertices in the graph in Figure 20-12, beginning at vertex *a*. In general, a breadth-first search will visit the same vertices as a depth-first search, but in a different order. In this example, the BFS traversal visits all of the vertices in this order: *a, b, f, i, c, e, g, d, h.*

A recursive version of BFS traversal is not as simple as the recursive version of DFS traversal. Exercise 19 at the end of this chapter asks you to think about why this is so.

FIGURE 20-14   The results of a breadth-first traversal, beginning at vertex *a*, of the graph in Figure 20-12

Node visited	Queue (front to back)
a	a
	(empty)
b	b
f	b f
i	b f i
	f i
c	f i c
e	f i c e
	i c e
g	i c e g
	c e g
	e g
d	e g d
	g d
	d
	(empty)
h	h
	(empty)

 Question 5   Use the breadth-first strategy to traverse the graph in Figure 20-6a, beginning with vertex 0. List the vertices in the order in which the traversal visits them.

20.4 Applications of Graphs

There are many useful applications of graphs. This section surveys some of these common applications.

20.4.1 Topological Sorting

A directed graph without cycles, such as the one in Figure 20-15, has a natural order. For example, vertex *a* precedes *b,* which precedes *c.* Such a graph has significance in ordinary life. If the vertices represent academic courses, the graph represents the prerequisite structure for the courses. For example, course *a* is a prerequisite to course *b*, which is a prerequisite to both courses *c* and *e*. In what order should you take all seven courses so that you will satisfy all prerequisites? There is a linear order, called a **topological order**, of the vertices in a directed graph without cycles that answers this question. In a list of vertices in topological order, vertex *x* precedes vertex *y* if there is a directed edge from *x* to *y* in the graph.

FIGURE 20-15   A directed graph without cycles

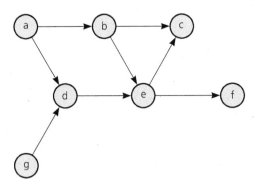

The vertices in a given graph may have several topological orders. For example, two topological orders for the vertices in Figure 20-15 are

> *a, g, d, b, e, c, f*

and

> *a, b, g, d, e, f, c*

If you arrange the vertices of a directed graph linearly and in a topological order, the edges will all point in one direction. Figure 20-16 shows two versions of the graph in Figure 20-15 that correspond to the two topological orders just given.

Arranging the vertices into a topological order is called **topological sorting**. There are several simple algorithms for finding a topological order. First, you could find a vertex that has no successor. You remove from the graph this vertex and all edges that lead to it, and add it to the

FIGURE 20-16   The graph in Figure 20-15 arranged according to two topological orders

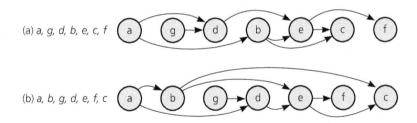

beginning of a list of vertices. You add each subsequent vertex that has no successor to the beginning of the list. When the graph is empty, the list of vertices will be in topological order. The following pseudocode describes this algorithm:

```
// Arranges the vertices in graph theGraph into a
// topological order and places them in list aList.
topSort1(theGraph: Graph, aList: List)
{
    n = number of vertices in theGraph
    for (step = 1 through n)
    {
        Select a vertex v that has no successors
        aList.insert(1, v)
        Remove from theGraph vertex v and its edges
    }
}
```

When the traversal ends, the list aList of vertices will be in topological order. Figure 20-17 traces this algorithm for the graph in Figure 20-15. The resulting topological order is the one that Figure 20-16a represents.

Another algorithm is a simple modification of the iterative depth-first search algorithm. First you push all vertices that have no predecessor onto a stack. Each time you pop a vertex from the stack, you add it to the beginning of a list of vertices. The pseudocode for this algorithm is

```
// Arranges the vertices in graph theGraph into a
// topological order and places them in list aList.
topSort2(theGraph: Graph, aList: List)
{
    s = a new empty stack
    for (all vertices v in the graph)
    {
        if (v has no predecessors)
        {
            s.push(v)
            Mark v as visited
        }
    }
    while (!s.isEmpty())
    {
        if (all vertices adjacent to the vertex on the top of the stack have been visited)
        {
            s.pop(v)
            aList.insert(1, v)
        }
        else
        {
            Select an unvisited vertex u adjacent to the vertex on the top of the stack
            s.push(u)
            Mark u as visited
        }
    }
}
```

When the traversal ends, the list aList of vertices will be in topological order. Figure 20-18 traces this algorithm for the graph in Figure 20-15. The resulting topological order is the one that Figure 20-16b represents.

FIGURE 20-17 A trace of `topSort1` for the graph in Figure 20-15

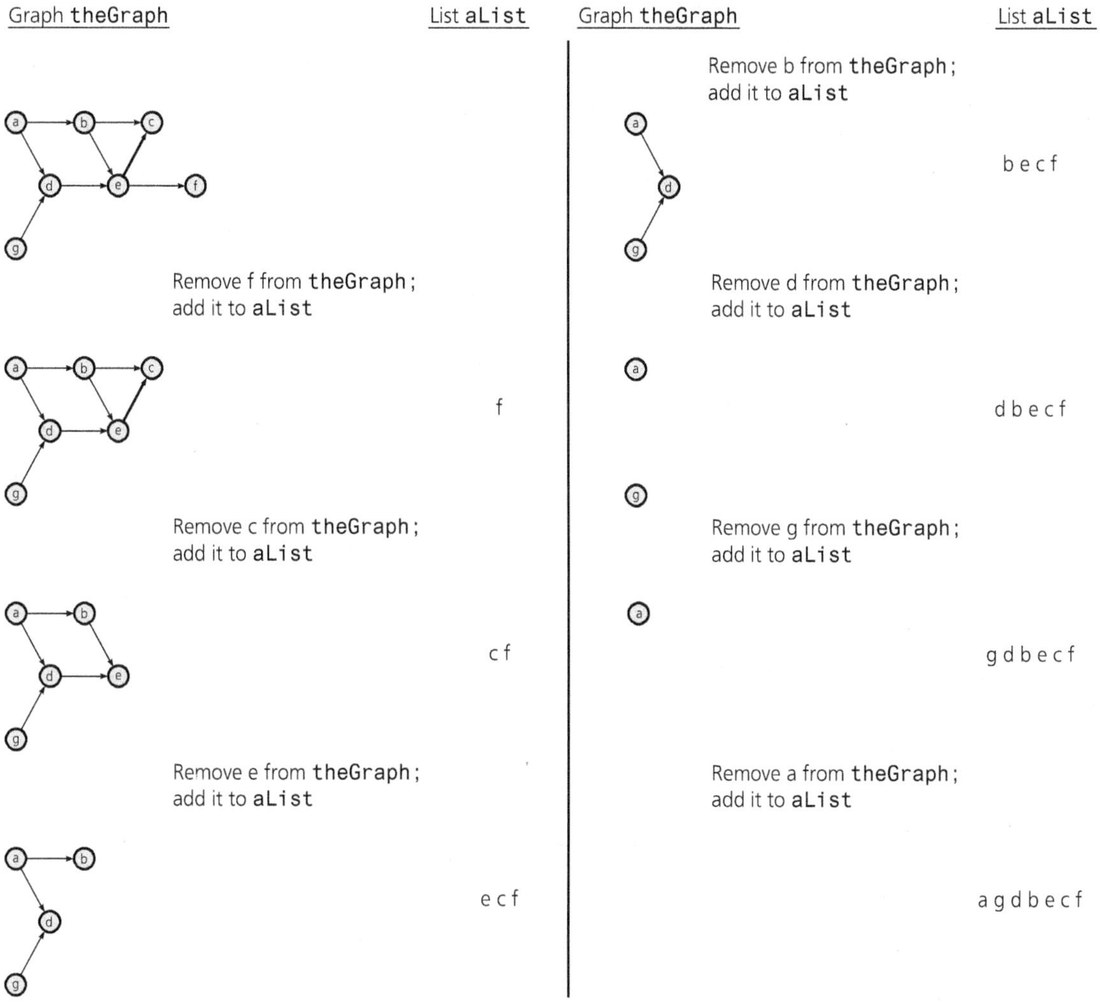

Graph `theGraph`	List `aList`	Graph `theGraph`	List `aList`

Remove b from `theGraph`;
add it to `aList`

b e c f

Remove f from `theGraph`;
add it to `aList`

f

Remove d from `theGraph`;
add it to `aList`

d b e c f

Remove c from `theGraph`;
add it to `aList`

c f

Remove g from `theGraph`;
add it to `aList`

g d b e c f

Remove e from `theGraph`;
add it to `aList`

e c f

Remove a from `theGraph`;
add it to `aList`

a g d b e c f

Question 6 Add an edge to the directed graph in Figure 20-15 that runs from vertex *d* to vertex *b*. Write all possible topological orders for the vertices in this new graph.

20.4.2 Spanning Trees

A tree is a special kind of undirected graph, one that is connected but that has no cycles. Each vertex in the graph in Figure 20-3a could be the root of a different tree. Although all trees are graphs, not all graphs are trees. The nodes (vertices) of a tree have a hierarchical arrangement that is not required of all graphs.

A tree is an undirected connected graph without cycles

FIGURE 20-18   A trace of `topSort2` for the graph in Figure 20-15

Action	Stack **s** (top to bottom)	List **aList** (beginning to end)
Push a	a	
Push g	a g	
Push d	a g d	
Push e	a g d e	
Push c	a g d e c	c
Pop c, add c to **aList**	a g d e	c
Push f	a g d e f	f c
Pop f, add f to **aList**	a g d e	e f c
Pop e, add e to **aList**	a g d	d e f c
Pop d, add d to **aList**	a g	g d e f c
Pop g, add g to **aList**	a	g d e f c
Push b	a b	b g d e f c
Pop b, add b to **aList**	a	a b g d e f c
Pop a, add a to **aList**	(empty)	

A **spanning tree** of a connected undirected graph G is a subgraph of G that contains all of G's vertices and enough of its edges to form a tree. For example, Figure 20-19 shows a spanning tree for the graph in Figure 20-12. The dashed lines in Figure 20-19 indicate edges that were omitted from the graph to form the tree. There may be several spanning trees for a given graph.

FIGURE 20-19   A spanning tree for the graph in Figure 20-12

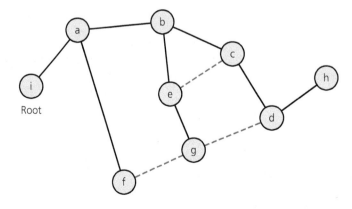

If you have a connected undirected graph with cycles and you remove edges until there are no cycles, you will obtain a spanning tree for the graph. It is relatively simple to see whether a graph contains a cycle. One way to do this is based on the following observations about undirected graphs:

FIGURE 20-20   Connected graphs that each have four vertices and three edges

1. **A connected undirected graph that has *n* vertices must have at least *n* – 1 edges.** To establish this fact, recall that a connected graph has a path between every pair of vertices. Suppose that, beginning with *n* vertices, you choose one vertex and draw an edge between it and any other vertex. Next, draw an edge between this second vertex and any other unattached vertex. If you continue this process until you run out of unattached vertices, you will get a connected graph like the ones in Figure 20-20. If the graph has *n* vertices, it has *n* – 1 edges. In addition, if you remove an edge, the graph will not be connected.

2. **A connected undirected graph that has *n* vertices and exactly *n* – 1 edges cannot contain a cycle.** To see this, begin with the previous observation: To be connected, a graph with *n* vertices must have at least *n* – 1 edges. If a connected graph did have a cycle, you could remove any edge along that cycle and still have a connected graph. Thus, if a connected graph with *n* vertices and *n* – 1 edges did contain a cycle, removing an edge along the cycle would leave you with a connected graph with only *n* – 2 edges, which is impossible according to observation 1.

2. **A connected undirected graph that has *n* vertices and more than *n* – 1 edges must contain at least one cycle.** For example, if you add an edge to any of the graphs in Figure 20-20, you will create a cycle within the graph. This fact is harder to establish and is left as an exercise. (See Exercise 17 at the end of this chapter.)

Observations about undirected graphs that enable you to detect a cycle

Thus, you can learn whether a connected graph contains a cycle simply by counting its vertices and edges.

It follows, then, that a tree, which is a connected undirected graph without cycles, must connect its *n* nodes with *n* – 1 edges. Thus, to obtain the spanning tree of a connected graph of *n* vertices, you must remove edges along cycles until *n* – 1 edges are left.

Count a graph's vertices and edges to see whether it contains a cycle

Two algorithms for finding a spanning tree of a graph are based on the previous traversal algorithms and are presented next. In general, these algorithms will produce different spanning trees for any particular graph.

 Question 7 Is it possible for a connected undirected graph with five vertices and four edges to contain a simple cycle? Explain.

The DFS spanning tree. One way to find a spanning tree for a connected undirected graph is to traverse the graph's vertices by using a depth-first search. As you traverse the graph, mark the edges that you follow. After the traversal is complete, the graph's vertices and marked edges form a spanning tree, which is called the **depth-first search (DFS) spanning tree**. (Alternatively, you can remove the unmarked edges from the graph to form the spanning tree.) Simple modifications to the previous iterative and recursive versions of dfs result in algorithms to create a DFS spanning tree. For example, the recursive algorithm follows:

DFS spanning tree
algorithm

```
//  Forms a spanning tree for a connected undirected graph
//  beginning at vertex v by using depth-first search:
//  Recursive version.
dfsTree(v: Vertex)
{
```
Mark v *as visited*

    for (*each unvisited vertex* u *adjacent to* v)
    {
       Mark the edge from u *to* v
```
        dfsTree(u)
    }
}
```

When you apply this algorithm to the graph in Figure 20-12, you get the DFS spanning tree rooted at vertex *a* shown in Figure 20-21. The figure indicates the order in which the algorithm visits vertices and marks edges. You should reproduce these results by tracing the algorithm.

FIGURE 20-21 The DFS spanning tree rooted at vertex *a* for the graph in Figure 20-12

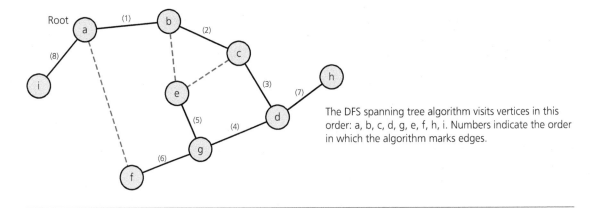

The DFS spanning tree algorithm visits vertices in this order: a, b, c, d, g, e, f, h, i. Numbers indicate the order in which the algorithm marks edges.

 Question 8 Draw the DFS spanning tree whose root is vertex 0 for the graph in Figure 20-22.

FIGURE 20-22 A graph for Checkpoint Questions 8, 9, and 10 and for Exercises 1 and 4

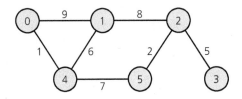

The BFS spanning tree. Another way to form a spanning tree for a connected undirected graph is to traverse the graph's vertices by using a breadth-first search. As you traverse the graph, mark the edges that you follow. After the traversal is complete, the graph's vertices and marked edges form a spanning tree, which is called the **breadth-first search (BFS) spanning tree**. (Alternatively, you can remove the unmarked edges from the graph to form the spanning tree.) You can modify the previous iterative version of bfs by marking the edge between w and u before you add u to the queue. The result is the following iterative algorithm to create a BFS spanning tree.

```
// Forms a spanning tree for a connected undirected graph
// beginning at vertex v by using breadth-first search:
// Iterative version.
bfsTree(v: Vertex)
{
    q = a new empty queue

    // Add v to queue and mark it
    q.enqueue(v)
    Mark v as visited

    while (!q.isEmpty())
    {
        q.dequeue(w)

        // Loop invariant: there is a path from vertex w to
        // every vertex in the queue q
        for (each unvisited vertex u adjacent to w)
        {
            Mark u as visited
            Mark edge between w and u
            q.enqueue(u)
        }
    }
}
```

When you apply this algorithm to the graph in Figure 20-12, you get the BFS spanning tree rooted at vertex *a* shown in Figure 20-23. The figure indicates the order in which the algorithm visits vertices and marks edges. You should reproduce these results by tracing the algorithm.

FIGURE 20-23 The BFS spanning tree rooted at vertex *a* for the graph in Figure 20-12

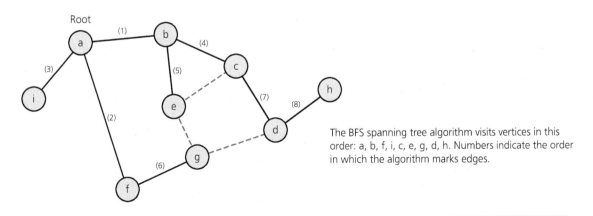

The BFS spanning tree algorithm visits vertices in this order: a, b, f, i, c, e, g, d, h. Numbers indicate the order in which the algorithm marks edges.

?
CHECK POINT **Question 9** Draw the BFS spanning tree whose root is vertex 0 for the graph in Figure 20-22.

20.4.3 Minimum Spanning Trees

Imagine that a developing country hires you to design its telephone system so that all the cities in the country can call one another. Obviously, one solution is to place telephone lines between every pair of cities. However, your engineering team has determined that due to the country's mountainous terrain, it is impossible to put lines between certain pairs of cities. The team's report contains the weighted undirected graph in Figure 20-24. The vertices in the graph represent n cities. An edge between two vertices indicates that it is feasible to place a telephone line between the cities that the vertices represent, and each edge's weight represents the installation cost of the telephone line. Note that if this graph is not connected, you will be unable to link all of the cities with a network of telephone lines. The graph in Figure 20-24 is connected, however, making the problem feasible.

FIGURE 20-24   A weighted, connected, undirected graph

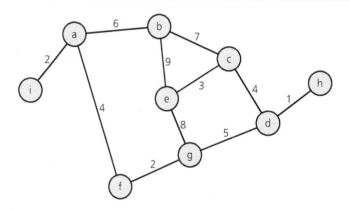

If you install a telephone line between each pair of cities that is connected by an edge in the graph, you will certainly solve the problem. However, this solution may be too costly. From observation 1 in the previous section, you know that $n - 1$ is the minimum number of edges necessary for a graph of n vertices to be connected. Thus, $n - 1$ is the minimum number of lines that can connect n cities.

If the cost of installing each line is the same, the problem is reduced to one of finding any spanning tree of the graph. The total installation cost—that is, the **cost of the spanning tree**—is the sum of the costs of the edges in the spanning tree. However, as the graph in Figure 20-24 shows, the cost of installing each line varies. Because there may be more than one spanning tree, and because the cost of different trees may vary, you need to solve the problem by selecting a spanning tree with the least cost; that is, you must select a spanning tree for which the sum of the edge weights (costs) is minimal. Such a tree is called a **minimum spanning tree**, and it need not be unique. Although there may be several minimum spanning trees for a particular graph, their costs are equal.

One simple algorithm, called **Prim's algorithm**, finds a minimum spanning tree that begins at any vertex. Initially, the tree contains only the starting vertex. At each stage, the algorithm selects a least-cost edge from among those that begin with a vertex in the tree and end with a

A minimum spanning tree of a connected undirected graph has a minimal edge-weight sum vertex not in the tree. The latter vertex and least-cost edge are then added to the tree. The following pseudocode describes this algorithm:

```
//  Forms a minimum spanning tree for a weighted,
//  connected, undirected graph whose weights are
//  nonnegative, beginning with any vertex r.
primsAlgorithm(r: Vertex)
{
    Mark vertex r as visited and include it in the minimum spanning tree
    while (there are unvisited vertices)
    {
        Find the least-cost edge (v, u) from a visited vertex v to some unvisited vertex u
        Mark u as visited
        Add the vertex u and the edge (v, u) to the minimum spanning tree
    }
}
```

Figure 20-25 traces `primsAlgorithm` for the graph in Figure 20-24, beginning at vertex *a*. Edges added to the tree appear as solid lines, while edges under consideration appear as dashed lines.

It is not obvious that the spanning tree that `primsAlgorithm` finds will be minimal. However, the proof that `primsAlgorithm` is correct is beyond the scope of this book.

Question 10 Draw the minimum spanning tree whose root is vertex 0 for the graph in Figure 20-22.

20.4.4 Shortest Paths

Consider once again a map of airline routes. A weighted directed graph can represent this map: The vertices are cities, and the edges indicate existing flights between cities. The edge weights represent the mileage between cities (vertices); as such, the weights are not negative. For example, you could combine the two graphs in Figure 20-5 to get such a weighted directed graph.

Often for weighted directed graphs you need to know the shortest path between two particular vertices. The **shortest path** between two given vertices in a weighted graph is the path that has the smallest sum of its edge weights. Although we use the term "shortest," realize that the weights could be a measure other than distance, such as the cost of each flight in dollars or the duration of each flight in hours. The sum of the weights of the edges of a path is called the path's **length** or **weight** or **cost**.

For example, the shortest path from vertex 0 to vertex 1 in the graph in Figure 20-26a is not the edge between 0 and 1—its cost is 8—but rather the path from 0 to 4 to 2 to 1, with a cost of 7. For convenience, the starting vertex, or origin, is labeled 0 and the other vertices are labeled from 1 to $n - 1$. Notice the graph's adjacency matrix in Figure 20-26b.

The following algorithm, which is attributed to E. Dijkstra, actually finds the shortest paths between a given origin and *all* other vertices. The algorithm uses a set *vertexSet* of selected vertices and an array *weight*, where *weight*[*v*] is the weight of the shortest (cheapest) path from vertex 0 to vertex *v* that passes through vertices in *vertexSet*.

If *v* is in *vertexSet*, the shortest path involves only vertices in *vertexSet*. However, if *v* is not in *vertexSet*, then *v* is the only vertex along the path that is not in *vertexSet*. That is, the path ends with an edge from a vertex in *vertexSet* to *v*.

FIGURE 20-25   A trace of `primsAlgorithm` for the graph in Figure 20-24, beginning at vertex a

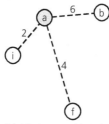

(a) Mark a, consider edges from a

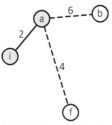

(b) Mark i, include edge (a, i)

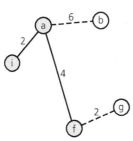

(c) Mark f, include edge (a, f)

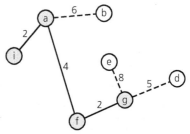

(d) Mark g, include edge (f, g)

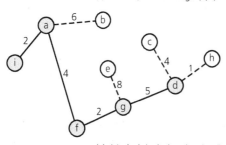

(e) Mark d, include edge (g, d)

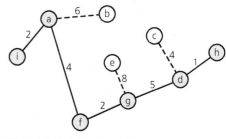

(f) Mark h, include edge (d, h)

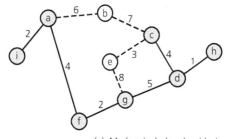

(g) Mark c, include edge (d, c)

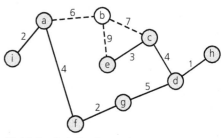

(h) Mark e, include edge (c, e)

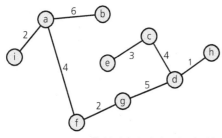

(i) Mark b, include edge (a, b)

FIGURE 20-26   (a) A weighted directed graph and (b) its adjacency matrix

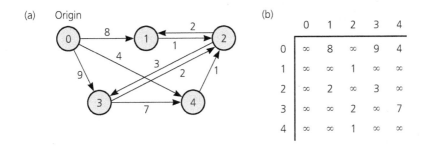

Initially, *vertexSet* contains only vertex 0, and *weight* contains the weights of the single-edge paths from vertex 0 to all other vertices. That is, *weight*[*v*] equals *matrix*[0][*v*] for all *v*, where *matrix* is the adjacency matrix. Thus, initially *weight* is the first row of *matrix*.

After this initialization step, you find a vertex *v* that is not in *vertexSet* and that minimizes *weight*[*v*]. You add *v* to *vertexSet*. For all (unselected) vertices *u* not in *vertexSet*, you check the values *weight*[*u*] to ensure that they are indeed minimums. That is, can you reduce *weight*[*u*]—the weight of a path from vertex 0 to vertex *u*—by passing through the newly selected vertex *v*?

To answer this question, break the path from 0 to *u* into two pieces and find their weights as follows:

$$weight[v] = \text{weight of the shortest path from 0 to } v$$
$$matrix[v][u] = \text{weight of the edge from } v \text{ to } u$$

Then compare *weight*[*u*] with *weight*[*v*] + *matrix*[*v*][*u*] and let

$$weight[u] = \text{the smaller of the values } weight[u] \text{ and } weight[v] + matrix[v][u]$$

The pseudocode for Dijkstra's shortest-path algorithm is as follows:

The shortest-path algorithm

```
// Finds the minimum-cost paths between an origin vertex
// (vertex 0) and all other vertices in a weighted directed
// graph theGraph; theGraph's weights are nonnegative.
shortestPath(theGraph: Graph, weight: WeightArray)
{
    // Step 1: initialization
    Create a set vertexSet that contains only vertex 0
    n = number of vertices in theGraph
    for (v = 0 through n - 1)
      weight[v] = matrix[0][v]

    // Steps 2 through n
    // Invariant: For v not in vertexSet, weight[v] is the
    // smallest weight of all paths from 0 to v that pass
    // through only vertices in vertexSet before reaching
    // v. For v in vertexSet, weight[v] is the smallest
    // weight of all paths from 0 to v (including paths
    // outside vertexSet), and the shortest path
    // from 0 to v lies entirely in vertexSet.
    for (step = 2 through n)
    {
        Find the smallest weight[v] such that v is not in vertexSet
        Add v to vertexSet
```

```
        // Check weight[u] for all u not in vertexSet
    for (all vertices u not in vertexSet)
        if (weight[u] > weight[v] + matrix[v][u])
            weight[u] = weight[v] + matrix[v][u]
    }
}
```

The loop invariant states that once a vertex v is placed in *vertexSet*, *weight*[v] is the weight of the absolutely shortest path from 0 to v and will not change.

Figure 20-27 traces the algorithm for the graph in Figure 20-26a. The algorithm takes the following steps:

FIGURE 20-27 A trace of the shortest-path algorithm applied to the graph in Figure 20-26a

					weight		
Step	v	vertexSet	[0]	[1]	[2]	[3]	[4]
1	–	0	0	8	∞	9	4
2	4	0, 4	0	8	5	9	4
3	2	0, 4, 2	0	7	5	8	4
4	1	0, 4, 2, 1	0	7	5	8	4
5	3	0, 4, 2, 1, 3	0	7	5	8	4

Step 1. *vertexSet* initially contains vertex 0, and *weight* is initially the first row of the graph's adjacency matrix, shown in Figure 20-26b.

Step 2. *weight*[4] = 4 is the smallest value in *weight*, ignoring *weight*[0] because 0 is in *vertexSet*. Thus, $v = 4$, so add 4 to *vertexSet*. For vertices not in *vertexSet*—that is, for $u = 1, 2$, and 3—check whether it is shorter to go from 0 to 4 and then along an edge to u instead of directly from 0 to u along an edge. For vertices 1 and 3, it is not shorter to include vertex 4 in the path. However, for vertex 2 notice that *weight*[2] = ∞ > *weight*[4] + *matrix*[4][2] = 4 + 1 = 5. Therefore, replace *weight*[2] with 5. You can also verify this conclusion by examining the graph directly, as Figure 20-28a shows.

Step 3. *weight*[2] = 5 is the smallest value in *weight*, ignoring *weight*[0] and *weight*[4] because 0 and 4 are in *vertexSet*. Thus, $v = 2$, so add 2 to *vertexSet*. For vertices not in *vertexSet*—that is, for $u = 1$ and 3—check whether it is shorter to go from 0 to 2 and then along an edge to u instead of directly from 0 to u along an edge. (See Figures 20-28b and 20-28c.)

Notice that

weight[1] = 8 > *weight*[2] + *matrix*[2][1] = 5 + 2 = 7. Therefore, replace *weight*[1] with 7.

weight[3] = 9 > *weight*[2] + *matrix*[2][3] = 5 + 3 = 8. Therefore, replace *weight*[3] with 8.

Step 4. *weight*[1] = 7 is the smallest value in *weight*, ignoring *weight*[0], *weight*[2], and *weight*[4] because 0, 2, and 4 are in *vertexSet*. Thus, $v = 1$, so add 1 to *vertexSet*. For vertex 3, which is the only vertex not in *vertexSet*, notice that *weight*[3] = 8 < *weight*[1] + *matrix*[1][3] = 7 + ∞, as Figure 20-28d shows. Therefore, leave *weight*[3] as it is.

Step 5. The only remaining vertex not in *vertexSet* is 3, so add it to *vertexSet* and stop.

FIGURE 20-28   Checking *weight*[u] by examining the graph

(a) *weight*[2] in step 2

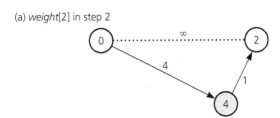

Step 2. The path 0–4–2 is
shorter than 0–2

(b) *weight*[1] in step 3

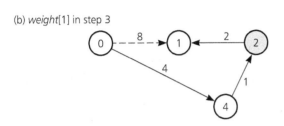

Step 3. The path 0–4–2–1 is
shorter than 0–1

(c) *weight*[3] in step 3

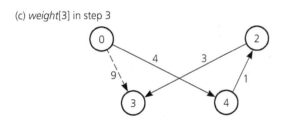

Step 3 continued. The path 0–4–2–3 is
shorter than 0–3

(d) *weight*[3] in step 4

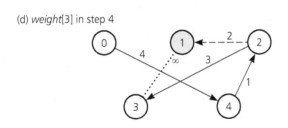

Step 4. The path 0–4–2–3 is
shorter than
0–4–2–1–3

The final values in *weight* are the weights of the shortest paths. These values appear in the last line of Figure 20-27. For example, the shortest path from vertex 0 to vertex 1 has a cost of *weight*[1], which is 7. This result agrees with our earlier observation about Figure 20-26. We saw then that the shortest path is from 0 to 4 to 2 to 1. Also, the shortest path from vertex 0 to vertex 2 has a cost of *weight*[2], which is 5. This path is from 0 to 4 to 2.

The weights in *weight* are the smallest possible, as long as the algorithm's loop invariant is true. The proof that the loop invariant is true is by induction on step, and is left as a difficult exercise. (See Exercise 20.)

Question 11 What are the shortest paths from vertex 0 to each vertex of the graph in Figure 20-26a? (Note the weights of these paths in Figure 20-27.)

20.4.5 Circuits

A **circuit** is simply another name for a type of cycle that is common in the statement of certain problems. Recall that a cycle in a graph is a path that begins and ends at the same vertex. Typical circuits either visit every vertex once or visit every edge once.

Probably the first application of graphs occurred in the early 1700s when Euler proposed a bridge problem. Two islands in a river are joined to each other and to the river banks by several bridges, as Figure 20-29a illustrates. The bridges correspond to the edges in the multigraph in Figure 20-29b, and the land masses correspond to the vertices. The problem asked whether you can begin at a vertex v, pass through every edge exactly once, and terminate at v. Euler demonstrated that no solution exists for this particular configuration of edges and vertices.

FIGURE 20-29   (a) Euler's bridge problem and (b) its multigraph representation

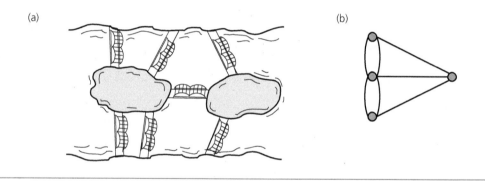

(a)

(b)

For simplicity, we will consider an undirected graph rather than a multigraph. A path in an undirected graph that begins at a vertex v, passes through every edge in the graph exactly once, and terminates at v is called an **Euler circuit**. Euler showed that an Euler circuit exists if and only if each vertex touches an even number of edges. Intuitively, if you arrive at a vertex along one edge, you must be able to leave the vertex along another edge. If you cannot, you will not be able to reach all of the vertices.

> An Euler circuit begins at a vertex v, passes through every edge exactly once, and terminates at v

Finding an Euler circuit is like drawing each of the diagrams in Figure 20-30 without lifting your pencil or redrawing a line, and ending at your starting point. No solution is possible for Figure 20-30a, but you should be able to find one easily for Figure 20-30b. Figure 20-31 contains undirected graphs based on Figure 20-30. In Figure 20-31a, vertices h and i each touch an odd number of edges (three), so no Euler circuit is possible. On the other hand, each vertex in Figure 20-31b touches an even number of edges, making an Euler circuit feasible. Notice also that the graphs are connected. If a graph is not connected, a path through *all* of the vertices would not be possible.

Let's find an Euler circuit for the graph in Figure 20-31b, starting arbitrarily at vertex a. The strategy uses a depth-first search that marks edges instead of vertices as they are traversed. Recall that a depth-first search traverses a path from a as deeply into the graph as possible. By

FIGURE 20-30   Pencil and paper drawings

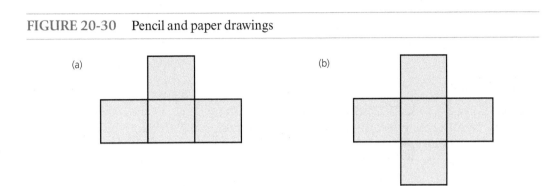

FIGURE 20-31   Connected undirected graphs based on the drawings in Figure 20-30

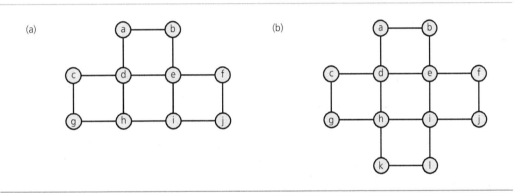

marking edges instead of vertices, you will return to the starting vertex; that is, you will find a cycle. In this example, the cycle is a, b, e, d, a if we visit the vertices in alphabetical order, as Figure 20-32a shows. Clearly this is not the desired circuit, because we have not visited every edge. We are not finished, however.

To continue, find the first vertex along the cycle a, b, e, d, a that touches an unvisited edge. In our example, the desired vertex is e. Apply our modified depth-first search, beginning with this vertex. The resulting cycle is e, f, j, i, e. Next you join this cycle with the one you found previously. That is, when you reach e in the first cycle, you travel along the second cycle before continuing in the first cycle. The resulting path is $a, b, e, f, j, i, e, d, a$, as Figure 20-32b shows.

The first vertex along our combined cycle that touches an unvisited edge is i. Beginning at i, our algorithm discovers the cycle $i, h, d, c, g, h, k, l, i$. Joining this to our combined cycle results in the Euler circuit $a, b, e, f, j, i, h, d, c, g, h, k, l, i, e, d, a$. (See Figure 20-32c.)

20.4.6 Some Difficult Problems

The next three applications of graphs have solutions that are beyond the scope of this book.

The traveling salesperson problem. A **Hamilton circuit** is a path that begins at a vertex v, passes through every vertex in the graph exactly once, and terminates at v. Detecting whether an arbitrary

A Hamilton circuit begins at a vertex v, passes through every vertex exactly once, and terminates at v

FIGURE 20-32   The steps to find an Euler circuit for the graph in Figure 20-31b

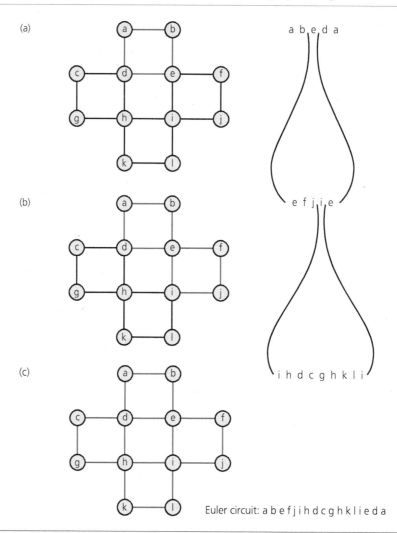

(a)

a b e d a

(b)

e f j i e

(c)

i h d c g h k l i

Euler circuit: a b e f j i h d c g h k l i e d a

graph contains a Hamilton circuit can be difficult. A well-known variation of this problem—the traveling salesperson problem—involves a weighted graph that represents a road map. Each edge has an associated cost, such as the mileage between cities or the time required to drive from one city to the next. The salesperson must begin at an origin city, visit every other city exactly once, and return to the origin city. However, the circuit traveled must be the least expensive.

Unfortunately for this traveler, solving the problem is no easy task. Checking every round-trip path to find the shortest one is quite slow, as it is O(n!). However, package delivery companies use approximate solutions to this problem to plan their daily routes.

The three utilities problem. Imagine three houses *A, B,* and *C* and three utilities *X, Y,* and *Z* (such as telephone, water, and electricity), as Figure 20-33 illustrates. If the houses and the utilities are vertices in a graph, is it possible to connect each house to each utility with edges that do not cross one another? The answer to this question is no.

FIGURE 20-33   The three utilities problem

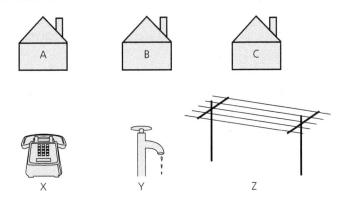

A graph is **planar** if you can draw it in a plane in at least one way so that no two edges cross. A generalization of the three utilities problem can test whether a given graph is planar. Performing this test has many important applications. For example, a graph can represent an electronic circuit where the vertices represent components and the edges represent the connections between components. Is it possible to design the circuit so that the connections do not cross? The solutions to these problems are also beyond the scope of this book.

A planar graph can be drawn so that no two edges cross

The four-color problem. Given a planar graph, can you color the vertices so that no adjacent vertices have the same color, if you use at most four colors? For example, the graph in Figure 20-12 is planar because none of its edges cross. You can solve the coloring problem for this graph by using only three colors. Color vertices *a, c, g,* and *h* red, color vertices *b, d, f,* and *i* blue, and color vertex *e* green.

The answer to our question is yes, but it is difficult to prove. In fact, this problem was posed more than a century before it was solved in the 1970s with the use of a computer.

SUMMARY

1. The two most common implementations of a graph are the adjacency matrix and the adjacency list. Each has its relative advantages and disadvantages. The choice should depend on the needs of the given application.

2. Graph searching is an important application of stacks and queues. Depth-first search (DFS) is a graph-traversal algorithm that uses a stack to keep track of the sequence of visited vertices. It goes as deep into the graph as it can before backtracking. Breadth-first search (BFS) uses a queue to keep track of the sequence of visited vertices. It visits all possible adjacent vertices before traversing further into the graph.

3. Topological sorting produces a linear order of the vertices in a directed graph without cycles. Vertex *x* precedes vertex *y* if there is a directed edge from *x* to *y* in the graph.

4. Trees are connected undirected graphs without cycles. A spanning tree of a connected undirected graph is a subgraph that contains all of the graph's vertices and enough of its edges to form a tree. DFS and BFS traversals produce DFS and BFS spanning trees.

5. A minimum spanning tree for a weighted undirected graph is a spanning tree whose edge-weight sum is minimal. Although a particular graph can have several minimum spanning trees, their edge-weight sums will be the same.

6. The shortest path between two vertices in a weighted directed graph is the path that has the smallest sum of its edge weights.

7. An Euler circuit in an undirected graph is a cycle that begins at vertex v, passes through every edge in the graph exactly once, and terminates at v.

8. A Hamilton circuit in an undirected graph is a cycle that begins at vertex v, passes through every vertex in the graph exactly once, and terminates at v.

EXERCISES

When given a choice of vertices to visit, the traversals in the following exercises should visit vertices in sorted order.

1. Give the adjacency matrix and adjacency list for
   a. The weighted graph in Figure 20-22
   b. The directed graph in Figure 20-34

2. Show that the adjacency list in Figure 20-9b requires less memory than the adjacency matrix in Figure 20-7b.

3. Consider Figure 20-35 and answer the following:
   a. Will the adjacency matrix be symmetrical?
   b. Provide the adjacency matrix.
   c. Provide the adjacency list.

FIGURE 20-34   A graph for Exercise 1

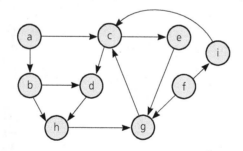

FIGURE 20-35   A graph for Exercise 3

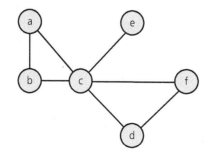

FIGURE 20-36   A graph for Exercise 10

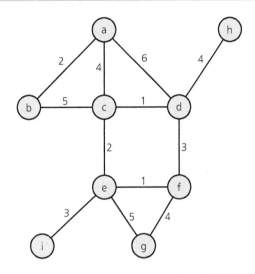

4. Use both the depth-first strategy and the breadth-first strategy to traverse the graph in Figure 20-22, beginning with vertex 0, and the graph in Figure 20-36, beginning with vertex *a*. List the vertices in the order in which each traversal visits them.

5. By modifying the DFS traversal algorithm, write pseudocode for an algorithm that detects whether a graph contains a cycle.

6. Using the topological sorting algorithm `topSort1`, as given in this chapter, write the topological order of the vertices for each graph in Figure 20-37.

7. Trace the DFS topological sorting algorithm `topSort2`, and indicate the resulting topological order of the vertices for each graph in Figure 20-37.

8. Revise the topological sorting algorithm `topSort1` by removing predecessors instead of successors. Trace the new algorithm for each graph in Figure 20-37.

FIGURE 20-37   Graphs for Exercises 6, 7, and 8

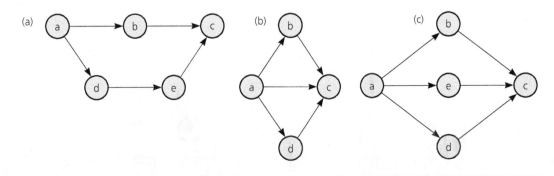

FIGURE 20-38   A graph for Exercise 11

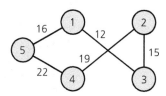

9. Trace the DFS and BFS spanning tree algorithms, beginning with vertex *a* of the graph in Figure 20-12, and show that the spanning trees are the trees in Figures 20-21 and 20-23, respectively.

10. Draw the DFS and BFS spanning trees rooted at *a* for the graph in Figure 20-36. Then draw the minimum spanning tree rooted at *a* for this graph.

11. For the graph in Figure 20-38,
    a. Draw all the possible spanning trees.
    b. Draw the minimum spanning tree.

12. Write pseudocode for an iterative algorithm that finds a DFS spanning tree for an undirected graph. Base your algorithm on the traversal algorithm dfs.

13. Trace Prim's algorithm to find the minimum spanning tree for the graph in Figure 20-24 when you start with
    a. Vertex *g*
    b. Vertex *c*

14. Trace the shortest-path algorithm for the graph in Figure 20-39, letting vertex 0 be the origin.

*15. Implement the shortest-path algorithm in C++. How can you modify this algorithm so that any vertex can be the origin?

FIGURE 20-39   A graph for Exercise 14

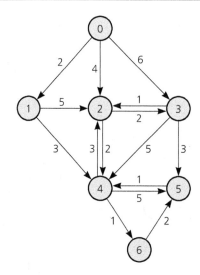

FIGURE 20-40   A graph for Exercise 16

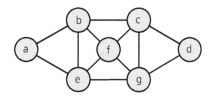

16. Find an Euler circuit for the graph in Figure 20-40. Why is one possible?

*17. Prove that a connected undirected graph with n vertices and more than $n - 1$ edges must contain at least one simple cycle. (See observation 3 in Section 20.4.2.)

*18. Prove that a graph-traversal algorithm visits every vertex in an undirected graph if and only if the graph is connected, regardless of where the traversal starts.

*19. Although the DFS traversal algorithm has a simple recursive form, a recursive BFS traversal algorithm is not straightforward.
   a. Explain why this statement is true.
   b. Write the pseudocode for a recursive version of the BFS traversal algorithm.

*20. Prove that the loop invariant of Dijkstra's shortest-path algorithm is true by using a proof by induction on `step`.

PROGRAMMING PROBLEMS

1. Write a C++ class derived from `GraphInterface`, as given in Listing 20-1. Use an adjacency matrix to represent the graph.

2. Repeat the previous programming problem, but represent the graph using an adjacency list instead of an adjacency matrix.

3. Repeat Programming Problems 1 and 2, but allow the graph to be either weighted or unweighted and either directed or undirected.

4. Extend Programming Problem 3 by adding ADT operations such as `isConnected` and `hasCycle`. Also, include operations that perform a topological sort for a directed graph without cycles, find the DFS and BFS spanning trees for a connected graph, and find a minimum spanning tree for a connected undirected graph.

5. The HPAir problem was the subject of Programming Problems 11 through 14 of Chapter 6. Revise these problems by implementing the ADT flight map as a derived class of the graph class that you wrote for Programming Problem 3.

Processing Data in External Storage

Contents

Prerequisites

Appendix G   Files
Chapter 11   Sorting Algorithms and Their Efficiency
Chapter 18   Dictionaries and Their Implementations
Chapter 19   Balanced Search Trees

All of the previous ADT implementations assume that the data items reside in the computer's internal memory. Many real-world applications, however, require a data collection so large that it greatly exceeds the amount of available internal memory. In such situations, you must store the data on an external storage device such as a disk and perform ADT operations there.

This chapter considers the problem of data management in an external environment by using a direct access file as a model of external storage. In particular, this chapter discusses how to sort the data in an external file by modifying the merge sort algorithm and how to search an external file by using generalizations of the hashing and search-tree schemes developed previously.

21.1 A Look at External Storage

You use external storage when your program reads data from and writes data to a C++ file. Also, when you use a word processing program, for example, and choose Save, the program saves your current document in a file. This action enables you to exit the program and then use it later to retrieve your document for revision. This is one of the advantages of external storage: It exists beyond the execution period of a program. In this sense, it is "permanent" instead of volatile like internal memory.

External storage exists after program execution

Another advantage of external storage is that, in general, there is far more of it than internal memory. If you have a collection of one million data items, each of which is an object of moderate size, you will probably not be able to store the entire collection in internal memory at one time. On the other hand, this much data can easily reside on an external disk. As a consequence, when dealing with collections of this magnitude, you cannot simply read all of the data into memory when you want to operate on it and then write it back onto the disk when you are finished. Instead, you must devise ways to operate on data—for example, sort it and search it—while it resides externally.

Generally, there is more external storage than internal memory

In general, you can create files for either sequential access or direct access. To access the data stored at a given position in a **sequential access file**, you must advance the file window beyond all the intervening data. In this sense, a sequential access file resembles a linked chain. To access a particular node in the chain, you must traverse the chain from its beginning until you reach the desired node. In contrast, a **direct access file** allows you to access the data at a given position directly. A direct access file resembles an array in that you can access the element at data[i] without first accessing the elements before data[i].

Without direct access files, it would be impossible to support the data-management operations efficiently in an external environment. Many programming languages, including C++, support both sequential access and direct access of files. However, to permit a language-independent discussion, we will construct a model of direct access files. This model will be a simplification of reality but will include the features necessary for this discussion.

Direct access files are essential for external data collections

Imagine that a computer's memory is divided into two parts: internal memory and external memory, as Figure 21-1 illustrates. Assume that an executing program, along with its nonfile data, resides in the computer's internal memory; the permanent files of a computer system reside in the external memory. Further assume that the external storage devices have the characteristics of a disk (although some systems use other devices).

A file consists of **data records**. A data record can be anything from a simple value, such as an integer, to an aggregate structure, such as an employee record. For simplicity, assume that the data records in any one file are all of the same type.

The records of a file are organized into one or more **blocks**, as Figure 21-2 shows. The size of a block—that is, the number of bits of data it can contain—is determined by both the hardware configuration and the system software of the computer. In general, an individual program has no control over this size. Therefore, the number of records in a block is a function of the size of the records in the file. For example, a file of integer records will have more records per block than a file of employee records.

A file contains records that are organized into blocks

FIGURE 21-1   Internal and external memory

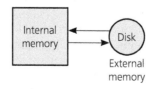

FIGURE 21-2   A file partitioned into blocks of records

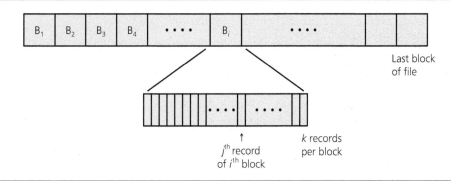

Much as you number the elements of an array, you can number the blocks of a file in a linear sequence. With a direct access file, a program can read a given block from the file by specifying its block number, and similarly, it can write data out to a particular block. In this regard a direct access file resembles an array of arrays, with each block of the file analogous to a single array element, which is itself an array that contains several records.

In this direct access model, all input and output is at the block level rather than at the record level. That is, you can read and write a block of records, but you cannot read or write an individual record. Reading or writing a block is called a **block access**.

Direct access input and output involves blocks instead of records

The algorithms in this chapter assume that commands exist for reading and writing blocks. The pseudocode statement

```
buf.readBlock(dataFile, i)
```

will read the ith block of file dataFile and place it in an object buf. This object must accommodate the many records that each block of the file contains. For example, if each block contains 100 employee records, buf must store at least 100 employee records. The object buf is called a **buffer**, which is a location that temporarily stores data as it makes its way from one process or location to another.

A buffer stores data temporarily

Once the system has read a block into buf, the program can process—for example, inspect or modify—the records in the block. Also, because the records in the object buf are only copies of the records in the file dataFile, if a program does modify the records in buf, it must write buf back out to dataFile, so that the file also reflects the modifications. We assume that the statement

```
buf.writeBlock(dataFile, i)
```

will write the contents of buf to the ith block of the file dataFile. If dataFile contains n blocks, the statement

```
buf.writeBlock(dataFile, n + 1)
```

will append a new block to dataFile, and thus the file can grow dynamically, just as a C++ file can.

Again, realize that these input and output commands allow you to read and write only entire blocks. As a consequence, even if you need to operate on only a single record of the file, you must access an entire block. For example, suppose that you want to give employee Smith a $1,000 raise. If Smith's record is in block i, you would perform the following steps:

Updating a portion of a record within a block

```
// Read block i from file dataFile into buffer buf
buf.readBlock(dataFile, i)
{
    Find the entry buf.getRecord(j) that contains the
      record whose search key is "Smith"

    // Increase the salary portion of Smith's record
    (buf.getRecord(j)).setSalary((buf.getRecord(j)).getSalary() + 1000)

    // Write changed block back to file dataFile
    buf.writeBlock(dataFile, i)
}
```

Reduce the number of block accesses

The time required to read or write a block of data is typically much longer than the time required to operate on the block's data once it is in the computer's internal memory.[1] For example, you typically can inspect every record in the buffer buf in less time than that required to read a block into the buffer. As a consequence, you should reduce the number of required block accesses. In the previous pseudocode, for instance, you should process as many records in buf as possible before writing it to the file. You should pay little attention to the time required to operate on a block of data once it has been read into internal memory.

Several programming languages, including C++, have commands to make it *appear* that you can access records one at a time. In general, however, the system actually performs input and output at the block level and perhaps hides this fact from the program. For example, if a programming language includes the statement

```
rec.readRecord(dataFile, i) // Reads the i-th record of file dataFile into rec.
```

the system probably accesses the entire block that contains the ith record. Our model of input and output therefore approximates reality reasonably well.

File access time is the dominant factor when considering an algorithm's efficiency

In most external data-management applications, the time required for block accesses typically dominates all other factors. The rest of the chapter discusses how to sort and search externally stored data. The goal will be to reduce the number of required block accesses.

 Question 1 Consider two files of 1,600 employee records each. The records in each file are organized into sixteen 100-record blocks. One file is sequential access and the other is direct access. Describe how you would append one record to the end of each file.

21.2 Working with External Data

VideoNote
Managing external data

This section discusses techniques for organizing records in external storage so that you can efficiently sort, traverse, retrieve, remove, or add to them. Although this discussion will only scratch the surface of this topic, you do have a head start if you studied Chapters 18 and 19.

21.2.1 Sorting Data in an External File

Consider the following problem of sorting data that resides in an external file:

A sorting problem

An external file contains 1,600 employee records. You want to sort these records by Social Security number. Each block contains 100 records, and thus the file contains 16 blocks B_1,

---

[1] Data enters or leaves a buffer at a rate that differs from the record-processing rate. (Hence, using a buffer compensates for the difference in the rates at which the two processes operate on data.)

B_2, and so on to B_{16}. Assume that the program can access only enough internal memory to manipulate about 300 records (three blocks) at one time.

Sorting the file might not sound like a difficult task, because you have already seen several sorting algorithms earlier in this book. There is, however, a fundamental difference here in that the file is far too large to fit into internal memory all at once. This restriction presents something of a problem because the sorting algorithms presented earlier assume that all the data to be sorted is available at one time in internal memory (for example, that it is all in an array). Fortunately, however, we can remove this assumption for a modified version of merge sort.

VideoNote
Sorting file data

The basis of the merge sort algorithm is that you can easily merge two sorted segments—such as arrays—of data records into a third sorted segment that is the combination of the two. For example, if S_1 and S_2 are sorted segments of records, the first step of the merge is to compare the first record of each segment and select the record with the smaller sort key. If the record from S_1 is selected, the next step is to compare the second record of S_1 to the first record of S_2. This process is continued until all of the records have been considered. The key observation is that at any step, the merge never needs to look beyond the *leading edge* of either segment.

This observation makes a merge sort appropriate for the problem of sorting external files, if you modify the algorithm appropriately. Suppose that the 1,600 records to be sorted are in the file F and that you are not permitted to alter this file. You have two work files, F_1 and F_2. One of the work files will contain the sorted records when the algorithm terminates. The algorithm has two phases: Phase 1 sorts each block of records, and phase 2 performs a series of merges.

Phase 1. Read a block from F into internal memory, sort its records by using an internal sort, and write the sorted block out to F_1 before you read the next block from F. After you process all 16 blocks of F, F_1 contains 16 **sorted runs** R_1, R_2, and so on to R_{16}; that is, F_1 contains 16 blocks of records, with the records within each block sorted among themselves, as Figure 21-3a illustrates.

External merge sort

Phase 2. Phase 2 is a sequence of merge steps. Each merge step merges pairs of sorted runs to form larger sorted runs. With each merge step, the number of blocks in each sorted run doubles, and thus the total number of sorted runs is halved. For example, as Figure 21-3b shows, the first merge step merges eight pairs of sorted runs from F_1 (R_1 with R_2, R_3 with R_4, ..., R_{15} with R_{16}) to form eight sorted runs, each two blocks long, which are written to F_2. The next merge step merges four pairs of sorted runs from F_2 (R_1 with R_2, R_3 with R_4, ..., R_7 with R_8) to form four sorted runs, each four blocks long, which are written back to F_1, as Figure 21-3c illustrates. The next step merges the two pairs of sorted runs from F_1 to form two sorted runs, which are written to F_2. (See Figure 21-3d.) The final step merges the two sorted runs into one, which is written to F_1. At this point, F_1 will contain all of the records of the original file in sorted order.

Given this overall strategy, how can you merge the sorted runs at each step of phase 2? The statement of the problem provides only sufficient internal memory to manipulate at most 300 records at once. However, in the later steps of phase 2, runs contain more than 300 records each, so you must merge the runs a piece at a time. To accomplish this merge, you must divide the program's internal memory into three arrays, in1, in2, and out, each capable of holding 100 records (the block size). You read block-sized pieces of the runs into in1 and in2 and merge them into the array out. Whenever an in array is exhausted—that is, when all of its entries have been copied to out—you read the next piece of the run into an in array; whenever the out array becomes full, you write this completed piece of the new sorted run to one of the files.

Merging sorted runs in Phase 2

Consider how you can perform the first merge step. You start this step with the pair of runs R_1 and R_2, which are in the first and second blocks, respectively, of the file F_1. (See Figure 21-3a.) Because at this first merge step each run contains only one block, an entire run can fit into in1 or in2.

FIGURE 21-3   Sorting a block of an external file F by merging the results of internal sorts and using two external work files F_1 and F_2

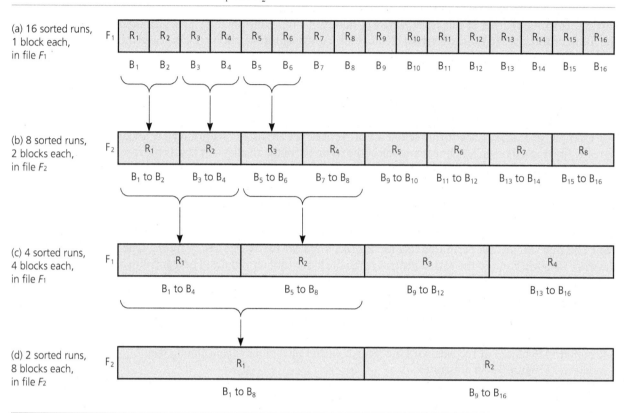

(a) 16 sorted runs, 1 block each, in file F_1

(b) 8 sorted runs, 2 blocks each, in file F_2

(c) 4 sorted runs, 4 blocks each, in file F_1

(d) 2 sorted runs, 8 blocks each, in file F_2

You can thus read R_1 and R_2 into the arrays in1 and in2, and then merge in1 and in2 into out. However, although the result of merging in1 and in2 is a sorted run two blocks long (200 records), out can hold only one block (100 records). Thus, when in the course of the merge out becomes full, you write its contents to the first block of F_2, as Figure 21-4a illustrates. The merging of in1 and in2 into out then resumes. The array out will become full for a second time only after all of the records in in1 and in2 are exhausted. At that time, write the contents of out to the second block of F_2. You merge the remaining seven pairs from F in the same manner and append the resulting runs to F_2.

This first merge step is conceptually a bit easier than the others, because the initial runs are only one block in size, and thus each can fit entirely into one of the in arrays. What do you do in the later steps when the runs to be merged are larger than a single block? Consider, for example, the merge step in which you must merge runs of four blocks each to form runs of eight blocks each. (See Figure 21-3c.) The first pair of these runs to be merged is in blocks 1 through 4 and 5 through 8 of F_1.

The algorithm will read the first block of R_1—which is the first block B_1 of the file—into in1, and it will read the first block of R_2—which is B_5—into in2, as Figure 21-4b illustrates. Then, as it did earlier, the algorithm merges in1 and in2 into out. The complication here is that as soon as you finish moving all of the records from either in1 or in2, you must read the next block from the corresponding run. For example, if you finish in2 first, you must read the next

FIGURE 21-4   Phase 2 of an external sort: Merging sorted runs

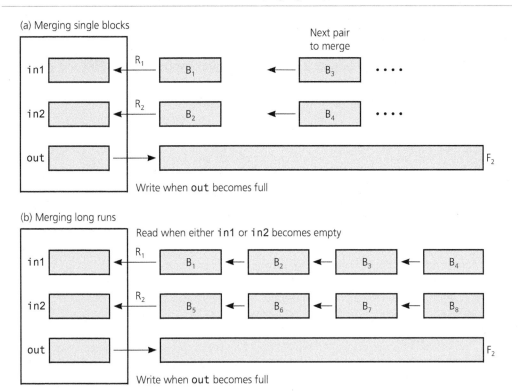

block of R_2—which is B_6—into in2 before the merge can continue. The algorithm thus must detect when the in arrays become exhausted as well as when the out array becomes full.

A high-level description of the algorithm for merging arbitrary-sized sorted runs R_i and R_j from F_1 into F_2 is as follows:

```
mergeRuns(R , R )
        i   j
{
    Read the first block of R into in1
                            i
    Read the first block of R into in2
                            j

    while (either in1 or in2 is not exhausted)
    {
        Select the smaller "leading" record of in1 and in2 and place it into
        the next position of out (if one of the arrays is exhausted, select the
        leading record from the other)

        if (out is full)
            Write its contents to the next block of F
                                                     2

        if (in1 is exhausted and blocks remain in R )
                                                   i
            Read the next block into in1

        if (in2 is exhausted and blocks remain in R )
                                                   j
            Read the next block into in2
    }
}
```

Pseudocode to
merge sorted runs

A pseudocode version of the external sorting algorithm follows. Notice that it uses `readBlock` and `writeBlock`, as introduced in the previous section, and assumes a function `copyFile` that copies a file. To avoid further complications, the solution assumes that the number of blocks in the file is a power of 2. This assumption allows the algorithm always to pair off the sorted runs at each step of the merge phase, avoiding special end-of-file testing that would obscure the algorithm. Also note that the algorithm uses two temporary files and copies the final sorted temporary file to the designated output file.

A pseudocode
mergesort function

```
// Sorts a file by using an external merge sort.
// Precondition: unsortedFileName is the name of an external
// file to be sorted. sortedFileName is the name that the
// function will give to the resulting sorted file.
// Postcondition: The new file named sortedFileName is sorted.
// The original file is unchanged. Both files are closed.
// Calls: blockSort, mergeFile, and copyFile.
// Simplifying assumption: The number of blocks in the
// unsorted file is an exact power of 2.
externalMergesort(unsortedFileName: string,
                   sortedFileName: string)
{
    Associate unsortedFileName with the file variable inFile
        and sortedFileName with the file variable outFile

    // Phase 1: Sort file block by block and count the blocks
    blockSort(inFile, tempFile1, numberOfBlocks)

    // Phase 2: Merge runs of size 1, 2, 4, 8,..., numberOfBlocks/2
    // (uses two temporary files and a toggle that tracks files for each merge step)
    toggle = 1
    for (size = 1 through numberOfBlocks/2 with increments of size)
    {
        if (toggle == 1)
            mergeFile(tempFile1, tempFile2, size, numberOfBlocks)
        else
        {
            mergeFile(tempFile2, tempFile1, size, numberOfBlocks)
            toggle = -toggle
        }
    }

    // Copy the current temporary file to outFile
    if (toggle == 1)
        copyFile(tempFile1, outFile)
    else
        copyFile(tempFile2, outFile)
}
```

Notice that `externalMergesort` calls `blockSort` and `mergeFile`, which calls `mergeRuns`. The pseudocode for these functions follows.

```
// Sorts each block of records in a file.
// Precondition: The file variable inFile is associated
// with the file to be sorted.
// Postcondition: The file associated with the file variable
// outFile contains the blocks of inFile. Each block is
// sorted; numberOfBlocks is the number of blocks processed.
// Both files are closed.
// Calls: readBlock and writeBlock to perform direct access
// input and output, and sortBuffer to sort an array.
```

```
blockSort(inFile: File, outFile: File, numberOfBlocks: integer)
{
    Prepare inFile for input
    Prepare outFile for output

    numberOfBlocks = 0
    while (more blocks in inFile remain to be read)
    {
        numberOfBlocks++
        buffer.readBlock(inFile, numberOfBlocks)

        sortArray(buffer)  // Sort with some internal sort

        buffer.writeBlock(outFile, numberOfBlocks)
    }

    Close inFile and outFile
}

// Merges blocks from one file to another.
// Precondition: inFile is an external file that contains
// numberOfBlocks sorted blocks organized into runs of
// runSize blocks each.
// Postcondition: outFile contains the merged runs of
// inFile. Both files are closed.
// Calls: mergeRuns.
mergeFile(inFile: File, outFile: File,
          runSize: integer, numberOfBlocks: integer)
{
    Prepare inFile for input
    Prepare outFile for output

    for (next = 1 to numberOfBlocks with increments of 2 * runSize)
    {
        // Invariant: Runs in outFile are ordered
        mergeRuns(inFile, outFile, next, runSize)
    }
    Close inFile and outFile
}
```

The following pseudocode is a refinement of the mergeRuns function given earlier:

```
// Merges two consecutive sorted runs in a file.
// Precondition: fromFile is an external file of sorted runs
// open for input. toFile is an external file of sorted runs
// open for output. start is the block number of the first
// run on fromFile to be merged; this run contains size blocks.
// Run 1: Block start to block start + size - 1
// Run 2: Block start + size to start + (2 * size) - 1
// Postcondition: The merged runs from fromFile are appended
// to toFile. The files remain open.
mergeRuns(fromFile: File, toFile: File, start: integer, size: integer)
{
    // Initialize the input buffers for runs 1 and 2
    in1.readBlock(fromFile, first block of Run 1)
    in2.readBlock(fromFile, first block of Run 2)

    // Merge until one of the runs is finished. Whenever an
    // input buffer is exhausted, the next block is read.
    // Whenever the output buffer is full, it is written.
    while (neither run is finished)
    {
```

```
      // Invariant: out and each block in toFile are ordered
      Select the smaller "leading edge" of in1 and in2, and
         place it in the next position of out

      if (out is full)
         out.writeBlock(toFile, next block of toFile)
      if (in1 is exhausted and blocks remain in Run 1)
         in1.readBlock(fromFile, next block of Run 1)
      if (in2 is exhausted and blocks remain in Run 2)
         in2.readBlock(fromFile, next block of Run 2)
   }

   // Assertion: Exactly one of the runs is complete

   // Append the remainder of the unfinished input
   // buffer to the output buffer and write it

   while (in1 is not exhausted)
      // Invariant: out is ordered
      Place next item of in1 into the next position of out

   while (in2 is not exhausted)
      // Invariant: out is ordered
      Place next item of in2 into the next position of out

   out.writeBlock(toFile, next block of toFile)

   // Finish off the remaining complete blocks

   while (blocks remain in Run 1)
   {
      // Invariant: Each block in toFile is ordered
      in1.readBlock(fromFile, next block of Run 1)
      in1.writeBlock(toFile, next block of toFile)
   }

   while (blocks remain in Run 2)
   {
      // Invariant: Each block in toFile is ordered
      in2.readBlock(fromFile, next block of Run 2)
      in2.writeBlock(toFile, next block of toFile)
   }
}
```

 Question 2 Trace externalMergesort with an external file of 16 blocks. Assume that the arrays in1, in2, and out are each one block long. List the calls to the various functions in the order in which they occur.

21.2.2 Basic Data Management Operations

A simple external implementation: records stored in search-key order

Suppose that you have a direct access file of records that have search keys like the records in Chapter 18 for the ADT dictionary. The file is partitioned into blocks, as described earlier in this chapter. Imagine that we store the records in order by their search key, perhaps sorting the file by using the external merge sort algorithm developed in the previous section. Once it is sorted, you can easily traverse the file in sorted order by using the following algorithm:

Sorted-order traversal

```
// Traverses the sorted file dataFile in sorted order,
// calling function visit once for each item:
traverse(dataFile: File, numberOfBlocks: integer,
         recordsPerBlock: integer, visit: FunctionType)
```

```
{
   // Read each block of file dataFile into an internal buffer buf
   for (blockNumber = 1 through numberOfBlocks)
   {
      buf.readBlock(dataFile, blockNumber)
      // Visit each record in the block
      for (recordNumber = 1 through recordsPerBlock)
         Visit record buf.getRecord(recordNumber - 1)
   }
}
```

To retrieve a record from the sorted file, you can use a binary search algorithm as follows:

```
// Searches blocks first through last of the file dataFile
// for the record whose search key equals searchkey
// Returns the record if found, else throws NotFoundException.
getItem(dataFile: File, recordsPerBlock: integer, first: integer, last: integer,
        searchKey: KeyType): ItemType
{
   if (first > last or nothing is left to read from dataFile)
      throw NotFoundException
   else
   {
      // Read the middle block of file dataFile into array buf
      mid = (first + last) / 2
      buf.readBlock(dataFile, mid)

      if ((searchKey >= (buf.getRecord(0)).getKey()) &&
          (searchKey <= (buf.getRecord(recordsPerBlock - 1)).getKey()) )
      {
         // Desired block is found
         Search buffer buf for record buf.getRecord(j) whose search key equals searchKey
         if (record is found)
            return buf.getRecord(j)
         else
            throw NotFoundException
      }
      // Else search appropriate half of the file
      else if (searchKey < (buf.getRecord(0)).getKey())
         return getItem(dataFile, recordsPerBlock, first, mid - 1, searchKey)

      else
         return getItem(dataFile, recordsPerBlock, mid + 1, last, searchKey)
   }
}
```

The retrieval algorithm recursively splits the file in half and reads the middle block into the internal object buf. Splitting a file segment requires that you know the numbers of the first and last blocks of the segment. You would pass these values as arguments, along with the file variable, to getItem.

Once you have read the middle block of the file segment into buf, you decide whether a record whose search key equals searchKey could be in this block. You can make this determination by comparing searchKey to the smallest search key in buf—which is in buf.getRecord(0)—and to the largest search key in buf, which is in buf.getRecord(recordsPerBlock-1). If searchKey does not lie between the values of the smallest and largest search keys in buf, you must recursively search one of the halves of the file (which half to search depends on whether searchKey is less than or greater than the search keys in the block you just examined). If, on the other hand, searchKey does lie between the values of the smallest and largest search keys of the block in buf, you must

FIGURE 21-5   Shifting across block boundaries

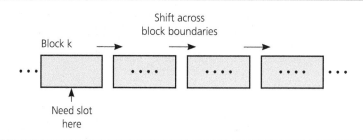

search `buf` for the record. Because the records within the block `buf` are sorted, you could use a binary search on the records within this block. However, the number of records in the block `buf` is typically small, and thus the time required to scan the block sequentially is insignificant compared to the time required to read the block from the file. It is therefore common simply to scan the block sequentially.

This external implementation is similar to the internal sorted array-based implementation of the ADT dictionary. As such, it has many of the same advantages and disadvantages. Its main advantage is that because the records are sorted sequentially, you can use a binary search to locate the block that contains a given search key. The main disadvantage of the implementation is that, as is the case with an array-based implementation, the add and `remove` operations must shift records. Shifting records in an external file is, in general, far more costly than shifting array entries. A file may contain an enormous number of large records, which are organized as several thousand blocks. As a consequence, the shifting could require a prohibitively large number of block accesses. If you add a new record to block k, for example, you must shift the records not only in block k, but also in every block after it. As a result, you must shift some records across block boundaries, as Figure 21-5 illustrates. Thus, for each of these blocks, you must read the block into internal memory, shift its records by using a statement such as

```
buf.setRecord(i+1, buf.getRecord(i))
```

and write the block to the file so that the file reflects the change. This large number of block accesses makes this external sorted implementation practical only for data collections for which additions and removals are rare.

21.2.3 Indexing an External File

Two of the best approaches to external data management utilize variations of the internal hashing and search-tree schemes presented in Chapters 18 and 19, respectively. The biggest difference between the internal and external versions of these approaches is that the external versions often have an **index** to the data file rather than an organization of the data file itself. An index to a data file is conceptually similar to other indexes with which you are familiar. For example, consider a library catalog. Rather than looking all over the library for a particular title, you can simply search the catalog. The entry for each book in the catalog contains either an indication of where on the shelves you can find the printed book or a link to the electronic version of the book (e-book).

Using a catalog to index the books in a library has at least three benefits:

* Because each catalog entry is much smaller than the book it represents, the entire catalog for a large library requires much less memory than the amount of memory occupied by the e-books.

FIGURE 21-6   A data file with an index

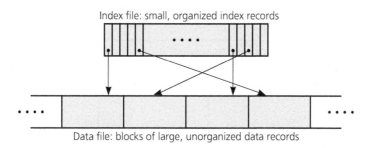

Index file: small, organized index records

Data file: blocks of large, unorganized data records

- The library can organize the printed books on the shelves or the e-books in electronic storage in any way, without regard to how easy it will be for a patron to find a particular book. To locate a particular book, the patron searches the catalog for the appropriate entry.
- The library can organize the catalog to facilitate different types of searches. For example, a patron can search the catalog by title or by author.

Now consider how you can use an index to a data file to much the same advantage as the library catalog. As Figure 21-6 illustrates, you can leave the data file in a disorganized state and maintain an organized index to it. When you need to locate a particular record in the data file, you search the index for the corresponding entry, which will tell you where to find the desired record in the data file.

An index to the data file is simply another file, called the **index file**, that contains an **index record** for each record in the data file, just as a library catalog contains an entry for each book in the library. An index record has two parts: a key, which contains the same value as the search key of its corresponding record in the data file, and a reference, which shows the number of the block in the data file that contains this data record. You thus can locate the block of the data file that contains the record whose search key equals searchKey by searching the index file for the index record whose key equals searchKey.

An index to a data file

Maintaining an index to a data file has benefits analogous to those provided by the library's catalog:

- In general, an index record will be much smaller than a data record. While the data record may contain many components, an index record contains only two: a key, which is also part of the data record, and a single integer pointer, which is the block number. Thus, an index file is only a fraction of the size of the data file. As you will see, the small size of the index file often allows you to manipulate it with fewer block accesses than you would need to manipulate the data file.

Advantages of an index file

- Because you do not need to maintain the data file in any particular order, you can add new records in any convenient location, such as at the end of the file. As you will see, this flexibility eliminates the need to shift the data records during additions and removals.

- You can maintain several indexes simultaneously. Just as a library catalog allows searches by title and by author, you can have one index file that indexes the data file by one search key (for example, an index file that consists of <name, pointer> records), and a second index file that indexes the data file by another search key (for example, an index file that consists of <socSec, pointer> records). Such **multiple indexing** is discussed briefly at the end of this chapter.

Organize the index file, but not the data file

FIGURE 21-7   A data file with a sorted index file

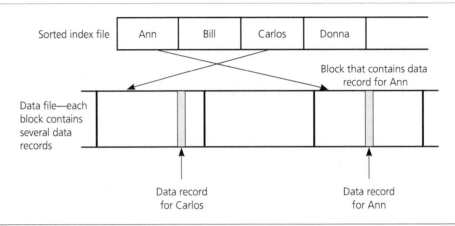

Although you do not organize the data file, you must organize the index file so that you can search and update it rapidly. Let's consider a simple organization that illustrates the concepts of indexing. In particular, let the index file simply store the index records sequentially, sorted by their keys, as shown in Figure 21-7.

To perform the retrieval operation, for example, you can use a binary search on the index file as follows:

```
// Searches the file dataFile for the record whose search key equals searchKey.
// Returns the record if found, else throws NotFoundException.
getItem(indexFile: File, dataFile: File, searchKey: KeyType): ItemType
{
    if (no blocks are left in indexFile to read)
        throw NotFoundException
    else
    {
        // Read the middle block of indexfile into object buf
        mid = number of middle block of indexFile
        buf.readBlock(indexFile, mid)

        if ((searchKey >= (buf.getRecord(0)).getKey()) &&
           (searchKey <= (buf.getRecord(indexrecordsPerBlock - 1)).getKey()))
        {
            // Desired block of index file found
            Search buf for index file record whose key value equals searchKey

            if (index record buf.getRecord(j) is found)
            {
                blockNum = number of the data-file block to which buf.getRecord(j) points
                data.readBlock(dataFile, blockNum)
                Find data record data.getRecord(k) whose search key equals searchKey
                return data.getRecord(k)
            }
            else
                throw NotFoundException
        }
    }
}
```

```
    // Else search appropriate half of index file
    else if (searchKey < (buf.getRecord(0)).getKey())
        return getItem(first half of indexFile, dataFile, searchKey)
    else
        return getItem(second half of indexFile, dataFile, searchKey)
  }
}
```

Because the index records are far smaller than the data records, the index file contains far fewer blocks than the data file. For example, if the index records are one-tenth the size of the data records and the data file contains 1,000 blocks, the index file will require only about 100 blocks. As a result, the use of an index cuts the number of block accesses in getItem down from about $\log_2 1000 \approx 10$ to about $1 + \log_2 100 \approx 8$. (The one additional block access is into the data file once you have located the appropriate index record.)

An index file reduces the number of required block accesses

The reduction in block accesses is far more dramatic for the add and remove operations. If you add a record to or remove a record from the first block of data, for example, you have to shift records in every block, requiring that you access all 1,000 blocks of the data file. (See Figure 21-5.)

However, when you add or remove a record by using the index scheme, you have to shift only index records. Because you do not keep the data file in any particular order when you use an index file, you can add a new data record into any convenient location in the data file. This flexibility means that you can simply add a new data record at the end of the file or at a position left vacant by a previous removal (as you will see). As a result, you never need to shift records in the data file. However, you do need to shift records in the index file to create an opening for a corresponding index entry in its proper sorted position. Because the index file contains many fewer blocks than the data file (100 versus 1,000 in the previous example), the maximum number of block accesses required is greatly reduced. A secondary benefit of shifting index records rather than data records is a reduction in the time requirement for a single shift. Because the index records themselves are smaller, the time required for the statement buf.setRecord(i+1, buf.getRecord(i)) is decreased.

Shift index records instead of data records

Removals under the index scheme reap similar benefits. Once you have searched the index file and located the data record to be removed, you can simply leave its location vacant in the data file, and thus you need not shift any data records. You can keep track of the vacant locations in the data file, so that you can insert new data records into the vacancies, as was mentioned earlier. The only shifting required is in the index file to fill the gap created when you remove the index record that corresponds to the removed data record.

Even though this scheme is an improvement over maintaining a sorted data file, in many applications it is far from satisfactory. The 100 block accesses that could be required to add or remove an index record often would be prohibitive. Far better implementations are possible when you use either hashing or search trees to organize the index file, as you will now see.

An unsorted data file with a sorted index is more efficient than a sorted data file, but other schemes are even better

Question 3 Trace the retrieval algorithm for an indexed external file when the search key is less than all keys in the index. Assume that the index file stores the index records sequentially, sorted by their search keys, and contains 20 blocks of 50 records each. Also assume that the data file contains 100 blocks, and that each block contains 10 employee records. List the calls to the various functions in the order in which they occur.

Question 4 Repeat Checkpoint Question 3, but this time assume that the search key equals the key in record 26 of block 12 of the index. Also assume that record 26 of the index points to block 98 of the data file.

21.2.4 External Hashing

You hash the index
file instead of the
data file

Hashing with an external file is quite similar to internal hashing, as described in Chapter 18. In the internal hashing scheme, each element of the array `table`—the hash table—contains a pointer to the beginning of a chain of data items that hash into that location. In the external hashing scheme, each element of `table` still contains a pointer to the beginning of a chain, but here each chain consists of *blocks of index records*. In other words, you hash an index file rather than the data file, as Figure 21-8 illustrates. (In many applications the array `table` is itself so large that you must keep it in external storage—for example, in the first K blocks of the index file. To avoid this extra detail, you can assume here that the array `table` is an internal array.)

FIGURE 21-8   A hashed index file

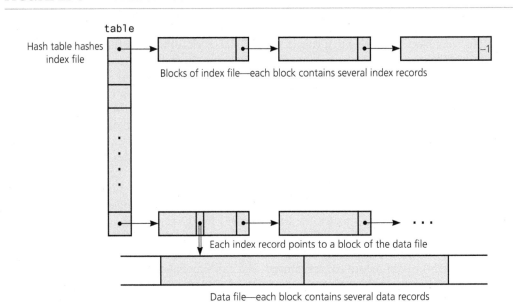

Associated with each entry `table[i]` is a linked chain of blocks of the index file, as you can see in Figure 21-8. Each block of `table[i]`'s linked chain contains index records whose keys (and thus whose corresponding data records' search keys) hash into location `i`. To form the linked chains, you must reserve space in each block for a block pointer—the integer block number of the next block in the chain—as Figure 21-9 illustrates. That is, in this linked chain the pointers are integers, not C++ pointers. A pointer value of -1 is used as a null pointer.

FIGURE 21-9   A single block with a pointer

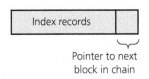

Retrieval when an index file uses external hashing. The retrieval operation appears in pseudocode as follows:

```
// Searches the data file for the record whose search key equals searchKey.
// Returns the record if found, else throws NotFoundException.
getItem(indexFile: File, dataFile: File, searchKey: KeyType): ItemType
{
   // Apply the hash function to the search key
   i = h(searchKey)

   // Find the first block in the chain of index blocks—
   // these blocks contain index records that hash into location i
   p = table[i]

   // if p == −1, no values have hashed into location i
   if (p != -1)
      buf.readBlock(indexFile, p)

   // Search for the block with the desired index record
   while (p != -1 and buf does not contain an index record whose key value equals searchKey)
   {
      p = number of next block in chain
      // if p equals −1, you are at the last block in the chain

      if (p != -1)
         buf.readBlock(indexFile, p)
   }
   // Retrieve the data item if present
   if (p != -1)
   {
      // buf.getRecord(j) is the index record whose key value equals searchKey
      blockNum = number of the data-file block to which buf.getRecord(j) points
      data.readBlock(dataFile, blockNum)
      Find data record data.getRecord(k) whose search key equals searchKey
      return data.getRecord(k)
   }
   else
      throw NotFoundException
}
```

Addition when an index file uses external hashing. The external hashing versions of the addition and removal operations are also similar to the internal hashing versions. The major difference is that, in the external environment, you must add or remove both a data record and the corresponding index record.

To add a new data record whose search key is searchKey, you take the following steps:

1. **Add the data record into the data file.** Because the data file is not ordered, the new record can go anywhere you want. If a previous removal has left a free slot in the middle of the data file, you can insert it there.

    If no slots are free, you place the new data record at the end of the last block, or, if necessary, you append a new block to the end of the data file and store the record there. In either case, let p denote the number of the block that contains this new data record.
2. **Add a corresponding index record into the index file.** You need to add to the index file an index record whose key value is searchKey and whose pointer value is p. (Recall that p is the number of the block in the data file into which you placed the new data record.) Because the index file is hashed, you first apply the hash function to searchKey, letting

    $$i = h(searchKey)$$

You then insert the index record <searchKey, p> into the chain of blocks that table[i] points to. You can insert this record into any block in the chain that contains a free slot, or, if necessary, you can allocate a new block and link it to the beginning of the chain.

Removal when an index file uses external hashing. To remove the data record whose search key is searchKey, you take the following steps:

1. **Search the index file for the corresponding index record.** You apply the hash function to searchKey, letting

   $i = h(searchKey)$

   You then search the chain of index blocks to which table[i] points for an index record whose key value equals searchKey. If you do not find such a record, you can conclude that the data file does not contain a record whose search key equals searchKey. However, if you find an index record <searchKey, p>, you remove it from the index file after noting the block number p, which indicates where in the data file you can find the data record to be removed.

2. **Remove the data record from the data file.** You know that the data record is in block p of the data file. You simply access this block, search the block for the record, remove the record, and write the block back to the file.

Observe that for each of the operations getItem, add, and remove the number of block accesses is very low. You never have to access more than one block of the data file, and at worst you have to access all of the blocks along a single hash chain of the index file. You can take measures to keep the length of each of the chains quite short (for example, one or two blocks long), just as you can with internal hashing. You should make the size of the array table large enough so that the average length of a chain is near one block, and the hash function should scatter the keys evenly. If necessary, you can even structure each chain as an external balanced search tree by using the techniques described in the next section.

The hashing implementation is the one to choose when you need to perform retrieval, addition, and removal operations on a large external data collection. As is the case with internal hashing, however, this implementation is not practical for certain other operations, such as sorted traversal, retrieval of the smallest or largest data item, and range queries that require ordered data. When these types of operations are needed, you should use a search-tree implementation—like the one in the next section—instead of hashing.

Choose external hashing for basic retrieval, addition, and removal operations

21.2.5 B-Trees

Another way to search an external data collection is to organize it as a balanced search tree. Just as you can apply external hashing to an index file, you can organize the index file, not the data file, as an external search tree. The implementation developed here is a generalization of the 2-3 tree of Chapter 19.

You can organize the blocks of an external file into a tree structure by using block numbers for child pointers. In Figure 21-10a, for example, the blocks are organized into a 2-3 tree. Each block of the file is a node in the tree and contains three child pointers, each of which is the integer block number of the child. A child pointer value of −1 plays the role of a null pointer, and thus, for example, a leaf will contain three child pointers with the value −1.

If you organized the index file into a 2-3 tree, each node (block of the index file) would contain either one or two index records, each of the form <key, pointer>, and three child pointers. The pointer portion of an index record has nothing to do with the tree structure of the index file; pointer indicates the block (in the data file) that contains the data record whose search key

Organize the index file as an external 2-3 tree

Working with External Data 683

FIGURE 21-10   An index file organized as a 2-3 tree

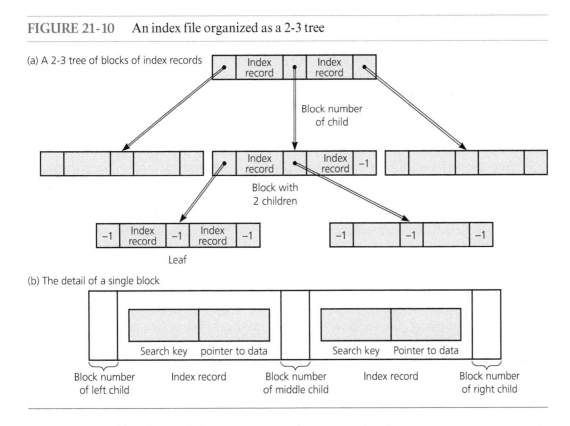

(a) A 2-3 tree of blocks of index records

Block number of child

Block with 2 children

Leaf

(b) The detail of a single block

Search key   pointer to data

Search key   Pointer to data

Block number of left child

Index record

Block number of middle child

Index record

Block number of right child

equals key. (See Figure 21-10b.) To help avoid confusion, the pointers in the tree structure of the index file will be referred to as child pointers.

You must organize the index records in the tree so that their keys obey the same search-tree ordering property as an internal 2-3 tree. This organization allows you to retrieve the data record whose search key has a given value, as follows:

```
// Searches the data file for the record whose search key equals searchKey.
// Returns the record if found, else throws NotFoundException.
// rootNum is the block number (of the index file) that contains the root of the tree.
getItem(indexFile: File, dataFile: File, rootNum: integer,
        searchKey: KeyType): ItemType
{
    if (no blocks are left in the index file to read)
        throw NotFoundException
    else
    {
        // Read from index file into internal array buf the block that contains the root of the 2-3 tree
        buf.readBlock(indexFile, rootNum)

        // Search for the index record whose key value equals searchKey
        if (searchKey is in the root)
        {
            blockNum = number of the data-file block that index record specifies
            data.readBlock(dataFile, blockNum)
            Find data record data.getRecord(k) whose search key equals searchKey
            return data.getRecord(k)
        }
```

```
                    // Else search the appropriate subtree
        else if (the root is a leaf)
            throw NotFoundException
        else
        {
            child = block number of root of appropriate subtree
            return getItem(indexFile, dataFile, child, searchKey)
        }
    }
}
```

You can perform additions and removals in a manner similar to those in the internal version, but you also must add records to and remove records from both the index file and the data file (as was the case in the external hashing scheme described earlier). In the course of adding to and removing from the index file, you must split and merge nodes of the tree just as you do for the internal version. You perform additions to and removals from the data file—which, recall, is not ordered in any way—exactly as described for the external hashing implementation. You thus can support these operations fairly well by using an external version of the 2-3 tree.

However, you can generalize the 2-3 tree to a structure that is even more suitable for an external environment. Recall the discussion in Chapter 19 about search trees whose nodes can have many children. Adding more children per node reduces the height of the search tree but increases the number of comparisons at each node during the search for a value.

In an external environment, however, the advantage of keeping a search tree short far outweighs the disadvantage of performing extra work at each node. As you traverse the search tree in an external environment, you must perform a block access for each node visited. Because the time required to access a block of an external file is, in general, far greater than the time required to process the data in that block once it has been read in, the overriding concern is to reduce the number of block accesses required. This fact implies that you should attempt to reduce the height of the tree, even at the expense of requiring more comparisons at each node. In an external search tree, you should thus allow each node to have as many children as possible, with only the block size as a limiting factor.

How many children can a block of some fixed size accommodate? If a node is to have m children, clearly you must be able to fit m child pointers in the node. In addition to child pointers, however, the node must also contain index records. Before you can answer the question of how many children a block can accommodate, you must first consider this related question: If a node N in a search tree has m children, how many key values—and thus how many index records—must it contain?

In a binary search tree, if the node N has two children, it must contain one key value K_1, as Figure 21-11a indicates. You can think of the key value in node N as separating the key values in N's two subtrees—all of the key values in N's left subtree are less than N's key value, and all of the key values in N's right subtree are greater than N's key value. When you are searching the tree for a given key value, the key value in N tells you which branch to take.

Similarly, if a node N in a 2-3 tree has three children, it must contain two key values, K_1 and K_2, with $K_1 < K_2$. (See Figure 21-11b.) These two values separate the key values in N's three subtrees—all of the key values in the left subtree are less than N's smaller key value K_1, all of the key values in N's middle subtree lie between N's two key values, and all of the key values in N's right subtree are greater than N's larger key value K_2. As is the case with a binary search tree, this requirement allows a search algorithm to know which branch to take at any given node.

In general, if a node N in a search tree is to have m children, it must contain $m - 1$ key values to separate the values in its subtrees correctly. (See Figure 21-11c.) Suppose that you denote the subtrees of N as S_0, S_1, and so on to S_{m-1} and denote the key values in N as K_1, K_2, and so on to K_{m-1} (with $K_1 < K_2 < \cdots < K_{m-1}$). The key values in N must separate the values in its subtrees as follows:

FIGURE 21-11   Nodes with two, three, and *m* children and their search keys

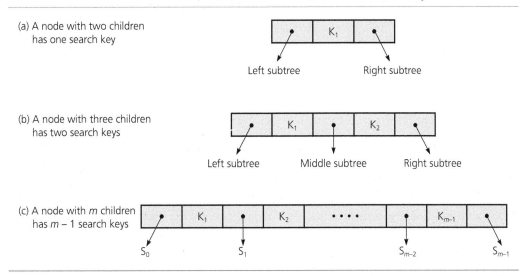

(a) A node with two children
has one search key

K_1

Left subtree   Right subtree

(b) A node with three children
has two search keys

K_1 K_2

Left subtree   Middle subtree   Right subtree

(c) A node with *m* children
has *m* − 1 search keys

K_1 K_2 · · · · · K_{m-1}

S_0 S_1 S_{m-2} S_{m-1}

- All the values in subtree S_0 must be less than the key value K_1.
- For all *i*, $1 \le i \le m - 2$, all the values in subtree S_i must lie between the key values K_i and K_{i+1}.
- All the values in subtree S_{m-1} must be greater than the key value K_{m-1}.

If every node in the tree obeys this property, you can search the tree by using a generalized version of a search tree's retrieval algorithm as follows:

```
// Searches the data file for the record whose search key equals searchKey.
// Returns the record if found, else throws NotFoundException.
getItem(indexFile: File, dataFile: File, rootNum: integer,
        searchKey: KeyType): ItemType
{
    if (no blocks are left in the index file to read)
        throw NotFoundException

    else
    {   // Read from index file into internal array buf the
        // block that contains the root of the tree
        buf.readBlock(indexFile, rootNum)

        // Search for the index record whose key value equals searchKey

        if (searchKey is one of the K_i in the root)
        {
            blockNum = number of the data-file block that index record specifies
            data.readBlock(dataFile, blockNum)
            Find data record data.getRecord(k) whose search key equals searchKey
            return data.getRecord(k)
        }

        // Else search the appropriate subtree
        else if (the root is a leaf)
            throw NotFoundException
```

Retrieval with a general external search tree

```
        else
        {
            Find the subtree Sᵢ to search
            child = block number of the root of Sᵢ
            return getItem(indexFile, dataFile, child, searchKey)
        }
    }
}
```

Now return to the question of how many children the nodes of the search tree can have—that is, how big can m be? If you wish to organize the index file into a search tree, the items that you store in each node will be records of the form <key, pointer>. Thus, if each node in the tree (which, recall, is a block of the index file) is to have m children, it must be large enough to accommodate m child pointers and $m - 1$ records of the form <key, pointer>. You should choose m to be the largest integer such that m child pointers (which, recall, are integers) and $m - 1$ <key, pointer> records can fit into a single block of the file. Actually, the algorithms are somewhat simplified if you always choose an odd number for m. That is, you should choose m to be the largest odd integer such that m child pointers and $m - 1$ index records can fit into a single block.

Number of children
per node
Ideally, then, you should structure the external search tree so that every internal node has m children, where m is chosen as just described, and all leaves are at the same level, as is the case with full trees and 2-3 trees. For example, Figure 21-12 shows a full tree whose internal nodes each have five children. Although this search tree has the minimum possible height, its balance is too difficult to maintain when adding or removing nodes. As a consequence, you must make a compromise. You can still insist that all the leaves of the search tree be at the same level—that is, that the tree be balanced—but you must allow each internal node to have between m and $[m/2] + 1$ children. (The [ ] notation means *greatest integer in*. Thus, [5/2] is 2, for example.)

FIGURE 21-12   A full tree whose internal nodes have five children

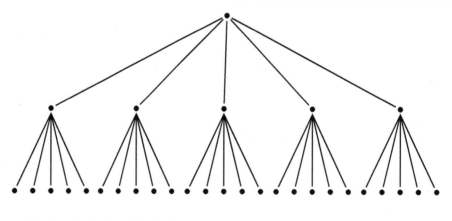

The format of each node in the above tree

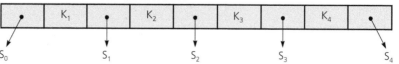

This type of search tree is known as a **B-tree of degree** *m* and has the following characteristics:

- All leaves are at the same level.
- Each node contains between $m - 1$ and $\lceil m/2 \rceil$ records, and each internal node has one more child than it has records. An exception to this rule is that the root of the tree can contain as few as one record and can have as few as two children. This exception is necessitated by the addition and removal algorithms described next.

Notice that a 2-3 tree is also a B-tree of degree 3. Furthermore, the manner in which the B-tree addition and removal algorithms maintain the structure of the tree is a direct generalization of the 2-3 tree's strategy of splitting and merging nodes. These algorithms are illustrated next by means of an example. Assume that the index file is organized into a B-tree of degree 5—that is, 5 is the maximum and 3 is the minimum number of children that an internal node—other than the root—in the tree can have. (Typically, a B-tree will be of a higher degree, but the diagrams would get out of hand!)

Adding a record to a B-tree.   To add a data record with search key 55 into the tree shown in Figure 21-13, you take the following steps:

1. **Add the data record to the data file.** First you find block p in the data file into which you can insert the new record. As was true with the external hashing implementation, block p is either any block with a vacant slot or a new block.
2. **Add a corresponding index record to the index file.** You now must add the index record <55, p> to the index file, which is a B-tree of degree 5. The first step is to locate the leaf of the tree in which this index record belongs by determining where the search for 55 would terminate.

   Suppose that this is the leaf *L* shown in Figure 21-14a. Conceptually, you insert the new index record into *L*, causing it to contain five records (Figure 21-14b). Since a node can contain only four records, you must split *L* into L_1 and L_2. With an action analogous to the splitting of a node in a 2-3 tree, L_1 gets the two records with the smallest key values, L_2 gets the two records with the largest key values, and the record with the middle key value (56) is moved up to the parent *P*. (See Figure 21-14c.)

FIGURE 21-13   A B-tree of degree 5

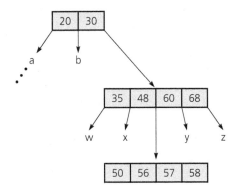

FIGURE 21-14 (a through d) The steps for adding 55 to a B-tree; (e) splitting the root

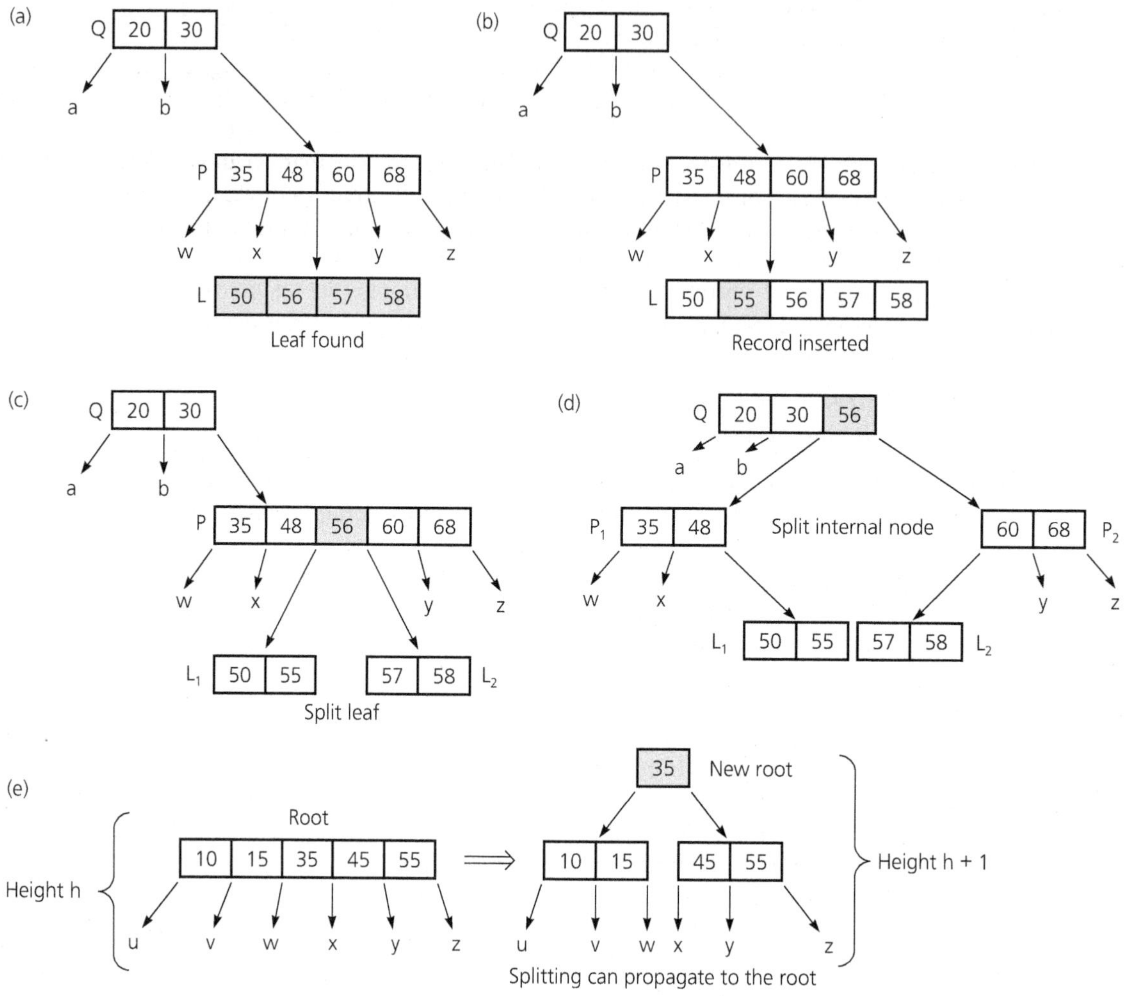

In this example, *P* now has six children and five records, so it must be split into P_1 and P_2. The record with the middle key value (56) is moved up to *P*'s parent, *Q*. Then *P*'s children must be distributed appropriately, as happens with a 2-3 tree when an internal node is split. (See Figure 21-14d.)

At this point the addition is complete, as *P*'s parent *Q* now contains only three records and has only four children. In general, though, an addition might cause splitting to propagate all the way up to the root (Figure 21-14e). If the root must be split, the new root will contain only one record and have only two children—the definition of a B-tree allows for this eventuality.

Removing a record from a B-tree. To remove a data record with a given search key from a B-tree, you take the following steps:

1. **Locate the index record in the index file.** You use the search algorithm to locate the index record with the desired key value. If this record is not already in a leaf, you swap the

record with its inorder successor. Suppose that the leaf L shown in Figure 21-15a contains the index record with the desired key value, 73. After noting the value p of the pointer in this index record (you will need p in step 2 to remove the data record), you remove the index record from L (Figure 21-15b). Because L now contains only one value (recall that a node must contain at least two values), and since L's siblings cannot spare a value, you merge L with one of the siblings and bring down a record from the parent P (Figure 21-15c). Notice that this step is analogous to the merge step for a 2-3 tree. However, P now has only one value and two children, and since its siblings cannot spare a record and child, you must merge P with its sibling P_1 and bring a record down from $P's$ parent, Q. Because P is an internal node, its children must be adopted by P_1. (See Figure 21-15d.)

After this merge, P's parent Q is left with only two children and one record. In this case, however, Q's sibling Q_1 can spare a record and a child, so you redistribute children and records among Q_1, Q and the parent S to complete the removal. (See Figure 21-15e.) If a removal ever propagates all the way up to the root, leaving it with only one record and only two children, you are finished because the definition of a B-tree allows this situation. If a future removal causes the root to have a single child and no records, you remove the root so that the tree's height decreases by 1, as Figure 21-15f illustrates. The removal of the index record is complete, and you now must remove the data record.

FIGURE 21-15   (a through e) The steps for removing 73 ; (f) removing the root

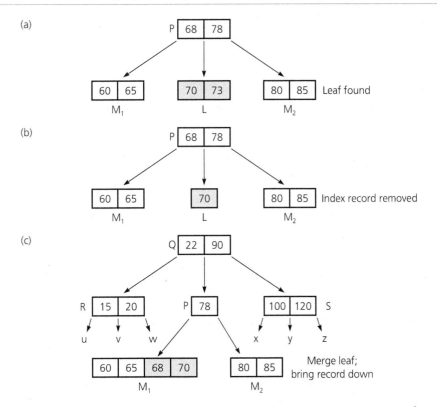

(continues)

FIGURE 21-15   (a through e) The steps for removing 73 ; (f) removing the root (*continued*)

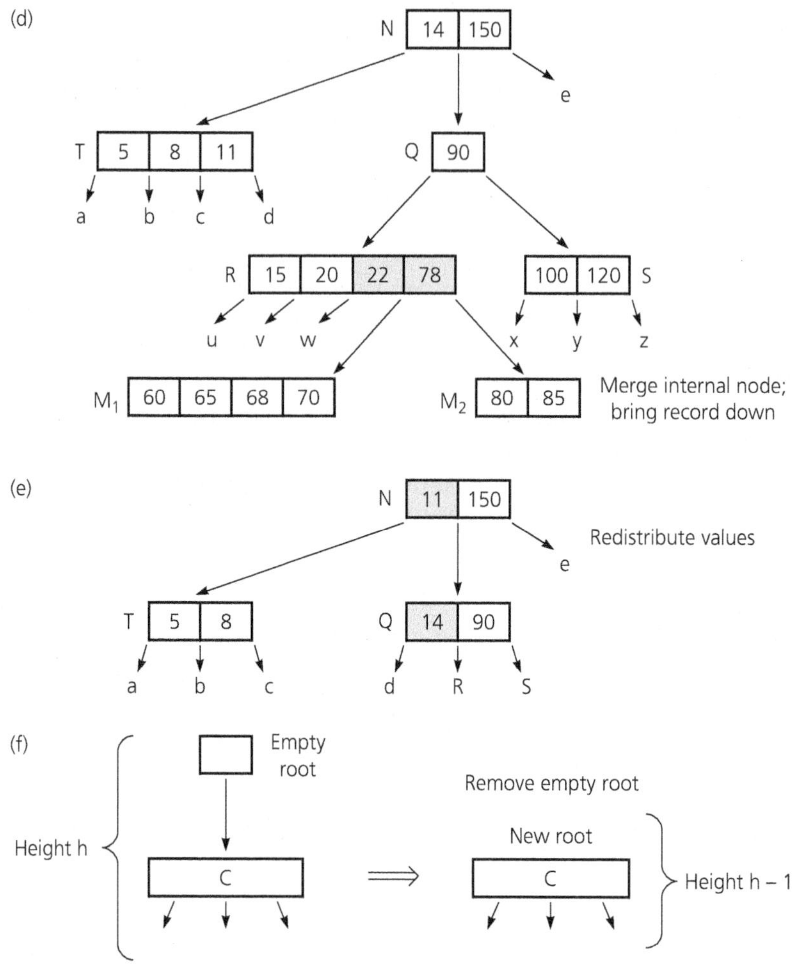

(d)

(e)

(f)

2. **Remove the data record from the data file.** Prior to removing the index record from the index file, you noted the value p of its pointer. You now know that block p of the data file contains the data record to be removed. Thus, you simply access block p, remove the data record, and write the block back to the file. The high-level pseudocode for the addition and removal algorithms parallels that of the 2-3 tree and is left as an exercise.

21.2.6 Traversals

Access the search key of each index record, but not the data record

Now consider the operation traverse in sorted order. Often an application requires only that the traversal display the search keys of the records. If such is the case, the B-tree implementation can efficiently support the operation, because you can access the search keys in the index file; that is, you do not have to access the data file.

You can visit the index file's search keys in sorted order by using an inorder traversal of the B-tree, as follows:

Inorder traversal of
a B-tree index file

```
// Traverses in sorted order the search keys in an index file that is organized as a B-tree of
// degree m. blockNum is the block number of the root of the B-tree in the index file.
traverse(blockNum: integer, m: integer): void
{
    if (blockNum != -1)
    {
        // Read the root into internal array buf
        buf.readBlock(indexFile, blockNum)

        // Traverse the children

        // Traverse S₀
        Let p be the block number of the 0-th child of buf
        traverse(p, m)

        for (i = 1 through m - 1)
        {
            Display key Kᵢ of buf

            // Traverse Sᵢ
            Let p be the block number of the i-th child of buf
            traverse(p, m)
        }
    }
}
```

This traversal accomplishes the task with the minimum possible number of block accesses because each block of the index file is read only once. This algorithm, however, assumes that enough internal memory is available for a recursive stack of h blocks, where h is the height of the tree. In many situations this assumption is reasonable—for example, a 255-degree B-tree that indexes a file of 16 million data records has a height of no more than 3. When internal memory cannot accommodate h blocks, you must use a different algorithm. (See Exercise 12.)

If the traversal must display the entire data record (and not just the search key), the B-tree implementation is less attractive. In this case, as you traverse the B-tree in the index file, you also must access the appropriate block of the data file. The traversal becomes

Accessing the entire
data record

Sorted-order
traversal of a data
file indexed with a
B-tree

```
// Traverses in sorted order a data file that is indexed with a B-tree of degree m.
// blockNum is the block number of the root of the B-tree.
traverse(blockNum: integer, m: integer): void
{
    if (blockNum != -1)
    {
        // Read the root into internal array buf
        buf.readBlock(indexFile, blockNum)
        // Traverse S₀
        Let p be the block number of the 0-th child of buf
        traverse(p, m)

        for (i = 1 through m - 1)
        {
            Let p_i be the pointer in the i-th index record of buf
            data.readBlock(dataFile, p_i)
            Extract from data the data record whose search key equals Kᵢ
            Display the data record

            // Traverse Sᵢ
            Let p be block number of the i-th child of buf
            traverse(p, m)
        }
    }
}
```

Generally, the previous traversal is unacceptable

This traversal requires you to read both the index file and the data file. Since you must read a block of the data file before you display each data record, the number of data-file block accesses is equal to the number of data records. In general, such a large number of block accesses would not be acceptable. If you must perform this type of traversal frequently, you probably would modify the B-tree scheme so that the data file itself was kept nearly sorted.

21.2.7 Multiple Indexing

Before concluding the discussion of managing external data, let's consider the multiple indexing of a data file. Programming Problem 6 in Chapter 16 asked you to support multiple organizations for data stored in internal memory. Such a problem is also common for data stored externally. For example, suppose that a data file contains a collection of employee records on which you need to perform two types of retrievals:

    // *Retrieves the data item whose search key contains the name* aName.
    retrieveN(aName: NameType): ItemType

    // *Retrieves the data item whose search key contains the Social Security Number* ssn.
    retrieveS(ssn: SSNType): ItemType

Multiple index files allow multiple data organizations

One solution to this problem is to maintain two independent index files to the data file. For example, you could have one index file that contains index records of the form <name, pointer> and a second index file that contains index records of the form <socSec, pointer>. These index files could both be hashed, could both be B-trees, or could be one of each, as Figure 21-16 indicates. The choice would depend on the operations you wanted to perform with each search key. Similarly, if an application required extremely fast retrievals by Social Security number and also required sorted traversals and range queries by Social Security number, it might be reasonable to have two index files—one hashed, the other a B-tree.

FIGURE 21-16   Multiple index files

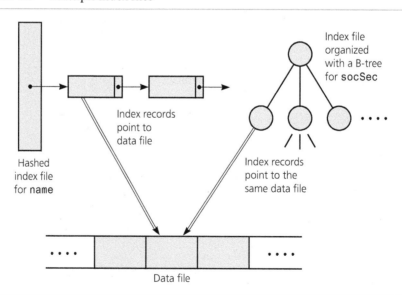

Although you can perform each retrieval operation by using only one of the indexes (that is, use the name index for retrieveN and the socSec index for retrieveS), addition and removal operations must update both indexes. For example, the remove-by-name operation removeN(jones) requires the following steps:

1. Search the name index file for jones and remove the index record.
2. Remove the appropriate data record from the data file, noting the socSec value ssn of this record.
3. Search the socSec index file for ssn and remove this index record.

A removal by name must update both indexes

In general, the price paid for multiple indexing is more storage space and an additional overhead for updating each index whenever you modify the data file.

This chapter has presented at a very high level the basic principles of managing data in external storage. The details of implementing the algorithms depend heavily on your specific computing system. Particular situations often mandate either variations of the techniques described here or completely different approaches. In future courses and work experience, you will undoubtedly learn much more about these techniques.

SUMMARY

1. An external file is partitioned into blocks. Each block typically contains many data records, and a block is generally the smallest unit of transfer between internal and external memory. That is, to access a record, you must access the block that contains it.

2. You can access the ith block of a direct access file without accessing the blocks that precede it. In this sense direct access files resemble arrays.

3. Before you can process (for example, inspect or update) a record, you must read it from an external file into internal memory. Once you modify a record, you must write it back to the file.

4. Block accesses are typically quite slow when compared to other computer operations. Therefore, you must carefully organize a file so that you can perform tasks by using only a few block accesses. Otherwise, response time can be very poor.

5. You can modify the merge sort algorithm, presented in Chapter 11, so that it can sort an external file of records without requiring all of the records to be in internal memory at one time.

6. An index to a data file is a file that contains an index record for each record in the data file. An index record contains both the search key of the corresponding data record and the number of the block in the data file that contains the data record.

7. If a record is added to or removed from a data file, you must make the corresponding change to the index file. If a data file has more than one index file, you must update each index file. Thus, multiple indexing has an overhead.

8. You can organize an index file by using either hashing or a B-tree. These schemes allow you to perform the basic data-management operations by using only a few block accesses.

9. Although external hashing generally permits retrievals, additions, and removals to be performed faster than does a B-tree, it does not support such operations as sorted traversals or range queries. This deficiency is one motivation for multiple indexing.

10. You can have several index files for the same data file. Such multiple indexing allows you to perform different types of operations efficiently, such as retrieval by name and retrieval by Social Security number.

Exercises

1. Assuming the existence of `readBlock` and `writeBlock` functions, write a pseudocode program for shifting data to make a gap at some specified location of a sorted external file. Pay particular attention to the details of shifting the last item out of one block and into the first position of the next block. You can assume that the last record of the file is in record `lastRec` of block `lastBlock` and that `lastBlock` is not full. (Note that this assumption permits shifting without allocating a new block to the file.)

2. The problem of managing the blocks of an external data file indexed by either a B-tree or an external hashing scheme is similar to that of managing memory for internal structures. When an external structure such as a data file needs more memory (for example, to add a new record), it gets a new block from a free list that the system manages. That is, if the file contains n blocks, the system can allocate to it an $(n + 1)^{th}$ block. When the file no longer needs a block, you can deallocate it and return it to the system.

   The complication in the management of external storage is that a block allocated to a file may have available space interspersed with data. For example, after you have removed a record from a data file, the block that contained that record will have space available for at least one record. Therefore, you must be able to keep track of blocks that have space available for one or more records as well as recognize when blocks are completely empty (so that you can return them to the system).

   Assuming the existence of the functions `allocateBlock` and `returnBlock` that get empty blocks from and return empty blocks to the system, write pseudocode implementations of the following external memory-management functions:

   ```
   // Determines the block number (blockNum) and record number (recNum) of an available slot in file
   // dataFile. A new block is allocated to the file from the system if necessary.
   getSlot(dataFile: File, blockNum: integer, recNum: integer): void

   // Makes record recNum in block blockNum of file dataFile available.
   // The block is returned to the system if it becomes empty.
   freeSlot(dataFile: File, blockNum: integer, recNum: integer): void
   ```

   What data structure is appropriate to support these operations? You may assume that you can distinguish slots of a block that do not contain a record from those that do. You can make this distinction either by having a convention for null values within a record or by adding an empty/full flag.

3. Describe pseudocode algorithms for adding a record to and removing a record from an external data file that has a hashed index file.

4. Execute the following sequence of operations on an initially empty B-tree of degree 5. Note that addition to an empty B-tree will create a single node that contains the added item.

   ```
   bTree.add(10)
   bTree.add(100)
   bTree.add(30)
   bTree.add(80)
   bTree.add(50)
   bTree.remove(10)
   bTree.add(60)
   bTree.add(70)
   bTree.add(40)
   bTree.remove(80)
   bTree.add(90)
   bTree.add(20)
   bTree.remove(30)
   bTree.remove(70)
   ```

5. Given a B-tree of degree 5 and a height of 3,

   a. What is the maximum number of nodes (including the root) in the B-tree?

   b. What is the maximum number of records that can be stored?

FIGURE 21-17   A B-tree for Exercise 6

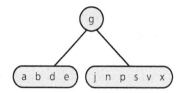

FIGURE 21-18   A B-tree for Exercise 7

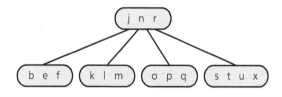

6. Given the B-tree of degree 7 in Figure 21-17, draw the B-tree that results after the addition of *m, o, y, r, c, i, k, w,* and *h.*

7. Given the B-tree of degree 7 in Figure 21-18, draw the B-tree that results after the removal of *s, t, p, m, k,* and *e.*

8. Describe a pseudocode algorithm for finding an item's inorder successor in an external B-tree.

9. Describe pseudocode algorithms for adding entries to and removing entries from an ADT dictionary implemented with an index file organized as a B-tree.

10. Write a rangeQuery function for a B-tree in pseudocode. (See Exercise 4 of Chapter 19.) Assume that only the search keys are needed (as opposed to the entire data record).

11. Integrate calls to the appropriate memory-management functions (see Exercise 2) into the pseudocode for add and remove under both the B-tree and hashing schemes. (See Exercises 3 and 9.)

12. The B-tree traversal algorithm presented in this chapter assumes that internal memory is large enough to accommodate the recursive stack that contains up to *h* blocks, where *h* is the height of the B-tree. If you are in an environment where this assumption is not true, modify the traversal algorithm so that the recursive stack contains block numbers rather than the actual blocks. How many block accesses does your algorithm have to perform?

13. Consider an external data file whose index file is organized as a B-tree.

    a. Write pseudocode B-tree implementations of traversals and range queries that need to access entire data records, not simply the search keys. How many block accesses do your functions require?

    b. To reduce the number of block accesses required by these operations, various modifications of the basic B-tree structure are frequently used. The central idea behind such structures is to keep the data file itself sorted. First, assume that you can keep the data file in sequential sorted order—that is, the records are sorted within each block and the records in block B_{i-1} are less than the records in B_i for $i = 2$, 3, and so on to the number of blocks in the file. Rewrite your implementations of the traversal and range-query operations to take advantage of this fact. How many block accesses do these operations now require?

c. Because it is too inefficient to maintain a sequentially sorted data file in the face of frequent additions and removals, a compromise scheme is often employed. One such possible compromise is as follows. If a data record belongs in block *B* and *B* is full, a new block is allocated and linked to *B*, allowing the new record to be inserted into its proper sorted location. The difficulty is that you must now view each index record in the B-tree as indicating the first of possibly several blocks in a chain of blocks that might contain the corresponding data record. Rewrite the `add`, `remove`, `getItem`, `traverse`, and `rangeQuery` operations in terms of this implementation. What is the effect on their efficiency?

14. Write an iterative (nonrecursive) version of the internal merge sort, as given in Chapter 11, that is based on the external version that this chapter describes.

PROGRAMMING PROBLEMS

1. Consider the `externalMergesort` algorithm given in Section 21.2.1.

   a. Implement the algorithm in C++ by using the functions `seekg` and `seekp`. Assume that the file to be sorted is a file of type `int` and that each block contains one integer. Further assume that the file contains 2^n integers for some integer *n*.

   b. Now assume that each block contains many integers. Write C++ functions that simulate `read-Block` and `writeBlock`. Implement `externalMergesort` by using these functions.

   c. Extend your implementation of `externalMergesort` by removing the restriction that the file contains 2^n blocks.

2. Implement the ADT dictionary by using a sorted index file, as described in Section 21.2.3.

3. Implement an ADT dictionary that uses a sorted index file using the STL `map` container.

4. Implement a simple dictionary application, such as the one described in Exercise 4 of Chapter 18, using the external dictionary of Programming Problem 3.

5. Implement the ADT dictionary by using a hashed index file, as described in Section 21.2.4.

6. Implement the ADT dictionary by using a B-tree, as described in Section 21.2.5.

7. Repeat Programming Problem 8 of Chapter 18, using an external dictionary.

C++
Interlude

8

The Standard Template Library

Contents

The STL contains many ready-made classes and functions and is included with any C++ library implementation. This interlude gives an overview of some useful methods available with each of the STL containers and in the STL algorithms library. It also highlights many of the similarities and differences in the various container classes, but does not attempt to describe the entire library.

VideoNote
C++ STL

C8.1 STL Containers

Throughout this text we have been designing and implementing classes of objects that hold collections of other objects. As Chapter 1 mentions, such objects are called *containers*. We will use the term **container class** to mean a class of containers. Each container was inspired by a problem to solve and was designed to efficiently solve that specific problem. While we can use each container in a variety of situations, we need to consider the strengths and weaknesses of each one when choosing which to use.

C++ comes with a library of container classes that implement many of the more commonly used ADTs. These classes are in the form of a **template**, or **class template**, and are defined in the **Standard Template Library**, or **STL**. A template defines a family of classes having similar functionality but various data types, such as List<int>, List<double>, and so on. Many of the ADTs that are presented in this text have a corresponding class template in the STL. For example, the STL defines a stack class that is similar to the class LinkedStack presented in Chapter 7. Just like the ADTs we designed, each template in the STL has strengths and weaknesses that you need to consider when deciding which one to use.

You may wonder why we spent so much time developing ADTs in this text if they are already provided in the STL. There are many reasons for doing so; here are just a few:

- Developing simple ADTs provides a foundation for learning to develop other ADTs, especially ones that are not in the STL.
- STL container classes are not part of a class hierarchy and so cannot take advantage of polymorphism in the same way our ADTs can.
- You might find yourself working in a language that does not provide any predefined classes. You need to have the ability to develop ADTs on your own, and hence you must understand the process.
- If the ADTs defined by the language you are using are insufficient, you may need to develop your own or enhance existing ones.

The STL provides support for predefined classes through the use of three basic items: containers, iterators, and algorithms. Containers are objects, such as a list, that hold other objects. Iterators provide a way to cycle through the contents of a container and are described in C++ Interlude 7. Algorithms, such as a sorting algorithm, act on containers. STL container classes are implemented as class templates, similar to the way we implemented the ADTs in this text.

You already are familiar with one STL class—the class vector—which we used in Chapter 3 to implement the ADT bag method toVector. Moreover, many programmers use the STL class template vector instead of arrays as a simple way to store multiple items of a similar type.

By using the STL, you can create three types of containers:

- **Container adapters** provide efficient, restricted, position-based access to the collection. They are considered adapters because they use other STL containers to implement their operations.
- **Sequence containers** provide efficient sequential access to the collection. The containers in this group provide various trade-offs in efficiency for additions and removals.
- **Associative containers** provide efficient key-based access to the collection. Each of these containers organizes and accesses the search keys to provide efficient groups of operations.

Each container type implements similar operations, but with a different emphasis in efficiency. You'll find that many of these operations have corresponding methods in the ADTs that we defined in this text, but the STL names might be different.

Two methods that all STL containers define are empty and size. These correspond to isEmpty and getLength, respectively, in this book's ADTs. The maximum number of entries that either a sequence container or an associative container can hold is known as the **container size**. If the container is empty, not only does it not have any entries, but it cannot hold any. To add a new entry to the container, you must either use one of the methods that increases the container size during the add operation or, in the case of sequence containers, resize the container using

OPERATIONS COMMON TO ALL STL CONTAINERS		
METHOD	DESCRIPTION	EFFICIENCY
Constructor	Creates a container; sequence containers allow the user to specify an initial size.	Varies
Destructor	Deallocates all entries in the container, and then deallocates the container.	$O(n)$
operator=	Assigns entries in the container on the right-hand side to the container on the left-hand side.	$O(n)$
bool empty()	Returns true if the container is empty (size is 0).	$O(1)$
uint[1] size()	Returns the number of locations in the container, that is, its capacity.	$O(1)$

[1] uint is the data type for an unsigned integer.

the `resize` method. Note that the behavior of removal operations is undefined when they fail, but most major C++ compilers throw an exception in this situation.

To use one of the STL classes, you must include the appropriate header file, which has the same name as the STL class. So to use the class `stack`, for example, your code must have the following statement:

```
#include <stack>
```

To instantiate an STL container, you must supply the type of item it will hold, just as we did for our ADTs. For example, the following statement creates a vector that can hold 10 strings:

```
vector<string> cities(10); // Create a vector to hold 10 strings
```

All STL containers are part of the `std::` namespace. Therefore, if you do not use the statement

```
using namespace std;
```

in your code, you must precede any reference to the container with `std::` as shown here;

```
std::vector<std::string> cities(10); // Create a vector to hold 10 strings
```

In our ADTs, we used `ItemType` to represent the data type of the item stored in the collection. The STL header files use `value_type` or simply `T` instead. If the entries in the collection have search keys and values, much like those in our ADT dictionary, the STL uses `key_type` and `mapped_type`, respectively, for their data types.

C8.1.1 STL Container Adapters

The STL container adapter classes are `stack`, `queue`, and `priority_queue`. These correspond to the ADTs stack, queue, and priority queue and are optimized so that the operations listed below perform at O(1). These containers grow to accommodate new entries as the entries are added. When entries are removed, the size of the container decreases. Thus, each of these containers has a size exactly equal to its current number of entries.

STL STACK OPERATIONS	
METHOD	DESCRIPTION
`value_type& top()`	Returns a reference to the top entry on the stack.
`void push(value_type& item)`	Adds `item` to the top of the stack.
`void pop()`	Removes the top entry from the stack.

STL QUEUE OPERATIONS	
METHOD	DESCRIPTION
`value_type& front()`	Returns a reference to the front entry in the queue.
`value_type& back()`	Returns a reference to the last (back) entry in the queue.
`void push(value_type& item)`	Adds `item` to the back of the queue.
`void pop()`	Removes the front entry from the queue.

STL PRIORITY_QUEUE OPERATIONS	
METHOD	DESCRIPTION
`value_type& top()`	Returns a reference to the front entry in the priority queue.
`void push(value_type& item)`	Adds `item` to the priority queue.
`void pop()`	Removes the front entry from the priority queue.

Listing C8-1 provides an example of how to use the STL `stack`.

LISTING C8-1 Example use of the STL `stack`

```cpp
1   #include <iostream>
2   #include <stack>
3
4   int main()
5   {
6      std::stack<int> aStack;
7
8      // Right now, the stack is empty
9      if (aStack.empty())
10        std::cout << "The stack is empty." << std::endl;
11
12     for (int j = 0; j < 5; j++)
13        aStack.push(j); // Places items on top of stack
14
15     while (!aStack.empty())
16     {
17        std::cout << aStack.top() << " ";
18        aStack.pop();
19     } // end while
20
21     return 0;
22  } // end main
```

Output

```
The stack is empty.
 4 3 2 1 0
```

C8.1.2 Sequence Containers

The entries in a sequence container are ordered in a linear sequence and can be accessed, added to, and removed by position. Similar to the arrangement in traditional arrays, the positions in sequence containers are numbered from 0 to $size - 1$. The **front** of these containers is at position 0, and the **back** is at position $size - 1$.

The STL sequence containers are: `array`, `vector`, `deque`, `list`, and `forward_list`. Let's consider each of these containers.

The sequence container `array`. As part of the C++11 standard, the STL array provides a fixed-size container that is implemented as a traditional array, so unlike other STL containers, an STL array container cannot grow or shrink in size. You can access individual elements in an STL array just as you access elements in a traditional array, by using the operator `[ ]`.

An advantage of an STL array over traditional C++ arrays is the method at that allows for range checking. For example, a traditional array declared as

```
int myArray[5];
```

permits the programmer to access elements beyond the memory allocated to the array by using an expression such as myArray[24]. This leads to unpredictable results and is a common source of errors in a program. Although an STL array declared as

```
std::array<int> mySTLArray(5);
```

would have the same issue if the programmer used the expression mySTLArray[24], the expression mySTLArray.at(24) would throw an out_of_bounds exception that you could catch. In this way, you could fix the error and allow the program to continue execution safely.

Two other important features of the STL array are its size method—which returns the array's capacity—and the availability of iterators for array traversal, as discussed in C++ Interlude 7.

STL ARRAY OPERATIONS		
METHOD	DESCRIPTION	EFFICIENCY
value_type& front()	Returns a reference to the first (front) entry in the array.	O(1)
value_type& back()	Returns a reference to the last (back) entry in the array.	O(1)
value_type& at(size_type n)	Behaves the same as [ ], but performs a bounds check.	O(1)
void fill(const value_type& val)	Fills array elements with the value val.	O(n)
iterator begin()	Returns an iterator that begins at the first element of the array.	O(1)
iterator end()	Returns an iterator that begins at the last element of the array.	O(1)
reverse_iterator rbegin()	Returns a reverse iterator that begins at the last element of the array.	O(1)
reverse_iterator rend()	Returns a reverse iterator that begins at the first element of the array.	O(1)

Other STL sequence containers have many methods in common but are optimized differently. For example, vector and deque permit efficient access to specific locations using the [ ] operator, but list is better for sorting and merging because it has methods to do so. Though these containers can be constructed with an initial capacity, they also grow and shrink as entries are added and removed. If you realize that you need to add a significant number of entries to the container, a resize method lets you adjust its capacity.

OPERATIONS COMMON TO STL SEQUENCE CONTAINERS		
METHOD	DESCRIPTION	EFFICIENCY
value_type& front()	Returns a reference to the first (front) entry in the container.	O(1)
value_type& back()	Returns a reference to the last (back) entry in the container.	O(1)

(continues)

`void push_back(value_type& item)`	Appends `item` onto the back of the container, and increases the container's capacity by 1.	O(1)
`void pop_back(value_type& item)`	Removes the back entry from the container, and decreases the container's capacity by 1.	O(1)
`void resize(uint newSize)`	Changes the container's capacity to `newSize`.	O(*n*)
`void clear()`	Deallocates all entries in the container, and changes its capacity to 0.	O(*n*)
`void insert(uint position,` `            value_type& item)`	Adds `item` to the container at the given position and increases the container's capacity by 1.	Varies
`void insert(iterator itPosition,` `            value_type& item)`	Adds `item` to the container at the current position of the iterator `itPosition` and increases the container's capacity by 1.	Varies
`void erase(uint position)`	Removes from the container the entry at the given position, and decreases the container's capacity by 1.	Varies
`void erase(iterator itPosition)`	Removes from the container the entry at the current position of the iterator `itPosition`, and decreases the container's capacity by 1.	Varies
`iterator begin()`	Returns an iterator that begins at the first element of the container.	O(1)
`iterator end()`	Returns an iterator that begins at the last element of the container.	O(1)
`reverse_iterator rbegin()`	Returns a reverse iterator that begins at the last element of the container.	O(1)
`reverse_iterator rend()`	Returns a reverse iterator that begins at the first element of the container.	O(1)

The STL class `vector`. The STL class `vector` is implemented using dynamic arrays so that it can increase in size as necessary. You access individual entries in a `vector` just as you do for an STL array by using either [ ] or at. Since vectors are stored as an array in a contiguous sequence of memory locations, vectors are good for accessing entries by either position or iteration, and for adding entries to or removing entries from the back.

ADDITIONAL STL VECTOR OPERATION		
METHOD	DESCRIPTION	EFFICIENCY
`value_type& at(size_type n)`	Behaves the same as [ ], but performs a bounds check.	O(1)

The STL container `deque`. The STL container `deque` allows access to individual elements using [ ] and enables the efficient addition and removal of entries at both its front and back. Unlike our ADT deque, the STL `deque` permits addition to (insert) and removal from (erase) the interior of the container.

The STL deque does not use contiguous memory locations, but stores sequences of its entries in multiple blocks of memory that it tracks internally. While this makes the STL deque more complex to implement, it enables it to grow in size more efficiently, since additional memory can be allocated without the need to copy all existing entries into the new elements.

ADDITIONAL STL DEQUE OPERATIONS		
METHOD	DESCRIPTION	EFFICIENCY
`value_type& at(size_type n)`	Behaves the same as `[ ]`, but performs a bounds check.	O(1)
`void push_front(value_type& item)`	Appends `item` onto the front of the deque, and increases the deque's capacity by 1.	O(1)
`void pop_front(value_type& item)`	Removes the first (front) entry from the deque, and decreases the deque's capacity by 1.	O(1)

The STL class `list`. The STL class `list` is typically implemented using some form of a doubly linked chain. It is optimized for the addition and removal of entries but does not provide subscripting, because element access would be inefficient. Bidirectional iterators are provided to access list entries. The STL `list` can efficiently add and remove entries at any location in the container. This performance is improved if an iterator, either forward or reverse, is used to indicate position. The nature of the STL `list` is well suited for sorting and merging operations, and it has methods that implement those algorithms. The STL `list` does not provide direct access to its elements by position. Access to elements other than the front or back must be done using an iterator.

The STL container `forward_list`. Another C++11 STL container is `forward_list`. It has the same methods as the STL `list` and similar efficiency. Since the STL `forward_list` is implemented as a singly linked chain, it both performs better with operations using forward iterators and requires less storage than the STL `list`. The STL `forward_list` offers the same functionality for sorting, merging, and element access as the STL `list`.

ADDITIONAL STL LIST AND FORWARD_LIST OPERATIONS		
METHOD	DESCRIPTION	EFFICIENCY
`void push_front(value_type& item)`	Appends `item` onto the front of the list, and increases the list's capacity by 1.	O(1)
`void pop_front(value_type& item)`	Removes the first (front) entry from the list, and decreases the list's capacity by 1.	O(1)
`void remove(value_type& val)`	Removes all items from this list that are equal to `val`, and adjusts the list's capacity.	O(n)
`void sort()`	Sorts the list in ascending order.	O(n)
`void merge(list<value_type>& rhs)`	Merges the list `rhs` with this list by placing entries in their correct sorted order, resulting in a sorted list of all entries.	O(n)

(continues)

`void slice(iterator position,` `        list<value_type>& rhs)`	Adds entries in the list `rhs` to this list by placing them at the current position of the given iterator. Note that other forms of this method specify the number of entries.	$O(n)$
`void reverse()`	Reverses the order of the entries in the list.	$O(n)$

Listing C8-2 contains an example that uses the STL `list` to maintain a list of groceries. Each entry is placed at the front of the list initially, and then the list is sorted.

LISTING C8-2 Example of using the STL `list`

```
1   #include <iostream>
2   #include <string>
3   #include <list>
4
5   int main()
6   {
7      std::list<string> groceryList; // Create an empty list
8      std::list<string>::iterator myPosition = groceryList.begin();
9
10     groceryList.insert(myPosition, "apples");
11     groceryList.insert(myPosition, "bread");
12     groceryList.insert(myPosition, "juice");
13     groceryList.insert(myPosition, "carrots");
14
15     std::cout << "Number of items on my grocery list: "
16              << groceryList.size() << std::endl;
17
18     groceryList.sort();
19
20     std::cout << "Items are:" << std::endl;
21     for (auto groceryItem : groceryList)
22     {
23        std::cout << groceryItem << std::endl;
24     } // end for
25  } // end main
```

Output

```
Number of items on my grocery list: 4
Items are:
apples
bread
carrots
juice
```

C8.1.3 Associative Containers

STL associative containers store their entries according to search keys, much as our value-based ADT dictionary does. There are two basic associative containers—`set` and `map`—with several variations of each. The STL `set` uses the entry to be stored as the search key and uses a binary tree for its structure. The STL `map` uses a separate entry as the search key, similar to the technique used by our ADT dictionary. The STL `set` and STL `map` both expect unique search keys, and they store entries in ascending order based on these keys.

The STL `multiset` and STL `multimap` are variations of the STL `set` and STL `map`, respectively, that permit multiple occurrences of the search keys. The STL containers `unordered_set`, `unordered_map`, `unordered_multiset`, and `unordered_multimap` are hash-based implementations of the corresponding ordered STL containers.[2]

Since they are hash based, the unordered associative containers are faster than their ordered counterparts for the direct access of an entry based on its search key. The ordered associative containers are more efficient for iterator-based access. The STL `map` and STL `unordered_map` containers permit direct access to entries using the [ ] operator.

OPERATIONS COMMON TO THE STL SET AND MULTISET		
METHOD	DESCRIPTION	EFFICIENCY
`void clear()`	Deallocates all entries in the container, and changes its capacity to 0.	$O(n)$
`void insert(value_type& item)`	Adds `item` to the container and increases the container's capacity by 1.	$O(\log n)$
`void erase(value_type& item)`	Removes all entries matching `item` from the container and adjusts the container's capacity.	$O(\log n)$
`void erase(iterator& position)`	Removes from the container the entry at the current position of the given iterator and adjusts the container's capacity.	$O(1)$
`iterator find(value_type& item)`	Returns the iterator referencing `item`.	$O(\log n)$
`uint count(value_type& item)`	Counts the occurrences of `item` in the container. For `set` this is at most 1; it can vary for `multiset`.	$O(\log n)$
`iterator lower_bound(value_type& item)`	Returns an iterator referencing the first entry not less than `item`.	$O(\log n)$
`iterator upper_bound(value_type& item)`	Returns an iterator referencing the first entry greater than `item`.	$O(\log n)$
`iterator begin()`	Returns an iterator that begins at the first element of the container.	$O(1)$
`iterator end()`	Returns an iterator that begins at the last element of the container.	$O(1)$
`reverse_iterator rbegin()`	Returns a reverse iterator that begins at the last element of the container.	$O(1)$
`reverse_iterator rend()`	Returns a reverse iterator that begins at the first element of the container.	$O(1)$

---

[2] The unordered hash-based containers are part of C++11.

Generally, the methods of the STL map and its variations have the same behavior as those of the STL set, though the parameters are different since the STL map uses a search key for each mapped value stored in the container. In particular, the insert method for the STL map expects a pair_type that contains both the search key and the entry value mapped to that key.

For example, the following code declares a map with a search key of type char and a mapped type of int. It then stores several values in the map and uses an iterator to display them:

```cpp
#include <iostream>
#include <map>

int main()
{
   std::map<char, int> myMap;
   myMap.insert(std::pair<char, int>('A', 100));
   myMap.insert(std::pair<char, int>('B', 200));
   myMap.insert(std::pair<char, int>('C', 300));

   for (auto mapIterator : myMap)
   {
      std::cout << "Key: " << mapIterator.first;
      std::cout << " Value: " << mapIterator.second << std::endl;
   }  // end for

   return 0;
}  // end main
```

As an alternative to the three insert statements, you can use the [ ] operator as follows:

```cpp
myMap['A'] = 100;
myMap['B'] = 200;
myMap['C'] = 300;
```

Other methods for the STL map use a parameter of key_type or an iterator to identify the entry to act upon.

OPERATIONS COMMON TO THE STL MAP AND MULTIMAP

METHOD	DESCRIPTION	EFFICIENCY
void clear()	Deallocates all entries in this container and changes its capacity to 0.	$O(n)$
void insert(pair_type& item)	Adds item to this container and increases its capacity by 1.	$O(\log n)$
uint erase(key_type& item)	Removes all entries matching item from this container, and changes the container's capacity to 0.	$O(\log n)$
void erase(iterator& position)	Removes from this container the entry at the current position of the given iterator and decreases the container's capacity by 1.	$O(1)$
iterator find(key_type& item)	Returns an iterator to item.	$O(\log n)$

`uint count(key_type& item)`	Counts the occurrences of `item` in this container. For an instance of `set`, this count is at most 1; it can vary for `multiset`.	O(log *n*)
`iterator lower_bound(key_type& item)`	Returns an iterator referencing the first entry not less than `item`.	O(log *n*)
`iterator upper_bound(key_type& item)`	Returns an iterator referencing the first entry greater than `item`.	O(log *n*)
`iterator begin()`	Returns an iterator that begins at the first element of the container.	O(1)
`iterator end()`	Returns an iterator that begins at the last element of the container.	O(1)
`reverse_iterator rbegin()`	Returns a reverse iterator that begins at the last element of the container.	O(1)
`reverse_iterator rend()`	Returns a reverse iterator that begins at the first element of the container.	O(1)

As mentioned earlier, the unordered versions of the associative containers are hash-based—they use a hashing function to either place a new entry or locate an existing entry in the container. When you instantiate an unordered associative container, you can use the default hash function for the type of your data or you can specify your own. Most often, the default hash function will produce acceptable results, but if you are testing your own hashing algorithm, you have the option to pass it to the constructor of an unordered associative container.

Since hash functions are difficult to write, it is often helpful to take advantage of one in the STL. The C++ standard does not provide a stand-alone hash function. An unordered associative container, typically an `unordered_map`, must be instantiated first. Then, the hash function for that container can be used to hash any key of the correct type. Section 18.4.1 in Chapter 18 contains a Programming Tip that demonstrates one way to use this hash function within the `getHashIndex` function.

Let's look at a slightly different way of implementing the `getHashIndex` function in the `HashedDictionary` class discussed in Chapter 18. We need to take two steps when using the `unorder_map` hash function within `getHashIndex`: Instantiate an `unordered_map` object, and create a variable to represent the hash function. We can accomplish both of these tasks within the header file of `HashedDictionary`. In the private section of the header file, we instantiate a `mapper` object:

```
std::unordered_map<KeyType, ItemType> mapper;
```

The sole purpose of the dummy object `mapper` is to give us access to its hash function.

We then call the method `hash_function` to get a reference to the hash function we use to hash the search keys. We store the returned reference in a variable of type `hasher`:

```
typename std::unordered_map<KeyType, ItemType>::hasher hashFunction =
                                        mapper.hash_function();
```

In the C++11 standard, hashing functions are of type `hasher`. They have a single parameter of generic type (`KeyType` in the previous example) and return an unsigned integer that represents the hash value of the key. The keyword `typename` is required so that the compiler understands that this statement is based on the template parameters.

The function `hash_function` returns an unsigned integer in the range 0 to UINT_MAX—the maximum unsigned integer. We must use the modulo operator to scale this return value to be within the range of the hash table. After the modulo operator is applied, we can cast the result to be the type of index we need. Thus, we have the following statement:

```
int hashIndex = std::static_cast<int>(hashFunction(searchKey) % hashTableSize);
```

Note that we use `hashFunction` instead of `mapper.hash_function`. Because `hashFunction` is defined and initialized in the header file, it is available to any method in the `HashedDictionary` class.

The code in Listing C8-3 gives an example of how to use a hash function when it is not part of an ADT. This example creates a hash function for `string` objects. Since the key type of the map determines the hash function, the type of the mapped value is not important; hence we use `int`.

LISTING C8-3 Alternative definition of a hashing function

```cpp
1   #include <iostream>
2   #include <string>
3   #include <unordered_map>
4
5   // Create a type since this is a long name to use (optional)
6   typedef std::unordered_map<std::string, int> StringKeyMap;
7
8   // Create a dummyMap object so we can get its hash function
9   StringKeyMap dummyMap;
10
11  // Capture the hash function for use in program
12  StringKeyMap::hasher myHashFunction = dummyMap.hash_function();
13
14  int main()
15  {
16     std::cout << "Hashing a String: " << myHashFunction("Hashing a String:")
17              << std::endl;
18     std::cout << "Smashing a String: " << myHashFunction ("Smashing a String:")
19              << std::endl;
20     return 0;
21  }  // end main
```

Output

```
Hashing a String: 2084157801917477989
Smashing a String: 14048775086903850803
```

C8.2 STL Algorithms

One of the strengths of the STL container library is the set of functions defined in the header `<algorithm>`. These functions are designed to operate on ranges of entries in any container that has iterators. In C++ Interlude 7, you saw a few of these functions: `for_each`, `find`, `count`, `advance`, and `distance`. In most cases, the type of container is not important, but it must support iterators. This makes possible the comparison of differing types of containers. For instance, the entries stored in a `vector` can be compared to those stored in a `map`.

The first group of algorithms search and compare items in a range. Though they may change a value, they do not modify the structure of the containers. Several algorithms, such as `for_each`, `find_if`, and `count_if`, apply helper functions to each entry during the traversal in a manner similar to the tree traversals presented in Chapter 15. The table below shows only one form of each function. Most functions have several forms that allow additional customization of the range of container entries to process and the functions to use for comparison. Also, STL map methods, such as upper_bound and lower_bound, can be used as functions and applied to other container types.

STL Search and Compare Algorithms	
FUNCTION	DESCRIPTION

`void for_each(iterator start,`
`              iterator end,`
`              Function fun)`
	Applies `fun` to the range specified by `start` and `end`.

`iterator find(iterator start,`
`              iterator end,`
`              value_type& val)`
	Returns an iterator to `val` in the range specified by `start` and end.

`iterator find_if(iterator start,`
`                 iterator end,`
`                 PredFunction fun)`
	Returns an iterator to the entry between `start` and `end` that makes the predicate function `fun` true.

`uint count(iterator start,`
`           iterator end,`
`           value_type& val)`
	Counts the number of occurrences of `val` between `start` and `end`.

`uint count_if(iterator start,`
`              iterator end,`
`              PredFunction fun)`
	Counts the number of entries between `start` and `end` that make the predicate function `fun` true.

`bool equal(iterator start1,`
`           iterator end1,`
`           iterator start2)`
	Compares the entries between `start1` and `end1` to those beginning at `start2`. Returns true if all items match.

`value_type& min(value_type& item1,` `                value_type& item2)`	Returns the minimum of `item1` and `item2`.
`value_type& min_element(iterator start,` `                        iterator end)`	Returns the minimum value in the range from `start` to `end`.
`value_type& max(value_type& item1,` `                value_type& item2)`	Returns the maximum of `item1` and `item2`.
`value_type& max_element(iterator start,` `                        iterator end)`	Returns the maximum value in the range from `start` to `end`.

The sequence-modification algorithms change the entries stored in a container within a range specified by two iterators. The entries can be either

- Replaced by a specific value using `fill`
- Copied or moved to new locations using `copy` or `move`
- Removed based on specified conditions using `remove`, or
- Have operations applied to them using `transform`

The following table lists a few of the more common algorithms and the syntax used to invoke them.

STL SEQUENCE MODIFICATION ALGORITHMS	
FUNCTION	DESCRIPTION

`iterator copy(iterator start1,`
`            iterator end1,`
`            iterator start2)`
	Copies the entries within the range `start1` to `end1` to the positions beginning at `start2` within the same or another container. Returns an iterator to the last entry copied.

`iterator copy_backward(iterator start1,`
`            iterator end1,`
`            iterator start2)`
	Copies the entries within the range `start1` to `end1` to the positions beginning at `start2` (used if ranges overlap in the same container). Copies entries starting at `end1 - 1`. Returns an iterator to the last entry copied.

`void swap(value_type& item1,` `        value_type& item2)`	Swaps the values of two objects, `item1` and `item2`.

`iterator transform(iterator start1,`
`            iterator end1,`
`            iterator start2,`
`            UnaryOperator op)`
	Applies the given unary operator `op` to items within the range `start1` to `end1` and places the result in elements beginning at `start2`. Returns an iterator to the last element in the resulting container.

`iterator transform(iterator start1,`
`            iterator end1,`
`            iterator operand2,`
`            iterator start2,`
`            BinaryOperator bop)`
	Uses entries within the range `start1` to `end1` as the left-hand operand for `bop` and the entries beginning at `operand2` as the right-hand operand. Places the result in elements beginning at `start2`. Returns an iterator to the last element in the resulting container.

`void fill(iterator start1,`
`        iterator end1,`
`        value_type& val)`
	Sets all entries within the range from `start1` to `end1` to the value `val`.

The STL algorithm library also provides a number of functions that perform sorting or heap operations on a range of elements in a container. It also includes functions, such as `partition` and `nth_element` that can be used to implement user-developed sorting algorithms.

STL SORTING AND HEAP ALGORITHMS	
FUNCTION	DESCRIPTION
`void sort(iterator start,` `        iterator end)`	Sorts entries within the range `start` to `end` into ascending order.
`void stable_sort(iterator start,` `        iterator end)`	Sorts entries within the range `start` to `end` into ascending order but has stability in ordering—that is, the relative order of equal values is maintained.

```iterator partition(iterator start, iterator end, PredFunction fun)```	Rearranges all entries within the range from start to end so that those that make the predicate function fun true are before those for which the function is false.
```iterator partition_stable(iterator start, iterator end, PredFunction fun)```	Behaves the same as partition, but has stability in ordering—that is, the relative order of equal values is maintained.
```void nth_element(iterator start, iterator nth, iterator end)```	Rearranges the entries within the range start to end so that the entry in position nth is in the correct sorted position—that is, it is in the nth position in the sorted sequence.
```void make_heap(iterator start, iterator end)```	Rearrange the entries in the range start to end to form a heap.
```void push_heap(iterator start, iterator end)```	Assumes that the entries within the range start to end − 1 form a heap and places the entry at position end into the correct location in the heap, extending the heap to position end.
```void pop_heap(iterator start, iterator end)```	Moves the value at position start to position end − 1 and rebuilds the heap in the range start to end − 2 inclusive.
```void sort_heap(iterator start, iterator end)```	Assumes that the entries within the range start to end − 1 form a heap and turns the heap back into a sorted container.

Review of C++ Fundamentals

Contents

Prerequisite

Knowledge of a modern programming language

This book assumes that you already know how to write programs in a modern programming language. If that language is C++, you can probably skip this appendix, returning to it for reference as necessary. If instead you know a language such as Python, Java, or C, this appendix will introduce you to C++. Also, Appendixes K and L compare C++ to Java and Python, respectively.

It isn't possible to cover all of C++ in these pages. Instead this appendix focuses on the parts of the language used in this book. First we look at the basics of data types, variables, expressions, operators, and simple input/output. We continue with functions, decision constructs, looping constructs, arrays, and strings. Various C++ Interludes, which appear throughout the book as needed, will cover classes, pointers, exceptions, iterators, and the Standard Template Library.

A.1   Language Basics

Let's begin with the aspects of the language that allow you to perform simple computations. For example, the C++ program in Figure A-1 computes the volume of a sphere. Running this program produces the following output, where the user's response appears in blue:

```
Enter the radius of the sphere: 19.1
The volume of a sphere of radius 19.1 is 29186.927734
```

A typical C++ program consists of several modules, some of which you write and some of which you use from standard libraries. C++ provides a **source-inclusion facility**, which allows the system to *include* the contents of a file automatically at a specified point in a program before the program is compiled. For example, our sample program uses a standard library to perform input and output operations. The first line of this program is an include **directive** that names a **standard header** iostream, which enables the program to use input and output statements.

Each C++ program must contain a function main

A C++ program is a collection of functions, one of which must be called main. Program execution always begins with the function main. The following paragraphs provide an overview of the basics of C++ and refer to the simple program in Figure A-1 by line number. Note that the only function this simple program contains is main.

A.1.1   Comments

Each comment line begins with two slashes

Each comment line in C++ begins with two slashes // and continues until the end of the line. You can also begin a multiple-line comment with the characters /* and end it with */. However,

FIGURE A-1   A simple C++ program

1. Enables input and output ------------>	`#include <iostream>`
2. Begins the function **main** ------------>	`int main()`
3. Begins body of function ------------->	`{`
4. A comment ---------------------------->	`// Computes the volume of a sphere of a given radius`
5. Defines a constant -------------------->	`const double PI = 3.14159;`
6. Declares a variable -------------------->	`double radius;`
7. Displays a prompt to the user ------->	`std::cout << "Enter the radius of the sphere: ";`
8. Reads **radius** ------------------------>	`std::cin  >> radius;`
9. Declares and computes **volume** --->	`double volume = 4 * PI * radius * radius * radius / 3;`
10. Displays results ------------------------->	`std::cout << "The volume of a sphere of radius "`
11. Statement continues ------------------>	`           << radius << " inches is " << volume`
12. Statement continues ------------------>	`           << " cubic inches.\n";`
13. Normal program termination ------->	`return 0;`
14. Ends body of function --------------->	`}  // end program`

a comment that begins with `/*` and ends with `*/` cannot contain another comment that begins with `/*` and ends with `*/`.

Appendix I talks about documentation comments that begin with `/**` and end with `*/`. We use this style of comment in this book at the beginning of classes, methods, and functions.

A.1.2 Identifiers and Keywords

A C++ **identifier** is a sequence of letters, digits, and underscores that must begin with either a letter or an underscore. C++ distinguishes between uppercase and lowercase letters, so be careful when typing identifiers.

You use identifiers to name various parts of the program. Certain identifiers, however, are reserved by C++ as **keywords**, and you should not use them for other purposes. A list of all C++ reserved keywords appears inside the cover of this book. The keywords that occur within C++ statements in this book appear in color.

C++ is case-sensitive

A.1.3 Primitive Data Types

The primitive data types in C++ are organized into four categories: boolean, character, integer, and floating point. With the exception of boolean, each category contains several data types. For most applications, you can use

`bool`	for boolean values
`char`	for character values
`int`	for integer values
`double`	for floating-point values

FIGURE A-2   Primitive data types

Category	Available Data Types by Category		
Boolean	bool		
Character	char	signed char	unsigned char
Signed integer	short	int	long
Unsigned integer	unsigned short	unsigned	unsigned long
Floating point	float	double	long double

Most of the data types are available in several forms and sizes. Although you will probably not need more than the four types given previously, Figure A-2 lists the available primitive data types for your reference.

A boolean value can be either true or false. Characters are represented by their ASCII integer values, which are listed in Appendix J. Integer values are either signed, such as −5 and +98, or unsigned, such as 5 and 98. The **floating-point types** are used for real numbers that have both an integer portion and a fractional portion. Boolean, character, and integer types are called **integral types**. Integral and floating-point types are called **arithmetic types**.

The size of a data type affects the range of its values. For example, a long integer can have a larger magnitude than a short integer. The sizes of—and therefore the specific ranges for—a data type depend on the particular computer and version of C++ that you use. C++, however, provides a way to determine these ranges, as you will see later in Section A.1.6.

A.1.4 Variables

A variable, whose name is a C++ identifier, represents a memory location that contains a value of a particular data type. You declare a variable's data type by preceding the variable name with the data type, as in

```
double radius; // Radius of a sphere
```

Note that you can write a comment on the same line to describe the purpose of the variable.

This declaration is also a definition in that it assigns memory for the variable radius. The memory, however, has no particular initial value and so is said to be uninitialized. The program in Figure A-1 declares radius without an initial value and later reads its value by using std::cin >> radius.

When possible, avoid uninitialized variables

When possible, you should avoid uninitialized variables of a primitive data type. That is, you should initialize a variable when you first declare its data type or, alternatively, declare a variable's data type when you first assign it a value. For example, volume appears for the first time in line 9 of Figure A-1 in the statement

```
double volume = 4 * PI * radius * radius * radius / 3;
```

Because we did not declare volume's data type earlier in the program—thus avoiding an uninitialized value—we declare its data type *and* assign it a value in the same statement.

A.1.5 Literal Constants

You use **literal constants** to indicate particular values within a program. The 4 and 3 in line 9 of Figure A-1 are examples of literal constants that are used within a computation. You can also use a literal constant to initialize the value of a variable. For example, you use true and false as the values of a boolean variable, as mentioned previously.

You write decimal integer constants without commas, decimal points, or leading zeros. The default data type of such a constant is either `int`, if small enough, or `long`.

Do not begin a
decimal integer
constant with zero

You write floating-point constants, which have a default type of `double`, with a decimal point. You can specify an optional power-of-10 multiplier by writing `e` or `E` followed by the power of 10. For example, `1.2e-3` means 1.2×10^{-3}.

Character constants are enclosed in single quotes—for example, `'A'` and `'2'`—and have a default type of `char`. You write a literal character string as a sequence of characters enclosed in double quotes.

Several characters have names that use a backslash notation, as given in Figure A-3. This notation is useful when you want to embed one of these characters within a literal character string. For example, the program in Figure A-1 uses the new-line character `\n` in the string `"cubic inches.\n"` to end the line of output. Any additional output will appear on the next line. You will see this use of `\n` in the discussion of output later in this appendix. You also use the backslash notation to specify either a single quote as a character constant (`'\''`) or a double quote within a character string.

> **Programming Tip:** Do not begin a decimal integer constant with zero. A constant that begins with zero is either an octal constant or a hexadecimal constant.[1]

FIGURE A-3   Some special character constants

Constant	Name
\n	New line
\t	Tab
\'	Single quote
\"	Double quote
\0	Zero

A.1.6 Named Constants

Unlike variables, whose values can change during program execution, **named constants** have values that do not change. The declaration of a named constant is like that of an initialized variable, but the keyword `const` precedes the data type. For example, the statement

The value of a
named constant
does not change

```
const double PI = 3.14159;
```

declares `PI` as a named floating constant, as is the case in the sample program in Figure A-1. Once a named constant such as `PI` is declared, you can use it, but you cannot assign it another value. By using named constants, you make your program both easier to read and easier to modify.

Named constants
make a program
easier to read and
modify

The standard header file `climits` contains named constants such as `INT_MIN` and `LONG_MAX` that specify installation-dependent maximum and minimum values for the integral data types. Likewise, the standard header file `cfloat` contains named constants that specify installation-dependent maximum and minimum values for the floating data types. You use the `include` directive to gain access to these header files.

---

[1] Octal and hexadecimal constants are also available, but they are not used in this book. An octal constant begins with `0`, a hex constant with `0x` or `0X`.

A.1.7 Enumerations

Enumeration provides another way to name constants

Enumeration provides another way to name integer constants. For example, the statement

```
enum {SUN, MON, TUE, WED, THU, FRI, SAT};
```

is equivalent to the statements

```
const int SUN = 0;
const int MON = 1;
    . . .
const int SAT = 6;
```

By default, the values assigned to the constants—called **enumerators**—begin with zero and are consecutive. You can, however, assign explicit values to any or all of the enumerators, as in

```
enum {PLUS = '+', MINUS = '-'};
```

You can create an integral data type by naming an enumeration

By naming an enumeration, you create a distinct integral type. For example,

```
enum Season {WINTER, SPRING, SUMMER, FALL};
```

creates a type Season. The variable whichSeason, declared as

```
Season whichSeason;
```

can have values WINTER, SPRING, SUMMER, or FALL. This use of named enumerations instead of int can make your program easier to understand.

A.1.8 The typedef Statement

You use the typedef statement to give another name to an existing data type. In this way, you can make your program easier to modify and to read. For example, the statement

```
typedef double Real;
```

The typedef statement gives another name to an existing data type, making your program easier to change

declares Real as a synonym for double and allows you to use Real and double interchangeably.
    Suppose that you revise the program in Figure A-1 by using Real as follows:

```
int main()
{
    typedef double Real;
    const Real PI = 3.14159;
    Real radius = 0.0;

    std::cout << "Enter the radius of the sphere: ";
    std::cin >> radius;
    Real volume = 4 * PI * radius * radius * radius / 3;
    . . .
```

At first glance, this program does not seem to be more advantageous than the original version, but suppose that you decide to increase the precision of your computation by declaring PI, radius, and volume as long double instead of double. In the original version of the program (Figure A-1), you would have to locate and change each occurrence of double to long double. In the revised program, you simply change the typedef statement to

```
typedef long double Real;
```

The typedef statement does not create a new data type

Realize that typedef does not create a new data type, but simply declares a new name for an existing data type. A new data type requires more than a name; it requires a set of operations. C++, however, does provide a way to create your own data types, as described in C++ Interlude 1.

A.1.9 Assignments and Expressions

You form an **expression** by combining variables, constants, operators, and parentheses. The assignment statement

```
volume = 4 * PI * radius * radius * radius / 3;
```

assigns to the previously declared variable `volume` the value of the arithmetic expression on the right-hand side of the **assignment operator** =, assuming that `PI` and `radius` have values. The assignment statement

```
double volume = 4 * PI * radius * radius * radius / 3;
```

which appears in line 9 of Figure A-1, also declares `volume`'s data type, since it was not declared previously.

The various kinds of expressions that you can use in an assignment statement are discussed next.

Arithmetic expressions. You can combine variables and constants with arithmetic operators and parentheses to form arithmetic expressions. The arithmetic operators are

- `+` Binary add or unary plus
- `–` Binary subtract or unary minus
- `*` Multiply
- `/` Divide
- `%` Modulo (remainder after division)

The operators `*`, `/`, and `%` have the same **precedence**,[2] which is higher than that of `+` and `–`; unary operators[3] have a higher precedence than binary operators. The following examples demonstrate operator precedence:

Operators have a set precedence

`a - b / c`	means $a - (b/c)$	(precedence of / over −)
`-5 / a`	means $(-5)/a$	(precedence of unary operator −)
`a / -5`	means $a/(-5)$	(precedence of unary operator −)

Arithmetic operators and most other operators are left-associative. That is, operators of the same precedence execute from left to right within an expression. Thus,

Operators are either left- or right-associative

```
a / b * c
```

means

```
(a / b) * c
```

The assignment operator and all unary operators are right-associative, as you will see later. You can use parentheses to override operator precedence and associativity.

Relational and logical expressions. You can combine variables and constants with parentheses; with the relational, or comparison, operators `<`, `<=`, `>=`, and `>`; and with the equality operators `==` (equal to) and `!=` (not equal to) to form a relational expression. Such an expression is true or false according to the validity of the specified relation. For example, the expression `5 == 4` is false because 5 is not equal to 4. Note that equality operators have a lower precedence than relational operators.

You can combine variables and constants of the arithmetic types, relational expressions, and the logical operators `&&` (and) and `||` (or) to form logical expressions, which are either true or false. C++ evaluates logical expressions from left to right and stops as soon as the value of

Logical expressions are evaluated from left to right

---

[2] A list of all C++ operators and their precedences appears inside the cover of this book.
[3] A unary operator requires only one operand; for example, the − in −5. A binary operator requires two operands; for example, the + in 2 + 3.

Sometimes the value of a logical expression is apparent before it is completely examined

the entire expression is apparent; that is, C++ uses **short-circuit evaluation**. For example, C++ determines the value of each of the following expressions without evaluating (a < b):

```
(5 == 4) && (a < b) // False since (5 == 4) is false
(5 == 5) || (a < b) // True since (5 == 5) is true
```

 Programming Tip: Remember that = is the assignment operator; == is the equality operator.

Conditional expressions. The expression

$expression_1$ **?** $expression_2$ **:** $expression_3$

has the value of either $expression_2$ or $expression_3$ according to whether $expression_1$ is true or false, respectively. For example, the statement

```
larger = ((a > b) ? a : b);
```

assigns the larger of a and b to larger, because the expression a > b is true if a is larger than b and false if not.

Conversions from one data type to another occur during both assignment and expression evaluation

Implicit type conversions. Automatic conversions from one data type to another can occur during assignment and during expression evaluation. For assignments, the data type of the expression on the right-hand side of the assignment operator is converted to the data type of the item on the left-hand side just before the assignment occurs. Floating-point values are truncated—not rounded—when they are converted to integral values.

During the evaluation of an expression, any values of type char or short are converted to int. Similarly, any enumerator value is converted to int if int can represent all the values of that particular enum; otherwise, it is converted to unsigned. These conversions are called **integral promotions**. After these conversions, if the operands of an operator differ in data type, the data type that is lower in the following hierarchy is converted to one that is higher (int is lowest):

int → unsigned → long → unsigned long → float → double → long double

For example, if a is long and b is float, a + b is float. Only a copy of a's long value is converted to float prior to the addition, so that the value stored at a is unchanged.

Use a static cast to convert explicitly from one data type to another

Explicit type conversions. You can explicitly convert from one data type to another by using a **static cast**, with the following notation:

```
static_cast<type>(expression)
```

which converts *expression* to the data type *type*. For example, static_cast<int>(14.9) converts the double value 14.9 to the int value 14. Thus, the sequence

```
double volume = 14.9;
std::cout << static_cast<int>(volume);
```

displays 14 but does not change the value of volume.

Other assignment operators. In addition to the assignment operator =, C++ provides several two-character assignment operators that perform another operation before assignment. For example,

```
a += b means a = a + b
```

Other operators, such as −=, *=, /=, and %=, have analogous meanings.

Two more operators, ++ and −−, provide convenient incrementing and decrementing operations:

a++ means a += 1, which means a = a + 1

The operators ++ and −− are useful for incrementing and decrementing a variable

Similarly,

a−− means a −= 1, which means a = a − 1

The operators ++ and −− can either follow their operands, as you just saw, or precede them. Although ++a, for instance, has the same effect as a++, the results differ when the operations are combined with assignment. For example,

b = ++a means a = a + 1; b = a

Here, the ++ operator acts on a *before* assigning a's new value to b. In contrast,

b = a++ means b = a; a = a + 1

The assignment operator assigns a's old value to b before the ++ operator acts on a. That is, the ++ operator acts on a *after* the assignment. The operators ++ and −− are often used within loops and with array indices, as you will see later in this appendix. When we use these operators with arithmetic variables, we write the operator after the variable.

In addition to the operators described here, C++ provides several other operators. A summary of all C++ operators and their precedences appears inside the cover of this book.

A.2   Input and Output Using `iostream`

A typical C++ program reads its input from a keyboard and writes its output to a display. Such input and output consist of **streams**, which are simply sequences of characters that either come from or go to an input or output (I/O) device.

The data type of an input stream is `istream`, and the data type of an output stream is `ostream`. The `iostream` library provides these data types and three default stream variables: `cin` for the standard input stream, `cout` for the standard output stream, and `cerr` for the standard error stream, which also is an output stream. Your program gains access to the `iostream` library by including the `iostream` header file. This section provides a brief introduction to simple input and output.

A.2.1   Input

C++ provides the input operator >> to read integers, floating-point numbers, and characters into variables whose data types are any of the primitive data types. The input operator has the input stream as its left operand and the variable that will contain the value read as its right operand. Thus,

The input operator >> reads from an input stream

```
std::cin >> x;
```

reads a value for x from the standard input stream. The >> operator is left-associative. Thus,

```
std::cin >> x >> y
```

means

```
(std::cin >> x) >> y
```

That is, both of these expressions read characters for x from the input stream and then read subsequent characters for y.

The input operator >> skips whitespace, such as blanks, tabs, and new-line characters, that might occur between values in the input data line. For example, after the program segment

```
int ia = 0;
int ib = 0;
double da = 0;
double db = 0;
std::cin >> ia >> da >> ib;
std::cin >> db;
```

reads the data line

```
21  -3.45  -6 475.1e-2 <eol>
```

the variable ia contains 21, da contains −3.45, ib contains −6, and db contains 4.751. A subsequent attempt to read from cin will look beyond the end of the line (<*eol*>) and read from the next data line, if one exists. An error occurs if no data exists for a corresponding variable processed by >> or if the variable's data type does not match the type of the data available. For example, after the previous program segment reads the data line

```
-1.23  456.1e-2  -7 8 <eol>
```

the variable ia contains −1, da contains 0.23, ib contains 456, and db contains 0.001. The rest of the data line is left for a subsequent read, if any. As another example, if the segment attempts to read a data line that begins with .21, the read would terminate because ia is int and .21 is not.

An expression such as std::cin >> x has a value after the read operation takes place. If the operation is successful, this value is true; otherwise the value is false. You can examine this value by using the selection and iteration statements that are described later in this appendix.

You can also use the >> operator to read individual characters from the input stream into character variables. Again, any whitespace is skipped. For example, after the program segment

```
char ch1 = '';
char ch2 = '';
char ch3 = '';
std::cin >> ch1 >> ch2 >> ch3;
```

reads the data line

```
xy  z
```

ch1 contains 'x', ch2 contains 'y', and ch3 contains 'z'.

You can read whitespace when reading individual characters into character variables by using the C++ method get. Either of the statements

```
std::cin.get(ch1);
```

or

```
ch1 = std::cin.get();
```

reads the next character, even if it is a blank, a tab, or a new-line character, from the input stream into the char variable ch1.

Section A.7, later in this appendix, describes how to read character strings.

A.2.2 Output

The output operator
<< writes to an
output stream

C++ provides the output operator << to write character strings and the contents of variables whose data types are any of the primitive ones. For example, the program segment

```
int count = 5;
double average = 20.3;
std::cout << "The average of the " << count
          << " distances read is " << average
          << " miles.\n";
```

produces the following output:

```
The average of the 5 distances read is 20.3 miles.
```

Subsequent output will appear on the next line. Like the input operator, the output operator is left-associative. Thus, the previous statements append the string "The average of the " to the output stream, then append the characters that represent the value of count, and so on.

Note the use of the new-line character \n, which you can conveniently embed within a character string. Observe also that the output operator does not automatically introduce whitespace between values that are written; you must do so explicitly. The following statements provide another example of this:

You need to explicitly introduce new-line characters and whitespace where desired in a program's output

```
int x = 2;
int y = 3;
char ch = 'A';
std::cout << x << y << ch << "\n"; // Displays 23A
```

Although you can use the output operator to display individual characters, you can also use the put method for this task. Further, you can specify a character either as a char variable or in ASCII. Thus, the statements

```
char ch = 'a';
std::cout.put(ch);    // Displays a
std::cout.put('b');   // Displays b
std::cout.put(99);    // Displays c, which is 99 in ASCII
std::cout.put(ch+3);  // Displays d
std::cout.put('\n');  // Carriage return
```

display abcd followed by a carriage return.

Section A.7, later in this appendix, provides further information about writing character strings.

A.2.3 Manipulators

C++ enables you to gain more control over the format of your output and the treatment of whitespace during input than the previous discussion has indicated. Most of these techniques apply to the format of output.

Suppose, for example, that you have computed your grade point average and you want to display it with one digit to the right of the decimal point. If the floating variable gpa contains 4.0, the statement

```
std::cout << "My GPA is " << gpa << "\n";
```

writes 4 without a decimal point. A number of **manipulators** affect the appearance of your output. You can use these with cout:

Use manipulators to specify the appearance of a program's output

```
std::cout << std::manipulator;
```

where *manipulator* has any of the values listed in Figure A-4. A manipulator is a predefined value or function that you use with the input and output operator. For example,

```
std::cout << std::showpoint;
```

uses the showpoint manipulator and causes all floating-point output to appear with a decimal point.

FIGURE A-4   Stream manipulators

Manipulator	Meaning
endl	Insert new line and flush stream
fixed	Use fixed decimal point in floating-point output
left	Left-align output
right	Right-align output
scientific	Use exponential (e) notation in floating-point output
setfill(f)	Set fill character to **f**
setprecision(n)	Set floating-point precision to integer **n**
setw(n)	Set field width to integer **n**
showpoint	Show decimal point in floating-point output
showpos	Show + with positive integers
ws	Extract whitespace characters (input only)

Even if you use the showpoint manipulator, gpa will likely appear as 4.00000 instead of 4.0. You can specify the number of digits that appear to the right of the decimal point by using the manipulator function setprecision, and you can insert a new-line character and flush the output stream by using the manipulator endl. Thus,

```
std::cout << std::showpoint;
std::cout << std::setprecision(1) << gpa << std::endl;
```

displays 4.0 followed by a carriage return.

The effect of setprecision on the output stream remains until another setprecision is encountered. Except for setprecision, however, a manipulator affects the appearance of only the next characters on which << (or >>) operates. For example,

```
std::cout << std::right; // Right-align output
std::cout << "abc" << std::setw(6) << "def" << "ghi";
```

displays

```
abc   defghi
```

Although manipulator values, such as endl, are available when you include iostream in your program, you must also include iomanip to use any of the manipulator functions setfill, setprecision, and setw. Note that all of the manipulators are in the C++ standard namespace.

A.3   Functions

A C++ program is a collection of functions

As was mentioned earlier in this appendix, a C++ program is a collection of functions. Usually, each function should perform one well-defined task. For example, the following function returns the larger of two integers:

A function definition implements a function's task

```
int maxOf(int x, int y)
{
   if (x > y)
      return x;
   else
      return y;
} // end maxOf
```

A function definition, like the one just given, has the following form:

type name(*parameter-declaration-list*)
{
   body
}

The portion of the definition before the left brace specifies a return type, the function name, and a list of **parameters**. The part of the definition that appears between the braces is the function's body.

The return type of a **valued function**—one that returns a value—is the data type of the value that the function will return. The body of a valued function must contain a statement of the form

```
return expression;
```

where *expression* has the value to be returned.

Each parameter represents either an input to or an output from the function. You declare a parameter by writing a data type and a parameter name, separating it from other parameter declarations with a comma, as in

```
int x, int y
```

When you **call**, or **invoke**, the function maxOf, you pass it **arguments** that correspond to the parameters with respect to number, order, and data type. For example, the following statements contain two calls to maxOf:

```
int a = 0;
int b = 0;
int c = 0;
std::cin >> a >> b >> c;

int largerAB = maxOf(a, b);
std::cout << "The largest of " << a << ", " << b << ", "
          << " and " << c << " is " << maxOf(largerAB, c) << ".\n";
```

As written, the definition of maxOf indicates that its arguments are **passed by value**. That is, the function makes local copies of the values of the arguments—a and b, for example—and uses these copies wherever x and y appear in the function definition. Thus, the function cannot alter the arguments that you pass to it. This restriction is desirable in this example because x and y are input parameters, which maxOf does not change.

Alternatively, arguments can be **passed by reference**. The function does not copy such arguments; rather, it references the argument locations whenever the parameters appear in the function's definition. This allows a function to change the values of the arguments, thus implementing output parameters.

For example, consider the following function computeMax:

```
void computeMax(int x, int y, int& larger)
{
    larger = ((x > y) ? x : y);
} // end computeMax
```

computeMax is a **void function** instead of a valued function. That is, its return type is void, and it does not return a value by using a return statement.[4] Instead, computeMax returns the larger of x and y in the output parameter larger. The & that follows larger's data type int indicates that larger

_____

[4] Whereas valued functions must contain a statement of the form return *expression*, void functions cannot contain such a statement. A void function can, however, contain return without an expression. Such a statement causes the function to return to the statement that follows its call. This book does not use return with void functions.

Marginal notes: A valued function must use return to return a value. When you call a function, you pass it arguments that correspond to the parameters in number, order, and data type. An argument passed by value is copied within the function. An argument passed by reference is not copied but is accessed directly within the function. A void function does not use return to return a value.

An output argument should be a reference argument

is a **reference parameter**. Thus, computeMax will access and alter the argument that corresponds to larger, whereas the function will make and use copies of the values of the arguments that correspond to the **value parameters** x and y.

The following statements demonstrate how to invoke computeMax:

```
int a = 0;
int b = 0;
int largerAB = 0;
std::cin >> a >> b;
computeMax(a, b, largerAB);
std::cout << "The larger of " << a << " and " << b
         << " is " << largerAB << ".\n";
```

An input argument should be either a value argument or a constant reference argument

If a function's input argument is a large object, like the objects you will encounter in this book, you might not want the function to copy it. Thus, you would not pass the argument by value. Because it is an input argument, however, you do not want the function to be able to alter it. A **constant reference parameter** is a reference parameter that is tagged as const. The function uses the actual argument that is passed to such a parameter, not a copy of it, yet cannot modify it.

For example, for the function f that begins

```
void f(const int& x, int y, int& z)
```

An argument that is both an input to and an output from a function is passed by reference

x is a constant reference parameter, y is a value parameter, and z is a reference parameter. Here x and y are suitable as input parameters because f cannot change them, while z is an output parameter. Note that z can also be an input parameter. That is, the argument corresponding to z can both provide a value to the function and return a value from the function. Such arguments must be passed by reference.

 **Note:** Use reference parameters with caution, as you might inadvertently change an argument. On the other hand, constant reference parameters are safe to use.

If you write another function f that calls computeMax, you must either place the definition of f after the definition of computeMax or precede f's definition with a **function declaration** for computeMax. For example, you can use either of the following statements to declare the function computeMax:

```
void computeMax(int x, int y, int& max);
```

A function declaration ends with a semicolon

or

```
void computeMax(int, int, int&);
```

A function declaration provides the data types of the function's parameters and its return type. Parameter names are optional in a function declaration, although they are helpful stylistically. However, parameter names are required in the function's definition. Although a function declaration ends with a semicolon, a semicolon does not appear in a function definition.

Declarations for each function usually appear at the beginning of a program

A typical C++ program contains a function declaration for every function used in the program. These declarations appear first in the program, usually with comments that describe each function's purpose, parameters, and assumptions. The program in Listing A-1 demonstrates the placement of a function declaration, function definition, and main function:

LISTING A-1 A program that contains a function declaration

```
1   #include <iostream>
2
3   /** Returns the larger of two given integers.
4    @param x  An integer.
5    @param y  An integer.
6    @return  The larger of x and y. */
7   int maxOf(int x, int y);          // A function declaration
8
9   int main()
10  {
11     int a = 0;
12     int b = 0;
13     std::cout << "Please enter two integers: ";
14     std::cin >> a >> b;
15
16     int largerAB = maxOf(a, b);
17     std::cout << "The larger of " << a << " and " << b
18             << " is " << largerAB << ".\n";
19  }  // end main
20
21  // A function definition
22  int maxOf(int x, int y)
23  {
24     return (x > y) ? x : y;
25  }  // end maxOf
```

A.3.1 Standard Functions

C++ provides many standard functions, such as the square root function sqrt and the input function get. Appendix H provides a summary of the standard functions and indicates which header file you need to include in your program to gain access to them. For example, the standard functions listed in Figure A-5 facilitate character processing and require the header file cctype. Thus, you need to include the statement

> Standard functions provide many common operations and require a specific header file

```
#include <cctype>
```

in your program when you want to use functions such as isupper and toupper. For the character variable ch, isupper(ch) is true if ch is an uppercase letter, and toupper(ch) returns the uppercase version of the letter ch without actually changing ch.

FIGURE A-5   A selection of standard functions

(a) Standard classification functions

Function	Returns true if ch is
isalnum(ch)	A letter or digit
isalpha(ch)	A letter
isdigit(ch)	A digit
islower(ch)	A lowercase letter
isupper(ch)	An uppercase letter

(b) Standard conversion functions

Function	Returns
tolower(ch)	Lowercase version of ch
toupper(ch)	Uppercase version of ch
toascii(ch)	int ASCII code for ch

A.4   Selection Statements

Selection statements allow you to choose among several courses of action according to the value of an expression. In this category of statements, C++ provides the `if` statement and the `switch` statement.

A.4.1   The `if` Statement

You can write an `if` statement in one of two ways:

> An `if` statement has two basic forms

```
if (expression)
   statement1
```

or

> Parentheses around the expression in an `if` statement are required

```
if (expression)
   statement1
else
   statement2
```

where *statement1* and *statement2* represent any C++ statement except a declaration. Such statements can be compound; a **compound statement**, or **block**, is a sequence of statements enclosed in braces. If the value of *expression* is true, *statement1* is executed. Otherwise, the first form of the `if` statement does nothing, whereas the second form executes *statement2*. Note that the parentheses around *expression* are required.

For example, the following `if` statements each compare the values of two integer variables a and b, and copy the larger value to the integer variable largerAB:

```
if (a > b)
   std::cout << a << " is larger than " << b << ".\n";
std::cout << "This statement is always executed.\n";

if (a > b)
{
   largerAB = a;
   std::cout << a << " is larger than " << b << ".\n";
}
else
{
   largerAB = b;
   std::cout << b << " is larger than " << a << ".\n";
}  // end if

std::cout << largerAB << " is the larger value.\n";
```

> You can nest `if` statements

You can nest `if` statements in several ways, since either *statement1* or *statement2* can itself be an `if` statement. The following example, which finds the largest of three integer variables a, b, and c, shows a common way to nest `if` statements:

```
if ((a >= b) && (a >= c))
   largest = a;
else if (b >= c) // a is not largest at this point
   largest = b;
else
   largest = c;
```

 Note: An arithmetic expression whose value is not zero is treated as true; one having a value of zero is false.

A.4.2 The switch Statement

When you must choose among more than two courses of action, the if statement can become unwieldy. If your choice is to be made according to the value of an integral expression, you can use a switch statement.

For example, the following statement assigns the number of days in a month to the previously defined integer variable daysInMonth. The int variable month designates the month as an integer from 1 to 12, and the boolean variable leapYear is true if the year is a leap year.

A switch statement provides a choice of several actions according to the value of an integral expression

```cpp
switch (month)
{
   // 30 days hath Sept., Apr., June, and Nov.
   case 9: case 4: case 6: case 11:
      daysInMonth = 30;
      break;

   // All the rest have 31
   case 1: case 3: case 5: case 7:
   case 8: case 10: case 12:
      daysInMonth = 31;
      break;

// Except February
   case 2: // Assume leapYear is true if a leap year, else is false
      if (leapYear)
         daysInMonth = 29;
      else
         daysInMonth = 28;
      break;

   default:
      std::cout << "Incorrect value for month.\n";
}  // end switch
```

Parentheses must enclose the integral switch expression—month, in this example. The case labels have the form

case *expression*:

where *expression* is a constant integral expression. After the switch expression is evaluated, execution continues at the case label whose expression has the same value as the switch expression. Subsequent statements execute until either a break statement is encountered or the switch statement ends.

Without a break statement, execution of a case will continue into the next case

Unless you terminate a case with a break statement, execution of the switch statement continues. Although this action can be useful, omitting the break statements in the previous example would be incorrect.

If no case label matches the current value of the switch expression, the statements that follow the default label, if one exists, are executed. If no default exists, the switch statement exits.

A.5 Iteration Statements

C++ has three statements that provide for repetition by iteration, that is, loops: the while, for, and do statements. Each statement controls the number of times that another C++ statement—the body—is executed. The body cannot be a declaration and is often a compound statement.

A.5.1   The `while` Statement

A `while` statement executes as long as the expression is true

The general form of the `while` statement is

```
while (expression)
    statement
```

As long as the value of *expression* is true, *statement* is executed. Because *expression* is evaluated before *statement* is executed, it is possible that *statement* will not execute at all. Note that the parentheses around *expression* are required.

Suppose that you wanted to compute the sum of positive integers that you enter at the keyboard. Since the integers are positive, you can use a negative value or zero to indicate the end of the input. The following `while` statement accomplishes this task:

```
int nextValue = 0;
int sum = 0;

std::cin >> nextValue;
while (nextValue > 0)
{
    sum += nextValue;
    std::cin >> nextValue;
} // end while
```

If 0 was the first value read, the body of the `while` statement would not execute.

Recall that the expression `std::cin >> nextValue` is true if the input operation was successful and false otherwise. Thus, you could revise the previous statements as

```
int nextValue = 0;
int sum = 0;
while ( (std::cin >> nextValue) && (nextValue > 0) )
    sum += nextValue;
```

This loop control is difficult to maintain, and so we do not recommend it.

A.5.2   The `for` Statement

A `for` statement lists the initialization, testing, and updating steps in one location

The `for` statement provides for counted loops and has the general form

```
for (initialize; test; update)
    statement
```

where *initialize, test*, and *update* are expressions. Typically, *initialize* is an assignment expression that initializes a counter to control the loop. This initialization occurs only once. Then if *test*, which is usually a logical expression, is true, *statement* executes. The expression *update* executes next, usually incrementing or decrementing the counter. This sequence of events repeats, beginning with the evaluation of *test*, until the value of *test* is false.

For example, the following `for` statement displays the integers from 1 to `n`:

```
for (int counter = 1; counter <= n; counter++)
    std::cout << counter << " ";
std::cout << std::endl; // This statement is always executed
```

If `n` is less than 1, the `for` statement does not execute at all. Thus, the previous statements are equivalent to the following `while` loop:

```
int counter = 1;
while (counter <= n)
{
```

```
    std::cout << counter << " ";
    counter++;
}  // end while
std::cout << std::endl; // This statement is always executed
```

In general, the logic of a `for` statement is equivalent to

initialize;
```
while (test)
{
    statement;
    update;
}
```

A `for` statement is equivalent to a `while` statement

Note that in a `for` statement the first expression *initialize* must have either an arithmetic type or a pointer type.[5] Note that `char` in the following example is considered an arithmetic type:

```
for (char ch = 'z'; ch >= 'a'; ch--)
// ch ranges from 'z' to 'a'
```

The *initialize* and *update* portions of a `for` statement each can contain several expressions separated by commas, thus performing more than one action. For example, the following loop raises a floating-point value to an integer power by using multiplication:

```
// Floating-point power equals floating-point x raised to int n;
// assumes int expon
for (power = 1.0, expon = 1; expon <= n; expon++)
   power *= x;
```

Both `power` and `expon` are assigned values before the body of the loop executes for the first time. The comma here is an example of the **comma operator**, which evaluates its operand expressions from left to right.

When compared to a `while` statement, the `for` statement can make it easier to understand how the loop is controlled because the initialization, testing, and updating steps of the loop are consolidated into one statement. C++ programmers use `for` statements for loops that process collections or sequences of data.

For counted loops, a `for` statement is usually favored over the `while` statement

A.5.3 The `do` Statement

Use the `do` statement when you want to execute a loop's body at least once. Its general form is

```
do
    statement
while (expression);
```

A `do` statement loops at least once

Here, *statement* executes until the value of *expression* is false.

For example, suppose that you execute a sequence of statements and then ask the user whether to execute them again. The `do` statement is appropriate, because you execute the statements before you decide whether to repeat them:

```
char response;
do
{
   // A sequence of statements
```

---

[5] C++ Interlude 2 introduces pointer types.

```
    . . .
    std::cout << "Do it again?";
    std::cin >> response;
} while ( (response == 'Y') || (response == 'y') );
```

A.6   Arrays

An array contains data that has the same type

You can access array elements directly and in any order

An array contains data items, or **entries**, that have the same data type. An array's memory locations, or **elements**, have an order: An array has a first element, a second element, and so on, as well as a last element. That is, an array has a finite, limited number of elements. Therefore, you must know the maximum number of elements needed for a particular array when you write your program and *before* you execute it. Because you can access the array elements directly and in any order, an array is a **direct access**, or **random access**, data structure.

A.6.1   One-Dimensional Arrays

When you decide to use an array in your program, you must declare it and, in doing so, indicate the data type of its entries as well as its **size**, or **capacity**. The following statements declare a one-dimensional array, maxTemps, which contains the daily maximum temperatures for a given week:

```
const int DAYS_PER_WEEK = 7;
double maxTemps[DAYS_PER_WEEK];
```

The bracket notation [] declares maxTemps as an array. This array can contain at most seven floating-point values.

Use an index to specify a particular element in an array

An array index has an integer value greater than or equal to 0

You can refer to any of the floating-point entries in maxTemps directly by using an expression, which is called the **index**, or **subscript**, enclosed in square brackets. In C++, array indices must have integer values in the range 0 to *size* − 1, where *size* is the number of elements in the array. The indices for maxTemps range from 0 to DAYS_PER_WEEK − 1. For example, the fifth element in this array is maxTemps[4]. If k is an integer variable whose value is 4, maxTemps[k] is the fifth element in the array, and maxTemps[k+1] is the sixth element. Also, maxTemps[k++] accesses maxTemps[k] before adding 1 to k. Note that you use one index to refer to an element in a one-dimensional array.

Figure A-6 illustrates the array maxTemps, which at present contains only five temperatures. The last value in the array is in maxTemp[4]; the elements maxTemps[5] and maxTemps[6] are not initialized and therefore contain unknown values.

You can use enumerators as indices because they have integer values. For example, consider the following definition:

You can use an enumerator as an array index

```
enum Day {SUN, MON, TUE, WED, THU, FRI, SAT};
```

Given this definition, maxTemps[THU] has the same meaning as maxTemps[4]. You can also use the enumerators within a loop that processes an array, as in the following for statement:

```
for (Day dayIndex = SUN; dayIndex <= SAT; dayIndex++)
    std::cout << maxTemps[dayIndex] << std::endl;
```

Clearly, before you access an element of an array, you must assign it a value. You must assign values to array elements one at a time by using the previously described index notation. Note that, if a and b are arrays of the same type, the assignment a = b is illegal.[6]

---

[6] C++ enables you to define your own array data type and array operators so that this assignment would be valid. To do so, you need to use classes (C++ Interlude 1) and overloaded operators (C++ Interlude 6).

FIGURE A-6   A one-dimensional array of at most seven elements

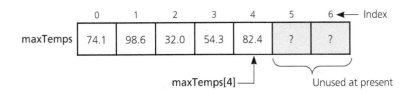

The data type of maxTemps is a **derived type**, which is a type that you derive from the primitive types by using a declaration operator such as [ ]. Naming a derived type by using a typedef is often useful. Thus, you can write

```
const int DAYS_PER_WEEK = 7;
typedef double ArrayType[DAYS_PER_WEEK];
ArrayType maxTemps;
```

and make ArrayType available for use throughout your program.

Initialization. You can initialize the elements of an array when you declare it for the first time. For example,

> You can initialize an array when you declare it

```
double maxTemps[DAYS_PER_WEEK] = {82.0, 71.5, 61.8, 75.0, 88.3};
```

initializes the first five elements of maxTemps to the values listed and the last two elements to zero.

Passing an array to a function. If you wanted a function that computed the average of the first *n* entries in a one-dimensional array, you could declare the function as

```
double getAverageTemp(double temperatures[], int n);
```

Because the compiler does not know the number of entries that the array can hold, you must also pass the function either the size of the array or the number of array entries to process. Traditionally, the array is listed as the first parameter and the number of entries as the second. You can invoke the function by writing, for example,

```
double avg = getAverageTemp(maxTemps, 5);
```

where maxTemps is the previously defined array.

An array is never passed to a function by value, regardless of how you write its parameter. *An array is always passed by reference.* This restriction avoids the copying of perhaps many array entries. Thus, the function getAverageTemp could modify the entries of the array maxTemps, even though it is an input to the function. To prevent such alteration, you can specify the array parameter as a constant reference parameter by preceding its type with const, as follows:

> Arrays are always passed by reference to a function

```
double getAverageTemp(const double temperatures[], int n);
```

A.6.2 Multidimensional Arrays

You can use a one-dimensional array, which has one index, for a simple collection of data. For example, you can organize 52 temperatures linearly, one after another. A one-dimensional array of these temperatures can represent this organization.

FIGURE A-7   A two-dimensional array

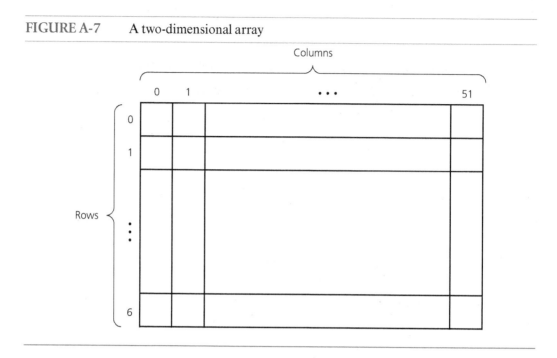

An array can have
more than one
dimension

You can also declare multidimensional arrays. You use more than one index to designate an element in a multidimensional array. Suppose that you wanted to represent the minimum temperature for each day during 52 weeks. The following statements declare a two-dimensional array, minTemps:

```
const int DAYS_PER_WEEK = 7;
const int WEEKS_PER_YEAR = 52;
double minTemps[DAYS_PER_WEEK][WEEKS_PER_YEAR];
```

These statements specify the ranges for two indices: The first index can range from 0 to 6, while the second index can range from 0 to 51. Most people picture a two-dimensional array as a rectangular arrangement, or matrix, of elements that form rows and columns, as Figure A-7 indicates. The first dimension given in the declaration of minTemps is the number of rows. Thus, minTemps has 7 rows and 52 columns. Each column in this matrix represents the seven daily minimum temperatures for a particular week.

In a two-dimensional
array, the first index
represents the row,
the second index
represents the
column

To reference an element in a two-dimensional array, you must indicate both the row and the column that contain the element. You make these indications of row and column by writing two indices, each enclosed in brackets. For example, minTemps[1][51] is the element in the 2nd row and the 52nd column. In the context of the temperature example, this element contains the minimum temperature recorded for the 2nd day (Monday) of the 52nd week. The rules for the indices of a one-dimensional array also apply to the indices of multidimensional arrays.

As an example of how to use a two-dimensional array in a program, consider the following program segment, which determines the smallest value in the previously described array minTemps. We use enumerators to reference the days of the week.

```
enum Day {SUN, MON, TUES, WED, THURS, FRI, SAT};

// Initially, assume the lowest temperature is first in the array
double lowestTemp = minTemps[0][0];
```

```
Day dayOfWeek = SUN;
int weekOfYear = 1;

// Search array for lowest temperature
for (int weekIndex = 0; weekIndex < WEEKS_PER_YEAR; weekIndex++)
{
   for (Day dayIndex = SUN; dayIndex <= SAT; dayIndex++)
   {
      if (lowestTemp > minTemps[dayIndex][weekIndex])
      {
         lowestTemp = minTemps[dayIndex][weekIndex];
         dayOfWeek = dayIndex;
         weekOfYear = weekIndex + 1;
      }  // end if
   } // end for
} // end for

// At this point, lowestTemp is the smallest value in minTemps and
// occurs on the day and week given by dayOfWeek and weekOfYear,
// that is, lowestTemp == minTemps[dayOfWeek][weekOfYear - 1].
```

Although you can declare arrays with more than two dimensions, generally more than three dimensions is unusual. The techniques for working with such arrays, however, are analogous to those for two-dimensional arrays.

 Programming Tip: When referencing an element of a multidimensional array, do not use comma-separated indices. For example, `myArray[3,6]` does not reference the array element `myArray[3][6]`. The expression 3,6 is a **comma expression** whose value is that of the last item listed, namely 6. Thus, although `myArray[3,6]` is legal, its meaning is `myArray[6]`, which references the element `myArray[0][6]`.

Initialization. You can initialize the elements of a two-dimensional array just as you initialize a one-dimensional array. You list the initial values row by row. For example, the statement

```
int x[2][3] = { {1, 2, 3},
                {4, 5, 6} };  // 2 rows, 3 columns
```

initializes the two-dimensional array x so that it appears as

```
1   2   3
4   5   6
```

That is, the statements initialize the elements `x[0][0]`, `x[0][1]`, `x[0][2]`, `x[1][0]`, `x[1][1]`, and `x[1][2]` in that order. In general, when you assign initial values to a multidimensional array, it is the last, or rightmost, index that increases the fastest.

A.7 Strings

Earlier, you saw that C++ provides literal character strings such as

```
"This is a string."
```

You can declare and use variables that contain such strings, and then manipulate the strings as naturally as you manipulate integers by using familiar operators. Our presentation includes only some of the possible operations on strings.

The C++ Standard Library provides the data type `string`. To use `string` in your program, you precede it with the statement

```
#include <string>
```

Note that `string` is in the `std` namespace. We will discuss libraries and namespaces later in this appendix.

You can declare a string variable `title` and initialize it to the empty string by writing

```
std::string title; // Initialization is provided by string's default constructor
```

You can initialize a string variable to a string literal when you declare it by writing

```
std::string title = "Walls and Mirrors";
```

You can subsequently assign another string to `title` by using an assignment statement such as

```
title = "J Perfect's Diary";
```

In each of the previous examples, `title` has a length of 17. You use either of the methods `length` or `size` to get the current length of a string. Thus, `title.length()` and `title.size()` are each 17.

You can reference the individual characters in a string by using the same index notation that you use for an array. Thus, in the previous example, `title[0]` contains the character J and `title[16]` contains the character y.

You can compare strings by using the familiar comparison operators. Not only can you see whether two strings are equal, but you can also discover which of two strings comes before the other. The ordering of two strings is analogous to alphabetic ordering, but you use the ASCII table instead of the alphabet. Thus, the following relationships are all true:

Examples of true expressions

```
"dig" < "dog"
"Star" < "star"    (because 'S' < 's')
"start" > "star"
"d" > "abc"
```

You can concatenate two strings to form another string by using the + operator. That is, you place one string after another to form a third string. For example, if

```
std::string str1 = "Com";
```

the statement

```
std::string str2 = str1 + "puter";
```

forms the string `"Computer"` and assigns it to `str2`. Similarly, you can append a single character to a string, as in

```
str1 += 's';
```

Use substr to access part of a string

You can manipulate a portion of a string by using the method

```
substr(position, length)
```

The first argument specifies the position of the beginning of the substring (remember that 0 is the position of the first character in the string). The second argument is the length of the substring. For example,

```
title.substr(2, 7)
```

is the string `"Perfect"`.

To perform input and output with C++ strings, you must include the library `iostream` by beginning your program with the statement

```
#include <iostream>
```

For example, you then can display the contents of a string variable by executing

```
title = "Walls and Mirrors";
std::cout << title << "\n";
```

You can use << to display a string

The result is `Walls and Mirrors`. The operator `<<` writes the entire string, including the blanks. You can read a string of characters into a string variable. For example, when the statement

```
std::cin >> title;
```

reads the data line

You can use >> to read a string without whitespace

```
Jamie Perfect's Diary
```

it assigns the string `"Jamie"` to `title`. Whitespace in the input line terminates the read operation for a string. To read the entire line of input, including its blank characters, you write

```
getline(std::cin, title);
```

A.8   Vectors

Another way to hold data items of the same type is by using a **vector**. A vector is similar to a one-dimensional array, but vectors provide additional features for the programmer not found in a simple array. A vector is an object of a standard C++ class named `vector`. This class is a part of the **Standard Template Library**, or **STL**. The STL is a library of template classes that provide data types you can use in your programs. These data types are not part of the official C++ language, but they have been added to the built-in data types. Section A.10 discusses libraries such as the STL and their usefulness. C++ Interlude 8 explores the STL in more detail.

To use a vector in your program, you must begin it with the following statement:

```
#include <vector>
```

You can declare a vector in one of three ways:

- If you know how many elements you want in the vector, you can place the type of data it will hold in angle brackets and the number of elements in parentheses:

```
std::vector<double> firstVector(10);    // Vector to hold 10 doubles
std::vector<std::string> myVector(12); // Vector to hold 12 strings
```

The size you specify when declaring the vector is only its initial size. As you will see, a vector can grow in size when you add entries. Note that both `vector` and `string` are in the `std` namespace. Section A.11 of this appendix discusses namespaces.

- You can place initial values into a vector when you declare it by writing a second argument:

```
std::vector<int> intVector(5, -1); // Vector to hold 5 integers, initially -1
```

When the elements in the vector are allocated, they are given the value of the second argument.

- You can also create an empty vector—a vector with no elements—by omitting its size and the parentheses:

```
std::vector<char> letterVector; // An empty vector of characters
```

Access vector
entries using [ ] just
as you would an
array

You can store or access the entries in a vector by using the [ ] operator, just as you would when using an array. As for an array, the subscripts that identify elements in a vector start at 0 and go to s − 1, where s is the current size of the vector. The following statements are examples of accessing an existing value in a vector and changing the value of an existing entry:

```cpp
double x = firstVector[5];                  // Gets sixth entry in x
myVector[3] = "This is a sample string."; // Sets fourth entry's value
```

Using [ ] stores a value in an *existing* element. If you are not sure how many elements the vector has, you can call the method size, as in the following example:

```cpp
std::cout << intVector.size() << std::endl; // Displays the capacity of intVector
```

size returns the
number of elements
in the vector

By calling the size method, you can find out whether the vector is full. This is an important advantage that a vector has over an array.

If the vector is either full or has no elements—that is, if it was created without elements, as letterVector was previously—you can still add new values by using the method push_back. The push_back method accepts an argument and adds it after the last element of the vector. In other words, it pushes the value onto the back of the vector.

Earlier, we declared a ten-element vector firstVector that could hold data of type double. If that vector was full, and we needed to add the additional values 2.3 and 3.4, we could use the push_back method:

push_back places
its argument into a
new element at the
back of a vector

```cpp
firstVector.push_back(2.3); // Grow vector and store value
firstVector.push_back(3.4); // Grow vector and store value
```

At this point, calling the size method would return 12, since two additional elements have been added to the vector.

pop_back removes
the last element
from a vector

You also can reduce the size of a vector by removing either its last element or all of its elements. To remove only the last element, you can use the pop_back method. This method shortens the vector but does not give you the entry in the removed element. You must save that entry before calling pop_back. For example, the following statements get the current size of the vector myVector, save the value in the last element, and then remove the last element from the vector:

```cpp
int length = myVector.size();               // Find the current number of elements
std::string last = myVector[length - 1]; // Get the string in the last element
myVector.pop_back();                        // Reduce the number of elements by 1
```

A subsequent call to myVector.size() would return length − 1, since the last element was removed.

clear removes all
elements from a
vector so it has a
size of 0

To remove all elements from a vector and leave the vector empty, you use the method clear:

```cpp
myVector.clear(); // myVector is now an empty vector
```

After a vector has been cleared, you must use the method push_back to add new entries.

C++ Interlude 8 provides more information about vector, including these and other methods.

A.9   Classes

Object-oriented programming, or **OOP**, views a program not as a sequence of actions but as a collection of components called **objects** that interact to produce a certain result. A group of objects of the same kind belong to a **class**, which is a programming construct that defines the object's data type. Chapter 1 talks more about OOP; here we want to discuss how to write a class in C++.

An object contains data and can perform certain operations on or with that data. The class associated with a particular object describes its data and its operations. That is, a class is like a blueprint for creating certain objects. An object's operations, or **behaviors**, are defined within the class by **methods**, which are simply functions within a class. These methods, together with the class's data are known as the class's **members**.

A C++ class defines a new data type

We could use a ball as an example of an object. Because thinking of a basketball, volleyball, tennis ball, or soccer ball probably suggests images of the game rather than the object itself, let's abstract the notion of a ball by picturing a sphere. A sphere of a given radius has attributes such as volume and surface area. A sphere as an object should be able to report its radius, volume, surface area, and so on. That is, the sphere object has methods that return such values.

In C++, a class has the following form:

```
class Sphere
{
private:
    <Declarations of private data members and methods>
    <Definitions of private methods>
    . . .

public:
    <Definitions of public methods>
    . . .
}; // Note the semicolon
```

By default, all members in a class are **private**—they are not directly accessible by any program that uses the class—unless you designate them as **public**. However, explicitly indicating the private and public portions of a class is a good programming practice and one that we will follow in this book. You should always declare a class's data members as private.

Most methods are public, but private methods—which only the class can call—can be helpful, as you will see. The definition of a class's method can call any of the class's other methods or use any of its data members, regardless of whether they are private or public.

Classes have special methods, called constructors and destructors, for the creation and destruction of its objects. A **constructor** creates and initializes new objects, or **instances**, of a class. A **destructor** destroys an object by freeing the memory assigned to it, when the object's lifetime ends. A typical class has several constructors, but only one destructor. For many classes, you can omit the destructor. In such cases, the compiler will generate a destructor for you. For now, the compiler-generated destructor is sufficient. C++ Interlude 2 discusses how and why you would write your own destructor.

An object is an instance of a class
A constructor creates and initializes an object

In C++, a constructor has the same name as the class. Constructors have no return type—not even void—and cannot use return to return a value. Constructors can have arguments. We discuss constructors in more detail shortly, after we look at an example of a class definition.

A destructor destroys an object

A.9.1 The Header File

You should place each class definition in its own **header file** or **specification file**—whose name by convention ends in .h. The header file Sphere.h shown in Listing A-2 contains a class definition for sphere objects.

LISTING A-2   The header file Sphere.h

Comments in the
header file specify
the methods

```cpp
1   /** @file Sphere.h */
2   const double PI = 3.14159;
3
4   /** Definition of a class of Spheres. */
5   class Sphere
6   {
7   private:
8      double theRadius; // The sphere's radius
9
10  public:
11     /** Default constructor: Creates a sphere and initializes its radius
12      to a default value.
13      Precondition:  None.
14      Postcondition:  A sphere of radius 1 exists. */
15     Sphere();
16
17     /** Constructor: Creates a sphere and initializes its radius.
18      Precondition:  initialRadius is the desired radius.
19      Postcondition:  A sphere of radius initialRadius exists. */
20     Sphere(double initialRadius);
21
22     /** Sets (alters) the radius of this sphere.
23      Precondition:  newRadius is the desired radius.
24      Postcondition:  The sphere's radius is newRadius. */
25     void setRadius(double newRadius);
26
27     /** Gets this sphere's radius.
28      Precondition:  None.
29      Postcondition:  Returns the radius. */
30     double getRadius() const;
31
32     /** Gets this sphere's diameter.
33      Precondition:  None.
34      Postcondition:  Returns the diameter. */
35     double getDiameter() const;
36
37     /** Gets this sphere's circumference.
38      Precondition:  PI is a named constant.
39      Postcondition:  Returns the circumference. */
40     double getCircumference() const;
41
42     /** Gets this sphere's surface area.
43      Precondition:  PI is a named constant.
44      Postcondition:  Returns the surface area. */
45     double getArea() const;
46
47     /** Gets this sphere's volume.
48      Precondition:  PI is a named constant.
49      Postcondition:  Returns the volume. */
50     double getVolume() const;
51
52     // The compiler-generated destructor is sufficient.
53  }; // end Sphere
54  // End of header file.
```

You should always place a class's data members within its private section. Typically, you provide methods—such as setRadius and getRadius—to access the data members. In this way, you control how and whether the rest of the program can access the data members. This design principle should lead to programs that not only are easier to debug, but also have fewer logical errors from the beginning.

A class's data members should be private

Some method declarations, such as

```
double getRadius() const;
```

are tagged with const. Such methods cannot alter the data members of the class. Making get-Radius a const method is a fail-safe technique that ensures that it will only return the current value of the sphere's radius, without changing it.

const methods cannot change a class's data members

A.9.2 The Implementation File

Let's begin implementing the class Sphere by examining its constructors.

Constructors. A constructor allocates memory for an object and can initialize the object's data to particular values. A class can have more than one constructor, as is the case for the class Sphere.

The first constructor in Sphere is the **default constructor**:

```
Sphere();
```

A default constructor has no arguments

A default constructor by definition has no arguments. Typically, a default constructor initializes data members to values that the class implementation chooses. For example, the implementation

```
Sphere::Sphere()
{
    theRadius = 1.0;
} // end default constructor
```

sets theRadius to 1.0. C++ Interlude 1 will show you another way to initialize data members within constructors that is preferable to using assignment statements.

Notice the qualifier Sphere:: that precedes the constructor's name. When you implement any method, you qualify its name with its class type followed by the **scope resolution operator** :: to distinguish it from other methods that might have the same name.

When you declare an instance of the class, you implicitly invoke a constructor. For example, the statement

```
Sphere unitSphere;
```

invokes the default constructor, which creates the object unitSphere and sets its radius to 1.0. Notice that you do not include parentheses after unitSphere.

The next constructor in Sphere is

```
Sphere(double initialRadius);
```

It creates a sphere object of radius initialRadius. This constructor needs only to initialize the private data member theRadius to initialRadius. Its implementation is

```
Sphere::Sphere(double initialRadius)
{
    theRadius = initialRadius;
} // end constructor
```

You implicitly invoke this constructor by writing a declaration such as

```
Sphere mySphere(5.1);
```

In this case, the object mySphere has a radius of 5.1.

We can make the previous constructor ensure that the given radius is not negative by writing its definition as follows:

```
Sphere::Sphere(double initialRadius)
{
   if (initialRadius > 0)
      theRadius = initialRadius;
   else
      theRadius = 1.0; // Set to default value, if bad input
}  // end constructor
```

Note: If you omit all constructors from your class, the compiler will generate a default constructor—that is, one with no arguments—for you. A compiler-generated default constructor, however, might not initialize data members to values that you will find suitable. If you define a constructor that has arguments but you omit the default constructor, the compiler will not generate one for you. Thus, you will not be able to write statements such as

```
Sphere defaultSphere;
```

The implementation file contains the definitions of the class's methods

Typically, you place the implementation of a class's constructors and other methods in an **implementation file** whose name ends in .cpp. Listing A-3 contains an implementation file for the class Sphere. Notice that within the definition of a method, you can reference the class's data member or invoke its other methods without preceding the member names with Sphere::. In particular, notice how the constructor calls the method setRadius to avoid duplicating the code that ensures a positive radius.

LISTING A-3   The implementation file Sphere.cpp

```
1   /** @file Sphere.cpp */
2   #include "Sphere.h" // Include the header file
3
4   Sphere::Sphere()
5   {
6      theRadius = 1.0;
7   }  // end default constructor
8
9   Sphere::Sphere(double initialRadius)
10  {
11     setRadius(initialRadius); // Sphere:: not needed here
12  }  // end constructor
13
14  void Sphere::setRadius(double newRadius)
15  {
16     if (newRadius > 0)
17        theRadius = newRadius;
```

```
18      else
19         theRadius = 1.0;
20   }  // end setRadius
21
22   double Sphere::getRadius() const
23   {
24      return theRadius;
25   }  // end getRadius
26
27   double Sphere::getDiameter() const
28   {
29      return 2.0 * theRadius;
30   }  // end getDiameter
31
32   double Sphere::getCircumference() const
33   {
34      return PI * getDiameter();
35   }  // end getCircumference
36
37   double Sphere::getArea() const
38   {
39      return 4.0 * PI * theRadius * theRadius;
40   }  // end getArea
41
42   double  Sphere::getVolume() const
43   {
44      double radiusCubed = theRadius * theRadius * theRadius;
45      return (4.0 * PI * radiusCubed) / 3.0;
46   }  // end getVolume
47   // End of implementation file.
```

A local variable such as radiusCubed should not be a data member

Note: Local variables
You should distinguish between a class's data members and any local variables that the implementation of a method requires. It is inappropriate for such local variables to be data members of the class.

A.9.3 Using the Class Sphere

The following simple program demonstrates the use of the class Sphere:

```
#include <iostream>
#include "Sphere.h"
int main()
{
   Sphere unitSphere;         // Radius is 1.0
   Sphere mySphere(5.1);      // Radius is 5.1
   mySphere.setRadius(4.2);   // Resets radius to 4.2
   std::cout << mySphere.getDiameter() << std::endl;

   return 0;
}  // end main
```

An object such as mySphere can, on request, reset the value of its radius; return its radius; and compute its diameter, surface area, circumference, and volume. These requests to an object are called **messages** and are simply calls to methods. Thus, an object responds to a message by acting on its data. To invoke an object's method, you qualify the method's name with the object variable. For example, we wrote mySphere.getDiameter() in the previous program.

Notice that the previous program included the header file Sphere.h, but did not include the implementation file Sphere.cpp. You compile a class's implementation file separately from the program that uses the class. The way you tell the operating system where to locate the compiled implementation depends on the particular system. Section A.10 of this appendix and C++ Interlude 1 provide more information about header and implementation files.

The previous program is an example of a **client** of a class. A client of a particular class is simply a program or module that uses the class. We will reserve the term **user** for the person who uses a program.

A.9.4 Inheritance

A brief discussion of **inheritance** is provided here, because it is a common way to create new classes in C++. Further discussions of inheritance occur in C++ Interludes 1 and 5, and as needed throughout the book.

A class derived from the class Sphere

Suppose we want to give our spheres a color, knowing that we have already developed the class Sphere. Instead of writing an entirely new class of spheres that have a color, we can reuse the Sphere implementation and add color characteristics and operations by using inheritance. Here is a declaration of the class SphereInColor that uses inheritance:

```cpp
#include "Sphere.h"
enum Color {RED, BLUE, GREEN, YELLOW};
class SphereInColor : public Sphere
{
private:
   Color sphereColor;

public:
   SphereInColor(Color initialColor);
   SphereInColor(Color initialColor, double initialRadius);
   void setColor(Color newColor);
   Color getColor() const;
}; // end SphereInColor
```

The class Sphere is called the **base class** or **superclass**, and SphereInColor is called the **derived class** or **subclass** of the class Sphere.

Any instance of the derived class is also considered to be an instance of the base class and can be used in a program anywhere that an instance of the base class can be used. Also, when the keyword public precedes the name of the base class in the new class's header, any of the publicly defined methods or data members that can be used with instances of the base class can be used with instances of the derived class. The derived class instances also have the additional methods and data members that are publicly defined in the derived class definition.

The implementation of the methods for the class SphereInColor is as follows:

```cpp
SphereInColor::SphereInColor(Color initialColor): Sphere()
{
   sphereColor = initialColor;
} // end constructor
```

```
SphereInColor::SphereInColor(Color initialColor, double initialRadius)
                                            : Sphere(initialRadius)
{
   sphereColor = initialColor;
}  // end constructor

void SphereInColor::setColor(Color newColor)
{
   sphereColor = newColor;
}  // end setColor

Color SphereInColor::getColor() const
{
   return sphereColor;
}  // end getColor
```

Notice how the constructors for the class `SphereInColor` invoke the base-class constructors `Sphere()` and `Sphere(initialRadius)`. The derived class needs the initialization of the data members in the base class that the base-class constructors can provide. The derived-class constructors then add initializations that are specific to the derived class.

Here is a function that uses the class `SphereInColor`:

```
void useSphereInColor()
{
   SphereInColor ball(RED);
   ball.setRadius(5.0);
   std::cout << "The ball diameter is " << ball.getDiameter();
   ball.setColor(BLUE);
   ...
}  // end useSphereInColor
```

An instance of a derived class can invoke public methods of the base class

This function uses the constructor and the method `setColor` from the derived class `SphereInColor`. It also uses the methods `setRadius` and `getDiameter` that are defined in the base class `Sphere`.

A.10 Libraries

One of the advantages of modular programming is that you can implement modules independently of other modules. You might also find it possible for several different programs to use a particular module. As a result, you can build a **library** of modules—that is, classes and functions—that you can include in future programs.

Any library—a C++ standard library or one that you write—has a corresponding header that provides information about the contents of the library. For standard libraries, the header is simply an abstraction that the compiler either maps to a filename or handles in a different manner. Thus, when using the standard libraries, you do not see the `.h` extension that ends the names of our own header files.

You have already seen some standard libraries, such as the one that provides input and output services. To use the modules contained in a library, you use the `include` directive with the name of the header associated with the library. For example, you write

```
#include <iostream>
```

Appendix H provides a list of some of the available headers.

User-defined libraries are typically organized into two files. One file, the header file, contains a definition for each class in the library that is available to your program. This file could also contain, for example, function declarations, constant definitions, `typedef` statements, enumerations, and other `include` statements. By convention, the name of a header file associated with a user-defined library ends in `.h`. The other file—the implementation file—contains definitions of the class methods that the header file declares. Typically, the name of an implementation file ends in `.cpp`.

The assumption, of course, is that the files are in source form—that is, they need to be compiled. It certainly would be more efficient to compile the method definitions once, independently of any particular program, and then later merge the results of the compilation with any program that you desire. In fact, you should compile the implementation file and then include the header file in source form in your program by using an `include` directive such as

```
#include "MyHeader.h"
```

You use double quotes instead of angle brackets to enclose the name of a header file that you have written. The mechanics of incorporating the compiled implementation file into your program are system dependent.

Thus, your program can use previously compiled C++ statements, which are no longer available to you in source form. Maybe you did not even write these statements, just as you did not write the standard C++ functions such as `sqrt`. That is, you use a library in the same spirit in which you use standard functions. Because the header file indicates what is available to you, you must think of a library in terms of what it can do for you and not how it is implemented. You should think of all of your modules in this way, even if you eventually implement them yourself.

Note: The C++ Standard Library

The C++ Standard Library is a collection of standard classes and functions that you can use in your C++ programs. This library provides us with such features as input and output services, strings, and functions to perform certain mathematical tasks.

Note: The C++ Standard Template Library (STL)

The C++ Standard Template Library, or STL, is a collection of classes and functions that is a part of the C++ Standard Library, and you can use in your C++ programs with any data type—either built-in or user-defined. To achieve this flexibility, this library uses templates, which are a construct that we will discuss in C++ Interlude 1. Note that `vector` is a template class within the STL.

A.11 Namespaces

Since different libraries can use the same names for their classes and functions, C++ organizes these names into namespaces. A **namespace** is a named group, or category, of identifiers that enables you to differentiate among identical identifiers. For example, if the namespaces x and y each contain the identifier z, `x::z` and `y::z` are different identifiers.

Earlier when we used strings in a program, we included the standard class of strings by writing

```
#include <string>
```

The names of the classes and functions in the C++ Standard Library are organized into the namespace std. You can write the directive

```
using namespace std;
```

to tell the compiler to look for string in the C++ Standard Library if it does not find its definition in our program. Another library might also contain a class named string, but it would be associated with a different namespace. Analogous comments apply to vector, as described in Section A.8, since it also is in the std namespace.

The following program contains a using directive for the namespace std:

```
#include <iostream>
#include <string>

using namespace std;

int main()
{
    string title = "Walls and Mirrors";
    cout << title << endl;

    return 0;
} // end main
```

The program can reference all of the classes in the std namespace, including iostream and string, without preceding their names with std::.

Programming Tip: The previous using directive lets the compiler see all of the names in the std namespace. You might use a name in your program that is also in the std namespace and defined in the C++ Standard Library. The compiler would be faced with two definitions for the same identifier, yours and the library's. To avoid this confusion and the chance for hard-to-detect errors, professional programmers do not use this directive; we will not use it within the chapters of this book.

One way to omit the using directive for the std namespace is to precede the identifiers in that namespace with the **namespace indicator** std::. For example, we can write the previous program as follows:

```
#include <iostream>
#include <string>

int main()
{
    std::string title = "Walls and Mirrors";
    std::cout << title << std::endl;

    return 0;
} // end main
```

Although writing a namespace indicator is often the best way to proceed, you might find it tedious. In such an event, you could write **using declarations** as follows:

```
#include <iostream>
#include <string>

int main()
{
```

```
using std::string; // string is in the std namespace
using std::cout;   // cout is in the std namespace

// You can use string and cout without an std:: prefix
string title = "Walls and Mirrors";
cout << title << std::endl;
return 0;
} // end main
```

After the `using` declarations, you can write `string` and `cout` without needing to precede them with `std::`.

SUMMARY

1. A comment in C++ can begin with

    *   `//` as a single line or at the end of a C++ statement.

    *   `/**`, end with `*/`, and occupy several lines at the beginning of a method, function, or class.

    *   `/*`, end with `*/`, and occupy several lines anywhere within a program.

2. A C++ identifier is a sequence of letters, digits, and underscores that must begin with either a letter or an underscore.

3. You can use a `typedef` statement to declare new names for data types. These names are simply synonyms for the data types; they are not new data types.

4. You define named constants by using a statement of the form

    `const` *type identifier* = *value*;

5. Enumeration provides another way to name integer constants and to define an integral data type, as in

    `enum Day {SUN, MON, TUE, WED, THU, FRI, SAT};`

6. C++ uses short-circuit evaluation for expressions that contain the logical operators `&&` (and) and `||` (or). That is, evaluation proceeds from left to right and stops as soon as the value of the entire expression is apparent.

7. The output operator `<<` places a value into an output stream, and the input operator `>>` extracts a value from an input stream. You can imagine that these operators point in the direction of data flow. Thus, in `cout << myVar`, the operator points away from the variable `myVar`—data flows from `myVar` to the stream— whereas in `cin >> myVar`, the operator points to the variable `myVar`—data flows from the stream into `myVar`.

8. The general form of a function definition is

    type name (*parameter-declaration-list*)
    {
      body
    }

    A valued function returns a value by using the `return` statement. Although a void function does not return a value, it can use `return` to exit.

9. When invoking a function, the actual arguments must correspond to the parameters in number, order, and type.

10. A function makes local copies of the values of any arguments that are passed by value. Thus, the arguments remain unchanged by the function. Such arguments are, therefore, input arguments. A function does not copy arguments that are passed by reference. Rather, it references the actual argument locations whenever the parameters appear in the function's definition. In this way, a function can change the values of the arguments, thus implementing output arguments. However, a function does not copy and cannot change a constant reference argument. If copying an input argument would be expensive, make it a constant reference argument instead of a value argument.

11. The general form of the `if` statement is

```
if (expression)
    statement₁
else
    statement₂
```

If *expression* is true, *statement₁* executes; otherwise *statement₂* executes.

12. The general form of the `switch` statement is

```
switch (expression)
{
    case constant₁:
        statement₁
        break;
    . . .
    case constantₙ:
        statementₙ
        break;
    default:
        statement
}
```

The appropriate *statement* executes according to the value of *expression*. Typically, `break` follows the statement or statements after each `case`. Omitting `break` causes execution to continue to the statement(s) in the next `case`.

13. The general form of the `while` statement is

```
while (expression)
    statement
```

As long as *expression* is true, *statement* executes. Thus, it is possible that *statement* never executes.

14. The general form of the `for` statement is

```
for (initialize; test; update)
    statement
```

where *initialize*, *test*, and *update* are expressions. Typically, *initialize* is an assignment expression that occurs only once. Then if *test*, which is usually a logical expression, is true, *statement* executes. The expression *update* executes next, usually incrementing or decrementing a counter. This sequence of events repeats, beginning with the evaluation of *test*, until *test* is false.

15. The general form of the `do` statement is

```
do
    statement
while (expression);
```

Here, *statement* executes until the value of *expression* is false. Note that *statement* always executes at least once. Also note the required semicolon.

16. An array contains items that have the same data type. You can refer to these items by using an index that begins with zero. Arrays are always passed to functions by reference.

17. You must be careful that an array index does not exceed the size of the array. C++ does not check the range of array indices. Similar comments apply to strings.

18. An object encapsulates both data and operations on that data. In C++, objects are instances of a class, which is a programmer-defined data type.

19. A string is an object of the standard C++ class `string`. It represents a sequence of characters. You can manipulate the entire string, a substring, or the individual characters.

20. A vector is an object of the standard C++ class `vector`. It holds items of the same data type. A vector behaves like a high-level array.

21. A C++ class contains at least one constructor, which is an initialization method, and a destructor, which is a cleanup method that destroys an object when its lifetime ends.

22. If you do not define a constructor for a class, the compiler will generate a default constructor—that is, one without arguments—for you. If you do not define a destructor, the compiler will generate one for you. C++ Interlude 2 and Chapter 4 describe when you need to write your own destructor.

23. Members of a class are private unless you designate them as public. The client of the class—that is, the program that uses the class—cannot use members that are private. However, the implementations of methods can use them. You should make the data members of a class private and provide public methods to access some or all of the data members.

24. Because certain classes have applications in many programs, you should take steps to facilitate their use. You can define and implement a class within header and implementation files, which a program can include when it needs to use the class.

25. A typical C++ program uses header files that you incorporate by using the `include` directive. A header file contains class definitions, function declarations, constant definitions, `typedef` statements, enumerations, and other `include` statements. The program might also require an implementation file of function definitions that have been compiled previously and placed into a library. The operating system locates the required implementation file and combines it with the program in ways that are system dependent.

Important Themes in Programming

Contents

Prerequisites

Appendix A   Review of C++ Fundamentals
Chapter 1   Data Abstraction: The Walls

W hat are the specific characteristics of good solutions? How can you construct good solutions? This appendix provides some answers to these very difficult questions.

The programming themes that we will discuss should be familiar to you. However, the novice programmer usually does not truly appreciate their importance. After the first course in programming, many students still simply want to "get the thing to run." The discussion that follows should help you realize just how important these themes really are.

People read programs, too

One of the most widespread misconceptions held by novice programmers is that a computer program is "read" only by a computer. As a consequence, they tend to consider only whether the computer is able to "understand" the program—that is, does the program compile, execute, and produce the correct output? The truth is, of course, that other people often must read and modify programs. In a typical programming environment, many individuals share a program. One person may write a program, which other people use in conjunction with other programs written by other people, and a year later, a different person may modify the program. It is therefore essential that you take great care to design a program that is easy to read and understand.

Key programming themes

You should always keep in mind the following seven themes of programming: modularity, style, modifiability, ease of use, fail-safe programming, debugging, and testing.

B.1   Modularity

As this book continually emphasizes, you should strive for modularity in all phases of the problem-solving process, beginning with the initial design of a solution. Many programming tasks become more difficult as the size and complexity of a program grows. Modularity slows the rate at which the level of difficulty grows. More specifically, modularity has a favorable impact on the following aspects of programming:

Modularity facilitates programming

- **Constructing the program.** The primary difference between a small modular program and a large modular program is simply the number of modules each contains. Because the modules are independent, writing one large modular program is not very different from writing many small, independent programs, although the interrelationships among modules make the design much more complicated. On the other hand, working on a large nonmodular program is more like working on many interrelated programs simultaneously. Modularity also permits team programming, in which several programmers work independently on their own modules before combining them into one program.

Modularity isolates errors

- **Debugging the program.** Debugging a large program can be a monstrous task. Imagine that you type a 10,000-line program and eventually get it to compile. Neither of these tasks would be much fun. Now imagine that you execute your program, and after a few hundred lines of output, you notice an incorrect number. You should anticipate spending the next day or so tracing through the intricacies of your program before discovering a problem such as an incorrect array index.

  A great advantage of modularity is that the task of debugging a large program is reduced to one of debugging many small programs. When you begin to code a module, you should be almost certain that all other modules coded so far are correct. That is, before you consider a module finished, you should test it extensively, both separately and in context with the other modules, by calling it with actual arguments carefully chosen to induce all possible behaviors of the modules. If this testing is done thoroughly, you can feel fairly sure that any problem is a result of an error in the last module added. *Modularity isolates errors.*

Formal theoretical techniques are available to verify the correctness of a program. Modular programs are amenable to this verification process.

- **Reading the program.** A person reading a large program may get lost in its details. Just as a modular design helps the programmer cope with the complexities of solving a problem, so too does a modular program help its reader understand how the program works. A modular program is easy to follow because the reader can get a good idea of what is going on without reading any of the code. A well-written function can be understood fairly well from only its name, initial comments, and the names of the other functions that it calls. Readers of a program need to study actual code only if they require a detailed understanding of how the program operates. Program readability is discussed further in the next section on style.

  Modular programs are easy to read

- **Modifying the program.** Modifiability is discussed in greater detail in Section B.3 of this appendix, but as the modularity of a program has a direct bearing on its modifiability, a brief mention is appropriate here. A small change in the requirements of a program should require only a small change in the code. If this is not the case, it is likely that the program is poorly written and, in particular, that it is not modular. To accommodate a small change in the requirements, a modular program usually requires a change in only a few of its modules, particularly when the modules are independent (referred to as being **loosely coupled**) and each module performs a single well-defined task (referred to as being **highly cohesive**). This point is of particular importance with iterative development techniques, which produce changes in program requirements at every iteration, as Appendix D will discuss.

  Modularity isolates modifications

  When making changes to a program, it is best to make a few at a time. By maintaining a modular design, you can reduce a fairly large modification to a set of small and relatively simple modifications to isolated parts of the program. *Modularity isolates modifications.*

- **Eliminating redundant code.** Another advantage of modular design is that you can identify a computation that occurs in many different parts of the program and implement it as a function or class method. Thus, the code for the computation appears only once, resulting in an increase in both readability and modifiability.

  Modularity eliminates redundancies

B.2   Style

We now consider the following seven issues of style in programming: the use of private data members, the proper use of reference arguments, the proper use of methods, avoidance of global variables in modules, error handling, readability, and documentation. Admittedly, much of the following discussion reflects the personal taste of the authors; certainly other good programming styles are possible. Most organizations that hire programmers publish style guides, so that each programming team can produce code that is easily read and maintained by other teams.

Seven issues of style

B.2.1   Use of Private Data Members

Each object has a set of methods that represents the operations that the object can perform. The object also contains data members for storing information. You should hide the exact representation of these data members from modules that use the object by making all of the data members private. Doing so supports the principle of information hiding. The details of the object's implementation are hidden from view, with methods providing the only mechanism for getting information to and from the object. When the only operations involved with a

Data members should always be private

particular data member are `retrieve` and `modify`, the object should provide a simple method—called an **accessor**—that returns the value of the data member and another method—called a **mutator**—that sets the value of the data member. For example, a `Person` object could provide access to the data member `theName` through the methods `getName` to return the person's name and `setName` to change the person's name.

B.2.2   Proper Use of Reference Arguments

A method interacts, in a controlled fashion, with the rest of the program via its arguments. Value parameters, which are the default in C++ when you do not write & after the parameter's data type, pass values into the method. The value of each argument corresponding to a value parameter is copied into the parameter, which is local to the method. Any change that the method makes to these parameters is not reflected in the actual arguments back in the calling program. This communication between the calling program and the method is one-way and supports the notion of an isolated module. Thus, you should use value arguments when possible. However, passing large objects by value is not very efficient because of the copying required.

> Reference arguments return values from a method

How and when is it appropriate to use reference parameters? Since a reference parameter becomes an **alias** (another name) for the corresponding argument, changes to the parameter within the method also occur in the argument in the calling module. The obvious situation requiring reference arguments is when a method needs to return several values to the calling module. Whenever you use a parameter to pass a value out of a method, the parameter must be a reference parameter.

Suppose that you are writing a method that requires access to a large object x, whose value should not be altered. You consider passing x by value; however, to increase the efficiency of your program, you would like to avoid the computer-time and storage requirements of making a copy of x. So what about passing x by reference? The problem with passing x by reference is that it conveys misinformation about the method's relation to the rest of the program. Since a reference parameter is used to communicate a value from the method back to its calling module, the program is more difficult to read if the parameter's value remains unchanged. The program also is more prone to errors if modifications are required. The situation is analogous to using a variable whose value never changes when you really should use a constant. The solution is to precede the parameter's declaration with `const`, which prevents the method from changing the corresponding argument. Thus, we have the efficiency of pass-by-reference (no copy is made) with the protection of pass-by-value (the argument is input only). This is called **pass-by-constant-reference**. If objects are large and complex, use pass-by-constant-reference; otherwise pass-by-value works fine.

> When copying the argument is expensive, use pass-by-constant-reference instead of pass-by-value

B.2.3   Proper Use of Methods

To reduce coupling among modules, you should restrict the calls that a method can make. A method should call only other methods:

> To reduce coupling, restrict what a method can do

- Defined within the same class
- Of argument objects
- Of objects created within the method
- Of objects contained within the same class as data members

For example, suppose we have the following code for three classes that represent a building, an appliance, and a lamp, respectively:

> Building is coupled to Lamp

```
// Original Solution
class Building
{
```

```
private:
   Appliance appliance;
public:
   void turnOnLight()
   {
       appliance.getLamp().turnOn(); // Improper method use
   } // end turnOnLight
}; // end Building

class Appliance
{
private:
   Lamp light;

public:
   Lamp getLamp()
   {
       return light;
   } // end getLamp
}; // end Appliance

class Lamp
{
public:
   void turnOn();
}; // end Lamp
```

Here, Building's method turnOnLight fails to follow these rules. It calls the method turnOn from the Lamp class, although a Lamp object is not part of the Building class and has not been passed to the turnOnLight method as an argument. This code has coupled the Building class to the Lamp class.

A much better design would decouple the Building and Lamp classes, as follows:

```
// Revised Solution
class Building
{
private:
   Appliance appliance;

public:
   void turnOnLight()
   {
       appliance.turnOnLamp();
   } // end turnOnLight
}; // end Building

class Appliance // Improved Appliance class
{
private:
   Lamp light;

public:
   void turnOnLamp()
   {
       light.turnOn();
   } // end turnOnLamp
}; // end Appliance

class Lamp
{
public:
   void turnOn();
}; // end Lamp
```

Building and Lamp are not coupled

Now the building asks the appliance to turn on the lamp, and the appliance turns on its light.

Suppose that the lamp's switch is replaced with a dimmer-type switch. We would need to give the turnOn method in the Lamp class an indication of how much to dim the light. Finding the call to turnOn in the original code segment might be difficult, because the Building class does not have explicit access to a Lamp object. You could search the Building class for instances of Lamp, and not find any. This type of dependency makes a solution more difficult to modify.

In the revised code segment, the Appliance class has a Lamp object as a data member. You can easily find the calls to this object, if necessary.

B.2.4 Avoidance of Global Variables in Modules

Do not use global variables

One of the main advantages of the concepts of encapsulation and information hiding is the creation of isolated modules. This isolation is sacrificed when a module accesses a global variable, because the effects of a module's action are no longer self-contained or limited to output arguments. That is, such a module has a **side effect**. Hence, the isolation of both errors and modifications is greatly compromised when global variables appear in modules.

B.2.5 Error Handling

In case of an error, methods should return a value or throw an exception, but not display a message

A program should check for errors in both its input and its logic and attempt to behave gracefully and consistently when it encounters them. A method should check for certain types of errors, such as invalid input or argument values. What action should a method take when it encounters an error? Depending on context, the appropriate action in the face of an error can range from ignoring erroneous data and continuing execution to terminating the program. A common technique is for a method to leave error handling to the calling module. In general, a method should either return a value to the calling module or throw an exception instead of displaying a message to indicate that it has encountered an error.

B.2.6 Readability

For a program to be easy to follow, it should have a good structure and design, a good choice of identifiers, good indentation and use of blank lines, and good documentation. These points are demonstrated in the programs throughout this book. You should avoid clever programming tricks that save a little computer time at the expense of much human time.

Choose identifiers that describe their purpose—that is, that are self-documenting. Distinguish between keywords, such as int, and user-defined identifiers. This book uses the following conventions:

Identifier style

- Keywords are lowercase and appear in color.
- Names of standard functions are lowercase.
- User-defined identifiers use both uppercase and lowercase letters, as follows:
  □ Class names are nouns, with each word in the identifier capitalized.
  □ Method names and function names are verbs or action phrases, with the first letter lowercase and subsequent internal words capitalized.
  □ Variables begin with a lowercase letter, with subsequent words in the identifier capitalized.
  □ Data types declared in a typedef statement and names of enumerations each begin with an uppercase letter.
  □ Named constants and enumerators are entirely uppercase and use underscores to separate words.

Two learning aids

- One other naming convention is suggested as a learning aid:
  □ Data types declared in a typedef statement end in Type.

Use a good indentation style to enhance the readability of a program. The layout of a program should make it easy for a reader to identify the program's modules. Use a blank line between method or function definitions. Also, within these definitions, you should indent individual blocks of code. These blocks are generally—but are not limited to—the actions performed within a control structure, such as a `while` loop or an `if` statement.

You can choose from among several good indentation styles. The four most important general requirements of an indentation style are:

- Blocks should be indented sufficiently so that they stand out clearly.
- Indentation should be consistent: Always indent the same kind of construct in the same manner.
- The indentation style should provide a reasonable way to handle the problem of **rightward drift**, the problem of nested blocks bumping against the right-hand margin of the page.
- In a compound statement, the open and close braces should line up, and each should appear on its own line:

Guidelines for
indentation style

```
{
    statement₁
    statement₂
        .
        .
        .
    statementₙ
}
```

- To prevent future errors, you should make the body of each control structure a compound statement, even if it consists of only one line of code. When you include open and close braces around the single-statement body of a control structure, you enable that control structure to contain multiple statements if needed in the future. A common programmer error is to include a second statement in the single-statement body of a control structure, thinking that it will execute within the body of that control structure. *Because of space restrictions, this book will not always follow this style.*

Within these guidelines there is room for personal taste. Here is a summary of the style you will see in this book:

- A `for` or `while` statement is written for a simple action as

Indentation style in
this book

```
while (expression)
    statement
```

and for a compound action as

```
while (expression)
{
    statements
}  // end while
```

- A `do` statement is written for a simple action as

```
do
    statement
while (expression);
```

and for a compound action as

```
do
{
    statements
} while (expression);
```

- An `if` statement is written for simple actions as

```
if (expression)
    statement₁
else
    statement₂
```

and for compound actions as

```
if (expression)
{
    statements
}
else
{
    statements
}  // end if
```

- One special use of the `if` statement warrants another style. Nested `if` statements that choose among three or more different courses of action, such as

```
if (condition₁)
    action₁
else if (condition₂)
        action₂
        else if (condition₃)
                action₃
```

are written as

```
if (condition₁)
    action₁
else if (condition₂)
    action₂
else if (condition₃)
    action₃
```

This indentation style better reflects the nature of the construct, which is like a generalized `switch` statement:

```
case condition₁: action₁; break;
case condition₂: action₂; break;
case condition₃: action₃; break;
```

- Braces are used to increase readability, even when they are not a syntactic necessity. For example, in the construct

```
while (expression)
{
    if (condition)
        statement₁
    else
        statement₂
}  // end while
```

the braces are syntactically unnecessary, because an `if` is a single statement. However, the braces highlight the scope of the `while` loop.

B.2.7   Documentation

A program should be well documented so that others can read, use, and modify it easily. Many acceptable styles for documentation are in use today, and exactly what you should include often depends on the particular program or your individual circumstances.

This book will use a special form of documentation comment, called a **javadoc-style comment** because it originated with the Java™ programming language. These comments start with `/**` and end with `*/` and contain **tags** that classify different parts of your documentation. Several utility programs are available to read these comments and generate HTML-based documentation. One of these programs is called **doxygen**.

Highly formatted, HTML-based documentation is easy to produce

The advantage of using javadoc-style comments—and a documentation system, like doxygen—is that you can edit the documentation for your source code as you make changes to that code. The documentation lives directly in the source code—as javadoc-style comments—making it very easy and convenient to keep your documentation up to date.

The following are the essential features of any program's documentation—with associated commenting tags in parentheses:

> **Note: Essential features of program documentation**
> 1. An initial comment at the top of each source code file that includes:
>   a. File name (`@file`)
>   b. Statement of purpose
>   c. Author (`@author`)
>   d. Date (`@date`)
>   e. Optional file version number (`@version`)
> 2. Initial comments for each class that includes:
>   a. Name of class and its header file (`@class`)
>   b. Statement of purpose
> 3. Initial comments for each method or function that includes:
>   a. Statement of purpose
>   b. Description of each parameter (`@param`)
>   c. Preconditions (`@pre`)
>   d. Postconditions (`@post`)
>   e. Exceptions thrown (`@throw`)
>   f. Return value (`@return`)
> 4. Standard C++ comments in the body of each method or function to explain important features or subtle logic

Beginning programmers tend to downplay the importance of documentation because comments do not affect a program's logic. By now, you should realize that people also read programs. Your comments must be clear enough for someone else to either use your module in a program or modify it. Thus, some of your comments are for people who want to use your module, while others are for people who will revise its implementation. You should be conscious of different kinds of comments.

Consider who will read your comments when you write them

Beginners also have a tendency to document programs as a last step. You should, however, write documentation as you develop the program. Because the task of writing a large program might extend over a period of several weeks, you may find that the module that seemed so obvious when you wrote it last week seems confusing when you try to revise it next week. Why not benefit from your own documentation by writing it now rather than later?

You benefit from your own documentation by writing it now instead of later

See Appendix I for more details on the use of the javadoc-style comments and the doxygen documentation system.

B.3   Modifiability

After each iteration in the development of a program, the design can change to some degree. This tendency requires that your program be written in a way that makes it easy to modify. This section offers two examples of how you can make a program easy to modify: named constants and typedef statements.

B.3.1   Named Constants

Named constants make a program easier to modify

The use of named constants is a way to enhance the modifiability of a program. For example, the restriction that an array must have a predefined, fixed size causes a bit of difficulty. Suppose that a program uses an array to process the test scores of the computer science majors at your university. When the program was written, there were 202 computer science majors, so the array was declared by

```
int scores[202];
```

The program processes the array in several ways. For example, it reads the scores, writes the scores, and averages the scores. The pseudocode for each of these tasks contains a construct such as

```
for (index = 0 through 201)
    Process the score
```

If the number of majors should change, not only do you need to revise the declaration of scores, but you also must change each loop that processes the array to reflect the new array size. In addition, other statements in the program might depend on the size of the array. A 202 here, a 201 there—which to change?

On the other hand, if you use a named constant such as

```
const int NUMBER_OF_MAJORS = 202;
```

you can declare the array by using

```
int scores[NUMBER_OF_MAJORS];
```

and write the pseudocode for the processing loops in this form:

```
for (index = 0 through NUMBER_OF_MAJORS - 1)
    Process the score
```

If you write expressions that depend on the size of the array in terms of the constant NUMBER_OF_MAJORS (such as NUMBER_OF_MAJORS - 1), you can change the array size simply by changing the definition of the constant and compiling the program again.

B.3.2   The typedef Statement

Suppose that your program performs floating-point computations of type float, but you discover that you need greater precision than float variables provide. To change the relevant float declarations to long double, for example, you would have to locate all such declarations and decide whether to make the change.

You can simplify this change by using a typedef statement, which gives another name to an existing data type. For example, the statement

```
typedef float RealType;
```

declares RealType as a synonym for float and allows you to use RealType and float interchangeably. If you declare all the relevant items in the previous program as RealType instead of float, you can make your program easier to modify and to read. To revise the precision of the computations, you would simply change the typedef statement to

```
typedef long double RealType;
```

B.4   Ease of Use

Another area in which you need to keep people in mind is the design of the user interface. Humans often process a program's input and output. Here are a few obvious points:

- In an interactive environment, the program should always prompt the user for input in a manner that makes it quite clear what it expects. For example, the prompt "?" is not nearly as enlightening as the prompt "Please enter your account number." You should never assume that the users of your program know what response the program requires.

Prompt the user for input

- A program should always echo its input. Whenever a program reads data from a user, the program should include the values it reads in its output. This inclusion serves two purposes: First, it gives the user a check on the data entered—a safeguard against typos and errors in data transmission. This check is particularly useful in the case of interactive input. Second, the output is more meaningful and self-explanatory when it contains a record of what input generated the output. When a program reads data from a large file, it can report the number of records read instead of displaying every data value.

Echo the input

- The output should be well labeled and easy to read. An output of

```
1800 6 1
Jones, Q. 223 2234.00 1088.19 N, J Smith, T. 111
110.23 I, Harris, V. 44 44000.00 22222.22
```

is more prone to misinterpretation than

```
CUSTOMER ACCOUNTS AS OF 1800 HOURS ON JUNE 1

Account status codes: N=new, J=joint, I=inactive

NAME        ACC#   CHECKING     SAVINGS      STATUS

Jones, Q.   223    $ 2234.00    $ 1088.19    N, J
Smith, T.   111    $  110.23    ─────────    I
Harris, V.   44    $44000.00    $22222.22    ─────
```

Label the output

These characteristics of a good user interface are only the basics. Several more subtle points separate a program that is merely usable from one that is user-friendly. Novices tend to ignore a good user interface, but by investing a little extra time here, you can make a big difference: the difference between a good program and one that only solves the problem. For example, consider a program that requires a user to enter a line of data in some fixed format, with exactly one blank between the items. A free-form input that allows any number of blanks between the items would be much more convenient for the user. It takes so little time to add code that skips blanks, so why require the user to follow an exact format? Once you have made this small additional effort, the code is a permanent part of both your program and your library of techniques, and the user of your program will never have to think about input format.

A good user interface is important

B.5   Fail-Safe Programming

A **fail-safe program** is one that will perform reasonably no matter how anyone uses it. Unfortunately, this goal is usually unattainable. A more realistic goal is to anticipate the ways that people might misuse the program and to guard carefully against these abuses.

Check for errors in input

This discussion considers two types of errors. The first type is an *error in input data*. For example, suppose that a program expects a nonnegative integer but reads −12. When a program encounters this type of problem, it should not produce incorrect results or abort with a vague error message. Instead, a fail-safe program allows the user to reenter the data by providing a message such as

```
-12 is not a valid number of children.
Please enter this number again.
```

Check for errors in logic

The second type of error is an *error in the program logic*. Although a discussion of this type of error belongs in the next section about debugging, detecting errors in program logic is also a characteristic of fail-safe programming. A program that appears to have been running correctly may at some point behave unexpectedly, even if the data that it reads is valid. For example, the program may not have accounted for the particular data that elicited the surprise behavior, even though you tried your best to test the program's logic. Or perhaps you modified the program and that modification invalidated an assumption that you made in some other part of the program. Whatever the difficulty, a program should have built-in safeguards against these kinds of errors. It should monitor itself and be able to indicate that something is wrong and that you should not trust the results.

B.5.1   Guarding Against Errors in Input Data

Suppose that you are computing statistics about the people in income brackets between $10,000 and $100,000. The brackets are rounded to the nearest thousand dollars: $10,000, $11,000, and so on to $100,000. The raw data is a file of one or more lines of the form

> *G   N*

where *N* is the number of people with an income that falls into the *G*-thousand-dollar group. *G* is an integer in the range 10 to 100, inclusive, and *N* is a nonnegative integer. If several people have compiled the data, several entries for the same value of *G* might occur. As the user enters data, the program must add up and record the number of people for each value of *G*.

As an example of how to guard against errors in input, consider an input function for this problem. The first attempt at writing this function will illustrate several common ways in which a program can fall short of the fail-safe ideal. Eventually you will see an input function that is much closer to this ideal than the original solution.

A first attempt at the function might be

```cpp
const int LOW_END    = 10;   // 10-thousand-dollar income
const int HIGH_END   = 100;  // 100-thousand-dollar income
const int TABLE_SIZE = HIGH_END - LOW_END + 1;
typedef int TableType[TABLE_SIZE];

/** Reads and organizes income statistics.
 @param incomeData A TableType of income statistics.
 @pre  The calling module gives directions to the user.
    Input data is error-free, and each input line has the form
    G N, where N is the number of people with an income in the
    G-thousand-dollar group and LOW_END <= G <= HIGH_END.
```

```
      An input line with values of zero for both G and N terminates the input.
   @post  incomeData[G - LOW_END] is the total number of people
      with an income in the G-thousand-dollar group for each G read.
      The values read are displayed. */
   void readData(TableType incomeData)
   {
      bool terminateInput = false;                                                    This function is not
      int group, number; // Input values                                             fail-safe

      // Clear array
      for (group = LOW_END; group <= HIGH_END; group++)
         incomeData[group - LOW_END] = 0;
      do
      {
         std::cout << "Please enter group and number of people in group, ";
         std::cout << "separated by a space: ";
         std::cin >> group >> number;
         terminateInput = (group == 0) && (number == 0);

         // Group and number are not both 0
         std::cout << "Income group " << group << " contains "
                   << number << " people.\n";
         incomeData[group - LOW_END] += number;
      } while (!terminateInput); // end do-while
   } // end readData
```

This function has some problems. If an input line contains unexpected data, the program will not behave reasonably. Consider two specific possibilities:

- The first integer on the input line, which the function assigns to group, is not in the range LOW_END to HIGH_END. The reference

  ```
  incomeData[group - LOW_END]
  ```

  is then incorrect, since it accesses an array element outside the array bounds. This error also will happen when the user tries to end the input by entering zeros for both group and number.
- The second number on the input line, which the function assigns to number, is negative. Although a negative value for number is invalid, because you cannot have a negative number of people in an income group, the function will add number to the group's array entry. Thus, the array incomeData will be incorrect.

After the function reads values for group and number, it must check to see whether group   Test for invalid input
is in the range LOW_END to HIGH_END and whether number is positive. If either value is not in that   data
range, you must handle the input error.

Suppose that instead of checking the value of number before you add it to the array element incomeData[group - LOW_END], you perform the addition and see whether the sum is positive. This approach is insufficient, since you might add a negative value to an entry of incomeData without that entry becoming negative. For example, if number is −4,000 and the corresponding entry in the array incomeData is 10,000, the sum is 6,000. Thus, a negative value for number could remain undetected and invalidate the results of the rest of the program.

One possible course of action when the function detects invalid data is for it to set an error flag and terminate. Another possibility is for it to set an error flag, ignore the bad input line, and continue. Which action is correct really depends on how the program uses the data once it is read.

The following readData function attempts to be as universally applicable as possible and to make the program that uses it as modifiable as possible. When the function encounters an error in input, it sets a flag, ignores the data line, and continues. By setting a flag, the function leaves it to the calling module to determine the appropriate action—such as abort or continue—when an input error occurs. Thus, you can use the same input function in many contexts and can easily modify the action taken upon encountering an error.

A function that
includes fail-safe
programming

```cpp
/** Reads and organizes income statistics.
 @param incomeData A TableType of income statistics.
 @pre  The calling program gives directions to the user.
    Each input line contains exactly two integers in the form G N,
    where N is the number of people with an income in the G-thousand-
    dollar group and LOW_END <= G <= HIGH_END. An input line with
    values of zero for both G and N terminates the input.
 @post  incomeData[G - LOW_END] is the total number of people with
    an income in the G-thousand-dollar group. The values read are
    displayed. If either G or N is erroneous (either G < LOW_END,
    G > HIGH_END, or N < 0), the function ignores the data line and
    continues execution.
 @return  False if either G or N are erroneous (either G < LOW_END,
    G > HIGH_END, or N < 0) for any data line read. In this case,
    the calling program should take action. The return value is
    true if the data is error-free. */
bool readData(TableType incomeData)
{
   int group = -1;
   int number = -1;          // Input values
   bool dataCorrect = true;  // No data error found as yet
   bool userFinished = false;

   for (group = LOW_END; group <= HIGH_END; group++)
      incomeData[group - LOW_END] = 0;
   do
   {
      std::cout << "Please enter group and number of people in group, ";
      std::cout << "separated by a space: ";
      std::cin >> group >> number;

      std::cout << "Input line specifies that income group "
                << group << "\ncontains " << number
                << " people.\n";
      if ((group >= LOW_END) && (group <= HIGH_END) && (number >= 0))
         // Input data is valid - add it to tally
         incomeData[group - LOW_END] += number;
      else if ((group == 0) && (number == 0))
         userFinished = true; // User signaled input is finished
      else
      {
         // Error in input data:
         // Set error flag and ignore input line
         dataCorrect = false;
      }  // end if
   } while( (dataCorrect && !userFinished ); // end do-while

   return dataCorrect;
}  // end readData
```

Although this input function will behave gracefully in the face of most common input errors, it is not completely fail-safe. What happens if an input line contains only one integer? What happens if an input line contains a noninteger? The function would be more fail-safe if it read its input character by character, converted the characters to an integer, and checked for the end of the input line. In most contexts, this processing would be a bit extreme. However, if the people who enter the data frequently err by typing nonintegers, you could alter the input function easily because the function is an isolated module. In any case, the function's initial comments should include any assumptions it makes about the data and an indication of what might make the program abort abnormally.

B.5.2   Guarding Against Errors in Program Logic

Now consider the second type of error that a program should guard against: errors in its own logic. These are errors that you may not have caught when you debugged the program or that you may have introduced through program modification.

Unfortunately, a program cannot reliably let you know when something is wrong with it. (Could you rely on a program to tell you that something is wrong with its mechanism for telling you that something is wrong?) You can, however, build into a program checks that ensure that certain conditions always hold when the program is correctly implementing its algorithm. For example, all integers in the array incomeData of the previous example must be greater than or equal to zero. We argued that the function readData should check that number is positive before adding it to an entry in incomeData instead of checking only the validity of the entries in incomeData. However, the function could check incomeData in addition to checking number. For example, if the function finds that an entry in the array incomeData is outside some range of believability, it can signal a potential problem to its users.

Functions should check conditions that should be true

Another general way in which you should make a program fail-safe is to make each function check its precondition. For example, consider the following function, computeFactorial, which returns the factorial of an integer:

Functions should enforce their preconditions

```
/** Computes the factorial of an integer.
 @param n The given integer.
 @pre  n >= 0.
 @post  None.
 @return  n * (n - 1) * ... * 1, if n > 0, or 1, if n == 0. */
int computeFactorial(int n)
{
   int fact = 1;
   for (int i = n; i > 1; i--)
      fact *= i;

   return fact;
}  // end computeFactorial
```

The initial comments in this function contain a precondition—information about what assumptions are made—as should always be the case. The value that this function returns is valid only if the precondition is met. If n is less than zero, the function will return the incorrect value of 1.

In the context of the program for which this function was written, it may be reasonable to make the assumption that n will never be negative. That is, if the rest of the program is working correctly, it will call computeFactorial only with correct values of n. Ironically, this last observation gives you a good reason for computeFactorial to check the value of n: If n is less than zero, the warning that results from the check indicates that something may be wrong elsewhere in the program.

Another reason the function computeFactorial should check whether n is less than zero is that the function should be correct outside the context of its program. That is, if you borrow the function for use in another program, the function should warn you if you use it incorrectly by passing it an n that is negative. A stronger check than simply the statement of the precondition in a comment is desirable.

> **Note:** A function should state its assumptions and, when possible, check whether its arguments conform to these assumptions.

Functions should check the values of their arguments

In this example, `computeFactorial` could check the value of `n` and, if it is negative, return zero, because factorials are never zero. The program that uses this function could then check for this unusual value. Alternatively, `computeFactorial` could abort execution if its argument is negative. Many programming languages, including C++, support a mechanism for error handling called an **exception**. A module indicates that an error has occurred by **throwing** an exception. A module reacts to an exception that another module throws by **catching** the exception and executing code to deal with the error condition. C++ Interlude 3 provides more information about exceptions.

C++ also provides a convenient function `assert(`*expression*`)` that both displays an informative message and aborts a program if *expression* is zero. You can use `assert` as a debugging tool to check for both error conditions and the validity of preconditions within your program. C++ Interlude 3 provides more information about `assert`.

B.6   Debugging

No matter how much care you take in writing a program, it will contain errors that you need to track down. Fortunately, programs that are modular, clear, and well documented are generally amenable to debugging. Fail-safe techniques, which guard against certain errors and report them when they are encountered, are also a great aid in debugging.

Use breakpoints, single-stepping, watches, and temporary cout statements to find logic errors

Without a systematic approach, finding a small mistake in a large program can indeed be a difficult task. Many people have difficulty in debugging a program, perhaps because they believe that their program is really doing what it is supposed to do. For example, on receiving an execution-time error message at line 1098, a person might say, "That's impossible. The statement at line 1098 was not even executed, because it is in the `else` clause, and I am positive that it was not executed." However, the proper approach is either to trace the program's execution by using available debugging facilities or to add `cout` statements that show which part of the `if` statement was executed. By doing so, you verify the value of the expression in the `if` statement. If the expression is 0, for example, when you expect it to be 1, the next step is to find out how it became 0.

How can you find the point in a program where something becomes other than what it should be? A typical **Integrated Development Environment**, or **IDE**, allows you to trace a program's execution either by **single-stepping** through the statements in the program or by setting **breakpoints** at which execution will halt. You also can examine the contents of particular variables by either establishing **watches** or inserting temporary `cout` statements. The key to debugging is simply to use these techniques to tell you what is going on. This may sound pretty mundane, but the real trick is to use these debugging aids in an effective manner. After all, you do not simply put breakpoints, watches, and `cout` statements at random points in the program and have them report random information.

Systematically check a program's logic to locate where an error occurs

A program's logic implies that certain conditions should be true at various points in the program. If the program's results differ from your expectations, an error occurs. To correct the error, you must find the first point in the program at which this difference is evident. By inserting either breakpoints and watches or `cout` statements at strategic locations of a program— such as at the entry and departure points of loops and functions—you can methodically isolate the error.

These diagnostic techniques should inform you whether things start going wrong before or after a given point in the program. Thus, after you run the program with an initial set of diagnostics, you should be able to trap the error between two points. For example, suppose that things are fine before you call method M_1, but that something is wrong by the time you call M_2. This kind of information allows you to focus your attention between these two points. You continue the process until eventually the search is limited to only a few statements. There is really no place in a program for an error to hide.

 Programming Tip: A statement of truth about some aspect of a program's logic is known as an **assertion**. You can express an assertion either as a comment or by using the `assert` macro. By including assertions in your program, you facilitate the debugging process.

The ability to place breakpoints, watches, and `cout` statements in appropriate locations and to have them report relevant information comes in part from thinking logically about the problem and in part from experience. Here are a few general guidelines.

B.6.1 Debugging Functions and Methods

You should examine the values of the arguments passed to a function or method at its beginning and end by using either watches or `cout` statements. Ideally, you should debug each major function or method separately before using it in your program.

B.6.2 Debugging Loops

You should examine the values of key variables at the beginnings and ends of loops, as the comments in this example indicate:

```
// Check values of start and stop before entering loop
for (index = start; index <= stop; index++)
{
    // Check values of index and key variables
    // at the beginning of iteration
    ...
    // Check values of index and key variables
    // at the end of iteration
}   // end for
// Check values of start and stop after exiting loop
```

B.6.3 Debugging `if` Statements

Just before an `if` statement, you should examine the values of the variables within its expression. You can use either breakpoints or `cout` statements to see which branch the `if` statement takes, as this example indicates:

```
// Check variables within expression before executing if
if (expression)
{
    std::cout << "Condition is true (value of expression is 1)." << std::endl;
    ...
}
```

```
else
{
    std::cout << "Condition is false (value of expression is 0)." << std::endl;
    ...
}   // end if
```

B.6.4 Using cout Statements

Sometimes cout statements can be more convenient than watches. Such cout statements should report both the values of key variables and the location in the program at which the variables have those values. You can use a comment to label the location, as follows:

```
// This is point A
std::cout << "At point A in the method computeResults:\n"
          << "x = " << x << ", y = " << y << std::endl;
```

Remember to either disable or remove these statements when your program finally works.

B.6.5 Using Special Dump Functions

Often the variables whose values you wish to examine are arrays or other, more complex data structures. If so, you should write dump functions to display the data structures in a highly readable manner. You can easily move the single statement that calls each dump function from one point in the program to another as you track down an error. The time you spend on these functions often proves to be worthwhile, as you can call them repeatedly while debugging different parts of the program.

Hopefully, this discussion has conveyed the importance of the effective use of diagnostic aids in debugging. Even the best programmers have to spend some time debugging. Thus, to be a truly good programmer, you must be a good debugger.

B.7   Testing

You can never test a program too much

Programs need to be tested to make sure that they correctly solve their current requirements. Good testing cannot happen without a plan. Software is complex, and making sure that it works correctly is not easy. Software testing is so important that some development processes argue that programming teams should design tests before writing any code.

B.7.1 Levels of Testing

Unit testing checks individual modules

Several levels of testing should take place. The first level of testing is called **unit testing**, and it happens on the individual modules. You should test individual methods first, and then test the classes. The second level of testing is called **integration testing**, and it tests the interactions among modules. The next level of testing is called **system testing**, in which the entire program is tested. Finally, a special type of testing called **acceptance testing** shows whether the system as a whole complies with its requirements.

Unit testing is something that you have probably done before. It is closely related to some of the ideas talked about in the previous debugging section. A function is tested to make sure that it conforms to its requirements. Often with small programs, testing does not go beyond this level.

One way to perform integration tests is to make sure that the various objects within a program correctly implement the interactions in your design. Integration testing can be challenging, because there are many ways in which the objects in a program can interact. It is difficult to make sure they do what they are designed to do and nothing more.

System testing entails running the program in the environment in which it was designed to work. Here the program is tested to make sure that it interacts with external systems correctly. The external systems might be other programs—such as a government tax collection system—or hardware devices.

B.7.2   Kinds of Testing

Two kinds of testing can be applied to a system:

- **Open-box testing.** With **open-box**, **white-box**, or **glass-box testing**, you design tests knowing how the modules work. You carefully choose a method's actual arguments in a way that exercises all lines of code in the method. For example, you must make sure that all branches of `if` and `switch` statements are executed.
- **Closed-box testing.** With **closed-box**, **black-box**, or **functional testing**, you know the name of the method being tested, as well as its parameter list, its return type, and its operation contract. Using only this information, you develop tests across a range of valid input, and then check the output against hand-calculated results. Choosing some actual arguments outside of their valid range tests how the module handles incorrect input.

B.7.3   Developing Test Data

The test data that you use must test a wide range of conditions. It should include valid, typical input and values at the extreme limits of valid data—called **boundary values**—as well as values that should never occur in normal execution. For example, suppose that you are testing a simple linear search algorithm:

```
for (int i = 0; i < size; i++)
{
    if (array[i] == target)
        return i;
}  // end for
```

You should use all of the following values of `target`:

- Just less than `array[0]` (boundary at the beginning of the array)
- Equal to `array[0]` (boundary at the beginning of the array)
- Equal to some entry in the middle of the array
- Within the range of values stored in the array, but unequal to any
- Equal to `array[size - 1]` (boundary at the end of the array)
- Just greater than `array[size - 1]` (boundary at the end of the array)

You should also test this algorithm with

- An empty array
- An array with one entry in it
- An array with many entries

For each of these tests, you should manually trace the data so that the results are known ahead of time. In this way, test data can be the input to a module, and you can compare the output with known results.

B.7.4   Testing Techniques

As indicated in the debugging section, `assert` statements can be useful for checking assertions. However, the `assert` statement is not powerful enough for the full-scale testing of a system. Other techniques need to be utilized.

Disable, but do not remove, testing code after use

A common technique is to write a block of code that tests a module. When you have finished testing the system, you can simply comment it out—rather than deleting it—as more testing will be required after you make modifications during the next iteration. Alternatively, you can turn these testing blocks of code on and off by using one of the techniques that we discuss next.

The first technique uses a boolean variable to grant access to testing code contained within the body of `if` statements. Setting the variable to false turns testing code "off," and setting it to true enables testing. For example, the following test is disabled:

```cpp
const bool TESTING = false; // Disables testing code
if (TESTING)
{
   ... // Testing code
} // end if
```

You could define several different boolean variables to turn different tests "on" and "off." All that is required is to change the value of the boolean variable and to recompile.

A second, more efficient, technique uses the **preprocessor** to the compiler. You define a symbol that affects the testing code. Then you place the test code within preprocessor directives that test whether that symbol has been defined. For example:

```cpp
#define TESTING

#ifdef TESTING
... // Testing code
#endif
```

To turn off testing, you comment out the definition of the macro (`// #define TESTING`) and recompile. Because the macro is no longer defined, the test code is not included in the executable. This has the advantage that the test code is completely removed from the executable, making it smaller. Again, you can define several different macros to enable you to turn different blocks of testing code "on" and "off."

A driver is a module that tests another module

A third way uses a function `main` to thoroughly test a class. Such a function is known as a **driver**. It does not do anything algorithmically interesting; it simply tests the class. For instance, the following function is a driver for the class `Example`:

```cpp
int main()
{
   Example anObject;
   anObject.initialize();
   anObject.dump();
   anObject.sortData();
   anObject.dump();
   return 0;
} // end main
```

This driver creates an instance of `Example` and then, calling `Example`'s methods, initializes the object, displays its data, sorts its data, and finally displays its data again.

B.7.5   Use of Stubs

Testing a class before implementing all of its methods is often useful. Instead of simply omitting some methods, you partially implement them so that each one acknowledges that it has been called. Such methods are called **stubs**. Stubs allow you to see that the method has been called in the correct place in the overall flow of a program.

A stub is an incomplete method that acknowledges that it has been called

For example, suppose that a class has an array `data` of integers as a data member and a method `sortData`. You could write the following stub for `sortData`:

```
void sortData() // Stub
{
    std::cout << "sortData has been called\n"
    data[0] = 1;
    data[1] = 2;
    data[2] = 3;
} // end sortData
```

sortData is a stub

The stub `sortData` not only indicates that it has been called, but also changes the data into a sorted form. Thus, this stub could be used for simple integration testing as well. Later, you could implement `sortData` by using an appropriate sorting algorithm.

Chapter 3 gives other examples of stubs and talks more about testing.

 Note: Testing takes a lot of planning and is not easy to do. Like many things in programming, testing well takes some time and experience.

The Unified Modeling Language

Contents

Prerequisites

The Unified
Modeling Language
visually represents
object-oriented
designs

The **Unified Modeling Language**, or **UML**, is a modeling language used to express object-oriented designs. The UML provides specifications for many types of diagrams and text-based descriptions that show various aspects of a design.

C.1 The Use Case

A use case is a
textual story; a
scenario describes
the system's
behavior under
certain conditions
from the perspective
of the user

A **use case** is a set of textual **scenarios** or stories that describe the proposed solution to a problem. A use case is not object-oriented, but it is an important part of the analysis of the problem. A single use case usually has several scenarios. The **main success scenario** (or "happy path") describes how the system satisfies the goals of the user when everything goes smoothly. Other **alternate scenarios** describe the interaction between the user and the system when specific things do not go well or when exceptional conditions apply.

For example, suppose that a customer wants to withdraw money from his or her checking account. A main success scenario might look like this:

An example of a
main success
scenario

Customer makes a request to withdraw money from a bank account. Bank identifies and authenticates the customer. Bank gets from the customer the type of account (savings or checking), the account number, and the amount of the withdrawal. Bank verifies that the account balance is greater than the amount of the withdrawal. Bank generates a receipt for the transaction. Bank counts out the correct amount of money for the customer. Bank gives the customer the receipt and money. Customer leaves the bank.

A scenario is written from the perspective of the user of the system. In this way, the analysis will focus on the *responsibilities* of the system to meet a user's needs. That is, the analysis will focus on *what* the system needs to accomplish to meet the goals of its users.

Notice that the scenario does not describe *how* the system works. For example, "Bank identifies and authenticates the customer" does not indicate *how* this will occur. The focus should be on the interactions between the user and the system but not on the user interface to the system, which will be explored during design.

Alternate scenarios should be written only for stories that are interesting or tricky. For example, one such scenario describes what happens when the customer fails authentication:

An example of an
alternate scenario

Customer makes request to withdraw money from a bank account. Bank identifies but fails to authenticate the customer. Bank refuses to process the customer request. Customer leaves the bank.

Other alternate scenarios could include the denial of a withdrawal request because insufficient funds are in the account or because the bank does not have sufficient cash on hand.

From the scenarios in the use case, you generate a list of objects by listing the nouns in the use case. (This is where the analysis becomes object oriented.) For example, bank, money, customer, account, account type, account number, transaction amount, and receipt are nouns all found in the main success scenario and could be objects in the solution. The final solution might not use all of the objects discovered.

> **Note:** **The use case during object-oriented analysis**
> 1. Describes the problem domain in terms of scenarios involving the solution that satisfies user goals
> 2. Discovers noteworthy objects, attributes, and associations within the scenarios

C.2 UML Sequence Diagrams

A UML sequence
diagram shows the
interactions among
objects over time

After you create a use case and list potential objects, you need to explore how these objects will interact with one another. You accomplish this by using a UML **sequence diagram**, or **interaction diagram**, that models your use case scenarios. Such a diagram shows how two or more objects will interact with one another over time within a single scenario. This diagram allows you to visualize the messages sent among the objects in a scenario and the order in which those messages happen. In addition to giving a sense of the flow of the logic, the diagram is important when defining the **responsibilities** of the objects: What must the object "remember," or keep track of, and what must the object do for other objects? Many of the responsibilities are described in the use case. Figure C-1 shows a UML sequence diagram for the main success scenario given previously.

Although the development of the use case is part of object-oriented analysis (OOA), the creation of sequence diagrams is part of object-oriented design (OOD). The sequence diagram shows a scenario's objects from left to right horizontally and their actions in order of occurrence vertically. The UML represents an object as a square-cornered box containing the name of the object—if it has one—followed by a colon and the type of the object, all underlined. In Figure C-1, the object of type Bank is named bank, and the objects of type Customer and Account are nameless.

A UML sequence
diagram represents
an object as a box

FIGURE C-1   Sequence diagram for the main success scenario

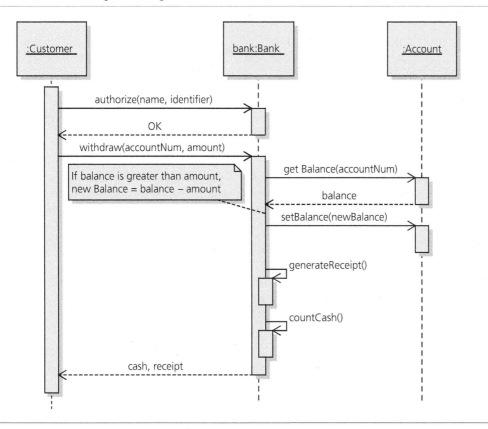

Each object in a sequence diagram has a **lifeline** denoted by a vertical dashed line below the object box extending forward in time. Each lifeline can have one or more **activation bars**, each represented by an open box on the lifeline. An activation bar indicates when an object is active—and represents a responsibility of the object's class. The class needs a method to handle that responsibility. To represent the sending of a message between objects, you draw a solid arrow from the activation bar of the calling object to the top of a new activation bar on the lifeline of the called object. Such arrows are labeled with a **message expression** indicating what task the object needs to perform. The message expression corresponds to the name of a method for handling that task. The message expression may also include **parameters** necessary for performing the task. Ultimately, these parameters will correspond to method arguments. When an object finishes a task, the activation bar associated with that task ends. If the task returns something of interest to the calling object, a dashed arrow may be shown pointing back to the calling object's activation bar. You can label this arrow with the name of the variable receiving the returned value.

> An activation bar on an object's lifeline represents a responsibility of the object's class

In Figure C-1, the customer asks the bank for authorization by giving its name and identifier—passed as arguments—to the `authorize` message. The bank then processes this message—as indicated by the activation bar associated with the `bank` object's lifeline—and then signals whether or not the customer has been authenticated by returning a value to the variable `OK` within the `Customer` object. Note that you should write the messages in a general, language-independent fashion. However, a `Bank` class could declare the `authorize` message as follows:

```
class Bank
{
public:
    ...

    bool authorize(string name, string identifier);
    ...

}; // end Bank
```

An object may also send messages to itself, as is done in the generateReceipt and countCash messages in Figure C-1. Notice the piggybacked activation bars, which indicate that the Bank class is calling its own member methods.

A sequence diagram can also show the creation of a new object. In Figure C-2, a new account is created. This diagram can represent a part of an alternate scenario in a use case, in which a customer comes into the bank but does not yet have an account. In the UML, the notation <<create>> is what is known as a **stereotype**. Stereotypes use left and right guillemets (<< and >>), but when drawing a sequence diagram by hand, you can simply label the message arrow with create. A stereotype is used to identify a unique characteristic of an element in any UML diagram.

> A stereotype identifies a special characteristic of an element

FIGURE C-2   Sequence diagram showing the creation of a new object

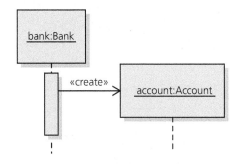

The UML sequence diagram is a design document that gives guidance on several levels to the programmer implementing a solution. It gives a view of how the objects will dynamically interact (collaborate) to solve a use case scenario. In particular, a sequence diagram shows

- Which objects *collaborate* to solve a particular use-case scenario
- The *synchronous* nature of the messages that are passed between the objects in the scenario, providing the order in which tasks are accomplished
- Which object is *responsible* for what task or tasks by handling a particular message

Note: UML sequence diagrams
- Provide a visual representation of the flow of messages sent between objects during a single scenario
- Indicate the responsibilities of an object
- Indicate the collaborations among objects

C.3   UML Class Diagrams

The last design element we will introduce is the UML **class diagram**, or **static diagram**. The class diagram shows the attributes and operations of an individual class and how multiple classes are related to one another. These design elements do not change after they have been created within a solution—that is, they are static, or unchanging.

A UML class diagram shows the unchanging relationships among classes of objects

The class diagram shown in Figure C-3 represents a class of banks. Each diagram consists of a square-cornered box containing the name of the class centered within its borders. Figure C-3a shows the simplest of class diagrams: a class with a name but no attributes or operations. Figure C-3b shows the bank's attributes in the middle section and its operations in the bottom section. If a class has no attributes, as in Figure C-3c, an empty middle section must be present.

FIGURE C-3   Three possible class diagrams for a class of banks

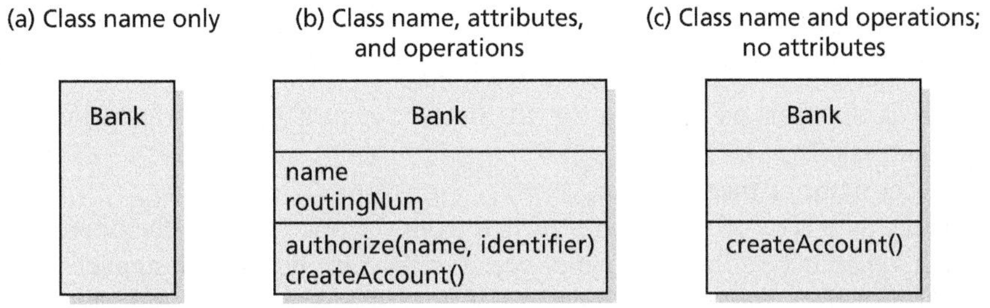

(a) Class name only

Bank

(b) Class name, attributes, and operations

Bank

name
routingNum

authorize(name, identifier)
createAccount()

(c) Class name and operations; no attributes

Bank

createAccount()

The class diagram represents a conceptual model of a class of objects in a language-independent way. That is, the diagram does not dictate how the class is implemented. It just gives you a design to work from. However, you can specify many qualities associated with the attributes and operations of the class as an option. These qualities are easily implemented in C++, and they increase the amount of information given in a design.

The UML syntax for the attributes of a class is

[*visibility*] *name* [: *type*] [= *default Value*] [{*property*}]

UML syntax for the attributes of a class

where

- All elements within square brackets are optional.
- *visibility* can be + for public accessibility, − for private accessibility, or # for protected accessibility. (C++ Interlude 5 covers protected accessibility.) If omitted, the visibility defaults to private accessibility.
- *name* is the name of the attribute.
- *type* is the data type of the attribute.
- *default Value* is the default value of the attribute.
- *property* indicates some property that applies to this attribute.

At a minimum, the *name* of an attribute should be given. The *default Value* is given only in situations where the design dictates that a default value is appropriate for that attribute. In certain cases it might be appropriate to omit the *type* of an attribute, leaving this detail until the implementation phase.

The UML specifies that programming-language-independent names be used for the *type* of an attribute. This text will follow the UML recommendations by using integer for integral storage, float for floating-point storage, boolean for boolean storage, and string for storing strings.

The *property* of an attribute can have one of the following values:

* changeable indicates a normal, modifiable attribute and is usually omitted.
* frozen indicates a constant or write-once attribute.

The attributes for the Bank class in Figure C-3b could now be written as

```
-name: string
-routingNum: integer
```

The visibility of these attributes is private and adheres to the object-oriented programming principle of information hiding.

The UML syntax for a class's operations is more involved:

UML syntax for the operations of a class

$$[\textit{visibility}] \; \textit{name} \; ([\textit{parameterList}]) \; [:\textit{type}] \; [\{\textit{property}\}]$$

where

* All elements within square brackets are optional.
* *visibility* is the same as specified for attributes, except if omitted operations default to public accessibility.
* *name* is the name of the operation.
* *type* is the data type of the result returned from the operation. If the operation returns nothing, *type* can be either omitted or specified as void. The same language-independent types apply here as for attribute types.
* *property* indicates some property that applies to this operation. The only property relevant to us is query, which indicates that the operation will not modify any of the data members in the calling object.
* *parameterList* is either empty—in which case the parentheses are still required—or contains a comma-delimited list of parameters to the operation. The syntax for each parameter looks like the following:

$$[\textit{direction}] \; \textit{name:type} \; [=\textit{defaultValue}]$$

where

□ All elements within square brackets are optional.
□ *direction* shows whether the parameter is used for input (in), output (out), or both input and output (inout).
□ *name* is the name of the parameter.
□ *type* is the data type of the parameter. The same language-independent types apply here as for attribute types.
□ *defaultValue* is the value of this parameter if no corresponding actual argument is provided when this operation is called.

In Figure C-3b, the Bank class operations could be written as

```
+authorize(in name: string, in identifier: string): void {query}
-createAccount()
```

The authorize operation has public accessibility, and the createAccount operation is private. Because the design of the authorize operation has the query property specified, this operation will not change any of the data in the calling object.

The UML provides for several types of relationships among the classes in a class diagram. For example, Figure C-4 shows a static (class) diagram for a banking system. Because the bank has both checking accounts and savings accounts for its customers, the diagram shows five classes of objects: a Bank class, a Customer class, an Account class, a Checking class, and a Savings class. These classes collaborate by sending each other messages. Through these collaborations, the classes are related to one another in various ways.

For example, the Bank and Customer classes have an **association** relationship indicated by the solid line with no arrowheads. The numbers at the ends of the association—and other relationships—are called **multiplicities** and are optional. Each bank object is associated with zero or more customers, but each customer is associated with one bank. Each customer can have multiple accounts of any type, but an account can belong to only one customer.

> An association indicates that the classes know about each other

The Bank and Account classes are in one kind of relationship called an **aggregation**, or **containment**, in which one class contains an instance of another class. This relationship is denoted by the open diamond arrowhead near the containing class. In an aggregation relationship, the lifetime of the containing object and the object contained are not necessarily the same. Banks "live" longer than the accounts that they contain. Another similar relationship, called **composition**, uses a filled-in diamond arrowhead near the containing class. This relationship denotes a stronger containment, where the lifetimes of the container and the contained objects are the same. For example, a ballpoint pen is a pen that has a ball at the tip. When the pen "dies," the ball "dies" with it. Thus, the pen and its ball are in a composition relationship. By also looking at the multiplicities, we can say that a bank stores—that is, contains—zero or more accounts. The Customer and Account classes also have an aggregation relationship.

> Aggregation indicates that one class contains an instance of another class

> Composition is a stronger form of aggregation; the lifetimes of the container and the contained objects are the same

FIGURE C-4   A UML class diagram of a banking system

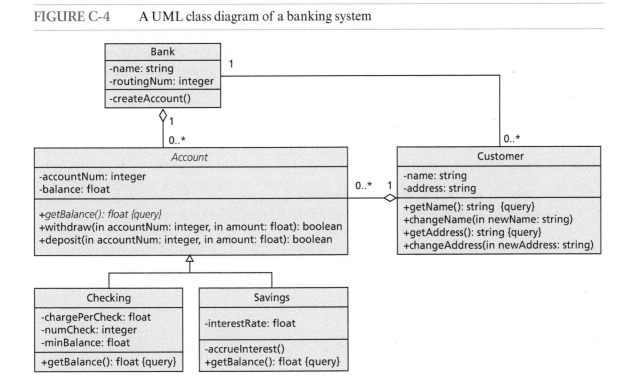

Each of the bank's accounts stores its account number and current balance and allows a customer to ask for the current balance, withdraw funds, and deposit funds. The Account class specifies these attributes and operations, and they are common to all accounts. The Account class is related to the Checking and Savings classes through a **generalization** relationship, indicated by the open triangular arrowhead pointing to the general (or parent) class. The generalization relationship denotes inheritance. The attributes and operations of the **ancestor class**, Account, are inherited by the **descendant classes**, Checking and Savings.

Note that the Account class name is in italic in Figure C-4. This denotes an **abstract base class**. The getBalance operation in the Account class is also in italic. This indicates that getBalance is not implemented in the Account class but must be implemented within the descendant class. In fact, the Checking and Savings classes each implement the inherited getBalance operation. This operation will take on polymorphic behavior when called from a **parent class** object. Many of these points, both in design and implementation, are covered in detail in C++ Interlude 5.

Note: UML Class (Static) Diagrams
- Show the attributes and operations of individual classes
- Show the unchanging relationships among the classes in the solution

C.4   Keeping the UML in Perspective

UML diagrams are not documentation

Although the UML can be thought of as a tool for documenting a solution to a problem, this is *not* how it should be used. Rather, you should use the UML to quickly draw various aspects of the current problem to better understand it during OOA and to create a set of objects during OOD that can collaborate to solve this problem. Often small teams of programmers will draw several UML diagrams on a whiteboard and, after working out the kinks in the diagrams, take digital pictures of them for future reference. These design diagrams are considered an **artifact**, or document, associated with the analysis and design. However, the ultimate implementation— that is, the solution—might not exactly match the original design. Thus, the design diagrams might not document the solution.

The UML is a tool for exploration and communication

The UML is a useful tool for creating a design for a solution. It enables programmers to explore and understand the problem domain and to develop a design that is close to the required solution. Although the UML will not necessarily make better designs than other techniques, it can conceptually model a problem domain in terms of software objects, independently of a programming language. Because the UML gives a visual representation of the proposed system, humans—as visual creatures—can benefit from using it. After all, a picture is worth a thousand words. The UML enables the members of a programming team to communicate visually with one another, thereby gaining a common understanding of the system that is being built.

The Software Life Cycle

Contents

Prerequisites

A general knowledge of software

The software life cycle describes the phases of software development

This appendix examines what a major piece of software "experiences" during its lifetime. The **life cycle** of software describes the phases through which software will progress from conception to replacement to deletion from a hard disk forever. We will look at the development phases, from project conception to deployment to end users. Beyond this development process, software will need maintenance to correct errors and add new features. Eventually the software will be retired.

The development of good software is a complex affair. Over the last several decades, many techniques have been developed in an attempt to control that complexity. Some of these techniques have been more successful than others.

Iterative development forms a solution after many iterations; each iteration builds on the previous iteration until a complete solution is achieved

D.1 Iterative and Evolutionary Development

An **iterative development** of a solution to a problem progresses through many short, fixed-length **iterations**, where each iteration cycles through the analysis, design, implementation, testing, and integration of a small portion of the problem domain. The early iterations establish the core of the system. Subsequent iterations build on that core. After many iterations, the entire solution is developed.

To manage the time spent on an iteration, each one is assigned a predetermined duration—called a **timebox**—at the beginning of the project. Typical timeboxes are two to four weeks in length. The portion of the system that can be developed in less than two weeks is typically too small to be meaningful. In more than four weeks, the partial system becomes too large. At the end of each iteration, the partial system should be functional and completely tested. Each iteration makes relatively few changes to the partial system produced by the previous iteration, so it can occur quickly. Thus, you do not expend too much effort on something that you may have misunderstood about the system requirements.

A critique of each iteration influences the next iteration

This process creates the solution incrementally. Thus, there are many places for end users and developers to check that it solves the correct problem. Because each iteration produces a functional but partial system, developers can engage end users to generate feedback. This feedback influences the next iteration and can change the direction of development so a more correct solution is reached. Figure D-1 illustrates the progress of an iterative development. We see that early iterations may be way off base, reflecting the fact that the requirements of the solution are not clearly understood. This is not anyone's fault; even the people that have requested the software to be built, the **domain experts**, may not be able to see what is required in the final system. Later iterations will probably not vary so much, as the requirements of the final system will have become more stable and in line with the correct solution. In an incremental fashion, the correct solution is created.

FIGURE D-1   Iterative development's progress toward the goal system

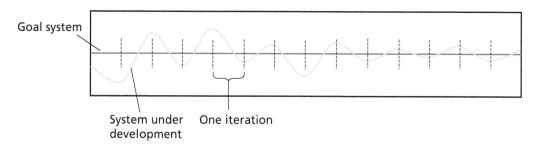

Iterative, incremental development gives a programmer the ability to let the requirements analysis and design evolve over time to meet a changing environment. Thus, the process is sometimes called **evolutionary development**.

Iterative development enables you to adapt a solution to a changing environment

Note: Iterative and Evolutionary Development
- Establishes timebox lengths at the start of a project
- Keeps timebox lengths short (two to four weeks)
- Gets end-user and domain-expert feedback from iteration n to influence the direction of iteration $n + 1$

D.2   Rational Unified Process Development

The RUP gives structure to the software development process

The **Rational Unified Process (RUP)** is widely used as a basis for examining the phases of the development process. The RUP will give structure to the use of the analysis and design tools you learned earlier. As the RUP is a large and complex process, most of its workings are beyond the scope of this text. Thus, we will simply introduce the process.

The RUP organizes development into four phases:

- **Inception**—feasibility study, project vision, rough estimates of time and cost
- **Elaboration**—refined project vision, iterative development of core system, development of system requirements, more accurate time and cost estimates
- **Construction**—iterative development of remaining system
- **Transition**—testing and deployment of the system

We will look at the characteristics of each phase. Figure D-2 shows how the RUP development phases relate to iterations.

FIGURE D-2   RUP development phases

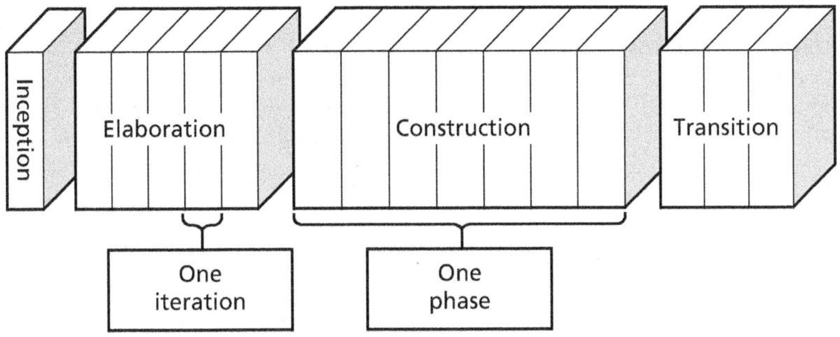

D.2.1   Inception Phase

During the inception phase, we define the scope of the project and decide whether the project is feasible. If a team has already implemented solutions for similar problems, and the solution is clearly feasible, the inception phase may be very brief.

The inception phase defines a project's scope and feasibility

   At a minimum, the inception phase must define an initial set of system requirements and choose the length of the iteration timebox. While defining the initial requirements, you generate a core set of use case scenarios and determine which elements of the solution involve the greatest risk. This set of scenarios and the highest-risk aspects of the solution are the focus of the first iterations in the elaboration phase. Note that the inception phase is not an iteration. You should not try to develop all—or even most—of the use case scenarios during inception. Usually only about 10 percent of the use case scenarios are written in any detail during the inception phase.

The elaboration phase develops a core system and addresses high-risk elements

D.2.2   Elaboration Phase

During the elaboration phase, the system's core architecture is iteratively developed, high-risk elements of the system are addressed, and most of the system requirements are defined. The **core architecture** is composed of those software components that are central to the system. For example, the objects represented in the Unified Modeling Language (UML) class diagram in Figure C-4 of Appendix C would make up the core architecture of that banking system.

   The elaboration phase extends over two or more iterations. If the elaboration phase has only one iteration, no feedback can come into play. Multiple iterations are necessary when developing the correct solution incrementally and adaptively.

   The usual reason for a solution to fail is that high-risk elements were not handled adequately. Early in the elaboration phase, high-risk elements need to be addressed and resolved. If these elements are irresolvable, either the scope of the project must be changed to remove them or the

The elaboration phase refines a system's requirements and cost

project must be abandoned. In either case, little time, money, and effort will have been wasted. Leaving the high-risk elements until later in the development of a project can lead to time and cost overruns—and poor time and cost estimates—because the resolution of the high-risk issues will consume considerable resources. Moreover, if these issues cause the project to fail, much is lost. Therefore, you should address high-risk issues early.

Each iteration starts with an object-oriented analysis of the system requirements and input from the testing of the previous iteration. This analysis leads to a set of use case scenarios to analyze, design, implement, and test. Those scenarios are examined for objects and attributes. UML sequence and class diagrams are drawn to clearly show the objects' collaborations, responsibilities to the system, and relationships to one another. This design is then coded and tested. If this iteration is not one of the first, the code may need to be integrated into the existing subsystem. After final testing, end users and domain experts use the system to produce feedback for subsequent iterations.

D.2.3   Construction Phase

The construction phase develops the remaining system

The construction phase begins once most of the system requirements have been formalized. Each iteration in this phase still consists of analysis, design, implementation, and testing. At this point in the development of the system, however, the analysis and design components require less attention, and increased effort is focused on implementation and testing.

D.2.4   Transition Phase

During the transition phase, beta testing and system development occur

The transition phase begins as the system is put into the environment in which it was designed to work. This may involve **beta testing** with advanced end users or one of several other techniques to move the system into a production environment.

Figure D-3 shows an example of the relative levels of work done during each of the phases in analysis, design, implementation, and testing. This example simply suggests the work levels; do not take them literally.

FIGURE D-3   Relative amounts of work done in each development phase

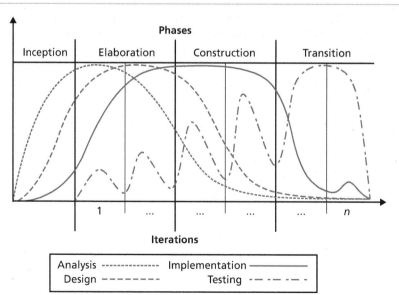

D.3   What About the Waterfall Method of Development?

The RUP is probably new to you, as is another development process—the **waterfall method**—in which the solution is developed by *sequentially* moving through phases such as requirements analysis, design, implementation, testing, and deployment. We think the waterfall method is inferior to the RUP. However, you doubtless will meet programmers during your career who know only the waterfall method. For this reason, you should know what it is.

The waterfall method often results in the following actions:

* Systems analysts produce a set of documents specifying the requirements of the proposed system.
* The requirements documents are passed to a design team that produces a set of design documents.
* The design documents are passed to programmers who code the design.
* The code is passed to a testing team.
* The testing team verifies that the code correctly implements the requirements of the system, as specified by the systems analysts at the beginning of the process.

Notice that the phases occur one after the other. If the systems analysts do not understand *everything* about all aspects of the system and its environment, it is likely that they will specify the wrong system. Such aspects include the system's end users and their needs, other computer systems that must be used, the global business environment, and so on. Incorrect requirements analysis will create a design that, when implemented, leads to a correct system for the wrong problem. In other words, the system solves the problem defined by the requirements analysis, but the requirements analysis describes the wrong problem.

The difficulty with trying to specify the requirements of the proposed system up front is that system requirements are not predictable. Most things in the world today, especially in the high-tech and business worlds, are highly speculative. Change is constant. This implies that the requirements of any system might change at any time. The development process must allow the system under development to evolve and adapt to the changing environment. The waterfall method requires analysts to be omnipotent. For a system to succeed, the waterfall method should not be used for its development. Using iterative, incremental, evolutionary development processes, however, allows feedback to guide the adaptation of the system to a correct solution.

The waterfall method is outdated and should not be used

Be careful not to impose the waterfall method on the RUP development phases. For example, the RUP's inception phase is not the same as the waterfall requirements phase. During the inception phase, some, but not all, system requirements are specified, and programmers also make sure the system is feasible, estimate how much the system will cost to develop, and identify the significant high-risk issues that might doom the project. Trying to develop all use case scenarios during the inception phase makes it the same as the waterfall method.

Further, the RUP's elaboration phase is not the same as the waterfall design phase. During the elaboration phase, some, but not all, design is done, and programmers also do analysis, coding, and testing. If the elaboration phase degrades to having only one iteration, the development process effectively becomes the waterfall method. Similarly, the RUP's construction phase is not only about implementation, and it is not the same as the waterfall implementation phase.

Mathematical Induction

Many proofs of theorems or invariants in computer science use a technique called mathematical induction, or simply **induction**. Induction is a principle of mathematics that is like a row of dominoes standing on end. If you push the first domino, all the dominoes will fall one after another. What allows us to draw this conclusion? If you know that when one domino falls the next domino will fall, you know that pushing the first domino will cause them all to fall in succession. More formally, you can show that all the dominoes will fall if you can show that the following two facts are true:

- The first domino falls.
- For any $k \geq 1$, if the kth domino falls, the $(k + 1)^{th}$ domino will fall.

The principle of mathematical induction is an axiom that is stated as follows:

Axiom E-1. The principle of mathematical induction. A property $P(n)$ that involves an integer n is true for all $n \geq 0$ if the following are true:

1. $P(0)$ is true.
2. If $P(k)$ is true for any $k \geq 0$, then $P(k + 1)$ is true.

A **proof by induction on n** is one that uses the principle of mathematical induction. Such a proof consists of the two steps given in Axiom E-1. The first step is called the *basis*, or *base case*. The second step is the *inductive step*. We usually break the inductive step into two parts: the *inductive hypothesis* ("if $P(k)$ is true for any $k \geq 0$") and the *inductive conclusion* ("then $P(k + 1)$ is true").

Example 1

The following recursive function, which is given here in pseudocode, computes x^n:

```
pow2(x: integer, n: integer)
{
    if (n == 0)
        return 1
    else
        return x * pow2(x, n-1)
}
```

You can prove that pow2 returns x^n for all $n \geq 0$ by using the following proof by induction on n.

Basis. Show that the property is true when $n = 0$. That is, you must show that pow2(x, 0) returns x^0, which is 1. As you can see from the definition of pow2, pow2(x, 0) is 1, which establishes the basis.

Now you must establish the inductive step. By assuming that the property is true when $n = k$ (the inductive hypothesis), you must show that the property is true when $n = k + 1$ (the inductive conclusion).

Inductive Hypothesis. Assume that the property is true when $n = k$. That is, assume that

$$\text{pow2(x, k)} = x^k$$

Inductive Conclusion. Show that the property is true when $n = k + 1$. That is, you must show that pow2(x, k + 1) returns the value x^{k+1}. By definition of the function pow2,

$$\text{pow2(x, k + 1)} = x \text{ * pow2(x, k)}$$

By the inductive hypothesis, pow2(x, k) returns the value x^k, so

$$\text{pow2(x, k + 1)} = x \text{ * } x^k$$
$$= x^{k+1}$$

which is what you needed to show to establish the inductive step.

The inductive proof is thus complete. We demonstrated that the two steps in Axiom E-1 are true, so the principle of mathematical induction guarantees that pow2 returns x^n for all $n \geq 0$. **(End of proof.)**

Example 2

Prove that

$$1 + 2 + \cdots + n = \frac{n(n + 1)}{2} \text{ when } n \geq 1$$

It will be helpful to let S_n represent the sum $1 + 2 + \cdots + n$.

Basis. Sometimes the property to be proven is trivial when $n = 0$, as is the case here. You can use $n = 1$ as the basis instead. (Actually, you can use any value of $n \geq 0$ as the basis, but a value of 0 or 1 is typical.)

You need to show that the sum S_1, which is simply 1, is equal to $1(1 + 1)/2$. This fact is obvious.

Inductive Hypothesis. Assume that the formula is true when $n = k$; that is, assume that $S_k = k(k + 1)/2$.

Inductive Conclusion. Show that the formula is true when $n = k + 1$. To do so, you can proceed as follows:

$$\begin{aligned}
S_{k+1} &= (1 + 2 + \cdots + k) + (k + 1) && \text{(definition of } S_{k+1}) \\
&= S_k + (k + 1) && \text{(definition of } S_k) \\
&= k(k + 1)/2 + (k + 1) && \text{(inductive hypothesis)} \\
&= (k(k + 1) + 2(k + 1))/2 && \text{(common denominator)} \\
&= (k + 1)(k + 2)/2 && \text{(factorization)}
\end{aligned}$$

The last expression is $n(n + 1)/2$ when n is $k + 1$. Thus, if the formula for S_k is true, the formula for S_{k+1} is true. Therefore, by the principle of mathematical induction, the formula is true when $n \geq 1$. **(End of proof.)**

Example 3

Prove that $2^n > n^2$ when $n \geq 5$.

Basis. Here is an example in which the base case is not $n = 0$ or 1, but instead is $n = 5$. It is obvious that the relationship is true when $n = 5$, because

$$2^5 = 32 > 5^2 = 25$$

Inductive Hypothesis. Assume that the relationship is true when $n = k \geq 5$—that is, assume that $2^k > k^2$ when $k \geq 5$.

Inductive Conclusion. Show that the relationship is true when $n = k + 1$—that is, show that $2^{k+1} > (k + 1)^2$ when $k \geq 5$. To do so, you can proceed as follows:

$$
\begin{aligned}
(k + 1)^2 &= k^2 + (2k + 1) &&\text{(square } k + 1) \\
&< k^2 + k^2 \text{ when } k \geq 5 &&(2k + 1 < k^2) \\
&< 2^k + 2^k \text{ when } k \geq 5 &&\text{(inductive hypothesis)} \\
&= 2^{k+1}
\end{aligned}
$$

Therefore, by the principle of mathematical induction, $2n > n^2$ when $n \geq 5$. (**End of proof.**)

Sometimes, the inductive hypothesis in Axiom E-1 is not sufficient. That is, you may need to assume more than $P(k)$. The following axiom is a stronger form of the principle of mathematical induction:

Axiom E-2.   The principle of mathematical induction (strong form). A property $P(n)$ that involves an integer n is true for all $n \geq 0$ if the following are true:

1. $P(0)$ is true.
2. If $P(0), P(1), \ldots, P(k)$ are true for any $k \geq 0$, then $P(k + 1)$ is true.

Notice that the inductive hypothesis of Axiom E-2 ("If $P(0), P(1), \ldots, P(k)$ are true for any $k \geq 0$") includes the inductive hypothesis of Axiom E-1 ("If $P(k)$ is true for any $k \geq 0$").

Example 4

Prove that every integer greater than 1 can be written as a product of prime integers.

Recall that a prime number is one that is divisible only by 1 and itself. The inductive proof is as follows:

Basis. The statement that you must prove involves integers greater than 1. Thus, the base case is $n = 2$. However, 2 is a prime number, and therefore it trivially is a product of prime numbers.

Inductive Hypothesis. Assume that the property is true for each of the integers $2, 3, \ldots, k$, where $k \geq 2$.

Inductive Conclusion. Show that the property is true when $n = k + 1$; that is, show that $k + 1$ can be written as a product of prime numbers.

If $k + 1$ is a prime number, then there is nothing more to show. However, if $k + 1$ is not a prime number, it must be divisible by an integer x such that $1 < x < k + 1$. Thus,

$$k + 1 = x \times y$$

where $1 < y < k + 1$. Notice that x and y are each less than or equal to k, so the inductive hypothesis applies. That is, x and y can each be written as a product of prime numbers. Clearly, the product $x \times y$, which is equal to $k + 1$, must be a product of prime numbers. Because the formula holds for $n = k + 1$, it holds for all $n \geq 2$ by the principle of mathematical induction. (**End of proof.**)

Example 5

Chapter 2 discusses the following recursive definition:

$rabbit(1) = 1$
$rabbit(2) = 1$
$rabbit(n) = rabbit(n - 1) + rabbit(n - 2)$ when $n > 2$

Prove that

$$rabbit(n) = (a^n - b^n)/\sqrt{5}$$

where $a = (1 + \sqrt{5})/2$ and $b = (1 - \sqrt{5})/2 = 1 - a$.

Basis. Because $rabbit(0)$ is undefined, begin at $n = 1$. Some algebra shows that $rabbit(1) = (a^1 - b^1)/\sqrt{5} = 1$. However, notice that $rabbit(2)$ is also a special case. That is, you cannot compute $rabbit(2)$ from $rabbit(1)$ by using the recurrence relationship given here. Therefore, the basis in this inductive proof must include $n = 2$.

When $n = 2$, some more algebra will show that $rabbit(2) = (a^2 - b^2)/\sqrt{5} = 1$. Thus, the formula is true when n is either 1 or 2.

Inductive Hypothesis. Assume that the formula is true for all n such that $1 \leq n \leq k$, where k is at least 2.

Inductive Conclusion. Show that the formula is true for $n = k + 1$. To do so, you can proceed as follows:

$$
\begin{aligned}
rabbit(k + 1) &= rabbit(k) + rabbit(k - 1) && \text{(recurrence relation)} \\
&= [(a^k - b^k) + (a^{k-1} - b^{k-1})]/\sqrt{5} && \text{(inductive hypothesis)} \\
&= [a^{k-1}(a + 1) - b^{k-1}(b + 1)]/\sqrt{5} && \text{(factorization)} \\
&= [(a^{k-1}(a^2) - b^{k-1})(b^2)/]\sqrt{5} && (a + 1 = a^2; b + 1 = b^2) \\
&= (a^{k+1} - b^{k+1})/\sqrt{5}
\end{aligned}
$$

Because the formula holds for $n = k + 1$, it holds for all $n > 2$ by the principle of mathematical induction. (**End of proof.**)

Note that the previous proof requires that you show that $a + 1 = a^2$ and $b + 1 = b^2$. Although simple algebra will demonstrate the validity of these equalities, exactly how did we discover them after the factorization step? Some experience with inductive proofs will give you the confidence to determine and verify the auxiliary relationships—such as $a + 1 = a^2$—that are necessary in a proof. Here, after we introduced the factors $(a + 1)$ and $(b + 1)$, we observed that if these factors were equal to a^2 and b^2, respectively, we could finish the proof. Thus, we tried to show that $a + 1 = a^2$ and $b + 1 = b^2$; indeed, we were successful. Inductive proofs often require adventurous algebraic manipulations!

Algorithm Verification

Prerequisite

$\mathbf{F}$ormal, theoretical techniques are available for proving that an algorithm is correct. Although research in this area is incomplete, it is useful to mention some aspects of the verification process.

An **assertion** is a statement about a particular condition at a certain point in an algorithm. Preconditions and postconditions are simply assertions about conditions at the beginning and end of methods and functions. An **invariant** is a condition that is always true at a particular point in an algorithm. A **loop invariant** is a condition that is true before and after each execution of an algorithm's loop. As you will see, loop invariants can help you write correct loops. By using invariants, you can detect errors before you begin coding and thereby reduce your debugging and testing time. Overall, invariants can save you time.

You can prove the correctness of some algorithms

Proving that an algorithm is correct is like proving a theorem in geometry. For example, to prove that a method or function is correct, you would start with its preconditions—which are analogous to the axioms and assumptions in geometry—and demonstrate that the steps of the algorithm lead to the postconditions. To do so, you would consider each step in the algorithm and show that an assertion before the step leads to a particular assertion after the step.

By proving the validity of individual statements, you can prove that sequences of statements, and then methods and functions, classes, and finally the program are correct. For example, suppose you show that if assertion A_1 is true and statement S_1 executes, then assertion A_2 is true. Also suppose you have shown that assertion A_2 and statement S_2 lead to assertion A_3. You can then conclude that if assertion A_1 is true, executing the sequence of statements S_1 and S_2 will lead to assertion A_3. By continuing in this manner, you eventually will be able to show that the program is correct.

Clearly, if you discovered an error during the verification process, you would correct your algorithm and possibly modify the analysis and/or design. Thus, when you use invariants, your algorithm will likely contain fewer errors *before* you begin coding. As a result, you will spend less time debugging your program.

You can formally prove that particular constructs such as `if` statements, loops, and assignments are correct. An important technique uses loop invariants to demonstrate the correctness of iterative algorithms. For example, we will prove that the following simple loop computes the sum of the first n values in the array `item`:

```
// Computes the sum of item[0], item[1], . . ., item[n-1] for any n >= 1.
int sum = 0;
int j = 0;
while (j < n)
{
    sum += item[j];
    j++;
}  // end while
```

Before this loop begins execution, `sum` is 0 and `j` is 0. After the loop executes once, `sum` is `item[0]` and `j` is 1. In general,

> `sum` is the sum of the values in `item[0]` through `item[j-1]`

Loop invariant

This statement is the invariant for this loop.

The invariant for a correct loop is true at the following points:

- Initially, after any initialization steps, but before the loop begins execution
- Before every iteration of the loop
- After every iteration of the loop
- After the loop terminates

For the previous loop example, these points are as follows:

```
int sum = 0;
int j = 0;
                        ◀──────  The invariant is true here
while (j < n)
{
                        ◀──────  The invariant is true here

  sum += item[j];
  j++;
                        ◀──────  The invariant is true here
}  // end while
                        ◀──────  The invariant is true here
```

You can use these observations to prove the correctness of an iterative (loop-controlled) algorithm. For the previous example, you must show that each of the following four points is true:

Steps to establish the correctness of an algorithm

1. **The invariant must be true initially,** before the loop begins execution for the first time. In the previous example, `sum` is 0 and `j` is 0 initially. In this case, the invariant states that `sum` contains the sum of the values in `item[0]` through `item[-1]`; the invariant is true because there are no array elements in this range.
2. **An execution of the loop must preserve the invariant.** That is, if the invariant is true before any given iteration of the loop, you must show that it is true after the iteration. In the example, the loop adds `item[j]` to `sum` and then increments `j` by 1. Thus, after an execution of the loop, the most recent value added to `sum` is in `item[j-1]`; that is, the invariant is true after the iteration.
3. **The invariant must capture the correctness of the algorithm.** That is, you must show that if the invariant is true when the loop terminates, the algorithm is correct. When the loop in the previous example terminates, `j` contains `n`, and the invariant is true: `sum` contains the sum of the values in `item[0]` through `item[n-1]`, which is the sum that you intended to compute.

4. **The loop must terminate.** That is, you must show that the loop will terminate after a finite number of iterations. In the example, j begins at 0 and then increases by 1 at each execution of the loop. Thus, j eventually will equal n for any $n \geq 1$. This fact and the nature of the while statement guarantee that the loop will terminate.

Not only can you use invariants to show that your loop is correct, but you can also use them to show that your loop is wrong. For example, suppose that the expression in the previous while statement was j <= n instead of j < n. Steps 1 and 2 of the previous demonstration would be the same, but step 3 would differ: When the loop terminated, j would contain n + 1 and, because the invariant would be true, sum would contain the sum of the values in item[0] through item[n]. Because this is not the desired sum, you know that something is wrong with your loop.

Notice the clear connection between steps 1 through 4 and **mathematical induction**.[1] Showing the invariant to be true initially, which establishes the **base case**, is analogous to establishing that a property of the natural numbers is true for 0. Showing that each iteration of the loop preserves the invariant is the **inductive step**. This step is analogous to showing that if a property is true for an arbitrary natural number k, the property is true for the natural number $k + 1$. After performing the four steps just described, you can conclude that the invariant is true after every iteration of the loop—just as mathematical induction allows you to conclude that a property is true for every natural number.

Identifying loop invariants will help you write correct loops. You should state the invariant as a comment that either precedes or begins each loop, as appropriate. For example, in the previous example, you might write the following:

```
// Invariant: 0 <= j <= n and
//            sum = item[0] + ··· + item[j-1]
while (j < n)
   ...
```

State loop invariants in your programs

You should confirm that the invariants for the following unrelated loops are correct. Remember that each invariant must be true both before the loop begins and after each iteration of the loop, including the final one. Also, you might find it easier to understand the invariant for a for loop if you temporarily convert it to an equivalent while loop:

```
// Compute n! for an integer n >= 0
int factorial = 1;
// Invariant: factorial == (j-1)!
for (int j = 1; j <= n; j++)
   factorial *= j;

// Compute an approximation of eˣ for a real x
double term = 1.0;
double series = 1.0;
int    k = 1;
// Invariant: term == xᵏ⁻¹/(k-1)! and
//            series == 1+x+x²/2!+···+xᵏ⁻¹/(k-1)!
while (k <= n)
{
   term *= x / k;
   series += term;
   k++;
}  // end while
```

Examples of loop invariants

---

[1] A review of mathematical induction appears in Appendix E.

C++ File Fundamentals

Contents

Prerequisite

G.1 File Input and Output

You have used files ever since you wrote your first program. In fact, your C++ source program is in a file that you probably created by using a text editor. You can create and access such files outside of, and independently of, any particular program. Files can also contain data that is either read or written by your program. It is this type of file that concerns us here.

A file is a sequence of bytes that resides in auxiliary storage, often a disk. Files are useful because they can be large and can exist after program execution terminates. In contrast, variables, for example, represent memory that is accessible only within the program that creates them. When program execution terminates, the operating system reuses this memory and changes its contents.

Because files can exist after program execution, they not only provide a permanent record for human users, they also allow communication between programs. Program A can write its output into a file that program B can use later for input. However, files that you discard after program execution are not unusual. Chapter 16 discusses one such file that can help balance a binary search tree. You can also use such a file as a scratch pad during program execution when you have too much data to retain conveniently in memory all at once.

Files are classified as follows. A **text file** is a file of characters that are organized logically into lines. The files that you create—by using an editor—to contain your C++ programs are text files. A file that is not a text file is called a **binary file** or, sometimes, a **general file** or **nontext file**.

G.2   Text Files

Text files are designed for easy communication with people. As such, these files are flexible and easy to use, but they are not as efficient with respect to computer time and storage as binary files.

A text file—like any other file—is a sequence of bytes. That is, a text file is a sequence of characters. One special aspect of text files is that they *appear* to be divided into lines. A special end-of-line character creates the illusion that a text file contains lines by making the file behave as if it were divided into lines. Typically, you process a text file sequentially a character, a group of characters, or a line at a time.

A text file contains lines of characters

When you create a text file by typing data at your keyboard, each time you press the Enter, or Return, key, you insert one end-of-line character into the file. When an output device, such as a printer or monitor, encounters an end-of-line character in a text file, the device moves to the beginning of the next line. In C++, this end-of-line symbol is the character \n.

Files end with a special end-of-file symbol

In addition, you can think of a special end-of-file character that follows the last data in a file. Such a symbol may or may not actually exist in the file, but C++ behaves as if one did. The predefined constant EOF, for "end of file," represents this symbol within your program. This book assumes that all text files—including the empty file—end with both an end-of-line symbol and an end-of-file symbol. Figure G-1 depicts a text file with these special symbols.

FIGURE G-1   A text file with end-of-line and end-of-file symbols

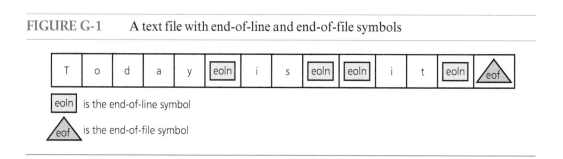

Any program that uses files must access the standard C++ file stream library. You enable this access by including the following statement in your program:

```
#include <fstream>
```

Use a stream variable to access a file

The C++ file stream library, fstream, provides three stream types: ifstream for input file streams, ofstream for output file streams, and fstream for file streams that are for both input and output. You use a **stream variable** of one of these types to access a file. Files are sometimes referred to as streams since you can think of a file as a stream of characters flowing into or out of your program.

To use a file in your program, there are three simple steps:

1. Open the file.
2. Read data from the file or write data to the file.
3. Close the file.

G.2.1   Opening and Closing Text Files

Opening a file. Before you can read from or write to a file, you need to **open** it. That is, you need to initialize the file and associate its name with a stream variable. One way to open a file is to provide the file's name when you declare the stream variable. For example,

You must initialize, or open, a file before you can use it

```
std::ifstream inFile("Ages.DAT"); // Input file
```

declares an input stream variable `inFile` and associates it with the file named `Ages.DAT`. The file name can be a literal constant, as it is here, or a string variable. Once the file is open, you no longer need the file's name; it is used only to link the file on the disk to the stream variable that you use in your program.

Alternatively, you can declare an input stream variable by writing

```
std::ifstream inFile;
```

and then later use the `open` method to associate it with the file's name:

```
inFile.open("Ages.DAT");
```

Regardless of how you open a file, you can check the stream variable to see if the process was successful by writing

You can check whether a file was opened successfully

```
if (!inFile)
    processError(); // Deal with failure to open file in a function that you write
```

Closing a file. You close a particular file—that is, disassociate it from a stream variable and free system resources—by using the `close` method:

Close a file when you are finished with it

```
myFile.close();
```

Once a file is closed, it is no longer available for input or output until a program opens it again.

G.2.2   Reading and Writing Text Files

Associated with each file in a program is a **file window**, which marks the current position within the file. Opening a file positions the file window over the first byte in the file, as Figure G-2 illustrates. Because each byte in a text file is a character, the file window for a text file moves from character to character. The following sections describe the behavior of the file window.

Opening a text file for input positions the file window over the first character in the file

---

FIGURE G-2   The file window after an existing text file is opened for input

---

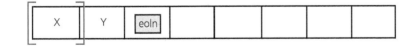

A file window marks the current position within a file

Character input. Suppose that you have declared an input stream variable `inFile` and associated it with the name of the text file by writing

```
std::ifstream inFile(fileName);
```

where `fileName` is a string variable. When you use a file for input, the file window is over the byte that you will read next. Thus, after you open a file, you are ready to read the first byte, as you saw in Figure G-2. As you read the characters from a text file, the file window advances sequentially

---

FIGURE G-3   A file window over the character to be read next

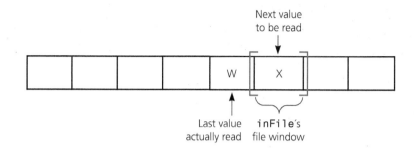

---

from one character to another. After reading several characters, you will see the file window shown in Figure G-3.

The input operator >> and methods such as `get`, whose use with `cin` was described in Appendix A, are also used with files. For the character variable `ch` and the stream variable `inFile`, either of the statements

```
inFile >> ch; // Preferred technique
```

or

```
inFile.get(ch);
```

means

ch = *the value at the file window*
Advance the file window to the next character

as Figure G-4 illustrates.

FIGURE G-4   The effect of `inFile >> ch` on a text file `inFile`

Before `inFile >> ch;`

| ch | ? |

| a | b | c | d | eoln | e | f | eoln | eof |

After `inFile >> ch;`

| ch | c |

| a | b | c | d | eoln | e | f | eoln | eof |

You can detect when the file window has reached either the end of a line or the end of the file by using the `peek` method. This method returns the character in the file window but does not advance the window to the next character. For example, the loop

```
while (inFile.peek() != '\n')   // Loop until end of line.
    std::cout << (inFile.get()); // Get character from inFile and display it.
```

displays a line of a text file, and the loop

```
while (inFile.peek() != EOF)   // Loop until end of entire file.
    std::cout << (inFile.get()); // Get character from inFile and display it.
```

displays the contents of an entire text file.

To summarize, consider the text file inFile that appears in Figure G-4. If ch is a character variable, the statements in the following sequence assign values to ch as indicated:

```
std::ifstream inFile(fileName);
inFile >> ch;               // ch = 'a'
inFile.get(ch);             // ch = 'b' — alternate technique 1
ch = inFile.get();          // ch = 'c' — alternate technique 2
inFile.ignore(10, '\n');    // Advance to end-of-line symbol
inFile >> ch;               // ch = 'e'
ch = inFile.peek();         // ch = 'f'
inFile >> ch;               // ch = 'f'
inFile >> ch;               // ch = '\n'
inFile >> ch;               // Error: attempted read beyond end of file
```

The method ignore advances the file window, thereby skipping characters, until it reaches a specified character as follows:

- ignore() skips characters until it reaches the end-of-line character.
- ignore(n) skips characters until it reaches either the nth character or the end-of-line character, whichever is first.
- ignore(n, 'c') skips characters until it reaches either the nth character, the character 'c', or the end-of-line character, whichever is first.

You also can read the characters in the file as strings by using getline in the same way that you used it with cin.

Character output. Suppose that you have declared an output stream variable outFile and associated it with the name of the text file, as in

```
std::ofstream outFile(fileName);
```

If you are creating a new file, the file window will be positioned at the beginning (and the end) of the new file, which is empty. If the file already exists, opening it erases the data in the file and positions the window at the beginning—and the end—of the now empty file.

The output operator << and methods such as put, whose use with cout was described in Appendix A, are also used with files. For the character variable ch and the stream variable outFile, either of the statements

```
outFile << ch; // Preferred technique
```

or

```
outFile.put(ch);
```

means

Write the value of ch *at the file-window position*
Advance the file window

Figure G-5 illustrates these steps when ch contains the character 'X'. Note that if ch contains '\n', either of the previous statements writes the end-of-line symbol to the file.

You can also write strings to a text file by using the operator <<.

FIGURE G-5   The effect of outFile << ch on a text file outFile when ch contains the character 'X'

Before outFile << ch;   After outFile << ch;

Numeric data within text files. As you know, you can read integer and floating-point values from the standard input stream into variables with arithmetic data types. You also know that the standard input stream is a sequence of characters. Likewise, a text file is a sequence of characters, so it should not surprise you that integer and floating-point values can be read from and written to a text file. Although this presentation uses int values to illustrate the concepts, the other arithmetic data types follow by analogy.

When your program reads from a text file into an int variable, the system expects a sequence of characters that it can convert into an integer. For example, if the text file contains the character sequence 234 and you read from the text file into the int variable x, the system will read three characters—2, 3, and 4—and convert them into the computer's internal representation for the integer 234 and assign this value to x. More precisely, the text file contains the ASCII codes for the characters 2, 3, and 4—which are, respectively, the decimal values 50, 51, and 52. However, these codes appear in the file in binary, as Figure G-6a indicates. If you read those characters into the integer variable x, x will contain the computer's internal representation for the integer 234, which appears in binary as shown in Figure G-6b. In other words, the representation of digits in a text file differs from the representation in memory of the number that those digits symbolize.

FIGURE G-6   (a) The ASCII characters 2, 3, and 4 represented in binary in a text file; (b) the internal binary representation of the integer 234

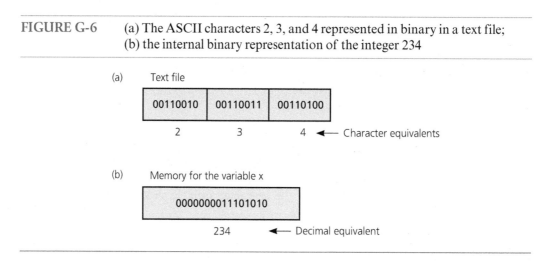

To summarize, if inFile is an input stream variable that is associated with a text file of valid integers, and x is an int variable, the statement

    inFile >> x;

has the following effect:

> *Skip to the first nonblank character*
> *Convert into an integer the sequence of characters that begins*
>   *at the current position of inFile's window and ends just before the next*
>   *character c that is not a digit*
> *Assign this integer value to x*
> *Advance the file window so that it is over the character c*

Figure G-7 illustrates these steps. Observe that if the sequence begins with a character other than +, –, or 0 through 9, reading will terminate. For example, the system cannot convert the sequence w123 into an integer. It will, however, read the integer 123 from the sequence 123wrt.

FIGURE G-7   Reading an integer from a text file

Before `inFile >> x;`

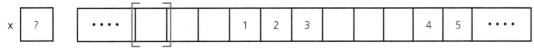

After `inFile >> x;`

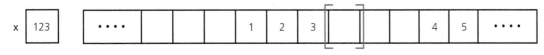

When your program writes an integer value such as 234 to a text file, the system first converts the integer from the computer's internal binary representation (0000000011101010) to the character sequence 2, 3, 4 and then writes these characters to the file. For the output stream variable outFile and the integer variable x, the statement

```
outFile << x;
```

has the following effect:

Convert the value of x *into a sequence of characters*
Append this sequence of characters to the file
Position the file window just past the last character written

The following function reads and displays the contents of an entire text file of integers:

```
void echoFile(string fileName)
{
   std::ifstream inFile(fileName);
   int x = 0;

   while (inFile >> x) // Read fails at end of file
      std::cout << x << " ";

   std::cout << std::endl;
   inFile.close();
} // end echoFile
```

The function ignores the end-of-line symbols in the file and displays the integers all on one line.

Suppose that you want to display each line in the file regardless of the number of integers per line. You can use the peek and ignore methods to skip the blanks between the integers. Note that you always pass a stream variable to a function as a reference argument.

```
// Skips blanks in a text file.
void skipBlanks(std::ifstream& inFile)
{
   while (inFile.peek() == ' ') // While the current character is a blank:
      inFile.ignore(1);          // Ignore character, advance file window
} // end skipBlanks
```

```cpp
// Displays one line of a text file containing integers.
void echoLine(std::ifstream& inFile)
{
   int x = 0;
   while (inFile.peek() != '\n')  // While the current character is not eol:
   {
      inFile >> x;                   // Read the next integer into x
      std::cout << x << " ";         // Display the number to user
      skipBlanks(inFile);            // Skip blanks following number
   }  // end while

   inFile.ignore(1);                 // Advance beyond \n
   std::cout << "\n";                // Move to next line
}  // end echoLine

// Displays the contents of a text file.
void echoFile(string fileName)
{
   std::ifstream inFile(fileName);

   skipBlanks(inFile);
   while (inFile.peek() != EOF)
      echoLine(inFile);

   inFile.close();
}  // end echoFile
```

G.2.3   Manipulating Text Files

Copying a text file. Suppose that you wanted to make a copy of the text file associated with the stream variable originalFile. Copying a text file requires some work and provides a good example of the statements you have just studied. The approach taken by the following function copies the file one character at a time, taking into account both the end-of-line symbols and the end-of-file symbol:

```cpp
/** Makes a duplicate copy of a text file.
 @pre  The name of an existing external text file and the name of the
   text file to be created are given as strings.
 @post  The original text file is duplicated.
 @param originalFileName  Name of file to copy.
 @param copyFileName  Name of duplicate file. */
void copyTextFile(std::string originalFileName, std::string copyFileName)
{
   std::ifstream originalFile(originalFileName); // Input file
   std::ofstream copyFile(copyFileName);         // Output file
   char ch = '';

   // Copy characters one at a time from given file to new file
   while (originalFile.get(ch))               // Fails at end of file
      copyFile << ch;                          // Write character to new file

   // Close the files.
   originalFile.close();
   copyFile.close();
}  // end copyTextFile
```

Notice that this function copies each end-of-line symbol just as it copies any other character. To do so, the expression

```cpp
originalFile.get(ch)
```

is necessary because

```
originalFile >> ch
```

skips whitespace, including the end-of-line symbol.

Adding to a text file. When you open a file, you can specify a second argument in addition to the file's name. This second argument has the form

```
std::ios::mode
```

where *mode* has values such as in, out, or app. Until now, this argument has been omitted because ifstream files are by default opened for input, whereas ofstream files are opened for output. However, we use this second argument to append a component to an ofstream file by first opening it in append mode. Either the statement

```
std::ofstream outFile("Sample.DAT", std::ios::app);
```

or the statements

```
std::ofstream outFile;
outFile.open("Sample.DAT", std::ios::app);
```

prepare the file outFile for output and position the file window after the file's last component. Thus, the old contents of the file are retained, and you can write additional components.

Searching a text file sequentially. Suppose that you have a text file of data about a company's employees. For simplicity, assume that this file contains two consecutive lines for each employee. The first line contains the employee's name, and the next line contains data such as salary.

Given the name of an employee, you can search the file for that name and then access the other information about this person. A sequential search examines the names in the order in which they appear in the file until the desired name is located. The following function performs such a sequential search. If the person is found, it returns that worker's salary; otherwise, it returns -1.0.

```
double getSalary(std::string fileToSearch, std::string desiredName)
{
   bool found = false;
   std::string nextName;
   double nextSalary = -1.0;
   std::ifstream inFile(fileToSearch);

   while ( !found && getline(inFile, nextName) )
   {
      inFile >> nextSalary; // Salary for nextName
      inFile.ignore();      // Ignores remaining whitespace in line
      if (nextName == desiredName)
         found = true;
   } // end while

   inFile.close();          // Always close file before return statement
   return nextSalary;
} // end getSalary
```

This function needs to look at all the names in the file before discovering that a particular name does not occur. If the names were in alphabetical order, you could detect when the search passed the place in the file that should have contained the desired name, if it existed. In this way, you could terminate the search before you needlessly searched the rest of the file.

Accessing a text file directly. Although you usually process a text file sequentially, you can access the character stored at a given position directly without first reading the preceding characters.

The characters in a text file are numbered sequentially in order of appearance in the file, beginning with zero. The `seekg` method provides access to any character in the file, given the character's number. For example,

```
myFile.seekg(15)
```

advances the file window to the character numbered 15, which is actually the 16th character in the file. Immediately following this operation, you can read the character.

You can also locate a character relative to either the beginning of the file, the current position in the file, or the end of the file by specifying—as the second argument to `seekg`—

```
std::ios::mode
```

where *mode* is one of `beg`, `cur`, or `end`. Thus,

```
myFile.seekg(2, std::ios::cur)
```

seeks the second character after the one at the present location of the file window.

G.3 Binary Files

Files that are not text files are called binary (or general or nontext) files. Like a text file, a binary file is a sequence of bytes grouped together into **file components**. It is important to emphasize that each file component is an indivisible entity. For example, each component of a binary file of integers is an integer in the computer's internal representation. If you write the integer value 234 to a binary file, the system would write the computer's internal representation of 234, which is 0000000011101010 in binary, to the file, rather than the three ASCII characters 2, 3, 4, which are, respectively, 00110010, 00110011, and 00110100 in binary. Similar comments are true for a binary file of floating-point numbers. If you could use a text editor to look at the file, you would see gibberish. You create a binary file not by using an editor—as you can for a text file—but rather by running a program.

The statement

```
std::ofstream outFile(myFileName, std::ios::binary);
```

associates the stream variable `outFile` with the external binary file whose name is in the string variable `myFileName`. A binary file has an end-of-file symbol at its end, just as a text file does. However, the notion of lines does not exist for a binary file, although a binary file might contain data that coincidentally looks like an end-of-line symbol. Except for the differences noted here, C++ treats binary files in the same way that it treats text files.

C++ Header Files and Standard Functions

Here is a list of commonly used C++ header files. Other header files are introduced in the chapters when needed.

cassert

This library contains only the function assert. You use

assert(*assertion*);

to test the validity of an assertion. If *assertion* is false, assert writes an error message and terminates program execution. You can disable all occurrences of assert in your program by placing the directive #define NDEBUG before the include directive.

cctype

Most functions in this library classify a given ASCII character as a letter, a digit, and so on. Two other functions convert letters between uppercase and lowercase.

The classification functions return a true value if ch belongs to the specified group; otherwise they return false.

isalnum(ch)	Returns true if ch is either a letter or a decimal digit
isalpha(ch)	Returns true if ch is a letter
iscntrl(ch)	Returns true if ch is a control character (ASCII 127 or 0 to 31)
isdigit(ch)	Returns true if ch is a decimal digit
isgraph(ch)	Returns true if ch is printable and nonblank
islower(ch)	Returns true if ch is a lowercase letter
isprint(ch)	Returns true if ch is printable (including blank)
ispunct(ch)	Returns true if ch is a punctuation character
isspace(ch)	Returns true if ch is a whitespace character: space, tab, carriage return, new line, or form feed
isupper(ch)	Returns true if ch is an uppercase letter
isdigit(ch)	Returns true if ch is a hexadecimal digit

toascii(ch)	Returns the ASCII code for ch
tolower(ch)	Returns the lowercase version of ch if ch is an uppercase letter; otherwise returns ch
toupper(ch)	Returns the uppercase version of ch if ch is a lowercase letter; otherwise returns ch

cmath

The C++ functions in this library compute certain standard mathematical functions. These functions are overloaded to accommodate float, double, and long double. Unless otherwise indicated, each function has one argument, with the return type being the same as the argument type (either float, double, or long double).

acos(x)	Returns the arc cosine
asin(x)	Returns the arc sine
atan(x)	Returns the arc tangent
atan2(x, y)	Returns the arc tangent of x/y
ceil(x)	Rounds up
cos(x)	Returns the cosine
cosh(x)	Returns the hyperbolic cosine
exp(x)	Returns e raised to the power x
fabs(x)	Returns the absolute value
floor(x)	Rounds down
fmod(x, y)	Returns x modulo y
log(x)	Returns the natural log
log10(x)	Returns the log base 10
modf(x, iptr)	For arguments x and iptr, returns the fractional part of x and sets iptr to point to the integer part of x
pow(x, y)	Returns x raised to the power y
sin(x)	Returns the sine
sinh(x)	Returns the hyperbolic sine
sqrt(x)	Returns the square root
tan(x)	Returns the tangent
tanh(x)	Returns the hyperbolic tangent

cstdlib

This library contains some miscellaneous but useful functions.

abort()	Terminates program execution abnormally
abs(x)	Returns the absolute value of an integer
atof(s)	Converts a string argument to floating point
atoi(s)	Converts a string argument to an integer

`exit(x)`	Terminates program execution, and returns x to the operating system
`rand()`	Returns a pseudorandom integer
`srand(x)`	Initializes, or seeds, the pseudorandom number generator to x
`srand()`	Initializes, or seeds, the pseudorandom number generator to 1

cstring

This library enables you to manipulate C strings that end in \0. Unless noted otherwise, these functions return a pointer to the resulting string in addition to modifying an appropriate argument. The argument ch is a character, n is an integer, and the other arguments are strings.

`strncat(toS, fromS, n)`	Copies at most n characters of fromS to the end of toS and appends '\0'
`strcmp(str1, str2)`	Returns an integer that is negative if str1 < str2, zero if str1 == str2, and positive if str1 > str2
`stricmp(str1, str2)`	Behaves like strcmp, but ignores case
`strncmp(str1, str2, n)`	Behaves like strcmp, but compares the first n characters of each string
`strncpy(toS, fromS, n)`	Copies n characters of fromS to toS, truncating or padding with '\0' as necessary
`strspn(str1, str2)`	Returns the number of initial consecutive characters of str1 that are not in str2
`strcspn(str1, str2)`	Returns the number of initial consecutive characters of str1 that are in str2
`strlen(str)`	Returns the length of str, excluding '\0'
`strlwr(str)`	Converts any uppercase letters in str to lowercase without altering other characters
`strupr(str)`	Converts any lowercase letters in str to uppercase without altering other characters
`strchr(str, ch)`	Returns a pointer to the first occurrence of ch in str; otherwise returns nullptr
`strrchr(str, ch)`	Returns a pointer to the last occurrence of ch in str; otherwise returns nullptr
`strpbrk(str1, str2)`	Returns a pointer to the first character in str1 that also appears in str2; othewise returns nullptr
`strstr(str1, str2)`	Returns a pointer to the first occurrence of str2 in str1; otherwise returns nullptr
`strtok(str1, str2)`	Finds the next token in str1 that is followed by str2, returns a pointer to the token, and writes nullptr immediately after the token in str1

fstream

Defines the C++ classes that support file I/O.

iomanip

The manipulators in this library affect the format of stream operations. Note that iostream contains additional manipulators.

setbase(b)	Sets number base to b = 8, 10, or 16
setfill(f)	Sets fill character to f
setprecision(n)	Sets floating-point precision to integer n
setw(n)	Sets field width to integer n

iostream

The manipulators in this library affect the format of stream operations. Note that iomanip contains additional manipulators.

dec	Tells the subsequent operation to use decimal representation
endl	Inserts the new-line character \n and flushes the output stream
ends	Inserts the null character \0 into an output stream
flush	Flushes an output stream
hex	Tells the subsequent I/O operation to use hexadecimal representation
oct	Tells the subsequent I/O operation to use octal representation
ws	Extracts whitespace characters from the input stream

stdexcept

Defines several exception classes that can be thrown or extended for specific exceptional conditions.

string

This library enables you to manipulate C++ strings. Described here is a selection of the methods that this library provides. In addition, you can use the following operators with C++ strings: =, +, ==, !=, <, <=, >, >=, <<, and >>. Note that positions within a string begin at 0.

erase()	Makes the string empty
erase(pos, len)	Removes the substring that begins at position pos and contains len characters
find(subString)	Returns the position of the substring subString within the string
length()	Returns the number of characters in the string (same as size)
replace(pos, len, str)	Replaces the substring that begins at position pos and contains len characters with the string str
size()	Returns the number of characters in the string (same as length)
substr(pos, len)	Returns the substring that begins at position pos and contains len characters

Appendix

I

C++ Documentation Systems

Documenting programs has never been a very enjoyable task. With the advent of the javadoc documentation system, commenting Java programs is at least less tedious. Inspired by javadoc, others have produced utility software to process documentation for other programming languages, including C++. Documentation tools like doxygen (doxygen.org) and DOC++ (docpp.sourceforge.net) read C++ source code and generate HTML-based documentation from javadoc-style comments embedded within the code. The comments in this book assume that doxygen will prepare the documentation.

The doxygen tool extracts the header for your class, the headers for all public methods, and comments that are written in a certain form. No method bodies and no private items are extracted.

For a comment to be extracted, the comment must satisfy two conditions:

- The comment must occur immediately before a public class definition or the header of a public method.
- The comment must begin with /** and end with */ and is a special form of the C++ multiline comment /* ... */.

Inside the comment, doxygen tags identify different aspects of the documentation, such as the programmer's name and a method's parameters and return value. Tags begin with the symbol @. We will describe only some of the available tags in this appendix. Note that some doxygen tags differ from the tags used by javadoc.

- @author lists the name of a class's programmer.
- @file identifies the name of the file containing a class.
- @param identifies a method's parameter by name and includes its description.
- @post identifies a method's postcondition.
- @pre identifies a method's precondition.
- @return describes a method's return value.
- @throw lists an exception that a method can throw.

You write a @param tag for each parameter in a method. You should list these tags in the order in which the parameters appear in the method's header. After the @param tag, you give the name and description of the parameter. For example, for the parameter customer, you might write

```
@param customer   The string that names the customer.
```

You write a @return tag for every method that returns a value, even if you have already described the value in the method's description. Try to say something more specific about this value here. This tag must come after any @param tags in the comment. Do not use this tag for void methods and constructors.

Next, if a method can throw an exception, you name it by using a @throw tag. You list multiple exceptions alphabetically by name, one per @throw tag.

Here is a sample comment for a method. We usually begin such comments with a brief description of the method's purpose. This is our convention; javadoc has no tag for it.

```
/** Adds a new entry to a roster.
 @param newEntry  The object to be added to the roster.
 @param newPosition  The position of newEntry within the roster.
 @pre  None.
 @post  If the addition is successful, the roster contains the new entry;
    otherwise, the roster is unchanged.
 @throw  PrecondViolatedExcept if newPosition is out of range.
 @return  True if the addition is successful, or false otherwise. */
```

Here is the beginning of a sample class definition that is in the file someClass.h:

```
/** An example of a class.
 @file  someClass.h
 @author  Ima Student */
```

Programming Tip: Comments

- Use /** ... */ comments before the headers of classes and methods to document their use and specifications. Use tags within a comment to identify aspects of the documentation.
- Use // for comments within the body of a class declaration or method definition that describe the details of the implementation.
- Use /* ... */ during debugging to temporarily disable a portion of your code.

ASCII
Character Codes

Code	Character	Code	Character	Code	Character	Code	Character
0	NUL	32	(blank)	64	@	96	` (reverse quote)
1	STX	33	!	65	A	97	a
2	SOT	34	"	66	B	98	b
3	ETX	35	#	67	C	99	c
4	EOT	36	$	68	D	100	d
5	ENQ	37	%	69	E	101	e
6	ACK	38	&	70	F	102	f
7	BEL	39	' (apostrophe)	71	G	103	g
8	BS	40	(	72	H	104	h
9	HT	41	)	73	I	105	i
10	LF	42	*	74	J	106	j
11	VT	43	+	75	K	107	k
12	FF	44	, (comma)	76	L	108	l
13	CR	45	–	77	M	109	m
14	SO	46	.	78	N	110	n
15	SI	47	/	79	O	111	o
16	DLE	48	0	80	P	112	p
17	DC1	49	1	81	Q	113	q
18	DC2	50	2	82	R	114	r
19	DC3	51	3	83	S	115	s
20	DC4	52	4	84	T	116	t
21	NAK	53	5	85	U	117	u
22	SYN	54	6	86	V	118	v
23	ETB	55	7	87	W	119	w
24	CAN	56	8	88	X	120	x
25	EM	57	9	89	Y	121	y
26	SUB	58	:	90	Z	122	z
27	ESC	59	;	91	[	123	{
28	FS	60	<	92	\	124		
29	GS	61	=	93	]	125	}
30	RS	62	>	94	^	126	~
31	US	63	?	95	_ (underscore)	127	DEL

Note: The codes 0 through 31 and 127 are for control characters that do not print.

C++ for Java Programmers

Contents

This appendix covers some of the differences between Java and C++ that a beginning programmer may encounter. While there are many additional differences, they either are not applicable to the code and examples used in this text or are explained when needed. This appendix should be used in conjunction with Appendix A to fully understand the features provided in C++.

K.1 General Concepts

Transitioning from Java to C++ is not too difficult, since most of the syntax and many of the concepts are the same. C++ gives you much greater control of how and where you create variables and objects. Thus, a C++ programmer can create programs that are flexible and efficient in speed and use of storage. This flexibility and greater control require you to take great care in managing data and memory, because C++ does not provide garbage collection.

Both Java and C++ are compiled languages. While Java programs are compiled into byte-code for the Java Virtual Machine (JVM), C++ programs are compiled into object code that is specific to an operating system. This means that you need to recompile your C++ code for each operating system that you want your program to run on. The code in this book follows the recent ANSII C++11 and C++14 standards, so you should be able to compile and run your programs on whichever operating system you choose if your compiler supports those standards.

Java classes and interfaces can be grouped into packages that are stored in the same directory hierarchy. When your Java code is compiled, the compiler searches this hierarchy for classes that you use. Any class or method in the package is automatically found by the compiler and later the JVM during program execution. If you need a class outside of the package, you must import it using the Java import statement.

The C++ compiler is stricter and requires the programmer to declare all functions, classes, and variables in a file before they are used. Because classes and constants are often used in multiple programs and multiple locations in a program, C++ provides a mechanism called the **preprocessor** that lets you specify classes and data in a separate **header file** and then include that file in your program. Commands, or **directives**, to the preprocessor are lines that begin with the character #, such as

```
#include <iostream>  // Include the declaration of the iostream classes
#include "MyClass.h" // Include the declaration of MyClass
```

Notice that system files use < >, while user-defined files use " ", to delimit the file name. Section A.8.1 of Appendix A, C++ Interlude 1, and Section K.4 of this appendix show how to develop C++ class declarations.

Although both Java and C++ are object-oriented languages, C++ has many elements that reflect its roots in the imperative language C. An imperative programming language does not use classes to group data and operations on that data. Instead, it is a sequence of statements and functions—methods that are not part of a class. As such, variables, constants, and functions in a C++ program can be declared anywhere in a file; you are not forced to declare them within a class, as you are in Java. The only restriction to this capability is that you cannot declare or define a function within another function.

Comments. Comments are an important part of any program, and C++ supports the same commenting standards as Java:

```
// This is a comment that appears on its own line.
int sum = 0; // This is a comment that appears within a C++ statement
// The following two multiline comments end in */.
/** This is a special multiline comment used for documentation systems
    such as doxygen. It begins with /**. See Appendix I for details. */
/* This is a multiline comment that begins with /*.
   This style is often used to temporarily disable a group of
   statements during debugging. */
```

K.2   Data Types, Variables, Constants, and Arrays

C++ uses primitive data types and variable declarations that are similar to those in Java. The Java types char, int, float, and double are used in C++ and behave the same as in Java. In C++, int can be modified with short, long, signed, and unsigned. All Java variables are initialized to either zero, if a primitive data type, or null, if an object reference. In contrast, you must initialize all C++ variables. If you do not, and an uninitialized variable is used, the result of the statement is unpredictable.

Boolean types. One very important difference between Java and C++ data types occurs with boolean variables. In Java, boolean is a distinct type that has the value true or false. In C++, the analogous data type is bool. It also has a value of true or false, but in C++, true and false are special integers. That is, variables of type bool are actually integers. This affects the type of statement that is used as the predicate or test clause in an if statement, for loop, or while loop, as you will see in the next section. The C++ value of `false` is 0, and an integer value of 0 can be considered `false` in a boolean test. The value of `true` is 1, and any non-zero integer is considered `true`.

String types. Java has a special class `String` to represent character strings. C++ also provides a special class `string` (note the lower case `s`) that implements many of the same features. To use this class, you must write

```
#include <string>
```

as one of the first lines in your program. More information on the C++ class `string` is in Section A.7 of Appendix A.

Constants. Constants in Java are declared within a class or method using the syntax

```
public static final int MAX_SIZE = 20;
```

which creates a publicly accessible constant `MAX_SIZE` with the value 20. A similar statement in C++ uses the keyword `const` to indicate a constant value:

```
const int MAX_SIZE = 20;
```

Constants in C++ are available anywhere within the scope of their declaration. If a constant is declared outside of a class or file, that constant is available to any function or class defined after it in the file and is said to be **global**, even though it is restricted to that file.

Java has a constant `null` that is used to indicate that an object has not been assigned to a variable. C++ uses `nullptr` for this purpose.

Arrays. Although you declare and reference arrays in Java and C++ using similar statements, their implementations are very different. Arrays in Java are objects and have a public data field `length` that contains the number of locations in the array. If a program attempts to access a position beyond the end of the array, an exception is thrown.

C++ arrays are not objects, but are sequences of memory locations of the data type declared for the array. Entries in a C++ array are accessed using `[ ]`, just as they are in Java. C++ arrays have no data field that tracks the number of positions in the array, and most importantly, C++ permits the programmer to reference positions in the array that do not exist. This is a very common source of errors in a C++ program and is one of the areas where you must take great care. The STL class `vector`, which is discussed in Section A.6.3 of Appendix A, is an alternative to C++ arrays that provides some of the features of the Java array.

The following statement declares an array of 20 integers in Java, where `MAX_SIZE` is an integer constant whose value is 20:

```
int[] myArray = new int[MAX_SIZE];
```

This statement does the same thing in C++:

```
int myArray[MAX_SIZE];
```

You can also declare a C++ array by using syntax similar to that of Java:

```
int myArray[] = new int[MAX_SIZE];
```

One difference is the location of the square brackets, but you must also take responsibility for deallocating the array when you are finished using it. You do so with the `delete` statement:

```
delete[] myArray;
```

Notice the `[ ]` following the `delete` operator to indicate that `myArray` is an array. In C++ Interlude 2, we discuss the use of the operators `new` and `delete` in C++.

K.3   Flow Control and Functions

Flow control. Since the syntax of Java is derived from C++, the structure of flow-control statements in C++ is the same as those you are familiar with in Java. This is true for the selection statements if, if-else, and switch. It is also true for loop statements while, do-while, and for. The significant differences in C++ are related to the **test expression** that controls the selection or repetition.

Consider the following Java if-else statement that compares the integer x to 6 and increments y by 10 if x is 6, and by 20 otherwise:

```
if (x == 6)
    y += 10;
else
    y += 20;
```

Because the syntax for an if-else statement is the same in C++, we could place this statement in a C++ program and it would behave in the same way.

The test x == 6 is a **predicate expression** that returns true if the variable x is equal to 6 and false otherwise. In Java, a predicate expression such as this returns a value of type boolean. A Java flow-control statement requires its test expression to have a boolean value, so you must use a predicate expression as the test expression.

A C++ flow-control statement does not restrict the data type of its test expression. Flow-control decisions are made based on whether the expression returns zero or nonzero. If the test expression returns zero, the test is false. Any nonzero value is considered true. The equality operator in the example above returns true, which is 1, if x has the value of 6. Otherwise, it returns false, which is 0. The if-else statement chooses its course of action based on these values.

This behavior of the C++ if-else statement gives you great flexibility in constructing tests for flow-control statements. It also can create confusion and subtle logic errors. For example, consider the following if-else statement:

```
if (x = 6)
    y += 10;
else
    y += 20;
```

At first glance, this may appear to be the same as the earlier example, but upon closer inspection you can see that the test expression is the assignment statement x = 6. The Java compiler will reject this as an error, since it is not a predicate expression. The C++ compiler will accept this statement, and when the program runs, the if-else statement will be evaluated as follows:

```
if (x = 6)   // The variable x is assigned the value of 6.
    y += 10; // 6 is non-zero, so it is "true"; increment y by 10.
```

Every time this code executes, x will be assigned the value 6, and y will be incremented by 10. The original value of x is overwritten by the if clause's test expression and is never used! Tracking down subtle errors, such as this one, has caused your authors many sleepless nights. When performing equality tests in C++ flow-control statements, always check that the test uses == and not =.

Functions. As mentioned earlier, C++ functions do not need to be part of a class. Thus, you do not need to precede C++ functions with access modifiers, as you would for Java methods. Otherwise, the syntax for the declaration and invocation of a C++ function is similar to that of a Java method. Functions can be defined anywhere inside a C++ file, except inside another function.

Here is an example of a C++ function, computeRealCube, that has a parameter of type double and returns the cube of a number:

```
double computeRealCube(double x)
{
   return x * x * x;
} // end computeRealCube
```

Any function defined after `computeRealCube` in the file can invoke `computeRealCube`. But what if a function is defined before `computeRealCube` and needs to call it? In this case, the compiler would issue an error stating that `computeRealCube` was not defined. C++ requires that each function, constant, variable, or class be defined before it can be called.

In a simple program with a few functions, it is easy to order the function definitions so that the compiler sees each one before it encounters the function call. In more complex programs, this order is more difficult or even impossible to achieve. However, the compiler needs only the header of a function before processing a call to it, and C++ provides a way for you to satisfy the compiler. You simply write the function's header followed by a semicolon—that is, its **prototype**—at the beginning of the program that calls it.

For example, the prototype of the function `computeRealCube` is

```
double computeRealCube(double x);
```

You now can place the function's definition anywhere within your program.

In larger programs, function prototypes are placed in header files, as mentioned in C++ Interlude 1 and Section K.1. You then include the header files in your program. Prototypes are also important in the creation of classes, as you will see in the next section. Section A.9.1 of Appendix A also discusses header files.

Note that you can pass a function as an argument to another function or method. This feature is used in Sections 15.2.1 and 15.2.3 of Chapter 15.

K.4 Classes

Many object-oriented concepts implemented in Java classes also apply to C++ classes. This appendix covers only some of the syntax differences that you may encounter in a simple class. Additional information about C++ classes appears in Section A.9 of Appendix A and in C++ Interludes 1 and 5.

Consider the Java class given in Listing K-1. You would write it in one file whose name is the name of the class followed by `.java`. In this case, the class `PlainBox` is in the file named `PlainBox.java`. Though is it possible to define a class in C++ in a single file, we will use two files, since this is a more common and flexible approach. The first file—the class **header file**—contains the data fields for the class and the prototypes of all methods defined in the class. It is a description of the class and does not normally contain executable code.

LISTING K-1 The Java class `PlainBox`

```
1  public class PlainBox
2  {
3     private String item;
4
5     public PlainBox()
6     {
7     } // end default constructor
8
9     public PlainBox(String theItem)
10    {
11       item = theItem;
12    } // end constructor
```
(continues)

```
13
14      public void setItem(String theItem)
15      {
16         item = theItem;
17      }  // end setItem
18
19      public String getItem()
20      {
21         return item;
22      }  // end getItem
23   }  // end PlainBox class
```

The name of a header file is the name of the class followed by .h. For example, Listing K-2 contains the header file for the C++ class PlainBox. Private data members and methods are grouped together, and public methods are grouped with each other. Each of these two groups is preceded by an access modifier—private or public—followed by a colon. In this way, data members and methods do not need their own access modifiers. The class declaration must end with a semicolon after the closing brace, as shown in line 15 of the listing.

LISTING K-2   **The header file for the C++ class** PlainBox

```
1    /** @file PlainBox.h */
2    #include <string>       // Needed because we use string objects
3                            // Strings are part of the system std library
4    class PlainBox          // This is a class declaration for PlainBox
5    {
6    private:                // Items defined below have private access
7       std::string item;
8
9    public:                 // Items defined below have public access
10      // Prototypes for constructors and methods
11      PlainBox();
12      PlainBox(std::string theItem);
13      void setItem(std::string theItem);
14      std::string getItem();
15   }; // end PlainBox - Note semicolon after close brace
```

The **implementation file**, or **source file**, for the class typically has the same name as the header file, but ends in .cpp to indicate that it is a C++ file. The implementation file contains the definitions for the methods declared in the accompanying header file. For example, the implementation file for the C++ class PlainBox is given in Listing K-3. It begins by including

LISTING K-3   **The implementation file for the C++ class** PlainBox

```
1    /** @file PlainBox.cpp */
2    #include "PlainBox.h" // We need to tell the compiler about our data
3                          // fields and methods.
4    PlainBox::PlainBox()
5    {
6    }  // end default constructor
```

```
 7
 8   PlainBox::PlainBox(std::string theItem)
 9   {
10      item = theItem;
11   }  // end constructor
12
13   void PlainBox::setItem(std::string theItem)
14   {
15      item = theItem;
16   }  // end setItem
17
18   std::string PlainBox::getItem()
19   {
20
21      return item;
22   }  // end getItem
```

the header file, so that the compiler has the class declaration and knows the data fields and methods of this class. We then define each method in the implementation file. No "master" set of braces encloses all of the methods. Each method is individually defined. To let the compiler know that a method belongs to the PlainBox class, we added the prefix PlainBox:: to the method name. Observe that the prefix is immediately before the method's name and after the method's return type.

To create a PlainBox object in Java, you could use the following statement:

```
PlainBox myBox = new PlainBox("Jewelry");
```

C++ provides several forms for creating objects:

```
PlainBox myBox = PlainBox("Jewelry");
PlainBox myBox("Jewelry");
```

These statements are equivalent in C++ and create a PlainBox object that is local to the function or method in which it is created. In these examples the C++ keyword new is not used.

The following example does use the keyword new to create a PlainBox object that exists until the programmer specifically deletes it:

```
PlainBox* someBoxPtr = new PlainBox("Jewelry");
```

The syntax is very similar to Java's, except that PlainBox is followed by the * character. The * indicates that someBoxPtr is a pointer to a PlainBox object and is not the object itself. Pointers are discussed in more detail in C++ Interlude 2.

If an object in C++ is instantiated using the new operator, as in the previous example, it is the responsibility of the programmer to delete that object from memory when it is no longer needed, because C++ does not provide garbage collection. To delete the object pointed to by someBoxPtr, use the statements

```
delete someBox;     // Frees memory used by the object.
someBox = nullptr;  // A safety precaution.
```

Note: Each time you use the new operator to create an object, you must write a corresponding delete operator to free the object's memory. Otherwise, your application will have a memory leak. C++ Interlude 2 discusses this problem.

Additional information about C++ classes appears in Section A.9 of Appendix A and in C++ Interludes 1 and 5.

K.5   Basic Input and Output

Although at the system level, Java and C++ treat keyboard input and console-display output similarly, the high-level constructs used to accomplish these tasks differ greatly.

For a Java application to accept input from the keyboard, you create a `Scanner` object with `System.in` and use it to accept input from the user. Output to the display is accomplished by calling either the `print` or `println` method of the `System.out` object. The following code creates a `Scanner` object, displays a prompt for the user, accepts a response from the user, and echoes the response back to the user:

```
Scanner keyboard = new Scanner(System.in);
System.out.print("How many apples are in a box? ");
int applesPerBox = keyboard.nextInt();
System.out.print("You entered " + applesPerBox + " apples per box. ");
```

C++ does not have a `System.in` or `System.out` object; instead you use `cin` and `cout` objects for keyboard input and console-display output, respectively. To use `cin` and `cout`, you include the statement

```
#include <iostream>
```

at the start of your program. You also must write `std::` before each occurrence of `cin` and `cout`.

The following C++ statements are equivalent to the previous Java statements:

```
std::cout << "How many apples are in a box? ";
int applesPerBox = 0;
std::cin >> applesPerBox;
std::cout << "You entered " << applesPerBox << " apples per box. " << std::endl;
```

Notice the use of the output stream operator << to send string literals and variables to the output object `cout`. Similarly, the input stream operator >> sends input from the input object `cin` to a variable. It is easy to remember which operator to use if you imagine them as arrows pointing in the direction of the data flow.

The constant `endl` is defined in `iostream` and represents the new-line character. Additional information about the `iostream` library, and about basic input and output in C++, is in Section A.2 of Appendix A.

C++ for Python Programmers

Contents

This appendix covers some of the differences between Python and C++ that a beginning programmer may encounter. While there are many additional differences, they either are not applicable to the code and examples used in this text or are explained when needed. This appendix should be used in conjunction with Appendix A to fully understand the features provided in C++.

L.1   General Concepts

Transitioning from the Python programming language to C++ is similar to graduating from high school and going through basic training in the military. Python is a weakly typed, interpreted language with a readable syntax. C++, on the other hand, is a strongly typed, compiled language that follows strict punctuation rules for its syntax. The good news is that after completing boot camp, you have the chance to become an Army Ranger or Navy Seal. This text can help you be all you can as a computer scientist and C++ programmer.

Python programs are interpreted and can execute on any computer that has a Python interpreter. Python interpreters have even been written in JavaScript, so that you can run Python code inside a window in your web browser! C++ programs, on the other hand, are compiled into object code that is specific to an operating system. This means that you need to recompile your C++ code for each operating system that you want your program to run on. The code in this book follows the recent ANSII C++11 and C++14 standards, so you should be able to compile and run your programs on whichever operating system you choose if your compiler supports that standard.

L.2   Comparison of Language Elements

When it comes to writing a C++ program, there are several important differences you need to keep in mind.

Comments. Comments are an important part of any program, and C++ supports single and multiline comments with different delimiters:

```
// This is a comment that appears on its own line.
int sum = 0; // This is a comment that appears at the end of a C++ statement.
// The following comment begins with /** and ends with */.
/** This is a special multiline comment used for documentation systems
    such as doxygen. See Appendix I for details. */
// The following comment begins with /* and ends with */.
/* This is a multiline comment that is often used to temporarily
    disable a group of statements during debugging. */
```

Statements. White space and indentation in C++ have no significance. C++ statements end with a semicolon. Statements in a block, known as a compound statement, are analogous to a suite in Python and are grouped together by braces { }.

Variables. In Python, a variable can be used as soon as it is assigned a value. Variables in C++ must be declared and given a type before they can be used. Though the C++ compiler does not require it, variables should also be given an initial value before being used. Once a variable has been declared with a given a type, it maintains that type throughout the scope in which it was declared.

Relational operators. Variables in C++ can be used only with one relational operator at a time. Python expressions such as 5 < x < 10 must be written as (5 < x) && (x < 10) in C++. The operator && is used for a logical AND, and || is used for a logical OR.

Predicate expressions. Predicate expressions in conditional and iteration flow-control statements must be in parentheses.

Assignment statements. Multiple assignment is not allowed in C++. Python statements such as x,y = 5,6 cannot be used.

Iteration statements. C++ has a while statement that behaves like the Python while statement. The C++ for statement is a special case of the while statement. To use a C++ for statement as you would use a Python form statement, you must use iterators, which are explained in C++ Interlude 7. C++ has a do-while statement, which is a post-test loop. Python has no equivalent statement.

Basic input and output. In a Python application, you use the raw_input function to accept input from the keyboard. This function returns a string. If you need an integer or a value of some other data type, you must use another function to transform the string into the desired input. Output to the display is accomplished by calling the print function. For example, the following Python code displays a prompt for the user, accepts a response as an integer, and echoes the response back to the user:

```
userNumber = int(raw_input ("How many apples are in a box? "))
print "You entered %d apples per box." %(userNumber)
```

C++ uses two objects, cin and cout, for keyboard input and console display output, respectively. To use cin and cout, you should include the following statement at the start of your program:

```
#include <iostream>
```

The following C++ statements are equivalent to the previous Python statements:

```
std::cout << "How many apples are in a box? ";
int applesPerBox = 0;
std::cin >> applesPerBox;
std::cout << "You entered " << applesPerBox << " apples per box." << std::endl;
```

Notice the use of the output stream operator << to send string literals and variables to the output object cout. Similarly, the input stream operator >> sends input from the input object cin to a variable. It is easy to remember which operator to use if you imagine them as arrows pointing in the direction of the data flow.

The constant endl is defined in iostream and represents the new-line character. Additional information about the iostream library and basic input and output in C++ is in Section A.2 of Appendix A.

Example. Listing L-1 gives a short interactive Python program using the statements and expressions just discussed. Listing L-2 shows the equivalent program in C++. C++ programs begin execution at the main function. You can see some of the differences in user input and output in this example also.

LISTING L-1   Short Python program to test and modify a user-entered value

```
1   small, large = 1, 1000
2   print "Your number was between %d and %d large." %(small, large)
3   userNumber = int(raw_input ("Enter something: "))
4
5   if small < userNumber < large :
6       print "Your number was between %d and %d large." %(small, large)
7
8   elif userNumber < small :
9       while userNumber <= small :
10          userNumber = userNumber + 1
11  else :
12      while True :
13          userNumber = userNumber - 1
14          if userNumber < 1000 :
15              break
16          print "I fixed your number to be between %d and %d!" %(small, large)
```

LISTING L-2 Short C++ program equivalent to the Python program in Listing L-1.

```
1   #include <iostream>
2   int main()
3   {
4       int small = 1;
5       int large = 1000;
6       int userNumber = 0;
7       std::cout << "Enter something: ";
8       std::cin >> userNumber;
9       if ( (small < userNumber) && (userNumber < large) )
10      {
```
(continues)

```
11          std::cout << "Your number was between " << small << " and ";
12          std::cout << large << std::endl;
13       }
14       else if (userNumber < 1)
15       {
16          while (userNumber <= 1)
17          {
18             userNumber++;
19          }
20       }
21       else
22       {
23          do
24          {
25             userNumber--;
26          } while (userNumber >= 1000);
27          std::cout << "I fixed your number to be between " << small << " and ";
28          std::cout << large << std::endl;
29       }
30    }
```

L.3   Functions

As with its variables, C++ functions are strongly typed. When a C++ function is defined, the parameters are given a type. If the function returns a value, the function must indicate the type of the return value. This information is given in the header, that is, the first line, of the function. If a function does not return a value, its return type is void. The definition of the function follows the header and is enclosed in { }, as in other C++ blocks.

Here is a short Python function that computes the cube of its single parameter:

```
def computeRealCube(x):
    return x * x * x
```

Here is the equivalent C++ function:

```
double computeRealCube(double x)
{
    return  x * x * x;
}
```

Notice that the C++ function and its parameter are each given a type. C++ functions are discussed in greater detail in Section A.3 of Appendix A.

Any function defined after computeRealCube in the file can invoke computeRealCube. But what if a function is defined before computeRealCube and needs to call it? In this case, the compiler would issue an error stating that computeRealCube was not defined. C++ requires that each function, constant, variable, or class be defined before it can be called.

In a simple program with a few functions, it is easy to order the function definitions so that the compiler sees each one before it encounters the function call. In more complex programs, this order is more difficult, or even impossible, to achieve. However, the compiler needs only the header of a function before processing a call to it, and C++ provides a way for you to satisfy the compiler. You simply write the function's header followed by a semicolon—that is, its **prototype**—at the beginning of the program that calls it. For example, the prototype of the function computeRealCube is

```
double computeRealCube(double x);
```

You now can place the function's definition anywhere within your program.

In larger programs, function prototypes are placed into one or more header files, as mentioned in C++ Interlude 1 and Section K.1 of Appendix K. You then include the header files in your program. Prototypes are also important in the creation of classes, as you will see in the next section. Section A.9.1 of Appendix A also discusses header files.

Note that you can pass a function as an argument to another function or method. This feature is used in Sections 15.2.1 and 15.2.3 of Chapter 15.

L.4 Classes

Python classes permit clients of the classes to access all data fields and methods. In C++, this is called **public access** and is not recommended for data fields. In Python, when you create a class member that should be used only by class methods, you typically begin the member's name with two underscores, __. This convention is only a signal to the programmer; the Python interpreter does not enforce it. C++ permits the class designer to restrict access to certain data fields and methods by labeling them as **private**, and the compiler enforces this restriction by permitting only class methods to access private members.

Classes in C++ have constructors that are similar to the __init__ method in a Python class. When writing a method in a Python class, you precede the names of data fields by self to indicate that they are instance variables of the class. Instance variables in a C++ class do not need a special prefix, if they are referenced from within a method of the class.

Here is a simple Python class, PlainBox:

```
class PlainBox

    def init__(self, theItem):
        self.item = theItem

    def setItem(self, theItem):
        self.item = theItem

    def getItem(self):
        return  self.item
```

You also can define the same class in a form that is closer to that of a C++ class:

```
class PlainBox

    __item = " "

    def __init__(self, theItem):
        self.__item = theItem

    def setItem(self, theItem):
        self.__item = theItem

    def getItem(self):
        return  self.__item
```

Though is it possible to define a class in C++ in a single file, we will use two files, since this is a more common and flexible approach. The first file is the class header file; it contains the data fields for the class and prototypes for all methods defined in the class. It is a description of the class and does not normally contain executable code. The name of a header file is the name of the class followed by .h. For example, Listing L-3 contains the header file for the C++ class PlainBox:

LISTING L-3   The header file for the C++ class PlainBox

```
1   /** @file PlainBox.h */
2   #include <string>         // Needed because we use string objects
3                             // Strings are part of the system std library
4   class PlainBox            // This is a class declaration for PlainBox
5   {
6      private:               // Items defined below have private access
7         std::string item;
8
9      public:                // Items defined below have public access
10        // Prototypes for constructors and methods
11        PlainBox();
12        PlainBox(std::string theItem);
13        void setItem(std::string theItem);
14        std::string getItem();
15   }; // end PlainBox - Note semicolon after close brace
```

Private data members and methods are grouped together, and public methods are grouped with each other. Each of these two groups is preceded by an access modifier—private or public—followed by a colon. In this way, data members and methods do not need their own access modifiers. The class declaration must end with a semicolon after the closing brace, as shown in line 15 of the previous listing.

The **implementation file**, or **source file**, for the class typically has the same name as the header file, but ends in .cpp to indicate that it is a C++ file. The implementation file contains the definitions for the methods declared in the accompanying header file. For example, the implementation file for the C++ class PlainBox is given in Listing L-4. It begins by including the header file, so that the compiler has the class declaration and knows the data fields and methods of this class. We then define each method in the implementation file. No "master" set of braces encloses all of the methods. Each method is individually defined. To let the compiler know that a method belongs to the PlainBox class, we added the prefix PlainBox:: to the method name. Observe that the prefix is immediately before the method's name and after the method's return type.

LISTING L-4   The implementation file for the C++ class PlainBox

```
1   /** @ file PlainBox.cpp */
2   #include "PlainBox.h"  // We need to tell the compiler about our data
3                          // fields and methods
4
5   PlainBox::PlainBox()
6   {
7   }  // end default constructor
8
```

```
 9   PlainBox::PlainBox(std::string theItem)
10   {
11      item = theItem;
12   }  // end constructor
13
14   void PlainBox::setItem(std::string theItem)
15   {
16      item = theItem;
17   }  // end setItem
18
19   std::string PlainBox::getItem()
20   {
21      return item;
22   }  // end getItem
```

To create a PlainBox object in Python, you could use the following statement:

```
myBox = PlainBox("Jewelry");
```

C++ provides several forms for creating objects:

```
PlainBox myBox = PlainBox("Jewelry");
PlainBox myBox("Jewelry");
```

These statements are equivalent in C++ and create a PlainBox object that is local to the function or method in which it is created. In these examples, the C++ keyword new is not used.

The following example uses the keyword new to create a PlainBox object that exists until the programmer specifically deletes it:

```
PlainBox* someBoxPtr = new PlainBox("Jewelry");
```

Notice that PlainBox is followed by the * character to indicate that someBoxPtr is a pointer to a PlainBox object and is not the object itself. Pointers are discussed in more detail in C++ Interludes 2 and 4.

If an object in C++ is instantiated using the new operator, as in the example above, it is the responsibility of the programmer to delete that object from memory when it is no longer needed. In Python, garbage collection deletes unused objects and frees the memory that was used by those objects. C++ does not provide garbage collection, so you must free unused memory. To delete the object pointed to by someBoxPtr, use the statements

```
delete someBox;     // Frees memory used by the object.
someBox = nullptr;  // A safety precaution.
```

 Note: Each time you use the new operator to create an object, you must write a corresponding delete statement to free the object's memory. Otherwise, your application will have a memory leak. C++ Interlude 2 discusses this problem.

Additional information about C++ classes appears in Section A.9 of Appendix A and in C++ Interludes 1 and 5.

Index